HOLT McDOUGAL

UNITED STATES
Government

★ ★ PRINCIPLES IN PRACTICE ★ ★

Luis Ricardo Fraga

Developed in Partnership with

 Center for
Civic Education

DIVISION FOR
PUBLIC
EDUCATION
AMERICAN BAR ASSOCIATION

Charles N. Quigley
John Hale
Maria Gallo
Robert Leming
Kari Coppinger
Mark Stritzel
Mark Gage

HOLT McDOUGAL
a division of Houghton Mifflin Harcourt

Author

LUIS RICARDO FRAGA

Dr. Luis Ricardo Fraga is a Russell F. Stark University Professor of Political Science, Associate Vice Provost for Faculty Advancement, and Director of the Diversity Research Institute at the University of Washington. A native of Corpus Christi, Texas, Dr. Fraga received his A.B. from Harvard University and his M.A. and Ph.D. from Rice University.

Dr. Fraga's primary interests are urban politics, education politics, voting rights policy, and the politics of race and ethnicity. He has published extensively in scholarly journals and edited volumes including the *American Political Science Review,* the *Journal of Politics, Urban Affairs Quarterly, Dubois Review,* and the *Harvard Journal of Hispanic Policy.*

Dr. Fraga served as the Secretary of the American Political Science Association (APSA) in 2006–2007. He has also served on the APSA standing committee on Civic Engagement and Education and as president of the Western Political Science Association.

Dr. Fraga has served on the faculty at Stanford University, the University of Notre Dame, and the University of Oklahoma. He has received numerous teaching awards, including the Rhodes Prize for Excellence in Undergraduate Teaching and the Dinkelspiel Award for Distinctive Contributions to Undergraduate Education.

Printed in the United States of America

ISBN-13 978-0-03-093028-7

ISBN 0-03-093028-6

4 5 6 7 0914 12 11 10   4500229850

Program Consultants

Contents

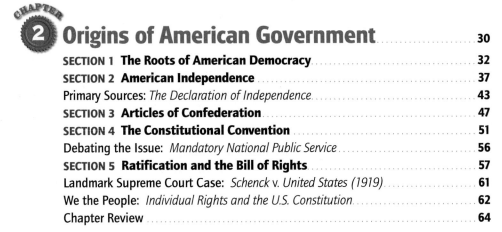

PART 1 Essentials of United States Government 2

Reference Section R1

Features

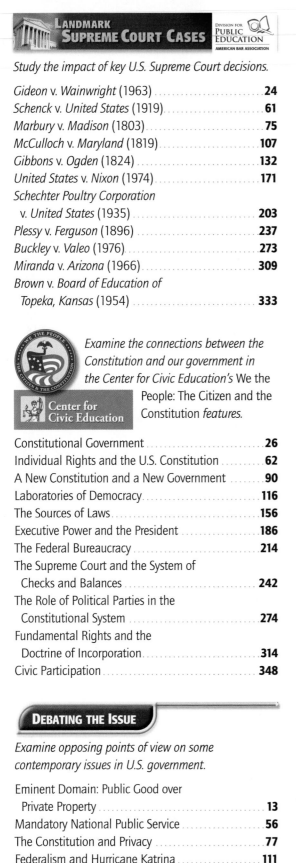

CASE STUDIES

Examine major topics in government through Case Studies.

REAL-WORLD EXAMPLE

Explore more about a key government topic through Real-World Examples.

WEBQUEST

Go online to explore Webquests relating to key government topics.

SIMULATIONS

Apply your knowledge of topics in government by taking part in simulations.

Interactive Feature ✳

Go online to extend your learning with interactive features that focus on key topics in government.

POLITICAL CARTOONS

Interpret and analyze political cartoons to learn more about the role of government.

QUICK FACTS

Analyze key facts and concepts about government.

Primary Sources

Explore government through eyewitness accounts, court decisions, and other major documents.

Charts, Graphs, Maps, and Time Lines

Analyze information presented visually to learn more about government.

Charts

Graphs

Maps

Time Lines

How to Use Your Textbook

Holt McDougal United States Government: Principles in Practice was created to make your study of U.S. government an enjoyable, meaningful experience. Take a few minutes to become familiar with the book's easy-to-use structure and special features.

Essentials of United States Government

Chapters 1–11 present the central concepts of U.S. government, including chapters on the origins of American government and on each branch of the national government.

Each chapter in **Part 1** begins with a **Chapter at a Glance** feature that summarizes the key points from each section.

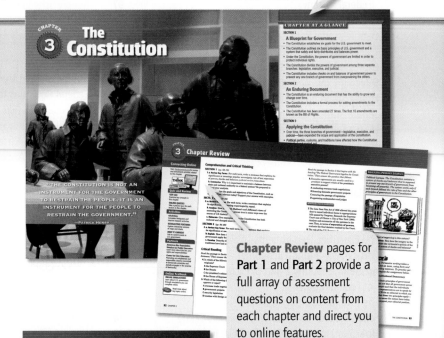

Chapter Review pages for **Part 1** and **Part 2** provide a full array of assessment questions on content from each chapter and direct you to online features.

Interactive United States Government

Chapters 12–16 examine key topics in U.S. government through engaging Case Studies, Real-World Examples, Webquests, and Simulations.

A **Case Study** begins each section in **Part 2** and examines a real-life situation that relates to the content of the section.

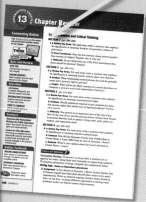

Before You Read features at the beginning of each section in **Part 1** highlight the section's Main Idea, Reading Focus questions, and Key Terms.

A New Constitution and a New Government

What are Congress's constitutional powers?

SECTION 2 **An Enduring Document**

BEFORE YOU READ

Main Idea
The Constitution is both a product of its time and a document for all time. It can be changed as society's needs change.

Reading Focus
1. How did Jefferson and Madison differ in their views on amending the Constitution?
2. Why might the Constitution be called a document for all time?
3. By what processes can the Constitution be amended?
4. What types of amendments have been added to the Constitution over the last 220 years?

Key Terms
supermajority
repeal

A Blueprint that Would Last

WHY IT MATTERS A Constitution for All Generations

| 1870 15th Amendment | 1920 19th Amendment | 1971 26th Amendment |

78 CHAPTER 3

We the People features from the Center for Civic Education focus on in-depth constitutional issues relating to each chapter in **Part 1**.

THE CONSTITUTION 83

Reading Check questions throughout each section in **Part 1** and **Part 2** provide opportunities to review and assess your understanding of what you read.

These sections also end with a **Section Assessment** which allows you to check your understanding of the main ideas and key content.

In **Part 2** **What You Need to Know** presents section content, key terms, and special features such as Real-World Examples and Webquests.

WHAT YOU NEED TO KNOW

Freedom of Religion

Key Terms
freedom of expression
redress of grievances
right of assembly

The Establishment Clause

Your First Amendment Freedoms

SUPREME COURT CASES 393

Student Assembly

Section 1 Assessment

SUPREME COURT CASES 399

SIMULATION

The Play's the Thing

Will students from Home City High School be allowed to stage their play?

Student Casebook

① The Situation

Roles
- Federal judge
- Jurors
- Plaintiffs' attorneys
- Defendants' attorneys
- Attorney for Civil Liberties Association (CLA)
- Attorney for Center for Free Student Press (CFSP)
- Attorney for Association of United Churches (AUC)
- Attorney for Association of School Administration (ASA)
- Drama club members
- School principal
- School newspaper editor

Background

400 CHAPTER 11

Simulations at the end of each section in **Part 2** highlight government activities or scenarios.

Real-World Examples in **Part 2** point out relevant and interesting cases that relate to the content.

REAL-WORLD EXAMPLE
CASE STUDY LINK

Webquests in **Part 2** point you to engaging online activities linked to the topic.

WEBQUEST

XV

Basic Principles of the U.S. Constitution

The U.S. Constitution outlines six fundamental principles that have guided American government for more than 200 years. The Framers of the Constitution established these six principles—popular sovereignty, limited government, separation of powers, checks and balances, judicial review, and federalism—as the basis of our national government.

POPULAR SOVEREIGNTY

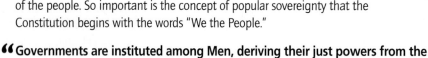

Popular sovereignty is the concept that a government's power comes from the people it rules. Our government was created by and for the people of the United States, and power remains in the hands of the people. So important is the concept of popular sovereignty that the Constitution begins with the words "We the People."

❝Governments are instituted among Men, deriving their just powers from the consent of the governed.❞

—Declaration of Independence, 1776

LIMITED GOVERNMENT

The Constitution also established a limited government to guide the United States. In order to protect the people from an all-powerful government, much of the Constitution deals with setting limits on the powers and functions of government. This idea that government is limited by the laws is one of the fundamental principles of our nation.

❝A sacred respect for the constitutional law is the vital principle, the sustaining energy of a free government.❞

—Alexander Hamilton, letter III to the *American Daily Advertiser*, 1794

JUDICIAL REVIEW

The principle of judicial review is designed to ensure that the government obeys the laws set forth in the Constitution. Judicial review grants courts the power to review government actions and judge their constitutionality. Although not specifically mentioned in the Constitution, judicial review is a concept that has been promoted since the early days of the United States.

❝The interpretation of the laws is the proper and peculiar province of the courts.❞

—Alexander Hamilton, *Federalist Paper* No. 78, 1788

CHECKS AND BALANCES

To prevent any branch from exercising too much power, the Framers of the Constitution established a system of checks and balances. This system gives each branch certain powers to change or negate acts of the other two branches. The system of checks and balances prevents any one branch from dominating the national government.

❝ The powers of government should be so divided and balanced among several bodies . . . as that no one could transcend their legal limits. ❞

—James Madison, *Federalist Paper* No. 48, 1788

SEPARATION OF POWERS

Another way to ensure that the powers of government are limited was to create three distinct branches with separate duties and powers. This separation of powers among the legislative, executive, and judicial branches is designed to prevent any one person or branch from becoming too powerful.

❝ The first principle of a good government is certainly a distribution of its powers into executive, judiciary and legislative. ❞

—Thomas Jefferson, letter to John Adams, 1787

FEDERALISM

In order to protect the power of individual states and strengthen the national government, the Framers of the Constitution established a federal system. The principle of federalism divides power between the national government and state governments.

❝ The federal and State governments are in fact but different agents and trustees of the people. ❞

—James Madison, *Federalist Paper* No. 46, 1788

To the Student

The opportunity that citizens have to participate in public affairs and to influence government decision making is the most important feature of American government. Active participation in the political and social life of the United States is essential to maintaining a vibrant democracy. As such, citizen participation is an act of leadership.

One cannot understand—or participate effectively in—the structure and operation of American government without a full appreciation of three dimensions of leadership: the leadership of ideas, the leadership of decision making, and leadership in learning.

The leadership of ideas was the type of leadership that the Framers of the Constitution demonstrated when they adopted untried ideas such as individual liberty, limited government, and federalism to guide how our government should be structured.

The leadership of decision making reflects the type of leadership required to make difficult choices about how governmental power should be used. When making these choices, leaders have always decided who wins and who loses in American politics, as well as by how much and how often.

Leadership in learning represents the type of leadership shown when one learns from what has worked well in American government—as well as from what has failed—and then uses this learning to fashion future public policy.

Taken together, these dimensions of leadership in ideas, decision-making, and learning make up what I call the **responsibilities of leadership.**

The goal of this textbook is to help you understand how our nation, through both its leaders and its people, has accepted the responsibilities of leadership—from the founding of the nation to the present day. My hope is that by focusing your study of American government on these responsibilities, you are each more fully informed and able to accept the responsibilities required of all citizens and residents who are effectively engaged in American politics today.

All of us, whatever our ideological positions and policy preferences, must accept responsibility for the ideas, choices, and consequences that we choose to support in our collective life as a nation. If more of us accept the responsibilities of leadership to propose new ideas, make informed choices, and learn from the consequences of those choices, our nation will be better prepared to confront the complex, ever-changing challenges that confront it today and in the future.

Luis Ricardo Fraga

To maximize your study and understanding of United States government, use the Skills Handbook to review and practice a variety of key skills.

Distinguishing Fact from Opinion

Define the Skill

In order to be a critical thinker, you must know how to distinguish fact from opinion as you read. A **fact** is a statement that can be proved or disproved. An **opinion** is a personal belief or attitude, so it cannot be proved true or false. Distinguishing fact from opinion can help you make reasonable judgments about what you read.

Learn the Skill

Use the following strategies to distinguish between fact and opinion.

1 **Examine the source carefully.** Look at the language the author uses. Consider which statements may be facts and which may be opinions.

In 1776 Thomas Paine wrote the pamphlet Common Sense, *arguing against British rule in the American colonies.*

❝In short, monarchy and succession have laid (not this or that kingdom only) but the world in blood and ashes . . .

If we inquire into the business of a king, we shall find that in some countries they have none; and after sauntering away their lives without pleasure to themselves or advantage to the nation, withdraw from the scene, and leave their successors to tread the same idle round. In absolute monarchies the whole weight of business, civil and military, lies on the king; the children of Israel in their request for a king, urged this plea "that he may judge us, and go out before us and fight our battles." But in countries where he is neither a judge nor a general, as in England, a man would be puzzled to know what is his business.

The nearer any government approaches to a republic the less business there is for a king.❞

2 **Identify facts.** Consider what evidence the author uses to support his or her statements. If a statement can be proved, it is a fact. Check other sources to determine if a statement is a fact. Be careful with statistics. They can be used incorrectly to mislead the reader.

3 **Identify opinions.** Determine if a statement can be proved or not. If it cannot, it is an opinion. Opinions may use positive or negative words, such as *outstanding* and *poor* and phrases such as *I believe*, *probably*, and *should*.

Apply the Skill

1 What language does the author use that might indicate facts or opinions?
2 What facts does the author cite?
3 What opinions does the author cite?

Identifying Cause and Effect

Define the Skill

Identifying cause and effect can help you to become a critical thinker and to better understand what you read. A **cause** is something that brings about an action or condition. Often, a cause will be directly stated in the text, but sometimes it will be implied, or stated indirectly. An **effect** is an event that happens as the result of a cause. A cause may have more than one effect. Similarly, an effect may have several causes. By identifying causes and effects, you will be able to determine why certain events occurred, whether certain events are related, and what the relationship is between events.

Learn the Skill

Use the following strategies to identify cause and effect.

From Chapter 2, Section 2

The Stamp Act Congress The colonists' reaction to the Stamp Act of 1765, Parliament's first attempt to tax the colonists directly, should have been a warning sign of the rough times to come. The Stamp Act infuriated colonists, who responded with organized protest. Secret colonial societies called the Sons of Liberty sprang up across the colonies. Their goal was to intimidate the stamp agents charged with collecting Parliament's taxes. In many places, mobs forced stamp agents out of office. In Philadelphia, colonists even conducted a mock hanging of a stamp agent.

In October 1765 nine colonies sent delegates to the Stamp Act Congress in New York to craft a united response to the new tax measure. The congress was the colonies' first attempt at forging a plan to work together since the 1754 Albany meeting. It sent a petition to the king that declared their loyalty but voiced a strong protest, asserting that the power to tax colonies should belong solely to the colonial assemblies.

1 Identify the causes of events. Look for reasons that prompted a given event to occur. Words such as *since, because, so, therefore*, and *due to* can signal a causal relationship among events.

2 Identify the effects of events. Look for phrases and clue words that indicate consequences, such as *thus, brought about, led to, consequently*, and *as a result*.

3 Connect causes and effects. Consider why certain causes led to an event and why the event turned out as it did. Remember that an event can be both a cause and an effect.

Apply the Skill

1 What was the cause of the events described in the passage?

2 List the various effects described in the passage.

3 What is the ultimate outcome described in the passage? Why might that outcome have resulted from the cause you identified?

Analyzing Points of View and Frames of Reference

Define the Skill

A **point of view** is a person's outlook or attitude. It is the way that he or she looks at a topic or an issue. Each person's point of view is shaped by his or her frame of reference. A **frame of reference** refers to a person's background and experiences. Because people's frames of reference are different, so are their points of view. Understanding frames of reference can help you to better analyze a person's point of view and understand what you read.

Learn the Skill

Use the following strategies to analyze points of view and frames of reference.

Democratic Senator Hubert Humphrey, speech accepting nomination as the Democratic vice presidential candidate, June 1964

"We of the Democratic Party call upon all Americans to join us in making our country a land of opportunity for our young, a home of security and dignity for our elderly, and a place of compassion and care for our afflicted . . . Let us take those giant steps forward . . . to build the great society."

Republican Senator Barry Goldwater, speech announcing candidacy for the presidency, January 1964

"I've always stood for government that is limited and balanced and against the ever increasing concentrations of authority in Washington . . . I believe we must now make a choice in this land and not continue drifting endlessly down and down for a time when all of us, our lives, our property, our hopes, and even our prayers will become just cogs in a vast government machine."

1 Examine information about the author's background. Knowing the author's background can give you insight into his or her frame of reference. You may need to conduct research to learn more about the author.

2 Identify the author's opinions. A person's opinions can provide clues to his or her point of view.

3 Consider how the author's frame of reference might influence his or her beliefs. Consider such factors as age, occupation, education, personal experiences, and political affiliations, as they might indicate the author's point of view.

Apply the Skill

1 What can you determine about the frame of reference, or background, of each author?
2 What is the point of view of each author?
3 Why might the authors' frames of reference influence their opposing views?

Recognizing Bias and Propaganda

Define the Skill

Many sources you encounter may contain bias or propaganda. **Bias** is information that indicates a preference or an inclination that prevents a person from making an impartial judgment. Bias can be influenced by a person's political, social, or personal beliefs. **Propaganda** is information designed to persuade a person to think or act in a particular way. Propaganda can be used by governments or political parties to convince people to espouse a particular issue or course of action. In order to analyze documents effectively, you must be able to recognize the presence of bias or propaganda.

Learn the Skill

Use the following strategies to recognize bias and propaganda.

1 Identify facts and opinions stated by the author. Analyze the facts and opinions presented. Unsupported facts and opinions are often indicators of bias and propaganda.

2 Analyze the language the author uses. Look for emotional, persuasive, or exaggerated language that is trying to sway the reader to a particular point of view.

3 Examine the author's point of view. Analyze what beliefs the author is trying to convey to his or her audience. Bias and propaganda often provide one-sided information on a subject.

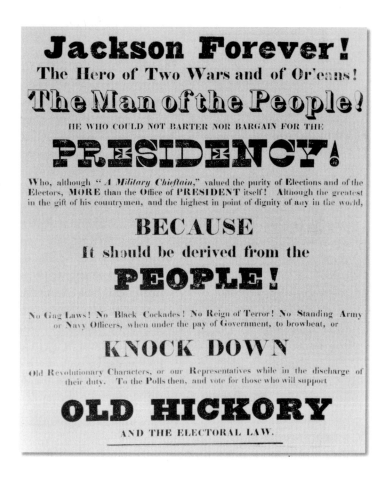

Apply the Skill

1 What is the subject of the poster?

2 What opinions and emotional language does the poster use? What purpose do they serve?

3 What point of view is presented by the poster?

4 Is there bias or propaganda in the poster? Explain.

Analyzing Primary Sources

Define the Skill

A **primary source** is a document or other artifact created by people who are present at historical events either as witnesses or participants. Usually, you can identify a primary source by reading for first-person clues, such as *I, we,* and *our.* Primary sources are valuable tools because they give firsthand information about an event or a time period and are the work of people who have created or witnessed history.

Learn the Skill

Use the following strategies to analyze primary sources.

1 Identify the author or creator of the primary source and when the source was created. The author and the date the primary source was created give you a historical context in which to place the document.

2 Compare details in the primary source to what you know about the historical event or time period. The time frame of the primary source allows you to make connections between your previous knowledge and the information the document provides.

3 Determine why the author created the primary source. Each document has a particular purpose and can be used by its author to inform, persuade, direct, or influence the audience.

In 1796 George Washington chose not to seek re-election for a third term as president. Washington gave the nation advice in his Farewell Address.

"I have already intimated to you the danger of parties in the State, with particular reference to the founding of them on geographical discriminations. Let me now take a more comprehensive view, and warn you in the most solemn manner against the baneful effects of the spirit of party generally.

This spirit, unfortunately, is inseparable from our nature, having its root in the strongest passions of the human mind. It exists under different shapes in all governments, more or less stifled, controlled, or repressed; but, in those of the popular form, it is seen in its greatest rankness, and is truly their worst enemy.

The alternate domination of one faction over another, sharpened by the spirit of revenge, natural to party dissension, which in different ages and countries has perpetrated the most horrid enormities, is itself a frightful despotism. But this leads at length to a more formal and permanent despotism. The disorders and miseries which result gradually incline the minds of men to seek security and repose in the absolute power of an individual; and sooner or later the chief of some prevailing faction, more able or more fortunate than his competitors, turns this disposition to the purposes of his own elevation, on the ruins of public liberty."

Apply the Skill

1 What was Washington's purpose in writing this portion of his Farewell Address?

2 Why might Washington have given the advice he did at this time?

3 What does this primary source tell you about the time in which it was written?

Analyzing Secondary Sources

Define the Skill

Produced after a historical event, a **secondary source** is an account created by people who were not present at the actual event. These people rely on primary sources in order to write their secondary source accounts. Secondary sources often contain summaries and analyses of events and time periods. Your textbook, for example, can be considered a secondary source. Before determining whether a document is a primary or secondary source, you must pay attention to how the document is presented.

Learn the Skill

Use the following strategies to analyze secondary sources.

1 Identify the source. Examine any source information to learn the origins of the document and its author.

From Chapter 9, Section 3

Criticisms of Political Parties Some critics argue that by trying to appeal to as many types of voters as possible, the major parties lack unity, discipline, and loyalty. As a result, parties may not be able to fulfill all the campaign promises they make.

Critics also charge that parties are full of office seekers who are interested more in their own personal success than in serving the public good. For example, a candidate may express support for a certain policy during a campaign because doing so helps the person get elected—even though in a previous campaign or office, the candidate had held, and stated, a position directly contrary to his or her new position.

Finally, some people are angered by the partisan bickering between the two major parties. They charge that parties offer simple, narrow solutions to complex problems and are more interested in winning public opinion—and votes—than in solving the complex issues confronting the nation.

2 Analyze the summary of historical events provided by the source. The author of a secondary source usually offers a summary of events or of a time period.

3 Identify the author's purpose. Look for clues that indicate the intention of the author.

Apply the Skill

1 What clues indicate that this passage is a secondary source?

2 What information about political parties does this source present?

3 What is the author's purpose and point of view?

H7

Analyzing Political Cartoons

Define the Skill

A **political cartoon** is a type of visual we can use to understand a particular time period or issue. Unlike other visuals such as photographs and fine art, the primary goal of political cartoons is to express a specific point of view. Political cartoons often use exaggerated characteristics of subjects or events in order to convey a specific message, either about politics in particular or society in general. To interpret a political cartoon, examine all the elements while considering the social, political, and historical context of the time in which it was created.

Learn the Skill

Use the acronym **BASIC** to analyze political cartoons.

Background Knowledge Place the political cartoon in its historical context. Use your prior knowledge of what is being depicted to analyze the cartoon's message about the particular issue, person, or event.

Argument Determine what message the artist is trying to convey. Analyze the message that the artist is sending to the audience.

Symbolism Analyze any symbols in the cartoon. Symbols can be used to represent large groups that cannot be depicted easily or to stand for a person or an event. Symbols can also be used to simplify the cartoon or make its message clearer to the audience.

Irony Examine any irony that is present in the cartoon. Irony is the use of words to express something other than, and often the opposite of, their literal meaning. Sometimes in political cartoons, examples of irony are implied through the various symbols and images.

Caricature Caricature, or exaggeration, is often used in political cartoons. Exaggerated facial features or figures are used to make a point. Analyze any caricature present in the cartoon and consider what the meaning of such exaggerations might be.

Apply the Skill

1 What symbols are used in the political cartoon? What do they mean?

2 What caricature does the artist use? What point do you think the artist is trying to make through the use of caricature?

3 What is the artist's message?

Making Inferences

Define the Skill

Sometimes reading effectively means understanding both what the writer tells you directly and what the writer implies. When you fill in the gaps, you are making inferences, or educated guesses. **Making inferences** involves using clues in the text to connect implied ideas with what is stated. You also draw on your own prior knowledge and use common sense to help make inferences.

Learn the Skill

Use the following strategies to practice making inferences.

Supreme Court Justice Robert H. Jackson, West Virginia State Board of Education *v.* Barnette, *1943*

"The very purpose of a Bill of Rights was to withdraw certain subjects from . . . political controversy, to place them beyond the reach of majorities and officials and to establish them as legal principles to be applied by the courts. One's right to life, liberty, and property, to free speech, a free press, freedom of worship and assembly, and other fundamental rights <u>may not be submitted to vote; they depend on the outcome of no elections</u> . . .

If there is <u>any fixed star in our constitutional constellation</u>, it is that <u>no official, high or petty, can prescribe what shall be orthodox in politics, nationalism, religion, or other matters of opinion</u> or force citizens to confess by word or act their faith therein. If there are any circumstances which permit an exception, they do not now occur to us."

1 **Identify the main idea and details in the passage.** Take note of stated facts and information in the reading passage.

2 **Identify implied ideas in the text.** Look for ideas that are suggested but not directly stated. Noting statistics and opinionated language can help you understand what is being implied.

3 **Compare stated and unstated ideas with your prior knowledge.** Use facts from the reading, your common sense, and what you already know about a topic or an event to make a valid inference about it.

Apply the Skill

1 What does the author believe about the purpose of the Bill of Rights?

2 What does the author mean by the statement "One's right to life, liberty, and property . . . may not be submitted to vote"?

3 Using the reading and your prior knowledge, what can you infer about the protections provided in the Bill of Rights?

Determining Relevance

Define the Skill

When conducting research, you will likely be faced with a great variety of different sources. Identifying which sources will help you is an important task. One step in identifying your sources is to determine their relevance. **Determining relevance** means deciding if a piece of information is related to your topic. It also involves identifying *how* something is related to your topic.

Learn the Skill

Use the following strategies to determine the relevance of information.

1 Identify the specific topic. Determine what types of sources address your research topic. Define your specific task to narrow down what types of information you need. Write down any questions for which you need answers.

2 Locate a variety of sources. Use several resources to track down sources. Textbooks, encyclopedias, periodicals, and electronic databases are just a few types of resources you can use.

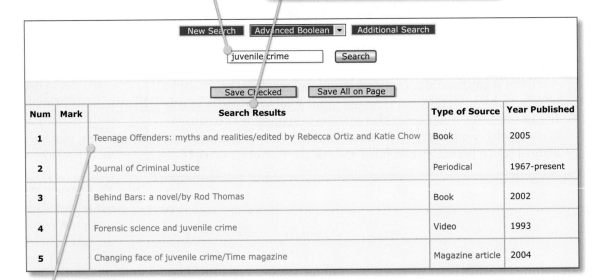

Num	Mark	Search Results	Type of Source	Year Published
1		Teenage Offenders: myths and realities/edited by Rebecca Ortiz and Katie Chow	Book	2005
2		Journal of Criminal Justice	Periodical	1967-present
3		Behind Bars: a novel/by Rod Thomas	Book	2002
4		Forensic science and juvenile crime	Video	1993
5		Changing face of juvenile crime/Time magazine	Magazine article	2004

3 Examine the sources carefully. Identify the purpose of the source and the information it provides.

4 Determine what information is useful for your topic. Decide if the information in the sources can help you answer the list of questions you created.

Apply the Skill

1 List several resources you might use to find information on the topic of juvenile crime.

2 How might you evaluate each of the sources listed above?

3 What sources from the list above would be relevant to your research? Explain.

Developing and Testing Hypotheses

Define the Skill

A **hypothesis** is a testable statement about the relationship between two or more factors. Hypotheses are possible explanations based on facts. Because they can be tested, hypotheses can be proved or disproved.

Learn the Skill

Use the following strategies to learn to develop and test hypotheses.

1 Identify the question. Examine the issue at hand to find the trend, relationship, or event that you want to explain.

Question: What has caused the drop in Monroeville's crime rate?

2 Examine the facts. Identify all the facts surrounding the question. The facts may support several different conclusions.

FACTS:
- Crime rates in the city of Monroeville have declined for five consecutive years.
- Monroeville's crime rate used to be the highest in the county.
- This year unemployment rates dropped to an all-time low.
- The population of Monroeville has increased by 26 percent since the new factory opened six years ago.
- Monroeville has hired three new police officers in the last three years.

3 Consider what you already know about the issue. Use your own prior knowledge to help you formulate a hypothesis.

Hypothesis: The availability of jobs in Monroeville has led to the drop in the town's crime rate.

FACTS THAT SUPPORT HYPOTHESIS: Monroeville's population has increased 25 percent in six years.

FACTS THAT REFUTE HYPOTHESIS: Monroeville has three new police officers.

4 Develop a hypothesis that addresses the question. Analyze the facts and your own knowledge to form a conclusion, explanation, or prediction.

5 Test your hypothesis. Conduct research to test your hypothesis. Identify facts that support or refute your conclusion. Depending on your findings, you may need to modify your hypothesis.

Apply the Skill

1 Develop a list of facts and a hypothesis that might explain why voter turnout rates among young voters has increased in recent years.

2 Use a graphic organizer like the one above to test your hypothesis.

Evaluating Sources

Define the Skill

Not all the sources you will come across in your research will be useful. By evaluating your sources, you can identify reliable and valid sources of information. Evaluating sources means that you determine the reliability and validity of the information in your sources. A **reliable** source is one that is trustworthy and verifiable. In other words, it is a respected source of information. A **valid** source is one that is accurate and free from error. Strive to use only sources that are both reliable and valid.

Learn the Skill

Use the following strategies to evaluate sources.

1 Identify the author of the source. Consider the author's background and determine if the author is an authoritative source on the topic.

2 Examine the language used in the source. Look for bias in the source. Sources that lack objectivity may not be reliable or valid.

3 Identify the author's purpose, point of view, and frame of reference. Information about the author and source may help you determine the source's reliability and validity.

4 Determine if the source is valid and reliable. Compare the source with other information on the topic to determine if the source is valid, or accurate. Use what you know of the author to determine if the source is reliable, or a respected source of information.

James Madison, Journal of the Constitutional Convention, *July 16, 1787*

"On the morning following before the hour of the Convention a number of the members from the larger States, by common agreement met for the purpose of consulting on the proper steps to be taken in consequence of the vote in favor of an equal Representation in the 2d branch, and the apparent inflexibility of the smaller states on that point. Several members from the latter States also attended. The time was wasted in vague conversation on the subject, without any specific proposition or agreement. It appeared indeed that the opinions of the members who disliked the equality of votes differed much as to the importance of that point, and as to the policy of risking a failure of any general act of the Convention by inflexibly opposing it. Several of them supposing that no good Governmt. could or would be built on that foundation, and that as a division of the convention into two opinions was unavoidable; it would be better that the side comprising the principal States, and a majority of the people of America, should propose a scheme of Govt. to the States, than that a scheme should be proposed on the other side, would have concurred in a firm opposition to the smaller States, and in a separate recommendation, if eventually necessary."

Apply the Skill

1 What is the purpose of this source?

2 Do you think this source presents a balanced or biased point of view? Explain your answer.

3 Is this source valid? Is it reliable? Explain your answers.

Using Electronic Media

Define the Skill

Much of your research will come from books and periodicals and also from electronic media. **Electronic media** are digital sources of information such as the Internet and electronic databases. Because a great deal of research information has been digitized, it is often available through electronic sources. The Internet is one such electronic medium. Electronic databases are digital collections of records, books, periodicals, and other reference material. They can be found in most libraries. Using both the Internet and databases requires that you employ careful search techniques.

Learn the Skill

Use the following strategies to learn to use electronic media.

1 Determine the information you need. Identify what specific information you need to search for. Write down keywords associated with your topics.

> Topic: State transportation projects
> Keywords: transportation costs, department of transportation, transportation projects, highway construction

2 Conduct a careful search. Use databases and Internet search engines to identify possible sources of information. Use your list of keywords to search for sources. Be sure to analyze the search results carefully to determine if they are appropriate for your needs. You may need to adjust your topic or keywords based on the information you find.

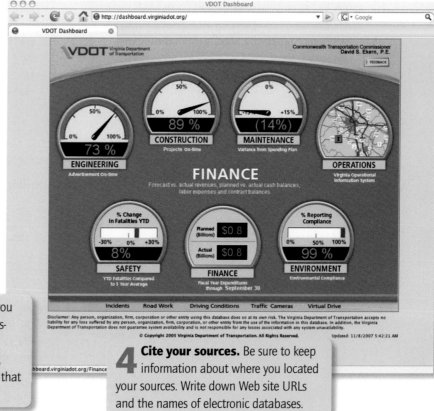

3 Evaluate your sources. Once you have located several sources, investigate who wrote or created each one. Determine if the sources are balanced, reliable, and valid. Do not use sources that are questionable.

4 Cite your sources. Be sure to keep information about where you located your sources. Write down Web site URLs and the names of electronic databases.

Apply the Skill

1 Who created the Web site pictured above?

2 Do you think the Web site above presents a balanced or biased point of view? How can you tell?

3 What other keyword search terms might you use to find information on state transportation projects?

Synthesizing Information from Multiple Sources

Define the Skill

An important critical thinking skill is synthesizing information. **Synthesizing information** means combining information from different sources. Each source you use might provide different information on a particular topic or issue. Synthesizing the information from all of your sources will help you to produce a new idea, point of view, or interpretation.

Learn the Skill

Use the following strategies to practice synthesizing information from multiple sources.

1 **Evaluate each source.** Analyze each source to determine if the source is valid and reliable. Determine if the various sources are comparable.

2 **Examine the information from each source.** Identify the key facts presented in each source separately. Make a list of the information each source provides.

3 **Compare the information from your various sources.** Identify similarities and differences between the sources and analyze relationships between the sources.

4 **Synthesize the information from the sources.** Draw conclusions based on the information from each of your sources. Use your conclusions to create your own interpretation, point of view, or idea on the topic.

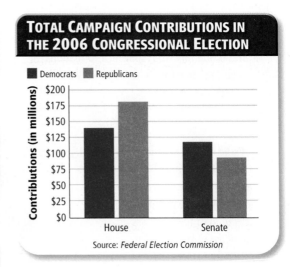

TOTAL CAMPAIGN CONTRIBUTIONS IN THE 2006 CONGRESSIONAL ELECTION

■ Democrats ■ Republicans

Source: *Federal Election Commission*

Chapter 12, Section 2

Contributions by PACs After individual donations, PACs are the most important source of campaign funding. In the 2006 House and Senate races, about 25 percent of the money raised came from PACs. This figure compares to about 60 percent that came from individuals' donations. Some candidates receive more PAC money than others, however. For example, in Tom DeLay's final race in 2004, almost half of his campaign funds came from PACs.

Apply the Skill

1 Are the sources above valid and reliable? How can you tell?

2 What similarities and differences exist between the two sources?

3 What conclusions can you draw based on the information in these two sources?

Creating a Multimedia Presentation

Define the Skill

A **multimedia presentation** is a speech or presentation that uses a variety of media to present information to an audience. Multimedia presentations are used to help speakers convey engaging messages to their audiences. These presentations might include text, graphics, audio, video, and even animation.

Learn the Skill

Use the following strategies to create a multimedia presentation.

1 Plan your presentation. Determine the main points of your presentation and conduct research to prepare. Write an outline or take notes on your key points.

2 Determine what types of media best suit your presentation. Music, audio, graphs, and charts are some of the media to consider. Keep in mind any time constraints you may have. Make a list of ways in which you might present certain information in your presentation.

3 Identify the media available to you. Consider what equipment and software are necessary to use the types of media you have identified. If necessary, revise your list of ways to present information.

4 Prepare and deliver the presentation. Use your outline to help guide your presentation. Use available resources to prepare the multimedia content. Practice your entire presentation before delivering it to your audience.

TOPIC: HOW A BILL BECOMES A LAW

NOTES FOR PRESENTATION	TYPES OF MEDIA	AVAILABILITY OF MEDIA
• Bill is introduced into the House and Senate.	• video of news report; computer animation	• video from school library
• Bill is assigned to committee.	• text; chart listing different committees	• word processor or spread sheet program in computer lab
• Committee debates bill, makes changes, and votes.	• graphic organizer showing the actions taken in committee	• computer graphics program in computer lab
• Bill reaches floor where it is debated and voted on.	• text; audio of floor debate; graph of results of floor vote	• audio recordings available on Internet
• Bill goes to conference committee.	• text listing changes and summarizing debate	• word processor in computer lab
• Approved bill goes to president for signature.	• video or photo of president signing bill into law	• video from school library
• If vetoed, bill goes back to Congress for further action.	• text; chart of bills that have been successfully overridden	• word processor or spread sheet program in computer lab

Apply the Skill

1 Use a table like the one above to prepare a multimedia presentation on the principles of the U.S. Constitution.

2 What types of media might help enhance your presentation? Why?

Making Decisions

Define the Skill

Making decisions is a skill that people use every day. **Making decisions** involves gathering information, weighing possible options, and deciding on a course of action. Making reasoned decisions is an important critical thinking and citizenship skill.

Learn the Skill

Use the following strategies to practice making decisions on a public policy issue.

Situation

Citizens in Lincoln City have petitioned the city to institute term limits for city council members.

1 **Identify the situation that calls for a decision.** Determine if the situation needs a decision and clarify what exactly needs to be decided.

Facts

- City council members in Lincoln City may serve an unlimited number of 4-year terms.
- Three current council members have each served for more than 15 years.
- All three council members in question are extremely popular among their constituents.
- Incumbents have more experience with city business than first-time council members.
- Council members with more tenure tend to have more say in what issues come up for discussion.

2 **Gather information.** Conduct research and ask questions to learn more about the situation.

3 **Analyze possible options.** Use your research to develop possible options to address the situation.

Option 1

Institute new rules limiting city council members to two three-year terms.
Possible consequences:
- The city council will have new, inexperienced members every few years.
- There will be less chance of members dominating city business.
- Citizens may feel that they are being prevented from electing experienced candidates.

Option 2

Do not institute any term limits.
Possible consequences:
- Experienced council members will strengthen city government.
- Council members could serve for many years, monopolizing city business.
- Citizens may feel they have no say in electing council members.

4 **Predict consequences of each option.** Consider possible outcomes associated with each option. Evaluate possible negative and positive effects.

Decision

Institute new rules limiting city council members to two three-year terms.

5 **Decide on a course of action.** Use the information you gathered and your analysis of possible options to help you reach a final decision.

Apply the Skill

Use a graphic organizer like the one above to make a decision regarding the need for campaign finance reform.

Solving Problems

Define the Skill

Solving problems is a process for finding solutions to difficult situations. It involves asking questions, identifying and evaluating information, analyzing a variety of solutions, and making judgments. Knowing how to solve problems is an important citizenship skill.

Learn the Skill

Use the following strategies to solve problems.

1 Identify the problem. Study the issue to learn about the problem.

2 Gather information. Research and ask questions to learn more about the problem.

3 Identify possible solutions. Based on your research, list possible options for solving the problem.

4 Evaluate your options. Weigh each possible option. Consider their advantages and disadvantages.

5 Choose and apply a solution. After comparing your options, choose the one that seems best and apply it to solve your problem.

6 Evaluate the solution. Once you have implemented your solution, evaluate whether it solves the problem. If this solution does not work, go back to your list of options and start again.

Problem

Voter turnout in local elections in the town of Blue River has dropped steadily in recent years.

Facts

- In 1997 voter turnout for local elections averaged 51 percent of registered voters.
- In 2007 voter turnout for local elections averaged 37 percent of registered voters.
- While the town's population has grown dramatically since 1997, the number of registered voters has only increased slightly.
- When local elections coincide with state or national elections, voter turnout increases dramatically.

Possible Options

Option 1: Start a campaign to encourage registered voters to vote in local elections.
Option 2: Move the date of all local elections to correspond with state or national elections.
Option 3: Start a campaign to increase the number of registered voters in the town.

Evaluation

Option 1: might persuade more people to vote, but could be expensive
Option 2: might help boost voter turnout, but might not always be possible
Option 3: might not substantially increase voter turnout and could be costly

Solution

An advertising campaign to encourage voters to participate in local elections increased voter turnout by 7 percent and cost an estimated $500,000.

Apply the Skill

1 Use a graphic organizer like the one above to address the problem of a rise in graffiti at a local park.
2 Do you think your solution would be successful in solving the problem? Explain.

Essentials of United States Government

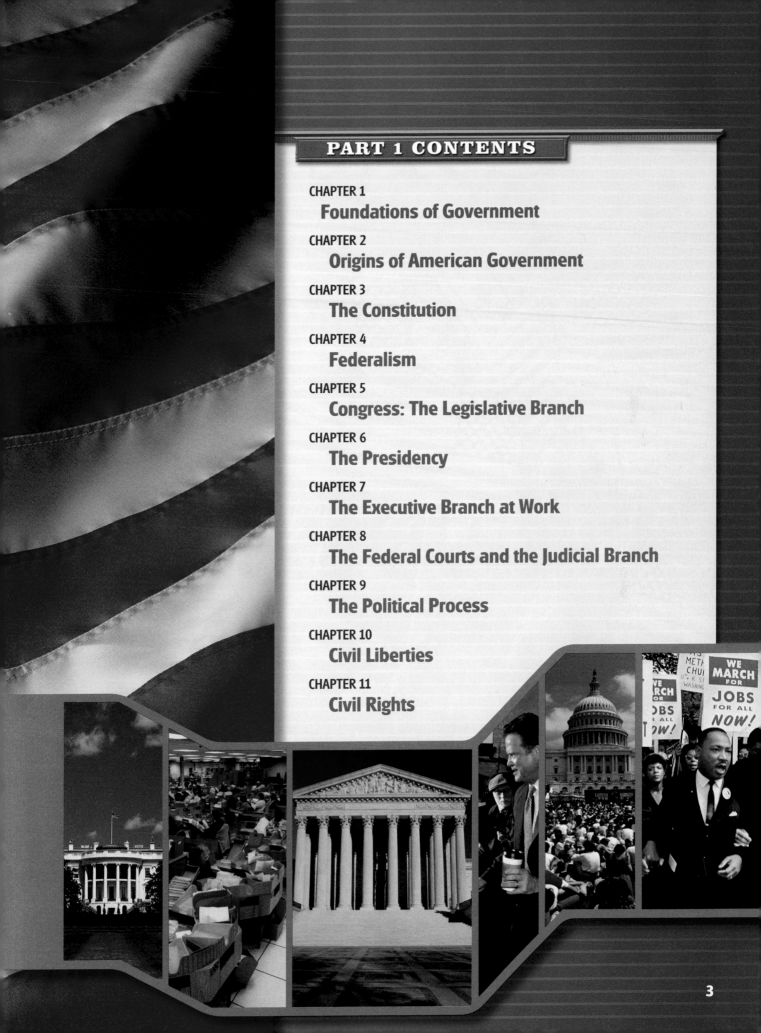

Foundations of Government

"THE WILL OF THE PEOPLE IS THE ONLY
LEGITIMATE FOUNDATION OF ANY
GOVERNMENT, AND TO PROTECT
ITS FREE EXPRESSION SHOULD
BE OUR FIRST OBJECT."

—THOMAS JEFFERSON, 1801

SECTION 1

The Purposes of Government

- Government is the formal structures and institutions through which decisions are made for a body of people.

- Most governments today exercise power within the context of a state.

- Governments function to ensure national security, maintain order, resolve conflict, provide services, and provide for the public good.

- Many theories have been put forth to explain why governments exist and the source of government's authority.

SECTION 2

Forms of Government

- Forms of government can be grouped into categories based on who exercises authority and how power is distributed.

- Within a government, how power is shared between a central government and local governments determines whether a government has a unitary, federal, or confederal system.

- Most democratic governments have either a presidential or parliamentary system of government. In presidential systems, power is divided between executive and legislative branches. In parliamentary systems, the functions of the executive and legislative branches are often combined.

SECTION 3

Democracy in the United States

- American democracy has been guided by a core set of democratic ideals—liberty, equality, and self-government—since our nation's earliest days.

- U.S. citizens ensure the continuation of democracy by committing to uphold basic principles of American democracy, including the worth of the individual, the rule of law, majority rule/minority rights, compromise, and participatory citizenship.

- Economic freedom and the free enterprise system have a special place in American democracy and help preserve liberties and limit government.

CONNECTING TO THE CONSTITUTION

Our nation's system of government is based on constitutional law established by the United States Constitution. See the "We the People: The Citizen and the Constitution" pages in this chapter for an in-depth exploration of why our nation's Founders chose constitutional government.

The Preamble to the Constitution boldly begins with "We the People . . ." With these three words, the Framers of the Constitution announced to the world that the will of the people was the foundation of government in the United States.

SECTION 1

The Purposes of Government

BEFORE YOU READ

Main Idea
Understanding major political ideas and classic forms of government will help you understand the purposes of government.

Reading Focus
1. What is government?
2. Which major characteristics do all states share?
3. What are the major functions of government?
4. What theories of rule have been put forth to explain government?

Key Terms
government
power
policy
state
sovereignty
politics
legitimacy
divine right of kings
social contract theory

 TAKING NOTES As you read, take notes on the purposes of government in a graphic organizer like this one.

Government

 WHY IT MATTERS

Life without Government In 1992 the world caught a glimpse of what life without government would be like when war broke out in what is today Bosnia-Herzegovina. The war was a result of the collapse of Yugoslavia. It pitted two once friendly ethnic groups—the Bosnians and the Serbs—against one another.

The Bosnian capital of Sarajevo was particularly hard hit. For 44 months, Serbian forces laid siege to the city, blocking all roads leading in and out of Sarajevo. Approximately 400,000 residents were trapped in the city, subjected to daily sniping and shelling and cut off from food, medicine, water, and electricity. Even United Nations peacekeepers were unable to stem the violence. By the end of the siege, nearly 12,000 civilians had died.

The daily terror in Sarajevo calls to mind a bleak vision put forth by the English philosopher Thomas Hobbes nearly 400 years ago. According to Hobbes, without government, people would find themselves in a "war of all against all" that made life "nasty, brutish, and short." Peace and security could only be achieved by establishing government. In fact, Hobbes argued, that achievement was government's primary purpose. ■

A Government Collapses

These photos show Sarajevo in 1992. At left, rubble and burned-out buildings line a city street. Above, UN peacekeepers take cover as residents run under sniper fire in Sarajevo's "Sniper Alley."

6

What Is Government?

Americans sometimes complain that the problem with government is that there is just too much of it. The collapse of Yugoslavia, however, makes clear just how much people count on government in their daily lives. Strong national defense, law and order, and clean water are just a few of the services that most people, Americans included, expect of "good" government.

Before examining the workings of the U.S. government, it is important to first understand a number of major political ideas. Top among these ideas is the concept of government itself. **Government** is made up of the formal institutions and processes through which decisions are made for a group of people. Most governments consist of three main components: people, powers, and policies.

In terms of people, government includes both elected officials who have authority and control over others as well as all of the public servants who carry out the day-to-day business of government. So the postal carrier on your block, the president, a paratrooper in the armed forces, a judge in traffic court, your state and national legislators—all these people and more—make up government.

Another component of government, **power**, refers to the government's authority and ability to get things done. The people in government exercise three basic types of power. First, a government must have legislative power, or the power to make laws. Second, government exercises executive power to carry out, enforce, and administer the law. Third, a government must have judicial power, which is the power to interpret the laws and to settle disputes between members of society.

Governments also carry out policies. A **policy** is any decision made by government in pursuit of a particular goal. A policy can take the form of a law, a government program, or even a set of government actions. Taxation, defense, environmental protection, health care, and transportation are just some of the policy areas that concern government.

READING CHECK **Summarizing** Describe the three main components of most governments.

Characteristics of a State

Today most governments exercise power within the context of a state. A **state** is a political unit with the power to make and enforce laws over a group of people living within a clearly defined territory. Used in this sense, the term *state* does not refer to one of the 50 states in the United States. Instead, it stands closer in meaning to the terms *country* and *nation-state*. All such states are characterized as having a population, a territory, a government, and sovereignty.

Population A state must have people, but the size of a population does not determine whether or not a place is a state. For example, Tuvalu, a group of nine tiny islands in the South Pacific with fewer than 12,000 people, is one of the world's smallest states. By contrast, more than 1 billion people live in Henan Province in China. Because its people, land, and government are subject to the laws of China, Henan is not an independent state.

Territory States must have clearly defined and recognized borders. Throughout history, border disputes, and the wars they often trigger, have shaped relations between states.

Origins of the State

Many theories have been put forth to explain how and why the state came into being. Among them are

Divine Right Theory
States are founded by God or the gods, and the ruler possesses a "divine right" to rule.

Evolution Theory
States form gradually over time, growing from family and extended kinship groups.

Social Contract Theory
States form when people reach a "contract" to surrender some power to a common authority in return for security.

Force Theory
States form when an individual or group uses force to make enough people submit to a central authority.

 Skills FOCUS **INTERPRETING CHARTS**

How do social contract theory and force theory differ in their explanations of the origins of the state?

Today members of the United Nations, the world's chief body for international cooperation, pledge to respect the territorial boundaries of every other member state.

Government All states are politically organized. In other words, they have governments that issue and enforce rules for the people living within their territories. These governments are recognized from within by their own people as well as by other nation states in the international community. The United States, France, Japan, China, Nigeria, Brazil, and Mexico are just a handful of the nearly 200 recognized states in the world today.

Sovereignty Every state is said to have **sovereignty**, or the supreme power to act within its territory and to control its external affairs. Sovereignty includes independence from other states as well as the freedom to establish a form of government. The individual states of the United States do not have this authority; therefore, they are not states in the sense of international law.

A state's sovereignty does not mean that its government is above the law. Most states limit the sovereign power of their governments with a set of rules that restricts the lawful use of power. Usually, these rules are outlined in a constitution, or a written plan of government.

READING CHECK **Identifying the Main Idea** Why is sovereignty important to a state?

Functions of Government

How does government function in people's everyday lives? What roles does it play? Most governments, including the U.S. government, perform a number of key functions.

Ensure National Security One of the most basic purposes of government is to guard its territory and its people against external threats, such as those posed by enemy states and terrorists. Toward this end, most states devote a great deal of their resources to national defense forces, including armies, navies, and air forces. For example, in 2007 the United States spent about $600 billion on defense. That paid for more than 2.5

million military personnel and their weaponry, active military operations, and numerous peacekeeping missions as well as the nation's intelligence-gathering activities.

Because national security also depends on maintaining good relations with other nations, the United States spent an additional $35 billion on diplomacy. This money helped support U.S. embassies, treaty negotiations, and other efforts to build strong relationships with foreign countries. In all, roughly one-fifth of our nation's 2007 federal budget was spent on national defense measures and international relations.

Maintain Order As you read in Why It Matters that opened this section, the philosopher Thomas Hobbes (1588–1679) asserted that life without government was like a war pitting each individual against the other. Universal war—who would want to live in such an environment?

Only when government was established, Hobbes argued, could order be brought to society. Indeed, one of the chief tasks of government is to establish and maintain order within its territory, thereby securing the safety of people and property. To do this, governments establish laws and a means to enforce those laws. Laws must set clear rules about unacceptable behavior. Stealing and killing, for example, are behaviors societies typically categorize as unlawful. Laws must also clearly set forth the consequences for violating the rules.

Ideas about lawful behavior differ from society to society and are often quite complicated. In the United States, for example, blatant bribery of a government official—such as giving a politician money with the intention of influencing his or her decision making—is illegal. Elected officials can, however, receive gifts, campaign contributions, and offers of employment so long as nothing is promised or expected in return. In some nations, all such gifts are unlawful.

Likewise, societies hold different ideas about what constitutes appropriate punishment. In the United States, the death penalty is a legally accepted punishment for murder in 36 states. By contrast, most European and Latin American countries no longer practice capital punishment.

Laws without enforcement serve little purpose, so governments have means to identify and punish wrongdoers. Usually, these functions are divided among three institutions. First, the police identify alleged wrongdoers. Then courts determine their guilt or innocence and assign a punishment. Lastly, in the penal system, or prisons, the punishment is carried out.

Resolve Conflict The ability of government to maintain order is closely tied to its ability to resolve conflict. Some governments maintain order through intimidation and force. Most governments, however, rely on other means—such as politics and the judicial system—for the peaceful resolution of conflict.

Politics is the process by which government makes and carries out decisions. The political process provides people with an arena for pursuing different and often competing interests. By participating in the political process, groups try to influence the decisions that government makes. Politics is also about debating issues and policies. In democratic societies, groups with different interests frequently must compromise with their opponents in order for government to make decisions. In this way, the political process helps resolve conflicts about what government should do—what laws it should create, what programs it should enact, and what policies it should pursue.

Government also establishes a system of justice in which conflicts can be resolved. Parties who feel they have been wronged can seek relief in courts. Courts determine whether a law has been broken or whether a party has been wronged and decide what should happen as a result.

Provide Services Today residents in most developed nations expect government to provide an array of services. The U.S. government, for example, spends billions of dollars every year on dozens of public policies and projects, ranging from building roads and providing parks and recreational facilities to delivering the mail and educating young people. The people of the United States pay local, state, and national taxes to fund these services.

FUNCTIONS OF GOVERNMENT

Ensure National Security	• Protect the nation's people and territory from external threats
Maintain Order	• Maintain internal order through police and the legal system
Resolve Conflict	• Provide means to resolve conflicts through politics and the legal system
Provide Services	• Provide a variety of services, ranging from education to public transportation, which are paid for by tax dollars
Provide for the Public Good	• Make decisions and policies that attempt to balance the public good with the needs of smaller segments of the population

Some U.S. government services, such as clean water, roads, and public parks, are available for everyone's use and cannot be denied to any particular person or group. Such services are called *public goods*. Other services, such as medical care, high schools, and public housing may be restricted to people who meet specific qualifications.

Provide for the Public Good The Preamble to the U.S. Constitution lays out as one of its goals the promotion of "the general welfare." Another name for the general welfare is the public good—the needs and interests of the people as a whole. In the United States, as in many countries, people believe that government must balance the public good with the needs of select groups within the population.

The notion of the public good is an abstract one. What does it mean? Who defines it? There may be agreement about some things considered in the public good. Building roads, for example, potentially benefits everyone, or at least everyone who uses the road. But what about the person whose house must be removed or whose land is taken by the government to make way for the road? Defining the public good involves making tough choices that often do not benefit everyone equally.

RESPONSIBILITIES OF LEADERSHIP

What might be the consequences to individuals and society if too great an emphasis is placed on protecting the public good at the expense of individual rights?

Education and the Public Good

An educated citizenry is key to the maintenance of democracy. In the United States, students start school as young as age three, and more than one-half of high school graduates continue to college.

The definition of the public good changes over time. Before 1900, for example, the United States had few national laws to ensure a safe supply of food. Surely there could be no clearer example of serving the public good than putting in place regulations designed to safeguard food. Still, at the time, many people disagreed, including members of the Supreme Court. In their view, the public good was better served by minimizing government regulations on business.

Even the definition of "public" can change. For much of our nation's history, most African Americans and Native Americans were not considered part of the "public," nor did the government consider their needs or desires when making decisions designed to meet the public good. Moreover, because of restrictions on voting rights, all women and many men had no voice in defining the public good.

Over time, however, the definition of "public" has expanded to become a more inclusive concept. In 1868 African Americans became citizens. In 1920 women gained voting rights. Still, the debate over who to include in the "public" continues. For example, are people convicted of crimes part of the public whose interests must be served? What about undocumented immigrants and their children, who may be U.S. citizens?

Because our government is a government of, by, and for the people, it is our job to address these difficult questions. We do this through the process of politics. Being effective citizens and civic participants requires a solid understanding of the government we have.

READING CHECK **Making Inferences** How might ideas about the public shape policy?

Theories of Rule

Political philosophers have long wondered why the majority of people allow others to rule them. Certainly, some governments rule through force and fear. But even in states ruled through force, rebellions can occur. What makes some forms of rule more acceptable than others?

To explain why people accept some forms of rule and not others, political philosophers have developed the idea that rulers often have **legitimacy**. That is, rulers are seen as right and proper by important segments of a nation's population. As a result, people voluntarily accept governance from those they see as their rightful leaders.

Divine Right Throughout history, the belief that a ruler is chosen by God or the gods has been a powerful source of legitimacy. In ancient China, emperors were said to rule with the "Mandate of Heaven." In ancient Egypt, in the Inca Empire, and in Japan until the mid-twentieth century, rulers were seen as divine, as gods on earth. Roman emperors, often merely successful generals, routinely declared themselves to be gods.

In seventeenth century Europe, to reinforce the absolute power they held over their kingdoms, kings often claimed that their power stemmed from the will of God. In the mid-1600s a French religious leader named Jacques-Bénigne Bossuet put forth a political and religious theory based on this idea. Bossuet argued that the French king Louis XIV possessed the **divine right of kings**. This made the king answerable only to God, not to the people he ruled. To disagree with the king was to disagree with God.

ACADEMIC VOCABULARY

absolute not limited by restrictions

Combining the power of earthly rule with divine sanction, or approval, can be a remarkably effective means of asserting legitimacy—at least for a while. About 100 years after Bossuet defended the French crown, King Louis XVI was beheaded during the French Revolution.

Natural Law and Natural Rights An alternate theory of rule rests on the idea of natural law, a system of rules derived from the natural world. As a system, natural law is said to provide a just and rational order to all things in the world, including human behavior. Following the logic of natural law, all people, by virtue of their being human, possess natural rights. Today these rights are commonly understood as human rights.

Notions of natural law have a long history. The ancient Greek philosopher Aristotle wrote of natural law, as did the ancient Roman leader Cicero. Medieval Christian thinkers, such as Augustine and Thomas Aquinas, linked the idea of natural law to their faith. Aquinas argued that since human nature comes from God, natural law, too, must come from the same divine source.

Natural law binds citizens and rulers alike. As a result, according to many philosophers, a legitimate government does not violate natural law. In this line of thinking, citizens are not obligated to follow a ruler who acts against natural law. "If the subjects have a government which commands unjust things," wrote Thomas Aquinas, "they have no obligation to obedience."

The Social Contract Beginning in the 1600s, a number of influential European thinkers contributed to a new theory of rule. **Social contract theory** holds that the first governments formed as a result of people agreeing among themselves to submit to the authority of a state. In return, the state would provide people protection and support. Under this theory, a government is legitimate only so long as the parties to the agreement hand over their power to the state.

The theory dates back to the English philosopher Thomas Hobbes. In his classic work *Leviathan* (1651), Hobbes argues that people originally lived in a "state of nature" without government or laws. In the state of nature, people enjoyed complete personal freedom but were also driven by self-interest and were constantly at war with one another over scarce resources:

> **❝** In such condition there is no place for industry, because the fruit thereof is uncertain . . . no arts, no letters, no society, and, which is worst of all, continual fear and danger of violent death, and the life of man solitary, poor, nasty, brutish, and short. **❞**
>
> —Thomas Hobbes, *Leviathan*, 1651

Because the state of nature is so violent, Hobbes reasons, humans decide to cooperate. That is, they enter into a social contract and form a government.

Hobbes argues that government must have great power to defend itself and compel people to obey its laws. To describe the enormous power wielded by such a state, Hobbes uses the metaphor of a leviathan, a monstrous and powerful biblical sea creature.

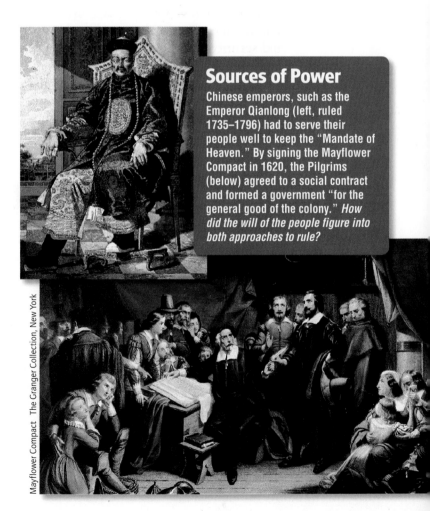

Sources of Power

Chinese emperors, such as the Emperor Qianlong (left, ruled 1735–1796) had to serve their people well to keep the "Mandate of Heaven." By signing the Mayflower Compact in 1620, the Pilgrims (below) agreed to a social contract and formed a government "for the general good of the colony." *How did the will of the people figure into both approaches to rule?*

Mayflower Compact The Granger Collection, New York

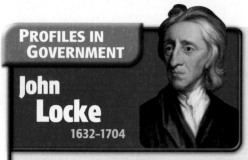
John Locke lived during one of the most turbulent political and intellectual periods in English history. During his lifetime, Locke saw great change, conflict, and experiment in governmental institutions—including debates over religious tolerance and the English monarchy being abolished and later restored—that culminated in the Glorious Revolution and the beginning of the end of the absolute power of the monarchy in Britain.

One of the most influential thinkers of his time, Locke was an inspiration to the Framers of the U.S. Constitution. In particular, the Framers took notice of Locke's social contract theory and his views on natural rights. Locke believed that people were naturally good and that they formed governments in order to preserve the public good. According to Locke, a government had a duty to protect its citizens' natural rights to life, liberty, and property.

Making Inferences How do you think Locke's view of human nature influenced his ideas about government?

The state's power is enormous because it contains all the power given up by the people. In exchange, the people gain peace and security. This, Hobbes asserts, works to everyone's advantage.

English philosopher John Locke (1632–1704) also saw government as the product of a social contract built on the consent of the governed. Locke, however, emphasized that people had natural rights. In his view of the state of nature, people are governed by natural law. They consent to government solely to protect their natural rights, including life, liberty, and property.

Locke believed that in order to protect natural rights from government interference government power had to be limited, or subject to certain restrictions. Any violation of the people's natural rights by government provided grounds for rebellion. In other words, people could withdraw their consent from government and start anew.

French philosopher Jean-Jacques Rousseau (1712–1778) introduced a third vision of the state of nature and the social contract. According to Rousseau, humans lived independent lives in the state of nature, but they were happy, good, and free. It was the formation of societies and government that corrupted the human condition and introduced inequality.

In *The Social Contract* (1762), Rousseau argues that the only way people could regain their freedom was by establishing a government that was both based on a social contract and responsive to the "general will" of the people. As you will read, Rousseau's ideas, as well as Locke's, would profoundly influence early American political leaders.

READING CHECK **Summarizing** What assumptions about human nature did Locke and Rousseau make?

SECTION 1 ASSESSMENT

THINK central **Online Quiz**
thinkcentral.com
KEYWORD: SGO BAS HP

Reviewing Ideas and Terms

1. **a. Describe** What is **government**?
   b. Make Inferences Why do you think larger complex communities require larger and more complex governments?

2. **a. Identify** What are the four characteristics of a **state**?
   b. Make Inferences What might happen if a state is not recognized by other states?

3. **a. Summarize** What are the major functions of government?
   b. Rate Which function of government do you think is most important? Explain.

4. **a. Explain** How is natural law related to natural rights?
   b. Compare How do Hobbes, Locke, and Rousseau understand the state of nature and the social contract differently?

Critical Thinking

5. **Compare and Contrast** Copy the diagram below to contrast theories of rule based on divine right and the social contract.

Divine Right | Social Contract

FOCUS ON WRITING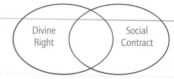

6. **Persuasive** Imagine what life would be like if you lived in the "state of nature" described by Thomas Hobbes. Write a speech to convince others to join with you and form a government.

Eminent Domain: Public Good over Private Property

What rights should the government have over private property?

In 2000 the city of New London, Connecticut, condemned Susette Kelo's house to make way for new housing, offices, and a marina that would generate more money for the city. Kelo fought the decision in court.

THE ISSUE

The Fifth Amendment to the U.S. Constitution guarantees "life, liberty, and property," and states that no person's property can be taken by the government for public use without just compensation. Still the national and state governments can exercise eminent domain, or the power to take private property for public use, presumably to serve the public good. In exchange, eminent domain compels the government to pay property owners a fair price for their land. In cases where the rights of property owners and the power of government are at odds, conflicts arise. Who decides what amounts to "the greater public good"? Whose rights are more important? Who determines a fair price?

VIEWPOINTS

Enabling Eminent Domain Do the economic benefits of private development constitute public use under the Fifth Amendment? In *Kelo* v. *City of New London* (2005), the Supreme Court ruled that private, for-profit development—in this case, tearing down private residences in order to build restaurants, shops, offices, apartments, a hotel—indeed qualifies as public use. The Fifth Amendment did not require a literal definition of public use, the Court held, but instead the "broader and more natural interpretation of public use as 'public purpose.'" The Court reasoned that because it benefited the economic development of the community, the plan did indeed fit the definition of public use.

Restricting Eminent Domain Many Americans worry that the *Kelo* ruling gave local government too much power to seize private property. Some states have already passed legislation to restrict the use of eminent domain. In November 2005, about four months after the *Kelo* decision, the U.S. House of Representatives overwhelmingly voted to pass the Private Property Rights Protection Act. The act specified that federal funds would be withheld from state and local governments that exercise eminent domain over property intended for private economic development. The bill makes allowances for public projects such as building hospitals and roads and in cases of abandoned private property.

What Is Your Opinion?

1. Should government exercise the power of eminent domain to boost a city's or a state's economy? What constitutes abuse of eminent domain?

2. Is the public good always best served through eminent domain? Under what circumstances, if any, might your opinion change?

THINK central **Practice Online**

thinkcentral.com
KEYWORD: SGO BAS

Forms of Government

BEFORE YOU READ

Main Idea
Different forms of governments are categorized based on who exercises authority and how power is organized.

Reading Focus
1. What are the classic forms of government?
2. How is national power organized differently in unitary, federal, and confederal systems?
3. In what ways do presidential and parliamentary systems differ?

Key Terms
monarchy
dictatorship
oligarchy
direct democracy
republic
unitary system
federal system
confederal system
presidential system
parliamentary system

TAKING NOTES As you read, take notes on different types of government systems using a chart like this one.

Form	Details

ONE PEOPLE Two Koreas

WHY IT MATTERS

The Power of Government More than 50 years ago, during the Korean War (1950–1953), the border between North Korea and South Korea was shut down. In the years since, the two countries have followed dramatically different paths.

In the 1980s South Korea developed into a vibrant multiparty democracy and an economic powerhouse. Today South Korea is the world's fourteenth-largest economy and a leading exporter of cars and personal electronics. It is also one of the most digitally connected countries in the world. Wireless Internet, cell phones, and online gaming dominate the nation's popular culture.

Meanwhile, North Korea turned to totalitarianism and communism and sank into poverty. Backed by nuclear capabilities and the world's fifth-largest army, the nation's dictator Kim Jong Il tightly controls all aspects of life in North Korea. Although information about life in North Korea is closely guarded, reports of mass famine, torture, slave labor, prison camps, and public executions have reached the outside world.

The divide between the two Koreas shows just how deeply forms of government affect people's lives. Put simply, it matters a great deal who rules a nation and what form of government is in place. ■

Despite their differences, South Korean president Roh Moo-hyun (above, with his wife) and North Korean dictator Kim Jong Il (right) signed a wide-ranging peace and prosperity pact on October 4, 2007.

The Classic Forms

"Democracy is the worst form of government," British politician Winston Churchill once commented, "except all others that have been tried." One might expect a democratic leader like Churchill to vigorously defend democracy. Instead, he suggests that all forms of government have their problems, and all have the power to do great harm or good to those under their rule. One way to understand how different forms of government affect people's lives is to ask: Who has the authority to rule?

Monarchy In a **monarchy** the government is headed by one person, such as a king or a queen, who exercises supreme authority. Monarchs inherit their position and their power by virtue of being born into a royal family. In an absolute monarchy, their powers are unlimited and unchecked.

Monarchies have been the most common form of rule in world history. Today though, monarchies are rare. In some nations, such as Saudi Arabia, the royal family still exercises ultimate authority. Most present-day kings and queens, however, are ceremonial heads of state for constitutional monarchies. The real power lies in another part of government, such as a legislative body. Spain, Great Britain, and Japan are just a few of the world's 30 constitutional monarchies.

Monarchy is an example of autocracy, any form of government in which a single individual—an autocrat—controls most governing decisions. Placing the bulk of government power in the hands of one person is risky business. As the British historian Lord Acton once commented, "Power tends to corrupt and absolute power tends to corrupt absolutely." In the modern world, Acton's maxim is most clear in nations under the rule of autocrats called dictators.

Dictatorship A **dictatorship** is a system of rule in which one person, a dictator, or a small group of people can hold unlimited power over government. Dictators often achieve power by violently overthrowing a government. They maintain power by force, stifling even peaceful opposition with varying degrees of repression and brutality.

CLASSIC FORMS OF GOVERNMENT

FORM	CHARACTERISTICS
Monarchy Example: Jordan	• Ruled by a monarch, usually a king or a queen, who belongs to a royal family • Power is inherited • Absolute monarchs have unlimited power
Constitutional Monarchy Example: United Kingdom	• Based on the idea that there are limits to the rightful power of a government over its citizens • Power of the monarch is limited by law; the real power lies in another branch of government • May coexist with other forms of government, such as representative democracy
Dictatorship Example: Cuba	• Single dictator or a small group holds absolute authority and makes all decisions • Violence and force used to maintain rule
Totalitarian Regimes Example: North Korea	• Dictator holds ultimate authority • Government tightly controls all aspects of life—political, social, and economic • No formal or informal limits on government
Oligarchy/ Aristocracy Example: ancient Greece (Sparta)	• Small group of powerful people make most government decisions for their own benefit • Membership in the ruling group may be based on wealth, family, or military power
Theocracy Example: Iran	• Rulers claim to represent and be directed by a set of religious ideas • Laws are rooted in a particular religion or religious doctrine • Government power is unlimited
Direct Democracy Example: ancient Greece (Athens)	• Government by the people; citizens are the ultimate source of government authority • Citizens come together to discuss and pass laws and select leaders • Works best in small communities
Republic/ Representative Democracy Example: ancient Rome, United States	• Government by the people; citizens are the ultimate source of government authority • Indirect form of democracy; citizens elect representatives to make government decisions on their behalf • Representatives elected for set terms

The Roman Republic

In 509 BC the Romans established a new form of government—the republic. The essence of the Roman Republic was the Senate, a body of 300 members who advised elected officials, controlled public finances, reviewed proposed laws, and handled all foreign relations.

Dictators may claim that they respond to the will of the people or even that they head democratic states. In reality, most dictators head authoritarian regimes, under which people are subject to various forms of state control. At its most extreme, authoritarianism becomes totalitarianism. Totalitarian governments seek to dominate all aspects of society—the government, the economy, and even people's personal beliefs and actions. Nazi Germany under Hitler, the Soviet Union under Joseph Stalin, China under Mao Zedong, and North Korea under Kim Jong Il are examples of totalitarian regimes.

Some dictatorships may be led by small groups of people, usually members of the military or the economic elite. This state of affairs is sometimes called an **oligarchy**, meaning rule by a few, or an aristocracy. Many dictatorships are secular governments, meaning that their laws and political institutions are independent of religion. Others, however, are theocracies, or governments under the rule of a small group of religious leaders.

Democracy The term democracy means "rule by the people." Strictly speaking, in a pure democracy, the people make major government decisions through a process of majority rule. Whatever the majority of voters wants becomes law.

Such was the state of affairs in Athens and other ancient Greek city-states. Athenian democracy was a **direct democracy**. Citizens met regularly in a popular assembly to discuss issues and vote for leaders. Athenians liked to boast that in their government everyone had equal say. In truth, Athenian democracy was an elite-based system. Only a small fraction of the male population was eligible to participate in political life. Neither women nor slaves, who formed the majority of the population, could participate.

Direct democracy works best in small communities, where people are able to meet face to face. For large, industrialized nations, however, direct democracy is an impractical option. For this reason, most of the world's democracies—the United States included—are republics. A **republic** is an indirect form of democracy that places political decision making at least one step away from the people. In a republic, the people elect representatives to make decisions on their behalf.

Still, forms of direct democracy persist within republics. In the United States, for example, a handful of New England towns govern by holding town meetings, in which all townspeople have a say in setting policy.

People often use the terms *republic* and *representative democracy* interchangeably to describe the U.S. political system. The main point about a representative democracy is that people are the ultimate source of government authority. In such a system, elected representatives closely follow the wishes of the people, elections are free and fair, and everyone has equal opportunity to participate in the political process.

READING CHECK **Identifying the Main Idea** Who holds political power in a representative democracy?

Organizing National Power

Most national governments consist of a number of smaller administrative units—states, cities, or provinces. The power to govern these units can be spread across different geographic regions or it can be centralized. In addition to understanding who governs, it is important to ask: How is national power organized across regions?

Unitary Systems The vast majority of the world's nations have unitary systems of government. In a **unitary system**, sovereignty, or ultimate authority, rests in a single, national government. The United Kingdom, France, and Japan are leading examples of unitary governments.

In unitary systems, local levels of government may be active and important agencies of rule, but the national government has ultimate authority. It also has the power to change or abolish local governments as it sees fit. In the United Kingdom, for example, the British Parliament still has authority to override and even dismantle the parliaments of Northern Ireland and Scotland.

Federal Systems A **federal system** of government divides power over people and territory between a national government and smaller, regional levels of government. As it exists today, the federal system is largely an American invention—the product of compromises made by the Framers of the U.S. Constitution over balancing national power and states' rights.

The U.S. federal system consists of two levels—an overarching national government and 50 state governments. Both levels have the power to make their own laws, elect officials, and create agencies. A significant feature of American federalism is that each level has the power to act independently of the other level, and neither level can abolish or reorganize the other level at will.

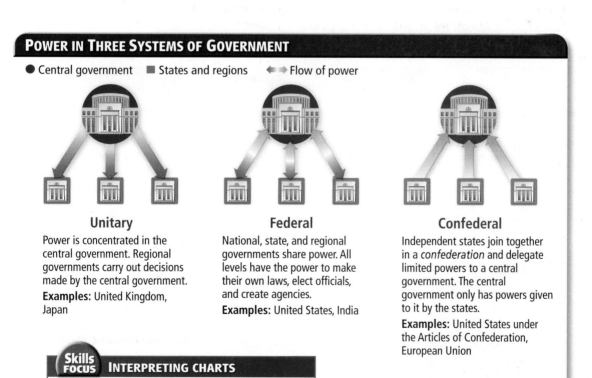

POWER IN THREE SYSTEMS OF GOVERNMENT

● Central government   ■ States and regions   ⬅➡ Flow of power

Unitary
Power is concentrated in the central government. Regional governments carry out decisions made by the central government.
Examples: United Kingdom, Japan

Federal
National, state, and regional governments share power. All levels have the power to make their own laws, elect officials, and create agencies.
Examples: United States, India

Confederal
Independent states join together in a *confederation* and delegate limited powers to a central government. The central government only has powers given to it by the states.
Examples: United States under the Articles of Confederation, European Union

Skills FOCUS **INTERPRETING CHARTS**

In which system of government do states and regions exercise the most power?

For example, Congress cannot redraw the boundaries of California to give more land to Oregon and Nevada.

While it is no longer uniquely American, the federal system is still a comparatively uncommon form of government. Only 25 of the world's 190 or so nations have federal systems. Among these are Canada, India, Germany, Mexico, Nigeria, and Brazil.

Confederal Systems In a **confederal system** independent states join forces by forming a central government, called a confederation. The states keep full control over their own territories and people. However, the states delegate limited powers to a central government to pursue areas of common interests, such as providing for national defense and regulating trade.

In its earliest days under the Articles of Confederation, the United States operated as a confederal system. With the exception of the United Arab Emirates and the European Union, present-day confederations are rare.

READING CHECK Comparing How is power divided in federal, unitary, and confederal systems?

Presidents and Parliaments

People often believe that their government is the only or even the best way of doing things. But, as the discussion of unitary, federal, and confederal systems shows, there is no one way for a nation to organize power. All governments are born out of unique historical circumstances, developing their own special features and institutions. This is true, too, for democracy. Today most countries have adopted some form of democratic government. Even as they follow their own particular paths, the world's democracies fall into two types of political systems—presidential and parliamentary.

Presidential Systems Many of the world's governments are modeled after the presidential system of the United States. In general, a **presidential system** is distinguished by having a president that is elected by the people for a limited term of office.

In addition to performing the symbolic duties of a head of state, the president is in charge of the executive branch of government.

Presidential and Parliamentary Systems

Many of the world's presidential systems have been modeled on the U.S. system, while the world's parliamentary systems have taken the British system as a model. In July 2007, President George Bush welcomed a newly elected British Prime Minister, Gordon Brown, on his first official visit to the United States.

Presidential	Parliamentary
ADVANTAGES	**ADVANTAGES**
• President is elected by the people for a fixed term and cannot be dismissed	• The legislative and executive branches are often united in purpose
• Separation of powers prevents abuses of authority	• Prime minister directly accountable to parliament
• Independent of other branches of government	• Easier to pass legislation
• President is able to make decisions quickly and independently	**DISADVANTAGES**
DISADVANTAGES	• Few checks and balances
• Difficult to remove an unsuitable president from office	• Prime minister selected by the legislative branch, not by the people
• Separation of powers may lead to gridlock	• Prime minister lacks independence
• Branches of government may have different agendas	
• Presidents may become too strong	
• Many presidential systems have become authoritarian	

Skills FOCUS INTERPRETING CHARTS

Which of the advantages and disadvantages listed in the chart might explain why more of the world's democracies follow a parliamentary system of government?

He or she appoints cabinet members to oversee major state bureaucracies, executes policy, serves as the head of the armed forces, and is responsible for setting foreign policy and initiating domestic legislation.

A key feature—and an important strength—of presidential systems is that the president's powers are balanced by a legislature, which is both popularly elected and independent of the president. This has important implications for how a president exercises power. Because the president and the legislature are independent of one another, they must work together to get things done. For example, in the United States, the president may be commander in chief of the armed forces, but only Congress can declare war. Similarly, Congress relies on the president to approve and carry out the laws that it passes.

Divided government can also be a drawback to presidential systems. In the United States, if the president and members of Congress hold opposing political views, they may refuse to cooperate. The result is political stalemate. In the worst of such situations, little gets accomplished—Congress is unable to pass laws without the president's support. Without Congress's support, an otherwise powerful president becomes immobilized.

Parliamentary Systems Most of the world's democracies, by contrast, are modeled after the British parliamentary system. In a **parliamentary system**, the executive and legislative branches of government are combined. In place of a popularly elected president, parliamentary systems have a prime minister, who is chosen by and from an elected legislature called parliament.

The prime minister is not only a member of parliament; he or she is also the leader of parliament's majority party. Once selected, the prime minister appoints cabinet members from the ranks of the majority party. Should the prime minister ever lose support of the majority party, he or she must resign immediately, as do the cabinet members. Members of parliament then choose another prime minister, or else a new election is called in which voters choose a new parliament.

Combining the executive and legislative branches is both an advantage and a disadvantage for parliamentary systems. Some observers argue that it is easier to pass laws in a parliamentary system. Others take issue with the fact that prime ministers are neither directly elected by the people nor able to effectively take a stand against parliament.

READING CHECK Contrasting How does electing a president differ from electing a prime minister?

WHAT DO YOU THINK?

What might happen in a government in which there was no agreed on or peaceful means for removing officials? Give a recent example to support your answer.

SECTION 2 ASSESSMENT

THINK central Online Quiz
thinkcentral.com
KEYWORD: SGO BAS HP

Reviewing Ideas and Terms

1. **a. Define** What is the meaning of the following terms: **direct democracy, republic, monarchy, dictatorship**?
   b. Compare and Contrast How are democracies and republics similar to and different from one another?
   c. Predict What circumstances might lead to people's rights being denied in a direct democracy?

2. **a. Identify** How is power organized in a **unitary system**?
   b. Draw Conclusions Why do you think a federal system replaced the confederal form of government that was first tried in the United States?

3. **a. Describe** What are the potential disadvantages of a **presidential system**?
   b. Design If you were designing a plan of government for a new democracy, would you plan for a presidential or parliamentary system? Explain.

Critical Thinking

4. **Compare and Contrast** Copy the graphic organizer below, and compare and contrast how power is shared and limited in presidential and parliamentary systems.

Presidential   Parliamentary

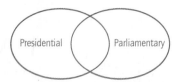
FOCUS ON WRITING

5. **Persuasive** Write a speech arguing in favor of a particular form of government for a newly founded nation. Be sure to address the question of who should hold power and how power should be organized.

Democracy in the United States

Main Idea

American democracy is characterized by core democratic ideals and principles, as well as by the free enterprise system.

Reading Focus

1. Why are the ideals of liberty, equality, and self-government important to American democracy?
2. What are the principles of American democracy?
3. Why is the free enterprise system important to American democracy?

Key Terms

ideal
liberty
equality
self-government
majority rule
minority rights
liberal democracy
free enterprise

TAKING NOTES As you read, take notes on democracy in the United States. Record your notes in a graphic organizer like this one.

Democracy in the U.S.

Small Steps toward Democracy

First-grade student Ruby Bridges leaves William Frantz Elementary School in New Orleans under protection of federal marshals in 1960.

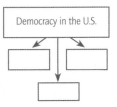

WHY IT MATTERS

Approaching an Ideal In 1954 the U.S. Supreme Court issued a ruling that struck down state-sponsored racial segregation in public schools. The ruling was hailed by many people as a bold step toward the realization of one of the most cherished ideals of American democracy—equality.

The next steps, however, would require much more courage. These steps were often taken by young African American children. In order to make the ruling a reality, these children would have to walk past crowds of angry white protestors and into the school.

In 1960 six-year-old Ruby Bridges, flanked by federal marshals, made this walk to reach her first-grade classroom. She was the only African American student assigned to the all-white school in her New Orleans, Louisiana, neighborhood.

Ruby and her family faced many challenges. People threatened them. Ruby's father lost his job and her grandparents, who lived in Mississippi, were forced to move when the white people who owned the land they farmed found out about the events in New Orleans. Still, the Bridges family supported Ruby through what they knew was a key battle in the struggle for social equality—school integration. Ruby, with the federal government and her family's support, bravely met the challenges. ■

Ideals of American Democracy

An **ideal** is a conception of something in its most perfect form. Liberty, equality, and self-government are the core ideals of American democracy. These ideals have been with us since the earliest days of our republic. They were put into words in our nation's founding documents, and they have guided the expansion of American democracy for more than two centuries.

At our nation's beginning, these ideals applied to only a small set of people. When the Framers of the Constitution set pen to paper on behalf of "We, the People," they did not speak for all Americans. If they had, women, free African Americans, men without property, and slaves would have had a voice in the political process.

American democracy has evolved over time, and it is still changing. As they have in the past, Americans continue to look to the ideals of liberty, equality, and self-government while shaping the democratic experiment.

Liberty More than anything, the Founders of our nation aspired to **liberty**, or the ability of people to act and think as they choose, so long as their choices do no harm to the liberty or well-being of others. Another word for liberty is freedom. It was for liberty that the American patriot Patrick Henry declared himself ready to die; it was in the name of "Life, Liberty, and the Pursuit of Happiness" that the 13 American colonies banded together to declare independence. And, once the Revolutionary War was over, the Framers of the Constitution crafted a new plan for government to "secure the Blessings of Liberty to Ourselves and our Posterity."

In the early days of the republic, liberty was thought of mainly as *freedom from* government control. The Framers carefully identified the basic rights of the people and then declared them off-limits from government interference. "Congress shall make no law," the First Amendment says, that restricts an individual's right to speak, assemble, publish, or worship freely.

Liberty also refers to a person's *freedom to* exercise the rights guaranteed to all U.S. citizens under the Constitution. In this sense, citizens are free to vote, free to exercise their right to counsel, free to experience equal rights and equal protection under the law, and free to fulfill their potential. In this last sense, liberty is clearly not defined by the absence of government restraints. Government intervention may in fact be required to protect the rights of citizens. For example, extensive government action was necessary to protect the right of Ruby Bridges to an education and to ensure her equal protection under the law.

Equality Like liberty, Americans have embraced equality as a worthy democratic pursuit. **Equality** is the principle that all people possess a fundamental, moral worth that entitles them to fair treatment under the law and equal opportunity in all aspects of life—political, social, and economic. It was in this sense that Thomas Jefferson eloquently argued that "We hold these truths to be self-evident, that all men are created equal, and they are endowed by their Creator with certain unalienable rights."

In *Democracy in America* (1835), the French noble Alexis de Tocqueville was among the first to seriously explore the meaning of equality in American culture. Tocqueville saw the United States leading "a great democratic revolution" that would sweep the world. In the 1830s, he travelled to the United States, where he set off on a journey that led him across the nation, from New York, down the Mississippi River, and into the lower South. Tocqueville deeply admired the widespread political and economic equality he observed. He saw this as American democracy's great promise but also worried that equality was incomplete and that it could even be a peril to liberty.

Tocqueville was among the first to note that the American quest for equality was unfinished business. On his travels, he witnessed firsthand glaring examples of inequality, including the poor treatment of Native Americans and what he called "the abomination of slavery."

> ## Ideals of American Democracy
>
> - **Liberty** All people have the ability or freedom to act and think as they choose.
> - **Equality** All people possess the same fundamental moral worth that entitles them to fair treatment.
> - **Self-Government** Ordinary people can rule themselves and do so as political equals.

Democracy in America

Alexis de Tocqueville took note of two aspects of American culture that he saw as central to self-government: participation in voluntary associations and a commitment to the common good.

❝ I must say that I have often seen Americans make great and real sacrifices to the public welfare; and I have noticed a hundred instances in which they hardly ever failed to lend faithful support to one another. The free institutions which the inhabitants of the United States possess, and the political rights of which they make so much use, remind every citizen, and in a thousand ways, that he lives in society. They every instant impress upon his mind the notion that it is the duty as well as the interest of men to make themselves useful to their fellow creatures; and as he sees no particular ground of animosity to them . . . his heart readily leans to the side of kindness. Men attend to the interests of the public, first by necessity, afterwards by choice; what was intentional becomes an instinct, and by dint of working for the good of one's fellow citizens, the habit and the taste for serving them are at length acquired. ❞

—Alexis de Tocqueville, *Democracy in America*, 1835

Skills FOCUS **INTERPRETING PRIMARY SOURCES**

Analyzing Primary Sources Why do you think Tocqueville thought that a commitment to the common good was essential to democracy?

See **Skills Handbook**, p. H6.

ACADEMIC VOCABULARY

despotism a political system in which the ruler exercises absolute power

Although Tocqueville applauded the goals of American democracy, he feared that people might give too much power to a central government to achieve equality. He called this democratic despotism, a subtle form of tyranny that could reduce a nation's people to a "herd of timid and industrious animals." This was democracy's peril. For democracy to truly work, equality had to be kept in balance with liberty.

Self-Government From the beginning of our republic, Americans have held fast to the ideal of **self-government**, or the belief that ordinary people could aspire to rule themselves and do so as political equals. The key to self-government is that people are the ultimate source of government authority.

The belief that the only just government was a government that derived its powers directly from the consent of the people set the American Revolution in motion. The Declaration of Independence plainly states this ideal: "Governments are instituted among Men, deriving their just powers from the consent of the governed." Moreover, the Declaration contends that, should a government lose consent, it is "the Right of the People to alter or to abolish it, and to institute new Government." In short, the people have a right to revolution. This is, of course, exactly what happened.

READING CHECK **Summarizing** What steps did the Founders take to protect liberty?

Principles of American Democracy

Today our sense of who we are as Americans is deeply bound—indeed, inseparable from—our belief in the democratic ideals of liberty, equality, and self-government. But ideals are goals, and democracy is not something that already exists or something that just happens. A commitment to uphold and act upon each of the following principles is necessary to maintain American democracy.

Worth of the Individual American democracy places a high value on individual freedom, personal responsibility, self-reliance, and individual achievement. The deep respect that Americans hold for the individual is strongly tied to the belief that, if left free to pursue their own path, people can reach their highest potential.

These beliefs are rooted in the values our nation's Founders held for the individual's natural capacity for reason, intellect, and self-determination. The words in the Declaration of Independence that express the Founders' sentiments bear repeating: "all men are created equal" and are born with rights to "Life, Liberty, and the Pursuit of Happiness." For the Founders, this positive estimation of human nature and natural rights was the foundation of self-rule.

Rule of Law The Framers of the U.S. Constitution aimed to create a government under the rule of law. John Adams described the United States as "a government of laws, not of men." In other words, the U.S. government and its officials are subject to recognized and enforced limits on their powers. These limits are spelled out in the U.S. Constitution. Ideally, the rule of law forces leaders to act according to the law and holds them accountable when they do not.

Majority Rule, Minority Rights A basic principle of democracy is that decisions are made by **majority rule**. Ideally, a candidate wins an election by a majority, by getting more than half of the votes cast. In fact, candidates typically win by a plurality, or by getting more votes than any other candidate.

The Framers fretted over granting any group—even a majority—too much political power. Any such imbalance, they believed, could pose a direct threat to the rights of individuals and to the common good. For this reason, they took measures to protect individual rights, such as freedom of speech, as well as government institutions, such as the Supreme Court, against what they called the "tyranny of the majority."

Americans believe strongly that a balance must be struck between majority rule and protecting minority rights. **Minority rights** are the political rights held by groups who make up less than half of the population. In a **liberal democracy**, such as the United States, the individual rights and liberties of all people, including those in the minority, are protected. In addition, all citizens have the right to express their opinions, even if their views are not popular. In turn, those in the majority have a responsibility to respect the views of the minority. Successful liberal democracies achieve balance between majority and minority groups through debate, political persuasion, and elections.

Compromise Another key principle of American democracy is compromise, the ability of two opposing groups to give up some of their demands and come to an agreement. In part, the necessity for compromise is a by-product of the diversity of the American people. In the American political system, there is rarely a shortage of political interests and issues. For example, some people may think that government should raise taxes to fund math and science training for young people entering today's competitive technological job market. Others might argue that they are taxed unfairly and that they should have their taxes cut. When such conflicts occur, compromise is necessary to keep the political process moving.

Citizen Participation To be successful, self-government requires participation from citizens. At the very least, citizens must be informed about public issues so that they can participate effectively, whether by voting or by running for office. In a strong democracy people participate in the political process at all levels. They become informed of the issues, speak their minds, serve on juries, debate public issues, hold their leaders accountable, attend community meetings, volunteer for military and social service, pay taxes, and join political parties. They must even be willing, on occasion, to stand in protest for what they believe. Yet participation must also be peaceful, respectful of the law, and tolerant of the rights and liberties of others.

READING CHECK **Drawing Conclusions** Why is it important to protect minority rights in a democracy?

Key Principles of American Democracy

- **Worth of the Individual** All people are created equal and deserve an opportunity to pursue their potential.
- **Rule of Law** Government is subject to recognized and enforced limits.
- **Majority Rule/Minority Rights** The majority rules but the rights of the political minority are protected.
- **Compromise** Despite their differences, opposing groups can reach agreements.
- **Citizen Participation** A healthy democracy requires active citizen participation at all levels.

Responsible Citizenship

Citizen participation at all levels of government and society is key to the success of American democracy. Below, volunteers working for AmeriCorps, a national service organization, help clear tree limbs from an Oklahoma neighborhood after an ice storm.

LANDMARK SUPREME COURT CASES

Constitutional Issue: Due Process

DIVISION FOR
PUBLIC
EDUCATION
AMERICAN BAR ASSOCIATION

Gideon v. Wainwright (1963)

WHY IT MATTERS *The U.S. Supreme Court has ruled on a number of cases concerning democratic ideals and principles. In* Gideon v. Wainwright, *the Court considered whether the right to counsel was necessary to guarantee a defendant's liberty and ensure equality under the law.*

Background

On June 3, 1961, someone broke into the Bay Harbor Pool Room in Panama City, Florida, and smashed a cigarette machine and a jukebox, stealing money from both machines. Later that day, Clarence Earl Gideon was arrested and charged with the crime of breaking and entering. Gideon, a known drifter, was found with change in his pockets and a bottle of wine. A witness later told police that he had seen Gideon in the pool-room on the day of the burglary.

Gideon could not afford a defense attorney, and a Florida judge refused to appoint him one. Forced to defend himself, Gideon was found guilty and sentenced to five years in a state penitentiary. In prison, Gideon studied the law. He determined that his lack of legal counsel was a denial of due process, meaning that without a lawyer, Gideon had been unfairly deprived of "life, liberty, and property." Armed with this argument, Gideon appealed his case to the Florida Supreme Court, but the lower court's decision was upheld. The U.S. Supreme Court agreed to review his case in 1963.

Arguments for Gideon

Gideon argued that the court's failure to appoint him counsel violated his right to a fair trial and due process of law as protected by the Sixth and Fourteenth Amendments of the U.S. Constitution. In prison, Gideon filed a petition with the Florida Supreme Court for release because of unjust imprisonment. The court denied his request. Gideon appealed to the U.S. Supreme Court, filing suit against the Secretary of the Florida Division of Corrections, Louie L. Wainwright.

Arguments for Wainwright

In *Betts* v. *Brady* (1942) the U.S. Supreme Court had previously ruled that, in criminal trials, states only had to provide defendants with counsel under special circumstances, including the complexity of the criminal charges as well as the defendant's mental state and ability to read and write. Since Gideon had not claimed any special circumstances, the Florida Supreme Court had upheld the lower court's decision. At the time, Florida state law only provided defendants with lawyers in capital cases, or cases in which the death penalty could be inflicted.

THE IMPACT TODAY On March 18, 1963, in a unanimous decision, the U.S. Supreme Court overturned *Betts* and ruled in favor of Gideon. The Court held that the right to counsel was essential to a fair trial. Thus, a person who could not afford legal counsel had to be provided with counsel by the state or the national government. Subsequent Court decisions extended the *Gideon* ruling to all felonies and misdemeanors that can result in prison time. Because the quality of state-provided defense counsel varies from state to state, the Court established in *Strickland* v. *Washington* (1984) a two-part test for determining the adequacy of any counsel, including a court-appointed one. Such rulings have changed the nation's perspective on the rights of criminal defendants.

CRITICAL THINKING

What Do You Think? Today all states are required to provide lawyers for criminal defendants who can not afford to pay for legal representation on their own. What measures do you think states should take to ensure quality legal representation for all criminal defendants?

Research Supreme Court cases at thinkcentral.com. **KEYWORD:** SGO SCC

Free Enterprise

Of all the freedoms held dear to American democracy—freedom of speech, religion, and the press—economic freedom holds a special place. This freedom is best expressed in the economic system of the United States, the free enterprise system. **Free enterprise** allows for people and businesses to make their own economic choices about how best to produce, distribute, and exchange goods and services with limited interference from government. It also protects rights of ownership to the results of one's labor and to one's property.

Our nation's Founders believed deeply that safeguarding economic freedom was key to preserving other freedoms. In this regard, they were influenced by John Locke, who asserted that people have a natural right to "life, liberty, and property." Equally important, the Founders believed that economic freedom allowed people to build wealth that would empower them to limit the power of government.

A free market—a market outside the control of government—is essential to free enterprise. If left alone, the thinking goes, individuals and businesses will compete with each other to offer better products at lower prices in a free market. Those who succeed in this competition will prosper. Their prosperity, in turn, will benefit society and the economy overall.

Like all freedoms, free enterprise is a matter of degrees. Over time, the U.S.

The Free Market and the Individual

The U.S. free enterprise system is based on the free market and driven by individuals. As president and Chief Executive Officer of eBay, Margaret Whitman leads businesses in a new frontier of the free market—the Internet.

government has often found it necessary to interfere in the economy. Today, in an age of globalization, Internet marketplaces, and nonrenewable resources, many people argue that a completely free market is unrealistic. Still, the U.S. economy holds true to basic principles of the free-enterprise system. The proper balance between government intervention in and noninvolvement with the economy is something that will continue to change over time.

READING CHECK **Summarizing** Why did the Founders think protecting economic freedom was important?

SECTION 3 ASSESSMENT

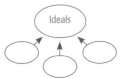
THINK central **Online Quiz**
thinkcentral.com
KEYWORD: SGO BAS HP

Reviewing Ideas and Terms

1. **a. Describe** What are the ideals of American democracy?
   b. Evaluate Which ideal of American democracy do you think is most important? Explain.

2. **a. Define** What is the rule of law?
   b. Predict What would happen to American democracy if citizens stopped participating in political and social life?

3. **a. Explain** Why was protecting economic freedom important to the Founders?
   b. Elaborate Under what circumstances do you think government involvement in the economy might be justified?

Critical Thinking

4. **Analyze** Copy the graphic organizer below, and identify and describe three core ideals of American democracy.

Ideals

FOCUS ON WRITING

5. **Expository** Write a letter to the editor urging either more or less government involvement in the U.S. economy. Draw on democratic ideals and principles to support your argument.

Constitutional Government

Our nation's Founders struggled with how best to prevent government abuse of power. Their answer was to establish a constitutional government that protected individual rights by placing limits on what government can do and how it can exercise power.

What is a constitution? As it is understood today, a constitution is a plan that sets forth the structure and powers of government. Constitutions specify the main institutions of government. In so doing constitutions state the powers of each of these institutions and the procedures that the institutions must use to make, enforce, and interpret law. Usually constitutions also specify how they can be changed, or amended. In the American conception of constitutional government the constitution is a form of higher, or fundamental, law that everyone, including those in power, must obey.

Many controversies surround written constitutions, including what the words mean, whether the understanding of the document should evolve or remain unchanged, and who should have the final say about what the document means. Nearly all constitutions are written. Only three of the world's major democracies have unwritten constitutions—that is, constitutions that are not single written documents. These are Britain, Israel, and New Zealand. In each of these nations, the constitution consists of a combination of written laws and precedents.

Constitutional government means limited government—government limited by the provisions of the constitution. Limited government is characterized by restraints on power as specified by the constitution. In democracies, for example, one restraint is the inclusion of free, fair, and regular elections. The opposite is unlimited government, in which those who govern are free to use their power as they choose, unrestrained by laws or elections. Aristotle described the unlimited government of a single ruler as tyranny. Today the terms autocracy, dictatorship, or totalitarianism often are used to describe such governments. Believing that they had been subjected to tyranny by the British king, the Founders also believed that government in the newly independent United States of America should be limited by the higher law of a written constitution.

How did the Founders characterize higher law? According to the founding generation, a constitution should function as a type of higher law. A higher law differs from a statute enacted by a legislature in these four ways:

- It sets forth the basic rights of citizens.
- It establishes the responsibility of the government to protect those rights.
- It establishes limitations on how those in government may use their power with regard to citizens' rights and responsibilities, the distribution of resources, and control or management of conflict.
- It can be changed only with the consent of the citizens and according to established and well-known procedures.

Adapted with permission from Lesson 1 of *We the People: The Citizen & the Constitution*. Copyright 2009, Center for Civic Education.

Why did the Founders fear government abuse of power? Given their knowledge of history and their experiences under British rule, it is not surprising that the Founders feared possible abuses of governmental powers.

> **❝**Give all power to the many, they will oppress the few. Give all power to the few, they will oppress the many.**❞**
>
> —Alexander Hamilton, 1787

> **❝**There are two passions which have a powerful influence on the affairs of men. These are ambition and avarice; the love of power and the love of money.**❞**
>
> —Benjamin Franklin, 1787

> **❝**From the nature of man, we may be sure that those who have power in their hands . . . will always, when they can . . . increase it. **❞**
>
> —George Mason, 1787

What kinds of governments may be constitutional governments? The Founders knew that constitutional government might take many forms. It is possible to have a constitutional government with one ruler, a group of rulers, or rule by the people as a whole so long as those in power must obey the limitations placed on them by the "higher law" of the constitution. Historically, constitutional governments have included monarchies, republics, democracies, and various combinations of these forms of government.

The problem for any constitutional government is to make sure that those in power obey constitutional limits. History provides many examples of rulers who ignored constitutions or tried illegally to increase their personal power. The Founders believed that direct democracy was more likely to ignore constitutional limits than representative government. Direct democracy makes it easy for momentary passions to inflame people and leads to passionate rather than reasoned judgments. The interests of the community as well as the rights of individuals in the minority may suffer as a result.

The Constitutional Convention that met in Philadelphia in 1787 wrote a plan of government for the United States that, after more than 200 years, remains strong.

Reviewing Ideas

1. **Recall** Why is a constitution considered a higher law, and what are the major characteristics of higher law?

2. **Explain** What is the difference between limited and unlimited government? Do you think the difference is important?

Critical Thinking

3. **Evaluate** Is it important that a constitution be written? What are the advantages and disadvantages of a written constitution? Of an unwritten constitution?

Chapter Review

Connecting Online

Visit **thinkcentral.com** for review and enrichment activities related to this chapter.

KEYWORD: SGO BAS

Quiz and Review

GOV 101
Examine key concepts in this chapter.

ONLINE QUIZZES
Take a practice quiz for each section in this chapter.

Activities

eActivities
Complete Webquests and Internet research activities.

INTERACTIVE FEATURES
Explore interactive versions of maps and charts.

KEEP IT CURRENT
Link to current events in U.S. government.

Partners

American Bar Association Division for Public Education
Learn more about the law, your rights and responsibilities.

Center for Civic Education
Promoting an enlightened and responsible citizenry committed to democratic principles and actively engaged in the practice of democracy.

Online Textbook

ONLINE SIMULATIONS
Learn about U.S. government through simulations you can complete online.

Comprehension and Critical Thinking

SECTION 1 *(pp. 6–12)*

1. a. Review Key Terms For each term, write a sentence that explains its significance or meaning: government, state, sovereignty, politics, legitimacy, divine right of kings, social contract theory.

b. Summarize According to philosophers such as Hobbes, Locke, and Rousseau, why are people willing to enter into a social contract?

c. Rate What type of government do you think is best suited to accomplish the purposes of government outlined in this section?

SECTION 2 *(pp. 14–19)*

2. a. Review Key Terms For each term, write a sentence that explains its significance or meaning: monarchy, dictatorship, oligarchy, direct democracy, republic.

b. Contrast What are the main differences between federal, unitary, and confederal systems?

c. Evaluate Which advantages and disadvantages might explain why there are more parliamentary than presidential systems?

SECTION 3 *(pp. 20–25)*

3. a. Review Key Terms For each term, write a sentence that explains its significance or meaning: ideal, liberty, equality, self-government, free enterprise.

b. Analyze Why do you think that the ideal of liberty is important to the free enterprise system?

c. Elaborate Under what circumstances do you think the government should regulate business in a free enterprise system?

Critical Reading

Read the passage in Section 2 that begins with the heading "The Classic Forms." Then answer the questions that follow.

4. Which of the following is an example of limited government?

A dictatorship

B authoritarian regime

C constitutional monarchy

D oligarchy

5. Which of the following forms of governments has elected representatives that make decisions on behalf of the people?

A monarchy

B authoritarian regime

C direct democracy

D representative democracy

Read the passage in Section 3 that begins with the heading "Principles of American Democracy." Then answer the questions that follow.

6. Which principle of American democracy holds government officials accountable to the law?

  A worth of the individual

  B rule of law

  C majority rule

  D minority rights

7. Why did the Framers of the U.S. Constitution fear majority rule?

  A Majority rule would ensure minority rights.

  B Majority rule could pose a threat to the rights of individuals.

  C Majority rule could lead to a theocracy.

  D Majority rule could not coexist with minority rights and democracy.

RESPONSIBILITIES OF LEADERSHIP

8. Create a four-column chart or spreadsheet contrasting **classic forms of government**. In the first column list forms of government: monarchy, dictatorship, totalitarian regime, theocracy, oligarchy, aristocracy, constitutional monarchy, republic/representative democracy, and direct democracy. In the second column include a definition and one historical or present-day example for each form. In the third column record details about how leaders are selected and identify the government as limited or unlimited. Use the fourth column to tell how each form affects people's private lives and describe the rights and responsibilities of citizens living under that government. Conduct library or Internet research as necessary to complete the chart or spreadsheet.

CONNECTING TO THE CONSTITUTION

9. Read the Preamble to the U.S. Constitution in the Reference Section at the end of your textbook. According to the Preamble, what is the main purpose of the Constitution? Explain the meaning of each of its stated purposes.

ANALYZING PRIMARY SOURCES

Excerpt *In* Leviathan *(1651), Thomas Hobbes argued that to create an effective government capable of imposing order, people had to agree to surrender power to a central authority.*

> "The only way to erect such a common power, as may be able to defend them from the invasion of foreigners, and the injuries of one another, and thereby to secure them in such sort as that by their own industry and by the fruits of the earth they may nourish themselves and live contentedly, is to confer all their power and strength upon one man, or upon one assembly of men, that may reduce all their wills, by plurality of voices, unto one will."

10. Analyze According to Hobbes, how do people benefit from giving their power to the state?

11. Draw Conclusions What is the source of the state's power?

FOCUS ON WRITING

Persuasive Writing *Persuasive writing takes a position for or against an issue, using facts and examples as supporting evidence. To practice persuasive writing, complete the assignment below.*

Writing Topic: Voting and Constitutional Democracy

12. Assignment The United States is the world's oldest constitutional democracy. However, research shows that American citizens vote less often than citizens of other nations. Based on what you have read in this chapter, write a paragraph persuading people to vote. Explain why voting is necessary to maintain constitutional democracy and American democratic ideals. Support your position with reasoning and examples from the chapter.

CHAPTER 2 Origins of AMERICAN GOVERNMENT

"WE DARE NOT FORGET TODAY THAT WE ARE THE HEIRS OF THAT FIRST REVOLUTION."

—JOHN F. KENNEDY, 1961

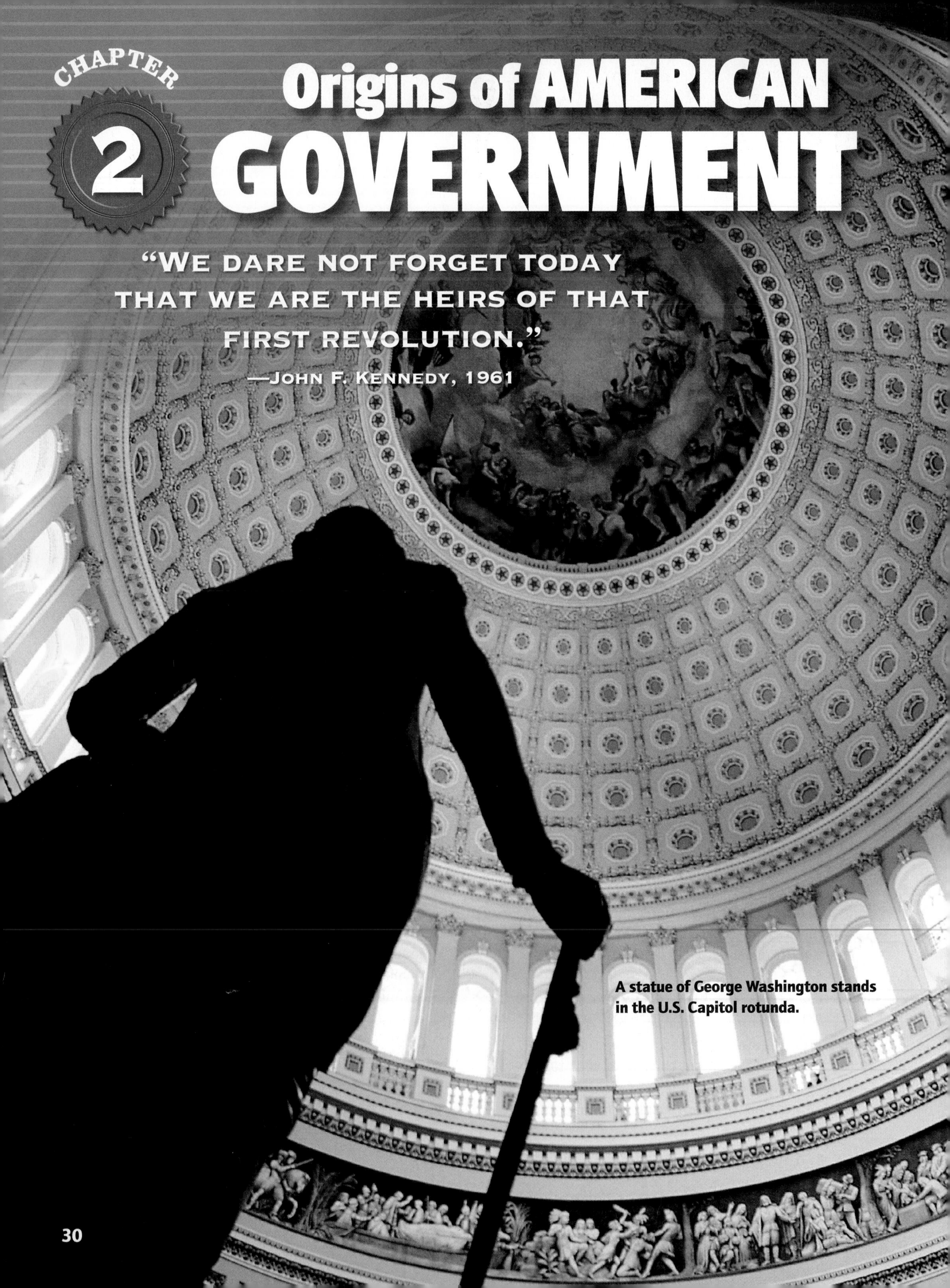

A statue of George Washington stands in the U.S. Capitol rotunda.

CHAPTER AT A GLANCE

SECTION 1

The Roots of American Democracy

- The English political heritage of representative government, limited government, and individual rights influenced the development of government in the United States.

- From the start, the English colonies in North America experimented with forms of self-government.

- The English colonists were influenced by ideas from various intellectual traditions, ranging from republicanism to natural rights theory, Judeo-Christian ideals and the work of Enlightenment thinkers.

SECTION 2

American Independence

- After the French and Indian War, the colonists rebelled against British attempts to assert control over the colonies and against new British taxes.

- In 1775 the Second Continental Congress called for the writing of a formal Declaration of Independence.

SECTION 3

Articles of Confederation

- In 1777 the Second Continental Congress passed the first official plan for national government, the Articles of Confederation.

- After the Revolutionary War, weaknesses in the Articles led to conflicts among the states, sparking calls for a stronger national government.

SECTION 4

The Constitutional Convention

- At the Constitutional Convention in Philadelphia, delegates debated competing plans—the Virginia Plan and the New Jersey Plan—for how the new government should be organized.

- To finalize the Constitution, delegates compromised on key issues.

SECTION 5

Ratification and the Bill of Rights

- Ratification of the Constitution involved a heated debate between those who supported the Constitution and those who opposed it.

- Antifederalists opposed the Constitution because it lacked a bill of rights.

- The *Federalist Papers* outlined the key ideas of the Federalists, who supported the Constitution.

- The struggle for ratification took place in every state.

CONNECTING TO THE CONSTITUTION

Our nation's system of government is based on constitutional law established by the United States Constitution. See the "We the People: The Citizen and the Constitution" pages in this chapter for an in-depth exploration of the national government and the Bill of Rights.

The Roots of American Democracy

Main Idea

American democracy was shaped by our English political heritage, colonial experiments in self-government, and a range of intellectual influences.

Reading Focus

1. Which American political ideas derived from an English political heritage?

2. How did colonial governments give English colonists experience in self-rule?

3. What intellectual influences shaped the development of American political philosophy?

Key Terms

bicameral
Magna Carta
Petition of Right
English Bill of Rights
Fundamental Orders of Connecticut
proprietary colony
royal colonies
charter colonies

TAKING NOTES As you read, take notes on the political ideas and historical events that shaped government in the English colonies. Record your notes in a chart like this one.

Ideas	Events

WHY IT MATTERS

Cradle of American Democracy In April 1607, more than 10 years before the Pilgrims landed at Plymouth Rock, three small wooden ships—the *Susan Constant*, the *Godspeed*, and the *Discovery*—landed on the marshy shores of coastal Virginia. The ships carried just over 100 English men and boys. In little over a month's time, they built a fort and founded Jamestown, the first permanent English settlement in North America.

Within six months, however, more than half of the colonists were dead, mostly from famine. These troubled early days are what most Americans know of Jamestown. But Jamestown should also be remembered for something more significant.

Jamestown was the birthplace of American democracy. In 1619 a series of reforms were made to attract more settlers to Jamestown. One of the reforms permitted the colonists to elect a representative body modeled after the English Parliament. On July 30, 1619, the first representative assembly in North America met at a church in Jamestown. The 22 burgesses, or representatives, in attendance passed laws concerning tobacco and taxes and took measures against drunkenness and gambling to preserve the common good of the colony. In time, the assembly gave rise to Virginia's colonial House of Burgesses, ultimately influencing the shape of the U.S. government. ■

Old Ideas, New World

The Virginia General Assembly (above), the legislative branch of the Commonwealth of Virginia, traces its origins to the House of Burgesses (left). In honor of Jamestown's 400th anniversary, Vice President Dick Cheney joined the Virginia General Assembly for a special session held in Jamestown on January 7, 2007.

English Political Heritage

The first English settlers did not arrive in North America with a master plan for democratic government, but they did not arrive empty-handed. Settlers brought with them a rich political heritage built on ideas of limited government, representative government, and individual rights. These seeds of democracy took root in the rough-and-ready wilderness of Jamestown and, in time, spread to the other English colonies.

Colonial government would never be an exact copy of the British system. Instead, it grew into a uniquely American form of democracy. What caused this development? According to historian Frederick Jackson Turner, it was the circumstances in which the colonists found themselves. Faced with landscapes and situations unknown in England, colonial leaders had to adapt old ideas to a new environment. The result was democracy that Turner said "came out of the American forest." To understand this new democracy, one must first explore the English traditions on which it is based.

Representative Government England's tradition of representative government dates to the eleventh century, when a council of religious leaders and nobles formed to advise the king. Gradually, the council's importance grew, and towns and villages began to send their own representatives to participate in the council's proceedings.

Over time, the king's advisory council evolved into a **bicameral**, or two-chamber, legislature called Parliament. Nobles composed the upper house, or House of Lords. Lesser officials and local representatives participated in the House of Commons, the lower house. As a representative assembly, Parliament worked to limit the power of the English monarchs.

Limited Government One of the earliest English efforts toward limited government dates to the year 1215, when English nobles forced King John to sign **Magna Carta**, or the "Great Charter." Weakened by military losses in France and in desperate need of funds, John demanded that nobles pay more taxes. The nobles rebelled and began to move a large army toward London. At Runnymede, near London, they forced John to sign Magna Carta, the document they had drawn up.

Magna Carta was a significant move from the "rule of man" to the "rule of law." By signing the document, King John conceded that even kings and queens had to obey English laws. The document also outlined a number of individual rights that the king could not violate. For example, the king was no longer able to levy taxes without approval from the nobles. The document also guaranteed people accused of crimes the right to a trial by a jury of their peers.

The original intent of Magna Carta was to protect the rights of nobles. In time, the rights protected by Magna Carta would be extended to most of the English people.

Individual Rights Alongside representative and limited government, a tradition of individual rights developed in England. When in 1628 a new confrontation between the king and Parliament put these rights at risk, England's legislature made King Charles I sign the **Petition of Right**. The document required monarchs to obtain Parliament's approval before levying new taxes. It also said that monarchs could not unlawfully imprison people, force citizens to house soldiers in their homes, or establish military rule during times of peace.

The Petition of Right was part of an extended conflict between Charles and Parliament. In 1642 the conflict erupted into the English Civil War, in which an army raised by Parliament defeated Charles and his supporters. In 1649 Charles was beheaded. England would not have another king until 1660, when Charles II assumed the throne.

Although the English monarchy appeared to have returned to normalcy, it was forever changed. Parliament had dramatically increased its power at the Crown's expense.

QUICK FACTS

Important English Ideas

Representative Government
The idea that people should have a say in their own government

Limited Government
The belief that government should be subject to strict limits on the lawful use of power

Individual Rights
The belief that government should protect individual and property rights

This was unusual for the time. The rest of Europe was entering the Age of Absolutism, a time when monarchs claimed the "divine right of kings" and wielded absolute power.

The extent of Parliament's new power would soon be made clear when James II, Charles's brother, took the throne in 1685. James II's enthusiastic promotion of his faith, Roman Catholicism, led to renewed conflicts between Crown and Parliament. Most of the English were Protestants and, fearing the king would impose the Catholic religion on the country, Parliament launched a rebellion.

ACADEMIC VOCABULARY

impose to force on another or others

The rebels rallied behind James's daughter, Mary, and her husband, William of Orange, who were Protestants. On November 5, 1688, William landed his army in England. With a force twice the size of William's army, James should have easily turned back the invaders. Many of his officers and soldiers, however, deserted to the other side, leaving James without a strong fighting force. The country had clearly abandoned its king.

On February 13, 1689, Parliament offered the English crown to William and Mary. Before taking the throne, the couple had to swear "to govern the people of this kingdom according to the statutes in Parliament." Moreover, Parliament passed the **English Bill of Rights** for the monarchs to sign. No longer would monarchs be able to enact laws, raise taxes, or keep an army without Parliament's consent. The document also guaranteed Parliament the privilege of free speech and gave all people protection from cruel and unusual punishment. Without a shot having ever been fired, what came to be called the Glorious Revolution was over.

The ultimate result of the Glorious Revolution was the establishment of a constitutional monarchy in England. As Magna Carta and the English Civil War had done before, the Glorious Revolution set clear limits on royal authority and shifted power to Parliament. At the same time, the English Bill of Rights set expectations about the "rights of Englishmen." English ideas about limited and representative government, as well as individual rights, were far-reaching. They spread beyond England itself.

READING CHECK **Summarizing** How did limited government develop in England?

The English Colonies

Beginning in the early 1600s—before the Petition of Right and the English Bill of Rights were signed—English colonists had begun to settle parts of North America. They brought with them English political theories and methods of governance.

Experiments in Early Governance From the start, the English settlers drew on their English heritage and tested new political forms. For example, the first meeting of Jamestown's House of Burgesses in 1619 was an early experiment with representative government. So too was the 1620 signing of the Mayflower Compact by all adult men on board the *Mayflower,* prior to their landing at Plymouth Rock. By signing, they agreed to form a society governed by majority rule and based on the consent of the people.

Other milestones quickly followed. In 1639 Connecticut colonists approved the **Fundamental Orders of Connecticut**, a set of laws that limited the power of government and gave all free men the right to choose people to serve as judges. The Massachusetts Body of Liberties of 1641, the first code of law in New England, protected the individual rights of citizens in the Bay Colony. For example, it protected personal property from seizure by colonial authorities.

Such experiments took place within a broader context of English rule. Each of the thirteen colonies was established by charter, an agreement whereby the English king gave settlers the right to establish a colony. Each charter guaranteed colonists the "rights of Englishmen," a promise that would trouble the monarchy during the Revolutionary era.

Types of English Colonies England established three types of colonies in North America: proprietary, royal, and charter. A **proprietary colony** was based on a grant of land by the English monarch to a proprietor, an individual or a group who financed the the start of the colony. The proprietor represented the Crown and could appoint all officials and make laws for the colony.

Nine colonies started as proprietary colonies. Maryland was originally granted to Lord Baltimore as a refuge for Catholics in

1632, and Pennsylvania was established by a charter granted to Sir William Penn in 1681. In 1701, Penn replaced his charter with the Charter of Privileges, which established a unicameral legislature, an elected assembly, and freedom of worship. In time, all proprietary colonies, except Pennsylvania and Maryland, became royal colonies.

Royal colonies were directly controlled by the king through an appointed governor. In time each royal colony had a two-house legislature. Members of the lower house were elected, but the king appointed members to the upper house. By the mid-1770s, Delaware, Georgia, Massachusetts, New Hampshire, New Jersey, New York, North and South Carolina, and Virginia were under the direct control of the Crown.

Charter colonies operated under charters agreed to by the colony and the king. Charter colonies enjoyed the most independence from the Crown. By the American Revolution, there were only two charter colonies left, Rhode Island and Connecticut. Each had an elected legislature that made laws for the colony and appointed the colony's governor. The charters for the Connecticut and Rhode Island colonies were so effective that they were later used as state constitutions.

READING CHECK **Contrasting** How were charter colonies and royal colonies different?

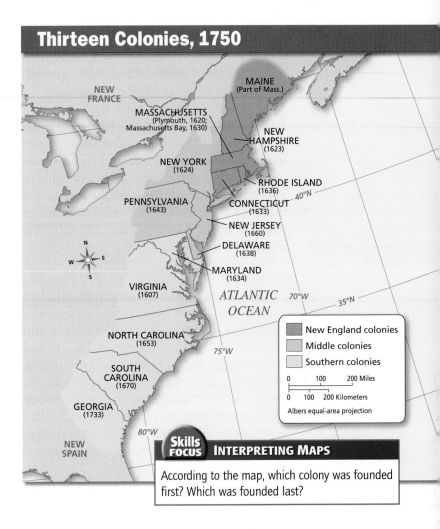

Thirteen Colonies, 1750

Skills FOCUS **INTERPRETING MAPS**

According to the map, which colony was founded first? Which was founded last?

Intellectual Influences

English traditions and colonial experiments in self-rule shaped American democracy, but there were other influences as well. Ideas would be key to transforming loyal English colonists first into revolutionaries and then into founders of a new nation.

Republicanism The term *republicanism* refers to a broad set of ideas about representative government that can be traced back to ancient Greece and Rome. Republican thinking highly values citizen participation, the public good, and civic virtue—the idea that people should place the common good over their private interests.

Such ideas were popular among the Framers of the U.S. Constitution. The Framers rejected the idea of monarchy and looked to the Roman Republic for a model of representative democracy. They were also well versed in classical Greek and Roman ideas about government, such as the Greek philosopher Aristotle's argument that unrestricted power vested in a king could easily lead to tyranny.

The Framers also came to republican ideas through the work of Renaissance scholars such as Niccolò Machiavelli. In his book *Discourses on Livy* (1513–17), Machiavelli put forth a theory of a republic based on civic virtue. He argued that a republic could survive only so long as its citizens actively participated in government and put the good of the republic before their own needs. For a republic to thrive, Machiavelli argued, it had to represent the interests of three levels of society: the monarch (the one), the aristocracy (the few), and the people (the many). At the time, asserting that government should be of and for the people was a radical suggestion.

Machiavelli's views helped undermine the idea that a monarch's power was God-given, one of the basic beliefs underlying feudalism, the reigning political order of his time.

For ideas about how to design a republican government, the Framers turned to the work of French philosopher Charles de Montesquieu. In *Spirit of the Laws* (1748), Montesquieu argued that government power had to be divided between the legislative, executive, and judicial branches of government. Montesquieu called this the separation of powers.

Judeo-Christian Influences The Framers' political thinking was influenced by a Judeo-Christian religious heritage, which includes traditions common to both Judaism and Christianity. These religions see the law and individual rights as being of divine origin. Moreover, the Framers benefited from the Protestant Reformation, a sixteenth-century Christian reform movement whose leaders developed ideas about individual responsibility, the freedom to worship as one chooses, and self-government.

Enlightenment Thinkers The Framers were deeply concerned with liberty and individual rights. These ideas had strong ties to the Enlightenment, an intellectual movement that took place in Europe during the eighteenth century, and are sometimes referred to as classical liberal concerns.

The Framers were particularly taken with Enlightenment ideas about people possessing natural rights to life, liberty, and property. They were equally influenced by the idea of a social contract—the belief that people agreed to form government to protect their rights. Such ideas were put forth by the British political thinker John Locke in *The Second Treatise on Government* (1690) and by the French philosopher Jean-Jacques Rousseau in *The Social Contract* (1762), both of whom you read about in Chapter 1.

Enlightenment thinkers also wrote about economic and civil liberties. In thinking about how best to protect economic freedom and rights to property, the Framers drew from the Scottish economist Adam Smith's work, *The Wealth of Nations* (1776). In defense of civil liberties, such as freedom of speech and religion, many of the Framers turned to an outspoken French philosopher named François Marie Arouet, better known by his pen name, Voltaire.

For ideas about how to use the law to protect people's natural rights to life, liberty, and property, the Framers looked to the English legal scholar William Blackstone. Blackstone's *Commentaries on the Laws of England* (1765–69) was a comprehensive overview of English law that became the basis for law in the colonies and influenced the writing of the U.S. Constitution.

READING CHECK Summarizing What intellectual influences shaped the Framers' views on republicanism?

SECTION 1 ASSESSMENT

Reviewing Ideas and Terms

1. a. Identify Which landmark English documents challenged the absolute authority of the monarchy?
b. Predict What ideas expressed in **Magna Carta** do you think would most influence the authors of the U. S. Constitution?

2. a. Define Which political philosopher is associated with the idea of the separation of powers?
b. Elaborate Why might colonists in a **proprietary colony** be unhappy if their colony were converted to a **royal colony**?

3. a. Recall How is civic virtue important to republicanism?
b. Rank Which of the natural rights—life, liberty, or property—do you think is most important? Explain.

Critical Thinking

4. Analyze Copy the chart below and list the major political ideas from each document that influenced the colonies.

Document	Major Political Ideas
Magna Carta	
Petition of Right	
English Bill of Rights	

FOCUS ON WRITING

5. Expository Write a paragraph explaining why the concept of civic virtue is still important today. Give at least one example of a private interest that people give up for the common good.

American Independence

Main Idea

The British imposed new policies on their American colonies, sparking rebellion and, in time, the American Revolution.

Reading Focus

1. How did British colonial policies lead to American independence?

2. What were the aims of the Continental Congresses?

3. Which ideas and events inspired the Declaration of Independence?

4. How did the first state governments reflect the conflict that led to the American Revolution?

Key Terms

New England Confederation
Iroquois Confederation
Albany Plan of Union
Stamp Act
First Continental Congress
Second Continental Congress
Virginia Declaration of Rights

 TAKING NOTES As you read, take notes on the causes and effects of the American Revolution. Record your notes in a graphic organizer like this one.

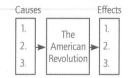

A Bold Declaration for Independence

John Hancock, the president of the Second Continental Congress, was the first to sign the Declaration of Independence on July 4, 1776.

WHY IT MATTERS

The Colonies Become States In hindsight, the American Revolution seems inevitable—the only course of action for the English colonies to take. In the summer of 1776, however, the way was not so clear. The course for revolution would not be set until a small group of delegates sent from each colony met at the Second Continental Congress in Pennsylvania. Together, they passed a bold resolution to sever ties with Great Britain, the world's most powerful empire.

The resolution was the Declaration of Independence. Written in flowing script on a large sheet of paper, the document outlined the delegates' reasons for seeking independence. Then, in the final paragraph, the authors made their radical declaration: "We . . . solemnly publish and declare, That these United Colonies are, and by Right ought to be Free and Inde-

pendent States." These were fighting words that the delegates pledged to back with "our Lives, our Fortunes, and our sacred Honor." The seven bloody years of revolution that followed would put their resolve to the test. ■

The Road to Independence

The road that led the American colonies to unite with one another and break with Great Britain was long and fraught with conflict. In part, the break was the result of the British government's failure to respect the English traditions of representative government, limited government, and individual rights—all of which had been transplanted to the colonies.

Events Leading to the American Revolution

Until the 1750s, Great Britain ruled its North American colonies with a light hand. As a result, the colonies grew used to a measure of political independence. Between 1754 and 1774 a series of events unfolded that led Great Britain to attempt to strengthen its control over the colonies. These events pushed the colonies in two directions at the same time: toward unity with one another and toward independence from Great Britain.

French and Indian War

The Stamp Act

British Actions	In 1754, the British and French forces battle for control of the Ohio River valley. The British win, gain control over North America, and tax the colonies to repay massive war debts.	In 1765 Parliament passes the Stamp Act, a tax on paper goods. The act requires all goods to bear a stamp to show that the tax had been paid.
Colonists' Actions	The war unites the colonies against a common enemy. Some colonists voluntarily join the war effort. Others resent having to shelter and supply British troops.	Outraged colonists boycott British goods, claiming Parliament had no right to tax them without their consent. Nine colonies send delegates to a Stamp Act Congress.

Early Attempts at Unity One of the earliest steps toward colonial unity came in 1643 when the Plymouth, Connecticut, Massachusetts Bay, and New Haven colonies formed the **New England Confederation**. Their common purpose was to defend against threats from Native Americans and from nearby Dutch colonies. Despite frequent disagreements, the confederation held together until 1684.

Nearly 70 years later, the outbreak of the French and Indian War (1754–1763) spurred a new drive toward unity in the colonies. The war pitted the British against the French in a struggle for control over the North American continent. In 1754, as fighting raged on the colonies' western frontier, Great Britain urged its colonies to sign a treaty with the **Iroquois Confederation**, a powerful alliance of six Native American nations—the Mohawk, Oneida, Onondaga, Cayuga, Seneca, and Tuscarora. Guided by a constitution and a council of leaders, the alliance had held strong for close to 200 years, keeping peace among its members.

To gain the support of the Iroquois in the fight against the French, the northern colonies invited Iroquois leaders to a meeting in Albany, New York. At the meeting, Benjamin Franklin, inspired by the Iroquois, proposed a plan that became known as the **Albany Plan of Union**. The plan called for a council of representatives appointed by the colonial assemblies and a president general appointed by the king. The proposed council would have the power to control trade, raise armies, build settlements, and equip fleets.

Although the delegates in Albany unanimously approved the Albany Plan, the colonial assemblies were quick to reject it. They feared that the plan gave too much power to the Crown. Likewise, the British, uneasy at the prospect of united colonies, rejected the plan. Franklin's plan, however, would not be forgotten. Less than a quarter of a century later, it became the basis for an early draft of the first official constitution for the newly born United States.

Growing Tensions By the mid-1700s the colonists had grown quite used to handling their own affairs with little interference from the British. The king and Parliament intervened mainly in colonial business having to do with trade and foreign relations. Soon after George III became king in 1760, however, the British government began to tighten its control over the colonies.

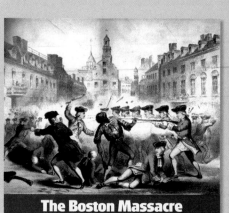

The Boston Massacre

On March 5, 1770, British soldiers in Boston are surrounded by an unfriendly crowd of colonists and accidently open fire, killing three and fatally wounding two colonists.

The colonists call the event the Boston Massacre. The killings stir opposition to British policies and lead to the withdrawal of British troops from Boston.

The Boston Tea Party

The British pass the Townshend Acts, taxing all paper, glass, lead, and tea. They send forces to the colonies to enforce the new taxes but shortly repeal all but the tea tax.

Insulted by the tea tax, a small band of patriots disguised as Native Americans board English ships in Boston Harbor and dump 342 chests of tea overboard.

The Intolerable Acts

As a response to the Boston Tea Party, the British pass a number of punitive measures in the spring of 1774. Boston Harbor is closed, and British troops are quartered.

The colonists call for a Continental Congress in 1774. The repeal of the Intolerable Acts would be the colonists' primary demand until independence.

Even though most colonists viewed themselves as loyal subjects of the British Crown, there was a growing attitude among members of Parliament that the colonies had become too independent. The real rise in tensions would follow the French and Indian War, when Parliament placed new financial burdens on the colonists.

Changes in British Policies

Through a series of spectacular and costly military engagements, the British emerged victorious in the French and Indian War. But the war left Great Britain with massive debts.

To offset the cost of the war and the ongoing defense of the colonies, Parliament looked to the colonists as a source of revenue. With George III's blessing, Parliament enforced trade restrictions that benefited Britain. Beginning in 1764 with the Sugar Act, Parliament imposed a series of taxes designed to alleviate Britain's debt.

The colonists, however, had no representation in Parliament, and they resented being taxed without their consent. "No taxation without representation" became a rallying cry throughout the colonies. The right to tax, the colonists argued, rightfully belonged to their elected colonial assemblies.

The Stamp Act Congress

The colonists' reaction to the **Stamp Act** of 1765, Parliament's first attempt to tax the colonists directly, should have been a warning sign of the rough times to come. The Stamp Act required a government tax stamp on paper goods and all legal documents, including contracts and licenses. Newspapers, almanacs, and even printed sermons and playing cards had to bear the official stamp.

The Stamp Act infuriated colonists, who responded with organized protest. Secret colonial societies called the Sons of Liberty sprang up across the colonies. Their goal was to intimidate the stamp agents charged with collecting Parliament's taxes. In many places, mobs forced stamp agents out of office. In Philadelphia, colonists even conducted a mock hanging of a stamp agent.

In October 1765 nine colonies sent delegates to the Stamp Act Congress in New York to craft a united response to the new tax measure. The congress was the colonies' first attempt at forging a plan to work together since the 1754 Albany meeting. It sent a petition to the king that declared their loyalty but voiced a strong protest, asserting that the power to tax colonies should belong solely to the colonial assemblies.

Colonial Protests Although Parliament repealed the Stamp Act in 1766, it continued to impose new taxes. The new measures stoked the flames of colonial resistance, and in some communities protests erupted into violence. On March 5, 1770, British soldiers fired into a crowd of colonial protestors in Boston, killing five people in an event known as the Boston Massacre.

A number of resistance groups began to organize, often in secret. They staged rallies, published pamphlets, and recruited community leaders to protest British policies they deemed unfair to the colonies. In 1772 colonial activist Samuel Adams formed the Committees of Correspondence to inform the other colonies of events in Boston. Through organized letter-writing campaigns with similar groups, a network of communication formed among the colonies.

When Parliament gave all rights to the American tea trade to one British company, the East India Company, Adams and other Boston colonists reacted by staging the Boston Tea Party. On December 16, 1773, a group of colonists disguised themselves as Native Americans, boarded three British ships and dumped the ships' tea cargo overboard into Boston Harbor.

For Parliament and George III, the Boston Tea Party was a brazen act of disrespect that had to be punished. "The Colonies must either submit or triumph," the king wrote. Parliament passed a new set of harsh laws in 1774. Called the Intolerable Acts in the colonies, the laws closed Boston Harbor, ended all forms of self-rule in Massachusetts, and called for the quartering of British troops in private homes. Thousands of British troops were dispatched to the colonies to enforce the new measures.

READING CHECK **Summarizing** What forms of protest did the colonists use to oppose British policies?

The Continental Congresses

Most American colonists held out hope for a compromise that would roll back the harshest tax measures. Toward this end, the Virginia and Massachusetts assemblies called for a general meeting of the colonies to be held in Philadelphia, Pennsylvania.

The First Continental Congress Every colony except Georgia sent delegates to the **First Continental Congress** in Philadelphia in fall of 1774. The delegates sent George III a document known as the Declaration and Resolves, demanding a repeal of the Intolerable Acts, an end to British military occupation, and the power of the colonies to impose their own tax laws. Congress also called for a boycott of British goods until its demands were met. The delegates agreed to meet again the following May should the king refuse to address their grievances.

The British rejected the colonists' demands. In April 1775, British troops clashed with colonial militia at Lexington and Concord in Massachusetts. The clashes became known as "the shot heard 'round the world," the first time the colonists met the British with armed resistance.

The Second Continental Congress Three weeks after Lexington and Concord, the **Second Continental Congress** met in Philadelphia. Again representatives from 12 of the 13 colonies attended. Many delegates no longer expected better treatment by the Crown. This time, they were resolved to take strong measures. One of the Congress's first actions was to organize the ragtag militia around Boston into an official Continental Army. By a unanimous vote, delegates then made George Washington its commander.

Still, some delegates clung to hopes of reconciliation. In July 1775, the Congress sent George III a final appeal. In the Olive Branch Petition, the delegates pledged continuing loyalty and begged the king to ask Parliament to repeal the new measures. George III refused to read the petition. On August 23, he proclaimed the American colonists to be in a full state of rebellion. Every effort would be made, he said, "to suppress such rebellion, and to bring the traitors to justice."

With the Revolutionary War now under way, the Congress assumed the role of a government. It had no legal grounds to do so, but it did so out of desperate necessity. During the Revolution, the Congress would raise troops, borrow money, send diplomats to Europe, and create a monetary system. Most importantly, it would declare the colonies independent from Britain.

ACADEMIC VOCABULARY

quartering
housing

The Common Sense of Democracy On January 10, 1776, a 47-page political pamphlet that would inspire widespread support for independence appeared in Philadelphia. The pamphlet was *Common Sense* by Thomas Paine, an Englishman who had arrived in America only a year earlier.

In plain language, Paine persuasively made the case for a break with England. He laid blame for colonial hostilities at Parliament's feet. Then he took the king in particular and monarchy in general to task, arguing that "a thirst for absolute power is the natural disease of monarchy." For Paine, independence was the only "common sense" course of action for the colonists to take.

Paine saw the history of the world hanging on the outcome of the colonies' rebellion. "We have it in our power," he wrote, "to begin the world over again." That new world would take the form of a republican government, in which people governed themselves through democratically elected representatives. Paine's message struck a chord. Within three months of its first printing, 150,000 copies of *Common Sense* had flown off colonial presses.

READING CHECK Making Inferences According to Paine, why was independence "common sense"?

The Declaration of Independence

The armed conflict continued for months before independence was officially declared. On June 7, 1776, Virginia delegate Richard Henry Lee stood before the Congress and proposed a resolution to officially declare independence from Great Britain. No longer concerned with restoring their "rights as Englishmen," the delegates passed Lee's resolution on July 2.

Congress appointed a committee of five to write a formal statement justifying the move for independence. The committee included John Adams, Benjamin Franklin, Robert Livingston, Roger Sherman, and a Virginian named Thomas Jefferson. Widely esteemed for his writing ability, Jefferson wrote most of the document in little more than two weeks.

Jefferson later claimed that he consulted "neither book nor pamphlet" to write the Declaration. However, Jefferson likely drew on the **Virginia Declaration of Rights** that the Virginia House of Burgesses had adopted just one month earlier. Inspired by the philosophy of John Locke and written mostly by George Mason, the Virginia Declaration proclaimed "all men are by nature equally free and independent and have certain inherent rights" that cannot be denied.

Likewise, echoing Locke's view on natural rights, Jefferson's Declaration states that people have "unalienable" rights to "Life, Liberty, and the pursuit of Happiness" that no government can take away because they are granted by "their Creator," or God. Jefferson also drew on Locke's idea that government is the result of a social contract based on the consent of the people. As Jefferson argued, governments derive "their just powers from the consent of the governed." If a government disregards the rights of its people, then the people have a legitimate right to change their government.

On the evening of July 4, 1776, the Congress adopted the Declaration of Independence. Britain's thirteen colonies ceased to exist. A new nation of united sovereign states had entered the world stage.

READING CHECK Summarizing How did John Locke's ideas inspire the Declaration of Independence?

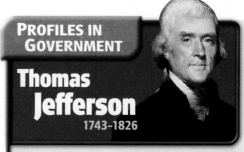

PROFILES IN GOVERNMENT

Thomas Jefferson
1743–1826

Thomas Jefferson was born into a family of wealthy Virginia planters. Upon graduating from the College of William and Mary, he practiced law before serving in the Virginia House of Burgesses. Jefferson had many roles in early American government. He served as governor of Virginia, ambassador to France, secretary of state, and as president of the United States. In addition, Jefferson was also a writer, philosopher, inventor, architect, slaveholder, scientist, musician, and astronomer.

Because of his writing ability, Jefferson was called upon to draft the Declaration of Independence. Next to the Declaration, Jefferson was most proud of writing the Virginia Statute of Religious Freedom (1786), which protected freedom of religion in Virginia and provided the basis for the First Amendment to the U.S. Constitution.

Summarizing How did Jefferson contribute to American government?

The State Constitutions

In May 1776 the Continental Congress passed a resolution encouraging each colony to draft its plan for government. By 1780, each of the 13 newly independent states had adopted its own written constitution. This was a remarkable feat. At that time, no nation in Europe had a written constitution. Moreover, the early state constitutions tested ideas about how to design a republican government that protected individual rights. These ideas would later influence the writing of the U.S. Constitution.

Self-Government All of the new state constitutions established republican governments with strong legislatures composed of elected representatives. Voting rights, however, differed from state to state. Seven states granted the right to vote to any adult male taxpayer, while other states set property qualifications for voting. Although slaves were denied the right to vote, free African American men could vote in some states if they met the requirements for voters. New Jersey was the only state to allow women who met property qualifications to vote.

Separation of Powers Each state established three branches of government: legislative, executive, and judicial. The new constitutions gave state legislatures the real power to govern, including the power to conduct foreign affairs and declare war. With the exception of Pennsylvania, all legislatures had two houses. In some states, the legislature elected the governor and state judges.

Limited Government The strong legislative bodies that the colonists created reflected their general distrust of monarchy. The colonists, however, were careful not to grant unlimited power to their legislative bodies. Annual elections, term limits, and separation of powers were established as checks on legislative power. Because colonists feared that a strong executive might undermine a republic, their state constitutions kept the power of the governors deliberately weak, and nine constitutions limited the governor's term to one year.

Individual Rights One way to protect people from the excesses of government power was to legally protect their rights. The Massachusetts constitution of 1780 was the first of seven state constitutions to include a bill of rights that protected individual liberties. These liberties included trial by jury, freedom of assembly, and freedom of speech. Almost all of the rights later included in U.S. Constitution's Bill of Rights were protected in some form in the early state constitutions.

READING CHECK **Summarizing** What ideas about government did state constitutions experiment with?

SECTION ② ASSESSMENT

THINK central **Online Quiz**

thinkcentral.com
KEYWORD: SGO ORI HP

Reviewing Ideas and Terms

1. **a. Explain** What ideas about government could early American leaders have learned from the **Iroquois Confederation**?
   b. Predict What might have happened if Parliament had allowed the colonists to rule and tax themselves?

2. **a. Recall** Why was the **First Continental Congress** called?
   b. Make Inferences Why was it necessary for Congress to assume the role of a national government during the war?

3. **a. Describe** What was the Congress's purpose in drafting the Declaration of Independence?
   b. Summarize What sources likely influenced Thomas Jefferson's draft of the Declaration of Independence?

4. **a. Identify** What principles expressed in state constitutions later influenced the writing of the U.S. Constitution?
   b. Explain How did state constitutions protect rights?

Critical Thinking

5. **Develop** Copy the graphic organizer below and use it to list in order and describe the events leading up to the writing of the Declaration of Independence.

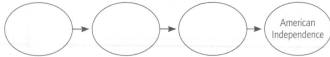

American Independence

FOCUS ON WRITING

6. **Descriptive** Imagine that you are a journalist working for a colonial American newspaper in 1776. Write an editorial describing the Declaration of Independence and explaining the ideas that influenced it.

The Declaration of Independence

In Congress, July 4, 1776
The unanimous Declaration of the thirteen united States of America,

When in the Course of human events, it becomes necessary for one people to dissolve the political bands which have connected them with another, and to assume among the Powers of the earth, the separate and equal station to which the Laws of Nature and of Nature's God entitle them, a decent respect to the opinions of mankind requires that they should declare the causes which **impel** them to the separation.

We hold these truths to be self-evident, that all men are created equal, that they are endowed by their Creator with certain unalienable Rights, that among these are Life, Liberty, and the pursuit of Happiness. That to secure these rights, Governments are instituted among Men, deriving their just powers from the consent of the governed, That whenever any Form of Government becomes destructive of these ends, it is the Right of the People to alter or to abolish it, and to institute new Government, laying its foundation on such principles and organizing its powers in such form, as to them shall seem most likely to effect their Safety and Happiness. Prudence, indeed, will dictate that Governments long established should not be changed for light and transient causes; and accordingly all experience hath shown, that mankind are more disposed to suffer, while evils are sufferable, than to right themselves by abolishing the forms to which they are accustomed. But when a long train of abuses and **usurpations**, pursuing invariably the same Object **evinces** a design to reduce them under absolute **Despotism**, it is their right, it is their duty, to throw off such Government, and to provide new Guards for their future security.—Such has been the patient sufferance of these Colonies; and such is now the necessity which constrains them to alter their former Systems of Government. The history of the present King of Great Britain is a history of repeated injuries and usurpations, all having in direct object the establishment of an absolute **Tyranny** over these States. To prove this, let Facts be submitted to a **candid** world.

He has refused his Assent to Laws, the most wholesome and necessary for the public good.

He has forbidden his Governors to pass Laws of immediate and pressing importance, unless suspended in their operation till his Assent should be obtained; and when so suspended, he has utterly neglected to attend to them.

EXPLORING THE DOCUMENT John Locke's thoughts about natural rights strongly influenced Thomas Jefferson and the founders. **How does the Declaration's mention of "the Laws of Nature" and "Life, Liberty, and the pursuit of Happiness" relate to Locke's views on the natural rights that people possess?**

EXPLORING THE DOCUMENT Thomas Jefferson wrote the first draft of the Declaration in a little more than two weeks. **How is the Declaration's idea about why governments are formed still important to our country today?**

Vocabulary

impel force

usurpations wrongful seizures of power

evinces clearly displays

despotism unlimited power

tyranny oppressive power exerted by a government or ruler

candid fair

He has refused to pass other Laws for the accommodation of large districts of people, unless those people would relinquish the right of Representation in the Legislature, a right **inestimable** to them and **formidable** to tyrants only.

He has called together legislative bodies at places unusual, uncomfortable, and distant from the depository of their Public Records, for the sole purpose of fatiguing them into compliance with his measures.

He has dissolved Representative Houses repeatedly, for opposing with manly firmness his invasions on the rights of the people.

He has refused for a long time, after such dissolutions, to cause others to be elected; whereby the Legislative Powers, incapable of **Annihilation**, have returned to the People at large for their exercise; the State remaining in the mean time exposed to all the dangers of invasion from without, and **convulsions** within.

He has endeavored to prevent the population of these States; for that purpose obstructing the Laws of Naturalization of Foreigners; refusing to pass others to encourage their migration hither, and raising the conditions of new **Appropriations of Lands.**

He has obstructed the Administration of Justice, by refusing his Assent to Laws for establishing Judiciary Powers.

He has made Judges dependent on his Will alone, for the tenure of their offices, and the amount and payment of their salaries.

He has erected a multitude of New Offices, and sent hither swarms of Officers to harass our people, and eat out their substance.

He has kept among us, in times of peace, Standing Armies without the Consent of our legislature.

He has affected to render the Military independent of and superior to the Civil Power.

He has combined with others to subject us to a jurisdiction foreign to our constitution, and unacknowledged by our laws; giving his Assent to their Acts of pretended legislation:

For **quartering** large bodies of armed troops among us:

For protecting them, by a mock Trial, from Punishment for any Murders which they should commit on the Inhabitants of these States:

For cutting off our Trade with all parts of the world:

For imposing taxes on us without our Consent:

For depriving us in many cases, of the benefits of Trial by Jury:

For transporting us beyond Seas to be tried for pretended offences:

EXPLORING THE DOCUMENT Here the Declaration lists the charges that the colonists made against King George III. **How does the language in the list appeal to people's emotions?**

For abolishing the free System of English Laws in a neighboring Province, establishing therein an **Arbitrary** government, and enlarging its Boundaries so as to **render** it at once an example and fit instrument for introducing the same absolute rule into these Colonies:

For taking away our Charters, abolishing our most valuable Laws, and altering fundamentally the Forms of our Governments:

For suspending our own Legislature, and declaring themselves invested with Power to legislate for us in all cases whatsoever.

He has abdicated Government here, by declaring us out of his Protection and waging War against us.

He has plundered our seas, ravaged our Coasts, burnt our towns, and destroyed the lives of our people.

He is at this time transporting large armies of **foreign mercenaries** to complete the works of death, desolation and tyranny, already begun with circumstances of Cruelty & **perfidy** scarcely paralleled in the most barbarous ages, and totally unworthy the Head of a civilized nation.

He has constrained our fellow Citizens taken Captive on the high Seas to bear Arms against their Country, to become the executioners of their friends and Brethren, or to fall themselves by their Hands.

He has excited domestic **insurrections** amongst us, and has endeavored to bring on the inhabitants of our frontiers, the merciless Indian Savages, whose known rule of warfare, is an undistinguished destruction of all ages, sexes and conditions.

In every stage of these Oppressions We have **Petitioned for Redress** in the most humble terms: Our repeated Petitions have been answered only by repeated injury. A Prince, whose character is thus marked by every act which may define a Tyrant, is unfit to be the ruler of a free People.

Nor have We been wanting in attention to our British brethren. We have warned them from time to time of attempts by their legislature to extend an **unwarrantable jurisdiction** over us. We have reminded them of the circumstances of our emigration and settlement here. We have appealed to their native justice and **magnanimity**, and we have **conjured** them by the ties of our common kindred to disavow these usurpations, which, would inevitably interrupt our connections and correspondence. They too have been deaf to the voice of justice and of **consanguinity**. We must, therefore, **acquiesce** in the necessity, which denounces our Separation, and hold them, as we hold the rest of mankind, Enemies in War, in Peace Friends.

We, therefore, the Representatives of the united States of America, in General Congress, Assembled, appealing to the Supreme Judge of the world for the **rectitude** of our intentions, do, in the Name, and by Authority of the good People of these Colonies, solemnly publish and declare, That these United

EXPLORING THE DOCUMENT How do the king's actions and the idea of arbitrary power go against the notion of limited government and the rule of law?

Vocabulary

arbitrary not based on law

render make

foreign mercenaries soldiers hired to fight for a country not their own

perfidy violation of trust

insurrections rebellions

petitioned for redress asked formally for a correction of wrongs

unwarrantable jurisdiction unjustified authority

magnanimity generous spirit

conjured gently called upon

consanguinity common ancestry

acquiesce consent to

rectitude rightness

EXPLORING THE DOCUMENT Here the Declaration describes how the colonies attempted to resolve issues with Great Britain. **Why do you think the authors included this information when announcing their separation?**

Colonies are, and of Right ought to be Free and Independent States; that they are Absolved from all Allegiance to the British Crown, and that all political connection between them and the State of Great Britain, is and ought to be totally dissolved; and that as Free and Independent States, they have full Power to levy War, conclude Peace, contract Alliances, establish Commerce, and to do all other Acts and Things which Independent States may of right do. And for the support of this Declaration, with a firm reliance on the Protection of Divine Providence, we mutually pledge to each other our Lives, our Fortunes and our sacred Honor.

EXPLORING THE DOCUMENT Here the document declares the colonies independent. **Whose authority does the Congress use to declare independence?**

EXPLORING THE DOCUMENT The Congress adopted the final draft of the Declaration of Independence on July 4, 1776. A formal copy, written on parchment, was signed on August 2, 1776.

EXPLORING THE DOCUMENT The following is part of a passage the Congress removed from Jefferson's original draft: "He has waged cruel war against human nature itself, violating its most sacred rights of life and liberty in the persons of a distant people who never offended him, captivating and carrying them into slavery in another hemisphere, or to incur miserable death in their transportation thither." **Why do you think the Congress deleted this passage?**

John Hancock	Benjamin Harrison	Lewis Morris
Button Gwinnett	Thomas Nelson, Jr.	Richard Stockton
Lyman Hall	Francis Lightfoot Lee	John Witherspoon
George Walton	Carter Braxton	Francis Hopkinson
William Hooper	Robert Morris	John Hart
Joseph Hewes	Benjamin Rush	Abraham Clark
John Penn	Benjamin Franklin	Josiah Bartlett
Edward Rutledge	John Morton	William Whipple
Thomas Heyward, Jr.	George Clymer	Samuel Adams
Thomas Lynch, Jr.	James Smith	John Adams
Arthur Middleton	George Taylor	Robert Treat Paine
Samuel Chase	James Wilson	Elbridge Gerry
William Paca	George Ross	Stephen Hopkins
Thomas Stone	Caesar Rodney	William Ellery
Charles Carroll of Carrollton	George Read	Roger Sherman
George Wythe	Thomas McKean	Samuel Huntington
Richard Henry Lee	William Floyd	William Williams
Thomas Jefferson	Philip Livingston	Oliver Wolcott
	Francis Lewis	Matthew Thornton

③ Articles of Confederation

Main Idea
The states' first attempt to build a national government, the Articles of Confederation, proved too weak to last.

Reading Focus
1. How was the first national government organized under the Articles of Confederation?
2. What were the weaknesses of the Articles of Confederation?
3. What events convinced some American leaders that a stronger national government was needed?

Key Terms
Articles of
  Confederation
ratified
Northwest Ordinance
Shays's Rebellion

TAKING NOTES As you read, take notes on the advantages and disadvantages of the Articles of Confederation. Record your notes in a chart like this one.

The Articles of Confederation	
Advantages	Disadvantages

First Plan of Government

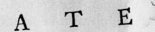

The Articles of Confederation declared the 13 former colonies to be sovereign states in a "perpetual union" called the United States of America.

WHY IT MATTERS

States Become Nation On June 7, 1776, Richard Henry Lee rose to the floor of the Second Continental Congress to make a dramatic proposal: "Resolved: These United Colonies are, and of right ought to be free and independent States, that they are absolved from all allegiance to the British Crown." Soon after, the Congress voted to do two things: to declare independence and to establish a confederation to govern the states.

As one committee of congressional delegates began work on the Declaration of Independence, a second committee acted quickly to organize a new government. They now had a revolution to win. The committee's delegates drew on a number of sources for their confederation. The product of their labors took its name, the *Articles of Confederation and Perpetual Union*, from Benjamin Franklin's plan. It was the first plan of government for the United States.

The new government would be strong enough to see the colonies through the American Revolution, but it would not last long. As the founders soon learned, their confederation was deeply flawed. By 1785 George Washington and other important leaders were discussing the need to reform the plan—or replace it. ■

First National Government

In June 1776, on the eve of independence, the Second Continental Congress turned its attention to creating a national government. The committee appointed to the task consisted of one delegate from each former colony. With John Dickinson, the delegate from Pennsylvania, serving as chief author, the committee drew up a new model of government. In their eyes, the United States was to be a confederation. The delegates aimed to build a "firm league of friendship" among 13 states that retained their "sovereignty, freedom, and independence."

On June 12, 1777, after six drafts and several months of debate, Congress adopted the nation's first constitution, the **Articles of Confederation**. Before it could go into force, it had to be **ratified**, or formally approved, by all of the states.

A Delay in Ratification Disputes over who would control the vast western lands that stretched between the Appalachian Mountains and the Mississippi River delayed the ratification process. Small states feared that large states with claims to western lands would become enormously powerful and overpower smaller states. For this reason, small states without land claims refused to approve the Articles. To win states' approval, the authors of the Articles changed their plan, granting the Confederation control over western lands. Maryland, the last state to pass the Articles, held out until 1781.

CONGRESS UNDER THE ARTICLES OF CONFEDERATION

QUICK FACTS

The Powers of Congress	The Limits on Congress
• Coin and borrow money • Admit new states and divide western lands • Request money from states • Raise an army • Appoint military officers • Establish a postal system • Declare war and make peace • Conduct foreign affairs	• No president or executive branch • No national court system • No power to tax or raise national funds • No power to regulate trade or currency • No power to prohibit states from conducting foreign affairs • Major laws required the approval of nine states to pass

Powers of the National Government The Articles of Confederation guarded state powers by creating a weak national government. Fearing the power wielded by a king, the authors of the Articles made no provision for an executive office. Nor did they provide for a national court system.

The Articles did call for a one-house Congress, in which each state had one vote. Delegates to the Congress were appointed and paid by their state legislatures. To pass any major legislation, nine states had to agree. Moreover, any change to the Articles required approval from all of the 13 states.

The Articles gave Congress the power to act on matters of common interest to the states. Congress could admit new states and organize the division of western lands. Congress could also settle disputes between states, organize a postal service, coin and borrow money, appoint military officers, and raise an army. The powers to declare war, make peace, and conduct foreign policy were also given to Congress by the Articles.

State Powers The states retained all powers not specifically given to Congress. According to Article II of the document, each state would retain "every power, jurisdiction, and right which is not by this confederation expressly delegated to the United States in Congress assembled." The states' powers included the ability to collect taxes and enforce national laws. It was also up to the states to contribute funds to the national government as they saw fit.

READING CHECK Summarizing How did national and state powers differ under the Articles?

Weaknesses of the Articles

On paper, the Confederation Congress looked powerful enough. The Articles had given Congress a number of key responsibilities. In reality, the Articles placed limits on Congress that kept it from effectively enforcing its laws and policies. For example, without a separate executive branch, the national government lacked the means to carry out Congress's laws. Without a national court system, Congress had to rely on the state courts to apply national laws.

More important, the Articles denied Congress the power to tax. Congress could ask the states for money, but the states often refused. This situation made it difficult to raise money for a national army. It also meant that Congress could not raise the funds necessary to repay money that the nation had borrowed during the Revolution. Nor could it pay many of the soldiers who had fought for independence.

Congress also lacked the authority to regulate commerce, or trade, between the states. For example, Congress was not able to intervene when one state passed laws taxing goods from other states in an effort to give an advantage to its local businesses.

Although Congress had the power to coin money, it did not have the *sole* power to do so. By the mid-1780s several different state currencies were in circulation. Some states refused to accept the currencies of other states. Such barriers to trade created major obstacles to the economic development of the young country.

Congress was further hindered by the degree of consensus required to pass laws. Rarely did 9 of the 13 states agree on any policy. Moreover, only one state had to raise an objection to block changes to the Articles. Such disagreement weakened Congress's ability to act swiftly and decisively.

READING CHECK **Summarizing** What were the weaknesses of the Articles of Confederation?

Pressures for Stronger Government

With independence from Britain secured by the Treaty of Paris in 1783, the United States faced a range of challenges that, for the most part, the national government was ill-equipped to meet. The shortcomings of the government created by the Articles of Confederation would lead to calls for a new plan of government to replace the Articles.

Northwest Ordinance One of Congress's greatest successes was the passage of the **Northwest Ordinance** of 1787. The ordinance established a plan for settling the Northwest Territory, which included areas that are now in Illinois, Indiana, Michigan, Ohio,

Minnesota, and Wisconsin. This territory included the disputed western lands that had delayed ratification of the Articles.

The Northwest Ordinance created a system for admitting new states to the Union. It banned slavery in the territory. It also included a bill of rights that guaranteed representative government, religious freedom, trial by jury, and other freedoms to settlers. For more than 125 years, the ordinance guided the nation's westward expansion.

Dangers and Unrest When Congress turned to other challenges—war debts, a sluggish economy, uncooperative states, and civil unrest—it largely floundered. Perhaps the most pressing problem was the war debts. Congress had borrowed heavily from foreign creditors and wealthy Americans to pay for the war. In addition, it owed back wages to soldiers. To meet its obligations, in 1783 Congress called on the states to approve a tax on imports. Unanimous consent was needed. With war debts of their own, the states balked. By 1787 only nine states had consented. Without a steady stream of income, the government was broke.

To make matters worse, the economy was slow to recover from a postwar depression. Farmers were particularly hard hit. Many fell into debt and faced losing their farms. Creditors in all states feared that borrowers would not make good on their loans.

Meanwhile, the states pursued their own interests. Some flouted laws passed by Congress and the terms of foreign treaties. Others negotiated directly with foreign powers and raised their own armed forces. In a 1786 letter to James Madison, George Washington likened the United States to "thirteen sovereignties pulling against each other and tugging at the federal head."

Shays's Rebellion In September 1786 a small band of Massachusetts farmers rebelled at the prospect of losing their land. Led by former Revolutionary War captain Daniel Shays, the farmers attacked courthouses to prevent judges from foreclosing on farms. By 1787, the ranks of **Shays's Rebellion** had swelled to nearly 2,500. Shays even stormed the Springfield military arsenal, where hundreds of guns were stored. The

WHAT DO YOU THINK?

What were the positive and negative consequences of a limited national government?

ACADEMIC VOCABULARY

flout ignore

Shays's Rebellion

Because news of Shays's uprising shocked the nation and led to calls for stronger government, Shays's Rebellion has been called the last battle of the American Revolution.

Massachusetts legislature asked Congress for help, but Congress had neither money nor forces to offer. Finally, a hastily assembled state militia scattered Shays and his angry mob.

Shays's Rebellion came at a sensitive time. It showed just how feeble the Confederation Congress was, and it hastened moves to revise the Articles of Confederation.

Calls to Revise the Articles In March 1785 George Washington invited representatives from Virginia and Maryland to his home at Mount Vernon. The purpose of the meeting was to discuss resolving a trade dispute between the two states.

The success of the Mount Vernon meeting convinced James Madison to organize a second, larger meeting at Annapolis, Maryland, to discuss regulating commerce between all of the states. At his urging, the Virginia General Assembly issued meeting invitations to the states. Nine states accepted, but delegates from only five states showed up. The poor attendance led to a call for yet another meeting—this time to discuss strengthening the Articles of Confederation.

The next meeting was to be held in May 1787 in Philadelphia. In an address to the states, Alexander Hamilton called on states to send delegates to discuss commerce and all matters necessary to make the national government "adequate to the exigencies [emergencies] of the union."

In February 1787 Madison persuaded the Confederation Congress to endorse the Philadelphia meeting "for the sole and express purpose of revising the Articles of Confederation." No mention was made of writing a new constitution.

READING CHECK Identifying Cause and Effect
What events caused leaders to want to revise the Articles of Confederation?

SECTION 3 ASSESSMENT

Reviewing Ideas and Terms

1. **a. Recall** What issue led to the delay of the ratification of the Articles of Confederation?
   b. Explain How did the Articles of Confederation reflect the colonists' fear of monarchy?

2. **a. Identify** What weakness in the Articles prevented Congress from financing its activities?
   b. Explain How did the distribution of powers under the Articles make the national government dependent on the states?

3. **a. Identify** What was Shays's Rebellion?
   b. Summarize Describe the events leading from Shays's Rebellion to the call for the Constitutional Convention.

Critical Thinking

4. **Compare and Contrast** Copy the chart below and take notes on the powers and limits of Congress under the Articles of Confederation.

Powers	Limits

FOCUS ON WRITING

5. **Expository** Write a paragraph explaining the impact of the Northwest Ordinance of 1787 on the United States, the Midwest, and your state.

SECTION 4
The Constitutional Convention

BEFORE YOU READ

Main Idea
Delegates at the Constitutional Convention compromised on key issues to create a plan for a strong national government.

Reading Focus
1. Why did the Constitutional Convention draft a new plan for government?
2. How did the rival plans for the new government differ?
3. What other conflicts required the Framers to compromise?

Key Terms
Framers
Virginia Plan
New Jersey Plan
Great Compromise
Three-Fifths
  Compromise

TAKING NOTES As you read, take notes on the writing of the U.S. Constitution. Record your notes in a graphic organizer like this one.

U.S. Constitution

Crafting a More Perfect Union There is a story often told of the closing day of the Constitutional Convention held in Philadelphia, Pennsylvania. As delegate Benjamin Franklin exited the convention, he was approached by a woman who asked him whether the delegates had created a republic or a monarchy. Franklin responded, "A republic, if you can keep it."

As one of the 55 delegates who toiled for four months to create a new framework for the government of the United States, Franklin understood the significance of a republican government. Because the U.S. Constitution granted unprecedented power to the people to choose their leaders, the new government's success or failure now rested in the hands of the American people. It was a brave, new experiment in self-rule.

For more than 220 years, the American people have kept the republic going strong. Today the United States is the world's oldest constitutional democracy. ■

A New Plan for Government

Throughout the summer of 1787, George Washington presided over the Constitutional Convention in Philadelphia.

Drafting a New Constitution

By May 1787 the United States was on the verge of a crisis. The weak central government created by the Articles of Confederation had proved inadequate to the social, diplomatic, and economic problems the new nation faced. Delegates from the states gathered at a convention in Philadelphia to revise the Articles of Confederation, which they unanimously agreed was too weak to meet the nation's needs. The result, however, was an entirely new plan for government.

The Convention Meets On May 25, 1787, after a quorum, or majority, of state delegations had arrived, the convention got under way. Representatives from 12 of the 13 states would eventually attend. Leaders in Rhode Island, fearful that the convention would strip power from the states, refused to send a delegation. Over the course of the next four months, the delegates to the convention worked together to draft the framework for a new government.

FRAMERS OF THE CONSTITUTION

DELEGATE	KEY ROLE AND CONTRIBUTIONS
Benjamin Franklin Pennsylvania	At age 81, the oldest and most admired delegate in attendance
Alexander Hamilton New York	Strongly advocated for passing the Constitution by co-authoring a series of essays known as the *Federalist Papers*
James Madison Virginia	Major author of the Virginia Plan and a supporter of a strong national government
William Paterson New Jersey	Proposed the New Jersey Plan, which called for a unicameral legislature with equal representation from each state
Edmund Randolph Virginia	Proposed the Virginia Plan, which called for a government with three separate branches based on each state's population or wealth
Roger Sherman Connecticut	Proposed the Great Compromise, which called for equal representation in the Senate and representation based on state population in the House

The delegates set some general guidelines for their proceedings. Each state would have one vote, and decisions would be made by a simple majority. To ensure their ability to speak their minds freely, delegates voted to meet in strict secrecy. The press and the public were not allowed to attend, and official records were limited.

Framers of the Constitution The 55 delegates who attended the Convention were a remarkable group. One-third of the delegates had served in the Continental Army. Eight had signed the Declaration of Independence. Almost all had experience in colonial, state, or local government. They ranged in age from 26-year-old Jonathan Dayton of New Jersey to 81-year-old Benjamin Franklin of Pennsylvania. Together, the delegates to the Constitutional Convention are known as the **Framers** of the Constitution for their efforts in drafting the framework of the new government.

Several of the Framers played key roles in guiding the convention. George Washington, for example, gave the meetings an air of dignity and authority in his role as president of the convention. Virginia's James Madison also played a pivotal role. Madison took the lead in planning the convention and in calling for a new government. Today Madison is hailed as the Father of the Constitution because of his influence on the outcome of the convention.

READING CHECK **Drawing Conclusions** Why did the delegates want to keep the proceedings secret?

Rival Plans

The delegates had been sent to Philadelphia to revise the Articles of Confederation, but many of them believed the Articles were irredeemably flawed. When the convention opened, delegates soon raised the idea of creating a new form of government. In the days that followed, two rival plans emerged— the Virginia Plan and the New Jersey Plan.

The Virginia Plan In the weeks before the Philadelphia convention, delegates from Virginia had gathered to discuss the problems of the existing government. It quickly became apparent to them that what was needed was not a revision of the Articles of Confederation, but an entirely different government. They formulated a proposal to that effect. On the fourth day of the Convention, Virginia delegate Edmund Randolph presented the group's proposal, known as the **Virginia Plan**, to the Philadelphia Convention.

Based largely on the ideas of James Madison, the Virginia Plan called for a central government divided into three branches—legislative, executive, and judicial—each with the power to check the other branches. Unlike the Articles of Confederation, Virginia's proposal called for a strong national government with the power to make laws, levy its own taxes, and control commerce between the states. The new government would also have the power to override state laws.

In addition, the Virginia Plan called for a bicameral legislature. Membership in both houses of Congress would be based on a state's population, with more populous states having a greater number of representatives. Members of the lower house would be directly elected by the people, while members of the upper house would be selected by state legislatures.

The New Jersey Plan Delegates from small states were concerned that the Virginia Plan gave too much power to the large states. After two weeks of discussion, the small states countered with a plan of their own, presented by William Paterson of New Jersey. Paterson's **New Jersey Plan** called for a strong central government made up of three branches. However, the plan was designed to stick closer to the Articles of Confederation.

It proposed a unicameral legislature. Each state would have one vote, giving equal representation to every state regardless of its population. As a result, each state—large or small—would have equal say in determining public policy.

After three days of vigorous debate, the Convention voted on the New Jersey Plan. Despite support from small states, the plan was ultimately rejected.

READING CHECK **Contrasting** How did the Virginia Plan and the New Jersey Plan differ?

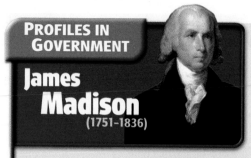

Often called the Father of the Constitution, James Madison played a central role in guiding discussion at the Convention and writing the final document. He carefully transcribed his notes from each day's proceedings into his diary at night; the results remain the best primary account of the Convention. In addition, Madison worked to help secure ratification of the Constitution and to help draft the Bill of Rights. Later, as president, Madison continued to pursue a balance between a strong national government and individual liberty.

Drawing Conclusions Why is James Madison considered the Father of the Constitution?

Conflict and Compromise

For weeks after the rejection of the New Jersey Plan, the Convention was deadlocked. Tempers flared, and at times it seemed the Convention would fall apart. In the end, a series of compromises saved the Convention.

The Great Compromise On June 30, 1787, Roger Sherman of Connecticut rose to present a plan he and a group of fellow delegates had devised. The Connecticut Compromise, now known as the **Great Compromise**, combined elements from both the Virginia and the New Jersey plans.

Like the Virginia Plan, the Great Compromise called for the creation of a bicameral legislature. Membership in the lower house, known as the House of Representatives, would be based on a state's population, thus pleasing the states with larger populations. Members of the lower house would be elected by popular vote.

In the upper house, known as the Senate, each state would have two members regardless of its population. Similar to the New Jersey Plan, this proposal would protect the smaller states by granting them equal representation. Members of the Senate would be selected by state legislatures.

Sherman's plan solved the dilemma over representation to the satisfaction of large and small states alike. On July 16, delegates to the convention approved the compromise. Their work, however, was not yet finished.

KEY ISSUE	VIRGINIA PLAN (Large-State Plan)	NEW JERSEY PLAN (Small-State Plan)	THE GREAT COMPROMISE (The Constitution)
What is the source of the national government's power?	The people	The states	The people
What is the structure of the legislature?	Bicameral Congress	Unicameral Congress	Bicameral Congress
What is the basis of representation in Congress?	Representation based on population	One vote for every state	Equal votes in the Senate; representation based on population in the House
How will Congress pass laws?	Simple majority	Extraordinary majority	Simple majority vote, with provision for a presidential veto
What powers will Congress have?	Power to regulate commerce and tax	Power to regulate commerce and tax	Power to regulate commerce and tax
What kind of executive is there?	Number of executives undetermined; elected and removed by Congress	More than one executive; removable by a state majority	One executive; elected by the people and removable by Congress
What kind of judicial branch?	National court system with power to overturn state laws	National court system with no power over states	National court system with power to overturn state laws
Who will approve the new plan for government?	The people	State legislatures	State ratification conventions

Skills FOCUS · INTERPRETING CHARTS

What features of the New Jersey Plan would have appealed to smaller states?

Compromises over Slavery The issue of slavery lay just below the surface of debates throughout the Philadelphia Convention. At issue was not whether slavery would be allowed to continue. Rather, delegates argued over two key points. The first point concerned whether or not enslaved people should be counted as part of a state's population. The second was whether the importation of enslaved people should be allowed to continue.

Counting enslaved people would greatly increase the population—and thus the power—of the southern states in the House of Representatives. Northern delegates argued that enslaved people should not be counted as part of a state's population since enslaved people were not allowed to vote. Southern delegates, however, insisted that enslaved people should be counted, even though they had no intention of extending the vote to slaves.

This dispute was settled by what came to be called the **Three-Fifths Compromise**. It provided that three-fifths of the enslaved people in a state would be counted when determining a state's population. Thus, for every five enslaved people, three would be added to the state's population total to determine the number of representatives a state would have in the House.

The Framers also took up the issue of the slave trade. By 1787 there was widespread agreement in the North that the slave trade was inhumane and many northern delegates wanted to ban the slave trade, but not the institution of slavery itself. Southern delegates warned that such a proposal would endanger the entire work of the Convention.

Once again, the Convention was saved by a last-minute compromise. The Atlantic slave trade would be protected for the next 20 years. A clause in Article I, Section 9, of the Constitution prohibited Congress from interfering with the importation of enslaved people until 1808. In exchange, the delegates agreed that a simple majority in both houses of Congress would be all that was needed to regulate commerce.

Presidential Election The delegates negotiated another compromise to settle how to select the president. Some delegates believed that the president should be elected directly by the people. Others wanted the president to be chosen by the state legislatures or by the national legislature.

The Framers created a system in which the president would be chosen by state electors. The number of a state's electors would match the number of representatives the state had in both houses of Congress. Many delegates assumed that state legislatures would choose the electors by popular vote. If no presidential candidate received a majority of electoral votes from the states, the House of Representatives would choose the president.

Finalizing the Constitution Throughout the hot summer of 1787, weary delegates debated a number of difficult issues. They settled disputes and made key decisions. In the middle of July, they set about writing a draft. By September, the delegates had only one thing left to do—show their approval by signing the final document.

Benjamin Franklin urged the delegates to overlook the parts of the document that they did not like because it was as close to a perfect Constitution as he thought possible.

PRIMARY SOURCE

> ❝ I confess that there are several parts of this constitution which I do not at present approve, but I am not sure I shall ever approve them . . . It therefore astonishes me, Sir, to find this system approaching so near to perfection as it does . . . Thus I consent, Sir, to this constitution because I expect not better, and because I am not sure that it is not the best. ❞
>
> —Benjamin Franklin, September 17, 1787

Franklin urged the meeting to "act heartily and unanimously" in signing the Constitution. Many who signed the document wholeheartedly supported the new plan, and others signed in spite of their misgivings. A handful of respected delegates, however, refused to sign the document because it lacked a bill of rights. They were George Mason and Edmund Randolph of Virginia and Elbridge Gerry of Massachusetts.

In all, 39 delegates from 12 states signed the Constitution. The Constitutional Convention adjourned on Monday, September 17, 1787. It was now time for the American people to approve the document.

READING CHECK **Summarizing** What compromises made the Constitution possible?

SECTION 4 ASSESSMENT

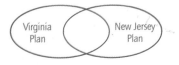

THINK central — Online Quiz
thinkcentral.com
KEYWORD: SGO ORI HP

Reviewing Ideas and Terms

1. **a. Recall** What was the original purpose of the 1787 Constitutional Convention?
   b. Summarize What qualifications did the Convention's delegates possess?

2. **a. Explain** How did the **Virginia Plan** aim to improve the structure of the national government?
   b. Contrast How did supporters of the Virginia Plan and New Jersey Plan differ?

3. **a. Summarize** What were the key issues involved in the compromises made over slavery?
   b. Predict What might have happened if the delegates were not able to agree to the terms of the Great Compromise?

Critical Thinking

4. **Compare and Contrast** Copy the diagram below and take notes comparing and contrasting the Virginia Plan and the New Jersey Plan.

   Virginia Plan — New Jersey Plan

FOCUS ON WRITING

5. **Descriptive** James Madison kept a journal recording the proceedings of the Constitutional Convention. Write a diary entry describing a pivotal event that happened at the convention from Madison's point of view.

Mandatory National Public Service

Should the national government institute new programs for mandatory national public service?

THE ISSUE

The Framers of the U.S. Constitution believed strongly that a representative democracy could not last without active citizen participation and a spirit of civic virtue, or people's ability to place the common good over their own self-interest. In their view, all citizens must be prepared to do their part to maintain democracy and the public good. In addition to voting and paying taxes at the local, state, and national levels, civic participation can also mean volunteering one's service and abilities at any one of these levels, either independently or as part of a group.

At present, the United States sponsors voluntary military service as well as voluntary public service opportunities. To ensure the future of our republic, however, some people have proposed that our national government should institute a mandatory public service plan.

Opponents of mandatory public service claim that it could rob volunteers for groups such as Teach for America (top, right) and individuals such as Geoffrey Canada (above, left), the founder of Harlem Children's Zone, of their initiative to volunteer.

VIEWPOINTS

Public service should be mandatory. Proponents of mandatory public service see it as the best way to cultivate civic virtue in our nation's youth. Young people could choose service in either the nation's military or a nationally funded public service program, such as Ameri-Corps, which sponsors community service programs ranging from public education to building public housing. In exchange, the government would offer money for college or other payment. Such a system would promote patriotism and tolerance of one's fellow citizens and would help our nation's future leaders develop the compassion and courage they need to maintain democracy.

Public service should remain voluntary. Many people argue that the needs of the people are better served by private volunteerism and civic organizations, not the government. Mandatory service runs contrary to personal liberty and takes away freedom of choice, a freedom most Americans are reluctant to give up. Moreover, mandatory service would diminish the spirit and quality of service, since people might perform it grudgingly. Lastly, paying for a mandatory public service program would be enormously expensive. Society would not be able to reap the benefits until years later, and the government would be footing the bill.

What Is Your Opinion?

1. Do you think that the government should institute mandatory public service? Explain.

2. Should Americans continue to care about civic virtue? Why or why not?

THINK central **Practice Online**

thinkcentral.com
KEYWORD: SGO ORI

SECTION 5

Ratification and the Bill of Rights

BEFORE YOU READ

Main Idea

Before the Constitution could take effect, a heated debate between those in favor of the Constitution and those who opposed it took place in all the states.

Reading Focus

1. What were the main points of disagreement between the Antifederalists and the Federalists?
2. What were the main arguments made by the authors of the *Federalist Papers*?
3. Why was the Bill of Rights important to the ratification of the Constitution?

Key Terms

Federalists
Antifederalists
Publius
Federalist Papers
Bill of Rights

TAKING NOTES As you read, take notes on the ratification debate in a graphic organizer like this one.

Ratifying the Constitution

A Government by Choice

WHY IT MATTERS **The Fight for Ratification** In the wake of the Constitutional Convention, a heated debate—between those who supported the new plan for government and those who opposed it—gripped the newly born American republic. For 10 months, the debate raged across the nation, spilling out of the state-level conventions specially called to consider the terms of the Constitution and into newspapers, pamphlets, sermons, speeches, and everyday conversations.

On October 27, 1787, the *New York Independent Journal* invited its readers to join the debate. Upon opening their newspapers, readers found *Federalist Paper* No.1, the first in a new series of essays written to defend the Constitution and to persuade New Yorkers to ratify it. The essays outlined the philosophy behind the Constitution and argued for a strong national government. Later, the essays were collected in a volume called *The Federalist* and circulated widely in other states.

The authors of *The Federalist* were not the only ones writing essays and pamphlets. Opponents of the Constitution weighed in on the debate with their own vigorous writings. After all, the stakes were high. For the first time in history, a people had a chance to prove, in the words of *Federalist Paper* No.1, that they could create a government "by reflection and choice" instead of having rule imposed on them by "accident and force." ■

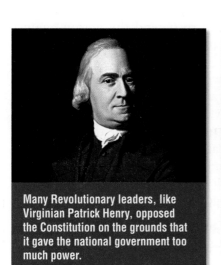

Many Revolutionary leaders, like Virginian Patrick Henry, opposed the Constitution on the grounds that it gave the national government too much power.

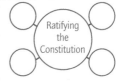

As one of the authors of the Federalist Papers, New Yorker Alexander Hamilton helped build support for the Constitution in New York State and in the rest of the nation.

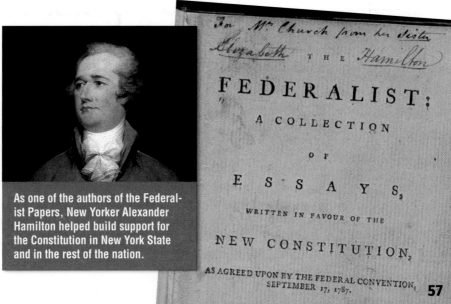

For Mr. Church from her sister Elizabeth Hamilton

THE FEDERALIST; A COLLECTION OF ESSAYS, WRITTEN IN FAVOUR OF THE NEW CONSTITUTION, AS AGREED UPON BY THE FEDERAL CONVENTION, SEPTEMBER 17, 1787.

57

Antifederalists versus Federalists

On September 17, 1787, the Constitutional Convention adjourned. The result of the Convention—the Constitution, an entirely new plan of government—went far beyond the delegates' original intention, to revise the Articles of Confederation. When the Constitution was finally published, the drastic changes surprised some and angered others. With the memory of British rule still fresh in the minds of Americans, many feared a too-powerful national government.

The Framers had anticipated resistance from Congress and the state legislatures. The new national government would not only greatly reduce the powers of state legislatures, but also would completely restructure Congress as established by the Articles of Confederation. Therefore, before concluding the Convention, the Framers outlined a process for ratifying the Constitution that bypassed these bodies. The process called for voters in each state to elect representatives to a state ratifying convention. To become the law of the land, the Constitution had to be ratified by 9 of the 13 states. In the fall of 1787, the battle for ratification began.

The battle would drag on for 10 months, pitting former allies against each other. On one side, there were the supporters of the Constitution, once called nationalists, now called **Federalists**. On the other side of the debate stood those who opposed the Constitution. They were called **Antifederalists**.

Were the delegates justified in creating new rules for the ratification of the proposed Constitution? Why or why not?

The Antifederalists Although they recognized the need for a stronger national government, the Antifederalists charged that the Constitution betrayed the democratic ideals of the American Revolution. In their view, representative government could only exist in a small territory. They saw the document as an assault upon state sovereignty, republicanism, and the liberty of the people. They believed that the national government called for by the Constitution would become too powerful and that the strong executive it described would be too similar to a king.

The Antifederalists' strongest criticism, however, was that the Constitution lacked something that every state constitution possessed—a bill of rights guaranteeing the people's civil liberties. In 1776, for example, Virginia had passed a bill of rights that protected free speech, the right to a trial by jury, the right of property owners to vote, and other individual liberties. Antifederalists believed that without explicit protections of those rights written into the Constitution, a national government could easily violate those rights.

The Federalists By contrast, the Federalists were enthusiastic supporters of a powerful and vigorous national government. Like the Antifederalists, the Federalists feared a central government that was too strong and too far away. Only one thing worried the Federalists more: a weak national government. The Federalists believed a sufficiently powerful national government would strengthen the fragile union and be able to promote the public good.

Such a government would have to be empowered to defend the nation against foreign enemies, regulate trade, and put down internal disturbances, like the mob violence witnessed during Shays's Rebellion. The Federalists believed that the Constitution would give the country the strong, orderly national government that the Articles of Confederation had failed to deliver. At the same time, they pointed out that the separation of powers in the Constitution put limits on government power.

READING CHECK Contrasting Over what issues did Antifederalists and Federalists disagree?

Antifederalist and Federalist Positions

Antifederalists	Federalists
• Opposed the Constitution	• Supported the Constitution
• Feared a too-strong national government	• Wanted a strong national government
• Believed only a small republic could protect rights	• Believed a large republic could best protect individual liberty
• Drew support from small farmers in rural areas	• Drew support from large farmers, merchants, and artisans
• Believed a bill of rights was necessary to protect individual liberties	• Believed a bill of rights was unnecessary

The Federalist Papers

Three of the most intellectually gifted Federalists—Alexander Hamilton, James Madison, and John Jay—teamed up to write a series of articles defending the Constitution for New York newspapers. They wrote under the pen name of **Publius** to honor one of the founders of the Roman Republic. Between fall 1787 and spring 1788, Publius authored a total of 85 essays.

The essays were collected into a single volume and circulated throughout the states. They proved hugely influential in the ratification debate. According to Thomas Jefferson, they were "the best commentary on the principles of government which was ever written." Today, the essays are collectively called the *Federalist Papers* and considered a classic statement of American political theory.

In the essays, Madison, Hamilton, and Jay defended the principles underlying the Constitution. In *Federalist Papers* No. 10 and 51, Madison argued that the Constitution would balance the influence of factions, or groups who attempt to bend the government to serve their own will at the expense of the common good. Other *Federalist Papers*, including No. 47, 48, 49, 50, and 51, explained how the Constitution used principles of government—namely checks and balances and separation of powers—to limit national authority and preserve liberty.

In response, the Antifederalists published essays of their own, under names such as Brutus and the Federal Farmer. Protecting liberty was one of their chief concerns. The Federal Farmer wrote: "There are certain unalienable and fundamental rights, which in forming the social compact . . . ought to be explicitly ascertained and fixed."

READING CHECK **Making Inferences** Why were the Federalist Papers written?

The Fight for Ratification

Because they did not trust government, the Antifederalists wanted the basic rights of the people spelled out in the Constitution. The struggle over a bill of rights became a key focus in the fight over ratification.

Winning over the States When the fight for ratification began, the Federalists, fresh from the Constitutional Convention, were better prepared than their opponents. They first targeted the small states. Attracted by equal representation in the Senate, the small states were quick to ratify. Delaware led the way, approving the Constitution on December 7, 1787.

In the largest and most powerful states—Massachusetts, Virginia, and New York—the ratification struggle was much harder. Strong leaders weighed in on both sides. The Federalists counted James Madison, George Washington, Alexander Hamilton, and Benjamin Franklin among their ranks. The Antifederalists countered with Samuel Adams, Patrick Henry, and Richard Henry Lee.

Patrick Henry was particularly passionate in his opposition. In a speech before the Virginia ratifying convention, Henry asked this question:

PRIMARY SOURCE

❝My political curiosity . . . leads me to ask, who authorized them to speak the language of, '*We, the People,*' instead of '*We, the States?*'❞

—Patrick Henry, June 4, 1788

Ratification of the Constitution

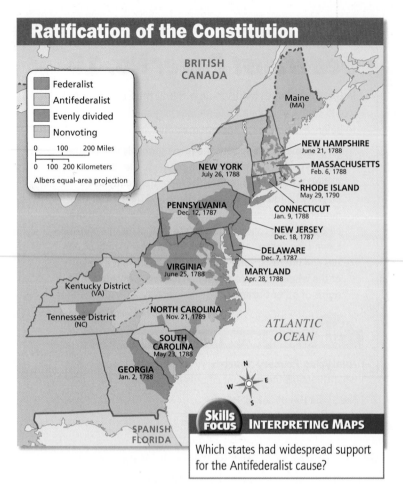

Federalist
Antifederalist
Evenly divided
Nonvoting

0   100   200 Miles
0 100 200 Kilometers
Albers equal-area projection

BRITISH CANADA

Maine (MA)

NEW HAMPSHIRE
June 21, 1788

MASSACHUSETTS
Feb. 6, 1788

RHODE ISLAND
May 29, 1790

CONNECTICUT
Jan. 9, 1788

NEW JERSEY
Dec. 18, 1787

DELAWARE
Dec. 7, 1787

MARYLAND
Apr. 28, 1788

NEW YORK
July 26, 1788

PENNSYLVANIA
Dec. 12, 1787

VIRGINIA
June 25, 1788

Kentucky District (VA)

Tennessee District (NC)

NORTH CAROLINA
Nov. 21, 1789

SOUTH CAROLINA
May 23, 1788

GEORGIA
Jan. 2, 1788

ATLANTIC OCEAN

SPANISH FLORIDA

Skills FOCUS INTERPRETING MAPS

Which states had widespread support for the Antifederalist cause?

Despite objections from noted patriots such as Patrick Henry, the Federalists continued to make progess toward ratification. After agreeing to add a bill of rights, the Federalists secured a victory in Massachusetts in February 1788. The vote was close, 89 to 79, but the win marked a shift in public opinion and helped convince both Maryland and South Carolina to ratify. On June 21, 1788, New Hampshire became the ninth state to ratify, and the Constitution officially went into effect.

Ultimately, the promise of a bill of rights was key to winning over other states—New York and Virginia included—where the Constitution was hotly debated. In the end, all 13 states ratified. North Carolina and Rhode Island were the final holdouts. Both withheld their approval until after the new government was already at work.

Bill of Rights During the First Congress, James Madison encouraged his fellow legislators to make a bill of rights one of the new government's first priorities. To this effect, he suggested a number of rights be protected in amendments, or official changes, to the Constitution. The ideas for these rights had been voiced before—in the English Bill of Rights, the Virginia Declaration of Rights, the Declaration of Independence, and in various state constitutions.

In September 1789 Congress proposed 12 amendments and sent them to the states for ratification. By December 1791 the states had ratified 10 of the amendments. Traditionally called the **Bill of Rights**, these amendments protect such rights as freedom of speech, press, and religion as well as due process protections, such as the right to a fair trial and trial by jury.

READING CHECK **Summarizing** How did the promise to add a bill of rights to the Constitution influence the ratification debate?

SECTION 5 ASSESSMENT

THINK central **Online Quiz**
thinkcentral.com
KEYWORD: SGO ORI HP

Reviewing Ideas and Terms

1. **a. Summarize** Why did the Framers establish a ratification process that bypassed Congress and the state legislatures?
   b. Compare and Contrast How did the **Antifederalists** and **Federalists** differ in their views on national government?

2. **a. Identify** Who were the authors of the *Federalist Papers*?
   b. Explain How did the *Federalist Papers* contribute to the ratification debate?

3. **a. Recall** Why did the Antifederalists insist on a bill of rights?
   b. Predict What might have happened if the Federalists had failed to make good on their promise of a bill of rights?

Critical Thinking

4. **Sequence** Copy the flowchart below and list the order of the events that led to ratification of the Constitution.

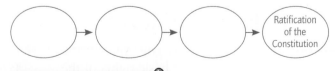

Ratification of the Constitution

FOCUS ON WRITING

5. **Persuasive** Write a letter from James Madison to Patrick Henry to convince him to support the Constitution.

DIVISION FOR
PUBLIC
EDUCATION
AMERICAN BAR ASSOCIATION

Schenck v. United States (1919)

WHY IT MATTERS Are the rights outlined in the Bill of Rights guaranteed absolutely? The Supreme Court's decision in Schenck v. United States considered what limits, if any, could be set on free speech without violating the individual freedoms outlined in the First Amendment.

Background

Shortly after the United States entered World War I, Congress passed the Espionage Act of 1917. The law aimed to silence opposition to the war and stop any activity that might undermine the nation's chances at victory. It made illegal any activity that might obstruct the recruiting or enlistment of soldiers. Congress amended the act with the Sedition Act of 1918, which made it a crime to "willfully utter, print, write or publish any disloyal, profane, scurrilous, or abusive language about the form of government of the United States or the Constitution of the United States."

Still, many people opposed the war, including Charles Schenck, the general secretary of the Socialist Party of America. Among his other antiwar activities, he distributed thousands of leaflets urging men to resist the draft. Schenck was arrested and charged with violating the Espionage Act, which made interfering with the draft illegal. He was found guilty and appealed his case to the Supreme Court.

Arguments for Schenck

Since political speech was protected under the First Amendment, Schenck argued that the Espionage Act was unconstitutional. He claimed his opposition to what he considered an immoral war was a protected right. If Congress could choose under what circumstances a citizen's rights could be diminished, Schenck warned, other First Amendment rights would also be in danger of being taken away.

Arguments for the United States

The United States argued that the case did not involve the First Amendment, but the draft policy. During a time of war, the nation must be able to take steps to defend itself, including against speech that threatens to jeopardize national security or the personal safety of American citizens. The Espionage Act was warranted and just, because criticisms of the government should not be allowed during a military crisis.

THE IMPACT TODAY In 1919 the Supreme Court issued a unanimous decision, upholding the Espionage Act and Schenck's conviction. Writing for the majority, Justice Oliver Wendell Holmes argued that the government could restrict freedom of speech in wartime if such speech posed "a clear and present danger" to national security. The court determined that Schenck's leaflets posed just such a danger. Today the question of how and if free speech should be limited in wartime continues to challenge American society. The right to disagree with government policy is considered an essential right by many Americans. Others feel that it is unpatriotic to oppose an ongoing war.

CRITICAL THINKING

What Do You Think? What is the policy on war protest and the draft today? Compare the Espionage Act of 1917 to current laws, such as the Patriot Act, that deal with treason, sedition, and subversive activities. What effect do you think the limitation of free speech has on American democracy today?

THE CITIZEN & THE CONSTITUTION

Individual Rights and the U.S. Constitution

The Framers of the Constitution believed that individual rights had to be protected from government interference. To ensure the adoption of the Constitution, they promised to add a bill of rights that would safeguard individual rights.

Who may hold rights? Rights may be held by individuals, classes (categories) of individuals, or institutions.

- **Individuals.** The idea that individuals can hold rights reflects the belief that humans should be considered autonomous and self-governing. This includes the belief that each individual should possess certain fundamental rights, such as those to freedom of thought and conscience, privacy, and movement. This emphasis on the rights of individuals is reflected in natural rights philosophy, exemplified in the Declaration of Independence by the statement that "all Men are created equal, that they are endowed by their Creator with certain unalienable Rights, that among these are Life, Liberty, and the Pursuit of Happiness."

- **Classes (categories) of individuals.** Under most legal systems members of certain classes or categories of individuals within a society are recognized in the law as holding certain rights. For example, laws may grant such rights to children, the mentally ill or disabled, veterans, and those who hold professional qualifications, such as teachers, doctors, attorneys, building contractors, and airplane pilots.

- **Institutions.** Institutions such as schools; governmental institutions at local, state, and national levels; unions; universities; business partnerships; and corporations also hold certain rights.

What are common categories of rights? Three common categories are personal rights, economic rights, and political rights.

- **Personal rights.** These rights provide for individual autonomy, including, among others rights, freedom of thought and conscience, privacy, and movement. The idea that humans are autonomous, self-governing individuals with fundamental rights is central to natural rights philosophy. The rights to life, liberty, property, and the pursuit of happiness often are said to be "God-given" or based on nature. Every person is believed to possess such rights at birth. The purpose of government is to protect those rights.

- **Economic rights.** These rights include choosing the work one wants to do, acquiring and disposing of property, entering into contracts, creating and protecting intellectual property such as copyrights or patents, and joining labor unions or professional associations. Like political rights, such rights can be created and protected by statutes, national or state constitutions, or both. Many people consider economic rights to be associated with ownership.

- **Political rights.** These are rights of individuals that address political participation and can be created and protected by statutes, national or state constitutions, or both. Examples are the rights to vote and to engage in political activities, such as supporting particular candidates for office or running for office.

What kinds of rights does the Bill of Rights protect? The Bill of Rights is commonly understood to contain specific guarantees of individual rights. In fact, the situation is more complicated because the Bill of Rights involves a number of different types of rights.

For example, the Second Amendment provides that "A well regulated Militia, being necessary to the security of a free State, the right of the people to keep and bear Arms, shall not be infringed." Some people argue that this amendment refers to the institutional rights of states to maintain militia units. Others contend that it refers to the individual right to keep and bear arms. The Supreme Court seemed to side with the institutional view in *United States* v. *Miller* (1939), but lower federal courts have continued to debate the issue. In 2007 the Court agreed to revisit the question by agreeing to rule on a case challenging the constitutionality of a District of Columbia ban on the possession of handguns by individuals.

What is the meaning and importance of the Ninth and Tenth Amendments? The first eight amendments to the U.S. Constitution contain specific guarantees of rights. By contrast, the Ninth and Tenth Amendments do not. There is ongoing debate about the meaning of these amendments.

The Ninth Amendment provides that "The enumeration in the Constitution of certain rights shall not be construed to deny or disparage others retained by the people." Theories about the Ninth Amendment include the following:

- It is simply an admission that it would be impossible to list all the rights and liberties that should be protected from government interference.
- It confirms that the Bill of Rights does not increase the powers of the national government in areas not mentioned in the first eight amendments. It does not guarantee any rights or impose any limitations on the national government.
- It commands judges and Congress to affirm rights not mentioned in the Constitution.

The Tenth Amendment states, "The powers not delegated to the United States by the Constitution, nor prohibited by it to the States, are reserved to the States respectively, or to the people." Of all the amendments the Anti-Federalists demanded in state ratifying conventions, one designed to reserve powers to the states was the most common. Two views of the Tenth Amendment are

- It states the nature of American federalism but adds nothing to the Constitution as originally ratified.
- It protects the powers of the states against the national government.

THE BILL OF RIGHTS

Amendment I	Safeguards freedom of religion, speech, press, and the right to assembly and to petition
Amendment II	Asserts the need for a militia and protects the right to keep and bear arms
Amendment III	Prevents soldiers from taking over private homes during peacetime or war unless authorized to do so by law
Amendment IV	Prohibits unreasonable searches and seizures
Amendment V	Protects the rights of accused persons
Amendment VI	Provides the right to a speedy, fair trial
Amendment VII	Guarantees the right to a trial by a jury of one's peers
Amendment VIII	Prohibits excessive bail and fines, prohibits cruel and unusual punishment
Amendment IX	Ensures that people's rights that are not specifically listed in the Constitution are retained by the people
Amendment X	Grants to the states and to the people powers that are not specifically listed in the Constitution

---

Reviewing Ideas and Terms

1. **Identify** Select three rights from the Bill of Rights. Are the rights you selected personal, economic, or political rights?

2. **Explain** What do you think is the meaning of the Ninth Amendment? the Tenth?

Critical Thinking

3. **Evaluate** What is the importance of the Bill of Rights to the preservation of individual rights in the American political system? How does the Bill of Rights serve the public good?

Connecting Online

Visit thinkcentral.com for review and enrichment activities related to this chapter.

THINK central

KEYWORD: SGO ORI

Quiz and Review

GOV 101
Examine key concepts in this chapter.

ONLINE QUIZZES
Take a practice quiz for each section in this chapter.

Activities

eActivities
Complete Webquests and Internet research activities.

INTERACTIVE FEATURES
Explore interactive versions of maps and charts.

KEEP IT CURRENT
Link to current events in U.S. government.

Partners

American Bar Association Division for Public Education
Learn more about the law, your rights and responsibilities.

Center for Civic Education
Promoting an enlightened and responsible citizenry committed to democratic principles and actively engaged in the practice of democracy.

Online Textbook

ONLINE SIMULATIONS
Learn about U.S. government through simulations you can complete online.

Comprehension and Critical Thinking

SECTION 1 *(pp. 32–36)*

1. **a. Review Key Terms** For each term, write a sentence that explains its significance or meaning: Magna Carta, Petition of Right, English Bill of Rights.

   b. Analyze How did the struggle between Parliament and the English monarch affect American ideas about government?

   c. Contrast How did royal, proprietary, and charter colonies differ from one another?

SECTION 2 *(pp. 37–42)*

2. **a. Review Key Terms** For each term, write a sentence that explains its significance or meaning: Iroquois Confederation, Albany Plan of Union, Stamp Act, delegates, First Continental Congress, Second Continental Congress.

   b. Analyze Why did the colonists object to Britain's Parliament placing taxes on the colonies?

   c. Contrast How did the goals of the delegates attending the First and Second Continental Congresses differ?

SECTION 3 *(pp. 47–50)*

3. **a. Review Key Terms** For each term, write a sentence that explains its significance or meaning: Articles of Confederation, ratify, Northwest Ordinance, Shays's Rebellion.

   b. Summarize What powers did states have under the Articles of Confederation?

   c. Explain What do you think was the most significant weakness of the Articles of Confederation?

SECTION 4 *(pp. 51–55)*

4. **a. Review Key Terms** For each term, write a sentence that explains its significance or meaning: Virginia Plan, New Jersey Plan, Great Compromise, Three-Fifths Compromise.

   b. Explain Who were the Framers?

   c. Contrast How did the New Jersey and Virginia plans differ?

SECTION 5 *(pp. 57–60)*

5. **a. Review Key Terms** For each term, write a sentence that explains its significance or meaning: Federalists, Antifederalists, Bill of Rights.

   b. Summarize What were the key points of the Antifederalists?

   c. Elaborate How did the *Federalist Papers* contribute to the ratification process?

   d. Identify What is the Bill of Rights and why was it important to the ratification process?

Critical Reading

Read the passages in Section 2 entitled "The Road to Independence." Then answer the questions that follow.

6. Which of the following meetings was the earliest example of an attempt at colonial unity?

A New England Confederation

B Albany Plan of Union

C Annapolis Convention

D Articles of Confederation

7. Which of the following events led colonial leaders to call for the First Continental Congress?

A French and Indian War

B Stamp Act

C Boston Tea Party

D Intolerable Acts

RESPONSIBILITIES OF LEADERSHIP

8. Conduct Internet or library research to find a current event that illustrates one of the following concepts: **rule of law**, **social contract**, **natural rights**, or **representative government**. Then write a paragraph describing the event or situation and how it illustrates the concept you selected. Be sure to explain the concept and, where possible, compare and contrast it to a similar event from English or U.S. history.

9. Choose one foundational document of American democracy, such as the **Declaration of Independence**, the **Constitution**, or the **Bill of Rights**. Explain how the document expresses basic political principles, such as popular sovereignty, the rule of law, the separation of powers, limited government, and representative government.

CONNECTING TO THE CONSTITUTION

10. Read the Bill of Rights to the Constitution, the English Bill of Rights, and the Virginia Declaration of Rights at the end of your textbook. Analyze each document and compare it to a copy of your state bill of rights. In what ways are the documents similar? How are the documents different? What factors might help explain these differences?

ANALYZING PRIMARY SOURCES

Political Cartoon *First published in May 1754, the cartoon below appeared in Benjamin Franklin's newspaper, the* Pennsylvania Gazette, *with an editorial Franklin wrote concerning the "disunited state" of the colonies.*

11. Analyze What is happening in this cartoon?

12. Draw Conclusions How does the imagery in the cartoon illustrate the cartoonist's opinion of the relationship between the colonies?

WRITING FOR THE SAT

Think about the following issue:

During ratification of the Constitution, the Antifederalists withheld approval of the Constitution until they secured a promise of a bill of rights. Consider what might have happened if the Antifederalists had lost this debate.

13. Assignment How might your life be different if you were not protected by the Bill of Rights? Write a three-paragraph narrative in the form of a story about someone who is not protected by the Bill of Rights. First, write an opening sentence that will catch the attention of your readers. Follow it up with interesting and believable details that will convey your story.

The Constitution

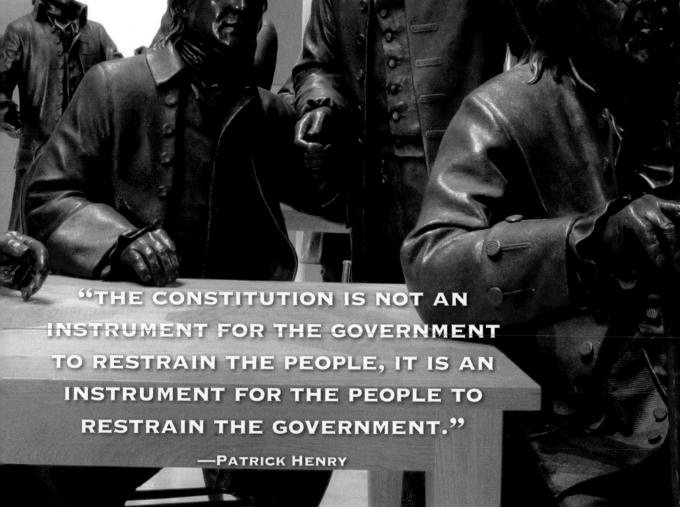

"THE CONSTITUTION IS NOT AN INSTRUMENT FOR THE GOVERNMENT TO RESTRAIN THE PEOPLE, IT IS AN INSTRUMENT FOR THE PEOPLE TO RESTRAIN THE GOVERNMENT."

—PATRICK HENRY

SECTION 1

A Blueprint for Government

- The Constitution establishes six goals for the U.S. government to meet.
- The Constitution outlines six basic principles of U.S. government and a system that safely and fairly distributes and balances power.
- Under the Constitution, the powers of government are limited in order to protect individual rights.
- The Constitution divides the powers of government among three separate branches: legislative, executive, and judicial.
- The Constitution includes checks on and balances of government power to prevent any one branch of government from overpowering the others.

SECTION 2

An Enduring Document

- The Constitution is an enduring document that has the ability to grow and change over time.
- The Constitution includes a formal process for adding amendments to the Constitution.
- The Constitution has been amended 27 times. The first 10 amendments are known as the Bill of Rights.

SECTION 3

Applying the Constitution

- Over time, the three branches of government—legislative, executive, and judicial—have expanded the scope and application of the Constitution.
- Political parties, customs, and traditions have affected how the Constitution is applied and carried out.
- Political scholars have debated what some see as disadvantages of the framework of government established by the Constitution.

CONNECTING TO THE CONSTITUTION

Our nation's system of government is based on constitutional law established by the United States Constitution. See the "We the People: The Citizen and the Constitution" pages in this chapter for an in-depth exploration of how the Constitution organized the new government.

Visitors to Signers' Hall at the Constitution Center in Philadelphia, Pennsylvania, can walk among the statues and feel as if they are taking part in the signing of the Constitution in 1787.

A Blueprint for Government

Main Idea

Drawing lessons from history, the Framers wrote a constitution that divided, limited, and balanced power among three branches of government.

Reading Focus

1. What are the six goals of the Constitution?
2. What are the six principles of government in the Constitution?
3. What is popular sovereignty?
4. What is limited government?
5. How does the Constitution create a separation of the powers of government?
6. How does the system of checks and balances limit the powers of government?
7. Why is the principle of judicial review so powerful?
8. Why is the principle of federalism still a topic of debate?

Key Terms

popular sovereignty
limited government
rule of law
separation of powers
checks and balances
veto
judicial review
unconstitutional
federalism

TAKING NOTES As you read, take notes on the principles of government set out in the Constitution. Record your notes in a graphic organizer like this one.

Principles of Government

WHY IT MATTERS

Checks and Balances The Constitution gives each branch of government certain powers. While citizens—the "We the People" in the Constitution's Preamble—are the ultimate source of all government power, it is the Constitution that divides, limits, and balances these powers among the three branches of government.

For example, the Constitution gives Congress the power to declare war and to raise, support, regulate, and fund the military. Congress has formally declared war only five times—the War of 1812, the Mexican-American War, the Spanish-American War, World War I, and World War II. At the same time, the president also has military powers—the Constitution names the president

commander in chief of the U.S. military. Presidents have used this singular power to send U.S. armed forces to places such as Korea, Vietnam, Grenada, Panama, Saudi Arabia and the Persian Gulf, Afghanistan, and Iraq.

Congress and a president may disagree on one issue or another. When they do, the Constitution's system of checks and balances keeps either branch from taking control or imposing its will on the other one. Sometimes, the judicial branch, including the Supreme Court, must decide the issue. Ultimately, however, we the people may settle the issue by exercising our political power by voting. ■

President George W. Bush, left, and Speaker of the House of Representatives Nancy Pelosi, right, at the president's 2007 State of the Union speech.

The Need to Balance Power

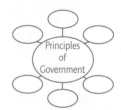

Goals of the Constitution

In the Preamble to the Constitution, the Framers stated the six goals they wanted the national government to accomplish: form a more perfect union, establish justice, ensure domestic tranquility, provide for the common defense, promote the general welfare, and secure the blessings of liberty to themselves and the generations that followed. Such a government would have to raise an army, pay its bills, and conduct relations with foreign countries to reach these goals. Many of the Framers, though, had strong reservations about—or were completely opposed to—a strong national government.

Governing after a Revolution To the Framers, the idea of government suppressing the liberty of citizens was not a fantasy. They had recently fought the American Revolution to stop the powerful British government from infringing on what they viewed as their natural rights. Many of the Framers were students of political philosophy and history. They knew of the achievements and failures of past governments—from Greek city-states to the Roman Empire to the European monarchies. Some of the Framers were also familiar with the constitution of the Iroquois League. As they gathered in Philadelphia in 1787, the Framers faced difficult choices about governing the new nation. They knew their decisions would have long-lasting consequences, and they were determined not to repeat the mistakes of the past. But how?

Addressing the Problem of Governing A dilemma of democratic government is how to allow people substantial freedom while controlling the worst aspects of human behavior. In *Federalist Paper* No. 51, the author described the dilemma as follows:

PRIMARY SOURCE

❝If men were angels, no government would be necessary. If angels were to govern men, neither external nor internal controls on government would be necessary. In framing a government which is to be administered by men over men, the great difficulty lies in this: you must first enable government to control the governed; and in the next instance oblige it to control itself.❞

—James Madison (probable author), 1788

GOALS OF THE CONSTITUTION — QUICK FACTS

GOAL	PURPOSE OF THE GOAL
1. Form a more perfect union	Strengthen the relationship among the states as part of a union and between the states and the national government as part of a new federal system
2. Establish justice	Provide laws that are reasonable, fair, and impartial and make sure that the administration of those laws is also reasonable, fair, and impartial
3. Ensure domestic tranquility	Keep peace and maintain order within the country
4. Provide for the common defense	Defend the nation against foreign enemies
5. Promote the general welfare	Allow all states and citizens to benefit militarily and economically from the protection of a strong national government
6. Secure the blessings of liberty	Protect the liberties recently won in the American Revolution and preserve them for the generations to come

Establishing a system of law was essential. The Framers agreed on this. They drew from the ideas of English philosopher John Locke, who wrote that "where there is no Law, there is no Freedom." Laws help maintain order in society. At all levels of government, they protect rights, property, and lives. Laws set standards of behavior for all citizens and for the society as a whole. Each citizen can know exactly what is expected of him or her.

But laws must also be enforceable. They can be enforced only if there is an explicit threat of punishment, such as imprisonment or fines. The problem is that when a government has the power to make laws and punish lawbreakers, what is to stop it from turning that power against law-abiding citizens? How, in Madison's words, could government be obliged "to control itself"?

READING CHECK **Identifying the Main Idea**
What problem of governing did the Framers face?

Principles of Government in the Constitution

The Framers' solution was to create a governing document, the Constitution, that divided, distributed, and balanced governmental power. In addition, the Constitution made almost all uses of government power subject to the will of the people through their power as voters. Finally, with the inclusion of the Bill of Rights in 1791, the Constitution placed specific restraints on the power of government to take actions that violate the basic rights of citizens.

The Constitution Is the Blueprint The original, unamended U.S. Constitution runs just over 4,500 words. In this brief document, the Framers offered a blueprint for governing that incorporated both ideas that had worked in the past and new, uniquely American principles of governing.

The Constitution we read and apply today consists of three main parts: the Preamble, the articles, and the amendments.

ACADEMIC VOCABULARY

concept an abstract or generic idea generalized from specific instances

---

PRINCIPLES OF THE CONSTITUTION
QUICK FACTS

POPULAR SOVEREIGNTY
The people establish government and are the source of its power.

LIMITED GOVERNMENT
Government powers are restricted to protect individual rights.

SEPARATION OF POWERS
The power to govern is divided among executive, legislative, and judicial branches to prevent the concentration and abuse of power by any one branch.

CHECKS AND BALANCES
Each branch of government has the authority to check, or restrain, some powers of the other two branches.

JUDICIAL REVIEW
The judiciary has the power to strike down laws and other government actions as invalid under the Constitution.

FEDERALISM
The rights of the states are protected by dividing powers between the national government and the state governments.

The Preamble, or introduction to the Constitution, states the broad goals for the new government established by the Constitution. The seven articles following the Preamble create, with little detail or elaboration, the structure of the U.S. government. These articles are remarkable in that only 27 changes, or amendments, have been added to the original Constitution during the nation's history.

Basic Principles of Governing In its structure and its language, the Constitution expressed six basic principles of governing. These principles are popular sovereignty, limited government, separation of powers, checks and balances, judicial review, and federalism. The Framers believed that if the federal government reflected and remained true to these principles, the goals of the U.S. Constitution could be accomplished.

> **READING CHECK** **Identifying the Main Idea**
> Describe how the Constitution provides a blueprint for governing the nation.

Popular Sovereignty

The concept that government gets its authority from the people and that ultimate political power remains with the people is known as **popular sovereignty**. The Framers made popular sovereignty the foundation upon which the Constitution rests.

PRIMARY SOURCE

❝We the People of the United States . . . do ordain and establish this Constitution for the United States of America.❞
—Preamble to the Constitution, 1787

By creating a republic—a national government in which people exercise their sovereignty by electing others to represent them—the Framers firmly established the people's authority. Still, much as the Framers despised the idea of an all-powerful king or central government, they had no intention of putting unlimited power in the hands of citizens, either. They established a republic, not a direct democracy. Moreover, they placed some constitutional limits on popular sovereignty, such as restricting how the Constitution can be amended.

A republic, according to James Madison, was also the best way to guard against the danger of factions, which Madison and other Framers saw as a serious outgrowth of unchecked popular sovereignty. Madison defined a faction as a number of citizens—whether a minority or a majority—united by a common interest who might act in a way that hurt the rights of other citizens or the interests of the nation. Madison argued that factions were certain to exist, so the way to deal with them was to limit their effects. A republican form of government in which elected leaders represent a broad and diverse group of citizens with competing interests would tend to create factions with broad, rather than narrowly partisan, interests.

Popular sovereignty still lies at the heart of our government. Each election, whether it is a local school board election that may affect taxes or a presidential campaign in full swing, is a chance for citizens to exercise their sovereignty. Every elected leader, from the president on down, works for you, and when you step into the voting booth, you can vote to "fire" them. That is an important power and an even more important responsibility. It places with citizens an obligation to exercise their sovereignty wisely, choosing leaders after thoughtful deliberation.

READING CHECK Identifying the Main Idea How is popular sovereignty expressed in the Constitution?

Limited Government

No matter what their political beliefs, most Americans oppose the government exercising too much control over their businesses or private activities. Likewise, the Framers believed that limited government would promote their goals and protect individual rights. **Limited government** is the principle that the powers and functions of government are restricted by the U.S. Constitution and other laws. This principle is also known as the **rule of law**, the concept that every member of society, including the ruler or government, must obey the law and is never above it.

The principle of limited government is spread throughout the Constitution. Article I, Section 8, for example, defines the powers of Congress, including the power to declare

Using Your Power

Voting, as this man is doing, is the most powerful and direct expression of popular sovereignty. Your vote is your voice to express your opinion on issues and to choose your representatives in our political system. *How can voting reinforce limited government and the rule of law?*

war, raise armies, and impose taxes. The list of powers is extensive, but the very act of listing permitted powers implies that any powers not listed are powers excluded. Moreover, Article I, Section 9, specifically denies Congress certain powers, such as the power to grant titles of nobility or pass laws that make criminal an act that was legal when it was committed. The Bill of Rights prohibits government from violating an individual's rights, such as free speech and to a jury trial. By spelling out the limits on government power, the Framers hoped to protect citizens from future abuses of power.

A vigorous civil society—voluntary civic and social groups that form around shared values, purposes, and interests—also works to constrain government power. Civil society groups often participate in the political process, helping educate and inform the citizenry. Informed citizens make better choices when they vote, and they may be more likely to hold government accountable when it exceeds its powers or fails to respond to and address society's needs.

READING CHECK Drawing Conclusions How might civil society support the principle of limited government?

Separation of Powers

WHAT DO YOU THINK?

Read Article II of the Constitution. Article II, Section 1, gives the president "executive power" but does not define what that power is. What other provisions of Article II give an indication of what the Framers meant by "executive power"?

Another way to ensure that the powers of government are not concentrated in the hands of a few officials or agencies is to create three distinct branches of government. Under the principle of **separation of powers**, the duties of governing are divided among three branches: legislative, executive, and judicial. The first three articles of the Constitution list the responsibilities and powers of each branch.

Article I creates and empowers Congress, the nation's lawmaking body, which is made up of the House of Representatives and the Senate. Although the two houses of Congress share responsibility for passing laws, each has its own special powers. For example, laws that fund government must begin in the House of Representatives. This gives the House, where members face voters every two years, significant "power of the purse."

Article II establishes the duties of the executive branch, which comprises the president, vice president, and many executive departments. The executive branch implements, or carries out, laws passed by the legislative branch. The president is also commander in chief of the nation's military.

Article III establishes the judicial branch, including the Supreme Court, to exercise the judicial power of the United States. It is the function of the judicial branch to interpret and apply the law—to say what the law is.

READING CHECK **Summarizing** How does the structure of the Constitution reflect the separation of powers of government?

Interactive Feature

Separation of Powers

The powers of government are divided among the legislative, executive, and judicial branches.

Legislative · Makes laws

Executive · Carries out laws

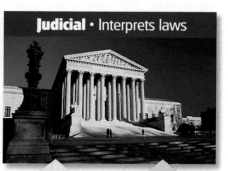

Judicial · Interprets laws

| Executive | Judicial | Legislative | Judicial | Executive | Legislative |

Checks and Balances
Each of the three branches of government has ways to check, or limit, the powers of the other branches.

• Can veto acts of Congress • Can call special sessions of Congress • Can suggest laws and send messages to Congress	• Can declare acts of Congress unconstitutional through the power of judicial review	• Can impeach and remove the president • Can override veto • Controls spending of money • The Senate approves or rejects certain presidential nominations. • The Senate must ratify all formal U.S. treaties.	• Can declare executive acts unconstitutional • Judges are appointed for life and are free from executive control.	• Appoints federal judges • Can grant reprieves and pardons for federal crimes	• Can impeach and remove federal judges • Establishes lower federal courts

Skills FOCUS **INTERPRETING CHARTS**

Analyzing How do checks and balances reinforce the separation of powers?

Checks and Balances

Under the principles of separation of powers and checks and balances, one responsibility of the legislative branch is to oversee the actions of the federal government. Congress's oversight authority is implied in the Constitution as part of its power to raise and spend federal funds. Does this authority extend to the executive branch? If so, does it extend to the president, or does the separation of powers exempt parts of the executive branch from any checks? In this cartoon, the systems of checks and balances seems to have broken down. A frightened Jack-and-the-Beanstalk character representing Congress tries to exercise oversight on an empowered giant.

SKILLS FOCUS **INTERPRETING PRIMARY SOURCES**

Making Inferences How does the artist represent the structure of the U.S. government? What does the cartoon say about the relationship among the branches of government at the time the cartoon was drawn?

See **Skills Handbook**, p. H9.

Checks and Balances

Under the Constitution, each branch of government has its own area of governmental responsibility. The three branches are not completely separate from each other, however. The Framers wanted to be sure that none of the branches, especially the executive, would become so powerful it dominated the other two. They feared that if one branch controlled the government, that branch could interfere with individual political rights and harm the "common good." The common good are those policies and actions that benefit all of society, such as health, safety, and defense programs.

The Framers constructed a system of checks and balances among the three branches of government. **Checks and balances** refers to the system that gives each branch of government the power to change or cancel acts of another branch. The system prevents any branch from exerting too much power.

For example, Congress can check the executive branch by controlling taxes and spending. First the House of Representatives, then the Senate, must pass all bills that spend money. As a result, Congress can limit or even cut the spending by the executive branch on hundreds of federal programs. In addition, the Senate can reject presidential nominations to top government jobs and must approve international treaties negotiated by the president by a two-thirds vote in order for the agreements to become law. Finally, Congress is given the power to declare war, which places limits on the president's power as commander in chief.

The executive branch has a check on the legislative branch by way of the president's power to **veto**, or reject, legislation. Sometimes the threat of a presidential veto is sufficient to push congressional leaders to revise legislation so that it has a better chance of being signed by the president and thus becoming law. Other times, the president must actually exercise the veto power and challenge the legislature's action.

The president's veto power is limited, however, because of a further constitutional check: Congress has the power to override a presidential veto if at least two-thirds of the members in both houses of Congress vote to do so. If Congress can muster the votes to override the president's veto, the bill passes.

The judicial branch can check the powers of the legislative and executive branches by declaring their acts unconstitutional. This is the power of judicial review. The Constitution also insulates federal judges from undue political influence by granting them lifetime terms. The Constitution balances the power of judicial review by giving the president the power to nominate, and the Senate the power to approve, all federal judicial nominations.

Congress and presidents have, at times, been frustrated by courts exercising judicial review. Perhaps the most famous example of presidential annoyance at the Supreme Court occurred in the 1930s. President Franklin Delano Roosevelt had convinced Congress to pass several measures to combat the Great Depression, only to have the Court declare some of his recovery measures unconstitutional. Roosevelt responded by introducing legislation to reorganize the federal judiciary. One part of the plan was to increase the size of the Court—which would have been constitutional—by adding up to six new justices. The result would have been a larger Supreme Court with a majority of the justices friendly to his programs.

Critics claimed that Roosevelt was trying to change the constitutional balance of power among the branches of government. Roosevelt's "court-packing" plan was bitterly opposed in Congress. The Senate removed the controversial language and passed a watered-down reorganization plan.

RESPONSIBILITIES OF LEADERSHIP

Leaders know that there may be several ways to reach a goal. Sometimes a compromise will help all parties reach an agreement. Other times, a leader may try to find another legal way to reach the goal.

Roosevelt's controversial plan was never implemented. However, in his second term, President Roosevelt was able to replace five of the Supreme Court justices, which gave him a sympathetic majority. The Court then ruled favorably on a number of the New Deal programs, such as Social Security.

READING CHECK Identifying Supporting Details Name at least one check or balance that each branch of government has on the others.

Judicial Review

Who decides if a government action or a new law agrees with the Constitution? In the United States, courts exercise **judicial review**, which is power to determine whether the actions of the legislative and executive branches of government are constitutional.

Any law or government action that is found to violate a part of the Constitution is said to be **unconstitutional**. Because the Constitution is the nation's highest law, an unconstitutional law or act is deemed illegal and cannot be enforced or carried out by the government. The U.S. Supreme Court is most often asked to decide the constitutionality of a federal statute or action, but under certain circumstances the Court may be asked to decide the validity of a state law or action.

Although judicial review plays a pivotal role in American democracy, it is not specifically mentioned in the Constitution. So how did courts get this power? The writers of the *Federalist Papers* made it clear that the courts were to have such power. For example, the author of *The Federalist* No. 51 (probably James Madison) wrote that the power of an independent judiciary would serve as a precaution against one branch of government becoming predominant over the others. In addition, Article III, Section 2, of the Constitution implies the power when it states that "the judicial power shall extend to all cases ... arising under" the Constitution. But it was not until 1803, in the landmark case *Marbury* v. *Madison*, that the principle of judicial review became firmly established by the Supreme Court.

READING CHECK Making Inferences How might the power of judicial review affect ordinary citizens?

PROFILES IN GOVERNMENT

The Granger Collection, New York

John Marshall
(1751–1836)

John Marshall was a prominent Federalist. In 1801, President John Adams named Marshall chief justice of the United States. Marshall served on the Supreme Court as chief justice for more than 34 years. No other justice has had a greater effect on U.S. constitutional law. Marshall wrote more than 500 opinions, including *Marbury* v. *Madison* (1803), which used the power of judicial review to make the Court an equal branch of government, and *McCulloch* v. *Maryland* (1819), which firmly established the principles of the implied powers of Congress and the supremacy of the federal government.

Summarize How did Marshall use the judicial power of the Supreme Court to make the Court an equal branch of government?

DIVISION FOR
PUBLIC
EDUCATION
AMERICAN BAR ASSOCIATION

Marbury v. Madison (1803)

WHY IT MATTERS

Marbury v. Madison **established the Supreme Court's power to decide whether laws are constitutional. This power, called judicial review, is a basic principle of American government.**

Background

The presidential election of 1800, pitting Democratic-Republican Thomas Jefferson against Federalist John Adams, was bitterly contested. Jefferson won the popular vote, but confusion over the electoral college vote threw the election into the House of Representatives. Eventually, Jefferson prevailed—by one vote—and took office in March 1801.

Before Jefferson's inauguration, outgoing President Adams quickly appointed 58 members of his own party, including William Marbury, to fill government posts created by the Federalist-majority Congress. Adams also nominated John Marshall, his secretary of state, to be chief justice of the Supreme Court.

As secretary of state, Marshall was responsible for delivering the commissions to the newly appointed officials. He signed and sealed the commissions, but did not deliver 17 of them before Adams left office. The appointees could not take office without their commissions in hand. Marshall thought that James Madison, the new secretary of state, would finish the job. However, when Jefferson took office, he instructed Madison not to deliver some of the commissions, including Marbury's. Marbury sued Madison to get his commission.

Arguments for Marbury

Marbury argued that he had a vested property right to receive his commission because once it had been signed and sealed, his appointment was complete. Delivering the commission, Marbury argued, was not part of the appointment process. Under Section 13 of the Judiciary Act of 1789, Marbury went directly to the Supreme Court to ask for a writ of mandamus—an order from a court requiring a government officer to take a particular action—ordering Madison to deliver his commission.

Arguments for Madison

Madison argued that President Jefferson had ordered him not to deliver Marbury's commission. President Jefferson believed that because the commission had not been delivered under President Adams, Marbury's appointment had not been completed and Marbury had no right to his commission. Jefferson also argued that under the Judiciary Act of 1789, the Supreme Court did not have the authority to order him to deliver the commission.

THE IMPACT TODAY In *Marbury* v. *Madison*, the Supreme Court ruled that Marbury did have a right to receive his commission. However, the Court ruled that Section 13 of the Judiciary Act extending the Court's jurisdiction to cases involving writs of mandamus was unconstitutional. With that ruling, the Supreme Court asserted its power of judicial review—and established the judiciary as a co-equal branch of the government.

Since the 1980s, presidents have sometimes issued written statements declaring that part of a bill they are about to sign is unconstitutional. Opponents say that signing statements violate the Constitution's separation of powers. The use of signing statements has raised an issue of who has the power—courts or the president—to declare laws unconstitutional. The Supreme Court has never addressed the issue of the constitutionality of presidential signing statements.

CRITICAL THINKING

What Do You Think? Judicial review is not expressly set out in the Constitution, but since 1803 it has been a powerful judicial check and balance on the executive and legislative branches. Should the president have a power similar to judicial review to declare laws unconstitutional? Why or why not?

Federalism

The final principle in the Constitution's blueprint is **federalism**, under which the powers of government are distributed between the national government and state governments. The Framers struggled to find an acceptable distribution of powers. They had to ensure that the national government had sufficient power to be effective without infringing on the rights of states.

Two clauses of the U.S. Constitution have been at the heart of the debate over how to strike the proper balance of state and national power. Article I, Section 8, concludes by giving Congress the power to "make all Laws . . . necessary and proper for carrying into Execution the foregoing Powers." In addition, Article VI of the Constitution contains the supremacy clause, which declares that the Constitution—together with U.S. laws passed under the Constitution and treaties made by the national government—is "the supreme law of the land." Advocates for state sovereignty found these clauses troubling. Where was the limit on federal power?

The Tenth Amendment to the Constitution addresses this issue. It states "The powers not delegated to the United States by the Constitution, nor prohibited by it to the states, are reserved to the states respectively, or to the people." This language allows the federal government the flexibility it needs to meet national problems at the same time it guarantees that states retain the powers and rights necessary to meet their needs.

Today most Americans accept strong federal authority on matters such as national defense, disaster response, and highway construction. Yet people disagree over which level of government has authority over many contemporary issues, from natural resources to health care to education.

READING CHECK **Drawing Conclusions** Why do supporters of states' rights refer to the Tenth Amendment to strengthen their arguments?

SECTION 1 ASSESSMENT

THINK central   **Online Quiz**
thinkcentral.com
KEYWORD: SGO CON HP

Reviewing Ideas and Terms

1. a. Describe What are the main goals of the U.S. Constitution?
b. Explain Why might the problems of governing keep the six goals from being achieved?

2. a. Identify Name the six basic principles of governing set out in the Constitution.
b. Summarize How is the Constitution a plan for government?

3. a. Define What is **popular sovereignty**?
b. Evaluate Is popular sovereignty important to a republic? Why or why not?

4. a. Recall What is **limited government**?
b. Elaborate How is the rule of law related to the principle of limited government?

5. a. Describe What problem of governing does the **separation of powers** address?
b. Make Inferences Which branch of government do you think received the most power under the Constitution? Explain your answer, including why the Framers may have done it this way.

6. a. Describe How do **checks and balances** in the Constitution control the powers of government and lead to the development of democratic government?
b. Explain How are the "common good" and individual political rights secured by checks and balances?

7. a. Identify What is the power of a court to declare a law unconstitutional called?
b. Evaluate Do you think the judiciary, which has the power of judicial review, is, as Alexander Hamilton called it, the "least dangerous" branch of government? Explain your answer.

8. a. Explain What is the necessary and proper clause?
b. Elaborate How is the necessary and proper clause related to federalism and states' rights? How might the clause lead to disputes between the federal government and individual state governments?

Critical Thinking

9. Analyze Copy the chart below and give one example of a check that each branch of government has on the other branches.

	Legislative	Executive	Judicial
Legislative	X		
Executive		X	
Judicial			X

FOCUS ON WRITING

10. Descriptive As a reporter in 1787, write an article describing the goals and structure of the newly created U.S. Constitution.

The Constitution and Privacy

As a matter of constitutional interpretation, does the right of privacy exist?

THE ISSUE

Does the Constitution protect your right of privacy? The Constitution does not explicitly mention such a right, but many people argue that the Constitution and Bill of Rights, when read as a whole, protect an implied right of privacy. This approach to constitutional interpretation is sometimes called "loose construction." Other people, calling for "strict construction," argue that the Constitution should be read literally: The words on the page mean exactly—and only—what they say. When the Constitution is read strictly, people argue, it is improper to protect a broad right to privacy.

Many cities now use surveillance cameras to help deter crime, monitor public places, and catch drivers running red lights.

VIEWPOINTS

Loose Construction The Fourth Amendment to the U.S. Constitution states that the right of the people to be "secure in their persons, houses, papers, and effects against unreasonable searches and seizures, shall not be violated . . . but upon probable cause." Justice Louis Brandeis wrote in his dissent in *Olmstead* v. *United States* (1928), a case considering the government's right to use evidence obtained by illegal wiretaps, that "the right to be let alone [is] the most comprehensive of rights and the right most valued by men. To protect that right, every unjustifiable intrusion by the government upon the privacy of the individual, whatever the means employed, must be deemed a violation of the Fourth Amendment." Brandeis argued that by looking at the Constitution and the Bill of Rights as a whole, an individual's privacy is protected. His position was affirmed in *Griswold* v. *Connecticut* (1965), in which the Court ruled that the various guarantees within the Constitution together create a general right to privacy.

Strict Construction Strict constructionists, beginning with Thomas Jefferson, argue that Congress should be able to exercise only the powers expressly given to it and only those implied powers that are absolutely necessary to carry out the expressed powers. Allowing the Court to interpret the Constitution broadly takes away the power of Congress to make laws. Since the word *privacy* does not appear in the Constitution or Bill of Rights, is it reasonable to infer that people have such a right? Justice Hugo Black, who believed that strict construction was necessary in order to rein in judicial power, argued in his dissent in *Griswold* that because an explicit right of privacy is not found in the Constitution, such an inference is improper. In his dissent, Black stated that he found nothing in the Constitution that gives the Court the power to set aside laws when it believes that the laws are "unreasonable, unwise, arbitrary, capricious or irrational." Black voted to uphold the Connecticut statute and found no protected general right of privacy.

What Is Your Opinion?

1. Do you agree with Justice Brandeis's statement from his *Olmstead* dissent, above? Why or why not?

2. Should the Constitution be interpreted more literally or more broadly? Write a short paragraph to support your opinion.

THINK central Practice Online

thinkcentral.com
KEYWORD: SGO CON

An Enduring Document

BEFORE YOU READ

Main Idea
The Constitution is both a product of its time and a document for all time. It can be changed as society's needs change.

Reading Focus
1. How did Jefferson and Madison differ in their views on amending the Constitution?
2. Why might the Constitution be called a document for all time?
3. By what processes can the Constitution be amended?
4. What types of amendments have been added to the Constitution over the last 220 years?

Key Terms
supermajority
repeal

 TAKING NOTES As you read, take notes on the amendment process. Record your notes in a chart like this one.

Proposing	Ratifying
1	1
2	2

A Blueprint that Would Last

WHY IT MATTERS

A Constitution for All Generations
When the Constitution was written, there was a question whether the plan for the new government it laid out would succeed. And if so, for how long? For a generation or two? Longer? What if future generations discovered flaws in it? What if the central government that it created turned out to be too strong or too weak? What if states decided that they wanted more powers? Thomas Jefferson argued that it was inevitable that any imperfections in the new

constitution would become apparent. After all, the document contained several compromises and was bound to have some weaknesses. Therefore, Jefferson argued, it was "imperative" to provide a means for amending, or changing, the Constitution.

Jefferson's instincts were correct, at least to a certain extent: A few imperfections in the Constitution have been discovered. Since 1789, Americans have changed the Constitution—but only 27 times. However, some of those changes do protect our most precious freedoms, as the examples below show. ■

1870
15th Amendment
The right of citizens to vote shall not be denied on account of race, color, or previous condition of servitude.

The Granger Collection, New York

1920
19th Amendment
The right of citizens to vote shall not be denied on account of gender.

1971
26th Amendment
The right to vote of citizens who are 18 years of age or older shall not be denied on account of age.

Jefferson and Madison on Amending the Constitution

In letters to friends, Thomas Jefferson expressed his belief that the Constitution should not be changed on a whim, but it should be able to be changed as society and circumstances changed. In fact, Jefferson saw change as inevitable and positive. He believed that each generation of Americans should be regarded as "a distinct nation," with the right to govern itself but not to bind succeeding generations. "The Earth belongs to the living, not to the dead," he declared. Therefore, Jefferson argued, the Constitution should be revised every generation or so.

PRIMARY SOURCE

❝Each generation is as independent as the one preceding . . . It has then, like them, a right to choose for itself the form of government it believes most promotive of its own happiness.❞

— Thomas Jefferson, letter to Samuel Kercheval, 1816

Jefferson made many of his arguments in an exchange of letters with fellow Virginian James Madison. For his part, Madison had concerns about Jefferson's point of view and wrote to his friend to express his concerns.

PRIMARY SOURCE

❝Would not a Government so often revised become too mutable [changeable] to retain those prejudices in its favor which antiquity inspires . . . ? Would not such a periodical revision engender [cause] pernicious [harmful] factions [groups of people] that might not otherwise come into existence?❞

—James Madison, letter to Jefferson, 1790

Madison is making two points: First, laws and constitutions grow in authority and acceptance the longer they go unchanged. Second, changing the Constitution too often could split the country into bitter factions. Some Framers feared that factions might reinforce sectional rivalries and leave the nation prey to foreign powers and influence. Madison also feared that if the government had to be rebuilt every so often, periods of chaos might occur between revisions.

READING CHECK **Summarizing** Why was Madison opposed to frequent changes to the Constitution?

A Document for All Time

The original Constitution was a product of its time. It reflects both the wisdom and the biases of the Framers. The relatively few changes the document has undergone over more than 220 years testify to its enduring wisdom. The Constitution has survived the Civil War, presidential assassinations, and economic crises to become the world's oldest written constitution.

Yet, as Jefferson suggested, the document that was ratified in 1789 was not perfect. By our standards, it perpetuated injustices. For example, the Framers forged compromises, which you read about in Chapter 2, permitting slavery and the slave trade. States were given the power to set the qualifications for voting, which meant that women, nonwhites, and poor people were denied the right to vote. These decisions reflected the attitudes of many in society at the time. Most people today, however, would find both the attitudes and the decisions unacceptable.

It would be up to future generations to amend the Constitution to address these problems. Many of the amendments, in fact, deal with voting rights and personal liberties. It is the Constitution's ability to incorporate changing ideas of freedom and liberty that has helped make the document relevant to each new generation since 1789.

READING CHECK **Drawing Conclusions** What makes the U.S. Constitution an enduring document?

The Amendment Process

The amendment process gives Americans the power to change the Constitution. But the Framers intentionally made the process difficult. If the process were too easy, they reasoned, the momentary passions and prejudices of the majority—or even an active minority—of the citizens might produce violations of the rights of the rest of the citizens and even threaten the democratic structure of government.

The process for amending the Constitution is described in Article V. Amendments must be proposed and then ratified, or approved. Article V provides two ways of proposing an amendment and two ways of ratifying it.

WHAT DO YOU THINK?

Read Article V of the Constitution. What are the advantages and disadvantages of each amendment process described in Article V?

That means there are four different methods of amending the Constitution, which the Quick Facts chart below illustrates. The different paths to amendments reflected several desires on the Framers' part. By creating a two-step process that required ratification by the states, they restricted the power of Congress to change the Constitution and ensured that any change would reflect the national will. This was in line with the principle of popular sovereignty.

The Framers also required that each step in the process—proposal and ratification—required a supermajority. A **supermajority** is a majority—such as three-fifths, two-thirds, or three-fourths—that is larger than a simple majority. Congress, by contrast, passes ordinary laws by a simple majority vote. The Framers wanted to ensure that the difficult process of changing the Constitution would weed out <u>frivolous</u> amendments.

Proposing an Amendment Constitutional amendments may be proposed in two ways:

1. by Congress, with the approval of at least two-thirds of the House and two-thirds of the Senate

2. by delegates at a national convention that is called by Congress at the request of at least two-thirds of the state legislatures

So far, however, all the amendments to the Constitution have been proposed the first way, by Congress. The required number of states for a national convention has been nearly reached twice, but convention supporters have never managed to persuade the last few needed states. Why not?

Many people point to the wording of Article V itself. Article V does not specify whether a convention can be limited to proposing only the amendment it was called to consider. So, for example, if a convention were called to consider an amendment on immigrants' rights, what would prevent the convention from opening the rest of the Constitution for reconsideration and change? Could the convention propose an amendment to repeal the First or Fourteenth amendments, two amendments that provide the foundation for many of the rights we enjoy today? Or what if the convention proposed an amendment that required every citizen to donate one year after high school to government service? Whatever the reason—whether because it is complicated or because of the uncertainty surrounding it—this method in Article V has remained unused.

AMENDING THE CONSTITUTION

Amendments can be proposed by

Congress

or

National Convention

with a two-thirds vote in each house

called by Congress at the request of two-thirds of the state legislatures

Amendments can be ratified by

Legislatures
of three-fourths of the states

or

Conventions
in three-fourths of the states

Amendment is added to the Constitution.

Skills FOCUS INTERPRETING CHARTS

What steps must be taken to amend the Constitution by using a national convention to propose the amendment? How could the amendment be ratified?

Ratifying an Amendment Once an amendment has been formally proposed by either method, Congress sends the proposed amendment to the 50 states for ratification. States can ratify an amendment in one of two ways—but it is Congress that determines which method of ratification is to be used for any particular amendment.

The two methods for ratifying an amendment are as follows:

1. The proposed amendment is voted on by state legislatures. Legislatures in at least three-fourths of the states must approve an amendment before it is added to the Constitution. In 1978 the Supreme Court ruled that a state legislature may call for an advisory vote by citizens before it votes on the amendment.

2. Citizens elect delegates to conventions called in each state specifically to consider the amendment. Passage by this method requires approval by conventions in at least three-fourths of the states.

The rise and fall of prohibition—a ban on the production, transportation, and sale of alcoholic beverages—illustrates the different ways amendments may be ratified. In the late 1800s and early 1900s, groups of reformers, such as the Woman's Christian Temperance Union (WCTU) and the Prohibition Party, campaigned to outlaw alcoholic beverages. These reformers argued that drinking alcohol led to idleness, violence against women and children, and an increase in crime.

By 1917, more than half the states had passed laws restricting alcohol use. Those laws, plus the need for grain (from which alcohol is made) during World War I strengthened calls for a national ban on alcohol. Responding to this public demand, Congress proposed a prohibition amendment in 1917. By 1919 enough state legislatures had ratified the proposal to make it the Eighteenth Amendment to the Constitution.

Despite the law, however, a widespread illegal trade in alcohol sprang up. After all, the law made it illegal to make, transport, and sell alcohol, but *drinking* alcohol was not banned. The <u>lucrative</u> trade in illegal alcohol spurred the growth of organized crime, political corruption, and violence. Prohibition became very unpopular. Once again, groups of citizens led the movement for reform. In fact, opponents of prohibition used many of the same arguments earlier reformers had used in support of it.

In 1933 Congress responded by proposing the Twenty-first Amendment to repeal prohibition and to give states the power to

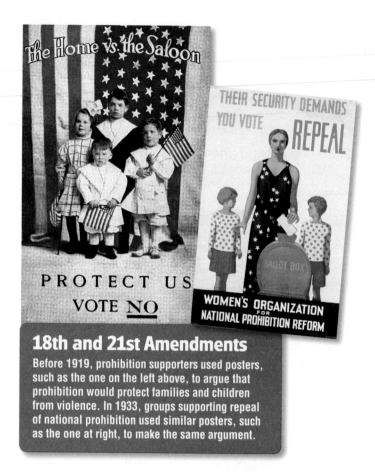

18th and 21st Amendments
Before 1919, prohibition supporters used posters, such as the one on the left above, to argue that prohibition would protect families and children from violence. In 1933, groups supporting repeal of national prohibition used similar posters, such as the one at right, to make the same argument.

regulate the transportation and distribution of alcoholic beverages. To **repeal** a law is to cancel or revoke it by a legislative act—in this case, the Twenty-first Amendment.

Every amendment before and since the Twenty-first Amendment has been approved by state legislatures, but not the Twenty-first Amendment. Supporters of the amendment in Congress thought it had a better chance of being ratified by state conventions of delegates elected specifically to vote on the issue. The strategy worked. Conventions in 36 states ratified the Twenty-first Amendment within the year. The Eighteenth Amendment was repealed.

The Fate of Amendments Undoing prohibition may seem to have been relatively easy, but in general, changing the Constitution is difficult—as the Framers intended it to be. In fact, more than 10,000 attempts to change the Constitution have been suggested or proposed in Congress. Imagine how long and confusing the Constitution would be today if those changes had succeeded.

ACADEMIC VOCABULARY
lucrative profitable; producing wealth

AMENDMENTS TO THE CONSTITUTION

AMENDMENT	SUBJECT	YEAR RATIFIED
1st–10th	Protected certain rights from government infringement; Bill of Rights	1791
11th	Made states immune from certain lawsuits	1795
12th	Changed electoral college	1804
13th	Abolished slavery	1865
14th	Defined citizenship, expanded due process, established equal protection	1868
15th	Prohibited denying right to vote because of race, color, or previous servitude	1870
16th	Permitted passage of income tax	1913
17th	Provided for direct election of U.S. senators	1913
18th	Prohibited production, transportation, and sale of alcohol	1919
19th	Gave women the right to vote	1920
20th	Changed dates for start of presidential and congressional terms	1933
21st	Repealed national Prohibition	1933
22nd	Created presidential term limits	1951
23rd	Gave District of Columbia vote in presidential elections	1961
24th	Banned poll tax (tax paid as voter qualification)	1964
25th	Established rules for presidential succession, filling presidential vacancy, vice presidential succession	1967
26th	Lowered voting age to 18	1971
27th	Provided rules for congressional pay	1992

In fact, only 33 amendments have been passed by Congress and sent to the states for ratification. Of those, 27 amendments have been adopted, while 6 others have been rejected.

READING CHECK **Summarizing** What are the four ways of amending the Constitution?

More than 200 Years of Amendments

The process of adding to the Constitution began almost immediately with the passage of the first 10 amendments, known as the Bill of Rights. Another 17 amendments have been added since then. Together, the amendments identify, support, and protect some of the most important rights that reflect the fundamental goals and principles in our democratic society.

The Bill of Rights In Chapter 2, you read that many Americans had concerns about the original Constitution because it lacked a bill of rights to protect specific individual freedoms. Following ratification of the Constitution, various states offered up a total of 210 suggestions for amendments. James Madison, who had opposed a bill of rights, drafted 12 amendments. Congress passed them and sent them to the states. Ten of the 12 amendments were ratified. The Bill of Rights was adopted in 1791.

The First Amendment set the tone for the other amendments in the Bill of Rights. It begins by forcefully declaring what the federal government may not do:

PRIMARY SOURCES

❝ Congress shall make no law respecting an establishment of religion, or prohibiting the free exercise thereof; or abridging the freedom of speech, or of the press; or the right of the people peaceably to assemble, and to petition the Government for a redress of grievances. ❞
—First Amendment to the U.S. Constitution, 1791

The First Amendment is intended to be a restriction on the power of the national government to interfere with an individual's exercise of certain basic freedoms, such as a person's right to practice religion freely.

The First Amendment also protects freedom of expression and the right to ask the government to correct injustices. You will read more about the protections of the First Amendment in Chapter 13.

The Bill of Rights contains other specific guarantees. For example, the Second Amendment gives citizens a right to bear arms. The Third Amendment prohibits government from forcing citizens to quarter, or shelter, military troops in their homes. The Fourth Amendment protects individuals against unreasonable searches and seizures of private property. The Fifth and Sixth Amendments guarantee that individuals cannot lose their life, liberty, and property without due process of law; are protected against self-incrimination; and have the right to a speedy trial and, in some cases, the right to an attorney. The Bill of Rights concludes with amendments prohibiting the national government from usurping rights or powers that belong to the states and to the people.

The Other Amendments Many of the amendments ratified since the Bill of Rights were proposed during periods of crisis or of social and political progress. For example, in the aftermath of the Civil War, Congress passed the Thirteenth, Fourteenth, and Fifteenth amendments, which banned slavery, recognized all African Americans as U.S. citizens, and gave African American men various rights, including the right to vote. In the South, however, these three amendments were not often enforced from 1877 to 1965. Most southern states passed Jim Crow laws—state laws that separated people on the basis of race—that minimized the effect of the post–Civil War amendments.

The amendments passed in the first two decades of the 1900s marked a time of vigorous social reform. The Eighteenth and Twenty-first amendments were passed during these years. In the same era, the Seventeenth and Nineteenth amendments extended democracy by providing for the popular election of senators—originally state legislatures chose senators—and by granting women the right to vote.

The Framers, however, could never have imagined the changes in the United States in the last 220 years, from the diversity of our population to our rail and highway systems, our ability to manipulate human genes, and our airport X-ray screening devices. Yet throughout the growth from young nation to global superpower, the Constitution has provided a stable, flexible government.

READING CHECK **Summarizing** What are five issues that constitutional amendments have addressed?

RESPONSIBILITIES OF LEADERSHIP

The Framers made some hard choices when they wrote the Constitution. Most of what they wrote has survived without changes. One exception is which citizens have the right to vote. Since the Bill of Rights was ratified in 1791, three amendments that expand the right to vote have been ratified. As society changes, citizens may be called upon to make new hard choices about privacy, security, and other issues.

SECTION 2 ASSESSMENT

THINK central — Online Quiz
thinkcentral.com
KEYWORD: SGO CON HP

Reviewing Ideas and Terms

1. **a. Describe** Why did Thomas Jefferson believe that the Constitution should be amended every generation or so?
   b. Compare How did James Madison's opinion about amending the Constitution differ from Jefferson's opinion?

2. **a. Recall** What is a constitutional amendment?
   b. Evaluate Do you think it should be easier to amend the Constitution today? Explain your answer.

3. **a. Identify** How can an amendment be repealed?
   b. Draw Conclusions How does the amendment process reflect the principle of popular sovereignty?
   c. Evaluate Do you think the Prohibition experience indicates that the Constitution is too flexible? Explain your answer.

4. **a. Explain** What is the purpose of the Bill of Rights?
   b. Make Inferences How do the 27 amendments reflect Americans' changing values and ideals? Give examples to support your answer.

c. Evaluate Why does the First Amendment declare what the U.S. Congress is not allowed to do?

Critical Thinking

5. **Rank** Copy the chart below and list the four amendments you think are most important. Explain your choice.

Amendment	Importance

FOCUS ON WRITING

6. **Expository** Do you think the methods the Framers created for amending the Constitution are still effective to provide for change today? Write two paragraphs stating your opinion.

Applying the Constitution

Main Idea
The scope and impact of the Constitution have expanded as it has been put into practice, interpreted, and applied to new or changing social and political challenges.

Reading Focus
1. How have the three branches of government applied the Constitution?
2. How have political parties, customs, and traditions changed how the Constitution is applied?
3. What criticisms have some people made of the Constitution?

Key Terms
executive agreements
political party
cabinet
gridlock
electoral college

TAKING NOTES As you read, take notes on how the reach of the Constitution has expanded. Record your notes in a graphic organizer like this one.

How the scope and application of the Constitution have expanded

4,540 words

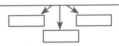

We the People of the United
insure domestic Tranquility, provide for the common defence, promote the
and our Posterity, do ordain and establish this Constitution for the United

Article. I.

Section. 1. All legislative Powers herein granted shall be vested in a Cong
of Representatives.

The original Constitution has changed very little since 1789, but its reach has been expanded to give us the government we have today.

Section. 2. The House of Representatives shall be composed of Members cho

WHY IT MATTERS

A Few Words, a Long Reach Including signatures, the original U.S. Constitution—the foundation and blueprint for the world's most powerful government—runs only about 4,540 words, or about the length of a 20-page term paper. In that short space, there is no mention of whether a teacher can, or cannot, search your backpack. Nor does the Constitution say anything about school prayer, sharing music over the Internet, or prohibiting the purchase of inexpensive medicines from Canada.

In fact, the Constitution is silent about most of the specific issues that you deal with in your life every day. However, in addition to protecting your basic rights, the Constitution also underlies the tens of thousands of laws and the hundreds of government agencies that can, and do, affect your life. How has so much government been derived from so few words? What processes have worked to shape or extend the meaning of the Constitution and change its application over time? How did we arrive at the government and laws we have today? ◼

The Federal Government Applies the Constitution

The Framers did not set out to define the nation's government in exhaustive detail, nor did they intend to regulate people's everyday activities. The Framers created a framework to be followed and filled in by citizens then and in later generations. Over time, the United States has grown in size, population, and complexity, and as it has grown, so has its government. In the process, the legislative, executive, and judicial branches have put the Constitution into action, extending its reach and meaning.

Legislative Action The Framers gave Congress the job of putting meat on the bones of the Constitution. For example, Section 1 of Article III, which created the Supreme Court, also authorized Congress to create "such inferior courts as the Congress may from time to time ordain and establish." This authority is quite general. So Congress passed the Judiciary Act of 1789, which created the system of lower-level federal courts. Article I, Section 8, gives Congress power to "constitute tribunals inferior to the Supreme Court." Over the years, Congress has used both Articles I and III to expand the judicial branch as needed.

Without congressional legislation, none of the departments and agencies that make up today's executive branch would exist. Yet Article II—which creates and defines the executive branch, describes the offices and powers of president and vice president as well as their election, impeachment, and compensation—makes only two passing references to executive departments.

When passing laws to meet new situations, Congress inevitably pushes into areas on which the Constitution is silent. Powerful new technologies, such as today's personal computers and cell phones, and threatening international circumstances, such as possible attacks by terrorists, are two factors that sometimes push Congress onto uncertain constitutional ground. If the Supreme Court strikes down a new law, the reach of the Constitution remains unchanged. If, however, the Court upholds the law, the application of the Constitution has been changed slightly.

THE ENDURING CONSTITUTION

QUICK FACTS

The application of the Constitution has been expanded as the three branches of government have interpreted the document through:

Legislative action
Congress passes minimum wage laws under its power to regulate commerce and immigration laws under its power to regulate naturalization.

Executive action
Presidents negotiate agreements with foreign leaders and foreign governments that create or change U.S. relationships with those governments.

Judicial review
Courts have upheld laws, such as laws that outlaw types of discrimination, as being constitutional.

Executive Implementation Presidents may sometimes exercise their authority in ways that the Constitution does not expressly state. For example, presidents often make **executive agreements**—arrangements or compacts with foreign leaders or foreign governments—even though this power is found nowhere in the Constitution's text. Presidents derive the power to fashion these executive agreements from the acknowledged constitutional powers: their inherent executive power; their power as commander in chief; their power to receive ambassadors and officials from other nations; and their duty to faithfully execute the laws.

Executive agreements are important in conducting foreign policy. In recent years, presidents have increasingly used their executive agreement power, especially when they are seeking to bypass the long, formal— and often contentious—treaty process. For example, in 1990 an executive agreement was used to create the international coalition that defeated the Iraqi invasion of Kuwait.

An executive agreement has the force of a treaty but does not require ratification by the Senate, as treaties do. In practice, however, Congress has authorized a majority of executive agreements in advance or has approved them after they have been signed.

ACADEMIC VOCABULARY

compact an agreement between two or more parties

Most executive agreements require subsequent congressional action—legislation giving an agency the necessary power or money—to be implemented.

Actions of the executive department and agencies also change the way the Constitution is applied or interpreted. Congress passes laws to create these bodies and sets broad goals for them to achieve. It is up to the agencies themselves, however, to define their operations and carry out the programs Congress has assigned to them. In doing so, they are applying the Constitution.

Executive branch agencies also usually have rule-making power, which they use to implement Congress's laws. These rules have the force of law. They affect everything from the medicine we take to the water that comes from our faucets. The Code of Federal Regulations, a collection of all the rules made by executive agencies, is about 135,000 pages long and fills more than 200 volumes. It is another extension of the Constitution.

Judicial Interpretation Can you imagine what it would be like to be a Supreme Court justice trying to apply the Constitution—a brief set of rules for the structure and operation of a new government written before the Industrial Revolution—to a mind-boggling range of modern-day cases? It is an extraordinary responsibility.

As noted in Section 1, the 1803 Supreme Court case of *Marbury* v. *Madison* established the principle of judicial review, the Court's power to determine if a law or other government action is constitutional. Court rulings, therefore, may affect the meaning of the Constitution—what the rights of citizens are and what the government is allowed to do or is prevented from doing.

For example, the Fourth Amendment prohibits "unreasonable searches and seizures." What does this phrase mean in an era of airport screening devices, cell phones, and wireless Internet access? The Framers could not have imagined how technology might change the concepts of "unreasonable," "searching," and "seizing." It is up to courts to interpret the Fourth Amendment in light of changing conditions, and judges are beginning to apply the Constitution's prohibitions to new technologies. Courts try to set legal standards that law-enforcement officers must follow when intercepting private conversations, monitoring e-mail, and using other "searching" methods.

The debate today is not about whether to interpret the words of the Constitution but how to interpret them. You may have heard discussions of "strict" versus "loose" construction of the Constitution. In general, a strict construction, or interpretation, of the Constitution means giving the words in the document only their literal meaning. A loose construction of the Constitution means following the words plus any reasonable inferences that can be drawn from them. For example, the Constitution gives Congress the power to lay and collect taxes. One way for the central government to lay and collect taxes is to establish a national bank.

A strict constructionist would argue, as Thomas Jefferson did, that because there is no provision for a national bank in the Constitution, the government has no power to create such a bank. The government would have to find another way to exercise its power to collect taxes and pay its bills.

A loose constructionist would respond, as Alexander Hamilton did, that because Congress has the important power to lay and

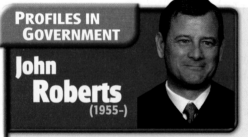

John Roberts did not plan to be a lawyer. However, after he graduated with a degree in history from Harvard University, Roberts decided to pursue a career in law and attended Harvard Law School. As a lawyer, he argued cases before the U.S. Supreme Court, where he earned the reputation of having an outstanding legal mind. In July 2005, President George W. Bush nominated Roberts to replace retiring justice Sandra Day O'Connor.

In September 2005, Bush named Roberts to fill the position of chief justice following the death of former chief justice William H. Rehnquist. On September 29, 2005, John Roberts was sworn in as the seventeenth chief justice of the United States. Roberts is described by most experts as a conservative justice who will be a "strict constructionist" in terms of Constitutional interpretation.

Make Inferences Why might a president appoint a strict constructionist like John Roberts to the Supreme Court?

collect taxes, it is therefore reasonable to think that the Framers intended Congress also to have the implied power to carry out these responsibilities. As a result, creating a national bank is both necessary and proper.

Two other methods of interpreting the Constitution—judicial activism versus judicial restraint and original intent versus evolutionary meaning—are frequently debated. They are similar to strict versus loose construction. Read more about interpreting the Constitution in Chapter 13.

READING CHECK **Identifying the Main Idea** How has each branch of government put the Constitution into action? Give one example for each branch.

Political Parties, Customs, and Traditions

You have read about how the Constitution has been expanded through amendments and how its language has been interpreted and applied by the actions of the three branches of government. Other factors—informal, yet quite important ones—also affect how the Constitution is interpreted, applied, and carried out. These factors include political parties and entrenched customs and traditions.

Political Parties Political parties have an impact on how the Constitution is interpreted and applied for one primary reason: They help determine the choice of candidates, policies, and programs presented to the voters. A **political party** is an organized group that seeks to win elections in order to influence the activities of government. Parties also help shape the judicial branch, whose job is to decide what the law is by supporting or opposing nominees to federal judicial positions, such as U.S. Supreme Court justices. Although they are not mentioned in the Constitution, political parties deeply affect how government operates.

Political parties have also at times led the drive to change the Constitution through the amendment process. The post–Civil War amendments mentioned in last section were largely the work of the Republican Party. The legacy of two political movements popular in the late 1800s and early 1900s

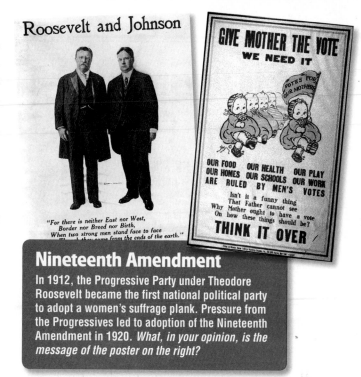

Roosevelt and Johnson

"For there is neither East nor West, Border nor Breed nor Birth, When two strong men stand face to face Tho' they come from the ends of the earth."

Nineteenth Amendment

In 1912, the Progressive Party under Theodore Roosevelt became the first national political party to adopt a women's suffrage plank. Pressure from the Progressives led to adoption of the Nineteenth Amendment in 1920. *What, in your opinion, is the message of the poster on the right?*

GIVE MOTHER THE VOTE
WE NEED IT

VOTES FOR OUR MOTHERS

OUR FOOD   OUR HEALTH   OUR PLAY
OUR HOMES OUR SCHOOLS OUR WORK
ARE   RULED   BY MEN'S   VOTES

Isn't it a funny thing
That Father cannot see
Why Mother ought to have a vote
On how these things should be?

THINK IT OVER

but around no longer, the Populists and Progressives, rests in the Constitutional amendments they helped get passed.

The Populists were a coalition of farmers, labor leaders, and reformers. Populists supported bank regulation; government ownership, or at least government regulation, of railroads; and the unlimited coinage of silver. They also called for the direct election of senators. Populism faded after the presidential elections of 1892 and 1896.

Progressives took up many of the same causes as Populists but also wanted to improve living conditions for the urban poor. As a result of Progressive influence in the early 1900s, Congress passed laws giving the federal government powers to regulate banks, food and drug safety, railroads, and business monopolies—powers upheld by the Supreme Court. Progressives were also instrumental in the passage of the Sixteenth, Seventeenth, and Nineteenth amendments to the Constitution (allowing the income tax, providing for popular election of senators, and giving women the right to vote).

Recently, groups and people—sometimes allied with political parties and sometimes not—also not mentioned in the Constitution have affected government policies. These groups and individuals range from interest group political action committees (PACs) to online political commentators and bloggers.

Gridlock in Government

Most presidents have a legislative agenda, a list of laws and programs they would like to see enacted. However, Congress—not the president—makes laws. The president, therefore, must work with Congress to get his or her agenda enacted. If, for any reason, Congress and the president cannot agree on legislation, the government may grind to a halt. When one political party controls Congress and the other party controls the presidency, the chances of a standoff are that much greater. This cartoon illustrates how party politics sometimes affect the Constitution's systems of separation of powers and checks and balances.

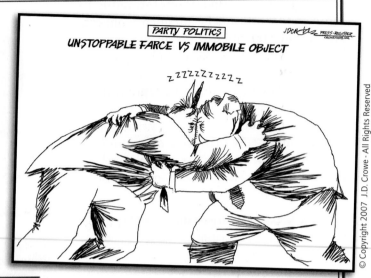

Skills Focus **INTERPRETING PRIMARY SOURCES**

Making Inferences According to this cartoon, who is responsible for government gridlock? Explain why you agree or disagree.

See **Skills Handbook,** p. H9.

Customs and Traditions The Framers might have expected that customs and traditions would help guide the practices of the government. After all, Great Britain had no written constitution—and still does not—but its government was anchored in practices handed down for nearly 1,000 years.

Customs and traditions are not mentioned in the Constitution, but they strongly influence how American government behaves. For example, the Constitution authorizes the president to "require the opinion, in writing, of the principal officer in each of the executive departments." President George Washington relied on this language in Article II to create a **cabinet**, a group of advisers consisting of the heads of the executive departments. Subsequent presidents followed Washington's custom, and the tradition of cabinet and cabinet meetings was born. Today, the cabinet is a firmly entrenched part of our government.

Some traditions have become law. For example, for more than 150 years, starting with Washington himself, no president served more than two terms in office. Franklin Roosevelt broke with tradition to run for and win third and fourth terms as president in the 1940s. The example of Roosevelt worried many Americans, who felt that such lengthy stays in office could lead to an unsafe concentration of power in the hands of one party. As a result, Congress passed the Twenty-second Amendment. It limits presidents to two terms, thus formalizing the custom that began with Washington.

READING CHECK **Identifying the Main Idea** How do political parties and traditions affect the functioning of government?

Criticisms of the Constitution

The U.S. Constitution commands respect around the world for its brevity, insight, and flexibility. Yet with the passage of time, some people have come to agree with Jefferson's prediction that "the imperfections of a written Constitution will become apparent." What are some criticisms that have been raised about the Constitution?

A System That Creates Gridlock In our system of checks and balances, power and decision making are distributed among the branches of government. Critics say that this diffusion of power makes it too easy for the president and congressional leaders to avoid responsibility for their actions.

Frequently, Congress and the president blame one another when they are unable to get things done. This inability to govern effectively due to separation of powers is called **gridlock**. Occasionally, gridlock has been so severe that it has brought government to a standstill. For example, in 1995 a budget dispute between the Republican-controlled Congress and Democratic president Bill Clinton shut down the entire federal government for 27 days.

Questions about Representation Some political observers argue that the Constitution falls short of truly representative democracy when judged by contemporary democratic standards. They are especially critical of the Senate, in which residents of states with small populations have far more relative influence than residents of states with large populations. Wyoming, a state with just over half a million people, elects the same number of senators as California, a state with about 37 million people. Thus, the influence of each voter in Wyoming is far greater than the influence of each voter in California.

The Electoral College You may already know that the president of the United States is not elected directly by voters. Instead, the president and vice president are elected by members of the **electoral college**, the body of 538 people elected from the 50 states and the District of Columbia. Critics of the electoral college point to the fact that the winner of the popular vote may not win the presidency, as happened most recently in the election of 2000. Supporters of the electoral college argue that this system requires candidates to generate support from a variety of states, large and small.

Winner-take-all Elections In elections for U.S. Congress, the candidate who receives the most votes is elected to the House or Senate. A candidate who comes in second or third goes home—even if he or she receives a large number of votes. This type of election is known as the winner-take-all system.

By contrast, many European parliaments use proportional representation. Voters choose from party lists of candidates. Seats are given to each party according to the percentage of the total votes they win. More-popular parties will have a larger number of seats, but less-popular parties will not be entirely shut out of the parliament.

Supporters of proportional representation say it allows a larger variety of viewpoints to gain representation in the legislature. Defenders of the U.S. system respond that proportional representation leads to fractured legislatures with many small parties, while the American process allows the party with the most support to govern.

READING CHECK **Contrasting** How does the winner-take-all election system differ from a system of proportional representation?

SECTION 3 ASSESSMENT

THINK central Online Quiz
thinkcentral.com
KEYWORD: SGO CON HP

Reviewing Ideas and Terms

1. **a. Recall** What is the difference between an executive agreement and a treaty?
   b. Explain How have the three branches of the federal government defined the scope of the Constitution?
   c. Evaluate Do you think the Framers intended for the government to expand as it has? Explain.

2. **a. Identify** What is the main goal of a political party?
   b. Make Inferences How can political parties affect judicial interpretation of the Constitution?

3. **a. Describe** What are three criticisms of the Constitution?
   b. Evaluate Which criticisms of the Constitution do you agree with, and which do you disagree with?

Critical Thinking

4. **Analyze** Copy the chart below. From most to least important in your opinion, list the formal and informal ways in which the U.S. Constitution has been expanded. Explain your reasoning.

Formal	Informal
1.	1.

FOCUS ON WRITING

5. **Expository** In your opinion, is government gridlock ever good for the country? Why or why not? Express your opinion in a brief letter, with examples, to your congressperson.

THE CITIZEN & THE CONSTITUTION

A New Constitution and a New Government

The Constitution was a plan for the new national government that described the new government, its powers, and the limits on it. The Framers wrote the Constitution as a general framework and left out details they knew would be added in the future.

What are Congress's constitutional powers? John Locke claimed that the legislature is the most powerful branch of government because it makes laws. Mistrusting any concentration of political power, the Framers carefully limited Congress's power:

- Article I, Section 8: The Constitution limits Congress's law-making powers to those "herein granted . . ." In addition to 17 specific powers, Congress has a generalized eighteenth power: "To make all Laws which shall be necessary and proper for carrying into Execution the foregoing Powers, and all other Powers vested by this Constitution in the Government of the United States, or in any Department or Officer thereof."

- Article I, Section 9: The Constitution identifies several matters on which Congress "shall not" legislate. For example, it cannot tax articles "exported from any state." It cannot grant titles of nobility. It cannot draw any money from the Treasury "but in Consequence of Appropriations made by Law."

Bill of Rights Added to the Constitution in 1791, the Bill of Rights lists rights upon which Congress "shall not" infringe. For example, the First Amendment states that "Congress shall make no law" establishing a national religion or abridging free speech or press. The Eighth Amendment prohibits Congress from levying "excessive fines" and imposing "cruel and unusual punishments" on convicted criminals.

Even with these limitations, Congress today has far-reaching powers, which include enumerated and implied powers.

Enumerated powers Enumerated, or express, powers are those listed in the Constitution. Article I, Section 8, for example, gives Congress power to "regulate Commerce with foreign Nations and among the several States, and with the Indian Tribes." Other parts of the Constitution also give Congress power:

- Article II: The Senate must advise and consent when the president makes treaties and appoints ambassadors, other public ministers, judges of the Supreme Court, and many other public officials.

- Article III: Congress has complete control over the appellate jurisdiction of the Supreme Court and authority to create lower federal courts.

- Article IV: Congress can admit new states and adopt all rules and regulations respecting U.S. territories and properties.

- Article V: Congress, like the states, can propose constitutional amendments. Congress has proposed all 27 amendments to the Constitution and many that have not been ratified.

Implied powers Some express grants of authority to Congress imply, or suggest, other powers. The "necessary and proper" clause in Article I gives Congress power to legislate on at least some subjects not expressly described in the Constitution.

Adapted with permission from Lessons 21, 23, and 25 of *We the People: The Citizen & the Constitution.* Copyright 2009, Center for Civic Education.

What are the president's constitutional responsibilities? Article II of the Constitution places "the executive Power," the powers of the executive branch of government, in the president of the United States. Unlike Article I, which gives Congress those powers "herein granted," Article II does not define executive power. The Constitution lists some of the president's powers, but those listed have never been thought to be the president's only powers. The listed powers include the following:

- commanding the army and navy (as commander in chief)
- heading the executive department (cabinet and executive departments)
- granting reprieves, or postponement of punishment, and pardons
- making treaties (subject to the advice and consent of the Senate)
- nominating ambassadors, public ministers, consuls, and judges of the Supreme Court and other federal courts
- recommending legislation to Congress
- reviewing legislation passed by Congress and returning bills to which the president objects
- receiving ambassadors and other public ministers (chief diplomat)

Presidents have asserted many reasons to justify a broad definition of executive powers, particularly in times of national emergency, such as the Great Depression, and war. The Constitution has proven flexible enough to adapt to changing understandings of presidential power.

What are the constitutional powers of the Supreme Court? Article III of the Constitution created the Supreme Court and gives Congress power to create other courts that are inferior to, or below, the Supreme Court. It gives courts created under the authority of Article III (called federal courts) jurisdiction, or power, to decide only certain cases. These are cases arising under national laws and involving citizens from more than one state. Finally, the article guarantees trial by jury in all criminal cases except impeachment. The Supreme Court also exercises the power of judicial review, deciding whether acts of Congress, the executive, state laws, and even state constitutions violate the U.S. Constitution.

The Constitution gives the Supreme Court jurisdiction to decide two categories of cases:

Original jurisdiction This term refers to the power of a court to pass judgment on both the facts of a case and the law. The Supreme Court has original jurisdiction in "cases affecting Ambassadors, other public Ministers and Consuls, and those in which a State shall be a Party." When the Supreme Court hears a case in its original jurisdiction, it is the only court to hear the case.

Appellate jurisdiction This term refers to the power of a superior, or higher, court to review and revise the decision of an inferior, or lower, court. The Supreme Court has appellate jurisdiction in all cases not in its original jurisdiction "with such Exceptions and under such Regulations as the Congress shall make."

Reviewing Ideas

1. **Explain** In your own words, explain what the Article I, Section 8, phrase "necessary and proper" means to Congress.

2. **Make Generalizations** Why do you think that Article II, Section 1, gives the president the "executive power" of the United States but does not specifically define what that power is?

Critical Thinking

3. **Elaborate** How does the power of judicial review make the judicial branch a co-equal branch of government?

Connecting Online

Visit **thinkcentral.com** for review and enrichment activities related to this chapter.

THINK central

KEYWORD: SGO CON

Quiz and Review

GOV 101
Examine key concepts in this chapter.

ONLINE QUIZZES
Take a practice quiz for each section in this chapter.

Activities

eActivities
Complete Webquests and Internet research activities.

INTERACTIVE FEATURES
Explore interactive versions of maps and charts.

KEEP IT CURRENT
Link to current events in U.S. government.

Partners

American Bar Association Division for Public Education
Learn more about the law, your rights and responsibilities.

Center for Civic Education
Promoting an enlightened and responsible citizenry committed to democratic principles and actively engaged in the practice of democracy.

Online Textbook

ONLINE SIMULATIONS
Learn about U.S. government through simulations you can complete online.

 Read more about key topics online.

Comprehension and Critical Thinking

SECTION 1 *(pp. 68–76)*

1. **a. Review Key Terms** For each term, write a sentence that explains its significance or meaning: popular sovereignty, rule of law, separation of powers, checks and balances, judicial review, federalism.

   b. Summarize Why is it important to maintain a balance between state and national authority in a federal system? Be prepared to defend your analysis.

   c. Evaluate Are the goals and objectives of the Constitution, such as the rule of law, relevant today? Support your answer with examples.

SECTION 2 *(pp. 78–83)*

2. **a. Review Key Terms** For each term, write a sentence that explains its significance or meaning: supermajority, repeal.

   b. Analyze How have both Madison's and Jefferson's views of amending the Constitution proven true in some ways over the course of U.S. history?

   c. Elaborate Give examples of how the Constitution has both endured and changed since it was ratified.

SECTION 3 *(pp. 84–89)*

3. **a. Review Key Terms** For each term, write a sentence that explains its significance or meaning: executive agreements, political party.

   b. Explain How does each of the three branches of government apply the Constitution to its job responsibilities?

   c. Develop Describe the impacts that political parties, customs, and traditions have had on the U.S. system of government.

Critical Reading

Read the passage in Section 1 that begins with the heading "Checks and Balances." Then answer the questions that follow.

4. In which of the following bodies must government-funding laws originate?

   A the Supreme Court

   B the Senate

   C the president's cabinet

   D the House of Representatives

5. Which of the following does the Senate have the sole authority to approve or reject?

   A overseas trade negotiations

   B government projects

   C security legislation

   D treaties with foreign countries

Read the passage in Section 3 that begins with the heading "The Federal Government Applies the Constitution." Then answer the question that follows.

6. Executive agreements are usually used by a president to support which of the president's executive powers?

   A conducting overseas trade negotiations

   B financing domestic government projects

   C ensuring the passage of legislation

   D appointing ambassadors and judges

RESPONSIBILITIES OF LEADERSHIP

7. The Line Item Veto Act of 1996 allowed the president to cancel individual items in appropriations bills passed by Congress. Research the Supreme Court case of *Clinton* v. *City of New York* (1998). Analyze and summarize all the opinions in the case. Then, in terms of **separation of powers,** evaluate the final decision reached by the Court.

8. The role of the U.S. Supreme Court is to say what the law is. The Court, however, is composed of nine individual justices. Select one justice and research his or her judicial philosophy. Evidence of the justice's philosophy may be found in his or her opinions in cases involving freedom of speech or religion; the commerce clause and states' rights; Fourth Amendment issues; and the death penalty. Create a spreadsheet to collect and sort your evidence. From these opinions, classify the justice as a **strict or loose constructionist** of the Constitution. Write a short biography of the justice. Using examples from the justice's opinions, describe his or her judicial philosophy, including whether the justice is considered conservative, liberal, or in the center of the Court's philosophical spectrum. Share your results with the class.

CONNECTING TO THE CONSTITUTION

9. Read Article I, Section 8, of the Constitution in the Reference Section at the end of your textbook. List any powers of Congress that are not included that you think should be. Also list which powers, if any, that are included but that you think should not be. Provide one or two sentences of support for each addition or deletion that you make.

ANALYZING PRIMARY SOURCES

Political Cartoon *The Constitution contains a system of checks and balances that is supposed to prevent any one branch of government from becoming all-powerful. The system works only if each branch follows the rule of law and the other principles of government in the Constitution.*

©2007 Lisa Benson. Reprinted with permission of Lisa Benson and the Washington Post Writers Group in conjunction with the Cartoonist Group.

10. **Analyze** What is happening in this cartoon?

11. **Draw Conclusions** How does the imagery in the cartoon illustrate the cartoonist's opinion of the constitutional system of checks and balances?

FOCUS ON WRITING

Persuasive Writing *Persuasive writing takes a position for or against an issue, using facts and examples as supporting evidence. To practice persuasive writing, complete the assignment below.*

Writing Topic: Constitutional Democracy

12. **Assignment** Two basic principles of government in the Constitution are that all government power comes from the people and that the individuals we elect to be our representatives are to speak for us in government. Write an editorial in which you convince people that these two principles apply—or do not apply—to issues the nation faces today. Give examples to support your editorial position.

4 Federalism

"THE QUESTION OF THE
RELATION OF THE STATES TO
THE FEDERAL GOVERNMENT IS
THE CARDINAL QUESTION OF OUR
CONSTITUTIONAL SYSTEM."

—WOODROW WILSON, 1917

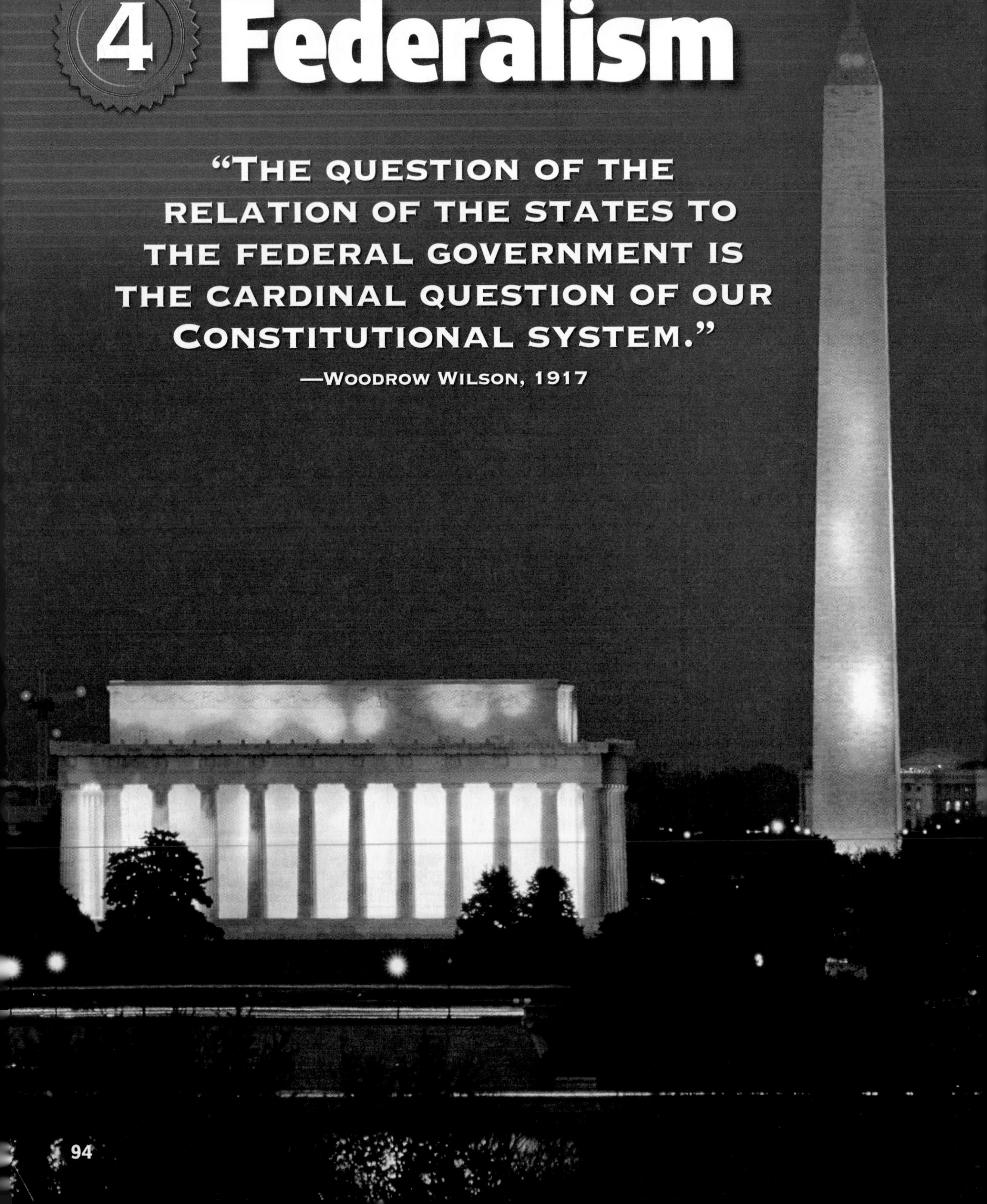

SECTION 1

Dividing Government Power

- After much debate, the Framers designed a federal system that they hoped would strengthen the national government and protect states' rights.
- The Constitution divides power between two levels of government: national and state governments.
- The Constitution delegates certain powers to the national government.
- The powers granted to state governments are called reserved powers.
- Concurrent powers may be exercised by the national and state governments.
- States must give full faith and credit to the laws of other states.

SECTION 2

American Federalism: Conflict and Change

- Federalism has changed over time to meet new political needs.
- The Supreme Court acts as a referee in the division of power between the national and state governments.
- Before the Civil War, American federalism was guided by the principle of dual federalism, or the idea that the national and state governments were equal in authority.
- Over the course of U.S. history, American federalism has experienced a steady expansion in national power.
- In recent years, a trend in American federalism called devolution has attempted to return power to the states.

SECTION 3

Federalism Today

- Fiscal federalism is a system in which the national government uses grants and mandates to influence state policy to achieve national ends.
- Grants-in-aid from the national government to the states have increased the influence of the national government.
- Today American federalism continues to evolve in the face of new issues.

CONNECTING TO THE CONSTITUTION

Our nation's system of government is based on constitutional law established by the United States Constitution. See the "We the People: The Citizen and the Constitution" pages in this chapter for an in-depth exploration of how states serve as "laboratories of democracy" in the American federal system.

Originally called the Federal City, Washington, D.C., was founded in 1791 to serve as our nation's capital.

Dividing Government Power

Main Idea

The Framers of the Constitution established a federal system that divides powers and responsibility between the national and state governments.

Reading Focus

1. Why did the Framers choose federalism?

2. What powers does the national government have?

3. What powers do state governments have?

4. What powers are shared by both the national government and the state governments?

5. How does the Constitution limit the powers of the state and national governments?

6. How does the Constitution guide the relationships between the nation and the 50 states?

Key Terms

expressed powers
implied powers
inherent powers
reserved powers
concurrent power
full faith and credit clause

TAKING NOTES As you read, take notes on the powers of the national, state, and shared powers in a graphic organizer like this one.

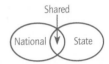

WHY IT MATTERS

Federalism in Action What do fish swimming in Idaho's Snake River have to do with American federalism? The Snake River runs more than 1,000 miles through Idaho. It provides water for power plants and local communities, irrigation for 3.8 million acres of farmland, and a vital habitat for endangered salmon.

For the last 20 years, the Snake River has been the subject of one of the longest-standing water disputes in the western United States. In May 2007 the state of Idaho, the U.S. government, and the Nez Percé finalized the terms of the Snake River Water Agreement. The agreement aimed to sort out more than 150,000 water claims, including those made by the Nez Percé, who in 1855 signed a treaty with the U.S. government that granted the tribe fishing rights in the river.

In exchange for giving up their claims, the Nez Percé will receive more than $95 million in U.S. funding. Idaho will be able to settle disputes and safeguard its water. Such complex, multi-level government action may be a far cry from what the Framers imagined, but it still takes place within a basic structure for federal government the Framers outlined in the Constitution. ■

A Basic Structure for Government

In 2004, Nez Percé tribal chair Anthony Johnson announced the proposed settlement of the Snake River Basin at a joint press conference held with then Idaho governor Dirk Kempthorne and former U.S. Secretary of the Interior Gale Norton.

Why Federalism?

American federalism was invented in Philadelphia in 1787. When delegates to the Constitutional Convention met to consider strengthening the national government, federalism was an obvious choice. As you have read, under the Articles of Confederation, the new nation struggled to function as a confederation, and it was failing. Without the power to raise funds, the national government was simply not strong enough to deliver the stability and economic unity that the young nation needed.

Moreover, unitary rule—rule in which all power is held by a strong central authority—was out of the question. This was the system the American colonies had known under the British monarchy. It left the nation's founders deeply suspicious of a powerful central government. Some found the idea so distasteful that they outright declined to attend the Philadelphia Convention. They worried that delegates were plotting to put in place a strong national government that would diminish states' rights. Virginian Patrick Henry claimed that he "smelt a rat."

The Framers did have in mind a few ways to prevent government abuse of power. As discussed in Chapters 2 and 3, the Framers sought to forge a republic. In so doing, they relied heavily on the writings of a number of philosophers—such as Thomas Hobbes, John Locke, Jean-Jacques Rousseau, and Adam Smith—who advocated self-rule and limited government.

They also drew ideas from the French philosopher Baron de Montesquieu. In Montesquieu's *Spirit of the Laws* (1748), he wrote extensively on the virtues of dividing power between different parts of government. According to Montesquieu, dividing power was the best way to defend people's freedom from a too-powerful government. This idea would be thoroughly absorbed by the Framers of the Constitution.

The Framers faced a difficult balancing act. How could the national government address the needs of the nation, preserve states' rights, and ensure a republican government? In the spring of 1787, echoing Montesquieu, James Madison described his idea for the new government.

After much debate and a series of compromises, the Framers devised a plan for government that balanced authority between the nation and the states. In other words, the new government was federal in form. The Framers carefully divided powers between two levels of government—state and national.

THE UNITED STATES: FROM CONFEDERATION TO FEDERAL SYSTEM

The United States as a Confederation

From 1781 to 1788, the states were united as a confederation under the Articles of Confederation. The national government received its power from the states, but it had no direct authority over the people.

The United States as a Federal System

Under the U.S. Constitution, the national and state governments are based on the consent of the people and exercise authority directly over the people.

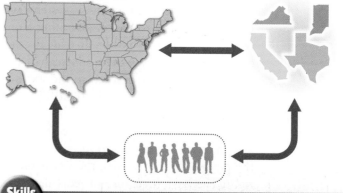

Skills FOCUS INTERPRETING CHARTS

In what ways was the United States as a confederation similar to and different from the United States as a federal system?

Powers of the National Government

The U.S. Constitution gives the national government the power to:

- Borrow and coin money
- Levy taxes
- Conduct foreign relations
- Raise armies, declare war, and make peace
- Regulate commerce with foreign nations and between states
- Establish post offices
- Regulate immigration and naturalization
- Establish and operate the federal court system
- Make laws necessary and proper to execute national powers

The Constitution specifically grants the national government the power to raise armed forces, such as the Coast Guard.

The Framers assigned all powers having to do with the states' common interests, such as national defense and control over currency, to the national government. All other powers remained with the states.

The arrangement was a practical solution to the nation's needs. In 1787 the nation's people were spread far apart, and its transportation and communications systems were far too primitive to make governing from a central location feasible. In the Framers' eighteenth century world, matters of local concern really were best left to the states.

The Framers deliberately avoided detailed provisions. They recognized that general rules stated briefly would give the nation and the states flexibility to meet the needs of the people. In this regard, the Framers were right. The basic structure of federalism crafted in Philadelphia remains in place today.

READING CHECK Identifying Supporting Details Why did the Framers choose federalism?

National Powers

The Constitution outlined a federal system that would provide strong national government and protect states' rights. In the U.S. federal system, some powers belong to the national government, others are reserved for the states, and still others are shared by both. Much of the Constitution deals with the expressed, implied, and inherent powers of the national government.

Expressed Powers The Constitution lists powers granted to the national government. These powers are called **expressed powers** and are sometimes referred to as enumerated powers. For example, Article I, Section 8, lists the expressed powers of the legislative branch. Congress has the power to issue money, collect taxes, pay government debts, regulate trade among the states and with other nations, declare war, and raise and maintain armed forces.

The expressed powers of the other two branches are listed in Articles II and III. Article II gives the president the power to command the armed forces and to conduct foreign relations. Article III gives the judicial branch the power to rule on constitutional issues, cases involving the U.S. government, and disputes among the states.

Implied Powers The national government also possesses **implied powers**. In contrast to expressed powers, implied powers are not specifically listed in the Constitution, but they are logical extensions of expressed powers. The constitutional source for implied powers is the last clause of Article I, Section 8, which is often referred to as the necessary and proper clause.

PRIMARY SOURCE

> ❝[Congress has the power] To make all Laws which shall be necessary and proper for carrying into Execution the foregoing Powers, and all other Powers vested by this Constitution in the Government of the United States.❞
>
> — U.S. Constitution, Article I, Section 8

The necessary and proper clause is also referred to as the elastic clause because it has been used to stretch the powers of Congress. Many congressional policies, ranging from building highways to regulating food are justified as implied powers. For example, the Sixteenth Amendment gives Congress the power to collect income taxes, but nowhere does the Constitution explain how taxes should be collected. Using its implied powers, Congress established the Internal Revenue Service, the agency that collects your taxes.

Inherent Powers The national government also has **inherent powers**, or powers that historically have been recognized as naturally belonging to all governments that conduct the business of a sovereign nation. In other words, the U.S. government has inherent powers simply because it is a national government. These powers include the power to acquire new territory and to conduct foreign affairs. The United States has done all of these things since its earliest years, even though these powers are not specifically granted by the Constitution.

READING CHECK Contrasting How do expressed, implied, and inherent powers differ from one another?

State Powers

The Constitution has considerably less to say about state powers. In the days leading up to the ratification of the Constitution, James Madison suggested that, although state powers were not listed in the Constitution, that did not mean they did not exist. In *Federalist Paper* No. 45, Madison explained that the constitutional powers granted to the national government were "few and defined." By contrast, the powers that remained with the states were "numerous and indefinite."

To protect states' rights, Madison's idea was worked into the Constitution in 1791 as part of the Bill of Rights.

PRIMARY SOURCE

❝The powers not delegated to the United States by the Constitution, nor prohibited by it to the States, are reserved to the States respectively, or to the people.❞

— U.S. Constitution, Tenth Amendment

This provision is often called the reserved powers clause. **Reserved powers** are not specifically mentioned in the Constitution, but they belong to the states because the

Powers of the State Governments

The U.S. Constitution gives state governments the power to:

- Draw electoral district lines
- Conduct elections
- Maintain state militias (the National Guard)
- Regulate commerce within the state
- Establish and operate state court systems
- Levy taxes
- Ratify amendments to the Constitution
- Exercise powers not specifically delegated to the nation or prohibited to the states

States have the power to draw electoral lines, like these proposed by Georgia state senator Tom Price in 2004.

Constitution neither delegates these powers to the national government nor prohibits them to the states.

State governments have drawn heavily on their reserved powers to regulate the health, public safety, morals, and general welfare of their citizens—the areas that most directly impact the day-to-day lives of people. For example, state laws tell you when you can get your license to drive a car and how fast you can drive on a highway.

Among the states' other reserved powers are the ability to regulate marriage, form local governments, conduct elections, control public school systems, and establish and enforce criminal laws. States also have the power to regulate businesses operating within their borders and to issue licenses to doctors, lawyers, and even the person you pay to cut your hair.

READING CHECK Summarizing What powers does the Tenth Amendment give to the states?

Powers Shared by the Nation and the States

The Constitution gives some powers to both state and national governments. These powers are called concurrent powers.

- Collect taxes
- Provide for the health and welfare of the people
- Build roads
- Conduct commerce
- Establish courts

- Borrow money
- Take private property for public use, with just compensation
- Pass and enforce laws
- Charter banks and corporations
- Regulate education

Both the states and the nation have the power to regulate public education.

WHAT DO YOU THINK?

Read the supremacy clause in Article VI, Section 2, and the Tenth Amendment to the Constitution. How do the two provisions help explain why the national government and the states seem to be locked in a perpetual struggle for power?

Shared Powers

In addition to their reserved powers, states may also share powers with the national government. If the Constitution does not specifically state that a power belongs *exclusively* to the national government, then the states may exercise that power, too. For example, when Americans file their income tax returns every April, many people file two forms, one for their state government and another for the national government. This is because the power to collect taxes is a **concurrent power**, or a power held by the national government and the state governments at the same time.

In addition to collecting taxes, both levels of government can establish courts, make and enforce laws, build roads, provide education, and borrow and spend money. Both the states and the national government perform these tasks, often at the same time and for the same people. In short, this means

that citizens are subject to two levels of authority. In the state of Texas, for example, you must follow both Texas laws and national laws.

What happens, though, if a national law and a state law come into conflict? Who prevails? The Framers considered these questions very carefully. They laid out their answer in Article VI of the Constitution. Often called the supremacy clause, Article VI states that the Constitution, national laws, and treaties form the "supreme Law of the Land." The clause specifically says that judges in every state have to obey the Constitution, even if it contradicts state laws. The supremacy clause establishes that national laws are supreme ovr state laws, so long as the national government acts within its constitutional limits.

READING CHECK Identifying Supporting Details Name three powers that are held by both the national government and the state governments.

The Limits of Power

In addition to granting powers, the U.S. Constitution denies certain powers to the national and state governments. As you have read, the Framers believed strongly in limited government. By placing limits on both levels of government, they hoped to prevent tyranny and protect individual liberties.

Limits on National Government Fearful of tyranny, the Framers included provisions in the Constitution to prevent the national government from growing too-powerful. These provisions aimed to protect the people of the United States from specific injustices that the colonists had experienced at the hands of the English monarchy.

For example, Article I, Section 9, states that the government cannot deny a citizen the right to trial by jury, grant titles of nobility, tax exports between states, pass laws favoring the trade of one state over another, or spend money unless authorized to do so by Congress. The national government also may not exercise powers that are reserved to the states, and it may not pass laws that threaten the federal system as established by the Constitution.

The power of the national government is further limited by the Bill of Rights. The Bill of Rights guarantees that the government cannot interfere with basic liberties such as freedom of speech and freedom of the press.

Limits on State Governments To prevent conflict between the states and the national government, Article I, Section 10, denies specific powers to the state governments. For example, states are not allowed to coin money or tax imports and exports from other states. States are also prohibited from having their own armies, separately engaging in wars, and entering into treaties with other states or nations. If states did such things, they would undermine national unity.

Powers Denied to Both Levels Other powers are specifically denied by the Constitution to both the national and state governments. Neither level, for example, can deny people accused of crimes the right to a trial by jury or grant titles of nobility. The Constitution also forbids both levels from passing ex post facto laws, or laws made "after the fact." This protects people from being convicted of an offense that was not a crime at the time the offense was committed.

READING CHECK **Summarizing** What limits did the Framers place on state governments?

Nation and State Relations

The Constitution does more than divide government power. It also describes the responsibilities that the national government and the states have toward one another. American federalism might never have worked had the Framers not included these guidelines for interaction.

The Nation and the Fifty States The Framers wanted to be sure that state governments would themselves be republics, democracies led by elected representatives of the people. Toward this end, Article IV, Section 4, of the Constitution states that the national government must "guarantee to every State in the Union a Republican form of government." In other words, the national government will only officially recognize representative state governments.

The national government is also responsible for protecting the states, both from foreign invasion and domestic uprisings. For example, when terrorists attacked the World Trade Center in New York City and the Pentagon in Washington, D.C., on September 11, 2001, the national government responded with military force to the crisis.

In addition, the Constitution ensures that the states be treated as equals by the national government. The national government must grant states equal representation in the Senate, and it cannot tax the people of one state more than another. Finally, although the national government can admit new states, it cannot split up states that already exist or change state boundaries in any way.

Relations between the States The Constitution gives states the right to manage affairs within their borders, and it also encourages states to cooperate with one another. Imagine the chaos that could result if states did not recognize each other's laws. A person could break a law in one state but escape punishment by fleeing to another state. The Constitution was designed to prevent this from happening. Although state laws differ and states are not required to enforce the criminal laws of other states, the Constitution says that states are required to extradite, or return, a person charged with a crime to the state in which the offense was committed for prosecution.

Article IV of the Constitution, often referred to as the **full faith and credit clause**, ensures that extradition can take place. Article IV requires that states give "full faith and credit," to the public acts, official records, and judicial proceedings of every other state. For example, this means that a contract signed in one state must be recognized and honored by officials in other states. It also means that state drivers' licenses are valid in any state, from Maine to California. Similarly, the full faith and credit clause ensures that if you marry someone in one state, the other states must recognize that marriage.

The Constitution also takes measures to prevent states from discriminating against the citizens of other states. It does this in a clause of Article IV, Section 2, that is often called the privileges and immunities clause.

This clause specifies that citizens of each state should receive all the "privileges and immunities" of any state in which they happen to be. This ensures, for example, that a New Yorker living in or visiting the state of North Carolina will pay the same sales tax and enjoy the same police protection as North Carolinians do.

Still, there are many exceptions to the privileges and immunities clause. A state can offer reduced state university tuition to residents, and it can charge its own residents less for services funded by taxes, such as public health facilities.

What about Local Government? The U.S. Constitution does not include a single word about local government. Thus, creating local governments is a power reserved for the states. Each state outlines a plan for local government in a state constitution. The relationship between state and local government, however, is quite different from the relationship between the national and state governments. The most important difference is that state government has the power to reorganize local government at any time to better address state needs.

Native American Sovereignty The Constitution says little about the sovereign Native American nations that existed in the United States long before the arrival of Europeans. However, Article I, Section 8, does grant the national government the power "to regulate Commerce . . . with the Indian Tribes." The national government used this power to make treaties with Native American nations.

When a Native American nation signed a treaty, it often agreed to give up some or all of its land as well as some of its sovereign powers. Signing also meant entering into a trust relationship with the United States, in which the U.S. government promised benefits and rights, such as fishing and hunting rights, to Native Americans in exchange for land.

In most cases, the treaties resulted in loss of land, sovereignty, and individual rights for native peoples. Moreover, Native Americans were not granted full citizenship until 1924. In Chapter 11 you will learn about how Native Americans have since worked to attain full civil rights.

READING CHECK **Summarizing** How does the full faith and credit clause affect relations among states?

THINK central **Online Quiz**

thinkcentral.com
KEYWORD: SGO FED HP

SECTION 1 ASSESSMENT

Reviewing Ideas and Terms

1. a. Recall What philosopher influenced the Framers' vision of a federal system?
b. Analyze Why did the Framers of the Constitution choose a federal system of government?

2. a. Define What are inherent powers?
b. Evaluate Do you think the necessary and proper clause was a good idea? Why or why not?

3. a. Identify What does the Tenth Amendment have to do with American federalism?
b. Contrast How does the Constitution delegate powers to the nation differently from how it gives powers to the states?

4. a. Recall Name two powers that are denied to both the states and the national government.
b. Explain Why did the Framers want to limit the powers of the national and state governments?

5. a. Define What is a concurrent power?
b. Predict Could the American federal system survive without the supremacy clause? Explain.

6. a. Define What is the full faith and credit clause?
b. Predict What might happen if the national government taxed citizens of one state more than others?

Critical Thinking

7. Compare Use the graphic organizer below to list the powers of the national government and the powers of the state governments. Which level of government do you think most affects your daily life? Provide support for your answer.

National Government	State Government
1.	1.
2.	2.

FOCUS ON WRITING

8. Expository Write a paragraph explaining the constitutional powers of the national government. Describe how expressed, implied, and inherent powers differ and give examples of each.

SECTION 2
American Federalism: Conflict and Change

BEFORE YOU READ

Main Idea

Over the past 200 years, conflicts over the balance of power between the national and state governments have led to changes in American federalism.

Reading Focus

1. What role does the Supreme Court play in American federalism?

2. How was government power divided in dual federalism?

3. What events caused the expansion of national power in the twentieth century?

4. What is new federalism?

Key Terms

dual federalism
doctrine of nullification
doctrine of secession
cooperative federalism
creative federalism
new federalism
devolution

TAKING NOTES As you read, take notes on the events that led to changes in American federalism. Record your notes in a diagram like this one.

WHY IT MATTERS

Crisis at Fort Sumter In the early hours of April 12, 1861, shots rang out at Fort Sumter, a U.S. fort in South Carolina, and continued for 34 hours. The attack did not come from a foreign army but from armed forces raised by a group of southern states that had decided to separate from the Union.

Calling themselves the Confederate States of America, the southern states claimed that since Fort Sumter lay in the South, it rightfully belonged to their Confederacy. On April 14, Fort Sumter surrendered to Confederate forces. President Abraham Lincoln readied U.S. troops to fight back. The War between the States—the Civil War—had begun.

Could the nation survive this challenge to its very union? In the end, the Union survived, but it was forever changed. Over the course of American history, the states and the national government had come into conflict many times. This was the first—and the only time since—that such a conflict escalated into war. The Union's victory restored the nation and redirected the course of American federalism.

One of the final outcomes of the war that pitted states against nation was that the nation emerged victorious over the states. The war put to rest the most extreme arguments for states' rights and established the supremacy of the national government in the American federal system. ■

States against Nation

As much as the Civil War was a struggle over slavery, it was also a contest between state and national authority.

Anne S.K. Brown Military Collection, Brown University Library

Role of the Supreme Court

Long before the Civil War, the Framers anticipated that the government they created might lead to conflicts between the states and the national government. They were concerned, for example, that states might pass laws that conflicted with laws passed by the national government. How did the Framers plan to resolve such conflicts?

In the previous section, you read about how the Framers disagreed over which level of government—the states or the nation—should have ultimate authority in the new nation. For this reason, they made no attempt to outline solutions for specific types of conflicts in the wording of the Constitution. Instead, the Framers came up with a problem-solving strategy. They gave the Supreme Court the power to resolve conflicts between the nation and the states.

Article III of the Constitution gives the judicial branch the authority to hear cases involving the Constitution, U.S. laws, and disputes between states. This gives the judicial branch, especially the Supreme Court, the power to act as a referee, sorting out conflicts between the nation and the states. In sports, referees make decisions based upon the rules of a game. Similarly, in the federal system, the courts make decisions based on the rules in the Constitution.

The Framers also addressed the question of how to resolve conflicts between the states and the national government in Article VI of the Constitution. As you read in Section 1, this article of the Constitution includes the supremacy clause, which declares that the Constitution, national laws, and treaties made by the national government are "the supreme law of the land."

Acting in the role of referee, the Supreme Court has influenced how power is divided between the nation and the states. For 200 years, the Court's interpretation of the supremacy clause and other articles of the Constitution has gradually increased the power of the national government. This trend would not be broken until the 1990s.

Over time, American federalism has continually changed to meet the needs of new generations. The changes in our federal system may best be understood in terms of four historical eras: dual federalism, cooperative federalism, creative federalism, and new federalism.

READING CHECK **Summarizing** How does the Supreme Court serve as a referee in the federal system?

Dual Federalism

The first era of American federalism, dual federalism, lasted from about 1789 to the 1930s. Under **dual federalism**, both state and national governments were equal authorities operating within their own spheres of influence, as defined by a strict reading of the Constitution. The powers of the national government included only those powers

Interactive Feature ✳

Eras of Federalism

American federalism has evolved over time. Until recently, one general trend has characterized American federalism—the expansion of national power.

Dual Federalism
1789–1930s
Dual federalism was guided by the idea that both the national and state governments were sovereign within their own spheres. During this era, leaders such as Supreme Court Chief Justice John Marshall (left) helped to gradually increase the power of the national government.

Cooperative Federalism
1930s–1960s
Cooperative federalism was marked by the belief that all levels of government should work together to solve problems, such as poverty. During the Great Depression, the national government created the Works Progress Administration (WPA) to give unemployed workers jobs. WPA workers (left) dig a well at Big Bend National Park in Texas.

listed in the Constitution. The Tenth Amendment reserved all other powers to the states. Political scientists often compare dual federalism to a layer cake, with each layer representing a distinct level of government.

The Great Debate From our nation's very beginning, dual federalism was at the center of a great debate. On one side of the debate stood nationalists, or advocates of a strong, centralized national government. They counted among their numbers George Washington and Alexander Hamilton. On the other side were proponents of states' rights, such as Thomas Jefferson, who held that the national government should not unduly intrude in state affairs.

In 1790 nationalists faced off against supporters of states' rights when President George Washington's secretary of the treasury, Alexander Hamilton, urged Congress to create a national bank. Thomas Jefferson objected to the bank, claiming it was unlawful because the national government had no constitutional power to establish banks. In response, Hamilton argued that because the national government had a constitutional power to regulate currency, it had an implied power to create a bank.

Congress sided with Hamilton and granted a 20-year charter for the First Bank of the United States. But the question of whether the bank was constitutional remained. When the bank's charter expired, Congress refused to renew it.

The dispute resurfaced in 1816 when Congress chartered the Second Bank of the United States. Maryland had imposed a tax on all banks operating within the state, but James McCulloch, an officer at a Maryland branch of the national bank, refused to pay the tax. Maryland pressed its case in court.

The Marshall Court The bank dispute reached the Supreme Court in the case of *McCulloch* v. *Maryland* (1819). At the time, the Court was under the leadership of Chief Justice John Marshall, a judge with strong nationalist leanings. Starting with *McCulloch*, the Court's rulings did much to expand the powers of the national government.

The Court ruled decisively in favor of the nation's authority to start a bank. Marshall argued that the bank's charter was justified by the Constitution's necessary and proper clause, which gives Congress the power to take actions necessary and proper to carrying out its expressed powers. In this case, Marshall concluded that it was reasonable for the nation to exercise an implied power to start a bank since it would help the nation properly execute its powers to regulate commerce and currency.

Furthermore, Marshall argued that Maryland could not tax the bank because "the power to tax involves the power to destroy." If states could tax a national institution, then they could weaken or destroy it. This, Marshall asserted, violated the supremacy clause of the Constitution.

Creative Federalism
1960s–1980s
In this era, the national government funded state and local programs that met national goals, such as fighting poverty. In the 1960s, First Lady Lady Bird Johnson (above) visited a school program funded by national grants.

New Federalism
1980s–2001
In the 1990s supporters of New Federalism and devolution, such as Newt Gingrich (above), argued that decreased national spending and returning power to the states would improve government.

THINK central Interactive
thinkcentral.com
KEYWORD: SGO FED

"A House Divided" In the years leading up to the Civil War, the United States became bitterly divided over the issue of slavery, a debate that was wrapped up in arguments about states' rights and the extent of national power. The slave states—the southern states—resisted all measures taken by the national government to outlaw slavery in new states and territories. They held fast to the notion that the states were sovereign and could make such decisions for themselves.

Politicians in some southern states believed that states had the right to <u>nullify</u> national laws that they believed contradicted or clashed with state interests. This was known as the **doctrine of nullification**. The idea of nullification was not new. From the nation's earliest years, proponents of states' rights—including James Madison and Thomas Jefferson—had argued that states could refuse to follow national laws they found objectionable and could even declare such laws "null and void."

In 1832, for example, the South Carolina legislature voted to nullify specific national tariffs, or taxes. The effort was led by South Carolinian John C. Calhoun, who believed the tariffs favored northern industry over southern plantations. Calhoun argued that because the national government was created by the states, the states had the right to challenge federal laws.

According to the doctrine of nullification, if a state challenged a national law, three-quarters of the other states would have to ratify an amendment allowing Congress to enact the law. At that point, the state that had challenged the law could either choose to follow the law or separate from the Union. The idea that states had the right to separate themselves from the Union was known as the **doctrine of secession**. <u>Secession</u> was the most extreme option for those who believed in state sovereignty.

The issue of state sovereignty would soon come to a head. In 1860 Abraham Lincoln was elected president. Southerners feared that President Lincoln would try to limit slavery or stop the practice altogether. Just a few years earlier, as the Republican nominee in a race for an Illinois Senate seat, Lincoln had made his views on the divisive nature of slavery clear.

ACADEMIC VOCABULARY
nullify to cancel

ACADEMIC VOCABULARY
secession a formal withdrawal or separation

PRIMARY SOURCE

❝A house divided against itself cannot stand. I believe this government cannot endure permanently half slave and half free. I do not expect the Union to be dissolved—I do not expect the house to fall—but I do expect it will cease to be divided.❞

—Abraham Lincoln, Senate nomination acceptance speech, 1858

After Lincoln's presidential election, events quickly led to secession and war. South Carolina was the first to secede, followed by 10 other states. These states united to form a confederation, a group of sovereign states, officially called the Confederate States of America. By 1861 the United States was divided by the Civil War. For four years, the Union and the Confederacy battled each other in the bloodiest war in U.S. history.

After the Civil War In 1865 the Confederacy surrendered and the Union was restored. The defeat of the Confederacy settled the matter of slavery in the United States once and for all. The war also profoundly changed the relationship between the states and the national government. The Union's victory firmly established national supremacy and put to rest the most radical interpretations of state sovereignty. No longer could states claim a right to nullify national laws or withdraw from the union.

The Civil War also led to expanded constitutional powers of the national government. After the war, Congress passed the Thirteenth, Fourteenth, and Fifteenth amendments to the Constitution, known collectively as the Reconstruction Amendments. These amendments abolished slavery, defined citizenship, prohibited the states from denying citizens' rights, and extended voting rights to African American men.

The Reconstruction Amendments were significant because they set national standards that states had to follow. In time, the national government would use its new constitutional powers to protect the rights of African Americans, women, and other groups of people from discrimination by state and local governments.

READING CHECK **Identifying Cause and Effect**
How did the Civil War resolve the issue of secession?

McCulloch v. Maryland (1819)

DIVISION FOR
PUBLIC EDUCATION
AMERICAN BAR ASSOCIATION

WHY IT MATTERS

In McCulloch v. Maryland *the Supreme Court had the first of many opportunities to influence the division of power in the federal system. The Court's decision led to the expansion of national power.*

Background

In 1791 Congress passed a law that established the First Bank of the United States. However, in 1811 an attempt to renew the bank's charter failed. At that time, a number of states took advantage of this situation by chartering their own banks.

After the War of 1812, the nation needed money to repay its war debts. Because there was no longer a national bank, Congress borrowed money from several state banks. As a result, Congress set up the Second Bank of the United States in 1816. The states generally opposed the National Bank. Some state banks, including the state bank of Maryland, placed a tax on all banks operating within their borders. When the Maryland branch of the National Bank refused to pay the tax, the state of Maryland sued the National Bank's cashier, James McCulloch.

In 1819 the legal battle reached the U.S. Supreme Court. According to Chief Justice John Marshall, the Court had two crucial questions to resolve. The first question was whether or not the Constitution gives Congress the power to establish a national bank. The second question involved whether or not the Constitution gives states the power to tax a national bank.

Arguments for McCulloch

The question of whether Congress had the power to establish a bank was not new. It had been asked in 1790, when President George Washington's secretary of the treasury, Alexander Hamilton, pushed Congress to establish the First Bank of the United States. Supporters of the First Bank claimed that, even though the Constitution did not specifically grant the national government the power to create a bank, Congress had an implied power to do so because it had the constitutional authority to regulate commerce.

Arguments for Maryland

Opponents of the National Bank argued that the Bank was unlawful because the national government had no constitutional power to start banks. Moreover, they argued that because the states are sovereign, self-governing entities, each state should have the right to impose taxes on businesses and institutions operating within its borders.

THE IMPACT TODAY Led by Chief Justice John Marshall, the Supreme Court unanimously ruled in favor of the Bank. Marshall asserted that Article I, Section 8, of the Constitution gave Congress the power to make all laws "necessary and proper" for carrying out its responsibilities, such as regulating commerce. Moreover, Marshall argued that Maryland's tax was invalid. "The power to tax," Marshall wrote, "involves the power to destroy." If a state could tax one of the national government's activities, then it would have power over the national government. The *McCulloch* decision set a precedent for the expansion of national power and for the role of the Court as a referee in the federal system.

CRITICAL THINKING

What Do You Think? Chief Justice Marshall's decision in *McCulloch* v. *Maryland* expanded the power of the national government. What might have happened if Marshall had ruled in favor of Maryland? What part of the Constitution could he have drawn upon to support his argument?

Expanding National Power

The Civil War reinforced the supremacy of the national government over the states. In the years following the war, new challenges—including those posed by business interests, the economy, and unfair social conditions—continued to shift the balance of power in favor of the national government.

Turn-of-the-Century Reforms The turn of the twentieth century was a time of tremendous change in the United States. New technology, such as railroads, the telegraph, and industrial machinery changed how Americans lived and worked. In addition, the country experienced unprecedented growth. Between 1870 and 1916 the population of the United States more than doubled, and hundreds of thousands of people flocked to the nation's cities.

These dramatic changes were accompanied by a range of social and economic problems. Cities grew overcrowded, and crime rates rose. Many laborers suffered from long workdays and dangerous working conditions. Powerful corporations developed great economic influence, often at the expense of working-class Americans. These issues grew so widespread that it became difficult to address them at the state level. The national government eventually stepped in, passing legislation to reform social conditions and business practices.

In 1887 Congress passed the Interstate Commerce Act to regulate the railroad industry. As new railroad lines crisscrossed the nation, railroad companies gained unprecedented power. In some areas, railroads were the only effective means of transportation, and companies realized that they could charge higher prices for their service. The Interstate Commerce Act set restrictions on the rates these companies could charge.

The government undertook other forms of regulation as well. In 1890 Congress passed the Sherman Antitrust Act to prevent monopolies, or the exclusive control of a good or service in a particular market, and to encourage fair competition in all industries. In the early 1900s the Sherman Antitrust Act was used to break up a number of large monopolies, including that of the American Tobacco Company.

PRIMARY SOURCES

Monopoly Busting

By the twentieth century, powerful companies had formed monopolies by establishing exclusive control over a good or service. As a result, they could eliminate competition and control prices, often at the expense of consumers. During the Great Depression, monopolies were of particular concern to the national government. In 1937 President Franklin Roosevelt vowed to make "every effort to end monopoly in business." This 1937 cartoon illustrates Roosevelt's determination to curb the power of monopolies.

Skills FOCUS **INTERPRETING PRIMARY SOURCES**

Analyzing Political Cartoons Why do you think the artist portrayed a monopoly in this way? Explain.

See **Skills Handbook**, p. H8.

Although these new laws did expand the national government's power to regulate business, several Supreme Court cases limited the reach of national power. For example, in *United States* v. *E.C. Knight Company* (1895) the Court ruled that a combination of sugar refining companies was not a monopoly under the Sherman Antitrust Act. The Court's decision explained that since the sugar companies operated locally, they could not be regulated by the national government.

The New Deal In the 1930s an economic crisis led to another expansion of the authority of the national government. In 1929 the American stock market crashed, triggering a major economic downturn known as the Great Depression.

As a result of the Great Depression, poverty and unemployment soon became widespread. Previously the job of helping the poor had fallen to the states and to local community groups. So great was this crisis, however, that local organizations were unable to respond adequately. It soon became clear that more help was needed.

In 1933 newly elected President Franklin Roosevelt responded with a plan to bring immediate relief. His program, known as the New Deal, created a series of national programs to address the needs of Americans. Some programs provided for the unemployed. For example, the Social Security program was established to assist the unemployed and the elderly. Other programs provided food, protected homeowners, and created jobs.

The New Deal marked a major change in the role of the national government. For the first time, the national government assumed responsibility for the social and economic welfare of the people. Since the national and state governments worked together to meet the crisis, federalism under the New Deal was known as **cooperative federalism**.

Because the New Deal was such a major shift, legislation was often challenged in the courts, and several cases reached the Supreme Court. Opponents argued that the constitutional powers to tax and regulate commerce did not give the national government the power to enact many New Deal programs. In time, however, the Supreme Court upheld most New Deal legislation.

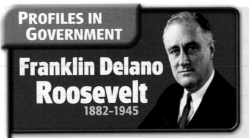

PROFILES IN GOVERNMENT

Franklin Delano Roosevelt
1882-1945

Franklin D. Roosevelt holds the distinction of being the only president elected to four terms of office. During his 12 years as president, he led the nation through two of its greatest crises, the Great Depression and World War II.

During his first term as president, the nation was in a severe economic depression and unemployment was at an all-time high. In response, Roosevelt proposed a series of far-reaching programs, collectively known as the New Deal. Although Roosevelt and the New Deal were popular, some argued that his programs extended the reach of the national government too far into state affairs. Roosevelt fought against critics that questioned the constitutionality of certain New Deal laws. He claimed the national government should have the authority to regulate industry and the economy. Eventually, many New Deal reforms achieved widespread national acceptance.

Making Inferences Why might the length of Roosevelt's presidency have concerned proponents of states' rights?

The Great Society In the 1960s President Lyndon Johnson further expanded the powers of the national government with his Great Society program, a series of initiatives aimed at eliminating poverty and social inequality. Johnson called his approach to solving national problems **creative federalism**. It involved releasing national funds, in the form of grants to state and local communities, to achieve national goals. For example, in July 1965, Congress authorized funds for states to set up Medicaid, a program that provides free health care for poor people.

These grants came with strings attached. If the national government thought that states were not fully cooperating, it would withhold funding. The threat of losing money was a powerful tool that spurred states into action against racial discrimination, hunger, unemployment, and pollution.

The grant system greatly increased the size and cost of national government. Grants for subsidized housing and urban renewal, for example, increased from $212 million in 1964 to more than $1 billion in 1970. Such spending soon raised concerns about the power of national government.

READING CHECK **Summarizing** How did New Deal and Great Society programs change federalism?

New Federalism

Throughout much of U.S. history, the powers of the national government expanded. Beginning in the 1980s, many political leaders worked to reverse this trend by returning authority to state governments. This era is known as **new federalism**.

The Reagan Years During the 1980s, President Ronald Reagan supported returning power to the states. He believed that the national government was less effective than state governments in providing services to the people. In his first inaugural address, Reagan promised to change the American federal system.

PRIMARY SOURCE

❝It is my intention to curb the size and influence of the federal establishment and to demand recognition of the distinction between the powers granted to the national government and those reserved to the states or to the people. All of us need to be reminded that the national government did not create the states; the states created the national government.❞

—Ronald Reagan, First Inaugural Address, January 20, 1981

As president, Reagan worked to reduce the size of government by cutting national grant money to the states. He relaxed national requirements that specified how states could use national grant money. States, he believed, were more effective than the national government in identifying the specific needs of their citizens.

The Devolution Revolution Following Reagan's example, Republican candidates in the 1994 congressional elections ran with a political message they called the Contract with America. The contract was a promise to achieve specific goals within 100 days of taking office. Central to the Contract with America was the idea of returning power to states, a concept known as **devolution**.

The Contract with America pledged to reduce the size and power of the national government by eliminating costly federal programs and by combining others. The Republicans also promised to force the government to review federal spending.

Some people, however, opposed devolution. They feared that it might result in increased social and economic inequality, or that states might be unable to adequately fund social programs. Still, concerns about the scope of the national government's powers extended across party lines, leading then Democratic President Bill Clinton to declare: "The era of big government is over."

READING CHECK **Identifying Supporting Details** How did Ronald Reagan attempt to reduce the influence of the national government?

SECTION 2 ASSESSMENT

THINK central **Online Quiz**
thinkcentral.com
KEYWORD: SGO FED HP

Reviewing Ideas and Terms

1. a. Identify What is the supremacy clause?
b. Explain How did the Framers plan to resolve conflicts that might arise between the states and the national government?

2. a. Recall What is dual federalism?
b. Analyze How did the southern states use the doctrine of nullification to support secession?

3. a. Recall Why was the Interstate Commerce Act passed?
b. Elaborate How did the Supreme Court limit the scope of the Sherman Antitrust Act?

4. a. Define What is devolution?
b. Contrast How did new federalism differ from previous trends in federalism?

Critical Thinking

5. Analyze Use a graphic organizer like the one below to identify the effects of historical events on the American federal system.

Civil War	→	
Great Depression	→	
Reagan Years	→	

FOCUS ON WRITING

6. Expository Write a letter to one of the Framers of the Constitution describing the relationship between the states and the national government during a specific era of American federalism.

Federalism and Hurricane Katrina

What roles should local, state, and national governments play in responding to natural disasters such as Hurricane Katrina?

Storm-related flooding covered more than 80 percent of New Orleans. Above, people make their way through high water in front of the Superdome, one of the designated storm shelters in New Orleans.

Photo by Mark Wilson/Getty Images

THE ISSUE

In August 2005 Hurricane Katrina devastated New Orleans, Louisiana, and the Gulf Coast. As the storm approached, officials at all levels of government prepared. Mayor Ray Nagin of New Orleans ordered a mandatory evacuation of the city. The governors of Louisiana and Mississippi declared a state of emergency. The national government authorized the Federal Emergency Management Agency to respond to the storm. On August 29, Katrina made landfall as a strong Category 4 storm. The results were catastrophic. Katrina and storm-related flooding took more than 1,800 lives and caused an estimated $81 billion in damages. In the storm's aftermath, there was widespread debate over government response to the disaster.

VIEWPOINTS

The national government should have done more. Many people blame the national government for not doing more to protect people from the storm. Some take issue with the failed flood protection system designed by the army and with officials who knew the system might fail if faced with a major hurricane. They argue that more could have been done to prevent New Orleans from flooding. Others argue that during the crisis, supplies, troops, and FEMA-sponsored buses for evacuees were slow to move into areas in need of assistance. They cite a lack of coordination among government agencies for confusion and delay. Lastly, critics of the Bush administration say that he and his advisers did not act quickly enough to respond to the disaster and save lives.

Local and state governments should be responsible for disaster relief. On the other side of the debate, people believe that the bulk of the responsibility lay with the state and local governments. These people argue that state and local officials should have been better prepared ahead of time and had more comprehensive plans in place to minimize danger to citizens. Moreover, the national government has traditionally only sent its military into a state at the request of that state's governor. Some people have criticized the governors of Louisiana and Mississippi for not immediately requesting such action. They also criticize the governors for not moving state National Guard troops into the hardest hit areas soon enough and for not coordinating efforts effectively.

What Is Your Opinion?

1. What might supporters of devolution say about the governmental response to Katrina?

2. Which level of government do you think should be primarily responsible for disaster relief? Explain your answer.

THINK central **Practice Online**

thinkcentral.com
KEYWORD: SGO FED

SECTION 3 Federalism Today

BEFORE YOU READ

Main Idea

Today the balance of power between the states and the national government is characterized by a system of grants and mandates, as well as by a number of key policy areas.

Reading Focus

1. What is fiscal federalism?

2. How does the national government use grants and mandates to influence state policies?

3. What issues most influence American federalism today?

Key Terms

fiscal federalism
grants-in-aid
categorical grants
block grants
federal mandates

TAKING NOTES As you read, take notes on the features of present-day federalism in a graphic organizer like this one.

Federalism Today

WHY IT MATTERS

A Need for National Power September 11, 2001, marked a new day in American federalism. The international terrorist attacks on the World Trade Center in New York City and on the Pentagon in Washington, D.C., that occurred on September 11 sparked calls for increased national security.

The American people and their representatives in Congress called on the national government to take the lead in securing the homeland. Under the leadership of President George W. Bush, the national government proposed a massive economic package to aid in homeland security.

Since the September 11 attacks, the national government has released billions of dollars to the states to fund a range of homeland security training measures, including disaster preparedness and emergency response training. The states also assumed enormous responsibilities on their own to protect electrical lines, ports, and the food and water supply.

The nation's response to terrorism is characteristic of today's brand of federalism. This newest phase in American federalism depends heavily on a complex web of financial ties to meet the needs of the nation. At the same time, our federal system remains flexible to deal with new issues as they arise. ◼

Since September 11, 2001, the national government has increased its spending on disaster preparedness training.

Facing New Challenges

Fiscal Federalism

The beginning of the twenty-first century marked yet another shift in relations between the states and the nation. In the wake of the September 11, 2001, terrorist attacks, the need for increased national security led to an expansion in the powers of government. This latest trend in federalism runs against the standard set by new federalism—the return of power to the states. Today the power of the national government to influence state policies occurs within a context of **fiscal federalism**, a system of spending, taxing, and providing aid in the federal system.

Fiscal federalism as we know it took shape during the 1900s. Examples of the national government providing aid to the states, however, may be found farther back in time. For example, under the Articles of Confederation, the Land Ordinance of 1785 set aside land for public schools in the Northwest Territory.

After the Constitution was ratified, the national government continued to give aid to states. The Morrill Act (1862) granted large tracts of land to states. In turn, the states sold the land and used the money to establish colleges. Seventy state universities, including Texas A&M and Ohio State University, originated from the Morrill Act.

During the twentieth century, the power of the national government expanded with increased use of grants-in-aid. **Grants-in-aid** include money and other resources that the national government provides to pay for state and local activities. This money is used to fund a range of services and policy areas, including low-income housing, community arts programs, energy assistance for the elderly, and disaster preparedness programs.

How does the national government get the money to pay for grants-in-aid? The Sixteenth Amendment, ratified in 1913, gave Congress the authority to set a federal income tax. Federal income taxes are the main source of the nation's income. The ability to give this money back to states, in the form of aid, is the national government's chief tool for aiding and influencing states.

READING CHECK **Making Inferences** How might grants-in-aid increase the national government's power?

Grants and Mandates

Fiscal federalism allows the national government to influence state policies in such a way that they support national priorities. Categorical grants, block grants, and federal mandates are among the national government's most important tools for influencing state policy.

Categorical Grants Most federal aid is distributed to the states in the form of **categorical grants**. These grants can only be used for a specific purpose, or category, of state and local spending, such as the building of a new airport or crime-fighting in a certain area. The national government also uses categorical grants to provide money to areas affected by natural disasters. The amount of money released in a categorical grant often depends on a state's population, and states may be required to contribute money in addition to the national money.

Block Grants In contrast to categorical grants, **block grants** are federal grants that are given for more general purposes or for broad policy areas, such as welfare, public health, community development, or education. States usually prefer block grants because they are designed to allow state officials to spend the money as they see fit. At the same time, Congress loses some control over how the money is spent.

In the 1980s President Ronald Reagan used block grants in an attempt to decrease the size and influence of the national government. In 1981, as part of a major revision of the federal budget, Congress combined many categorical grants into nine block grants to the states.

Federal Mandates State and local governments are usually pleased to receive money from the national government, but the national government often distributes money with strings attached. For example, the U.S. government may impose **federal mandates**, or demands on states to carry out certain policies as a condition of receiving grant money. In some cases, Congress has even imposed "unfunded mandates," or demands without funding.

WHAT DO YOU THINK?

How would you explain American federalism to a non-American?

RESPONSIBILITIES OF LEADERSHIP

The national government uses grants-in-aid to influence state and local policies. Why might it be a mistake for state and local leaders to depend on grants-in-aid for funding?

Tools of Fiscal Federalism

Categorical Grants

Categorical grants are national grants that state and local governments use for specific purposes. For example, categorical grant money is being used to protect the habitat of the whooping crane in Port Aransas, Texas.

Block Grants

State and local governments use block grants from the national government to address broad policy areas, such as home energy efficiency programs and health services. Block grants usually come with few or no strings attached.

Federal Mandates

The national government uses federal mandates to encourage state and local governments to comply with national policy. The Clean Air Act was an unfunded mandate that set automobile emissions standards in order to improve air quality.

Federal mandates have been particularly important in enacting civil rights and environmental policies. For example, a number of government actions taken during the civil rights movement, such as school busing, desegregation, and affirmative action resulted from federal mandates. In such cases, the national government often used the equal protection clause of the Fourteenth Amendment to justify its use of mandates.

Likewise, since air pollution, contaminated water, and acid rain can spill across state lines, many environmental regulations come from the national government. The Clean Air Act of 1970 was a national mandate that required states to meet national air-quality levels. In exchange for grant money, the states were required to create programs to reduce pollution. States that did not meet the air quality levels after a certain period of time risked losing federal funding.

As you can probably imagine, unfunded mandates have often been a source of conflict between the national government and the states. For example, in 1993 a federal mandate required states to change their voter registration procedures in an effort to increase the number of voters. Yet some states argued that they should not have to pay for a program they have not approved.

READING CHECK **Making Generalizations** What types of federal aid do the states generally prefer? Why?

Issues in Federalism Today

Along with the ongoing debates concerning the division of power and funding, new issues challenge American federalism. Today political debates over how the United States will best address key policy areas—poverty, homeland security, environmental protection, immigration, and health care—drive changes in our federal system.

Poverty In 1996 Congress passed a welfare reform law that gave the states the authority to manage their own welfare systems using federal block grants. This marked a major change from the previous welfare program—in existence since the New Deal—in which the national government had paid welfare recipients directly.

Since the 1996 reforms, the number of people on welfare in the United States has decreased. Some people credit this to the added flexibility and creativity that can come when programs to help the poor are handled at the state level. Others argue that the decrease only represents a strong economy and question whether the states will be able to continue to meet the needs of the poor.

Homeland Security Another policy area shaping federalism today is homeland security. The Department of Homeland Security was formed after the attacks of

September 11, 2001, to protect the nation from terrorism, natural disasters, and other emergencies. When Hurricane Katrina hit the Gulf Coast in 2005, local and state governments worked alongside the Department of Homeland Security to respond to the disaster. In the aftermath of the storm, people questioned whether better leadership and better cooperation between the levels of government might have saved lives.

Environment Government efforts to protect the environment are often seen as the responsibility of the national government. There are many practical reasons for this. For one, the environmental policies of one state might affect other states. In addition, a state government might hesitate to enact environmental regulations that might cause businesses to relocate to a different state that has fewer restrictions.

Still, some leaders believe that environmental protection is better handled at the state and local level. Members of Congress representing this view have asked to limit the reach of the national government's Environmental Protection Agency in favor of local recycling and conservation efforts.

Immigration In recent years, immigration has become an important issue testing our federal system. Although the national government handles immigration policies, such as citizenship and border protection, immigration is not just a national issue. Many states, including California, Texas, New Mexico, and Arizona, have international borders. Moreover, state governments often take on responsibility for a number of immigration-related issues, including increased education costs, health and social services, employment-related issues, and low-cost housing. For the past several years, Congress has considered various immigration reforms, but they have yet to resolve the issue at a national level.

Health Care More than ever, Americans are turning to their state and national governments for creative solutions to the rising costs of medical services, health insurance, and hospitalization. Many are concerned, for example, that in 2003 as many as 45 million Americans did not have health insurance. Some see the trend as an indicator that the United States may be on the verge of a health care crisis. If Americans cannot afford to pay for their own health care, should the government pick up the tab? Which level of government should take the lead, state or national? The answers to these questions will no doubt redirect the course of American federalism in the years to come.

READING CHECK **Making Inferences** Why do you think some people seek a federal solution to poverty?

SECTION 3 ASSESSMENT

THINK central **Online Quiz**
thinkcentral.com
KEYWORD: SGO FED HP

Reviewing Ideas and Terms

1. **a. Define** What are **grants-in-aid**?
   b. Evaluate Do you think **fiscal federalism** gives the national government too much power? Why or why not?

2. **a. Identify** For what purposes are **categorical grants** used?
   b. Contrast In what ways are categorical grants and **block grants** different?
   c. Elaborate How can the national government use categorical grants, block grants, and **federal mandates** to influence state policies? Which do you think is most effective?

3. **a. Identify** How has welfare reform affected the way state and national governments work together to fight poverty?
   b. Evaluate Which issue facing the United States today do you think poses the greatest challenge to the American federal system? Explain your answer.

Critical Thinking

4. **Analyze** Use the graphic organizer below to analyze how grants and mandates have been used to increase and decrease the influence of the national government.

Increase — Influence of National Government — Decrease

FOCUS ON WRITING

5. **Persuasive** Write a grant proposal from the viewpoint of a city official. In the proposal, ask the federal government for a block grant that will have a positive impact on your community.

Laboratories of Democracy

From health care to taxes and education, the states have a high degree of control over policy areas that affect the daily lives of their citizens. In American federalism, the states are often testing grounds for new approaches to meeting the needs of the people. Over time, many state polices have influenced national policy.

Why have the states been called "laboratories of democracy"? Supreme Court Justice Louis D. Brandeis observed that one of the principal values of American federalism is that "a single courageous State may, if its citizens choose, serve as a laboratory; and try novel social and economic experiments without risk to the rest of the country." There are many examples of governance experiments in states and localities. Some innovations catch on in other states or in the nation as a whole. For instance, many states, starting with Wyoming, began permitting women to vote at least in local and state elections well before 1900. Those experiments set the stage for the adoption of the Nineteenth Amendment in 1920, which guaranteed women the right to vote in all elections.

What democratic methods have been tested in the states? Initiative, referendum, recall. This trio of methods, begun during the Progressive Era of the late nineteenth century, allows citizens to participate in direct democracy in their states. Initiative, referendum, and recall describe discrete actions but they are related by the direct involvement of citizens.

- **Initiative** South Dakota was the first state to permit the initiative. There are two forms of initiative: direct and indirect. In a direct initiative an individual or a group proposes and drafts a law or a state constitutional amendment. Then the initiator gathers a prescribed number of signatures to place the proposal on the ballot for approval or rejection by the voters. In the indirect process proposals first go to the legislature. If legislators reject the proposal or take no action on it, then the proposal goes on the ballot. Twenty-four states today use the initiative.

- **Referendum** The referendum involves placing a measure that has been approved by a legislature on the ballot for popular vote. Some state constitutions require the legislature to refer certain kinds of measures to the people. Others permit citizens to demand a vote on a law that has been passed by the legislature by gathering a prescribed number of signatures. Twenty-four states now use the referendum.

- **Recall** is a process of removing elected officials from office. In the eighteen states that permit recall it is used most frequently at the local level. However, in 2003 enough California voters signed petitions to call an election to recall their governor and elect a new one.

How have states experimented with innovative environmental policies? In 1997 some 164 countries signed the Kyoto Accords, an international treaty aimed at reducing the level of carbon dioxide and five other greenhouse gasses

in the air. President Bill Clinton signed the treaty, but the U.S. Senate did not ratify it. When President George W. Bush took office, he withdrew the United States from the Kyoto Accords. In 2006 seven northeastern states entered into the Regional Greenhouse Gas Initiative aimed at achieving most of the emission standards set by the Kyoto Accords. The coalition of states also hoped to put pressure on the national government to commit the United States to the Kyoto Accords.

Also in 2006 California became the first state to impose a cap on the emission of carbon dioxide and other gasses. The Global Warming Solutions Act aims to cut California's emissions by 25 percent by 2020. Many of the nation's cities, from Seattle to New York, also are adopting measures aimed at reducing air pollution and global warming.

How have the states contributed to health care initiatives? By the mid-1990s soaring health care costs and increasingly large numbers of people without health insurance had become a major issue of public concern. Congress had not adopted legislation to address the problem. However, by 2006 several states had adopted programs seeking to offer nearly universal access to health insurance for all their residents, regardless of ability to pay. Several other states were considering programs at that time. A former Oregon governor, John Kitzhaber, initiated the Archimedes Movement in 2006, which aimed at mobilizing people at the grassroots level to find a solution to the health care problem that eventually would be accepted nationwide.

Supporters of the Oregon based Archimedes Movement work to improve health care in their state and for the nation as a whole.

Reviewing Ideas

1. **Recall** What is a referendum?
2. **Explain** Why have the states been called "laboratories of democracy"?

Critical Thinking

3. **Evaluate** Conduct research to find an example of an initiative, referendum, or recall effort in your state. Explain how this effort was a social, political, or economic experiment.

Connecting Online

Visit **thinkcentral.com** for review and enrichment activities related to this chapter.

THINK central

KEYWORD: SGO FED

Quiz and Review

GOV 101
Examine key concepts in this chapter.

ONLINE QUIZZES
Take a practice quiz for each section in this chapter.

Activities

eActivities
Complete Webquests and Internet research activities.

INTERACTIVE FEATURES
Explore interactive versions of maps and charts.

KEEP IT CURRENT
Link to current events in U.S. government.

Partners

American Bar Association Division for Public Education
Learn more about the law, your rights and responsibilities.

Center for Civic Education
Promoting an enlightened and responsible citizenry committed to democratic principles and actively engaged in the practice of democracy.

Online Textbook

ONLINE SIMULATIONS
Learn about U.S. government through simulations you can complete online.

Comprehension and Critical Thinking

SECTION 1 *(pp. 96–102)*

1. a. Review Key Terms For each term, write a sentence that explains its significance or meaning: expressed powers, implied powers, inherent powers, reserved powers.

b. Make Inferences Why do you think the Constitution denies both the state governments and the national government the power to grant titles of nobility?

c. Evaluate What are the main reasons that the Framers chose a federal system rather than a confederation?

SECTION 2 *(pp. 103–110)*

2. a. Review Key Terms For each term, write a sentence that explains its significance or meaning: dual federalism, doctrine of nullification, doctrine of secession, cooperative federalism, creative federalism, new federalism.

b. Analyze Why do you think the period of dual federalism was characterized by tension between the levels of government?

c. Rank Which event had a greater impact on federalism: the Civil War or the Great Depression? Support your answer with details.

SECTION 3 *(pp. 112–115)*

3. a. Review Key Terms For each term, write a sentence that explains its significance or meaning: fiscal federalism, grants-in-aid, categorical grants, block grants, federal mandates.

b. Summarize How does the federal government provide money and resources to the states?

c. Predict What trend do you think will characterize federalism in the near future—an expansion in national power or a return of power to the states? Explain your answer.

Critical Reading

Reread the passage in Section 2 that begins with the heading "The Marshall Court." Then answer the questions that follow.

4. On what two clauses of the Constitution did Supreme Court Chief Justice John Marshall base his decision in *McCulloch v. Maryland*?

A the commerce clause; the full faith and credit clause

B the necessary and proper clause; the supremacy clause

C the full faith and credit clause; the necessary and proper clause

D the privileges and immunities clause; the full faith and credit clause

5. What effect did John Marshall's Supreme Court have upon American federalism?

A It expanded the powers of the state and local governments.

B It determined that the full faith and credit clause was unconstitutional.

C It expanded the powers of the national government.

D It put an end to the process of judicial review.

RESPONSIBILITIES OF LEADERSHIP

6. To understand **important eras of American federalism**, create a time line that includes dual federalism, cooperative federalism, creative federalism, new federalism, and devolution. Begin your time line with the Articles of Confederation and end it with a recent event that illustrates how the relationship between the states and the national government is changing. Use your time line to prepare a brief presentation for the class. Be sure that your presentation answers the following questions: How has the American federal system changed over time? In what areas, if any, do you think the nation or the states should have more power and responsibility today?

CONNECTING TO THE CONSTITUTION

7. The term *federalism* is not defined in a single passage of the Constitution. Instead provisions for a federal form of government are scattered throughout the document. Use information from this chapter and from the Constitution presented at the end of your textbook to complete a three-column chart for "The Constitutional Foundations for Federalism." In the first column record information about provisions in the Constitution that deal with federalism, such as provisions for national powers, state powers, shared powers, and limits on the powers of each level of government. In the second column, record information about where you found each provision in the Constitution. Lastly, in the third column, write a brief description of what you think each provision means.

ANALYZING PRIMARY SOURCES

Political Cartoon *In 2005 the U.S. Supreme Court, against the wishes of many in Congress, upheld a Florida State Supreme Court decision in a controversial right-to-die case.*

8. Analyze What is happening in this cartoon?

9. Draw Conclusions How does the cartoonist portray the relationship between the state and the national governments in this cartoon?

WRITING FOR THE SAT

Think about the following issue:

Many people argue that American federalism, as it exists today, would be unrecognizable to the Framers of the Constitution.

10. Assignment Do you think the Framers of the Constitution would approve of American federalism today? Write a three-paragraph essay from the point of view of one the Framers of the Constitution that evaluates American federalism today. Be sure to identify whether your Framer was a supporter of states' rights or of a strong national government.

Congress: The Legislative Branch

"I HAVE SEEN IN THE HALLS OF
CONGRESS MORE IDEALISM, MORE
HUMANNESS, MORE COMPASSION,
MORE PROFILES OF COURAGE
THAN IN ANY OTHER INSTITUTION
THAT I HAVE EVER KNOWN."

—HUBERT H. HUMPHREY, 1965

The United States Capitol building in Washington, D.C.

CONNECTING TO THE CONSTITUTION

Our nation's system of government is based on constitutional law established by the United States Constitution. See the "We the People: The Citizen and the Constitution" pages in this chapter for an in-depth exploration of the sources of congressional legislation.

SECTION 1

Congress

BEFORE YOU READ

Main Idea

The voters elect members of Congress to represent them and to enact laws in their name. Congress plays a vital role in our government's system of checks and balances.

Reading Focus

1. How does Congress represent the people?
2. Why is the structure of Congress important?
3. What is the role of Congress in the system of checks and balances?

Key Terms

constituents
apportionment
appropriation
impeachment
oversight

TAKING NOTES

As you read, take notes on the powers and features of Congress. Record your notes in a chart like this one.

Representing the People	Structure	Checks and Balances

WHY IT MATTERS

The People's Representatives Every two years, in January, members of Congress—535 of them—convene in the Capitol to open a new Congress. They are people from different regions of the country and different walks of life. They bring different viewpoints and life experiences. They come to Washington, D.C., to speak for over 300 million of their fellow Americans.

Opening day of a new Congress is a relaxed time. The business of legislating has not begun. For returning members, it is a chance to meet old friends and congratulate them on winning re-election. For new members there is the satisfaction of

knowing they have two years to pursue the policies and agendas that motivated them to run for Congress.

Senate procedures on opening day are fairly routine. Newly elected and re-elected members, about a third of the Senate, take the oath of office, and the chamber passes resolutions on rules. In the House of Representatives, the clerk calls the House to order, checks the roll, and then the members-to-be formally elect a Speaker, who swears in the other 434 representatives.

The oath points to the serious purpose of the day. Before they begin to carry out the people's business, each member swears to "preserve, protect, and defend the Constitution." ■

Opening Day in Congress

Speaker of the House Nancy Pelosi (D, California) administers the oath of office to House members on January 4, 2007.

Congress and the People

The opening words of the Constitution—"We the People"—signal that, in our nation, it is the people who are sovereign. Yet the people do not take part in national government directly. They do so by electing representatives, whose job it is to make and carry out laws.

Article I of the Constitution gives the law-making power to Congress. It also specifies that the "people of the several States" shall choose the members of Congress in regularly scheduled elections. The U.S. Congress, then, is the body through which the will of the people is made into law.

Representing the People Each member of Congress represents the people of a particular geographic area. The people who live within that area are called the member's **constituents**. Thus, one way in which a member of Congress represents the people is by representing his or her constituents.

Most constituents have particular interests and concerns. Those interests may be economic—for example, related to their jobs and industries. Interests may also be philosophical or personal—for example, a constituent may have a strong belief in environmental protection. Indeed, constituents may hold a variety of interests. Sometimes these various interests are in conflict with each other, which complicates the job of a member of Congress pledged to represent the constituents' interests.

Members of Congress must also deal with the demands of organized groups of like-minded people who join together to influence government and its policies. These organized groups, called interest groups, may draw their membership from across the nation and represent only a small number of any one of a Congress member's constituents. Still, members of Congress must deal with pressure applied by interest groups as they attempt to represent "the people."

In addition to representing their constituents, members of Congress also keep in mind the needs of the country as a whole. They try to balance their constituents' special needs with a desire to promote the common good—the outcome that is best for all.

This can be a difficult task. Sometimes members seek to serve their constituents directly—for example, by working to bring federal funding to their home district or answering a query. In fact, each member employs a staff of assistants to act on queries from constituents. Other times, members may vote based on what they think is in the best interest of the nation, even if it conflicts with the views of their constituents. These are both ways in which members of Congress represent the people.

Members of Congress Who are these men and women representing the people of the nation? How did they get their jobs? Beyond certain minimal requirements of office, which will be explained in detail in Sections 3 and 4 of this chapter, the Constitution places few limits on who can be a member of Congress. Still, members of Congress tend to have more in common with each other than with the constituents they represent.

Members of Congress tend to be older than the average age of the general population. The average age of members in recent Congresses has been in the mid-to-upper fifties. Members of Congress are also much wealthier than the general population. In recent years there have been dozens of millionaires in Congress.

Most members of Congress are white men. The number who are women, African Americans, Hispanics, or members of other minority groups is low compared to these groups' percentage of the general population. In recent years, however, Congress has become more diverse. The numbers of women and African Americans in the 110th Congress (which began in 2007) were at an all-time high. The 110th Congress also elected the first female Speaker of the House, Nancy Pelosi (D, California).

READING CHECK Identifying the Main Idea
What groups do members of Congress represent?

The Structure of Congress

As you know, Congress is a bicameral legislature. Its two houses are the House of Representatives and the Senate. These houses differ significantly in key details.

WHAT DO YOU THINK?

How might members of Congress balance their roles as delegates of their constituents and trustees of the common good?

The House of Representatives The Constitution states that seats in the House "shall be apportioned among the several States . . . according to their respective Numbers." **Apportionment** means the distribution of House seats among the states based on population. Each House seat is meant to represent about the same number of people. The larger a state's population, the more representatives it has. Each state, however, is guaranteed at least one House member.

Today the total number of House seats is 435. That number was fixed by law in 1929. Congress has since added nonvoting delegates from the District of Columbia, Guam, the U.S. Virgin Islands, and American Samoa. House members serve two-year terms. All seats are contested at the same time. This can result in a rapid swing of control of the House from one party to another after an election.

The Senate The Constitution fixes membership in the Senate at "two Senators from each state." As a result, the Senate today has 100 members.

Originally, the Constitution gave the power to choose senators to state legislatures rather than to the voters. This changed in 1913, when the Seventeenth Amendment, requiring popular election of senators, was ratified. This amendment made the Senate a more democratic institution.

Unlike their colleagues in the House, senators serve six-year terms. These terms are staggered so that every two years, one-third of the seats are up for election. Staggered elections prevent major changes in Senate membership due to any one election.

The Two-House Structure Why did the Constitutional Convention create a bicameral legislature? The Framers were familiar with the two-house British Parliament. Several of the states also had bicameral legislatures. These models no doubt had an influence on the Framers' thinking. The decision at the Convention, however, was a result of the Great Compromise—one of the most important compromises of the Convention.

The Great Compromise combined elements of the Virginia Plan, which called for a bicameral legislature with representation based on state population, and the New Jersey Plan, which proposed a one-house legislature in which all the states would be represented equally. States with large populations favored the Virginia Plan, and those with small populations favored the New Jersey Plan. The plan accepted in the Great Compromise featured two houses, one in which small states and large states had equal representation and one in which representation was based on population.

The Great Compromise also settled a Convention debate over how much say to give the voting public. The House, with its frequent direct elections, would more closely reflect the people's will. The Senate, with no direct elections and longer terms, would be less subject to public passions. George Washington compared the two-house system to drinking a cup of hot coffee. "We pour legislation [from the House]," he explained to Thomas Jefferson, "into the senatorial saucer to cool it."

READING CHECK Summarizing What are the key features and purposes of the bicameral structure?

Interactive Feature

CONGRESSIONAL REPRESENTATION SELECTED STATES, 2007

State	Population*	House Members	Senate Members
California	36,457,549	53	2
Florida	18,089,888	25	2
Georgia	9,363,941	13	2
Illinois	12,831,970	19	2
Indiana	6,313,520	9	2
Texas	23,507,783	32	2
Virginia	7,642,884	11	2
Wyoming	515,004	1	2

*Census estimates, 2006

Skills FOCUS INTERPRETING CHARTS

Do you think having equal representation of every state in the Senate reflects the principle of federalism? Do you think it is fair?

THINK central Interactive

thinkcentral.com
KEYWORD: SGO CNG

Congress and Checks and Balances

As you have read, our constitutional system is built on a system of checks and balances. Governmental power is divided and separated into three different branches. As the legislative branch of government, Congress has potent checks on the powers of the executive and judicial branches.

The Power of the Purse Congress alone has the power to approve spending by the federal government. It exercises this power through a special type of act called an **appropriation,** or a bill that sets aside funds for a specific purpose. This congressional power is sometimes referred to as the "power of the purse." With it, Congress can prevent the executive branch from carrying out policies it disagrees with. The president can make budget requests, yet Congress can refuse to fund those requests.

Likewise, Congress can, in theory, withhold funding for military actions that the president has committed to. In reality, though, when troops are in the field, members of Congress find it politically difficult to withhold funding.

The Framers placed some limits on Congress's power of the purse. Congress cannot, for example, lower the pay of the president and judges during their time in office. The Framers wanted to make sure that Congress did not use salary as a means to put pressure on or undercut the authority of the other branches.

The Power of Advice and Consent The Constitution gives the president the job of making treaties with foreign governments and appointing key government officials. These officials include ambassadors, federal judges and Supreme Court justices, and other top government leaders. These presidential powers, however, are subject to the "advice and consent" of the Senate.

Any treaty negotiated by a president is put to a vote in the Senate. It must receive a two-thirds vote to become law. In fact, several treaties signed by U.S. presidents have never been enacted because the Senate chose not to approve them.

The Impeachment Power

Congress can impeach officials, including presidents, for "high crimes and misdemeanors." Presidents Andrew Johnson (top left) and Bill Clinton (top right) are the only two presidents to be impeached. Neither was convicted by the Senate.

The Senate can also reject top presidential appointees. In 1987, for example, the Senate rejected President Ronald Reagan's Supreme Court nominee Robert Bork after a lengthy confirmation battle.

The Impeachment Power Congress has the power to charge officials in the executive and judicial branches with wrongdoing and bring them to trial. This is known as the power of **impeachment**. If found guilty, impeached officials can be removed from office before the completion of their terms.

The impeachment process begins in the House of Representatives, which has responsibility for drawing up the charges against the official. A majority vote to approve the charges results in the formal impeachment of the official.

The Senate then holds a trial, with the vice president serving as the judge. In the event of the impeachment of a president or vice president, the Chief Justice of the United States serves as the judge. A two-thirds vote of the Senate is required to find the official guilty and remove him or her from office.

The Constitution calls for impeachment in cases of treason, bribery, or "high crimes and misdemeanors." The last phrase gives Congress wide freedom to decide when an official deserves impeachment. In fact, though, Congress has impeached only 17 officials. Most of these were federal judges. Two, however, were presidents—Andrew Johnson in 1868 and Bill Clinton in 1998.

In 1868 Congress and President Johnson were bitterly divided over Reconstruction. Congress had passed a law requiring Senate approval before the president could remove any top government official. Johnson felt the law was unconstitutional and disobeyed it. The House impeached him. Johnson avoided conviction in the Senate trial by one vote and served out the rest of his term.

In 1998 the House impeached President Bill Clinton. The charges included giving false testimony to a court in a civil case unrelated to the president's official duties. As in the Johnson case, the Senate fell short of the votes necessary to convict Clinton. He served out the remainder of his term.

Another president, Richard Nixon, faced almost certain impeachment in 1974. Embroiled in the Watergate scandal in which he was accused of covering up illegal activities by members of his re-election campaign staff, Nixon resigned before Congress had a chance to impeach him.

Other Checks and Balances Congress balances the powers of the other branches of government in several more ways. For example, Congress can check the power of the judicial branch by starting the process of amending the Constitution. The states have the final authority to ratify any amendments Congress proposes. The ability to help change the Constitution can serve as a check on the power of courts to declare acts of Congress unconstitutional.

Congress can also check the power of the executive branch by voting to override a presidential veto of a bill previously passed by Congress. An override is not easy to obtain. It requires a two-thirds vote of each chamber of Congress. About 100 presidential vetoes, 4 percent, have been overridden since the first Congress convened in 1789.

Congress has broad powers to review how the executive branch is operating and to make sure it is following the laws Congress has passed. This is called congressional **oversight**. Congress can hold hearings and force witnesses to appear, including officials from the executive branch. Congress can use its oversight power to bring great political pressure on the executive.

READING CHECK **Identifying Supporting Details** What are some examples of checks and balances Congress has over the executive branch?

SECTION 1 ASSESSMENT

THINK central **Online Quiz**
thinkcentral.com
KEYWORD: SGO CNG HP

Reviewing Ideas and Terms

1. **a. Recall** What is the term for the people represented by a member of Congress?
   b. Explain What are some of the ways in which members of Congress try to represent the people they serve?
   c. Elaborate How well do you think the members of Congress have reflected the people they represent in recent times?

2. **a. Describe** What are some of the key differences between the House of Representatives and the Senate?
   b. Evaluate How well do you think the structure of Congress addresses the concerns about the power of large states and the influence of public passions on legislation?

3. **a. Describe** What is **impeachment**?
   b. Make Inferences What can you infer from the fact that Congress has impeached just 17 officials in U.S. history?

Critical Thinking

4. **Rank** Using your notes and the graphic organizer below, rank the significance of checks on the other branches that Congress has.

Congressional Checks

FOCUS ON WRITING

5. **Persuasive** As a delegate at the Constitutional Convention, write a speech supporting the Great Compromise.

SECTION 2 The Powers of Congress

BEFORE YOU READ

Main Idea

The Constitution gives Congress many expressed powers, and it implies some others. The Constitution also places limits on the powers of Congress.

Reading Focus

1. What types of powers does Congress have?

2. What are the expressed powers of Congress?

3. What are the implied powers of Congress?

4. What are some of Congress's nonlegislative powers?

5. What are some of the limits on the powers of Congress?

6. How has the power of Congress changed during U.S. history?

Key Terms

necessary and proper clause
indirect tax
direct tax
deficit
commerce clause
subpoenas
writ of habeas corpus
bill of attainder
ex post facto laws

TAKING NOTES As you read, take notes on the powers of Congress. Record your notes in a graphic organizer like this one.

Powers of Congress

WHY IT MATTERS

A Fire Leads to Change In 1969 the Cuyahoga River, which runs through downtown Cleveland, Ohio, caught fire. Decades of unregulated dumping of industrial wastes had turned the river into a toxic—and flammable—brew of oil and chemicals. The fire that day was not the first time the Cuyahoga had burst into flames, nor was it the biggest to have broken out on the river. In 30 minutes the fire was out. The Cleveland newspapers did not even have time to send photographers to cover the story.

The fire on the Cuyahoga may have burned a short time, but for advocates of a cleaner environment, it came at the right time. A growing environmental movement, spurred by books like *Silent Spring*, was calling for change. A river catching fire

provided a vivid demonstration of why new laws safeguarding the environment were needed. The calls for reform reached the halls of Congress. In 1972 Congress passed the first of a series of environmental laws to protect the nation's waterways that today goes by the name of the Clean Water Act.

Where did Congress get the authority to pass laws protecting the environment? The word *environment* never appears in the Constitution. Nor does Social Security or interstate highways or many other programs we take for granted. Congress used its powers under generally worded clauses to create these programs. The Framers made the Constitution flexible enough to allow Congress to meet new challenges as they arise. ■

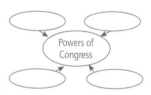

Congress and the Clean Water Act

The Cuyahoga River, afire in 1952, (above) is the scene of rowing races today (right).

Defining the Powers of Congress

As discussed in Chapter 4, the Constitution establishes the structure of Congress and lists its powers. It also includes language suggesting additional congressional powers.

- **Expressed Powers** Article I, Section 8, of the Constitution lists 18 specific powers that Congress is meant to wield, including coining money, collecting taxes, regulating commerce, raising and maintaining armed forces, and declaring war.

- **Implied Powers** Implied powers are those powers only suggested by the Constitution. Congress's implied powers derive from Article I, Section 8, Clause 18, which gives the national legislature the power to "make all Laws which shall be necessary and proper for carrying into execution the [expressed] Powers and all other Powers vested by this Constitution in the Government of the United States." This clause is known variously as the elastic clause or the **necessary and proper clause**.

- **Inherent Powers** Those powers that all governments of independent nations possess are known as inherent powers because they do not have to be spelled out. Examples of inherent power include the power to control borders and to make agreements with other nations. Just which branch of government—the legislative or the executive—holds these inherent powers has never been definitively determined. Because most inherent powers involve foreign affairs, presidents have been more forceful and more frequent in asserting a claim to them. However, Congress has often shown itself willing to contest, or at least modify, these claims.

- **Powers Denied Congress** Since the Framers believed in limited government overall and federalism specifically, they were careful to place some limits on congressional power. Article I, Section 9, lists powers specifically denied to Congress.

READING CHECK **Contrasting** What is the difference between an expressed power and an implied power?

ACADEMIC VOCABULARY

levy to impose or collect

Expressed Powers of Congress

The expressed powers of Congress—those powers explicitly listed in Article I, Section 8, and elsewhere in the Constitution—fall into three broad categories. There are powers relating to government finance and revenue, to the regulation of commerce, and to national defense. In addition, there are other powers that address specific issues of national importance, such as the creation of a postal service and coining money.

Financing Powers The Constitution gives Congress the power to raise money to run the government through two means—levying taxes and borrowing money. In giving Congress these powers, the Framers sought to address a major weakness of the Articles of Confederation. Under that document, the national government could ask the states for money, but it could not *force* the states to supply it. In practice, Congress had difficulty obtaining the funding it needed.

Article I, Section 8, Clause 1, of the Constitution expressly grants Congress the "power to lay and collect Taxes . . . to pay the Debts and provide for the common Defense and general Welfare of the United States." For much of the nation's history, the majority of tax revenue was generated by tariffs. A tariff is a tax on goods imported into the country. Another important source of revenue was the indirect tax. An **indirect tax** is a tax levied on one person but passed on to another for payment to the government. Today the federal government collects indirect taxes for products such as gasoline, liquor, and airline tickets. The seller simply includes the tax in the price of the product.

The Framers of the Constitution limited the use of the **direct tax**, or a tax an individual pays directly to the government. Article I, Section 9, Clause 4, says that direct taxes have to be levied in proportion to a state's population as determined by the census. This provision was meant to reassure slaveholding states, who feared having to pay taxes on their enslaved populations according to a one-to-one ratio instead of the three-fifths ratio used for counting slaves in the census.

In 1895 the Supreme Court used this clause to strike down a federal income tax law. In a sharply divided decision, the Court ruled that an income tax was a direct tax. Unless it was apportioned among the states according to population—something that would be unworkable—an income tax was unconstitutional.

The Sixteenth Amendment addressed this concern in 1913. It specifically empowered Congress to levy an income tax. The amendment also restricted the kinds of direct taxes that could be collected according to "apportionment among the several States." Today revenue generated by the income tax far outpaces revenue generated by tariffs and other indirect taxes.

The Constitution also gives Congress the power to borrow money on behalf of the United States. This power allows the government to function when there is not enough expected revenue to cover expenses— a budget **deficit**. Deficits can occur during times of emergency, such as during wars. In recent decades, deficit spending has become standard practice in Congress even during good economic times.

Commerce Power The Constitution gives the federal government the right to regulate interstate commerce. That is, Congress alone can pass laws affecting economic activity that takes place across state lines. Under the Articles of Confederation, Congress lacked this power, and individual states promoted their own businesses and penalized those of other states. States placed taxes on the goods of other states or even barred their entry. As a result, the nation's economy suffered.

Congress's commerce power is contained in Article I, Section 8, Clause 3, of the Constitution, known as the **commerce clause**. The commerce clause passed with little debate during the Constitutional Convention. The Framers were all too aware of the problems under the Articles of Confederation. Yet from 1789 to 1950, no clause in the Constitution was the subject of more litigation than the commerce clause. Through that litigation, and the Supreme Court decisions that resulted, the commerce clause became the single most important source of federal government power. The shape of our modern economy as well as many activities we take for granted today as the proper responsibility of government derive ultimately from the commerce clause.

An early Supreme Court case, *Gibbons* v. *Ogden* (1824), helped define the commerce clause. The case involved the right of a state legislature to award a monopoly to operate a steamship line for travel between two states, New York and New Jersey. The Supreme Court struck down the state law, ruling that only Congress has the right to regulate interstate commerce. You can read more about this case later in the section.

Using its commerce power, Congress has passed many laws that, on the surface, seem unrelated to regulating interstate commerce.

ACADEMIC VOCABULARY
litigation legal dispute

Expressed Powers of Congress

Article I, Section 8, of the Constitution lists 18 powers that Congress has. These powers are extensive, and some, such as the power to regulate interstate commerce, have been used to accomplish policy goals the Framers never imagined.

Clause 1 To levy taxes
Clause 2 To borrow money
Clause 3 To regulate foreign and interstate commerce
Clause 4 To establish uniform rules of citizenship

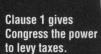

Clause 1 gives Congress the power to levy taxes.

Congress's power to regulate interstate commerce rests on Clause 3.

For example, as part of the Civil Rights Act of 1964, Congress used its commerce power to outlaw segregation in certain types of public establishments. The Heart of Atlanta Motel challenged the idea that the renting of rooms in its motel was an act of interstate commerce. The Supreme Court disagreed. In *Heart of Atlanta Motel, Inc., v. United States* (1964), the Court ruled that the availability of motel rooms affected interstate travel of truckers. Congress acted constitutionally when it used the commerce clause to attack racial segregation.

Defense-Related Powers The Constitution splits responsibility for national defense and foreign policy between Congress and the president. The Framers made the president commander in chief because they knew that having a single leader was important for effective military action. The president must also shape and carry out the nation's diplomatic efforts and relations with foreign countries. These duties give the president far-reaching powers to make decisions and take action in this arena.

The Framers reserved for Congress the power to declare war. A congressional declaration of war can send a strong message of resolve to the nation's enemies. In reality, however, a president can make war without a congressional declaration of war. The president simply commands troops into battle, and they go. This has happened frequently in U.S. history.

Following the Vietnam War, where U.S. troops were engaged in combat for nine years without a formal declaration of war, Congress moved to limit the president's ability to fight wars without such a declaration. It passed a joint resolution in 1973 known as the War Powers Resolution. The act requires a president to report to Congress anytime he or she sends troops into possible conflict without a declaration of war. Congress can then declare war or otherwise approve the continued use of U.S. forces. Without congressional agreement, the act requires the president to end the military action within 60 to 90 days, in most cases.

The ability of Congress to use the act to halt a president's use of military power is still unclear. Presidents have, however, made dozens of reports to Congress under the terms of the act. Some see this as proof that the act has increased Congress's involvement in the war-making power of the government.

The Constitution gives Congress the power to create an army and navy and to provide for their funding (Article I, Section 8, Clauses 12 and 13). At the time of the Constitution's writing, there was great fear of standing peacetime armies. The delegates discussed whether to forbid the maintenance of an army in times of peace. They finally chose to place a two-year limit on spending for the U.S. army. The two-year cap would prevent the army from becoming too powerful and independent of the control of Congress. This constitutional provision

Expressed Powers of Congress

Clause 5 To coin money; to set uniform weights and measures

Clause 6 To punish counterfeiters

Clause 7 To establish post offices and post roads

Clause 8 To make copyright and patent laws

Clause 9 To establish national courts inferior to the Supreme Court

Clause 10 To define and punish piracy and other violations of international law

Clause 11 To declare war

Clause 12 To raise and support armies

George Washington Carver Stamp Designs ©1998, United States Postal Service. Used with permission. All rights reserved. Written authorization from the Postal Service is required to use, reproduce, post, transmit, distribute, or publicly display these images.

Clause 5 covers the power to coin money.

Congress created the U.S. Postal Service using its powers under Clause 7.

Federal courthouses, like this one in New York City, exist because of Clause 9.

today gives the Congress the power of the purse over military activities. If Congress strongly opposed a president's use of the military, it could vote to deny funding.

Congress shares power with the states over the maintenance of the militia—today known as the National Guard. Congress has given the president the power to call out the National Guard in emergencies.

Other Expressed Powers Many of the other expressed powers aimed either to aid the development of a national economy or to safeguard national sovereignty. These were areas of policy the Framers believed belonged to the national government.

- **Coinage power** Under the Articles of Confederation, the individual states had the power to coin money, resulting in confusion and conflict. The Constitution gave this power to the national government.

- **National postal service** The creation of a fast, reliable postal system was seen as vital to the development of nation's economy.

- **Copyrights and patents** The Constitution gave Congress the power to write copyright and patent laws, which ensure writers and inventors "exclusive rights" to their respective writings and discoveries. The Framers believed that guaranteeing ownership rights and, with them, the chance to profit from one's work would encourage "the Progress of Science and useful Arts."

- **Weights and measures** Standardizing weights and measures—for example, gallons, pounds, and yards—gave people confidence that a pound of goods in one state would be a pound in another.

- **Bankruptcy** Bankruptcy was a major issue in the early days of the nation. Congress is constitutionally charged with the job of establishing laws on the subject of bankruptcy. The fair and clear settlement of bankruptcy cases is an aid to commerce.

- **Naturalization** The Constitution gives Congress the power to "establish an uniform Rule of Naturalization." Naturalization is the process by which an immigrant to this country becomes a citizen. This provision of the Constitution suggests that the Framers expected the country to grow and for immigrants to continue to move here.

- **Federal courts** The Constitution establishes the Supreme Court. Congress is charged, however, with establishing the federal courts beneath the Supreme Court. In Chapter 8, you will read how Congress has used this power.

- **Congressional elections** Congress has the power to make laws about the time, place, and manner of electing its members. In practice, it leaves the details to the states.

READING CHECK **Summarizing** How do Congress's expressed powers in finance, defense, and commerce give it a leading role in American life?

Clause 13 To raise and maintain a navy

Clause 14 To establish military laws

Clause 15 To call up a national militia in times of uprising or foreign invasion

Clause 16 To organize, arm, and discipline a militia when it is called into service

Clause 17 To exercise jurisdiction over the District of Columbia

Clause 18 To make all laws necessary and proper to the execution of any of the other expressed powers

Congress funds the construction and operation of naval vessels using its powers under Clause 13.

Clause 17 empowers Congress to create a local government and courts for Washington, D.C.

Over time, Clause 18, the necessary and proper clause, has become the source of authority for much of the congressional legislation that affects Americans' everyday lives.

LANDMARK SUPREME COURT CASES

Constitutional Issue: Federalism

Gibbons v. Ogden (1824)

WHY IT MATTERS *Gibbons v. Ogden was the first case in which the Supreme Court ruled on the Constitution's commerce clause, which concerns Congress's power to regulate interstate commerce.*

Background

In the early 1800s steamboat inventors Robert Fulton and Robert Livingston had a monopoly granted by the state legislature on steamboat travel in New York State. Their company later licensed Aaron Ogden to operate steamboat ferries between New York City and New Jersey. When Thomas Gibbons, who held a "coasting license" from the federal government, began to operate a competing ferry line between New York and New Jersey, Ogden sued to keep Gibbons out of New York waters. A New York court ruled that the Fulton–Livingston monopoly was legal and that Gibbons could not operate in New York under his federal license. Gibbons then appealed this decision to the Supreme Court.

Arguments for Gibbons

Gibbons argued that New York's grant of a steamboat monopoly to Fulton and Livingston conflicted with the congressional power to regulate interstate commerce outlined in Article I, Section 8, of the Constitution. Navigation, he said, was a distinct form of commerce, one that clearly fell under congressional authority. His steamboat ferry operated between two states; therefore, even though the New York monopoly affected only New York waters, it unfairly restricted him from engaging in interstate commerce.

Gibbons argued that the Court should confirm federal authority over interstate commerce in all its forms. Quite simply, federal regulations—in this case, Gibbons's federal coasting license—should take precedence over state and local regulations—in this case, New York's steamboat monopoly.

Arguments for Ogden

Ogden argued that the commerce clause should be read narrowly and that commerce should be defined as simply the buying and selling of goods. Since Ogden's steamboat line did not buy or sell goods, he argued that it could not be considered commerce and that steamboat travel could not be regulated by the federal government under the commerce clause. Even if steamboat travel were to be considered commerce, Ogden believed, the New York restrictions on steamboat traffic applied only to New York waters and should not be subject to congressional authority over interstate commerce. Instead, navigation should be regulated only by state or local governments.

THE IMPACT TODAY In an opinion written by Chief Justice John Marshall, the Court ruled strongly in favor of Gibbons, saying that the power to regulate commerce "is complete in itself [and] may be exercised to its utmost extent." Since the *Gibbons* ruling, the commerce clause has emerged as the most important source of federal power. Our modern economy and the federal regulation of any number of industries rest largely on the commerce clause. The commerce clause also frequently underlies congressional action on many issues of morality, criminal activities, the minimum wage, racial discrimination in hotels, restaurants, and other public places, and other areas seemingly unconnected to interstate commerce.

CRITICAL THINKING

What Do You Think? Congress and the Supreme Court have interpreted the commerce clause broadly, expanding the areas open to federal action. Do you think this is appropriate? Explain your answer.

Research Supreme Court cases at **thinkcentral.com**. **KEYWORD:** SGO SCC

Implied Powers of Congress

The Constitution's list of expressed powers is long. Nonetheless, the Framers knew that they could not list all possible powers that a future Congress would need. Therefore, they concluded the list of congressional powers with a final clause, known as the necessary and proper clause, that would allow Congress to take actions needed to carry out the expressed powers.

From the nation's founding, the necessary and proper clause has stirred controversy. How should these words, and by implication, the Constitution itself, be interpreted?

Loose and Strict Constructionists On one side of the issue, strict constructionists argue that Congress should exercise only those powers clearly granted to it in the Constitution. In the early days of the republic, strict constructionists were known as Antifederalists because they wanted to preserve power for the states as much as possible. Loose constructionists, known as Federalists, wanted Congress to have freedom to act vigorously. If something were "necessary and proper" to the exercise of one of Congress's expressed powers, they argued, then Congress could do it.

Thomas Jefferson and Alexander Hamilton led the opposing sides in the debate over what "necessary and proper" meant. As advisers to President George Washington in 1791, they fought bitterly over the issue. As a strict constructionist, Jefferson argued that "to take a single step beyond the boundaries . . . drawn around the powers of Congress is to take possession of a boundless field of power." The Federalist reading of "necessary and proper," Jefferson said, "would reduce the whole instrument to a single phrase."

Hamilton countered for the Federalists. He argued that because the needs of the nation were "of such infinite variety, extent, and complexity," the national government had to have freedom to meet those needs.

The setting for this conflict was a proposal for Congress to create a national bank. Hamilton thought a bank was a necessary and proper tool for regulating commerce. Jefferson countered that the Constitution said nothing about Congress creating a bank, so one should not be created.

Hamilton won the debate, though to get Jefferson and other southerners who opposed the bank to compromise he had to agree to support their plan to move the capital to an area on the Potomac River, site of Washington, D.C., today. In 1791 a national bank was created.

The debate did not end there. The bank's charter ended in 1811, and a new bank was created in 1814. In 1816, however, Maryland imposed a tax on the activities of the national bank. Maryland's actions led to a Supreme Court case—*McCulloch* v. *Maryland* (1819). The Court's opinion addressed Maryland's actions. It also addressed the question of whether the necessary and proper clause gave Congress the power to create the bank in the first place. In his opinion, Chief Justice John Marshall wrote:

PRIMARY SOURCE

❝We admit, as all must admit, that the powers of the government are limited, and that its limits are not to be transcended [surpassed]. But we think the sound construction of the constitution must allow to the national legislature that discretion, with respect to the means by which the powers it confers [gives] are to be carried into execution, which will enable that body to perform the high duties assigned to it, in the manner most beneficial to the people.❞

—John Marshall, *McCulloch v. Maryland*, 1819

The Necessary and Proper Clause Today In general, Marshall's interpretation of the necessary and proper clause has prevailed in American government. Since the Court's decision, the doctrine of implied powers has been an important source of federal authority. Congress has relied on this view to create programs and laws in a wide variety of areas. For example, Social Security and Medicare are not directly related to any expressed power. They are considered reasonably related to the constitutional duty to preserve the general welfare. Because the necessary and proper clause has led to the stretching of congressional power, it is sometimes referred to as the elastic clause.

SELECTED EXPRESSED AND IMPLIED POWERS

Expressed Power	Implied Power
To collect taxes to support the general welfare	• To create the Internal Revenue Service (IRS) to collect taxes • To spend revenue on education, roads, housing, etc.
To raise and support armies	• To create a draft or selective service requirement • To create the air force • To create the interstate highway system, easing troop transportation
To make all laws necessary and proper . . .	• To create Social Security, unemployment insurance, and Medicare as means to protect the general welfare
To regulate commerce	• To pass minimum wage and overtime pay laws • To set health standards for foods • To establish laws regulating labor unions • To prohibit job discrimination based on age, race, or gender • To break up anticompetitive monopolies • To restrict the use of child labor

Skills FOCUS INTERPRETING CHARTS

Implied powers have to be based in specific expressed powers. How can Social Security, Medicare, and unemployment insurance be considered appropriate use of congressional implied powers?

While it is generally agreed that the necessary and proper clause gives Congress and the federal government implied powers, the extent and nature of those powers remains a matter for debate and contention. What policies are truly reasonable extensions of expressed congressional powers? It is a ever-present question of American politics, one that the Supreme Court is often called on to address but one that perhaps can never be resolved definitively. New conditions call for new solutions, which must be tested against the Constitution.

READING CHECK Identifying Cause and Effect
How did the Supreme Court's decision in *McCulloch* v. *Maryland* lead to extension of Congressional power?

Nonlegislative Powers

Congress has a variety of powers that are not directly related to the making of laws. Some of these are held by both houses, some only by the House or the Senate.

Powers Common to Both Houses Both houses of Congress together share the power to propose amendments to the Constitution. This requires a two-thirds majority vote of both houses. Congress can, if requested by two-thirds of the states, also call a convention to propose a constitutional amendment. Final amendment power, though, rests with the states, three-fourths of which must approve an amendment for it to be ratified.

Both houses of Congress have the power to conduct investigations. It is their job to oversee the programs they create and the activities of other branches of the national government. To do this work, members of Congress have the power to call witnesses. It can issue **subpoenas**, which are legal documents that require a person to testify in a certain matter. One limit to this power is the president's claim of executive privilege.

You have read also about the roles of the House and Senate in impeachment proceedings. In the case of wrongdoing by a government official, the House can vote to impeach. A trial is then held in the Senate. If two-thirds of the Senate votes to convict, the person can be removed from office.

The Twenty-fifth Amendment states that if the vice presidency is vacant, the president will nominate a replacement. It is the job of both houses of Congress to confirm the choice by majority vote.

Powers of the House The House has the sole power of choosing a president if no candidate gets a majority of votes in the electoral college. The House vote is by state—each state gets one ballot. That is, each state delegation would decide how to cast that state's ballot. The House has had to choose a president on two occasions, in 1800 and in 1824.

The current method by which the House votes is defined in the Twelfth Amendment, which was passed to correct a flaw in the Constitution's original method. Electors were originally supposed to cast two presidential ballots. The top vote-getter would become president, and the second-place finisher the vice president. The Framers did not, however, foresee party tickets, which list presidential and a vice presidential candidates running together. That flaw became apparent during the election of 1800.

That year, Thomas Jefferson was the presidential candidate and Aaron Burr was his running mate. Electors supporting their Democratic-Republican ticket cast ballots for each man, leading to the tie. The election then went to the House, which was controlled by the Federalists: The party that had just lost the presidential race now got to choose the president. The Federalists chose Jefferson, whom they preferred to Burr.

The Twelfth Amendment eliminated this problem. It created two separate electoral college votes, one for president and one for vice president. The House retained the power to choose the president in the event of no majority in the electoral college.

Powers of the Senate The Twelfth Amendment also gave the Senate the power to choose a vice president if no candidate gets a majority of the electoral college vote. Each senator takes part in this vote.

The Senate also has the job of providing advice and consent on executive and judicial branch appointments made by the president. The Senate must also approve treaties that the president may negotiate in order for them to go into effect.

READING CHECK **Making Inferences** Why do you think the subpoena power is important for Congress?

Limits on the Powers of Congress

The Constitution was meant to create a stronger federal government, correcting the weaknesses of the Articles of Confederation. Still, the Framers included a number of checks on congressional power.

The separation of powers, which distributes government powers among three branches, is the strongest check on congressional power. The Supreme Court's power of judicial review, which is implied if not spelled out in the Constitution, checks the power of Congress to pass laws deemed unconstitutional. The president's veto power, although subject to override, also checks Congress's lawmaking powers. Moreover, because Congress relies on the executive branch to carry out the laws, a president who is not pleased with an act of Congress can limit the effect of congressional action through lax enforcement of the law. A president may also apply his or her own interpretation of a law. These interpretations are sometimes expressed in presidential signing statements when a president signs a bill into law. Presidential signing statements are discussed in more detail in Section 5.

In addition to the limitations inherent in the system of checks and balances, the Constitution specifically denies Congress certain powers. These are detailed in Article I, Section 9. For example, Congress was forbidden from prohibiting the slave trade until 1808. It was also forbidden from making laws that might favor one or another state's ports or from placing a tax on articles exported from any state.

The Constitution includes several clauses that protect people's basic civil rights. Article I, Section 9, Clause 2, bars Congress from suspending the **writ of habeas corpus**, a court order that forces the police to present a person in court to face charges, except in cases of rebellion or invasion. Habeas corpus is a Latin phrase meaning "you have the body." The purpose of the writ is to prevent a government from holding people in secret or without charge. When President Abraham Lincoln suspended habeas corpus during the Civil War, a federal court declared the action unconstitutional because Congress had not taken it.

Congress cannot pass a **bill of attainder**—a law that punishes a person without a trial. **Ex post facto laws**, which criminalize an action that took place in the past and that were legal at that time, are likewise forbidden by the Constitution. *Ex post facto* is another Latin phrase, meaning "from after the fact."

READING CHECK **Identifying Supporting Details** What are some of the limitations on the powers of Congress?

The Changing Power of Congress

The scope of Congress's activities and the range of powers it exercises have grown greatly since the days when Hamilton and Jefferson argued over what the phrase *necessary and proper* means. In response to changing domestic and international conditions, Congress has repeatedly expanded the role of the federal government.

During the Great Depression of the 1930s, for example, Congress responded to the severe economic crisis by passing dozens of far-reaching laws urged on it by President Franklin Roosevelt. These new programs expanded the reach of government into the everyday lives of people as never before—for example, providing Social Security retirement benefits for older people and cash payments to the unemployed.

After World War II, Congress responded to the new status of the United States as a dominant world power by creating new military and intelligence-gathering bodies, such as the U.S. Air Force and the Central Intelligence Agency. Congress created NASA—the National Aeronautics and Space Administration—in the 1950s to catch and surpass the Soviet Union's program of space exploration.

Significantly, to accomplish these goals, Congress has delegated some of its powers to new federal agencies it created. These agencies are part of the executive branch, and while Congress retains oversight and budgetary authority over these agencies, the job of monitoring them has proved a huge task. Congressional staffs, both for individual members and for committees and subcommittees, have grown to aid members in this task. Congress has used these expanded resources to defend its position against what it perceives as potential encroachments by an empowered executive branch.

In some sense, this is just what the Framers intended. The system of checks and balances means the legislative and executive branches will always be sparring for power.

READING CHECK **Identifying the Main Idea** What has happened to the powers of Congress over time?

SECTION 2 ASSESSMENT

THINK central **Online Quiz**

thinkcentral.com
KEYWORD: SGO CNG HP

Reviewing Ideas and Terms

1. a. Describe What are the main powers given to Congress?
b. Design What constitutional solution might be devised to resolve the uncertainty about which branch possesses government's inherent powers?

2. a. Describe What is an **indirect tax**?
b. Analyze Is the division of responsibility for national security between the legislative and the executive branch a good idea?

3. a. Identify What is the key constitutional clause that lies behind most of the implied powers of Congress?
b. Rate Consider the arguments of both Hamilton and Jefferson and explain which one seems the most compelling to you.

4. a. Describe What is the significance of **subpoenas** to the work of Congress?
b. Evaluate Why do you think the Constitution gives the House of Representatives the job of picking a president in the event of a tie vote in the electoral college?

5. a. Recall Why did the founders of the nation want to limit the powers of Congress?
b. Evaluate Why do you think the Constitution includes particular mention of **bills of attainder**, **ex post facto laws**, and suspension of the **writ of habeas corpus**?

6. a. Identify What are some areas of American life that Congress is involved in today that it was not at the time of the writing of the Constitution?
b. Predict What might have happened if Congress had not become involved in modern-day concerns, such as space exploration?

Critical Thinking

7. Analyze Copy and fill in the graphic organizer below and use it to compare and contrast the powers of the House and Senate.

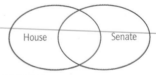

House   Senate

FOCUS ON WRITING

8. Narrative Prepare a five-minute lecture on the history of Congress, explaining its original purpose, the early debates about its function, and the changes in its role throughout history.

The House of Representatives

Main Idea

The House of Representatives, with its frequent elections and regular reapportionment, is the more representative chamber of Congress. Its members carry out much of their work in committees.

Reading Focus

1. What are the key features of the House of Representatives and its membership?
2. What are some of the challenges that reapportionment and redistricting raise?
3. How is the leadership of the House organized?
4. What is the role of committees in the operation of the House?

Key Terms

reapportionment
gerrymandering
Speaker of the House
bills
floor leader
whips
party caucus
standing committees
select committees
joint committees

TAKING NOTES As you read, take notes on the features of the House of Representatives. Record your notes in a graphic organizer like this one.

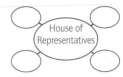

House of Representatives

The Iron Duke

THE POLITICAL CHESS-BOARD

This 1910 political cartoon satirizes the control that Joseph Cannon had over Congress as Speaker of the House.

WHY IT MATTERS **The Power of the Speaker** The House of Representatives has given rise to some of the most powerful—and colorful—figures in U.S. history. Perhaps no one illustrates this better than Joseph Gurney Cannon (R, Illinois), whose reign over the House in the early 1900s inspired both affection and fear. To some, he was Uncle Joe, a man beloved by his colleagues. To others, he was Czar Cannon or the Iron Duke.

Cannon won his reputation while serving as the Speaker of the House, the chamber's presiding officer and most powerful member. From that post, Cannon controlled much of what happened in Congress—and in the U.S. government. No bill came up for a vote if he did not want it to. "Not a cent for scenery," he once scoffed at a proposal to protect forests. He decided who would serve on committees. He chaired the Rules Committee himself, which gave him power over the flow of legislation.

In 1910 the House finally revolted against Cannon's iron rule. "The . . . minority," he said, "is now in the majority." The House stripped him of key powers, making changes in the role of the Speaker that would become a permanent part of the office. Indeed, today's House of Representatives is in no small part a result of, and a reaction to, Cannon's years in power. ■

Membership in the House

The Framers intended the House of Representatives to be the chamber most closely in touch with the people. That is why the Constitution calls for House members to be chosen by direct popular vote.

HOUSE OF REPRESENTATIVES: TERMS, SALARY, BENEFITS AND PRIVILEGES

QUICK FACTS

	House Members	Speaker of the House	Majority and Minority leaders
Salary	$165,200	$212,100	$183,500
Term	2 years		
Benefits and Privileges	• Tax deduction for two residences • Travel allowances • Staff • Health and retirement benefits • Franking privilege: free mail to constituents • Free printing • Use of gym, restaurants, and other amenities in the Capitol • Legal immunity for statements made while Congress is in session		

Source: Congressional Research Service, 2007

The idea of popular election of House members concerned some of the delegates to the Constitutional Convention. John Rutledge, for example, questioned whether voters could be counted on to elect qualified people. Rutledge's position did not prevail, but the delegates decided to restrain the House with a Senate. James Madison assured worried delegates that senators, chosen by state legislatures, would act as a "necessary fence" against reckless representatives.

Formal Qualifications Since it is intended as the people's house, the House of Representatives has less stringent qualifications for membership than the Senate. Article I, Section 2, of the Constitution gives these basic job qualifications. Members must be

- at least 25 years old
- a U.S. citizen for at least seven years
- a resident of the state he or she represents

According to custom, representatives live in the districts they represent, but that is not required under the Constitution.

The Constitution states that the House is judge of the "Elections, Returns, and Qualifications of its own Members." The power to determine qualifications, however,

is limited. In *Powell v. McCormack* (1969) the Supreme Court ruled that the House could only exclude members if they failed to meet the specific standards of Article I, Section 2. The Court wished to grant a high degree of respect to the wishes of the voters.

While Congress can exclude a person only for specific reasons, it can expel a sitting member for any reason. Expulsion, however, requires a two-thirds majority vote. This has happened only five times in U.S. history, most recently in 2002, when James Traficant (D, Ohio) was expelled after being convicted of taking bribes and income tax evasion.

Informal Qualifications The most important informal qualification for anyone who wants to be a member of the House is the ability to appeal to the voters in his or district. The qualities needed for this vary by time and place. People with military backgrounds are sometimes popular. Famous people—actors and athletes—have enjoyed success. Today however, the ability to raise money—or have a lot of your own—is vital. In 2006, the winning and losing candidates for each seat in the House spent a combined average of more than $1.5 million.

READING CHECK Identifying Supporting Details
What are the formal and informal qualifications for membership in the House?

Reapportionment and Redistricting

As you read Section 1, there are 435 members of the House. They represent more than 300 million Americans, for an average of about 690,000 people per representative.

Some House members represent considerably more or fewer people than the average. One reason is that each state must have at least one representative regardless of its population. For example, Wyoming, with about 500,000 residents, has one representative. At the same time, Montana, with more than 900,000 residents, falls short of the population needed for two representatives. As you can see, Montana's one representative serves nearly twice as many people as Wyoming's representative.

Changes in Population The Constitution requires that every 10 years, the House must undergo **reapportionment**, in which seats are redistributed among the states based on the results of the census. Once census results are available, Congress reapportions the congressional seats among the states. States that gain population may gain seats, and states that lose population may lose them.

Before the number of seats was fixed in 1929, Congress simply added seats as the nation's population grew. Fixing the number of seats, however, transformed reapportionment. Now, if a state loses population or grows too slowly, it may lose seats to another state. After the 2000 census 10 states, mainly in the North and East, lost seats. Eight states in the South and West added them.

Gerrymandering The Constitution gives Congress the responsibility to reapportion seats among the states. It leaves redistricting, the job of creating district boundaries within the states, however, to state governments. Not surprisingly, the party in power in each state tends to draw the boundaries to its own political advantage—boundaries that divide and weaken the opponents' strength or that cluster together areas of support. The goal is simple: Give your party the best chance to win as many elections as possible. Drawing district boundaries for political advantage is known as **gerrymandering**.

One Person, One Vote For much of U.S. history, the Supreme Court largely ignored gerrymandering. In a series of cases over the last 50 years, however, the Court has placed restrictions on the practice.

For example, the 1964 case of *Wesberry v. Sanders* focused on a congressional district in Georgia that had several times as many people as other districts in the state. The Court observed that this arrangement "contracts [shrinks] the value of some votes and expands that of others." This violates the Constitution, which requires that one person's vote be worth as much as another's. To remedy the problem, the Supreme Court ruled that future congressional districts within a state must be of roughly equal population.

Gerrymandering Past and Present

Gerrymandering takes its name from nineteenth century Governor Elbridge Gerry of Massachusetts. In 1812 Gerry enacted a law that created new state senatorial districts. The shape of one district was said to resemble a salamander. A political cartoonist added wings, claws, and a head to create a "Gerry-mander." Gerrymandering continues today. One example is the Seventeenth Illinois Congressional District shown on the map.

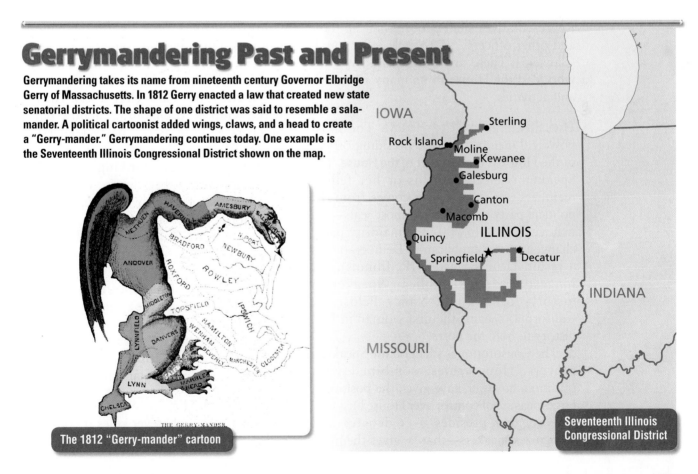

The 1812 "Gerry-mander" cartoon

Seventeenth Illinois Congressional District

The Court has struggled to define how much consideration should be given to race in determining district boundaries. It has struck down districts purposely drawn to <u>disenfranchise</u> racial minorities. Likewise, the Court has ruled against districts drawn *solely* to benefit racial minorities. Most recently, the Court has sought a middle position, ruling that race can be a factor in drawing boundaries, just not the main one.

In 1986 the Court addressed political gerrymandering. In *Davis* v. *Bandemer* it held that gerrymandering that causes actual harm to a political party may violate the constitutional guarantee of equal protection of the law. Proving that harm has resulted from gerrymandering, though, has been difficult.

Despite these court decisions, gerrymandering is alive and well. The stakes—control of the House—are too high for either party to surrender an advantage to the other.

READING CHECK **Sequencing** What are the steps by which House seats are assigned to different states?

Leadership in the House

The Constitution says that the "House of Representatives shall choose their speaker and other officers . . ." (Article I, Section 2, Clause 5). These are the men and women who lead the House in its many functions and activities.

The Speaker of the House The most powerful member and the presiding officer of the House is the **Speaker of the House**. The Speaker is elected by his or her fellow members of Congress and comes from the political party that holds the most seats—the majority party. In 2007 the majority party changed from Republican to Democratic. As a result, Dennis Hastert (R, Illinois), the longest-serving Republican Speaker in history, lost his job. Nancy Pelosi (D, California) became the first woman in U.S. history to hold the post.

The Constitution is silent on the Speaker's powers. House rules, combined with tradition, however, have given the position a large measure of control over House business. The Speaker presides over debates and recognizes speakers—that is, gives them the authority to speak on the House floor. As presiding officer, the Speaker also rules on points of order. The Speaker assigns **bills**, or proposed laws, to particular committees. The Speaker determines when, or if, a measure comes up for debate and how it is debated. Finally, the Speaker assigns individual House members to certain committees, which gives the Speaker great power over a member's political career. With the power to shape events in one house of Congress, the Speaker can play a large role in the fate of a party's political agenda.

The Speaker of the House is also second in the line of succession to the presidency. If both the president and vice president were to die or be unable to perform, the Speaker of the House would become president.

Other Leadership Posts Each party also elects a **floor leader** to help manage the actions and strategy of the party in the House. The floor leader of the majority party, known as the majority leader, serves as the assistant to the Speaker. The floor leader of the minority party is known as the minority leader. He or she acts as the chief spokesperson for the minority party in the House. Minority leaders try to keep their party members united behind common positions. This unity will help to increase the minority's bargaining position with the majority.

The two parties also elect **whips**. The job of the whip is to encourage fellow party members to vote as the party leadership wants. Whips collect information about what members are thinking—and alert leaders about members whose vote cannot be counted on. The name *whip* suggests that sometimes the form of encouragement borders on force. In addition to the whips, each party has upwards of 100 assistant whips reporting to the whip.

The election of party officers—whips, floor leaders, and, for the majority party, the Speaker—takes place at a party caucus at the beginning of a congressional term. A **party caucus** is a meeting of all the House members from a particular political party.

House Rules The Constitution allows the House to make whatever rules it considers necessary to carry out its business. As you

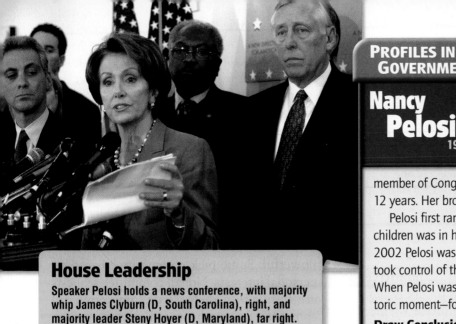

House Leadership
Speaker Pelosi holds a news conference, with majority whip James Clyburn (D, South Carolina), right, and majority leader Steny Hoyer (D, Maryland), far right.

PROFILES IN GOVERNMENT

Nancy Pelosi
1940–

The first woman to serve as Speaker of the House, Nancy Pelosi comes from a family with a tradition of public service. Her father was a five-term member of Congress from Maryland and the mayor of Baltimore for 12 years. Her brother also served as mayor of Baltimore.

Pelosi first ran for office herself after the youngest of her five children was in high school. She was elected to the House in 1987. In 2002 Pelosi was chosen as House minority leader; after Democrats took control of the House in 2007, she became Speaker of the House. When Pelosi was sworn in as Speaker, she called the occasion "a historic moment—for the Congress, and for the women of this country."

Draw Conclusions Why did Pelosi say that her election as Speaker was "a historic moment"?

have read, the House can judge its own members' behavior and expel a member for almost any reason. In addition, the House can vote to issue a reprimand. A stronger statement of House disapproval of a member's actions is called a <u>censure</u>.

In addition, the House has a separate Rules Committee. This powerful committee acts as the "traffic cop" for the House, setting the rules for when, how, and under what conditions debate on a bill will take place. For example, a rule may limit the time spent debating a particular bill or place limits on how it can be amended. By setting the rules under which a bill can be considered, the Rules Committee can speed up or delay passage of a bill. For this reason, the chair of the Rules Committee is often a key ally of the Speaker.

READING CHECK **Making Inferences** What role does the leadership play in running the House?

The Role of Committees

Think about the challenge of making laws for the entire country. No member could possibly have or acquire all the knowledge needed on the topics the House considers. To help provide this sort of expert analysis, the House has a system of committees and subcommittees, each concentrating on a specific area of public policy.

Standing Committees The House has 20 **standing committees**, or permanent committees. Standing committees address the major areas in which most proposed laws fall, such as agriculture, the budget, and the armed services. For a list, see the next page.

The House Committee on Ways and Means deals with taxes and other revenue-raising measures. Ways and Means also exercises oversight on big programs such as Social Security. Because the Constitution says that all bills dealing with taxes and revenue begin in the House, the Committee on Ways and Means is a congressional powerhouse.

Standing committees typically have at least four subcommittees. The Appropriations Committee has 13. Subcommittees take an even narrower focus than a committee. So, for example, the Armed Services Committee may have subcommittees dealing with air and land power, sea power, and more.

Other Committees The House sometimes creates **select committees** to carry out specific tasks not already covered by existing committees, such as investigations. Select committees are usually created to serve for a limited duration. The Speaker, with advice from the minority leader, appoints all members of select committees.

The House and Senate sometimes form **joint committees**. Such committees address broad issues that affect both chambers.

House Standing Committees

Agriculture	Homeland Security	Small Business
Appropriations	House Administration	Standards of Official
Armed Services	Judiciary	Conduct
Budget	Natural Resources	Transportation and
Education and Labor	Oversight and	Infrastructure
Energy and Commerce	Government Reform	Veterans' Affairs
Financial Services	Rules	Ways and Means
Foreign Affairs	Science and Technology	

For example, the Joint Committee on Taxation advises Congress on tax policy.

Another type of committee formed by both chambers of Congress is the conference committee. You will read more about conference committees in Section 5.

Committee Chairs Each committee is headed by a chair. Because so much of the work of the House takes place in committee, committee chairs have great power.

Chairs are always chosen by the majority party. Historically, the job went to the committee member with the most seniority—that is, the person who had served on the committee the longest. In the 1970s, however, Congress began to change the seniority system. Hoping to encourage new leadership and new ideas, Congress began holding elections for the committee chairs. Seniority remains a factor in who becomes chair, but it is no longer the *only* factor.

In 1995 Republicans won control of the House and voted to impose term limits of six years on committee chairs. When Democrats regained control of the House in 2007, they agreed to keep the six-year term limit.

Committee Membership Members request committee assignments. They may seek a certain post because it is important to their constituents or because it is politically powerful. Some pick a committee based on personal interests. Not all committee requests are fulfilled. In the case of some powerful committees, a member may have to campaign among his or her colleagues for a spot. Final assignments are made by a vote of the party caucus or conference.

In general, House members can serve on up to two standing committees and four subcommittees. There are exceptions to these rules.

While members do important work in their committees, paid staff members do much of the information gathering and background work. A typical committee has a team of managers, lawyers, policy experts, and office staff. The House Appropriations Committee, for example, has a staff of over 150 to assist its members.

READING CHECK **Identifying the Main Idea** What is the advantage of having committees in the House?

SECTION 3 ASSESSMENT

THINK central Online Quiz
thinkcentral.com
KEYWORD: SGO CNG HP

Reviewing Ideas and Terms

1. **a. Describe** What are the formal qualifications for the House?
   b. Evaluate Do you think that there should be more formal requirements for a House member? fewer? Explain your answer.

2. **a. Identify** What is **gerrymandering**?
   b. Explain What limits has the Supreme Court placed on gerrymandering?

3. **a. Describe** What are the roles of the **Speaker of the House**, **floor leader**, and **whips**?
   b. Elaborate What role do political parties play in the organization of the House?

4. **a. Recall** What is the term for the regular committees that exist to evaluate **bills**?
   b. Explain How do committees help the House function?

Critical Thinking

5. **Evaluate** Using your notes and the graphic organizer below, evaluate the role, powers, and duties of the Speaker of the House.

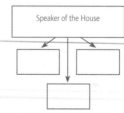

Speaker of the House

FOCUS ON WRITING

6. **Persuasive** Write a letter to the editor urging an end to gerrymandering in your state. Provide reasons for your position.

The Senate

Main Idea

Senators represent entire states, have longer terms, and follow different rules of debate. These features help give the Senate its reputation as a more weighty and careful body than the House.

Reading Focus

1. What are the major features of the Senate and its membership?
2. What are the Senate's leadership posts?
3. What is the role of committees in the Senate?
4. What are some of the distinctive rules and traditions of the Senate?

Key Terms

president of the Senate
president pro tempore
Senate majority leader
seniority rule
filibuster
cloture

TAKING NOTES As you read, take notes on the features of the Senate. Record your notes in a graphic organizer like this one.

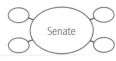

Senate

WHY IT MATTERS

Debate in the Senate A crowd of photographers jostles for position to get the best shot. Through their lens they see tomorrow's front page photo—beds being set up in the Senate chambers. Are guests expected? In a way, yes. There is an all-night debate scheduled, and the senators won't be going home tonight.

The senators are participating in one of the distinctive traditions of the Senate: the filibuster. This tradition of nearly unlimited debate gives a minority of the Senate, even a single senator, the power to hold up the passage of bills favored by the majority. This creates leverage—to get the bill killed or modified or to receive favorable consideration on some other bill altogether.

Senators have used the tactic for momentous and minor occasions alike. In 1954 Strom Thurmond (D, North Carolina) set the record for the longest speech in Senate history when he opposed a civil rights bill. In 1986 Alfonse D'Amato (R, New York) made the second-longest speech when he protested the cutting of funding to a defense factory in his home state.

Since 1917, the Senate has been able to bring debate to a close, but it requires the votes of 60 senators to achieve that. In 2005, Senate Republicans threatened to change the rules that allowed this tactic. But a compromise was reached. As long the tactic gives each senator outsized leverage, the Senate is not likely to do away with its distinctive tradition of talk. ■

Getting Ready to
Talk All Night

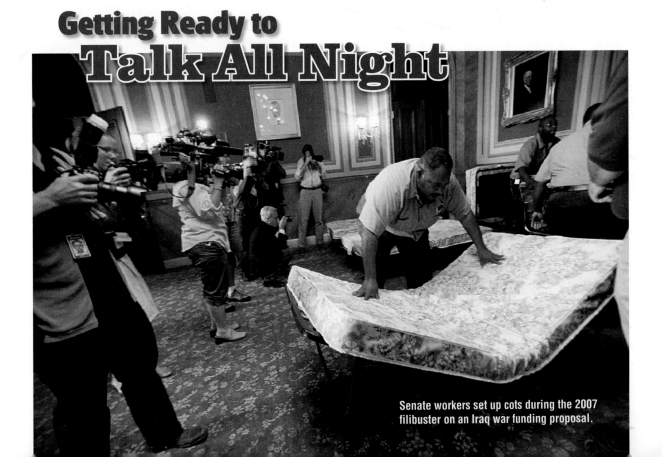

Senate workers set up cots during the 2007 filibuster on an Iraq war funding proposal.

SENATE: TERMS, SALARY, BENEFITS AND PRIVILEGES

QUICK FACTS

	Senators	President Pro Tempore	Majority and Minority Leaders
Salary	$165,200	$183,500	$183,500
Term	6 years		
Benefits and Privileges	• Tax deduction for two residences • Travel allowances • Staff • Health and retirement benefits • Franking privilege: free mail to constituents • Free printing • Use of gym, restaurants, and other Capitol amenities • Legal immunity for statements made while Congress is in session		

Source: Congressional Research Service, 2007

WHAT DO YOU THINK?

What are the advantages of having a representative body like Congress made up of seasoned and experienced lawmakers? What are the disadvantages of allowing members of Congress to serve as long as their constituents re-elect them?

The Senate and Its Membership

The Senate is often called the upper house. The term reflects the greater prestige and power that individual senators have compared to their House colleagues. It also reflects the special powers, such as the power to reject presidential appointments, that the Constitution gives to the Senate.

Senators tend to be better known than members of the House, if only because they must win statewide election. In addition, the smaller number of senators allows them to become nationally known figures more easily. Perhaps that is why it is common for House members to try to "move up" to a Senate seat. From there, many an ambitious politician has launched a run for the White House, although only a few have succeeded.

Formal Qualifications Delegates at the Constitutional Convention thought the Senate required a different type of leader than the House. If the Senate were to fulfill its role as a break on the House, the chamber for ordinary citizens, than it would need to be filled with experienced, knowledgeable politicians. James Madison explained the reasoning in a *Federalist Papers* essay.

❝The propriety [appropriateness] of these distinctions [between the Senate and House] is explained by the nature of the senatorial trust, which, requiring greater extent of information and stability of character, requires at the same time that the senator should have reached a period of life more likely to supply these advantages.❞

—James Madison, *Federalist Papers* No. 62

Article I, Section 3, of the Constitution sets out the basic job qualifications for the Senate. A person seeking to be a senator must be

- at least 30 years old—five years older than House members
- a U.S. citizen for at least nine years—as compared to seven for House members
- a resident of the state he or she represents

To further encourage a calmer, more thoughtful chamber, the Framers gave senators a longer term of office than representatives and staggered their election so that only one-third of the seats come up for election every two years. The longer term of office—six years compared to a House member's two years—is thought to make it easier for senators to focus on serving the nation rather than on pleasing the public. Staggered elections ensure that the Senate membership does not undergo major, rapid shifts and lose experienced political leaders.

Election of Senators As you read in Section 1, the Constitution originally gave state legislatures the power to choose senators. This was another feature intended in part to shield senators from public pressure and to help ensure that only the best people would be chosen.

In fact, selection of senators by state legislators proved troublesome. Politically divided legislatures sometimes had trouble reaching a decision, and Senate seats occasionally went unfilled for months or longer. Accusations of corrupt elections undermined trust in the Senate. In the early 1900s, some states adopted popular election of senators, with the results ratified by state legislatures. In 1913 the Seventeenth Amendment made direct popular election of senators part of the Constitution.

Informal Qualifications Typically, voters tend to elect older people to the Senate than to the House. Senators tend to be wealthier both than their House colleagues and the general population. That is why the Senate is sometimes referred to as a "millionaires' club." The wealth of the senators is helpful, because running for Senate is very costly. In a recent election, Senate candidates spent over $400 million in 33 races.

While Congress overall has become much more diverse, the Senate has lagged behind the House in reflecting the diversity of the general population. In 2007, only 16 women, one African American, two Asian Americans, and three Hispanic Americans were serving in the Senate—not an accurate reflection of U.S. population.

READING CHECK **Contrasting** How do requirements for a senator's seat differ from those for a House member?

Senate Leadership

Like the House, the Senate has a leadership structure that helps the chamber do its work. The Senate's leadership, however, is generally less powerful than the House leadership.

Constitutional Positions Article I, Section 3, Clause 4, of the Constitution assigns the job of **president of the Senate** to the vice president of the United States. The position is largely ceremonial. As president of the Senate, the vice president may preside over debate in the chamber, acknowledging speakers and making sure everyone follows the rules of debate. But the president of the Senate cannot take part directly in debate. Nor can the president of the Senate vote, except to break a tie. The position's greatest influence is felt on those rare occasions when Senate membership is divided equally among both parties. When that occurs, the party affiliation of the vice president determines which party will be in the majority.

The Constitution also directs the Senate to choose a **president pro tempore**—the person who presides in the absence of the president of the Senate. By tradition, this position goes to the senator from the majority party who has the longest record of service

in the Senate. The president pro tempore is third in line, behind the Speaker of the House, to succeed the president.

Party Leaders Like the House, the Senate has party leaders who guide the work of the majority and minority parties. In the Senate, the most powerful position belongs to the **Senate majority leader**. As the name suggests, this figure is chosen by a vote of the majority party. This vote takes place at a party caucus at the start of each term.

The Senate majority leader serves as the spokesperson and main strategist for the majority party in the Senate. He or she works to carry out the party's agenda in the Senate. A majority leader must be willing to work for his or her party members—for example, helping them get desired committee assignments. In return, the majority leader expects cooperation and support from the senators. The power of this position and the importance of the Senate make the majority leader a major national political figure.

The Senate also has a minority leader. Both the minority and majority party have whips who help the leaders assess how senators are planning to vote.

READING CHECK **Identifying the Main Idea and Details** What is the Senate leadership structure?

RESPONSIBILITIES OF LEADERSHIP

Party leaders in the Senate need to couple the power of persuasion with an acute ear for the needs of their caucus members. Since the 1970s, they have also been expected to be effective advocates of their party's position on television and in the media.

Styles of Leadership
Senate majority leaders use different styles to unite their parties. Shown on the left in the photo above, current majority leader Harry Reid prefers to listen to his fellow senators. At right, Lyndon Johnson, leader from 1953–1961, was known for giving senators the "treatment."

Committees in the Senate

As in the House, the Senate performs much of its work in committees, reviewing and refining the bills that will become the laws of the nation. Committee assignments allow senators to study an area of public policy in depth. As in the House, Senate committees hire professional staffers who bring additional skills and knowledge to the lawmaking process.

Types of Senate Committees

The Senate has a similar array of committees to the House. It has 16 standing committees and many dozens of subcommittees. The Senate also has select and special committees. These may be temporary in nature, though that is not always the case. They generally exist to examine a particular issue, to advise the Senate, and to provide oversight of government agencies. They are not generally involved in making laws.

Of course, senators participate in joint committees with members of the House. As you will read in Section 5, they also take part in conference committees.

Membership in Committees

Senate rules limit the number of committees and subcommittees a senator may serve on. In general, senators serve on no more than three committees and five subcommittees.

Senators seek assignments that align with their interests and the needs of their state. As in the House, committee assignments in the Senate are determined by the party conference or caucus at the beginning of each session. In general, party caucuses try to accommodate the preferences of individual members, with a priority given to members who have served in the Senate longer. The proportion of seats each party receives on a committee reflects its numbers in the overall Senate.

Committee Chairs

Like their House counterparts, Senate committee chairs hold considerable power. They set the committee's schedule, decide what bills will be discussed and when, and call hearings. No senator chairs more than one committee. Chairs are always a member of the majority party.

Traditionally, the chair of a committee has gone to the most senior majority senator on a committee, following the so-called **seniority rule**. When Republicans took control of the Senate in 1995, however, they announced that they would hold secret ballots within each committee to choose the chair. In addition, they placed six-year term limits on committee chairs. When the Democrats gained control of the Senate in 2007, they continued the term-limit rules for committee chairs.

Senate Committee Power

Senate committees have some functions that are unique to that chamber. Recall that the Senate alone has the job of providing advice and consent on certain top presidential nominees. Nominees are usually first examined by the relevant Senate committee—for example, the Senate Judiciary Committee examines nominees for federal judges. Typically, the full Senate follows the recommendation of the Senate committee.

The Senate also debates and votes on any treaties that the government negotiates. A two-thirds majority vote is required for a treaty to become law. This gives the Senate—and in particular, the Senate Foreign Relations Committee—great influence. If a treaty fails to win the support of a powerful chair of the Senate Foreign Relations Committee, its chances of passage are slim. In 1919, for example, opposition from Senator Henry Cabot Lodge helped defeat the Versailles Treaty, which President Woodrow Wilson had helped negotiate at the end of World War I.

READING CHECK Contrasting How do committee assignments differ in the House and Senate?

WHAT DO YOU THINK?

Throughout American history, deliberative bodies have used committees to facilitate their work. How does the use of committees in Congress promote or undermine the principles of representation, majority rule, and limited government?

Senate Standing Committees

Agriculture, Nutrition, and Forestry	Foreign Relations
Appropriations	Health, Education, Labor, and Pensions
Armed Services	
Banking, Housing, and Urban Affairs	Homeland Security and Governmental Affairs
Budget	
Commerce, Science, and Transportation	Judiciary
	Rules and Administration
Energy and Natural Resources	Small Business and Entrepreneurship
Environmental and Public Works	
Finance	Veterans' Affairs

Rules and Traditions

As you read in the "Why It Matters," the Senate is a keen guardian of its rules and traditions. It is these rules and traditions that give the Senate its special character, one very different from the House.

The Filibuster Perhaps the greatest difference between the Senate and the House is that the Senate places few limits on debate. This rule allowed for the development of a practice called the **filibuster**. A filibuster occurs when opponents of a measure take the floor of the Senate and refuse to stop talking in an effort to prevent the measure coming up for a vote. The tactic is used when a minority knows that a measure is likely to pass if it ever comes to a vote. Filibusterers hope that if they can stall action long enough, the rest of the Senate will eventually be forced to move on to other business.

In 1917 the Senate moved to place some limit on the filibuster. It adopted a rule by which a two-thirds vote would impose **cloture**—an end to debate. Though difficult to achieve, cloture has been accomplished on a number of occasions. In 1975 the cloture rule was revised. It now requires 60 votes to achieve cloture.

Discipline in the Senate Like the House, the Senate has the constitutional right to judge the conduct of its own members. On 15 occasions it has voted to expel a member. Expulsion requires a two-thirds majority vote. The first expulsion took place in 1797, when Tennessee senator William Blount was expelled for conspiring with Britain to seize Florida from the Spanish. All the other expulsions involved senators who supported the Confederacy in the Civil War.

The Senate has on nine occasions voted to censure, or officially denounce, a senator. The most recent such incident was the 1990 censure of David Durenberger (R, Minnesota) for unethical conduct, including using campaign funds for personal use.

Filling Vacancies When a Senate seat becomes vacant due to the retirement or death of a senator, the Seventeenth Amendment calls for the governor of that senator's state to appoint a replacement, provided the state's legislature has given the governor the power to do so. The replacement senator serves until a special election can be held to choose a permanent replacement. Governors usually choose replacement senators from their own party.

READING CHECK **Summarizing** What are some of the unique traditions of the Senate?

SECTION 4 ASSESSMENT

THINK central | Online Quiz
thinkcentral.com
KEYWORD: SGO CNG HP

Reviewing Ideas and Terms

1. a. Recall What are the constitutional requirements to become a member of the Senate?
b. Evaluate How do the Senate's unique formal and informal requirements support the notion that it is a more exclusive body than the House?

2. a. Identify What are the roles of the **president of the Senate**, the **president pro tempore**, and the **Senate majority leader**?
b. Elaborate How is the Senate majority leader similar to and different from the Speaker of the House?

3. a. Recall How many standing committees exist in the Senate?
b. Rate In your opinion, which Senate committee—the Judiciary Committee or the Foreign Relations Committee—has a greater influence on American life?

4. a. Define What is the meaning of the terms **filibuster** and **cloture**?

b. Evaluate What are the benefits and drawbacks of having nearly unlimited debate in the Senate?

Critical Thinking

5. Compare and Contrast Copy the diagram below and compare and contrast the main features of the House and Senate.

House   Senate

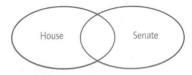

FOCUS ON WRITING

6. Expository You are working on a brief guide to Congress for use by foreign exchange students visiting your school. Write a brief section that compares and contrasts the House and the Senate—their functions, organization, and stature.

The Seniority System

Should seniority be a determining factor for committee chairs in the House of Representatives and the Senate?

THE ISSUE

For most of the twentieth century, committee chairs were chosen strictly according to the seniority system, which reserved these posts for the long-serving committee members of the majority party. A series of reforms in the 1970s and 1990s empowered party conferences to elect their committee chairs through secret ballots and set term limits on a chair's service. Still, committee chairs and ranking minority party members are almost always the longest-serving members of their respective parties on a committee.

Collectively, senators Orrin Hatch (R, Utah), Arlen Specter (D, Pennsylvania), and Patrick Leahy (D, Vermont) have more than 85 years of senatorial experience.

VIEWPOINTS

Committee chairs should be chosen solely on merit, not seniority. The seniority system is an outdated relic. It lost what little validity it had in the 1940–1950s, when long-serving committee chairs routinely killed civil rights legislation. Even today, there is still too much consideration given to seniority in choosing committee chairs. A senator's accomplishments and skills as a legislator, not longevity, should guide the decision of who serves as committee chairs. In fact, the skills needed to convince fellow party members that you should be chair or ranking minority party member—persuasion, deal-making, and charisma—are just the skills needed to be an effective chair.

Seniority should be a factor in choosing a committee chair. Seniority is still a valuable measure of a member's ability to be a committee chair. Long-serving members acquire extensive policy experience and procedural knowledge, both of which are important for conducting committee work and getting bills passed. This knowledge and experience should be rewarded with greater authority. The current system allows for the removal of chairs who do not take the needs of their fellow party members on the committee or the party's policy agenda sufficiently into account. This makes chairs more accountable, without losing the experience that seniority brings.

What Is Your Opinion?

1. Should the length of tenure be a factor in choosing a congressional committee chair? Why or why not?

2. Though in theory committee chairs are elected, more often than not the position goes to the most senior member of that committee. Explain how the process might be reformed.

THINK central Practice Online
thinkcentral.com
KEYWORD: SGO CNG

5 Congress at Work

Main Idea

The main job of Congress is to make laws. The process of making laws is well established and orderly.

Reading Focus

1. How are bills introduced in Congress?

2. What happens to a bill in committee?

3. What happens to a bill on the floor of the House and Senate?

4. What is a conference committee?

5. What actions can a president take on a bill?

Key Terms

rider
joint resolution
concurrent resolutions
discharge petition
Committee of the Whole
quorum
roll-call vote
conference committee
pocket veto

TAKING NOTES As you read, take notes on the process of making law in Congress. Record your notes in a graphic organizer like this one.

☐→☐→☐→

WHY IT MATTERS

Purpose of Laws Congress is the nation's lawmaking branch of government. But what, exactly, are laws? You can think of some examples. For example, you know that there are laws against driving under the influence of alcohol. You know that it is against the law for one person to kill another.

Federal laws, however, do more than define what is right or wrong. They also establish new government programs, set government policy, and allocate funding to pay for government activities and services.

The U.S. Congress makes all kinds of laws. For example, in its two sessions the 109th Congress considered bills for extending formal recognition to certain Native American groups, pro-

tecting portions of specific rivers, authorizing the U.S. Mint to produce dollar coins featuring likenesses of U.S. presidents, and appropriating money for all manner of government activities, and much, much more. All told, the House and the Senate of the 109th Congress considered almost 11,000 bills. Just under 400 became law. In this way, Congress helped determine exactly what actions the federal government will take in a wide variety of areas.

For each action taken by Congress, the members of the House and Senate follow an organized procedure. This procedure ensures a careful, thorough consideration of the nation's legislative business. ■

From Bills to Laws

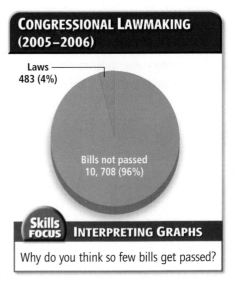

CONGRESSIONAL LAWMAKING (2005–2006)

Laws 483 (4%)

Bills not passed 10,708 (96%)

Skills FOCUS INTERPRETING GRAPHS

Why do you think so few bills get passed?

Representative Thelma Drake (R, Virginia) holds a copy of a bill she co-sponsored, just one of thousands introduced in the 110th Congress.

CONGRESS: THE LEGISLATIVE BRANCH **149**

Bills in Congress

Laws start out as bills introduced by members of Congress. Ideas for bills come from many different sources. Some are suggested by constituents or by interest groups. The president is another major source of proposed legislation. In addition, members of Congress also come up with ideas for bills. Regardless of a bill's origin, only a member of Congress can introduce a bill for consideration.

Introducing Bills Both senators and House members introduce bills. The one exception is that, according to the Constitution, any bill for raising revenue—that is, tax bills—must begin in the House (Article I, Section 7, Clause 1). In addition, by custom, appropriations bills also begin life in the House.

Introducing a bill is a simple matter. House members simply place the required documents in a wooden box called a hopper. A senator hands the paperwork to a clerk.

In the 109th Congress, nearly 6,500 bills were first submitted in the House. More than 4,100 were submitted in the Senate. Bills submitted in the House are assigned the letters "H.R." and a number. Senate bills are labeled with an "S.," followed by a number.

Bills may be public or private. A private bill affects only a particular person, family, or small group. A common example is a bill granting permanent residency to an illegal immigrant. A public bill is one affecting all of society. Most bills are public bills.

A bill may deal with a single subject or many. As they make their way through the legislative process, some bills get riders attached to them. A **rider** is a provision that bears little relationship to the bill's main topic. The goal of a rider is to add an unpopular provision to a bill that is likely to be passed in order to allow the unpopular provision to "ride" in on the broader bill's popularity. In some cases, however, riders are added in hopes of killing a bill. Such a rider, called a "poison pill," makes the bill too unpopular to pass.

Other Types of Action Bills make up the large share of the legislative work of Congress. But House members and senators also deal with other types of measures. For example, they sometimes consider joint resolutions. A **joint resolution** is much like a bill—it follows the same procedures as a bill, and it has the force of law if it is passed by both houses of Congress and is signed by the president. Joint resolutions are used for certain out-of-the-ordinary circumstances. For example, Congress used a joint resolution to authorize President George W. Bush to use military force against Iraq in late 2002. Joint resolutions are also used to propose constitutional amendments. The amendment process is described in Chapter 3.

Congress also sometimes considers **concurrent resolutions,** by which both houses of Congress address matters that affect the operations of both chambers or express an opinion. These are not signed by the president and do not have the force of law.

Finally, each chamber passes resolutions that apply to matters of concern just within that chamber, such as the election to leadership offices or members' committee assignments. Such resolutions can also be used as a means for members of Congress to express their opinion on an important subject. They do not have the force of law.

READING CHECK Summarizing What are some of the legislative actions that Congress takes?

Bills in Committee

Committees act as the filter of Congress. Most of the bills submitted to Congress simply die in committee and never receive the attention of Congress as a whole. Most of the work on bills, including the decision to kill them, takes place in committee, where bills are studied and adjusted.

Referral Bills are assigned to a committee by a process known as referral. In the House, the Speaker is mainly responsible for determining which committee is most appropriate for a given bill. In the Senate, the majority leader performs this role. In both chambers, written rules help govern the referral process. A bill may go to one or more committees. This happens if the subject matter of the bill falls into the areas of expertise of more than one committee.

How a Bill Becomes a Law

Bills must be passed by both houses of Congress before going to the president. At what point do the different versions of the bill get unified into one bill?

HOUSE

Bill is introduced
H.R. 1 is introduced in the House.

Bills in Committee
1. H.R. 1 is referred to standing committee.
2. Assigned to subcommittee for study, hearings, revisions, and approval. Subcommittee reports to full committee.
3. Markup: H.R. 1 returns to full committee for more hearings and revisions.
4. H.R. 1 goes to Rules Committee, which sets conditions for debate and amendments.

Bill on the Floor
H.R. 1 is debated, then passed or defeated. If passed, H.R. 1 goes to Senate.

SENATE

Bill is introduced
S. 1 is introduced in the Senate.

Bills in Committee
1. S. 1 is referred to standing committee.
2. Assigned to subcommittee for study, hearings, revisions, and approval. Subcommittee reports to full committee.
3. Markup: S. 1 returns to full committee for more hearings and revisions.

Bill on the Floor
S. 1 is debated, then passed or defeated. If passed, S. 1 goes to House.

Conference Committee
Conference Committee negotiates a compromise version of House and Senate bills.

Congressional Approval
House and Senate vote on final version of the bill. If passed, the bill goes to the president.

PRESIDENT

The Bill with the President
The president signs, vetoes, or allows the bill to become law without signing it.

Vetoed bills return to Congress, where a two-thirds vote of each house can override the veto.

Once in committee, the bill may be assigned to a subcommittee of the main committee. As you have read, committees and subcommittees are controlled by the majority party in each house. This control can help determine the fate of the bill.

Committee and Subcommittee Hearings Committees or subcommittees often hold hearings to seek input from interested parties on the bills they are considering. The hearings are open to the public. Witnesses may include other members of the House or Senate, officials from the executive branch, and representatives from special interest groups. Witnesses may appear voluntarily, but the committee can use a subpoena to force them to appear. At the hearing, witnesses usually make a statement and then answer members' questions.

In general, the chair of the committee or subcommittee has considerable control over who appears at the hearings. Minority-party members have only limited ability to call witnesses. The chair can use his or her power over hearings to help shape other people's views of the bill.

Ways and Means Committee
All revenue-raising bills must pass through the House Ways and Means Committee, making its chair, Charles Rangel (D, New York, at left), among the most influential members of Congress. *Why do you think Congress concentrates such power in one committee?*

The Subcommittee's Report Following the hearings, a subcommittee must report on the bill to the full committee. A subcommittee may report a bill favorably, unfavorably, or without comment. The subcommittee may also recommend that the full committee take no further action on the bill, effectively killing it. The subcommittee's report is based on a vote of the members.

In general, House subcommittees may also make amendments to a bill. In the Senate, this task is left to the full committee.

The Markup Process The markup is a meeting of the full committee. Here, the committee hears any subcommittee reports, debates the bill further, and considers possible amendments to the bill. It is during the markup process that the bill is reviewed in close detail to ensure that every aspect of the proposed legislation is in order.

When the markup is complete, committee members vote on how to report the bill to the full chamber. As in the subcommittees, reports may be favorable, unfavorable, or without recommendation. If the bill has been heavily amended, the committee may submit an entirely new bill to the House or Senate that includes all the amendments. This new piece of legislation is called a clean bill.

The committee may also decide to take no further action on the bill. Such a step has the effect of killing the bill. In the House, however, a majority of members may sign a **discharge petition**, forcing the bill out of committee. Though rare, discharge petitions have been used successfully. In 1970, for example, Representative Martha Griffiths (D, Michigan) began a discharge petition to get a proposed constitutional amendment on equal rights for women out of the Judiciary Committee. The proposed amendment had been there for more than two decades.

House Rules As you read in Section 3, the House has a separate "traffic cop" committee called the Rules Committee. Its members are chosen by the Speaker and the minority leader. Most bills must pass through this committee before reaching the full House. The rules assigned by the Rules Committee govern how a bill can be debated or amended by the full House.

Rules can vary from bill to bill, but there are three main types: open, closed, and modified rules. Open rules allow amendments to the bill. Closed rules mean that there can be no amendments. Modified rules limit amendments to certain parts of the bill. Rules also limit the time available for debate.

The Rules Committee has significant power. By limiting debate or the ability to amend a bill, for example, it can prevent opponents of a bill from mounting a successful attack on it. The Rules Committee can in some cases even prevent a bill from being considered by the full House. Bills in the Rules Committee are, however, subject to a discharge petition.

Some privileged bills can bypass the Rules Committee. Examples include major budget or appropriations bills. In addition, the House can agree to <u>suspend</u> the rules for some minor bills that are not controversial. If two-thirds of the House agrees, "suspensions" come to the floor for quick debate and with no option for amendment. Suspension of the rules is a way for the chamber to dispose of many bills quickly.

READING CHECK **Sequencing** What are the steps a bill follows while it is in committees?

The Bill on the Floor

Once a bill leaves a committee and receives a rule, it goes to the full House or Senate for consideration. Depending on the nature of the bill, this may be an involved and dramatic piece of political theater—or a simple, routine procedure. The process differs somewhat in the two chambers.

The Bill in the House The first step in the process is the adoption of the rules put forward by the Rules Committee. This is accomplished by a vote of the House.

Sometimes, the whole House then debates the bill. In many cases, however, the House forms itself into a **Committee of the Whole**. In effect, all House members become members of a single committee. The Speaker of the House names a member of the majority party to serve as chair of the committee.

Why does the House take this step? According to the Constitution, the full House can only conduct business when at least half its members are present. Today that means 218 representatives. But for the Committee of the Whole, the **quorum**, or the number needed to legally conduct business, is only 100. The Committee of the Whole, then, allows the House to function even when many members are at hearings or are otherwise absent.

The rule for the bill regulates the debate in the Committee of the Whole. The available time is divided equally between the two parties. Members discuss the substance of the bill and any amendments made in committee. Members can also recommend amendments, and debate on these is limited to ten minutes—five minutes for, five minutes against. When the time for debate is over, the chair asks the speaker to stop talking.

According to House rules, amendments must be related to the subject matter of the bill in question. Indeed, this rule applies to all amendments made in the House. As you will read, however, this rule does not always succeed in preventing unrelated amendments from becoming attached to bills.

The Committee of the Whole cannot pass a bill. Instead, when it has completed its work, it dissolves. Then the full House votes on the measure and any amendments to it. The House votes first on the amendments. Then it votes on the bill itself, along with the amendments it has passed.

The most important votes are usually called record votes, in which each member is required to publicly state his or her vote. Such a vote is sometimes also called a **roll-call vote**. According to the Constitution, a roll-call vote must take place when one-fifth of the lawmakers present demand it.

The Bill in the Senate What happens when a bill leaves a Senate committee and heads to the Senate floor? Unlike the House, the Senate does not have a Rules Committee. Nor does it use a Committee of the Whole. Further, Senate rules generally do not limit debate or the right to offer amendments.

A senator *can* request that limits be placed on a particular bill, including limits on debate and restrictions on amendments. To take effect, however, such requests require the unanimous consent of the Senate.

ACADEMIC VOCABULARY
suspend to set aside or make temporarily inoperative

The unanimous consent requirement to limit debate opens the door to a filibuster, the delaying tactic discussed in Section 4. The Senate can end debate, however, with a three-fifths majority vote, or 60 senators, on a cloture motion.

When the Senate completes debate, it votes on the amendments and the bill. As in the House, important bills are often subject to roll-call votes.

READING CHECK **Comparing and Contrasting** How does floor debate on a bill differ in the House and Senate?

The Conference Committee

Bills can become law only after they are passed in identical form by both houses of Congress. If the House passes a measure that is then changed and passed by the Senate, the two houses must agree on a common version of the bill. For minor bills, the two sides might work informally before passage to reach agreement over differences in wording and amendments. But for major bills, resolving the differences between the House and Senate versions is the job of a **conference committee**.

Members of a conference committee are drawn from each chamber, usually from among the committees that handled the bill. The presiding officer of the Senate names the Senate representatives. The Speaker of the House names the House conferees.

House and Senate members in conference committee discuss the differences between the two versions of the bill. There are no formal rules for these meetings. The chair often rotates from one chamber to the other.

A conference committee sometimes fails to reach an agreement. In such a situation, the bill may die. Usually, though, there is strong desire on both sides to find a solution. After all, each chamber has passed a version of the bill, hoping it would become law.

When the conference committee reaches agreement, it issues a conference report. Both chambers receive this report. Debate on the report is allowed, but amendment of it is not. In some cases, one or the other house may request that the conference committee make further changes. One or the other house can also reject the report. But if and when both sides accept the report, the bill moves to the president's desk.

READING CHECK **Identifying the Main Idea** What is the purpose of a conference committee?

Pork-Barrel Spending

Getting a majority of members of Congress to agree on a bill can involve a lot of bargaining. Often, a member will agree to support something that will benefit the constituents of another member provided the other member supports something benefiting the first member's constituents. Multiply that sort of bargaining by 535 members, and there is a lot of room in the federal budget for what is known as pork-barrel spending, or spending on projects that target a small constituency but that all taxpayers fund. Large bills, such as highway or farm bills, are particular targets for pork-barrel spending because so many members have highways or farms in their districts. Recent years have seen a rise in the use of earmarks, in which individual members insert provisions into bills mandating specific sums of money to be spent on specific projects of interest to them.

Skills FOCUS **INTERPRETING PRIMARY SOURCES**

Understanding Points of View What do you think the cartoonist is trying to say by drawing the Capitol with a pig's nose?

See *Skills Handbook*, p. H4.

Presidential Action on a Bill

When the president receives a bill that both houses have passed, there are several possible outcomes:

- The president can sign the bill, which makes it law.
- The president may choose not to sign the bill. After 10 days (excluding Sundays), if Congress remains in session, the bill becomes law. But, if during those 10 days Congress adjourns—ends its session—the bill does not become law. This last tactic is known as a **pocket veto**.
- The president may veto the bill. The president does this by returning the bill to the chamber where it began its life. The president may also include a "veto message" that outlines specific objections.

Different presidents have taken different approaches to vetoes. Some presidents veto many bills, some hardly any—or none at all. George Washington, for example, vetoed just two bills. John Adams vetoed none. Franklin D. Roosevelt, on the other hand, tops all presidents. During his three full terms and part of a fourth in the 1930s and 1940s, he issued 635 vetoes. In the little over two years that he was president, Gerald Ford logged in 66 vetoes.

Congress can attempt to override a veto. This requires a two-thirds majority vote in each chamber. As a result, overrides are rare. There have been just 106 overrides in U.S. history out of a total of over 2,500 vetoes.

From 1996 to 1998, congressional legislation gave the president line-item veto power. This tool allowed a president to veto any part of a spending bill. Many state governors have this power. The Supreme Court ruled, however, that presidential line-item veto violated the Constitution, which prescribes specific veto procedures not including the line-item veto.

President George W. Bush has issued few vetoes, but he has made frequent use of signing statements. These are formal statements in which a president declares an intention to enforce a law in a certain way. Bush was not the first president to issue signing statements, but his use of them has been considered controversial. For some, it is a proper assertion of presidential power. For others, it amounts to an encroachment on the lawmaking powers of the legislative branch and on the interpretive powers of the judicial branch.

READING CHECK **Summarizing** What are the different ways a president has to reject a bill?

RESPONSIBILITIES OF LEADERSHIP

Presidents need to evaluate laws, but so do ordinary citizens. Developing criteria by which you determine whether or not you support a law is one part of being an informed and engaged citizen.

THINK central Online Quiz

thinkcentral.com
KEYWORD: SGO CNG HP

SECTION 5 ASSESSMENT

Reviewing Ideas and Terms

1. a. Recall What are the types of measures considered by Congress?
b. Make Inferences What advantages might there be for Congress in passing a **joint resolution** instead of a typical bill?

2. a. Identify What is the purpose of a **discharge petition**?
b. Evaluate Do you think committees and subcommittee chairs should have more or less power over the progress of bills? Explain your answer.

3. a. Describe What is the significance of the **Committee of the Whole** in the legislative process in the House?
b. Evaluate What do you think about the House's use of the Committee of the Whole? Is it a prudent efficiency or an unrepresentative maneuver?

4. a. Recall Who makes up a **conference committee**?
b. Evaluate Why do you think that neither house of Congress is allowed to amend conference reports?

5. a. Recall What can a president do to make a bill into a law?
b. Elaborate Why do you think the Constitution grants the president the power only to pass or veto a whole bill—not just parts of it?

Critical Thinking

6. Compare and Contrast Copy the chart below and fill in the details of how the lawmaking process is similar and different in the House and Senate.

Similarities	Differences
1.	1.

FOCUS ON WRITING

7. Narrative Write a paragraph that describes in narrative form the story of a bill as it travels through Congress.

The Sources of Laws

Where do members of Congress get ideas for legislation and information in deciding which bills to introduce or support? As the people's representatives, they must be open to ideas from a number of sources.

Members of Congress often initiate legislation based on campaign promises to constituents, responses to problems or crises, or their own analysis of what laws are needed. They also introduce legislation at the request of others and must decide whether to support bills that are submitted by others. The Library of Congress through its Congressional Research Service frequently assists Congress by providing information and analyzing issues. The Congressional Budget Office will provide an analysis of the budget for a bill and its projected costs. In addition, information and requests for legislation often come from the following sources:

The executive branch Article II, Section 2, instructs the president to give Congress information on the "State of the Union" and to "recommend to their Consideration such Measures as he shall judge necessary and expedient." The president delivers an annual state of the union address to Congress that outlines the president's legislative agenda, among other things. This agenda can include creating, consolidating, or eliminating departments or agencies. Members of the president's party in Congress usually sponsor the president's legislative proposals.

Executive departments and agencies are another regular source of legislative proposals. Most proposals from the executive branch are aimed at improving the functions of the departments or agencies that Congress already has created. These proposals usually are carefully crafted and ready for a member of Congress to introduce.

Constituents Many of those who live in a representative's district or a senator's state communicate with their elected officials, recommending the enactment of new laws or the repeal of existing laws. They make telephone calls, respond to public opinion polls, send faxes and e-mail, write personal letters, participate in letter-writing campaigns, and use blogs to inform their elected representatives and to persuade them about the need for particular legislation. Sometimes constituents ask their representative to introduce special legislation to address an individual problem or situation.

Interest groups Thousands of individuals and groups seek to influence members of Congress and legislation through lobbying, the practice of trying to affect legislation on behalf of organizations, industries, or interest groups through contact with legislators. Groups that participate in lobbying include businesses, civic organiza-

Adapted with permission from Lesson 22 of *We the People: The Citizen & the Constitution.* Copyright 2009, Center for Civic Education.

tions, professional associations, and nongovernmental organizations. The Lobbying Disclosure Act of 1996 requires some lobbyists to disclose the interests they represent, the issues in which they are interested, and how much they spend annually. The act does not limit the amount of lobbying in which any individual or group may engage. The activity of lobbying reflects the First Amendment rights to speak, assemble, and petition. Effective lobbyists, whether individuals or groups, must be

- **Well informed** Members of Congress must be able to rely on the information they receive from lobbyists. Information must be able to withstand scrutiny, and it must be timely.

- **Knowledgeable** Lobbyists need to know not only their own issues but also the intricacies of the legislative process, key players, and which groups support and oppose particular proposals.

- **Organized** Interest groups must convey a consistent message and must be persistent. They must be able to explain how an issue affects their members and clients. And they must use various forms of communication effectively, including personal contact with members of Congress.

- **Cooperative** Successful interests groups, like members of Congress, must be able to build coalitions with other interest groups in the search for workable majorities.

Left, Representative Lincoln Diaz-Balart (R, Florida) met with students in 2007. Right, Former U.S. senator Barack Obama (D, Illinois) listened to the concerns of senior citizens in 2005.

Reviewing Ideas

1. **Explain** What are some sources of legislative ideas for members of Congress?

2. **Analyze** Do you think an individual constituent is more likely to be able to influence a senator or a representative? Why or why not?

Critical Thinking

3. **Evaluate** Interest groups employ full-time paid lobbyists to convey their points of view to members of Congress. Do you think this gives them too much influence over legislation? Explain your answers.

CHAPTER 5 Chapter Review

Connecting Online

Visit **thinkcentral.com** for review and enrichment activities related to this chapter.

THINK central

KEYWORD: SGO CNG

Quiz and Review

GOV 101
Examine key concepts in this chapter.

ONLINE QUIZZES
Take a practice quiz for each section in this chapter.

Activities

eActivities
Complete Webquests and Internet research activities.

INTERACTIVE FEATURES
Explore interactive versions of maps and charts.

KEEP IT CURRENT
Link to current events in U.S. government.

Partners

American Bar Association Division for Public Education
Learn more about the law, your rights and responsibilities.

Center for Civic Education
Promoting an enlightened and responsible citizenry committed to democratic principles and actively engaged in the practice of democracy.

Online Textbook

ONLINE SIMULATIONS
Learn about U.S. government through simulations you can complete online.

 Click for More Read more about key topics online.

Comprehension and Critical Thinking

SECTION 1 *(pp. 122–126)*

1. a. Review Key Terms For each term, write a sentence that explains its significance or meaning: constituents, apportionment, appropriation, impeachment, oversight.

b. Summarize What is the role of Congress in the system of checks and balances?

c. Elaborate What are the main goals and purposes of the bicameral structure of Congress?

SECTION 2 *(pp. 127–136)*

2. a. Review Key Terms For each term, write a sentence that explains its significance or meaning: necessary and proper clause, indirect tax, direct tax, deficit, commerce clause, subpoenas, writ of habeas corpus, bill of attainder, ex post facto laws.

b. Make Inferences What did Thomas Jefferson infer from the necessary and proper clause?

c. Predict How do you think the powers of Congress will change in the future?

SECTION 3 *(pp. 137–142)*

3. a. Review Key Terms For each term, write a sentence that explains its significance or meaning: reapportionment, gerrymandering, Speaker of the House, bills, floor leader, whips, party caucus, standing committees, select committees, joint committees.

b. Explain Why did single-member districts evolve in the House?

c. Elaborate In what ways is the House closer to the people than the Senate?

SECTION 4 *(pp. 143–147)*

4. a. Review Key Terms For each term, write a sentence that explains its significance or meaning: president of the Senate, president pro tempore, Senate majority leader, seniority rule, filibuster, cloture.

b. Analyze How does the size of the Senate affect its operation?

c. Elaborate How does the practice of the filibuster reflect the special character and structure of the Senate?

SECTION 5 *(pp. 149–155)*

5. a. Review Key Terms For each term, write a sentence that explains its significance or meaning: rider, joint resolution, concurrent resolutions, Committee of the Whole, quorum, roll-call vote, conference committee, pocket veto.

b. Draw Conclusions What can you conclude from the numbers of bills submitted and the numbers of bills passed in Congress?

c. Evaluate Do you think the process of making law should be made more difficult or easier? Explain your answer.

Critical Reading

Read the passage in Section 2 that begins with the heading "Implied Powers of Congress." Then answer the questions that follow:

6. Which of the following was the central issue in the debate over implied powers?

A the War Powers Resolution

B the commerce power

C the necessary and proper clause

D the state of Maryland

7. The Supreme Court's decision in the case of *McCulloch* v. *Maryland* most closely lined up with the position of which of the following?

A Alexander Hamilton

B Thomas Jefferson

C the Antifederalists

D the strict constructionists

RESPONSIBILITIES OF LEADERSHIP

8. Select an **issue of public concern** that interests you. The issue should be something for which federal action is an appropriate solution, rather than state or local action. Write a draft of a bill addressing an aspect of that issue. Make sure your bill is constitutional. Share your bill with the class.

9. Identify your **congressional representative**. Visit the representative's Web site or call his or her office. Learn the key issues the representative is interested in, the committees and subcommittees the representative serves on, and the constituent services the representative provides. Select one of the items you learned about and write a paragraph describing it. Share your paragraph with the class.

CONNECTING TO THE CONSTITUTION

10. Review Article I, Section 8, of the Constitution in the Reference Section at the end of your textbook. Then read the Preamble to the Constitution. Relate each of the powers listed in Article I, Section 8, to the general purposes of government that are found in the Preamble.

ANALYZING PRIMARY SOURCES

Political Cartoon *Because of the rising costs of campaigning for office, members of Congress spend a great deal of their time raising money. The law places limits on how much money an individual, business, or group can donate. Still, much of the money comes from interest groups, leading some people to question whether members of Congress are "for sale."*

11. Evaluate Where is the poll being taken?

12. Draw Conclusions What do you think the cartoonist means to suggest by having members of Congress willing to talk in return for money?

FOCUS ON WRITING

Expository Writing *Expository writing gives information, explains why or how, or defines a process. To practice expository writing, complete the assignment below.*

Writing Topic: Congress and the Common Good

13. Assignment Based on what you have read in this chapter, write a paragraph about how the structure and practices of Congress help to achieve the common good for the people of the United States.

The **Presidency**

"NO ONE WHO HAS NOT HAD THE
RESPONSIBILITY CAN REALLY UNDERSTAND
WHAT IT IS LIKE TO BE PRESIDENT...
THERE IS NO END TO THE CHAIN OF
RESPONSIBILITY THAT BINDS HIM."

—HARRY S TRUMAN, 1955

SECTION 1

The President

- The Constitution names the president as the head of the executive branch of the U.S. government.

- The president's official and unofficial roles include: chief executive, chief administrator, commander in chief, foreign policy leader, chief agenda setter, chief of state, party leader, and chief citizen.

- The Constitution and its amendments set the presidential term of office, the process of electing the president, the line of succession to the presidency, and the president's salary.

- There are few formal qualifications for the president, but there are many informal ones.

SECTION 2

The Powers of the Presidency

- The Constitution grants the president specific executive, diplomatic, military, judicial, and legislative powers. The president also has some informal powers that are not expressly stated in the Constitution.

- The powers of the president are checked by both the legislative and the judicial branches.

- Presidential power has grown and changed since the Constitution was adopted.

SECTION 3

The President's Administration

- The Executive Office of the President works closely with the president to determine domestic, economic, and foreign policy.

- The role of the vice president has grown a great deal. Nine vice presidents have had to assume the title of president when the position has been left vacant.

- Over the years, the cabinet has increased in size, and presidents have varied in how much they rely on the cabinet for counsel.

CONNECTING TO THE CONSTITUTION

Our nation's system of government is based on constitutional law established by the United States Constitution. See the "We the People: The Citizen and the Constitution" pages in this chapter for an in-depth exploration of how the Constitution gives power to the president.

The White House, Washington, D.C.

The President

Main Idea

The Constitution gives only a brief description of the president's qualifications and powers. Yet the job is vast and complex, as the president must fulfill many roles.

Reading Focus

1. What are the roles of the president?
2. What are the formal characteristics of the presidency?
3. What are the informal qualifications for the presidency?

Key Terms

chief executive
commander in chief
foreign policy
diplomacy
chief of state
succession

TAKING NOTES As you read, take notes on the duties and qualifications of the president. Record your notes in a graphic organizer like this one.

The President	
Formal	Informal

WHY IT MATTERS

Responsibilities of a President

President Lyndon Johnson once said, "A president's hardest task is not to do what is right, but to know what is right." Presidents make hundreds and hundreds of decisions that affect the nation, and, in making these decisions, they must try to consider what is in the best interest of the country and act accordingly.

When Richard Nixon became president in 1969, the Cold War was at its height. American military forces were fighting Communist forces in Vietnam, and the United States and the Soviet Union were locked in a nuclear arms race. The

Communist government of China seemed to be a solid ally of the Soviet Union. Nixon, however, believed that China and the Soviet Union were not as friendly as they appeared. So he took a risk. Nixon decided that improved relations with China would give the United States an advantage in the Cold War against the Soviet Union.

In 1972 Nixon made an historic trip to China, meeting with China's Communist leader, Mao Zedong. In doing so, Nixon officially recognized the People's Republic of China, causing many other nations to do the same.

Presidents make countless decisions every day. Some are historic and have long-lasting consequences, like Nixon's decision to visit China. Some are routine. Each decision is a part of the full-time, 24-hour-a-day job of leading a nation. ■

LEADING A Nation

Commander in Chief
Franklin Roosevelt visits American troops in Morocco during World War II.

Foreign Policy Leader
Richard Nixon and his wife Patricia meet with Chinese diplomats at the Great Wall.

Roles of the President

The presidency is one of the most complex jobs in the world. The person who sits in the Oval Office must fill a variety of roles in order to lead the nation. Some of these roles are stated in the Constitution. Others have developed over time.

Official Roles Article II of the Constitution outlines the executive branch of the federal government and, in particular, the presidency. It assigns the president the following duties:

- chief executive
- chief administrator
- commander in chief
- foreign policy leader
- chief agenda setter

The Constitution states, "The executive power shall be vested in a President of the United States . . ." (Article II, Section 1, Clause 1). "Executive power" means the power to execute, or carry out, the nation's laws. The president carries out this duty as **chief executive**. It is the president's responsibility to see that government programs are carried out and that the laws passed by Congress are implemented.

In running the government, the president does not act alone. The Constitution assumes that the president will have assistance. It states that the president "may require the opinion, in writing, of the principal officer in each of the executive departments." As the leader of the executive branch, the president acts as the chief administrator, or manager, of the fifteen executive departments and the numerous federal agencies that help carry out government policy.

Today the job of chief administrator is an enormous task. The executive departments employ about 1.8 million people while the postal service and other government agencies employ millions more.

The Constitution also names the president **commander in chief** of the nation's military. As commander in chief, the president has the authority to order troops into action and to call them back home. This power is a significant one. While it is Congress's duty to declare war on other nations, more often than not, U.S. forces go into action at the direction of a president and not because Congress has declared war.

As **foreign policy** leader, the president has the job of formulating the nation's plans and procedures for dealing with other countries. This can involve negotiating treaties and receiving foreign ambassadors. The president also directs the activities of the country's ambassadors and its diplomatic efforts. **Diplomacy** is the art of negotiating with foreign governments.

The Constitution specifies that the president will set the government's agenda, or outline of things to do, during an annual State of the Union address. This duty makes the president the nation's chief agenda setter. Often, the State of the Union address includes a number of specific programs for Congress to consider enacting into law.

As chief agenda setter, the president also helps Congress prepare the annual federal budget. You will read more about the budget process in Chapter 7.

Unofficial Roles In addition to the official duties, a president also fills other key roles in the federal government. These unofficial roles include:

- chief of state
- party leader
- chief citizen

As **chief of state**, also known as the head of state, the president takes on the role of the symbolic figurehead of the United States.

Chief Agenda Setter
Bill Clinton gives the State of the Union address.

When a president represents the country at the funeral of a foreign leader or at a major international sporting event, for example, it is in the role of chief of state. The role of chief of state often overlaps with other roles. For example, the president may host a foreign leader at a formal state dinner. In this particular instance, the president is acting as both chief of state and foreign policy leader.

The president is also recognized as the official party leader of his or her political party. The president takes the lead in shaping and then promoting the party platform—the important issues for which the party stands. At election time, the president may also help raise money and build support for party members around the country.

The president and vice president are the only two nationwide elective positions in the government. As such, they are said to be chief citizens, or the primary representatives of all the American people. They should be seen as models of good citizenship and are often held to a high standard of personal behavior by the American public.

READING CHECK **Comparing** How are the president's roles as chief of state and foreign policy leader similar?

ACADEMIC VOCABULARY

ensure make certain

Formal Characteristics of the Presidency

In addition to describing the roles of the president, the Constitution lists the qualifications, term of office, election, succession, and benefits for the position. These topics are covered in only a few short paragraphs.

Formal Qualifications As outlined in the Constitution, there are three formal qualifications for the presidency. Presidents must:

- be at least 35 years old
- have lived in the country for 14 years
- be a natural-born U.S. citizen

A natural-born citizen is a person who has been born a citizen of a country. Natural-born U.S. citizens also include persons born of U.S. citizens overseas or people who are born on U.S. soil, territories, or military bases overseas. No naturalized citizen—a person made a citizen by law, after his or her birth—can become president.

Why did the Framers restrict the presidency to natural-born citizens? They saw it as a way to safeguard the gains of the American Revolution. They feared that, without such a restriction, a rich duke or king could come to the United States and assume the presidency. That person might use the presidency to overthrow representative government. "The safety of a republic," observed Alexander Hamilton, "depends essentially . . . on that love of country, which will almost invariably be found to be closely connected with birth."

Some Americans today feel that the requirement unnecessarily blocks qualified people from the presidency and call for an amendment to the Constitution to eliminate it. Some of the people interested in re-evaluating this requirement cite the example of California governor Arnold Schwarzenegger, who is not allowed to run for president because he was born in Austria.

Term of Office Today a president can serve two four-year terms. At the Constitutional Convention, the Framers considered several different term lengths for the president, including a single six- or seven-year term. They also debated whether to allow a president to seek multiple terms. They wanted to ensure that a president had enough time in office to govern effectively without granting the officeholder too much power. In the end, they compromised on a four-year term with the chance for re-election.

George Washington, the first president, served two terms and declined to seek another because he felt himself beginning to weaken physically and desired some leisure time free from political stresses. Washington's decision established an unofficial two-term limit that guided future presidents for nearly a century and a half.

In 1940, however, Franklin Roosevelt broke this tradition and ran for a third term. At the time, World War II was raging in Europe, and Roosevelt believed the nation needed experienced leadership to help it get through this tumultuous time. While some criticized his decision, the voters returned him to office. Four years later, with American troops fighting in the war, Roosevelt sought and won a fourth term.

Roosevelt died in office in 1945. Two years later, Congress proposed a constitutional amendment to limit a president to two full terms and no more than 10 years in office. Proponents felt the amendment was necessary in order to prevent one person or party from gaining a dangerous hold on government. Opponents argued that it weakened a second-term president's authority, since Congress and foreign leaders knew that the president would soon be leaving office. Despite the opposition, the states ratified the Twenty-second Amendment in 1951.

Election to Office The formal process for electing the president of the United States is outlined in the Constitution. As discussed in Chapter 3, voters do not directly elect the president and vice president. Instead, voters are actually choosing electors, or people pledged to support the candidates that the voters choose. Taken together, these men and women are known as the electoral college.

The electoral college was a product of a Constitutional Convention compromise. Some of the Framers wanted direct popular election of the president while others worried that the public would be unable to make a wise choice and wanted Congress to select the president. The resulting compromise was the electoral college. The electoral college would help to maintain the balance between the small and large states. It would also ensure that a president would be elected by a cross-section of the country's voters.

Under the Constitution, every state is granted a number of electors equal to the number of its members in the House and the Senate. These electors represent the voters of the state. Additionally, Washington, D.C., has three electors. Today there are 435 representatives and 100 senators, which adds up to 535. Add in the three electors from Washington, D.C., for a total of 538 electors.

Each state has a different number of representatives, so those states with more representatives, such as California, New York, and Texas, have more electoral votes. This fact makes a win in these states a big advantage for a presidential candidate.

The Constitution gives states the power to decide how to pick their electors. Historically, some states chose their electors

THE ELECTORAL COLLEGE

JUNE/JULY: Electors are Selected

Electors are nominated by state political parties the summer before the election.

States nominate electors through different means:
- Primary elections
- Party conventions
- Named by campaign committees

Names from each political party are submitted to the secretaries of state at least one month prior to the election.

NOVEMBER: Election Day

Voters cast ballots for presidential and vice presidential candidates. Each vote is awarded to a slate of voters who represent the candidates.

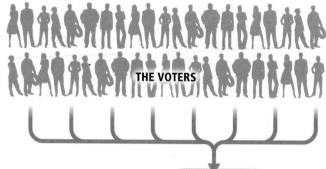

THE VOTERS

In all but two states, the slate of electors representing the candidate who wins the popular vote become members of the electoral college. *

* Maine and Nebraska elect two electors by statewide ballot, and the remainder are chosen by district.

ELECTORS

DECEMBER: Electoral Votes Counted

At separate meetings in each state 41 days following the election, electors cast one ballot for president and one for vice president. Six days later, the current vice president officially counts the electoral votes during a joint session of Congress. The candidate who receives the majority of electoral college votes–270–wins the election.

PRESIDENT

Skills FOCUS INTERPRETING CHARTS

What political issues are raised by the use of the electoral college? Explain.

by popular vote; others through their state legislatures. Today all states use the popular vote. Electors can be nominated through a primary election or at the party's convention. Electors can also be named by campaign committees who work on behalf of a certain presidential candidate.

Today electors have little or no discretion in deciding for whom to vote. Each political party chooses a slate of electors pledged to represent its candidate. In most states, if that candidate wins the popular vote, then the party's electors cast their votes for that candidate. This "winner-take-all" rule is required by 48 states. However, two states, Maine and Nebraska, pick some of their electors by congressional district. In these states there could be a split in electoral votes since their electors are pledged to choose the popular candidate in their district only.

As discussed earlier in Chapter 3, there are criticisms of the electoral college system. The original purpose of the electoral college, that of having more enlightened people select the president, no longer exists. What remains is a system that gives small states unequal representation but requires candidates to campaign broadly across the country in order to win electoral votes.

Succession According to the Constitution, the vice president is the first in the line of succession to the presidency. **Succession** is the process of succeeding, or coming after, someone. The Constitution's wording, however, was unclear as to whether a vice president becomes president, or just acts as president, if there is a presidential vacancy.

This question was first tested in 1841, when William Henry Harrison died in office. Vice President John Tyler assumed not just Harrison's duties but also the title of president. The nation followed this custom for more than a century. In 1967 the Twenty-fifth Amendment formally incorporated it into the Constitution.

The Twenty-fifth Amendment not only set guidelines for succession but it also created the procedures for handling presidential disability, such as temporary illness. In such cases the vice president assumes the role of acting president until the president is no longer disabled.

The Constitution gives Congress the power to decide the order of succession. In 1947 Congress passed the Presidential

Presidential Succession

QUICK FACTS

Following the president pro tempore, the executive departments heads are next in the line of succession. The order is determined by the order in which Congress established each department.

1. Vice President
2. Speaker of the House
3. President Pro Tempore of the Senate
4. Secretary of State
5. Secretary of the Treasury
6. Secretary of Defense
7. Attorney General
8. Secretary of the Interior
9. Secretary of Agriculture
10. Secretary of Commerce
11. Secretary of Labor
12. Secretary of Health and Human Services
13. Secretary of Housing and Urban Development
14. Secretary of Transportation
15. Secretary of Energy
16. Secretary of Education
17. Secretary of Veterans Affairs
18. Secretary of Homeland Security

Vice President Lyndon Johnson takes the oath of office following the assassination of President John F. Kennedy. On the right is Jacqueline Kennedy, President Kennedy's widow.

Succession Act. It establishes the Speaker of the House as the person next in the line of succession after the vice president. President Truman, who signed the act, pushed for the Speaker of the House to be the next in line because the Speaker is elected by his or her district and is the chosen leader of the House. The Speaker, Truman argued, was a true representative of the people.

Salary and Benefits Compared to the average American's income, the president and vice president make quite a lot of money. The president makes $400,000 per year, and the vice president makes $208,100 per year. The Constitution states that a president's salary is not to be altered during his or her term in office. This clause stops Congress from threatening to cut a president's salary as a bargaining tool or from rewarding a popular president.

In addition to a salary, presidents receive other benefits. The president has a large staff that includes chefs, butlers, and doctors who are on call whenever the president may need them. Presidents live with their family in a mansion in Washington, D.C., the White House, for the duration of their term and receive health and retirement benefits along with special tax deductions. The president also has access to numerous cars and *Air Force One*, the president's private plane.

READING CHECK **Summarizing** How did the current plan for presidential succession come to be?

Informal Qualifications for the Presidency

The constitutional requirements for the presidency are few. However, the informal qualifications—the experience and personal qualities that the public looks for in a president—are many.

Presidential Backgrounds The backgrounds of the people who have become president share many common features. Most presidents have been well-educated white men from middle- to upper-class families. In 1984, though, Geraldine Ferraro became the first woman to run for vice president on a major party ticket. Several

QUICK FACTS

PRESIDENT AND VICE PRESIDENT: TERMS, SALARY, AND BENEFITS

Title	Term	Salary
President	Four years	$400,000
Vice President	Four years	$208,100

Benefits

- Travel allowances
- Staff including Secret Service officers for protection
- Tax deduction for two residencies
- Health and retirement benefits

Source: Congressional Research Service, 2007

African American men and women have sought the presidency, none winning a major party's nomination until 2008. That year, Barack Obama made history when he was elected the first African American president of the United States, after winning the Democratic Party's nomination.

All presidents to this point have had a religious background in some Christian denomination. There has only been one Roman Catholic president thus far—John F. Kennedy, who was elected in 1960. Al Smith, who lost to Herbert Hoover in 1928, was the first Roman Catholic to be a major presidential candidate. In the 2000 election, Joe Lieberman made history as the first Jewish person to run for vice president.

Three-fourths of the presidents have had some background in the military. George Washington established a pattern followed by such men as Andrew Jackson, Zachary Taylor, and Ulysses S. Grant.

In recent years, Americans have tended to favor former governors for the White House. For example, four recent presidents—Jimmy Carter, Ronald Reagan, Bill Clinton, and George W. Bush—have served as governors.

Personal Qualities A president does not get the position by filling out an application. Instead, a president must win the support and eventually the votes of the American public. While the backgrounds of potential presidents are important, presidents must also possess appealing personal qualities.

The Great Communicator
Ronald Reagan was a very well-spoken and charismatic president. He was known as the "Great Communicator" for his speaking skills and ability to communicate effectively with the people.

significant. A president needs to appear dignified, confident, and poised, and should demonstrate a certain degree of charisma.

Presidents must continue to demonstrate these qualities in the faces of constant challenges. As President Harry Truman soon realized, there is no relaxing as president.

PRIMARY SOURCE

❝Within the first few months I discovered that being a President is like riding a tiger. A man has to keep on riding or be swallowed. . . . [A] President either is constantly on top of events or, if he hesitates, events will soon be on top of him. I never felt that I could let up for a single moment.❞

—Harry S Truman, *Memoirs, Volume Two: Years of Trial and Hope*, 1956

Successful presidents are likeable and possess evident qualities of leadership. They are also able to communicate their ideas effectively. They should be persuasive at a minimum and, if possible, inspiring.

In the age of television and the Internet, when public access to the president is at an all-time high, a president's appearance is also

Day in and day out, presidents must work well with friends and foes alike. They must effectively manage the vast workings of a huge executive department. They must be able to present a clear vision of what they plan to do for the nation and how they plan to do it. When a crisis strikes, they must exhibit calm and control, and they must do all of this under constant scrutiny and enormous pressure.

READING CHECK Identifying Supporting Details What are some of the personal qualities that presidents have possessed?

SECTION 1 ASSESSMENT

THINK central Online Quiz
thinkcentral.com
KEYWORD: SGO PRE HP

Reviewing Ideas and Terms

1. **a. Define** What is **diplomacy**?
   b. Contrast What are the differences between the president's jobs as **commander in chief** and **chief of state**?
   c. Rank Which of the presidential roles do you think is the most important? Explain your answer.

2. **a. Describe** What are some of the benefits that the president and vice president receive?
   b. Explain Why do you think that the presidential requirement of natural-born citizenship is still in effect today?
   c. Evaluate What is your opinion about the arguments for and against the electoral college?

3. **a. Describe** What are some informal job requirements for the presidency?
   b. Make Generalizations In what ways have presidents past and present been similar?
   c. Design What are some possible features and qualities that you think an ideal president should have?

Critical Thinking

4. **Make Generalizations** Copy the graphic organizer below and use information from the section to identify characteristics of the presidency. What are the main features of the American presidency?

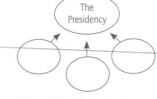

The Presidency

FOCUS ON WRITING

5. **Persuasive** Write a speech in which you, as a presidential candidate, try to persuade your audience that you have the qualities necessary to be a good president. Think about the qualities of past presidents that made them effective leaders.

The Powers of the Presidency

Main Idea

The powers of the presidency, outlined in Article II of the Constitution, are vast and have grown throughout the history of the United States. They are, however, checked by the other branches of government.

Reading Focus

1. What are the executive powers of the president?
2. What are the diplomatic and military powers of the president?
3. How does the president exercise legislative and judicial powers?
4. What are some of the informal powers of the president?
5. How are the president's powers checked by the other branches?
6. In what ways has presidential power changed over the years?

Key Terms

executive orders
executive privilege
diplomatic recognition
reprieve
pardon
amnesty
commute

 TAKING NOTES As you read, take notes on the powers of the presidency. Record your notes in a graphic organizer like this one.

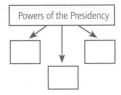

Powers of the Presidency

WHY IT MATTERS

The Burden of Power With great power comes great responsibility—and the pressure that goes with it. The president of the United States is one of the most powerful people in the world, and the decisions that he or she makes affect not only American citizens but also people throughout the world.

In 1962 President John F. Kennedy experienced the full weight of presidential responsibility during the Cuban missile crisis. Government intelligence revealed that the Soviet Union was stockpiling missiles in Cuba, just 90 miles off the coast of Florida. For Kennedy, the stakes could not have been higher: One wrong move might plunge the world into nuclear war.

With the world nervously watching and waiting, Kennedy enlisted the counsel of his top advisers. Some suggested an air strike on Cuba, others a naval blockade. In the end, Kennedy chose the blockade and a course of vigorous diplomacy with Soviet leaders. The crisis ended with neither country attacking the other—and with Soviet missiles being withdrawn from Cuba.

Presidents today continue to confront challenges. Their office grants them an incredible array of powers. They must use these powers with care and in the best interest of the nation. ■

Great Power and Great Responsibility

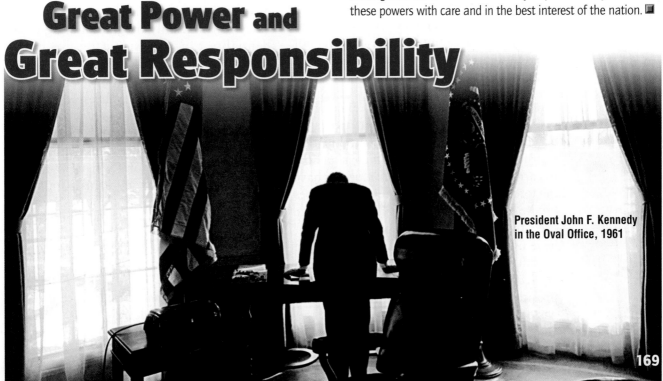

President John F. Kennedy in the Oval Office, 1961

Executive Powers

When presidents take the oath of office, they pledge to "preserve, protect and defend the Constitution of the United States." This pledge includes exercising the powers of their office in a constitutional manner. As chief executive, the president has three main powers: appointment and removal of key executive branch officials, issuing executive orders, and maintaining executive privilege.

Appointment and Removal Powers The Constitution gives the president power to appoint people to fill the top posts in the executive branch. These officials help presidents carry out their duties as chief executive. Presidents today directly appoint some 3,000 people.

Oftentimes, a president will use the power to nominate and appoint as a political tool, rewarding political supporters and winning new ones. This power also allows presidents to place in key positions people who support their policies.

Of the many jobs a president fills, about a third are subject to the "advice and consent" of the Senate. Such posts include Supreme Court justices and federal judges, the ambassadors who represent the United States in foreign countries, members of the cabinet, and top military advisers.

Most presidential appointees serve "at the pleasure of the president," which means a president may remove these people at any time for any reason. However, there are some exceptions. For example, a president is not allowed to fire federal judges, who serve for life. Only Congress can impeach them.

Executive Orders As chief executive, presidents also have the power to issue executive orders—a formal rule or regulation instructing executive branch officials on how to carry out their jobs. Executive orders have the force of law. While the Constitution does not specifically permit presidents to issue executive orders, presidents past and present have used this tool as a way of taking "care that the laws be faithfully executed" (Article II, Section 3). Executive orders give the president great power to interpret laws passed by Congress.

Executive orders are used for a variety of purposes. A president may use an executive order to clarify a law's application. In October 2006 President George W. Bush issued an executive order announcing penalties against the nation of Sudan under the terms of existing laws.

An executive order may also establish rules and regulations for the operation of an executive agency. In 2000, for example, President Clinton ordered that all executive agencies make appropriate accommodations to employees with disabilities.

As discussed in Chapter 5, presidents also issue signing statements, which have grown increasingly controversial. Signing statements differ from executive orders in that they are issued at the time of the law's signing and often specify some provision in the law that the president plans to ignore or modify.

Executive Privilege The final power that presidents claim as chief executive is the right of **executive privilege**. This power allows a president to refuse to release information to Congress or a court. This power, though, is often disputed by the other branches.

Presidents claim the right of executive privilege in order to shield information in the interest of national security. They argue that being able to keep sensitive information secret is vital to the safety of the nation.

Presidents have also argued that they must be able to hold private discussions with advisers in order to make good decisions. They feel that only by guaranteeing confidentiality can a president receive honest feedback from his or her advisers.

The Constitution does not mention executive privilege. Nevertheless, courts have generally supported the concept—within limits. During the Watergate scandal of the early 1970s, for example, President Richard Nixon was accused of covering up crimes committed by members of his administration. The courts and Congress sought audiotapes about specific White House conversations, which Nixon refused to turn over, claiming executive privilege. The case eventually went to the Supreme Court.

READING CHECK **Summarizing** What are the extent of and the limits of a president's right to hire and fire?

LANDMARK SUPREME COURT CASES

Constitutional Issue: Powers of the President

United States v. *Nixon* (1974)

DIVISION FOR
PUBLIC
EDUCATION
AMERICAN BAR ASSOCIATION

WHY IT MATTERS

The Supreme Court's decision in United States v. Nixon *was a major ruling on the concept of executive privilege and the limits to presidential power.*

Background

During the 1972 presidential election campaign, administration officials of President Richard Nixon helped plan and cover up an illegal break-in at the Democratic Party's campaign headquarters at the Watergate Hotel in Washington, D.C. After the break-in was discovered, President Nixon had to appoint a special prosecutor to conduct a criminal investigation. Congress began hearings on the matter. In those hearings, a former presidential aide revealed that Nixon had tape-recorded conversations in the Oval Office. Investigators realized that these tapes revealed whether Nixon knew of the Watergate burglary, so the special prosecutor subpoenaed Nixon to force him to turn over the tape recordings. Nixon refused. The special prosecutor, representing the U.S. government, and Nixon's attorneys took the case to the Supreme Court.

Arguments for the United States

The special prosecutor needed access to certain audiotapes in order to establish the credibility of witnesses and to determine whether or not any criminal activity had taken place. Under claims of executive privilege, past presidents had generally been allowed to keep official presidential conversations and meetings private. In this case, however, the special prosecutor argued that the taped discussions concerned only political matters related to Nixon's re-election committee, not to presidential business. These political conversations, he said, were not protected by executive privilege. Furthermore, Nixon had already released edited transcripts of portions of some tapes, which weakened any claim to confidentiality.

Arguments for Nixon

Nixon and his attorneys argued that the Supreme Court had no jurisdiction over the matter, claiming that the constitutional separation of powers prevented the courts from stepping into what was a dispute among departments within the executive branch. They compared the matter to a disagreement among congressional committees, which would be resolved by Congress without any involvement by the Supreme Court. Furthermore, they argued that under the right of executive privilege, Nixon was completely within his power to refuse to give the tapes to the special prosecutor and Congress.

THE IMPACT TODAY The Supreme Court's decision in favor of the United States was a constitutional landmark that established limits to executive privilege and presidential immunity that are still recognized today. While the president does have some privileges that are not granted to other citizens, these rights have conditions. The president must recognize the legitimate claims of the other two branches of government and understand that these branches may have valid reasons to seek information from the executive branch. In criminal proceedings, for example, the courts' need for information may outweigh the president's right to confidentiality.

CRITICAL THINKING

What Do You Think? All presidents exert executive privilege at some point during their presidency. Under what circumstances, if any, is such a claim legitimate? Can you think of a case in which they are not legitimate? Explain your answer.

Research Supreme Court cases at **thinkcentral.com. KEYWORD: SGO SCC**

THE PRESIDENCY **171**

Diplomatic and Military Powers

The president is foreign policy leader, chief of state, and the commander in chief of the United States. These roles give the president wide, but not unlimited, diplomatic and military powers.

Diplomatic Powers As foreign policy leader, the president represents the United States in its interactions with foreign governments. The Constitution gives the president the power to negotiate treaties, or formal agreements between two or more countries that are used to end conflicts, form alliances, and establish trade relationships.

The president's treaty-making power is limited by Congress. Two-thirds of the Senate must vote to approve any treaty, making any amendments it sees fit to in the process. On some occasions, Senate opposition has even blocked treaties. For example, the Treaty of Versailles, the peace settlement following World War I, was never approved by the Senate. In addition, even after a treaty is ratified, Congress can still pass laws that alter or override parts of it.

In addition to their treaty-making powers, presidents also have the power to make executive agreements. Executive agreements are agreements between a president and the head of a foreign government. Unlike a treaty, an executive agreement does not require the advice and consent of the Senate. However, executive agreements are similar to treaties in that they have the effect of law.

In general, presidents employ executive agreements for simple or routine interactions with foreign governments. Yet, executive agreements have sometimes been used for more far-reaching ends. The North American Free Trade Agreement, or NAFTA, is an example of an executive agreement. NAFTA is now a congressional-executive agreement (see Chapter 14).

The president also has the power to formally recognize the legitimacy of a foreign government. This power is known as **diplomatic recognition**, and it can have a major impact on international relations. President Truman's recognition of Israel's government in 1948, for example, was vitally important to that nation's survival because the United States, as a world power, held great influence over other nations in the region. If the United States recognized Israel, other nations would, and did, follow.

Military Powers As commander in chief, the president has the responsibility to ensure the defense and security of the nation and its interests around the world. The Constitution gives Congress the power to declare war, but from the beginning, presidents have claimed the power to take military action without a formal declaration of war from Congress.

Presidents have called out the armed forces more than 200 times in American history. In fact, on only five occasions in U.S. history has Congress actually declared war—the War of 1812, the Mexican-American War, the Spanish-American War, World War I, and World War II. Both the Korean War and the Vietnam War were fought without a formal declaration of war.

Following the Vietnam War, Congress decided to restrain the president's power to commit troops. Over President Richard Nixon's veto, Congress passed the War Powers Resolution in 1973. This law calls on

PROFILES IN GOVERNMENT

George WASHINGTON
1732-1799

As the nation's first president, George Washington set precedents that defined the office for generations. In serving only two terms, Washington established the unofficial two-term limit. Washington also established the first cabinet and instituted financial concepts such as the National Bank and the federal debt.

Washington declined to serve a third term as president. He then set the precedent for giving a farewell address upon taking leave from office. In his eloquent address, published in September 1796, he counseled Americans to shun political parties and factionalism, and he warned of the dangers of foreign alliances, a principle that guided America for nearly 100 years. Washington's dignity, reserve, and measured use of presidential power exemplified what the Framers believed the chief executive should be.

Draw Conclusions Why do you think Washington believed foreign alliances and political parties were dangerous to Americans?

Declaring War

The Constitution grants Congress the power to declare war. However, citing their constitutional role as commander in chief, presidents throughout history have taken it upon themselves to call troops into action without getting a formal declaration of war from Congress. Despite the efforts of Congress to clarify war-making responsibility with the passage of the War Powers Resolution in 1973, there remains tension between Congress and the president when it comes to the use of U.S. troops. According to this political cartoon, the tension is grounded in the Constitution itself.

Courtesy William Costello

Skills FOCUS INTERPRETING PRIMARY SOURCES

Making Inferences What does this cartoon say about the war-making powers of Congress?

See **Skills Handbook**, p. H9.

---

the president to consult with Congress before and during any possible armed conflict involving U.S. military forces.

Under the terms of the resolution, if a president must commit forces without congressional authorization, he or she must report to Congress within 48 hours to explain the reasons for the action. Unless Congress then declares war or approves continued action, U.S. forces must be withdrawn within 60–90 days. The law allows Congress to force a president to end the use of armed forces at any time if Congress passes a concurrent resolution to that effect.

Since the law's enactment, presidents have contested its constitutionality. They have also frequently ignored its requirement for congressional consultation prior to committing troops. Still, presidents have submitted 118 reports to Congress about military actions. For its part, Congress has not forced the issue by demanding troop withdrawals.

The war in Iraq in 2002 dramatized the constitutional standoff. In authorizing the use of force, Congress explicitly required the president to comply with the stipulations of the War Powers Resolution. However, in his signing statement, President George W. Bush

was careful to assert that his "signing . . . does not constitute any change in the long-standing positions of the executive branch on either the President's constitutional authority to use the Armed Forces . . . or on the constitutionality of the War Powers Resolution."

READING CHECK **Sequencing** Under the War Powers Resolution, what must a president do first?

Legislative and Judicial Powers

The Constitution calls for a separation of powers among the branches. However, in order to make the system of checks and balances effective, the Framers gave the president some powers in both the legislative and judicial branches of the government.

Legislative Powers The president has great power to influence the work of Congress in the role of chief agenda setter. Through the annual State of the Union address and the federal budget proposal, the president proposes legislation to Congress.

Furthermore, the president is permitted to suggest legislation at any time. It is common, in fact, for a president to work closely with lawmakers on a legislative agenda.

The president's main legislative power is the veto. While the Framers gave supreme lawmaking power to the legislative branch, they also wanted the president to have a voice in the process. That "voice" is the veto. After Congress passes a bill, a president can either sign it or veto it, meaning the president does not sign the bill into law.

Congress has the power to override the veto if two-thirds of the members of each house vote to do so. Overriding a veto is difficult since it can be hard to obtain enough votes. Because it is so hard to override a veto, veto power is a significant check on Congress. The threat of a veto can also hold power. If lawmakers believe that a president is going to veto a bill, they will change parts of the bill in order to gain presidential approval.

As discussed in Chapter 5, for a brief time, Congress allowed the president to use the line-item veto, which gave the president the power to cancel certain provisions in a bill without vetoing the entire bill. This procedure was made legal in 1996 but was struck down by the Supreme Court in 1998.

Judicial Powers The Constitution gives presidents two means of exercising judicial power. First, presidents may nominate the people who become federal judges and justices. Second, they may alter the sentences of people convicted of crimes through their powers of clemency, or mercy.

The Constitution grants the president the power to nominate federal judges and justices. With this power, a president can place men and women on the Supreme Court and other high courts who have similar political beliefs. The nomination power is checked by the Senate, which must approve and confirm all presidential nominees.

Nominating judges and justices is a great responsibility, especially in the case of the Supreme Court. Supreme Court justices serve a lifetime term. In most cases a president's appointment will remain on the bench for years after the president's term. The justice may continue to rule on cases in a way that supports a president's agenda, allowing a president to have an influence on government long after his or her term has ended.

In addition to the appointment of justices and judges, the Constitution says that the president "shall have the power to grant reprieves and pardons for offences against the United States." A **reprieve** postpones the carrying out of a sentence, or the length of time a person is put in jail. It is sometimes granted for humanitarian reasons or to give a person the chance to present new evidence. A **pardon** releases a convicted criminal from having to fulfill a sentence.

The president can also offer **amnesty**, which grants a group of offenders a general pardon for offenses committed. Though the

The President's Legislative and Judicial Powers

President George W. Bush (above) performs a presidential legislative power by signing the "No Child Left Behind" bill into law in 2002. Following the resignation of Richard Nixon, President Gerald Ford (right) pardoned Nixon for crimes during the Watergate scandal. President Ford reads the pardoning statement to the American public in a live television broadcast. *Why is pardoning an important presidential power?*

exact words do not actually appear in the Constitution, included in the power to pardon is the power to **commute**, or reduce, a person's sentence.

A president can issue reprieves, pardons, or commutations for federal crimes. The president has no authority over state cases, and clemency is not allowed in cases of impeachment. Once issued, however, a president's grant of clemency cannot be overturned by Congress or the courts.

Presidents may issue clemency in order to free a person wrongly convicted or for prior or current service to the nation. For example, following the assassination of President Abraham Lincoln, one of the alleged assassination conspirators, Dr. Samuel Mudd, was convicted and sent to prison. Mudd, who claimed that he had no ties to the assassination, served four years of a life sentence. In 1869 President Andrew Johnson pardoned Mudd after he helped stop a yellow fever epidemic that claimed the life of the prison doctor and many other prisoners.

Presidential pardons can be very controversial. President Gerald Ford was widely criticized for pardoning former president Richard Nixon after he resigned from office in 1974. President Bill Clinton also aroused anger for pardoning 140 people on his final day in office.

READING CHECK **Contrasting** What is the difference between a reprieve and a pardon?

Informal Powers

The informal powers of the president are those powers that are not directly stated in the Constitution but, nonetheless, play a major part in the success of a presidency. The two main sources of a president's informal powers are access to the media and the president's position as party leader.

Today a president is followed everywhere by a large group of reporters. Television and radio coverage is available to the president at any time. Presidents can easily present their case to the public at a media press conference. They also employ a professional staff of media experts dedicated to helping them shape their message and present it most effectively to the public.

A president who is skilled in using the media has greater success in persuading the public and building support. You have read about President Ronald Reagan's skills as a communicator. President John F. Kennedy was also able to charm reporters and voters with his easy manner at press conferences. A president who lacks such skills can find the job of leading the nation very difficult.

Another source of informal power comes from the president's position as party leader. Fellow party members in Congress are expected to follow the president's agenda and work for its passage. The president's staff works to ensure that there is a unified message among all members of the party. In return, the president offers support to fellow party members at election time.

A president's ability to take advantage of these informal sources of power varies. Presidents strive for high approval ratings, which are determined by national polls that rate how Americans feel about the president. A president who has a high approval rating and the support of the public is better able to command respect and lead effectively than a president with low approval ratings.

READING CHECK **Identifying the Main Idea** What is meant by the term *informal powers*?

Checks on the President's Powers

The Constitution places checks on the president and the executive branch. Though the nature of the presidency has changed over the years, these checks on the president remain powerful.

Formal Checks Presidential actions are subject to judicial review. Sometimes, a president's actions violate the Constitution. For example, in *Clinton* v. *City of New York* (1998) the Supreme Court ruled that the use of the line-item veto by President Clinton violated the Presentment Clause of the Constitution, since it gave the president undue power to amend or repeal parts of laws that had already been passed by Congress. This decision took away the right of the president to use the line-item veto.

RESPONSIBILITIES OF LEADERSHIP

Presidential pardons are clear examples of leaders doing what they think is necessary, rather than what is known to be popular. Citizenship calls for the same responsibility.

Presidential power is also checked by Congress. The Senate, for example, can block a president's choice for certain top positions. Congress can also choose to override a presidential veto if two-thirds of the members of each house vote to do so.

Informal Checks The media is the primary source of informal checks on presidential power. The media can keep the American public informed and alert to potential abuses of power. The Framers thought this task important enough to grant it special protection in the First Amendment. The importance of media scrutiny of government was demonstrated during the Nixon administration. The *New York Times* published the Pentagon Papers, revealing how the government had misled the nation about the Vietnam War. Without the media, the public would not have known of this information.

Public approval is another check on presidential power. Presidents today draw much power from their public image. Successful presidents have strong public support and can sometimes bully Congress to follow them. At the same time, presidents who lose public support have a harder time getting Congress to follow them.

READING CHECK Identifying Supporting Details
What are some of the informal checks on a president?

Changes in Presidential Power

The power and influence of the presidency has grown significantly over the years. Two factors have driven this change: the growth of government itself in response to new challenges and changing situations, and the growth of the nation as a world power.

The First 100 Years The Framers created a government based on a separation of powers, and they gave the majority of government power to Congress. They believed, in the words of James Madison in *Federalist Paper* No. 51, that "in a republican government, the legislative authority necessarily predominates."

Early presidents largely shared this belief and acted accordingly, deferring to Congress on most matters of domestic policy. Neither Presidents John Adams nor Thomas Jefferson vetoed a single piece of legislation during their collective 12 years in office. Jefferson believed that vetoes should be reserved for cases where a president doubts the constitutionality of a measure.

A few early presidents, however, did challenge congressional predominance in the 1800s. Jefferson stretched the boundaries of presidential power when he authorized the

Interactive Feature

Growth of Presidential Power

Throughout history, presidents have increased presidential power as they deemed necessary. *In what ways has presidential power grown from 1789 to the present?*

1789
George Washington sets the precedent for the two-term limit and creates a cabinet.

1803
Thomas Jefferson authorizes the purchase of Louisiana from France.

1829–1837
Andrew Jackson expands the powers of the presidency; he vetoes more bills than all six previous presidents combined.

1861–1865
Abraham Lincoln uses the power of the presidency to preserve the Union during the Civil War.

BORN TO COMMAND
OF VETO MEMORY
HAD I BEEN CONSULTED
KING ANDREW the FIRST

Andrew Jackson portrayed as King Andrew the First in a political cartoon

Boundaries of the United States following the purchase of Louisiana

purchase of Louisiana from France in 1803, even though the Constitution gave him no clear authority to do so. Andrew Jackson, who was president from 1829 to 1837, viewed the president as the one true representative of the people. To Jackson, this gave a president power that even Congress could not claim. He thus reserved for himself the right to veto acts of Congress simply because he disagreed with them. Most presidents since Jackson have taken a similar position.

Congress did not take Jackson's assertiveness kindly. When he withdrew government funds from the congressionally chartered Second Bank of the United States, Congress censured, or reprimanded, him.

Presidential Power Expands The Civil War marked a turning point in presidential power. Not only did government itself expand to meet the emergency, but President Abraham Lincoln also took on great powers. Lincoln believed that the threat to the nation endangered the Constitution, which he was sworn as president to preserve. Therefore, any steps he took that were necessary to defend the nation were legal.

Interestingly, Lincoln's relations with Congress were friendly. He deferred to it on most domestic issues and rarely used his veto. Once the war and Reconstruction had ended, Congress resumed its traditional leading role in national affairs. But Lincoln's actions were to prove a model for later presidents intent on vigorous action.

President Theodore Roosevelt was one such person. He saw the presidency as a "bully pulpit" that shaped public opinion and, if necessary, pressured Congress to pass legislation he supported. Roosevelt believed that the rise of big business presented the nation with new challenges and that government needed new tools to meet those challenges. He convinced Congress to give the executive branch stronger powers to regulate commerce, to protect park lands, and to ensure the safety of the food supply.

The Great Depression offered President Franklin Roosevelt an opportunity to expand presidential powers even further. To meet the economic crisis, he convinced Congress to create a host of new government programs, including Social Security. These New Deal programs represented a shift in the way Americans thought about government and its responsibility. People now looked to the government, and to the executive branch, to help solve problems in society.

By the 1960s and 1970s, some observers began to worry about the growth of presidential power. For conservatives, the government had simply become too big.

One of Franklin Roosevelt's New Deal programs, the Works Progress Administration (WPA) provided public-works jobs to Americans in need of relief during the Great Depression.

THINK central Interactive

thinkcentral.com
KEYWORD: SGO PRE

1901–1909
Theodore Roosevelt uses presidential power to break up trusts, establish conservation lands, and gain control of the Panama Canal.

1933–1938
Franklin Roosevelt expands the power of the executive branch with New Deal programs he establishes during the Great Depression.

1981–1989
Ronald Reagan greatly increases defense spending in order to fight the Cold War.

2001–2009
George W. Bush expands the national security powers of the presidency in an effort to protect the nation from terrorist threats.

Theodore Roosevelt uses his "Big Stick" over big businesses and trusts.

NO MOLLY-CODDLING HERE

The Granger Collection, New York

As unofficial leader of the free world, Reagan calls for the dismantling of the Berlin Wall.

THE PRESIDENCY **177**

Liberals felt the presidency had taken on qualities resembling those of a monarchy. Citing conerns for national security, they talked about an *imperial presidency* in which executive power went virtually unchecked.

These concerns were not unfounded. Government today is vastly more powerful than it was at the time of the founding of the nation, and most of that power is vested in the executive branch. Moreover, following victories in World Wars I and II, the United States became the most powerful nation in the world. Again, much of that power is concentrated in the executive branch, with the president at its head. By virtue of the nation's economic and military strength, American presidents are today the most powerful leaders in the world.

Presidential Power and the Media One of the ways modern presidents project that power is through the media. This is nothing new. Though the technology has changed, presidents have long relied on the media to get their message out. Presidents in the early 1800s used posters, pamphlets, and friendly newspapers. Franklin Roosevelt used radio in his famous "fireside chats." Modern presidents use television and the Internet. The goal is the same: to convince voters—and Congress—to support their plans.

As you read earlier, the media can scrutinize and criticize a president. Presidents go to great efforts to control how their message and image is presented. They prepare rigorously for press conferences and major speeches. They employ experts, often from the media itself, to help them craft their presentations. Choosing the right phrase or backdrop can mean the difference between voter acceptance or indifference. Even "town hall meetings" are carefully scripted to avoid anything embarrassing or unexpected.

Despite these efforts, the power available to modern presidents through the media can also work against them. Intense media scrutiny can quickly damage less popular presidents and, as a result, decrease their power as president.

READING CHECK Summarizing How have the people's expectations of presidents changed over time?

RESPONSIBILITIES OF LEADERSHIP

In using the media, presidents balance how much to promise the public with the risk of raising its expectations far beyond what he or she can actually do.

SECTION 2 ASSESSMENT

THINK central **Online Quiz**
thinkcentral.com
KEYWORD: SGO PRE HP

Reviewing Ideas and Terms

1. **a. Define** What are **executive orders** and **executive privilege**?
   b. Explain Why do you think it is necessary for a president to be involved in the hiring of so many people?

2. **a. Define** What is an **executive agreement**?
   b. Predict What might happen if a president were unable to commit military forces without first getting the approval of Congress?

3. **a. Define** What is the meaning of the terms **reprieve**, **pardon**, and **commute**?
   b. Draw Conclusions In what circumstances do you think a president might rightfully use a veto?

4. **a. Describe** What is the role of the media as a source of a president's informal powers?
   b. Predict How do you think popularity and public approval ratings affect a president's ability to use the informal powers of the office?

5. **a. Identify** What are some formal checks on the president's power?
   b. Analyze Why do you think a popular president is able to push Congress into following an agenda?

6. **a. Define** What is meant by the term *imperial presidency*?
   b. Elaborate How do you think the growing military power of the United States has given it more power in general? Explain your answer.

Critical Thinking

7. **Rank** Copy the chart below and identify examples of the powers given. Which power do you feel is the most important? Which is the least important? Explain your answer.

Executive	
Diplomatic	
Military	
Legislative	
Judicial	
Informal	

FOCUS ON WRITING

8. **Expository** Review the ideas of the early presidents regarding the proper relationship among the president, the people, and Congress. Think about the ways in which these ideas have changed and how they have remained constant. Write a brief article that evaluates this relationship.

The Presidential Power to Make War

Are the chief executive's expanding war powers constitutionally sound?

U.S. soldiers talk to a local Afghani farmer through an interpreter while on patrol in the Nuristan Province of Afghanistan.

THE ISSUE

The president of the United States is arguably the most powerful person in the world. Over the years, presidential powers—especially those involving war and national security—have increased. As part of the War Powers Resolution, enacted to check increasing executive power after the Vietnam War, Congress required the president to seek its approval before committing U.S. troops abroad for longer than 60 days. Presidents have disputed the constitutionality of the law. The legislative and executive branch have yet to resolve the issue once and for all.

VIEWPOINTS

The power to make war is a vital and constitutional presidential power. The Constitution names the president commander in chief of the armed forces in Article II, Section 2. As commander in chief, one of the president's primary duties is to protect the immediate security interests of the country. To fulfill their oath to "preserve, protect, and defend the Constitution," presidents have at times been forced to act in secrecy or without the full support of Congress. Citing reasons of national security, presidents sometimes decide that it is necessary to bypass certain channels or checks on their war-making powers. In fulfilling the responsibility as the commander in chief, a president must make quick and effective decisions for the good of the nation. Limiting this power would undermine the authority of the presidency.

The scope of presidential war powers is too expansive and is overstepping its constitutional bounds. The Framers did not intend for the chief executive to have as much power as is commonly accepted today. Critics of expanding executive power say that recent presidents have misinterpreted the implicit rights of the president outlined in the Constitution to commit troops to war. Committing a nation to war without the approval of the people or their representatives is characteristic of a monarchy or dictatorship, not a democracy. Congress has been criticized in recent years for giving the president unusual unilateral, or one-sided, powers following the terrorist attacks of September 11, 2001. Since then, some in Congress have worked to check presidential war-making powers. So far, they have been unsuccessful.

What Is Your Opinion?

1. Why do you think presidential power has expanded over time? Explain your answer.

2. Should the president be able to commit troops without congressional approval? Why or why not?

THINK central **Practice Online**

thinkcentral.com
KEYWORD: SGO PRE

The President's Administration

BEFORE YOU READ

Main Idea

The president leads a large team of people who help carry out the duties of the office. This team includes a staff of advisers, the vice president, and members of the cabinet.

Reading Focus

1. What is the Executive Office of the President, and what are its duties?

2. How has the role of the vice president changed over time?

3. What is the cabinet, and how does it work with the president?

Key Terms

administration
Executive Office of the President
White House Office
chief of staff
National Security Council
Council of Economic Advisers
Office of Management and Budget
executive departments

TAKING NOTES As you read, take notes on the president's administration. Record your notes in a graphic organizer like this one.

The President's Administration

WHY IT MATTERS

The President's Staff Early presidential staffs were small, consisting of little more than personal secretaries who performed a variety of tasks, such as communicating with Congress or dealing with job seekers. As late as 1900, President William McKinley had a staff of fewer than 30 people, including a gardener and telephone operator. But in 1902, in order to accommodate this ever-expanding presidential staff, President Theodore Roosevelt had a new wing, the West Wing, added to the White House. In 1933 President Franklin Roosevelt remodeled the West Wing in order to accommodate even more presidential staff members.

The West Wing today is the nerve center of the executive branch. The president's office, known as the Oval Office, is situated in one corner of the West Wing and is attached to the Cabinet Room, which is where the cabinet holds meetings. The

vice president, press secretary, White House counsel, national security adviser, congressional liaison, and the chief of staff all have offices and conduct their daily work within the West Wing. The West Wing also has a press briefing room where the president can meet with the press at any time or have the press secretary share the president's ideas.

In the West Wing, the president is surrounded by key staffers ready to assist with the daily work of the executive branch as well as handle unexpected emergencies. The West Wing is a symbol of how the scope of presidential power, and the presidency itself, has grown since the Framers first created the position of president of the United States. ◼

Inside THE West Wing

The West Wing undergoes construction in 1934. George W. Bush's cabinet (inset) meets in the Cabinet Room of the West Wing.

Executive Office of the President

A president's **administration** is made up of all the people who work for the executive branch—from your local mail carrier on up to the president. Most of these people are career government employees. But the top ranks of an administration are filled by people appointed to their posts by the president. These people usually change when a new president is elected.

Many of the top administration officials belong to the **Executive Office of the President** (EOP). The EOP consists of a number of separate offices that help the president formulate policy. Among them are the White House Office—the center of much of the daily business in the White House—the National Security Council, the Council of Economic Advisers, and the Office of Management and Budget. You will read more about each of these offices below.

The Formation of the EOP The now-vast organization known as the EOP did not exist 100 years ago. Early presidents had small personal staffs. They also relied on a circle of informal, unpaid advisers. Until the turn of the last century, most presidents continued to look to the cabinet as their primary source of advice and assistance.

Starting with the presidency of Theodore Roosevelt, an era of activist government led to an expansion of the president's staff. During the Great Depression in the 1930s, President Franklin Roosevelt and Congress created many new government programs and agencies.

In 1939 Roosevelt asked Congress to authorize a new organizational structure to help manage these new agencies—the Executive Office of the President. Since then, new challenges—global leadership following World War II, the threat posed by nuclear weapons, the need to manage an ever-rising tide of information flooding into the White House—have spurred further growth of the Executive Office of the President.

With some significant exceptions, members of the EOP are nominated by the president and confirmed by the Senate.

Today they are often some of the most influential people in a president's administration. As one top staff member of the Clinton White House has said, "In a very fast-moving world . . . staff in the closest proximity to the President can have the greatest degree of power in influencing the decisions of that President."

The White House Office At the heart of the EOP is the **White House Office**. The White House Office consists of the president's key personal and political staff. They are, in short, the White House staff. Most work in the White House itself or across the street in the Old Executive Office Building. They serve without Senate confirmation.

The president determines the size of his or her White House Office. President George W. Bush, for example, has had more than 400 people on his White House staff. This is a bit larger than President Clinton's staff, but smaller than the nearly 600 employed in President Nixon's White House Office.

To manage the White House Office the president appoints a **chief of staff**. The precise role of the chief of staff varies from president to president. In some cases, the chief of staff focuses on managing the everyday operations of the White House Office. In other cases, the chief of staff is a primary presidential adviser who controls all access to the president and helps map political strategy. President Ronald Reagan's first chief of staff, James Baker, took an active role. In the first term of Reagan's presidency, Baker exercised a great deal of influence with the president over domestic policy.

The president's personal secretary and legal counsel report to the chief of staff. In addition to directing these two key staffers, the chief of staff also oversees teams charged with political tasks such as handling relations with Congress and the cabinet, dealing with presidential mail, planning presidential appearances, and hiring other members of the president's staff.

The chief of staff also manages the work of the staff offices that are responsible for getting out the president's message. These offices include the professional speechwriters who work in the Office of Speechwriting.

SELECTED WHITE HOUSE OFFICES

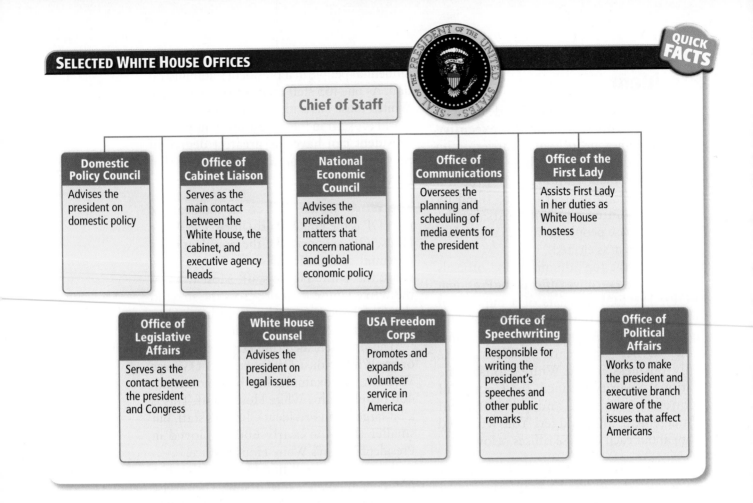

Chief of Staff

Domestic Policy Council
Advises the president on domestic policy

Office of Cabinet Liaison
Serves as the main contact between the White House, the cabinet, and executive agency heads

National Economic Council
Advises the president on matters that concern national and global economic policy

Office of Communications
Oversees the planning and scheduling of media events for the president

Office of the First Lady
Assists First Lady in her duties as White House hostess

Office of Legislative Affairs
Serves as the contact between the president and Congress

White House Counsel
Advises the president on legal issues

USA Freedom Corps
Promotes and expands volunteer service in America

Office of Speechwriting
Responsible for writing the president's speeches and other public remarks

Office of Political Affairs
Works to make the president and executive branch aware of the issues that affect Americans

The White House press secretary, whose job it is to handle relations with news reporters, is also a part of the communications staff. This particular position has taken on increasing importance in recent decades as mass media, including television and the Internet, has become more and more important to the success of a presidency.

National Security Council One of the most important parts of the EOP is the **National Security Council** (NSC). The National Security Council brings together the top military, foreign affairs, and intelligence officials in the administration to coordinate U.S. national security policy.

The NSC was created in 1947. At the dawn of the Cold War rivalry with the Soviet Union, it became apparent that national security required more than maintaining strong military forces. A coordinated plan combining vigorous diplomatic efforts, military preparedness, and secret intelligence-gathering activities was now essential. Congress established the National Security

Council to manage these coordinated planning efforts. Eventually, the NSC became part of the Executive Office of the President.

The president chairs the National Security Council. The activities of the NSC are coordinated by the assistant to the president for national security affairs, also known as the national security adviser. This person is a presidential appointee who does not require Senate approval.

Presidents have differed in how much they rely on their national security advisers. In some cases, the national security adviser has ranked among the most powerful people in the administration. President Richard Nixon, for example, relied heavily on his national security adviser, Henry Kissinger, sending him as a secret envoy to negotiate agreements with foreign nations, often bypassing his secretary of state.

NSC meetings include the vice president, the secretaries of state, treasury, and defense, the director of national intelligence, and the chairman of the Joint Chiefs of Staff. The latter is a group composed of the heads of each major branch of the armed forces. The president's chief of staff, chief counsel, and the attorney general may also be involved in NSC meetings. Other members of the cabinet, including the secretary of homeland security, or senior executives may be invited, depending on the matters under discussion.

Council of Economic Advisers Congress created the **Council of Economic Advisers** (CEA) as a part of the EOP in 1946. The CEA provides the president with expert analysis of the economy. Its members examine the economy to see how <u>trends</u> and events may affect the president's economic policy as well as how economic policy is affecting the economy. The CEA also assists the president in forming economic policy.

The Council of Economic Advisers consists of three members nominated by the president. These members must be confirmed by the Senate. In addition to these three advisers, the CEA has its own staff of assistants and advisers. The CEA helps the president prepare the annual *Economic Report*. This report is a detailed study of the nation's economy, published soon after the president submits his or her budget.

It is important to note that the CEA is not the same as the National Economic Council, which is a part of the White House Office. That office is focused on coordinating government-wide economic policies.

The OMB Another key component of the EOP is the **Office of Management and Budget** (OMB). The purpose of the OMB is to help develop the federal budget and to oversee its execution by the agencies in the executive branch. The OMB also gathers information and sets policies regarding the management of government finances and the purchase of goods, services, and property for the entire government. The OMB works not only with the president and other members of the executive branch but also with Congress.

The OMB is the largest organization in the EOP, employing more than 500 people. It is headed by an appointed director, who is nominated by the president and confirmed by the Senate. Many of the remaining OMB employees are not political appointees but rather are career staff. That is, they are

people with specialized skills who are not replaced when a new president comes to office. You will read more about the Office of Management and Budget in Chapter 7.

READING CHECK Summarizing What are some of the primary offices located within the Executive Office of the President?

The Vice President

The vice president is also a part of the president's administration. This position is unique in that it is the only other elected position in a president's administration.

The Constitution assigns the office of the vice president three major duties: presiding over the Senate, opening and counting the electoral votes in presidential elections, and serving as president if the president cannot do the job. To date, nine vice presidents have had to perform this last duty. Presidents John Tyler, Millard Fillmore, Andrew Johnson, Chester Arthur, Theodore Roosevelt, Calvin Coolidge, Harry Truman, and Lyndon Johnson all became president after the death of a president. President Gerald Ford became president after Richard Nixon resigned.

The Early Vice Presidency In the 1800s, the vice president's role did not amount to much more than carrying out the duties outlined above. They generally did not attend cabinet meetings or help make policy. The very first vice president, John Adams, did not even run for office with George Washington. Adams came in second in the presidential election and was thus made vice president. In 1804, however, Congress passed the Twelfth Amendment, requiring separate ballots for president and vice president.

Besides assuming the presidency in the event of a vacancy, the main role of the vice president in the past was to help elect the president. A vice presidential candidate can help balance the ticket—bring in votes from a certain political group or particular geographical areas that the presidential candidate cannot get on his or her own.

For example, Abraham Lincoln's first vice president was Hannibal Hamlin, from Maine. When it came time for re-election, Lincoln felt secure in winning Maine's vote.

ACADEMIC VOCABULARY

trends tendencies or developments

The Vice Presidency

Then

Many early vice presidents felt as though the job was not challenging and that the position held little prestige. The first vice president, John Adams, said of the position:

"My country has in its wisdom contrived for me the most insignificant office that ever the invention of man contrived or his imagination conceived."

Now

Today's vice presidents, in comparison to earlier ones, have taken a far more active role. As vice president in the Bush administration, Dick Cheney demonstrated this active role during his two terms in office by:

- Attending cabinet meetings and sitting on the National Security Council
- Making several visits to foreign nations as one of President Bush's foreign policy liaisons
- Serving as a key adviser to the president

How was Dick Cheney's role as vice president different from that of John Adams?

So he chose Andrew Johnson, from the less-certain state of Tennessee, for his second running mate.

The few formal duties for the vice president have both pleased and troubled the people who held the office. Thomas Jefferson had a positive outlook on the position:

PRIMARY SOURCE

❝A more tranquil and unoffending station could not have been found for me. It will give me philosophical evenings in the winter [while at the Senate] and rural days in the summer.❞

—Thomas Jefferson, letter to Benjamin Rush, 1797

On the other hand, Theodore Roosevelt, who served under William McKinley, called the vice presidency a "steppingstone to . . . oblivion" and complained, "I would a great deal rather be anything . . . than Vice President." John Nance Garner, who was vice president under Franklin Roosevelt, called it the "spare tire on the automobile of government."

The Modern Vice Presidency Since the 1970s presidents have begun to rely more heavily on their vice presidents to help make policy and carry out their programs. Jimmy Carter's vice president, Walter Mondale, established a tradition of weekly lunch meetings with the president. Some recent vice presidents have also been given special assignments. Bill Clinton charged Vice President Al Gore with a project to reform the organization of the executive branch. Similarly, President George W. Bush relied heavily on his vice president, Dick Cheney, who took an extremely active role in assisting the president with foreign policy and energy programs.

To help them carry out their duties, vice presidents today have their own staffs. Additionally, the vice president's office is in close proximity to the Oval Office in the West Wing, which allows for more interaction between the two offices.

READING CHECK **Making Generalizations** How has the role of the vice president changed over time?

The Cabinet

Another key part of the president's administration is the cabinet. As discussed in Chapter 3, the cabinet is an organization made up of the heads of the executive departments. The **executive departments** are responsible for carrying out laws, administering programs, and making regulations in their particular area of responsibility. You will take a look at the departments in more detail in Chapter 7.

The main task of each department head, or secretary, is to run his or her department, helping to formulate and carry out the president's policies. When assembled as the cabinet, though, the secretaries can act as an advisory body to the president. Cabinet members are nominated by the president, but they must be confirmed by the Senate. In recent years, presidents have given other administrative officers, like the director of the OMB and the chief of staff, cabinet rank.

The Cabinet's History The Articles of Confederation called for committees similar to what we know today as the executive departments. But these departments were a part of the legislative branch of government, not the executive branch.

The Constitution does not directly mention the term *cabinet*. It does say, though, that a president "may require the opinion, in writing, of the principal officer of each of the executive departments." From these words, as well as the ideas from the Articles of Confederation, came the plan for creating an advisory body of "principal officers," or a cabinet. President George Washington created the first cabinet, which consisted of only four members—the secretaries of state, war, and treasury, and the attorney general.

Historically, cabinets provided valuable guidance to presidents. In order to receive the best advice, some presidents choose people with varying political views to serve as members of their cabinet. Abraham Lincoln, for example, assembled a cabinet that included many top figures from his political party. This cabinet, however, included bitter political rivals, many of whom had run against Lincoln for the Republican presidential nomination in 1860. There was often disagreement and dissent between these cabinet members. Despite these differing views, or perhaps, because of them, Lincoln got much useful advice and input from his cabinet.

Some presidents choose a different course, placing skilled administrators on their cabinets rather than powerful political figures. Presidents also often choose cabinet members with strong ties to the business community—an important source of funding during election campaigns.

The Cabinet Today Today's cabinets are nearly four times as large as the first cabinet. As new executive departments have been created, the size of the cabinet has increased. Today there are 16 official cabinet positions, including the vice president. As you read earlier, some presidents choose to invite other high-ranking officials to sit on the cabinet, such as the chief of staff.

Recent presidents have varied in how much they relied on their cabinet for advice. President Dwight Eisenhower, for example, made heavy use of his cabinet. Most of his successors, however, have used it less. As you read earlier, the role of other advisory bodies, such as the Executive Office of the President, has increased.

READING CHECK **Identifying the Main Idea** How has the cabinet and the degree to which a president relies on it changed over time?

SECTION 3 ASSESSMENT

THINK central **Online Quiz**
thinkcentral.com
KEYWORD: SGO PRE HP

Reviewing Ideas and Terms

1. **a. Define** What is the **Executive Office of the President**?
   b. Make Inferences What has led to the growth of the Executive Office of the President?
   c. Evaluate Why do you think a president might rely more on the **White House Office** than on the cabinet for counsel?

2. **a. Identify** What are the formal duties of the vice president?
   b. Summarize How have presidents traditionally regarded the role of vice president?
   c. Elaborate What qualities do you think a presidential candidate should look for in a vice president?

3. **a. Identify** Who makes up the cabinet?
   b. Make Generalizations Besides the job of running the **executive departments**, what have presidents expected their cabinet members to do for them?
   c. Rank What do you think would be the most important quality to have in a cabinet member?

Critical Thinking

4. **Compare and Contrast** Copy the Venn diagram below and use information from the section to compare and contrast the roles and functions of the Executive Office of the President, vice president, and the cabinet.

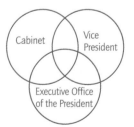

Cabinet — Vice President — Executive Office of the President

FOCUS ON WRITING

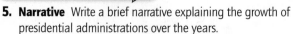

5. **Narrative** Write a brief narrative explaining the growth of presidential administrations over the years.

Executive Power and the President

Deciding how to organize the executive branch and check the power of the president was a difficult decision for the Framers. Read to explore the limitations that the Framers placed on the presidency.

How did the delegates think about executive power, and what questions did organizing the executive branch raise? The Articles of Confederation did not provide for an executive branch, but the Confederation Congress had found it necessary to create executive officials for specific purposes, including coordination of foreign affairs and management of the treasury. The Framers wanted to give the executive branch of the new government enough power and independence to fulfill its responsibilities. In contrast to the deliberative nature of Congress, the executive needed "energy"—the capacity to act quickly when necessary for the common defense, to preserve the public peace, and in international relations. However, the delegates did not want to give the executive any power or independence that could be abused.

The Philadelphia Convention did not discuss the executive branch until after it had resolved most issues concerning Congress. No delegate had come with a plan for organizing the executive. The Virginia Plan said only that the national executive should be elected by the national legislature, not what the executive branch should look like, or what its powers should be.

To achieve the balance between an energetic executive and limited government, the delegates had to resolve a number of questions. Each question concerned the best way to establish an executive strong enough to check the power of the legislature but not so powerful that it would endanger republican government. Three key matters needed to be decided.

First, would there be more than one chief executive? Many Framers agreed that there should be a single executive to avoid conflict between two or more leaders of equal power. Some delegates argued also that it would be easier for Congress to keep a watchful eye on a single executive. Others argued for a plural executive, claiming that such an arrangement would be less likely to become tyrannical. The Framers agreed that there would be one president of the United States. They also assumed that there would be an executive branch composed of departments.

Second, how long should the chief executive remain in office? The Committee on Detail recommended a seven-year term for the president, but many delegates thought seven years too long. The Committee on Postponed Matters changed the term to four years, and the convention adopted that proposal.

Third, should the executive be eligible for re-election? Under the Committee on Detail's proposal for a seven-year term of office the president would not have been eligible for re-election. When the term was reduced to four years, the Framers decided to allow the president to serve more than one term. The Constitution originally set no limit on the number of times a president could be re-elected.

How did the Framers envision the presidency?

The Framers envisioned the president as an official above partisan politics. Publius explained in *Federalist Paper* No. 68 that they wanted the president to be a person who had earned the esteem and confidence of the entire nation, with a character "pre-eminent for ability and virtue." They designed the electoral college to identify people of such character. There was no expectation that candidates would campaign for the office. The Framers thought that the president should remain above partisan politics. But their expectations were unmet even during President Washington's administration, when factions arose that led to the development of political parties.

The Framers did not want the president to have the powers of a monarch. But they did want the president to be "energetic," a quality they contrasted with legislative "deliberation." "Energy" refers to the capacity of one person to act efficiently and vigorously on behalf of the nation. The Framers feared what they called a "feeble executive." As Hamilton argued in *Federalist Paper* No. 70, "A feeble execution is but another phrase for a bad execution; and a government ill executed, whatever it may be in theory, must be, in practice, a bad government."

How do the president's powers expand in war and emergency?

During wars and emergencies, presidents commonly exercise powers not granted by the Constitution. Grover Cleveland (in office, 1885–1889 and 1893–1897) deployed federal troops without congressional authorization in 1894 to put down a strike among Pullman train car workers. President Franklin Roosevelt transferred destroyers to Great Britain in 1940, a year before the United States entered World War II. Harry Truman (in office, 1945–1953) ordered the secretary of commerce to operate the nation's steel mills during a strike to ensure an adequate supply of steel during the Korean War.

On occasion Congress and the Supreme Court have tried to rein in the president. In 1952 the Supreme Court held that President Truman exceeded his authority in seizing the steel mills. Congress debated withdrawing funding for the Vietnam War when the war began to lose public support in the 1970s. In 2006 the Court held that President George W. Bush's creation of special military commissions to try alleged terrorists violated the Uniform Code of Military Justice passed by Congress in 1950 and the 1949 Geneva Convention, an international treaty that the United States had signed. These examples aside, during wars and national emergencies both Congress and the courts tend to defer to the president.

Reviewing Ideas and Terms

1. **Identify** What issues did the delegates have to decide regarding the organization of the executive branch?

2. **Make Generalizations** How is the system of checks and balances designed to limit the exercise of presidential power?

Critical Thinking

3. **Evaluate** How would you define a "feeble" executive? In what ways might a feeble executive be as dangerous as an overly "energetic" executive?

Connecting Online

Visit thinkcentral.com for review and enrichment activities related to this chapter.

THINK central

KEYWORD: SGO PRE

Quiz and Review

GOV 101
Examine key concepts in this chapter.

ONLINE QUIZZES
Take a practice quiz for each section in this chapter.

Activities

eActivities
Complete Webquests and Internet research activities.

INTERACTIVE FEATURES
Explore interactive versions of maps and charts.

KEEP IT CURRENT
Link to current events in U.S. government.

Partners

American Bar Association Division for Public Education
Learn more about the law, your rights and responsibilities.

Center for Civic Education
Promoting an enlightened and responsible citizenry committed to democratic principles and actively engaged in the practice of democracy.

Online Textbook

ONLINE SIMULATIONS
Learn about U.S. government through simulations you can complete online.

 Click for More Read more about key topics online.

Comprehension and Critical Thinking

SECTION 1 *(pp. 162–168)*

1. **a. Review Key Terms** For each term, write a sentence that explains its significance or meaning: chief executive, commander in chief, diplomacy, foreign policy, succession.

   b. Explain How has the term of office of the presidency changed over the years?

   c. Evaluate Do you think presidents should be judged by their personal qualities as shown in their behavior in public?

SECTION 2 *(pp. 169–178)*

2. **a. Review Key Terms** For each term, write a sentence that explains its significance or meaning: executive orders, executive privilege, reprieve, pardon, commute.

   b. Make Inferences What does a president need in order to effectively exercise the informal powers of the presidency?

   c. Predict What might happen if the president alone did not have the power to negotiate with foreign governments?

SECTION 3 *(pp. 180–185)*

3. **a. Review Key Terms** For each term, write a sentence that explains its significance or meaning: Executive Office of the President, chief of staff, National Security Council, Council of Economic Advisers, Office of Management and Budget.

   b. Contrast How does the cabinet differ from the Executive Office of the President?

   c. Evaluate How do you think the growth in the size of presidential administrations affects the president's power?

Critical Reading

Read the passage in Section 1 that begins with the heading "Election to Office." Then answer the questions that follow.

4. Which group of people casts the official vote for the candidates running for president of the United States?

   A American citizens

   B electors chosen by each state

   C the cabinet

   D members of the Senate

5. How do most states today choose their electors to the electoral college?

   A The governor selects the representatives.

   B State legislatures appoint representatives.

   C Representatives are elected by popular vote.

   D The current vice president chooses representatives.

Read the passage in Section 2 that begins with the heading "Diplomatic Powers." Then answer the questions that follow.

6. What is one way that a president can enter into an agreement with a foreign country?

A by exercising the right of executive privilege

B by issuing executive agreements

C by nominating judges and justices to the Supreme Court

D through the use of line-item vetoes

7. What are the purposes of treaties?

A to make agreements between the United States and foreign countries that do not require the advice and consent of the Senate

B to ensure the president's right to declare war on another country

C to end conflicts, form alliances, and establish trade relationships

D to formally recognize the existence of a foreign government

RESPONSIBILITIES OF LEADERSHIP

8. Select a president from any time period in U.S. history and conduct research on how that particular president asserted **presidential authority and power**. Consider how that president used executive, diplomatic, military, legislative, judicial, and informal powers while in office. Use your research to write a short biography of that president. Be sure to discuss the ways your president exercised each of the powers of the presidency. Then create a bar graph that illustrates the six areas of presidential power. Rate on a scale of 1 to 5 (5 being the highest rating and 1 being the lowest) how you think that particular president executed presidential power in each area. Share your graph results with the class, using examples from your biography. Be prepared to support your conclusions.

CONNECTING TO THE CONSTITUTION

9. Go to your school or community library and research some of the suggested alternatives to the present term of office of the president. What advantages and disadvantages do these alternatives have?

Political Cartoon *The electoral college is the constitutional framework for electing the president and vice president of the United States. Critics of the electoral college system today are opposed to it because the winner in the electoral vote may not be the winner of the popular vote. Others think that the system provides a more equal voice to less densely populated areas of the country.*

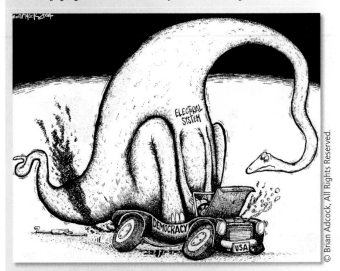

10. Analyze What is happening in this cartoon?

11. Draw Conclusions How does the imagery in the cartoon illustrate the cartoonist's opinion of the U.S. electoral system?

WRITING FOR THE SAT

Think about the following issue:

The power and responsibilities of the president have grown and changed a great deal since 1790. Today some people consider the president to be among the most powerful people in the world. This power is not something that should be taken lightly or abused.

12. Assignment Do presidents today have too much power? Should there be greater limitations placed on presidential power? Write a short essay in which you develop your position on this issue. Support your point of view with reasoning and examples from your reading and studies.

CHAPTER 7

The Executive Branch at Work

> "IF GOVERNMENT IS TO SERVE
> ANY PURPOSE IT IS TO DO FOR OTHERS
> WHAT THEY ARE UNABLE TO
> DO FOR THEMSELVES."
> —LYNDON JOHNSON, 1964

CHAPTER AT A GLANCE

SECTION 1

The Federal Bureaucracy

- The federal bureaucracy is made up of all of the agencies, departments, and bureaus of the federal government.
- Members of the civil service are responsible for carrying out the work of the federal government.
- Jobs in the federal bureaucracy were once filled through the use of the spoils system. Today's civil service system guarantees that qualified people are placed in government jobs.

SECTION 2

Executive Departments and Independent Agencies

- The executive departments, headed by the members of the cabinet, are charged with administering a broad range of government programs and services.
- As the size and power of the United States has grown, so too have the number of executive departments and their responsibilities.
- Independent agencies, outside the executive departments, focus on particular aspects of governing that cannot be attended to by the executive departments.
- Bureaucrats, members of Congress, and outside interest groups sometimes collaborate to protect and advance mutual interests.

SECTION 3

Financing Government

- The government funds its operations through various taxes and loans.
- Government spending is divided into two main types: mandatory spending and discretionary spending.
- The president works with Congress to create a budget to fund the vast number of government programs and activities.
- The government's fiscal and monetary policies can affect the economy.

CONNECTING TO THE CONSTITUTION

Our nation's system of government is based on constitutional law established by the United States Constitution. See the "We the People: The Citizen and the Constitution" pages in this chapter for an in-depth exploration of how the Constitution allows for the establishment of departments and agencies in the federal bureaucracy and the bureaucracy's role in the executive branch.

Internal Revenue Service tax return–processing center in Cincinnati, Ohio

The Federal Bureaucracy

Main Idea

The federal bureaucracy includes all the organizations and agencies of the executive branch. The civil service system is used to place qualified civilians into positions within the agencies of the federal bureaucracy.

Reading Focus

1. What is the federal bureaucracy?

2. What is the civil service, and how has it changed over the years?

Key Terms

bureaucracy
bureaucrats
civil service
spoils system

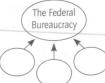

TAKING NOTES As you read, take notes on what makes up the federal bureaucracy. Record your notes in a graphic organizer like this one.

The Federal Bureaucracy

The Nation's
Largest Employer

WHY IT MATTERS

Working for the Federal Government

The federal government is the largest employer in the United States. More than 2.7 million people work for the government, excluding military personnel. That number translates into 1 out of every 50 nonmilitary workers in the United States. The vast majority of these workers are members of the executive branch.

Only a fraction of this gigantic workforce is located in the nation's capital. In fact, about 300,000 federal employees actually work in the Washington, D.C., area. Because different jobs require employees to work in different areas, this vast enterprise is spread across all 50 states and in more than 200 countries. It is divided into hundreds of different organizations, each devoted to a specific task. Taken together, this collection of agencies, bureaus, commissions, and departments is known as the federal bureaucracy. ■

What Is the Federal Bureaucracy?

A **bureaucracy** is any organization, either in government or the private sector, having the following features: a clear formal structure, a division of labor, and a set of rules and procedures by which it operates. The bureaucracy associated with the U.S. executive branch is called the federal bureaucracy.

The federal bureaucracy contains all the agencies and departments of the executive branch, including the office of the vice president, the Executive Office of the President, the executive departments, and the independent agencies. As the chart on the next page shows, there are three types of independent agencies: independent executive agencies, independent regulatory commissions, and government corporations. You will read more about each type in Section 2.

The federal bureaucracy is large and has grown throughout U.S. history—although it is actually smaller today than it was a few decades ago. In the late 1960s it employed about 2.9 million people. By the early 1990s it had topped 3 million. Today about 2.7 million people work for the federal bureaucracy.

Some of this recent reduction is due to an increase in the federal government's use of outside contractors. Contractors are private businesses who are paid to perform specific jobs. However, numerous state and local government employees have jobs that are paid

The Executive Branch

The executive branch, led by the president, consists of hundreds of departments and agencies whose employees make up the federal bureaucracy.

PRESIDENT

Executive Office of the President

Executive Departments
The 15 executive departments have broad administrative responsibilities. The Department of State has embassies all over the world, including this one in Santiago, Chile.

Independent Regulatory Commissions
Independent regulatory commissions regulate specific areas of the economy. The Nuclear Regulatory Commission, for example, is responsible for regulating all nuclear facilities and materials.

Vice President

Independent Executive Agencies
Independent executive agencies manage particular aspects of the federal government. For example, the Environmental Protection Agency works to safeguard the environment, which this EPA worker demonstrates by collecting water samples.

Government Corporations
Government corporations, which are run like businesses, provide Americans with a variety of services. Amtrak provides passenger rail service to all areas of the continental United States.

Skills FOCUS **INTERPRETING CHARTS**

What are the three types of independent agencies and their primary functions?

---

for largely, if not entirely, through federal funds. Taking these people into account adds additional millions to the total number of government employees.

In the federal bureaucracy, the top administrators are political appointees. That is, they are nominated by the president and approved by the Senate, or they are directly appointed by the president. These direct appointees most often leave office when a president's term ends. However, most of the **bureaucrats**—the administrators and skilled, expert workers who carry out many specific tasks of the federal bureaucracy—are career employees. These people are hired through a competitive process, and they stay in their jobs as presidents come and go. By having so many career employees, the bureaucracy is able to build expertise so it can implement legislation and executive orders.

READING CHECK **Summarizing** How many people work for the federal bureaucracy today?

ACADEMIC VOCABULARY

implement to fulfill or carry out

The Civil Service

The **civil service** is made up of the civilians who carry out the work of the federal government. Unlike the few top-level policy makers—such as the heads of the executive departments and independent agencies—who are appointed by the president, civil service workers are hired through competitive processes. This hiring system, however, was not always in place in the United States.

WHAT DO YOU THINK?

What are the advantages and disadvantages of the spoils system? of civil service?

The Spoils System In the nation's early years, government jobs were given out by the president, usually as political rewards to people who supported the president's policies or the president's election campaign. This practice is known as the **spoils system**.

Both George Washington and John Adams selected federal workers from the Federalist Party. When Thomas Jefferson took office, he replaced many Federalists with people from his own party, the Democratic-Republicans, which set a precedent for using the spoils system. This system remained in place through many early presidencies.

In 1829 Andrew Jackson took office and replaced more than 2,200 federal employees with Jacksonian Democrats. In 1832 Senator William L. Marcy defended Jackson's actions when he said, "To the victor belong the spoils of the enemy." Marcy implied that Jackson was justified in his appointments because, as the victorious candidate, he had a right to the spoils, or rewards, of his election victory.

In time, the spoils system began to come under scrutiny. Critics believed that it led to government corruption, with political appointees rewarding an administration's supporters with contracts for work on federal projects. Additionally, with so much turnover in government jobs as presidents came and went, the federal bureaucracy remained inexperienced and inefficient.

Changes in the Spoils System In the late 1800s, reformers began to push for changes in government appointments. In 1871 Congress created a Civil Service Advisory Board to write new rules governing federal hiring. Inadequately funded, it accomplished little in its three years and was disbanded.

PRIMARY SOURCES

The Spoils System

For most of its first 100 years, the United States relied on the spoils system as the primary method for choosing federal workers. This system, however, often led to corruption and the appointment of people who were not qualified to perform their duties. The Pendleton Civil Service Act of 1883 began a process of reform. However, the spoils system remained difficult to kill: Too many political figures still benefited from it. This cartoon from 1889 illustrates the struggle between the old system and the forces of reform.

THIS IS THE "PULL" THAT CIVIL SERVICE "REFORM" HAS WITH THIS ADMINISTRATION.

Benjamin Harrison sits atop the Republican Party elephant, whose trunk holds tight to the spoils system, as Civil Service Commissioners Theodore Roosevelt, Hugh S. Thompson, and C. Lyman pull the elephant back toward civil service reform.

Skills FOCUS **INTERPRETING PRIMARY SOURCES**

Making Inferences Why might some politicians push for others to follow civil service–reform legislation?

See **Skills Handbook**, p. H9.

A tragedy spurred new reform efforts. In 1881 Charles Guiteau, a disappointed office seeker, assassinated President James Garfield. Garfield's successor, Chester A. Arthur, used the assassination to convince Congress to pass civil service–reform legislation.

In 1883 Arthur signed the Pendleton Civil Service Act into law. This law was the first in a series of laws that would eventually put an end to the spoils system. The Pendleton Act based hiring and promotions for certain government jobs on merit and not on a person's party affiliation. The act created a Civil Service Commission to administer exams as an objective assessment of a person's qualifications and to grant jobs only to qualified applicants.

The Civil Service Today The Pendleton Civil Service Act initially applied to only 10 percent of positions within the federal bureaucracy. With subsequent presidents, however, Congress broadened the scope of the act to include other jobs. Today more than 90 percent of federal government jobs are protected by civil service legislation.

The Civil Service Reform Act of 1978 created the agencies that manage today's civil service. The Office of Personnel Management (OPM) conducts competitive exams, places applicants in jobs, and maintains the administrative functions of the civil service. The Federal Labor Relations Authority handles federal employees' complaints regarding unfair labor practices and works to resolve

The Civil Service Exam

For many years, in order to get a job with the government, people had to pass a civil service exam. Today, however, the majority of people obtain federal jobs through an interview process.

employee concerns. The U.S. Merit Systems Protection Board protects civil service employees and the system of hiring them from partisan practices and abuses by the executive branch.

Many civil service jobs today require specialized technical or professional qualifications not covered by a standardized examination. For this reason, Congress has allowed a number of agencies to devise their own hiring criteria with OPM approval.

READING CHECK **Identifying Problems and Solutions** What were the problems with the spoils system, and how did civil service reform help solve them?

SECTION 1 ASSESSMENT

THINK central **Online Quiz**

thinkcentral.com
KEYWORD: SGO EXE HP

Reviewing Ideas and Terms

1. a. Define What is the federal **bureaucracy**?

b. Explain How has the size of the federal bureaucracy changed over time?

c. Evaluate Why do you think the bureaucracy has shrunk in recent years?

2. a. Describe What is the **spoils system**, and what is its relationship to the **civil service**?

b. Summarize How did the spoils system for selecting government workers benefit presidents?

c. Rate How important do you think the civil service system is to the overall organization and operation of the federal bureaucracy?

Critical Thinking

3. Analyze Copy the graphic organizer below and use it to record the causes and effects of civil service reform. In what ways did civil service reform change the federal bureaucracy?

Causes

1.
2.
3.

Civil Service Reform

Effects

1.
2.
3.

FOCUS ON WRITING

4. Expository Write a brief lecture that describes the major features of the federal bureaucracy.

Executive Departments and Independent Agencies

BEFORE YOU READ

Main Idea

Executive departments and independent agencies provide key services and regulate important industries for the American people.

Reading Focus

1. What is the purpose of the executive departments?
2. What are the primary functions of executive departments today?
3. What are independent agencies?
4. What are some issues regarding power and accountability in the federal bureaucracy?

Key Terms

independent agencies
independent executive agencies
independent regulatory commissions
bipartisan
government corporations

TAKING NOTES As you read, take notes on the executive departments and independent agencies. Record your notes in a graphic organizer like this one.

Independent Agencies

Executive Departments

WHY IT MATTERS

The Organizations of the Federal Government The federal bureaucracy is made up of hundreds of individual departments and agencies—both large and small, well-known and obscure. Some, such as the U.S. Postal Service, employ hundreds of thousands of people and are visible parts of Americans' everyday lives. Others—such as the Federal Communications Commission, which licenses and monitors the content of TV and radio stations—employ far fewer people but play no less a part in our everyday lives. You may not know it, but you regularly interact with the federal bureaucracy, whether you are mailing a letter or sitting down to watch your favorite television show.

The federal bureaucracy was not always as extensive as it is today. But as Americans' ideas about the proper role and responsibility of government changed, particularly since the 1930s, the bureaucracy grew to meet the changing demands. The primary organizations of the federal government are the executive departments and independent agencies. ■

GOVERNMENT IN Our Daily Lives

A U.S. Postal Service employee helps a customer resolve a zip code issue.

Executive Departments

The executive departments are the major units of administration and policy making in the executive branch. Because the heads, or secretaries, of these departments make up the cabinet, the executive departments are sometimes called cabinet-level departments. In the U.S. government today, there are 15 executive departments, and they employ about 60 percent of all federal government employees.

Each executive department oversees a broad area of government responsibility. Within each department, there are often smaller, more narrowly focused agencies. The Federal Highway Administration, for example, is an agency within the Department of Transportation.

Congress and the president share responsibility for the executive departments. When establishing a new executive department, Congress spells out the department's general duties and powers. Congress must also approve the budgets and expenditures for each executive department. The president nominates the secretaries, top officials, and heads of the smaller agencies of each department, but the Senate must give advice and consent on these selections.

Early Departments George Washington established the first executive departments in 1789 when he created the Departments of State, Treasury, and War. Although the post of attorney general was also established at this time, the Department of Justice was not officially created until 1870.

In the 1800s and 1900s, Congress created new executive departments to meet new needs. In 1849, for example, the new lands and responsibilities that the nation acquired as a result of the Mexican-American War led Congress to create the Department of the Interior. Its purpose was to manage the country's public lands, its resources, and its relationships with Native American groups.

Congress also created new departments to show the federal government's changing priorities. For example, the Department of Labor was created in 1913, which reflected the increased power and importance of organized labor.

New Departments since 1950 In the post–World War II era, Congress created seven executive departments. The new departments reflected the expanded role government now played in Americans' lives. Increasingly, Americans expected the federal government to take action when a problem confronted society. Congress created the Department of Housing and Urban Development in 1965, for example, shortly after riots in the Watts section of Los Angeles and in other cities dramatized how economic decline and racial unrest had begun to undermine U.S. cities. Likewise, Congress created the Department of Energy in response to the 1973 Arab oil embargo, which led to gasoline shortages and skyrocketing prices.

READING CHECK Identifying Supporting **Details** What were the first three executive departments established by Congress?

The Departments Today

The table on pages 198 and 199 lists each of the executive departments and its goals and functions. Below, we will take a closer look at three of these departments: the Department of Health and Human Services, which oversees a number of health-related agencies; the Department of Defense, which has the largest budget of any government agency; and the most recently created department, the Department of Homeland Security.

Health and Human Services It is the job of the Department of Health and Human Services (HHS) to protect the health of the American people. It is also the main federal provider of social services. Originally a part of the Department of Health, Education, and Welfare (HEW), the Department of Health and Human Services was restyled into its present state in 1980, when Congress created a separate Department of Education.

HHS employs more than 65,000 people. Key HHS programs include Social Security, Medicare, and Medicaid. Medicare provides medical insurance to people age 65 and older, while Medicaid provides medical insurance to low-income people of all ages. Together these programs help supplement health care for about one-fourth of the U.S. population.

ACADEMIC VOCABULARY
supplement
supply what is missing from

THE EXECUTIVE DEPARTMENTS

DEPARTMENT (YEAR CREATED)	GOALS AND FUNCTIONS
Department of State (1789)	• Protect and assist U.S. citizens living and traveling abroad • Help advance the global interests of the United States • Coordinate and provide support for American international activities
Department of Defense* (1789)	• Provide military forces and domestic security • Deliver humanitarian aid and disaster relief and provide peacekeeping forces
Department of the Treasury (1789)	• Manage federal finances and supervise national banks • Print and coin U.S. currency • Collect money due to the United States and pay the bills of the United States • Develop domestic and international financial policy
Department of the Interior (1849)	• Protect the nation's resources—both natural and cultural • Manage resource use • Provide recreation opportunities
Department of Agriculture (1862)	• Protect farmland by promoting sustainable development • Work to end hunger and improve health in the United States • Keep food safe for the consumer
Department of Justice (1870)	• Represent the United States in the Supreme Court and other courts • Control federal law enforcement • Manage the legal affairs of the United States
Department of Commerce (1903)	• Promote international trade • Ensure effective use of American technological and scientific resources by U.S. citizens • Assist states, groups, and individuals through economic progress
Department of Labor (1913)	• Work to improve working conditions; set standards for wages and overtime pay • Protect retirement and health care benefits • Protect employees from discrimination

*When established in 1789, the Department of Defense was known as the War Department. In 1947 an act of Congress created the National Military Establishment, which established the Department of Defense and the cabinet-level position of secretary of defense.

Similar to other executive departments, HHS has many smaller agencies that work within the larger department. The Centers for Disease Control and Prevention (CDC) and the Food and Drug Administration (FDA), for example, are divisions of HHS.

The CDC monitors health trends and helps prevent disease outbreaks. It also warns the nation of influenza outbreaks and plans for possible bioterrorism attacks. The FDA inspects and sets safety standards for food, food additives, and medicinal drugs. It also approves new drug and food products and makes sure that they are safe for the public.

Department of Defense The Department of Defense (DOD) oversees U.S. military forces charged with protecting the nation. First known as the Department of War, it was one of three departments created by Congress in 1789. In the nation's early years, the Department of War housed several smaller departments, each responsible for managing a specific branch of the armed services, such as the army or the navy.

During World War II, however, a new defense strategy emerged: Officials believed that military operations would be more successful if the various branches of the

DEPARTMENT (YEAR CREATED)	GOALS/FUNCTIONS
Department of Health and Human Services (1953)	• Conduct and fund health-related research; responsible for food and drug safety • Monitor and prevent disease outbreaks • Provide health care to low-income citizens (Medicaid) and senior citizens (Medicare)
Department of Housing and Urban Development (1965)	• Work to increase access to affordable housing • Ensure fair housing laws are followed • Assist in developing public-housing programs for low-income citizens
Department of Transportation (1966)	• Form national transportation policy and oversee safety of air and rail travel • Assist states in building new highway systems • Develop programs for improvement of public transportation systems
Department of Energy (1977)	• Promote reliable, clean, and affordable energy sources and assist in environmental protection • Develop nuclear weapons and energy technologies • Ensure the safety of the nation's nuclear weapons • Promote scientific discovery and improve the quality of life through technological innovations
Department of Education (1980)	• Establish policies for federal financial aid for educational purposes • Collect data and research on American schools • Focus national attention on major educational issues • Enforce laws that ban discrimination in educational programs that receive federal funding
Department of Veterans Affairs (1989)	• Assist disabled veterans • Help veterans returning from military service to transition back into civilian life • Honor veterans in life and memorialize them in death
Department of Homeland Security (2003)	• Identify and assess threats to the safety of the United States • Coordinate the national response to and lead recovery efforts after acts of terrorism, natural disasters, and other emergencies • Work to prevent possible attacks to the United States

Skills FOCUS INTERPRETING CHARTS

Why do you think Congress created so many executive departments following World War II?

military served under a unified command. As a result, in 1947 Congress created the DOD, which brought all branches of the military under a single secretary of defense.

The DOD is a massive enterprise. It employs more than 1.3 million men and women on active duty in the armed forces and another 1.1 million in the National Guard and Reserve. These armed forces are supported by another 670,000 civilian employees. The DOD has a larger budget than any other department. The proposed 2008 DOD budget was $480 billion. Salary and housing make up about a third of this amount. <u>Procurement</u> of equipment and supplies costs about $100 billion, and about $75 billion is spent on research and testing.

Homeland Security The Department of Homeland Security is a prime example of how the changing world can bring about changes in, or additions to, the executive departments. In 2003 Congress created the Department of Homeland Security, two years after the attacks of September 11, 2001.

ACADEMIC VOCABULARY

procurement the act of getting something through special means

This department differs from some of the others in that it was not an entirely new organization but, rather, a reorganization of several agencies that were already in place.

The purpose of this reorganization was to refocus government efforts involving law enforcement, border security, transportation, immigration, emergency preparedness, and other issues, in order to prevent further attacks on U.S. soil. The Secret Service—the organization charged with protecting the president and other high government officials—and the U.S. Coast Guard are also under the jurisdiction of the Department of Homeland Security.

READING CHECK Identifying Cause and **Effect** Why was the Department of Homeland Security established?

Independent Agencies

In addition to the executive departments and their many smaller offices and agencies, the federal bureaucracy includes about 140 **independent agencies**—government agencies that operate separately from the executive departments. Creating an independent agency requires an act of Congress. For the most part, Congress establishes independent agencies to address certain issues that have become too complicated or require too much specialized knowledge to handle through regular legislation.

For example, Congress established the Environmental Protection Agency, or EPA, in 1970 to address the issue of protecting the environment. The EPA is in charge of all government programs that are related to safeguarding the environment, such as the Energy Star program, which promotes the reduction of energy consumption and greenhouse gases.

Congress retains power over independent agencies. It must approve the funding that allows the agencies to operate. Congress can also pass laws to direct an agency to do something and can change the scope of an agency's authority whenever it wishes.

Congress grants certain independent agencies powers that go beyond the scope of executive functions. In doing so, Congress gives these agencies quasi-legislative and quasi-judicial powers, which means these agencies have not only the power to make regulations that have the force of law but also the authority to decide disputes over their regulations. While these agencies have the power to enforce the laws that they have created, Congress maintains the authority to override any of those laws.

Independent agencies vary greatly in size. On one hand, the U.S. Postal Service, which has more employees than any of the executive departments, employs more than 700,000 people. On the other hand, some of the smaller agencies, such as the Defense Nuclear Facilities Safety Board, have fewer than 100 full-time employees.

There are three main types of independent agencies: independent executive agencies, independent regulatory commissions, and government corporations. We will examine each in closer detail below.

Independent Executive Agencies The purpose of **independent executive agencies** is to oversee and manage a specific aspect of the federal government. These agencies are given executive powers similar to those of the executive departments. However, the heads of independent executive agencies are not cabinet members.

Although Congress establishes these agencies and retains ultimate authority over them, the president exercises much of the control over their operation. For example,

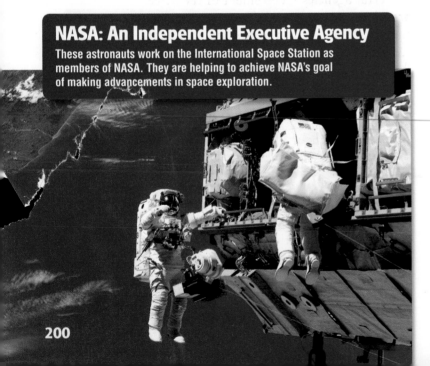

NASA: An Independent Executive Agency
These astronauts work on the International Space Station as members of NASA. They are helping to achieve NASA's goal of making advancements in space exploration.

the president nominates the top officials of independent executive agencies. These nominees must be confirmed by the Senate, but they report directly to the president.

The structure of the National Aeronautics and Space Administration (NASA) is typical of that of the larger independent executive agencies. Like many such agencies, NASA has one head administrator who oversees the entire agency. This person is nominated by the president and confirmed by the Senate. In addition, NASA is divided into program offices that are responsible for particular parts of the agency. These smaller offices are in charge of all the various aspects of space exploration—from research into the origins of the universe to continuing human exploration of space.

Presidents may push for the creation of certain independent executive agencies to help fulfill their particular vision. An example of such an agency is the Peace Corps, which was created in 1961 at the urging of President John F. Kennedy. In his inaugural address, Kennedy encouraged Americans to fulfill their civic duties and to "ask not what your country can do for you—ask what you can do for your country."

This historic speech laid the foundation for a change in people's ideas about political involvement and gave individuals a new role to play in world affairs. People could fulfill this new role through federal agencies like the Peace Corps, which places American volunteers in developing nations in order to help those nations address their economic and social problems.

Other independent executive agencies include the General Services Administration (GSA) and the National Archives and Records Administration (NARA). The GSA helps other government agencies buy goods and services, while the NARA organizes and maintains government records.

Independent Regulatory Commissions
The purpose of **independent regulatory commissions** is to regulate some aspect of the economy. These commissions are, in a sense, separate from the branches of government. Their job is to set and enforce rules that have the force of law, and most have quasi-judicial powers to settle disputes arising from

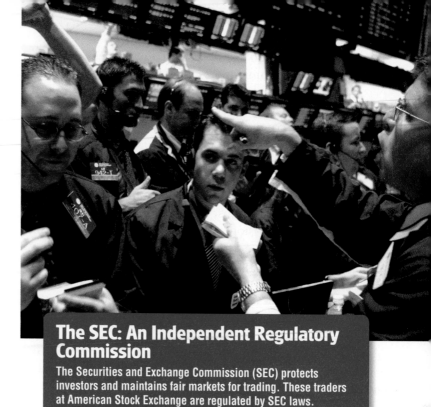

The SEC: An Independent Regulatory Commission
The Securities and Exchange Commission (SEC) protects investors and maintains fair markets for trading. These traders at American Stock Exchange are regulated by SEC laws.

their rules. They are led by a three- to seven-person board, whose members are nominated by the president and confirmed by the Senate. In most such commissions, the members of the board serve fixed terms and cannot be removed by the president. By law, this board must be **bipartisan**, or include members from both major political parties. For example, on a five-person board, only three members can be from the same party.

Why would Congress want to create such powerful agencies independent of the three branches of government? The answer can be found by looking at the first independent regulatory commission Congress created—the Interstate Commerce Commission (ICC).

Congress created the ICC in 1887 for three main reasons. Many in Congress believed that (1) a group of specialists was better equipped than Congress to regulate the railroads; (2) there could be more continuity in legislation if a permanent commission, rather than an elective legislative body, oversaw regulation of certain aspects of the economy; and (3) an independent body would be free of undue political influence. Although abolished in 1995, the ICC set the template for later independent regulatory commissions.

An example of an independent regulatory commission that is still active is the Federal Communications Commission, or the FCC. Congress created the FCC in 1934. The commission now regulates radio, television, wire, satellite, and cable communications.

The FCC gives licenses to broadcasters and sets and enforces broadcast rules. One of its primary responsibilities is to limit the use of obscene or offensive language on television and radio. Violations of FCC rules can lead to fines and even a loss of license.

As with all independent regulatory commissions, Congress can override FCC rules. In 1996, for example, Congress passed legislation that lifted many FCC restrictions on the ownership of media outlets, such as TV and radio stations. The new law allows any business to enter the communications industry. The goal is to increase competition and thus encourage the development of new TV and radio services. By passing this new law, Congress asserted its role as the primary communications policy maker.

The powers of regulatory commissions have at times proved controversial. For example, during the 1930s, issues arose over the constitutionality of some of the new regulatory agencies. One such controversy involved the Schechter Poultry Corporation and the National Recovery Administration (NRA), an independent agency created by the National Industrial Recovery Act (NIRA). The purpose of the NIRA was to help regulate economic activity and foster economic growth. The Schechter Poultry Corporation was found in violation of NRA regulations, and the case eventually went to the Supreme Court.

Government Corporations The third type of independent agency is a government corporation. **Government corporations** are organized and run like businesses but are owned in whole or in part by the federal government.

In general, Congress creates a government corporation to achieve a public goal that private business may not be able to address for a sufficient profit. An example of a government corporation is the U.S. Postal Service (USPS). Through the USPS, anyone can send a letter anywhere in the United States for a fixed price. The USPS follows the principles of a business in order to operate as efficiently as possible. The USPS is not expected to make a profit, although it is supposed to break even.

Unlike a private business, however, the USPS does not focus on the most profitable areas of business. As an agent of the federal government, the USPS has a responsibility to see that all areas of the country, no matter how remote, have affordable and equitable mail services.

Another government corporation is the National Railroad Passenger Corporation, or Amtrak. Amtrak is a government-run passenger rail service. It was formed in 1971 when the growth of air and auto travel made it less profitable for private companies to provide rail service in most parts of the country.

Amtrak has come under criticism in recent years for its significant financial losses. To compensate for these losses, Amtrak has had to rely on government subsidies, which are government payments aimed at achieving a public benefit. Today Amtrak continues to struggle just to break even.

READING CHECK **Identifying the Main Idea** What is the purpose of independent agencies?

The TVA: A Government Corporation

The Tennessee Valley Authority (TVA) provides electric power and flood control to parts of seven southern states that had previously been underserved. The Apalachia Dam in western North Carolina, shown below, is one of many dams and reservoirs run by the TVA.

Schechter Poultry Corporation v. United States (1935)

WHY IT MATTERS

In Schechter, the Court examined whether the federal government overstepped its authority in regulating commerce and business practices, giving the president an unconstitutional extension of power.

Background

During the Great Depression, Congress and President Franklin D. Roosevelt worked together to pass various reform bills intended to pull the nation out of its economic slump. At the heart of Roosevelt's New Deal legislation was the National Industrial Recovery Act of 1933 (NIRA), which aimed to stimulate the economy and reduce unemployment. The act set up the National Recovery Administration (NRA), which in turn created industry-specific boards whose purpose was to enforce codes for production, prices, wages, and working hours. The NIRA allowed these boards to draft the codes that the president would then sign into law. The goal of these boards was to create jobs for many unemployed Americans and to promote fair production and competition among industries and businesses.

The Schechter Poultry Corporation sold chickens at wholesale prices and fell under the jurisdiction of the Live Poultry Code, which was part of the NIRA. In addition to convictions against Schechter for the sale of unfit and uninspected chickens, among other charges, a federal district court found the company guilty of violating the minimum wage and maximum hours specifications set forth by the NRA for the live poultry industry. Schechter appealed the ruling and lost. The "Sick Chicken" case eventually came before the Supreme Court in 1935.

Arguments for Schechter

Schechter argued that Congress had acted unconstitutionally by relinquishing too much legislative authority to independent regulatory commissions like the NRA. The defendants also argued that because they were local operators who sold their product only locally, their employees' wages and hours did not affect interstate commerce. The defendants held that their business should be free from federal regulations. Schechter also argued that since it operated within New York State boundaries, the commerce clause was not implicated and federal jurisdiction was not created.

Arguments for United States

The government argued that Schechter Poultry Corporation broke federal regulations and violated the poultry code. The government argued that the NIRA, and by extension the poultry code, was constitutional and necessary for the good of the nation. The government maintained further that Congress could delegate lawmaking power to the executive branch under the NIRA because the NIRA only dealt with businesses and industries that participated in interstate commerce.

THE IMPACT TODAY In a unanimous decision, the Court ruled that the NIRA was an unconstitutional delegation of Congress's legislative powers to the executive branch. Later decisions by the Court, however, reversed this holding, paving the way for the many independent agencies of the executive branch that regulate various aspects of business and industry, including minimum wage standards.

CRITICAL THINKING

What Do You Think? Congress creates regulatory agencies that have control over some areas of the economy. At what point is it necessary for Congress to overrule these agencies? When might it be appropriate for Congress to take some power away from these agencies? Explain your answer.

Power and Accountability in the Federal Bureaucracy

The Constitution provides a number of tools for ensuring the accountability of the federal bureaucracy. Presidents, for example, can shape the direction of the bureaucracy through their appointment powers and by issuing executive orders. Likewise, congressional oversight committees and subcommittees routinely demand answers from federal agencies. By boosting or cutting funds to a federal department or agency, congressional appropriations committees can affect its operations.

Over the years Congress has taken some additional steps to ensure that agencies remain accountable. In 1946, for example, it passed the Administrative Procedure Act. This law and its various revisions set clear guidelines for agency rule making, including a lengthy period for public comment and participation. In addition, the Freedom of Information Act, passed by Congress in 1965 and later strengthened, allows citizens access to written records kept by federal agencies. Presidents can exempt certain information in the interest of national security or for other reasons. Together, these measures place a check on an agency's freedom of action.

One danger these measures do not address is what happens when bureaucratic agencies, congressional oversight committees, and outside interest groups form an unofficial alliance. An interest group will support members of Congress who support legislation that the group wants. The bureaucrats, hoping to obtain the necessary funding from Congress, may in turn shape their policy recommendations to Congress in ways that favor the interest group. Thus, each group benefits from the actions of the others.

Political scientists label this three-sided relationship an *iron triangle*. The triangle is "iron" because outsiders, including the president, cannot seem to penetrate or disrupt it. The danger is that policy making becomes a closed loop, for and in the interests of specific interest groups.

Iron triangles may not be as prominent as they once were. Issues are so complex that multiple congressional committees and federal agencies, each with a different agenda, have a hand in making policy. In addition, interest groups on both sides of an issue compete vigorously for influence, canceling each other out.

READING CHECK **Summarizing** What are some of the ways the federal bureaucracy is held accountable?

SECTION 2 ASSESSMENT

THINK central **Online Quiz**
thinkcentral.com
KEYWORD: SGO EXE HP

Reviewing Ideas and Terms

1. a. Recall How many executive departments are there today?
b. Elaborate What possible reasons explain the growth in the number of executive departments that occurred in the 1900s?

2. a. Identify In 1980 what change took place within the Department of Health, Education, and Welfare?
b. Develop What do you think about the Department of Defense's having the largest budget of all the executive departments? Explain your answer.

3. a. Define What are **independent executive agencies**, **independent regulatory commissions**, and **government corporations**?
b. Make Generalizations How are independent agencies beneficial to the federal bureaucracy as a whole?

4. a. Define What is an *iron triangle*?
b. Explain Do you think it was necessary for Congress to step in and further regulate independent agencies?

Critical Thinking

5. Elaborate Using a graphic organizer like the one below, identify the main features of the executive departments and independent agencies. What functions do the executive departments and independent agencies serve as a part of the federal bureaucracy?

The Federal Bureaucracy	
Executive Departments	*Independent Agencies*

FOCUS ON WRITING

6. Persuasive Write an editorial in which you analyze the consequences of the political decisions made by different independent agencies and the effect of these decisions on society.

The Size of the Federal Bureaucracy

Is the federal bureaucracy too large?

THE ISSUE

The federal bureaucracy is made up of numerous agencies and departments. More than 2.7 million employees work in these various organizations, and many people feel that the bureaucracy has grown too large. Supporters of the bureaucracy, on one hand, claim that a large bureaucracy is necessary because as a major world leader, the United States needs all of these agencies and departments to successfully run the country. Opponents, on the other hand, feel that a large bureaucracy impedes the efficiency of the federal government.

DUNAGIN'S PEOPLE

11-15

"Gentlemen, we must streamline the bureaucracy . . . I don't care how many people it takes."

This cartoon comments on the size of the federal bureaucracy and the challenge of shrinking it.

VIEWPOINTS

The federal bureaucracy is the right size for accomplishing the many tasks that are set before it. A large bureaucracy does not impede government actions; it helps government function better. Our nation needs a large bureaucracy to run all of the programs that benefit the American people. Having agencies that specialize in very specific aspects of the federal government is in the greatest interest of U.S. citizens, as Congress—the main overseer of all government actions—does not have the management capacity or expertise that the federal bureaucracy does. Furthermore, while the bureaucracy does spend a lot of money, U.S. government spending is not high compared to government spending in other economically developed countries. Most of the money that the bureaucracy spends goes back into the economy in the form of salaries for employees. This funding also makes it possible for certain businesses to run.

The federal bureaucracy has grown too large and needs to be downsized considerably. The term *bureaucracy* is just another word for *waste* and *inefficiency*. The chain of command is so complicated, with larger agencies overseeing so many smaller agencies, that it takes a long time to get anything accomplished. Even when an agency succeeds in implementing a program, the time when that program was needed may have already passed, making the program obsolete. There are too many people working for the bureaucracy to make it an efficient body. A smaller bureaucracy would allow the various agencies to function at a higher level because there would be fewer channels to go through. With fewer channels, work would get done faster and programs would reach more people. The government would also have more money to spend on other aspects of government that are in need, such as Social Security.

What Is Your Opinion?

1. Is a large bureaucracy beneficial to a powerful nation like the United States? Defend your position.

2. Should the federal bureaucracy be decreased to help it run more efficiently? Explain your reasoning.

THINK central   Practice Online

thinkcentral.com
KEYWORD: SGO EXE

SECTION ③ Financing Government

BEFORE YOU READ

Main Idea
By collecting taxes and borrowing money, the federal government is able to generate the funds it needs to run the nation. The government then assigns these funds to create a federal budget for the upcoming year.

Reading Focus
1. How does the federal government pay for its operations?
2. What are the two types of government spending?
3. How does the federal budget process work?
4. How do fiscal and monetary policy affect the nation's economy?

Key Terms
income tax
progressive tax
payroll tax
regressive tax
proportional tax
bond
federal debt
mandatory spending
discretionary spending
fiscal policy
monetary policy

 **TAKING NOTES** As you read, take notes on financing the federal government. Record your notes in a graphic organizer like this one.

Financing Government

WHY IT MATTERS

The Federal Budget In February 2007 President George W. Bush presented his proposed budget for the upcoming fiscal year. This proposed budget called for $2.9 trillion to spend on government programs.

How can we make sense of a number that large? To put it another way, take the average U.S. Navy aircraft carrier. The total unit cost for just one of these massive ships is about $4.5 billion. In order to equal the $2.9 trillion proposed in the president's 2008 budget, you would need a fleet of more than 644 of these ships.

The federal budget represents approximately one-fifth of the country's overall gross domestic product—the total market value of all the goods and services produced within a country in a given year. This number translates to more than $9,300 for every single man, woman, and child living in the United States.

The proposed budget also reveals how much the federal government plans to receive in revenue. The 2008 budget projected that the government would receive about $240 billion less than it planned to spend. That is also a big number. It represents a debt of about $800 for each person in the country.

The budget, in part, tells the story of the bureaucracy—what the different agencies and departments will receive and how they plan to spend the money. In effect, the budget is a story about our government and the way it works. ■

The number below illustrates what $2.9 trillion looks like when it is written out. Including the decimal places, there are 13 zeros in 2.9 trillion.

BIG NUMBERS

$2,900,000

Paying for Government

To pay for its operations—the programs and services it provides—the federal government relies on collecting revenue, or income, and borrowing. The revenue comes in the form of taxes, fees, and other nontax sources.

Income Taxes The Constitution grants Congress the power to "lay and collect" taxes. However, this power was limited to excise taxes, or taxes on the sale of a specific item. In 1913 the Sixteenth Amendment gave Congress the power to levy an **income tax**, which is a tax on a person's or corporation's income. Most people's income consists almost entirely of wages or a salary from a job and people are obligated to pay income taxes each year.

Today the income tax brings in the largest share of the federal government's revenue. Individual income taxes account for about 47 percent of federal revenue. Corporate income taxes make up another 12 percent.

The income tax is a **progressive tax**—a tax whose rates increase as the amount that is subject to taxation increases. Therefore, the income tax rates are higher for those who earn more. The federal individual income tax rates range from 10 percent for very low-income earners to 35 percent for high-income earners.

Payroll Taxes Another big source of federal revenue is payroll taxes, which are collected to help pay for Social Security, Medicare, and other forms of social insurance. A **payroll tax**, which makes up about 34 percent of federal revenues, is money that is withheld from a person's paycheck by his or her

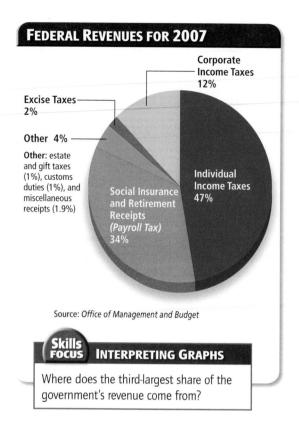

FEDERAL REVENUES FOR 2007

- Corporate Income Taxes 12%
- Excise Taxes 2%
- Other 4%
  Other: estate and gift taxes (1%), customs duties (1%), and miscellaneous receipts (1.9%)
- Individual Income Taxes 47%
- Social Insurance and Retirement Receipts *(Payroll Tax)* 34%

Source: *Office of Management and Budget*

Skills FOCUS **INTERPRETING GRAPHS**

Where does the third-largest share of the government's revenue come from?

employer. The payroll tax is a **regressive tax**, or a tax that has a greater impact on lower-income earners than on upper-income earners. The Social Security tax is a good example of a regressive tax because it applies to income only up to a certain amount. In 2007 this amount was $97,500. As a result, people who earned more than that sum paid a lower share of their income for the tax than did people who earned less. For example, a person who earned $200,000 per year paid the same Social Security tax as someone earning $97,500. In effect, the higher earner paid the tax at about half the rate of the lower earner.

The Medicare tax is a **proportional tax**, or a tax that is applied at the same rate against all income. Since this rate does not change according to the amount earned, the Medicare tax is also a regressive tax.

Other Sources of Revenue The federal government collects several other taxes and nontax revenues. Together, these revenues make up 6 percent of all federal funds.

Other taxes include excise taxes and tariffs. Tariffs are taxes on imported goods. They are also referred to as customs duties. Customs duties were once a major part of federal revenues, but the government has been trying to move toward "free trade"— trade without tariffs or with reduced tariffs.

Another federal tax is the estate tax. This tax is placed on money and property that is passed on to the heirs of someone who dies. In 2007 the government taxed estates valued at more than $2 million. Like estate taxes, gift taxes are placed on property that is given from one person to another. The difference between gift taxes and estate taxes is that gift taxes are placed on items that are passed on by a living person. Gift taxes exist so that people will not avoid paying estate taxes by giving property away before they die.

The federal government also collects nontax revenue from several sources, such as entrance fees at national parks. The largest source, however, is earnings by the Federal Reserve System. This system loans money to banks and charges interest. You will read more about this system later in the section.

Borrowing Money The federal government does not always cover its expenses by collecting revenue. When it does not, it borrows money. The Constitution gives Congress the power to borrow money, and the federal government does so by selling bonds. A **bond** is a financial instrument by which a borrower agrees to pay back borrowed money, plus interest, at a future date. Thus, a person may buy a $50 bond based on the promise of getting $100 back at some later date.

Historically, the government borrowed money only in emergencies. A war, for example, could place heavy financial strains on the government. Economic depressions could also cause a steep drop in government revenues, leading to budget deficits. A deficit occurs when government revenues are lower than expenses. In such cases, the government might borrow money until the emergency has passed.

In recent decades, the federal government has been running a deficit as a matter of course. Since 1970 the country has only had a surplus—more revenue than spending— from 1998 to 2001.

THE FEDERAL DEFICIT AND DEBT

Federal Deficits and Surpluses, 1940–2008* (in 2007 dollars)

Gross Federal Debt, 1940–2008* (in 2007 dollars)

*Estimate

Source: *Office of Management and Budget*

Skills Focus INTERPRETING GRAPHS

Why does the gross federal debt graph dip slightly when the federal deficits and surpluses graph peaks in 2000?

The total sum of money that the federal government has borrowed and not yet repaid is known as the **federal debt**. Today the federal debt has surpassed $9 trillion. In years of deficit, the government pays only the interest on the federal debt. The interest alone, however, amounts to hundreds of billions of dollars a year—now about 9 percent of the total annual budget.

The federal debt and interest expenses are growing sharply just as the demands on Social Security and Medicare are increasing because of the aging of the baby boomer generation—those people born between 1946 and 1960. This situation presents major difficulties for government officials:

PRIMARY SOURCE

❝One such challenge is putting the federal budget on a [path] that will be sustainable as our society ages. Under current law, federal spending for retirement and health programs will grow substantially in coming decades.❞

—Ben Bernanke, speech, 2006

Some observers fear that unless the debt is reduced, there will not be enough money to pay benefits to this aging population.

READING CHECK **Summarizing** What are the main sources of government revenue?

Government Spending

Each year, Congress creates a budget that tells how much the government will spend to fund its various programs. The two types of spending are mandatory and discretionary.

Mandatory Spending The first type of federal spending is known as mandatory spending. **Mandatory spending** is spending required by laws and not subject to the annual budget process. A large percentage of mandatory spending goes to entitlement programs, or government programs that people are entitled to by law, such as Social Security. Government cannot deny funding to such programs without changing the law.

The part of the budget used for mandatory spending has risen steadily in recent decades. In 1962 the government spent 26 percent of the budget on mandatory programs. Today the number is about 69 percent.

FEDERAL SPENDING 2008 (PROPOSED)

■ Mandatory Spending ■ Discretionary Spending

Other Discretionary Spending

Education, Training, Employment, and Social Services	3%
Transportation	3%
Administration of Justice	2%
International Affairs	1%
Natural Resources and Environment	1%
Other	>1%*

National Defense 21%
Social Security 21%
Other 10%
Income Security 13%
Net Interest Payments on the Debt 9%
Medicare 13%
Health 10%
Veterans' Benefits and Services 3%

* Other includes general science, space and technology, energy, agriculture, commerce and housing credit, community and regional development, general government; allowances.

Source: Office of Management and Budget

Skills FOCUS **INTERPRETING GRAPHS**

1. What percentage of the budget is spent on mandatory programs?
2. What does this graph tell you about how discretionary funds are spent?

Discretionary Spending The second type of federal spending is discretionary spending. **Discretionary spending** is spending subject to the annual budget process. Congress is able to use its own judgment when deciding how to allocate discretionary funds. It is from this pool of funds that the government must pay for any optional program or activity. Discretionary spending today makes up about 31 percent of the entire budget.

The budget process deals with how to allocate the discretionary funds. Recall that once the president proposes the budget, it must still be passed by Congress. Creating the budget, therefore, is a collaborative effort between the legislative and the executive branches. The pool of discretionary money is limited, though, and disputes often arise between Congress and the president. When the president's plan for the discretionary funds does not match that of Congress, approving the budget becomes a long and often laborious process.

READING CHECK **Contrasting** What is the difference between mandatory and discretionary spending?

ACADEMIC VOCABULARY

allocate to set aside for a particular purpose

The Budget Process

More than a plan for bringing in and spending money, the federal budget is a reflection of the nation's priorities. It also illustrates how the branches of government compromise. The president and Congress must decide which programs receive funds and how much funds they should receive.

The federal budget lasts for one fiscal year. The term *fiscal* means "financial" or "having to do with money." The government's fiscal year begins on October 1 and runs to September 30 of the next calendar year. A fiscal year is given the number of the calendar year in which it ends. So, fiscal year 2008, or FY2008, would go from October 1, 2007, to September 30, 2008.

The President's Budget The creation of the federal budget begins with the president. In 1921 an act of Congress formally gave the president the job of preparing and presenting a budget. This proposed budget reflects the president's legislative priorities, highlighting the areas of the federal government that he or she feels are most in need of funding.

As discussed in Chapter 6, the Office of Management and Budget (OMB) assists the president in creating the budget. Once the president sets broad budget and policy guidelines, the OMB director works over a period of about four months with the various government departments and agencies. Each department and agency submits its budget requests to the OMB, which reviews them and makes adjustments according to presidential priorities. A department or agency can make a case for its funding requests, but the OMB has the final word on which requests make it into the president's budget proposal.

By the January prior to the start of the fiscal year, in time for the State of the Union address, the president's budget is complete. In addition to offering spending proposals, the massive document estimates revenues and spending several years into the future. These estimates show the long-term effects of all the president's recommendations.

The Budget in Congress The president must present the budget to Congress by the first Monday in February. From that point on, budget work takes place in Congress. Congress uses the president's proposed budget as a guide for its discussions. Congress reviews the president's proposal and makes any changes that it deems necessary.

The Congressional Budget Office (CBO) assists Congress in this work. The nonpartisan CBO was created to provide expert economic analysis to Congress. Congress can then make its own judgments about the economic effects of various proposals and ideas.

Congress's first steps are to agree on the grand totals for revenue and spending and to pass a concurrent resolution, which will guide its future budget work. The resolution is not signed by the president and does not have the force of law. In order to write this resolution, the House and Senate Budget Committees hold hearings to gather input on the budget from the members of Congress.

Budget Milestones

The annual federal budget process lasts for seven months. *Why does the budget process take so long to complete?*

Senate Budget Committee staff unload the president's proposed budget. Congress then begins its review of the president's budget, making the changes that it sees fit.

First Monday of February
The president's budget proposal is submitted to Congress. The House and Senate Budget Committees and Appropriations Committees begin analyzing the budget.

April 15
The House and Senate Budget Committees send a concurrent resolution on spending and taxation to the floor of each house.

May 15
The entire Senate and House pass the concurrent resolution.

Congress then deals with the hundreds of individual funding and revenue resolutions contained in the budget. This work takes place in the House and Senate Appropriations Committees. The Appropriations Committees are committees that have authority over the discretionary spending of the budget.

The difference between the Appropriations Committees and the Budget Committees is that the Appropriations Committees actually write the budget legislation. Whereas the Budget Committees devise the concurrent resolution, which does not have the force of law, the Appropriations Committees have the power to determine precisely how the discretionary funds are to be spent.

The final product of the entire effort by the Appropriations Committees is a series of appropriations bills. Together, these bills formalize the spending decisions of the federal budget. These bills are then sent to the president.

Congress is supposed to complete its budget work by the beginning of the fiscal year. In recent years, Congress has often failed to meet this deadline. In such cases, Congress passes a continuing resolution for the president's approval to allow temporary funding of the government. Congress and the president have occasionally quarreled over such continuing resolutions. This quarreling has sometimes led to the shutdown of government programs while Congress and the president worked out a solution.

READING CHECK **Sequencing** What are the steps, in order, for creating the federal budget?

Fiscal and Monetary Policy

Each year the government takes in an amount of money equal to about 20 percent of the gross domestic product. It also spends and borrows a similar amount. Government spending and borrowing have a huge effect—both positive and negative—on the economy. Increasing taxes, increasing government spending, and borrowing money can all cause the economy to shift.

By creating the federal budget and tax laws, Congress and the president are making a **fiscal policy** for the United States. When the government alters the amount of money in circulation and the interest rates at which money is borrowed, it is creating a **monetary policy** for the United States. Together, fiscal and monetary policies help the federal government work toward a four-part economic goal, which includes economic growth, low unemployment, stable prices for goods and services, and a balanced budget.

Fiscal Policy The goal of fiscal policy is to provide adequate funds for government without adversely affecting the overall economy. In some circumstances, fiscal policy can even be used to boost the economy.

When the economy is growing slowly or shrinking, the government can do one of two things: spend more money or cut taxes. Through targeted government spending, sectors of the economy can be stimulated to produce more goods and hire more workers. By cutting taxes, though, the government can leave more money in taxpayers' pockets.

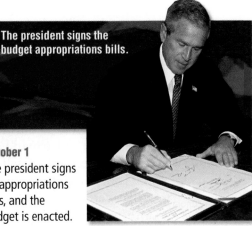

The president signs the budget appropriations bills.

The Senate and House Budget Committees discuss the federal budget. This task can often be a long and arduous process.

May–September
The House and Senate Appropriations Committees continue to hold hearings and debate any conflicts they have with the concurrent resolution.

September
Conference committees form to decide on any issues the House and Senate Appropriations Committees cannot resolve. Appropriations bills are passed by the House and Senate.

October 1
The president signs all appropriations bills, and the budget is enacted.

FISCAL POLICY AND THE ECONOMY

To counteract a slowing economy, the government can adjust fiscal policy by:

1. **Cutting Taxes** Consumers have more money to buy goods and services.

2. **Increasing Government Spending** The government buys more goods and services.

3. **Cutting Taxes and Increasing Government Spending**

Such government actions can cause one of two scenarios:

IF the economy grows so much that tax revenue increases

THEN

- The deficit closes
- Government borrowing decreases
- Interest rates drop
- Businesses can afford to expand

AND the economy continues to grow

IF the economy fails to grow enough to increase tax revenues

THEN

- The deficit does not close
- Government continues to borrow money
- Interest rates rise
- Businesses can not afford to expand

AND the economy begins to decline

Skills FOCUS INTERPRETING CHARTS

What are some of the effects that fiscal policy can have on the economy?

This action spurs consumer spending and business investment. In either case, the goal is to stimulate the economy by increasing the public demand for goods and services and by promoting long-term economic growth.

However, increasing government spending while cutting taxes can sometimes create large budget deficits, which the government must then cover by borrowing money. As you read earlier, the government borrows money by selling bonds to investors.

As the government borrows more, it must often pay higher interest on government bonds to continue to attract investors. This action triggers a rise in the rates at which businesses borrow money. With borrowing more expensive, businesses borrow less, build less, and expand more slowly. As a result, the economy itself begins to slow.

Too much government spending can, under certain conditions, trigger inflation—a rise in prices for goods and services. Inflation cuts into the purchasing power of people and businesses. People must buy less with the same amount of money, which reduces their standard of living. Government can combat inflation by reducing spending, raising taxes, or raising interest rates.

Monetary Policy The federal government can also influence the economy through its monetary policy, which controls the amount of money in circulation and the interest rates at which money is borrowed. This policy is set and carried out by the Federal Reserve System, or the Fed.

Created in 1913, the Fed is an independent regulatory commission that acts as the nation's central banking system. It has a seven-person board with one member acting as chairperson. The Fed Board is nominated by the president and confirmed by the Senate. The Fed chairperson holds a powerful position, as his or her decisions have a great impact on the U.S. economy.

RESPONSIBILITIES OF LEADERSHIP

The Federal Reserve uses all the information it can to try to set interest rates at a level that will best serve the American economy, businesses, and consumers.

The Fed carries out the monetary policy of the federal government in several ways. First, it sets rules for how much money banks must have in reserve. If it raises the reserve requirement, the Fed keeps more money out of circulation. If the Fed lowers the reserve requirement, it increases the amount of money in circulation.

The Fed also carries out monetary policy by adjusting the interest rates it charges its customers—the nation's other banks. These banks borrow money from the Fed at rates set by the Fed. Raising the rate discourages borrowing and reduces the amount of money in circulation. Lowering interest rates has the opposite effect.

Finally, the Fed can affect the money supply by buying or selling government bonds. When the Fed buys bonds, it puts money in circulation. When the Fed sells bonds, it reduces the amount of money in circulation.

Creating a successful monetary policy is a balancing act. In general, more money in circulation will foster economic growth, but it can also trigger inflation. Less money in circulation may reduce inflation, but it can also slow economic growth.

There are limits to what government can achieve with its fiscal policy and monetary policy. For example, any change in policy takes time to put in place. As a result, the effect of the change may not begin for months. By then, the nature of the problem itself may have changed—requiring yet another change in policy. This cycle could continue while the economy slows and becomes unstable.

READING CHECK **Identifying Supporting Details** Why is inflation bad for the economy?

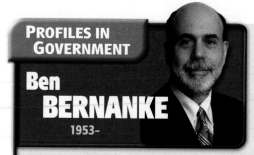

PROFILES IN GOVERNMENT

Ben BERNANKE
1953–

Ben Shalom Bernanke, whose middle name literally means "peace," has an affinity for diplomacy. Paired with his diplomatic nature, Bernanke's strong academic background prepared him well for his current role as the Federal Reserve chairman, a position he has held since February 2006. After graduating with a B.A. in economics from Harvard in 1975 and a Ph.D. in economics from the Massachusetts Institute of Technology in 1979, Bernanke went on to teach at several universities, including Stanford and Princeton. He has published numerous articles and books on economic theory and policy. Much of his scholarly work has also focused on the political and economic causes of the Great Depression.

Infer How do you think Bernanke's background helps him perform his duties as America's leading economist?

SECTION 3 ASSESSMENT

THINK central Online Quiz
thinkcentral.com
KEYWORD: SGO EXE HP

Reviewing Ideas and Terms

1. a. Define What is a **bond**?
b. Develop Defend the current practice of the federal government's methods of obtaining revenue by taxing the American people and borrowing money.

2. a. Define What is meant by the terms **mandatory spending** and **discretionary spending**?
b. Make Generalizations How do discretionary spending choices affect the budget process?

3. a. Recall How often must the federal government prepare a budget?
b. Contrast How do the roles of the president and Congress differ with regard to the budget process?

4. a. Identify What are the main goals of the federal government's **fiscal policy** and **monetary policy**?
b. Elaborate Do you think it is accurate to label maintaining a successful monetary policy a "balancing act"?

Critical Thinking

5. Compare and Contrast Copy the chart below and record key information about monetary policy and fiscal policy. In what ways are monetary policy and fiscal policy similar? In what ways are they different?

Monetary Policy	Fiscal Policy

FOCUS ON WRITING

6. Narrative Imagine you are trying to explain to a visitor from another country the government's budget process. Write a brief narrative explanation of the process.

The Federal Bureaucracy

The First Congress set up executive departments and agencies to carry out the business of the executive branch. Learn why Congress creates executive departments and agencies and identify some of the checks on the exercise of administrative power.

Why does Congress create administrative organizations, and what powers do they exercise? Laws usually are written in general terms. Congress cannot anticipate and does not have the expertise to resolve problems that arise when general laws are applied to specific circumstances. Almost from the beginning Congress has had to delegate some of its lawmaking powers to those who administer the laws. Administrative units exercise quasi-legislative powers by adopting rules to implement broad congressional mandates. Rules are published in the *Federal Register*. Many administrative units also exercise quasi-judicial powers by holding hearings to resolve disputes that involve parties claiming to have been injured by administrative policies or procedures.

The Internal Revenue Service (IRS) provides an example. The Sixteenth Amendment gives Congress the power to "lay" (establish) and collect taxes on income. Congress enacts general income tax laws. It has delegated to the IRS the responsibility to make and enforce rules about tax collection, including income tax forms, deadlines, and penalties for late filing. The IRS holds quasi-judicial proceedings, including hearings and opportunities to present evidence to a neutral hearings officer, for taxpayers who are accused of violating tax rules.

In 1946 Congress adopted the Administrative Procedure Act that established guidelines for administrative units to follow when they make rules to implement laws. Among other things the act requires public notice and an opportunity for the public to be heard before a rule goes into effect. The act also permits judicial review of the decisions of administrative units in federal court after someone has gone through, or exhausted, all quasi-judicial proceedings within the administrative unit.

How do checks and balances affect administrative agencies? Administrative agencies are subject to many checks on the exercise of their powers. Those who exercise checks include the following:

The president Presidents use their appointment power to reward political loyalists and advance their policy agendas. Presidential appointees usually are required to pursue the president's policies in administering government programs, thereby checking the power of civil service career employees.

Presidents also check the exercise of administrative power through the use of executive orders, which direct agency heads and cabinet members

to take particular actions. Executive orders have become more common in recent years as a means of forcing agencies to adjust administrative policies and procedures. For example, soon after he took office President George W. Bush issued executive orders creating Faith-Based and Community Initiatives offices in several departments and agencies to help ensure that faith-based groups would receive government contracts to provide social services.

Congress Congress can control the bureaucracy in many ways. It is responsible for the creation, consolidation, and elimination of administrative agencies. The Senate must confirm high-level presidential appointees. Many statutes direct agencies to undertake certain actions and refrain from others. Congress also must appropriate the money required for agencies to operate. Congressional committees are responsible for overseeing the actions of administrative agencies. They review agency budgets, require administrators to justify expenditures, hold investigative hearings about agency activities, and require agencies to submit their proposed rules, which Congress has the power to "veto." The Supreme Court declared the congressional veto unconstitutional in 1983, but Congress has continued to use it and has found other ways, including joint resolutions, to prohibit agencies from implementing rules with which Congress disagrees.

Courts Courts decide whether agency operations follow the Fourteenth Amendment requirements of due process and equal protection. Courts also determine whether Congress has delegated too much legislative authority to administrative agencies. The Supreme Court has never questioned Congress's power to permit administrative agencies to "fill in the details" of statutes, but the Court has insisted that Congress clearly identify the standards that agencies must meet.

Federalism If a state policy differs from a national policy—as has occurred in areas such as education, welfare, and environmental protection—then national bureaucrats can encounter resistance or refusal to comply with the national standards. Sometimes acting alone, and almost always when acting with others, states can have a significant effect on the national bureaucracy.

Citizens, interest groups and the media Those who are directly affected by administrative policies or who are interested in particular areas of public policy also check the exercise of administrative power. Many Social Security recipients, for example, monitor actions of the Social Security Administration and report complaints to the agency or to members of Congress. Environmental activists, welfare recipients, and many other individuals and groups keep a close watch over various administrative agencies. Media investigations also can alert the public and elected officials to problems and miscarriages of justice in the bureaucracy.

Reviewing Ideas and Terms

1. Describe What are the limits on the exercise of administrative power?

2. Explain How do both Congress and the president rely on administrative agencies?

Research Activity

3. Develop Find an example of how the media or a citizens' group in the United States or in your community has brought to light a problem in the bureaucracy.

Comprehension and Critical Thinking

SECTION 1 *(pp. 192–195)*

1. a. Review Key Terms For each term, write a sentence that explains its significance or meaning: bureaucracy, bureaucrats, civil service, spoils system.

b. Draw Conclusions Why do you think the federal bureaucracy today is so large?

c. Evaluate What do you think about the end of the spoils system and the implementation of a civil service?

SECTION 2 *(pp. 196–204)*

2. a. Review Key Terms For each term, write a sentence that explains its significance or meaning: independent executive agencies, independent regulatory commissions, bipartisan, government corporations.

b. Summarize In what ways have the executive departments changed since 1789?

c. Analyze What is your opinion about the legislative and judicial powers given to certain independent agencies? Should they be allowed to have such powers? Explain your answer.

SECTION 3 *(pp. 206–213)*

3. a. Review Key Terms For each term, write a sentence that explains its significance or meaning: progressive tax, regressive tax, proportional tax, bond, federal debt.

b. Contrast What is the difference between fiscal policy and monetary policy?

c. Predict What might happen if current budget patterns continue as they have over the past 50 years?

Critical Reading

Read the passage in Section 2 that begins with the heading "Independent Regulatory Commissions." Then answer the questions that follow.

4. What is the primary purpose of the Federal Communications Commission (FCC)?

A to regulate passenger trains

B to regulate radio, television, wire, satellite, and cable communication

C to regulate print media

D to regulate communication with foreign countries

5. What is distinctive about independent regulatory commissions?

A They are not a part of the federal bureaucracy.

B They only regulate commerce.

C They all have a bipartisan board of directors.

D They have only executive functions.

Read the passage in Section 3 that begins with the heading "The Budget in Congress." Then answer the questions that follow.

6. What is Congress's role in the budget process?

A Congress is legally bound to follow the president's proposed budget.

B Congress is able to change nearly any aspect of the president's proposed budget.

C Congress is required to produce an entirely different budget.

D Congress is bound by the advice of the Congressional Budget Office.

7. What is the main role of the Budget Committees in the House and the Senate?

A to approve the president's proposed budget

B to debate the concurrent resolution

C to cut the budget

D to establish spending and revenue guidelines

RESPONSIBILITIES OF LEADERSHIP

8. How much do you know about the **purpose and function of independent agencies**? Select an independent agency and research its purpose and function. Use your research to write an editorial on whether this agency is an important part of the federal bureaucracy today. Use persuasive arguments and language in order to convey your point.

9. The federal government takes an active role in many public health issues. The National Institute on Alcohol Abuse and Alcoholism, for example, is an agency that works to reduce alcohol-related problems in the United States. Using the library and the Internet, research examples of how **federal, state, and local governments take a role in substance abuse programs**. Write a report detailing the agency and explain why this agency is important to the prevention of substance abuse.

CONNECTING TO THE CONSTITUTION

10. Go to the periodicals section of your library and select articles from newspapers or magazines that show examples of actions taken by the executive departments and agencies. Use these articles to explain how the actions of these organizations relate to the purposes of republican government.

ANALYZING PRIMARY SOURCES

Political Cartoon *The federal budget determines the levels of funding that the agencies and organizations of the federal bureaucracy will receive each year. With every new fiscal year, the budget continues to grow. As budgets become bigger, the amount of tax revenue and additional government borrowing increases, which creates a strain on Americans and also increases the size of the federal debt.*

By permission of Bob Gorrell and Creators Syndicate, Inc.

11. Analyze What is the message of this cartoon?

12. Make Inferences How does the cartoon use the notion of weight loss to illustrate the size of the federal budget?

FOCUS ON WRITING

Expository Writing *Expository writing gives information, explains why or how, or defines a process. To practice expository writing, complete the assignment below.*

Writing Topic: The Executive Departments

13. Assignment How has the increasing number of executive departments affected the bureaucracy? Write a short essay in which you develop your position on this issue. Support your point of view with reasoning and examples from your reading and studies.

CHAPTER 8

The Federal Courts and the Judicial Branch

"THE GENERAL LIBERTY OF THE PEOPLE CAN NEVER BE ENDANGERED . . . SO LONG AS THE JUDICIARY REMAINS TRULY DISTINCT FROM BOTH THE LEGISLATURE AND THE EXECUTIVE."

—ALEXANDER HAMILTON, *FEDERALIST PAPER* NO. 78

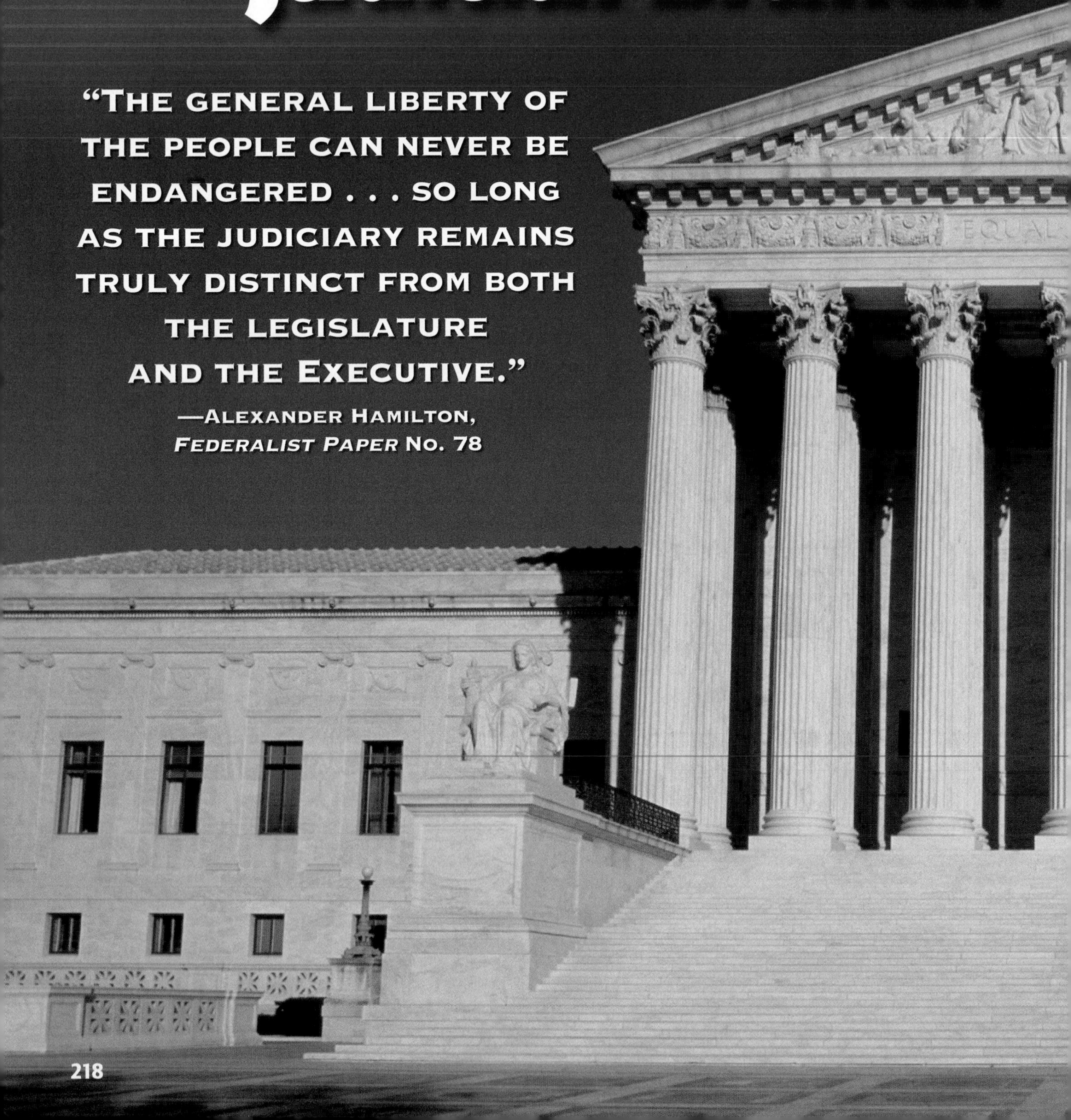

CHAPTER AT A GLANCE

SECTION 1

The Federal Court System

- The United States has a dual court system.

- The Judiciary Act of 1789 organized the federal courts into three tiers. Today these tiers consist of the district courts, the courts of appeals, and the Supreme Court.

- Through its powers of judicial review, the judicial branch plays a critical role in the system of checks and balances.

SECTION 2

Lower Federal Courts

- The courts in the 94 federal judicial districts have original jurisdiction over most federal and civil cases. They handle more than 300,000 cases a year.

- The 12 federal courts of appeals have appellate jurisdiction only.

- Under its Article I powers, Congress has established a number of specialized lower courts to hear cases of limited subject-matter jurisdiction.

SECTION 3

The Supreme Court

- The importance of the Supreme Court has grown since the Court's early days. As it gained in stature, the Court also tended to experience political shifts mirroring those in society at large.

- Supreme Court justices are nominated by the president and must undergo a lengthy Senate confirmation process.

- The Supreme Court meets from October to June or July, studying briefs, hearing oral arguments, discussing cases in conference, and issuing opinions on about 100 cases a year.

CONNECTING TO THE CONSTITUTION

Our nation's system of government is based on constitutional law established by the United States Constitution. See the "We the People: The Citizen and the Constitution" pages in this chapter for an in-depth exploration of the importance of judicial review and the checks on the Supreme Court's power.

The U.S. Supreme Court building in Washington, D.C.

The Federal Court System

Main Idea

The Framers created an independent judicial branch as part of the separation of powers of the national government. At the federal level, the judicial branch consists of three tiers of courts, each performing a different function.

Reading Focus

1. How is jurisdiction determined in the American court system?

2. How is the federal court system structured?

3. How are federal judges appointed?

4. What is the judicial branch's role in the system of checks and balances?

Key Terms

jurisdiction
exclusive jurisdiction
concurrent jurisdiction
plaintiff
defendant
original jurisdiction
appellate jurisdiction
judicial restraint
judicial activism
precedent
senatorial courtesy

TAKING NOTES As you read, take notes on the federal court system. Record your notes in a graphic organizer like this one.

A Dramatic CONFRONTATION

WHY IT MATTERS

Judicial Independence The Constitution makes the Supreme Court the ultimate interpreter of the law. The Constitution also gives Congress the power to impeach Supreme Court justices. Are these two powers compatible? If Congress can remove a Supreme Court justice for his or her opinions, how can the Supreme Court be free to rule on cases before it? Does the threat of impeachment undermine judicial independence?

That very question was at stake in a dramatic confrontation that shook Washington, D.C., in 1805. The majority party in Congress, the Democratic-Republicans, tried to impeach a sitting Supreme Court justice, Samuel Chase. Chase was a committed Federalist with a habit of speaking out on political issues and involving himself in party politics. That behavior prompted Democratic-Republicans to question his fairness. The House of Representatives, which was controlled by the Democratic-Republicans, brought impeachment charges against Chase, alleging judicial misconduct. John Randolph, leader of the Democratic-Republicans in the House, was appointed manager of the subsequent trial in the Senate.

Randolph presented an unconvincing case for conviction. Justice Chase mustered an impressive array of legal talent in his defense. Even better for Chase, some of Randolph's allies began to wonder if impeachment would set a dangerous precedent. In the end, too few senators voted to convict Chase, and the justice managed to save his job.

Historians count Chase's acquittal as a victory for judicial independence. Judges today rule without fear of politically motivated impeachment charges. There is a consensus that judges can only be removed for serious misconduct. Judicial independence remains the cornerstone of our federal court system. ■

Supreme Court justice Samuel Chase

The American Court System

Judicial independence is a cornerstone of our judicial system because it helps to safeguard the rule of law—the belief that no person is above the law and all persons are entitled to equal justice under the law. If people are to have confidence in the law's impartiality, they must know that judges cannot be unduly influenced by those in power.

The courts are where people go to settle disputes according to the law. In fulfilling this function, courts perform three basic tasks. They determine whether a law has been broken and what penalties can be applied. They decide how to provide relief for those who have been harmed by the actions of another. If necessary, they determine the meaning of a particular law or of the Constitution itself.

A Dual Court System Before the Constitution was written, there were no national courts. State courts decided how to interpret laws passed by Congress. Frequently, the decisions of the state courts contradicted each other, leaving people uncertain about what the law really was. The Framers sought to clarify the situation by creating a federal court system and defining what types of cases would be handled by it.

The Constitution created a dual court system: Alongside each state's court system, there is a national court system. It is important to note that state courts hear the vast majority of cases in the United States. Their powers flow from state constitutions and state laws. In contrast, the powers of the federal court system flow directly from the U.S. Constitution and federal laws.

Jurisdiction There are clear, if complicated, rules outlining which has **jurisdiction** over what types of cases. Jurisdiction means the authority to hear and decide a case. In general, state courts hear matters of state law and federal courts hear cases that involve the Constitution or other federal laws.

The Constitution gives federal courts **exclusive jurisdiction**—the sole right to hear a case—over certain types of cases, depending either on the subject matter of a case or the parties involved. Look at the chart on this

ARTICLE III, SECTIONS 2 AND 3: EXCLUSIVE JURISDICTION OF FEDERAL COURTS

SUBJECT MATTER	PARTIES INVOLVED
• Interpretation or applications of the Constitution, federal laws, or treaties • Admiralty and maritime law (law pertaining to maritime activities)	• The United States or one of its agencies • A representative, such as an ambassador, of a foreign country • A state government suing another state government, one of its residents, a foreign government, or one of its subjects • Citizens from the same state who claim lands in another state

page for the types of cases in which the federal courts have exclusive jurisdiction.

Concurrent jurisdiction refers to cases that fall under both state and federal jurisdiction. Concurrent jurisdiction applies when cases involve residents of different states and the amount of money involved exceeds $75,000. The **plaintiff**, or person making the legal complaint, can file his or her case in federal or state court. Under certain circumstances, the **defendant**, the person against whom the complaint is filed, can insist that the case be tried in federal court.

Whether a case is heard in state or federal court, the court that first hears it is said to have **original jurisdiction**. If the case is appealed to a higher court, it then moves to the court that has **appellate jurisdiction**.

READING CHECK **Making Inferences** Why is jurisdiction complicated by the nation's dual court system?

Structure of the Federal Court System

The Constitution does not go into great detail about the judicial branch or its structure. Article III, Section 1, states simply that "the judicial power of the United States, shall be vested in one Supreme Court, and in such inferior courts as the Congress may from time to time ordain and establish."

The Framers' brevity was partly strategic. Since the proper power of federal courts was a matter of debate and controversy, it made sense to be vague. Providing too many details might trigger opposition, which could delay or even prevent ratification. The Framers, therefore, left it to Congress to decide what kinds of courts were needed.

Judiciary Act of 1789 In its first session, Congress passed the Judiciary Act of 1789. This act fleshed out the details of the Supreme Court. It also proposed a three-tiered structure for the federal courts. The three tiers were the district courts, circuit courts, and the Supreme Court. While the federal judicial system has been altered in various ways over the years, the basic three-tiered structure laid out in the Judiciary Act of 1789 has remained intact.

District Courts District courts are spread throughout the country and serve as the trial courts of the federal system. That means they have original jurisdiction over nearly all the criminal and civil cases heard in the federal system. Criminal cases involve violations of criminal laws, such as those against murder or kidnapping. Civil cases involve disputes between private individuals or groups, such as over money or property.

There are 94 federal judicial districts—89 in the 50 states and one each in Washington, D.C.; Puerto Rico; Guam; the Virgin Islands; and the Northern Mariana Islands. There must be at least one court in every state.

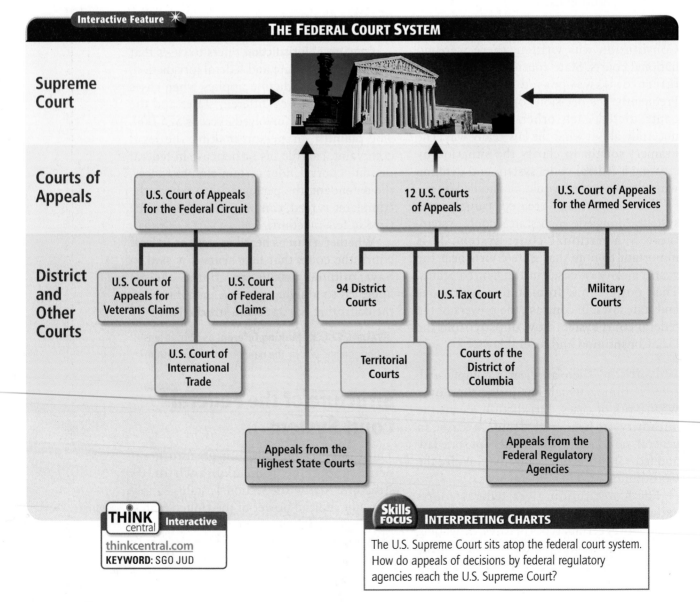

Interactive Feature

THE FEDERAL COURT SYSTEM

Supreme Court

Courts of Appeals

- U.S. Court of Appeals for the Federal Circuit
- 12 U.S. Courts of Appeals
- U.S. Court of Appeals for the Armed Services

District and Other Courts

- U.S. Court of Appeals for Veterans Claims
- U.S. Court of Federal Claims
- U.S. Court of International Trade
- 94 District Courts
- U.S. Tax Court
- Territorial Courts
- Courts of the District of Columbia
- Military Courts

Appeals from the Highest State Courts

Appeals from the Federal Regulatory Agencies

THINK central Interactive

thinkcentral.com
KEYWORD: SGO JUD

Skills FOCUS **INTERPRETING CHARTS**

The U.S. Supreme Court sits atop the federal court system. How do appeals of decisions by federal regulatory agencies reach the U.S. Supreme Court?

Courts of Appeals The Judiciary Act of 1789 established a layer of courts above the district courts called circuit courts. The term *circuit* referred to the fact that the courts originally had no fixed location. Judges would literally travel through the circuit, or designated region, going from district to district to hear cases.

When they were created, the circuit courts had original jurisdiction over some types of federal cases. They also heard appeals from cases from the district courts. The Judiciary Act of 1891 transformed the circuit courts into strictly appellate courts. Hence, their current name: the courts of appeals.

Courts of appeals hear appeals from district courts and also from those federal agencies that have rule-making and rule-enforcement powers. The United States is currently divided into 12 different circuits. Within each circuit is a court of appeals. In addition, there is now a Court of Appeals for the Federal Circuit. This court has nationwide appellate jurisdiction over certain types of cases decided by one of the specialized courts you will read about below.

The Supreme Court The U.S. Supreme Court occupies the top tier of the federal court system. The Supreme Court is mainly an appellate court—the ultimate appellate court, as a matter of fact. Article III, Section 2, of the Constitution does list a few instances in which the Supreme Court has original jurisdiction: "Cases affecting Ambassadors, other public Ministers and Consuls, and those in which a State shall be Party."

The Judiciary Act of 1789 and later acts of Congress formalized details of the Court's organization. Originally, the Court had one chief justice and five associate justices. Since 1869, the Court has had a chief justice and eight associate justices. Congress has also passed legislation that has altered the Court's appellate jurisdiction.

The Court receives some 8,000 petitions, or requests to review a case, each year. The Court chooses which cases it wants to hear. The cases usually involve major questions about the meaning of the Constitution or about federal law. On average, the Court hears and issues full opinions on about 100 cases a year.

Other Courts Over the years, Congress has created a number of other courts. Since the power to create these courts is outlined in Article I of the Constitution, these courts are often referred to as "Article I courts." The jurisdiction of these courts is limited to certain types of cases specified by Congress.

Because the jurisdiction of Article I courts is limited, their judges are not subject to the provisions regarding appointment, pay, and term length outlined in Article III. In other words, they are not appointed for life, and their pay is not guaranteed from reduction during their terms. You will read more about these courts in Section 2.

READING CHECK **Summarizing** What are the three tiers of the federal court system?

Appointing Federal Judges

The Constitution gives the president the power to nominate all federal judges, whom the Senate must then approve. Presidents typically take four factors into consideration when making nominations: legal expertise, party affiliation, a judge's judicial philosophy, and the approval of the Senate.

Legal Expertise Though the Constitution does not require it, most federal judges have been trained lawyers. Since 1952, the American Bar Association (ABA), a leading professional organization for the legal community, has issued reports on the integrity and professional competence of federal judicial nominees. The reports refrain evaluating a nominee's judicial philosophy or party affiliation. Presidents, senators, the media, and the public have often used these reports to assess a nominee's legal expertise.

Party Affiliation Presidents usually nominate judges with whom they share a party affiliation. Not only is it good politics—rewarding one's supporters with judges of like mind—it also satisfies a president's urge to leave a stamp on the nation. Judges will serve long after a president has left office. Justice William O. Douglas, for example, served 36 years. Appointed by President Roosevelt, he retired when President Ford was in office.

Judicial Philosophy Presidents also want to appoint judges who share their judicial philosophy. Definitions of judicial philosophy often come down to where a judge lands on a spectrum with **judicial restraint** on one end and **judicial activism** on the other end. Judicial restraint is the concept that a judge should interpret the Constitution according to the Framers' original intention. According to this view, laws should be overturned only when the violation of the Constitution's original meaning is absolutely clear.

The concept of judicial activism holds that judges can adapt the meaning of the Constitution to meet the demands of contemporary realities. According to this view, the Constitution should be interpreted more broadly, as an evolving document, something that subsequent generations can interpret consistent with changing values and circumstances.

Respect for **precedent**, or previous court rulings on a given legal question, can limit a judge's ability to interpret laws in innovative ways. A judge who respects precedent subscribes to the idea of *stare decisis*, which means "let the decision stand" in Latin. That is, the judge is likely to rule based on precedent rather than overturn earlier decisions. Virtually all judges agree to respect precedent to some degree. The question is how much and over which issues. Moreover, not all precedents are consistent with one another, and different precedents can be cited to support opposing interpretations of a law.

Opinions of the Senate The Senate must approve any nominee to the federal courts. For nominations to the federal district courts, the tradition of **senatorial courtesy** plays a large role. According to this tradition, a senator from the same state as the nominee and the same political party as the president can block a nomination for virtually any reason. The other senators simply respect his or her opposition to the nomination and refuse to support it. For this reason, presidents either consult with senators before making a nomination to the district courts or simply nominate candidates whom senators suggest.

Senatorial courtesy plays no role in nominations to courts of appeals or to the Supreme Court. Those courts hear cases originating in more than one state. Giving a single senator veto power over such nominations would unduly restrict the process.

Still, most presidents consult with senators, particularly those from their own party, when making nominations to the courts of appeals and to the Supreme Court. It is usually in a president's interest to avoid long, drawn-out confirmation battles in the Senate. Presidents know that senators can resort to filibusters and other tactics to block a nomination. Then again, sometimes presidents decide that a high-profile battle over a judicial nomination translates into good politics: It can stir up members of the president's party.

READING CHECK Drawing Conclusions How does the appointment process ensure that voters have some input on the selection of judges and justices?

FEDERAL JUDICIARY: TERMS OF OFFICE AND SALARY

COURT AND YEAR CREATED	JUDGES	TERMS	PAY
Supreme Court (1789)	9	Life	$203,000-$212,100
District courts (1789)	677	Life	$165,200
Courts of Appeals (1891)	179	Life	$175,100
Trade Court (1926)	9	Life	$165,200
Court of Appeals for the Armed Forces (1950)	5	15 years	$175,100
Tax Court (1969)	19	15 years	$165,200
Court of Appeals for the Federal Circuit (1982)	12	Life	$175,100
Court of Federal Claims (1982)	16	15 years	$165,200
Court of Appeals for the Veterans Claims (1988)	7	15 years	$165,200

Checks and Balances

The judicial branch plays a key role in the constitutional system of checks and balances. It both checks and is checked by the legislative and executive branches.

Judicial Review The primary judicial check on the legislative and executive branches is the power of judicial review. As discussed in Chapter 3, judicial review was established in 1803 by *Marbury* v. *Madison*. Because of *Marbury*, the Supreme Court has the power to rule on whether laws or executive actions violate the Constitution.

Checks on the Judiciary The appointment process—involving both the executive and legislative branches—is an important check on the judiciary, giving the people a say, through their elected representatives, on who will be their judges. But what happens once judges are in office? Can they be removed?

Congress has the power to impeach and remove judges from office, but it is not easy. The Constitution says that "Judges, both of the supreme and inferior courts, shall hold their terms of office during good behavior" (Article III, Section 1). Article III judges have no set terms and may serve for life.

The Framers thought that making judgeships permanent would help ensure judicial independence. It would free judges from being bullied by other branches of government or by the public. Even when it has set term limits for Article I courts, Congress has been careful to make the terms outlast any president's term of office.

Since the failure to impeach Samuel Chase, discussed earlier in this section, it has been understood that political views are not sufficient grounds for removing a judge from office. Seven judges have been removed, all for serious misdeeds such as taking bribes.

The Constitution further protects judicial independence by saying that judges' pay cannot be reduced during their term. This helps to protect the judiciary from undue political pressure or influence.

The amendment power offers another way for Congress and the states to check the judiciary. An amendment can make a formerly unconstitutional act constitutional. Both impeachment and the amendment power are difficult processes. The Framers made them that way to build a strong barrier protecting judicial independence.

READING CHECK **Summarizing** What is the judiciary's primary check on the other two branches?

WHAT DO YOU THINK?

What are the advantages and disadvantages of having federal judges appointed, not elected, to serve "during good behavior"?

SECTION 1 ASSESSMENT

THINK central Online Quiz

thinkcentral.com
KEYWORD: SGO JUD HP

Reviewing Ideas and Terms

1. **a. Describe** What is the purpose of courts?
   b. Elaborate How is the dual court system consistent with the principles of federalism?

2. **a. Identify** What is the only court specifically established in the Constitution?
   b. Elaborate How does the structure of the federal court system ensure that Americans have ample opportunities to seek justice?

3. **a. Compare** What are **judicial restraint** and **judicial activism**?
   b. Rank What do you think is the most important quality a president can consider in choosing a judge?

4. **a. Describe** What are two ways the Constitution helps ensure judicial independence?
   b. Predict How might the judiciary be different if judges served only limited terms?

Critical Thinking

5. **Analyze** Copy the graphic organizer below, and complete it using details from the section. Using the completed graphic organizer, analyze how the organization and processes of the judicial branch are or are not suitable for meeting its purposes.

Main Idea	Supporting Details
The American Court System	
Structure of the Federal Courts	
Appointment of Judges	
Checks and Balances in the Judiciary	

FOCUS ON WRITING

6. **Persuasive** Suppose you are a member of the first Congress. Write a brief summary of the judicial branch, and then take a stand defending how you and your fellow members of Congress designed it.

Judicial Activism or Judicial Restraint?

Should judges be guided by a philosophy of judicial activism or judicial restraint?

THE ISSUE

The question of how much power the judiciary should have in interpreting the Constitution is not one that is likely to have a final answer anytime soon. Most judges declare their belief in judicial restraint. But the power of judicial review, the fundamental power of the judiciary, demands that judges be willing to overturn the acts of the legislative and executive branches—in other words, that they be judicial activists. The tension between judicial restraint and judicial activism is built in to the fabric of judicial decision-making.

I PLEDGE ALLEGIANCE TO THE FLAG OF THE UNITED STATES OF AMERICA AND TO THE REPUBLIC FOR WHICH IT STANDS, ONE NATION UNDER DOPEY JUDICIAL ACTIVISM, DIVIDED, WITH LIBERTY AND JUSTICE FOR SOME....

Bruce Beattie/CNS/NewsCom

Critics saw judicial activism behind a 2005 ruling by a federal district court judge that said requiring public school students to recite the phrase "under God" was an unconstitutional endorsement of religion.

VIEWPOINTS

Judges should interpret the Constitution to address changing realities. Judicial activists argue that the Constitution should be seen as a living document, without fixed interpretation, in order to best meet the needs of the present day. Relying on the Framers' original intent, they argue, is unrealistic. Original intent is difficult, if not impossible, to determine: Different Framers had different intentions, and the Constitution reflected the political compromises needed at the time, not some fixed position for all time. Besides, the Framers never imagined the things we live with today—from electronic surveillance to the Internet. Morever, it is through the intervention of activist judges that key rights have been secured and the interests of all Americans protected. If it had been left to democratically elected legislatures, segregation, for example, might still exist.

Judges should interpret the Constitution according to the Framers' original intentions. Those who favor judicial restraint are not opposed to innovations to meet new situations, but they believe that legislatures are the proper forum to pursue such changes. Indeed, proponents of judicial restraint show great deference to the acts of legislatures and believe a law should be overturned only when it is clearly unconstitutional according to the Framers' original intent. They acknowledge the difficulty in determining original intent but believe that other criteria are too subjective. They argue that abandoning the Constitution—or creatively interpreting it—allows judges to place their personal views and opinions before sound legal reasoning and the actions of the legislative branch, violating the principle of separation of powers.

What Is Your Opinion?

1. Current Chief Justice John Roberts has said, "Judges are like umpires. Umpires don't make the rules; they apply them." In your own words, explain what you think he meant.

2. Do you think judges or justices should take a more restrained or a more activist approach? Are there situations in which your opinion might change? Explain your reasoning.

THINK central **Practice Online**

thinkcentral.com
KEYWORD: SGO JUD

Lower Federal Courts

Main Idea

Congress has created a system of lower courts for the federal judicial system. Each court has a specific role to play in the judicial branch.

Reading Focus

1. What are the roles, jurisdiction, and officers of the federal district courts?

2. What are the roles, jurisdiction, and procedures of the federal courts of appeals?

3. What are the functions of some of the other federal courts?

Key Terms

- grand juries
- bankruptcy
- magistrate judges
- misdemeanor
- public defenders
- marshals
- appellant
- briefs
- sovereign immunity
  courts-martial

TAKING NOTES As you read, take notes on the federal court system. Record your notes in a graphic organizer like this one.

District Courts	Courts of Appeals	Other Courts

WHY IT MATTERS

The Importance of the Lower Federal Courts The lower federal courts may not get the attention that the Supreme Court does, but they are equally as important. In any one year, for example, the lower federal courts handle about 99 percent of all federal cases. From bankruptcy to taxes, from kidnapping to terrorism, the lower federal courts have literally heard it all.

Their importance is told by more than numbers alone. In the absence of a Supreme Court ruling to the contrary, the lower federal courts determine what the law is. Their rulings set precedents to which other courts refer. Also, over the years, the lower courts, especially the district courts, have been

the scene of some dramatic—and historic—cases, including the treason trials of former vice president Aaron Burr (1807) and the Communist spy trials of Julius and Ethel Rosenberg (1951). These and many other moments of courtroom drama, as well as countless more routine cases, help illustrate the role of the lower courts in our federal judicial system. ■

Foundation of Justice

FEDERAL COURTS CASELOAD, 2006

Federal Courts of Appeal
66,618

Supreme Court
8,521*

District Courts
328,401

*Filed during 2005 Term

Source: *2006 Year-End Report on the Federal Judiciary*

Skills FOCUS **INTERPRETING CHARTS**

About what percentage of federal district court decisions get appealed?

Most federal trials take place in district court buildings like the Richard Sheppard Arnold U.S. Courthouse in Little Rock, Arkansas.

Federal District Courts

As discussed in Section 1, the federal court system consists of three basic tiers. The district courts occupy the lowest tier. As the trial courts of the federal system, with original jurisdiction for most federal cases, district courts are the workhorses of the federal court system, handling over 300,000 cases a year.

There are 94 federal court districts. Each judicial district has at least two judges, though some districts have many more. The U.S. Judicial District for Southern New York, which includes New York City, is the most active federal court district in the country. To handle its large caseload, it has 44 judges, the most of any federal district.

The Jurisdiction of District Courts What sorts of cases are tried before federal courts? The Constitution explicitly assigns some types of cases to the federal courts, such as those involving residents of different states or the United States and a foreign government. In addition, Congress has classified a number of offenses as violations of federal law. Civil offenses include violations of civil rights statutes and employment laws. Criminal offenses range from the destruction of aircraft to making false statements in a legal proceeding to murder. All told, district courts handle about 215,000 civil cases and 70,000 criminal cases each year.

In serious criminal cases, district courts convene panels of citizens known as **grand juries** to hear evidence of a possible

U.S. Federal Court Circuits and Districts

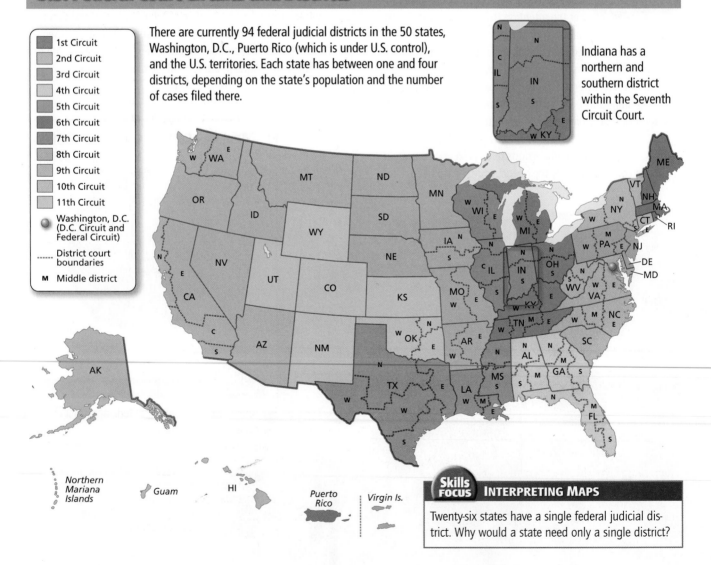

There are currently 94 federal judicial districts in the 50 states, Washington, D.C., Puerto Rico (which is under U.S. control), and the U.S. territories. Each state has between one and four districts, depending on the state's population and the number of cases filed there.

Indiana has a northern and southern district within the Seventh Circuit Court.

Legend:
- 1st Circuit
- 2nd Circuit
- 3rd Circuit
- 4th Circuit
- 5th Circuit
- 6th Circuit
- 7th Circuit
- 8th Circuit
- 9th Circuit
- 10th Circuit
- 11th Circuit
- Washington, D.C. (D.C. Circuit and Federal Circuit)
- District court boundaries
- **M** Middle district

Skills FOCUS INTERPRETING MAPS

Twenty-six states have a single federal judicial district. Why would a state need only a single district?

crime and to recommend whether the evidence is sufficient to file criminal charges. Grand juries consist of 16 to 23 people. Grand juries are not used in civil cases.

Bankruptcy cases fall under federal jurisdiction as well. Bankruptcy is a legal process by which persons who cannot pay money they owe others can receive court protection and assistance in settling their financial problems. Each district court includes a separate bankruptcy court with its own judges and procedures that handles only bankruptcy cases. The Bankruptcy Court for the Southern District of New York has 11 bankruptcy judges.

Court Officials Judges are the primary official in any court. The judge's main job is to preside over trials. He or she makes sure trials follow proper legal procedures to ensure fair outcomes. The judge also instructs juries about the matters of law they are to decide. In some cases, the participants in a trial may agree not to have a jury. In such cases, the judge decides the case.

As you read in Section 1, district court judges are nominated by the president and must be approved by the Senate. As Article III judges, they have no set term and can serve until they die or retire. Bankruptcy judges, however, are named by the courts of appeals for the circuit in which the district court is located. As Article I judges, bankruptcy judges serve 14-year terms.

District courts also have officials who are known as **magistrate judges**. These officials are responsible for overseeing some of the early hearings of a criminal trial when routine matters are carried out. They may also hear **misdemeanor**—minor criminal cases punishable by one year or less of prison time—and certain civil cases. Magistrate judges are appointed by the district court judges to terms of eight years.

Each district court has a clerk of the court. This person performs such nonjudicial jobs as maintaining court records, handling money received in fines and fees, and overseeing the jury recruitment process.

Other Courtroom Officials Each judicial district has a number of other officials who are not employees of the court but who are

vital to its operations. The most prominent of these is the U.S. attorney.

Each judicial district has one U.S. attorney. The U.S. attorney's job is to represent the United States government in federal court. When a person is charged with a federal crime, for example, the U.S. attorney, or an assistant, acts as prosecutor. That is, he or she tries to win a guilty verdict. If the United States is involved in a civil suit, U.S. attorneys represent the government.

U.S. attorneys oversee an office with numerous assistant U.S. attorneys and other staff. For the Southern District of New York, for example, there are more than 220 assistant U.S. attorneys. U.S. attorneys and their assistants are employees of the U.S. Department of Justice, making them part of the executive branch. U.S. attorneys are appointed by the president, subject to Senate approval, and serve a four-year term—though a president has the power to replace them before their term's end.

In criminal cases, the federal courts provide lawyers to defendants who cannot afford to hire one. Such lawyers are known as **public defenders**. Public defenders are appointed by the panel of the judges who make up the court of appeals.

Each judicial district is also home to an office of the United States Marshals Service.

ACADEMIC VOCABULARY

preside to hold or exercise authority

Among other duties, U.S. **marshals** provide security and police protection at federal courthouses. Marshals also transport prisoners, help track down and arrest people accused of crimes, and provide protection to witnesses in federal cases. The head of each U.S. Marshals office is appointed to a four-year term by the president, with the advice and consent of the Senate. These appointees are employees of the Department of Justice.

READING CHECK **Identifying Supporting Details** Aside from district court judges, who are some of the other officials who make up a district court?

Federal Courts of Appeals

The middle tier of the federal court system is made up of the courts of appeals. Today there are 13 of these courts. Twelve are scattered among the 12 regional circuits into which the country is divided. Washington, D.C., is both a judicial district and a circuit. In other words, it has a district court and a court of appeals. One court of appeals—the Court of Appeals for the Federal Circuit—has nationwide jurisdiction to hear certain types of cases.

Purpose of the Courts of Appeals The courts of appeals are, as their name suggests, appellate courts. They hear cases on appeal from the district courts within their circuit. They also hear appeals from various administrative agencies of the federal government. For example, people dissatisfied by a ruling by the Social Security Administration about retirement benefits may appeal to a court of appeals.

Each year, the courts of appeal hear about 65,000 cases. The vast majority—about three of four—are criminal and civil cases. In criminal cases, the appeal will be filed by a defendant who was found guilty. The federal government cannot appeal a verdict of "not guilty." In civil cases, either side can appeal.

Regardless of who files the appeal, few appeals are successful. In 2006, for example, fewer than 4 percent of filed cases were successfully appealed.

Appeals Court Procedure A person who files an appeal—the **appellant**—usually has

to show that the original ruling was based on a legal mistake. In almost all cases, the court of appeals will overturn a case only if the original court or agency followed an improper procedure.

Courts of appeals do not retry cases. They do not permit new evidence to be introduced or hear testimony from witnesses. Instead, they rely on the factual record as established by the trial court. Only in rare instances will an appeals court rule that the original court or agency misconstrued or drew a wrong conclusion from the evidence.

Most appeals are heard by a randomly chosen panel of three circuit judges. Usually the panel reviews the trial court record and reads written arguments, or **briefs**, from both sides in the case. In some cases, the court may listen to oral arguments from each side as well. When that happens, the government's side of the case is presented by the U.S. attorney who originally tried the case.

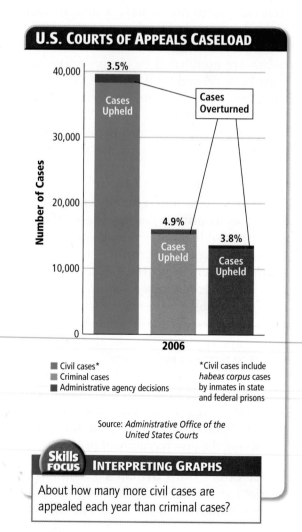

U.S. COURTS OF APPEALS CASELOAD

Number of Cases

40,000 — 3.5% — Cases Upheld — Cases Overturned

30,000

20,000 — 4.9% — Cases Upheld

10,000 — 3.8% — Cases Upheld

0

2006

■ Civil cases*
■ Criminal cases
■ Administrative agency decisions

*Civil cases include *habeas corpus* cases by inmates in state and federal prisons

Source: *Administrative Office of the United States Courts*

Skills FOCUS **INTERPRETING GRAPHS**

About how many more civil cases are appealed each year than criminal cases?

In reaching a decision, the panel of judges is guided both by Supreme Court precedent and precedents set by previous rulings within its own circuit. Decisions of one circuit court are not binding on other circuit courts.

After the Ruling The ruling of a court of appeals is usually the final word on a particular case. In some cases, though, the court might send the case back to the district court for additional hearings. If the panel finds in favor of a criminal defendant, the prosecutor may decide to retry the case, though that is rare.

The case may on occasion get further review from a larger panel of judges. This type of review is called an *en banc* review, and it often involves all the judges of a specific court of appeals.

In a small number of cases, the ruling of the court of appeals may undergo review by the U.S. Supreme Court. You will read more about this process in Section 3.

The Federal Circuit In 1982 Congress created the Court of Appeals for the Federal Circuit. This court has nationwide appellate jurisdiction for cases involving certain areas of law, such as international trade, government contracts, patents, and trademarks. Appeals come to the court from the federal district courts, from government agencies, and from some specialized federal courts that you will read about below.

READING CHECK Sequencing What is the path by which a case travels through a court of appeals?

Other Federal Courts

In addition to the district and circuit courts, Congress has created other Article III and Article I courts. These courts generally have a very limited jurisdiction to deal only with certain types of cases.

U.S. Court of International Trade This court hears cases involving disputes over laws and rules governing international trade. For example, an importer who believes he or she has been wrongly denied the right to bring a product into the country may seek relief from this court.

The U.S. Court of International Trade is located in New York City because the city has traditionally been the nation's most active port for international trade.

Because it is an Article III court, its judges, nominated by the president and approved by the Senate, can serve for life. The cases from this court can be appealed to the Court of Appeals for the Federal Circuit.

U.S. Tax Court The U.S. Tax Court hears disputes over federal taxes. If a citizen disagrees with a judgment by the Internal Revenue Service, he or she can seek redress in this court. Tax court decisions can be appealed in a federal court of appeals.

U.S. Court of Appeals for Veterans Claims Congress created the Department of Veterans Affairs to administer programs for the men and women who served in the military. Sometimes, disputes arise over a veteran's benefits, disability payments, or some other matter. The Court of Appeals for Veterans Claims hears these cases. It is located in Washington, D.C.

U.S. Court of Federal Claims In general, a sovereign nation is immune from being sued unless it agrees to be sued. This general principle is known as **sovereign immunity**. Congress, however, has identified circumstances in which parties can bring complaints against the U.S. government. To hear cases in which money claims are more than $10,000, Congress established the U.S. Court of Federal Claims, located in Washington, D.C., across from the White House. Rulings of this court can be appealed to the Court of Appeals for the Federal Circuit.

U.S. Court of Appeals for the Armed Forces Members of the military are subject to the Uniform Code of Military Justice. This code addresses the special and unusual need for order and discipline in the military. In cases of violation of the code, the military holds hearings called **courts-martial** to decide the cases. Congress has created a court to hear appeals from these courts-martial. The five judges of this court are civilian, not military, personnel. They serve fifteen-year terms. As civilians, they are not subject to the military command structure.

National Security Courts Congress has created two special courts charged with balancing the demands of national security with the rights of U.S. residents. The Foreign Intelligence Surveillance Court was established in 1978. Its job is to review and authorize requests by the government to conduct spying operations on American soil if it determines that the target of the investigation is an "agent of a foreign power." The court is made up of 11 district court judges appointed by the chief justice of the United States. They serve for seven-year terms.

The Alien Terrorist Removal Court, which Congress created in 1996, reviews requests by the U.S. attorney general to remove from the country an individual suspected of being a terrorist. Judges are appointed to this court by the Chief Justice of the Supreme Court and serve five-year terms.

Military Commissions During combat operations in Afghanistan following the terrorist attacks of September 11, 2001, U.S. military forces captured many individuals whom they classified as "enemy combatants." President George W. Bush created special military commissions to try these individuals. Modeled on U.S. military tribunals set up during World War II to try war criminals from Nazi Germany and Japan, the commissions were outside the normal judicial system. Their legality was challenged in federal court. In *Hamdan* v. *Rumsfeld* (2006), the Supreme Court struck down the procedures, methods, and powers under which these military commissions operated, forcing Congress and the president to draft new rules. These new rules are themselves being challenged in federal court.

Washington, D.C., and Territorial Courts Congress has governing responsibility for Washington, D.C., and the U.S. Territories of Guam, the Virgin Islands, and the Northern Mariana Islands. Accordingly, Congress has authorized the creation of local trial and appellate courts in each of these places to try local cases. These courts are distinct from the federal district court and the federal court of appeals in these jurisdictions, which hear federal cases.

READING CHECK **Summarizing** What are some of the reasons why Congress created additional courts?

SECTION 2 ASSESSMENT

THINK central Online Quiz
thinkcentral.com
KEYWORD: SGO JUD HP

Reviewing Ideas and Terms

1. a. Describe What kinds of cases are heard in federal district courts?
b. Elaborate How does membership of U.S. attorneys in the executive branch allow voters to have a voice in the judicial process?

2. a. Identify What is an **appellant**?
b. Evaluate Why do you think courts of appeals generally limit their review of cases to questions of the law rather than to matters of fact?

3. a. Describe What is the purpose of the Court of Appeals for the Armed Forces?
b. Evaluate How do the national security courts created by Congress balance individual rights and national security?

Critical Thinking

4. Compare and Contrast Copy and fill in the graphic organizer below. Then use it to compare and contrast the main features of the federal district courts and courts of appeals.

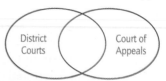
District Courts — Court of Appeals

FOCUS ON WRITING

5. Descriptive Prepare a brief job description for each of the courtroom officers, including the judges, who staff the federal district courts.

③ The Supreme Court

Main Idea

The Supreme Court is the highest court in the nation and the most important component of the judicial branch. It serves as the final word on questions of federal law and the Constitution.

Reading Focus

1. What are some of the highlights of Supreme Court history?

2. How are Supreme Court justices chosen?

3. What are the typical procedures of the Supreme Court?

Key Terms

writ of certiorari
docket
majority opinion
concurring opinions
dissenting opinions

TAKING NOTES As you read, take notes on the Supreme Court. Record your notes in a chart like this one.

History	Appointment	Procedures

WHY IT MATTERS

Interpreters of the Constitution They command no police force or army. Their budget is miniscule compared to the budgets of the other two branches of government. What they get they must petition Congress for, like any other government agency. Yet the nine justices of the U.S. Supreme Court have extraordinary power. They have the last word, the final word, about what the Constitution means.

The significance of that power was clear even 175 years ago, when French political observer Alexis de Tocqueville noted in his book *Democracy in America* that "a more imposing judicial power was never constituted by any people." The Constitution is the supreme law of the land, and the authority to interpret it gives the Supreme Court the final say over what is legal and illegal, what can be done and what cannot. In a nation in which, as de Tocqueville noted, "scarcely any political question arises . . . which is not resolved, sooner or later, into a judicial question," this power—the power of the final word—puts the Court's efforts at the very heart of our government. It is a power that the Court must strive to exercise for the common good. ■

THE Final Word

Supreme Court Justices

Supreme Court Milestones

Key rulings in Supreme Court history have defined the powers of the federal government and the rights of Americans.

	Marbury v. *Madison* (1803)	*Worcester* v. *Georgia* (1832)	*Scott* v. *Sandford* (1857)	*Plessy* v. *Ferguson* (1896)
Decision	Declares parts of Judiciary Act of 1789 unconstitutional; denies Marbury's claim to government post	Upholds Cherokee lands ownership against claims by the state of Georgia	Rules Dred Scott still a slave and Missouri Compromise unconstitutional	Rules separate facilities for blacks and whites do not imply inequality
Significance	Established the Court's power of judicial review	President Andrew Jackson's refusal to enforce ruling demonstrated limits of the Court's authority.	Furthered tensions that led to the Civil War	Led to an expansion of Jim Crow segregation

Justice John Marshall

Dred Scott

Highlights of Supreme Court History

The Supreme Court was not always the powerful institution it is today. In its early years, it was held in low esteem, and a number of prominent figures turned down the job of chief justice as unworthy of their interest. Over time, however, the Supreme Court gained in prestige and authority.

Even as it gained in prestige, the Court also underwent political shifts that mirrored—slowly and often belatedly—the shifts in society at large. This process of evolution continues today.

Early Visions The Constitution says little about the Supreme Court, leaving even its structure for Congress to define. But Alexander Hamilton, writing in *The Federalist* No. 78–83, gave a lengthy explanation of the federal judiciary and the powers of the Supreme Court. His writings have become a touchstone for constitutional scholars and Supreme Court justices trying to determine the intent of the Framers.

Hamilton began by reassuring those suspicious of a newly created federal judiciary that the judicial branch was "the weakest of the three departments of power." At the same time, Hamilton foresaw the critical role the Supreme Court had to play in providing judicial review of the acts of Congress and the executive branch.

PRIMARY SOURCE

❝ Limitations [on the powers of government] . . . can be preserved in practice no other way than through . . . courts of justice, whose duty it must be to declare all acts contrary to the manifest tenor [obvious meaning] of the Constitution void. Without this, all the reservations of particular rights or privileges would amount to nothing. ❞

—Alexander Hamilton, *The Federalist* No. 78

The Marshall Court It took a few years after the founding of the new government for the Supreme Court to fulfill Hamilton's vision. The change began with the 1801 appointment of John Marshall as chief justice. Marshall was a Federalist and as such took an expansive view of the power of both the Supreme Court and the national government in general. By the end of his 34 years on the Court, the judiciary had become an equal partner and a full participant in the system of checks and balances.

In the landmark case *Marbury* v. *Madison* (1803), Marshall cleverly negotiated perilous political waters to arrive at a decision that asserted the Court's power of judicial review. William Marbury had received a last-minute

	Court Packing Scheme (1937)	Brown v. Board of Education, Topeka, Kansas (1954)	Miranda v. Arizona (1966)	Hamdan v. Rumsfeld (2006)
Decision	Not a case, but FDR's plan to expand the Court in order to get support for New Deal programs	Rules separate educational facilities for blacks and whites are inherently unequal	Rules law enforcement must inform criminal suspects of their rights before questioning	Rules military commissions to try "enemy combatants" illegal
Significance	Integrity of Court protected, even as Court begins approving FDR's New Deal laws	Led to the end of de jure segregation in public schools	Expanded defendants' rights and restricted law enforcement's actions	In 2006 President George W. Bush and Congress passed new legislation clarifying military commission procedures. These procedures have been challenged in court.

FDR "packs" the Court.

Detainee at U.S. base at Guantanamo Bay, Cuba

appointment as justice of the peace by outgoing President John Adams, a Federalist. Incoming President Thomas Jefferson, a Democratic-Republican, ordered his Secretary of State James Madison not to deliver Marbury's commission. Marbury sued under provisions of the Judiciary Act of 1789. Marshall's decision denied Marbury's suit, giving a victory to Jefferson. But in doing so, Marshall had also declared part of the Judiciary Act of 1789 unconstitutional. In other words, Marshall had asserted the Court's right to review—and strike down—acts of the legislature. For Jefferson, who thought the legislature should be supreme, the *Marbury* decision amounted to winning the battle but losing the war.

Other key Marshall Court decisions helped shape the basic structure of the federal government and the economy. For example, in *McCulloch* v. *Maryland* (1819), the Court's decision made the necessary and proper clause a powerful mechanism to expand the implied powers of Congress. *Gibbons* v. *Ogden* (1824) helped assert the federal government's power to regulate interstate commerce. The Marshall Court also upheld the contracts clause (Article I, Section 10), laying the legal groundwork for the rapid growth of the nation's economy.

Dred Scott Democrats dominated the presidency and the Senate for much of the first half of the 1800s. Not surprisingly, the Supreme Court under Chief Justice Roger Taney began to reflect that party's concern for states' rights and protection of slavery.

The Taney Court's most famous decision came in *Dred Scott* v. *Sandford* (1857). Scott, an enslaved African American, sued for his freedom. Scott's slaveholder had taken him and his wife to live in the free state of Illinois and the free territory of Wisconsin, where Congress had outlawed slavery by the Missouri Compromise of 1820. Scott argued that because he and his wife had lived in free areas, they were free. The Supreme Court declared Scott was still a slave. Moreover, it argued that while blacks might be citizens of a particular state, the Constitution never envisioned that they could become U.S. citizens. Finally, the Court declared that Congress lacked the power to outlaw slavery in the territories, thus striking down the Missouri Compromise as unconstitutional.

The *Scott* decision set off violent partisan reaction, contributing to the atmosphere that led to the Civil War. One later scholar summed up its impact by labeling the decision as "the greatest disaster the Supreme Court has ever inflicted on the nation."

From Reconstruction to *Plessy* Following the Civil War, Republicans became the leading political party for the next 60 years, and their appointees dominated the Court. Two issues preoccupied the Court in this period: the civil rights of the newly freed African Americans and economic regulation.

The Republican-controlled Congress passed and the states ratified—in the case of the southern states, reluctantly ratified—a series of constitutional amendments. The Thirteenth, Fourteenth, and Fifteenth amendments outlawed slavery, established citizenship and equal protection of the law for African Americans, and guaranteed voting rights for African American males.

The Court, however, narrowly interpreted these amendments as they related to civil rights. In the *Civil Rights Cases* (1883), the Court struck down the Civil Rights Act of 1875, which had sought to give blacks federal protection from discrimination. The Court held that African Americans should look to state legislatures or courts for redress. The problem was that state legislatures in the South were passing discriminatory laws, and southern courts showed little interest in upholding the rights of African Americans. The Supreme Court's hands-off approach to discrimination came to a head in *Plessy* v. *Ferguson* (1896). You can read more about that case on the next page.

At the same time, the Court interpreted these Civil War amendments in a way that made much regulation of the economy unconstitutional. In the *Slaughterhouse Cases* (1873), for example, the Court struck down a state law regulating the sanitary slaughtering of livestock. It ruled that such regulations violated the Fourteenth Amendment's prohibition against state laws infringing federal rights—in this case, the property rights of slaughterhouse operators.

The Court and the New Deal The Court's tendency to view economic regulation as an assault on property rights persisted into the twentieth century. From 1899 to 1937, the Court struck down state laws in 184 cases, most of them involving efforts at economic regulation. In *Lochner* v. *New York* (1905), for example, the Court struck down a law limiting bakers to a 10-hour workday.

In the 1930s the Court clashed with President Franklin Roosevelt over an ambitious set of programs to help fight the Great Depression. The Court found that some of these New Deal programs violated the Constitution. In response, Roosevelt proposed a law that would let him add six new justices to the Court. Roosevelt clearly wanted to "pack the Court" with justices who would support his programs.

Roosevelt's plan sparked sharp criticism, but it also may have convinced the Court to defer to legislatures on matters of economic regulation. Roosevelt withdrew his plan. By then the Court had begun to reject challenges to New Deal legislation. In the years to come, moreover, because of his lengthy tenure as president, Roosevelt reshaped the Court through his many appointments. A liberal era on the Court had begun.

From the 1950s to the Present The liberal era on the Court reached its height during the chief justiceship of Earl Warren, former governor of California named to the Court by President Dwight D. Eisenhower in 1953. For the next 16 years, the Warren Court produced some of the most dramatic and controversial decisions in U.S. history.

In 1954 the Warren Court issued the unanimous decision of *Brown* v. *Board of Education of Topeka, Kansas*. This landmark ruling called for the desegregation of public schools. In *Gideon* v. *Wainwright* (1963) and *Miranda* v. *Arizona* (1966), the Warren Court expanded the rights of people accused of crimes. In *Tinker* v. *Ohio* (1969), the Court held that schools could not prevent students from protesting the Vietnam War. The Warren Court also halted religious prayer in public schools. Critics of the Warren Court accused it of overjealous judicial activism.

Since 1953, Republican presidents have appointed 16 of the last 22 Supreme Court justices. Over time, these appointments have resulted in a more conservative Court. The Court's 5–4 decision in *Bush* v. *Gore* (2000), assuring the presidency for George W. Bush, was along partisan lines, reflecting the deep ideological divide on the Court.

READING CHECK **Making Generalizations** How has the Supreme Court been shaped by politics?

DIVISION FOR
PUBLIC
EDUCATION
AMERICAN BAR ASSOCIATION

Plessy v. Ferguson (1896)

In Plessy v. Ferguson, the Supreme Court examined a Louisiana state law requiring racial segregation on public transportation and determined whether it violated the equal protection clause of the Fourteenth Amendment.

Background

By the early 1870s, support for Reconstruction was waning. Following the disputed presidential election of 1876, the federal troops that had been enforcing the Reconstruction laws in the South were withdrawn. Soon, many southern states began to pass laws that restricted the rights of African Americans, requiring that blacks use separate facilities, such as schools or public transportation, from whites.

Homer Adolph Plessy was active in a small group of African American and creole professionals seeking to overturn Louisiana's Separate Car Act of 1890. The law required nonwhites to sit in a separate train compartment and required that railroad companies "provide equal but separate accommodations for the white, and colored races."

The group chose Plessy, who was one-eighth African, to see if he could board the whites-only compartment on the East Louisiana Railway. The group wanted to challenge the act and used Plessy's light skin color to illustrate their belief that the law was subjective and unconstitutional. Railway officials also objected to the law. It meant an extra expense for their companies, so they agreed to cooperate with the group and arranged for Plessy to be arrested safely before the train left New Orleans. The case eventually came before the Supreme Court.

Arguments for Plessy

Plessy argued that the Separate Car Act violated the Thirteenth and Fourteenth Amendments. Plessy claimed that the Separate Car Act was unconstitutional because it imposed on him a "badge of servitude" (a reference to the Thirteenth Amendment) and deprived him of his right to equal protection as a citizen of the United States. Plessy lost his case and appealed to the Louisiana State Supreme Court. The state supreme court upheld the lower court's ruling, and Plessy took his case to the Supreme Court.

Arguments for Ferguson

Judge John Howard Ferguson presided over Plessy's original trial. At that trial, he ruled that Louisiana could regulate its railways as it saw fit within its borders and that, therefore, the Separate Car Act was constitutional. Because he was considered black under the law, Plessy was required to sit in the specified compartment, and when he refused to do so, he had committed a crime.

THE IMPACT TODAY The Supreme Court ruled against Plessy. Separation of the races, the Court ruled, did not imply inequality. This separate-but-equal doctrine helped perpetuate segregation until it was overturned by *Brown* v. *Board of Education of Topeka, Kansas* (1954). *Plessy's* greatest impact today might lie in the inspiration provided by the stinging dissent of Justice John Marshall Harlan. "Constitution," Harlan wrote, "is color-blind, and neither knows nor tolerates classes among citizens."

CRITICAL THINKING

What Do You Think? Are there some instances in which distinctions between classes, or groups, of citizens are legitimate? Support your reasoning with examples.

Choosing Supreme Court Justices

Choosing a Supreme Court justice is one of the most significant decisions a president and the Senate can make. Because they have such a long tenure in office, justices can profoundly affect the nation for many years. Not surprisingly, the process of choosing a Supreme Court justice can become a high-stakes political battle.

Choosing a Nominee Presidents use the same basic criteria in choosing a Supreme Court nominee as they do in choosing any federal judge—legal expertise, party affiliation, judicial philosophy, and a sense of the nominee's acceptability to the Senate. But under the intense scrutiny of the media and interest-groups, presidents act cautiously.

The Constitution gives no formal requirements for the job of Supreme Court justice. Throughout history, however, all Supreme Court justices have had a background in law. Most have served as federal judges. A few have served as state governors, as judges on state courts, or in various other government posts. One, William Howard Taft, was president of the United States before serving on the Supreme Court as chief justice from 1921 to 1930.

Presidents typically nominate individuals who are affiliated with their own political party. Sometimes, however, party membership is not enough. Party activists may impose a so-called "litmus test" on a candidate to ensure that he or she holds their position on some key issue, such as abortion. (The term refers to a scientific test that clearly shows the presence of acid in a solution.) Those who fail the test are rejected regardless of their other qualifications.

Presidents also seek to choose justices whose share their own judicial philosophy. This is not always as easy as it sounds. President Eisenhower, for example, once remarked that nominating Earl Warren was the biggest mistake of his presidency. Eisenhower expected Warren to be more conservative than he turned out to be.

No president wants to fight a losing battle with the Senate. So presidents often try to assess the level of Senate support or opposition to a nominee before making a public announcement. Presidents facing a Senate controlled by the opposition party are less likely to nominate a candidate whose beliefs reflect the extremes of their own party.

Confirmation Hearings The confirmation process begins with hearings in front of the Senate Judiciary Committee. The hearings are usually televised. The nominee often faces intense direct questioning, especially from senators who may oppose the nomination. Nominees have their judicial beliefs and record inspected in great detail. Senators may consult a report on the nominee's qualifications issued by the American Bar Association. Opponents bring up past writings or decisions, called the paper trail, to hint at how the nominee may rule on the Supreme Court. If the nominee lacks a record, that fact will be explored, too.

Sometimes senators raise issues aside from a nominee's legal background. For example, Douglas Ginsburg's admission at his hearings that he once used illegal drugs helped end his nomination in 1987.

PROFILES IN GOVERNMENT

Sandra Day O'Connor
1930–

Sandra Day O'Connor was the first female justice of the Supreme Court, serving from 1981 until she retired in 2006. A brilliant student, O'Connor graduated third in her class at Stanford University's law school at the age of 22.

Despite her accomplishment, no California law firm would hire O'Connor, so she entered government service. In 1958, she moved to Arizona, where she eventually served in all three branches of state government. In 1981 President Ronald Reagan nominated O'Connor as associate justice, fulfilling a campaign promise to place a woman on the Supreme Court. During her years on the Court, O'Connor tempered firm conservative principles with a commitment to a case-by-case analysis of the facts. In her later years, she often served as a crucial "swing vote" on a deeply divided Court.

Since leaving the Court, O'Connor has served as chancellor of the College of William and Mary and developed an educational Web site that helps students learn about the federal judiciary. "We are born free, but liberty is something we have to learn," she has said.

Drawing Conclusions How does O'Connor's career illustrate changing attitudes toward women in the workplace?

Confirmation Hearings

Over the last 20 years, Senate confirmation hearings for Supreme Court justices have become highly charged events. Opponents of Robert Bork's nomination in 1987 placed ads on TV denouncing what they saw as Bork's extreme conservative views. The hearings for Clarence Thomas in 1991 were dominated by accusations of sexual harrassment. More recent nominees, such as John Roberts, have prepared for hearings by trying to make themselves invulnerable to political attack.

Skills FOCUS INTERPRETING PRIMARY SOURCES

Making Inferences What is the confirmation process for Supreme Court nominations being compared to? Do you think the cartoonist approves of this situation?

See **Skills Handbook**, p. H9.

Often, however, hearings prove uneventful. Recent nominees generally say little about how they might rule on controversial issues—to the frustration of some senators. Moreover, presidents are careful to nominate candidates with a minimal paper trail.

When the Senate Judiciary Committee has completed its work, it votes on the nomination. The outcome of this vote nearly always guides the vote in the full Senate and predicts its outcome. While the full Senate may debate the nomination, little new ground is broken in most cases. Only rarely do problems arise at this point.

Most nominees are confirmed, but confirmation is no certainty. The Senate has rejected, put off, or forced the removal of 28 nominations since 1789.

READING CHECK **Sequencing** What is the process a nominee undergoes to join the Supreme Court?

Supreme Court Procedures

Once they are on the Supreme Court, what do the justices do? What are the processes and procedures they follow? How do justices go about their jobs?

The Term Begins The Supreme Court term begins each year on the first Monday in October. The Court remains in session until June or July. During this time, the Court hears cases, writes opinions, and carries out other duties.

In general, the Court session is divided into blocks of about two weeks. During one block, the justices sit on the bench, listening to lawyers present their cases. This period is followed by another block in which the justices work behind closed doors to make rulings, decide what cases they will hear in the future, and issue orders on minor cases.

Helping the justices in their work are several dozen clerks. These are recent law-school graduates who help do research, evaluate requests to have cases heard, and write drafts of opinions. Today, each justice typically has four clerks to assist him or her.

Selecting Cases A key task facing the Supreme Court is deciding which cases it will consider. In general, the Court chooses which cases it wants to hear. These cases come from three categories.

The Court typically hears only a few cases each year in which it has original jurisdiction.

How Supreme Court Decisions Get Made

A Supreme Court case typically follows a three-step process. Selecting and hearing cases proceeds according to a relatively fixed calendar. The drafting of final opinions, however, usually takes longer. *Why do you think the opinions stage often takes longer?*

Selecting Cases

Petition for a Writ of Certiorari One party to a dispute requests a review of a ruling made by either a federal appeals court or a state supreme court.

Granting Certiorari During conference, justices review petitions. If four of nine judges agree to review a case, certiorari is granted.

Briefs and Arguments

Briefs Parties file briefs explaining their side of the case. Outside parties may file additional briefs known as amicus curiae, or "friend of the court," briefs.

Oral Arguments Justices may decide to hear oral arguments. Each side is limited to 30 minutes to present its case. Justices usually vigorously question counsel.

Opinions

Conference Justices meet to discuss and decide the case by a vote. The most senior judge voting in the majority assigns the writing of the majority opinion to another judge in the majority. Majority opinion sets out the legal reasoning behind the decision. Individual justices may write concurring opinions or dissenting opinions.

Opinions Drafted With the assistance of their law clerks, justices draft written opinions and circulate them to other justices. Opinions sometimes change votes.

Opinions Announced Opinions are published by the Court. Opinions can include the following:
- majority opinion
- concurring opinion
- dissenting opinion

---

the Supreme Court to issue a **writ of certiorari** (suhr-shuh-RAR-ee), an order seeking review of the lower court case. If the Court grants certiorari, it agrees to hear the case. If the Court denies certiorari, the ruling of the lower court stands.

A less common route to the Supreme Court is through the highest state courts. If a state case has exhausted all appeals and involves a question about the Constitution or federal law, the Supreme Court may grant certiorari. Otherwise, the ruling of the state court stands.

Today, the Court chooses about 100 or so cases to hear each term. Four justices have to vote in favor of hearing a case on appeal before it is placed on the Court's **docket,** or list of cases to be heard. Cases are selected from what are now about 8,000 requests for certiorari. Usually, cases are chosen because they represent major questions about the Constitution or federal law.

Briefs and Oral Arguments What is involved in the Court "hearing" a case? The first step is reading briefs—the written arguments prepared and submitted by each side in the case. A good brief identifies past cases that support a particular point of view. It lays out a clear and convincing legal argument in favor of a specific judgment.

Justices may also consider so-called *amicus,* or "friend of the court," briefs. These are legal briefs prepared by outside parties that have an interest in a case.

After studying briefs, the justices listen to oral arguments. Oral argument takes place before the seated, robed panel of nine Supreme Court justices. The chief justice presides. During oral arguments, lawyers representing each side have precisely 30 minutes to present their case. This sometimes dramatic presentation usually involves sharp questioning from the justices, who probe for weaknesses in each side's argument.

Opinions After reading briefs and hearing oral arguments, the justices meet privately in conference to discuss the case. The chief justice leads these discussions, but all justices have the chance to speak. Based on these discussions and on the justices' own study, the Supreme Court eventually produces a

Such cases are those involving foreign ambassadors or the U.S. government, disputes between states, and disputes between one state and citizens of another state or country.

The most common way for a case to come to the Supreme Court is on appeal from a federal court of appeals. When a party is unhappy with an appeals court ruling, it asks formal, written opinion. Opinions are issued throughout the session but often come in a flurry near the end, in May or June, when the more difficult and divisive cases finally get resolved.

A Supreme Court opinion is a long, carefully worded exploration of the major issues, judicial precedents, and legal reasoning behind a decision. It explains in detail why the Court has overturned or supported a lower court's decision. The opinion serves as the formal judgment of the Supreme Court.

Court opinions take several forms. A **majority opinion** is one that is signed by at least five of the nine members of the Court. The majority opinion represents the Court's actual ruling in the case.

Majority opinions are sometimes accompanied by **concurring opinions**. These agree with the overall conclusion in the case but stress some different or additional legal reasoning. **Dissenting opinions** are those held by the minority of the justices who do not agree with the ruling in the case. Dissenting opinions do not have a direct legal impact on the case. They can, however, influence future judgments.

Court Orders The Court's full review of cases, complete with briefs, oral arguments, and written decisions, is called plenary review. In addition to the 100 or so cases that the Court gives full plenary review each year, the Court also disposes of some 50 to 60 cases with brief, unsigned court orders. For example, a court order may direct a lower court to reconsider a certain case in light of a specific Court decision. In these instances, the Court does not read briefs, hear oral arguments, or issue a written opinion explaining its reasoning.

READING CHECK Identifying Supporting **Details** What are the three main stages that cases before the Supreme Court typically must go through?

Influences on Judicial Decisions

Ultimately, judges and justices must be guided by the facts of a case and by the law. However, other considerations often play a part in their decisions.

- **Public Opinion** Courts take account of changing community standards, such as those related to the role of women or the definition of obscenity.

- **Legislative Opinion** Courts consult the intent of the legislatures as expressed in legislative findings and other documents submitted in support of a law.

- **Executive Opinion** Courts may consult presidential executive orders and signing statements.

- **Desire for Impartiality** Courts strive to be impartial, deciding cases on their merits and not favoring either party.

- **Judicial Ideology** Judges' own political beliefs may influence their decisions.

SECTION 3 ASSESSMENT

THINK central Online Quiz
thinkcentral.com
KEYWORD: SGO JUD HP

Reviewing Ideas and Terms

1. **a. Describe** Describe the background and significance of *Plessy* v. *Ferguson*.
   b. Explain Why is the Marshall Court considered so central to the nation's history?

2. **a. Identify** What are the main factors a president may look for in selecting a Supreme Court nominee?
   b. Evaluate Do you think the Congress should establish formal qualifications of Supreme Court justices? Why or why not?

3. **a. Define** What is the meaning of the terms **majority opinion**, **concurring opinions**, and **dissenting opinions**?
   b. Elaborate Why do you think it is important for justices who disagree with a majority opinion to record their opposition and present their arguments?

Critical Thinking

4. **Design** Copy and fill in the graphic organizer below, then describe an alternate Supreme Court nominating process that would avoid some of the current problems.

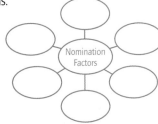

Nomination Factors

FOCUS ON WRITING

5. **Descriptive** Write a statement that describes the qualities you think would be most important in a Supreme Court justice.

The Supreme Court and the System of Checks and Balances

Because its members do not stand for election, the Supreme Court is considered the least democratic of the three branches of government. What is the source of its power, and how does the Constitution place checks on that power?

What is judicial review? In 1803, in the case of *Marbury* v. *Madison*, Chief Justice John Marshall, writing for a unanimous Supreme Court, ruled that judges have the power to decide whether acts of Congress, the executive branch, state laws, and even state constitutions violate the United States Constitution. The justices of the Supreme Court have the final say about the meaning of the Constitution. The power to declare what the Constitution means, and whether the actions of government officials violate the Constitution, is known as the power of judicial review.

The Constitution does not mention the power of judicial review. However, both Federalists and Antifederalists assumed that the Supreme Court would exercise judicial review. The practice traces its roots to the seventeenth-century English system of law. It was well known and used by most state courts before adoption of the Constitution and even by the Supreme Court before being officially acknowledged in *Marbury*. Alexander Hamilton defended the power in *Federalist* No. 78:

> *A constitution is, in fact, and must be regarded by the judges, as a fundamental law. It therefore belongs to them to ascertain its meaning.*

Judicial review was neither immediately nor universally accepted. Antifederalists such as Brutus feared that the Court would use judicial review to eliminate the power of state courts. Andrew Jackson argued against it and threatened not to enforce Supreme Court decisions with which he disagreed. Not even all judges accepted the validity of judicial review. In *Eakin* v. *Raub* (1825), Pennsylvania Supreme Court justice John B. Gibson identified several arguments against it:

- Legislatures are the repository of the people's sovereignty, and the exercise of judicial review is an act of sovereignty, which should reside with the legislatures or the people.

- Judicial review could lead to political turmoil if the other branches of government, or the states, refuse to acquiesce to the Court's interpretation of the Constitution.

- Judicial review makes the judiciary equal or even superior to the legislature, even though judges were not elected.

- All officers of the government take an oath to support the Constitution; therefore, all must consider the constitutionality of their actions.

- The judiciary is not infallible. Judges' errors in interpreting the Constitution cannot be corrected at the ballot box, only by constitutional amendment.

Today, judicial review is accepted almost universally in the United States and increasingly throughout the world. Controversy swirls around how the Court uses the power in particular cases.

What checks exist on the power of the Supreme Court? The Supreme Court exercises immense power when it interprets the Constitution. However, there are many checks on the exercise of judicial power, including limitations that the Supreme Court has imposed on itself. Following are checks on the Court's power:

Self-imposed limits. The Court avoids partisan politics by refusing to decide "political questions," or questions that it believes should properly be decided by other branches or levels of government. The Court decides only cases in controversy. The Supreme Court does not issue advisory opinions. That is, the Court will not offer an opinion about how a law should be interpreted unless there is a specific case before the Court where the interpretation of the law is actually in dispute.

Presidential appointments. Presidents seek to influence future Supreme Court decisions with their nominees to the Court. By changing Court personnel, presidents seek to change approaches to constitutional interpretation and attitudes about the role of the Court in the constitutional system.

Executive enforcement. Presidents and administrative agencies are responsible for enforcing the Court's decisions. Occasionally presidents have threatened to refuse to enforce Supreme Court decisions or have enforced them only reluctantly. For example, in 1974 Americans anxiously waited to see if Richard Nixon would comply with the Supreme Court's order in *United States v. Nixon*. The Court had ordered the president to turn over White House tape recordings to prosecutors. Once revealed, the tapes implicated Nixon and his aides in the Watergate scandal.

Congressional powers. Congress determines the Supreme Court's appellate jurisdiction and controls its budget. Congress has threatened to use those powers in response to Supreme Court decisions with which it disagrees. If the Supreme Court declares a congressional statute unconstitutional, Congress may pass the statute in another form to demonstrate its resolve on the issue. Congress also can alter the size of the Court, as it has done several times over the years. It even can determine when the Court meets or suspend a term of the Court, as it did in 1802. Finally, Congress can initiate constitutional amendments in response to unpopular Court decisions, such as a decision in 1895 that struck down an income tax statute. The Sixteenth Amendment, ratified in 1913, subsequently gave Congress the power to lay and collect taxes on income.

Federalism. States, like the executive branch, are responsible for implementing Supreme Court decisions. Sometimes state enforcement is lax. For example, 50 years after the Supreme Court ordered public school desegregation, several states still have found ways to evade that ruling.

Reviewing Ideas

1. Explain How did the Supreme Court acquire the power of judicial review?

2. Draw Conclusions Why do you think it is in the interests of the Supreme Court to refuse to decide "political questions"?

Critical Thinking

3. Evaluate What are the advantages and disadvantages in having the Supreme Court make judgments only about specific cases rather than issuing advisory opinions as constitutional questions arise?

Connecting Online

Visit <u>thinkcentral.com</u> for review and enrichment activities related to this chapter.

THiNK central

KEYWORD: SGO JUD

Quiz and Review

GOV 101
Examine key concepts in this chapter.

ONLINE QUIZZES
Take a practice quiz for each section in this chapter.

Activities

eActivities
Complete Webquests and Internet research activities.

INTERACTIVE FEATURES
Explore interactive versions of maps and charts.

KEEP IT CURRENT
Link to current events in U.S. government.

Partners

American Bar Association Division for Public Education
Learn more about the law, your rights and responsibilities.

Center for Civic Education
Promoting an enlightened and responsible citizenry committed to democratic principles and actively engaged in the practice of democracy.

Comprehension and Critical Thinking

SECTION 1 *(pp. 220–225)*

1. a. Review Key Terms For each term, write a sentence that explains its significance or meaning: original jurisdiction, appellate jurisdiction, judicial activism, judicial restraint, precedent.

b. Explain What factors made the creation of a federal judiciary controversial in the 1780s?

c. Evaluate What are the benefits and drawbacks of the constitutional system for protecting the independence of judges?

SECTION 2 *(pp. 227–232)*

2. a. Review Key Terms For each term, write a sentence that explains its significance or meaning: grand juries, bankruptcy, misdemeanor, public defenders, appellant, briefs, sovereign immunity.

b. Contrast What is the difference between federal district courts and federal courts of appeals?

c. Develop What are the advantages in having specialized courts for certain types of cases?

SECTION 3 *(pp. 233–241)*

3. a. Review Key Terms For each term, write a sentence that explains its significance or meaning: writ of certiorari, docket, majority opinion, concurring opinions, dissenting opinions.

b. Make Generalizations What is the relationship between the country's political climate and the makeup and rulings of the Supreme Court?

c. Evaluate What do you think should be the most important factor a president considers when picking a Supreme Court justice?

Critical Reading

Read the passage in Section 2 that begins with the heading "Purpose of the Courts of Appeals." Then answer the questions that follow.

4. In most instances, what must a party order do to bring an appeal to a court of appeals?

A have won the case in the lower court

B be a U.S. citizen

C be prepared to argue that the lower-court case involved a serious legal error

D have jurisdiction over the case

5. The 12 U.S. circuit courts of appeals hear appeals from what types of courts?

A state supreme courts

B criminal conviction or a civil ruling from a federal district court

C military courts

D U.S. Supreme Court

Read the first two paragraphs in Section 3 that begin with the heading "Choosing a Nominee." Then answer the questions that follow.

6. What previous jobs have most Supreme Court justices had?

   A president of the United States

   B state governor

   C federal court judge

   D army general

7. Why do party activists impose so-called "litmus tests" on potential Supreme Court nominees?

   A to determine a nominee's chemical composition

   B to determine where the nominee stands on an issue or issues vital to the activists

   C to determine if a nominee will support school-testing programs

   D none of the above

RESPONSIBILITIES OF LEADERSHIP

8. Research cases from the **current or most recent Supreme Court term**. Choose a case that interests you and write an editorial opinion column in support of or against the Court's decision in the case. Be sure to support your position with facts and logical arguments.

9. Create a political cartoon illustrating your point of view on one of the issues involving the **judicial branch**, such as judicial activism, a politicized nominating process, national security courts and military commissions, or senatorial courtesy.

CONNECTING TO THE CONSTITUTION

10. Research each of the cases below. Then write a paragraph explaining the Court's decision in each case and the significance of the decision to contemporary events.

    Fletcher v. *Peck* (1810)

    Dartmouth College v. *Woodward* (1819)

ANALYZING PRIMARY SOURCES

Political Cartoon *Decisions of the Supreme Court are binding on the lower federal courts. Sometimes, however, lower federal courts need further clarification. The cartoon depicts what happened in the wake of the Supreme Court's decision in* United States *v.* Booker (2005), *which made previously mandatory sentencing guidelines discretionary and gave the courts of appeals responsibility for reviewing sentences for "reasonableness."*

"I'm using this till the Supreme Court settles the sentencing guidelines issue."

Bruce Beattie/CNS/NewsCom

11. **Analyze** What is the judge using to determine a sentence?

12. **Draw Conclusions** What does the cartoonist mean to suggest about the result of the Supreme Court's decision in *United States* v. *Booker* (2005)?

WRITING FOR THE SAT

Think about the following issue:

Judicial activism has been a significant issue in recent decades. Some people believe that judges should interpret the Constitution rigidly and resist opportunities to issue rulings that make significant changes to government policy. Others argue that all parties support judicial activism when it promotes a goal they support.

13. **Assignment** Is judicial activism good or bad? Do we want judges that mainly let the legislature and executive branch determine policy? Write a brief essay in which you develop your position on this issue. Support your view with reasoning and examples from your reading and studies.

The Political Process

"IT IS NOT THE FUNCTION
OF OUR GOVERNMENT TO KEEP THE
CITIZEN FROM FALLING INTO ERROR;
IT IS THE FUNCTION OF THE CITIZEN
TO KEEP THE GOVERNMENT
FROM FALLING INTO ERROR."

—SUPREME COURT JUSTICE ROBERT H. JACKSON, 1950

CHAPTER AT A GLANCE

SECTION 1
Public Opinion

- Public opinion is the collection of views that large numbers of people hold about issues of public concern.
- Public opinion helps direct public policy.
- Individual opinion is influenced by such factors as family, friends, and age.
- The media can help shape public opinion.
- Polls can measure public opinion.

SECTION 2
Interest Groups

- People who share similar views and goals may form an interest group.
- Interest groups represent a wide variety of attitudes and opinions.
- Interest groups can affect public policy.

SECTION 3
Political Parties

- Political parties are groups of people organized to elect their members to public office.
- The United States has a two-party system.
- Political parties contribute to the public good by selecting candidates and educating voters.

SECTION 4
The Electoral Process

- Candidates for public office can be chosen in a variety of ways.
- Political parties and political candidates conduct political campaigns to try to win public office.
- Voters may be influenced by several factors, such as their religion, experiences, and age.

CONNECTING TO THE CONSTITUTION

Our nation's government is based on constitutional law established by the United States Constitution. See the "We the People: The Citizen and the Constitution" pages in this chapter for an in-depth exploration of the origins of American political parties.

Flanked by the news media, Senator Jim Webb (D, Virginia) greets supporters.

SECTION 1

Public Opinion

BEFORE YOU READ

Main Idea

Public opinion is the collection of views that people hold on public issues. Public opinion is important because it often influences the political process and affects the actions the government takes.

Reading Focus

1. What is public opinion?
2. How is public opinion formed?
3. How does the media affect public opinion?
4. How is public opinion measured?

Key Terms

public opinion
public policy
political socialization
mass media
propaganda
poll
sample
sampling error
bias
objectivity
exit poll

TAKING NOTES As you read, take notes on factors that shape public opinion. Record your notes in a chart like this one.

Factor	How it shapes public opinion

The Vietnam War and Public Opinion

The Living Room War In the late 1950s and early 1960s in Vietnam, a civil war was raging. On one side were Communist Viet Cong guerrillas and their North Vietnamese supporters. On the other side was the anti-Communist government of South Vietnam, supported by the United States. American public opinion was generally in favor of U.S. efforts in Vietnam, which were seen at the time as a way to stop the spread of communism.

As early as 1963, however, some Americans began to protest U.S. involvement in South Vietnam. In 1965, U.S. military activity in Vietnam increased greatly. By 1968, more than 540,000 U.S. troops were in Southeast Asia, fighting a fierce and bitter war.

As U.S. involvement in Vietnam increased, so did media coverage of the war. For the first time in history, people at home saw scenes of war unfolding as they watched the evening news on television. Many people believe that this nightly "living room war" coverage was responsible for a change in public opinion. Perhaps influenced by media coverage, the public began to believe that the war's cost in terms of lives, money, and material was greater than its perceived rewards. Public opposition to the war increased. In 1975, after 12 years of direct involvement and faced with mounting public opposition to the war, the United States withdrew its last military forces from Vietnam. Today the Vietnam War is an example of how public opinion may affect public policy. ■

In the late 1960s, reports about the Vietnam War appeared frequently on nightly newscasts.

What Is Public Opinion?

The aggregation of views shared by a segment of society on issues of interest or concern is called **public opinion**. These views may focus on foreign policy, such as the Vietnam War, or on domestic or local policy issues, such as reducing health care costs or debating the need for a new high school.

Public opinion is complex. For example, many people believe that human actions lead to global warming. Others disagree: They see global warming as a natural phenomenon. So public opinion on this issue is divided. Also, people who agree on one issue, such as global warming, may differ with each other on another issue, such as gun control.

Public Opinion and Public Policy Public opinion helps leaders shape **public policy**—that is, the choices the government makes and the actions it takes in response to a particular issue or problem. Public opinion also indicates how well the government is responding to the will of the people.

Public opinion can be viewed in two ways. The first is to consider the "public" as a single, centralized body—a large group of people concerned about public issues. In this view, public opinion *may be led*, or formed, by the decisions and actions of important political or social leaders.

For example, in 2002 and early 2003, President George W. Bush stated that intelligence reports indicated Iraqi president Saddam Hussein had weapons of mass destruction, which posed a threat to U.S. national security. Based on those claims, most Americans supported the president's policy of a U.S.-led invasion of Iraq in 2003. By November 2006, however, public opinion about Iraq had changed enough to negatively affect the president's party in the midterm congressional elections.

The second view of public opinion is that the public is many separate, individual "publics," each with its opinion on one or a few issues. Each "issue public" interacts with one or more decision makers. In this view of public opinion, people's attitudes *lead* public policy and the public agenda. For example, a neighborhood group's concerns might lead the city council to reduce traffic in the area.

Expressing Public Opinion Responsible citizens try to shape public opinion. They may express their opinions by writing Web logs or letters to the mayor or testifying at a public hearing. Active citizens may take part in marches or demonstrations. During the Vietnam War, for example, thousands of antiwar protesters marched in cities and on college campuses.

Many citizens also join and support groups or organizations that represent their views, such as Mothers Against Drunk Driving and Friends of the Earth. Many of these organizations have committees that donate money to political campaigns or provide information to try to influence local, state, or federal legislation—public policy issues—important to the group.

Finally, responsible citizens express their opinions by voting. The outcome of any election—local, state, or federal—reflects overall public opinion about the candidate or issue being voted on. But voting behavior, whether in a presidential election or a town's mayoral race, is complex. People may vote for a candidate because he or she agrees with their general views, is the incumbent, shares their view on a single issue—such as cutting taxes—or just seems more friendly or likable than the other candidates.

READING CHECK **Identifying the Main Idea** How is public opinion related to public policy?

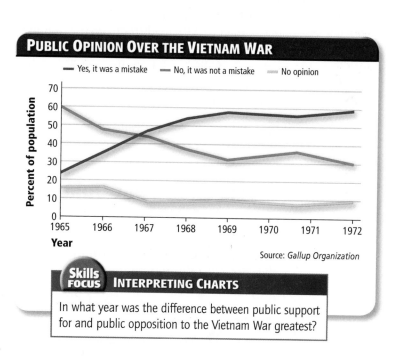

PUBLIC OPINION OVER THE VIETNAM WAR

— Yes, it was a mistake   — No, it was not a mistake   — No opinion

Percent of population — Year (1965–1972)

Source: *Gallup Organization*

Skills FOCUS **INTERPRETING CHARTS**

In what year was the difference between public support for and public opposition to the Vietnam War greatest?

Forming Public Opinion

People's opinions are influenced by several factors, including their family and friends; school and work experiences; and personal factors such as age, gender, race, and religion. The process by which people acquire political beliefs is called **political socialization**.

Family A person's family often has the most direct influence on his or her views. As children, we hear family members talk about political issues and current events. Even if we do not always understand what we hear and even if we disagree with other family members, the conversations help shape our attitudes about race, religion, politics, and other important social issues.

School and Work School is where we formally learn about government, citizenship, and other values. You know from your own experience that peer groups influence opinions about what to wear, what music to listen to, and whether something is fair.

Experiences in the late teens and early twenties also help shape personal opinions. At that stage, people are more independent of family influences. They may also face new influences at their place of employment.

Other Personal Factors Age, race, gender, and religion are also factors in shaping opinions. For example, a younger person's opinion about Social Security benefits and retirement plans may differ from the opinions of someone older. In some cases, a person's religious beliefs might influence his or her opinions about marriage, abortion, prayer in school, and other public policy issues.

READING CHECK **Summarizing** What personal factors shape a person's political socialization?

Media and Public Opinion

Public opinion and the public agenda may be shaped or determined by the mass media. **Mass media** are means of communication that provide information to a large audience. Your daily routine is probably filled with mass media. Mass media include magazines, television news, news on the Web, and the latest viral video on the Internet.

ACADEMIC VOCABULARY

enduring lasting, durable

Media Impact The media's effect on public opinion and public policy is most visible in two areas: It monitors, shapes, and determines the public agenda, and it covers electoral politics. The media reports and comments on issues that political leaders and the public consider important. It also reports when officials ignore public opinion. The media does not force people to take sides, but it focuses attention on important issues.

The Growth of Mass Media The most enduring form of mass media is print media—newspapers and magazines. In this country, the relationship between the press and public opinion—and politics—goes back to at least 1789. It was then that John Fenno published a Federalist paper, the *Gazette of the United States*. To counter this Federalist paper, Thomas Jefferson and the Whigs supported the *National Gazette*, which began in 1791. Bitter partisan battles to capture public opinion were often waged in the party press. Following are other examples of print media's influence on public opinion:

- The **"penny press."** These inexpensive newspapers covered issues of interest to working class people.
- **"Yellow journalism."** This type of journalism uses sensationalism, scandals, and appeals to patriotism to attract and influence readers. The height of yellow journalism was from 1895 to 1898.

Although average daily newspaper readership among adults has declined since its peak in the 1960s and 1970s, about 40 percent of American adults 18 years and older report reading a newspaper daily.

Radio was the first form of electronic media. In the 1920s radio stations broadcast news and entertainment to millions of homes. In the 1950s television replaced radio as the most influential form of electronic media. Today, even with the growth of the Internet, political candidates at all levels rely on radio and TV ads to deliver their messages.

The Internet has also changed mass media. In 1996, just 1 in 50 Americans depended on the Internet as a daily source for news. Today, 1 person in 3 regularly gets his or her news online. At the same time, only two-thirds as many people today watch network TV news as watched it in 1996.

However, most print media, such as the *New York Times* and the *Wall Street Journal*, have an online edition, and broadcast and cable TV networks also have online news sites.

Roles of Media The media shapes public opinion in several ways, such as by the issues it covers and the ones it ignores. For example, TV newscasts may choose not to cover a particular issue. However, if bloggers talk about the issue, newscasts may then pick it up and the public may start discussing it.

The type of coverage a topic receives is also important. For example, stories that describe a political candidate's experience create a different picture of the candidate than reports that focus on issues that have nothing to do with his or her experience.

Criticism of the Media All kinds of mass media—print, broadcast, electronic, and the Internet—are subject to criticism from a variety of sources. The most common criticisms include the following:

- **Bias in reporting.** Reporting may be slanted toward a certain point of view. For example, print and television news media are often described as being mostly liberal, while talk radio shows are described as almost always conservative.
- **Bias in story selection.** A media outlet may focus on one issue and ignore or downplay others. Media defenders say that because the time or space available to cover news is limited, journalists must decide what issues to cover at a particular time.
- **Factual inaccuracy.** Critics warn that news sources, especially non-traditional sources such as blogs or other Internet news sites, may be careless about factual accuracy. For example, standards for and ways to check accuracy on the Internet are still evolving.
- **Media consolidation.** About two dozen companies own most U.S. media outlets today. Critics argue that this media concentration destroys the independent sources of information our democracy needs.

Get Your Daily News

Traditional sources for daily news are declining in popularity. At the same time, online sources, such as Web logs (or blogs), are being used by more people for their daily news. The blogger shown below reports from the United Nations.

SOURCE OF NEWS IN DAILY LIFE

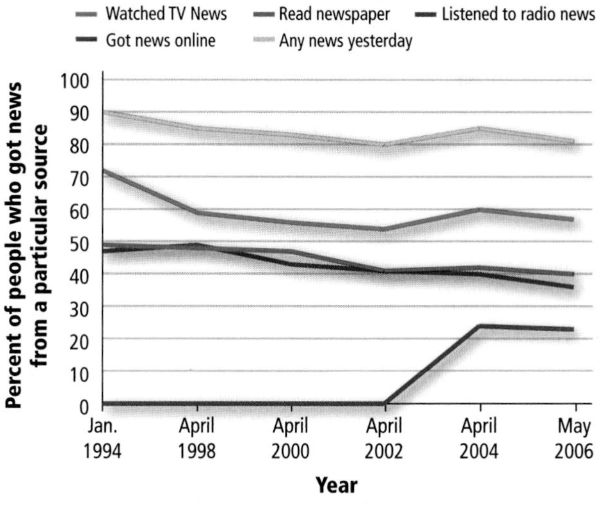

Legend:
— Watched TV News   — Read newspaper   — Listened to radio news
— Got news online   — Any news yesterday

Y-axis: Percent of people who got news from a particular source (0–100)
X-axis (Year): Jan. 1994, April 1998, April 2000, April 2002, April 2004, May 2006

Source: *Pew Research Center for the People & the Press Survey Reports, July 30, 2006*

Skills FOCUS **INTERPRETING CHARTS**

Has the increased popularity of blogs, RSS feeds, and other online news sources caused the declining popularity of traditional news sources? Why or why not?

The Future of the Media News and information can now be delivered instantly to your cell phone, home computer, or PDA. Many Americans go online everyday to get some or all of their news. Blogs, RSS feeds, and podcasts have grown rapidly as sources of daily news. People—not just journalists—share ideas without the limits of TV or print.

However, just because news is more accessible does not mean it is more accurate.

PRIMARY SOURCE

❝At its best, the Internet can educate more people faster than any media tool . . . At its worst, it can make people dumber faster than any media tool . . . Because the Internet has an aura of 'technology' surrounding it, the uneducated believe information from it even more.❞

—Thomas Friedman, *The New York Times* (2002)

Today, even with media consolidation, you have a choice of a wide variety of information sources. It is important not to rely on a single source. Using multiple sources will help you get accurate information and avoid **propaganda**, or statements meant to influence public opinion or promote a cause or viewpoint.

READING CHECK **Summarizing** Why should you consult more than one source for your news?

Measuring Public Opinion

Sooner or later, you may be asked to share your opinions about new products or an upcoming presidential election. You may be part of a public opinion **poll**—a survey of people scientifically selected to provide opinions about something. Scientific polling is a way to determine public attitudes or preferences about consumer products, social issues, and political candidates. Most surveys today are scientific polls.

The Polling Process A well-designed poll is an accurate measure of public opinion. The accuracy of a poll depends on the number of people answering the questions, how those people are chosen, how the questions are asked, and the absence of bias.

The first key to a poll's accuracy is the **sample**, or the group of people who take part in the poll. The size of the sample is important. For example, mathematically, a sample of about 1,500 people is sufficient to reflect the opinions of a sample universe of 230 million potential voters accurately. Second, for poll results to be accurate, the sample must be chosen at random from the sample universe. The sample universe is the total population or market of interest.

SCIENTIFIC POLLING

A scientific poll is a tool, based on mathematics, used to learn people's opinions about something, whether it is a new product, a public policy issue, or a political candidate.

1. SAMPLE UNIVERSE
"Sample universe" is the set of individuals, items, or data from which a statistical sample is taken.

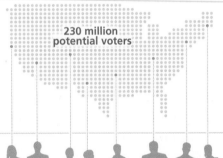

230 million potential voters

2. RANDOM SAMPLE
To be truly random, each member of the sample universe, and each geographical location, must have an equal chance of being selected for the poll.

3. THE POLL
Accurate poll results also depend on the way questions are worded and the order in which they are asked.

YES   NO

4. RESULTS AND MARGIN OF ERROR

The margin of error, expressed in percentage points, is a measure of the poll's accuracy. It gives the range within which the poll's results may vary from the true value in the entire population.

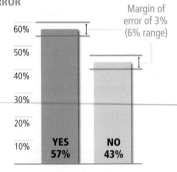

Margin of error of 3% (6% range)

YES 57%   NO 43%

Have higher gas prices caused economic hardship?

Skills FOCUS **INTERPRETING CHARTS**

Why is it necessary for a polling sample to be truly random?

Finally, the way questions are worded or the order in which they are asked can affect a poll's accuracy. For example, "Do you think the president is doing a good job?" may produce results different from "Is your overall opinion of the president very favorable, somewhat favorable, somewhat unfavorable, or very unfavorable?" Also, asking that question after questions about controversial issues, rather than as the first question, may change how people answer it and, therefore, affect the poll's accuracy.

A reliable poll states its margin of error, or uncertainty level. The margin of error, or **sampling error**, indicates a poll's accuracy, and is given as a percentage above and below the poll's results. For example, a poll with a margin of error of 3 percent may show that 37 percent of the respondents have a certain opinion. In the total population, then, between 34 percent and 40 percent of people are likely to hold that opinion.

Evaluating Polls Properly conducted polls produce reliable, accurate, objective, and bias-free results. In polling, **bias** refers to errors introduced by polling methods that lead to one outcome over others. **Objectivity** is freedom from bias and outside factors, such as timing, that may influence results.

Polls and Public Opinion Most major polls are created and conducted scientifically. However, polls are sometimes conducted in ways that produce certain results. For example, asking, "Do you favor or oppose the death penalty for those convicted of murder?" produces a different result than asking, "Which penalty do you prefer for people convicted of murder, the death penalty or life in prison?" Either result might be used to shape public opinion in support of a particular group's political or social agenda.

Exit Polls Another common type of scientific poll is the exit poll. Used on election day, an **exit poll** surveys a randomly selected fraction of voters after they have voted and tells pollsters how people voted before the official vote count. People may use exit poll results to predict the winners of all but very close races. Critics of exit polls argue that these predictions may discourage people from voting and may alter the result of some state and local races. Supporters of exit polls respond that studies show that very few voters are influenced by exit poll results. Today, to be safe, exit poll results are not usually announced until voting has ended.

READING CHECK **Summarizing** What factors can affect the accuracy of poll results?

SECTION 1 ASSESSMENT

THINK central **Online Quiz**
thinkcentral.com
KEYWORD: SGO POL HP

Reviewing Ideas and Terms

1. **a. Define** What is **public policy**?
   b. Explain In your own words, explain how public policy and **public opinion** are related.
   c. Elaborate What are the two views of public opinion, and what role does each view play in setting public policy?

2. **a. Describe** What is **political socialization**?
   b. Compare Do you think family and friends are similar in the way they influence a person's opinions? Why or why not?

3. **a. Explain** How does the media help determine public policy?
   b. Predict Will media consolidation affect public opinion or limit access to a variety of viewpoints? Why or why not?
   c. Elaborate What is the meaning and importance of a free and responsible press to our democracy?

4. **a. Recall** How is public opinion determined?
   b. Elaborate Why do you think it is important to know a poll's **sampling error** when evaluating its results?

Critical Thinking

5. **Elaborate** Copy and complete the web below. Then use it to explain how each of the four factors contributes to the accuracy of a public opinion poll.

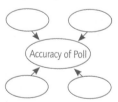

Accuracy of Poll

FOCUS ON WRITING

6. **Persuasive** Write a comment for posting to a Web log in which the following statement appeared: "It is not possible for television media to report the news objectively." Your comment should explain why you agree or disagree with the blogger.

BEFORE YOU READ

Main Idea

Interest groups are private organizations that try to influence public opinion and convince public officials to accept their goals and views. They give political power to segments of society that have similar views.

Reading Focus

1. What are interest groups, and what role do they play in the political process?
2. What different types of interest groups exist?
3. How do interest groups work?
4. Do interest groups serve the public good?

Key Terms

interest group
political action committee
trade association
labor unions
endorse
lobbying
grass roots

TAKING NOTES As you read, take notes on the different types of interest groups. Record your notes in a graphic organizer like this one.

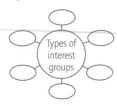

Types of interest groups

WHY IT MATTERS

Taking Interest, Taking Action For almost any significant public policy issue being considered by a legislative body, one or more groups of people are likely trying to convince public officials to support their ideas and policy solutions. Groups may call themselves clubs, associations, or committees. They may represent issues such as animal rights or tax reform, or they may represent groups such as workers or students. Whatever a group calls itself or whoever it represents, its goal is usually to influence public opinion and shape public policy.

For example, in Texas, as in most states, most political office-holders are men. In Texas, also as in most states, women have formed groups to elect more women to public office. One of those groups is Annie's List, a group of activists that endorses Democratic Party candidates, makes political campaign contributions, and recruits qualified Democrat women to run for state-wide elected offices and the Texas legislature. Another group is the Texas Federation of Republican Women (TFRW), whose purposes are very similar to those of Annie's List, including encouraging Republican women to run for office and supporting Republican Party candidates.

Annie's List and TFRW are interest groups. These two groups are part of a more general category of groups called cause-based interest groups. All interest groups, whatever their label, have one goal in mind: to shape public policy in a way that promotes their particular interests. ∎

Annie's List helped get these women elected to the Texas legislature.

Interest Groups and What They Do

Annie's List and the TFRW are two of the thousands of interest groups in the United States. An **interest group** is an association of people who hold similar views or goals. Interest groups, also called advocacy groups, represent those views and goals and try to influence public policy and the public agenda to achieve them. Interest groups are especially important to people who feel their views are overlooked in policy discussions.

Interest groups work at every level—local, state, and national—in our representative democracy. These groups give people a way to monitor government actions, express themselves about government policies, and participate in social action. Interest groups

- organize people who share concerns
- provide members with a means of political participation
- supply information to the public and to policy makers

Many interest groups also have political action committees (PACs) that support candidates for political office who agree with the group's position on the issues. A **political action committee** is an organization created to raise and contribute money legally to the campaigns of political candidates.

Organizing Interests Individual citizens can initiate, influence, or change public policy or the public agenda in several ways. In fact, part of the responsibility of being a good citizen is to try to influence public policy. People can write letters to the editor or their state or federal representatives; they can give speeches or testify at legislative hearings; and they can vote. They may also join others and march in demonstrations. Sometimes, however, one person's actions are not enough. Joining an interest group gives each person's opinion more impact than it had when the person acted alone. People join interest groups knowing that working with others strengthens their cause.

People who join groups to promote their common concerns include environmentalists, business owners, musicians, teachers, and members of minority groups. Sometimes interest groups form on different sides of the same issue. For example, the American Immigration Control Foundation is a group that wants to limit immigration; the Coalition for Comprehensive Immigration Reform is a group that supports broad immigration reform. Both groups give their members political impact that the members would not have as individuals.

Encouraging Participation People who feel strongly about an issue often want to do more than just vote for candidates who share their views. Being a member of a group gives individuals a way to take part in the political process—at every level of government—and helps the group to influence public policy.

Active membership in interest groups seems to have declined in recent years. According to recent studies, Americans are joining fewer social groups and organizations than in the past, whether because of technological changes or for other reasons. However, although active membership in interest groups may be down, "checkbook memberships"—financial contributions to such groups—have increased.

Supplying Information Greater resources, such as more money, have allowed many interest groups to hire experts and engage in new kinds of activities, such as lobbying campaigns or creating interactive Web sites to present their views. As a result, many interest groups can now exert influence in ways that exceed the power that results from membership alone.

An interest group's influence often comes more from the information it provides than from the activities of its members. Even a small group, such as the Swift Boat Veterans for Truth in 2004, can be powerful if it effectively delivers its message to policy makers and the public. The 2004 presidential election provided an example of this: The group's television ads attacked Democratic presidential candidate Senator John Kerry and hurt his campaign. Since that election, "swiftboating" has come to mean an attack on a candidate's truthfulness and patriotism.

READING CHECK **Identifying the Main idea** How are interest groups and public opinion related?

RESPONSIBILITIES OF LEADERSHIP

By knowing and exercising rights such as voting and influencing public opinion, responsible citizens help government serve the public good. Responsible citizens have other obligations as well, such as treating others with dignity and respecting the law.

Interest Groups

Although there are thousands of interest groups in the United States, they can generally be grouped into six basic categories. Examples of each category are shown below.

Agricultural

Agricultural groups represent the interests of people and businesses who grow and produce food and other crops.

Business

Most business groups follow issues such as taxes, energy prices, and consumer protection laws.

Labor

Labor unions protect the interests of workers, such as fair wages and salaries, safe workplaces, and a variety of employee benefits.

Types of Interest Groups

Many of the thousands of interest groups in the United States represent economic interests and issues. Other groups, such as the TFRW, form around political, social, cultural, or religious issues. Still other interest groups focus on foreign policy issues.

Agricultural Groups Many interest groups represent the nation's farmers and agricultural industry. Some, such as the large American Farm Bureau Federation, represent farmers as a whole. Others, such as the much smaller National Potato Council, are commodity groups that represent certain types of farmers or a particular agricultural product. The National Potato Council represents U.S. potato growers on legislative, regulatory, environmental, and trade issues.

Business Groups Organizations such as the U.S. Chamber of Commerce and the National Federation of Independent Business (NFIB) are examples of business interest groups. The Chamber of Commerce represents business interests in general, while the NFIB represents the rights of small and independent business owners.

Another type of business group, called a **trade association**, represents certain industries or parts of industries. For example, when you select a bag of pretzels from a vending machine, your choice matters to the Snack Food Association, a trade association that represents the snack food industry. Similarly, the American Wind Energy Association promotes the production of electricity from wind power facilities by supporting tax credits and other pro-growth policies.

In general, trade associations support laws and policies that benefit their industry and oppose laws and policies that harm their interests. Most business groups and trade associations also have their PACs make campaign contributions to political parties and candidates.

Labor Groups Most labor interest groups are also **labor unions**—groups of workers who do the same job or work in related industries. For example, the Brotherhood of Locomotive Engineers and Trainmen exists to make sure that train engineers, conductors, and the people who control the brakes and switches work under safe conditions. Another group, the Service Employees International Union (SEIU), represents people who work in health care, building cleaning and security, and public service jobs. Like business and trade association groups, unions and union members contribute to political campaigns. Many unions have a committee on political education (COPE) that directs the union's political activities, including fund-raising and support for political candidates.

Cause-based

Cause-based groups usually focus on a particular problem, such as endangered wildlife, children's health, or strengthening the nation's borders.

Societal

Societal groups, such as the American Muslim Alliance, educate the public about a particular segment of society, their views, and their issues of importance.

Professional

Professional groups often set the standards for practicing that profession, and they protect the economic interests of their members.

Cause-Based Groups Some groups, including many political interest groups, represent or promote a cause rather than the interests of a segment of society. For example, Mothers Against Drunk Driving (MADD) is a single-issue group devoted to fighting drunk driving and its causes. Another example is Common Cause, a group that works to strengthen public participation and confidence in the institutions of government. Finally, the Center for Civic Education is a national organization dedicated to promoting an enlightened and responsible citizenry.

Societal Groups Some groups represent religious, social, racial, ethnic, and other segments of the population, rather than economic or professional interests. Examples of societal groups include the National Organization for Women (NOW), the Eagle Forum, the Mexican American Legal Defense and Education Fund (MALDEF), the American Muslim Alliance, and AARP, which represents older Americans.

Professional Groups Some interest groups represent a particular profession, such as the American Medical Association (AMA) and the American Bar Association (ABA), which represent doctors and attorneys, respectively. Such groups establish standards for their profession, influence the licensing and training of those who enter the profession,

and educate the public and government about their professional interests and issues of concern to the profession.

READING CHECK **Contrasting** How do cause-based groups differ from other interest groups?

How Interest Groups Work

Interest groups do not change laws, but they do affect public opinion and public policy at every level of government. A group's success is based on hard work, accurate and timely information, effective and frequent communication, and money. Groups support candidates and engage in lobbying to influence public officials and public policy.

Endorsing Candidates One way groups influence public policy and legislation is to help elect candidates who support their views. An interest group may **endorse**—publicly declare its support for—a particular candidate in an election. For example, certain social, religious, or labor groups often endorse Democratic Party candidates, just as other business, social, or religious groups usually endorse Republican Party candidates. Whether a group endorses a particular candidate usually depends on the candidate's position on, and support for, the group's interests. Voters may use a candidate's list of endorsements to make voting decisions.

Interest groups also participate in elections by having their PACs contribute money to the campaigns of candidates. PACs usually contribute to candidates who have supported the group's views in the past. In some cases, PACs give money to both candidates for an office, hoping that whoever wins will support the group's interests. For example, in the 2006 congressional elections, the National Association of Realtors split $3.7 million in campaign contributions, giving 48 percent to Democrats and 51 percent to Republicans.

Lobbying Interest groups participate in government at every level by **lobbying**, or contacting a public official to persuade the official to support the group's interests. Groups lobby decision makers in government agencies as well as legislators.

A lobbyist may visit with city council members about changing the zoning along a city street or talk to state representatives about reducing taxes. Lobbyists now use technology, such as e-mail campaigns, to inform and influence officials, but their most effective tools are telephone calls and face-to-face conversations.

Informing Public Opinion Interest groups often provide someone to testify—whether at a city council meeting, a state agency, or congressional hearing—to express and explain the group's interests. This public testimony generates support for the group and may influence lawmakers.

Many groups and lobbyists practice grassroots politics. **Grass roots** is the name given to the lowest level of an organization or society. In grassroots politics, a group may organize a demonstration or march or get a large number of individual voters to contact a legislator or other official. The legislator may be influenced by this strong showing of support for a particular position.

Filing Lawsuits Another way interest groups influence public policy is through the legal system. Perhaps the best-known lawsuit occurred in the 1950s when a group of parents in Topeka, Kansas, sued to end legal racial segregation in public schools. In 1954, in the landmark case of *Brown* v. *Board of Education of Topeka, Kansas*, the Supreme Court ruled that racially segregated schools were illegal. The Court also ordered that the African American students be admitted to public schools "with all deliberate speed."

READING CHECK **Summarizing** What methods do interest groups use to influence public policy?

Interest Groups and the Public Good

American democracy includes both the principle of majority rule and the requirement that minority rights be protected. As you might expect, interest groups that represent majority interests and others that represent minority interests actively try to influence public policy and political issues.

Benefits of Interest Groups An important benefit of interest groups is that they give minority interests a voice in the political process. The civil rights movement of the 1950s and 1960s is a good example. Thousands of African Americans and their supporters united to draw society's attention to segregation's violence and discrimination against African Americans.

PROFILES IN GOVERNMENT

Fannie Lou Hamer
1917–1977

Fannie Lou Hamer, born in Mississippi, was the granddaughter of slaves and the youngest of 20 children. In the 1950s and 1960s, Hamer was a civil rights activist who worked with the Student Nonviolent Coordinating Committee to register African Americans to vote. In 1971, she ran for the Mississippi state senate, but was unsuccessful.

From the late 1960s until her death in 1977, Hamer devoted much of her energy to developing programs to help needy families in her community. These programs included the Delta Ministry, a community development program that focused on economic aid for poor and minority residents. In 1969 Hamer organized the Freedom Farms Corporation, a nonprofit land cooperative that provided poor and needy families land on which to raise food and livestock—land they could later purchase. Her focus was always on her community, where she fought against school segregation, organized child day care centers, and supported low-income housing projects.

Make Inferences Would you describe Fannie Lou Hamer as a "grassroots organizer"? Why or why not?

Other political minorities, such as neighborhood associations or hunters, may form their own interest groups. For example, rural landowners may unite to oppose a state's plan to build a major new highway.

Criticism of Interest Groups Some critics believe that interest groups have too much influence. A well-funded group, such as the Swift Boat group mentioned earlier, can have an impact even with a small membership.

Interest groups are also criticized for focusing on one narrow issue and ignoring broader social needs and policies. Critics also argue that interest groups often use appeals to people's emotions, rather than finding reasoned—and reasonable—solutions to the social problems they are addressing. Finally, critics sometimes argue that, with effective interest groups on all sides of an issue, Congress may decide not to act.

Limits on Interest Groups In 2007, in the wake of a number of highly publicized lobbying scandals, Congress passed ethics and lobbying reform legislation. These new rules tightened House and Senate ethics rules for legislators and limited some types of activities by lobbyists.

Although the reforms were extensive, critics note that Congress has, in the past, passed rules and laws that tried to weaken the links between elected officials, interest

AFTER THAT SCRUMPTIOUS FREE DINNER AND DRINKS WITH the LOBBYISTS, I'VE DECIDED TO VOTE AGAINST THE ETHICS BILL.

ME, TOO. URP!

STATE LAWMAKERS

Interest Groups and Their Impact
One goal of most interest groups is to elect candidates who support the group's point of view. *What does this political cartoon say about the relationship between interest groups and elected officials?*

groups, contributions, and political influence. Many of these reform efforts have only temporary success. Interest groups find ways to use their resources to continue to influence the political process. As a result, citizens should learn what they can about who is supporting or opposing major public issues.

READING CHECK **Summarizing** How do interest groups affect democracy?

SECTION 2 ASSESSMENT

THINK central **Online Quiz**
thinkcentral.com
KEYWORD: SGO POL HP

Reviewing Ideas and Terms

1. **a. Recall** What is an **interest group**, and what are its goals?
   b. Elaborate Describe the roles that interest groups play in our representative democratic political system.

2. **a. Define** What is a **trade association**?
   b. Compare In what ways are **labor unions** and professional groups alike?

3. **a. Describe** How do interest groups influence elections?
   b. Elaborate How do you think interest groups influence public policy at the local level? How would you use these groups to resolve a local issue?

4. **a. Explain** How did Congress try to limit the influence of interest groups in 2007? Why did it do so?
   b. Elaborate Do you agree with critics who charge that interest groups are harmful to the public good? Explain.

Critical Thinking

5. **Analyze** Copy and complete the web. Then use it to explain why some people believe that interest groups have too much power. Do you agree or disagree with that point of view? Explain.

How interest groups influence government

FOCUS ON WRITING

6. **Expository** Suppose that Congress is considering a ban on all interest group activities. Create a one-page "fact sheet" to be distributed at a rally in support of the role of interest groups in society and government.

SECTION 3 Political Parties

BEFORE YOU READ

Main Idea
Political parties are formal organizations that work to elect candidates to public office. Our political system is dominated by two major parties, but other parties are actively involved in the system.

Reading Focus
1. What are political parties, and what role do they play in the political process?
2. How does the American two-party political system work?
3. How are political parties organized?
4. Do political parties serve the public good?

Key Terms
political party
political spectrum
nomination process
electorate
one-party system
two-party system
multiparty system
third party
independent candidate
precinct
ward

TAKING NOTES As you read, take notes on how political parties serve the public good. Record your notes in a graphic organizer like this one.

How parties serve the public good

WHY IT MATTERS

Political Parties and Democracy In the United States, political parties have been around since James Madison used his quill pen to write letters to Thomas Jefferson. Parties began to form almost as soon as the Constitution was ratified. Today the United States has one of the oldest systems of popularly based political parties in the world. Some scholars suggest that this system has contributed to the long-term success of American democracy.

Yet to the Framers of the Constitution, factions, as political parties were called, were a new development—one that many of them opposed. Madison, whose thoughts and writings helped shape the form of government we have today, defined a faction as a group of citizens, whether a majority or a minority, that pursues its own interests at the expense of the common good. In *Federalist Paper* No. 10, Madison wrote the following:

> *The public good is disregarded in the conflicts of rival parties, and . . . measures are too often decided, not according to the rules of justice and the rights of the minor party, but by the superior force of an interested and overbearing majority.*

Despite his reservations, Madison would go on to form one of the nation's first political parties. A longtime tradition? Yes. However, what Madison wrote in 1787 still rings true today. The issue of how best to incorporate the will of the majority and the rights of the minority in public policy decisions is one political parties struggle with and why they matter today. ■

A Tradition Steeped in History

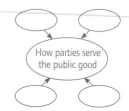

A photo of the 1920 Republican Party convention

The Role of Political Parties

The Constitution establishes a republican form of government, our representative democracy. Political parties are important to our system—they are the way we nominate, elect, and monitor our representatives. A **political party** is an organization that tries to elect its members to public office so that its views can become public policy.

Party Ideology Each political party has a basic set of ideas, theories, and aims about society and government that its members and supporters generally share. When a party unites its ideas and goals into a social and political program, that program is the party's ideology. This ideology is what sets one party apart from others. It also determines the party's place on the **political spectrum**, or the continuum of general political beliefs.

On the political spectrum, the Democratic Party is considered liberal and the Republican Party is considered conservative. Liberals generally support government action to change social, political, or economic policies that are believed to be unfair. Conservatives generally support limited government, lower taxes, and traditional social values.

Parties' Three Main Roles Wherever they are on the spectrum, parties—and party leaders—play three main roles in the political system: nominating candidates for political office, assisting the electoral process, and helping to operate the government.

The **nomination process**, or naming candidates for elective office, is a party's main function. A party's candidates may have their own views on specific issues, but their views must generally fit the party's beliefs to receive the party's support. Parties bring money, campaign workers, and other support to candidates, especially at state and local levels. In this and their other roles, parties train members to be future leaders.

Second, in addition to nominating candidates, political parties aid the electoral process in the following ways:

- Each party has a position on all major issues—a position that is connected to its ideology. Parties educate people about issues and try to motivate people to vote.

- Parties provide a "brand name." When a candidate is affiliated with a party, voters have an indication of his or her political views. Voters know that if a party usually offers candidates they support, a new candidate will meet those expectations.

- Parties help the **electorate**—the body of people entitled to vote—register to vote, learn about the issues and the party's position, and find out where they vote. Informed voters may make better choices.

- Parties watch how officeholders perform. Each party tries to ensure that its own officeholders—at every level—do the public's business well. At the same time, parties act as "watchdogs" on other officials. They criticize the actions and the mistakes of officeholders from the other parties. Parties use their successes and the mistakes of other parties to attract voters to their own candidates in the next election.

Finally, party leaders and party members help run the government. For example, in each house of Congress, one party usually is in the majority and thus controls that house. People appointed to positions in the executive and judicial branches are usually members of the president's party. If one or both houses of Congress are controlled by one party and the presidency is held by a different party, parties may provide ways for the branches to work out their differences.

Because they participate in government, political parties differ from interest groups, which pressure government from the outside. Also, most political parties address a variety of issues, but each interest group focuses on one issue and does not address others.

READING CHECK Summarizing What are the functions of political parties in elections and government at the state and local levels?

The American Two-Party System

The role that political parties play in a nation's political system or government depends on the type of party system the country has. Generally, the more parties there are, the smaller the role and influence of any particular party.

ACADEMIC VOCABULARY

ideology
the integrated assertions, theories, and aims that make up a social or political program

continuum
a continuous succession or sequence of values or elements that vary only by minute degrees

Party Systems There are three basic types of party systems. They are the one-party, two-party, and multiparty systems.

- **One-party system** A single political party controls government. Other parties may or may not be allowed to operate, but they usually have no power.
- **Two-party system** Two major parties compete to control government. Other parties may exist and may affect elections, but they rarely have enough support to elect a national leader or control the legislature. The United States has a two-party system.
- **Multiparty system** Several parties compete for control. For example, India has about 12 major parties, while Italy's government has about 15 parties. Multiparty systems are the most common party system.

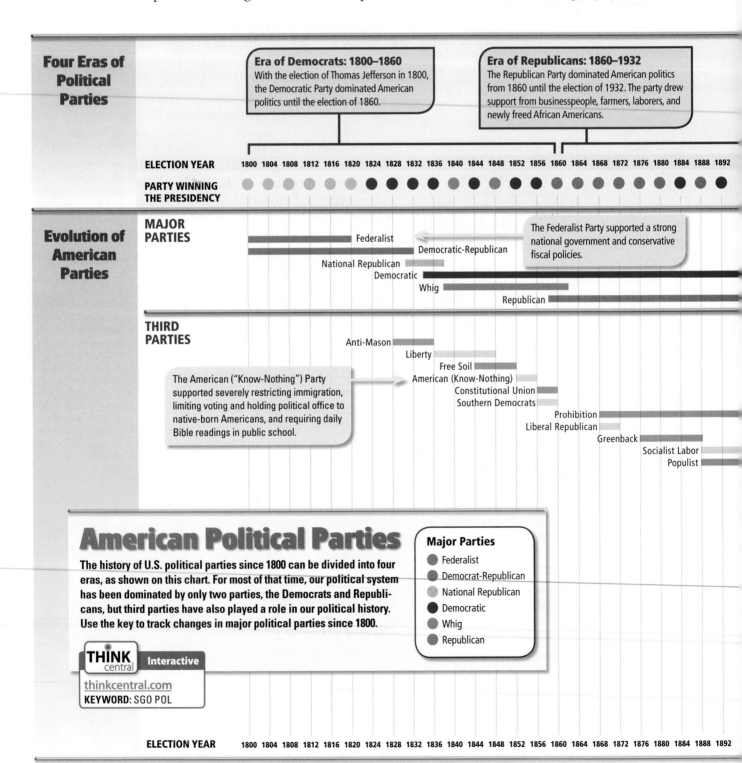

Four Eras of Political Parties

Era of Democrats: 1800–1860
With the election of Thomas Jefferson in 1800, the Democratic Party dominated American politics until the election of 1860.

Era of Republicans: 1860–1932
The Republican Party dominated American politics from 1860 until the election of 1932. The party drew support from businesspeople, farmers, laborers, and newly freed African Americans.

ELECTION YEAR 1800 1804 1808 1812 1816 1820 1824 1828 1832 1836 1840 1844 1848 1852 1856 1860 1864 1868 1872 1876 1880 1884 1888 1892

PARTY WINNING THE PRESIDENCY

Evolution of American Parties

MAJOR PARTIES
- Federalist
- Democratic-Republican
- National Republican
- Democratic
- Whig
- Republican

The Federalist Party supported a strong national government and conservative fiscal policies.

THIRD PARTIES
- Anti-Mason
- Liberty
- Free Soil
- American (Know-Nothing)
- Constitutional Union
- Southern Democrats
- Prohibition
- Liberal Republican
- Greenback
- Socialist Labor
- Populist

The American ("Know-Nothing") Party supported severely restricting immigration, limiting voting and holding political office to native-born Americans, and requiring daily Bible readings in public school.

American Political Parties

The history of U.S. political parties since 1800 can be divided into four eras, as shown on this chart. For most of that time, our political system has been dominated by only two parties, the Democrats and Republicans, but third parties have also played a role in our political history. Use the key to track changes in major political parties since 1800.

Major Parties
- Federalist
- Democrat-Republican
- National Republican
- Democratic
- Whig
- Republican

THINK central **Interactive**
thinkcentral.com
KEYWORD: SGO POL

ELECTION YEAR 1800 1804 1808 1812 1816 1820 1824 1828 1832 1836 1840 1844 1848 1852 1856 1860 1864 1868 1872 1876 1880 1884 1888 1892

Generally, when no party has a consistent majority, unstable government can result. Often, several parties join to form a coalition, or temporary alliance, to create a majority. If one party leaves the coalition, the government may collapse. New elections may be needed.

American Political Parties The first American political parties emerged soon after the Constitution was ratified. They were the Federalist Party (not related to the Federalist supporters of the Constitution) and the Democratic-Republican Party.

Members of the Federalist Party were supporters of Alexander Hamilton, who believed that the nation's future lay in a strong central government, large cities, and a strong manufacturing base.

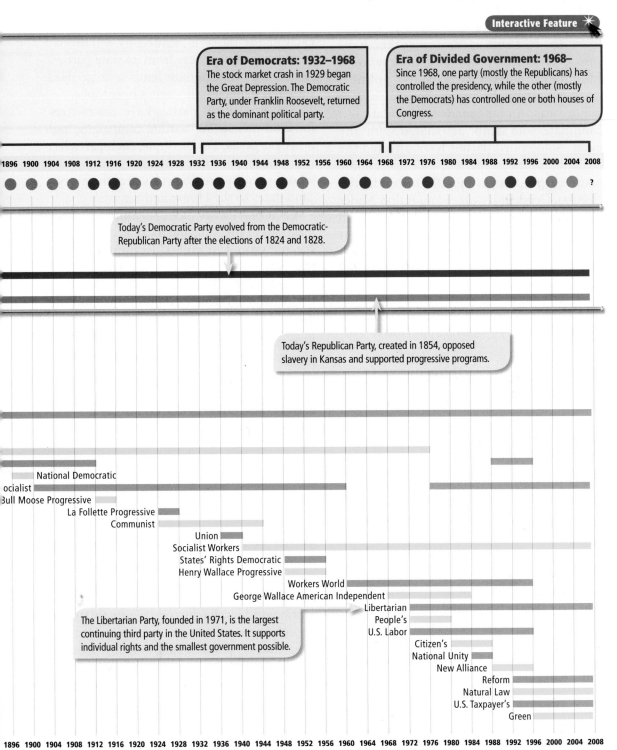

Interactive Feature

Era of Democrats: 1932–1968
The stock market crash in 1929 began the Great Depression. The Democratic Party, under Franklin Roosevelt, returned as the dominant political party.

Era of Divided Government: 1968–
Since 1968, one party (mostly the Republicans) has controlled the presidency, while the other (mostly the Democrats) has controlled one or both houses of Congress.

1896 1900 1904 1908 1912 1916 1920 1924 1928 1932 1936 1940 1944 1948 1952 1956 1960 1964 1968 1972 1976 1980 1984 1988 1992 1996 2000 2004 2008 ?

Today's Democratic Party evolved from the Democratic-Republican Party after the elections of 1824 and 1828.

Today's Republican Party, created in 1854, opposed slavery in Kansas and supported progressive programs.

National Democratic
Socialist
Bull Moose Progressive
La Follette Progressive
Communist
Union
Socialist Workers
States' Rights Democratic
Henry Wallace Progressive
Workers World
George Wallace American Independent
Libertarian
People's
U.S. Labor
Citizen's
National Unity
New Alliance
Reform
Natural Law
U.S. Taxpayer's
Green

The Libertarian Party, founded in 1971, is the largest continuing third party in the United States. It supports individual rights and the smallest government possible.

1896 1900 1904 1908 1912 1916 1920 1924 1928 1932 1936 1940 1944 1948 1952 1956 1960 1964 1968 1972 1976 1980 1984 1988 1992 1996 2000 2004 2008

Opposing the Federalist Party was the Democratic-Republican Party, which was led by Thomas Jefferson and James Madison. Jefferson believed that the nation's strength was in its agricultural base and in ordinary citizens living in small communities. After 1824, the party split. The two factions evolved into today's two major U.S. political parties, the Democrats and the Republicans.

These two parties have now dominated American politics for more than 150 years. Even so, in some elections voters have supported third-party and independent candidates. A **third party** is any political party in a two-party system besides the two major ones. An **independent candidate** is a candidate who is not associated with any party. Some third parties have affected the outcome of elections. For example, some people argue that in the 2000 presidential election, Green Party candidate Ralph Nader may have won enough votes in Florida to keep Democrat Al Gore from winning that state and its electoral votes, with the result that Republican George W. Bush was elected the new president.

READING CHECK **Drawing Conclusions** Why do you think the United States has only two major parties?

Party Organization

Political parties are organized at all levels, from small local committees to the large national committees. Each level contributes to the success of the party.

Local Parties Local party structures vary from state to state. The most common local organization is the county party, which is usually run by a committee. A county chairperson handles the party's daily affairs. His or her—and the local party's—main job is to select candidates for local offices and to help elect the party's candidates at all levels.

The county committee is usually selected by party members from precincts in the county. A **precinct** is the smallest unit for administering elections and local voting. Some cities have voting units, usually used for city council elections, called wards. A **ward** is a voting district made up of several precincts.

WHAT DO YOU THINK?

If political parties had not arisen, how might the constitutional system have accommodated America's tradition of free and open political debate?

State Parties Each state party is run by a central committee made up of representatives from the party's county committees. The state committee appoints a chairperson to manage the party's daily operations. Party leaders and party members in each state support and try to elect local, state, and national candidates—especially the party's presidential candidate—in their state.

National Parties The national party of each major party is headed by a national committee of members from its state parties. A national chairperson leads a large paid staff and manages the party's operations.

Major national parties have committees for fund-raising, supporting campaigns, and other purposes. For example, each party has two congressional campaign committees, whose primary mission is to elect the party's candidates to the House and Senate.

Each party also sponsors affiliated organizations at the state and local level to attract specific groups of voters. Examples include the National Federation of Republican Women, the College Democrats of America, the National Teenage Republicans, and the Young Democrats of America.

READING CHECK **Making Inferences** Why do political parties sponsor affiliated organizations?

Political Parties and the Public Good

Despite Madison's concerns, political parties have benefited American democracy in a number of ways. At the same time, however, parties are often the objects of criticism.

Benefits of Political Parties Some political scientists suggest that one way the two-party system serves the public good is that both parties filter out extreme or unconventional ideas. Each party wants to attract enough voters to win and keep a majority in government. As a result, parties provide stability against rapid and disruptive change.

In their effort to maximize their votes, parties try to include as broad a base of support as they can. The two major parties are made up of distinct groups, or constituencies, each with its own range of views.

Generally, Democratic Party constituencies include labor unions, women, racial and ethnic minorities, and educated urban voters. Republican constituencies, in general, include religious conservatives, corporate and business interests, and white men. Parties try to accommodate the diverse views of their constituents. The result of parties' efforts to include a variety of opinions may be an increase in political and social stability.

Because each major party represents a variety of groups and views, supporters who agree with most of the party's positions will not abandon the party over one issue with which they might disagree. This party loyalty also promotes stability by discouraging frequent, short-term shifts in power that might make government less stable.

Finally, parties provide a political "brand name" in much the same way a soft-drink company does for its products. Voters may not need to know everything about the candidates to reach political decisions. They might vote for a party's candidate because, overall, they support the party's views.

Criticisms of Political Parties Some critics argue that by trying to appeal to as many types of voters as possible, the major parties lack unity, discipline, and loyalty. As a result, parties may not be able to fulfill all the campaign promises they make. It is true that in the United States, officeholders from the same party stick together on issues less often than those in most other countries.

Some people note that interest groups give money for campaigns and other party activities. These contributions, people argue, influence parties and their officeholders to act in ways that benefit narrow interests rather than serve the larger public good.

Critics also charge that parties are full of office seekers who are interested more in their own personal success than in serving the public good. For example, a candidate may express support for a certain policy during a campaign because doing so helps the person get elected—even though in a previous campaign or office, the candidate had held, and stated, a position directly contrary to his or her new position. Voters and other candidates often call this reversal of position a flip-flop.

Finally, some people are angered by the partisan bickering between the two major parties. They charge that parties offer simple, narrow solutions to complex problems and are more interested in winning public opinion—and votes—than in solving the complex issues confronting the nation.

READING CHECK **Summarizing** How is a party's broad base both a benefit and a detriment to society?

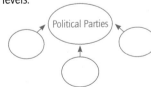

THINK central Online Quiz
thinkcentral.com
KEYWORD: SGO POL HP

SECTION 3 ASSESSMENT

Reviewing Ideas and Terms

1. **a. Identify** What is a **political party**?
   b. Evaluate Why are political parties important to the American political system?

2. **a. Recall** Why were the Federalist, Democratic-Republican, Democratic, and Republican parties created?
   b. Make Inferences Which type of party system produces the most stable government? Explain why.

3. **a. Summarize** What is the main purpose of a political party at all levels of its organization?
   b. Evaluate How important is each level of political party organization to achieving a party's goals? Explain how each level supports the others.

4. **a. Recall** What are some criticisms of political parties?
   b. Evaluate Do political parties promote the public good? Why or why not?

Critical Thinking

5. **Analyze** Copy and fill out the graphic organizer to illustrate how political parties are organized. Then identify opportunities for citizens to participate in political party activities at local, state, and national levels.

Political Parties

FOCUS ON WRITING

6. **Persuasive** The national chairperson of a party wants to eliminate the party's state and local organizations and conduct all operations at the national level. You are a national committee member. Write a memo to other national committee members explaining why this proposal is or is not a good idea.

Voting for a Third-Party Candidate

Is voting for a third-party candidate a meaningful use of your political voice?

THE ISSUE

Third parties and independent candidates have long played an important role in American politics, despite the fact our political system has been dominated by two major political parties for well over a century. Whether in a national election or a local election, third parties have been an important catalyst for positive change in our society. Whether you vote for a third-party candidate or a candidate from one of the two main parties, it's important to research the issues thoroughly and identify which ones really matter to you. It's important to exercise your right to vote, whatever party you support.

Third-party candidates do not usually win major political office, but some, such as Jesse Ventura, are successful. Ventura was elected governor of Minnesota in 1998.

VIEWPOINTS

Your vote will not count or will not be meaningful. Many people argue that if you vote for a third-party candidate, especially in a presidential race, you are squandering your vote. According to this view, most voters will choose one of the major-party candidates. Even if the third-party candidate has made it through all the primary elections, it is unlikely that he or she will win enough electoral votes to be elected president. Voting for a third-party candidate can also sway the outcome of an election in favor of a major candidate. One slogan used by the Democratic Party during the 2000 presidential campaign was "A vote for Nader is a vote for Bush." Even if a third-party candidate wins a significant portion of the popular vote, as Ross Perot did in 1992, the fact that the candidate lost means that he or she will not have any influence on public policy in the winner's administration.

A vote for a third-party candidate is both meaningful and worthwhile. Third parties play an important role in the U.S. political system as critics and innovators. Many people choose to vote for a third-party candidate because they feel that their interests are not being addressed by the major-party candidates. Because they are vying for the broad support of many diverse groups, both major parties are considered relatively conservative in their views, and their stances on major issues often overlap. In addition, third parties bring to the table issues not addressed by the big parties. For example, many ideas that we may take for granted today, such as women's suffrage and government regulation of food and drug safety, were first introduced and made popular by third parties. By not voting for a good third-party candidate, you ensure that the only voices that influence public policy are the same voices we always hear.

What Is Your Opinion?

1. Do you think third-party candidates have a greater chance of winning a national election or a state or local election? Explain your reasoning.

2. Would you ever vote for a third-party candidate? Why or why not?

THINK central **Practice Online**

thinkcentral.com
KEYWORD: SGO POL

The Electoral Process

Main Idea

The Constitution creates a system in which citizens elect representatives to public office. Each citizen has the responsibility to help make this system work. Citizens can affect the electoral process in many ways, but the most powerful is by voting on election day.

Reading Focus

1. How is a political campaign organized and financed?

2. How are candidates chosen for an election?

3. What are four factors that may influence voting and voter behavior?

4. What is the difference between a general election and a special election?

5. Do political campaigns serve the public good?

Key Terms

hard money
soft money
write-in candidates
caucus
direct primary
closed primary
open primary
plurality
absentee ballot

TAKING NOTES As you read, take notes on some factors that may influence voter behavior. Record your notes in a graphic organizer like this one.

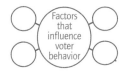

Factors that influence voter behavior

WHY IT MATTERS

Your Vote, Your Voice Voting is the most basic exercise of the constitutional principle of popular sovereignty. American author Louis L'Amour observed that "to make democracy work, we must be a nation of participants, not simply observers. One who does not vote has no right to complain." What does that mean today? Our democratic system depends on citizens being actively involved in the political process. In our democratic republic, we elect people to represent us at all levels of government. These people pass laws and make other decisions that affect the potholes in our streets and the security at our ports—everything from health care to warfare.

Candidates and their campaigns, political parties, and all kinds of interest groups spend hundreds of millions of dollars to influence opinions and votes. The decisions you make as a voter—or do not make by choosing not to vote—can impact you, your community, and your nation. ■

THE POWER TO Choose

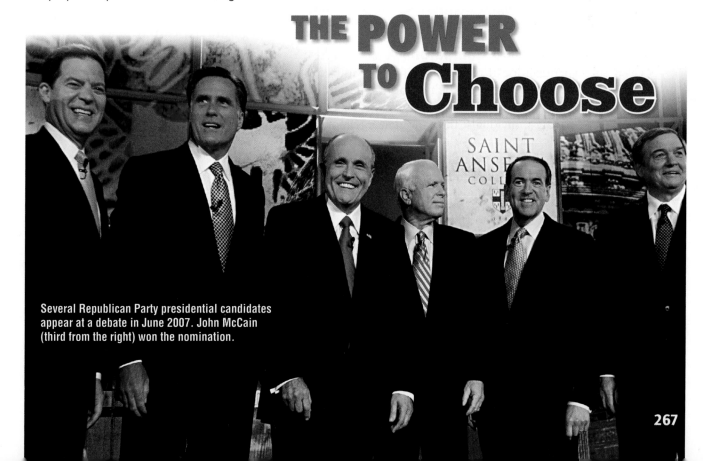

Several Republican Party presidential candidates appear at a debate in June 2007. John McCain (third from the right) won the nomination.

Organizing and Financing Campaigns

Political campaigns are expensive in both time and money. A person who wants to run for office must determine if he or she can raise the money for a campaign and if he or she is willing to spend the time it will take. So why do people bother to run for office?

First, holding elective office is considered an honor in our society. Also, most candidates are public-minded people who want to contribute to society. They are fulfilling a citizen's responsibility to act for the common good in public affairs. Finally, some people run for office because they want the power.

Political Campaigns Campaigning is hard work. Local candidates may spend hours walking door-to-door and attending local functions to meet voters. Presidential candidates travel from state to state to appear at rallies, fund-raisers, and meetings.

Candidates are trying to reach and attract enough voters to win. Candidates rely heavily on the media, especially television, to spread their message. They buy air time to run political ads or stage events to get free TV coverage. Today most candidates have Web sites and Web logs, and they hold virtual town meetings where voters e-mail or instant message questions to the candidate.

Money and Campaigns A candidate spends a lot of time raising money. Sources of campaign funds include political action committees (PACs), the candidate's party, private individuals, the candidate's personal funds, and, in some cases, public funds.

Money donated to an individual campaign is known as **hard money**. State and federal laws limit how much money individuals and organizations can give to candidates. Candidates must file reports with state or federal officials, listing how much hard money they have received and spent.

Contributions called soft money are a way to get around the limits on hard money contributions. **Soft money** is money given to a party, rather than to a specific candidate.

READING CHECK **Summarizing** Where do candidates get the funds to pay for their campaigns?

Choosing Candidates

How does a person get his or her name on the ballot as a candidate? Nomination is the first step in the electoral process. As you read in Section 3, nominating candidates is one of the functions of a political party. Parties select candidates by either primary elections or caucuses. Either way, a candidate usually makes an announcement in the company of party officials. The nominating process varies from state to state, but it usually involves one or more of the following methods.

Self-announcement The first step to becoming a candidate is to announce that you are running for a certain office. You might announce that you are seeking a specific party's nomination for the office, or you may decide to run as an independent candidate. Sometimes, people who fail to get their party's support will run as a self-announced candidate.

Self-nomination usually involves a registration process, such as paying a filing fee or circulating a petition—signed by a certain number of registered voters—to get on the ballot. Nomination by petition is often used at the local level. Candidates for local offices must submit petitions with the signatures of a certain number of qualified voters who reside in the election district.

A candidate can run as a write-in candidate and avoid the petition process. **Write-in candidates** announce they are running for an office, usually as an independent candidate or as a challenger to the party's preferred candidate, and ask voters to write in their name on the ballot. Write-in candidates almost always lose: If they had more support, they would not run as a write-in.

One of the most famous—though unsuccessful—write-in candidates was Eugene V. Debs, who ran for president in 1920. Debs, a leader of the Socialist Party, had been convicted under the Espionage Act of 1917 for a speech he gave in 1918. Although his conviction made him ineligible to hold office, Debs ran a write-in campaign from his prison cell in Atlanta, Georgia. Debs received almost 1 million write-in votes out of approximately 26 million votes cast.

Caucuses In some states candidates are chosen by caucus. A **caucus** is a meeting of party members who select the candidates to run for election. The caucus system began in the early 1800s, before today's election process existed. State party leaders would meet and select all the candidates for office.

When national party conventions first appeared in 1831 and 1832, state party leaders still met in state-level caucuses where, in addition to selecting candidates, they chose delegates to the national convention. Party leaders controlled both who went to the convention and how they voted when they got there. In the 1890s, reformers began to take the nominating power out of the hands of party leaders and let party members vote for the candidate of their choice.

Caucuses are still used in a few states, such as Iowa. Precinct caucuses—the lowest level—are open to all party members in the precinct. Starting in the precincts, caucuses endorse candidates for local offices and select delegates to the caucus or convention at the next level, such as the county or district. Caucus members select the delegates based on each delegate's stated preference for a particular candidate. The candidate with the most votes at the precinct level generally has the most delegates at the next level.

Conventions Caucuses and conventions are similar in some ways and different in others. Only party members take part in both, and both are ways to nominate candidates. However, a convention is open to the public. Also, delegates to a convention represent party members who are not there.

Local conventions choose delegates to the party's state convention and may nominate candidates for local offices. State conventions choose candidates for statewide offices, and in presidential election years, select delegates to the party's national nominating convention, which chooses the party's candidates for president and vice president.

Primary Elections If more than one member of a political party seeks the same office, a direct primary (meaning "first") election is held. In a **direct primary**, the party's candidate for office is chosen directly

Presidential Candidate Selection

From self-announcement to national party conventions, the process of presidential-candidate selection can last from about nine months to a year and a half.

SELF-ANNOUNCEMENT
Candidates for political office almost always self-announce, or declare publicly that they are running for office.

Bill Clinton announced his candidacy for president in October 1991.

PAY FILING FEE
Candidates usually pay a filing fee in each state to get their names placed on that state's election ballot.

COLLECT SIGNATURES
Candidates who lack funds to pay the filing fee may get their names on the ballot by collecting enough signatures on a petition.

WRITE-IN CANDIDATES
A candidate who can neither raise the money nor collect enough signatures may ask voters to write his or her name on the ballot.

PARTY PRIMARY ELECTION
In most states, if two or more candidates from the same party are running for president, the party conducts a primary election to choose a candidate.

NOMINATING CAUCUS
Several states use a party caucus, or a "meeting of neighbors," to choose the party's candidates.

NATIONAL PARTY CONVENTION
Delegates to each party's national convention officially select the party's presidential candidate.

In July 1992 Bill Clinton won the Democratic Party's presidential nomination. Clinton was elected president in 1992 and again in 1996.

Skills FOCUS **INTERPRETING CHARTS**

How does having the support of a political party make it easier for a candidate to run for president?

by voters. There are two types of direct primary elections: closed and open. In a **closed primary**, only voters registered as party members can vote in selecting that party's candidates. In an **open primary**, any registered voter may vote in either party's primary election, but only in one of them.

Most states hold presidential primary elections, which allow voters in each party to express their preference for their party's presidential candidate. The primary may also choose some or all of the state party members who will be delegates to the party's national convention. Each party's presidential candidate is chosen *after* all the states have held their primary elections.

The 2008 presidential primary season ran from January to June 2008. The primary process was long and, because each state has its own rules for selecting delegates, very confusing. For both major parties, primaries—not party leaders or nominating conventions—play the greatest role in determining who their candidates for president will be. As a result, candidates want to win the early primaries to show their strength with voters and build momentum for their nomination. Many states, therefore, want to hold their primaries as early as possible. States with early primaries attract candidates—as well as the money and media coverage that come with them—and can influence the nomination process.

READING CHECK **Summarizing** Why are primary elections an important part of the electoral process?

Voting and Voter Behavior

After the candidates have run their campaigns, it is time for voters to choose. Voting is a right, and to many people a duty, in our democracy. It is a person's most direct and powerful act of popular sovereignty.

In recent presidential elections, however, fewer than two-thirds of eligible voters voted. In years with no presidential election, turnout may reach the mid-40 percent range. In state and local elections, voter turnout is usually even lower. Why don't people vote? They offer a number of reasons, such as difficulty in registering to vote or believing that their vote will not make any difference.

ACADEMIC VOCABULARY
incumbent person who currently holds an office or position

Voting Requirements To qualify to vote, a person must be a U.S. citizen at least 18 years of age and a resident of the state in which he or she wishes to vote. Except in North Dakota, you cannot vote unless you are registered to do so. The registration requirement prevents ineligible people from voting. It also keeps people who have not registered from voting, even if they are eligible.

Some experts believe that the registration process is the main reason the voting rate in the United States is so low. In recent years, governments have made registration easier. States are required to let citizens register by mail or when they renew their driver's licenses. Some states are considering Internet registration and registration at the polls on election day.

Voter Behavior Many factors, from being the <u>incumbent</u> to being considered likable, can influence the way a voter votes. Campaigns address as many factors as they can so voters will feel that the candidate deserves to win. Four main factors influence why people vote the way they do:

- **Party Identification.** Some voters rely greatly on and respond to a candidate's party affiliation. About a third of voters identify themselves either as strong Republicans or strong Democrats.
- **Issues.** Voters' views on issues that are important to them—such as abortion, health care, or taxes—can affect their choice of candidates.
- **A candidate's background.** A voter's evaluation of a candidate's record, personality, integrity, age, and character affects the choices the voter makes.
- **The voter's background.** A voter's age, gender, race, family beliefs, and income and education levels all affect how he or she chooses candidates.

READING CHECK **Identifying the Main Idea** What factors affect voter behavior?

More About Elections

Primary elections are one kind of election. Two other kinds of elections are general elections and special elections. All elections are held according to state and federal laws. In addition, each Native American nation establishes its own procedures, rules, and requirements for electing its leaders.

General Elections The end of a campaign is the general election, in which one candidate is elected to each office. In most states, only a plurality is required for election. A candidate wins by a **plurality** if he or she has more votes than anyone else. In some states, however, a candidate must get a majority — more than 50 percent—of the votes to win. Otherwise, a runoff election is held.

Special Elections Special elections are sometimes held at the local or state level to let the people, rather than government leaders, decide an issue—for example, whether to raise taxes. A special election also might be called to replace an officeholder who has died in or resigned from office.

Holding an Election The dates of general elections are set by law. Federal elections take place on the first Tuesday following the first Monday in November of every even-numbered year. Most states hold statewide elections on the same day, and more than half the states require that local elections take place on this day as well.

On election day, voters go to the polling place in the precinct where they live. The polling place is usually run by workers paid by the local election authority. Occasionally, there will be a number of poll watchers from one or more political parties.

Voters cast a secret ballot—that is, they vote in private and no one knows for whom any individual voted. Votes may be cast on paper ballots or on some type of voting machine. Many voting machines are now electronic. Electronic voting is controversial because some machines do not keep a paper record of votes cast. Critics fear that using such machines increases the chance for inaccurate or unfair results due to system failure or illegal tampering.

Some voters are not able to vote at their polling place because they are seriously ill or, as with many members of the armed forces, are away from home. These voters can request an **absentee ballot**, which is a ballot submitted on or before election day by a voter who cannot be present on election day. A voter fills out this ballot and mails it in by the date set by law. All states now allow absentee voting by mail, but 22 states require voters to provide the reason they are using the vote-by-mail provision.

More than 30 states now allow voters to vote early, whether they will be absent on election day or not. Early voting rules vary by state. The early voting period may be as long as 45 days, but most states limit it to about 14 or 21 days before election day.

READING CHECK **Contrasting** How does a special election differ from a general election?

PRIMARY SOURCES

Politics and the Net

These excerpts from a July 2007 Rock the Vote blog were written after YouTube sponsored a televised presidential debate.

Was the YouTube Debate the Debate for Young Voters?

Did you catch the CNN/YouTube Democratic Presidential Debates . . . ? We sure hope you did, because a good portion of the media coverage has been emphasizing that this was the debate where young voters finally were heard. This debate, held in Charleston, South Carolina, was a bit more nontraditional, for the questions were asked not by a famous news personality, but rather by average Americans who submitted their queries over the popular video website YouTube . . . Though many newspapers and blogs posted varied opinions about the candidates' performances or the technology used in the debate . . . many of the articles agreed that young voters had a disproportionate role in the debates.

Skills FOCUS **INTERPRETING PRIMARY SOURCES**

Making Inferences How will Web logs and online videos influence politics and public policy in the future?

See **Skills Handbook**, p. H9.

Campaigns and the Public Good

Political parties, interest groups, and individuals all play a part in determining who represents us in our local, state, and national government. Parties nominate candidates and help define the public issues and public agenda the campaign will cover. Interest groups lend their voices to the public debate and support or oppose candidates and issues. Individuals vote, and the results of the vote determine which issues are important and which policies should continue and which policies should change.

Elections and the Public Good Elections serve the public good by allowing citizens to express their opinion on how the country should be run. Election campaigns spend a lot of time and money to inform voters about the candidates and call attention to important issues. Both functions can help voters make informed choices on election day.

Criticism of Campaigns On the other hand, the way that many campaigns are conducted has generated criticism. Some dislike campaigns' reliance on TV advertising. How much useful information, critics ask, is provided in a 30-second TV spot? Critics also charge that campaign advertising may distort or omit information, which leaves voters misinformed rather than informed.

Many campaigns are criticized for their negative ads. Voters often tell pollsters that they oppose negative campaigning. However, campaigns continue to "go negative" because a candidate who feels that he or she has been attacked usually feels the need to respond in a similar fashion. In addition, some candidates have found that criticizing an opponent is more effective in terms of influencing voter behavior.

Critics blame these factors, along with voter-registration requirements and today's reduced role of political parties, for the low level of voter turnout. These factors may also help explain why one-third of Americans claim to have little or no interest in politics and public affairs.

Whatever people think of political campaigns, the issues facing the country, such as health care, terrorism, and national security, will not go away. Your vote is your voice. Voting will help you shape the future of your community, state, and country.

READING CHECK **Summarizing** What are two criticisms that some people have about political campaigns?

SECTION 4 ASSESSMENT

THINK central **Online Quiz**
thinkcentral.com
KEYWORD: SGO POL HP

Reviewing Ideas and Terms

1. a. Describe How does a person become a candidate?
b. Evaluate How important to a candidate is a strong campaign organization?

2. a. Identify What is a candidate's main activity during an election campaign?
b. Make Inferences Why do you think election laws place limits on hard-money contributions?

3. a. Recall What two basic requirements must a person meet to be eligible to vote?
b. Evaluate What are some reforms that might increase the voting rate? How effective do you think those reforms might be in increasing voter turnout?

4. a. Recall What is the federal general election date?
b. Make Inferences Why might political parties station poll workers at polling places on election day?

5. a. Describe How do elections and election campaigns serve the public good?
b. Explain What are some steps government might take to improve public attitudes about election campaigns?

Critical Thinking

6. Summarize Copy and complete the graphic organizer. Then use it to describe each type of primary election and its uses.

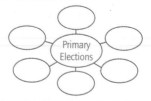

Primary Elections

FOCUS ON WRITING

7. Expository Create a pamphlet that a nonpartisan civic group could distribute to educate citizens about voting and why it is important.

Buckley v. Valeo (1976)

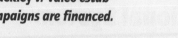

WHY IT MATTERS *Campaign finance laws aim to limit the influence that wealthy individuals and organizations might exert over elections and public officials. The Court's decision in Buckley v. Valeo established the basic rules that govern how modern presidential campaigns are financed.*

Background

When corrupt campaign finance practices came to public attention following the Watergate scandal and the 1972 presidential election, Congress passed several amendments to the 1971 Federal Election Campaign Act (FECA). Among other provisions, the amendments limited the amount individuals and political action committees could contribute to federal election campaigns. The amendments also placed limits on the amount candidates could spend on their campaigns and created the Federal Election Commission (FEC) to enforce federal campaign laws.

Shortly following the passage of the legislation, a group led by New York senator James Buckley filed suit against the FEC, charging that the new FECA amendments were unconstitutional because they violated rights protected under the First and Fifth amendments to the Constitution. The U.S. District Court of Appeals for the District of Columbia upheld the spending limitations enacted by Congress, and the case proceeded to the Supreme Court.

Arguments for Buckley

The plaintiffs argued that limiting campaign contributions and expenditures violated the right to freedom of speech under the First Amendment, because "virtually all meaningful political communications in the modern setting involve the expenditure of money." Limiting contributions and expenditures, they said, would restrict the speech of some in order to enhance the speech of others and would be unconstitutional.

Arguments for Valeo

Proponents for Valeo and the 1974 FECA amendments argued that placing limits on campaign contributions and expenditures would not restrict a citizen's ability to participate in the political process. These limits would, in fact, make the process more fair by equalizing the influence that wealthy and nonwealthy individuals could exert. If wealthy individuals were allowed to contribute more, then in effect, they would be given a stronger voice in the political process and more rights than the nonwealthy.

THE IMPACT TODAY After *Buckley* limited contributions to campaigns, soft-money contributions began to flow to the two parties and related organizations. Millions of dollars ended up in presidential and congressional campaigns. Legislation, such as the 2002 Bipartisan Campaign Reform Act (BCRA, or the McCain-Feingold Act), tried to limit soft-money contributions. Parts of the BCRA were upheld by the Court in 2003, but other provisions of the act were ruled unconstitutional in 2007. The impact of *Buckley* and later cases today depends on how the Federal Election Commission interprets and enforces these opinions.

CRITICAL THINKING

What Do You Think? In *Buckley*, the Court effectively said that in politics, "money is speech." It upheld limits on campaign contributions but not on campaign spending. Should either campaign contributions or campaign expenditures be limited in any way? Why or why not? Give examples to support your position.

THE CITIZEN & THE CONSTITUTION

The Role of Political Parties in the Constitutional System

Soon after the Constitution was ratified, there was an unforeseen development to which most of the Framers were opposed: the formation of political parties. Learn about the Framers' views on political parties and how parties became an essential component of the American political system by helping to address challenges that the Constitution left unresolved.

How did the Framers think about political parties? James Madison's argument that the new Constitution would control the effects of "factions" was part of an ongoing debate within Anglo-American political thought about political parties. Some British writers, as well as Americans such as Alexander Hamilton, used the words *faction* and *party* as synonyms and viewed them as an evil to be eradicated in the society at large. Others, such as the Scottish political philosopher David Hume (1711–1776), had argued that parties were the inevitable result of diverse interests. In fact, James Madison followed this reasoning in *Federalist Paper* No. 10 and believed that factions could be controlled. Ireland's Edmund Burke (1729–1797), another important political thinker, contended that open opposition expressed through political parties was a good thing. Without parties, Burke believed, opponents of the ruler would resort to conspiracy and intrigue. Political parties motivated by self-defined guiding principles provided a crucial service to the body politic by fostering open debate.

No major eighteenth-century American leaders echoed Burke's arguments. However, Americans were accustomed to factional politics in their colonial and new state governments, often because of differing regional or economic concerns. Some of the Framers recognized the potential value of political parties. For example, Alexander Hamilton argued in *Federalist Paper* No. 70 that parties within a legislature could "promote deliberation and circumspection, and serve to check excesses in the majority." But once a decision was made, Hamilton continued, opposition should cease.

Hamilton, Madison, and the other delegates to the Constitutional Convention had no experience with an ongoing party system, that is, a system of organized, relatively durable political parties that accept one another's right to exist and to compete in elections and within government.

Political parties developed within a decade of the ratification of the Constitution. Ironically Madison and Hamilton became leaders within those parties—on opposite sides. Several issues contributed to divisions within the national government and the nation as a whole. Those divisions became the basis for the first parties.

Adapted with permission from Lesson 16 of *We the People: The Citizen & the Constitution*. Copyright 2009, Center for Civic Education.

The presidential election of 1800 was the first to feature candidates for president and vice president who were openly supported by political parties. Federalists supported the re-election of John Adams. Republicans supported Thomas Jefferson. The candidates themselves did not campaign because it was considered undignified for presidential candidates to seek the office actively. But the election heightened the bitter party disagreements.

What part do political parties play in today's political system?

Today political parties play an essential role in the American political system. Since the 1860s, the Democratic party and the Republican party (founded in 1854) have been the two major parties in the United States, although the agendas and constituencies of each have changed dramatically over the years as new issues have created new coalitions and new divisions.

Political parties serve several important purposes:

- They mobilize popular participation in the nomination and election of candidates for public office.
- They connect the executive and legislative branches of government. Presidents generally work most closely with members of their own party in Congress, and governors do the same with those in their state legislatures.
- Political parties connect the national government with state governments. However, each major party has enough internal variation to remain viable in states with very different political climates.
- By joining a political party people indicate their support for a particular platform, the label given to the priorities and policies of that party.

- Political parties provide forums for deliberating about public policies. In a sense they work in a way that is opposite from what Madison suggested about factions. Rather than fracture the citizenry and promote passion and interest over reason and the common good, parties can help organize and channel passions and interests into the system. Each major party is like a large tent, under which a variety of interests and issues can coexist. Like the "large republic" that Madison envisioned, political parties actually could work against the most divisive tendencies of faction and passion.
- In times of rapid political change political parties can provide a way of ensuring that people demand a change of government, not a change of constitution. Parties can be an agent of stability.

In recent years many commentators also have observed less favorable aspects of the political party system:

- The longstanding dominance of the Democratic and Republican parties, entrenched through campaign finance laws and other structures, makes it difficult for parties espousing truly alternative views and agendas to gain lasting political support. In most other nations, especially those with parliamentary systems, there usually are many more parties, each representing a particular set of policies and values. Voters in such systems may feel as though they have a wider range of choices.
- American "third parties" tend to be short-lived expressions of discontent with the two major parties (such as Ross Perot's Reform party in 1992), to be small and oriented toward a narrow set of issues, or to be local or state-based. They have little chance of becoming new major parties that are competitive nationally and over the long haul with the Republicans and the Democrats.
- If a single set of interests, or a particularly passionate interest, gains dominant power within a party, then the party is subject to the same threat of majority tyranny that Madison and other Framers feared in small republics and from political factions.

Reviewing Ideas and Terms

1. **Identify** For Alexander Hamilton, what purpose might political parties serve within a legislature?

2. **Explain** What are six important functions that political parties serve in today's electoral system?

Critical Thinking

3. **Elaborate** In what ways does America's two-party system promote or thwart America's constitutional principles?

Chapter Review

Connecting Online

Visit thinkcentral.com for review and enrichment activities related to this chapter.

THINK central

KEYWORD: SGO POL

Quiz and Review

GOV 101
Examine key concepts in this chapter.

ONLINE QUIZZES
Take a practice quiz for each section in this chapter.

Activities

eActivities
Complete Webquests and Internet research activities.

INTERACTIVE FEATURES
Explore interactive versions of maps and charts.

KEEP IT CURRENT
Link to current events in U.S. government.

Partners

American Bar Association Division for Public Education
Learn more about the law, your rights and responsibilities.

Center for Civic Education
Promoting an enlightened and responsible citizenry committed to democratic principles and actively engaged in the practice of democracy.

Online Textbook

ONLINE SIMULATIONS
Learn about U.S. government through simulations you can complete online.

Click for More Read more about key topics online.

Comprehension and Critical Thinking

SECTION 1 (pp. 248–253)

1. a. Review Key Terms For each term, write a sentence that explains its significance or meaning: public opinion, public policy, mass media, poll, sampling error.

b. Make Inferences How might the media influence policy or regulatory decisions made by a government agency or institution? Give a recent example from the news.

c. Elaborate In what ways can the techniques used to conduct a poll affect its results?

SECTION 2 (pp. 254–259)

2. a. Review Key Terms For each term, write a sentence that explains its significance or meaning: interest group, political action committee, lobbying, grass roots.

b. Summarize What are the six basic types of interest groups? Provide an example of each.

c. Evaluate Do you think that political action committees and lobbying should be illegal? Explain why or why not.

SECTION 3 (pp. 260–265)

3. a. Review Key Terms For each term, write a sentence that explains its significance or meaning: political party, political spectrum, two-party system, third party, precinct.

b. Contrast What are the basic differences between a one-party, two-party, and multiparty system?

c. Elaborate Why are political parties important to the political system in the United States?

SECTION 4 (pp. 267–272)

4. a. Review Key Terms For each term, write a sentence that explains its significance or meaning: soft money, caucus, direct primary.

b. Explain How does the purpose of a general election differ from the purpose of a primary election?

c. Evaluate What is your opinion about why so many eligible voters do not take part in elections?

Critical Reading

Read the passage in Section 4 that begins with the heading "Choosing Candidates." Then answer the following questions.

5. Why did many states replace the caucus system with conventions?

A Caucuses were too expensive.

B Conventions are open to the public.

C Party leaders largely controlled the outcome of caucus decisions.

D Reformers wanted party leaders to have more power.

6. Political parties can affect our political system as well as individuals and elected officials. Research the **roles political parties play** and describe the changing influence of parties on elections and elected officials. Include in your analysis the roles of formal and informal party memberships, the development of party machines and regional party strongholds, the rise of independent voters, and disillusionment with the party system.

7. Political communications come from various sources. Select any **public policy issue**, such as health care, taxes, or privacy. Research one blog, one political speech, and one interest group dealing with that issue. Create a spreadsheet and compare the three sources of information, using the following criteria: logical validity, appeal to emotions, factual accuracy, factual omissions, distorted evidence, and appeals to prejudice or bias. Analyze your results. Explain which type of communication you would use to decide on a public issue.

8. One of the responsibilities of a leader is to help **resolve conflicts between groups**. At the local level—at school, in your neighborhood, or at the city council—your political behavior, such as writing letters or making speeches, might help resolve such conflicts. Give an example of a conflict in your community. Describe what steps you could take to resolve it. Assess how successful your leadership might be in helping the parties reach a satisfactory result to the dispute.

9. Under the Constitution, **you are entitled to equality, justice, certain freedoms, and individual rights**. Select one of these ideas. Research and evaluate how changes in economic, geographical, technological, and social forces have affected the topic you chose. For example, how have economic, geographic, technological, and social changes affected, if at all, your individual rights or the idea of justice?

CONNECTING TO THE CONSTITUTION

10. Research third-party movements in the United States. In two or three paragraphs, describe their influence and the policies that have resulted.

ANALYZING PRIMARY SOURCES

Political Cartoons *Each of the two major political parties has a wide and different base of support. Many people feel that the two-party system gives voters clear choices on election day. However, others accuse the two parties of holding similar views on many issues.*

Peter Bono/Images.com/NewsCom

11. Analyze In your opinion, who is "feeding" the two parties?

12. Elaborate Do you think that contributions from special interest groups make the two parties more alike or reinforce their differences? Explain your answer.

FOCUS ON WRITING

Persuasive Writing *Persuasive writing takes a position for or against an issue, using facts and examples as supporting evidence. To practice persuasive writing, complete the assignment below.*

Writing Topic: Money and Politics

13. Assignment Some people think that money plays too great a role in politics and that donations to campaigns should be limited or banned. Defenders of the system say that campaign finance laws and ethics laws for officeholders make the process fair and open. Write an editorial explaining and defending your position on campaign finance. Give examples to support your position.

CHAPTER 10

Civil Liberties

"EQUAL LAWS, PROTECTING EQUAL RIGHTS, ARE . . . THE BEST GUARANTEE OF LOYALTY AND LOVE OF COUNTRY."

—JAMES MADISON, 1820

CONNECTING TO THE CONSTITUTION

Our nation's system of government is based on constitutional law established by the United States Constitution. See the "We the People: The Citizen and the Constitution" pages in this chapter for an in-depth exploration of fundamental rights and the doctrine of incorporation.

The right to assemble peacefully is a civil liberty cherished by many Americans. In this photograph, a crowd gathers at an Earth Day celebration at the U.S. Capitol.

SECTION 1 Protecting Constitutional Rights

Main Idea

The United States was formed out of a belief that individuals had certain important liberties and rights. The Constitution's Bill of Rights protects these liberties and rights.

Reading Focus

1. What is the Bill of Rights, and what does it protect?

2. What are the limitations on civil liberties and rights?

3. How does the Fourteenth Amendment help protect civil liberties?

Key Terms

civil liberties
civil rights
due process
incorporation doctrine

 As you read, take notes on how the Bill of Rights protects Americans' civil liberties and rights. Record your notes in a graphic organizer like this one.

Guarding OUR Liberties

WHY IT MATTERS

The Importance of the Bill of Rights In the early years of World War II, as German troops swiftly conquered the democratic nations of Europe, President Franklin D. Roosevelt gave an eloquent speech in which he predicted a brighter future for the world. Roosevelt's historic "Four Freedoms" speech, delivered before Congress in January 1941, predicted a time when American ideals of liberty had spread to the farthest reaches of the earth. To Roosevelt, the essential human freedoms that every person should possess include the freedom of speech and expression and the freedom to worship as he or she chooses.

Why are liberties such as those promoted by Roosevelt so important to Americans? Simply put, civil liberties—including religious freedom, freedom of speech, and personal security—are the fundamental safeguards that protect us from government actions. The Bill of Rights guards these freedoms.

Respecting and protecting civil liberties is among the most important responsibilities of a democratic government. The principle behind the Bill of Rights—that government may not restrict freedoms and liberties without good reason—is why the United States has long been a symbol of freedom to people around the world. Without these protections, American society would be very different. ■

For many Americans, the Statue of Liberty symbolizes the rights and freedoms that we hold dear.

The Bill of Rights

It was a firm commitment to their personal freedoms that drove American colonists to break from Great Britain in the Revolutionary War. The Declaration of Independence explains the colonists' actions as an effort to protect their rights, including "Life, Liberty, and the pursuit of Happiness." Eventually, this quest to protect these rights led to the creation of the Bill of Rights.

After Independence Once independent from Great Britain, states adopted their own constitutions, most of which protected the liberties Americans had fought so hard to win. Virginia, for example, approved a Declaration of Rights that protected many freedoms, including freedom of religion.

Yet when delegates gathered in 1787 to draft a new national constitution, there was little talk of specifically protecting individual rights until the very end of the Constitutional Convention. At that time, George Mason—who had written the Virginia Declaration of Rights—proposed including a bill of rights in the Constitution. Other delegates argued that state constitutions and a separation of powers were enough to protect Americans' rights, and Mason's proposal was defeated. As a result, the Constitution included few specific protections of individual rights.

The Ratification Battle During the national debate over the ratification of the Constitution, it quickly became clear that the lack of a bill of rights could doom the Constitution. After years of British rule, the American people simply did not trust any government's commitment to protecting liberties and rights. Thomas Jefferson expressed concern over the Constitution.

PRIMARY SOURCES

> **❝** A bill of rights is what the people are entitled to against every government on earth, general or particular, and which no just government should refuse. **❞**
>
> —Thomas Jefferson, letter to James Madison, 1787

The Ten Amendments In order to win ratification of the Constitution, supporters of the Constitution agreed to add a bill of rights as soon as the new national government

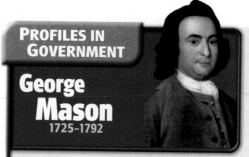

PROFILES IN GOVERNMENT

George Mason
1725–1792

George Mason, sometimes called the Father of the Bill of Rights, was a Virginia political leader and an early advocate of the constitutional protection of individual rights.

In 1776 Mason helped write the first Virginia constitution and the Virginia Declaration of Rights, a document that listed the inalienable rights of Virginians and called for independence from Great Britain. The Declaration influenced Thomas Jefferson's draft of the Declaration of Independence later that year.

Mason was a member of the Constitutional Convention that met in 1787, although he refused to sign the Constitution, believing that it did not do enough to protect individual liberties against government abuse. Later, as a delegate to the Virginia convention that met to ratify the Constitution, Mason urged delegates to demand a bill of rights as a condition of ratification. The Bill of Rights that was eventually adopted is based largely on Mason's Virginia Declaration of Rights.

Draw Conclusions Why is George Mason called the Father of the Bill of Rights?

met in 1789. When the government gathered, James Madison began drafting amendments to the Constitution. Members of Congress changed some of his proposals and rejected others. They also debated the very existence of a bill of rights. Some members of Congress feared that listing individual rights might imply that the government would protect only those rights. To address this concern, they added an amendment stating that listing specific rights did not mean that other rights were denied to the people.

Ultimately, 10 amendments were ratified by the states. These amendments—the Bill of Rights—became part of the Constitution in December 1791.

The amendments in the Bill of Rights protect both civil liberties and civil rights. **Civil liberties** are basic freedoms to think and to act that all people have and that are protected against government abuse. For example, the First Amendment's guarantee of religious freedom protects a civil liberty. **Civil rights** are rights of fair and equal status and treatment and the right to participate in government. The First Amendment's guarantee of the right to petition government helps protect a civil right.

RESPONSIBILITIES OF LEADERSHIP

James Madison and the other Framers had to make difficult decisions about what should be included in a bill of rights. In all, the states proposed a total of 210 amendments, 10 of which eventually became the Bill of Rights.

BILL OF RIGHTS

First Amendment Protects freedom of speech and expression and forbids Congress from making laws that establish religion or limit the free exercise of religion.

Second Amendment Protects the right to bear arms.

Third Amendment Prevents government from forcing someone to house troops in his or her home except in specific circumstances.

Fourth Amendment Prohibits government from searching a building or person, or seizing a person, without first meeting specific legal standards or getting a court order.

Fifth Amendment Protects people accused of a crime:
• requires a grand jury indictment for most serious crimes;
• prevents "double jeopardy"—an individual cannot be tried more than once for the same offense;
• prevents people from being forced to testify against themselves.

Protects people from unfair government actions:
• requires due process before government deprives anyone of life, liberty, or property;
• prohibits government from confiscating property without making proper payment.

Sixth Amendment Protects people accused of a crime:
• requires speedy and public trial by jury;
• requires that accused persons be told of charges against them;
• permits accused to question witnesses against them and to call their own witnesses;
• requires that accused persons be given legal assistance.

Seventh Amendment Guarantees trial by jury in federal civil cases involving more than $20.

Eighth Amendment Protects against excessive bail or fines in criminal cases and against "cruel and unusual punishments."

Ninth Amendment Protects other rights that are not specifically mentioned in the Constitution.

Tenth Amendment Reserves to the states or to the people powers not given to the federal government.

Skills FOCUS **INTERPRETING CHARTS**

1. What fundamental freedoms are protected by the First Amendment?
2. How does the Fifth Amendment protect Americans?

THINK central Interactive

thinkcentral.com
KEYWORD: SGO CLB

Despite the language of the Bill of Rights, civil liberties and rights were not originally guaranteed for all Americans. Women and slaves, for example, had their freedoms severely restricted. Over time, the protections of liberties and rights have been expanded to cover all American citizens. Today debate on this issue centers on the rights of aliens—citizens of other countries who are living in or visiting the United States.

READING CHECK **Sequencing** List the sequence of events that led to the creation of the Bill of Rights.

Limits on Civil Liberties and Rights

The Bill of Rights sets limits on government, but people do not have complete freedom to do whatever they choose. To protect the common good—the welfare of all—there are limits on individual liberties and rights.

When Rights Conflict To the Framers of the Constitution, the ideal government would be one that limited liberties as little as possible. Yet in some cases the government does limit personal freedoms. That is because one person's exercise of a certain freedom—such as smoking in a public place—can sometimes harm another person or conflict with civic responsibilities. In other words, individual liberties and rights can conflict. In that case, the government must decide if liberties and rights should be limited for the sake of the common good.

Take, for example, the freedom of speech. The right to express ideas publicly is widely considered to be necessary for democracy, and the First Amendment limits the government's power to deny this right. Yet the Supreme Court has found that when speech is likely to lead to immediate lawless action, government can limit free speech. For example, during wartime the government may be able to limit speech that aids the enemy, such as publishing information about the tactics of American soldiers. The Court has examined the limits of different constitutionally protected freedoms over the years. You will read more about the Court's decisions later in this chapter.

The Role of the Courts Balancing the protection of civil liberties and the protection of the common good is an enormous challenge for government. One way government maintains this balance is through the courts, which can strike down laws that they determine violate individual liberties and rights.

The courts, however, cannot bring action on their own. They can only issue rulings when cases are brought before them. Early in the history of the United States, few such cases were brought before the courts, in part because many of the people and groups who most needed their rights protected did not have access to the courts. African Americans, for example, could not readily bring a case against white people who were denying them rights. As a result, most Supreme Court cases that have protected civil liberties and rights have occurred since the early 1900s.

Some of the cases involving civil liberties and rights have come to the courts through the actions of interest groups such as the National Association for the Advancement of Colored People (NAACP), the American Civil Liberties Union (ACLU), and the Mexican American Legal Defense and Educational Fund (MALDEF). The groups' involvement in these cases has had an important impact on the courts' decisions about liberties and rights.

READING CHECK **Summarizing** Why are individual liberties and rights sometimes limited?

Civil Liberties and the Fourteenth Amendment

The Bill of Rights was intended to limit the actions of the federal government. This does not mean, of course, that state and local governments can deny individuals their civil liberties and rights. For one thing, many state constitutions have their own bills of rights. Article I of the Indiana state constitution, for example, clearly outlines the basic freedoms that residents of the state possess. In addition, the U.S. Supreme Court has ruled that most protections in the Bill of Rights apply not only to the federal government but also to state and local governments.

The Due Process Clause The Supreme Court's rulings that much of the Bill of Rights applies to state and local governments are based upon the Fourteenth Amendment. Ratified in the aftermath of the Civil War, the Fourteenth Amendment was intended to protect the rights of formerly enslaved African Americans. The amendment forbade states from passing laws that would "deprive any person of life, liberty, or property without due process of law." **Due process** means following established and complete legal procedures.

The Court has held that the Fourteenth Amendment's due process clause means that many of the guarantees of the Bill of Rights apply to the states. Thus, the Court has incorporated, or merged, much of the Bill of Rights into the Fourteenth Amendment. The Court's reasoning for incorporating these rights—the **incorporation doctrine**—holds that certain protections are essential to due process of the law. Thus, states cannot deny these protections to the people.

Key Cases The process of incorporation has taken place through a number of Supreme Court cases over many years. The first such case was *Chicago, Burlington & Quincy Railroad Company* v. *Chicago* (1897). In this case, the Court held that the Fourteenth Amendment's due process clause incorporated the Fifth Amendment's "just compensation" clause, thus requiring the states to give owners fair compensation when taking private property.

Starting in the 1920s, a flurry of cases led to the incorporation of the First Amendment freedoms. In *Gitlow* v. *New York* (1925) the Court agreed that New York State could forbid a man from plotting to overthrow the government. Using the due process clause, however, the Court ruled for the first time that states must respect the First Amendment's guarantee of freedom of speech.

Six years later, in *Near* v. *Minnesota* (1931), the Court incorporated the freedom of the press. *DeJonge* v. *Oregon* (1937) incorporated freedom of assembly and petition. *Everson* v. *Board of Education of Ewing Township* (1947) incorporated the First Amendment's limits against government establishment of religion.

WHAT DO YOU THINK?

How is due process related to the principle of limited government?

PROCESS OF INCORPORATION

AMENDMENT, PROVISIONS	SUPREME COURT DECISIONS
First, Establishment clause	*Everson* v. *Board of Education*, 1947
First, Free exercise clause	*Cantwell* v. *Connecticut*, 1940
First, Freedom of speech	*Gitlow* v. *New York*, 1925
First, Freedom of the press	*Near* v. *Minnesota*, 1931
First, Assembly and petition	*DeJonge* v. *Oregon*, 1937
Fourth, Exclusionary rule	*Mapp* v. *Ohio*, 1961
Fifth, Double jeopardy	*Benton* v. *Maryland*, 1969
Fifth, Self-incrimination	*Malloy* v. *Hogan*, 1964
Sixth, Speedy trial	*Klopfer* v. *North Carolina*, 1967
Sixth, Trial by impartial jury	*Duncan* v. *Louisiana*, 1968
Sixth, Confront witnesses	*Pointer* v. *Texas*, 1965
Sixth, Right to counsel	*Gideon* v. *Wainwright*, 1963
Eighth, Cruel and unusual punishments	*Robinson* v. *California*, 1962

Other Supreme Court rulings have addressed other Bill of Rights amendments—sometimes in painstaking detail. For example, it has taken at least a dozen cases to incorporate each aspect of the Sixth Amendment. The Court has also issued multiple rulings incorporating parts of the Fourth, Fifth, and Eighth Amendments.

The Supreme Court has not incorporated all of the Bill of Rights into the Fourteenth Amendment. The Court's deliberate decision to incorporate only certain rights is known as selective incorporation. In *Hurtado* v. *California* (1884), for example, the Court chose not to apply the Fifth Amendment's grand jury requirement to the states.

Note that the Supreme Court so far has not incorporated the Second Amendment's protection of the right to bear arms. Nor has it ruled on the incorporation of the Third or Seventh Amendments. Still, the incorporation of many rights into the Fourteenth Amendment has proved critically important for the protection of the rights and liberties that Americans hold dear.

READING CHECK **Summarizing** How has the incorporation of the Bill of Rights into the Fourteenth Amendment affected the protection of civil liberties?

SECTION 1 ASSESSMENT

Reviewing Ideas and Terms

1. a. Recall What is the difference between **civil liberties** and **civil rights**?
b. Make Inferences What do you think the desire for a bill of rights that some Americans felt during the 1780s suggests about their attitude toward the new national government?

2. a. Describe How do the courts help to protect civil liberties and rights?
b. Explain How can individual rights and the common good come into conflict?
c. Elaborate "My right to swing my fist ends where it meets your nose." What do you think this statement means?

3. a. Define Define the following terms:
due process, incorporation doctrine.
b. Explain How has the incorporation doctrine affected Americans' civil liberties?
c. Evaluate Do you believe that each state should be bound by all guarantees and protections of the Bill of Rights?

Critical Thinking

4. Rate Use a graphic organizer like the one below to list the civil liberties and civil rights protected by the Bill of Rights. You may need to add more boxes to your chart. In your opinion, which of these liberties and rights are most important today? Why?

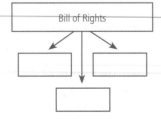

Bill of Rights

FOCUS ON WRITING

5. Persuasive Write a newspaper editorial from the perspective of an American in the 1780s, arguing either for or against the addition of a bill of rights to the U.S. Constitution.

SECTION 2

First Amendment Freedoms

BEFORE YOU READ

Main Idea

The First Amendment protects five fundamental freedoms that are central to the American notion of liberty: the freedoms of religion, speech, the press, assembly, and petition.

Reading Focus

1. How does the First Amendment guarantee religious freedom?

2. What are the guarantees of and limits on the freedoms of speech and of the press?

3. What are the guarantees of and limits on the freedoms of assembly and petition?

Key Terms

establishment clause
free exercise clause
slander
libel
treason
sedition
prior restraint
symbolic speech
freedom of association

TAKING NOTES

As you read, take notes on the five freedoms protected by the First Amendment. Record your notes in a diagram like this one.

First Amendment Freedoms

 WHY IT MATTERS

The First Amendment Today the five rights protected by the First Amendment—freedom of religion, speech, the press, assembly, and petition—are such a basic part of American government and society that many Americans take them for granted. The Framers of the Constitution had vivid memories of British restrictions on these freedoms, including forcing colonial support for the Church of England, punishing writers for criticizing public officials and laws, and limiting public demonstrations. The First Amendment was intended to prevent similar government abuses of Americans' rights.

The First Amendment is only 45 words long, covering barely two lines in the original handwritten copy of the Bill of Rights.

Yet despite its short length, the amendment is a cornerstone of the nation's liberty and is fundamental to our concept of what it means to be an American.

These rights are the freedoms that many Americans cherish above all others. With few exceptions, government cannot tell you what to believe in matters of religion, what you may or may not say, what the press may write or publish, or with whom you may gather. In short, the First Amendment gives us the freedom to live our lives as we see fit. ◼

FUNDAMENTAL Freedoms

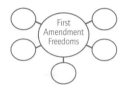

People gather at a rally in support of education funding, exercising their constitutional right to assemble peacefully.

285

Religious Freedom

Chief among the freedoms guaranteed by the First Amendment is the freedom of religion. The search for religious freedom was a central factor in the development of the United States. In colonial times, many people came to the American colonies for the freedom to practice their faith without the discrimination they faced in their home countries. As a result, protecting religious freedom was a major goal for the Framers.

The First Amendment guarantees religious freedom in two ways. First, it forbids the government from establishing an official religion. This portion of the amendment has been tested in court cases involving public religious displays and schools. Second, the First Amendment guarantees people's right to a "free exercise" of their own religion.

The Establishment Clause

"Congress shall make no law respecting an establishment of religion." This part of the First Amendment, called the **establishment clause,** declares that government cannot take actions that create an official religion or support one religion over another. Through the incorporation doctrine, discussed in Section 1, state governments face the same prohibition.

The idea behind the establishment clause was famously expressed in 1802 by Thomas Jefferson, a firm defender of religious freedom. In a letter to a religious group in Connecticut, Jefferson wrote that "religion is a matter which lies solely between Man & his God." He then cited the establishment clause, which he said built "a wall of separation between Church & State."

Jefferson's notion of the "wall of separation" has become a common metaphor for the separation of church and state. But while the First Amendment limits government support of religion, there is much disagreement about just how separated church and state should be. As a result, the courts have faced difficult questions about the proper role of government in religion. For example, can cities allow religious displays on public property? Can public money be used to support religious schools? Rather than issuing rigid guidelines, the courts have taken a case-by-case approach.

Public Displays One issue the courts face under the establishment clause is the legality of government-sponsored religious displays. In *Lynch* v. *Donnelly* (1984), for example, the Supreme Court evaluated a Rhode Island display that included both religious and nonreligious symbols, such as a Christmas tree, a scene depicting Jesus's birth, and colored lights. The Court decided 5–4 that the display did not intend to benefit a particular religion. Acknowledging religion, the decision said, does not necessarily mean the government is promoting it.

In 2005 a divided Supreme Court issued two 5–4 decisions about government displays of the Ten Commandments, which are part of the Christian and Jewish traditions. In one case, government officials in Kentucky hung framed copies of the Ten Commandments in two courthouses. After a lawsuit, they modified these displays to include other historical documents, such as the Declaration of Independence. Government officials claimed that their goal was to show that the Commandments were part of the foundation of U.S. law and government. The Court, in *McCreary County* v. *ACLU of Kentucky* (2005), held that this display was an unconstitutional government promotion of a particular religious belief because it had no legitimate secular purpose. That is, the Court felt that the display focused excessively on the religious aspects of the Ten Commandments.

On the same day, however, the Court's decision in *Van Orden* v. *Perry* (2005) allowed the display of the Ten Commandments at the Texas state capitol. In Texas, the Ten Commandments were carved into a stone marker and were part of a larger display that included other markers representing aspects of Texas history. For this reason, the Court found that the Texas display of the Ten Commandments did not primarily promote a religion. Rather, it was part of a historical and educational display.

Religion and Education Perhaps the strongest debate over the meaning of the establishment clause has to do with education. Indeed, the first Supreme Court case exploring the limits of the establishment clause was based on educational issues.

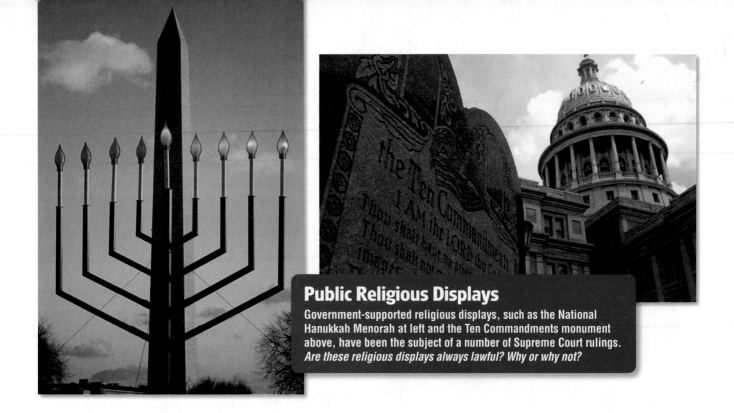

Public Religious Displays

Government-supported religious displays, such as the National Hanukkah Menorah at left and the Ten Commandments monument above, have been the subject of a number of Supreme Court rulings. *Are these religious displays always lawful? Why or why not?*

Everson v. *Board of Education* (1947) centered on a New Jersey school district's plan to use public money to bus students to private schools. In a 5–4 decision, the Court narrowly upheld the New Jersey plan, observing that the plan applied to students of all private schools. Because it did not single out students attending religious schools, the plan did not violate the establishment clause. The busing plan, said the Court, was similar to the use of public money for fire departments that protect all schools—public and private alike.

The Court again tackled the issue of religion in public schools in *Engel* v. *Vitale* (1962). New York school officials had written a prayer that public school students were asked to recite at the start of each day. The prayer was not based on any specific religion and students were not forced to participate, but the Court held that the prayer violated the establishment clause.

PRIMARY SOURCES

❝We think that the constitutional prohibition against laws respecting an establishment of religion must at least mean that in this country it is no part of the business of government to compose official prayers for any group of the American people to recite.❞

—Hugo L. Black, *Engel* v. *Vitale,* 1962

The *Engel* decision drew sharp criticism from some Americans who noted that the practice of beginning the school day with prayer had a long history in the United States. Others, however, supported the ruling. The public debate over prayer in public schools continues today.

The Supreme Court again took up a case involving public support for religious schools in *Lemon* v. *Kurtzman* (1971). In *Lemon*, the Court struck down a law that allowed public funding for the teaching of non-religious subjects at private schools, including religious schools. In its ruling, the Court established the so-called Lemon Test for use in future establishment clause cases. According to this test, a law must meet all three of the following standards in order to be found constitutional:

• It must have a secular, or nonreligious, purpose.
• Its major effects must neither advance nor inhibit religion.
• It must not encourage "excessive government entanglement with religion."

The Supreme Court applied the Lemon Test in the case *Wallace* v. *Jaffree* (1985). At issue in this case was an Alabama law requiring that the public school day begin with "silent meditation or voluntary prayer."

Separation of Church and State

The separation of church and state can be a controversial issue. **What do you think the cartoonist believes about the current condition of the "wall of separation" between church and state?**

In *Wallace*, the six-justice majority applied the Lemon Test and found that the Alabama law had a religious purpose. Therefore, the law was unconstitutional.

Free Exercise of Religion The First Amendment also protects freedom of religion through what is known as the **free exercise clause**, which guarantees each person the right to hold any religious beliefs they choose. Simply put, the government cannot tell a person what he or she must believe in matters of religion.

The free exercise clause does not give people a clear right to behave in any way they wish, however. Courts have ruled that religious practices can be limited in some cases. For example, the Supreme Court found in *Employment Division of Oregon* v. *Smith* (1990) that government can punish illegal drug use even if the drug use is part of a religious practice. Yet deciding when government may limit religiously based behavior has been a difficult challenge for the courts.

The Supreme Court first took on the issue of limiting religiously based behavior in *Reynolds* v. *United States* (1878). The case involved a Mormon religious practice that the faith now prohibits—polygamy, or the marriage of a man to more than one woman. The Court held that even though some Mormons saw polygamy as a religious duty, government could forbid it. Government had a strong interest in preserving certain social norms, the Court held. Toward that goal, laws regulating behavior could be constitutional, even if the result was to outlaw a religious practice—as long as those laws were neutral and did not target a specific religious group.

Similarly, in *Minersville School District* v. *Gobitis* (1940), the Court ruled that a child could be expelled from public school for refusing to salute the American flag or recite the Pledge of Allegiance, even though these actions violated the child's religious beliefs as a Jehovah's Witness. The Court held that government had an interest in encouraging national unity and that the flag-saluting requirement was therefore constitutional.

Three years later, though, the Supreme Court reversed itself. *West Virginia State Board of Education* v. *Barnette* (1943) also involved a Jehovah's Witness family and a state law requiring a flag salute. In *Barnette*, the Court decided that the state's interest in national unity was not strong enough to force people to act against their beliefs. Why the change? The beginning of American involvement in World War II in 1941 had made any refusal to salute the flag appear dangerously unpatriotic. As a result, Jehovah's Witnesses across the country had been physically assaulted, their meeting places burned to the ground. Recognizing the harmful consequences of the *Gobitis* decision, the Court interpreted the matter differently in *Barnette*, this time taking the side of religious freedom.

The *Barnette* ruling was later followed by the case of *Wisconsin* v. *Yoder* (1972). In this case the Court heard a challenge to a state law requiring school attendance until age 17, which conflicted with Amish religious beliefs. The Supreme Court again found that the state interest in forcing school attendance was not strong enough to justify the law at the expense of religious beliefs.

READING CHECK **Identifying the Main Idea** What two main guarantees regarding religion are protected by the First Amendment?

Freedom of Speech and of the Press

The First Amendment forbids Congress from making any law abridging freedom of speech or press, but courts have not treated these freedoms as absolute. The Supreme Court has ruled that government may place limits on freedom of speech and press, especially concerning issues of national security.

Why Freedom of Speech and of the Press?

In the U.S. system of government, decisions are made by representatives chosen by the people. If Americans are to make thoughtful decisions and participate fully in the democratic process, they must have access to a full range of opinions, beliefs, and information. They must also be able to discuss and criticize government policies without fear of punishment.

This principle of free political debate has led to the adoption of open meeting laws by states and the federal government. These laws generally require government bodies to debate and act in public, rather than behind closed doors. Furthermore, under the Freedom of Information Act, the federal government must release government documents—except for certain secret or private records—to the press and the public upon request.

Protecting freedom of speech and of the press is especially challenging in the case of unpopular ideas. Few people, for example, would agree with racist or offensive speech, and it would be relatively easy for government to outlaw such speech. Yet the First Amendment exists especially to protect unpopular ideas.

Limits on Freedoms

While the First Amendment protects even unpopular ideas, it does have limits. The ability to speak and to print ideas can be limited by government for a variety of reasons. For example, government can limit speech or printed material that is judged obscene. You will read more about government restrictions on the media later in this section. Government can also regulate what businesses say about their products. False advertising, for example, can be outlawed.

As with other basic rights, freedom of speech and of the press does not give a person the right to knowingly harm another person. As Supreme Court justice Oliver Wendell Holmes wrote in *Schenck* v. *United States* (1919), "The most stringent [strict] protection of free speech would not protect a man in falsely shouting fire in a theatre and causing a panic."

The Supreme Court has also ruled that the Constitution does not protect defamation, or false statements about a person that cause harm to that person. A spoken defamatory statement is called **slander**. Defamation in print is called **libel**.

Individuals who believe that they have been slandered or libeled may take legal action to defend themselves. In the landmark case *New York Times* Co. v. *Sullivan* (1964), however, the Supreme Court ruled that public officials have fewer legal protections against libel than do private citizens.

PRIMARY SOURCES

The Fundamental Rights

Supreme Court justice Robert H. Jackson wrote the majority opinion for *West Virginia State Board of Education* v. *Barnette* (1943), a decision that struck down a law that forced schoolchildren to salute the flag. The end of Jackson's opinion, excerpted here, is an eloquent defense of personal freedom.

" The very purpose of a Bill of Rights was to withdraw certain subjects from . . . political controversy, to place them beyond the reach of majorities and officials and to establish them as legal principles to be applied by the courts. One's right to life, liberty, and property, to free speech, a free press, freedom of worship and assembly, and other fundamental rights may not be submitted to vote; they depend on the outcome of no elections . . .

If there is any fixed star in our constitutional constellation, it is that no official, high or petty, can prescribe what shall be orthodox in politics, nationalism, religion, or other matters of opinion or force citizens to confess by word or act their faith therein. If there are any circumstances which permit an exception, they do not now occur to us. "

Skills FOCUS   **INTERPRETING PRIMARY SOURCES**

Understanding Points of View What does Jackson believe about the government's ability to restrict the freedoms mentioned in the excerpt?

See *Skills Handbook*, p. H4.

The *Times* case involved a full-page advertisement in the *New York Times* in which civil rights leaders described racial discrimination in the South. Some of the statements in the advertisement were false, and an elected official in Montgomery, Alabama, brought suit for libel.

In its decision, the Court rejected the libel suit. To be libelous, the Court ruled, a false statement about a public official must be shown to demonstrate "actual malice." That is, the author must have known that the statement was false or recklessly disregarded whether or not it was false. The Court noted that trying to prevent all false statements involving public officials would have a chilling effect on free speech.

PRIMARY SOURCES

❝Thus we consider this case against the background of a profound national commitment to the principle that debate on public issues should be uninhibited, robust, and wide-open, and that it may well include vehement [forceful], caustic [biting], and sometimes unpleasantly sharp attacks on government and public officials.❞

—William J. Brennan,
New York Times Co. v. Sullivan, 1964

PROFILES IN GOVERNMENT

Louis Brandeis
1856–1941

Louis Brandeis was a Supreme Court justice from 1916 to 1939. As a successful lawyer in Boston, Massachusetts, Brandeis developed what came to be known as the "Brandeis brief," a technique in which he used economic and sociological data and expert opinions to help support his case in court. This was a revolutionary idea at the time, although it is now a common practice.

Brandeis was nominated to the Supreme Court by President Woodrow Wilson in 1916, becoming the first Jewish member of the Court. As a justice, Brandeis was a firm supporter of individual rights and believed that "the unlimited exercise of governmental power in the name of the people" was dangerous to the American way of life. In his opinions and votes, he consistently worked to expand protections of civil liberties and to limit the exercise of governmental power. Brandeis retired from the Court in 1939. Brandeis University in Massachusetts is named after him.

Summarizing What did Brandeis believe about civil liberties and governmental power?

As with laws against slander and libel, the government may limit First Amendment freedoms in the name of national security, such as to prevent treason or sedition. **Treason** is the crime of making war against the United States or giving "aid and comfort" to its enemies. During wartime, certain speech or writings may be treasonous—for example, publishing information about the location or tactics of American forces that aids the enemy.

Sedition is a legal term for speech or actions that inspire revolt against the government. Courts have upheld laws banning seditious speech. Attempts to define seditious speech and to analyze whether or not it has been protected by the First Amendment have caused controversy throughout American history.

The Alien and Sedition Acts In 1798 the United States was on the verge of war with France. The Federalist Party, which controlled Congress and the presidency, passed the Alien and Sedition Acts. The acts were supposedly intended to protect the country from domestic dissent during a war; among other things, the acts outlawed "false, scandalous, and malicious" statements about the U.S. government. In reality, the new laws seemed designed to silence the Federalists' political rivals, the Democratic-Republicans.

Widespread public anger at the acts helped bring about the defeat of President John Adams, a Federalist, in the election of 1800. Three of the four acts were later repealed or allowed to expire, but the Alien Enemies Act, which authorizes the president to deport resident aliens if their home countries are at war with the United States, remains in effect today.

A "Clear and Present Danger" During World War I, the federal government again passed laws—the Espionage Act and the Sedition Act—targeting criticism of the government and interference with the American war effort. Charles Schenck, who opposed the war, printed a flyer urging men to refuse to serve in the military and was convicted of interfering with the war effort. In *Schenck* v. *United States* (1919), the Supreme Court upheld his conviction.

The *Schenck* decision, written by Justice Oliver Wendell Holmes, established the idea that speech can be limited if it creates a "clear and present danger" of an outcome that government has a right to prevent. Yet Holmes soon changed his view. In *Abrams* v. *United States* (1919), Holmes argued for a specific definition of dangerous speech. "It is only the present danger of immediate evil or an intent to bring it about," he wrote, "that warrants [justifies] Congress in setting a limit to the expression of opinion."

The Court continued to struggle with the "clear and present danger" standard in later years. In *Whitney* v. *California* (1927), the Court went even further than it had in *Schenck*: The majority opinion held that the state has the power to punish those whose words *might* encourage crime, disturb the peace, or otherwise harm the public welfare.

On the eve of the entry of the United States into World War II, Congress passed the Smith Act, which outlawed calling for the forceful overthrow of the United States. Organizing or joining a group that held such views was also outlawed. The Smith Act remains in force today, although it has been severely limited by the Court's rulings in cases such as *Yates* v. *United States* (1957).

In 1969 the Court issued a new standard for determining when government can outlaw seditious speech. In *Brandenburg* v. *Ohio* (1969), the Court overturned its *Whitney* decision and ruled that speech must be allowed unless it is *likely* to lead to immediate lawless action.

The First Amendment and the Media

Just as the First Amendment protects the freedom of speech, it also protects the freedom of the press. This protection acknowledges the importance of a free media in a democratic society. The press is vital to the free spread of information and ideas. As with speech, government has tried to balance the need for media freedom, the rights of others, and issues of national security.

Radio and television broadcasters have fewer First Amendment protections than print media, as the courts have allowed government to regulate the public airwaves over which radio and TV programs are broadcast. Congress created the Federal Communications Commission (FCC) to carry out this regulation. The FCC grants licenses to those wishing to use the public airwaves. Under FCC rules, certain language and content are limited or prohibited.

Because cable systems do not use public airwaves, they are given greater freedom than broadcasters. The Internet is also less subject to government regulation. The government has tried to limit pornography on the Internet, but this effort has been largely unsuccessful. In one case, *Reno* v. *American Civil Liberties Union* (1997), the Supreme Court rejected a law that sought to regulate Internet pornography, in part because users are not likely to encounter offensive content by accident. Instead, the Court ruled that the law violated the First Amendment's guarantee of free speech.

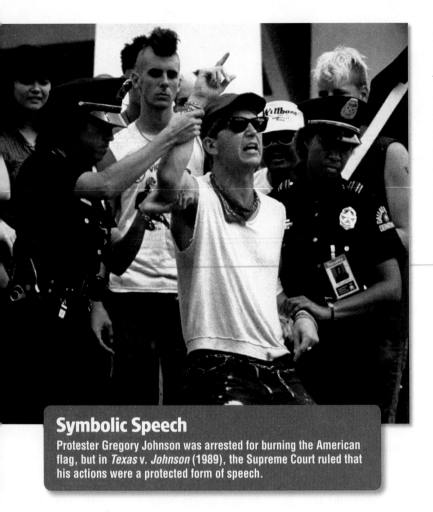

Symbolic Speech

Protester Gregory Johnson was arrested for burning the American flag, but in *Texas* v. *Johnson* (1989), the Supreme Court ruled that his actions were a protected form of speech.

New York Times publication of the Pentagon Papers. These were classified documents about the history of U.S. involvement in the Vietnam War. The White House argued that publishing the papers would threaten national security and the peace process, but in reality the Nixon administration realized that publication would reveal that U.S. officials had long misled the public about the war. The Court ruled that the government had failed to prove a need for prior restraint, and the papers were published.

Symbolic Speech In general, the Supreme Court has granted some First Amendment protections to **symbolic speech,** or the communication of ideas through symbols and actions. The Court has held that some symbolic speech deserves protection as long as the speech does not pose a major threat to property or public order.

An early case in which the Court protected symbolic speech was *Stromberg* v. *California* (1931). In *Stromberg*, the Court ruled on the case of a young woman who had been convicted under a California law that prohibited the display of a red flag, which according to the law was a symbol of opposition to organized government. The Court overturned her conviction, ruling that the California law was an overly vague and unconstitutional restriction on free speech.

Another important symbolic speech case was *Tinker* v. *Des Moines Independent Community School District* (1969). The Court ruled in *Tinker* that an Iowa school district could not prevent students from wearing black armbands to protest the Vietnam War. You will read more about the *Tinker* case in Chapter 13.

In the case *Texas* v. *Johnson* (1989) the Supreme Court ruled that burning the American flag as part of a political protest was a protected act of free speech. "If there is a bedrock principle underlying the First Amendment," the ruling said, "it is that Government may not prohibit the expression of an idea simply because society finds the idea itself offensive or disagreeable."

Prior Restraint Another issue related to the freedom of the press is **prior restraint,** or government action that seeks to prevent materials from being published. Consider the case of Jay Near, a Minnesota newspaper publisher in the 1920s who printed articles accusing local officials of corruption. The state of Minnesota tried to stop Near from publishing his paper. The state was not seeking to punish him for a past crime but was instead trying to restrict him from printing similar articles in the future. The Supreme Court ruled in *Near* v. *Minnesota* (1931) that prior restraint is almost always unconstitutional. Minnesota could punish Near if he violated a law, but the state could not prevent him from publishing his paper merely because officials believed he might violate a law in the future.

The Court addressed another case involving prior restraint in *New York Times Co.* v. *United States* (1971), in which President Richard Nixon tried to halt the

READING CHECK Drawing Conclusions Why are freedom of speech and freedom of the press so important in our democratic system?

Freedoms of Assembly and Petition

The First Amendment's final two protections prohibit government from denying people the right "peaceably to assemble, and to petition the Government for a redress of grievances." In other words, people have the right to meet together and express their views peacefully. This right helps ensure that Americans can share ideas with each other and make their opinions known to their government, including through measures known as initiatives, or petitions designed to force government to consider an issue or allow a vote. Still, there are limits to the right of assembly and petition.

Landmark Cases The Supreme Court has affirmed the freedoms of assembly and petition in several major decisions over the years, including *DeJonge* v. *Oregon* (1937). That case involved a man named Dirk DeJonge, who had attended a meeting of the American Communist Party. At the time, the party called for a revolution against the U.S. government. Oregon state law prohibited participation in meetings held by such organizations. DeJonge, however, argued that the meeting he attended was peaceful, did not involve discussion of any illegal actions, and was thus protected by the First Amendment. The Court agreed. The ruling recognized the right to peaceably assemble as a basic civil liberty and incorporated it into the Fourteenth Amendment, making it illegal for state governments to deny this right.

Edwards v. *South Carolina* (1963) was another important case involving the rights of assembly and petition. This case involved a group of 187 African American students in South Carolina who had gathered to protest racial injustice in the state. Though the assembly was peaceful, local police told the students to leave the area, fearing that the crowd gathering to watch the protest might become violent. When the students did not end their protest, they were arrested. In the *Edwards* decision, the Court declared that the students had been denied their constitutional right to assemble and petition for a redress of grievances. If an assembly is peaceful, the ruling said, it cannot be stopped simply because bystanders are disorderly.

Peaceful Protests

The First Amendment protects Americans' right to meet and express their views peacefully, even when those views are offensive to others. These photos show police officers protecting members of the Ku Klux Klan at a white supremacy rally as a crowd of anti-Klan demonstrators protests. *When may the right to assemble be limited by the government?*

Limits on Assembly and Petition In general, government cannot limit the right of assembly and petition based on protesters' points of view. Only in extreme cases, such as protesters encouraging others to commit violent acts, does government have strong enough reason to limit this important First Amendment freedom.

Government can more easily limit the right of assembly and petition for reasons other than the ideas expressed by protesters. For example, governments can place reasonable restrictions on the time, manner, and place of a gathering. Courts have found, for example, that citizens can be required to obtain a permit for holding a demonstration. They can be denied the right to make excessive noise. They can be kept off of private property or prevented from invading the privacy of others. But any such rules must serve a clear and valid purpose, and government must apply them evenly and without regard to the content of the demonstrator's message.

Freedom of Association The phrase *freedom of association* does not appear in the First Amendment. Still, the Supreme Court has determined that the freedoms guaranteed by the amendment together establish the right to **freedom of association**—the right to join with others, share ideas, and work toward a common purpose.

A major case involving the freedom of association is *National Association for the Advancement of Colored People* v. *Alabama ex rel. Patterson* (1958). The state of Alabama had tried to force the National Association for the Advancement of Colored People (NAACP) to give the state a list of its members. At the time, however, the NAACP was involved in a bitter fight to improve civil rights in Alabama and feared that publicizing the names of its members would lead to violence and other harmful consequences.

The Supreme Court agreed with the NAACP. In a unanimous ruling, the Court stated that "It is beyond debate that freedom to engage in association for the advancement of beliefs and ideas is an inseparable aspect of the 'liberty' assured by the Due Process Clause of the Fourteenth Amendment, which embraces freedom of speech." Forcing the release of the names of the NAACP's members, the Court felt, would harm the freedom to associate. Alabama's actions, therefore, violated the Constitution.

READING CHECK **Drawing Conclusions** What are the purposes of the freedoms of assembly and petition?

SECTION 2 ASSESSMENT

THINK central Online Quiz
thinkcentral.com
KEYWORD: SGO CLB HP

Reviewing Ideas and Terms

1. **a. Define** What are the **establishment clause** and the **free exercise clause**?
   b. Contrast What is the difference between government acknowledgment of religion and government endorsement of religion?
   c. Evaluate Why do you think so many questions of religious freedom have involved schools and public education?

2. **a. Describe** Under what conditions can the freedoms of speech and of the press be limited?
   b. Draw Conclusions Why do you think the courts are reluctant to allow **prior restraint**?
   c. Predict What might happen if the freedoms of speech and of the press were rights that could never be restricted or limited by government?

3. **a. Describe** What are time, manner, and place restrictions?
   b. Make Inferences How is the **freedom of association** implied by the First Amendment?

Critical Thinking

4. **Analyze** Use a chart like the one below to explain how civil liberties are protected by the First Amendment and limited by the government. Are the limits on these freedoms reasonable? Why or why not?

	Protections	Limits
Religion		
Speech and Press		
Assembly and Petition		

FOCUS ON WRITING

5. **Descriptive** Write a short essay that evaluates how interpretations of the First Amendment have changed over time. In your essay, include a time line that lists major Supreme Court rulings on the First Amendment. You may wish to focus on one of the freedoms protected by the amendment.

Prayer in Public Schools

Does the Constitution permit prayer in public schools?

THE ISSUE

The First Amendment states that "Congress shall make no law respecting an establishment of religion, or prohibiting the free exercise thereof." This protection of religious freedom both forbids the government from establishing an official religion and guarantees Americans' right to freely exercise their own religious beliefs. But what about prayer in public schools? Some Americans believe that allowing prayer in public schools is an unconstitutional government support for religion. Others believe that the right to pray in public schools is an essential religious freedom.

This 1990 photo of a coach leading his team in prayer predates court rulings that have declared this practice unconstitutional.

VIEWPOINTS

Prayer in public schools should be prohibited.

State-sponsored prayer implies that only one form of prayer—and of religion—is approved of by the state. American public school students come from families with many different religious beliefs or with no religious beliefs at all. As a result, any state-sponsored prayer will differ from some students' beliefs and will interfere with parents' right to influence their children's religious upbringing. Furthermore, the First Amendment forbids any government action to establish an official religion or support one religion over another. This separation between church and state is an important protection of religious freedom. In *Engel* v. *Vitale* (1962), the Supreme Court held that government-sponsored prayer in public schools violates the establishment clause, even if students are not forced to take part in the prayer. There should be no praying in public schools.

Prayer should be allowed in public schools.

Prayer has been a part of American classroom life since colonial times, and religion has had and continues to have an important role in American public life. The influence of religion in the United States should be acknowledged in the classroom. Fortunately, the *Engel* decision does not actually forbid prayer in public schools; it merely says that *government-sponsored* prayer is unconstitutional, not prayer of any kind. In fact, students may pray alone or in groups on school property, including in classrooms outside of regular class hours. Furthermore, students may form religious clubs, wear clothing with religious messages, or hand out religious materials to classmates. So long as the government—in this case, the school—takes no action to promote one religion over another, there is no violation of the First Amendment. Prayer should continue to be allowed in public schools.

What Is Your Opinion?

1. Do you agree with the Supreme Court's interpretation of the establishment clause in *Engel* v. *Vitale*? Why or why not?

2. Should beginning the official school day with prayer be permitted in public schools? Why or why not?

THINK central **Practice Online**

thinkcentral.com
KEYWORD: SGO CLB

Protecting Individual Liberties

Main Idea

A key purpose of the Bill of Rights is to protect individuals from government abuses. Several amendments limit the government's power and protect individual rights against government actions.

Reading Focus

1. What are the purposes of and limits on the right to keep and bear arms?

2. How does the Bill of Rights guarantee the security of home and person?

3. How has the right to privacy developed?

4. How and why does the Constitution guarantee due process of law?

Key Terms

probable cause
search warrant
exclusionary rule
police power
procedural due process
substantive due process

TAKING NOTES As you read, take notes on the different amendments discussed in this section. Record your notes in a chart like the one below.

Amendment	Protections
Second	
Third	
Fourth	
Fifth	

Following THE Rules

The actions of government authorities, such as these FBI agents seizing evidence during a terrorism investigation, are limited by rules and laws.

WHY IT MATTERS

Limits on Government What would life be like if police could enter your home for no reason at any time, day or night? What if the government could use illegally obtained evidence against you in court to convict you of a crime you did not commit? Thanks to the Constitution, these events cannot legally happen in the United States.

We all follow many rules and laws each day. Some of these rules are social customs, such as shaking someone's hand when you first meet him or her. Others are rules set by your school, such as no running in the hallway or no speaking loudly in the library. Still others are laws established by government, such as those regarding speed limits. These rules all restrict your actions in some way.

You may think of rules and laws as being things that only people have to obey, but it is important to know that governments also have rules they must follow. The government must act according to established rules and laws that are designed to protect the American people's rights and liberties. Many of these limits on government actions are established by the Bill of Rights, which guards Americans' right to live freely without government interference. ◼

The Right to Keep and Bear Arms

Today one of the most heavily debated amendments in the Bill of Rights is the Second Amendment, which reads, "A well regulated Militia, being necessary to the security of a free State, the right of the people to keep and bear Arms, shall not be infringed." This amendment was included in the Bill of Rights to protect the right of states to form militias and to ease the fears of those who worried about the power of a standing army controlled by the federal government.

Some Americans believe that the Second Amendment protects an individual right to own all kinds of firearms. Others believe that the amendment was intended only to protect the rights of states to form militia units, and that government can therefore place many limits on gun ownership.

The Supreme Court has issued only two major rulings on the Second Amendment, which has not been incorporated into the Fourteenth Amendment. In *United States* v. *Miller* (1939), the Court upheld a law that placed some restrictions on possession of automatic weapons and sawed-off shotguns, the types of guns that were then often used by criminals. The Court ruled that the Second Amendment was not meant to protect the right to have all types of weapons. Instead, it protected only those guns that might be used by people in a militia.

Nearly 70 years after *Miller,* the Supreme Court again addressed the issue of gun control in *District of Columbia* v. *Heller* (2008). *Heller* concerned a Washington, D.C., law that banned almost all ownership of handguns or rifles. A federal appeals court had overturned portions of this law, ruling that it was too strict. In *Heller,* the Court agreed with the appeals court's decision, ruling for the first time that the Second Amendment protects an individual's right to possess a gun and is not merely a protection of state militias. The Court did hold, however, that the right to own a gun is not unlimited and that the government may impose some reasonable restrictions on gun ownership.

READING CHECK **Summarizing** What is the controversy over the Second Amendment?

Security of Home and Person

Much of the Bill of Rights reflects Americans' desire to protect their rights from the kind of government abuses they had seen during their years under British rule. Together, the Third and Fourth Amendments help protect Americans' rights to be secure in both home and person.

The Third Amendment In colonial times, the British military sometimes quartered—housed—its soldiers in colonists' homes. Although the British occasionally paid homeowners for the food and shelter, they often did not. As tensions between Great Britain and the colonies rose during the years leading up to the Revolutionary War, more British soldiers were sent to the colonies—and many of them occupied private homes. As a result, the Declaration of Independence listed the quartering of troops among the many American complaints against the British government.

The Third Amendment forbids the government from housing troops in private houses during times of peace without the consent of the owner. During war, troops can only occupy private houses as prescribed by law. In other words, military forces cannot simply take over a house for no reason or without due process.

Today the Third Amendment is largely forgotten by most Americans. The forced quartering of troops has never been the subject of a Supreme Court case, and the amendment has not been incorporated into the Fourteenth Amendment.

The Fourth Amendment Like the Third Amendment, the Fourth Amendment was a result of a hated British practice during colonial days: the use of writs of assistance. A writ was a legal document that gave British authorities wide power to search private homes and businesses. British officials could conduct their searches without first showing **probable cause**, or the strong likelihood that they would find evidence of a crime. To show probable cause, authorities must explain what evidence they are looking for and why they believe they will find it in that location.

With a writ of assistance, however, the British could enter anyone's home at any time and search for as long as they wanted.

The Fourth Amendment was written to protect Americans against similar government abuses. It has proved to be an important guarantee of personal security.

Search and Seizure The purpose of the Fourth Amendment is to ensure that people are "secure in their persons, houses, papers, and effects." The amendment forbids "unreasonable searches and seizures." It also sets terms for issuing a **search warrant**, a document that gives police legal authority to search private property. The Fourth Amendment says government can issue a search warrant only after authorities have proved to a judge that there is probable cause for a search. The warrant must describe what will be searched and seized.

In most cases, authorities today need a search warrant to enter and search a building without the owner's consent. Officials can enter in an emergency situation without a warrant, but they must follow strict rules. They can only search for evidence directly related to the crime they are investigating. They may seize any other evidence they come across, but only if it is in "plain view," and only if the officer does not search for it.

The issue of "plain view" came before the Supreme Court in *Arizona* v. *Hicks* (1987), a case in which police entered an apartment without a warrant after a gun was fired there. The police then noticed some expensive stereo equipment in the apartment. Suspecting it had been stolen, officers moved the equipment to locate the serial numbers, which helped them determine that the equipment was indeed stolen property. The Court held that by moving the equipment, police had conducted a warrantless search without probable cause.

As a result of the warrantless search in *Hicks*, police could not use the stereo equipment as evidence. This rule that evidence obtained illegally may not be used against a person in court is known as the **exclusionary rule**. The rule was established in *Weeks* v. *United States* (1914), in which the Court decided that the Fourth Amendment prevents such government actions.

The Court expanded the exclusionary rule to state actions in *Mapp* v. *Ohio* (1961). In *Mapp*, police had forcibly entered Dollree Mapp's home in Cleveland, Ohio, to look for gambling evidence. They did not have a warrant for the search and found no evidence of gambling, but they did find several allegedly obscene books. Mapp was convicted of violating obscenity laws. The Court overturned her conviction, finding the books had been seized in an illegal search.

The Fourth Amendment does not always require police to obtain a warrant before a search or seizure of evidence. For example, a person's right to be free from police searches does not reach outdoors. The Court has held that police can search through a person's trash without a warrant.

Pedestrians and Cars What about situations in which police stop people on the street to arrest or question them? Legally speaking, stopping a person is considered seizure. Police can stop someone on the basis of a reasonable suspicion—if, for example, the person is acting oddly. Once stopped, police may frisk, or search, the person if there is concern for the safety of the police officer or others. The frisk is meant to find concealed weapons, though police may seize other evidence in some cases. To arrest a person, however, the police must be able to show probable cause.

The Fourth Amendment also relates to the stopping and searching of vehicles. Under some circumstances, police can stop and search automobiles without a warrant. For example, police can stop drivers who are observed committing traffic violations. If the police have stopped a vehicle based on probable cause, they may seize any evidence that is in plain view and may search any place that is within reach or control of the vehicle's occupants. In some cases officers can also search the vehicle's trunk without a search warrant.

Electronic Communications The Fourth Amendment also protects a person's "papers." With the invention of the telegraph, telephone, and Internet, the courts have had to decide whether the Fourth Amendment applies to new means of communication.

Government Surveillance

After the September 11, 2001, terrorist attacks on the United States, President George W. Bush authorized the National Security Agency (NSA) to monitor certain telephone calls, e-mails, and other communications without first obtaining a warrant. The controversial program was intended to help officials prevent future terrorist attacks, but it was widely criticized by people who believed it sacrificed important civil liberties protections.

SKILLS FOCUS — INTERPRETING PRIMARY SOURCES

Analyzing Political Cartoons Does the artist support or oppose the NSA's warrantless surveillance program? How can you tell?

See **Skills Handbook**, p. H8.

The Supreme Court first addressed this issue in *Olmstead* v. *United States* (1928). In *Olmstead*, agents had used evidence obtained by wiretapping, or using a concealed listening device to monitor telephone calls. The Court did not view wiretapping as an illegal search. But the Court reversed itself in *Katz* v. *United States* (1967). In *Katz*, the Court ruled that the Fourth Amendment protects a person's privacy as well as his or her personal space. After *Katz*, wiretapping has usually required a warrant based on probable cause.

The treatment of electronic communications became a major issue after the September 11, 2001, terrorist attacks on the United States. The USA PATRIOT Act, passed by Congress after the attacks, gave law enforcement agencies wide power to prevent future attacks. Among other things, the act gave officials more freedom to search telephone and e-mail communications and business, medical, and library records. Critics charge that the PATRIOT Act weakens important civil liberties protections. In 2007 a federal judge struck down part of the act, ruling that it gave officials too much power to search phone and Internet records without court oversight.

In late 2005, during President George W. Bush's second term, Americans learned about a secret program under which the National Security Agency (NSA) was authorized to monitor telephone calls, e-mails, and other communications to U.S. residents made by people outside the United States with suspected terrorist links. The NSA did not obtain warrants before intercepting these conversations. As a result, there was widespread public debate about whether the program violated the Fourth Amendment.

Testing for Drugs Another modern-day Fourth Amendment question involves testing people for the use of illegal drugs. Are such tests a violation of the Fourth Amendment's protections of personal security? In general, courts have held that private employers have wide freedom to test their workers in order to discourage drug use. Governments, however, face limits in their ability to test workers. Courts have ruled that governments cannot test all employees to screen for drug use. They can, however, test employees whose jobs may affect public safety, such as airline crews and mechanics, bus and truck drivers, or railroad workers.

Protections for Students The Supreme Court has ruled that public school students have fewer Fourth Amendment protections than does the general population. While students do have some rights to privacy, the Court has ruled that a school's need to ensure a safe learning environment can override privacy concerns. For example, school officials may search students for drugs or weapons. In *New Jersey* v. *T.L.O.* (1985), the Court permitted an official's search of a student's purse without probable cause.

In another case, *Vernonia School District* v. *Acton* (1995), the Court ruled that schools could randomly test student athletes for drug use. The *Vernonia* decision held that the school's interest in fighting drug use overrode student privacy concerns. The Court later extended this ruling in *Board of Education*

of Pottawatomie County v. *Earls* (2002), in which the Court held that schools may require students participating in extracurricular activities to be tested for drugs.

READING CHECK **Summarizing** How do the Third and Fourth Amendments protect Americans' security?

The Right to Privacy

Throughout this section you have read references to the Supreme Court's protection of a right to privacy. Yet the Constitution makes no explicit reference to such a right. Where does this unstated right come from?

Those who believe in a right to privacy say that it is implied in several amendments. For example, the Fourth Amendment implies that people can expect not to have their privacy violated by unreasonable searches. Some scholars argue that a right to privacy should be considered part of the concept of liberty guaranteed by the due process clauses of the Fifth and Fourteenth Amendments.

In *Olmstead* v. *United States*, the case involving the use of wiretaps on telephones, Justice Louis Brandeis wrote a dissent in which he argued for the existence of a "right to be let alone." Nearly 40 years later, the Court finally embraced a right to privacy in *Griswold* v. *Connecticut* (1965).

Griswold involved an organization that provided information about birth control to married couples. At the time, providing such information violated Connecticut law. The Court's decision stated that several constitutional amendments, including the Third and Fourth Amendments, create "zones of privacy." Within these zones of privacy, the Court held, was the right of married couples to make decisions about birth control.

Surely the most controversial Court decision concerning the right to privacy is *Roe* v. *Wade* (1973). This case centered on the question of whether state law could deny a woman the right to end a pregnancy by abortion. The Court, citing the right to privacy, said that the state could not do so in the first three months of the pregnancy.

The decision in *Roe* v. *Wade* has met with both approval and disapproval. Some critics have sought to bring cases to the Court that might lead to a reversal of *Roe*. In *Planned*

Students and the Fourth Amendment

The Supreme Court has ruled that public school students have fewer privacy rights under the Fourth Amendment than the general public. Officials can search students, their lockers, and their belongings for drugs or weapons. *Why do students have limited Fourth Amendment rights?*

At right, a police officer and a drug-sniffing dog search student lockers. Below, students enter a school through metal detectors intended to prevent students from bringing weapons into the building.

Surveillance and the Right to Privacy

Surveillance cameras in public places—such as the Lower East Side of Manhattan, New York City—can help reduce crime, but civil liberties advocates worry that the growth of surveillance has harmed the right to privacy.

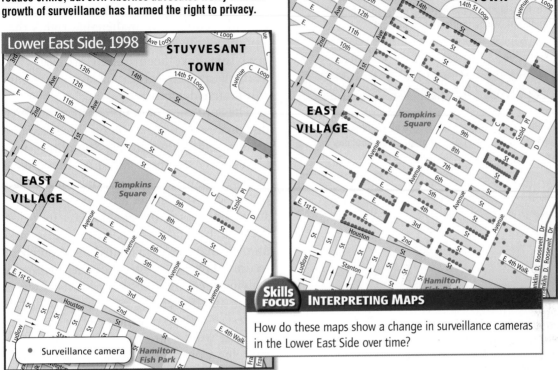

Skills Focus **INTERPRETING MAPS**

How do these maps show a change in surveillance cameras in the Lower East Side over time?

Parenthood of Southeastern Pennsylvania v. *Casey* (1992), the Court upheld some requirements of a law that allowed abortion only after a woman met several requirements, including parental consent for pregnant minors. The basic privacy right identified in *Roe* v. *Wade*, however, was left in place.

READING CHECK **Drawing Conclusions** Where does the concept of the right to privacy come from?

Due Process of Law

The concept of due process is key to the protections provided by the Bill of Rights. The Fifth Amendment forbids the federal government from depriving people of "life, liberty, or property, without due process of law." The Fourteenth Amendment gives the same protections against state governments.

As you read earlier, due process requires that government act fairly and reasonably in accordance with established laws. Due process limits the government's **police power**,

or its ability to regulate behavior for the common good. There are two different components of due process: procedural due process and substantive due process.

Procedural Due Process As the term suggests, **procedural due process** requires that government follow certain procedures before punishing a person. You will read more about these procedures in Section 4.

As with all rights, the right to procedural due process can be limited when government has a strong reason to do so. For example, the Supreme Court ruled in *Mackey* v. *Montrym* (1979) that a state could take away a driver's license if the driver refused to take tests to show if he or she had been drinking alcohol. The state's action in this case involved penalizing people without finding them guilty—that is, without going through a process. Yet the Supreme Court decided that the state's interest in getting drunk drivers off the road was strong enough to deny due process.

RESPONSIBILITIES OF LEADERSHIP

The police power is one of the greatest powers the government has. Using it wisely is an important responsibility.

Due Process

Due process requires that government act fairly and reasonably in accordance with established rules if it seeks to deprive a person of life, liberty, or property. This important concept has two sources: the Fifth Amendment, which limits the actions of the national government, and the Fourteenth Amendment, which limits state and local governments.

Fifth Amendment

"No person shall . . . be deprived of life, liberty, or property, without due process of law . . ."

Fourteenth Amendment

"No State shall . . . deprive any person of life, liberty, or property, without due process of law . . ."

Due Process

Federal, state, and local governments must act fairly and reasonably, in accordance with fair, established laws and policies.

Substantive Due Process Procedural due process involves questions about whether or not legal procedures are fair. **Substantive due process,** on the other hand, concerns whether the laws themselves are fair and just. Substantive due process is based on the idea that all people have inalienable rights that cannot be taken away from them, even by laws that have been passed properly. For example, a racial segregation law may violate substantive due process.

The Supreme Court addressed substantive due process in its decision on three lawsuits collectively known as the Slaughterhouse Cases (1873). These lawsuits involved a Louisiana law that allowed only one slaughterhouse to operate in a certain part of the state. The Court upheld the law in a 5–4 decision, but Justice Stephen Field dissented, arguing that the law violated most butchers' inalienable rights by unconstitutionally denying them the right to work. This was a violation, he wrote, of substantive due process. Field's opinion, joined by three other justices, would later become the basis for Supreme Court rulings that further defined due process.

READING CHECK **Contrasting** What is the difference between procedural and substantive due process?

SECTION 3 ASSESSMENT

THINK central **Online Quiz**
thinkcentral.com
KEYWORD: SGO CLB HP

Reviewing Ideas and Terms

1. a. Identify What right does the Second Amendment protect?
b. Predict What might happen if there were no Second Amendment?

2. a. Define Define the terms **probable cause**, **search warrant**, and **exclusionary rule**.
b. Explain Why must search warrants clearly explain what items the police are looking for?
c. Evaluate Do you believe that the NSA wiretapping program violates the Fourth Amendment? Why or why not?

3. a. Recall How does the Fourth Amendment imply a right to privacy?
b. Evaluate Do you think that it is proper for the courts to infer rights—such as the right to privacy—that are not explicitly mentioned in the Constitution? Explain your answer.

4. a. Define What are **procedural due process** and **substantive due process**?
b. Elaborate How does due process limit government's police power?

Critical Thinking

5. Interpret Use a graphic organizer like the one below to explain how the Second, Third, Fourth, and Fifth Amendments imply the existence of a right to privacy.

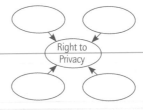

Right to Privacy

FOCUS ON WRITING

6. Persuasive The Supreme Court has ruled that students in public schools have fewer Fourth Amendment protections than the rest of the population. Do you agree or disagree with the Court? Write an opinion essay for your school newspaper in which you explain your position.

Crime and Punishment

Main Idea

The Constitution contains many features that help ensure that people accused of a crime receive fair and reasonable treatment—from arrest to trial to punishment.

Reading Focus

1. How does the U.S. justice system address both civil law and criminal law?

2. How does the Constitution guarantee the rights of those accused of a crime?

3. What are the major constitutional guarantees for ensuring fair trials?

4. How does the Constitution address the punishment of persons convicted of crimes?

Key Terms

civil law
criminal law
indictment
bail
capital punishment
Miranda warnings
bench trial
double jeopardy

TAKING NOTES As you read, take notes on the protected rights of people accused of crimes. Record your notes in a graphic organizer like the one below.

Rights of the Accused

WHY IT MATTERS

Protections for the Accused Even a child understands the fundamental concept of fairness. A child playing a game with friends, for example, quickly learns about fairness and the importance of playing by the rules. Fairness is at the heart of the U.S. justice system, which sets rules to protect the rights of those accused of crimes and to ensure a fair outcome to a trial. The Constitution offers many protections for persons accused of crimes as well as for those convicted and sentenced to be punished.

Why are there so many protections for those accused of crimes? While it is important to punish people who have committed crimes, it is also important to be sure that innocent people are not wrongly convicted. It is a core principle of American justice that a person accused of a crime is innocent until proven guilty. It can be difficult to balance the rights of the accused and society's interest in preventing and punishing crime, but under American law all people, no matter how terrible their crimes or how long their criminal records, are entitled to justice. ■

All persons accused of crimes have certain rights to ensure a fair trial and to prevent innocent people from being wrongly convicted. In addition to guaranteeing a fair trial, the Constitution also includes protections for those convicted of crimes.

Fairness and the Justice System

The U.S. Justice System

In this chapter you have read about the importance of civil liberties in American life. These basic freedoms to think and to act as we choose are guarded by the U.S. justice system, which also provides protections for persons accused of crimes and for those convicted of crimes. The justice system seeks fair and impartial outcomes for disputes of all kinds. It follows rules and guidelines established in the Constitution and in U.S. law in order to resolve lawsuits, criminal trials, and other disputes.

Types of Law The law is commonly classified into two categories: civil law and criminal law. **Civil law** covers private disputes between people over property or relationships. People who violate civil law are often fined or otherwise punished, but they are not usually subject to imprisonment. **Criminal law** is the system for dealing with crimes and their punishments. People who violate criminal law may be fined, imprisoned, or even executed.

Civil Law The field of civil law consists of several categories, including contracts, tort law, property law, and family law. A contract is a legal agreement, or promise, between two or more parties that makes clear what each party must do and when he or she must do it. Contracts may be verbal or written agreements, but all are legally binding. Failure to follow the contract—known as breach of contract—may lead to legal action against one or more parties.

Another category of civil law is called tort law. A tort is an action that harms another person, such as medical malpractice, wrongful death, or a civil rights violation. Personal injury cases are a common example of tort law.

Property law, as the name suggests, involves the purchase and sale of property, such as a house or an automobile. Family law addresses issues related to families, such as marriage, divorce, and child custody.

Civil Lawsuits As you read in Chapter 8, a case in civil law is called a lawsuit. In a lawsuit, a plaintiff brings the suit against a defendant, often seeking damages, or financial compensation from the defendant to correct the alleged wrong. The plaintiff does not have to demonstrate the defendant's guilt beyond a reasonable doubt. Instead, a defendant may be found guilty based on a preponderance—majority—of evidence.

Not all civil lawsuits go to trial. In some cases, parties in civil suits may seek—or may be ordered to seek—alternative dispute resolution outside of the government judicial process. The alternative dispute resolution process is similar to a trial, but it is less formal and less costly. There are three basic types of alternative dispute resolution:

- Mediation, in which a trained negotiator works with both sides to reach a compromise agreement acceptable to everyone;

- Arbitration, in which a third party listens to both sides and issues a ruling that both sides have agreed in advance to accept;

- Negotiation, in which the sides discuss ways to resolve the issue without the involvement of a third party.

000007

IG TOBACCO   DATE 12/14/1999   80-555/5552

$ **99,700,000.00**

The Commonwealth of Massachusetts

Nine Million Seven Hundred Thousand   DOLLARS

o Settlement

1": 1 1007": 56819 24 568 11":

Settling a Civil Lawsuit

In 1999 five tobacco manufacturers, sometimes referred to as Big Tobacco, settled a civil lawsuit brought by 46 states. The suit accused the companies of hiding smoking's harmful effects.

Justice Delayed

Edgar Ray Killen was first tried for the 1964 murder of three civil rights workers in 1967, but the all-white jury could not agree on a verdict. It was not until 2005, after years of increasing public pressure, that Killen—at 80 years old—was finally tried again. He was convicted of manslaughter. Below, Killen consults with his attorney; at right, he faces the judge at a hearing.

Civil lawsuits that are not settled by alternative dispute resolution go to trial. Both federal and state courts hear civil cases, and procedures can vary. In general, though, cases follow the same basic steps:

- The plaintiff hires a lawyer and files a complaint with the court.
- The two sides can seek to settle the dispute before trial.
- If the trial goes forward, the two sides exchange information about evidence and witnesses in a process known as discovery.
- The trial may be heard by a jury or, in some cases, by a judge alone.
- The jury or judge issues a ruling.
- Decisions may be appealed.

Criminal Law While civil law deals with private offenses and disagreements, criminal law deals with crimes, or offenses against the public. In general, a crime occurs when a person breaks a law passed by a local, state, or federal government.

There are two types of crimes—misdemeanors and felonies. A misdemeanor is a relatively minor offense for which a person may receive a minor fine or may be imprisoned for less than a year. Trespassing, traffic violations, and petty theft are examples of misdemeanor crimes. A felony is a more serious crime, such as murder, sexual assault, or grand theft, that carries a harsher sentence.

Criminal Case Processes The Fifth Amendment guarantees that people cannot face trial for most federal crimes without first facing a grand jury. Remember that a grand jury is a group of 16 to 23 citizens who gather in secret to decide whether there is enough evidence to send an accused person to trial. The grand jury hears and collects evidence about alleged crimes. It calls witnesses and can use subpoenas, court orders requiring people to appear in court or to produce certain evidence in court. If the grand jury believes there is enough evidence to charge a person with a crime, it issues a formal complaint of criminal wrongdoing called an **indictment**. If the defendant waives his or her right to be indicted by a grand jury, a prosecutor can bring charges in what is called an information, an official report of the offense for which the person is charged.

Next, the accused is arrested, or taken into custody by police. Arrest may happen before indictment or after, depending on the circumstances of the alleged crime.

After indictment and arrest, the accused may face several hearings before trial. Among these hearings is the arraignment, the formal reading of charges against the accused. At this time, the accused enters a plea—guilty or not guilty. Other hearings may involve motions, or requests, by the prosecutor or the defense—for example, to move the location of the trial or to block certain evidence from being considered.

The court also may hold a hearing to discuss the setting of bail. **Bail** is money pledged by the accused as a guarantee that he or she will return to court for trial. If the accused appears in court at the proper time, the money is returned. If he or she flees, the money is forfeited. Bail helps ensure that innocent people are not imprisoned unnecessarily before trial.

Often, a defendant will plead guilty before a trial takes place. This may occur as the result of a plea bargain, by which the defendant agrees to plead guilty to a lesser charge. Government may accept the plea bargain to ensure a conviction or to obtain the defendant's assistance in another criminal matter, such as testifying against another person involved in the crime. In U.S. courts, the vast majority of criminal cases are settled through plea bargain.

If a defendant does not plead guilty or accept a plea bargain, the trial takes place. This complex process usually involves jury selection, which you will read about later in this section. Both sides present evidence and witnesses to support their claims, and the judge or jury decides the case. Either side may appeal the decision to a higher court.

If a defendant pleads guilty or is found guilty in a trial, sentencing takes place at a separate hearing. Sentences depend on the severity of the crime and other factors. Some convicted people receive probation, meaning they remain free but are under close supervision by authorities. Other convicted people are sent to prison. A small number receive **capital punishment**—punishment by death. You will read more about sentencing and punishment later in this section.

READING CHECK Comparing and Contrasting
In the U.S. justice system, how are civil and criminal cases similar and different?

Rights of the Accused

In our justice system, we presume that people accused of crimes are innocent until they are proven guilty beyond a reasonable doubt. Balancing the rights of the accused with the need to protect society from criminals is a major challenge. Yet the Framers recognized that people can need protection from government, especially when a person's freedom is at stake.

Habeas Corpus The writ of habeas corpus, which you read about in an earlier chapter, is one such protection from government actions. Remember that the writ of habeas corpus is a legal order requiring that an imprisoned person be brought before a court so that a judge may determine whether or not the imprisonment is legal. Sometimes referred to as the "writ of liberty," the writ of habeas corpus is an important protection against the government abusing its police power. Without this protection, the government could arrest and hold people for any length of time without ever having to defend its actions in court.

Article I, Section 9, of the Constitution provides that: "The Privilege of the Writ of Habeas Corpus shall not be suspended, unless when in Cases of Rebellion or Invasion the public Safety may require it." Citing these words, President Abraham Lincoln suspended habeas corpus in certain parts of the country during the Civil War. Under Lincoln's order, people faced arrest merely for criticizing the government. In addition, prisoners faced military trials, not trial by jury.

Lincoln's action was—and remains—controversial. In the decision *Ex parte Merryman* (1861), a federal court ruled that his order was unconstitutional. In response, Congress passed a law approving of Lincoln's action. After the war, in *Ex parte Milligan* (1866), the Supreme Court ruled that neither Lincoln nor Congress had the power to suspend habeas corpus in this case, noting that Milligan was a civilian, the civil courts were functioning, and Milligan's activities did not take place in the theater of war.

The writ of habeas corpus has received much public attention in the aftermath of the September 11, 2001, terrorist attacks on the United States. In the years following the attacks, the United States and its allies captured a number of suspected terrorists in Afghanistan and Iraq. Many of these people—labeled unlawful enemy combatants by the Bush administration—were being held by the U.S. military several years after their capture without receiving any formal hearing or judicial process. Most were held in a U.S.-run facility at Guantánamo Bay, Cuba.

Several court cases, including three Supreme Court decisions, challenged the legality of the detentions. In *Hamdi* v. *Rumsfeld* (2004) and *Rasul* v. *Bush* (2004), the Supreme Court ruled that unlawful enemy combatants detained by the United States did have limited rights to challenge their imprisonment in a federal court. In 2006 Congress passed a law establishing a system for trying unlawful enemy combatants in military tribunals. A federal court in Washington, D.C., however, ruled that the law stripped detainees of the right to habeas corpus. A third Supreme Court case, *Boumediene* v. *Bush* (2008), ruled that detainees have a constitutional right to challenge their detentions in U.S. courts.

Grand Juries As you read earlier, the Fifth Amendment includes the guarantee that people cannot be tried for most federal crimes without first being indicted by a grand jury. The grand jury guarantee has not been incorporated into the Fourteenth Amendment, and some states do not have grand jury systems. In many states today, criminal charges are brought by a prosecutor in an information.

Self-Incrimination The Fifth Amendment provides another valuable safeguard for persons accused of crime, protecting the accused from being "compelled in any criminal case to be a witness against himself." This means that a person cannot be forced to give evidence or testimony that is incriminating—that is, evidence or testimony that suggests his or her own guilt. This protection covers any government proceeding that might lead to criminal charges, such as pre-trial questioning by police as well as criminal trials themselves.

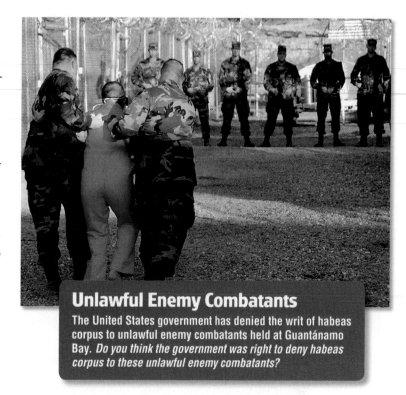

Unlawful Enemy Combatants
The United States government has denied the writ of habeas corpus to unlawful enemy combatants held at Guantánamo Bay. *Do you think the government was right to deny habeas corpus to these unlawful enemy combatants?*

The protection against self-incrimination exists only for spoken testimony, however. Government can force people to be searched or to have blood samples or fingerprints taken as evidence, among other things.

Government can also force people to give testimony against themselves by giving them immunity. That is, the government can agree not to prosecute a person for a crime. In return, the person can be forced to testify.

The protection against self-incrimination was the subject of *Miranda* v. *Arizona* (1966). The issue in *Miranda* was a suspect's confession to a crime after being questioned by police, who had not told him that he had the right to consult with an attorney before or during questioning. The Supreme Court ruled that the questioning of suspects under such circumstances violated the Fifth Amendment and that the resulting confession could not be used at trial.

PRIMARY SOURCE

❝ We hold that when an individual is taken into custody or otherwise deprived of his freedom by the authorities in any significant way and is subjected to questioning, the privilege against self-incrimination is jeopardized. Procedural safeguards must be employed to protect the privilege. ❞
—Earl Warren, *Miranda v. Arizona*, 1966

The Miranda Warnings

The Miranda warnings (left) are the result of the Supreme Court's ruling that Ernesto Miranda (above right) had not been properly told of his rights before he confessed to committing a crime. *Why did the Court strike down Miranda's conviction?*

WARNING AS TO YOUR RIGHTS

You are under arrest. Before we ask you any questions, you must understand what your rights are.

You have the right to remain silent. You are not required to say anything to us at any time or to answer any questions. Anything you say can be used against you in court.

You have the right to talk... question you and to have h...

If you cannot afford a lawy... provided for you.

If you want to answer ques... ent you will still have the... time. You also have the r... until you talk to a lawyer.

The *Miranda* decision requires police to read the Miranda warnings to a suspect before the suspect is questioned. The **Miranda warnings** are a list of certain constitutional rights possessed by those accused of crimes. Suspects must be told that:

- They have the right to remain silent.
- Anything they say can be used against them in court.
- They have the right to have an attorney present.
- If they cannot afford an attorney, one will be provided for them.

If the police fail to advise a suspect of these rights, the courts may refuse to consider a confession as evidence. As a result, the Miranda warnings are controversial. Critics argue that some guilty people go unpunished simply because a police officer did not inform them of their rights. Others, however, believe that the warnings protect innocent people from being tricked or forced into confessing to crimes they did not commit.

Bail The Eighth Amendment provides that "excessive bail shall not be required." Courts have ruled that bail is excessive if it is greater than the amount judged necessary to ensure a suspect's appearance at trial. The Eighth Amendment does not mean, however, that all people accused of crimes must be allowed to post bail. Some people charged with particularly serious crimes, such as murder, are not allowed to post bail.

Bills of Attainder Article I, Sections 9 and 10, of the Constitution prohibit Congress and the states from passing bills of attainder. As you read in Chapter 5, a bill of attainder is a law that declares a certain person guilty of a crime. In practice, a bill of attainder takes away a person's right to a trial and violates the system of separation of powers by allowing a legislative body to convict and punish a person without trial.

Bills of attainder were common during the colonial era, but they are rare today. Still, cases involving bills of attainder occasionally arise. In *United States* v. *Lovett* (1946) the Supreme Court overturned part of an appropriations bill that forbade the use of appropriated money to pay the salaries of three specific people. The Court found that this bill was legislative punishment without benefit of trial and thus was an unconstitutional bill of attainder.

Ex Post Facto Laws The Constitution also outlaws ex post facto laws in Article I, Sections 9 and 10. Ex post facto laws are laws that apply to events in the past. If not prohibited, such laws would make it possible to punish a person for actions that were legal at the time they were committed.

Victims' Rights Although the Bill of Rights and other parts of the Constitution provide many protections for people accused of crime, some people feel that the Constitution does not sufficiently protect victims of crimes. As a result, in recent years a number of states have passed laws designed to protect victims' rights. These laws often defend the victim's right to be treated with fairness and respect; to be present at court proceedings related to the offense; and to be informed about the conviction, sentence, imprisonment, and release of the accused.

READING CHECK **Making Inferences** Why do persons accused of crimes need special protection against possible government abuse?

LANDMARK SUPREME COURT CASES

Constitutional Issue: Due Process

DIVISION FOR
PUBLIC EDUCATION
AMERICAN BAR ASSOCIATION

Miranda v. Arizona (1966)

Miranda v. Arizona **protects the rights of criminal suspects during police interrogations. Suspects in police custody must be informed of their rights before questioning.**

Background

In 1963 Ernesto Miranda was arrested and brought to a Phoenix, Arizona, police station, where he was accused of committing a serious crime. The victim identified Miranda as responsible for the crime, but Miranda claimed to be innocent. After two hours of police questioning, however, Miranda confessed. At trial, prosecutors used Miranda's signed confession as evidence, and he was convicted and sentenced to jail.

After Miranda appealed his conviction, the police acknowledged that they had never told Miranda he had the right to consult with an attorney before or during questioning. It was unclear, however, whether Miranda had been warned that anything he said during interrogation could be used against him in court.

Arguments for Miranda

In Miranda's appeal to the Supreme Court, his attorney argued that Miranda's conviction was unconstitutional, violating aspects of the Fifth, Sixth, and Fourteenth Amendments. In *Brown* v. *Mississippi* (1936), the Court had ruled that confessions obtained through coercion, or force, by state or local officials violated the due process clause of the Fourteenth Amendment. As a result of *Brown*, coerced confessions were not admissible in court. Miranda's attorney also argued that Miranda's conviction violated the Court's recent decision in *Gideon* v. *Wainwright* (1963), in which the Court held that the Sixth Amendment protects a criminal defendant's right to an attorney. Furthermore, Miranda's attorney claimed that Miranda's conviction violated the Fifth Amendment protection against self-incrimination.

Arguments for Arizona

The state of Arizona argued that there was no reason that Miranda's confession could not be used in court. Arizona argued that Miranda's confession had been given freely with no coercion. He had not been beaten or otherwise mistreated by police, as the suspect had been in *Brown* v. *Mississippi*. Although Phoenix police had not told Miranda of his right to consult with an attorney, Arizona claimed that this did not make his confession any less admissible.

THE IMPACT TODAY In a 5–4 decision, the Court ruled that Miranda's rights had been violated and struck down his conviction. Today the issues of due process and the rights of criminal suspects are still highly debated. Some people worry that providing too many protections for suspects would mean that criminals might escape punishment for their crimes simply because of police mistakes over legal technicalities. On the other side of the debate are those who worry that having too few protections for people accused of crimes would result in police abuse of power. They believe that innocent people would be coerced, through violence, intimidation, or trickery, into making false confessions to crimes they did not commit. Courts must balance the rights of those accused of crimes with the rights of society to be protected from criminals.

CRITICAL THINKING

What Do You Think? Did the Supreme Court make the correct decision in ruling that Miranda's rights had been violated or did the Court go too far in protecting the rights of persons accused of crimes?

PROTECTIONS FOR THE ACCUSED

PROTECTION AND SOURCE	MEANING
Habeas Corpus, Article I, Section 9	• Prisoner has right to court hearing to determine legality of imprisonment.
No Self-Incrimination, Fifth Amendment	• Person cannot be forced to give testimony that suggests his or her own guilt.
Grand Jury, Fifth Amendment	• Person cannot face trial for most federal crimes unless indicted by a grand jury.
No Bills of Attainder, Article I, Sections 9 and 10	• Congress and states cannot pass laws declaring a specific person guilty of a crime.
No Ex Post Facto Laws, Article I, Sections 9 and 10	• Congress and states cannot pass laws that apply to past actions.
Speedy and Public Trial, Sixth Amendment	• Trial must take place soon after arrest or indictment and must be open to the public.
Trial by Jury, Sixth Amendment	• All those facing criminal charges must be tried by a jury.
Adequate Defense, Sixth Amendment	• Defendants must be informed of charges, be able to confront witnesses in court, and have adequate legal representation.
No Double Jeopardy, Fifth Amendment	• No person may be made to stand trial twice for the same offense.

Guarantees of a Fair Trial

The Constitution provides many safeguards for the rights of those accused of crimes. Portions of the Fifth, Sixth, Seventh, and Eighth Amendments, as well as Article I, guarantee the basic courtroom protections that define the American legal system.

Speedy and Public Trial The Sixth Amendment says, in part, "In all criminal prosecutions, the accused shall enjoy the right to a speedy and public trial." This guarantee also applies to the states through the incorporation doctrine.

The courts have never defined what the word *speedy* means, and there is no set time in which a trial is required to take place. But if a trial takes place soon after an arrest or indictment, an innocent person will spend less time confined in jail. Furthermore, the memories of witnesses will be fresher, helping ensure that their testimony is more accurate.

When considering complaints about the lack of a speedy trial, a court will examine the reasons for any delay and the delay's impact on a defendant. In general, delays that harm a defendant or that give the prosecutor an advantage may violate the Sixth Amendment. In such cases, the charges against the accused may be dropped.

A public trial is another important element of a fair trial. Opening a trial to the public and the press helps prevent abuses of the law by allowing the public to monitor the proceedings and make sure everything is done according to law. Press access to the courtroom, however, is controversial. Some argue that press coverage—especially television coverage—may influence jurors and affect the outcome of a trial. In *Chandler v. Florida* (1981), however, the Supreme Court ruled that televising a trial does not necessarily prevent a fair trial.

Courts do have the power, however, to place limits on public access to courtrooms. For example, television cameras can be blocked if the judge feels the fairness of a trial is threatened. A judge may also keep some people out of a courtroom in order to maintain order and to prevent unfair influence of witnesses or the jury. Indeed, in extreme cases, trials may even be closed to the public. This can only happen, however, if there is no other way to ensure that a defendant gets a fair trial or to protect important public interests.

Trial by Jury The Sixth Amendment also says that those facing criminal charges have a right to trial by a jury. This right has been incorporated into the Fourteenth Amendment and applies to state as well as federal criminal trials. In the federal system and in most states, a trial jury—sometimes called a petit jury—is made up of 12 people. It is the responsibility of all citizens to serve as members of a jury, if called to do so.

A defendant may waive his or her right to a jury trial. If no jury is used, the judge conducts a **bench trial**, in which he or she alone hears and decides the case. The Supreme Court has held that jury trials are unnecessary for minor criminal offenses in which the possible punishment is less than six months' imprisonment.

The Sixth Amendment says that jury trials shall take place in the district in which the crime took place. Jurors must be impartial, or unbiased, and must come from the area where the crime was committed. Defendants are allowed to request that the trial be moved to another location if finding an impartial jury in the area would be difficult.

Under the Seventh Amendment, jury trials are guaranteed for certain types of civil cases, including those involving money damages. The right to a jury trial in civil cases has not been incorporated into the Fourteenth Amendment, and the states have different rules on this subject.

Right to an Adequate Defense The Sixth Amendment includes several features that help a defendant present an adequate defense at trial. All have been incorporated into the Fourteenth Amendment. These rights help guarantee that the judicial process is fair.

Under the Sixth Amendment, all defendants have the right to be informed of the charges against them. Simply put, the government must make clear what a defendant is accused of doing.

Defendants also have the right to be confronted with the witnesses against them. In general, a prosecutor cannot use as evidence something said by a person outside of the courtroom. The defendant must have the chance to cross-examine all witnesses and to expose errors or weaknesses in their testimony. This right is considered essential in building a defense. The courts sometimes need to use a subpoena, a legal document that requires a person to appear in court, to ensure that witnesses appear at trial.

Adequate legal representation is another important element of a fair trial. In *Powell* v. *Alabama* (1932), the Supreme Court ruled that state criminal defendants charged with a capital offense (a crime punishable by death) could not receive a fair trial unless

The Right to an Attorney

Clarence Gideon was a poor, uneducated man who was convicted of a crime when he could not afford to hire a lawyer to defend him. His handwritten appeals to the Supreme Court, such as the excerpt below, contain many misspellings and grammatical errors, but the Court ultimately ruled in his favor in *Gideon* v. *Wainwright*. "Petitioner [Gideon] will attempt to show this Court that a citizen of the State of Florida cannot get a just and fair trial without the aid of counsel . . ."

❝ Respondent [Florida's attorney general] claims that I have no right to file petition for writ of Habeus Corpus. Take away this right to a citizen and there is nothing left.

It makes no differense how old I am or what color I am or what church I belong to if any. The question is I did not get a fair trial. The question is very simple. I requested the court to appoint me a attorney and the court refused. All countrys try to give there Citizens a fair trial and see to it that they have counsel. ❞

Skills FOCUS | **INTERPRETING PRIMARY SOURCES**

Understanding Points of View Why does Gideon believe that his trial was unfair?

See **Skills Handbook**, p. H4.

they were represented by a lawyer. The Court went farther in *Gideon* v. *Wainwright* (1963), ruling that *all* defendants accused of serious crimes have the right to an attorney. Anyone who cannot afford legal help must be given a lawyer at public expense.

In addition, courts have ruled that a lawyer's failure to meet professional standards when representing his or her clients may violate a defendant's Sixth Amendment rights. Defendants have the right to act as their own legal counsel, but judges may take away this right if the judge determines that a defendant is incapable of defending him- or herself properly.

Double Jeopardy Another protection provided by the Fifth Amendment is that no person shall be "twice put in jeopardy of life or limb." This means that no person will be subject to **double jeopardy**, or made to stand trial twice for the same offense. This restriction prevents government from trying repeatedly to convict a person for allegedly committing a crime.

Protection against double jeopardy has been incorporated into the Fourteenth Amendment, but it is not considered double jeopardy for a state and the federal government to try a person for the same offense. It is also not double jeopardy if a jury fails to reach a verdict and the government tries the case again.

READING CHECK **Summarizing** How does the Bill of Rights help ensure a fair trial for defendants?

Punishment

The Constitution also includes protections for those convicted of crimes. As always, the Framers were anxious to protect the American people from the possible abuse of government powers.

Excessive Fines The Eighth Amendment prohibits government from imposing excessive fines. The Supreme Court has issued few rulings on the subject, although it has made clear that the limit applies only to government. It does not limit, for example, jury awards in civil cases.

Cruel and Unusual Punishments The Eighth Amendment also bans cruel and unusual punishments. This restriction comes nearly word-for-word from the English Bill of Rights, which prohibited torture and other cruel practices. The Supreme Court extended this prohibition to the states in *Robinson* v. *California* (1962) when it overturned a California law criminalizing drug addiction.

The Court has never defined what *cruel and unusual* means, although in *Wilkerson* v. *Utah* (1879), it did say that torture and "atrocities" such as burning at the stake would be considered cruel and unusual. In general, lower courts have been left to decide what constitutes cruel and unusual punishment on a case-by-case basis. As a result, the debate over these few words from the Eighth Amendment has figured into numerous cases involving the death penalty.

Capital Punishment

Since the Supreme Court's decision in *Furman* v. *Georgia* (1972), the majority of states have passed laws permitting the death penalty. Public concern over the fairness of capital punishment, however, remains an important issue.

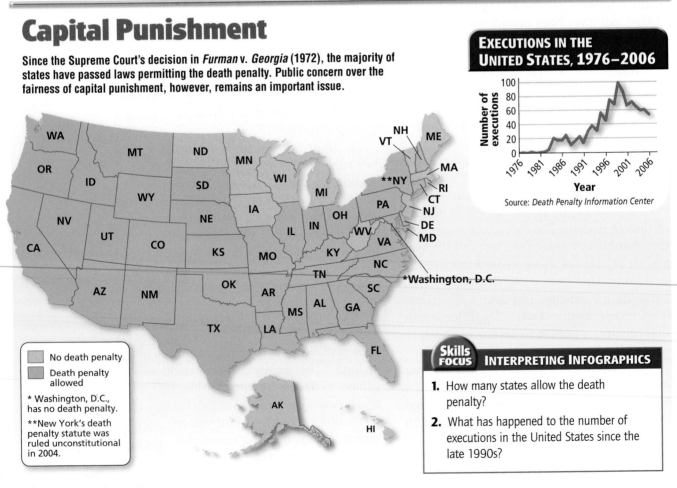

EXECUTIONS IN THE UNITED STATES, 1976–2006

Source: *Death Penalty Information Center*

No death penalty

Death penalty allowed

* Washington, D.C., has no death penalty.

**New York's death penalty statute was ruled unconstitutional in 2004.

*Washington, D.C.

Skills FOCUS **INTERPRETING INFOGRAPHICS**

1. How many states allow the death penalty?

2. What has happened to the number of executions in the United States since the late 1990s?

Capital Punishment The death penalty was practiced in the early days of the United States, at the time the Bill of Rights was written. Some opponents of the practice have argued that it is an inherently cruel and unusual punishment. The Supreme Court, however, has consistently ruled that capital punishment is constitutional.

Still, over the years the federal government and the states have greatly reduced the number of crimes for which capital punishment may be applied. Some states have abolished the practice entirely.

In recent years the Supreme Court has focused on ensuring a just application of the penalty. In *Furman* v. *Georgia* (1972), the Court found that the application of capital punishment in Georgia was <u>arbitrary</u>. Noting that Georgia executed some criminals while sparing others convicted of similar crimes, Justice Potter Stewart wrote, "These death sentences are cruel and unusual in the same way that being struck by lightning is cruel and unusual." Others on the Court noted that the death penalty in Georgia appeared to be applied far more often against African Americans and the poor than against others.

After *Furman*, Georgia reworked its capital punishment system. Four years later, the revised system again came before the Court in *Gregg* v. *Georgia* (1976). The new Georgia system involved two steps—the trial itself and a separate sentencing process. Other safeguards, including a review by the highest state court of all death sentences, helped ensure that capital punishment was applied fairly and evenly. The Supreme Court found Georgia's new system constitutional.

Gregg did not end the national debate over capital punishment. Most states still allow the death penalty, but some Americans have concerns over how fairly capital punishment is applied and about the nature of methods of execution. For example, new technology such as DNA analysis has helped prove the innocence of some convicted criminals who had been executed or who were scheduled to be executed. Lethal injection, which is used in 37 of the 38 states that have the death penalty, has also become the subject of controversy. In late 2007, the Supreme Court effectively halted the use of lethal injections as a means of execution until the Court ruled on whether that method constitutes cruel and unusual punishment. The Court's decision on lethal injection is expected in 2008.

ACADEMIC VOCABULARY

arbitrary random or unreasonable

READING CHECK **Summarizing** What issues involving capital punishment are controversial?

SECTION 4 ASSESSMENT

THINK central **Online Quiz**

thinkcentral.com
KEYWORD: SGO CLB HP

Reviewing Ideas and Terms

1. a. Describe What is the difference between **civil law** and **criminal law**?
b. Elaborate Why do you think there are so many steps in the civil and criminal processes?

2. a. Recall What is the purpose of the **Miranda warnings**?
b. Make Inferences Why did the Supreme Court rule that police must inform people of their constitutional rights before questioning them?
c. Elaborate How do the constitutional protections for the accused reflect the idea that people are innocent until proven guilty?

3. a. Identify Which amendments help ensure a fair trial?
b. Analyze Why do you think the Constitution seeks to protect the right to an adequate defense at trial?
c. Elaborate How can a jury both help and hurt an accused person's right to a fair trial?

4. a. Identify Which amendment to the Constitution seeks to ensure fair punishment?
b. Summarize Why was Georgia's capital punishment system found to be "cruel and unusual" in *Furman* v. *Georgia*?
c. Evaluate What do you think would make a punishment "cruel and unusual"?

Critical Thinking

5. Analyze Using a graphic organizer like the one below, analyze the ways in which the Constitution protects people at all stages of the judicial process.

| Arrest or Accusation | → | Trial | → | Punishment |

FOCUS ON WRITING

6. Persuasive Does the Constitution do too much, too little, or just enough to protect the rights of people suspected, accused, or convicted of crimes? Write a newspaper editorial that expresses your opinion on the subject.

We the People

THE CITIZEN & THE CONSTITUTION

Fundamental Rights and the Doctrine of Incorporation

Next to the preservation of the Union and the abolition of slavery, the most important constitutional development of the post-Civil War era was the passage of the Fourteenth Amendment. Originally intended to protect the rights of newly freed African Americans, the amendment has become a principal guarantee of the fundamental rights of all Americans, as important as the Bill of Rights itself.

What is procedural due process? Historically, due process of law meant that government officials must follow recognized procedures and not act arbitrarily when they make and enforce laws. This is called procedural due process, which requires government officials to act in certain ways before they regulate or take life, liberty or property. In England due process requirements initially focused on the rights of criminal defendants. For a criminal proceeding to be fair, for example, the laws must be clear. The defendant must know the charges that the government seeks to prove and be given a fair trial by a jury of his or her peers and the right to confront witnesses.

In the United States due process guarantees apply to both criminal and noncriminal (civil) matters. For example, the due process clause of the Fourteenth Amendment addresses property, in addition to life and liberty. Property is a broad term. It refers to everything that a person can own, from tangible things such as land and buildings to intangible things such as copyrights and patents. People also have property interests in other intangibles, such as their jobs, welfare or

unemployment benefits, and their reputations. In addition to constitutional guarantees, many laws enacted by state legislatures and Congress also contain provisions ensuring due process in matters such as public school discipline. Due process guarantees include the requirement of notice, the opportunity for a fair hearing, the opportunity to present evidence, and the opportunity to appeal an initial decision.

What is substantive due process? In the United States due process of law has two meanings. Procedural due process, described above, refers to the processes that governments must follow when they make and enforce laws. The second meaning of due process is known as substantive due process. It means that the Constitution usually prohibits some kinds of laws altogether, no matter how popular those laws may be with legislatures, executives, or even the people. Substantive due process is based on the idea that some rights are so fundamental that government must have a "compelling," or exceedingly important, reason to regulate or interfere with them. It is the role of the courts, interpreting the Constitution, to determine

Adapted with permission from Lesson 18 of *We the People: The Citizen & the Constitution.* Copyright 2009, Center for Civic Education.

whether a law is unconstitutional because it violates a fundamental right, and whether a governmental regulation of a fundamental right is justified by a compelling government interest.

The idea of fundamental rights traces to natural rights philosophy. Social contract theorists such as John Locke argued that people have natural rights that predate government. Some of those rights are so fundamental, or basic, that governments may not interfere with them or regulate them. One of the most difficult roles the Supreme Court plays is to identify which rights are fundamental and which are not. The justices' views of fundamental rights have changed over time.

For many years, for example, the Court held that the right to buy and sell a person's labor is so fundamental that state and Congressional laws establishing minimum wages and limiting the number of hours in a workday or work week were unconstitutional. This was known as the era of economic substantive due process. In 1937 the Court abandoned the view that economic rights are fundamental rights.

However, the Court did not abandon its effort to identify other fundamental rights. It has continued to try to identify rights that are so basic that Congress or states must have a "compelling interest" in order to pass laws that interfere with or regulate such rights. The Court has identified the following rights as "fundamental" (note that some but not all such rights are listed in the Constitution or Bill of Rights):

- the right to marry and have children,
- the right to purchase and use birth control,
- the right to custody of one's own children and to rear them as one sees fit,
- the right of mentally competent adults to refuse medical treatment,
- the right to free speech,
- the right to travel interstate,
- the right of legal voters to vote,
- the right to associate, and
- the right to religious freedom.

Whether any or all of these rights are indeed fundamental, and thus prohibit most governmental regulations, remains a topic of intense controversy throughout the United States.

What is the doctrine of "incorporation"? For the first few decades after ratification of the Fourteenth Amendment the Supreme Court continued to rely on the states to be the principal protectors of individual rights. All the state constitutions contained bills of rights. The Court was leery of interpreting the Fourteenth Amendment in a way that would upset the balance of power between the national government and the states.

However, not all states interpreted their bills of rights to ensure due process and to protect the fundamental rights of everyone within their boundaries. In 1925 the Supreme Court began to examine the due process clause of the Fourteenth Amendment with an eye to identifying the rights in the Bill of Rights that the states, like the national government, must protect. In *Gitlow* v. *New York* (1925) the Court recognized that the rights of free speech and free press are among the personal rights to liberty protected by the due process clause. States could not infringe on these rights.

Reviewing Ideas

1. **Summarize** How have Supreme Court justices' views of fundamental rights changed over time?
2. **Identify** What is substantive due process?

Critical Thinking

3. **Evaluate** Has incorporation of the Bill of Rights against the states validated the fears of the Antifederalists regarding the power of the national judiciary? Explain.

Connecting Online

Visit **thinkcentral.com** for review and enrichment activities related to this chapter.

THINK central

KEYWORD: SGO CLB

Quiz and Review

GOV 101
Examine key concepts in this chapter.

ONLINE QUIZZES
Take a practice quiz for each section in this chapter.

Activities

eActivities
Complete Webquests and Internet research activities.

INTERACTIVE FEATURES
Explore interactive versions of maps and charts.

KEEP IT CURRENT
Link to current events in U.S. government.

Partners

American Bar Association Division for Public Education
Learn more about the law, your rights and responsibilities.

Center for Civic Education
Promoting an enlightened and responsible citizenry committed to democratic principles and actively engaged in the practice of democracy.

Online Textbook

ONLINE SIMULATIONS
Learn about U.S. government through simulations you can complete online.

Comprehension and Critical Thinking

SECTION 1 *(pp. 280–284)*

1. a. Review Key Terms For each term, write a sentence that explains its significance or meaning: civil liberties, civil rights, due process.

b. Explain When may government limit civil liberties and rights?

c. Elaborate Since state constitutions generally contain the same guarantees as the Bill of Rights, why is the incorporation doctrine important to securing individual rights and liberties?

SECTION 2 *(pp. 285–294)*

2. a. Review Key Terms For each term, write a sentence that explains its significance or meaning: establishment clause, free exercise clause, slander, libel, prior restraint.

b. Draw Conclusions Does a public school that prohibits prayers in classrooms during the school day deny students their right to a free exercise of religion? Explain your answer.

c. Predict Americans' understanding of the First Amendment has changed over the years. How do you think our current interpretations of the Bill of Rights might change in the future?

SECTION 3 *(pp. 296–302)*

3. a. Review Key Terms For each term, write a sentence that explains its significance or meaning: probable cause, exclusionary rule, police power, procedural due process, substantive due process.

b. Interpret Should the Constitution be interpreted as protecting a right to privacy? Why or why not?

c. Rank Which do you think is more important: individual privacy or public security? Explain your answer.

SECTION 4 *(pp. 303–313)*

4. a. Review Key Terms For each term, write a sentence that explains its significance or meaning: capital punishment, double jeopardy.

b. Analyze How do the guarantees of a public trial and a fair trial sometimes conflict?

c. Rate Which do you think is worse: An innocent person being punished or a guilty person going free? Explain your answer.

Critical Reading

Read the passage in Section 3 that begins with the heading "Substantive Due Process." Then answer the questions that follow.

5. Which of the following is true about substantive due process?

A It involves questions about whether legal procedures are fair.

B It involves questions about whether the Constitution is fair.

C It involves questions about whether duly passed laws are fair.

D It involves questions about whether amendments are fair.

6. Substantive due process is based on which of the following ideas?

   A States should have more rights than the federal government.

   B All people have certain rights.

   C Inalienable rights can be denied in some cases.

   D As long as a law follows proper procedures, it is fair.

Read the passage in Section 1 that begins with the heading "When Rights Conflict." Then answer the questions that follow.

7. When can civil liberties and rights be limited by the government?

   A when the exercise of a liberty or right can harm another person

   B when the exercise of a liberty or right can harm the common good

   C when the exercise of a liberty or right can conflict with the liberties and rights of others

   D All of the above.

RESPONSIBILITIES OF LEADERSHIP

8. In a short essay, identify and examine the nature and causes of crime in your community, explaining the effects that these criminal acts have on their victims. Evaluate your local government's **attempts to prevent crime**. In your opinion, what other steps should the government take to help stop crime? A good source of information on crime is the annual report that many local governments produce; you may be able to find reports for your community online or in a library. You may wish to speak to a local police officer or government official to get their perspective on crime issues.

CONNECTING TO THE CONSTITUTION

9. Describe a situation that raises a question of procedural due process affecting young people. For example, the situation might be a story about students who were dismissed without a hearing from a school sports team. The students were reported to have been drinking at a party, thus breaking their team contract, which prohibited smoking and drinking by team players.

ANALYZING PRIMARY SOURCES

Political Cartoon *The National Security Agency's warrantless surveillance program led to widespread debate about whether the secret program violated Fourth Amendment guarantees of personal security.*

10. **Analyze** What is happening in this cartoon?

11. **Draw Conclusions** Does the cartoonist believe that the NSA program is monitoring the right people?

WRITING FOR THE SAT

Think about the following issue:

An editorial in a high school newspaper criticizes the principal of the school. In response, the principal announces that all future issues of the newspaper must be approved by school administrators before publication.

12. **Assignment** Was the principal's action a violation of the students' First Amendment rights or a reasonable measure to preserve order in the school? Write a short essay in which you develop your position on the issue. Defend your position with reasoning and examples from your reading and studies.

"INJUSTICE ANYWHERE IS A THREAT TO
JUSTICE EVERYWHERE."
—MARTIN LUTHER KING JR., APRIL 16, 1963

CONNECTING TO THE CONSTITUTION

Our nation's system of government is based on constitutional law established by the United States Constitution. See the "We the People: The Citizen and the Constitution" pages in this chapter for an in-depth exploration of the importance of civic participation in American constitutional democracy.

Martin Luther King Jr. (center) and other civil rights leaders at the March on Washington in 1963

SECTION 1

Civil Rights and Discrimination

BEFORE YOU READ

Main Idea

The Constitution is designed to guarantee basic civil rights to everyone. The meaning of civil rights has changed over time, and many groups have been denied their civil rights at different times in U.S. history.

Reading Focus

1. What are civil rights, and how have civil rights in the United States changed over time?
2. How has a pattern of discrimination affected the civil rights of some groups in U.S. history?

Key Terms

prejudice
racism
reservation
Japanese American
   internment

TAKING NOTES As you read, take notes on the meaning and importance of civil rights and on how discrimination has affected different groups. Record your notes in a chart like this one.

Civil Rights	Discrimination

Signs of Discrimination

Legalized discrimination against certain groups was common for much of U.S. history. Like many businesses in the 1950s, this store posted "white only" signs.

WHY IT MATTERS

The Importance of Civil Rights Picture this: you walk into a restaurant with your friends and the manager says that you have to sit in a different section simply because you are a member of a certain racial group. That would be unfair, illegal discrimination, right? What if you were prevented from voting, fired from your job, or harassed by the government? You would probably go to court to protect your rights and to hold those who violated them accountable. But what if the courts ruled that it was legal for the government and private businesses to treat you and other people so unfairly?

The type of unfair treatment described above used to be common in this country. Certain racial and ethnic groups, women, and others were denied basic civil rights for much of U.S. history. They were prevented from voting, they were discrimi-

nated against by the government and by businesses, and they were kept in an inferior position in society.

So what has changed? Over time, some groups that have been treated so unequally organized, protested, and challenged these discriminatory practices. New laws and court decisions attempted to limit and end such unfair treatment. These changes in government and laws extended many civil rights protections to more and more people.

The redefinition and expansion of civil rights led to dramatic changes in American society. There are now important legal limits that guard against actions by government officials or private citizens that would discriminate against you or deny your basic civil rights. You have the right to be treated equally and fairly and the right to use the law and government to ensure that your civil rights are protected. ■

Civil Rights in the United States

Civil rights are some of the most basic and important rights we have in the United States today. However, the meaning and application of civil rights have changed greatly over time as society's ideas about fairness and equal treatment have changed.

What Are Civil Rights? Civil rights are rights that involve equal status and treatment and the right to participate in government. One of the most basic civil rights is the right to be treated equally regardless of race, ethnicity, sex, or other personal characteristics. In other words, every citizen has the right to be free from discrimination—the act or practice of treating people unfairly based on their race, national origin, sex, religion, age, or other factors. This includes discrimination sponsored by the government. For example, a person cannot be denied admission to a school or a movie theater simply because he or she is African American.

Another basic civil right is the right to equal opportunities in voting and running for political office. Voting and holding office allow people to have a say in their government's decisions. Without this basic right to vote or participate in government, people can be unfairly subjected to a government and legal system that they have little or no power to influence or change.

Civil rights like the right to vote are guaranteed and protected by law. The government establishes these laws and has the duty and responsibility of enforcing them. In the United States, laws that guarantee civil rights include the Constitution and its amendments, federal and state laws, and Supreme Court decisions.

The idea that individuals have basic civil rights that government cannot violate is a more fundamental principle of American society than it has been in the past. We now recognize that *all* people in the United States are entitled to certain fundamental rights and freedoms, including many civil rights. In the past, however, that was not always the case, as you will read in this chapter.

How Have Civil Rights Changed?

The meaning of civil rights in the United States has changed greatly over time. This is because civil rights are about fairness and equal treatment, and people's ideas in the past about what is fair and who deserves equal treatment were very different from what they are today.

The Declaration of Independence, for example, states that "all men are created equal." Note that women were not included in this statement. At the time the Declaration was written, society viewed women's participation in government and politics as unnecessary. In addition, not all men were considered to be truly equal—in general, only white men of European ancestry were given equal treatment. Racial minorities, such as African American and Native American men, were viewed as unequals who were not entitled to the right to participate in government or enjoy its freedoms.

Much has changed since the Declaration of Independence was written, however. Groups that were denied equal treatment by the government, including women and ethnic and racial groups, fought for their rights nonetheless, inspired by the ideal of equality. In the course of their struggles, these groups succeeded in pushing for the passage of constitutional amendments, federal and state laws, and legal decisions that redefined the meaning of civil rights, fairness, and equal treatment. As a result, women and racial and ethnic groups won the right to vote, participate in government, and be free from discrimination. In this chapter, you will learn about the story of these struggles and how they changed our laws and government to protect, redefine, and extend civil rights.

READING CHECK Contrasting How is the meaning of civil rights today different from in the past?

Civil Rights

Key Civil Rights
- The right to fair and equal treatment
- The right to be free from discrimination
- The right to vote, run for office, and participate in public life

Legal Sources of Civil Rights
- Constitutional amendments, including the 1st, 5th, 13th, 14th, 15th, 19th, 24th, and 26th amendments
- Federal laws, including the Civil Rights Act of 1964 and Voting Rights Act of 1965
- Supreme Court rulings, such as *Brown* v. *Board of Education of Topeka, Kansas* (1954)
- State civil rights laws

A Pattern of Discrimination

ACADEMIC VOCABULARY

legalize to give legal sanction or validity to

The United States has a long history of inequality and unfair treatment of certain groups. In the past, the government even legalized and supported discrimination. Those in power viewed members of certain groups with **prejudice**, a negative opinion formed without just grounds. Widespread prejudice in society was often caused by **racism**—discrimination and unfair treatment based on race.

Because of racism and prejudice, women and racial minorities suffered unequal treatment in areas such as voting rights, housing, education, employment, and access to public facilities. Religious minorities such as Catholics, Jews, and Mormons as well as immigrants have also experienced widespread discrimination.

African Americans Perhaps no group has suffered more unfair treatment in American history than African Americans. African Americans were first brought here against their will to be sold as slaves. Over a period of some 250 years, generations of African Americans suffered inhumane treatment, including violence, forced labor, and separation from their families and culture.

Because enslaved African Americans were viewed as property, the government denied them any civil rights protections. In the Supreme Court case *Dred Scott* v. *Sandford*, Chief Justice Roger Taney wrote in 1857 that African Americans, whether slaves or free, could never be citizens of the United States. According to Taney, they historically had "no rights which the white man was bound to respect." Taney argued that the authors of the Declaration of Independence did not have African Americans in mind when they wrote that all men were created equal.

PRIMARY SOURCE

❝ But it is too clear for dispute, that the enslaved African race were not intended to be included, and formed no part of the people who framed and adopted this declaration. ❞

—Roger Taney, *Dred Scott v. Sandford*, 1857

After the Civil War, the United States abolished slavery with the Thirteenth Amendment. The Fourteenth and Fifteenth Amendments were then passed in an attempt to protect the civil rights of former slaves by granting them citizenship and the right to vote. But these amendments did not result in fair and equal treatment for African Americans. In many places, former slaves were kept from taking part in civic life by threats and physical attacks. In addition, new laws and judicial decisions legalized discrimination against African Americans.

Native Americans Native Americans have also suffered from long and intense discrimination. Like African Americans, Native Americans were viewed in the past as separate peoples that were not a part of American society and therefore not deserving of any rights at all.

As soon as Europeans began colonizing North America, Native Americans began losing territory. Introduced diseases from Europe and conflicts with colonists weakened many Native American groups, allowing settlers to seize their land. The United States

Discrimination in America

For much of American history, certain racial and ethnic groups and women have suffered widespread discrimination.

African Americans ▶
First brought to the United States as slaves, African Americans had essentially no rights for generations.

Native Americans ▶
Discrimination against Native Americans included sending their children to "Americanization" schools, where they were stripped of their native culture and taught "American" culture and values.

government also signed hundreds of treaties with Native Americans to acquire their land and then consistently violated these treaties, taking even more land.

As the American population grew and more settlers began moving west, the government faced increasing pressure to take yet more Native American land. In the mid-1800s the government began a policy of removing Native Americans from their traditional lands and forcing them onto reservations. A **reservation** is an area of public land set aside by the government for Native Americans. Throughout the 1800s many Native American groups were forced further and further west or onto reservations.

In addition to losing their land, many Native Americans were prevented from speaking their native languages or from maintaining their traditional ways of life. For example, some children were removed from their families and forced to go to "Americanization" schools, where they were isolated from their native language, dress, religion, and customs.

Asian Americans Asian Americans have come to this country from places such as China, Japan, Korea, South Asia, and Southeast Asia. Like many other racial minorities with their own languages, culture, and customs, Asian Americans faced significant discrimination almost from the moment they arrived.

Chinese workers first began to arrive in the United States in large numbers in the mid-1800s. They worked in mines and on railroads in the West. Many white Americans resented these new immigrants, who competed against them for jobs. As a result, white Americans discriminated against Chinese workers in jobs, housing, and access to public services. In fact, the United States government even passed a law to effectively end Chinese immigration—the Chinese Exclusion Act of 1882.

The Chinese were not the only Asian group to face discrimination. In the early 1900s widespread anti-Japanese feelings led to an agreement with Japan to end Japanese immigration to the United States. In return, the United States promised not to allow racial segregation of Japanese already living in America.

Japanese Americans suffered one of the most blatant civil rights violations during World War II. Fearing that Japanese Americans could aid a Japanese attack against the United States, President Franklin D. Roosevelt signed Executive Order 9066 in 1942. The order required all people of Japanese descent on the West Coast to report to War Relocation Centers. This event is known as the **Japanese American internment**. About 120,000 people, more than 60 percent of whom were American citizens, were forced to leave their homes and businesses, and about 80,000 people were confined to internment camps for the rest of the war. Many lost their homes, jobs, and businesses, in addition to their personal freedom. When some Japanese Americans challenged this internment in court, the Supreme Court upheld the program as a military necessity, ruling that it was acceptable to curtail the civil rights of a racial group when there was a "pressing public necessity."

Asian Americans ▲
Discrimination toward Asian Americans resulted in the internment of Japanese Americans during World War II.

Hispanics
Hispanics have faced widespread discrimination in housing, education, voting, and other areas.

Women
Discrimination toward women included the lack of voting rights and limited job opportunities.

Hispanics Hispanics, or Latinos, are people who have a Spanish-speaking background. They come from places such as Mexico, Puerto Rico, Cuba, and Central and South America. Like other groups with culture and language differences, Hispanics have faced discrimination in jobs, voting, education, and other areas.

In the 1840s the United States took control of what are now the states of Texas, New Mexico, Arizona, and California, and parts of Colorado, Nevada, and Utah. Mexican Americans in these areas were viewed as conquered peoples and suffered discrimination and violence. For example, their land was often taken under questionable circumstances. In addition, Mexican Americans were often forced to live in segregated communities.

From the mid-1800s to today, there have been several waves of Hispanic immigration to the United States. Mexican immigrants originally came to work on farms, ranches, and mines. Today they work in many areas of the economy. Puerto Ricans emigrated to places like New York after Puerto Rico became part of the United States in 1898. Cubans fled political turmoil in their country to settle in Florida in the 1960s. All of these groups have faced discrimination as a result of being culturally different.

Women Although women are not a numerical minority in the United States, they were historically denied equal treatment. Before 1920 most women could not vote or shape the laws that they were required to follow. They also could not serve on juries and had unequal property and custody rights compared to men. Socially, women were assigned an inferior position in society and were expected to marry, raise children, and work in the home. Also, women did not have access to most education and job opportunities.

This view was given legal justification by the Supreme Court in *Bradwell* v. *Illinois* (1873), when it upheld a law barring women from becoming attorneys. The Court said the law was legal because the "domestic sphere" was the proper area for women. In the words of one justice, "The paramount destiny and mission of woman are to fulfill the noble and benign offices of wife and mother."

Like many other groups in American history, women suffered a pattern of discrimination that denied them their civil rights. Eventually, however, women and other groups fought for and won the right to equal justice under the law.

READING CHECK Summarizing What groups have experienced civil rights violations in the past?

SECTION 1 ASSESSMENT

THINK central **Online Quiz**
thinkcentral.com
KEYWORD: SGO CRT HP

Reviewing Ideas and Terms

1. a. Define What are civil rights? Give two examples.
b. Explain How has the meaning of civil rights in the United States changed over time?
c. Predict What legal changes do you think happened to help minorities and women eventually win their civil rights?

2. a. Define Define the following terms: **prejudice, racism.**
b. Make Inferences How do you think people used the legal system to discriminate against members of ethnic and racial groups and women?
c. Predict What do you think are some possible contemporary effects of persistent discrimination against ethnic and racial minorities?

Critical Thinking

3. Compare and Contrast Copy the graphic organizer below and use it to describe how discrimination and the denial of civil rights were both similar and different for ethnic and racial groups and women.

Racial and Ethnic Groups   Women

FOCUS ON WRITING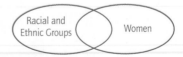

4. Persuasive Write a newspaper editorial reacting to the announcement in 1942 that Japanese Americans will be evacuated from the West Coast and moved to internment camps. Be sure to address the issue of civil rights.

Equal Justice under Law

Main Idea

The Fourteenth Amendment was designed to bolster civil rights by requiring states to guarantee to freed slaves "the equal protection of the laws." However, African Americans and women still struggled to win equal treatment in American society.

Reading Focus

1. What is meant by equal protection of the law?

2. What civil rights laws were passed after the Civil War, and why did they fail to end segregation?

3. How did women fight for and win voting rights?

4. What events began to roll back racial and ethnic segregation in the United States?

Key Terms

equal protection clause
suspect classification
segregation
Jim Crow laws
separate-but-equal doctrine
suffrage
Seneca Falls Convention
de jure segregation
desegregation
de facto segregation

TAKING NOTES As you read, take notes on the meaning of equal protection and its effects on the struggle of African Americans and women for equal rights.

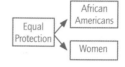

WHY IT MATTERS

Equal Protection On July 28, 1868, three years after the Civil War ended, the Fourteenth Amendment became part of the Constitution. At that time, the U.S. military occupied the defeated South. The federal government, as part of the South's Reconstruction, was responsible for ensuring law and order—and for protecting the rights of newly freed slaves. The Fourteenth Amendment promised to protect those rights by guaranteeing that no state could deny "the equal protection of the laws" to anyone. This promise of equal protection established for the first time in the Constitution a new idea of equality—that *all* Americans were entitled to equal rights.

It took a long time, however, for many Americans to begin to truly attain equal rights and fair treatment. Despite the passage of the Fourteenth Amendment, as well as other amendments and civil rights laws, African Americans and other groups continued to suffer from widespread racism and discrimination. Even though the Fourteenth Amendment promised equal protection, state governments passed racially discriminatory laws, and federal courts declared them to be constitutional. In fact, it took nearly 100 years for the government to ban many forms of racial discrimination.

Today, the idea of equal protection contained in the Fourteenth Amendment is much more accepted as one of the main legal foundations for civil rights. The Fourteenth Amendment holds the promise of equal treatment and equal justice—for everyone. ■

A New Idea of Equality

The ideal of legal equality is enshrined on the Supreme Court building in Washington, D.C.

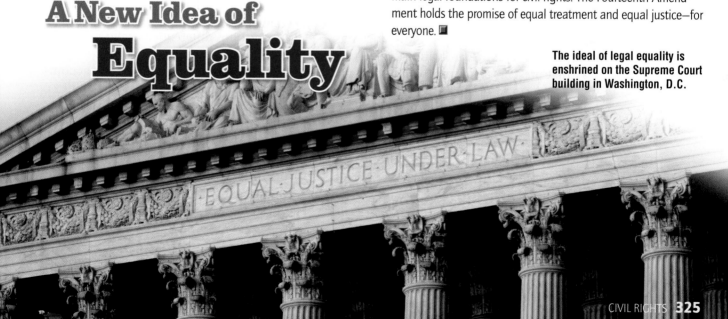

Equal Protection of the Law

Much of the progress against discrimination has been made in the courts. Over time, judges have used the equal protection clause of the Fourteenth Amendment to ban discrimination by the government and to extend equal protection of the law.

The Equal Protection Clause

The Fourteenth Amendment says that "No State shall . . . deny to any person within its jurisdiction the equal protection of the laws." This statement is known as the **equal protection clause**. The equal protection clause requires states to apply the law the same way for one person that they would for another person in the same circumstances.

You might have noticed that the equal protection clause is targeted specifically at the states. The Fourteenth Amendment was passed after the Civil War to protect the rights of newly freed slaves, especially in the South where they were the victims of severe and widespread discrimination by state governments.

By targeting the states directly, the equal protection clause and the rest of the Fourteenth Amendment marked a major change in the Constitution. Before the Fourteenth Amendment, the Bill of Rights protected people only from abuses by the federal government. The Fourteenth Amendment required state governments for the first time to protect the basic civil rights of all people and to provide them with equal treatment.

Although it was originally intended mainly to protect the rights of newly freed slaves, over time the Supreme Court has interpreted the equal protection clause in a way that prevents states from classifying any group of people unfairly or from making unreasonable distinctions between groups. As a result, the clause has been a vital tool in the fight for civil rights.

As the meaning of the equal protection clause has expanded over time, it has become increasingly important to society as a foundation for civil rights. In fact, the Fourteenth Amendment's equal protection clause is one of the main sources of civil rights protection today.

ACADEMIC VOCABULARY

rational based on reason

The equal protection clause, however, does not mean that all people must be treated the same in every respect. There are many times when it is legal to distinguish between different groups of people. This is known as reasonable distinction, and the courts have developed several tests to determine if reasonable distinction exists.

Reasonable Distinction

In many situations, the government can distinguish between different groups of people. For example, state governments may charge visitor fees at state parks. In this case, the government has reasonably distinguished between two groups of people—park visitors and nonvisitors.

Governments cannot, however, distinguish between different groups unreasonably. For example, while state governments can charge fees to park visitors, they could not charge only people with green eyes or red hair.

So when is distinguishing between different groups reasonable, and when is it unreasonable? This is an issue that the courts, among others, decide; and standards can change depending on the views of judges, social attitudes, and the facts of each case. Generally, classifications that seem random or without a valid purpose are not allowed.

Federal courts use three main guidelines to decide if the government has made fair distinctions between groups. These are the rational basis test, intermediate scrutiny test, and strict scrutiny test.

Rational Basis Test

Governments often have a rational basis, or good reason, to treat different groups of people differently. Treating groups differently is valid under the rational basis test if the law in question establishes reasonable methods of accomplishing a legitimate goal of government.

For example, states have laws that establish a minimum age, such as 16, for driving a car. Are these laws reasonable? Legislators believe that people below the minimum age may not have enough experience and maturity to drive a car safely. The courts have agreed. In this case, the legitimate goal of government is to ensure public safety, and the government may treat people below a certain age differently.

Applying Equal Protection

United States v. Virginia (1996)

Test Applied: Intermediate scrutiny

Background: The Virginia Military Institute (VMI), a public military college, denied admission to women. In 1990 the U.S. Department of Justice sued the state of Virginia to force an end to this policy, arguing that it violated the equal protection clause of the Constitution.

Decision: In a 7–1 decision, the Supreme Court ruled that VMI failed to show a persuasive justification for excluding women and was in violation of the equal protection clause. It ordered VMI to admit women.

Male and female cadets at VMI listen to a lecture in 2007.

Intermediate Scrutiny Test Sometimes courts impose a higher standard to determine if laws violate the equal protection clause. For example, the intermediate scrutiny test has been used in cases involving classifications based on sex. In such cases, the government must show an important reason for treating people differently. Using this test, the Court has upheld treating men and women differently in some military matters, such as the requirement that only men register with the Selective Service in preparation for any future drafts for military service.

Strict Scrutiny Test The highest standard is known as strict scrutiny. It is applied when (1) a fundamental right is being restricted, such as the right to free speech or the right to vote, or (2) a classification is made based on race or national origin. A classification based on race or national origin is called a **suspect classification**. The courts are inherently suspicious that such classifications might violate the equal protection clause.

The standard of strict scrutiny is often very hard for the government to meet. Under strict scrutiny, the government must show that a law that classifies a group of people is more than just a reasonable method to accomplish a legitimate role of government.

The government must show that there is "a compelling reason" that is in the public interest for the group classification.

The case of *Korematsu* v. *United States* (1944) is an example of the Supreme Court applying the strict scrutiny test to a law—and ruling that the law met the test. Fred Korematsu was a Japanese American who refused to evacuate California as ordered during World War II. His argument, based on the equal protection clause, was that the internment of people of Japanese descent simply because the United States was at war with Japan was unfair racial discrimination. But in a 6–3 decision, the Court ruled against Korematsu, saying that the government's compelling interest to protect the public against sabotage outweighed Korematsu's civil rights, as well as the rights of other Japanese Americans.

An example of a law that failed to meet strict scrutiny came in *Loving* v. *Virginia* (1967). In that case, the Supreme Court struck down a Virginia law outlawing marriage between whites and African Americans. The Court ruled that Virginia had no legitimate or compelling interest in preventing such marriages.

READING CHECK **Identifying the Main Idea** How does the Court interpret the equal protection clause?

Laws and Segregation after the Civil War

The Fourteenth Amendment was one of the laws passed in the aftermath of the Civil War to protect the rights of African Americans. However, the new laws and amendments failed to extend equal treatment to African Americans for many years. While the laws had changed, the discriminatory views of society had not. In fact, when Reconstruction effectively ended in 1877, state governments in the South began to pass new laws against African Americans in direct violation of the new constitutional amendments and laws.

Post–Civil War Laws The first major civil rights laws in the United States were passed after the Civil War. These laws included three new constitutional amendments and the first federal civil rights laws.

The Thirteenth, Fourteenth, and Fifteenth amendments were passed between 1865 and 1870. They are sometimes referred to as the Reconstruction Amendments. The Thirteenth Amendment banned slavery in the United States. The Fourteenth Amendment made all people born in the United States citizens and required states to guarantee "due process" and "equal protection of the laws" to all people. The Fifteenth Amendment guaranteed the right to vote to African American men.

In addition to these three amendments, Congress passed a series of federal civil rights laws. These federal laws attempted to provide African Americans some of the most basic rights that they had long been denied by white society. These new laws protected such rights as the right to own private property, the right to be a witness in court, and the right to fair treatment in public accommodations such as restaurants and theaters.

Despite these attempts to legally protect African Americans, civil rights discrimination continued. Racism and prejudice were so deeply rooted that new constitutional amendments and federal laws were not enough to end discrimination. Adding new words to the Constitution, it turned out, was not enough to transform society and create true equality.

Racial Segregation In the years after the passage of the Reconstruction Amendments and the federal civil rights laws, state governments began to set up a new system of racial inequality. Two key factors allowed state governments to create these unequal systems: the end of Reconstruction in the South and Supreme Court decisions that upheld racial discrimination.

During the era of Reconstruction, which lasted from 1865 to 1877, African Americans in the South made much political progress.

Early Civil Rights: Reconstruction Amendments and Laws

The first civil rights laws attempted to guarantee basic civil rights to African Americans.

Thirteenth Amendment (1865)	Civil Rights Act of 1866	Fourteenth Amendment (1868)	Fifteenth Amendment (1870)	Civil Rights Act of 1871	Civil Rights Act of 1875
Outlawed slavery in the United States	Sought to guarantee African Americans the right to sue, own property, and be a witness in court	Granted citizenship to African Americans and required states to provide all people "due process" and "equal protection"	Granted African American men the right to vote	Sought to protect African Americans from Ku Klux Klan violence Allowed individuals to sue state officials for civil rights violations	Sought to grant African Americans equal access to public places Overturned by the Supreme Court in the Civil Rights Cases of 1883

Many African Americans voted, and some ran and were elected to office. But then a disputed presidential election led to the Compromise of 1877, which gave Republican candidate Rutherford B. Hayes the presidency on the condition that he remove the remaining federal troops from the South.

The end of military occupation in the South led to a breakdown in the rule of law. Free from federal interference, extremist groups such as the Ku Klux Klan used violence to keep African Americans from pursuing their civil rights. African Americans were prevented from voting and running for office. Eventually, white-dominated governments began to pass segregation laws and laws reducing or barring participation in government by African Americans. **Segregation** is the separation of racial groups.

Most of these segregation laws, known as **Jim Crow laws** after a popular racist song, were passed in the late 1800s and early 1900s and were aimed mainly at African Americans. Other racial segregation laws were aimed at other groups, such as Hispanics, Asian Americans, and Native Americans. No matter their target, Jim Crow laws were designed to accomplish the same goal: maintain power and privilege for whites and relegate nonwhites to an inferior position.

Jim Crow laws segregated nearly all areas of life, including schools, public transportation, public restrooms and water fountains, hotels, restaurants, and theaters. To comply with the letter of the law, separate facilities were established for whites and nonwhites.

In addition to legalized segregation, white society in general discriminated against African Americans to the point that they were virtually unprotected by the law. Whites controlled all of the powerful institutions of society, such as police forces, courts, judgeships, and other institutions of local government. They used these institutions to harass African Americans who challenged authority by asserting their civil rights.

The discriminatory laws put in place by state governments were given clear legal justification by the Supreme Court. In 1883 the Court ruled that the Civil Rights Act of 1875 was unconstitutional because the Fourteenth

Violence after the Civil War

Violence against African Americans was commonplace in the decades after the Civil War. To raise public awareness of the issue, the NAACP, an African American civil rights group, often flew this flag outside its headquarters in New York City.

Amendment only prohibited discrimination by governments, not by private individuals. Chief Justice Joseph Bradley even suggested that African Americans had received enough federal help. "When a man has emerged from slavery . . ." he wrote, "there must be some stage in the progress of his elevation when he takes the rank of a mere citizen, and ceases to be the special favorite of the laws."

The Supreme Court also ruled that Jim Crow laws were constitutional in *Plessy* v. *Ferguson* (1896). In this landmark case, the Court upheld by an 8–1 decision a Louisiana law requiring African Americans to ride in separate railway cars from whites. The Court's ruling in the *Plessy* case established the **separate-but-equal doctrine**, the policy that laws requiring separate facilities for racial groups could be legal so long as the facilities were "equal," thereby effectively sanctioning racial discrimination.

Despite the *Plessy* ruling, in reality, separate facilities were almost never equal—facilities for African Americans and other racial groups were almost always inferior to facilities for whites. Fighting the separate-but-equal doctrine became one of the main goals in the struggle for African Americans' civil rights.

READING CHECK **Sequencing** What events after the Civil War led to legalized segregation in the South?

Voting Rights for Women

The struggle for African Americans' civil rights in the 1800s influenced another civil rights struggle: the fight for women's rights. Many women in the North had taken part in the battle to end slavery. As they fought for equal rights for African Americans, they also began to demand equal rights for women. One of the main goals of this struggle was women's **suffrage**, or the right to vote.

The Women's Movement Begins In 1848 a group of people led by Lucretia Mott and Elizabeth Cady Stanton held the **Seneca Falls Convention**, the first national women's rights convention in the United States. Delegates to the convention called for voting rights for women, along with equal rights in other areas like education and property. They also adopted a Declaration of Sentiments, modeled on the Declaration of Independence, that called for equal rights for women.

Despite these early calls for women's rights, when the Fifteenth Amendment gave African American men the right to vote in 1870, women were still denied that right. In fact, women's rights advocates lobbied to have women included in the language of the amendment. However, their efforts failed, and women were purposely excluded from the language of the amendment. In response, women formed several organizations to lobby for women's suffrage. These organizations had their roots in the abolition movement to end slavery.

Some activists, such as Susan B. Anthony, refused to support the Fifteenth Amendment because it failed to extend voting rights to women. Others supported the Fifteenth Amendment and worked to win women's suffrage on a state-by-state basis. Their first success came in the Wyoming Territory in 1869, where American women were first granted the right to vote. Over the next 50 years, more western states and territories passed laws giving women the right to vote. The populations of the West were more open to the great social change that suffrage represented. Still, despite progress at the state level, the lack of any federal laws meant that many women were still denied the right to vote by the late 1800s.

Winning the Vote In the early 1900s, some 50 years after the Seneca Falls Convention, a renewed effort was made to win women's suffrage. Women's rights activists used marches, picketing, and hunger strikes to fight for suffrage. Some activists even chained themselves to the White House fence to protest for the right to vote.

Finally, in 1920 the United States ratified the Nineteenth Amendment, giving all women in the United States the right to vote. The language of the amendment was short and to the point:

PRIMARY SOURCE

❝The right of citizens of the United States to vote shall not be denied or abridged by the United States or by any State on account of sex . . . Congress shall have power to enforce this article by appropriate legislation.❞

After a 70-year struggle, all American women finally had the vote. However, there were still many more battles ahead in the fight for civil rights.

READING CHECK **Sequencing** What were some key events in the fight for women's suffrage?

Rolling Back Segregation

While women had won an important civil rights victory, African Americans and other groups still suffered from segregation and a denial of civil rights. The *Plessy* ruling had laid the foundation for **de jure segregation**, segregation by law, and segregation remained legal for the first half of the 1900s. Eventually, however, African American activists began to pursue a legal strategy of challenging segregation in court. As a result, the courts began to chip away at legalized segregation and, eventually, overturned it.

Early Legal Challenges In the 1930s the National Association for the Advancement of Colored People (NAACP) launched a campaign to end legal segregation. It focused first on segregation in education and was led by two brilliant attorneys, Charles Hamilton Houston and Thurgood Marshall. The NAACP's approach was not to challenge the idea of "separate but equal" but to insist on true equality.

The first case to successfully challenge segregation was *Gaines* v. *Canada* (1938) in Missouri. Lloyd Gaines, an African American, was refused admission to the University of Missouri law school. The state offered him no alternative—no separate law program existed for African Americans. The Supreme Court ruled that the equal protection clause required states to either provide equal educational facilities for African Americans or admit them to white schools.

Another case, *Sweatt* v. *Painter* (1950), further rolled back segregation. Heman Sweatt applied to the University of Texas law school and, like Gaines, was denied admission. Texas offered Sweatt admission to a separate, all-black law school, but the facilities were far inferior. In a 9–0 ruling, the Court found that the segregated nature of the Texas law school for African Americans affected the quality of the education it provided. As a result, Sweatt was being denied equal protection of the law.

These two rulings were important steps in the battle to overturn segregation. The *Gaines* decision required states to provide separate facilities for African Americans, and the *Sweatt* decision required those facilities to be truly equal. While neither case reversed the separate-but-equal doctrine, the Court was approaching the recognition that, in fact, separate facilities could never be equal.

Brown v. Board of Education of Topeka, Kansas A huge victory in the fight to end segregation, and to guarantee civil rights to everyone, came in the case of *Brown* v. *Board of Education of Topeka, Kansas* (1954). The case was a class action lawsuit—a lawsuit filed by one or more plaintiffs on behalf of themselves and everyone else who has suffered from an alleged wrong. The *Brown* case was filed for all African American students who were denied entry to public schools and directly challenged the legality of the separate-but-equal doctrine.

In a dramatic 9–0 decision, the Court overturned *Plessy* and declared segregation in public schools illegal under the equal protection clause. It ruled that a racially segregated school "generates a feeling of inferiority" among African American students "that may affect their hearts and minds in a way unlikely ever to be undone." Chief Justice Earl Warren stated:

PRIMARY SOURCE

66 Does segregation of children in public schools solely on the basis of race . . . deprive the children of the minority group of equal educational opportunities? We believe that it does . . . We conclude that, in the field of public education, the doctrine of 'separate but equal' has no place. Separate educational facilities are inherently unequal. 99

—Earl Warren, *Brown v. Board of Education of Topeka, Kansas,* 1954

PROFILES IN GOVERNMENT

Thurgood MARSHALL
1908-1993

Thurgood Marshall spent most of his life fighting against inequality and racial discrimination. From the 1930s to the 1950s, Marshall led the NAACP's campaign against segregation. He argued more than 30 cases before the Supreme Court and won almost all of them, distinguishing himself as one of the nation's top lawyers. Marshall's victory in *Brown* v. *Board of Education of Topeka, Kansas* (1954) solidified his reputation as a lawyer and civil rights leader. In 1967 President Lyndon B. Johnson nominated Marshall for the Supreme Court, where he became the first African American justice.

Make Inferences What do you think were some reasons that President Johnson selected Marshall to serve on the Supreme Court?

Mrs. Nettie Hunt explains the significance of the *Brown* decision to her daughter, Nickie.

The News

HIGH COURT BANS SEGREGATION IN PUBLIC SCHOOLS

For the first time in U.S. history, one of the branches of government, the federal judiciary, endorsed a new concept of equality. According to this concept, it was now illegal for state or local governments to provide separate facilities based solely on race.

School Desegregation After the *Brown* ruling, the Supreme Court ordered schools to end segregation "with all deliberate speed." As a result, school districts began the process of **desegregation**, or ending the formal separation of groups based on race.

In many places, however, whites actively resisted desegregation and defied federal law. For example, some schools in Virginia closed for several years to avoid desegregation. In 1957 in Little Rock, Arkansas, the governor ordered Arkansas National Guard troops to stop African American children from attending white schools. After a three-week standoff, President Dwight Eisenhower sent more than 1,000 federal troops to Little Rock to escort the students to school.

Despite resistance, many schools were desegregated through a host of local court cases against individual school districts. As a result, by the 1970s de jure segregation in public schools had ended.

Another type of segregation, known as de facto segregation, still exists, however.

De facto segregation is segregation in fact, even without laws that require segregation. It is usually caused by school attendance rules and housing patterns that reflect social and economic differences among groups. For example, when whites live mainly in certain neighborhoods and racial minorities live mainly in others, schools will be segregated if students are required to attend schools in their neighborhood, even though laws requiring segregation are illegal.

How then, are schools supposed to end segregation? One attempted remedy was to bus students from one area to another within a school district. While the Supreme Court has upheld busing within districts, it has also placed sharp limits on using race and ethnicity to determine school attendance assignments. In 2007 the Court argued that there is no justification—including the goal of ensuring diversity and integration—to base school assignments primarily on race.

Despite the continuing challenges of desgregating both schools and society, the *Brown* decision caused important changes in this country. After *Brown*, calls for further civil rights protections, such as new civil rights laws, grew.

READING CHECK **Summarizing** How did legalized segregation in the United States finally end?

SECTION 2 ASSESSMENT

THINK central   Online Quiz
thinkcentral.com
KEYWORD: SGO CRT HP

Reviewing Ideas and Terms

1. **a. Identify** State the purpose of the Fourteenth Amendment.
   b. Explain Explain how the Supreme Court applies the **equal protection clause** to laws through the use of tests.

2. **a. Define** Define the following terms: **segregation, Jim Crow laws, separate-but-equal doctrine.**
   b. Draw Conclusions Why do you think the new amendments and laws passed after the Civil War failed to end segregation?

3. **a. Identify** Which amendment gave women the right to vote in the United States, and when was it passed?
   b. Make Inferences Why do you think **suffrage** was the main goal for women's rights activists?

4. **a. Describe** What legal strategy did the NAACP use to roll back segregation in the United States?
   b. Evaluate How successful was the *Brown* decision in ending segregation? Explain your answer.

Critical Thinking

5. **Rank** Copy the time line below and use it to list three key events in the struggle for equal protection of the law by African Americans and women. Then rank the events in order of importance and explain your ranking for each one.

1800   2000

FOCUS ON WRITING

6. **Narrative** Suppose that you are a student in 1955, just after the *Brown* decision. Write a short paragraph describing how the decision will affect your school.

DIVISION FOR
PUBLIC
EDUCATION
AMERICAN BAR ASSOCIATION

Brown v. Board of Education of Topeka, Kansas (1954)

WHY IT MATTERS

In this case the Supreme Court ruled that de jure segregation violated the equal protection clause of the Constitution. This decision led to desegregation and helped spark the civil rights movement.

Background

In the 1950s many states had laws that required or allowed segregation in public places. While separate facilities for whites and other groups were supposed to be equal, they almost never were, and segregation was entrenched in many communities around the country. When the parents of third-grader Linda Brown requested a transfer for her to an elementary school closer to home, their request was denied solely on the basis of race. The NAACP filed a class action lawsuit against the local school board on behalf of the Browns and other African American residents of Topeka, Kansas. In its 1951 ruling on the case, the U.S. District Court in Kansas found that segregation did have a negative effect on African American students. However, the court still held that segregated schools did not violate the Fourteenth Amendment because other factors like teachers, facilities, and transportation were equal. The Supreme Court ruled on *Brown* in 1954 in combination with four similar cases from around the country.

Arguments for Brown

NAACP counsel Thurgood Marshall argued that school segregation was a violation of civil rights protected by the Fourteenth Amendment. Marshall presented evidence from social scientists that segregation instilled a sense of inferiority in African American children, which in turn affected their motivation and academic performance. He argued that racially segregated schools stigmatized minority children by setting them apart and caused them permanent psychological damage.

Arguments for Board of Education of Topeka, Kansas

The board of education argued that the Kansas law requiring whites and nonwhites to attend different schools was legally based on the separate-but-equal doctrine established in *Plessy* v. *Ferguson*. The board contended that, to the best of its knowledge and ability, the quality of education provided in both white and nonwhite schools was equal. The board of education denied that school segregation harmed minority children or implied that they were inferior.

THE IMPACT TODAY The Court's unanimous ruling in the *Brown* case was a huge victory for civil rights activists. The NAACP's broad goal with *Brown* was to secure equal protection under the law in all areas of public life, and the *Brown* decision was a major step in that direction. It struck down *Plessy* and was an early step toward dismantling the legal framework of segregation. After *Brown,* segregation in other areas was outlawed as well, based on the principles established in *Brown*, including segregated golf courses, state parks, and public transportation. Although the battle to end segregation would still require many more years of struggle, the *Brown* case marked the beginning of the end for segregation in this country.

CRITICAL THINKING

What Do You Think? The *Brown* case involved the segregation of children in public education. How do you think this fact influenced the Court's decision?

Civil Rights Laws

Main Idea

In the 1950s and 1960s, an organized movement demanding civil rights changed American society and led to a series of new federal laws that protected the civil rights of African Americans and other groups.

Reading Focus

1. What was the civil rights movement, and what effects did it have on American society?

2. What new federal laws were passed in response to the civil rights movement?

3. How were civil rights extended to women, minorities, and people with disabilities?

4. How are affirmative action policies a part of the civil rights movement?

Key Terms

civil rights movement
civil disobedience
poll tax
affirmative action
reverse discrimination
quota

TAKING NOTES As you read, take notes on the civil rights movement and how it led to new civil rights laws.

WHY IT MATTERS

Standing Up for Your Rights What would you do if someone prevented you from going to school, and the government failed to do anything about it? Would you stand up and fight for your right to equal treatment? Would you demonstrate, march, or go on a hunger strike to demand equal rights? Would you risk your personal safety—and your life—by confronting those who were determined to keep you powerless and even use violence against you?

A Courageous Walk

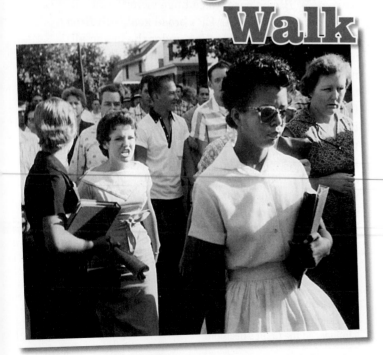

Elizabeth Eckford walks to Little Rock's Central High School in 1957.

In 1957 a 15-year-old high school student named Elizabeth Eckford did just that. Eckford was one of nine African American students who attempted to enter the all-white Central High School in Little Rock, Arkansas. On their first attempt, the students were prevented from entering by hostile white parents, students, and even Arkansas National Guard troops.

A famous photograph of Eckford being harassed by white students helped bring attention to the struggle for civil rights and the hostility that African Americans faced. In the photograph, a white student named Hazel Massery yells at Eckford, who keeps her composure and dignity. In 1963 Massery apologized to Eckford, and the two women became friends. But on that day in 1957, Eckford refused to be intimidated by intolerance and abuse. Would you have had the courage to join her? ■

The Civil Rights Movement

Elizabeth Eckford's attempt to enter Central High School was part of the **civil rights movement**—a mass movement in the 1950s and 1960s to guarantee the civil rights of African Americans. Civil rights activists used nonviolent protests to fight against injustice and segregation and to work toward the passage of new federal civil rights laws.

A key event in the civil rights movement came in 1955 when Rosa Parks, an African American, was arrested for refusing to give up her seat to a white person on a public bus in Montgomery, Alabama.

Her refusal violated the city's segregation laws, which had not been overturned by *Brown*, since the case applied only to segregation in public education.

Civil rights leaders in Montgomery responded by organizing a boycott against the city's buses. The boycott was led by Martin Luther King Jr., a minister and Southern Christian Leadership Conference (SCLC) civil rights leader. Despite the boycott, the city refused to integrate its buses. The NAACP filed suit, arguing that in accordance with the new legal principles of *Brown*, laws that segregated public facilities were also unconstitutional, based on the equal protection clause. The NAACP won in federal district court, and the Supreme Court upheld the decision, resulting in one of the first major successes of the civil rights movement.

Nonviolent protests became a major strategy of civil rights activists. Boycotts, sit-ins, demonstrations, marches, and other acts of **civil disobedience**, or nonviolent refusals to obey the law as a way to advocate change, spread across the country.

But despite the use of nonviolence, protesters were often attacked and brutalized by those resistant to change, including state and local officials. As images of violent attacks on peaceful protesters spread around the country, support for the civil rights movement grew.

In 1963 more than 200,000 people gathered in Washington, D.C., to show their support for the civil rights movement. This large, peaceful event, known as the March on Washington, focused national attention on the civil rights movement. On the steps of the Lincoln Memorial, Martin Luther King Jr. gave his "I Have a Dream" speech, now considered one of the greatest speeches in American history.

One of the most important victories of the civil rights movement came in 1965 with the Selma to Montgomery marches. African Americans in Alabama who had been intimidated from voting organized a march from Selma to the capitol building in Montgomery. Local sheriffs and Alabama state troopers responded by brutally attacking the peaceful protesters in an event now known as Bloody Sunday. Images of the attacks were shown on national television news programs and shocked the country. Bloody Sunday helped lead to the passage of new federal laws designed to protect the civil rights of African Americans and other minorities.

READING CHECK **Sequencing** What were the key events of the early civil rights movement?

PRIMARY SOURCES

"I Have a Dream"

Martin Luther King Jr. spoke at the March on Washington on August 28, 1963. His speech became one of the defining moments of the civil rights movement.

❝I say to you today my friends so even though we face the difficulties of today and tomorrow, I still have a dream. It is a dream deeply rooted in the American dream.

I have a dream that one day this nation will rise up and live out the true meaning of its creed: 'We hold these truths to be self-evident, that all men are created equal.'

I have a dream that one day on the red hills of Georgia the sons of former slaves and the sons of former slave owners will be able to sit down together at the table of brotherhood.

I have a dream that one day even the state of Mississippi, a state sweltering with the heat of injustice, sweltering with the heat of oppression, will be transformed into an oasis of freedom and justice.

I have a dream that my four children will one day live in a nation where they will not be judged by the color of their skin but by the content of their character. . . .❞

Skills FOCUS **INTERPRETING PRIMARY SOURCES**

Making Inferences What effect do you think King's speech had on people's ideas about their rights and about political involvement?

See **Skills Handbook**, p. H9.

New Federal Laws

In response to the civil rights movement, Congress passed a series of federal laws in a renewed attempt to guarantee all Americans' civil rights. By the mid-1960s these new federal laws began to transform the legal protections of everyone in the country.

Civil Rights Laws under Eisenhower In 1957 Congress passed, and President Dwight D. Eisenhower signed into law, the first civil rights legislation since Reconstruction. The Civil Rights Act of 1957 included several features to help the federal government fight discrimination. A key part of the law created the Civil Rights Commission, which had the power to investigate cases of discrimination and suggest remedies.

The next piece of federal civil rights legislation was the Civil Rights Act of 1960. This law empowered the federal government to actively engage in voter registration in places where voting discrimination had been found. It also made it illegal for anyone to obstruct a person's right to vote.

Both of these laws marked important advances in civil rights. However, they also faced powerful opposition, especially from southerners in Congress. As a result, both laws were weak and ineffective. One reason for this ineffectiveness was that the laws enabled the federal government to fight discrimination only on a case-by-case basis.

Civil Rights Act of 1964 A breakthrough in the civil rights movement came with the Civil Rights Act of 1964. This law, passed over the strong opposition of many southern lawmakers, was one of the most far-reaching civil rights laws in American history.

The Civil Rights Act of 1964 banned discrimination based on race, color, religion, sex, or national origin in voting, employment, and public accommodations. Age was added in 1967. The act also allowed the federal government to cut off federal funds from any program that allowed discrimination.

One of the reasons the Civil Rights Act of 1964 was so powerful was that it was passed under the authority of the Constitution's commerce clause. You may remember that the Fourteenth Amendment and its equal protection clause applied only to actions by states—they did not prevent discrimination by individuals or businesses. By passing this new law under the commerce clause, however, Congress was able to ban discrimination by any person or business that engaged in interstate commerce. As a result, businesses such as hotels, gas stations, restaurants, and many others were now barred from practicing discrimination.

Voting Rights Laws One of the main goals of the civil rights movement was to guarantee African Americans' voting rights. For decades, southern states had used a variety of means

---

Interactive Feature *

Modern Civil Rights: Federal Laws

THINK central | Interactive

thinkcentral.com
KEYWORD: SGO CRT

In response to the civil rights movement, Congress passed a series of federal laws in a renewed attempt to guarantee all Americans' civil rights.

Civil Rights Act of 1957	Civil Rights Act of 1960	Twenty-fourth Amendment (1964)	Civil Rights Act of 1964	Voting Rights Act of 1965	Civil Rights Act of 1968
Established the Civil Rights Commission to investigate civil rights violations; created a civil rights division in the Department of Justice to enforce civil rights laws	Gave the federal government the power to inspect local voter registration rolls and penalize anyone who obstructs a person's right to vote	Banned the use of poll taxes in federal elections	Banned discrimination based on race, color, national origin, or sex in voting, employment, and public accommodations; created the Equal Employment Opportunity Commission	Banned unfair tests in voting, such as literacy tests; allowed federal agents to help register African American voters	Banned discrimination in the sale, rental, or financing of housing

to keep African Americans from voting. These ranged from restrictive legislation that denied them the right to register to vote to violence and intimidation.

By the 1960s some of the unfair laws used to prevent African Americans from voting had been struck down by the courts. For example, the Supreme Court outlawed the use of grandfather clauses. Some of these laws limited voting to people whose descendants had the right to vote prior to the Fifteenth Amendment. The Court had also struck down white primaries—primary elections in which only whites could vote.

In 1964 the country took another step toward guaranteeing voting rights with the ratification of the Twenty-fourth Amendment. It banned the use of poll taxes to prevent people from voting. A **poll tax** is a tax levied on someone who wants to vote. Poll taxes were used to keep poor people, especially African Americans, from voting.

Still, despite these new laws and court decisions, few African Americans in the South could exercise their right to vote. The 1964 murder of civil rights workers in Mississippi who were trying to register African Americans to vote and the events of Bloody Sunday in 1965 showed how determined some people were to prevent African Americans from voting. These events showed that still more had to be done.

As a result, President Lyndon B. Johnson spearheaded the effort to have Congress enact the Voting Rights Act of 1965. This far-reaching law banned literacy tests, another device widely used against African American voters. The law also specifically targeted places where Congress believed discrimination was widespread. It gave the federal government power to review all changes to voting laws in these places, take part in voter registration, and monitor elections.

Effects of New Federal Laws The effects of the civil rights laws of the 1950s and 1960s were dramatic. For the first time, the new laws gave the federal government real power to stop discrimination by states and individuals. African Americans now had a powerful ally in the battle for desegregation, fair treatment in jobs and housing, and the right to vote. Finally, after many years, it was no longer legal to discriminate against people in voting, hiring, housing, or access to public accommodations based on race, national origin, religion, or sex.

READING CHECK Summarizing What major federal civil rights laws were passed in the 1950s and 1960s?

Extending Civil Rights

The progress that African Americans made in their fight for civil rights inspired other groups who were victims of discrimination as well. While many of the civil rights laws passed in the 1950s and 1960s were enacted largely to protect African Americans, they prohibited discrimination against *anyone* based on race, national origin, religion, or sex. In addition, other new laws and court decisions extended civil rights protections specifically to women, Hispanics, Native Americans, and people with disabilities.

ACADEMIC VOCABULARY

prohibit to forbid by authority

Women The Equal Pay Act of 1963 required employers to offer equal pay to men and women doing the same work. The Civil Rights Acts of 1964 and 1968 banned discrimination against women as well as members of racial and ethnic groups. In 1972 Title IX of the Education Amendments banned discrimination against women in areas such as admissions, athletics, and educational programs by schools and colleges that received federal funds. The Equal Credit Opportunity Act of 1975 prohibited banks, stores, and other businesses from discriminating against women in making loans or granting credit.

The courts have also helped women expand their rights. In 1973, for example, the Supreme Court ruled in *Roe* v. *Wade* that women had the constitutionally protected right to an abortion. According to the Court, this right was unlimited in the first three months of pregnancy, though it could be limited thereafter. A 1986 Supreme Court ruling declared that sexual harassment is a form of discrimination outlawed by the Civil Rights Act of 1964. The Court also struck down laws giving preference to fathers over mothers in administering their children's estates and excluding women from serving on juries.

Extending Civil Rights

Civil rights protections were extended to Hispanic workers through the efforts of activists like César Chávez (left). Disabled Americans lobbied successfully for the passage of the Americans with Disabilities Act in 1990 (right). *How are activists in these photographs trying to effect change?*

Hispanics Hispanics used legal challenges, walkouts, and marches in their fight for civil rights. Three court cases were particularly important in extending Hispanic civil rights. In 1946 a federal court in California ruled in *Mendez* v. *Westminster* that the state's segregation of Hispanic students was illegal. This case led to the end of racial segregation in California's public schools and facilities. In *Hernandez* v. *Texas* (1954) the Supreme Court ruled that the equal protection clause applied not only to African Americans but to Hispanics and other racial groups as well. In 1973, in the case of *Keyes* v. *Denver Unified School District*, the Court ruled that de facto segregation of Hispanics in public education was also unconstitutional.

Hispanics also made gains at the ballot box. In 1975 the Voting Rights Act was expanded to require that ballots be printed in Spanish and other languages in communities that had large numbers of non-English speakers.

The Hispanic labor and civil rights leader César Chávez also helped extend civil rights to Hispanics. He led marches and hunger strikes to fight for the rights of migrant farm workers, many of whom were Hispanic.

ACADEMIC VOCABULARY

accessible
capable of being reached

Native Americans Native Americans also used protests to demand new laws and better protection of their civil rights. The American Indian Movement (AIM) used aggressive and symbolic protests and takeovers to call attention to the inferior status of Native Americans in society. For example, in 1972 AIM and other Indian-rights groups took over the Bureau of Indian Affairs building in Washington, D.C., to demand a review of treaty violations as well as more education and economic help for Native Americans.

In response to these demands, Congress passed several laws, including the Indian Self-Determination and Education Assistance Act of 1975. The goal of this act was to allow Native American groups to control federally funded programs in their communities. In 1978 Congress passed the American Indian Religious Freedom Act, which declared that Native Americans have the same freedom of religion rights as other Americans.

People with Disabilities In 1990 Congress passed the Americans with Disabilities Act, which prohibited discrimination against people with disabilities. It also required that public buildings and transportation facilities be accessible to people with disabilities. As a result, wheelchair ramps, elevators, and other features are now common in public buildings. A court case in Alabama, *Wyatt* v. *Stickney* (2003), led to improved conditions for patients in state-run psychiatric facilities around the country.

READING CHECK **Summarizing** How were civil rights extended to groups besides African Americans?

Affirmative Action

Thanks to the civil rights movement and the laws it generated, discrimination is illegal today, and victims of discrimination have tools to fight injustice in court. But is that enough? Because of past discrimination, women and members of racial and ethnic groups are still underrepresented in many areas and have many obstacles to overcome. These groups suffer from entrenched disadvantages caused by generations of discrimination and unequal access to education, employment, and social opportunities. For example, if a person's parents suffered from discrimination, he or she might not live in a good school district or be able to afford to go to a highly ranked university.

One policy that has attempted to address the effects of past discrimination is **affirmative action**—a policy that requires employers and institutions to provide opportunities for members of certain historically underrepresented groups. Supporters of affirmative action believe that government should not just ban discrimination; it should actively promote equality for members of racial and ethnic groups and women. Opponents argue that such efforts lead to special privileges for members of targeted groups and are unfair to whites.

Early Affirmative Action Efforts

The federal government first began using affirmative action policies in the 1960s. These policies required businesses that contracted with the federal government and educational institutions that received federal funds to work to achieve more diverse workforces and student bodies.

In 1965 President Lyndon Johnson expanded that effort with Executive Order 11246, which declared that the government's policy was to "promote the full realization of equal employment opportunity through a positive, continuing program." Under this order, contractors were required to "take affirmative action" in their employment practices. An office in the Labor Department oversaw compliance with the order among large construction contractors. These employers were required to set goals and timetables for minority hiring.

By the late 1970s, however, affirmative action policies had become controversial. Some people charged that they were a form of **reverse discrimination**, or discrimination against the majority group. These people argued that giving preference to someone based on his or her race or sex was wrong, even if the intentions are good.

The *Bakke* Case The first major challenge to affirmative action was *Regents of the University of California* v. *Bakke* (1978). Allan Bakke, a white student, was denied entry to the University of California–Davis Medical School. The school had a **quota**—a fixed number or percentage—of minorities needed to meet the requirements of an affirmative action program.

Under this quota, each year 16 of the 100 places in the medical school were held for nonwhite students who were admitted under a separate process. Bakke, who believed that he was highly qualified, was not able to compete for admission for those 16 places. He sued, arguing that he was being discriminated against solely because of his race.

Major Supreme Court Rulings on Affirmative Action

Ruling: Race can be used as one factor in college admissions, but quota systems are unconstitutional.

Case: *Regents of the University of California* v. *Bakke* (1978)

Ruling: Consideration of sex as a factor in promotions is acceptable.

Case: *Johnson* v. *Transportation Agency*, Santa Clara County, California (1987)

Ruling: Affirmative action must be targeted at specific problems of past discrimination, not general discrimination by society as a whole.

Case: *Adarand Constructors, Inc.* v. *Peña* (1995)

Ruling: Reaffirmed that race can be used as one factor in admissions, but overturned a system that awarded points to minorities

Case: *Gratz* v. *Bollinger* and *Grutter* v. *Bollinger* (2003)

In its decision, the Supreme Court ruled in favor of Bakke and ordered the university to admit him. Although nonminorities held almost all of the other 84 admissions slots in the entering class, the Court decided that the strict quota system was invalid because it did not allow nonminorities to compete for any of the 16 places. However, a majority of the justices also held that race could be used as a factor in determining university admissions.

The Michigan Cases Some 25 years after the Bakke ruling, the Supreme Court again addressed the question of affirmative action in higher education. In 2003 the Court ruled on two Michigan cases—*Gratz* v. *Bollinger* and *Grutter* v. *Bollinger*.

Both Gratz and Grutter were white women who had applied to and been rejected by two different programs at the University of Michigan. Some minority applicants with lower test scores and grade point averages had been admitted, however. Both women sued, arguing that using race as a factor in admissions was discriminatory.

In its ruling, the Court overturned Gratz's rejection but upheld Grutter's. The difference was how race had been used in each case. In Gratz's case, the admissions policy awarded points to minorities based solely on the fact that they were minorities. This policy was mechanical and formulaic, so the Court rejected it because it was not carefully targeted to achieve the goal of diversity. In Grutter's case, however, there was no automatic award of points. Rather, race was just one factor taken into account in the admissions process.

Ballot Measures In addition to court rulings, several states have passed ballot measures restricting affirmative action policies. In 1996 California voters approved Proposition 209, the California Civil Rights Initiative. The measure amended the state constitution to forbid state and local agencies, including universities, from giving preferential treatment to any person or group based on race, color, ethnicity, or sex. The only exceptions are when the federal government requires affirmative action. Following California's lead, Washington and Michigan passed similar measures in 1998 and 2006, respectively.

READING CHECK **Summarizing** How have affirmative action policies changed over time?

SECTION 3 ASSESSMENT

Reviewing Ideas and Terms

1. **a. Identify** Which two key events in the **civil rights movement** took place in Alabama?
   b. Predict How do you think the civil rights movement and federal laws led to changes in American society and politics?

2. **a. Describe** What were three major civil rights laws or actions passed or taken in the1960s, and what did each do?
   b. Evaluate Why were the civil rights laws of the 1960s more effective in protecting people's rights than earlier legislation?

3. **a. Identify** Which groups besides African Americans benefited from the civil rights movement?
   b. Make Inferences How did some groups use democratic principles to resolve issues relating to their civil rights?

4. **a. Define** Define each of the following terms: **affirmative action, reverse discrimination, quota.**
   b. Evaluate In your opinion, when are affirmative action policies justified? When are they not justified?

Critical Thinking

5. **Compare and Contrast** Copy the graphic organizer below and use it to compare three major federal civil rights laws and their effects. How were the laws similar and different?

1.	→	
2.	→	
3.	→	

FOCUS ON WRITING

6. **Descriptive** Write two short paragraphs: one describing what society and discrimination laws were like before the civil rights movement, and one describing what they are like after the civil rights movement. Use the images in this section to add descriptive details to your paragraphs.

Affirmative Action

Should the government promote affirmative action to help address the effects of past discrimination?

THE ISSUE

Since 1965 federal law has required many public institutions and private companies to institute affirmative action policies to provide more opportunities for members of historically underrepresented groups, such as racial minorities and women. Affirmative action policies vary widely, employing methods such as recruitment, quotas, and proportional representation. However, these policies have been controversial, drawing both praise and criticism. Although the Supreme Court has ruled on a number of affirmative action cases, it has overturned about as many policies as it has upheld.

Students at the University of Michigan debate affirmative action in the university's admissions policies.

VIEWPOINTS

Government should promote affirmative action policies. Affirmative action was created to provide people with greater opportunity. Minority applicants are not selected solely on the basis of race. Affirmative action is not about choosing less-qualified applicants, but about giving all applicants a fair chance to succeed. President Lyndon B. Johnson once said, "You do not take a person who, for years, has been hobbled by chains and liberate him, bring him up to the starting line of a race and then say, 'you are free to compete with all the others,' and still justly believe that you have been completely fair." Overall, white males remain at the top of the power structure and represent the majority in positions of power and in economic status. Accusations of reverse discrimination are unfounded.

Affirmative action is unfair, and government should not promote it. Is a diverse workforce more important than a qualified workforce? By requiring private companies and state and local governments to follow affirmative action policies, the federal government is saying that a diverse workforce is more important. Employment or admissions decisions should be based solely on merit, not on race or gender. Giving minority or female applicants any kind of preferential treatment is a form of reverse discrimination. All applicants should be given equal consideration based on their individual merits and qualifications. Failure to do so results in exclusionary practices and goes against the very principles on which affirmative action supporters claim to stand.

What Is Your Opinion?

1. Is racial preference in employment or admissions practices equitable? Why or why not?

2. What are some ideas about how certain affirmative action programs could be revised?

THINK central **Practice Online**

thinkcentral.com
KEYWORD: SGO CRT

Citizenship and Immigration

Main Idea

Being a U.S. citizen includes certain rights and responsibilities. The federal government regulates citizenship through its immigration and naturalization policies.

Reading Focus

1. In what ways do people receive U.S. citizenship, and what civic responsibilities do citizens have?

2. What immigration policies has the federal government adopted in its history?

3. How has the federal government responded to the challenge of illegal immigration?

Key Terms

jus soli
jus sanguinis
naturalization
denaturalization
expatriation
undocumented alien
deportation

 TAKING NOTES As you read, take notes on American citizenship and immigration issues in a chart like this one.

Citizenship	Immigration

 U.S. Citizenship Many Americans think only now and then about their citizenship— what it means, what rights and responsibilities it involves, and why it is so important. But for hundreds of thousands of immigrants who come to this country each year hoping to become Americans, citizenship is a vital matter.

Citizenship is the key to full participation in the American system of government. Only citizens, for example, have the right to vote and run for office. In addition, American citizens have duties and responsibilities. For example, they must obey the law, pay taxes, and be loyal to the government and its principles.

The Most Important Office

Immigrants are sworn in as U.S. citizens during a ceremony in California.

Our government draws its power from its citizens and works to protect their rights. That is why Supreme Court Justice Louis Brandeis called citizenship "the most important office" and added that "the only title in our democracy superior to that of President is the title of citizen."

Some people who were born in the United States or have been citizens for a long time might take these rights and responsibilities for granted. But many newcomers are keenly aware of the meaning and importance of citizenship. As one new U.S. citizen said, "To be an American to me means to be free in my thinking, in my religious beliefs, and to be who I am." It is a freedom and a responsibility that all Americans share. ◼

U.S. Citizenship

For the most part, civil rights in the United States are guaranteed to everyone in the country, both citizens and noncitizens, or aliens. A major exception is the right to vote, which is denied to aliens. To fully participate in American democracy requires citizenship. There are several ways to become a citizen.

Citizenship by Birth The vast majority of Americans become citizens by birth. People can become citizens by birth in two ways: by being born in the United States or a U.S. territory, or by being born on foreign soil to parents who are U.S. citizens.

Most people born in the United States or a U.S. territory automatically become U.S. citizens.

This principle of citizenship by birthplace is known as **jus soli** (YOOS SOH-lee), a Latin phrase that means "law of the soil." The Fourteenth Amendment affirms the principle of jus soli by stating that "All persons born or naturalized in the United States, and subject to the jurisdiction thereof, are citizens of the United States." The main exception to jus soli is people who are born in the United States but are not subject to U.S. control, such as the children of foreign diplomats.

The second way to become a citizen by birth is to be born on foreign soil to parents who are U.S. citizens. This principle of citizenship by parentage is known as **jus sanguinis** (YOOS SANG-gwuh-nuhs), a Latin phrase meaning "law of the blood." However, there are many restrictions and rules on gaining citizenship in this way. Congress, applying its constitutional authority over the matter of citizenship, has spelled out these rules in the Immigration and Nationality Act.

Citizenship by Naturalization Another way to gain citizenship is by **naturalization**, the legal process by which an immigrant becomes a citizen. In general, naturalized citizens enjoy the same rights and privileges as native-born citizens. One major exception to this rule is that naturalized citizens cannot become president or vice president of the United States. Under the Constitution, those offices are reserved for "natural born" citizens only.

Naturalization typically begins after someone enters the country legally and meets certain requirements, including

- a period of continuous lawful residence and physical presence in the United States
- the ability to read, write, and speak English
- good moral character
- a belief in the principles of the U.S. Constitution
- a favorable disposition toward the United States

After meeting these and some other basic requirements, an applicant for citizenship must pass a citizenship exam administered by the government and take an oath of allegiance to the United States.

The U.S. government may also grant citizenship to an entire group of people through collective naturalization. For example, the Fourteenth Amendment granted immediate citizenship to all African Americans. Collective naturalization has also been used when the United States gained new territories, such as the Louisiana Purchase, Texas, Hawaii, and Puerto Rico.

Losing Citizenship The loss of citizenship is rare, but some Americans do choose to give up their citizenship voluntarily. Only the federal government can take someone's citizenship away involuntarily, however. The Supreme Court has ruled that in most situations, the government cannot take someone's citizenship away because it would be cruel and unusual punishment. For example, people who illegally avoid military service or desert the military in wartime cannot lose their citizenship as a result.

There are several main ways that a person can lose his or her citizenship. First, a court can take citizenship away from someone who became a citizen through fraud. For example, if someone lies or provides false information during the naturalization process, he or she can lose citizenship through a process called **denaturalization**. Second, someone can lose citizenship by committing serious crimes against the U.S. government, such as treason. Third, citizenship can be lost if someone swears an oath of loyalty to, or serves in a high-level position in, another country's government or military. Fourth, one can voluntarily give up citizenship. The legal process of giving up one's citizenship is called **expatriation**. It usually happens if someone chooses to live in and vote in another country and to be a part of another country's government.

Civic Responsibilities As you know, with citizenship comes certain rights—including civil rights. But citizenship also carries duties and responsibilities. These are known as civic responsibilities.

Citizens have a duty to respect and obey the law and accept responsibility for the consequences of their own actions. They also must respect the rights of others and be willing to defend the rights of everyone.

WHAT DO YOU THINK?

Review the list of criteria for naturalization today. Are there other or different criteria you think Congress should adopt? Explain.

Citizens have a basic duty to be loyal to the government and to the principles on which it is based. If called upon, they must serve in the armed forces to protect the nation. Citizens must pay taxes and are expected to take part in the political system by voting and by being informed about key issues. Citizens also must serve on juries when called upon.

Meeting these responsibilities is part of each citizen's civic life. By participating in the civic life of their country and communities, citizens help preserve and protect society for everyone. In addition, citizens may choose to participate directly in the political process by running for office or supporting a political cause. Such activities are part of a citizen's political life, along with voting. Citizens also have a personal life, which is devoted to the pursuit of private interests. The personal lives of citizens might include activities such as joining a business association, alumni group, or other private organization.

Civic Identity A commitment to civic responsibilities is one of the features that helps Americans share a common civic identity. A devotion to key ideas such as democracy, individual liberties, civil rights, and tolerance are also part of our civic identity. These ideas are expressed in the nation's key historic documents such as the Declaration of Independence, the U.S. Constitution, and Abraham Lincoln's Second Inaugural Address.

READING CHECK **Identifying Supporting Details** What are the two main ways of achieving citizenship in the United States?

Immigration Policies

Throughout our history, many people from other countries have come here to live and become citizens. This long history of immigration has had a huge influence on American society and culture. The United States is often described as "a nation of immigrants." Early in our history, there were few barriers to immigration, and it was generally encouraged. Over time, however, the government began to restrict immigration and to create national immigration policies.

Encouraging Immigration The federal government has the power to regulate immigration and to set immigration policies. This power is an inherent power that comes from a country's right to control and protect its borders.

Despite this power, Congress did little to regulate immigration during the first 100 years of the country's history. With abundant land and resources, immigration was generally encouraged. For example, the U.S.-Mexico border was quite open throughout the 1800s, and many workers and families moved back and forth across the border with little concern about whether or not they had the necessary papers. So many immigrants arrived in our early history that by 1870 about one in seven Americans had been born outside the country.

By the late 1800s however, the country's population had grown dramatically. With less land available for settlers, tensions between some immigrants and native-born Americans increased. In addition, the major sources of immigration changed. Previously, most immigrants had come from northern and western Europe. By the late 1800s, most immigrants came from southern and eastern Europe. Differences in language and cultural traditions between these new immigrants and the country's native-born population contributed to rising tensions.

Restricting Immigration In 1875 Congress enacted the first major restriction on immigration when it barred entry to criminals. Then, in 1882 Congress passed the Chinese Exclusion Act, effectively ending immigration from China for 10 years.

In the 1920s new laws began to restrict immigration even further. The Quota Law of 1921 and National Origins Quota Act of 1924 restricted immigration by country and established a total number of immigrants allowed into the United States annually— 165,000. Each European country was given an exact number of immigrants that could be admitted. The quotas were based on the national origin of the U.S. population in 1890. The largest group of residents at that time had ancestors from northern and western Europe, so Congress allowed more immigration from those regions.

Immigrants arrive in the United States in the early 1900s.

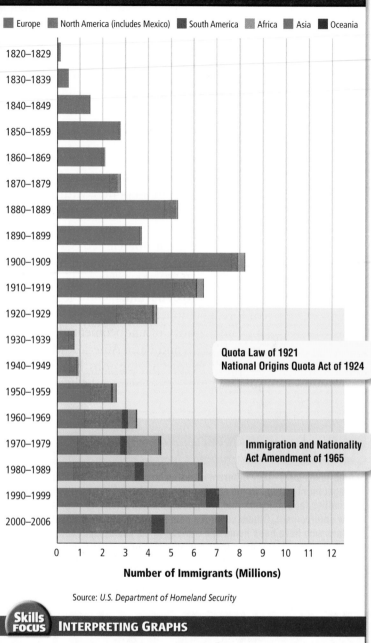

LEGAL IMMIGRATION TO THE UNITED STATES, 1820–2006

■ Europe ■ North America (includes Mexico) ■ South America ■ Africa ■ Asia ■ Oceania

Quota Law of 1921
National Origins Quota Act of 1924

Immigration and Nationality Act Amendment of 1965

Number of Immigrants (Millions)

Source: *U.S. Department of Homeland Security*

Skills FOCUS **INTERPRETING GRAPHS**

How did immigration laws in the 1920s and 1960s change the source and number of legal immigrants to the United States?

The new laws also effectively banned immigration from Asia and Africa and placed heavy restrictions on immigration from Latin America. The result of these new restrictions was a major drop in immigration, because the countries in Europe with the highest quotas did not have enough people who wanted to emigrate to the United States.

The national quota system that was developed in the 1920s remained in place until Congress passed the Immigration and Nationality Act Amendment of 1965. This law, inspired in part by the civil rights movement, did away with the country-based quota system that had favored immigration from Europe over that from non-European countries. Instead, the new law allowed 290,000 total immigrants annually without regard to national origin, with 120,000 from the Western Hemisphere and 170,000 from the Eastern Hemisphere. The law gave special preference to people with certain job skills and the relatives of U.S. citizens and legal residents.

The 1965 law led to a dramatic increase in immigration. In addition, the national origin of the majority of immigrants changed, as more immigrants arrived from Asia and Latin America. In 1990 the law was updated, and the total number of immigrants allowed was increased to about 675,000 annually.

Political Asylum and Refugees The federal government has separate immigration policies for refugees and people seeking political asylum, many of whom come fleeing wars or political persecution in their home country. The United States accepts far more refugees than any other country in the world. It accepted more than 50,000 in 2005.

READING CHECK **Sequencing** How has immigration policy in the United States changed over time?

Illegal Immigration

In addition to legal immigration, many people enter the United States illegally each year. Illegal immigration has been one of the most difficult challenges facing the country. Despite attempts to solve the problem, undocumented immigrants continue to enter the country in large numbers.

The Situation Today An unauthorized immigrant, or **undocumented alien**, is someone living in a country without authorization from the government. No one knows exactly how many undocumented aliens there are in the United States, but in 2007 the number was estimated to be about 12 million. If caught, undocumented aliens are subject to **deportation**—the legal process of forcing a noncitizen to leave a country.

The majority of undocumented aliens are from Mexico and Latin America. Most come to work in low-paying jobs because these jobs pay more than many jobs in their home countries. Some undocumented aliens travel back home after working here for a few months at a time or send part of their earnings back to relatives in their home countries. Others try to stay permanently.

About half of all unauthorized immigrants enter the United States by crossing the U.S.-Mexico border. Most of the rest enter legally, such as with tourist or student visas but then stay after their visas have expired. Once they are here, undocumented aliens work in such industries as agriculture, construction, and domestic services. Although the federal government makes efforts to apprehend and deport these immigrants, it has been unable to keep track of most of them.

The Debate over Illegal Immigration The large number of undocumented aliens in the United States is a concern to many citizens. Some people are concerned that undocumented aliens take jobs away from U.S. citizens and are a drain on government services like schools and hospitals, especially in states such as California, Arizona, Texas, and Florida, where the number of undocumented aliens is high. Others state that it is simply wrong for people to enter this country illegally with the intention of staying permanently.

On the other hand, undocumented aliens and their supporters argue that most are hardworking people who are trying to build a better life for themselves and their families. They resent that undocumented aliens are sometimes viewed as criminals. In addition, they say that undocumented workers contribute to the U.S. economy by paying taxes, buying American goods and services, and filling low-paying jobs that most Americans choose not to do.

Illegal Immigration Policies In the early 1900s, the United States began efforts to patrol the nation's borders with an eye toward preventing illegal immigration. This effort eventually led to the creation of the Border Patrol in the 1920s.

In 1954 the Border Patrol took part in a large-scale effort to identify illegal immigrants from Mexico and deport them. The operation resulted in an estimated 1 million undocumented aliens being

Views on Illegal Immigration

Americans have many different views on how to solve the problem of illegal immigration. Some support increased border security, tougher penalties for employers that hire undocumented aliens, or improved law enforcement. Others support a path to citizenship for undocumented aliens who have been living and working in the country for years. In 2006, as Congress was debating the issue of immigration reform, hundreds of thousands of people marched in cities such as Los Angeles (below) in support of undocumented aliens. *Why do you think the issue of illegal immigration has been so difficult for the government to solve?*

removed to Mexico. However, the operation also drew many complaints of discrimination against Mexican Americans who were also deported, and it was soon ended.

As illegal immigration continued to rise in later years, the federal government adopted new policies. In 1986 Congress passed the Immigration Reform and Control Act. This law gave undocumented aliens a one-time amnesty, or general pardon from the government for people who have broken the law. The law also gave undocumented aliens a path to citizenship. An estimated 2.7 million people used this law to become citizens. Another major provision of the law made it illegal for employers to hire undocumented workers, in the hope that reducing job opportunities would decrease illegal immigration. These employer sanctions were rarely enforced, however.

Despite the 1986 law, illegal immigration continued to increase. The federal government responded with the Illegal Immigration Reform and Immigrant Responsibility Act of 1996. This law increased the size of the Border Patrol, made it easier to deport undocumented aliens, and increased the penalties for smuggling people into the country.

The terrorist attacks of September 11, 2001, led to renewed demands for improved border security. Three of the hijackers had expired visas and were here illegally at the time of the attacks, and two others could have been denied admission to the country based on immigration laws. In yet another attempt to control the nation's borders, the Border Patrol was increased and began to conduct more patrols and deportations. Border security measures, such as fencing and barriers, also increased, especially in large border cities like San Diego and El Paso. In 2006 President George W. Bush ordered more than 6,000 National Guard troops to assist the Border Patrol.

Still, illegal immigration has continued, and despite prodding by the Bush administration, Congress has been unable to pass comprehensive immigration reform. Members of both parties are divided over issues such as whether to allow undocumented aliens to legalize their status or whether to create a guest worker program, as well as how to secure the borders.

ACADEMIC VOCABULARY

comprehensive covering completely or broadly

READING CHECK **Summarizing** What policies has the federal government created to deal with illegal immigration?

SECTION 4 ASSESSMENT

THINK central **Online Quiz**

thinkcentral.com
KEYWORD: SGO CRT HP

Reviewing Ideas and Terms

1. **a. Define** Define the following terms: **jus soli, jus sanguinis, naturalization, denaturalization, expatriation.**
   b. Explain What duties and responsibilities do citizens have, and why are they important?
   c. Evaluate What do you think about the Supreme Court's rulings that, in most cases, taking someone's citizenship away would be cruel and unusual punishment?

2. **a. Recall** When did the United States first make laws restricting immigration?
   b. Analyze How did the Immigration Act of 1965 change the nation's immigration policies and society?
   c. Evaluate How do you think national immigration policies affect local communities and states?

3. **a. Describe** What are some of the basic issues concerning illegal immigration today?

b. Rate What policies toward illegal immigration has the U.S. government created, and why do you think these policies have failed to stop illegal immigration?

Critical Thinking

4. **Analyze** Copy the chart below and use it to list three key facts about both citizenship and immigration. Then explain how each fact affects people in the United States.

Citizenship	Immigration

FOCUS ON WRITING

5. **Expository** The United States is becoming an increasingly diverse society. How might these changes affect our representative democracy? Write a short paper stating your opinion.

We the People

THE CITIZEN & THE CONSTITUTION

Civic Participation

Our system of government depends on the active participation of citizens. Citizens, after all, have the ultimate power and responsibility to govern. This lesson outlines the importance of civic participation in our constitutional democracy.

Why should Americans participate in the civic life of the country? America's constitutional democracy has often been called an experiment in self-government. Sovereignty resides with the people. How the people use their power directly affects the society in which they live and the vibrancy of their civic institutions. The people also determine which problems they can solve for themselves and which problems require governmental responses.

Participation in civic life does more than address problems. Participation helps individuals become attached to their communities, regions, states, and the country as a whole. Such attachment is necessary for Americans to develop pride in their communities and country and to understand that they share a common destiny. For many people, civic engagement includes recommitting to the ideals they have set for themselves and understanding how those ideals relate to the fundamental principles of American constitutional democracy.

Those who participate actively in civic life are more likely to vote. They also are more likely to become well-informed voters.

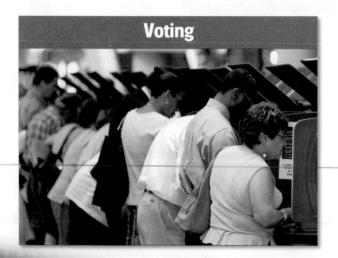

Voting

Contributing Community Service

Adapted with permission from Lesson 34 of *We the People: The Citizen & the Constitution.*
Copyright 2009, Center for Civic Education.

How is civic participation connected to self-interest? Many Americans engage in civic activities and vote because they realize it is in their self-interest to do so. Business people, for example, serve on local boards and commissions or run for county commission or city council because they know that healthy communities are good for business. Parents volunteer their time to create and maintain parks because they want safe places for their children to play. Homeowners join neighborhood associations because they care about the value of their property.

Civic engagement has other personal benefits, including:

- acquiring skills, such as organizing groups, speaking and debating in public, and writing letters
- becoming more self-confident
- learning how to affect decisions
- building a reputation as an important member of the community
- making new friends
- developing important contacts

Volunteering with Senior Citizens

Self-interest is not necessarily a narrow concept. French noble and historian Alexis de Tocqueville (1805–1859) observed that Americans often demonstrate "enlightened" self-interest as well as narrow self-interest. Many Americans sacrifice time, money, and effort to strengthen their communities and their country because they realize that the good of the whole benefits them as individuals.

How is civic participation related to advancing the common good? Working with others in civic activities frequently makes people aware of other perspectives and leads to a concern for the common good. Commitment to the common good is a central feature of classical republicanism. Concern for the common good requires individuals to see themselves as part of a larger whole and to modify their behavior to serve the needs of the whole.

Civic participation is one of the ways Americans strengthen the network of interdependence and contribute to the common good. Sometimes acting on behalf of the common good simply requires providing opportunities for others to have a voice in their community. At other times acting on behalf of the common good requires a more significant action, such as voting to increase taxes even though one receives no direct personal benefit from the increase.

Reviewing Ideas

1. **Describe** How can civic participation help develop life skills?

2. **Explain** What is the difference between narrow self-interest and enlightened self-interest?

Critical Thinking

3. **Develop** Imagine that you were asked to speak to a group of citizens about the importance of civic participation. Write a short paragraph outlining three main reasons why citizens should participate in the civic life of their communities.

Comprehension and Critical Thinking

SECTION 1 *(pp. 320–324)*

1. a. Review Key Terms For each term, write a sentence that explains its significance or meaning: discrimination, prejudice, racism.

  b. Compare and Contrast How has the ideal of civil rights compared to the reality of civil rights in United States history?

  c. Evaluate What factors do you think explain why only certain groups have endured widespread discrimination in U.S. history?

SECTION 2 *(pp. 325–332)*

2. a. Review Key Terms For each term, write a sentence that explains its significance or meaning: equal protection clause, suspect classification, de jure segregation, de facto segregation.

  b. Summarize What major civil rights laws were passed during Reconstruction, and what effects did they have?

  c. Evaluate In your view, what was the most significant aspect of the Court's ruling in the *Brown* decision?

SECTION 3 *(pp. 334–340)*

3. a. Review Key Terms For each term, write a sentence that explains its significance or meaning: civil rights movement, civil disobedience, affirmative action, reverse discrimination.

  b. Analyze How might the Civil Rights Act of 1964 be viewed as a crowning achievement of the civil rights movement?

  c. Elaborate How do you think supporters of affirmative action would justify reverse discrimination?

SECTION 4 *(pp. 342–347)*

4. a. Review Key Terms For each term, write a sentence that explains its significance or meaning: jus soli, jus sanguinis, naturalization, undocumented alien, deportation.

  b. Explain What factors caused the United States to begin to change its immigration policies in the late 1800s?

  c. Elaborate What are three factors that make illegal immigration such a difficult issue to solve?

Critical Reading

Read the passage in Section 2 that begins with the heading "The Equal Protection Clause." Then answer the questions that follow.

5. Why was the equal protection clause targeted at the states?

  A States were not upholding rights guaranteed by the Bill of Rights.

  B States refused to recognize the equal status of women.

  C States were discriminating against newly freed slaves.

  D States applied the strict scrutiny test to all claims of discrimination.

6. Why has the equal protection clause been a vital tool in the fight for civil rights?

   A because the Supreme Court has interpreted it to require the fair treatment of all groups

   B because it was so effective at protecting the civil rights of newly freed slaves

   C because it requires that people be equal in all respects

   D because it helped overturn the Fourteenth Amendment

RESPONSIBILITIES OF LEADERSHIP

7. One of the most basic civil rights, and a duty of citizenship, is **voting**. Find out what steps you would need to take to register to vote in your community, including the location of your polling place. Then gather information about the next election. What issues or candidates will be on the ballot? Share the information you gather with the class.

8. Identify and research a **civil rights issue** discussed in this chapter—for example, illegal discrimination. Locate and analyze primary and secondary sources that support an argument on this issue. Evaluate these sources and use them to construct and support your own persuasive argument on the issue.

CONNECTING TO THE CONSTITUTION

9. Take the activity above a step further. Students in your school may be eligible to register to vote. As a service learning project, work with your school to organize a voter registration drive. Contact your local chapter of the League of Women Voters for help in organizing and publicizing the event. Reflect upon the experience by writing an article for your school or local newspaper on the outcome of the drive. What constitutional principles does a voter registration drive endorse?

10. Pericles was an Athenian statesman who helped develop democracy in ancient Greece. Pericles once said "We . . . do not call a man who takes no part in public life quiet or unambitious; we call such a man useless." Do you agree or disagree with this statement? Write a short letter to Pericles explaining why you agree or disagree.

ANALYZING PRIMARY SOURCES

Photograph *This photograph was taken in 1968 in Memphis, Tennessee. In the photo, striking sanitation workers are blocked from a demonstration route by members of the National Guard.*

11. **Analyzing** Why do you think the protesters are wearing signs that say "I Am a Man"?

12. **Drawing Conclusions** What about this photograph symbolizes the struggle for civil rights?

FOCUS ON WRITING

Expository Writing *Expository writing gives information, explains why or how, or defines a process. To practice expository writing, complete the assignment below.*

Writing Topic: Civil Rights and the Law

13. **Assignment** Based on what you have read in this chapter, write a paragraph that explains how the struggle for civil rights in U.S. history has been tied to the law and to attempts to change the law.

Interactive United States Government

INTERACTIVE CHAPTER

12 Understanding Elections

Why are elections so important in the United States? Every year, thousands of elections are held in the United States—from those that elect council members for a town of 500 to those that elect the nation's president. Your school may also hold elections for student council and other organizations that require leadership.

Filling offices by election allows people to have a say in who will represent their needs and interests. Holding elections also gives citizens the power to change leadership on a regular basis. In this chapter, you will learn about election campaigns and the important role that citizens play as voters.

Table of Contents

Student Casebook Use your Student Casebook to take notes on the chapter and to complete the simulations.

President-elect Barack Obama waves to the crowd during an election night celebration in Chicago on November 4, 2008. Obama made history as the first African American to be elected president.

Election Campaigns

Student Casebook

Use your Student Casebook to take notes on the section and to complete the simulation.

Reading Focus

The purpose of election campaigns is to help the public learn about the candidates, so that voters can make an informed decision on election day. Candidates today take advantage of media exposure and polling in order to influence the voters and get elected to public office.

(CASE STUDY) **Television and the 1960 Election** Learn about the campaign that led to the election of President John F. Kennedy.

(WHAT YOU NEED TO KNOW) Learn about what is needed to run a successful election campaign and about the importance of the media and polling in today's elections.

(SIMULATION) **Running a Presidential Campaign** Use your knowledge to run an election campaign for someone running for president of the United States.

Kennedy and Nixon participate in the first televised presidential debate.

The 1960 Kennedy-Nixon debates took place in this television studio in Chicago, Illinois.

Television and the 1960 Election

In the 1960 presidential race, Vice President Richard M. Nixon ran against Senator John F. Kennedy. The first televised debates between presidential candidates took place during this campaign. This groundbreaking event changed the face of election campaigns and began a tradition that is still practiced today.

Nixon, Kennedy, and the Cold War

During the presidential election of 1960, the Cold War rivalry between the United States and the Soviet Union defined many of the campaign issues. Following an impressive string of firsts in Soviet space exploration in the 1950s, a Soviet-backed Communist government led by Fidel Castro came to power in Cuba. Americans viewed these events as a threat to the security of the United States.

During the campaign, Senator Kennedy, a Democrat from Massachusetts, used such concerns to criticize the administration of President Dwight D. Eisenhower and his vice president, Richard M. Nixon, a Republican from California. Kennedy accused Eisenhower of not being firm enough in his policies toward the Soviet Union. A loyal Nixon defended President Eisenhower's policies.

Voters perceived that they had a choice between two very different candidates. At age 43, Kennedy portrayed himself as the candidate for the future. Nixon was only 47, but his connection to Eisenhower made some people view him as a part of America's past.

The Presidential Debate

The voter perception of the candidates was strengthened by the nation's first televised presidential debate on September 26, 1960.

Kennedy, tanned from campaigning in California, looked fit and well-rested in a dark suit. In comparison, Nixon, who chose a gray suit and refused the makeup that people usually wear on camera, looked pale and tired from a long campaign swing through 25 states.

According to polls taken afterward, most people who listened to the debate on the radio thought that Nixon had won. But most television viewers gave Kennedy the victory. This reaction showed that in the age of television, how a candidate looks can sometimes make a greater impression than what he or she says.

The Debate's Aftermath

The presidential election that followed was one of the closest in U.S. history. Kennedy won by fewer than 120,000 votes, out of nearly 69 million cast. Although some historians question how much the debate affected the final outcome, political scholars agree that the influence of television on elections cannot be disputed.

Seeing the candidates and how they handle themselves on television has a great effect on voters. Election campaigns strengthen the notion that appearances matter, and the way a person presents himself or herself can leave a strong impression. Many voters also warm to candidates to whom they can relate, and television plays a key role in showing a candidate's personality.

Today voters gain a great deal of their knowledge of the candidates from television. Candidates are well aware of this fact and use it to their advantage whenever possible.

What Do You Think?

1. Why do you think Kennedy tried to link Nixon to Eisenhower?
2. Did the debate benefit Kennedy's campaign strategy? Why or why not?
3. Do you think television has a positive or a negative influence on election campaigns? Explain.

Campaign Planning

Election campaigns are an important part of the electoral process at every level of government. A campaign helps voters get to know the candidates and informs the public about each party's **platform**—the party's stand on important issues and the party's general principles. When a candidate is backed by a political party, the candidate's views usually coincide with the platform of that party.

Campaign Staff

Major election campaigns today have formal organizational structures. A variety of experts play significant roles in campaigns.

The size and salaries of a campaign staff vary from campaign to campaign. In presidential campaigns some positions, like campaign manager, are occupied by a full-time staffer who is paid for his or her work. In smaller campaigns, some or all of the jobs may be filled by unpaid volunteers. In some cases, campaign organizations hire part-time consultants to carry out key campaign functions. The members of a campaign staff include a campaign manager, finance chair, pollster, media coordinator, scheduler, issue advisers, and other staff, such as a treasurer, press secretary, and volunteers.

Campaign Manager The campaign manager coordinates and oversees the entire campaign. He or she is responsible for

- developing and executing the campaign plan

- supervising the other key staffers and resolving any differences that develop among the staff

- presenting any ideas or changes to the candidate for approval

The campaign manager is usually closer to the candidate than any other staffer. For that reason, the individual who fills this post is often a trusted adviser or a personal friend of the candidate.

Finance Chair The person in charge of raising money to pay for the campaign is called the finance chair. He or she is responsible for putting together and carrying out the campaign's fund-raising plan. This plan will likely include getting supporters to hold fund-raising events as well as asking political action committees (PACs) to contribute to the candidate's campaign.

Pollster The campaign's strategy is planned and monitored mainly according to polling results. For this reason, large campaign staffs often include a full-time polling expert, or pollster. This person obtains information on voters and their opinions by creating and

Key Terms

platform
focus group
swing states
stump speech
negative campaigning
sound bite
demographic

REAL-WORLD EXAMPLE

CASE STUDY LINK

Managing Victory Senator Kennedy had many trusted advisers and reliable staff on his campaign team during the 1960 campaign. One such person was Lawrence O'Brien, a key player in Kennedy's narrow victory over Nixon. O'Brien campaigned on behalf of Senator Kennedy in key states, convincing voters that Kennedy's Catholic faith would not conflict with his duties as president. His work helped win Kennedy the election. Following the election, O'Brien served as Kennedy's liaison to Congress.

Applying Information Why might a campaign staffer become an adviser to a president he or she helped win that office?

The Campaign Team

The campaign staff are key to a successful election campaign. The candidate relies on these people to help manage the campaign and make important decisions.

Candidate

Campaign Manager
Oversees all aspects of the campaign and campaign staff

Scheduler
Manages the candidate's time

Pollster
Creates and conducts polls for the campaign

Issue Advisers
Advises the candidate on important issues

Finance Chair
Creates and carries out the fund-raising plan

Media Coordinator
Gets the candidate's message out to the voters

Volunteer Coordinator
Oversees campaign volunteers

Treasurer
Handles the money that the campaign raises and reports the money spent

Press Secretary
Monitors media coverage and writes campaign press releases

Volunteers
Assists with fund-raising, polling, and other campaign-related areas

conducting scientific polls for the campaign. Even small campaigns often conduct polls. A campaign may also choose to hire an independent polling company to conduct its polls.

Media Coordinator The media coordinator is responsible for getting the candidate's message to the greatest number of potential supporters in the most effective ways possible. The media coordinator also handles paid advertising for the candidate as well as free advertising through media coverage of speeches, rallies, and any nonpolitical events that the candidate might attend.

Scheduler The job of the scheduler is to manage the candidate's time in ways that meet the strategy and goals of the campaign. Tasks include arranging for the candidate to get from place to place, handling invitations from groups that request the candidate to appear, and maintaining contact with persons who plan campaign events that require an appearance by the candidate.

Since about half of a candidate's time is spent raising money, the scheduler must work closely with the finance chair to make sure that the candidate attends fund-raising events during the campaign.

The Brain Trust Presidential candidates throughout the years have relied on issue advisers to help steer their campaigns. For example, in 1932 when Franklin D. Roosevelt first ran for president, the nation was in the middle of the Great Depression. Roosevelt asked some professors and other experts in economics and welfare policy to develop a strategy for combating the Depression. The press referred to these advisers as the Brain Trust. Roosevelt presented their ideas to the nation during the campaign. Some of those ideas later formed the basis of President Roosevelt's New Deal.

Applying Information What types of issue advisers would a presidential candidate need today?

The scheduler also works with the media coordinator to ensure that the candidate is available for interviews, press conferences, and other media activities.

▶ **Issue Advisers** Experts in certain fields who advise the candidate on various campaign issues are known as issue advisers. Their main function is to educate the candidate and write position papers that present the campaign's point of view on each issue. This group may include labor and business leaders, representatives of ethnic groups, religious leaders, and so on. Many are professors or other scholars who have spent years studying a particular issue.

Other Campaign Staff Each campaign has a treasurer to handle the funds it raises and spends. In addition, the treasurer files the financial disclosure reports required by state and federal election laws. Most campaigns also have a volunteer coordinator who recruits and manages campaign volunteers. The campaign's press secretary writes press releases for the media and monitors media coverage of the campaign. A campaign may also have a speech writer who writes and reviews the candidate's various speeches.

Campaign Strategy

Once a candidate has decided to run, the first two questions his or her staff must ask are how many votes will it take to win the election and where the candidate is likely to receive the most votes. The answers to these questions guide the entire campaign. They help determine to whom the campaign will direct the candidate's message, what that message will be, and how it will be delivered.

Identifying Supporters Many candidates conduct polls to determine where their support is greatest. This information helps to shape the entire course of the campaign—from the issues emphasized and how campaign funds are raised and spent, to places the candidate

Campaign Volunteers
Campaign volunteers are the backbone of a successful campaign. Volunteers help get information to voters in areas that candidates are unable to visit themselves.

visits during the campaign and what he or she says on the campaign trail. Contrary to popular belief, most campaigns make minimal effort to simply change voters' minds. Instead, they concentrate on getting the votes of people who either like the candidate or who are undecided.

Targeting the Message Once potential supporters have been identified, the campaign must find out what issues are most important to these supporters. In addition to polling, campaign staffers use focus groups to identify these issues. A **focus group** is a small gathering of people whose response to something is studied and used to predict the response of a larger population. Campaigns hire experts to select and lead focus groups and to discuss the participants' views on certain issues. The expert may also have the participants discuss how they feel about the candidate and his or her positions on the issues. The information gathered from focus groups can be very useful in shaping the campaign's message.

Once the message is determined, it is then delivered through various types of advertising and by the candidate through speeches, interviews, and other appearances. A 30-second television advertisement or a 10-minute speech, though, cannot present the candidate's views on all the issues. Therefore, the information in these ads and speeches is usually focused on or tailored to a specific group of voters. This strategy is known as targeting the message.

Packaging Candidates Critics often question the value of today's campaigns. Modern campaign organizations will routinely bring in experts to manage a candidate's image, message, and coverage by the news media. The effect, critics claim, is candidates who are "packaged" to fit what voters want and whose views may be more determined by poll results than by the candidate's own beliefs. As a result of such packaging, some people wonder if campaigns serve more to educate voters or to manipulate them. John F. Kennedy is a good example of a candidate who was "packaged" for voters. Because he and his family were viewed as charming and glamorous, his presidential campaign utilized this "Kennedy style" in order to gain supporters.

READING CHECK **Identifying Supporting Details** How do campaign organizations determine which issues and messages to emphasize?

Conducting a Campaign

Once a campaign strategy has been created, it is the job of the campaign team to carry it out. At the same time, both the candidate and the staff must be ready to adapt to any developments that may require the campaign strategy to <u>evolve</u>.

Election Platforms A political party's platform helps shape a candidate's message. Candidates running for office at all levels of government use their party's platform as a guide for their campaign.
Visit **thinkcentral.com** to begin a Webquest on political party platforms and the candidates running for office in your state or local government.

thinkcentral.com
KEYWORD: SGO ELE

ACADEMIC VOCABULARY

evolve change

REAL-WORLD
EXAMPLE

Choosing the Campaign Trail In the 2004 presidential election, Democratic candidate John Kerry paid little attention to Texas, the state with the second-largest number of electoral votes. Not only was Texas the home state of Kerry's opponent, President George W. Bush, but no Democratic candidate had won its electoral votes since 1976. In 2004 Kerry beat Bush in only 16 of the state's 254 counties, while Bush pulled 61 percent of the total vote.

Applying Information Do you think Kerry was right to not campaign heavily in Texas? Explain your answer.

▶ On the Campaign Trail

A campaign devotes most of its attention to places where the greatest number of potential votes exists. In presidential campaigns a candidate can spend a large amount of time and money in states that have the greatest number of electoral votes, like California. Sometimes, though, a campaign will avoid a populous state where support for the opponent is strong. The candidate will instead focus on states where he or she has a better chance of winning. States where support for each candidate is about equal, or **swing states**, may also experience intense campaigning because they are seen as being "up for grabs" by any candidate.

The candidate's stand on certain issues may also influence where he or she campaigns the hardest. For example, candidates with poor records on environmental issues may spend less time in places where these issues are important. And, when their campaign does bring them to these places, they may emphasize other aspects of their platform that will resonate more with people in these areas.

Tackling the Issues Throughout their campaigns, candidates are required to make speeches. Most candidates have a **stump speech**, or a standard speech that they give during the campaign. In this speech the candidate shares his or her views on the basic issues.

Candidates also use other speeches that serve a specific function for the campaign. Some of these speeches are meant to provoke listeners to action. Others address one particular issue and are given to groups who have a special interest in that issue. Candidates' speeches are usually short—rarely more than 20 minutes at the most. Candidates tend to speak in short sentences since no candidate wants to bore, confuse, or "lose" his or her audience. Speeches often use techniques to keep listeners' attention and help the audience identify the key points of the candidate's speech.

In addition, many campaigns use slogans to help deliver their message. A slogan is a short phrase designed to summarize the campaign's overall message and to give people a simple reason to vote for the candidate. In 1960, for example, with tensions growing between the United States and the Soviet Union, the campaign of Richard Nixon and his running mate, Henry Cabot Lodge, adopted the slogan "They understand what peace demands."

Negative Campaigning While designing their campaign strategy, candidates and their staffs may choose to run a campaign that does not focus so much on the candidate's platform as it does on the weaknesses of his or her opponent. In recent years, voter complaints about the mean-spirited nature of election campaigns have grown. However, **negative campaigning**—attacking the opponent during a campaign—is very common. Studies have even shown that "going negative" actually energizes the attacker's supporters and decreases support for his or her opponent.

WEBQUEST

The Impact of Campaign Ads Since the 1952 election, television has played a major role in presidential campaigns. Negative campaigning has increased with the use of TV. Two examples are shown here. In 1988 the George H. W. Bush campaign attacked opponent Michael Dukakis's stance on defense with an ad showing Dukakis riding in a tank. In 1964 the Lyndon Johnson campaign ran the "Daisy Girl" ad implying that Johnson's opponent, Barry Goldwater, would lead the nation into nuclear war. Visit **thinkcentral.com** to begin a Webquest on TV ads from presidential elections and how ads have changed over the years.

THINK central Webquest
thinkcentral.com
KEYWORD: SGO ELE

George H. W. Bush's 1988 "Dukakis in a tank" campaign ad

Another benefit of negative campaigning is that the opponent must take time to respond to the attack, which takes attention away from his or her original campaign message. At the same time, candidates who use negative campaigning as their main campaign strategy may not spend as much time on their own positions.

Campaigns and the Media

As discussed in Chapter 9, a person's age is often a good indicator of which form of media he or she uses to get news and information. Using this knowledge, a campaign's media coordinator must determine the types of voters the candidate should be trying to reach and must choose the best media form with which to reach them. For example, a candidate running for the House of Representatives in a district with an older population will probably focus more on television and print media than on the Internet, which often carries more appeal with younger voters.

Broadcast Media Because television is the main source of information for voters of all ages, most campaigns put as many ads on TV as they can afford. Campaigns also try to get the candidate on television talk shows and make him or her available for televised interviews. Since the election of 1960, presidential candidates have had to debate on national television, and many voters learn about the candidates from these debates.

Another way campaigns use television is by creating photo opportunities. Photo opportunities are media events the campaign arranges to show the candidate in a favorable manner, such as visiting wounded soldiers in a military hospital. Campaigns also offer candidates as guests on radio talk shows. Radio is a good way to reach the 30-to-64 age group. In addition, radio ads help get the candidate's message out. Radio ads probably reach fewer people than those on television, but they cost much less than TV ads.

Lyndon Johnson's 1964 "Daisy Girl" campaign ad

Sound Bites

Sound bites can sometimes have a negative effect on a candidate's campaign. They can also be positive. In some instances, the sound bite is noteworthy for its humor or its colorful jab at an opponent. Here are some memorable sound bites from past elections.

"There you go again."
Ronald Reagan, critical remark to President Jimmy Carter during their 1980 presidential debate

"Senator, you are no Jack Kennedy."
Lloyd Bentsen, 1988 vice presidential debate in which opponent Dan Quayle compared his own congressional service to that of John F. Kennedy (sometimes called Jack)

"Read my lips: no new taxes."
George H. W. Bush, 1988 Republican National Convention

"It's the economy, stupid."
Slogan of Bill Clinton's 1992 presidential campaign

"Yeeeahhhhhh!"
Howard Dean, 2004 campaign speech

A candidate's media coordinator and other staff, however, do not always get to control how a candidate is portrayed by the media. On television news, viewers often receive a candidate's message in a **sound bite**, a very brief segment of a speech or statement. In many cases, political sound bites have a great influence on the public's opinion of that candidate.

For example, in 2004 Howard Dean, a Democratic presidential-nominee candidate, let out a scream at a campaign event. This moment was shown on television 633 times in the four days following the event and repeated over the radio countless times. It is possible that Dean's overenthusiastic delivery marked the collapse of his campaign, as it portrayed him in a bad light to many voters.

Print Media Newspapers and magazines are especially effective at reaching voters over the age of 50. In the very close 2000 presidential race, 90 percent of all newspaper readers cast a ballot. Many campaigns use newspaper ads to clarify the candidate's stand on the issues and to compare the candidate to his or her opponent. Journalists may also write influential editorials on the candidates and their campaigns. Because of the format, print media are able to give more detailed information than broadcast media.

The Internet In recent years, the Internet has become a major media form in election campaigns. Political blogs, online editions of newspapers and magazines, and online TV news coverage are all key sources of information, especially for voters younger than 50.

Most candidates today have Web sites, which allow candidates to provide information about themselves and their views without the time, space, or editorial controls that exist in broadcast and print media. Candidates write Web logs, or blogs, on their own Web sites as well as on popular political Web sites. A candidate's Web site can also broadcast the campaign's own videos of campaign events. It can deliver the campaign's message directly to voters who live in areas where the candidate will not be making personal appearances.

Polls and Polling

As discussed earlier, polls can have a great influence on campaigns. Polls taken early in the campaign, for example, can reveal areas where support for the candidate is weak. The campaign will then target those areas for heavy advertising or personal appearances by the candidate. Or polls may suggest that a particular **demographic**—a population group defined by a specific characteristic or set of characteristics—might support the candidate. The campaign can then be geared toward attracting these voters.

During a campaign, polling can detect changes in voter attitudes. A presidential candidate's schedule may be changed if, for example, polls show that voter support in an important state is declining or wavering. Also, the candidate's positions on certain issues may be adjusted if polls show that public opinion is changing.

Polls can also influence voter behavior. Some voters who are undecided may choose to vote for the candidate the polls say is ahead, because he or she is the candidate the public seems to want.

READING CHECK **Identifying the Main Idea** What are some of the major decisions that candidates and their staffs have to make when deciding what kind of election campaign they want to run?

REAL-WORLD EXAMPLE

Targeting Demographics In the 1996 presidential election, campaigns targeted a demographic that pollsters labeled the Soccer Moms: upper-middle-class suburban mothers. In 2004, pollsters targeted so-called NASCAR Dads: small-town and rural white men, especially in the South, to whom family, religion, and patriotism were important ideals. Targeting this demographic proved helpful to Republican candidates in the South, as exit polls after the 2004 election showed that 70 percent of this demographic voted for President Bush.

Applying Information How does targeting a demographic help a campaign?

Section 1 Assessment

THINK central Online Quiz

thinkcentral.com
KEYWORD: SGO ELE HP

Reviewing Ideas and Terms

1. **a. Identify** What are five major staff positions in a candidate's campaign organization?
   b. Explain Why is identifying the candidate's supporters so important to campaign strategy?
   c. Rate Do you agree that the media coordinator is the most important staff member in an election campaign? Explain why or why not.

2. **a. Describe** What is the meaning of the term **demographic**?
   b. Summarize How do candidates use the Internet during election campaigns?
   c. Evaluate What do you think about judging a candidate based on a **sound bite**? Should the media take better care to not judge a candidate based on a sound bite? Explain your answer.

Critical Thinking

3. **Elaborate** What is your opinion of negative campaigning and the effects it has on an election?

CASE STUDY LINK You answered the following questions at the end of the Case Study. Now that you have completed Section 1, think about and answer the questions again. Then compare your answers with your earlier responses. Are your answers the same, or are they different?

4. Why do you think Kennedy tried to link Nixon to Eisenhower?

5. Did the debate benefit Kennedy's campaign strategy? Why or why not?

6. Do you think television has a positive or a negative influence on election campaigns? Explain.

SIMULATION

Running a Presidential Campaign

Who will win the presidential election?

Student Casebook

Use your Student Casebook to complete the simulation.

In order to run smoothly and successfully, election campaigns depend on the hard work and expertise of many different people. Using what you have learned in Section 1, complete the simulation to plan a campaign that will elect the next president of the United States.

Roles

- Presidential candidate Charles Smith
- Presidential candidate Nancy Carlson
- Campaign manager (one for each campaign)
- Finance chair (one for each campaign)
- Pollster (one for each campaign)
- Media coordinator (one for each campaign)
- Volunteers (three for each campaign)
- Voters of varying demographics

❶ The Situation

Democrat Ohio senator Charles Smith and Republican Texas senator Nancy Carlson each gained their party's nomination for president at the national conventions in July. Now they must work with their campaign staffs in order to win the general election.

Polls show that the Social Security system is the main issue on voters' minds. The system has been in crisis for years, and widespread disagreement over how to reform it exists among the American public and in Congress. The system will run out of money soon unless drastic action is taken during the next president's term. However, Americans are divided over whether to "save" Social Security by raising the Social Security tax (called FICA) or by cutting benefits to retirees.

Key Facts

- More than 12 percent of Americans are older than 65. Nearly all of these people are retired. Many depend on the monthly Social Security checks they get from the government to make ends meet.

- In the past, Smith has supported a proposal in Congress to double the FICA tax to 30 percent. Carlson, on the other hand, once backed a proposal to cut monthly Social Security benefits by half.

- Many labor unions and trade associations oppose increases in FICA to save Social Security. The American Association of Retired Persons (AARP), one of the nation's largest and most powerful interest groups, opposes cutting retirees' benefits—the proposal once favored by Carlson.

- Each campaign plans to raise and spend a total of $100 million.

- There are 100 days remaining until the November election.

The Electoral College

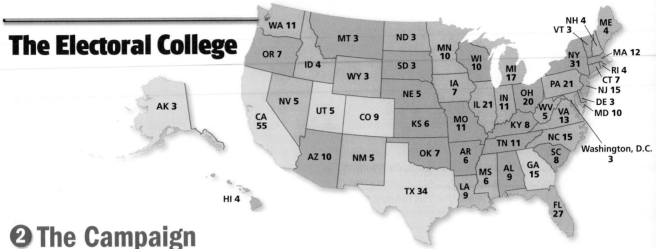

Percent of Population Age 65 and Over

	Under 11%
	11%–12.5%
	12.6%–14%
	Over 14%
11	Number of Electors

❷ The Campaign

The voters must decide for which candidate they will vote. First, however, the candidates and their campaign staffs must develop and implement a strategy that will gain the support needed to win.

- Each **candidate** will write and deliver a stump speech as well as a speech that addresses the Social Security issue and that targets a specific demographic.

- The **candidates** will debate each other on their positions on Social Security.

- The **campaign managers** will develop the campaign's slogan and coordinate the other tasks to make sure the campaign is carrying out its strategy and speaking with a unified voice.

- The **finance chairs** will decide where and how to raise the money needed and how it will be spent. They will propose a budget and will develop targeted fund-raising letters to be sent to selected demographics, geographic areas, and groups.

- The **pollsters** will develop a poll to assess how voters feel about the Social Security issue and the candidates' record on it. They will then analyze the poll results and report them to the staff.

- The **media managers** will decide which states each candidate will visit, how much time he or she will spend there, and how and where to spend the campaign's advertising budget.

- **Volunteers** will conduct the pollsters' poll with the voters, create campaign brochures, and assist the campaign staffers.

- Each **voter** will decide what demographic he or she represents, follow the campaigns of each candidate, cast his or her vote, and explain why he or she made that decision.

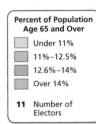

FICA Facts

- The FICA tax is 15 percent of each worker's earnings.

- Half of FICA is paid by the worker and half by his or her employer.

- The tax on current workers' earnings pays the benefits of current retirees.

❸ Debriefing

After the votes have been tallied, discuss ways in which the campaigns succeeded and areas where they could have been improved. Then write a report assessing how well these campaigns applied the knowledge of campaigning gained from Section 1.

Campaign Funding and Political Action Committees

Reading Focus

Money plays a major role in election campaigns. Candidates and their staff must carefully decide where the campaign will get money and how it will use this money.

CASE STUDY **Controversies over Campaign Funding** Learn about two politicians who became involved in campaign-funding controversies.

WHAT YOU NEED TO KNOW Learn about the funding that goes into an election campaign and the role that political action committees play in campaign funding.

SIMULATION **Deciding to Back a Candidate** Use your knowledge to decide if a political action committee should give funds to a candidate's election campaign.

Student Casebook

Use your Student Casebook to take notes on the section and to complete the simulation.

"IT TAKES A VILLAGE TO RAISE A PRESIDENTIAL CANDIDATE...

EVERYBODY OUT! WE NEED YOUR VILLAGE!

caglecartoons.com

This cartoon comments on the importance of money in election campaigns.

Controversies over Campaign Funding

In the early to mid-2000s, two members of Congress—one from Ohio and one from Texas—faced serious charges of campaign finance violations. Although both men denied the charges, their cases reveal the difficulties that can arise in campaign-funding operations and the need for laws to control election campaign contributions and spending.

James Traficant

James Traficant, a Democrat from Ohio, served in the House of Representatives from 1985 to 2002. A former star football player at the University of Pittsburgh, he was sheriff of Ohio's Mahoning County from 1981 to 1985.

As sheriff, Traficant encountered his first brush with accusations of federal corruption. In 1983 he was charged with racketeering—a system of organized crime that extorts money from businesses through illegal means—and accepting bribes. Although he was not a lawyer, Traficant represented himself at the trial. He won the case and was acquitted of all charges. He was elected to Congress in 1984.

While in the House, Traficant cast himself as a "man of the people" and a "regular guy." He became widely known for his independent and eccentric style. His unruly gray toupee and his colorful plaid suits made him a recognizable figure on Capitol Hill.

When Traficant made a speech in the House, many people tuned in to C-SPAN to watch his often controversial remarks. One regular remark was "Beam me up," a phrase from the show *Star Trek*. Traficant used the phrase to show his disapproval of and disgust for some government action. Many in his district loved him. He was reelected eight times without serious opposition.

In early 2002 Traficant was charged with federal corruption. These charges included taking funds donated to his campaigns and spending them for his personal use. Once again, Traficant represented himself at the trial. He strongly denied all charges of wrongdoing but was convicted on 10 felony counts, including bribery and tax evasion. He was sentenced to eight years in federal prison.

In July 2002 the House voted 420–1 to expel Traficant. He showed his defiance by seeking reelection. From his prison cell, Traficant ran for election as an independent candidate. Still recognizable in his former district, he received 15 percent of the vote.

James Traficant delivers his closing statement to the House ethics committee in 2002.

Tom DeLay

Tom DeLay served in the House of Representatives from 1985 to 2006. A Houston-area businessman, DeLay's political career began in 1978 when he was elected to the Texas state legislature as a Republican.

In 1984 DeLay was elected to the House of Representatives and rapidly rose to a position of leadership among House Republicans. His strict enforcement of party discipline earned him the nickname the Hammer. DeLay also formed a series of political action committees (PACs). One such committee, Texans for a Republican Majority (TRMPAC), was created to raise money for Republican candidates in Texas. Another DeLay PAC, Americans for a Republican Majority (ARMPAC), gave nearly $1 million to Republican congressional candidates in 2004.

Such success in raising money ultimately contributed to DeLay's downfall. Financial donations and other gifts from powerful Washington lobbyist Jack Abramoff focused attention on DeLay in 2005. Abramoff and several other lobbyists were indicted for crimes related to Abramoff's lobbying activities. Abramoff and one former member of DeLay's staff pleaded guilty. Abramoff then agreed to help with the government's investigation into the illegal activities of other members of Congress.

In May 2005, TRMPAC was found guilty of not reporting all the money it had raised. In September TRMPAC and DeLay himself were indicted in Texas for making illegal campaign contributions. Both were charged with illegally moving corporate donations from the National Republican Party to Republican candidates in Texas. All corporate contributions to state campaigns are illegal in Texas.

After being indicted on criminal charges of violating campaign finance laws, DeLay stepped down from his post as House majority leader. In January 2006, after weeks of pressure from fellow Republicans, DeLay resigned from the House of Representatives.

Campaign-Funding Challenges

The cases of Traficant and DeLay are just two examples of the problems that can arise with campaign funding. These cases show the need to regulate campaign spending in order to make sure that the funds candidates raise during their campaigns are used for their intended purpose.

Tom DeLay resigned from the House of Representatives after being charged with campaign-funding violations.

What Do You Think?

1. Should Traficant have been expelled from the House? Explain.
2. Was it right for House members to pressure DeLay to resign? Explain your answer.
3. Should concealing the source of any campaign contribution be illegal? Explain.

Funding Election Campaigns

Election campaigns can be very expensive. Running for mayor or city council in even a medium-sized city can require tens of thousands of dollars. Races for a state legislative seat or a statewide office often cost significantly more.

The candidate who won James Traficant's House seat in 2002 spent nearly $550,000 to do so. Tom DeLay's final House race in 2004 cost more than $3 million. Senate races involve even greater sums. Of the 33 Senate seats decided in 2006, spending in 10 different campaigns exceeded $27 million each. Estimates of total spending in the 2008 presidential election, including the primary races, come close to $1 billion.

Where the Money Comes From

The huge sums that candidates spend while running for office come from four main sources:

- **Individual donations** Individual Americans make contributions to the candidate or the candidate's political party.

- **Contributions by PACs** Political action committees (PACs) make contributions to the candidate or the candidate's party.

- **Political party contributions** The candidate's political party makes contributions to the candidate.

- **Public funding for presidential campaigns** Presidential candidates may receive public funds provided by the government.

The U.S. system of funding elections has fewer limits than any other major Western democracy. Germany, France, and the United Kingdom all put limits on what candidates may spend on campaigns. While U.S. election laws limit the amount that an individual or group may contribute, there are no limits on what a candidate may spend.

Critics of campaign funding complain that it makes money too important to campaigns. The Supreme Court has ruled, though, that limiting campaign spending is a restriction on freedom of speech.

Individual Donations The largest source of contributions to election campaigns comes from individual donations. These donations can build to great amounts over the course of a campaign. Because campaign finance laws require candidates, parties, and PACs to report only donations of $200 or more, there is no way of knowing how many small donations are given to a candidate's campaign.

Key Terms

Federal Election Commission
party-building activities
issue ads
leadership PACs
527 group

The Rise in Campaign Spending In recent years, the amount of money that candidates spend on both national and state elections has grown significantly.

Visit **thinkcentral.com** to begin a Webquest on the increase in spending for national and state elections and the effect that this increase has on election campaigns.

thinkcentral.com
KEYWORD: SGO ELE

TOTAL CAMPAIGN CONTRIBUTIONS IN THE 2006 CONGRESSIONAL ELECTION

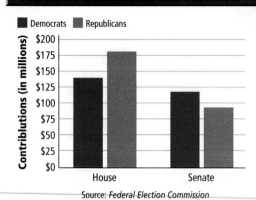

■ Democrats ■ Republicans

Source: *Federal Election Commission*

Skills FOCUS INTERPRETING GRAPHS

Which group had the largest amount of contributions during the 2006 congressional election? What was that contribution amount?

Senator Robert Menendez gives out autographed bowling pins at a campaign fund-raiser.

Candidates seek individual donations in a variety of ways. They request contributions by mailing letters to possible supporters or ask for donations on their Web sites. A candidate may choose to host a fund-raiser to obtain more individual donations. Additionally, candidates may contribute some of their own personal money to their campaigns.

Contributions by PACs After individual donations, PACs are the most important source of campaign funding. In the 2006 House and Senate races, about 25 percent of the money raised came from PACs. This figure compares to about 60 percent that came from individuals' donations. Some candidates receive more PAC money than others, however. For example, in DeLay's final race in 2004, almost half of his campaign funds came from PACs. The Democrat elected to Traficant's seat in 2002 got about 70 percent of his money from PACs.

Political Party Contributions A candidate may also receive funding from the political party that he or she represents. Committees that represent a political party and that party's interests are allowed to contribute money directly to a candidate's campaign. However, campaign finance laws limit how much the parties may contribute.

Public Funding Presidential candidates may also receive money from the federal government to help finance their campaigns. Public funding comes from individuals who check a box on their income tax return that allows the government to use $3 of their taxes for this purpose. This money is only available to qualified presidential candidates and not to those running for state or local office.

Public funding is voluntary for both the taxpayers and the candidates. To qualify, candidates must agree to certain limits on the other money they raise and spend. In the past, most candidates have refused public funding in their primary campaigns so that they would not have to limit their other fund-raising, which had brought in the largest amount of money at that point in the campaign. In the 2008 general election, Barack Obama became the first major party candidate to refuse public funds.

Campaign Finance Laws

Critics of election campaigns have long charged that a campaign's dependence on money exposes democracy to corruption. They note that candidates must either be rich themselves or be indebted to interest groups and wealthy donors. These criticisms have lead to major reforms in campaign finance.

Early Campaign Finance Reform The first serious attempt to decrease the connection between "big money" and election politics took place in 1907, when Congress banned corporations and national banks from making campaign contributions. In the 1940s the ban was extended to include contributions from labor unions. These restrictions were strengthened in 1971 when Congress passed the Federal Election Campaign Act (FECA). The FECA requires all candidates, PACs, and political parties to report contributions they receive that exceed a specified amount. The report must list the name, address, and occupation or business of each contributor.

- setting limits on campaign contributions by individuals, political parties, and PACs

- creating the system of public funding for presidential elections

- creating the **Federal Election Commission** (FEC) to enforce the FECA and administer the public-funding program

FECA Amendments In 1974 Congress strengthened the FECA by Congress amended the FECA again in 1976 and 1979. The 1979 changes allowed parties to spend unlimited sums of money on activities that did not support specific candidates. Such activities are known as **party-building activities**. Examples of party-building activities include voter registration drives, party bumper stickers, and television ads supporting the party's principles.

Soft Money Partly because of the easing of restrictions on party-building activities, a new type of donation was created—soft money. As discussed in Chapter 9, since soft money is not given directly to specific candidates, it is not regulated by the FEC. As a result, there is no limit to the amount of soft money a donor may contribute.

ACADEMIC VOCABULARY

regulate to keep under the control of

THE HISTORY OF CAMPAIGN FINANCE LAWS

QUICK FACTS

YEAR	LAW	PROVISIONS
1907	Tillman Act	Forbade corporations and banks from contributing to election campaigns
1947	Taft-Hartley Act	Banned unions from making campaign contributions
1971	Federal Election Campaign Act (FECA)	Required political campaigns to report all individual contributions over a certain amount of money
1974	FECA Amendments	Set limits on campaign contributions; created system of public funding for presidential elections; created the Federal Election Commission (FEC)
1976	FECA Amendment	Eliminated limits on campaign contributions except for presidential candidates who accept public funding
1979	FECA Amendment	Allowed political parties to spend unlimited amounts of money on party-building activities
2002	Bipartisan Campaign Reform Act (BCRA)	Banned soft-money contributions for political party ads and regulated how much interest groups could spend on issue ads

Some donors make soft-money contributions of hundreds of thousands of dollars. A great deal of this money comes directly from corporations, which federal law prohibits from contributing to candidates. Both major political parties use soft money to make issue ads. **Issue ads** are advertisements that support or oppose candidates' views without specifically calling for their election or defeat. In addition, paying for legitimate party-building activities with soft money frees up other funds to be used for direct support of candidates.

RESPONSIBILITIES OF LEADERSHIP

Some of the strongest leadership in American politics has appeared when Democrats and Republicans work together. The McCain-Feingold Campaign Reform Act (also known as the BCRA) is one such example.

Bipartisan Campaign Reform Act Between 1996 and 2002, the Democratic and Republican parties raised about $1.5 billion in soft money, much of which was spent on issue ads in election campaigns. In response to this massive use of soft money, Congress passed the Bipartisan Campaign Reform Act (BCRA) in 2002. The BCRA banned soft-money contributions to political parties for advertising. It also limited the ability of interest groups to air issue ads of their own. Opponents of these changes challenged the BCRA, but the Supreme Court upheld the law's major provisions.

READING CHECK **Making Generalizations** What is the largest source of money for most candidates' campaigns?

Interest Groups and Election Campaigns

In Chapter 9 you read about interest groups and their general role in politics and government. Their function in the election process is quite different, mainly because of the limits that federal election laws put on their direct involvement in campaigns. Political action committees arose out of interest groups' desire to avoid such limitations. However, as new laws and limits were put in place—such as the BCRA—new types of groups and new practices arose to take advantage of loopholes found in such laws.

Political Action Committees

Political action committees (PACs) are organizations that interest or other groups create to raise and donate money to candidates and political parties. The first PACs were formed by labor unions in the 1940s to get around the Taft-Hartley Act, which banned unions from making campaign contributions. Today, interest groups of every type have formed PACs. Not all interest groups have a PAC, but a large number do.

How PACs Function A PAC collects donations from members of an interest group or from others who support the PAC's cause. The PAC then distributes these funds to political parties, candidates, or other PACs that it supports. Donations to a national PAC are limited to $5,000 per donor per year. But many states place no limits on donations to, or contributions by, PACs organized in that particular state. Nor do many states limit the transfer of money from one PAC to another.

Leadership PACs In recent years, officeholders have formed **leadership PACs**, which are separate from the officeholder's campaign organization. Leadership PACs are groups that take advanatge of a loophole in campaign finance law, which allows them to raise unlimited sums of money. Officeholders can then use their leadership PACs to donate to other candidates' campaigns.

Influence of PACs Supporters of PACs claim that they give interest groups and their members a greater voice in politics than they would have if PACs did not exist. Political observers agree but question whether PAC money gives special interests undue influence on candidates who become officeholders. A $5,000 contribution from a PAC may weigh much more heavily on an elected official than the small contributions of many individual voters. Many critics believe this situation gives interest groups too much power. But as long as campaigns remain costly, PACs—and the groups they represent—will play an important role in campaign financing.

REAL - WORLD EXAMPLE
CASE STUDY LINK

Leadership PACs More than half of the 535 members of the House and Senate had a leadership PAC in 2006. Tom DeLay's ARMPAC and TRMPAC are both examples of leadership PACs. The Freedom Project of Representative John Boehner (R, Ohio) gave more than $1 million to Republican candidates in 2006. Representative Steny Hoyer's (D, Maryland) AmeriPAC dispensed $916,000. In all, 19 leadership PACs—14 Republican and 5 Democrat—gave at least $500,000 during the 2006 campaign.

Applying Information Do you think that leadership PACs should be allowed to contribute to a candidate's campaign? Why or why not?

THINK central **Online Link**

thinkcentral.com
KEYWORD: SGO ELE

Elections and 527 Groups

The limitations the BCRA put on soft money and issue ads have caused the growth of another type of group, known as the 527 group. A **527 group** is a tax-exempt organization created to influence an election. These organizations are named for a section of the U.S. tax code that allows certain kinds of groups to pay no taxes. A 527 group tries to influence voters' opinions about candidates or issues without directly calling for a candidate's election or defeat.

If a 527 group is connected to a political party or a PAC, it must obey campaign finance laws. But 527s that operate independently and do not make donations to a candidate or party are not bound by these restrictions. These groups can raise and spend unlimited sums of money without disclosing their income, spending, or contributors to the FEC.

Controversies over 527 Groups The existence of 527s came to the public's attention in the 2004 presidential election. Issue ads paid for by a group called the Swift Boat Veterans for Truth attacked Democratic presidential candidate John Kerry's claims of Vietnam War service. Another 527 group called MoveOn.org posted on its Web site an ad that compared President George W. Bush, the Republican candidate, to Adolf Hitler. Both ad campaigns aroused great controversy and, even though they were not explicitly endorsed by either candidate, accusations were made by both campaigns that their opponent supported the ads.

Impact of 527 Groups During the 2004 presidential campaign, 527 groups spent millions of dollars on issue ads. Nearly all of these ads were direct attacks on candidates. Political observers blame 527 groups for increasing the already negative tone of many election campaigns. These critics also question the wisdom of allowing small groups of wealthy persons or companies to buy influence over voters with such large, unregulated contributions. Supporters of 527s respond that the groups promote freedom of speech. They claim that limiting contributions to 527 groups violates donors' right to express their views.

Campaign Reform and the Media

Among its other reforms, the BCRA tightened requirements on campaign advertising in the media. One of the major reforms that the BCRA brought to campaign advertising is known as the stand-by-your-ad disclaimer. This law requires that all media advertisements

THE LARGEST INDEPENDENT 527 GROUPS IN 2006

Group	Money Raised	Money Spent
America Votes	$14,391,893	$14,108,355
Progress for America	$6,175,025	$13,000,574
September Fund	$5,230,500	$4,950,861
College Republican National Committee	$3,720,110	$10,260,343
Americans for Honesty on Issues	$3,030,221	$2,830,148

Source: The Center for Responsive Politics

Skills FOCUS INTERPRETING CHARTS

1. How much did the September Fund spend?
2. Which independent 527 group spent twice as much money as it raised in 2006?

include a visual or oral message that identifies who is paying for the ad. Furthermore, in the case of a television ad aired by a candidate's campaign, the ad must also contain a picture of the candidate and audio of the candidate saying something like "I'm [the candidate's name], and I approve of this message." This statement usually comes at the end of the ad.

Supporters of the BCRA media reforms hoped that the stand-by-your-ad disclaimer would lead to less negative advertising. They reasoned that campaigns would be less likely to air attacks on their opponents if the candidate had to appear in and openly approve the campaign advertisement. In some cases, this reasoning proved to be true and the attacks on a candidate's opponents decreased as the candidate was forced to stand behind everything that he or she said.

However, many voters found television advertising in the 2004 election campaign to be even more negative than ever before. One candidate even managed to turn her stand-by-your-ad disclaimer into an attack on her opponent. Representative Stephanie Herseth (D, South Dakota) closed one of her ads with the words, "I approved this message because I'm committed to a truthful campaign. It's clear that Larry Diedrich [her opponent] is not."

READING CHECK **Identifying Supporting Details** Explain why many interest groups have PACs and the roles that these PACs play in election campaigns.

THE TOP DONORS TO 527 GROUPS IN 2006

Contributor and Organization or Business	City, State	Contributions
Bob Perry, Perry Homes	Houston, TX	$9,750,000
Jerry Perenchio, Chartwell Partners	Los Angeles, CA	$5,000,000
George Soros, Soros Fund Management	New York, NY	$3,542,500
Linda Pritzker, Sustainable World Corporation	Houston, TX	$2,101,000
Jon R. Hunting, philanthropist	Grand Rapids, MI	$1,647,000

Source: The Center for Responsive Politics

Skills FOCUS **INTERPRETING CHARTS**

1. Who was the top donor to 527 groups in 2006?
2. Why do you think that the top donors are from states such as Texas, California, and New York?

Section 2 Assessment

THINK central Practice Online

thinkcentral.com
KEYWORD: SGO ELE HP

Reviewing Ideas and Terms

1. **a. Identify** From what four sources do most candidates get the money they need to run for political office?
   b. Summarize What campaign finance requirements did the FECA and its amendments establish?
   c. Predict Under what circumstances do you think presidential candidates might refuse public funding in a general election?

2. **a. Define** What is a **leadership PAC**?
   b. Analyze What do you think are factors that influence an individual's political attitudes and actions in regard to donating to PACs or **527 groups**?
   c. Design What are some possible ways that the current method of campaign funding could be improved? Explain your answer.

Critical Thinking

3. **Elaborate** If you decided to run for office, would you accept PAC money to help pay for your campaign? Explain why or why not.

CASE STUDY LINK The questions you answered at the end of the Case Study are given below. Now that you have completed Section 2, think about and answer the questions again. Then compare your answers with your earlier responses.

4. Should Traficant have been expelled from the House? Explain.

5. Was it right for House members to pressure DeLay to resign? Explain your answer.

6. Should concealing the source of any campaign contribution be illegal? Explain.

Deciding to Back a Candidate

Who will CleanEarthPAC support for election to the Senate?

Student Casebook

Use your Student Casebook to complete the simulation.

Before donating money to a candidate's campaign, a political action committee (PAC) must evaluate whether the candidate supports the goals of the PAC's interest group. Follow the steps below to simulate the process a PAC uses to decide which candidate to give money to in an election campaign.

Roles

- Candidate Laura Fox
- Candidate Andrew Flores
- Candidate Kenneth Jones
- Candidate Shelly Jackson
- CleanEarthPAC director
- CleanEarthPAC finance chair
- ACE executive committee (board members who will make the final decision)
- ACE members

❶ The Situation

CleanEarthPAC, the PAC of the environmental interest group Americans for a Cleaner Environment (ACE), must decide which candidates to support for the U.S. Senate. Thirty-three Senate seats are up for election this year. CleanEarthPAC will make contributions to campaigns in nearly all of these races. ACE has identified the elections in two states, California and Pennsylvania, as especially important to its interests.

Background

- ACE is a national organization that works to combat global warming. Its members believe that global warming is largely due to exhaust emissions from motor vehicles, air pollution from industrial activity, and the destruction of forests.

- ACE has about 10,000 members. The majority live in western states. Most are college educated and well-off financially. They are active voters and most often belong to at least one other environmental interest group.

- Democrat senator Laura Fox from California is running for reelection to her fifth term in the U.S. Senate. In her previous races, she has never earned less than 60 percent of the vote. Fox opposes government controls on auto and factory emissions. She was among the minority of senators who opposed renewal of the Clean Air Act.

- Republican Andrew Flores is opposing Fox. Flores is president of Earth Comes First, the nation's largest environmental interest group. He has never held a public office. This is his first election campaign. California has not elected a senator from his political party in almost 50 years.

- Democrat Kenneth Jones is the current three-term mayor of Philadelphia. This is his second run for the Senate. In his first attempt, he was defeated by the senator who is now retiring. Jones has received strong financial support from the Pennsylvania Manufacturers' Association in all his past campaigns.

● Republican Shelly Jackson is a former governor of Pennsylvania who was prevented by the state constitution from seeking a third term. As governor, she vetoed a bill passed by the state legislature requiring auto emissions testing in the state. Jackson is currently president of Pennsylvania College, where she supports the work of the school's famous climate study program.

❷ The Task

ACE must officially endorse a candidate in each race. Its PAC must then decide how much money to raise for these two races.

● Each **candidate** will prepare a statement for CleanEarthPAC, explaining why he or she is deserving of the PACs financial support.

● **ACE members** will use the "Factors to Consider" data sheet and vote for the candidate the group should endorse in each race.

● The **ACE executive committee** will take the members' views into account as well as the "Factors to Consider" data sheet and endorse one candidate in each race. The executive committee will also assist the CleanEarthPAC director and finance chair in deciding how to distribute the PAC's contributions among the candidates.

● **CleanEarthPAC's director** and **finance chair**, with advice from the ACE executive committee, will decide what contribution to make to each candidate. The director will announce and explain the PAC's funding decisions to the ACE members.

❸ Debriefing

After the CleanEarthPAC director has announced how much the organization will give to each candidate, discuss and evaluate the decision. Think about the factors a PAC needs to consider when making such decisions. Then write a paragraph about the importance of evaluating a candidate before deciding to give money to his or her campaign.

Factors to Consider

● How well does the candidate represent the values of ACE?

● How persuasive were the candidate's appeals for support?

● How strong is the candidate's record on environmental issues?

● What other endorsements does the candidate have?

● How likely is the candidate to carry out ACE's goals if elected?

● How likely is the candidate to win the election?

● Will it serve the group's interests for the PAC to back both candidates in a race?

● What campaign finance laws apply in this situation?

The major environmental interest groups have rated each candidate according to how well his or her record supports the group's goals and views. The highest possible rating is 100. An asterisk (*) next to a rating means that the group has endorsed the candidate.

CANDIDATE RATINGS

Group	Candidates			
	Fox	Flores	Jones	Jackson
Clean Air Coalition	5	100*	30*	20
Earth Comes First	20	100*	40*	40
Friends of the Forest	60	100*	40	50*
ACE	40	100	40	50
The Earth Society	40	100*	40	40*

Election Day and the Voters

Reading Focus

Voting is one of the main responsibilities of U.S. citizenship. Being a part of the voting process and taking an active role in electing public officials helps give all Americans a voice in their government.

CASE STUDY **Election 2000** Learn about the events of the presidential election in 2000 and its controversial aftermath.

WHAT YOU NEED TO KNOW Learn about the responsibilities of voters, the process of voting, and other events that affect outcomes on election day.

SIMULATION **Planning Election Day Strategies** Use your knowledge to plan and carry out election day strategies in a local election.

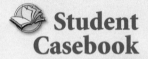

Student Casebook

Use your Student Casebook to take notes on the section and to complete the simulation.

George W. Bush (center) awaits results on election night.

Al Gore speaks to the press the day after the election.

Interactive Feature ✶
2000 Election

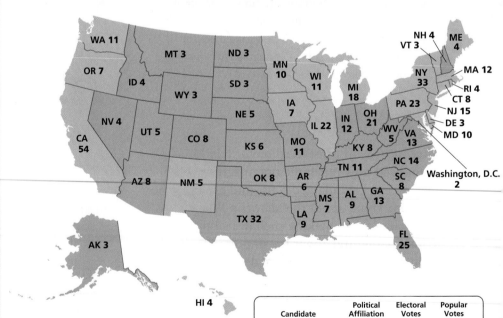

WA 11
MT 3
ND 3
MN 10
NH 4
VT 3
ME 4
OR 7
ID 4
WY 3
SD 3
WI 11
NY 33
MA 12
MI 18
RI 4
CT 8
NE 5
IA 7
IN 12
OH 21
PA 23
NJ 15
DE 3
NV 4
UT 5
CO 8
IL 22
WV 5
VA 13
MD 10
CA 54
KS 6
MO 11
KY 8
NC 14
AZ 8
NM 5
OK 8
AR 6
TN 11
SC 8
Washington, D.C. 2
MS 7
AL 9
GA 13
TX 32
LA 9
FL 25
AK 3
HI 4

THINK central **Interactive**

thinkcentral.com
KEYWORD: SGO ELE

Candidate	Political Affiliation	Electoral Votes	Popular Votes
George W. Bush	Republican	271	50,459,211
Albert A. Gore	Democrat	266	51,003,894
TOTAL		537	105,323,464

Election 2000

On the night of the 2000 presidential election, Republican George W. Bush and Democrat Al Gore awaited the results of their long and hard-fought campaigns for president. Unfortunately, the results would not be final on election night. A close race and a ballot recount in Florida delayed the election outcome for more than a month.

A Historic Election Night

As election day 2000 approached, polls showed that the race between George W. Bush and Al Gore would be very close. These predictions turned out to be quite accurate. As results came in on election night, it became clear that the race would hinge on the outcome in Florida. Whoever won Florida's 25 electoral votes would become the next president.

By about 8:00 p.m. EST, based on analysis of the votes counted so far in Florida, the major news media announced that Gore would win the state. About two hours later, the media retracted that announcement and said that Florida was too close to call. Then, at about 2:00 a.m., they declared Bush the winner in Florida. That news was soon replaced by bulletins that the Florida result was uncertain again. In the end, it would be more than a month before the outcome in Florida—and the next president of the United States—was officially known.

The Recount Controversy

Florida officials immediately started using machines to recount the ballots, which was required by state law in the event that the initial outcome was close. The recount showed Bush the winner by about 1,500 votes out of about 6 million votes cast. Democrats objected to this recount, claiming that the machines had failed to count thousands of ballots. Many ballots required voters to make their choice by punching a hole in the ballot. But if the hole was not big or clean enough, the machine could not read it as a vote. This malfunction proved to be a major recount obstacle.

Democrats asked for a recount of the ballots by hand. They hoped that the uncounted ballots would provide enough votes to overcome Bush's lead. Republicans opposed a hand recount, mainly because they did not want the recount to show that Gore had won in more districts. Over the next few days, each party filed lawsuits to force or prevent recounts.

Bush v. Gore

On December 8, 2000, Gore won an important legal victory. The Florida Supreme Court ordered hand recounts in Florida to take place statewide. The Bush campaign appealed the ruling to the U.S. Supreme Court, which issued its ruling in *Bush* v. *Gore* on December 12, 2000. In a 5–4 decision, the Court ruled that the Florida Supreme Court's order was unconstitutional because it did not include standards for how the votes should be recounted. The justices also ruled that there was not enough time before the deadline for these controversies to be resolved according to Florida state law.

The next day, Gore publicly accepted his defeat. That evening President-elect Bush went on television to ask Americans to put the controversy behind them and to unite for the good of the nation.

What Do You Think?

1. Do you think the media was helpful or harmful to the 2000 election results? Explain.
2. Were there flaws with the Florida ballots? Explain.
3. Should there have been a recount in Florida? Why or why not?

Political Participation

Key Terms
poll workers
poll watchers
redistricting

The United States is a democratic republic—a nation with a form of government in which political power belongs to the people. In order for a republic to function effectively, its citizens must participate in politics. There are many ways to participate in politics, such as being informed about important issues; volunteering, including volunteering in election campaigns; contributing money to candidates' campaigns; or seeking office oneself. However, the most basic and perhaps the most important form of political participation in a republic is voting.

Voting Rights and Responsibilities

Although most Americans older than 18 can register to vote, voter turnout rates in the United States today are lower than in any other democracy in the world. The right to vote is one that many Americans do not exercise and for much of the nation's history, voter turnout rates have been higher than they are today.

Until about 1830 most states granted the right to vote only to white men who owned property. By about the mid-1850s the property requirement was dropped by all states. In 1870, African American men gained the right to vote. Not until 1920 did all women receive the right to vote. For African American women—and men too—voting rights did not truly exist in many states until the 1960s because of discriminatory state laws. No American under age 21 could vote until 1971. With each extension of voting rights, the number and the diversity of people who were able to influence public policy decisions expanded.

Voting Rates The struggle to expand suffrage makes the right to vote very precious. Yet many people today still do not exercise it. In presidential-election years, an average of 45 percent of U.S. citizens who are eligible to vote do not do so. In non-presidential years, fewer than half of all eligible voters cast ballots. In some local elections, fewer than 20 percent of people vote.

Besides the type of election, a voter's age also influences his or her likelihood of voting. For example, fewer than half of all eligible voters

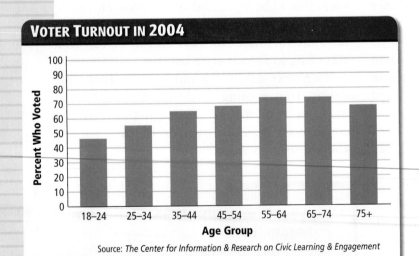

VOTER TURNOUT IN 2004

Percent Who Voted (y-axis: 0–100)
Age Group (x-axis): 18–24, 25–34, 35–44, 45–54, 55–64, 65–74, 75+

Source: *The Center for Information & Research on Civic Learning & Engagement*

Skills FOCUS INTERPRETING GRAPHS

1. Which two age groups have the highest percentages of voters?
2. Why do you think that the percentage of people who vote, which steadily increases as people get older, eventually begins to decline?

younger than 25 voted in the 2004 presidential election. On the other hand, nearly three-fourths of those age 65 and older went to the polls. In the 2006 midterm congressional elections, just 24 percent of eligible Americans younger than 30 cast a vote.

Impact of Voting Although the likelihood that one vote will determine the outcome of an election is slim, every vote is important. In the election of 2000, for example, the popular vote was very close and yet many people chose not to vote. If more votes were cast for Bush or if more votes were cast for Gore, making a final electoral decision in Florida might not have been so difficult.

Exercising the right to vote can have a great effect in local elections, where voter participation is generally the lowest. Local races often have the greatest direct influence on people's lives, and a number of local offices have been won or lost by a single vote.

Beyond the Right to Vote

Voting is the main means by which citizens participate in the political process. People who want to become more involved, however, can do so in a number of ways.

Working on Campaigns Some people give their time as well as their vote to support a candidate or issue. They do this by working on a campaign for a candidate or an issue. Unlike campaigning for a candidate, campaign organizations that form around issues on the ballot often involve two campaigns—one conducted by those who support an issue and the other by those who oppose it.

Every political campaign seeks and needs volunteers. Volunteer activities include working in the campaign office, making phone calls, going door to door to talk with voters or pass out literature, putting up yard signs, and helping supporters get out and vote on election day. It is a rare campaign that will be successful without the hard work of dedicated volunteers.

Working at the Polls Besides the voters, two other kinds of people are at the polls—poll workers and poll watchers. **Poll workers** are hired by local election officials to manage voting on election day. Each polling place has several poll workers. Their job is to verify voters' identification, compare voters' names to voter rolls, hand out ballots, and assist voters who need help voting. Although they may have to attend some advanced training, poll workers serve only on election day. They are paid for their service.

Poll watchers are mostly volunteers that a party or candidate sends to polling places to ensure that the election there is run fairly. In some states, poll watchers are allowed to check a polling place's list of registered voters to determine who has not yet voted. Other party workers can then contact those voters and urge them to vote.

Paths to the Presidency In the election of 2000, both candidates came from political backgrounds. Al Gore served in the House of Representatives from 1977 to 1985 and in the Senate from 1985 to 1993 before becoming vice president in 1993. George W. Bush served as governor of Texas from 1994 until he was elected president in 2000. Both men chose to become active participants in the political process by running for not only the presidency but other elected offices as well. **Applying Information** How might previous legislative experience be beneficial to a presidential candidate?

THINK central   **Online Link**

thinkcentral.com
KEYWORD: SGO ELE

▶ **Becoming a Candidate** Some citizens choose to become even more involved in politics by running for office themselves. They assume leadership positions and hope to effect change through their office. Many leaders begin their career as a public official in a state or local government office and later run for higher offices, like senator or president.

READING CHECK **Contrasting** What is the difference between poll workers and poll watchers?

The Voting Process

While not all citizens choose to take advantage of the right to run for office, they should still vote. Exercising the right to vote is necessary to ensure that the person who is elected will truly be the choice of a large number of citizens. Candidates who win elections are then responsible to all people—supporters and nonsupporters alike—to carry out the pledges they made in their campaign.

Steps to Voting

The first step in voting is gathering information. Voters should be familiar with the major duties and responsibilities of each office being contested. They should also be aware of each candidate's experience, other background information, and the candidates' stands on the important issues. This knowledge will help voters choose the best candidate to fill each position.

Phases of Voting

Learn about the candidates and the issues. The Internet is one way to gain information about candidates and campaign issues.

Register to vote. In most states, you must register to vote a specific number of days before election day.

Registering to Vote Unlike those of most other democratic countries, the U.S. government does not accept the responsibility of registering citizens to vote. Americans have to take the initiative to register.

Voter qualifications and voter registration vary from state to state. In New Mexico, for example, in order to qualify to vote, a citizen must have lived in the state for a year, in the county for 90 days, and in the precinct that he or she wishes to vote in for 30 days prior to election day. In many states, citizens can register to vote at a public library, by mail, at drivers' license agencies, or at the polls on election day. People can also access voter registration information online.

When registering, citizens may be asked to declare a political party. This information is necessary in many states if the voter wants to cast a ballot in primary elections. This declaration is not required, and people who do not choose a party are listed as independents.

Casting a Ballot As with registration, the act of voting is regulated by the individual states. In some places, citizens vote by marking paper ballots. In others, they use mechanical voting machines. This method of voting, though, can make certifying elections—declaring the official vote tally—difficult, as it can lead to inexact results.

One Person, One Vote

Every citizen in the United States should have an equal voice in government. Thus, every vote must have equal weight. However, if one member of a legislature represented 5,000 voters and another represented 500,000, equal weight would not be given. Therefore, the law requires that every district in a legislative body, other than the Senate, contain about the same number of people.

Skills FOCUS INTERPRETING CHARTS

Why is researching the candidates and the issues the first phase in the voting process?

Choose a political party affiliation. You can choose to be a member of the Republican or Democratic parties or be an independent.

Cast your vote. Voting machines vary from place to place. Some places use paper ballots, while others use electronic voting machines.

REAL-WORLD EXAMPLE

The Texas Eleven In 2003 a group of 11 Democratic state senators left Texas for 46 days. They were trying to block a plan to change the districts of five Democratic legislators into districts that would have Republican majorities. With the "Texas Eleven" absent, the Republican-controlled state senate did not have enough members to conduct business. Eventually, one of the Texas Eleven was convinced to return, which allowed the controversial redistricting bill to pass. In 2006 the Supreme Court upheld the right of a legislature to redistrict between censuses.

Applying Information What is your opinion about the actions of the Texas Eleven? Were their actions justified?

Reapportionment Populations change over time. Certain cities, states, or regions might have a surge in population growth, while others have a decrease in population. The U.S. Constitution requires a census to be taken every 10 years to keep track of such changes. The Constitution also requires that the seats in the House of Representatives be reassigned among the states to reflect the census results. The redistribution of seats in a legislative body is known as reapportionment. In the 1964 *Reynolds* v. *Sims* case, the Supreme Court ruled that reapportionment also applies to state legislatures.

▶ **Redistricting** Reapportionment requires redistricting. **Redistricting** is the process of drawing new boundaries for legislative districts. These boundaries must create districts that are relatively equal in population. For some voters, redistricting means that they will be represented by a different officeholder and that they will vote in a different legislative race in the next election.

The Voting Rights Act prohibits the drawing of districts that lessen the voting strength of minorities. Sometimes, though, state legislatures draw boundaries so the majority of voters in a district favor one political party over another. This practice is known as gerrymandering.

Campaigns on Election Day

For voters, the election is over once they have cast their ballots. For the candidates and their organizations, work continues until the polls are closed and the last vote is counted. In fact, election day is usually one of the busiest days of the entire campaign.

Election Day Activities Whether a race is local, state, or national, a campaign staff will know three things before election day arrives:

➊ the places where the candidate has strong support

➋ the places where support for the candidate's opponent is strong

➌ the places where the voting could go either way

Election day activities differ in each type of place. In places where polling shows the race is close or a large number of voters are undecided, the campaign may make a final appeal for votes. The candidate may visit key polling places to ask voters for support. In many states, laws prohibit campaigning at the polls but the candidate is allowed to stand a few hundred feet away and greet voters. Volunteers may also pass out sample ballots with their candidate's name marked on them.

As you read earlier, less work will take place where the candidate's opponent is expected to win. Efforts here may be limited to trying to get the candidate's supporters to vote instead of staying home. In presidential races, the organization may "write off" these states in order to concentrate its resources on swing states, where the state's electoral votes are still up for grabs.

Getting Out the Vote In places where the candidate's support is strong, the strategy will be to make sure that voters actually go to the polls. This effort is called getting out the vote, or GOTV for short. Most of a campaign's election day activities are usually devoted to GOTV. Historically and today, GOTV campaigns have been a way for citizens to maintain the continuity of a representative democracy by getting their fellow citizens to vote.

The telephone is the basic tool of GOTV. Calls playing a recorded message from the candidate may be made by computer from a database of phone numbers, or volunteers might make calls from the campaign office or a call center. Because of time and resource constraints, areas to be called are targeted beforehand. In the areas where the candidate has strong support, all voters from his or her party and all independents are called. Callers may even ask voters if they need a ride to the polls. In swing areas, usually only voters of the candidate's party will be contacted because campaigns do not want to risk encouraging voters who might support the opponent.

If poll watchers are allowed at the polls, they will report the number of voters to GOTV headquarters at <u>intervals</u> throughout the day. In areas with low turnout, resources may be redirected to make a second call to voters. Volunteers may even be sent door-to-door to ask people if they have voted or to take voters to the polls.

GOTV has become a very methodical operation. In many campaigns the GOTV coordinator is an expert hired specifically to plan GOTV strategy and to carry it out on election day.

READING CHECK **Identifying Supporting Details** What is the reason for reapportionment?

GOTV Get out the vote campaigns are just one of the many ways that people can get involved in election campaigns beyond simply casting a vote. Visit **thinkcentral.com** to begin a Webquest on GOTV campaigns and the different types of GOTV organizations that exist in the United States today.

THINK central **Webquest**

thinkcentral.com
KEYWORD: SGO ELE

ACADEMIC VOCABULARY

interval period of time between two events

THINK central **Online Quiz**

thinkcentral.com
KEYWORD: SGO ELE HP

Section 3 Assessment

Reviewing Ideas and Terms

1. **a. Identify** What age group has the lowest voting rate?
   b. Analyze Why do you think voting rates in the United States are so low?
   c. Rank Which form of political participation do you think is most important in a democratic republic? Explain your answer.

2. **a. Define** What is **redistricting**?
   b. Draw Conclusions Why do you think it is important for congressional districts in a given state to contain approximately the same number of people?
   c. Elaborate Why do you think a candidate's campaign might not conduct GOTV activities in all areas on election day?

Critical Thinking

3. **Analyze** Why are get out the vote campaigns important to the maintenance of a democratic republic?

CASE STUDY LINK The questions you answered at the end of the Case Study are given below. Now that you have completed Section 3, think about and answer the questions again. Then compare your answers with your earlier responses.

4. Do you think the media was helpful or harmful to the 2000 election results? Explain.

5. Were there flaws with the Florida ballots? Explain.

6. Should there have been a recount in Florida? Why or why not?

Planning Election Day Strategies

Who will be elected to the city council?

Student Casebook

Use your Student Casebook to complete the simulation.

Planning and carrying out election day activities require that a campaign team knows the voters, knows how and where it should concentrate campaign efforts, and is able to adapt to the day's events. In this simulation, two campaign teams will plan and carry out election day strategies to win a race for a seat on the city council.

Roles

- Two opposing candidates (Paul Green and Allison White)
- Campaign manager for each candidate
- Campaign workers for each candidate
- GOTV staff for each candidate
- GOTV coordinator for each candidate

❶ The Situation

Paul Green and Allison White both seek the tenth ward's seat on the city council. Each candidate has support in certain neighborhoods. Polls show that the race is close but that a large number of voters are still undecided. The outcome will depend on which candidate's team does the best job of getting out the vote on election day.

Key Facts

- The city's tenth ward consists of seven precincts. Each precinct has its own polling place. (To review the meaning of the terms *ward* and *precinct*, see Chapter 9.)

- All polling places are open from 6:00 a.m. to 9:00 p.m.

- Both campaigns have a poll watcher at each polling place. At 9:00 a.m., 1:00 p.m., and 6:00 p.m., the poll watchers contact campaign headquarters to report how many people have voted.

- Each candidate has 30 volunteers to pass out campaign literature at the polls, call voters, or go door-to-door. A plan of action must be created for these volunteers.

- Each campaign office has 10 phones to use for calling voters.

❷ The Task

Each candidate's campaign team must plan election day strategies to help its candidate win the election. Tasks include creating election day flyers that volunteers can pass out at the polls, writing scripts for volunteers to use when calling voters, and deciding how and where to use those volunteers on election day. At intervals during the simulation, your teacher will provide data on voter turnout at each polling place, as the poll watchers report in. Each campaign team will then have to decide whether to adjust its strategy based on these developments.

- Each **campaign manager** will supervise all election day planning and activities. The campaign manager and the candidate will decide at which polling places the candidate will appear and whether to change that plan as the day progresses. The campaign manager will also direct the campaign staff, approve the GOTV coordinator's plans, and fill out a GOTV chart.

- Each **candidate** will work with the campaign manager on the appearance schedule. The candidates will also write one or more scripts for a five-second greeting to use as they meet voters at each polling place.

- The **campaign workers** will create a flyer for volunteers to hand out at the polls and the phone script that the callers will use. Workers and the campaign manager will decide if different flyers or scripts are needed for the different types of precinct demographics. They will also decide if flyers or scripts should be changed throughout the day.

- The **GOTV coordinator** and **GOTV staff** will plan the campaign's election day GOTV activities, using the Precincts of the Tenth Ward Fact Sheet below. This task will include targeting specific activities—volunteers making phone calls, volunteers distributing flyers at polling places, volunteers going door-to-door—for specific precincts and the number of volunteers to assign to each. The GOTV coordinator and staff will also decide, with the campaign manager's approval, how to adjust the plan as voter turnout information comes in during the day.

❸ Debriefing

When the simulation ends, each campaign team will record its completed GOTV chart on the board. As a class, discuss how each team allocated its resources throughout the day and why it did so. Then write a one-page report explaining which candidate likely won the election, based on each team's GOTV activities.

PRECINCTS OF THE TENTH WARD FACT SHEET			
PRECINCT	**REGISTERED VOTERS**	**POLL RESULTS**	**DEMOGRAPHIC INFORMATION**
A	2,500	White: 60% Green: 15% Undecided: 15%	These are working class neighborhoods where most of the residents are employed at a large auto plant nearby. Work hours at the plant are 7:00 a.m. to 4:00 p.m., with an hour break for lunch between 11:00 a.m. and noon. About 80 percent of residents are registered voters.
B	2,300	White: 30% Green: 30% Undecided: 40%	
C	1,200	White: 20% Green: 20% Undecided: 60%	This is a poor neighborhood with high unemployment. Of residents who have jobs, most work part-time or work at night and sleep during the day. Less than half of the residents are registered to vote.
D	1,700	White: 20% Green: 50% Undecided: 30%	These are middle-class neighborhoods consisting largely of two-income families. Most of the residents commute to office jobs downtown. Their workday generally runs 9:00 a.m. to 5:00 p.m., with an hour off for lunch at noon. About two-thirds of residents are registered to vote.
E	1,800	White: 25% Green: 55% Undecided: 20%	
F	1,500	White: 25% Green: 25% Undecided: 50%	These are well-to-do neighborhoods. Large numbers of residents are older and retired. Of those still in the workforce, most are one-income families. Most of the working men own businesses, and most of the women are at home. Nearly all residents are registered voters.
G	1,500	White: 20% Green: 25% Undecided: 55%	

Connecting Online

Visit **thinkcentral.com** for review and enrichment activities related to this chapter.

THINK central

KEYWORD: SGO ELE

Quiz and Review

GOV 101
Examine key concepts in this chapter.

ONLINE QUIZZES
Take a practice quiz for each section in this chapter.

Activities

eActivities
Complete Webquests and Internet research activities.

INTERACTIVE FEATURES
Explore interactive versions of maps and charts.

KEEP IT CURRENT
Link to current events in U.S. government.

Partners

American Bar Association Division for Public Education
Learn more about the law, your rights and responsibilities.

Center for Civic Education
Promoting an enlightened and responsible citizenry committed to democratic principles and actively engaged in the practice of democracy.

Online Textbook

ONLINE SIMULATIONS
Learn about U.S. government through simulations you can complete online.

STUDENT CASEBOOK
Take notes electronically on Interactive Chapters.

Click for More Read more about key topics online.

Comprehension and Critical Thinking

SECTION 1 *(pp. 354–363)*

1. a. Review Key Terms For each term, write a sentence that explains its significance or meaning: stump speech, negative campaigning, sound bite, demographic.

b. Draw Conclusions How might negative campaigning affect voter attitudes about elections?

c. Rank Which position on a campaign staff do you think is the most important? Which position do you think is least important? Explain the reasons for your ranking.

SECTION 2 *(pp. 366–375)*

2. a. Review Key Terms For each term, write a sentence that explains its significance or meaning: party-building activities, issue ads, leadership PACs, 527 group.

b. Analyze What is the relationship between interest groups, PACs, and candidates in an election campaign? How might this relationship change over the course of the election campaign?

c. Predict How might a PAC ensure that an interest group is influential no matter which candidate wins?

SECTION 3 *(pp. 378–385)*

3. a. Review Key Terms For each term, write a sentence that explains its significance or meaning: poll workers, poll watchers, redistricting.

b. Explain In what ways does a GOTV campaign increase a candidate's chance of being elected? Do you think a candidate could win without the help of volunteers like those that take part in a GOTV campaign? Explain your answer.

c. Predict How might low voting rates among young people affect the influence young people have on society?

WRITING FOR THE SAT

Think about the following issue:

Laws limit the amount of money that individuals and PACs can contribute to the campaigns of persons running for elected office. Laws also limit contributions to political parties as well as the ability of some interest groups to air political ads during campaigns. Opponents of these limits have attacked them as restrictions on the freedom of speech that is guaranteed in the Bill of Rights.

4. Assignment Do you think that these limits are really a free speech issue? Are such limits on political activity appropriate in a democracy? Are any limits appropriate? Write a short essay in which you develop your position on this issue. Support your point of view with reasoning and examples from your reading and studies.

13 Supreme Court Cases

Why should you care about the Supreme Court? One of the purposes of the Constitution and its amendments is to protect your rights against government interference. The Constitution, however, is a collection of words. Someone—the justices of the Supreme Court—must say what those words mean and what the law is. But Supreme Court justices are not elected officials—they are appointed to the Court for life. Their decisions can affect your freedom of speech, your right to privacy, your right to a fair trial, and other aspects of your personal life.

Table of Contents

John Roberts was sworn in as the seventeenth chief justice of the United States in September 2005.

Student Casebook | Use your Student Casebook to take notes on the chapter and to complete the simulations.

The First Amendment: Your Freedom of Expression

Reading Focus

Your freedom of expression—the right to practice your religious beliefs; to hold, express, and publish ideas and opinions; to gather with others; and to ask the government to correct its mistakes—is the cornerstone of our democracy. Through its power to interpret the Constitution, the Supreme Court can expand—or limit—your rights.

CASE STUDY **Students' Right of Expression** Do students who are not being disruptive lose their constitutional right to freedom of speech or expression when they enter the schoolhouse door?

WHAT YOU NEED TO KNOW Learn about the fundamental freedoms guaranteed by the First Amendment to the Constitution.

SIMULATION **The Play's the Thing** Use your knowledge to prepare and argue a case in federal district court alleging a violation of freedom of speech. Your arguments must be guided by both the First Amendment and Supreme Court decisions on this subject.

Student Casebook

Use your Student Casebook to take notes on the section and to complete the simulation.

Mary Beth and John Tinker display the black armbands they wore to school in 1965 to protest the war in Vietnam.

Students' Right of Expression

In the mid-1960s public opinion about the Vietnam War was divided. Many Americans strongly supported the war, but sentiment against the war had been growing. By 1963, protests and demonstrations against the war began to spread, especially on college campuses. Within a couple of years, some high school and middle school students also began to protest the Vietnam War.

The Black Armband Case

In 1965 John Tinker, his sister Mary Beth, their friend Christopher Eckhardt, and a few other friends decided to protest the Vietnam War by wearing black armbands in their Des Moines, Iowa, school. John Tinker was 15 and Christopher Eckhardt was 16 at the time. Mary Beth Tinker was 13. Little did the teenagers know that their decision would result in a landmark Supreme Court case that defined students' First Amendment rights. The decision established a test for determining whether a school's actions violate students' rights to freedom of expression.

School officials heard rumors of the planned protest, and they feared that school would be disrupted. As a result, the school board adopted a policy banning the wearing of armbands.

Several students violated the policy and wore their armbands in school. Five students, including Mary Beth, John, and Christopher, were suspended. Their parents sued the school district, claiming that the children's First Amendment right to free expression had been violated.

In 1966 a U.S. district court ruled in favor of the school system. In 1967 a tie vote in the Court of Appeals for the Eighth Circuit meant that the district court's decision stood. The Tinkers and Eckhardts appealed directly to the U.S. Supreme Court.

The Supreme Court Decision

Before the Supreme Court, the Tinkers and other plaintiffs argued that the school's ban on armbands violated their right to free speech under the First and Fourteenth amendments. The armbands, they argued, were a form of symbolic speech protected by the Constitution.

The school district argued that the ban was intended to prevent classroom disruption, not to suppress expression. The district saw the rule as a reasonable use of its power to preserve order.

In 1969 the Supreme Court handed down its decision in *Tinker* v. *Des Moines School District*. By a 7–2 vote, the Court reversed the lower courts' ruling. Writing the Court's majority opinion, Justice Abe Fortas first reinforced the principle that neither "students [n]or teachers shed their constitutional rights to freedom of speech or expression at the schoolhouse gate."

The Court agreed that school authorities have a right to maintain order but observed that the protesters "neither interrupted school activities nor sought to intrude in the school affairs or the lives of others." Fortas wrote that "we do not confine the permissible exercise of First Amendment rights . . . to supervised and ordained discussion in a school classroom." The opinion concluded that, regarding the students in this case, "our Constitution does not permit officials of the State to deny their form of expression."

According to the Court, schools can regulate student speech when that speech would be disruptive or interfere with the rights of other students. The ruling created the Tinker test: if the expression does not substantially interfere with school operation, regulating that speech violates the Constitution's protection of free expression.

Justice Hugo Black wrote a blistering dissent. He argued that school officials had a right and a duty to control the learning environment so that students could focus on their studies without being distracted by other students' protests.

Schools "are operated to give students an opportunity to learn, not to talk politics," Black noted. "If the time has come when pupils of state-supported schools . . . can defy and flout [show contempt for] orders of school officials to keep their minds on their own schoolwork," he warned, "it is the beginning of a new revolutionary era in this country fostered by the judiciary."

After *Tinker*

The *Tinker* case, with its Tinker test, remains the leading case dealing with the free-expression rights of public school students. By the 1980s, however, the times and the Court's membership had changed. Only three of the nine justices who heard *Tinker* remained on the Court. With six new justices, the Court gradually modified and expanded the concept of school disruption. Over time, the Court has narrowed the limits of acceptable student expression.

For example, in 1986 in *Bethel School District* v. *Fraser,* the Court ruled 7–2 to uphold the suspension of a student for giving a speech at a school assembly that contained vulgar sexual references. The Court further limited students' freedom of expression in 1988. By a 6–3 vote in *Hazelwood School District* v. *Kuhlmeier,* the justices upheld the right of school officials to censor a journalism-class newspaper if school officials believe the paper's contents are inconsistent with a legitimate educational purpose.

In 2006 the Court took up a school's power to limit student expression off campus. In Juneau, Alaska, student Joseph Frederick was suspended for displaying a banner—bearing what Frederick claimed was a nonsense message—during a rally for the Winter Olympics across the street from his high school. The school principal, however, interpreted the banner as referring to and encouraging the use of illegal drugs.

Although students do have a protected right to free speech at school under certain conditions, that right is not absolute. The Supreme Court has limited student speech in a variety of ways.

Although Frederick and his friends were not being disruptive and despite the fact that the rally was neither on school property nor at a school-sponsored event, the principal suspended them for violating the school's antidrug policy.

In June 2007 the Supreme Court ruled 6–3 in *Morse* v. *Frederick* that because schools must take steps to protect students in their care, a principal may prohibit speech that a reasonable person might read as encouraging drug use. In this case, the Court said, it would not be unreasonable to read the banner that way. School officials did not, therefore, violate Frederick's First Amendment rights by confiscating his banner and suspending him for 10 days.

What Do You Think?

1. Are protests like the Tinkers' disruptive of school activities? Explain your point of view.

2. Should school authorities have the right to censor student speeches or newspapers? Why or why not?

3. Is the Tinker test an adequate way to handle issues related to students' freedom of expression? Why or why not?

Freedom of Religion

The First Amendment guarantees your right to **freedom of expression,** the right of citizens to hold, explore, exchange, express, and debate ideas. The First Amendment states that "Congress shall make no law respecting an establishment of religion, or prohibiting the free exercise thereof." These two guarantees are known as the establishment clause and the free exercise clause. Disputes over the meaning of these few words have led to many court cases over the years. In addition, a possible conflict between the establishment clause and the free exercise clause has aroused a debate that continues today.

The Establishment Clause

Thomas Jefferson called for a "wall of separation between church and state." As the Quick Facts chart on the next page shows, the Supreme Court has tried to maintain such a wall between religion and government. But disagreement exists over how high that wall should be or if it should even exist at all. For example, take the matter of student prayer in public schools.

School Prayer Some of the greatest controversy surrounds the issue of prayer in public schools. In 1962, in *Engel* v. *Vitale,* the Supreme Court banned a prayer required in New York public schools. The Court ruled that it is not "the business of government to compose official prayers . . . to recite as part of a religious program carried on by government." The next year, in *Abington School District* v. *Schempp,* the Court struck down a Pennsylvania requirement that each school day start with Bible readings and the Lord's Prayer.

In 1985, in *Wallace* v. *Jaffree,* the Court went further and rejected Alabama's required minute set aside each morning for silent meditation or prayer. In *Santa Fe Independent School District* v. *Doe* (2000), it banned a student-led prayer over the public address system before high school football games. The Court applied the three-prong Lemon test (see Chapter 10) in these two cases and concluded that both enforced silent prayer and public prayer before school athletic events violate the establishment clause—each activity comes too close to providing official support for religion.

Note that the Court has not banned private, voluntary school prayer. In fact, the Court requires high schools to allow students to form private religious groups if the school allows other groups not related to the curriculum—such as a chess club—to meet on school property (*Westside Community Schools* v. *Mergens,* 1990, and *Good News Club* v. *Milford Central School,* 2001). However, no school employees may take part in student religious groups. What the Court has prohibited are school-sponsored religious practices.

Key Terms

freedom of expression
redress of grievances
right of assembly

Your First Amendment Freedoms

QUICK FACTS

Freedom of religion
- The right to practice your religion is a basic form of self-expression.

Freedom of speech
- The right to express your ideas freely and to hear the ideas of others is fundamental to democracy.

Freedom of the press
- Freedom of the press extends the freedom of speech to printed words and other published works.

Freedom of assembly
- The right to associate or join with whomever you wish and express your opinions is also a basic right.

Freedom of petition
- The right to petition the government—to ask the government to correct a wrong—is protected.

RELIGION IN PUBLIC PLACES

YEAR	CASE	SUPREME COURT RULING
1984	*Lynch* v. *Donnelly*	A Christmas nativity scene in a public park was permitted because the display also contained Santa Claus and other nonreligious symbols.
1989	*Allegheny County* v. *Greater Pittsburgh ACLU*	A display that contained a Christmas tree and a Hanukkah menorah outside a county courthouse was allowed, but a nativity scene that stood alone inside the courthouse was not.
1995	*Capitol Square Review Board* v. *Pinette*	A private group was allowed to display a cross outside the Ohio state capitol on land that was traditionally open to use by the public.
2005	*Van Orden* v. *Perry*	A monument of the Ten Commandments, set among other historical monuments at the Texas state capitol, was allowed because in that context it did not indicate state endorsement of the religious message.
2005	*McCreary County* v. *ACLU*	A copy of the Ten Commandments displayed alone inside a Kentucky courthouse was not in that context religiously "neutral" and therefore violated the establishment clause.

REAL-WORLD EXAMPLE

Voluntary Prayer In 2007, seniors at three high schools in Round Rock, Texas, voted to have a public prayer at their graduation. Seniors at a fourth school voted against having a prayer.

The school district follows a state policy prohibiting school officials from having prayers at graduation unless students request it. The goal of the policy is to avoid conflicts involving separation of church and state.

Applying Information If students vote to have any prayer at graduation, should they have to allow as many different prayers as students want to offer? Why or why not?

THINK central **Online Link**

thinkcentral.com
KEYWORD: SGO SUP

Religion and Instruction Teaching about religion or the Bible in school is also allowable, as long as the instruction is done in a nonreligious manner. However, the Court has drawn the line when it comes to including religious beliefs in instruction. For example, in *Epperson* v. *Arkansas* (1968), it overturned a law that prohibited the teaching of evolution, a scientific theory that is contrary to many people's religious beliefs. The Court also voided a Louisiana law that required a religious view called creation science to be taught alongside evolution (*Edwards* v. *Aguillard*, 1987).

The Free Exercise Clause

The First Amendment seems to make freedom of religious belief an absolute right: "Congress shall make no law . . ." However, the Court has drawn a distinction between your right to believe whatever you want and your right to express those beliefs through actions. This difference was noted in the first case the Supreme Court heard that involved the free exercise clause.

In 1879, in *Reynolds* v. *United States,* the Supreme Court upheld the conviction of George Reynolds for having more than one wife, a practice known as polygamy. Reynolds belonged to the Mormon Church, which allowed polygamy at that time, but federal law prohibited the practice. The Court ruled that the free exercise clause did not protect religious practices that were "subversive of good order," even if those practices reflected religious beliefs.

The Court developed this principle into what is known as the "compelling interest test," which requires government to have a compelling, or very strong, reason for banning a religious practice as necessary to protect society. The Court has used this test to allow expression of religious beliefs in some situations but not in others.

West Virginia State Board of Education v. Barnette In 1943 the Court upheld students' right to refuse to salute the flag and recite the Pledge of Allegiance if it violated their religious beliefs. The case involved students who were Jehovah's Witnesses. Their faith teaches that the salute and pledge are a type of idol worship, which is forbidden by the Ten Commandments. The justices noted that making patriotic ceremonies voluntary instead of required did no great harm to society. The decision also established people's right to *not* take part in a practice that violates their religious beliefs as a protected form of religious expression.

Sherbert v. Verner In 1963 the Court extended this right when it reversed South Carolina's denial of unemployment benefits to a woman who had been fired for refusing to work on Saturdays, the day of worship in her religion. It applied the same principles again in 1972 in *Wisconsin v. Yoder,* when it exempted Amish children from Wisconsin's law that requires school attendance until a certain age. In both cases the justices ruled that what society gained from these requirements did not outweigh a person's freedom to follow his or her religious beliefs.

Goldman v. Weinberger The Court reached the opposite conclusion in this 1986 case that involved a Jewish member of the air force who wore a yarmulke (a skullcap worn by religious Jews) while on duty. The justices upheld the air force's ban on wearing nonmilitary apparel, given the military's need to foster unity and group spirit.

Employment Division v. Smith The Court stretched the compelling interest test in 1990 when it upheld Oregon's right to deny unemployment benefits to two Native Americans who had been fired for ingesting peyote in a religious ceremony. Peyote use is illegal in Oregon. The Court ruled that states may enforce laws that incidentally interfere with people's religious practices.

Charging that the *Smith* decision limited religious freedom, Congress passed the Religious Freedom Restoration Act (RFRA) in 1993. This law created a tougher compelling interest test for the courts to apply. However, the Supreme Court, exercising its power of judicial review, ruled the RFRA itself unconstitutional in 1997, in *City of Boerne, Texas v. Flores.*

READING CHECK Contrasting How did the Court's position on religious expression in *Sherbert v. Verner* differ from its position in the *Smith* case?

REAL-WORLD EXAMPLE

Religious Studies The state of Washington gave Joshua Davey a college scholarship. Under the Washington state constitution and the terms of the scholarship, Davey was prohibited from using the money to obtain a theology degree if the program was for "devotional theology majors." Davey lost his scholarship when he decided to get a degree in pastoral ministries. In 2004 in *Locke v. Davey,* the Supreme Court rejected Davey's claim that cancelling his scholarship violated the free exercise clause of the First Amendment.

Applying Information What state interest might Washington have in prohibiting the use of public funds for religious education?

Freedom of Speech

The First Amendment states, "Congress shall make no law . . . abridging freedom of speech, or of the press . . ." As with the freedom of religion, that seems pretty simple and straightforward. But what is "speech"? For example, is speech only spoken words, or does it include other forms of expression, such as dancing? Are there limits to this freedom? Is obscenity protected, for example? Or can you make statements about other people that are not true?

Protected and Unprotected Speech

The Supreme Court has observed in *Chaplinsky* v. *New Hampshire* (1942) that "the right to free speech is not absolute at all times and under all circumstances." Speech that has little or no social value is generally not protected by the First Amendment. In *Chaplinsky*, the Court named some classes of expression that are not protected:

- **Fighting words** Speech that insults or angers people so much that violence may result

- **Defamatory speech** False statements that damage a person's reputation and that are published in print or other media, called *libel*, or that are just spoken, called *slander*

- **Lewd and profane speech** Speech that is vulgar or obscene

TYPES OF PROTECTED AND UNPROTECTED SPEECH

QUICK FACTS

TYPE OF SPEECH	CASE	SUPREME COURT RULING
Fighting words, defamatory speech, and lewd and profane speech	*Chaplinsky* v. *New Hampshire* (1942)	Not protected by the First Amendment
Nondisruptive student political speech	*Tinker* v. *Des Moines* (1969)	Protected by the First Amendment
Student vulgar and obscene speech	*Bethel School District* v. *Fraser* (1986)	Not protected by the First Amendment
Content in student newspapers	*Hazelwood School Dist.* v. *Kuhlmeier* (1988)	Not protected by the First Amendment if not consistent with legitimate educational purpose
Off-campus student speech	*Morse* v. *Frederick* (2007)	Not protected by the First Amendment if a reasonable person might interpret speech as advocating use of illegal drugs

Student Speech

The Supreme Court has declared that students "do not shed their constitutional rights of . . . expression at the schoolhouse gate." Even so, students do not enjoy the same free speech rights as other Americans. For example, the Court has ruled that schools can regulate the time, place, and even the content of student expression.

Political Speech The Court has set the fewest limits on student speech that expresses political ideas or opinions. The standard for regulating student political speech is the *Tinker* case. In general, if student expression does not disrupt school activities, officials must allow it. And just *believing* that student speech might be disruptive does not pass the Tinker test. School officials must expect that the speech will cause a major disruption in order to <u>censor</u> it.

There are exceptions to this principle, however. School officials may ban speech that is vulgar, hateful, interferes with the rights of others, or, as of 2007, might be interpreted as promoting drug use.

Vulgar and Obscene Speech The case of *Cohen* v. *California* (1971) permits vulgar and obscene speech in public, but the Court has not allowed such speech in school. In the *Bethel School District* case, a student made vulgar statements in a speech supporting a friend running for student government. The Court upheld the speaker's suspension, writing that "freedom to advocate . . . views in schools and classrooms must be balanced against the society's . . . interest in teaching students the boundaries of socially acceptable behavior."

Speech Codes Recently many schools have adopted speech codes, or policies against—and limits on—speech that violates the right of all students to a safe learning environment. For example, schools have banned wearing Confederate flag patches on clothing because the flag is offensive to some students. In other cases, students have been punished for artwork or writing assignments containing content that officials found troubling. The Court has not yet ruled on speech codes but may, eventually, decide these issues.

Cyberspeech Student speech on the Internet is also an area of uncertainty. The Court has said that cyberspeech generally has the same protections as printed material. If so, students may be free to express themselves online when they use their own computers, are off campus, and are on their own time. However, some schools have suspended students for using home-based Web pages to criticize school officials. Officials argued—and some courts have agreed— that the off-campus pages' content so disrupted the learning environment that the pages had to be restricted or prohibited. In other cases, courts have rejected this argument and reversed students' suspensions.

READING CHECK **Summarizing** What limits are placed on student speech?

ACADEMIC VOCABULARY

censor to suppress or delete something as objectionable

REAL-WORLD EXAMPLE

CASE STUDY LINK

Mixed Messages In 2002 the Pennsylvania Supreme Court upheld the expulsion of a student who created a Web site that obscenely ridiculed his algebra teacher. But in 2005 a federal judge overturned the suspensions of two Arkansas students whose Web site contained comments made by other students ridiculing their school's athletes and band members. The judge ruled that because others had posted the comments on the Web site, the two students should not be punished for them.

Applying Information How is this case similar to *Tinker* v. *Des Moines*? How is it different?

Freedom of Petition and Assembly

The First Amendment also recognizes and protects Americans' right to petition government for a **redress of grievances**—that is, to remove the cause of a complaint and make things right. Freedom of petition is the right to ask the government to act to correct an injustice without fear of punishment for making the request. The rights of assembly and petition often go hand in hand. For example, people may join an association or a demonstration to publicize their grievances and to call on the government for redress.

The **right of assembly** means that you have the right to join and form groups, such as such as clubs, interest groups, or labor unions, and to gather for any peaceful and lawful purpose. Like other First Amendment rights, the right of assembly has limits. For example, the assembly must be peaceful, and people have no right to gather on private property without the owner's consent. Government may, however, make reasonable regulations about the time, place, and behavior of assemblies on public property.

The Supreme Court has also set limits on the kinds of groups to which people may belong. In *Whitney* v. *California* (1927) the Court upheld the conviction of a woman for her membership in the Communist Labor Party, an organization that supported the overthrow of the government by acts of violence. Today, such limits allow authorities to arrest suspected terrorists or members of armed groups that may pose a threat to society.

READING CHECK **Drawing Conclusions** How do the freedoms of petition and assembly support a republican form of government?

Freedom of Assembly

Schools may not ban student organizations, such as this prayer group, because of their religious or philosophical beliefs.

Student Assembly

The limits that apply to the public's right of assembly also apply to students in school. Here, too, the Court has often been more restrictive of student rights. For example, school officials have the right to control the time, place, and manner of student gatherings. They also have the right to set restrictions on school clubs. Finally, within certain limits, they have the right to deny some types of clubs permission to form.

The Equal Access Act of 1984 prohibits schools and school districts from forbidding or discriminating against any club because of its religious or philosophical viewpoint. In 1990 the Court ruled this law was constitutional in *Westside Community Schools* v. *Mergens*, discussed earlier in this section. Students may also distribute religious and political literature in school, but school officials may regulate this activity.

School officials do not have to allow any student organization that preaches hate or violence or that engages in illegal activity. However, they cannot restrict students from forming other clubs just because the clubs might be controversial. For example, a school could refuse to allow a neo-Nazi club that advocated racial or religious violence. But a club formed to promote tolerance of gays and lesbians would be permissible, although such clubs have sometimes aroused controversy.

READING CHECK **Making Generalizations** What kinds of school clubs are not protected by the right of assembly?

Section 1 Assessment

Reviewing Ideas and Terms

1. **a. Identify** What is the difference between the free exercise clause and the establishment clause?
   b. Make Generalizations What limitation exists on religious practices?

2. **a. Describe** What are three types of speech not protected by the First Amendment?
   b. Elaborate Why do you think the Supreme Court limits student speech more than the speech of adults? Give examples to support your answer.

3. **a. Describe** What are the requirements for a lawful assembly on private property?
   b. Make Inferences For what reasons might the right to assemble be limited on public property?

4. **a. Identify** What kinds of clubs are not allowed in schools?
   b. Analyze Why do school officials have the right to limit students' **right of assembly**?

Critical Thinking

5. **Predict** How can the change of one Supreme Court justice affect the outcome of a decision? In your opinion, is a president's choice of a nominee for justice important? Why or why not?

CASE STUDY LINK You answered the following questions at the end of the Case Study. Now that you have completed Section 1, think about and answer the questions again. Then compare your answers with your earlier responses. Are your answers the same or are they different?

6. Are protests like the Tinkers' disruptive of school activities? Explain your point of view.

7. Should school authorities have the right to censor student speeches or newspapers? Why or why not?

8. Is the Tinker test an adequate way to handle issues related to students' freedom of expression? Why or why not?

SIMULATION

The Play's the Thing

Will students from Home City High School be allowed to stage their play?

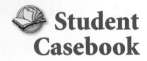

Student Casebook

Use your Student Casebook to complete the simulation.

Issues of student free speech can take many forms, including plays performed by student drama groups. Using what you have learned in Section 1, complete the simulation about a fictional lawsuit seeking permission to perform a student play.

Roles

- Federal judge
- Jurors
- Plaintiffs' attorneys
- Defendants' attorneys
- Attorney for Civil Liberties Association (CLA)
- Attorney for Center for Free Student Press (CFSP)
- Attorney for Association of United Churches (AUC)
- Attorney for Association of School Administrators (ASA)
- Drama club members
- School principal
- School newspaper editor
- Other witnesses

❶ The Situation

The drama club of Home City High School wants to stage a play on the life, teachings, and impact of the historical founder of an Eastern religion. Club members asked the principal for permission to present their play to an all-school assembly. When permission was denied, club members offered to present the play during the lunch period, so students could choose whether or not to attend. The principal also rejected this alternative.

A student who supported the play started a petition to demand that it be permitted. The petition was seized when the principal heard about it, and the student responsible for it was suspended. When the school newspaper prepared a story on the controversy, school officials refused to allow it to be published. Students filed a lawsuit in federal court, and trial of the case is ready to begin.

Background

- Three drama club members, their parents, and the suspended student have sued the school district. They are the plaintiffs in this case. They claim violations of First Amendment rights.

- The school district is the defendant in the case. School officials claim that the play would violate the establishment clause. They also claim that their actions were all within their power, and were taken, to maintain order.

- The Civil Liberties Association (CLA), the Center for Free Student Press (CFSP), the Association of United Churches (AUC), and the Association of School Administrators (ASA) have all filed legal briefs in this case.

- Home City has a population of 10,500 people. There are 26 Protestant churches, one synagogue, and one Roman Catholic church in Home City.

- The *Bugle*, Home City's weekly newspaper, carried a story about the play, its subject matter, and the subsequent dispute at the school.

❷ The Trial

The attorneys for the plaintiffs and defendants will present their case. The plaintiffs' case is presented first, followed by the defense. Each side calls its witnesses, including expert testimony, at the trial. The organizations present their arguments at the conclusion of the appropriate side's case. After each side's case has been heard, the jury will render a decision for the plaintiffs or for the defendant.

The Judge The judge will be in charge of the trial. He or she will keep order, recognize the attorneys for each side when it is that side's turn to speak, call witnesses, and cross-examine the other side's witnesses. The judge will rule on any objections to the evidence made by attorneys. The judge may also question witnesses if he or she chooses to do so.

The Parties' Attorneys Each side will have at least two attorneys. These attorneys will do the research needed to prepare their side's case, plan the case, and plan what witnesses to call. They will also be responsible for writing their side's opening and closing statements to the jury. The attorneys for each side will question their side's witnesses and cross-examine the other side's witnesses at the proper time.

The Amicus Attorneys A group may work with either side in the case. The list below is a suggestion. An attorney for each organization will write its amicus curiae brief—on whichever issue it chooses—to assist the court. Each organization's attorney will present the organization's position at the conclusion of testimony from the side the organization supports. The organizations' attorneys may work with the attorneys for the side they support to prepare that side's case.

The Witnesses The drama club members, school principal, and school newspaper editor will be witnesses for plaintiffs or defense. They will testify about the controversy and events that led to the lawsuit. Other witnesses, such as students who were not directly involved in the dispute, townspeople, or historians may be called by each side. These witnesses must have information relevant to one or more of the issues.

The Jurors Jurors will listen to opening statements, testimony, and closing arguments. They may take notes and, with the judge's permission, ask questions of any witness. The jury members, based on the evidence and First Amendment principles, will decide the case in favor of one side, the other, or both. The judge will read the jury's decision in court.

Amici Curiae for the Plaintiff	Amici Curiae for the Defense
● Civil Liberties Association (CLA)	● Association of School Administrators (ASA)
● Center for a Free Student Press (CFSP)	● Association of United Churches (AUC)

❸ Debriefing

After the jury has reached its verdict, discuss the jury's findings as a class. Assess whether the jury, the attorneys, and expert witnesses for each side correctly applied the First Amendment and case law to the facts in this trial. Then write a one-page summary explaining whether you agree with the verdict and why or why not.

Amicus Curiae Briefs *Amicus curiae* (plural, *amici curiae*) is Latin for "friend of the court." The term refers to a person or organization that files a legal brief, with the court's permission, to express views on one or more issues in a case involving other parties because it has a strong interest in the subject matter of the action.

The Fourth Amendment: Your Right to Be Secure

Reading Focus

The Fourth Amendment guarantees your right to be secure against unreasonable searches and seizures—in other words, it guarantees that you have rights to some sorts of privacy. As with First Amendment rights, Fourth Amendment rights are not absolute and are subject to judicial interpretation. In this cyber age, protection of these rights is perhaps more important than ever.

CASE STUDY **The Right to Privacy**
Learn about a 2005 case in which the police used a "sniffer" dog to search for illegal drugs during a routine traffic stop.

WHAT YOU NEED TO KNOW Learn about the privacy protections the Fourth Amendment provides and the circumstances under which the government can infringe upon your right of privacy.

SIMULATION **Have You Been Seized?** Use your knowledge to argue a case involving an alleged search and seizure violation.

Student Casebook

Use your Student Casebook to take notes on the section and to complete the simulation.

Specially trained dogs are often used by law enforcement agencies to search for illegal drugs or explosives. Here, police use dogs to search a van and a subway train.

The Right to Privacy

Should authorities be able to search a car or home with "sniffer" dogs? What about using an electronic sensor that detects chemical traces from illegal drugs or heat coming from a house? Neither method requires authorities to enter the car or building, so are these really searches? When, if ever, should such a search be legal?

A Canine Alert

On a rainy day in 1998, Roy Caballes was driving along the highway, headed for Chicago. Illinois state trooper Daniel Gillette clocked Caballes doing 71 miles per hour in a 65-mile-per-hour zone. Gillette pulled Caballes over to give him a ticket for speeding.

Gillette called police headquarters to check for any outstanding arrest warrants. Caballes was not wanted anywhere, but the check revealed that he twice had been arrested for selling drugs.

At the same time, another state trooper, Craig Graham, heard the call on his police radio. Because he was nearby, he decided to go to the location with his drug-sniffing dog. He arrived while Gillette was writing the ticket.

When Trooper Graham walked the dog around Caballes's car, it barked at the trunk. When the troopers opened the trunk, they found a large quantity of marijuana inside. The troopers arrested Caballes for drug trafficking.

Caballes's lawyer tried to prevent the drugs from being introduced as evidence at the trial, claiming that they were the product of an illegal search. The judge disagreed. Caballes was convicted and sentenced to 12 years in prison.

In 2003 the Illinois Supreme Court reversed Caballes's conviction. It ruled that using a drug-sniffing dog at a routine traffic stop violated Caballes's Fourth Amendment rights. The state appealed this ruling to the Supreme Court, creating the case *Illinois* v. *Caballes*.

The Court Hears *Illinois* v. *Caballes*

The Supreme Court heard oral arguments in *Illinois* v. *Caballes* in late 2004. Illinois attorney general Lisa Madigan claimed that Trooper Graham's actions were proper. She cited *United States* v. *Place* (1983), in which the Court ruled that dog sniff searches are not a search under the Fourth Amendment. Madigan pointed out that a dog sniff is not a search because a sniff does not violate anyone's privacy.

Justice David Souter replied that he agreed a sniff was not a full-blown search. But if it was constitutional, he asked, what would prevent police from walking dogs around the foundation of every private home, just to see if they get a "sniff of something"?

Madigan again said that dog sniffs were not searches. "Is that your answer?" responded Justice Ruth Bader Ginsburg. "That police can parade up and down the streets of the country with dogs?" Madigan replied that Illinois did not have the resources to be able to do that.

Justice Antonin Scalia noted that the law allows dogs to sniff at bus depots "and the republic seems to have survived." He also pointed to *Kyllo* v. *United States* (2001), in which the Court ruled that police violated Fourth Amendment rights when they used thermal-imaging devices to see if people were growing marijuana in their homes. Madigan replied that the scanners could detect all kinds of human activity—including perfectly legal behavior—inside a home, while a drug-sniffing dog would detect only drugs.

Caballes's attorney argued that the sniff was actually a search because, like the scanner, it revealed something that was hidden from view. He also noted that the Court's earlier decision in *Place* was based on a *suspicion* of illegal activity. He pointed out that in this case police had no reasonable suspicion of Caballes that would allow a search of his car.

Thermal-imaging devices, such as the camera shown here, use sensors to detect heat. In colored images produced by the device, the warmest areas are orange, red, and white.

The *Caballes* Decision

The Supreme Court ruled on *Illinois* v. *Caballes* in 2005. In a 6–2 decision (Chief Justice William Rehnquist took no part), the Court reversed the Illinois Supreme Court and upheld Caballes's conviction. Justice John Paul Stevens wrote the majority opinion and began by stating that a person has no legitimate privacy interest in possessing drugs or other contraband. Any government action that indicates possession of contraband—but nothing more—does not violate a protected Fourth Amendment privacy interest.

The Court agreed with the state's argument that a dog sniff is not a search. As long as the traffic stop itself was lawful, the Court said, the police had the right to use the dog. A sniffer dog only establishes the presence or absence of something. Once the dog alerted on the car, the police had the reasonable suspicion they needed to conduct their search.

Justices Ginsburg and Souter each wrote dissenting opinions. Souter pointed out that dogs can be wrong, as a result of poor training, errors by their handler, or a dog's limited ability. He argued that the dog's bark thus was not probable cause to search the car.

"Every traffic stop could become an occasion to call in the dogs," Ginsburg wrote, "to the distress and embarrassment of the law-abiding population." She worried that the decision "clears the way for . . . police with dogs, stationed at long traffic lights, circl[ing] cars waiting for the red signal to turn green."

What Do You Think?

1. Is a trained dog's sniff of someone or something a search of that person or thing? Explain why or why not.

2. Do you agree with the majority of the Court in the *Caballes* case or with the dissenting opinions? Explain why.

3. Would your opinion in the *Caballes* case be different if it had involved a bomb-sniffing dog instead? Explain why or why not.

WHAT YOU NEED TO KNOW

Understanding Search and Seizure

The Fourth Amendment to the Constitution states that "the right of the people to be secure in their persons, homes, papers and effects, against unreasonable search and seizure, shall not be violated." Perhaps the first thing to know about this guarantee is that it applies only to searches and seizures *made by the government*. In *United States* v. *Jacobsen* (1984), the Supreme Court ruled that the Fourth Amendment does not protect against unreasonable searches and seizures by private organizations or citizens. In addition, the Fourth Amendment did not apply to the actions of state governments until 1949 (*Wolf* v. *Colorado*). Finally, the Court did not apply the exclusionary rule (discussed in Chapter 10) to state courts until 1961 in the case of *Mapp* v. *Ohio*.

Searches and Seizures

Within the meaning of the Fourth Amendment, the definition of a **search**—any action by government to find evidence of criminal activity—is very broad. It includes everything from searching someone's property, to listening in on phone conversations, to stopping suspicious-looking persons and frisking them for weapons.

A **seizure** occurs when authorities keep something. That something can be an object or a person. For example, police officers might seize an item from a home that they think is evidence in a murder. They might take drugs or a weapon from a person they have stopped and frisked. Or they can seize a person.

A person, such as Roy Caballes in the case study, is seized when his or her movement is restricted by physical force or by someone's authority. Arrest is a seizure. But not all seizures involve arrests. For example, if a police officer tells you, "Stay here until I come back," have you been "seized"? It depends: If you believe you can leave, you have not been seized, but if you have the impression you will be arrested if you try to leave, your person has been "seized" under the Fourth Amendment (*United States* v. *Mendenhall*, 1980).

Probable Cause and Warrants

The Fourth Amendment also states that "no warrant shall issue, but upon probable cause." To obtain a warrant—a court order to search for something or seize someone—there must be probable cause, or good reason, to believe that the search will produce evidence of a crime or that the person to be seized committed the crime.

Note that nowhere in the Fourth Amendment is a warrant *required* for every instance of government search, seizure, or arrest.

Key Terms

search
seizure
plain view doctrine
Terry stop
special needs test
cyber-surveillance
National Security Letter

REAL-WORLD EXAMPLE

Seizure without Arrest One example of a seizure under the Court's application of the Fourth Amendment in *Mendenhall* is traffic stops. When police stop a car, the driver is not under arrest. But if the driver tries to drive away while the officer is in the police car, the driver can reasonably expect that he or she would be arrested. Since the driver likely knows that he or she cannot leave, even though he or she is not under arrest, that makes the traffic stop a seizure.

Applying Information If you are a passenger in a car that has been stopped, have you been "seized" along with the driver? Why or why not?

In fact, many Supreme Court cases have held that warrants are not always necessary. However, whether a warrant is required or not, probable cause is usually needed to make a search. Probable cause is always needed to make an arrest.

Unreasonable Searches The Fourth Amendment bans "unreasonable search and seizure." But what is "unreasonable"? The Court answered this question in *Katz* v. *United States* (1967) when it ruled that searchers must respect a person's right to privacy. In general, this means that a search warrant is needed to look inside something. The warrant must state what is being searched and what authorities are looking for. They cannot just look through all of someone's property and see what turns up. That would be an unreasonable invasion of privacy and therefore an unreasonable search under the Fourth Amendment.

Warrantless Searches There are many instances in which a search warrant is not required, however. If an object is in plain view, the law assumes that the owner does not consider it private. If the owner wanted to keep it private, he or she would have put it somewhere out of sight. This is known as the **plain view doctrine**. For example, if police have a warrant to search a home for stolen computers and see illegal drugs in plain view on the table, they can seize the drugs as evidence even though such items are not listed on the search warrant.

READING CHECK **Summarizing** How are search and seizure related?

QUICK FACTS

Warrantless Searches

According to the Supreme Court, no search warrant is necessary in some emergency situations or when protecting the safety of the police or the public.

Voluntary consent
If a person consents to a search, police do not need a warrant, even if the person does not know that he has the right to refuse (*Schneckloth* v. *Bustamonte*, 1973).

Lawful arrests ▶
Police may conduct a search limited to the person placed under arrest and the area immediately nearby for hidden weapons and evidence (*Chimel* v. *California*, 1969).

Hot pursuit
If police are chasing a suspect, they can follow him or her into a building and seize any evidence they find (*Ker* v. *State of California*, 1963).

Emergency circumstances
Police do not need a search warrant in life-threatening situations—for example, to search a building after a bomb threat or to enter a home after hearing a shot fired inside (*Payton* v. *New York*, 1980).

Automobile searches
In general, police do not need a warrant to search a car or anything inside it. However, they must still have probable cause to suspect that the car holds evidence of a crime (*California* v. *Acevedo*, 1991).

When police arrest a person lawfully, they may conduct a warrantless search of the person and of the area within "lunging distance" of the person. *Why do you think the Supreme Court allows a search of the area near a suspect?*

The Fourth Amendment and Privacy

In *Katz* v. *United States* the Court held that the Fourth Amendment protects people, not just places. Wherever a person is, his or her right to privacy is protected if he or she has exhibited a reasonable expectation of privacy. The level of privacy a person can expect depends, at least in part, on where the person is. You do not, for example, expect as much privacy in a coffee shop as you do inside your own home. No matter where a person is, however, he or she has *no* expectation of privacy in the possession of illegal drugs.

The Court has also said that a search or seizure that is lawful when it begins can subsequently violate the Fourth Amendment if the way the search is carried out unreasonably infringes upon interests protected by the Constitution (*United States* v. *Jacobsen*, 1984). The Court has used all of these principles to decide when and how far protections under the Fourth Amendment apply.

Searches of Homes

The Supreme Court applies the highest expectation of privacy to people's homes, including their yards. In most cases, a search warrant is required to conduct searches of homes. Over the years, though, the Court has relaxed even this requirement. In one case, police officers looking into an apartment through the window blinds saw two men bagging illegal drugs. The men did not live in the apartment but were there to buy and sell drugs. Police entered the home, arrested the men, and seized the drugs. The Court ruled that no search warrant was required because the men had no reasonable expectation of privacy in an apartment they were visiting for commercial purposes only (*Minnesota* v. *Carter*, 1998).

In *California* v. *Greenwood* (1988) the Court ruled that a person's garbage cans could be searched without a warrant. The justices held that a person has no expectation of privacy for items that he or she has thrown away.

In another case, police flying in a plane spotted marijuana plants growing in a yard. The Court allowed an arrest even though the yard had a high fence around it for privacy (*California* v. *Ciraolo*, 1986). But in *Kyllo* v. *United States* (2001), the case mentioned in the Case Study, the justices drew the line at the use of devices that "look" through the walls of homes from the outside. Police arrested Kyllo after a thermal scan of his home revealed that he was growing marijuana inside. The Court threw out his arrest because a thermal scan reveals information that would normally be available only with an actual intrusion into the house and is therefore a search requiring a warrant. Because authorities did not have a warrant, the seizure of evidence and Kyllo's arrest were unconstitutional.

REAL-WORLD EXAMPLE
CASE STUDY LINK

Public Safety Searches
The idea that society may need—to protect public safety—certain types of searches that might not be reasonable under the Fourth Amendment is shown by the Court's willingness to allow police to set up roadblocks to catch drunk drivers (*Michigan Dept. of State Police* v. *Sitz*, 1990) or to try to intercept illegal aliens near the border (*United States* v. *Martinez-Fuerte*, 1976). Laws also allow the screening of all airline passengers and their carry-on luggage, as well as random searches of automobiles at border crossings.

Applying Information
Should it be permissible for police to use a dog to sniff your carry-on luggage at an airport? Why or why not?

**Terry Stop
Search Prior to Arrest**

Before *Terry* v. *Ohio,* police had to have probable cause to arrest a person before they could search the suspect. If police searched the person and found evidence before an arrest was made, the evidence could be excluded from the trial. Law enforcement agencies argued that there were circumstances, such as when they had reasonable suspicion that a person had committed a crime, in which a search prior to an arrest was necessary to protect their safety and the safety of the public. The Supreme Court agreed in *Terry* and said that a brief detention and search of a person, based on reasonable suspicion, does not violate the protections of the Fourth Amendment. This search is called the Terry stop.

Personal Privacy

The Fourth Amendment provides that people will be secure in their persons from unreasonable search and seizure. The Supreme Court has interpreted this guarantee in a variety of ways and has applied it differently in a number of circumstances.

Stop and Frisk In general, police do not have the right to stop people randomly on the street and search them. In *Terry* v. *Ohio* (1968) the Court ruled that police could stop people who seem to be acting suspiciously and pat them down for weapons. Neither a warrant nor even probable cause is needed for what is now called a **Terry stop**. Under *Terry*, a reasonable suspicion will support an officer's "serious intrusion upon the sanctity of the person." The need for public safety outweighs the individual's privacy right.

In 1993 the Court widened the Terry stop in *Minnesota* v. *Dickerson* to allow police to seize other contraband that they find during a pat down. However, in 2000 the Court took a big step back from *Terry* in *Florida* v. *J.L.* In that case, the justices ruled that an anonymous tip that a man was carrying a gun was not sufficient reason to stop and search him. The same Court also decided that anyone who flees upon seeing the police can be stopped and searched (*Illinois* v. *Wardlow*, 2000).

Intrusive Searches The degree to which authorities may go in searching a person's body depends on the situation. In general, the Court seems to consider three questions in deciding whether such a search is reasonable under the Fourth Amendment:

1. What is the legal status of the person being searched? Is he or she in custody, suspected of a crime, or a "free" person?
2. How invasive is the search? Does it involve intrusions beyond the body's surface?
3. Does the search serve some safety or security need for society? This standard has been called the **special needs test**.

For example, strip searches of prisoners are permissible because of the obvious need to keep weapons and contraband out of jails—and because prisoners have few constitutional rights. Fingerprinting persons who have been arrested is also allowable because the arrest provides probable cause. But taking the fingerprints of people who are not under arrest requires the police to have probable cause to believe, or at least a reasonable suspicion, that the person has committed a crime (*Hayes* v. *Florida,* 1985).

Testing a person's blood or DNA is considered more invasive than fingerprinting, so for free persons such tests generally require a search warrant. Taking blood from a person who is under arrest requires only probable cause (*Schmerber* v. *California,* 1966).

Drug Testing Drug tests are also considered to be intrusive searches because they require blood or urine samples. In most cases they also require a warrant or at least probable cause. The Court has removed this requirement for certain groups of people in society. For example, it has ruled that the government can require workers in some jobs where public safety is important, such as in aviation, trucking, railroads, and other transportation industries, to be tested without probable cause or even the suspicion that they are on drugs (*Skinner* v. *Railway Labor Executives' Association,* 1989).

The Court has expanded the special needs test to public schools. In *Vernonia School District* v. *Acton* (1995), it ruled that schools may require random drug testing of athletes, even if no one is suspected of drug use. "Deterring drug use by our nation's school-children is at least as important as . . . deterring drug use by engineers and trainmen," the justices observed in their decision.

Students' Fourth Amendment Rights

As with First Amendment rights and freedoms, the Court has generally limited students' Fourth Amendment rights. The Court's reasoning is basically the same—students' rights may be restricted in order to preserve a proper learning environment in schools.

In *New Jersey* v. *T.L.O.* (1985) the Court ruled that probable cause is not needed for school officials to search students as long as the circumstances make the search reasonable. In the *T.L.O.* case a teacher found a girl smoking in a restroom. When brought before the vice principal, the girl denied that she smoked at all. Searching her purse, the vice principal found not only cigarettes but also a small amount of marijuana. The Court ruled that the vice principal's search of the purse was not unreasonable under the circumstances.

After the ruling in *T.L.O.*, most cases involving student searches, such as locker searches, were decided at the state level. Some cases have concluded that lockers are school property and students have no expectation of privacy. Other cases have held that students do have at least some privacy rights in their lockers. Any search conducted by police officers still requires a search warrant.

Private Communication

The landmark Supreme Court decision on wiretapping and other forms of electronic surveillance is *Katz* v. *United States* (1967). Since the *Katz* decision, however, the use of computers, cell phones, personal digital assistants, and other wireless devices has created new kinds of searches to which the Fourth Amendment must be applied. Cases involving what is called **cyber-surveillance**—searches of wireless communications—have yet to reach the Supreme Court.

The Fourth Amendment since 9/11 After the September 11, 2001, attacks on the World Trade Center and the Pentagon, Congress worried that terrorists might be plotting more attacks. In October 2001 Congress passed the USA PATRIOT Act, a law that greatly relaxed privacy protections and controls on searches and seizures. Among the law's controversial sections is a provision that allows government agencies to search a variety of information about Americans. For example, the FBI can require almost anyone—including phone companies, Internet service providers, libraries, and bookstores—to turn over records on their customers.

What troubles civil liberties advocates is that some of these searches do not require a warrant. Instead, they are authorized by a document called a **National Security Letter** (NSL). Unlike warrants, NSLs are not issued by a judge, and probable cause is not needed to obtain them. They are pieces of paper signed, issued, and used by the Federal Bureau of Investigation and other government agencies. The PATRIOT Act also contains a gag order—the recipient of an NSL is prohibited from disclosing that the letter was ever issued.

Wireless "Searches" Many of today's computers, phones, and other communication devices use wireless communication. Anyone with a scanner tuned to the proper frequencies can intercept these signals.

Limiting the Right to Privacy

Following the terrorist attacks on September 11, 2001, Congress passed laws, such as the USA PATRIOT Act, that expanded the authority of government agencies to take actions to protect the lives and safety of American citizens. *How would you resolve the conflict between the Fourth Amendment's search and seizure protections and the threat of terrorist attacks?*

Some personal items may be seized by airport security guards.

Government agencies may monitor some electronic communications.

The government may obtain a list of the books you borrow from a library.

Federal law makes this interception illegal, except for law enforcement agencies. In fact, federal law requires that all wireless equipment sold in the United States is able to be monitored. Authorities usually must obtain a warrant to monitor wireless or electronic communications. But under the PATRIOT Act and the government terrorist-surveillance programs, some standards for obtaining warrants have been relaxed or eliminated. The Supreme Court may one day be asked to rule on these programs.

National Security and the Courts Several Fourth Amendment challenges to government surveillance programs are before federal courts. In *United States* v. *Arnold* (2006) a federal court ruled that authorities violated Arnold's Fourth Amendment rights when they searched the contents of his laptop computer as he went through airport security. The authorities argued that the search was routine and did not require reasonable suspicion. The court ruled the search inadmissible, and the government has appealed the ruling.

In 2006 the Electronic Frontier Foundation, a communications watchdog group, filed a class-action suit in federal court against AT&T. The suit accuses AT&T of turning over the phone records of millions of Americans to the National Security Agency. A federal court also has ordered a halt to the government's 20-year practice of secretly obtaining stored e-mails from e-mail service providers without a warrant (*Warshak* v. *United States*, 2007).

The government has argued strongly that its actions are necessary to protect national security, and it has appealed these cases. It is likely that the Supreme Court will be asked to decide these Fourth Amendment issues as well as other similar cases.

READING CHECK **Summarizing** Why are National Security Letters controversial?

Section 2 Assessment

thinkcentral.com
KEYWORD: SGO SUP HP

Reviewing Ideas and Terms

1. **a. Describe** What is the **plain view doctrine**?
   b. Summarize In what situations can police conduct a **search** without a warrant?
   c. Elaborate Should searches of motor vehicles require police to have a warrant? Why or why not?

2. **a. Explain** What is **cyber-surveillance**?
   b. Evaluate What do you think is the most important factor in deciding whether a search is reasonable? Explain your answer.

Critical Thinking

3. **Evaluate** Why is it possible for people to agree on a fundamental value such as the right to privacy but disagree over the meaning of that right in specific situations? Give examples that illustrate your answer.

CASE STUDY LINK You answered the following questions at the end of the Case Study. Now that you have completed Section 2, think about and answer the questions again. Then compare your answers with your earlier responses. Are your answers the same or are they different?

4. Is a trained dog's sniff of someone or something a search of that person or thing? Explain why or why not.

5. Do you agree with the majority of the Court in the *Caballes* case or with the dissenting opinions? Explain why.

6. Would your opinion in the *Caballes* case be different if it had involved a bomb-sniffing dog instead? Explain why or why not.

Have You Been Seized?

How will the Supreme Court rule in *State* v. *Martin*?

Student Casebook

Use your Student Casebook to complete the simulation.

Issues relating to Fourth Amendment searches and seizures have been brought before courts for many years, and still not every question has been resolved. In this simulation, you will argue one such Fourth Amendment issue before the Supreme Court.

Roles

- Chief justice of the United States
- Eight associate justices
- Plaintiff's attorneys
- Defendant's attorneys
- Attorneys from the National Association of Law Enforcement Members (NALEM)
- Attorneys from the Foundation for Fourth Amendment Freedoms (FFAF)

❶ The Situation

In a pat-down search during a traffic stop, police discovered a small amount of illegal drugs on the person of 18-year-old Greg Martin. Martin was convicted in state district court for drug possession. He appealed his conviction to the state supreme court. Martin claimed that under the Fourth Amendment the search that discovered the drugs was illegal—because he was a passenger in the car and there was no probable cause to search him. The state supreme court agreed and overturned his conviction. The state has now appealed the ruling to the Supreme Court of the United States.

Background

- Eighteen-year-old Joel Anderson (the driver) was giving his friend Greg Martin (a passenger) a ride home after school.

- Joel Anderson was pulled over by the police because his taillight was burned out.

- Officer William Gibson told Anderson that he would get a written warning and asked to see Anderson's driver's license. At that point Anderson admitted that he did not have a license because it had been suspended.

- Officer Gibson ordered both men out of the car. He arrested Anderson and told him that the car was impounded and would be towed.

- At that point, Martin told Officer Gibson that he was going to a nearby grocery store to call someone to pick him up and walked away from the car.

- Officer Gibson ordered Martin to return to the car. Martin did so without comment or objection. Officer Gibson patted Martin down and found a small amount of illegal drugs.

- Officer Gibson placed Martin under arrest as well and transported both men to the police station.

❷ The Hearing

Attorneys for both the plaintiff and defendant will present their oral arguments to the Court. The plaintiff's case is presented first, followed by the defendant's. Justices may interrupt each argument at any time to ask the attorneys questions. After each side has made its argument, the Court will rule, either upholding or reversing the state supreme court's ruling that overturned Martin's conviction at trial.

The Chief Justice The chief justice will be in charge of the trial. He or she will read each side's amicus curiae brief and recognize the attorneys when it is their turn to speak. He or she will preside over the Court's deliberations at the end of the hearing and will assign one of the associate justices to write the Court's opinion. The chief justice will then "publish" the Court's decision by reading it aloud to the class.

The Associate Justices The associate justices will also read each side's amicus brief and listen to oral arguments. Along with the chief justice, they may interrupt each argument to ask the attorney questions about it. At the end of the hearing, all the justices will discuss the case and vote on how the Court should rule. Justices who disagree with the majority decision may write a dissenting opinion. If there is a dissenting opinion, the author will read it after the majority opinion has been read.

The Parties' Attorneys Each side's attorneys will prepare their oral argument and present it to the Court.

The Amicus Attorneys Attorneys representing each organization will write their amicus brief for the Court. They will also help the attorneys for whichever side they support in researching and preparing that side's case.

State v. Martin

Parties to the case

- The plaintiff: The State

- The defendant: Greg Martin

Amici curiae

- For the plaintiff: National Association of Law Enforcement Members (NALEM)

- For the defendant: Foundation for Fourth Amendment Freedoms (FFAF)

---

❸ Debriefing

While the Supreme Court is deliberating its decision, write a one-page decision of your own, revealing how you would decide the case if you were on the Court. After the Court's decision is read, discuss whether you agree or disagree with the Court's opinion or opinions.

Amicus Curiae Briefs *Amicus curiae* (plural, *amici curiae*) is Latin for "friend of the court." The term refers to a person or organization that files a legal brief, with the court's permission, to express views on one or more issues in a case involving other parties because it has a strong interest in the subject matter of the action.

Due Process and the Fourteenth Amendment

Reading Focus

The Fourteenth Amendment requires that states provide due process and equal protection under the law. These requirements have made this amendment one of the most important parts of the Constitution.

CASE STUDY **Due Process and Public Schools**
Learn about how the Fourteenth Amendment right to due process applies to public schools.

WHAT YOU NEED TO KNOW Learn about how the Supreme Court has used the due process clause of the Fourteenth Amendment to expand and protect people's rights.

SIMULATION **Terrorists and Due Process** Use your knowledge to argue a case involving due process issues before the Supreme Court.

Student Casebook

Use your Student Casebook to take notes on the section and to complete the simulation.

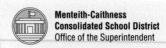
Menteith-Caithness Consolidated School District
Office of the Superintendent

Notice of Student Rights and Responsibilities

Student and Parent Complaints or Grievances

1. The student or parent may designate a representative through written notice to the District at any level of this process. "Representative" shall mean any person who or organization that is designated by the student or parent to represent the student or parent in the complaint process.

School boards may conduct student disciplinary proceedings that require that student due process rights—such as the right to notice and a hearing—be protected.

Due Process and Public Schools

What due process rights, if any, do students have if they are facing suspension from public school? The Supreme Court addressed the issue in *Goss* v. *Lopez* in 1975.

The School Suspension Case

In 1971 school officials in Columbus, Ohio, suspended a number of high school students for up to 10 days for student misconduct. One of the students, Dwight Lopez, asserted that he was an innocent bystander. Lopez filed a lawsuit claiming he had been denied his due process rights because school officials suspended him without a hearing. Joining Lopez as plaintiffs in the lawsuit were eight other students. They asked a federal district court to order that their suspensions be removed from their school records.

The district court ruled that the suspensions were unconstitutional because Lopez and the other plaintiffs had been denied due process. The court held that at a minimum the school system should have given the students notice of their suspension and held a hearing either before suspending them or shortly afterward. The school system appealed to the Supreme Court.

The Court Hears *Goss* v. *Lopez*

School system official Norval Goss argued that because there was no constitutional right in Ohio to a public education, there was no requirement that the school district provide students with due process—notice of their suspension and a hearing—before suspending them.

The attorneys for Lopez and the other plaintiffs pointed to Ohio law, which requires the state to provide a free education for all students. They argued that suspending students without due process unconstitutionally deprived students of this right.

The Supreme Court's Decision

The Court decided *Goss* v. *Lopez* in 1975. It said in a 5–4 decision that because Ohio offered public education to its citizens, students could not be deprived of the right to that education without due process of law.

Justice Byron White wrote the opinion for the majority. He agreed with Goss that the Ohio Constitution did not require the state to educate its citizens. But by creating a full K–12 (kindergarten through grade 12) education system and requiring students to attend school, Ohio had made an education a property right. Taking away that valuable right "unilaterally and without process," White wrote, "collides with the requirements of the Constitution."

The Court ruled that either before a suspension or soon thereafter, students must be given a hearing and allowed to explain their version of the events at issue. The Court stopped short, however, of allowing students to call or cross-examine witnesses.

The Aftermath

Student due process issues still arise. Lower courts continue to address questions left unanswered by *Goss*, such as how specific the notice must be. In general, courts defer to school officials when issues involving student procedural due process issues arise. However, courts have consistently interpreted *Goss* to mean that students who are suspended for longer than 10 days must be granted more due process rights.

What Do You Think?

1. Do you agree that a public education is a property right? Why or why not?

2. Should students suspended for fewer than 10 days for a rule violation have a right to a hearing? Why or why not?

3. Should students who are expelled receive more due process than those who are suspended? Explain why or why not.

Due Process and Equal Protection

Key Terms

unenumerated rights

REAL-WORLD EXAMPLE

Damages and Due Process In *Philip Morris* v. *Williams*, a jury found that Jesse Williams's death was caused by smoking and that the Philip Morris tobacco company should pay his widow $79.5 million in damages. Part of that award was for similar harm caused by Philip Morris to other people who were not parties to this lawsuit. Philip Morris appealed the damage award to the Supreme Court. In 2007, the Court ruled for Philip Morris, saying that due process forbids punishing a defendant for injury inflicted upon persons who are not even parties to the litigation.

Applying Information How would making Philip Morris pay damages to nonparties violate requirements of due process?

ACADEMIC VOCABULARY

doctrine a principle of law established through past decisions

The Fourteenth Amendment provides that no state shall "deprive any person of life, liberty, or property, without due process of law; nor deny to any person within its jurisdiction the equal protection of the laws." As you read in Chapter 10, this language has been interpreted by the Supreme Court to apply many of the guarantees in the Bill of Rights to actions of state governments through the doctrine of incorporation.

Equally important, the Fourteenth Amendment has enabled the Court to incorporate and apply the idea of "equal protection" against actions of the federal government. Nowhere in the Constitution or the Bill of Rights is the right to equal treatment under the law by the federal government guaranteed.

The part of the Fourteenth Amendment that guarantees "due process of law" is called the due process clause. The language that guarantees the equal protection of the laws is known as the equal protection clause. These two clauses are related, but the Supreme Court has given each clause its own meaning. To have due process of law, both the laws themselves and the process and procedures of applying and enforcing the law must be fair. Equal protection means that, all other circumstances being equal, the law is applied the same way to each person. In other words, each person in the same or similar circumstances stands before the law equally.

Applying the idea that both the law and legal procedures must be fair, the Court has defined the two types of due process. The first type is called procedural due process. Procedural due process requires that certain *procedures* must be followed in carrying out and enforcing the law. For example, the city cannot use eminent domain to take your property for a new city hall without giving you notice and an opportunity to contest the taking.

The second form is known as substantive due process, which stems from the belief that if the way that laws are carried out must be fair, the laws themselves should be fair, too. That is, what laws say and require—their content or *substance*—must be fair. The doctrine of substantive due process arose following the addition of the Fourteenth Amendment in 1868. It is part of the larger idea that people have natural rights that are not listed in the Constitution, and that to be fair, a law cannot violate people's natural rights. The Quick Facts chart on the next page highlights the differences between procedural and substantive due process.

READING CHECK **Summarizing** Explain how procedural due process and substantive due process ensure that a person will have a fair trial.

THINK central — Interactive

thinkcentral.com
KEYWORD: SGO SUP

Understanding Due Process

Under the Fifth and Fourteenth amendments to the Constitution, no government action may deprive a person of "life, liberty, or property, without due process of law." Due process requires the government to act fairly when carrying out government actions. Courts have separated due process into two parts: procedural due process and substantive due process. The difference between these two concepts is not always clear. To help you understand the difference, read the explanations below.

QUICK FACTS

PROCEDURAL DUE PROCESS

Procedural due process is based on the concept of "fundamental fairness." It ensures that government *application* of a law is fair and does not restrict a person's constitutional rights. Due process applies to both civil and criminal law. It generally requires:

- notice to the person of the action being taken
- an opportunity to be heard regarding the action
- an impartial decision maker
- the right to confront and cross-examine adverse evidence, parties, and witnesses
- a decision on the record
- assistance of counsel

SNYDER v. MASSACHUSETTS (1934): A PROCEDURAL DUE PROCESS CASE

Mr. Snyder and two other men were accused of murder. During Snyder's trial, the judge, the jury, a bailiff, the court reporter, and attorneys for both sides went to view the scene of the crime. Snyder requested that he be allowed to attend, but the judge denied his request. Snyder was convicted of murder. He appealed his conviction to the Supreme Court, asserting that under the Constitution, he had a due process right to view the crime scene as part of his defense.

The Court ruled against Snyder. It said that procedural due process is violated when an action "offends some principle of justice so rooted in the traditions and conscience of our people as to be ranked as fundamental." In this case, denying Snyder the right to attend the viewing did not violate his right to due process because the judge controlled the viewing and Snyder's counsel was present.

In a dissenting opinion, Justice Owen Roberts wrote that due process requires that "certain fundamental rules of fairness be observed; forbids the disregard of those rules; and is not satisfied though the result is just, if the hearing was unfair." In Roberts's opinion, everyone else was at the viewing, so Snyder should have been, too.

QUICK FACTS

SUBSTANTIVE DUE PROCESS

The principle of substantive due process is used to examine whether the *content* of a government action—a criminal or civil law—is fair and reasonable and does not unjustly restrict a person's constitutional rights. Substantive due process applies to both natural persons and corporations. It applies to:

- police power, as in regulations to promote the public health, safety, and morals
- laws regulating worker safety, wages, hours, and places of work
- government taxing, zoning, and eminent domain powers
- noneconomic rights such as privacy, family relationships, the right to die, the right to travel, the right to personal dignity, and other unenumerated rights

WASHINGTON v. GLUCKSBERG (1997): A SUBSTANTIVE DUE PROCESS CASE

The state of Washington bans physician-assisted suicide and makes it a crime. Dr. Harold Glucksberg, four other physicians, three terminally ill patients, and a nonprofit organization sued the state, arguing that the ban violated a terminally ill person's right of privacy and right to die under the Fourteenth Amendment's due process clause.

The federal district court ruled in favor of the plaintiffs. The Ninth Circuit Court of Appeals affirmed the district court's ruling. Washington appealed to the Supreme Court.

The Supreme Court focused on two due process clause issues: protecting our nation's fundamental, historically rooted rights and liberties; and defining what constitutes a due process liberty interest. The Court held that the right to assisted suicide is not a fundamental liberty interest protected by the due process clause since its practice has been, and continues to be, offensive to our national traditions and practices. Moreover, the Court held that Washington's ban was rationally related to the state's legitimate interest in protecting medical ethics, shielding disabled and terminally ill people from prejudice that might encourage them to end their lives, and preserving human life.

Substantive Due Process

One way of interpreting the Constitution, including the Bill of Rights, is to understand that the Constitution does not create or grant rights. Instead, it protects and guarantees those "unalienable rights" referred to in the Declaration of Independence. Under this interpretation, the purpose of the Ninth Amendment, when it states that "the enumeration in the Constitution of certain rights shall not be construed [understood] to deny . . . others retained by the people," is to recognize and protect those rights that are not explicitly stated. These unstated rights are known as **unenumerated rights**. The Supreme Court has used the doctrine of substantive due process to decide what some of these rights are, including certain property rights, the right to travel, the right to privacy, the right to personal autonomy, and the right to personal dignity.

ACADEMIC VOCABULARY

autonomy
personal sovereignty, independence, self-direction

Protecting Property Rights

At first, the Court used the doctrine of substantive due process mainly to define and protect property rights and other economic rights. Among the most famous examples of this use is *Lochner* v. *New York* (1905), also known as the Bakeshop Case.

The Bakeshop Case In 1895 the New York legislature passed the Bakeshop Act. This law prohibited bakery workers from being required to work more than 10 hours a day or 60 hours a week. Labor reformers believed that spending more time in such a dusty

The Bakeshop Case

Lochner v. *New York* (1905)

Significance: This case limited the states' ability to regulate labor and industry, such as limiting the number of hours per week a person could work.

Background: Bakery owner Lochner claimed the law violated his Fourteenth Amendment due process rights by depriving him of his freedom to make contracts with his employees.

Decision: Lochner won. The Supreme Court ruled that the Fourteenth Amendment includes the implicit individual property right to buy and sell labor. The Court ruled that any state law restricting that right is unconstitutional.

A photo of a bakery from the *Lochner* period

environment could harm people's health. Bakery owner Joseph Lochner was arrested for requiring an employee to work more than 60 hours a week. He appealed his conviction to the Supreme Court.

Lochner claimed that New York's law violated the Fourteenth Amendment's equal protection clause because it applied only to bakery workers. Lochner also argued that since the law prevented him from running his business as he chose, it violated the amendment's due process clause by depriving him of his property rights—an individual's right to negotiate an employment contract—without due process of law. The state countered that its law was a proper exercise of its power to protect the well-being of its citizens.

The Decision and the Dissent In a 5–4 decision, the justices agreed with Lochner. They overturned his conviction and ruled the Bakeshop Act unconstitutional. Justice Rufus Peckham wrote the majority opinion. When considering whether an exercise of a state's police power to safeguard the public health is constitutional, Peckham wrote, the Court must ask if the regulation is reasonable and necessary, or unreasonable, unnecessary, and arbitrary. In this case, the Court did not believe that working long hours in a bakery was unhealthy. As a result, the Court ruled that the New York law was unconstitutional because it was "an illegal interference with the rights of individuals, both employers and employees, to make contracts regarding labor upon such terms as they may think best."

Justices John Marshall Harlan and Oliver Wendell Holmes wrote strong dissents. Both argued that the Court's majority should have respected the legislature's judgment instead of following their own point of view on this issue. "A constitution is not intended to embody a particular economic theory," Holmes wrote. "I think that the word liberty in the Fourteenth Amendment is perverted when it is held to prevent the natural outcome of a dominant opinion."

Lochner's Effect After the *Lochner* decision the first criticisms of substantive due process began to be heard. Critics attacked the Court for using the doctrine to impose its views and values on the nation. As the Court continued to apply substantive due process to laws that affected property rights, criticism grew.

Finally, in *United States* v. *Carolene Products Company* (1938), the Court announced that it would apply only a rational basis test to economic regulations. The rational basis test meant that for a law to be upheld, the government would have to show only that it had a good reason—a rational basis—for passing the law. When the Court is called upon to review a law, the rational basis test is the least strict standard it can apply.

The practical result of the Court's announcement was that it nearly stopped applying substantive due process to property rights. However, the Court said in the *Carolene* decision that it would apply a stricter test to laws that affected personal rights.

REAL-WORLD EXAMPLE

Minimum Wages for Women In 1918 Congress enacted a law requiring that women in the District of Columbia be paid a minimum wage. The Children's Hospital of the District of Columbia challenged the constitutionality of the law. In *Adkins* v. *Children's Hospital* (1923), the Supreme Court, following the *Lochner* rule, declared the law unconstitutional as an infringement on an employer's right to negotiate employment contracts with the female employees.

Applying Information Should employers and employees have unlimited freedom to enter into employment contracts? Why or why not?

Protecting Personal Rights

After *Carolene*, the Court did begin to use substantive due process to define basic personal rights, none of which are expressly listed in the Constitution. For example, the Court recognized the rights to privacy, of autonomy, and to travel and establish a residence. The Court also guaranteed freedom of association.

Right to Privacy The privacy right was first recognized by the Court in *Griswold* v. *Connecticut* (1965), a case in which the Court struck down an 1879 law that banned the use of contraceptive devices. Eight years later the Court expanded the privacy right in the case of *Roe* v. *Wade* (1973). In *Roe* the Court ruled that the right to privacy gave women the right to decide whether or not to have an abortion.

As justices have died or retired and the makeup of the Court has changed, it has pulled back somewhat on the connection between privacy rights and abortion in cases such as *Webster* v. *Reproductive Services* (1989) and *Planned Parenthood of Southern Pennsylvania* v. *Casey* (1993). At the same time, however, the Court applied the privacy right to a new area—the right to die.

Determining the Right to Die In 1983 Missouri resident Nancy Beth Cruzan was critically injured in an auto accident. Paramedics restored her breathing and heartbeat at the scene, but she remained in what doctors call a "persistent vegetative state"—unconscious, unresponsive, and fed through a tube placed into her stomach. Doctors told Cruzan's parents she would never recover. In 1987 Cruzan's parents asked that the feeding tube be removed and that Nancy be allowed to die. The hospital refused, relying on a state policy that required "clear and convincing evidence" of what choice Nancy would make. The parents sued, arguing that their daughter would never want to live in such a condition.

Protecting Unenumerated Rights

The Constitution does not list all the rights that individuals have. The Supreme Court has used the due process clause of the Fourteenth Amendment to recognize and protect unenumerated, or unlisted, rights, such as Lochner's right to contract and the ones shown here. *Why has the Supreme Court recognized unenumerated rights?*

Travel

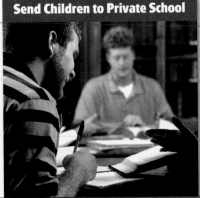

Send Children to Private School

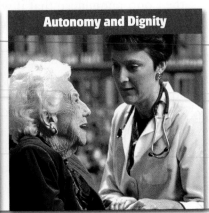

Autonomy and Dignity

The "Right to Die" Case

Cruzan v. Director, Missouri State Department of Public Health (1990)

Significance: Under the due process clause a person has a constitutional right to refuse treatment and to die.

Background: Nancy Cruzan was left in a vegetative state by a car accident. Her parents requested that she be allowed to die. The hospital refused.

Decision: In its 5–4 decision, the Court upheld the principle that incompetent persons are able to exercise the right to refuse medical treatment—and to die—under the due process clause. However, the Court ruled in favor of the Missouri Department of Health because there was no "clear and convincing evidence" of what Nancy Cruzan wanted. The Court upheld the state's policy and withdrawing Cruzan's life support was not allowed.

Nancy Cruzan before her car accident

The *Cruzan* Decision The trial court ruled for the parents. Yet the Missouri Supreme Court overturned the lower court, holding that there was no clear and convincing evidence that Nancy Cruzan wished to die. Her parents appealed to the U.S. Supreme Court.

In *Cruzan* v. *Director, Missouri State Department of Public Health* (1990), the Court ruled that the right to refuse medical treatment was a privacy right protected by the Fourteenth Amendment. However, at the same time, it also upheld the ruling of the Missouri Supreme Court. In a 5–4 decision, the justices noted that there was no strong evidence of what Cruzan wanted. To end her life-sustaining medical treatment without such evidence would violate her right to due process, the Court said.

The Effect of *Cruzan* Although the Court ruled against Cruzan's parents, this case established a person's right to refuse medical treatment and to die. It also set the due-process standard by which someone else can make that decision if the patient is unable to.

Following the Supreme Court's ruling, Cruzan's parents went back into state court in Missouri in 1990. There, they produced evidence of conversations with her friends in which Cruzan had said that she would never want to "live like a vegetable." The court ordered her feeding tube removed, and Cruzan died 12 days later.

Since the *Cruzan* decision, the Court has ruled that the right to die does not include a Fourteenth Amendment right to commit suicide. In 1997 it upheld laws banning physician-assisted suicide (*Washington* v. *Glucksberg* and *Vacco* v. *Quill*). As the population of the United States ages and medical care becomes more expensive, the Court may be asked to consider new "right-to-die" issues.

READING CHECK **Identifying the Main Idea** How has the Court's theory and use of substantive due process changed?

Due Process and the Right to Die The *Cruzan* right-to-die case followed a 1976 case in the New Jersey Supreme Court involving Karen Ann Quinlan. More recently, the 2005 case of Terri Schiavo involved many of the same issues. Assisted suicide cases include not only the *Washington* and *Vacco* cases but also a 2006 case, *Gonzales v. Oregon*. Visit **thinkcentral.com** to begin a Webquest on due process and the right to die with dignity.

THINK central Webquest

thinkcentral.com
KEYWORD: SGO SUP

Procedural Due Process

Procedural due process has a very different history from substantive due process. While substantive due process is a fairly new concept, the idea of procedural due process is an old one. It grew out of Magna Carta, the document signed in 1215 in which English nobles required the king to follow the law of the land.

Procedural Due Process and Property Rights

Most of the attention given procedural due process focuses on life and liberty issues—mainly as due process applies to the arrest and prosecution of persons accused of crimes. Property issues typically involve depriving people of their personal property or land.

In the 1970s, however, the Supreme Court expanded the concept of property to include other things to which people are entitled—including certain benefits, such as an education and statuses. In two landmark cases, it established minimum standards for procedural fairness before government can deprive people of these rights.

▶ *Goldberg v. Kelly* (1970) John Kelly and other New York residents receiving federal financial assistance challenged the constitutionality of procedures for termination of their aid. The state of New York originally offered no official notice or opportunity for hearings to those whose aid was about to be terminated. Recipients were allowed to file a written protest or to attend a hearing *after* their benefits had been cut off. Kelly argued that he should be entitled to a hearing *before* he was terminated. When his request was denied, he sued the city, which administered the programs. After Kelly filed his suit, New York state implemented procedures for hearings.

When local courts ruled in Kelly's favor, the city appealed to the Supreme Court. They argued that giving all aid recipients the right to a full evidentiary hearing would be too expensive.

In 1970 the Court ruled 5–3 that Kelly was entitled to a full hearing before his benefits were terminated. The justices ruled that he or his attorney had the right to appear at the hearing, to present evidence and arguments, and to cross-examine witnesses. The Court rejected the city's argument that a hearing after benefits were cut off satisfied Kelly's Fourteenth Amendment rights. "Termination of aid pending resolution of a controversy over eligibility may deprive an eligible recipient of the very means by which to live while he waits," wrote Justice William Brennan for the majority.

The *Goldberg* decision changed the way that all government payments, such as disability benefits or pensions, are administered. Before this case such payments were often viewed as charity or a privilege. In *Goldberg* the Court recognized aid payments as a form of property, and, the Court said, government cannot deprive people of this kind of property without due process of law.

REAL-WORLD EXAMPLE
CASE STUDY LINK

How Much Process Is Due? George Eldridge began receiving Social Security disability benefits in 1968. In 1972 the government stopped Eldridge's benefits without a pre-termination hearing. Eldridge sued, claiming that his Fifth Amendment right to due process was violated. In *Mathews* v. *Eldridge* (1976), the Supreme Court ruled that even though Eldridge had a property right in his benefits, no pre-termination hearing was required. The Court ruled that the interests of, and possible harm to, the individual must be balanced against the additional costs and benefits to the government of the additional procedures.
Applying Information How can *Mathews* and *Goldberg* both be right? Give examples to explain your answer.

The Unwed Father Case

Stanley v. Illinois (1972)

Significance: Established, in general, the minimum procedural steps required under the Constitution.

Background: Stanley was a father but not, under Illinois law, a parent. When his children were made wards of the state, Stanley sued, arguing that he had been denied the due process that married fathers had under state law.

Decision: The Supreme Court agreed with Stanley and ordered that unwed fathers are entitled to the same due process notice and hearing that married fathers get.

In cases involving family law issues, every parent is entitled to due process fairness.

Stanley v. Illinois (1972) Illinois resident Peter Stanley was not married to Joan Stanley, the mother of their three children. Illinois law defined a "parent" as the father and mother of a child born to a married couple and the mother—but not the father—of a child born to an unmarried couple. When Joan Stanley died, the state removed the children from Stanley's home because, according to the state's definition, Peter Stanley was not their parent. Stanley thought that the Illinois law was unfair—he had never been shown to be an unfit parent—and sued to regain custody of his children. The state court ruled that Stanley's fitness or unfitness as a parent was not relevant. Once it was shown that he was not married to the children's mother, state law allowed the removal of his children.

Stanley appealed the ruling to the Supreme Court. He argued that he had been denied due process because the state had never held a hearing to determine his fitness as a father. He also claimed that treating unwed fathers differently from other fathers violated the Fourteenth Amendment's equal protection clause. In 1972 the justices, by a 5–2 vote (two justices did not participate in the decision), agreed with both of Stanley's arguments. The Court held that unwed fathers are entitled to due process hearings—just like married fathers and unwed mothers—to determine their fitness as a parent before their children can be declared wards of the state.

The *Stanley* case is also important beyond the area of family law. In its decision, the Supreme Court established what the Constitution requires in the way of due process for any person. In general, the Court said, before government at any level can deprive a person of rights or property, the person must at least be given formal notice and a hearing to meet the requirements of procedural fairness.

Procedural Due Process and Juvenile Justice

By 1899 states recognized that juvenile offenders should be treated differently from adult criminals. Unfortunately, juvenile proceedings were often informal and did not include the due process protections of the Fifth and Fourteenth amendments. In the 1967 landmark case *In re Gault*, the Supreme Court extended many of the due process requirements of adult proceedings to the juvenile justice system.

Background to *Gault* The mother of 15-year-old Gerald Gault came home from work to find him missing from their Gila County, Arizona, home. She later discovered that Gerald had been taken into custody by the sheriff, following a complaint by a woman that someone had made an lewd phone call to her. The woman believed the caller to be Gerald.

Mrs. Gault went to the juvenile center where Gerald was being held. Only then did she learn that Gerald would have a juvenile court hearing the next afternoon—although she was never told clearly what Gerald was charged with. Neither Gerald nor his parents were advised he could have an attorney. During the hearing, the judge took no testimony from Gerald's family, no one testified under oath, and no record was made of the proceedings. The woman who complained was not required to appear, denying Gerald his Sixth Amendment right to confront and cross-examine his accuser. The judge found Gerald guilty and sentenced him to the state industrial school until he was 21—a period of six years.

The Juvenile Justice Case

In re Gault (1967)

Significance: The Supreme Court extended many of the requirements of fundamental fairness to juvenile criminal proceedings.

Background: Gerald Gault, 15, was accused of making obscene telephone calls and was taken into custody by the police. At his hearing, neither Gerald nor his parents were told he could have an attorney, nor was the complaining party present for Gerald to cross-examine. After the hearing, the family had no right to appeal Gerald's punishment.

Decision: Juveniles accused of crimes are entitled to most of the procedural safeguards—such as the right to notice and hearing, the right to an attorney, and the right to cross-examine witnesses—that adult criminal defendants are guaranteed.

Juvenile defendants are entitled to due process.

The *Gault* Decision Under Arizona law, Gerald Gault had no right to appeal his conviction or his punishment, so his parents petitioned the Supreme Court for his release. Gault's attorneys claimed that Arizona's juvenile code violated the Fourteenth Amendment protection of due process and that minors should have the same rights as adults in judicial procedures. The state argued that its juvenile justice system was deliberately informal so that the courts could do what was in the best interests of delinquent children.

In an 8–1 decision the justices rejected the state's argument. "Neither the Fourteenth Amendment nor the Bill of Rights is for adults alone," wrote Justice Abe Fortas in the majority opinion. Fortas said, "Under our Constitution, the condition of being a boy does not justify a kangaroo court." Gerald Gault, the Court said, is entitled to his due process protections.

***Gault's* Impact** The most important result of the *Gault* decision is that it gave juveniles most of the same due process rights—such as the rights to know what they are charged with, to counsel, and to confront witnesses—as adult defendants. States had to change their juvenile court systems and procedures to provide these rights.

As far as it went, though, *Gault* did not give juvenile defendants all the same rights as adult defendants. For example, in most states juvenile defendants still do not have a constitutional right to trial by jury. In addition, in *Schull* v. *Martin* (1984), the Court ruled that due process for juveniles does not include the right to be released from custody while they are awaiting trial.

READING CHECK **Summarizing** What is procedural due process?

Section 3 Assessment

THINK central **Online Quiz**
thinkcentral.com
KEYWORD: SGO SUP HP

Reviewing Ideas and Terms

1. **a. Identify** What does the Fourteenth Amendment's due process clause state?
   b. Compare How are the due process clause and equal protection clause related?

2. **a. Define** What are **unenumerated rights**?
   b. Explain Why is the doctrine of substantive due process controversial?
   c. Elaborate Do you think there should be a right to privacy? Why or why not?

3. **a. Recall** From when and where did the doctrine of procedural due process originate?
   b. Analyze How does procedural due process differ from substantive due process? How is it the same?
   c. Evaluate Do you think juvenile offenders should receive the same treatment as adults who are accused of crimes? Explain.

Critical Thinking

4. **Evaluate** Should the Supreme Court create and protect rights that are not specifically set out in the Constitution? Explain why or why not.

CASE STUDY LINK You answered the following questions at the end of the Case Study. Now that you have completed Section 3, think about and answer the questions again. Then compare your answers with your earlier responses. Are your answers the same or are they different?

5. Do you agree that a public education is a property right? Why or why not?

6. Should students suspended for fewer than 10 days for a rule violation have a right to a hearing? Why or why not?

7. Should students who are expelled receive more due process than those who are suspended? Explain why or why not?

SIMULATION

Terrorists and Due Process

Student Casebook

Use your Student Casebook to complete the simulation.

Should suspected terrorists receive due process of law?

The Fifth and Fourteenth Amendments guarantee that Americans may not be denied life, liberty, or property without due process of law. However, the Supreme Court has applied this protection in some very different ways. Use what you have learned in Section 3 to complete this simulation about a fictional procedural due process case being argued in the Supreme Court.

Roles

- Chief justice of the United States
- Associate justices
- Attorneys for the defendant
- Attorneys for the plaintiff
- Attorneys for the American Center for Civil Justice (ACCJ)
- Attorneys for Terrorism Victims and Survivors for Justice (TVSJ)

❶ The Situation

A number of people suspected of plotting or having committed terrorist acts against the United States are imprisoned at a U.S. military base in another country. These individuals have not been charged with a crime. They have never had a hearing or been brought to trial. They also have not been allowed to hire attorneys to represent them. Several of these individuals have been imprisoned for more than two years. Two individuals are U.S. citizens. The rest are citizens of other countries. A civil rights group has appealed on the detainees' behalf to the Supreme Court, asking that the prisoners receive due process of law.

Key Facts

- The civil rights group acting on the detainees' behalf is named Americans Protecting Civil Liberties (APCL).
- The group is seeking due process for the detainees, including the two U.S. citizens.
- All detainees were arrested outside the United States.
- Most of the detainees do not live in the United States.
- Americans Protecting Civil Liberties is the plaintiff in this case. The United States is the defendant.
- Another civil liberties group, the American Center for Civil Justice (ACCJ), has filed an amicus curiae brief with the Court in support of the plaintiff.
- A victims rights group, Terrorism Victims and Survivors for Justice (TVSJ), has filed an amicus curiae brief with the Court supporting the United States.

❷ Oral Arguments

Attorneys for plaintiff and defendant will present their oral arguments to the Supreme Court. The plaintiff's argument is presented first, followed by the defendant's argument. Any justice may interrupt any presentation at any time to ask questions of the attorneys. After both sides have concluded their arguments, the Court will rule on the question of what, if any, due process rights under the Fifth and Fourteenth amendments the detainees may be entitled to. The Court may order due process for all, some, or none of the detainees.

The Chief Justice The chief justice will be in charge of the proceeding, including recognizing the attorneys when it is their turn to speak. He or she will read all the briefs submitted in the case and will preside over the Court's deliberations at the end of the hearing. The chief justice may assign one of the justices to write the Court's opinion. The justice who writes the opinion will then "publish" it by reading it to the class.

The Associate Justices The associate justices will read all the briefs submitted and listen to oral arguments. Justices may interrupt any argument to ask the attorney questions about it. At the end of the hearing, all of the justices will discuss the case and reach the Court's decision. Justices who disagree with the majority decision may write a dissenting opinion if they wish. If there is a dissenting opinion, the author will read it to the class after the majority opinion has been read.

The Parties' Attorneys Each side's attorneys will prepare their argument and present it orally to the Court.

The Amicus Attorneys The attorney for each organization will write its amicus curiae brief for the court. They also will help the attorneys for the side they support in researching the case and in preparing its oral argument.

APCL v. United States

The parties to this case are:
- Plaintiff: Americans Protecting Civil Liberties
- Defendant: United States

Amici Curiae
- For the plaintiff: American Center for Civil Justice
- For the defendant: Terrorism Victims and Survivors for Justice

---

❸ Debriefing

"Those who would give up essential liberty to purchase a little temporary safety, deserve neither Liberty nor Safety," is a quote attributed to Benjamin Franklin. Use what you have learned about due process to discuss the trade-off between liberty and safety today.

Amicus Curiae Briefs *Amicus curiae* (plural, *amici curiae*) is Latin for "friend of the court." The term refers to a person or organization that files a legal brief, with the court's permission, to express views on one or more issues in a case involving other parties because it has a strong interest in the subject matter of the action.

Federalism and the Supreme Court

Reading Focus

In Chapter 4 you read that federalism is a system of government in which power is divided between a central government and regional governments. The Constitution gives the national government power over some issues and reserves to the state governments power over other issues. The balance of power between the national government and the states shifts from time to time as a result of legislation and Supreme Court decisions.

CASE STUDY **Treaties and States' Rights** Learn about the relationship between federal law, such as treaties with other countries, and state laws.

WHAT YOU NEED TO KNOW Learn about the distribution of power between the federal and state governments.

SIMULATION **Arguing a Federalism Case** Use your knowledge to argue a Supreme Court case involving the commerce clause, states' rights, and the Eleventh Amendment.

Student Casebook

Use your Student Casebook to take notes on the section and to complete the simulation.

State boundaries have no meaning to migratory birds such as snow geese. Federal law, adopted as part of an international treaty, protects migratory bird species against state hunting laws.

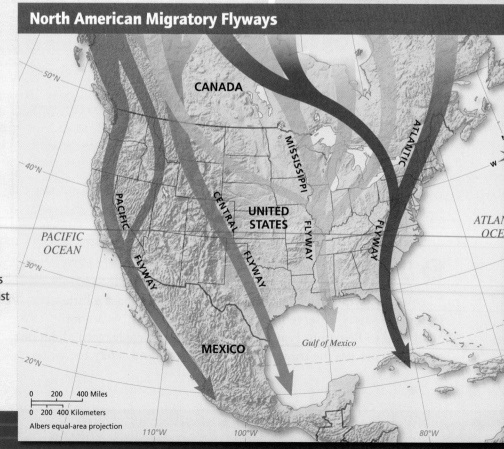

North American Migratory Flyways

50°N

CANADA

40°N

PACIFIC
FLYWAY

MISSISSIPPI

ATLANTIC

UNITED
STATES

CENTRAL
FLYWAY

FLYWAY

FLYWAY

PACIFIC
OCEAN

ATLAN
OCE

30°N

MEXICO

Gulf of Mexico

20°N

0   200   400 Miles

0   200   400 Kilometers

Albers equal-area projection

110°W   100°W   80°W

Treaties and States' Rights

Hunting and fishing are typically regulated by state governments. Should the federal government have any power over state-regulated activities, such as restricting the hunting of certain animals within a state's borders?

Protecting Migratory Birds

For many years, wild animals were considered to be the property of the states in which they lived. However, wild animals, especially birds, move across state and international boundaries freely. The federal government used this fact in trying to protect migratory birds by regulating bird hunting. Until 1920, however, the courts struck down such federal laws as unconstitutional.

The United States and the United Kingdom signed a treaty in 1916 to protect birds that migrated between the United States and Canada. Two years later Congress passed the Migratory Bird Treaty Act to implement the treaty. The law prohibited the killing or capturing of bird species covered by the treaty.

In Missouri, state authorities tried to prevent Ray Holland, a federal game warden, from enforcing the act. They claimed that the act was an unconstitutional exercise of federal power. A federal district court ruled the act constitutional and dismissed Missouri's lawsuit. Missouri appealed the decision to the Supreme Court.

The Court Hears *Missouri* v. *Holland*

Attorneys for the U.S. government argued that Article II, Section 2, of the Constitution gives the president the express power to make treaties. They also noted the supremacy clause in Article VI, which makes the Constitution, federal laws, and treaties—including the Migratory Bird Treaty—the supreme law of the land.

Missouri's attorneys claimed that the Migratory Bird Treaty Act violated the Tenth Amendment and was an unconstitutional intrusion into Missouri's sovereign powers. They noted that regulating hunting was not a power expressly granted to Congress in the Constitution, which therefore made it a power reserved to the states by the Tenth Amendment. They argued that Congress should not be able to use the president's treaty power to pass a law that would be unconstitutional if it were passed directly.

In *Missouri* v. *Holland* (1920), the Court upheld the lower court's decision. The Court observed that some matters require national action and that the national government must have the power to deal with those matters. As a result, the federal government can, under an international treaty, regulate activities within states that it might otherwise have no power to control. The supremacy clause allows Congress to pass laws necessary to implement treaty agreements to deal with such matters. The Court also ruled that migratory birds, which do not recognize borders, are not the property of anyone.

Holland's Impact

Holland was important because it clarified, and expanded, the limits of federal power to conduct international relations. Cases after *Holland* have continued to recognize the federal government's expanded authority over state laws when the nation is dealing with international issues.

What Do You Think?

1. Should the hunting of migratory birds be controlled by the states, which license hunters, or by federal authorities? Explain your point of view.
2. Was the Migratory Bird Treaty Act a proper expansion of federal power over the states? Why or why not?
3. Could the federal government amend the Constitution by making a treaty with another country? Explain.

Expanding Federal Authority

Key Terms

selective exclusiveness

The commerce clause of the Constitution (Article I, Section 8, Clause 3) states that Congress has the power "to regulate commerce with foreign Nations, and among the several States, and with the Indian Tribes." Congress's use of this clause and the Supreme Court's interpretation of it have significantly defined the balance of power between the national government and the states. As a result, it has also helped to shape American life.

One way Congress has used its power to regulate commerce is in trying to end racial discrimination in the United States. The Supreme Court upheld this use of the power in the *Heart of Atlanta Motel* v. *United States* (1964). That case involved a federal law, Title II of the Civil Rights Act of 1964. The Court held that Congress could force private businesses—such as a large motel in downtown Atlanta, Georgia—not to discriminate against African Americans. The Court ruled that the motel was engaged in interstate commerce (75 percent of the motel's guests were from out of state) and that racial discrimination had a disruptive effect on interstate commerce.

READING CHECK **Identifying the Main Idea** What part of the Constitution has had the greatest impact on changing the Constitutional system of federalism?

REAL-WORLD EXAMPLE

***Daniel* v. *Paul* (1969)** In *Daniel* v. *Paul*, the Supreme Court applied Title II of the Civil Rights Act of 1964 to a family business in a rural area. The Pauls, husband and wife, owned and operated a small private recreational park in Arkansas. Most of their customers were white residents of Arkansas. African Americans were denied admission to the park. However, the park advertised in a way to attract travelers from other states and items sold at the park's snack bar had moved in interstate commerce. Therefore, the Court said, the park was subject to the Civil Rights Act. As a result, the Court ruled, the Pauls could not bar anyone from the park because of their race.

Applying Information Should having snack food items that moved in interstate commerce be enough to make the Pauls subject to the Civil Rights Act? Why or why not?

The Commerce Clause and the Court

The Supreme Court's first interpretation of the commerce clause in *Gibbons* v. *Ogden* (1824) is discussed in Chapter 5. After *Gibbons*, Congress rarely used the commerce clause to expand federal government power until the late 1800s. But the Supreme Court laid the groundwork for this use in 1852 in *Cooley* v. *Board of Wardens*. That case was the first time the Court used the doctrine of selective exclusiveness. **Selective exclusiveness** means that when the commerce at issue requires national, uniform regulation, only Congress may regulate it. But if the commerce does not need exclusive national regulation and can be regulated locally, the states may regulate it.

The *Cooley* decision has never been overruled. But as the following two cases illustrate, the doctrine of selective exclusiveness has not been applied automatically or uniformly. Other factors, such as the political leanings of the justices or the Court's desire to expand or contract federal power, have often had more influence than has the idea of selective exclusiveness.

The Guns in School Case

In 1992 Alfonso Lopez arrived at his high school in San Antonio, Texas, carrying a concealed handgun. Acting on a tip, school authorities confronted Lopez. He admitted he had a .38-caliber revolver and five bullets. Lopez was arrested and charged under Texas law with firearm possession on school premises.

A day later, the state charges were dropped when federal officials charged Lopez with violating Section 922(q) of the Gun-Free School Zones Act of 1990. This federal law makes it illegal for anyone to have a firearm in a school zone. Lopez was convicted in federal district court and sentenced to six months in jail. When the Fifth Circuit Court of Appeals reversed the conviction, federal authorities appealed to the Supreme Court.

The Arguments Lopez's attorneys argued that Section 922(q) was an unconstitutional exercise of Congress's power to regulate interstate commerce. Having a gun at school, they argued, may be a criminal offense, but it has nothing to do with interstate commerce.

Government attorneys argued that guns in school zones could lead to violent crime, making people afraid to travel in the area. They also argued that fear of violent crime might interfere with students' learning, leading to less productive citizens. Both results could affect the economy. As a result, Congress could reasonably regulate firearms at schools under the commerce clause.

The Court's Ruling In the case of *United States* v. *Lopez* (1995), the Court ruled 5–4 that the Gun-Free School Zones Act of 1990 was unconstitutional. "The possession of a gun in a local school zone is in no sense an economic activity that might . . . substantially affect any sort of interstate commerce," wrote Chief Justice William Rehnquist for the majority. Rehnquist noted that "Section 922(q) is a criminal statute that by its terms has nothing to do with 'commerce' or any sort of economic enterprise."

The Guns in School Case

United States v. *Lopez* (1995)

Significance: *Lopez* is the first Supreme Court case since the 1930s to limit Congress's power under the commerce clause.

Background: Twelfth-grade student Alfonso Lopez was charged with a violation of the Gun-Free School Zones Act of 1990.

Decision: The 1990 act was unconstitutional as an exercise of Congress's commerce clause power.

Schools have posted signs like the ones shown here to notify everyone that carrying a gun is prohibited in a school zone.

The Medical Marijuana Case

Gonzales v. Raich (2005)

Significance: The federal Controlled Substances Act is constitutional under the commerce clause.

Background: Federal law makes marijuana illegal. California enacted a program for the sale and use of medical marijuana. Two California residents sued the federal government when authorities acting under federal law destroyed their marijuana plants.

Decision: The Supreme Court ruled that the Controlled Substances Act is a constitutional use of Congress's power under the commerce clause. Federal authorities may enforce the law against a state-approved program for the sale and use of medical marijuana.

Angel Raich, left, and Diane Monson, right, are shown standing outside the U.S. Supreme Court building.

Lopez was important because the case is the first to limit Congress's use of the commerce clause since the 1930s. Chief Justice Rehnquist stated that the Court had a duty to prevent the federal government from further expanding its powers to regulate the conduct of a state's citizens. "Admittedly, some of our prior cases have taken long steps down that road . . . ," he wrote. "The broad language in these opinions has suggested the possibility of further expansion, but we decline here to proceed any further."

The Medical Marijuana Case

Using marijuana has been illegal under federal law since 1937. In 1996, however, California voters approved marijuana use for medical purposes. Two California residents, Diane Monson and Angel Raich, began using home-grown marijuana to treat chronic pain. Raich's pain was so severe that her doctor said that without marijuana to relieve it she could die.

In 2002 federal authorities seized and destroyed six marijuana plants Monson was growing. Monson and Raich sued the federal government to stop it from interfering with their right to grow and use medical marijuana under California law. The court of appeals ruled in Monson and Raich's favor, and the government appealed the decision to the Supreme Court (*Gonzales* v. *Raich*, 2005).

The Arguments Raich and Monson claimed that, as applied to them, the federal law allowing the seizure was a violation of the commerce clause because they were not engaged in interstate commerce. Raich and Monson argued that their marijuana was home grown and that the seeds, soil, and equipment used to grow it were from the state in which they lived. Therefore, they argued, the marijuana they grew and used was a product entirely of intrastate commerce. The federal government's enforcement action—the destruction of Monson's plants—was therefore unconstitutional.

The government based its argument on the supremacy clause. It argued that federal law does not recognize the medical use of marijuana and that the Constitution makes federal law supreme over state law. They also argued that the use of home grown marijuana for medical purposes affected the illegal trade in marijuana coming into California from other states and countries. They claimed that this gave the government the right, under the commerce clause, to regulate home grown marijuana.

The *Raich* Decision In 2005 the Supreme Court ruled 6–3 to uphold the government's use of the commerce clause to seize home grown marijuana plants. The Court accepted the government's argument that home grown medicinal marijuana affects interstate commerce. Writing for the majority, Justice John Paul Stevens noted that marijuana is a popular part of commerce and that the commerce clause applies whether the commerce is legal or not. If Monson and Raich were not growing their own marijuana, they would have to purchase their supply somewhere else, which would ultimately have an impact on the interstate commerce that Congress can regulate.

In a strong dissent joined by Chief Justice Rehnquist, Justice Sandra Day O'Connor first cited the *Lopez* case and then wrote, "Federalism promotes innovation by allowing . . . a single courageous state, if its citizens choose . . . [to] try novel social and economic experiments without risk to the rest of the country." She then noted that this case makes growing and using small amounts of marijuana at home for medical purposes a federal crime. That, O'Connor said, is an unconstitutional use of Congress's power under the commerce clause. The principles of federalism, she said, should protect California's experiment from federal regulation.

READING CHECK **Summarizing** How did Justice O'Connor think the decision in *Gonzales* v. *Raich* affected federalism?

Section 4 Assessment

thinkcentral.com
KEYWORD: SGO SUP HP

Reviewing Ideas and Terms

1. **a. Identify** What is the commerce clause?
   b. Analyze Why has the federal government been able to use the commerce clause to regulate many private businesses?

2. **a. Describe** What is the supremacy clause?
   b. Evaluate In your opinion, how well did the Court apply the doctrine of **selective exclusiveness** in *United States* v. *Lopez* and *Gonzales* v. *Raich*? Explain.

Critical Thinking

3. **Analyze** Do you support the majority view or the dissent in the Court's ruling on the commerce clause and federalism in *Gonzales* v. *Raich*? Explain why.

CASE STUDY LINK You answered the following questions at the end of the Case Study. Now that you have completed Section 4, think about and answer the questions again. Then compare your answers with your earlier responses. Are your answers the same or are they different?

4. Should the hunting of migratory birds be controlled by the states, which license hunters, or by federal authorities? Explain your point of view.

5. Was the Migratory Bird Treaty Act a proper expansion of federal over state power? Why or why not?

6. Could the federal government amend the U.S. Constitution by making a treaty with another country? Explain.

Arguing a Federalism Case

Student Casebook

Use your Student Casebook to complete the simulation.

Should Native Americans be able to operate casinos on reservations in states where such gambling violates state law?

Native American groups are considered "domestic dependent nations" within the United States. Each group has the right to have its own government on a reservation that operates mostly independently of the laws of the state within which the reservation is located. Using what you have learned, complete this simulation involving issues of federalism and having a casino on a reservation.

Roles

- Chief justice
- Associate justices
- Attorneys for plaintiff, Native American Nation
- Attorneys for defendant, the State
- Attorneys for the National Native American Council, a Native American civil rights group
- Attorneys for the American Association for Family Values, a group that opposes casinos and gambling

❶ The Situation

Native American Nation asked the state to allow it to open a casino on its reservation in order to make money from tourists who would visit the reservation to gamble. When the state refused, the Native Americans sued the state in federal court under the provisions of the Indian Gaming Regulatory Act of 1988. The state filed a motion to dismiss the case.

The federal district court denied the state's motion, and the state appealed the ruling to the circuit court of appeals. The court of appeals granted the state's motion and dismissed the case, citing requirements of the Eleventh Amendment. Native American Nation appealed this decision to the Supreme Court. The appeals court considered, but did not address, any issue under the commerce clause of Article I of the Constitution.

Key Facts

- The Indian Gaming Regulatory Act (IGRA) requires that states negotiate agreements with tribal governments allowing Native Americans to offer various types of gambling on their reservations.

- If a state will not negotiate with a Native American nation, the IGRA allows the nation to sue the state in federal court, to ask the court to force the state to negotiate an agreement.

- Congress passed the IGRA using its power under the Constitution's commerce clause.

- The Eleventh Amendment to the Constitution states that citizens of a foreign country who sue a state must do so in the courts of that state.

❷ The Hearing

The attorneys for the plaintiff and the defendant will present their oral arguments to the Supreme Court. The plaintiff's position will be presented first, followed by the defense position. The justices will be able to interrupt each presentation to ask questions of the attorney. After each side's argument has been heard, the Court will rule on the plaintiff's request that it reverse the court of appeals and allow its suit in district court to proceed.

The Chief Justice The chief justice will be in charge of the proceeding. He or she will read each side's amicus curiae brief and recognize the attorneys when it is their turn to speak. He or she will preside over the Court's deliberations at the end of the hearing and assign one of the justices to write the Court's opinion. The chief justice will then "publish" the Court's decision by reading it aloud to the class.

The Associate Justices The associate justices will read each side's amicus curiae brief and listen to its oral argument. Along with the chief justice, the associate justices may interrupt each argument to ask the attorney questions about it. At the end of the hearing, all the justices will discuss the case and vote on how to decide it. Justices who disagree with the majority decision may write a dissenting opinion if they wish. If there is a dissenting opinion, the author will read it after the majority opinion has been read.

The Parties' Attorneys Each side's attorneys will prepare an argument and present it orally to the Court.

The Amicus Attorneys The amici curiae in this case are the National Native American Council and American Association for Family Values. Representatives from each organization will write the organization's amicus curiae brief for the court. They also will help the attorneys for the side they support in researching the case and in preparing its oral argument.

Native American Nation v. State

Parties to the case
- The plaintiff: Native American Nation
- The defendant: State

Central Issue
Should the commerce clause or the Eleventh Amendment be the determining factor in deciding this case?

❸ Debriefing

While the Supreme Court is deliberating its decision, write a one-page opinion of your own, revealing how you would decide the case if you were on the Court. After the Court's decision is read, discuss with the class and the justices any differences you see between the decision and any separate opinions the justices may have written and which opinion, if either, you think is better reasoned.

> **Amicus Curiae Briefs** *Amicus curiae* (plural, *amici curiae*) is Latin for "friend of the court." The term refers to a person or organization that files a legal brief, with the court's permission, to express views on one or more issues in a case involving other parties because it has a strong interest in the subject matter of the action.

Connecting Online

Visit **thinkcentral.com** for review and enrichment activities related to this chapter.

THINK central

KEYWORD: SGO SUP

Quiz and Review

GOV 101
Examine key concepts in this chapter.

ONLINE QUIZZES
Take a practice quiz for each section in this chapter.

Activities

eActivities
Complete Webquests and Internet research activities.

INTERACTIVE FEATURES
Explore interactive versions of maps and charts.

KEEP IT CURRENT
Link to current events in U.S. government.

Partners

American Bar Association Division for Public Education
Learn more about the law, your rights and responsibilities.

Center for Civic Education
Promoting an enlightened and responsible citizenry committed to democratic principles and actively engaged in the practice of democracy.

Online Textbook

ONLINE SIMULATIONS
Learn about U.S. government through simulations you can complete online.

STUDENT CASEBOOK
Take notes electronically on Interactive Chapters.

 Read more about key topics online.

Comprehension and Critical Thinking

SECTION 1 (pp. 390–399)

1. **a. Review Key Terms** For each term, write a sentence that explains its significance or meaning: freedom of expression, redress of grievances.

   b. Draw Conclusions Does the free exercise clause protect people's free exercise of religion? Explain why or why not.

   c. Elaborate Do you think that any of the First Amendment freedoms should be absolute? Explain.

SECTION 2 (pp. 402–411)

2. **a. Review Key Terms** For each term, write a sentence that explains its significance or meaning: search, seizure, plain view doctrine.

   b. Analyze What relationship exists between the need for probable cause and a person's right to privacy?

   c. Predict What will be the likely outcome of a search that does not recognize a person's reasonable expectation of privacy?

SECTION 3 (pp. 414–425)

3. **a. Review Key Terms** For each term, write a sentence that explains its significance or meaning: unenumerated rights.

   b. Evaluate Should schools be required to give students the same due process rights that adults have in legal proceedings? Explain your answer.

   c. Elaborate Due process is an important part of the rule of law. How do the rule of law and due process protect citizens from threats to personal liberties such as perjury (lying under oath), police corruption, and organized crime?

SECTION 4 (pp. 428–433)

4. **a. Review Key Terms** For each term, write a sentence that explains its significance or meaning: selective exclusiveness.

   b. Contrast How did the Supreme Court's view of federalism in *United States* v. *Lopez* differ from its view in *Gonzales* v. *Raich*?

   c. Evaluate What is your opinion about the Court's decision in *United States* v. *Lopez*?

FOCUS ON WRITING

Persuasive Writing *Persuasive writing takes a position for or against an issue, using facts and examples as supporting evidence. To practice persuasive writing, complete the assignment below.*

Writing Topic: States as Federalism Laboratories

5. **Assignment** In her dissent in *Gonzales* v. *Raich*, Justice Sandra Day O'Connor argued that federalism should allow states to try social experiments. Write an editorial arguing whether states should be free—or not free—to adopt different approaches to solving social problems under our federal system of government.

14 Making Foreign Policy

Why do U.S. government leaders care about events in Iraq or North Korea? After all, these nations are thousands of miles across the globe from the United States. Similarly, why does a political crisis in a foreign country draw the attention of U.S. and other world leaders?

No country is truly isolated from events outside its borders. Nations rely on their relationships with other nations of the world to ensure their own security. In addition, an increasingly interconnected world market and a need for global environmental protections bring nations closer together each day. In this chapter, you will learn how the United States creates its foreign policy.

German chancellor Angela Merkel and President Bush talk during a 2007 summit.

Table of Contents

Student Casebook | Use your Student Casebook to take notes on the chapter and to complete the simulations.

Foreign Policy Choices in a Complex World

Reading Focus

Foreign policy is a nation's plans and procedures for dealing with other countries. Although U.S. foreign policy has changed over time, it has been guided by five basic goals and formulated through a set of theories, tools, and strategies.

CASE STUDY **Genocide in Rwanda**
Learn about how the United States responded to genocide in the African country of Rwanda.

WHAT YOU NEED TO KNOW Learn about the goals, theories, and tools of U.S. foreign policy.

SIMULATION **Deciding Whether to Use Military Intervention** Use your knowledge to make a foreign policy decision about a simulated crisis in another country. Your decision must be guided by the basic goals and tools of U.S. foreign policy.

Student Casebook

Use your Student Casebook to take notes on the section and to complete the simulation.

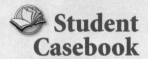

Photographs of some of the 800,000 victims of the genocide in Rwanda are displayed at a memorial in the Rwandan capital of Kigali.

Genocide in Rwanda

On April 6, 1994, a plane carrying Rwandan president Juvénal Habyarimana exploded over the capital, Kigali, killing both him and the president of neighboring Burundi. Habyarimana's death set in motion a swift and certain genocide.

Background to Genocide

Rwanda, once under Belgian control, gained its independence in 1962. The Hutu are the country's largest ethnic group, and the Tutsi are the chief minority. By 1962 the Hutu ethnic group had overthrown the Tutsi king, killing or exiling thousands of Tutsis in the process. Because a republic was established, the Hutu majority was able to control the government. In 1990 a Tutsi rebel group, the Rwandan Patriotic Front (RPF), attempted to overthrow the Hutu government. The following year, the RPF was conducting peace negotiations with the Rwandan government, led by Hutu leader Juvénal Habyarimana. Hutu extremists, however, opposed any peace deals with the RPF.

When Habyarimana's plane crashed, many people assumed he was killed by Hutu extremists. They opposed the president's peace deal with the Tutsi leaders, which included a transition to a multiparty government. The extremists used Habyarimana's death as an opportunity to take power.

One Hundred Days of Killing

Over the next 100 days, the Rwanda Armed Forces began systematically killing moderate Hutu politicians. Radio broadcasts urged Hutus to rid Rwanda of so-called *inyenzi*—"cockroaches"—a Hutu extremist name for a Tutsi. Hutu militia groups called the *interahamwe* ("those who attack together") roamed the streets, rounding up and killing Tutsis by the thousands. By the end of July, Hutus had taken machetes and slaughtered 800,000 of their Tutsi neighbors, colleagues, and Tutsi sympathizers.

The United States Responds

On April 7, 1994, President Bill Clinton issued an official statement expressing his shock about the thousands already dead. Although the killing continued, the United States did not come to Rwanda's aid, nor did any other nation. The United States had signed a United Nations convention against genocide, declaring it a crime under international law and committing itself to both "prevent and punish" those responsible. The United States and the UN, however, avoided publicly using the term *genocide* to describe the situation. If the events themselves did not obligate the United States to intervene, acknowledging that genocide was taking place would.

On May 3, 1994, Clinton signed a presidential decision directive (PDD) that established guidelines limiting U.S. military involvement in international peacekeeping operations. The Clinton administration had drafted the guidelines in response to the deaths of 18 U.S. soldiers during a peacekeeping operation in Somalia in 1993. After Somalia, Americans were wary of losing any more troops in humanitarian peacekeeping missions. On July 29, after the RPF rebels gained control in Rwanda, Clinton sent 200 troops to Rwanda for the "sole purpose of humanitarian relief." By that time, the genocide was over. An estimated 800,000 Rwandans had been killed in 100 days.

What Do You Think?

1. Why do you think the United States chose to limit its military involvement in international peacekeeping missions?
2. Did the United States do enough to help stop genocide in Rwanda? Explain your answer.
3. What could the United States have done to stop the killing?

SECTION 1

The Basics of Foreign Policy

Key Terms

foreign policy
isolationism
internationalist
embassies
defense alliance
collective security
economic sanctions
just war theory

How does the United States relate to the rest of the world? By creating foreign policy. **Foreign policy** is a nation's set of plans and procedures for dealing with foreign countries. U.S. foreign policy is not set in stone—no two situations are alike, and making the "right" decision is never simple. Not everyone agrees on how foreign policy should be used, and each presidential administration must balance U.S. foreign policy goals according to its priorities. However, U.S. foreign policy can be distilled into five basic goals.

The Five Goals of Foreign Policy

❶ **National security** National security is perhaps the primary priority of any government, and the United States is no exception. U.S. foreign policy strives to create a balance between the interests of national security and the protection of citizens' rights, freedoms, and property.

❷ **Establishing free and open trade** The free exchange of goods and services between countries provides markets for U.S. goods and allows the United States to import desired goods from overseas.

❸ **Promoting world peace** Tied closely to national security is world peace. The greater the number of countries that are at peace, the less likely the United States is to be drawn into conflicts.

❹ **Supporting democracy** Beyond the stability world peace brings, supporting democratic governments serves U.S. interests by further stabilizing the world. With the economic underpinnings needed for democracy, new democracies open new markets for American goods.

❺ **Providing aid to people in need** The United States spends around $27 billion annually on humanitarian and other aid in the form of money, food, or military assistance, not including the additional billions it is spending on reconstruction in Iraq.

REAL-WORLD EXAMPLE

CASE STUDY LINK

Aid to Rwanda After the genocide in Rwanda, the United States provided humanitarian aid totaling about $400 million, including food assistance. In recent years, U.S. aid to Rwanda has been targeted at helping the country develop rather than at relief measures.

Applying Information
Why might more U.S. aid to Rwanda be focused on development now?

How Should Foreign Policy Be Applied?

Several schools of thought have developed on how active a role the United States should take in foreign affairs. Until World War I, the United States mostly followed a policy of **isolationism**. The nation's leaders looked after domestic issues and believed that staying out of world affairs would keep the country from war. Today other principles guide our foreign policy, and the United States is an active participant in world affairs.

Realism Opposite of the isolationist stance is the **internationalist** approach to foreign policy, which promotes cooperation between nations. Internationalism is a component of the school of realism. Realists believe that an active role in international affairs is the best way to pursue national security. Realists perceive many countries or their leaders as dangers to U.S. security or U.S. economic interests and believe a show of force is sometimes necessary to protect national security. They look at past events and what they perceive as human nature as a guide, taking a more practical look at national security. Realists support the United States forging alliances with any nation that will serve our national interest, or the country's economic, military, or cultural goals.

A woman votes during Afghanistan's 2005 parliamentary elections. The United States was active in helping the country realize the first free and fair parliamentary elections in more than three decades.

Neoisolationism A new brand of isolationism, or neoisolationism, holds that U.S. involvement with foreign countries should be kept to a minimum for the benefit of both the United States and foreign countries themselves. We should let countries determine their own fates, neoisolationists believe. Moreover, they argue, history has shown that our interference is not always welcome overseas or popular at home. Many neoisolationists feel obligated to avoid war and believe <u>intervention</u> in another country's affairs may lead the United States into prolonged military conflict.

Idealism Idealists take an internationalist approach to foreign policy. Unlike realists, however, they consider not only the interests of the United States but also those of other countries as well when considering foreign policy. Defense of human rights is the guiding light of this doctrine. An idealist opposes alliances with tyrannical governments, no matter how useful such an alliance might be to U.S. interests. Allying with oppressors would not achieve their goals of promoting democracy and supporting human rights. Some idealists approve of military intervention in foreign affairs, while others do not.

ACADEMIC VOCABULARY

intervention an attempt to directly influence the politics and policy-making of another country

READING CHECK **Comparing and Contrasting** How are the doctrines of realism and idealism similar? How do they differ?

The Tools of Foreign Policy

The United States often relies on persuasion and power to pursue its foreign policy goals. The nation also relies on three types of foreign policy tools: diplomatic, economic, and military. Diplomatic tools help build peaceful relationships with other nations and promote national security. Economic tools can be used to bring social or political change. Military tools are used when force is called for, oftentimes if other means have been tried without success.

Diplomatic Tools

Diplomacy allows the United States to protect its interests at home by advancing its global presence and promoting international understanding. The United States currently maintains more than 160 **embassies**, or diplomatic centers, around the world. The United States has used its position as an active world citizen to help foreign nations settle conflicts peacefully.

The U.S. Constitution gives the president the power to negotiate treaties with foreign nations, subject to approval by the Senate. A treaty is a formal agreement between nations. The Senate must ratify, or approve, all treaties by at least a two-thirds vote. The United States currently has hundreds of treaties with nations all around the globe, from Afghanistan to Zimbabwe.

The United States also enters into defense alliances with other nations. A **defense alliance** is an agreement to come to another nation's aid in the event of an attack. The guaranteed mutual defense is one example of **collective security**, or attempts at keeping international peace and order.

SOME MAJOR U.S. DEFENSE ALLIANCES

QUICK FACTS

ALLIANCE	ESTABLISHED	TYPE	MEMBERS
NATO North Atlantic Treaty Organization	1949	Military	Belgium , Bulgaria, Canada, Czech Republic, Denmark, Estonia, France, Germany, Greece, Hungary, Iceland, Italy, Latvia, Lithuania, Luxembourg, Netherlands, Norway, Poland, Portugal, Romania, Slovakia, Slovenia, Spain, Turkey, United Kingdom, United States
OAS Organization of American States	1948	Economic	35 independent nations of the Americas
Rio Pact Inter-American Treaty of Reciprocal Assistance	1947	Military	23 of the 35 nations in the Organization of American States

Economic Tools

Money is a powerful tool in the pursuit of foreign policy goals. By giving financial aid to developing nations, the United States is attempting to both spread democracy and expand free markets. The United States Agency for International Development (USAID) carries out the government's nonmilitary foreign aid programs. USAID has an annual budget of more than $9 billion, or less than 0.5 percent of the overall U.S. budget. The United States also provides more than $10 billion in military aid to finance, train, and equip other nations' military forces.

Withholding money, or the use of **economic sanctions**, is also a powerful tool. Sometimes countries, individually or in groups, put pressure on other countries by imposing economic sanctions. By restricting imports, exports, or financial transactions, or by banning trade, a country and its allies try to bring about social or political change in the target country.

Sanctions have their supporters and detractors. The benefit of sanctions is that they are a low-cost, nonmilitary option, and they have sometimes proved effective in the past. But humanitarian groups have argued that sanctions harm the target nation's civilians, particularly the poor, more than its government by depriving people of basic goods, such as food and medical supplies.

Military Tools

The decision to use military force is not one that is arrived at easily. Despite this, military action can be an effective foreign policy tool. Although the Constitution names the president as commander in chief, Congress has the power to declare war. This has not, however, stopped presidents from taking military action without declarations of war. The vast majority of U.S. military interventions have not been declarations of war. It has generally been accepted that the Constitution grants the president this power, since the president can respond more quickly than Congress in the event of attack.

The United States has imposed sanctions on Cuba for nearly 50 years and retains no diplomatic ties with the country. ***Based on the photograph, how might economic sanctions have affected life in Cuba?***

Economic Sanctions

What are economic sanctions?

Economic measures taken against a country to force it to change its policies

Why might the United States impose economic sanctions?

- To show it condemns such practices as military aggression, development of weapons of mass destruction, human rights violations, communism, or terrorism
- To force a change in such practices
- To limit economic assistance that could be used to continue such practices

What are some types of economic sanctions?

- Total ban on trade or restrictions on certain trade items
- No foreign aid or restrictions on foreign aid
- No arms sales or limits on arms sales
- No loans or investments or limits on loans and investments

What are some pros and cons to economic sanctions?

Pros
- They provide a peaceful, nonmilitary foreign policy tool.

Cons
- Sanctions that ban or limit trade can hurt the economy of the sanctioning country.
- Long-term sanctions can harm the target country's civilian population when food and medical supplies are withheld.

The United States has used economic sanctions against:

NORTH KOREA
SYRIA
IRAN
CUBA
SUDAN
IRAQ

A president has many advisers when considering military options. In addition to the secretary of state, who as head of the Department of State can advise on diplomatic relations, the president hears advice from the secretary of defense and the nation's top five military leaders, the Joint Chiefs of Staff. The Central Intelligence Agency (CIA) gathers and processes information about foreign governments. Part of its job is to learn about the defense systems of other nations. The National Security Council (NSC) was created to manage the government departments that deal with national security. The national security adviser heads the NSC and has become a top military adviser. As you will read, the decision to go to war is never an easy one and depends on many factors.

READING CHECK **Summarizing** How does the United States use economics to advance its foreign policy goals?

Structure and Control of the U.S. Military

Civilian control is one of the key elements of the U.S. military system. The president is commander in chief of the armed forces. The chart below shows the chain of command that starts with the president.

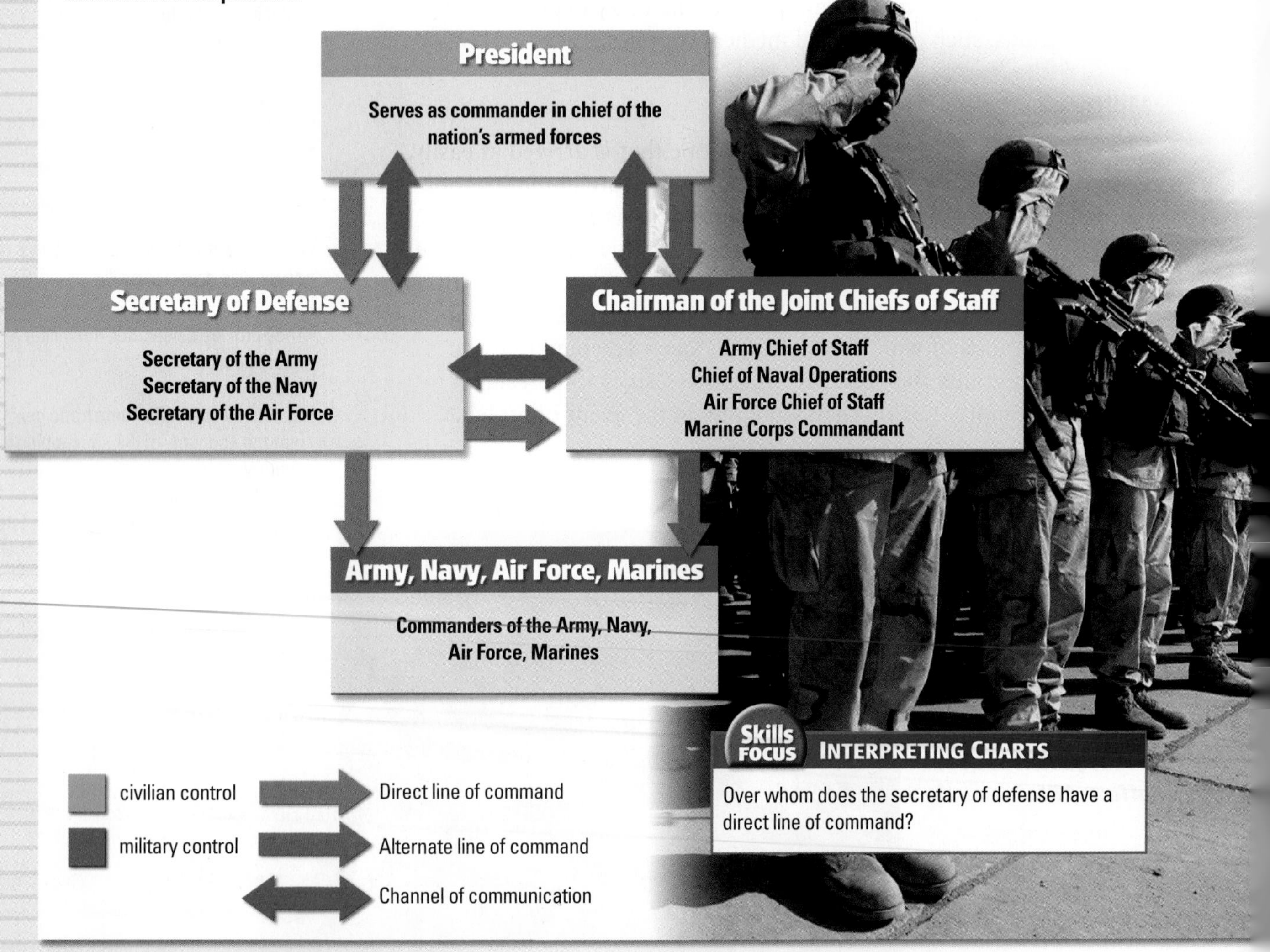

President

Serves as commander in chief of the nation's armed forces

Secretary of Defense

Secretary of the Army
Secretary of the Navy
Secretary of the Air Force

Chairman of the Joint Chiefs of Staff

Army Chief of Staff
Chief of Naval Operations
Air Force Chief of Staff
Marine Corps Commandant

Army, Navy, Air Force, Marines

Commanders of the Army, Navy, Air Force, Marines

civilian control — Direct line of command

military control — Alternate line of command

— Channel of communication

Skills FOCUS **INTERPRETING CHARTS**

Over whom does the secretary of defense have a direct line of command?

Just War Theory

There is a theory of warfare that has roots in Western thought—just war theory. According to **just war theory**, a state may justly go to war under certain specific circumstances and must limit its conduct according to certain standards. *Just* in this sense means "moral," "fair," or "proper."

Just war theory provides a moral context for deciding when to wage and how to conduct war. Justification for war is referred to by just war theorists as *jus ad bellum*, which is Latin for "justice of war." How the war should be conducted is called *jus in bello*, which is Latin for "justice in war."

As described by *jus ad bellum*, four principles define the decision to declare war. First, a state must openly declare a war for it to be just. In addition, the state must have a just cause for declaring war. For example, self-defense is a just cause. Second, the state must also have just intentions. Justice, rather than self-interest, must be the purpose for war. Third, the state must consider the following: Is there a reasonable chance of winning the war? Do the expected benefits of the war outweigh the costs? Have all other means of resolution been exhausted? Finally, *jus ad bellum* limits the war's goal to an outcome of a just peace.

Even with the doctrine of *jus ad bellum*, the decision to go to war is never simple. What defines a "just cause"? Under international agreements, countries follow certain standards of conduct in war. For example, *jus in bello* limits the conduct of war to necessary military targets only. Civilian targets are not allowed, nor is action beyond what is necessary to achieve the desired goal. Excessive, needless violence, such as torture and genocide, is not permitted.

READING CHECK **Summarizing** How does just war theory guide the decision to declare war?

War in Iraq In March 2003 President George W. Bush ordered the invasion of Iraq, citing the goals of regional stability and national security when he informed Congress. Visit **thinkcentral.com** to begin a Webquest to compare the consequences of choosing and implementing different tools of U.S. foreign policy in regards to the War in Iraq.

THINK central **Webquest**
thinkcentral.com
KEYWORD: SGO FOR

Section 1 Assessment

THINK central **Online Quiz**
thinkcentral.com
KEYWORD: SGO FOR HP

Reviewing Ideas and Terms

1. **a. Identify** What is **foreign policy**?
   b. Analyze What are the five basic goals of U.S. foreign policy?

2. **a. Recall** What are the tools of foreign policy?
   b. Explain Which foreign policy tools do you think the United States used in the Rwanda genocide?

3. **a. Define** What is **just war theory**?
   b. Explain What are the four principles underlying *jus ad bellum,* or the justification for war?

Critical Thinking

4. **Draw Conclusions** Which foreign policy tool do you think is most effective? Why?

CASE STUDY LINK You answered the following questions at the end of the Case Study. Now that you have completed Section 1, think about and answer the questions again. Then compare your answers with your earlier responses. Are your answers the same or are they different?

5. Why do you think the United States chose to limit its military involvement in international peacekeeping missions?

6. Did the United States do enough to help stop genocide in Rwanda? Explain your answer.

7. What could the United States have done to stop the killing?

Deciding Whether to Use Military Intervention

Will the United States intervene in the crisis in Branislava?

Student Casebook

Use your Student Casebook to complete the simulation.

Foreign policy issues often involve choices our nation's leaders need to make. Using what you have learned in Section 1, complete the simulation to make a foreign policy decision about a conflict in another country.

Roles

- President
- National security adviser
- Secretary of state
- Secretary of defense
- Ambassador to Branislava
- Chairman of the Joint Chiefs of Staff

❶ The Situation

The president is meeting with top advisers to decide whether the United States should intervene to stop widespread human rights violations in the fictional European nation of Branislava.

Background

- Branislava is a small landlocked nation with five international borders.

- The two major ethnic groups in Branislava are the Sellers and the Growers.

- The Growers are the segment of the population living at subsistence level. They live in poverty and are harshly oppressed by the relatively wealthy Sellers.

- The Sellers are the majority ethnic group that controls the government. The Sellers prevent the Growers from voting and sending their children to school.

- The Growers inhabit Branislava's richest, most fertile farmland and are ultimately responsible for producing the country's largest commercial crops.

- Separatist leaders in the Grower community are again threatening an uprising. The separatist movement is gaining support, both domestically among the Growers and internationally.

- Branislava's natural resources include petroleum, but reserves are undeveloped. These reserves are on Grower land.

- The country north of Branislava is governed by an authoritarian oligarchy that is funding the Growers' rebellion. This country is interested in exploiting Branislava's oil reserves.

- The country south of Branislava is one of Branislava's trading partners. This country buys 50 percent of Branislava's main commercial crop. The remainder is used internally or sold to other countries in Europe.

❷ The Crisis

The conflict has escalated into physical violence. Human rights abuses are taking place on both sides.

- A Growers' rebellion has broken out. Groups of armed Growers are attacking Sellers with knives.

- The Sellers have struck back by ordering the wholesale slaughter of Grower villages.

- Based on just a few days of fighting, U.S. aid workers project that death toll figures could rise as high as 35,000 if the fighting continues for several weeks. They predict that continued damage from the civil war will put the population in danger of starvation.

❸ The Decision

The president must decide whether to intervene in Branislava, and how. The advisers must give the president as much information as possible so he or she can make an informed decision.

- Should the United States use diplomacy to stop the violence?

- Would economic sanctions help stop the violence?

- Are U.S. aid workers in danger?

- Is military intervention justifiable?

- What would the costs—in both money and lives—of going to war be?

- What would the costs of not going to war be?

❹ Debriefing

After the president announces his or her decision, reconsider the responses of the United States to the crisis in Rwanda. Do you think the United States made the right decisions?

Branislava Fact Sheet

Population: 20 million

Area: 80,000 square miles

Type of government: Oligarchy (rule by few)

Number of U.S. aid workers: 1,200

Location of U.S. aid workers: 1,000 in rural areas and the rest in the country's capital

Number of Americans at the U.S. Embassy: 60

Number of U.S. troops in Branislava: None

U.S. Foreign Policy Goals

Your decision must reflect the main goals of U.S. foreign policy. Keep these goals in mind as you complete the simulation.

- National security

- Establishing free and open trade

- Promoting world peace

- Supporting democracy

- Providing aid to people in need

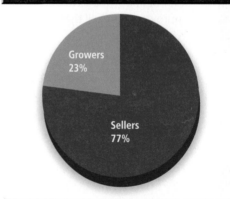

BRANISLAVA'S GDP BY SECTOR

Growers 23%

Sellers 77%

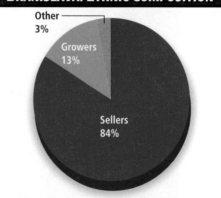

BRANISLAVA: ETHNIC COMPOSITION

Other 3%

Growers 13%

Sellers 84%

How Domestic Actors Affect Foreign Policy

Reading Focus

U.S. foreign policy is directed and shaped by the executive branch and Congress and is carried out by a large bureaucracy. Domestic influences such as interest groups also play a role in foreign policy.

CASE STUDY **Elián González** Learn about how the custody case of a Cuban boy involved key players in U.S. foreign policy.

WHAT YOU NEED TO KNOW Learn about the nation's foreign policy bureaucracy, how foreign policy is shaped, and the forces that can influence it.

SIMULATION **Senate Trade Bill Vote** Use your knowledge to decide whether to approve a trade bill that affects foreign policy.

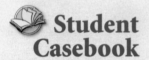

Student Casebook

Use your Student Casebook to take notes on the section and to complete the simulation.

JANUARY 17, 2000 $3.50 www.time.com

GORE v. BRADLEY: INSIDE THE WAR

TIME

The battle over ELIAN GONZALEZ sparks a debate about custody laws and what's best for kids

WHERE DOES HE BELONG?

The Cuban boy's arrival in the United States began a foreign policy saga that ended when U.S. immigration agents forcibly removed the boy and returned him to his homeland.

Elián González

In 1999 a young Cuban boy named Elián became the central character in a foreign policy saga that involved the United States, Cuba, Elián's relatives in both countries, and the state of Florida. Elián's story commanded top news headlines over a period of seven months. It also involved many of the key players who have a role in shaping U.S. foreign policy.

Rescued at Sea

On November 25, 1999—Thanksgiving Day—two Americans were fishing in a boat two miles off the coast of Fort Lauderdale, Florida. They discovered a most unusual catch: a six-year-old boy floating in an inner tube. The men rescued the boy and soon learned he was a Cuban named Elián González. Cuba is a Communist nation located 90 miles south of Florida. Elián was one of a group of refugees who had attempted to flee Cuba by sea. Their attempt ended in tragedy when their motorboat capsized. Elián's mother and stepfather were among 11 who drowned. Only Elián and two other people survived.

Cubans have been fleeing their country since 1959, when revolutionary leader Fidel Castro took over and set up a Communist government. Many Cuban refugees settled in the United States, particularly in parts of southern Florida. Since then, many Cuban Americans have remained staunchly anti-Castro.

Should He Stay in the United States or Be Returned to Cuba?

After an overnight stay in a Florida hospital, Elián was released into the custody of Cuban American relatives in Miami. Elián's relatives strongly opposed Elián's return to Cuba, where Elián's father was living. The Cuban American community in southern Florida rallied around Elián's relatives. The same day Elián was turned over to his Miami relatives, however, the Cuban government and Elián's father requested that Elián be returned to Cuba.

Many Cuban Americans are very politically motivated, and they form an influential voting bloc attractive to politicians. Elián's arrival in the United States became a powerful political symbol for some Cuban Americans. The daily demonstrations, candlelight vigils, and rallies almost immediately became food for a media feeding frenzy. Elián's fate also became a political issue for candidates in the 2000 presidential election.

In Cuba, Elián's father, Juan Miguel González-Quintana, claimed Elián had been kidnapped. He continued his demands for the boy's return. Cuban president Fidel Castro spoke out on the issue, saying that Elián belonged with his father on both legal and moral grounds.

A Custody Battle Like No Other

Under the U.S. legal system, a child with a living parent ordinarily would be released into that parent's custody. However, Elián was not a U.S. citizen, and his case was anything but ordinary. The United States and Cuba were—and are—engaged in a cold war. At the time, some conservative Cuban Americans were lobbying to keep in place a strict embargo against Cuba. Elián became the symbolic rope in a tug-of-war between Fidel Castro and many Cuban Americans. Despite the fact that Elián lost his mother in the attempt to come to the United States, Elián had entered the country illegally.

Elián's Cuban American relatives made several attempts to keep Elián in the United States, such as requesting political asylum on his behalf and attempting to have an uncle in the United States declared Elián's legal guardian. Neither attempt held up in court. Some members of the U.S. Senate even introduced legislation to grant citizenship and permanent residency to Elián.

▼ **November 1999** Elián González was placed in the care of his Cuban American uncle in Miami.

▲ **April 2000** After Elián was removed from his uncle's home by federal agents, hundreds of Cuban Americans protested in Miami.

▲ **June 2000** Elián returned to Cuba with his father, who received permission to come to the United States from the Department of State.

In early January 2000, the U.S. Immigration and Naturalization Service (INS) announced that Elián's father was responsible for Elián's custody. In April 2000 the U.S. Department of State permitted Elián's father to travel to the United States. After meeting with him, U.S. Attorney General Janet Reno announced on April 7 that U.S. officials would transfer Elián to his father. Five days later, on April 12, Reno met with Elián's relatives in Miami to begin the process of bringing Elián to his father. However, the Miami relatives did not agree to a transfer. They claimed Elián belonged in the United States, the country his mother died trying to reach.

Federal Agents Seize Elián

Shortly before dawn on April 22, armed INS agents stormed the home of Elián's uncle and retrieved Elián from a closet, where he was found hidden in the arms of one of the men who had rescued him. Elián was reunited with his father a few hours later. Protests erupted in Miami's Little Havana neighborhood immediately following Elián's seizure, resulting in some 250 arrests.

Elián's Miami relatives appealed to the Supreme Court to keep Elián in the United States. But Elián left the United States with his father and stepmother, arriving in Cuba in late June 2000. His departure came just hours after the Supreme Court rejected the case brought by the Miami relatives to keep him in the country.

What Do You Think?

1. Should Elián González have been allowed to stay in the United States or been returned to Cuba? Explain your reasoning.

2. Did the United States make the right foreign policy decision about Elián? Why or why not?

3. How might Elián's life have turned out differently if he had been ordered to remain with his relatives in the United States? How might that have affected U.S.–Cuba relations? Explain your answer.

The Foreign Policy Bureaucracy

The story of Elián González is undeniably dramatic. He survived a capsize that took the life of his mother. Once rescued, he became the central focus in a bitter debate that raged in two countries. Viewed through the perspective of the American government, however, we can see that Elián's story involved important players in our nation's foreign policy bureaucracy. Recall that a bureaucracy is a highly organized administrative structure that carries out policy on a day-to-day basis, regardless of changes in leadership.

Department of State

The leading U.S. foreign policy agency is the Department of State. The chief diplomatic institution of the nation, it manages international relations and coordinates the foreign policy efforts of other executive departments. The State Department maintains embassies and consulates around the world. The secretary of state, the highest-ranking member of the president's cabinet, is the head of the agency.

The Department of State comprises numerous bureaus and offices, each relating to a different region of the world or to a specific foreign policy issue, such as women's issues or refugees. More than 33,000 people work for the State Department. About 20,000 work overseas in what is known as the **foreign service**. These foreign service officers, or diplomats, not only carry out U.S. foreign policy but also provide crucial information for the policy makers back home. Such information covers a wide range of U.S. national interests, including issues of national security and economics.

Department of Defense

By far the largest of the executive departments, the Department of Defense (DOD) supervises the military activities of the nation and advises the president on military issues. More than 675,000 civilians work for the Defense Department. About 1.4 million military personnel are on active duty.

The secretary of defense heads the Department of Defense and is a member of the president's cabinet. The secretary is part of the National Security Council and also the North Atlantic Council, which directs NATO actions. He or she works closely with the secretary of state.

One key element of the Defense Department is the Joint Chiefs of Staff. The joint chiefs include the chiefs of staff of the army and the air force, the navy's chief of naval operations, and the commandant of the marine corps. These members of the military advise the secretary of defense, the National Security Council, and the president.

Key Terms

foreign service
presidential doctrines
diplomatic recognition

REAL-WORLD EXAMPLE
CASE STUDY LINK

State Department Responsibilities The State Department withdrew itself from considering Elián's custody and left the issue up to the Florida courts. Recall that the agency did give approval for Elián's father to travel from Cuba to the United States. Why? Under U.S. law, the Department of State is responsible for issuing visas. A visa is a permit allowing a foreign citizen to apply for entry into the United States.
Applying Information Why would the State Department issue a visa to Elián's father but not make a decision about parental custody?

FOREIGN POLICY BUREAUCRACY

ORGANIZATION	FUNCTION	NUMBER OF EMPLOYEES (2006)
Department of State	Formulates, represents, and implements the president's foreign policy	• 13,181 civil service • 20,764 foreign service
Department of Defense	Controls the army, navy, air force and marine corps and advises the president on military issues	• 675,111 civilian reserve • 1.42 million active-duty military personnel
Central Intelligence Agency	Collects, evaluates, and distributes foreign intelligence to help the president and top government officials make decisions relating to national security	• The number of employees is not made public.

REAL-WORLD EXAMPLE
CASE STUDY LINK

Domestic Pressures
Florida Democratic senator Bob Graham cosponsored legislation to grant Elián González U.S. citizenship and permanent residency. Senator Graham's constituents included the Cuban Americans who dominate the Hispanic population of south Florida. Graham said that granting Elián citizenship would be the only way to allow the custody question to be settled in a forum designed to determine what would be in the boy's best interests.
Applying Information How did Graham's position align with that of many Cuban Americans in south Florida?

Central Intelligence Agency

The third arm of the nation's foreign policy bureaucracy is the Central Intelligence Agency (CIA), which collects and analyzes information about foreign nations and implications for national security. The CIA also engages in covert, or secret, activities to advance U.S. foreign policy goals. Covert actions must be approved by the National Security Council, which oversees the CIA.

Domestic Influences

Policy makers have thousands of dedicated civil servants and military personnel working in the United States and around the world to help them craft sensible foreign policy, but other forces are also at work. Congress creates foreign as well as domestic policy, but sometimes these interests collide.

Since elected officials are responsible to their constituents, they must consider how their decisions will affect the folks back home. However, members of Congress also feel a loyalty to their political party. Because of this partisanship, a politician often feels pressure not to break with his or her party when making policy decisions.

Politicians also face pressure from lobbyists. Lobbyists can be hired by corporations, foreign governments, unions, and other interest groups. Although criticized by many as being an improper influence, lobbying is protected by the Constitution under the "right to petition the government."

READING CHECK **Identifying Supporting Details** How do members of the foreign policy bureaucracy act together to shape U.S. foreign policy?

The President, Congress, and Foreign Policy

The Constitution grants specific roles to the executive and legislative branches regarding the creation of U.S. foreign policy. Cooperation between the executive and legislative branches is necessary for strong and effective U.S. foreign policy. In some cases, though, these roles overlap, and who has the final say on the matter is not always clearly defined. Though the judicial branch does not have any constitutional powers related to foreign relations, courts continue to recognize its importance as a shared power.

Executive Powers

Traditionally, presidents have exercised greater power than Congress over foreign policy. Although general acceptance makes the president the leader in foreign policy, Congress provides checks and balances on presidential power.

Foreign Policy Leader As head of state, the president is not only the public face of U.S. foreign policy but also its chief architect. Practical considerations largely make the chief executive a leader in foreign policy—a president can make decisions more speedily than can a large, deliberative body such as Congress.

The president is our country's ambassador to the world. He or she meets with foreign leaders, engaging in diplomacy and building the international ties that further U.S. economic and security interests.

The Constitution gives the president, as chief diplomat, the power to negotiate treaties, such as peace agreements, trade agreements, and alliances, with foreign nations. The Constitution requires, however, that these treaties be ratified by a two-thirds majority of the Senate. The president also has the power to issue foreign policy statements, or **presidential doctrines**, which guide the direction of U.S. foreign policy.

The president can make executive agreements, or informal agreements with the heads of other nations, without congressional approval. However, Congress must be officially notified of an agreement within 60 days. Historically, executive agreements have covered a broad range of topics, such as educational and scientific exchange programs, joint economic ventures, and economic assistance.

The president also retains the right to establish **diplomatic recognition**. As chief of state, he or she determines whether the United States will officially acknowledge a government as the proper representative of its country's people. Once a country is officially recognized, the United States can engage in official relations with that nation's government.

RESPONSIBILITIES OF LEADERSHIP

Compare the actions of recent presidents in the handling of similar diplomatic or foreign policy issues. Which were more effective, and why?

Military Leader As you have read, the Constitution bestows upon the president the role of commander in chief of the armed forces. It also requires the president to take an oath to "preserve, protect, and defend" the Constitution. These are powerful clues that the Framers intended the chief executive to have a special role in national security. The Constitution balances the president's power as commander in chief with Congress's power to declare war, to raise and support armies, and to provide and maintain a navy.

It is generally accepted, however, that the president has the power to commit troops to military action outside of a formal declaration of war. Presidents have used this power for both short-term military strikes and also for what have been called undeclared wars. The Korean War and the Vietnam War were two such undeclared wars, or wars undertaken without a congressional declaration of war.

Some critics say that presidents' ongoing use of this option, called independent action, has upset the balance of power between the executive and legislative branches. This imbalance was keenly felt during the Vietnam War. In an attempt to check the presidency,

The President as Chief Diplomat

Nixon in China, 1972

Carter in the Middle East, 1979

Clinton signs NAFTA, 1993

The President as Commander in Chief

Johnson and the Vietnam War, 1968

Reagan with troops in South Korea, 1983

Bush and the War in Iraq, 2005

▲ Two of the roles of the president are chief diplomat and commander in chief. Each president has carried out these roles in many different situations, as shown by the examples above.

Congress passed the War Powers Resolution in 1973. The War Powers Resolution states that if a president sends troops into action, he or she must inform Congress within 48 hours. Unless Congress then issues a declaration of war or approves continued action, U.S. forces must be withdrawn within 60–90 days.

Legislative Powers

The Constitution grants Congress the power to declare war, appropriate or deny funds, ratify treaties, and <u>confirm</u> presidential appointments. Although Congress usually supports the foreign policy actions undertaken by the president, it has the power to make significant changes to presidential initiatives during the approval process.

ACADEMIC VOCABULARY

confirm establish or validate

Resolutions and Directives Like the president, Congress can introduce resolutions concerning foreign policy. These resolutions serve as a vehicle of communication with foreign nations and can lend support to the president. Since Congress cannot enforce policy, such resolutions are routinely ignored by the executive branch.

Congress can also initiate foreign policy by establishing programs, setting guidelines, directing the executive branch, and making funding requests. In the late 1990s Congress advanced legislation that made fighting religious persecution around the world a U.S. foreign policy objective. Conversely, Congress can influence foreign policy and attempt to sway the executive branch by threatening to pass legislation.

Funding Restrictions and Denials Perhaps Congress's greatest influence on foreign policy is the "power of the purse." The Constitution grants Congress the authority to appropriate funds, including money for national defense and for financial aid to foreign countries. Unlike other legislative actions, funding restrictions or denials are not subject to serious challenge by the president. When such restrictions are passed despite the president's opposition, confrontation between the branches is common.

Advice and Oversight Congress is also able to shape foreign policy by simply advising the executive branch. Informal advice given at meetings and discussions can help the president gauge reactions to policy initiatives before they are brought to the attention of the public.

Oversight of the executive branch is another important function of Congress that impacts foreign policy. Congress conducts hearings and investigations into the ability of executive agencies to effectively carry out foreign policy legislation.

READING CHECK **Making Inferences** How does Congress's funding authority serve as a check on the president's foreign policy authority?

Interest Groups and Foreign Policy

As you have read, the president and Congress often work together to shape and influence foreign policy. Many individual Americans also attempt to influence the government and its policies through the activities of various interest groups.

For example, Cuban Americans make up just 0.4 percent of the total U.S. population and just 3.5 percent of the nation's Hispanic population. But interest groups provide a way for minority viewpoints to be heard.

Information and Influence

Interest groups supply information to the public and to policy makers. In 2005, for example, Congress ratified the Dominican Republic–Central America Free Trade Agreement, a trade agreement with five Central American nations and the Dominican Republic. The agreement, known as CAFTA, was hotly debated not only in Congress but also by business groups, farmers' alliances, the sugar industry, labor unions, and environmentalists.

In the fight over CAFTA, many interest groups supplied members of Congress and the public with their analysis of how CAFTA

SOME FOREIGN ADVOCACY GROUPS

GROUP	PURPOSE
ATLANTIC COUNCIL OF THE UNITED STATES	To promote constructive U.S. leadership and engagement in international affairs, stimulate dialogue and discussion of critical international issues
CITIZENS FOR GLOBAL SOLUTIONS	To educate Americans about global interdependence and develop programs to create, reform, and strengthen international institutions
UNION OF CONCERNED SCIENTISTS	To achieve practical environmental and health solutions by securing changes in government policy, corporate practices, and consumer choices
PHYSICIANS FOR SOCIAL RESPONSIBILITY	To protect human life from the gravest threats to health and survival
PEACE ACTION	To move forward peace legislation through active citizen campaigning

Skills Focus INTERPRETING CHARTS

Domestic interest or advocacy groups, such as those noted above, attempt to effect change in U.S. foreign policy by uniting like-minded citizens to lobby Congress to initiate or reform legislation. Why might politicians take into account the interests of lobbyists when creating foreign policy legislation?

would affect their areas of interest, hoping to influence the final vote. The Sierra Club, for example, is a large interest group that promotes the enjoyment and protection of the environment. It studied the language of CAFTA and how it provided for protection of the environment. Despite Bush administration claims that CAFTA required member countries to enforce environmental laws, the Sierra Club made a case for how CAFTA actually weakened environmental protections. Information and influence from groups like the Sierra Club helped sway many Democrats—who had voted in favor of NAFTA, the North American Free Trade Agreement, in 1993—to oppose CAFTA.

The Media, Public Opinion, and Policy

President Franklin D. Roosevelt once said, "No president who badly misguesses public opinion will last very long." Indeed, all politicians are sensitive to public opinion. Interest groups are well aware of this. They not only make use of paid advertisements through various media but also use the news media to generate public awareness.

The Elián González case demonstrates the ever-increasing role the media play in shaping public opinion. The media's demand for images of Elián was fed by his Cuban American family's desire to bring attention to their cause. Some people accused the family and their supporters of manipulating both Elián and the media. The media, too, began to examine their own role in the affair.

READING CHECK **Identifying Supporting Details** Give an example of how the Elián González case gave interest groups a means of political participation.

NAFTA Critics argue that the North American Free Trade Agreement actually impedes free trade because it imposes strict governmental controls. Others claim that the overall effects of NAFTA have been positive. Visit **thinkcentral.com** to begin a Webquest on the economic and environmental impact of NAFTA on member countries.

THINK central **Webquest**
thinkcentral.com
KEYWORD: SGO FOR

Section 2 Assessment

THINK central **Online Quiz**
thinkcentral.com
KEYWORD: SGO FOR HP

Reviewing Ideas and Terms

1. **a. Identify** What are the duties and functions of the Department of State?
   b. Make Inferences Why is a large civil service needed to do policy work?

2. **a. Identify** What foreign policy powers does the Constitution give the president?
   b. Summarize Give three examples of checks and balances that Congress has over the president's foreign policy powers.

3. **a. Recall** What is CAFTA?
   b. Summarize How do interest groups affect foreign policy?

Critical Thinking

4. **Draw Conclusions** Do you think interest groups help or harm the formation of U.S. foreign policy? Explain your answer in a brief paragraph.

CASE STUDY LINK The questions you answered at the end of the Case Study are given below. Now that you have completed Section 2, think about and answer the questions again. Then compare your answers with your earlier responses.

5. Should Elián González have been allowed to stay in the United States or been returned to Cuba? Explain your reasoning.

6. Did the United States make the right foreign policy decision about Elián? Why or why not?

7. How might Elián's life have turned out differently if he had been ordered to remain with his relatives in the United States? How might that have affected U.S.–Cuba relations? Explain your answer.

SIMULATION

Senate Trade Bill Vote

Will the Senate approve the Solana trade bill?

Student Casebook

Use your Student Casebook to complete the simulation.

Congress can play a major role in foreign policy decisions. Using what you have learned in Section 2, complete the simulation to decide whether the United States should sign an agreement that would increase its trade with the fictional country of Solana.

Roles

- Democratic senators
- Republican senators
- Food industry lobbyist
- Manufacturing lobbyist
- Human rights group lobbyist
- Labor union representative
- Members of the media

Facts About Solana

- Population: 10 million
- Area: 45,000 square miles
- Government: Dictatorship

❶ The Situation

The Senate is about to vote on an important trade agreement with Solana. Labor and human rights groups oppose the agreement, while business groups support it.

Background

- Solana is a Caribbean nation governed by an elected president. Supported by the military, the president refused to hold elections or leave office when his legal term expired.

- The president suspended Solana's constitution 25 years ago. Since then, the president has ruled as a dictator.

- Solana has a weak economy. Its main export crops are sesame seeds and sesame oil. It also produces rubber and latex.

- The trade bill would lift a ban on imports from Solana and allow U.S. businesses to operate there.

- Senators are facing mid-term elections, so they are very aware of how their votes will be viewed by their constituents.

- The multibillion-dollar food industry in the United States favors the trade bill. The food industry desires a cheap and dependable supply of sesame products.

U.S. Labor Union Data

According to one economic think tank, the United States has lost more than 750,000 jobs since the North American Free Trade Agreement (NAFTA) went into effect in 1994.

Food Industry Data

Sesame is a key ingredient in a variety of foods and baked goods. Sesame oil is used as a cooking oil and in margarine. Sesame seeds are used to flavor and garnish foods.

The United States imports about 40,000 tons of seed and 2,200 tons of oil annually, primarily from South America and the Caribbean.

There is a worldwide shortage of sesame. The current price of 44 cents per pound is expected to increase to 58 cents per pound.

- Manufacturers also favor the trade bill. For example, latex glove manufacturers want to establish factories in a nearby nation that has a good supply of natural latex.

- Human rights advocates and labor unions oppose the trade bill. They fear that the bill will only serve to expose the citizens of Solana to exploitation. The country has few worker protection laws and a poor human rights record. It is in desperate need of democratic reform. Labor unions also fear that American jobs will be lost to cheaper labor in Solana.

❷ Senate Hearing

Your teacher will act as chairperson of a Senate hearing.

- At the hearing, lobbyists from the interest groups will give their opinions of the Solana trade bill.

- Senators will listen to the concerns and opinions of each speaker and may ask questions of them in turn.

- Lobbyists should prepare a summary of their talking points before the Senate hearing.

- Senators should take notes on lobbyists' arguments and review them before casting their votes.

- After the hearing is over, the Senate votes on the bill.

- Members of the media will give a report on the hearing and the results of the vote.

❸ Debriefing

Think about the factors to be considered before senators must cast their votes. Then write a paragraph about why it is important to examine all sides of an issue before making a decision.

Human Rights Data

Solana's citizens have limited civil liberties. The president suspended the constitution 25 years ago and has also suspended elections.

Solana has one opposition political party. It is leading a movement to bring democratic reforms to the government.

Solana's workers have the right to join unions. Workers are not allowed to strike.

Manufacturing Industry Data

Natural rubber is a key raw material used to make more than 40,000 consumer and industrial products.

The United States imports all of its natural rubber from Southeast Asia and Africa. It buys more than 1 million tons each year.

Analysts predict a serious shortage of natural rubber in the next five years. Prices are expected to increase from about $1 per kilogram to $2 per kilogram.

The U.S. rubber industry is working to develop domestic or nearby sources of natural rubber.

Foreign Policy and International Institutions

Reading Focus

The United States is a member of international organizations that work to maintain peace and political stability around the world.

CASE STUDY **Making the Case for War**
Learn about the events that led the United States to take military action against Iraq in 2003.

WHAT YOU NEED TO KNOW Learn about the purpose of the United Nations and the role of international economic organizations and international courts.

SIMULATION **Crisis at the UN Security Council** Use your knowledge to respond to a simulated nuclear disarmament crisis.

Student Casebook

Use your Student Casebook to take notes on the section and to complete the simulation.

United Nations weapons inspectors in Iraq in 2003 (top and bottom).

Making the Case for War

The United States regularly interacts with a host of international organizations. In March 2003 the United States entered into its second war with Iraq, citing violations of UN resolutions. However, unlike the first war, the United States bypassed UN approval.

The Persian Gulf War

In 1990 Iraq invaded the neighboring country of Kuwait. The immediate response of the United Nations (UN) was to impose economic sanctions against Iraq. The UN also passed a resolution authorizing member states in the UN to use force against Iraq if it refused to withdraw from Kuwait. Soon after Iraq failed to meet the deadline for removing its forces from Kuwait, a U.S.-led coalition began attacks on Iraq. The campaign used conventional, non-nuclear war tactics. Coalition forces soon returned Kuwait's government to power. As part of the cease-fire agreement at the war's end, the UN required Iraq to end its weapons of mass destruction (WMD) program and stop developing nuclear weapons.

The Iraq War

In October 2002 both houses of Congress voted to authorize President George W. Bush to send troops to Iraq if it violated the UN requirement that it abandon its WMD program. "The Congress has spoken clearly to the international community and the United Nations Security Council," President Bush stated after the vote. "Saddam Hussein and his outlaw regime pose a grave threat to the region, the world and the United States. Inaction is not an option, disarmament is a must."

The message from the White House was directed as much at the UN and the international community as it was at Saddam Hussein, Iraq's leader. The United States was prepared to take action against Iraq, even if the UN was not. While Congress invoked the enforcement of UN resolutions as justification for action against Iraq, it did not require the UN to make any resolutions for its member nations to attack Iraq before the United States could launch a strike.

The United Nations Weighs In

By November 2002 the UN issued a resolution giving Iraq its "final opportunity to comply" with its obligation to disarm or face "serious consequences." The United States continued to leave weapons inspections to the UN. The wording of the resolution was vague, and the U.S. representative to the UN Security Council pointed out that nothing in the resolution prevented any member state from taking individual action to defend itself or enforce the UN resolutions unilaterally.

Despite this resolution, it became clear that the UN Security Council was not ready to back military action against Iraq. The Security Council

UN headquarters in New York City

The United Nations Security Council in session at UN headquarters in New York City ▼

The U.S.-led invasion of Iraq began in March of 2003 with heavy bombing in Baghdad, Iraq's capital. ▼

is primarily responsible for maintaining international peace and security. Five permanent members (China, France, the Russian Federation, the United Kingdom, and the United States) and 10 nonpermanent members must vote a super-majority, or 9 out of 15 votes, to pass a resolution. Any permanent member may veto a resolution. France had already stated it would veto any resolution to attack Iraq.

President Bush Takes Action

President Bush decided not to go before the UN Security Council for a vote to take military action against Iraq. Nor did he seek to take advantage of U.S. alliances. Instead, Bush put together what he described as a "coalition of the willing," with Great Britain being the principal ally, to launch an invasion of Iraq. On March 18, 2003, he invoked the resolution passed by Congress the previous October, stating that diplomacy and other peaceful means would not protect the national security "nor lead to enforcement of all relevant United Nations Security Council resolutions regarding Iraq."

UN aid workers and weapons inspectors were given 48 hours to leave Iraq. Diplomatic relations with many American allies, particularly France, soured. Many saw the actions of the United States as marginalizing international organizations such as the UN and NATO and resented U.S. unilateralism.

What Do You Think?

1. Why did President Bush decide that the use of military force was necessary in Iraq?
2. How does the U.S.-led invasion of Iraq align with the foreign policy goals of the United States?
3. Why do you think President Bush decided not to go before the UN Security Council before attacking Iraq? Explain your reasoning.

The United Nations

The United Nations is an international organization of peace and cooperation. Established in 1945, it succeeded the League of Nations, which was formed at the end of World War I. Nearly the entire world—192 nations—belongs to the United Nations. According to its charter, the UN's purpose is

- "to maintain international peace and security"

- "to develop friendly relations among nations based on respect for the principle of equal rights and self-determination of peoples"

- "to achieve international co-operation in solving international problems of an economic, social, cultural, or humanitarian character"

- "to be a centre for harmonizing the actions of nations in the attainment of these common ends"

Within the UN's six main divisions, outlined below, dozens of agencies carry out a wide range of functions.

General Assembly

UN member states meet in the UN General Assembly to discuss pressing international matters, such as globalization, human rights, and armed conflict. Each member state gets one vote. Votes on critical matters—regarding international security, for example—require a two-thirds majority. Less urgent matters need only a simple majority. The General Assembly is an advisory body only. It cannot force any member state to follow its recommendations.

Security Council

Fifteen member states of the General Assembly serve on the **UN Security Council**, which is charged with maintaining international peace and security. Unlike the General Assembly, the Security Council has the authority to impose economic sanctions, order arms embargoes, and engage in peacekeeping and collective military action. Any country, even a nonmember state, may bring a dispute or situation to the attention of the General Assembly or Security Council. Security Council decisions require a supermajority, or nine "yes" votes, in order to pass.

China, France, the Russian Federation, the United Kingdom, and the United States are permanent members of the Security Council.

Key Terms

UN Security Council
trust territory

REAL-WORLD EXAMPLE

Universal Declaration of Human Rights After World War II, many people thought that the UN Charter did not fully define the human rights it outlined. To address this, the General Assembly adopted the Universal Declaration of Human Rights on December 10, 1948. All UN member states were encouraged to publicly display and disseminate the text, which advocates "universal respect for and observance of human rights and fundamental freedoms."
Applying Information
What are some ways that governments preserve and protect the rights, liberties, and responsibilities of their citizens?

NGOs and the UN ECOSOC partners with a number of nongovernmental organizations (NGOs) devoted to improving public health and providing disaster relief, aid, and economic development. Perhaps two of the most well-known NGOs are the International Red Cross and Amnesty International. There are also many smaller or religiously affiliated NGOs, such as the World Council of Churches and the Catholic Relief Services. **Applying Information** How do actions of NGOs reflect the characteristics of American democracy?

These permanent members were the victorious powers at the end of World War II. The remaining 10 members are elected by the General Assembly for two-year terms.

Economic and Social Council

Addressing issues related to human welfare and human rights, the Economic and Social Council (ECOSOC) coordinates the efforts of dozens of UN organizations and more than 2,700 nongovernmental organizations, or NGOs. Much of ECOSOC's focus is directed toward raising living standards in developing countries and encouraging universal respect for human rights. The UN also has a working relationship with a number of independent international organizations working for better global health. The World Health Organization (WHO) is one such body. It works to fight disease and improve public health in developing countries.

International Court of Justice

The International Court of Justice (ICJ), also known as the World Court, is a body of the UN, which means that all UN member states are also parties to the World Court. The General Assembly and the Security Council jointly elect 15 judges to serve on the World Court. Judges serve nine-year terms, and no two may be from the same country. Only states may be parties in cases before the World Court. Nonmember states may also become parties. Participation is voluntary, but if a state agrees to settle a dispute in the World Court, it is bound by the court's decision. The court rules on the basis of international law. All verdicts are final, with no appeals.

The Public Face of the United Nations

The UN's eighth secretary-general, Ban Ki-moon of the Republic of Korea, began his term in January 2007.

Trusteeship Council

The Trusteeship Council suspended operation in 1994, when Palau, the last remaining United Nations trust territory, gained independence. A **trust territory** is a colony or territory placed under administration by another country or countries. The UN came to administer 11 trust territories as it replaced the League of Nations as a world body. The UN charter originally charged the Trusteeship Council with administering the UN trust territories. The five permanent members of the Security Council at present make up the Trusteeship Council, which now only meets on an as-needed basis.

ACADEMIC VOCABULARY
administer manage or supervise

Secretariat

Administration and coordination of UN efforts takes place in the Secretariat. As part of an international civil service, staff members take an oath to take instructions from the organization only—not from any government or outside authority. The Secretariat is headed by the secretary-general, who is elected by the General Assembly on the recommendation of the Security Council to a five-year, renewable term. All five permanent members of the Security Council must approve the selection. The secretary-general is the chief administrative officer at all meetings of the General Assembly, the Security Council, the Economic and Social Council, and the Trusteeship Council, and is the public face of the United Nations.

READING CHECK **Making Inferences** Analyze possible reasons for differences between the civic values expressed in the Universal Declaration of Human Rights and the realities of everyday political, social, and economic life around the world.

Other International Institutions

Several large institutions govern the world's economic and judicial systems. Though they are affiliated with the UN, these organizations are not officially part of the General Assembly or the Security Council. The International Criminal Court, however, is an independent, permanent court based on a treaty signed by 105 nations as of 2008.

International Economic Organizations

Together, the World Trade Organization, the International Monetary Fund, and the World Bank set the agenda for world trade and global economic development. These organizations are considered intergovernmental agencies related to the United Nations.

World Trade Organization The World Trade Organization (WTO) is the premier international trade organization. Its 151 members accounted for roughly 97 percent of the world's trade by mid-2007.

Globalization The world economy is moving toward greater globalization—the international production, distribution, and marketing of goods and services. Visit **thinkcentral.com** to begin a Webquest about how international economic institutions like the World Trade Organization, the International Monetary Fund, and the World Bank shape trade and development.

THINK central **Webquest**
thinkcentral.com
KEYWORD: SGO FOR

The WTO is the successor to the U.S.-sponsored 1947 General Agreement on Tariffs and Trade (GATT), which operated in effect as an international trade organization.

In order to protect the financial interests of smaller, weaker countries and to discourage discriminatory trade practices among larger, stronger countries, WTO members must agree to grant equal market access to all member countries. This equal-access trade, previously known as most-favored nation status, is called normal trade relations. While the WTO works toward the liberalization of trade—that is, the unrestricted flow of goods and services—it does allow some tariffs and some forms of protectionism. The WTO gives greater allowances to less-developed countries in scheduling the reduction of existing tariffs.

International Monetary Fund Established in 1944, the International Monetary Fund (IMF) was originally founded to help the world economy recover from the effects of World War II and to prevent the conditions that had led to the economic collapse of the Great Depression. Today, the IMF boasts near-global membership and focuses primarily on loaning money to less-developed countries.

Many less-developed countries are trapped in a cycle of debt. The effort to repay loans to foreign, industrialized nations can overburden the economies of less-developed nations. Resources needed to develop their economies end up being funneled into debt repayment. The IMF attempts to help such countries end this cycle and stop them from defaulting on their loans. It offers short-term loans and technical assistance to turn around the economies of debtor nations.

One function of the World Bank today is to provide development loans for agricultural projects like this tea plantation in India.

World Bank Developed alongside the International Monetary Fund, the World Bank was created to address the reconstruction needs of post–World War II Europe as well as aid developing nations in Asia, Africa, and Latin America. It provides long-term loans and technical assistance to developing nations for specific development projects, such as road building or teacher training, or for specific sectors of the economy, such as agriculture. The World Bank works closely with the IMF, formulating policy and developing programs to aid countries in improving their economies.

International Judicial Organizations

As you have read, the International Court of Justice, also know as the World Court, is the official judicial body of the United Nations.

In 2002, the International Criminal Court was established to prosecute individuals for genocide, crimes against humanity, and war crimes. Both the ICJ and the ICC base their rulings on established international laws and customs. The courts are headquartered in The Hague, The Netherlands.

International Criminal Court The International Criminal Court (ICC) is considered "a court of last resort." Unlike the World Court, the ICC is treaty-based and prosecutes individuals, not states. Its purpose is "to promote the rule of law and ensure that the gravest international crimes do not go unpunished." Terrorism is prosecuted only as it falls under these categories. The ICC investigates and prosecutes such crimes only if a member state is unwilling or unable to do so itself. The UN Security Council may also refer cases to the ICC. The United States is not a member of the ICC.

International Tribunals To address atrocities committed in the former Yugoslavia in the early 1990s and in Rwanda in 1994, the Security Council established the International Criminal Tribunal for the former Yugoslavia (ICTY) in 1993 and the International Criminal Tribunal for Rwanda (ICTR) in 1994. These tribunals were established in the absence of an international criminal court and will expire when their work is complete. The ICTR delivered the world's first international court judgment on genocide in 1998.

READING CHECK **Contrasting** In what ways does the International Criminal Court differ from the World Court?

THINK central Online Quiz
thinkcentral.com
KEYWORD: SGO FOR HP

Section 3 Assessment

Reviewing Ideas and Terms

1. **a. Identify** What is the purpose of the United Nations according to its charter?
   b. Contrast What are the differences between the General Assembly and the Security Council?

2. **a. Identify** Name the three organizations related to the UN that set the agenda for world trade and global economic development.
   b. Explain Why were international economic organizations founded after World War II?

3. **a. Describe** What are the functions of the International Court of Justice?
   b. Interpret In what ways does the International Court of Justice contribute to international security?

Critical Thinking

4. **Draw Conclusions** What determined which nations are permanent members of the UN Security Council? Why do you think there is debate over this today?

CASE STUDY LINK You answered the following questions at the end of the Case Study. Now that you have completed Section 3, think about and answer the questions again. Then compare your answers with your earlier responses. Are your answers the same or are they different?

5. Why did President Bush decide that the use of military force was necessary in Iraq?

6. How does the U.S.-led invasion of Iraq align with the foreign policy goals of the United States?

7. Why do you think President Bush decided not to go before the UN Security Council before attacking Iraq? Explain your reasoning.

SIMULATION

Crisis at the UN Security Council

Will the Security Council succeed in making Aridstan give up its nuclear weapons?

Student Casebook

Use your Student Casebook to complete the simulation.

Foreign policy issues that threaten world peace often become a matter of discussion for the UN Security Council. Using what you have learned in Section 3, you will play a Security Council member state and decide how to respond to a fictional country set on developing nuclear weapons.

Roles

Permanent members of the Security Council

- China
- France
- Russian Federation
- United Kingdom
- United States

Nonpermanent members of the Security Council

- Brazil
- Ecuador
- Germany
- Iceland
- Mozambique
- Nigeria
- Pakistan
- Poland
- Japan
- Tanzania

❶ The Situation

The fictional Central Asian country of Aridstan has long made clear its intentions to develop a nuclear arsenal. Hoping to prevent this, the Security Council passed sanctions in order to limit Aridstan's economic activity, though the country has been allowed to sell oil to Russia and China to prevent hardship among its people. Despite economic sanctions, Aridstan continued to pursue development of nuclear weapons.

Background

- Aridstan is a dry, landlocked country that borders Russia and China.
- Aridstan's economy is controlled by a Soviet-style government led by a dictator.
- Political parties in Aridstan are banned, but there is a growing movement toward a democratic government.
- Aridstan's most abundant natural resource is petroleum. Although it is a small country, its land lies atop rich reserves of oil.
- Russia and Aridstan have agreed to jointly operate an oil pipeline that delivers oil to Russia. Russia is a main buyer of oil and also provides economic aid to Aridstan. China is Aridstan's second-largest oil buyer.

❷ The Crisis

This week Aridstan's leader made a bold claim that the country succeeded in developing nuclear weapons. On display this week at a parade in the capital were rockets capable of launching a nuclear warhead from Aridstan to cities throughout Europe and Asia. World intelligence agencies, however, are unable to confirm or deny Aridstan's claim.

Sensing the need for a swift and powerful response, China has drafted a resolution to present to the Security Council.

China Prepares a Resolution

China calls for the creation of a military force that would be authorized to invade Aridstan. The invasion force would have two tasks:

- Secure any nuclear warheads
- Destroy Aridstan's capability to produce nuclear weapons

Russia, France, and Pakistan Raise Objections

Russia, France, and Pakistan all have objections to the proposed resolution. Russia and France have both threatened to veto any resolution that fails to take their objections into account. Each country proposes an amendment to the resolution.

- Russia has invested a lot of money in an oil pipeline running through Aridstan. Russia proposes an amendment to the resolution stating that it would be compensated for any damage to the pipeline caused by an invasion.

- France is not convinced that Aridstan actually has nuclear weapons. The French delegation proposes an amendment that would allow for an invasion only after a six-month cooling-off period has passed.

Pakistan, a rival of both Russia and China in the region, has a desire to see the entire resolution fail. Its delegation will attempt to build enough support among the nonpermanent members of the Security Council to prevent passage of the final resolution.

❸ Security Council Meeting

Each of the 15 countries on the Security Council should be represented in the Security Council meeting. Use the agenda at right to role-play the meeting. Representative(s) from the United Kingdom, which currently holds the rotating presidency of the Security Council, will chair the meeting.

Debate and vote on the amendments first. Security Council members may vote for one amendment only. Nine "yes" votes are needed to pass an amendment. Then vote on the final resolution. In order for the final resolution to pass, nine "yes" votes are also needed.

❹ Debriefing

Reflect on the consensus-building process. Write a short essay in which you discuss how the need to build a consensus is both an important check on the Council's power and a possible hindrance to its ability to take decisive action.

Agenda

- **The Russian Amendment**

  A. Russia presents arguments for its amendment.

  B. Open debate is held on the amendment.

  C. The Council votes on the amendment.

- **The French Amendment**

  A. France presents arguments for its amendment.

  B. Open debate is held on the amendment.

  C. The Council votes on the amendment.

- **The Final Resolution**

  A. China presents its resolution, including the amendments if either were passed.

  B. Open debate is held on the resolution.

  C. The Council votes on the resolution.

Foreign Policy Challenges

Reading Focus

Helping countries make the transition to democracy and overcome poverty are some foreign policy challenges facing the United States.

CASE STUDY **The Czech Republic** Learn about the events that led to the end of Communist government in Czechoslovakia.

WHAT YOU NEED TO KNOW Learn about the changes in U.S. foreign policy over time, transitions to democracy in different world regions, and ways in which the United States is working to overcome poverty through humanitarian aid.

SIMULATION **Negotiating an Environmental Treaty** Use your knowledge to complete a simulation on a global summit meeting on environmental concerns.

Student Casebook

Use your Student Casebook to take notes on the section and to complete the simulation.

Václav Havel, shown above, led a democracy movement that ended Communist rule in Czechoslovakia in 1989.

The Czech Republic

"None of us know all the potentialities that slumber in the spirit of the population, or all the ways in which that population can surprise us when there is the right interplay of events." So said Czechoslovakia's leading dissident, Václav Havel, in his 1986 work *Disturbing the Peace*. Despite all efforts to suppress it, the spirit of the Czechoslovak people awoke to throw off the shackles of a Soviet-dominated Communist government.

From Democracy to Soviet Bloc

The nation of Czechoslovakia did not start out with a Communist government. Formed in 1918 after World War I, the nation brought together the Czechs and Slovaks, who were eager to be free of the Austrian monarchy that had dominated them for centuries. For about 20 years Czechoslovakia stood as the lone democracy of eastern Europe. The aftermath of World War II brought a Soviet presence that changed the course of Czechoslovak politics. By 1948 the Czechoslovak Communist Party took control of the government. Under Soviet pressure, the government increasingly conformed to the Soviet model. Political opposition was restricted. As it underwent centralization, Czechoslovakia's once healthy economy began to stagnate.

A Reform Movement

As the economy reached a crisis point in the 1960s, a reform movement within the Communist Party emerged. The strongest leader in that movement was Alexander Dubček. He called not only for economic reforms but also for democratic reforms. His "Prague Spring" reforms received wide public support. Alarmed by this turn of events, Soviet leaders ordered troops to invade Czechoslovakia in 1968 and instituted a period of so-called "normalization."

Normalization returned the country to its pre-reform status by ridding the Communist Party of all reform-minded members, censoring the media, banning religion, and arresting dissidents.

One prominent dissident who was repeatedly thrown in jail was the playwright Václav Havel. He became a leading figure in a growing human-rights movement during the 1970s and 1980s. In 1977 Havel and more than 240 other leading dissidents signed Charter 77, a statement demanding that the government of Czechoslovakia allow its citizens the civil and political rights that existed for Czechoslovaks "on paper alone." He also came to lead the Civic Forum, a loose antigovernment coalition of various reform groups. Millions of Czechs supported the Civic Forum and its Slovak counterpart, Public Against Violence.

The Velvet Revolution

The security forces of Czechoslovakia's Communist government were no match for the massive popular and peaceful demonstrations in Czechoslovakia in mid-November 1989. With communism collapsing in the neighboring countries of Poland, Hungary, and East Germany, Czechoslovakia's Communist government had no choice but to dissolve. By December Havel was elected interim president of Czechoslovakia. The nearly bloodless defeat of the Communist Czech government has been named the Velvet Revolution. In 1992 the Czech and Slovak republics agreed to separate as independent states. This peaceful separation went into effect on January 1, 1993.

What Do You Think?

1. What roles did individual citizens play in the overthrow of Czechoslovakia's Communist government?

2. How did the Velvet Revolution align with U.S. foreign policy goals?

3. Why was the Velvet Revolution successful? Explain your answer.

Key Terms

Monroe Doctrine
deterrence
containment
détente
preemptive strike
democratization
food security

REAL-WORLD EXAMPLE

Imperialist Era During the late nineteenth and early twentieth centuries, the European powers, Japan, and the United States practiced imperialism—aggressive expansion in the forms of military, political, and economic control over other nations. Motivations for countries practicing imperialism varied from altruistic (having unselfish concern for others) to exploitative to benign.

Applying Information
Brainstorm with your classmates current variations of imperialism.

Past Foreign Policy Challenges

U.S. foreign policy must be fairly flexible to adapt to the changing needs of the United States and of other countries. Outlined on the following pages are highlights of major developments in U.S. foreign policy since our nation's beginning.

Independence to World War II

U.S. foreign policy was largely isolationist for many years. However, the outbreak of wars and a desire for territorial expansion caused the United States to take a more active role in international affairs.

Isolationist Beginnings Neutrality was a guiding principle in foreign relations during the early years of our nation. Both Presidents Washington and Jefferson formally took an isolationist stance, stating that the United States should avoid making any permanent alliances with foreign nations. In 1823 President Monroe issued the Monroe Doctrine proclaiming America's intentions to remain neutral during European conflicts. However, the doctrine also stated that the United States would view any European colonization attempts occurring in the Americas as hostile and worthy of retaliation.

Rise to World Power By the late 1800s the United States had become a strong, industrialized nation. The U.S. desire for global markets necessitated a shift toward internationalism. The Spanish-American War of 1898 marked the beginning of this shift.

Cuba was one of the last of Spain's holdings in the Americas, and Cubans had long been unhappy with Spanish rule. Americans' sympathy with Cuba's struggle for independence, as well as growing public support for U.S. expansion in other areas of the world, led the United States to declare war on Spain in 1898. After a swift victory, the United States emerged from the war a world power, gaining possession of Guam, Puerto Rico, and the Philippines as well as securing independence for Cuba.

World War I Rivalries among European nations culminated in war in 1914. Public sentiment was deeply divided about U.S. intervention. Though the United States was a colonial power, many Americans preferred neutrality concerning European affairs. German militarism had begun to take the form of attacks against U.S. shipping and a proposed German-Mexican alliance. In 1917 the United States entered the war. In the words of President Woodrow Wilson, it was a war to make the world "safe for democracy." Wilson argued that a peace settlement should be followed by the creation of a League of Nations, an international organization dedicated to stopping further aggression.

World War II Antiwar and isolationist sentiment ran high after America witnessed the brutality of World War I. However, Germany and Japan posed a possible threat to U.S. security with their military aggressions in Europe and the Pacific, and public support for U.S. involvement in the second world war increased after a time.

Though President Franklin D. Roosevelt announced U.S. neutrality at the outset of war in Europe, when Japanese planes attacked the U.S. naval base at Pearl Harbor on December 7, 1941, Roosevelt called for, and received from Congress, a declaration of war on Japan. The United States and the other Allies won the war in 1945, but Europe and Japan were left in ruins. The United States again emerged from world war as a first-class power.

New Policies Returning to isolationism ceased to be an option for the United States. World War II solidified the nation's role as a major player on the world stage.

The United States began to practice collective security, or working with other countries to keep international peace and order. With the hopes of preventing future wars and furthering international cooperation, the United States helped found the United Nations in 1945.

Another U.S. foreign policy that came as a result of World War II is that of deterrence. **Deterrence** is the policy of building up the U.S. armed forces in order to discourage acts of military aggression by other nations. The policy of deterrence remains in effect today.

◄ **REAL-WORLD EXAMPLE**

Propaganda of War Both the public and private sectors have long relied on propaganda to convey information to the public. During wartime, propaganda is seen as especially important to the national interest. World War I marked the first of the large-scale propaganda campaigns by the U.S. government in order to gain public support during wartime.
Applying Information How does propaganda promote a government's national interests?

Major Shifts in Foreign Policy (1823–1945)

Social, political, cultural, and economic exchanges and scientific and technological advances—those originating domestically and internationally—have influenced life in the United States and U.S. foreign policy.

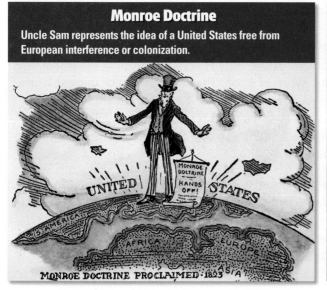

Monroe Doctrine
Uncle Sam represents the idea of a United States free from European interference or colonization.

World War II Troops
U.S. troops march down the Champs-Élysées in Paris, France, during the liberation of Paris from German forces in 1944.

The Cold War to the Collapse of the Soviet Union

The United States and the Soviet Union were temporary allies during World War II, but the two nations had never been friendly. The Communist political system was sharply at odds with American democratic ideals. After World War II, relations between the two nations became increasingly strained.

Origins of the Cold War In March 1947 President Harry S. Truman gave a speech that set forth what came to be known as the Truman Doctrine. With this speech, Truman set in motion the strategy of containment, a policy that remained in place for the next 40 years. Containment was based on the view that communism threatened democratic values and that Soviet expansion must be stopped.

By 1949 the Soviet Union had taken control of Eastern Europe. In September of that year President Truman announced that the Soviet Union had exploded an atomic bomb. Preventing nuclear war became the primary concern of U.S. foreign policy makers.

By that time the Cold War had expanded beyond Europe. Communists led by Mao Zedong seized control of China in 1949. Communist governments in North Korea, Cuba, and North Vietnam soon challenged U.S. containment efforts as well.

The Korean War After World War II, Korea was divided into two countries: a Communist north and a non-Communist south. Following a 1950 invasion of the South, troops from the United States and other nations were sent by the United Nations to help defend South Korea. Within a few months UN troops had repelled the attack and pushed into North Korea. Communist China, worried by the approach of U.S. troops near its border, sent its own soldiers to aid North Korea. After three bloody years, an armistice, or cease-fire, was signed in 1953. However, no peace treaty was signed, and relations between the two Koreas remain tense.

Cuban Missile Crisis In 1958 Cuba's pro-American dictator was overthrown by a group of rebels led by Fidel Castro. Opposed by the United States, Castro turned to the Soviet Union for help.

In 1962 the Soviet Union began secretly installing nuclear weapons in Cuba. Worried about the implications of nuclear arms so close to U.S. soil, President John F. Kennedy ordered a naval blockade to stop Soviet ships from transporting missiles to Cuba. Six days after the blockade began, the Soviet Union agreed to withdraw the missiles.

The Vietnam War Communist forces helped Vietnamese nationalists secure independence from France in 1954. The cease-fire agreement divided Vietnam into a non-Communist South Vietnam and a Communist North Vietnam. U.S. aid to South Vietnam began in the mid-1950s and increased under the Kennedy administration. In 1965 President Lyndon Johnson further escalated U.S. involvement.

REAL-WORLD EXAMPLE

Presidential Powers The first direct confrontation between nuclear-armed powers occurred during the Cuban missile crisis. In order to avoid war, Kennedy used his authority as president to enact military action. Other presidents who have had to respond to crisis situations with military intervention include George H. W. Bush during the Gulf War after Iraq invaded Kuwait and Bill Clinton in Bosnia after the breakup of Yugoslavia.
Applying Information Why is the ability to enact military action included in the scope of presidential power?

Johnson committed more U.S. troops and ordered the bombing of North Vietnam.

Bombing against North Vietnam increased under President Richard Nixon, though opposition to the undeclared war increased at home. U.S. troops finally left Vietnam in 1973. In 1975 the U.S.-backed South Vietnamese government surrendered. More than 58,000 Americans had been killed or were missing in action.

End of the Cold War The late 1980s marked perhaps the most dramatic shift in global relations in modern history—the collapse of the Soviet Union. Fear of Communist expansion had dominated U.S. foreign policy for decades. Throughout the 1970s, the Soviet Union continued its aggressive policies and arms buildup. However, the United States and the Soviet Union also began practicing in earnest the policy of **détente**, or a relaxing of tensions.

When Mikhail Gorbachev became Communist Party leader in 1985 and later Soviet president, he instituted a wave of market and policy reforms. One of the most influential foreign policy reforms was the withdrawal of the long-standing threat of Soviet military intervention in the internal affairs of Soviet satellite countries. These reforms sparked similar movements across Eastern Europe, and Communist governments began to fall. Within two years, the Soviet Union itself had dissolved. After a failed coup to oust Gorbachev, 10 of the 15 former Soviet republics formed a new union in December 1991.

READING CHECK **Summarizing** How has U.S. foreign policy changed over time?

Major Shifts in Foreign Policy (1945–1989)

Though peace agreements were reached after World War II, tensions between the Communist East and democratic West escalated for decades. The fall of the Berlin Wall symbolically ended the Cold War and smoothed the path for German reunification efforts.

Yalta Conference
Churchill, Roosevelt, and Stalin (from left to right) represent the UK, U.S., and the Soviet Union respectively at a 1945 conference in Yalta to discuss governing a post-war Germany.

Fall of the Berlin Wall
Built in 1961, the Berlin Wall was a powerful reminder of Soviet domination in Germany. After East Germany opened the wall in November 1989, East Berliners flooded past the border and tore down parts of the wall.

Contemporary Foreign Policy Challenges

Though most Communist governments had fallen by the 1990s, the United States still faced a number of other challenges. The post–Cold War era presented the United States with a new global agenda.

Post–Cold War to the Present

The United States today faces a number of pressing issues concerning foreign policy. These include ending the spread of nuclear weapons. The United States itself is a nuclear power, as are all five permanent members of the UN Security Council. Most of the world's nations have signed a Nuclear Non-Proliferation Treaty. Only India, Israel, Pakistan, and North Korea have not signed the treaty, which aims to limit the spread of nuclear weapons. The nation's top foreign policy priority, however, is U.S. involvement in regional conflicts in the Middle East.

Shifting Alliances in the Middle East The political climate in the Middle East has become increasingly complex in recent years. The relationship between the United States and Saudi Arabia is but one example of the complexity of foreign policy challenges in the Middle East.

The United States has maintained diplomatic relations with Saudi Arabia since 1933, despite cultural and ideological differences. Saudi Arabia's location on the oil-rich Arabian Peninsula—it possesses the world's largest oil reserves—and its position in the Islamic world has made Saudi Arabia a valuable U.S. ally. The United States is Saudi Arabia's largest trading partner, and Saudi Arabia remains the largest market for American exports to the Middle East. American companies also form the largest group of foreign investors in the country. Apart from U.S. economic and political interests in the region, the two countries share a number of other concerns, such as regional security and development.

Because of Saudi Arabia's influential status as a member of the Organization of Petroleum Exporting Countries (OPEC) and the current and projected U.S. needs for foreign supplies of oil, maintaining favorable relations with the country remain essential to American economic prosperity. Saudi Arabia's system of government, a monarchy, does not align with the American goal of spreading democracy. Legal gender discrimination and accusations of human rights abuses have also strained U.S.–Saudi relations. However, foreign policy leaders weigh carefully the costs and benefits of each alliance. Depending on perspective, U.S. foreign policy interests—and those of any nation—can be seen through many different lenses.

REAL-WORLD EXAMPLE

Global Economic Challenges Another pressing foreign policy issue facing the United States is how to best position U.S. interests to compete in a global economy. In 1992 the European Union (EU) emerged as a strong political unit, and the European Monetary Unit (EMU) is a powerful competitor with U.S. markets. Growing numbers of multinationals—large corporations with operations in several countries—present additional challenges in the marketplace.

Applying Information How might increasing global competition impact U.S. foreign policy concerning trade?

Arab-Israeli Conflict Though political instability has long troubled the region, Arab rejection of the State of Israel has been at the center of violent conflicts in the Middle East for more than 60 years. Efforts toward peace have been made throughout the conflict. The United States helped achieve peace between Israel and Egypt and Jordan. However, there has not yet been a complete solution.

In 1947 the UN proposed that the British mandate of Palestine be divided into a two-state, Arab and Jewish, partition. The Jews accepted, but the Arab countries refused the proposal. U.S. support of Israel began in 1948 when the State of Israel was created. Five Arab nations attacked Israel, and the resulting war <u>displaced</u> thousands of Arabs and Jews (from Arab countries), the cause of much of the region's current unrest. Israel and the United States maintain close ties, and that relationship underlies much of U.S. dealings in the Middle East.

The United States remains committed to peace negotiations, including working toward the creation of an independent Palestinian state alongside Israel. Palestinians and Israelis are meeting and discussing issues. However, Palestinian terrorist attacks against Israel and Israeli military reprisals continue.

ACADEMIC VOCABULARY

displace to compel a person or group to leave their home or country

9/11 and the War on Terror After terrorists attacked the United States on September 11, 2001, the United States demanded that Afghanistan turn over Osama bin Laden, alleged mastermind of the attacks. Bin Laden's network had found refuge under Afghanistan's government, led by the Taliban. The Taliban is an Islamic movement that controlled most of the country from 1996 to 2001. The attacks killed thousands and prompted heightened security measures throughout the nation and U.S. military action in Afghanistan.

Soon after, President George W. Bush began a campaign to stop the spread of terrorism, known as the War on Terror or the War on Terrorism. In September 2002 the administration shifted U.S. foreign policy toward a more aggressive approach with regard to counterterrorism, one that justified the use of a preemptive strike. The **preemptive strike** doctrine, or the potential use of force before an attack occurs, is a departure from the previous U.S. strategies of deterrence and containment. Some critics claim that preemptive war does not adhere to the theory of just war and that it violates international law.

In October 2002 the Bush administration announced the extension of the campaign against terror into Iraq, citing Iraq's alleged possession of weapons of mass destruction and state sponsorship of terror. As you have read, U.S. troops invaded Iraq in March 2003. As of 2008, no exit strategy or timetable for troop withdrawal is in place. Efforts to rebuild Iraq are ongoing. The U.S. and international communities will likely be involved in security and reconstruction efforts in the country for quite some time.

The Attacks of 9/11

On September 11, 2001, terrorists crashed planes into the World Trade Center towers in New York City, into the Pentagon in Washington, D.C., and in southwestern Pennsylvania.

The World Trade Center attack

The destruction at the Pentagon

REAL-WORLD
EXAMPLE

Communist Dissent The Soviet Union and the countries it dominated were good at stifling dissent. However, detractors of the regime still found ways to get their messages out. Aleksandr Solzhenitsyn wrote vivid and powerful accounts of his time as a political prisoner in books such as *One Day in the Life of Ivan Denisovich*. Pope John Paul II is noted, among his many other accomplishments, for speaking out against the repressive Communist environment and promoting religious freedom for all.

Applying Information How did Solzhenitsyn and the Pope express dissent with the Communist system?

Transitions to Democracy

Support of **democratization**, the establishment of democratic governments, has become a cornerstone of U.S. foreign policy. But the transition to democracy is often a long and difficult process. Nations making the transition to democracy face enormous challenges. The switch from a centralized economy to free enterprise can result in unemployment. Many nations often lack a middle class and instead have a ruling elite that controls most of the wealth. Countries emerging from recent conflicts often find themselves overwhelmed by constant tensions between ethnic or religious groups.

Eastern Europe The collapse of communism brought forth a period of democratization throughout Eastern Europe. It began in the mid-1980s, when Soviet Communist Party leader Mikhail Gorbachev instituted a program of economic and political restructuring called *perestroika* and a policy of *glasnost*, or "openness."

Russia, the largest of the former Soviet republics, faced economic hardships as it tried to establish a market economy. It was also troubled by ethnic conflict, particularly with the breakaway republic of Chechnya. In recent years the progress Russia has made toward democratic reforms has begun to falter.

Latin America Following World War II, Latin America was characterized by revolutionary activity and military dictatorships. This unrest eventually culminated in Castro's takeover of Cuba. When communism seemed to threaten Latin America, the United States took an interventionist role, which included supporting some authoritarian dictators. But with the Cold War over, U.S. efforts have turned toward supporting the democracies that emerged by the 1990s. The persistent gap between the rich and poor and the challenges of global economic competition in these nations continues to slow democratic progress, however.

Struggles for Democracy

South Africa is one example of a country that has established a democratic government. In other countries, such as Cambodia, the process of democratization is not yet complete.

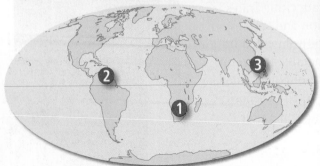

1 South African women wait in line to vote in the country's first all-race election held in April 1994.

Asia Throughout Asia are many examples of new democracies. China has adopted market-oriented reforms in recent decades, though it has not instituted democratic political reforms and remains a Communist nation. In terms of U.S. foreign policy concerns, the most critical challenges in recent years involve government upheavals in Afghanistan and Iraq.

Largely in response to the attacks of September 11, 2001, U.S. and British forces drove out the Taliban government in Afghanistan later that year. Afghan political and tribal leaders formed a council to rule temporarily until the nation could hold democratic elections, which took place in 2004. One of the major difficulties facing the new democracy is recovering from more than 20 years of civil war.

One of the biggest challenges for Iraq, according to the U.S. Agency for International Development (USAID), is that the various ethnic and sectarian religious groups of Iraq must form a common vision for their country based on tolerance and other democratic principles. The best course of action for U.S. support and promotion of Iraqi democracy remains a subject of great debate.

Africa According to Freedom House, an independent nongovernmental organization that promotes democratic reform, only 11 out of 48 nations in Africa can be considered free, while 23 are considered "partly free." A country's level of freedom is gauged by examining the political rights and civil liberties afforded its citizens.

Many African nations face huge development challenges, including conflicts, ethnic tension, and issues of poverty and health. As you have read, establishing and following the rule of law—the belief that a government must be accountable to its citizens—is key to effective democratic rule. This process often proves most challenging to developing democracies, as it did with early American democracy. U.S. foreign aid to transitional democracies in Africa includes substantial funds dedicated to programs aimed at supporting democracy and creating frameworks for governance.

REAL-WORLD EXAMPLE

Pakistan Since 2001, Pakistan has been a partner in the U.S.-led war on terror, even though the United States is concerned about its nuclear weapons program and political turmoil that has troubled the nation. Pakistan tested a nuclear bomb in 1998 in response to nuclear tests made by India. In 1999 General Pervez Musharraf took power in a military coup, becoming president and remaining head of the army. Pakistan's largest political parties opposed Musharraf because he stalled a return to democracy. In 2007 former prime minister Benazir Bhutto returned to Pakistan after years of self-imposed exile. A leader in the effort to restore democracy, she was assassinated in late 2007.

Applying Information What advice would you give to the U.S. president regarding Pakistan?

2 Venezuelans protest the removal of the nation's oldest TV station in mid-2007 by authoritarian president Hugo Chavez.

3 Freedom of the press is not yet fully guaranteed in Cambodia. Here, a radio station director is arrested in 2005 for a broadcast that offended the government.

Interactive Feature ⭑

Goals of Foreign Policy Today

The goals of U.S. foreign policy are interconnected and work together to support each other. Stable, secure, and democractic nations are more likely to support free trade and less likely to pose security threats to the United States.

Goals

● National Security

● Establish Free and Open Trade

● Promote Peace

● Promote Democracy

● Provide Aid

Walk-through security portals, such as this one in New York's JFK airport, help detect explosives.

Well over half the trade conducted at this Oakland, California, container port is with Asian countries.

THINK central **Interactive**
thinkcentral.com
KEYWORD: SGO FOR

Overcoming Poverty

For more than six decades, foreign aid has been part of U.S. policy. Foreign aid is aimed at bolstering the economies of struggling nations and helping to strengthen our alliances. The United States supports a number of development programs, largely through USAID. The programs must tackle a variety of problems that can limit economic progress, such as poverty, hunger, illiteracy, and inadequate health care.

Hunger Each year, malnutrition claims the lives of more than 1.5 million children. Poor nutrition can also lead to reduced growth and intellectual function. Malnutrition also weakens the immune system, exposing people to greater risk of disease.

Together, the United States and other developed nations help combat starvation and malnutrition by promoting food security. **Food security** is an adequate food supply at the national, household, and individual level. Food security is best achieved through a combination of improved agricultural practices and improved economic polices and the promotion of education, property rights, and other civil rights.

Literacy Literacy has long been an indicator of economic development. Improved literacy rates have been linked with benefits such as lower infant mortality rates, higher agricultural productivity, and increased political participation, among others.

An estimated 1 billion adults lack basic literacy skills. Due to unequal access to education, two-thirds of them are women. Worldwide, about 115 million children do not have access to even the most basic primary education. In developing countries, far more boys than girls receive a primary school education, and that gap widens at the secondary level. The United States has designed literacy programs aimed specifically at supporting gender equality in education in the developing world. Equal access to an education is seen not only as a basic right but also as a powerful engine for social progress.

Health Care The global health care community is trying to wipe out three deadly diseases: malaria, tuberculosis (TB), and HIV/AIDS. Malaria is a potentially fatal blood infection caused by a parasite. Transmitted by mosquito bites, it kills 1 million people each year, mostly children. Though malaria is treatable, the most effective treatments must be administered within 24 hours of infection.

TB is an infectious disease that affects the lungs. It infects one-third of the world's people, or 2 billion people, mostly in less-developed nations where poor nutrition, lack of health care, and other factors make people more vulnerable to disease.

HIV, or human immunodeficiency virus, causes a disease that attacks the immune system. AIDS, or acquired immunodeficiency syndrome, exists when the body's immune system is so weakened it cannot fight off other diseases. More than 40 million people are infected with HIV worldwide, and more than 2 million of them are children under the age of 15. People with HIV are also far more vulnerable to diseases such as malaria and TB.

READING CHECK Identifying Problems and Solutions What are the pros and cons of U.S. participation in world affairs? Give support for your reasoning.

REAL-WORLD EXAMPLE

Water and Disease Access to clean drinking water and adequate sanitation are keys to combating the spread of disease. About 17 percent of the world, or 1.1 billion people, lack access to safe drinking water. Some people who have access to clean water end up contaminating it by handling it or storing it improperly. Unsafe water supplies and poor sanitation and hygiene claim 1.8 million lives each year.

Applying Information How might improved sanitation boost a country's economy?

Section 4 Assessment

Reviewing Ideas and Terms

1. **a. Identify** What is **democratization**?
   b. Analyze How did the collapse of communism help encourage the process of democratization?
   c. Predict How might strengthening the rule of law help developing democracies?

2. **a. Define** What is **food security**?
   b. Explain How do hunger and malnutrition contribute to poverty, not just result from it?
   c. Develop In your opinion, which poverty issue presents the biggest challenge to a developing country? Develop a rationale for your position.

Critical Thinking

3. **Analyze** Write a paragraph that summarizes the U.S. approach to foreign policy over time.

THINK central Online Quiz

thinkcentral.com
KEYWORD: SGO FOR HP

CASE STUDY LINK You answered the following questions at the end of the Case Study. Now that you have completed Section 4, think about and answer the questions again. Then compare your answers with your earlier responses. Are your answers the same or are they different?

4. What roles did individual citizens play in the overthrow of Czechoslovakia's Communist government?

5. How did the Velvet Revolution align with U.S. foreign policy goals?

6. Why was the Velvet Revolution successful? Explain your answer.

SIMULATION

Negotiating an Environmental Treaty

Can world leaders agree on the terms of a global treaty?

Student Casebook

Use your Student Casebook to complete the simulation.

Foreign policy makers must address issues of global interdependence and the environment. Using what you have learned in Section 4, complete the simulation to discuss solutions to combat the impacts of climate change.

Roles

Regional representatives, including

● Australia

● Brazil

● China

● Germany

● India

● Russia

● United States

● Environmental and industrial scientists

● Nongovernmental environmental organizations

❶ The Situation

Prenegotiations for a multilateral—involving more than two nations—environmental treaty have already taken place. Now, the proposed signers will meet to address the provisions of the draft treaty and attempt to strike a balance between global environmental protection and economic stability.

Background

● Climate change is a global issue, but it affects regions in different ways.

● A comprehensive global environmental treaty addressing the effects of climate change exists but will expire in five years.

● The international scientific community is not in full agreement about the causes and consequences of climate change.

● Many leaders are concerned about the treaty's implications on global trade and development. Less-developed countries believe that since wealthier nations are responsible for more emissions and pollution worldwide, these countries should be responsible for the costs incurred by treaty restrictions.

● Developing countries are especially sensitive to the effects of climate change. Often, such countries lack the infrastructure to effectively adapt to changes in precipitation and temperature or to respond to disasters caused by extreme weather.

● The United States, Russia, and China are lobbying heavily against the treaty. They believe it will hurt industry in their countries.

❷ Proposed Terms of the Treaty

Consider the following broad provisions of the draft, and work with your fellow representatives to narrow its focus.

● Enact standards to reduce emissions and enforce stricter industrial regulations within a specific time frame.

- Continue to fund research on causes and effects of global warming, as well as alternative and renewable energy research and development.

- Develop an incentive plan for companies to create environmentally friendly consumer goods and to use energy-efficient technologies and production methods.

- Develop an incentive plan to reward participating countries for their efforts to promote and implement energy-efficient technologies at all levels of domestic government.

❸ Summit Meeting

Your teacher will act as meeting chairperson.

- Regional representatives will discuss current international legislation, such as the Kyoto Protocol, and listen to testimony of environmental and industrial scientists.

- Regional representatives will openly debate each of the topics introduced.

- Regional representatives will vote on whether to accept the terms of the treaty.

❹ Debriefing

Think about all of the factors each country must consider before it can make an informed recommendation. Write a short paragraph to outline your opinion on the necessary course of action. What position should U.S. foreign policy makers take on the issue of climate change?

Issues to Consider

- How will the treaty be enforced? Who will be responsible for enforcing it?

- How long should the treaty remain in effect?

- How could the treaty affect global trade and individual nations' economies?

Some Effects of a Warmer Planet

- Rising temperatures worldwide increase energy demands, which depletes Earth's natural resources.
- Changes in climate can permanently alter ecosystems, putting animal and plant habitats at risk and threatening the planet's biodiversity. Changing ecosystems also affect the type and amount of crops a country can grow, which affects that nation's food security.
- Increased instances of extreme weather events related to climate change, such as tsunamis or hurricanes, can severely depress a country's economy by damaging the tourist industry.

Views of the Scientific Community

- The scientific community is not in full agreement about the issue of climate change. Some scientists argue that human processes do not significantly affect the earth's climate. Others dispute the accuracy of the scientific measurements and data gathered.
- Those scientists backing the human-caused theory argue that the temperature changes noted are out of range for the normal, cyclical changes in the earth's temperature.

Comprehension and Critical Thinking

SECTION 1 *(pp. 438–445)*

1. a. Review Key Terms For each term, write a sentence that explains its significance or meaning: foreign policy, isolationism, just war theory.

b. Make Generalizations How are defense alliances important to the principle of collective security?

c. Evaluate Evaluate the effectiveness of the various tools of U.S. foreign policy. Select and defend the tools you think are more effective in promoting the national interest.

SECTION 2 *(pp. 448–457)*

2. a. Review Key Terms For each term, write a sentence that explains its significance or meaning: foreign service, presidential doctrines, diplomatic recognition.

b. Summarize Briefly review the foreign policy powers of Congress.

c. Predict How might the influence of the media and public opinion affect decisions of U.S. foreign policy makers in the future?

SECTION 3 *(pp. 460–467)*

3. a. Review Key Terms For each term, write a sentence that explains its significance or meaning: UN Security Council, trust territory.

b. Make Inferences How do the purposes of the UN align with the goals of U.S. foreign policy?

c. Elaborate Do efforts to liberalize world trade always benefit developing nations? Defend your answer.

SECTION 4 *(pp. 470–481)*

4. a. Review Key Terms For each term, write a sentence that explains its significance or meaning: deterrence, containment, democratization.

b. Interpret In what ways have decisions of foreign governments influenced U.S. actions in matters of international concern?

c. Predict How might past U.S. foreign policy decisions affect future international relationships?

WRITING FOR THE SAT

Think about the following issue:

The United States has a strong voice in the global community and is a member of a number of large international bodies, such as the UN, NATO, NAFTA, and the WTO. Often, U.S. alliances are trade-based or are otherwise strategic.

5. Assignment What are the costs and benefits of the U.S. government maintaining relationships with foreign nations? With international organizations? Explain your answer in a short paragraph. Give support for your reasoning.

INTERACTIVE CHAPTER 15

Comparative Political and Economic Systems

Why study the world's political and economic systems? Building knowledge about how other nations function is essential for you as a citizen. Our government deals with other nations every day. Studying different types of political and economic systems can help you understand how our nation interacts with other countries. In this interactive chapter, you will learn about the different ways in which the world's nations structure their governments and economies.

Table of Contents

Student Casebook Use your Student Casebook to take notes on the chapter and to complete the simulations.

The world's different systems of government include the constitutional monarchy of the United Kingdom (top) and the presidential democracy of Brazil (bottom).

Democratic Governments

Reading Focus
Today many of the world's countries are democracies. Democracies consist of two basic forms of government: presidential and parliamentary. All democratic governments share certain characteristics, but no two governments are exactly alike.

(CASE STUDY) **Emerging Democracy in Nigeria**
Learn about the difficult transition to democracy in Nigeria.

(WHAT YOU NEED TO KNOW) Learn about the different ways in which democratic governments can be organized, including those of Mexico, Brazil, the United Kingdom, and Japan. You will also learn about some of the world's emerging democracies.

(SIMULATION) **Choosing a System of Government** Use your knowledge to decide which form of government is best for an emerging democracy.

 **Student Casebook**

Use your Student Casebook to take notes on the section and to complete the simulation.

Nigerian voters cast their ballots in the historic 2007 presidential election.

Emerging Democracy in Nigeria

Many nations have adopted or are currently adopting some form of democratic system of government. Nigeria is one such country. Nigeria's history shows that the transition to democracy can be long and difficult.

Colonization and Independence

The West African nation of Nigeria has the largest population of any other African country and is one of the fastest growing nations on earth. Like other African countries, Nigeria has faced great political change in recent decades.

In the early 1900s, Nigeria was a colony controlled by Great Britain. The British largely left local government to Nigerian officials, but British governors made all important decisions—decisions that often ignored existing Nigerian culture and practice. The years of British control brought many changes to Nigeria: Christianity and the English language spread; railroads and roads were built; and the nation's economy was converted to the export of cash crops such as cocoa, cotton, and peanuts.

Nigeria eventually gained its independence in 1960. Nigeria's first government had a parliamentary system in which representatives from multiple parties sought election to a parliament, or legislature. The majority party in control of parliament then selected a chief executive. Often no party held a majority in the parliament, and alliances had to be formed from among competing political groups.

A Fragile Democracy

Nigeria was politically unstable for decades following independence, in large part because of tensions among its different regional, ethnic, and religious groups. In the 1960s regional conflict led to a bloody civil war, which was in turn followed by a series of military dictatorships and assassinations of national leaders.

Nigeria developed a new constitution in the 1970s, changing its system of government to one that more closely resembles that of the United States. Nigeria now has three independent branches of government—legislative, executive, and judicial. The nation's leader is a president elected by voters in a national election.

Despite the new system, Nigeria saw a series of fraudulent elections, military takeovers, and assassinations in the 1980s and 1990s as the nation's rulers and military leaders sought to gain and keep power. Multiple new constitutions failed to stabilize the country's government.

At last, a series of elections in 1998 and 1999 led to the election of General Olusegun Obasanjo as president. Obasanjo had served as military ruler of Nigeria in the late 1970s, but in his two terms as elected leader, he led efforts to reform government and improve human rights.

The nation has made slow progress toward political stability. In 2007 Nigerian voters elected a new president, marking the first peaceful transition from one civilian leader to another since Nigeria became independent.

Yet Nigeria's history of political turmoil is still placed firmly in the minds of Nigerians. In a poll taken after the 2007 election, 67 percent of Nigerians believed that the election was not conducted fairly. The high number suggests that Nigeria's leaders must continue to work hard to establish trust among the people that their government is truly committed to free, open, and fair elections that can result in democratic self-rule by the Nigerian people.

What Do You Think?

1. How did democracy cause change within Nigeria?
2. What signs give reason for hope for Nigeria's political future?
3. What system of government does Nigeria have today?

Democratic Systems

Key Terms

authoritarian
coalition
apartheid

Nigeria established a presidential form of democracy, but there are many ways to organize a government. We categorize governments based on who holds governmental power as well as by how power is distributed among the branches that make up government. In a democracy, much power rests with the voters and the leaders they elect to act on their behalf. In an **authoritarian** government, however, power is concentrated in the hands of a single leader or small group.

Democracies may have one of two different types of governmental systems: presidential or parliamentary. Recall that presidential systems have an executive branch that is largely separate from the legislative branch. In this system, presidents generally serve both as head of state—symbolic leader—and as chief executive—head of government—and are usually elected by the people. In a parliamentary system, power is centered in the legislative branch, which chooses the chief executive. As a result, parliamentary governments avoid the conflict between executive and legislative branches that can be a problem in presidential systems. This structure also means, however, that parliamentary governments do not have many of the checks and balances of presidential governments.

Democracy has spread in recent decades. Today nearly half of the more than 190 countries in the world are democratic or partly democratic. Although the level of personal and political freedom in these nations varies widely, they share some basic features:

REAL-WORLD EXAMPLE

CASE STUDY LINK

The Office of President Just because a country has a president does not mean it has a presidential system of government like that of Nigeria or the United States. Israel, for example, has a president who is not the chief executive or head of the government. Rather, Israel's president serves in the largely ceremonial role of head of state. A number of other countries, such as Germany and Ireland, have similar systems.
Applying Information Why might some nations have heads of state with little real power?

- Democratic systems tend to have social welfare policies that seek to improve the quality of their citizens' lives.

- Most democratic governments protect basic human rights such as freedom of expression and freedom from unlawful imprisonment.

- Strong democratic countries can generally withstand national crises such as war, economic trouble, or civil unrest without major changes to their basic systems or structures.

READING CHECK Summarizing What are the basic features of democratic systems?

Mexico and Brazil

As you know, the United States is a democracy with a presidential system of government. Mexico and Brazil are two examples of other nations with presidential systems. The governments of these countries have much in common with our own.

Mexico's Government

After three centuries of control by Spain, in 1810 Mexican revolutionaries rose up against Spanish authority. In 1821 Mexico declared independence. The country's current governmental structure and constitution were established in 1917, after a civil war that began as a series of uprisings against the dictator Porfirio Díaz.

Mexico's federal government, like the government of the United States, has three branches: legislative, executive, and judicial. In a federal system, powers are divided between central and state governments. Mexico's central government is based in Mexico City, and its 31 states make up its state government.

The Three Branches Mexico's legislative branch has two houses. Three-fifths of the legislators are elected, but the remaining seats are distributed to the major political parties in proportion to the parties' overall share of the popular vote. That is, if a political party wins 60 percent of the popular vote in an election, it may select legislators to fill 60 percent of the seats of this type.

The executive branch is headed by a president elected directly by the people, who serves one six-year term. By law, voting is mandatory for people over age 18, although there is no formal penalty for not voting. Mexico does not have the office of vice president.

Mexico has an independent judicial branch. Its highest court is the Supreme Court of Justice. The judges on this court are appointed by the president and must be approved by one of the houses of the legislature.

REAL-WORLD EXAMPLE

The Mexican Revolution
Widespread fighting among various rebel groups in Mexico broke out in 1910 and continued for ten years. In the chaos of the revolution, Mexico had four leaders between 1911 and 1914. The revolution finally came to an end in 1920, several years after the new constitution was established.

Applying Information Why might fighting have continued after the new constitution was passed?

THINK central **Online Link**

thinkcentral.com
KEYWORD: SGO PES

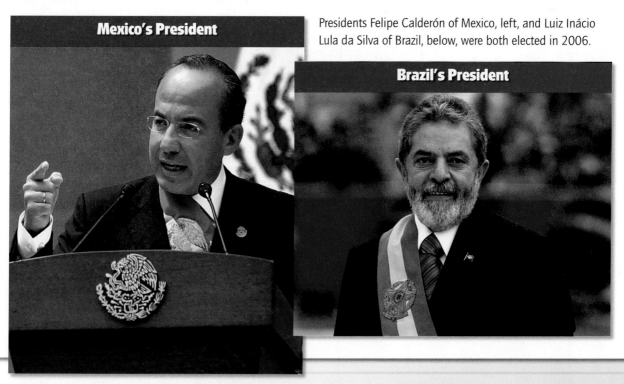

Mexico's President

Brazil's President

Presidents Felipe Calderón of Mexico, left, and Luiz Inácio Lula da Silva of Brazil, below, were both elected in 2006.

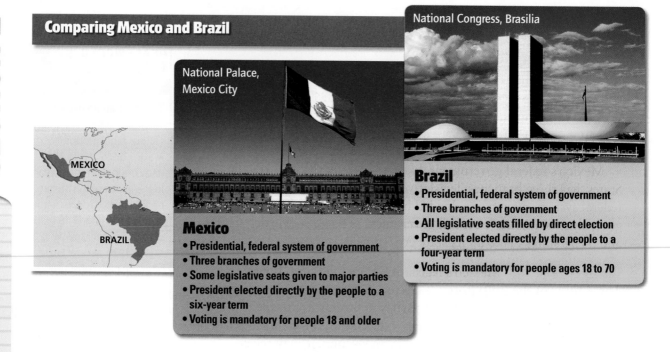

Comparing Mexico and Brazil

National Palace, Mexico City

Mexico
- Presidential, federal system of government
- Three branches of government
- Some legislative seats given to major parties
- President elected directly by the people to a six-year term
- Voting is mandatory for people 18 and older

National Congress, Brasilia

Brazil
- Presidential, federal system of government
- Three branches of government
- All legislative seats filled by direct election
- President elected directly by the people to a four-year term
- Voting is mandatory for people ages 18 to 70

ACADEMIC VOCABULARY

dominant most important, controlling

Politics and Economy The political party known as the Institutional Revolutionary Party, or PRI, was the <u>dominant</u> party in Mexican politics for more than 80 years. The PRI's hold on the presidency finally ended in 2000 with the election of Vicente Fox of the National Action Party, or PAN. In 2006 the PAN candidate, Felipe Calderón, was elected president in an extremely close election. His main rival challenged the election results but was unsuccessful.

In recent years, Mexico's leaders have worked to improve the nation's infrastructure, expand free trade, and reduce poverty. Although today the nation has a relatively stable economy, Mexico still faces the challenges of modernization, global competitiveness, job growth, income inequality, and poverty that face many developing nations. The heavy reliance of the Mexican economy on trade with Canada and the United States is also a concern.

Brazil's Government

Brazil was a Portuguese colony for 300 years before gaining independence in 1822. The nation became a republic in 1889, but wealthy coffee planters held much of the political power until a series of military-led uprisings began in the 1920s. In 1930 Getúlio Vargas took power in a nonviolent revolution; by 1937 Vargas ruled as a dictator. After alternating attempts at democracy and at military rule, in 1985 the military finally turned over power to a civilian government. Three years later, Brazil enacted a revised constitution that is still in effect today.

Brazil has a federal system with 26 states and a federal district. In many ways, Brazil's government is similar to that of Mexico and the United States, with three branches and a separation of powers.

The Three Branches Brazil's legislature is bicameral and includes a senate and a chamber of deputies. All members are elected.

The executive branch is led by the president, who is both head of state and chief executive. The president is elected by a direct vote of the people, which takes place every four years. At the same time, voters elect a vice president. Voting is mandatory for literate Brazilians between the ages of 18 and 70, and those who do not vote may be fined.

The judicial system is comprised of state-level courts, federal appeals courts, and the Supreme Court. The Supreme Court is made up of two courts: the Superior Court of Justice, which is the nation's highest court for nonconstitutional issues, and the Supreme Federal Court, which handles cases involving constitutional interpretation.

Politics and Economy Politics in Brazil features four major political parties and other smaller parties. This diversity means that Brazilian leaders often must work with rival politicians to achieve their goals.

Brazil is a large country with a large workforce and a rich supply of natural resources. This combination of factors offers promise for the future. Yet Brazil also struggles with modernization, environmental issues, economic growth, and income inequality.

READING CHECK **Comparing and Contrasting** How are the governments of Mexico and Brazil similar and different?

ACADEMIC VOCABULARY

comprise to be made up of

The United Kingdom and Japan

Democracy's most common form of government is the parliamentary system, in which the legislature is the most powerful branch. In addition to making laws, the parliamentary legislature chooses the chief executive—a prime minister or a premier—from its own membership. Parliamentary systems often feature multiple parties, and even small parties may have some role in government.

The United Kingdom and Japan are typical examples of nations with parliamentary systems. Their governments have characteristics in common, but they also have key differences.

The United Kingdom's Government

The United Kingdom, which includes Great Britain and Northern Ireland, is the source of many of our basic concepts of modern democratic government. Over the centuries, documents such as the Magna Carta and the English Bill of Rights limited the king's powers and protected the rights of the English people.

Unlike the United States and some other nations, the United Kingdom's government is not based on a single written constitution. The government has developed over centuries into its current form.

REAL-WORLD EXAMPLE

Australia's Government
Like the United Kingdom and Japan, Australia has a parliamentary system headed by a prime minister. Australia was once part of the British Empire and its formal head of state is still the British monarch, although today Australia is independent. Australia's constitutional division of power is similar to that of the United States, with much power given to state governments.
Applying Information Given Australia's history as a British colony, why do you think its division of power is more like that of the United States?

Comparing the United Kingdom and Japan

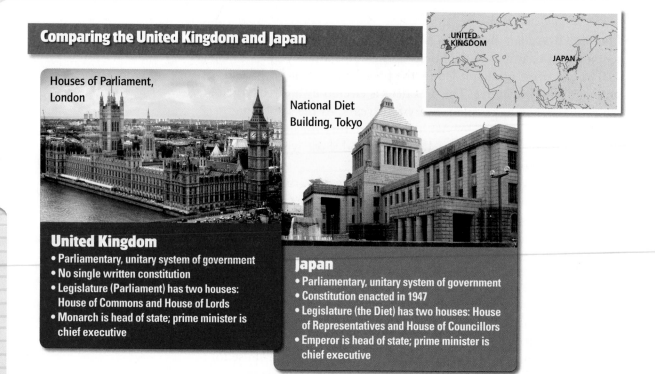

Houses of Parliament, London

National Diet Building, Tokyo

UNITED KINGDOM

JAPAN

United Kingdom

- Parliamentary, unitary system of government
- No single written constitution
- Legislature (Parliament) has two houses: House of Commons and House of Lords
- Monarch is head of state; prime minister is chief executive

Japan

- Parliamentary, unitary system of government
- Constitution enacted in 1947
- Legislature (the Diet) has two houses: House of Representatives and House of Councillors
- Emperor is head of state; prime minister is chief executive

The United Kingdom is a constitutional monarchy with a unitary government. Unlike federal systems, unitary systems are those in which local governments have only the powers given to them by the central government. The head of state is the hereditary monarch, but today the role of monarch is largely ceremonial. Power is held by the legislature, known as Parliament, and by the prime minister.

Parliament and the Prime Minister Parliament consists of two houses: the House of Lords and the House of Commons. Most members of the House of Lords are chosen by political parties or are members of the British nobility who have inherited their seats. The House of Lords has a limited role in lawmaking, although it does serve as the highest court of appeal in the United Kingdom's judicial system. The House of Commons is the main legislative body. Members are elected by the British people for terms that last up to five years. All British citizens age 18 or older may vote.

The seats in Parliament are typically held by a number of political parties. The 2005 elections, for example, saw 12 different parties elected to Parliament. As a result, parties often join together to form a **coalition**, or a temporary alliance for political purposes.

The leader of the party or coalition that holds the majority in Parliament is the prime minister. He or she serves as the nation's chief executive and can be a powerful figure—after all, the prime minister represents the majority party or coalition. At the same time, he or she depends on Parliament's support. The majority party or coalition can force a prime minister from office by choosing another leader. If a coalition breaks apart—from internal conflict, for example—the prime minister may be forced out as well.

REAL-WORLD EXAMPLE

Key British Leaders Since parliamentary systems such as the United Kingdom's ensure that the legislative and executive branches are controlled by the same party, a forceful leader can accomplish much. William Gladstone in the late 1800s and Margaret Thatcher in the late 1900s are examples of prime ministers who drove the policy-making efforts of their governments.

Applying Information Why can a leader have great power in a parliamentary system?

Japan's Government

Japan's government underwent enormous change following the nation's defeat in World War II. Under the guidance of the United States, which occupied Japan in the postwar years, the former empire enacted a new democratic constitution in 1947. This constitution still shapes Japan's government today.

Like the United Kingdom, Japan has a unitary system of government and a bicameral legislature. Japan's legislature is called the Diet. The Diet consists of the House of Representatives and the House of Councillors. Japanese voters—any person age 20 or older—elect candidates to most seats in the Diet, but some seats are distributed based on the share of the popular vote each party receives. This means even small parties can have seats in the Diet.

The head of the Japanese government is the prime minister. He or she is chosen from the majority party or coalition in the House of Representatives. As in the United Kingdom, the prime minister depends on the support of the legislature to remain in power.

The head of state in Japan is the emperor. As with the United Kingdom's monarch, the emperor's position is largely ceremonial.

READING CHECK **Comparing** In what ways is Japan's government similar to that of the United Kingdom?

Emerging Democracies

Democratic governments are more widespread today than at any other point in human history. In recent years, human rights and prodemocracy movements have led to change in many nations as people have sought to overthrow authoritarian regimes and establish democratic governments.

Yet democracy places many demands on people. As you have read, the United States has faced challenges to live up to its own democratic ideals in the years since the nation was founded. The world's emerging democracies face similar challenges and struggles as they shape their democratic futures.

Latin America

Latin America was once dominated by European powers. In the early 1800s, revolutionary leaders such as Simon Bolívar started independence movements, inspired by the American Revolution and by the democratic values and principles expressed in the Declaration of Independence and the French Declaration of the Rights of Man and of the Citizen. Their dreams of democracy went largely unfulfilled. When European nations were forced to leave the region, many Latin American countries came under the control of wealthy landowners—including some Americans—or authoritarian leaders.

Democracy and Iraq One of the goals of the 2003 U.S.-led invasion of Iraq was to replace Iraq's authoritarian government with a democracy. Violence in Iraq has complicated this plan. How can plans to promote democracy develop problems? Visit **thinkcentral.com** to begin a Webquest on the challenge of democracy in Iraq.

thinkcentral.com
KEYWORD: SGO PES

The Growth of Democracy

Democracy has spread throughout the world in recent decades. Today many nations once ruled by authoritarian regimes are working to build stable constitutional democracies.

1 Chilean voters elected Michelle Bachelet as the nation's first female president in January 2006.

THINK central Interactive

thinkcentral.com
KEYWORD: SGO PES

In recent years, many countries in the region, such as Argentina, Chile, and Bolivia, have moved toward establishing constitutional democracies. In Guatemala, a lengthy civil war led to the establishment of democracy in 1996. In other places, such as Colombia, the struggle for democracy is ongoing. These nations are in different stages of democratic development, but they all must overcome their history of authoritarianism and protect their fragile democracies.

Africa

The story of Nigeria, which you read in the Case Study, is common in Africa. The continent spent decades under European control, and a number of African nations won their independence only after World War II. By the end of the 1960s, most of these newly independent nations had adopted authoritarian governments. Many of these countries have since struggled to establish democracies.

South Africa is among Africa's democratic success stories. Before the 1990s, South Africa's white minority dominated the country in a system of racial segregation and oppression known as **apartheid**. The end of apartheid and the establishment of democracy led to the historic 1994 election of Nelson Mandela as South Africa's first black president. South Africa still faces challenges, including economic growth, global competitiveness, and high rates of HIV and AIDS infections, but the transition to democracy is promising.

Asia

Several countries in Asia have also made the difficult transition from colony to independent democracy. As in Africa and Latin America, Asian countries such as Indonesia and the Philippines have experienced periods of authoritarian rule.

The Southeast Asian country of Cambodia also fits this pattern. Along with its neighbor Vietnam, Cambodia won independence

2 Under Cambodia's constitutional monarchy, King Norodom Sihamoni holds only symbolic power.

3 Evo Morales was elected president of Bolivia in 2005, becoming Bolivia's first indigenous president.

from French colonial rule in the 1950s. A Communist group known as the Khmer Rouge took control of the country in 1975, having gained power during the turmoil caused by the Vietnam War. Led by Pol Pot, the Khmer Rouge murdered more than 1 million Cambodians in an attempt to destroy the influences of modern life.

Vietnam forced Pol Pot from power in Cambodia in 1979, but he led a guerrilla campaign in a civil war that raged throughout the 1980s. Eventually, with international support, Cambodia established a constitution in 1993. Today Cambodia is a constitutional monarchy with a democratically elected parliament.

READING CHECK **Summarizing** Give examples of emerging democracies in Latin America, Africa, and Asia.

Section 1 Assessment

Reviewing Ideas and Terms

1. **a. Describe** What are the two customary roles of the president in a presidential system?
   b. Make Generalizations What basic features do democratic nations share?

2. **a. Recall** What system of government do Mexico and Brazil have?
   b. Compare and Contrast What challenges do Mexico and Brazil face?

3. **a. Recall** What system of government do the United Kingdom and Japan have?
   b. Compare and Contrast How do small political parties play a role in the United Kingdom and Japan?

4. **a. Describe** What has happened following the end of colonial rule in many parts of the world?
   b. Elaborate Why do you think democracy is difficult for newly independent nations to establish?

Critical Thinking

5. **Contrast** Which system of government, presidential or parliamentary, is more likely to permit a small political movement to be involved in government? Explain your answer.

CASE STUDY LINK You answered the following questions at the end of the Case Study. Now that you have completed Section 1, think about and answer the questions again. Then compare your answers with your earlier responses. Are your answers the same or are they different?

6. How did democracy cause change within Nigeria?

7. What signs give reason for hope for Nigeria's political future?

8. What system of government does Nigeria have today?

Student Casebook

Use your Student Casebook to complete the simulation.

SIMULATION

SIMULATION

Choosing a System of Government

What system of government is best for an emerging democracy?

A nation emerging from a period of authoritarian rule or control by another country must decide which form of democratic government to establish. Using what you learned in Section 1, complete the simulation to make a decision about whether to establish a presidential system or a parliamentary system in a fictional nation.

Roles

- Interim president, who will serve as the convention's moderator
- Delegates to the constitutional convention

❶ The Situation

In the nation of Centralia, a group of delegates has gathered at a constitutional convention. The delegates' purpose is to form a strong and stable democratic government for their country, which has suffered from years of civil war.

Background

- For years, Centralia was ruled by a series of dictators.
- Civil war broke out two decades ago. During the war, there were multiple factions involved in the fighting.
- During the civil war, Centralia did not have an effective central government. Instead, areas of the country were controlled by competing warlords.
- The civil war ended several months ago. Since then, Centralia has been governed by an interim president.
- The interim president called the constitutional convention and will serve as moderator.
- The delegates to the convention have been elected from all different parts of Centralia.
- Centralia has few established political parties.
- There are many different ethnic groups in Centralia.

❷ The Convention

All delegates agree that a democratic system is necessary, but some delegates favor a presidential system and others support a parliamentary system. They will debate the issue at the convention.

- Delegates who favor a presidential system believe that Centralia needs a strong central government to unite the nation and fight the warlords.

- Delegates who favor a parliamentary system worry that establishing a strong president will lead to a return of authoritarian rule.

- The interim president supports the idea of the presidency—and hopes to become president. The interim president will moderate the discussion at the convention.

- All delegates have an opportunity to raise points and to debate ideas presented.

PRESIDENTIAL AND PARLIAMENTARY SYSTEMS: STRENGTHS AND WEAKNESSES

SYSTEM	STRENGTHS	WEAKNESSES
Presidential	• Strong leader • Separation of powers with checks and balances	• One party controls executive branch • Possible conflict between executive and legislative branches
Parliamentary	• Multiple parties have power • United executive and legislative branches	• Encourages political factions • Few checks on executive or legislative powers

❸ The Decision

After debate and discussion, the delegates must vote on whether to support a presidential or a parliamentary plan. They must consider questions such as the following:

- What are the biggest threats to the success of democracy in Centralia?

- What are the strengths and weaknesses of a presidential system?

- What are the strengths and weaknesses of a parliamentary system?

- How do conditions in Centralia right now affect the suitability of one or another type of government?

❹ Debriefing

After the delegates vote, consider Nigeria's choice of a parliamentary system of government after gaining independence. Do you think Nigeria made the right decision?

Authoritarian Governments

Reading Focus
Democracy has spread throughout the world in recent decades, but some countries are still under the rule of authoritarian governments. Citizens in these countries have little control over their own government and, in some cases, over their very lives.

CASE STUDY **Totalitarian Rule in North Korea** Learn about life under North Korea's authoritarian government.

WHAT YOU NEED TO KNOW Learn about essential features of authoritarian systems, including past governments in the Soviet Union, Chile, Italy, and Germany, and contemporary governments in China and Saudi Arabia.

SIMULATION **Overthrowing a Dictator** Use your knowledge to determine how best to remove a dictator from power.

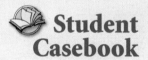
Student Casebook

Use your Student Casebook to take notes on the section and to complete the simulation.

At top, a massive statue of Kim Il Sung, North Korea's first leader, towers above children in Pyongyang, the capital. The government often holds large political rallies, as in the photo at right, in which soldiers stand in front of a display formed by thousands of children holding up colored cards.

Totalitarian Rule in North Korea

North Koreans live under the authoritarian rule of Kim Jong Il, their so-called "Dear Leader." Kim dominates all aspects of life in his nation of 23 million people.

A Totalitarian Dictatorship

North Korea's official name is the Democratic People's Republic of Korea. Its constitution establishes democratic processes, and all North Koreans age 17 and up are eligible to vote. In reality, though, North Korea is about as far from a democracy as one can imagine.

North Korea was formed in the aftermath of World War II when the United States and the Soviet Union split Korea into two regions. North Korea, which was occupied by the Soviet Union, established a government based in part on the Soviet Communist system. Kim Il Sung was the nation's first president.

Kim Il Sung was a totalitarian dictator who sought control over all aspects of North Korean life. Kim controlled government, education, and the media. He told North Koreans what to do and what to think, and he built a cult of personality that encouraged adoration of his carefully constructed public image.

After Kim Il Sung's death in 1994, North Korea's calendar was changed to begin with the year of Kim's birth. An official period of mourning lasted for three years, during which time North Koreans could be punished for not expressing adequate grief over Kim's death. Today his preserved body lies in state for public viewing.

Kim's son Kim Jong Il took power after his father's death. Like his father, Kim Jong Il rules as a totalitarian dictator with his own cult of personality. His rule is fully supported by the North Korean military.

An Isolated Nation

North Korea has long been closed off from much of the rest of the world. Its secretive government allows little contact with people from other nations, and much of what the outside world knows about North Korea comes from citizens who have escaped the country.

North Korea is infamous for its abuses of civil and human rights. Although the constitution protects citizens' right to vote, North Korean elections list only one candidate for each open position: the candidate chosen by North Korea's ruling political party, the Korean Workers' Party. Anyone who criticizes the government is subject to imprisonment and torture. Some 200,000 political prisoners are reportedly held in North Korean jails.

Many North Koreans live in extreme poverty. Although the government spends heavily on the military, a combination of failed economic policies and natural disasters has led to between 2 and 3 million deaths from starvation since the mid-1990s. The collapse of the Soviet Union, a major supporter of North Korea, also harmed the nation. Today North Korea's largest trading partners are China and South Korea.

In spite of its serious economic problems, North Korea rarely accepts much foreign aid. In addition, its efforts to develop nuclear weapons have harmed its diplomatic relations with other nations, most notably after its leaders announced a successful test of a nuclear weapon in 2006. In the fall of 2007, however, North Korea agreed to end its nuclear program by the end of the year in return for fuel and economic aid.

What Do You Think?

1. How does the North Korean constitution's promise of democratic processes match with reality?
2. What role does the cult of personality surrounding North Korea's leader play in the country's system of government?
3. Why is North Korea isolated from other nations?

WHAT YOU NEED TO KNOW

Authoritarian Systems

An authoritarian system of government such as North Korea's is one in which all power rests with a single leader or a small group. Citizens are expected to follow all government decisions and policies. They have no way to influence or change the government.

Authoritarian governments sometimes maintain the appearance of democratic rule. For example, they may hold elections and have a written constitution. But these displays of democracy are nothing more than exhibitions to deceive the nation's people or outside observers. As you read in the Case Study, elections in North Korea do not offer voters any choices. In Nazi Germany under Adolf Hitler (1933–1945) and in the Soviet Union under Joseph Stalin (1928–1953), constitutions did not prevent leaders' abuse of power.

Types of Authoritarian Systems

Authoritarian systems come in many forms. One form of authoritarian government is a **theocracy**, which is a government that is ruled by religious leaders. That is, the nation's leaders believe that government authority rests with God or some divine power rather than with the people. Iran is an example of a modern-day country that has some theocratic features. While Iran does have an elected president, the country's supreme leader is Ayatollah Ali Khamenei, a Muslim cleric who serves for life.

The most common form of authoritarian government is a dictatorship. Dictators often take power by overthrowing a previous government. For example, Idi Amin, the former dictator of Uganda, led a military takeover of the government in 1971. Cuba's Fidel Castro used force to gain power in 1959. Other dictators may first gain power through legitimate elections, as Adolf Hitler did.

Some authoritarian governments develop into totalitarian systems. **Totalitarianism** is authoritarian rule that controls nearly

---

Authoritarian Rulers

Authoritarian rulers have great power over their people. Rarely limited by laws or constitutions, they often control nearly every aspect of life in a country.

1 Communist Fidel Castro seized power in Cuba in 1959.

every aspect of public and private life in a country. In a nation with a totalitarian government, such as the Soviet Union under Stalin or North Korea under Kim Jong Il and his predecessors (1948–present), there are no areas in which ordinary citizens can exercise freedom of choice. The government controls everything—all economic planning, all organizations, all media, all industry, and so on. Often, totalitarian governments enforce a cult of personality surrounding the nation's ruler. For example, portraits and statues of the leader decorate public areas, or streets and towns are named after the leader.

Features of Authoritarian Systems

Although the forms of authoritarian systems vary, they all share certain features. In authoritarian systems, ordinary citizens' civil rights and human rights are rarely recognized or protected, and citizens cannot effectively take part in government or express their views openly. Authoritarian rulers often use force to put down opposition, such as human rights or prodemocracy movements demanding change.

Authoritarian governments are not limited by law. In the United States, the Constitution governs what government can and cannot do. Authoritarian rulers, however, may simply change or ignore constitutions or laws that restrict their power. Before Saddam Hussein of Iraq was overthrown in a 2003 U.S.-led invasion, for example, he used torture and violence against his political opponents, even though torture was officially banned under Iraqi law.

Authoritarian systems have obvious disadvantages for ordinary citizens. At the same time, authoritarian power can help a government face an emergency or make rapid changes to a society.

READING CHECK Summarizing What are the types and features of authoritarian governments?

Characteristics of Authoritarian Systems

- Citizens have few or no protections for civil rights or human rights.

- Citizens cannot effectively take part in government.

- Citizens cannot express their views freely.

- Rulers often use force to put down opposition.

- Rulers are not limited by law.

2 Army officer Idi Amin ruled Uganda from 1971 to 1979.

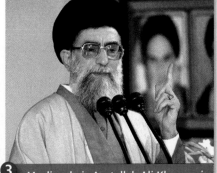
3 Muslim cleric Ayatollah Ali Khamenei is the supreme leader of Iran.

4 Saddam Hussein ruled Iraq from 1979 to 2003.

The Soviet Union and China

In the second half of the 1900s, two authoritarian nations rose to world prominence. The histories of the Soviet Union and China give insight on the nature of authoritarian governments.

The Soviet Union

In 1917 the people of Russia overthrew their ruler, Czar Nicholas II. Five years later, revolutionaries led by Vladimir Lenin formed a new country called the Soviet Union. Lenin and his followers believed in **communism**—an economic and political system in which government owns all property and controls economic planning.

The structure of the Soviet government reflected Communist ideas. The Soviet constitution did not limit government power or protect basic rights such as free speech, and it allowed only one political party: the Communist Party of the Soviet Union (CPSU). The CPSU was headed by the Central Committee, which in turn elected the smaller Politburo, the chief decision-making body. The Politburo was headed by the general secretary, the Soviet leader.

Joseph Stalin became the new Soviet leader in 1928, several years after Lenin's death, and called for the government to make all economic decisions. Intent on controlling every aspect of daily life and crushing all opposition, Stalin worked to turn the Soviet Union into a totalitarian state. Millions of Soviet citizens were killed or imprisoned if they were thought to be disloyal to Stalin. At the same time, heroic portraits of Stalin decorated public places throughout the Soviet Union, creating an idealized image of the dictator.

Stalin died in 1953. Later Soviet leaders eased some restrictions but continued to limit freedoms in the Soviet Union and other nations under their control. Yet Soviet power ultimately weakened. As discussed in Chapter 14, political and economic reforms in the 1980s led to the collapse of the Soviet government in 1991.

China

The People's Republic of China was established in 1949. Like the leaders of the Soviet Union, Chinese leader Mao Zedong created an authoritarian Communist system, imprisoning or killing those who spoke out against his policies. He quickly put in place Soviet-style five-year plans for industrial development. Early efforts had some success, but widespread food shortages led to the deaths of tens of millions of Chinese by 1961. Later, in 1966, Mao began the Cultural Revolution, a violent effort to rid China of its pre-Communist customs, beliefs, and culture.

China after Mao As in the Soviet Union after Stalin's death, Mao's death in 1976 saw a gradual retreat from many of his policies. Deng Xiaoping eventually became China's leader and slowly introduced

Democracy in the Former Soviet Union The breakup of the Soviet Union seemed to represent a victory for democracy. Some former Soviet republics have flourishing democracies, but others have had difficulty putting their authoritarian past behind them. How has democracy fared in Russia and the other former Soviet republics? Visit **thinkcentral.com** to begin a Webquest on democracy in the countries of the former Soviet Union.

thinkcentral.com
KEYWORD: SGO PES

Propaganda and Reality in China and the Soviet Union

In China and the Soviet Union, propaganda differed sharply from the reality of life under an authoritarian government.

China

A 1971 propaganda poster contrasts with prodemocracy demonstrators confronting Chinese troops in Tiananmen Square, Beijing, in 1989.

Soviet Union

In a 1932 poster, Joseph Stalin gazes over Soviet farmland. In a photo taken the same year, Soviet political prisoners build a canal in northern Russia.

many economic and a few political reforms. There were limits to what Chinese officials would allow, however. In 1989 the Chinese government violently crushed a peaceful prodemocracy student demonstration in China's capital, Beijing, in what became known as the Tiananmen Square Massacre.

China's leaders today are balancing authoritarian rule, economic growth, and slow political reform. China continues to limit its citizens' basic freedoms and rights, including free speech and religious freedoms, and the government exercises strict control over the media and the Internet. Political protesters can be jailed.

China's Government Today As in the Soviet Union, China's Communist Party (CCP) effectively rules the country, with high-ranking CCP members holding all powerful government and military positions. The CCP meets every five years to hold a national congress and elect a Central Committee of about 350 people. In turn, the Central Committee elects the Politburo, a small committee that holds decision-making power. The Politburo is led by the general secretary, who, in recent decades, has also served as China's president. Currently, Hu Jintao holds both positions.

REAL-WORLD EXAMPLE

The Problem of Taiwan After the Communists took over China, the defeated Chinese government fled to the nearby island of Taiwan. Today the United States has close ties to Taiwan, which is now democratic, but Taiwan's desire for full independence from China has complicated this relationship.

Applying Information Why might Taiwan's desire for independence from China harm its relationship with the United States?

The Chinese government consists of two main bodies, the State Council and the National People's Congress. The State Council is China's chief executive body and is headed by the premier, who is chosen by the president. The National People's Congress consists of representatives elected for five-year terms by local people's congresses throughout China. While the Congress has the constitutional power to make laws and elect the president, in practice it simply carries out State Council and CCP decisions.

READING CHECK **Comparing and Contrasting** How is China's government similar to and different from the Soviet Union's government?

Other Authoritarian Nations

Recent history includes many authoritarian governments. Some, including Chile's government during most of the 1970s and 1980s and governments in Italy and Germany during World War II, are no longer in power. Others, like Saudi Arabia's government, still exist.

Chile Today Chile is a democratic nation, but its history includes several periods of authoritarian rule. The most recent authoritarian period began in 1973, when the Chilean military, with U.S. support, overthrew the country's Socialist leader, Salvador Allende, and General Augusto Pinochet came to power. Pinochet's government committed widespread human rights abuses. Thousands of Chileans who opposed Pinochet were killed or tortured.

Eventually, however, Pinochet loosened his iron grip on Chile. In 1988 he allowed voters to determine whether he would continue in power. They rejected his rule in favor of open elections. Since that time, Chile's president has been elected by the people.

Fascist Italy and Nazi Germany The early 1920s saw the rise of the Italian dictator Benito Mussolini, who promoted a philosophy he called fascism. Fascism placed the glorification of the state above all

Pinochet's Chile

At right, a woman stands with images of people allegedly tortured or killed by the Chilean government under General Augusto Pinochet, shown below.

else, including individual needs. Mussolini sought to develop a self-sufficient economy and used threats, violence, and propaganda to establish a totalitarian dictatorship. His desire to build a powerful empire caused Italy's entrance into World War II, but Italy's battlefield defeats led to Mussolini's overthrow in 1943.

Italy had entered World War II on the side of another fascist regime: Adolf Hitler's Nazi Germany. Hitler's version of fascism included racism and anti-Semitism, or hostility toward or prejudice against Jews. During World War II, the Nazis murdered 6 million Jewish men, women, and children. Millions of other people were killed by Hitler's armies before Germany was defeated in 1945.

Saudi Arabia Saudi Arabia is an example of a modern authoritarian nation. The nation holds no regular elections and has no political parties. The Saudi government is headed by a monarch who is chosen by the ruling family from among its members. The monarch has near-absolute power, including the right to ratify legislation, to select high-ranking government officials and judges, and to act as the nation's highest court of appeals. The Saudi monarch, however, is bound to follow the Qur'an, the sacred text of Islam, and the laws of that faith.

The government keeps strong control over the Saudi economy—which is largely reliant on the oil industry—and spends heavily on social programs and the military. Human rights groups express concern about human rights abuses in Saudi Arabia, but Saudi Arabia is one of the strongest U.S. allies in the Middle East, in part because of U.S. dependence on Saudi oil production.

READING CHECK **Making Inferences** Why do you think that many authoritarian governments are no longer in power?

REAL - WORLD EXAMPLE

CASE STUDY LINK

Germany's Changing Government When Adolf Hitler took power in 1933, the German legislature passed laws that essentially abolished the constitution and turned the nation into an authoritarian state. After World War II, Germany was partitioned into two countries, Communist East Germany and democratic West Germany, much as Korea was divided in two after the Korean War. Germany was reunited in 1990 and today has a democratic parliamentary government based on the 1949 West German constitution. **Analyzing Information** How has Germany's government changed since 1933?

Section 2 Assessment

THINK central **Online Quiz**

thinkcentral.com
KEYWORD: SGO PES HP

Reviewing Ideas and Terms

1. **a. Describe** What are the features of an authoritarian system of government?
   b. Explain How can a government have democratic features such as elections yet still be authoritarian?

2. **a. Define** Write a sentence explaining the meaning of the term **communism**.
   b. Compare and Contrast Compare and contrast the efforts of Joseph Stalin and Mao Zedong to gain and keep political power.
   c. Predict China's government limits citizens' rights and strictly controls the media. How might human rights movements or the free flow of information lead to political change within China?

3. **a. Describe** How did Pinochet rule Chile?
   b. Summarize In what ways is Saudi Arabia's government authoritarian?

Critical Thinking

4. **Draw Conclusions** Why do you think that the United States openly supports and works with some authoritarian governments? Should it do so?

CASE STUDY LINK You answered the following questions at the end of the Case Study. Now that you have completed Section 2, think about and answer the questions again. Then compare your answers with your earlier responses. Are your answers the same or are they different?

5. How does the North Korean constitution's promise of democratic processes match with reality?

6. What role does the cult of personality surrounding North Korea's leader play in the country's system of government?

7. Why is North Korea isolated from other nations?

SIMULATION

Overthrowing a Dictator

Student Casebook

Use your Student Casebook to complete the simulation.

What is the best way to get rid of a tyrant?

Even in an authoritarian system, the people sometimes can have great political power. Using what you have learned in Section 2, complete the simulation to determine the best way to remove a dictator from power.

Roles

- Prodemocracy activists who oppose Mendoza's dictator

- Officers in the Mendoza army who oppose the ruler and who control roughly half of the country's armed forces

- Leaders of Mendoza's major religious organizations who have protested the dictator's human rights abuses

- Historian with knowledge of recent uprisings against dictators

❶ The Situation

Citizens of Mendoza, a fictional island nation, are meeting secretly to decide how to force Mendoza's authoritarian dictator from power.

Background

- Mendoza is a poor country. Many people live in the capital city, but the rest are scattered among dozens of islands.

- The country has a long history of democracy and is an ally of the United States.

- For years, a small Communist rebel group has sought to overthrow the government.

- The current ruler, Edward Gray, was first elected 10 years ago to a four-year term as president. The election was fair and democratic.

- Midway through his term, Gray used the excuse of Communist rebel attacks to declare a national emergency and to give himself dictatorial powers.

- Gray's authoritarian rule has included mass arrests of his political opponents and the torture and assassination of opposition leaders.

- The U.S. government has strongly condemned Gray's actions.

❷ The Crisis

International pressure finally forced dictator Edward Gray to agree to hold new nationwide elections for the office of president. Neutral election observers believed that Gray's opponent easily won the election, but Gray nevertheless claimed victory and declared that he would remain in power.

- After Gray's announcement that he had won the election, large public protests immediately broke out in Mendoza's capital city.

- Some members of the military took part in the protests.

- Military forces loyal to Gray violently crushed the protest.

❸ The Decision

Opposition leaders—including prodemocracy activists, army officers, and religious leaders—are meeting secretly to discuss overthrowing Gray. A majority vote will determine their actions. A historian at the meeting can give advice based on how past uprisings in other countries have succeeded or failed. The leaders must consider questions such as:

● Should they lead an armed uprising against Gray?

● Should they work for international economic and political pressure against Gray, hoping to force him to step down or hold a fair election?

● Should they appeal for assistance from the United Nations?

● Should they seek to convince the military to overthrow Gray?

● Would the military and the public support or resist an uprising?

RECENT EXAMPLES OF UPRISINGS AGAINST DICTATORS

COUNTRY (DATE)	METHOD	OUTCOME
The Philippines (1986)	A peaceful civilian and military uprising forced dictator Ferdinand Marcos, a U.S. ally, from power.	• A working democracy was established, although corruption remains a problem. • Antigovernment rebels remain a problem.
Romania (1989)	A popular uprising ended Nicolae Ceausescu's Communist dictatorship, leaving 1,500 civilians dead.	• Political parties previously banned under communism were reorganized, and elections were held. • A working democracy was established.
Haiti (1994)	A U.S.-led military force replaced the military dictatorship with elected leader Jean-Bertrand Aristide.	• A period of instability and unrest followed Aristide's return to Haiti. • Haiti still struggles to establish a democracy.
Liberia (2003)	Civil war led to the resignation of dictator Charles Taylor under strong pressure from the United States.	• The country held successful democratic elections in 2005.
Myanmar (2007)	Buddhist monks and prodemocracy activists took part in widespread protests against the military dictatorship.	• The military cracked down on the protestors, killing an unknown number of people and ending the demonstrations.

❹ Debriefing

After the people at the secret meeting agree upon their course of action, write a detailed explanation of the group's reasoning. What was the thinking behind the decision?

Economic Systems

Reading Focus

Economic systems can be characterized by three basic types: traditional, market, and command. Nearly all nations today have mixed economies, meaning they have some combination of traditional, market, and command features.

CASE STUDY **A Changing India** Learn about the impact of recent economic changes in India.

WHAT YOU NEED TO KNOW Learn about the world's different economic systems.

SIMULATION **Negotiating a Trade Agreement** Use your knowledge to negotiate a trade agreement between two fictional countries.

Student Casebook

Use your Student Casebook to take notes on the section and to complete the simulation.

India's rapid economic growth in recent years has led to the rise of a middle class and to a booming construction industry.

A Changing India

India has the second-largest population in the world. It has long been troubled with high poverty rates, but in recent decades sectors of the Indian economy have undergone dramatic change and rapid growth.

Independence and Beyond

India was under the colonial domination of the British for well over 100 years. The British used India's large population as a market for their own manufactured goods, deliberately preventing Indian industry from developing and competing with British businesses. After years of struggle, India finally won its independence in 1947.

After independence, the Indian people faced a difficult economic situation. The country was very poor. Most Indians relied on agriculture, forestry, or fishing to earn a living, and industry made up just 10 percent of the economy.

In order to encourage economic growth, India's leaders favored socialist policies. Socialism is a system in which government owns or controls key parts of the economy. In theory, socialism allows government to directly control the economy and to spread wealth more equally among the people.

India's government made all major economic decisions and soon took control of key industries, including railroads, steel, aircraft manufacturing, and more. In other industries, the government set strict rules and regulations.

India and the Free Market

At first, the government's policies did help the country's economy to grow. But when economic growth rates slowed in the 1960s and 1970s, many Indians blamed India's complicated system of government ownership and regulation.

Beginning in the 1970s, India began to take a new approach to its economy, moving away from socialism and toward an economy based more on free markets. Little by little, government reduced its direct control over industries and the economy, giving individuals and businesses the freedom to make more of their own economic decisions. This strategy worked. Certain sectors of India's economy grew quickly in the 1980s.

These economic changes accelerated in the 1990s. Among the many reforms made by the Indian government was the lowering of barriers to trade with other countries, including tariffs, or taxes on imported goods. The growth of free trade has meant more competition with foreign companies, and Indian businesses have been forced to become more efficient in the production of goods and services in order to compete with foreign countries. India also began to encourage more foreign investment. Foreign investors soon started building businesses in India, providing jobs and helping the Indian economy grow.

The result of these new policies has been dramatic. By 2000 the Indian economy was booming and the nation had a quickly growing middle class—people with enough money to buy consumer goods such as televisions and cell phones.

India's move toward free-market policies has brought many benefits to certain segments of its population, but India still has many challenges to face. Nearly 30 percent of the population lives in poverty. India's infrastructure—its transportation and communications systems, water and power lines, and other basic facilities and services—can barely meet the nation's needs. Still, the country's economic future looks solid.

What Do You Think?

1. How did British colonialism affect Indian industry?
2. Why did India choose socialist policies after independence?
3. How has the Indian economy responded to the move toward free-market policies?

Making Economic Decisions

Key Terms

factors of production
traditional economy
market economy
command economy
mixed economy
capitalism
laissez-faire
socialism
proletariat
bourgeoisie

ACADEMIC VOCABULARY

factor an element that contributes to a result or outcome

Economics is the study of how people produce, distribute, and consume goods and services. Different economic systems create and distribute goods and services in different ways, but every economy requires certain basic resources. The basic resources that make up an economy are called the **factors of production**. The three main factors of production are land and natural resources, labor, and capital, although some economists also recognize the entrepreneur as a factor of production. An entrepreneur is someone who decides how to use the factors of production in effective ways.

How do the factors of production work? Consider this example: a farmer uses tools to grow crops on a farm. In this example, the farmer represents labor, the tools represent capital, and the farm represents land. The farmer has combined the three main factors of production to create goods and services, or, in this case, crops.

When deciding how to use resources to provide goods and services, all societies must address three basic economic questions:

- What should be produced?

- How should it be produced?

- For whom should it be produced?

A society or country answers these questions through its economic system. In a **traditional economy**, people answer the basic questions by custom. People choose what to produce, how to produce it, and who to produce it for based on what people in their community have always done. This economic system is rare today.

Another type of economic system is the market economy. In a **market economy**, individuals and businesses make most economic decisions. They base their choices on their own understanding of the needs and wants of others. In a **command economy**, on the other hand, the government makes most economic decisions.

REAL-WORLD EXAMPLE

CASE STUDY LINK

The World's Largest Economies The United States is by far the world's largest economy, with a gross domestic product (GDP) estimated at over $13 trillion in 2006. India has the fourth-largest economy, with an estimated 2006 GDP of just over $4 trillion.

Applying Information In terms of GDP, what are the world's 10 largest national economies?

THINK central **Online Link**

thinkcentral.com
KEYWORD: SGO PES

FACTORS OF PRODUCTION

QUICK FACTS

ENTREPRENEUR + LAND, LABOR, CAPITAL = GOODS AND SERVICES

Each of these economic systems takes a distinct approach to such goals as freedom, efficiency, fairness, stability, and sustainability. Today most countries combine elements of traditional, market, and command economic systems into what is called a **mixed economy**.

READING CHECK **Identifying the Main Idea** How do different economic systems influence nations' economic decisions?

Mixed Economies

There are three main types of mixed economies: capitalism, socialism, and communism. Capitalism is closest to the market economy model while communism is closest to the command economy model. Socialism falls between the market and command models.

Capitalism

Capitalism is familiar to Americans because it is the system on which the U.S. economy is largely based. In **capitalism**, people and businesses make most economic decisions.

Capitalism in Theory In a capitalist economy, individuals and businesses own the factors of production. They act in their own interest, and no central government authority tells them what to do.

Philosopher Adam Smith is the founder of capitalist theory. In *The Wealth of Nations* (1776), Smith popularized a concept known as **laissez-faire**, which is French for "to let alone." At that time, many European governments followed the economic theory of mercantilism, which held that a nation's power depended on its wealth. As a result, leaders exercised great control over national economies. Smith's laissez-faire theory, however, called for minimal government involvement in economic affairs.

Capitalism stresses the freedom of the individual, but it also promotes efficiency through the effects of competition. The economic pressures of a capitalist system, in theory, are constantly pushing people to make better products at lower prices. Not everyone can win in this competitive environment, but capitalists believe the overall effect is good for most people.

Capitalism in Practice Even Adam Smith acknowledged that government has a role to play in an economy. Indeed, in capitalist countries today, government is highly involved in the economy. In the United States, for example, the government acts to encourage job creation, stable prices, and economic growth and justice.

TYPES OF ECONOMIC SYSTEMS

ECONOMIC SYSTEM	FEATURES
Traditional	Individuals make economic decisions based on custom or habit.
Market	Individuals and businesses make most economic decisions based on their understanding of others' needs and wants.
Command	Government makes most economic decisions.
Mixed	System combines traditional, market, and command economies.

REAL-WORLD EXAMPLE

Mercantilism Mercantilists believed that a nation had to take wealth away from other nations in order to increase its power. As a result, many European countries established colonies, which Europeans used for raw materials and as markets for manufactured goods. European powers were unconcerned with colonists' welfare or human rights— only wealth mattered.
Applying Information How did mercantilism influence economic and human rights practices?

Capitalism

In a capitalist system, individuals and businesses make most economic decisions. Governments may take certain actions to regulate or otherwise control the economy, but capitalists generally believe that individual freedom, competition, and free trade will best lead to efficiency and economic growth. *What is the government's role in a capitalist system?*

Adam Smith is the founder of capitalist theory.

Economic officials meet at an international trade conference.

RESPONSIBILITIES OF LEADERSHIP

The expansion of global trade has created a significant new challenge for the United States: how to properly balance free trade's benefits for Americans, such as low-cost imported goods, and free trade's negative effects, such as the loss of jobs.

Recent Developments In recent years, the United States and many other countries have moved to reduce government involvement in international trade and encourage global competition. Free trade agreements such as the North American Free Trade Agreement (NAFTA), signed by the United States, Mexico, and Canada in 1994, reduce government-imposed barriers to international trade. The World Trade Organization (WTO) helps countries work toward free trade. Most of the world's nations belong to the WTO, but some opponents of free trade argue that it benefits wealthy developed nations at the expense of less developed nations.

Socialism

Some countries have command economies in which the government exercises a great deal of control. In recent years, many of the world's command economies have been socialist. **Socialism** is an economic and political system in which the state controls most productive resources—factories, land, and so on. One of the key goals of socialism is to distribute a nation's wealth throughout society for the benefit of the majority of its citizens.

Marx and Socialism The founder of modern socialism was German political and economic theorist Karl Marx. During the mid-1800s, Marx and fellow German Friedrich Engels wrote important works that criticized capitalism. Under capitalism, Marx argued, the **proletariat**, or working class, was treated unfairly by the **bourgeoisie**, or the people who own the means of production in a capitalist system. Capitalism, he believed, placed too strong an emphasis on profit. Marx advocated the overthrow of the capitalist system by force, arguing that socialism would best protect workers' rights.

Socialism

In a socialist system, the government controls most productive resources and makes most economic decisions. Many socialists believe that government is responsible for the welfare of its citizens and should provide them with a range of basic social services. *What is the government's role in a socialist system?*

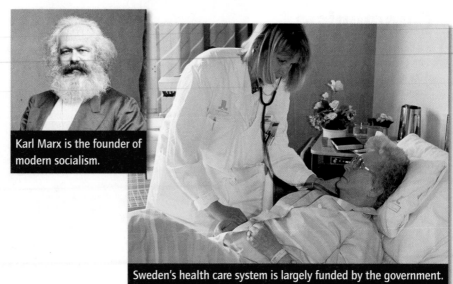

Karl Marx is the founder of modern socialism.

Sweden's health care system is largely funded by the government.

Socialism and Democracy Socialist nations today are generally democratic. Unlike pure socialism, which seeks to eliminate capitalism, these social democracies use state regulation and social services to ease any economic injustices caused by capitalism. Sweden is an example of a social democracy, but many other European nations—including the United Kingdom, Denmark, and Germany—are also democracies with strong socialist features.

Socialism varies from nation to nation, but it usually involves certain common characteristics. Many socialists believe that government should take primary responsibility for the individual and social welfare of its citizens. Accordingly, a socialist nation often provides a broad range of basic social services to its people, such as retirement benefits, health insurance, unemployment benefits, child care, and so on. Some socialist governments also take control of key industries, such as transportation and public utilities, in a process known as nationalization.

Advantages and Disadvantages Critics of socialism point out that comprehensive social programs often lead to high taxes. One consequence of high taxes, they argue, is that workers and companies have little incentive to produce more efficiently. Why work harder when most of your income is taken by the government in the form of taxes, critics ask, especially when the government also provides for most of your basic needs? The economic controls of socialism, critics believe, discourage private economic development and innovation.

Defenders of socialism argue, however, that the inequalities of capitalism harm the greater good and that it is fairer to provide everyone with their basic needs. Economic democracy, they believe, should go hand-in-hand with political democracy.

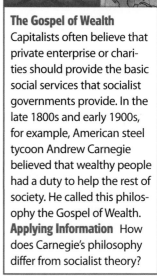

REAL-WORLD EXAMPLE

The Gospel of Wealth
Capitalists often believe that private enterprise or charities should provide the basic social services that socialist governments provide. In the late 1800s and early 1900s, for example, American steel tycoon Andrew Carnegie believed that wealthy people had a duty to help the rest of society. He called this philosophy the Gospel of Wealth. **Applying Information** How does Carnegie's philosophy differ from socialist theory?

Communism

In a Communist system, the government owns or controls all areas of the economy. Unlike a socialist democracy, however, a Communist nation has an authoritarian government that has complete control over the nation's economy, politics, and society. *What is the government's role in a Communist system?*

Although China has made a number of market reforms, many Chinese workers still work in state-run factories.

Communism Today

Communism of the type followed in the Soviet Union and Mao Zedong's China is rare today. Only a few countries, such as North Korea and Cuba, still have government-controlled economic planning and rigid one-party Communist rule. Visit thinkcentral.com to begin a Webquest on communism in the twenty-first century.

THINK central   **Webquest**

thinkcentral.com
KEYWORD: SGO PES

Communism

Like socialism, communism developed from the ideas of Karl Marx. Communism is an economic and political system in which the government owns all property and controls economic planning. Unlike a socialist democracy, however, Communist nations have authoritarian governments.

Marx and Communism Marx was convinced that the proletariat—the workers—would rise up in a violent revolution against the bourgeoisie, overthrowing the capitalist system. After this revolution, he believed, a global society would emerge in which there were no class distinctions and government would slowly wither away. Marx used the term *Communist* to describe this classless society.

The Soviet Union The Soviet Union was the first Communist nation, and its leaders adopted many of Marx's ideas. The state took control of many businesses and of the means of production. The Communist Party held complete political power and made decisions about all aspects of the Soviet economy.

Economically, communism brought mixed results. Under the protection of the government, the economy underwent rapid industrialization and the Soviet military became one of the two most powerful militaries in the world, along with that of the United States. But the inefficiencies of central planning and the increasing costs of military competition with the United States eventually destroyed the Soviet economy. By the 1980s, widespread shortages of food and consumer goods led to increasing public unhappiness with the government. As you have read, the inability of the government to meet the needs and wants of its people helped destroy the Soviet empire.

China After Communist China was established in 1949, its early attempts at central planning had mixed results. Beginning in the late 1970s, however, China's authoritarian government began to slowly reform the economy, moving away from communism and giving businesses new freedom to make economic decisions. Eventually the government allowed foreign investors to enter the Chinese market; today many international companies manufacture goods in China.

The result of these market reforms has been spectacular economic growth and a decline in China's poverty rate. By 2006, China's economy was projected to be the second largest in the world, behind only that of the United States. This growth has placed great demands on China's resources and environment, with industrial expansion leading to widespread air and water pollution.

Advantages and Disadvantages Communism shares some of the advantages and disadvantages of socialism. After all, communism is essentially just an extreme authoritarian form of socialism. One advantage is that a command economy may allow countries to develop their economies quickly, as in the Soviet Union and China.

Recall, though, that economic competition can be helpful. Without competition, there is little reason to create new and better products. As a result, poor product quality is a common problem in command economies. The shortage of consumer goods can be another issue, as central planners are carrying out a larger economic plan in which consumer desires often have little influence on economic decisions.

READING CHECK Comparing and Contrasting How are capitalism, socialism, and communism alike and different?

Section 3 Assessment

Reviewing Ideas and Terms

1. **a. Recall** What are the three basic economic questions that all countries must answer?
   b. Contrast What are the differences among **traditional**, **market**, **command**, and **mixed economies**?
   c. Evaluate Why might a traditional economy not work well in a modern, complex society like our own?

2. **a. Recall** Are most of today's economic systems traditional, market, command, or mixed?
   b. Compare and Contrast Compare and contrast **socialism** and communism.
   c. Elaborate Why might some people prefer to live and work in a capitalist economic system? Why might others prefer a socialist system?

Critical Thinking

3. **Draw Conclusions** Explain how a command economy and the absence of competition might affect workers in a government-run automobile factory in a Communist nation.

CASE STUDY LINK You answered the following questions at the end of the Case Study. Now that you have completed Section 3, think about and answer the questions again. Then compare your answers with your earlier responses. Are your answers the same or are they different?

4. How did British colonialism affect Indian industry?

5. Why did India choose socialist policies after independence?

6. How has the Indian economy responded to the move toward free-market policies?

SIMULATION

Negotiating a Trade Agreement

Student Casebook

Use your Student Casebook to complete the simulation.

What role does free trade play in an economy?

Even nations with very different economic and political systems often work together to encourage trade. Using what you have learned in Section 3, complete the simulation to make a decision about a trade agreement.

Roles

- Moderator, a representative from the Global Trade Council

- Trade representatives of Atlantica, a democratic nation with a highly developed capitalist economy

- Trade representatives of Pacifica, a Communist nation with a less-developed centrally planned economy that has recently begun to make substantial free-market reforms

➊ The Situation

Representatives of two fictional nations, Atlantica and Pacifica, are meeting to negotiate a free trade agreement, with each country trying to ensure the economic well-being of its own people. Under the agreement, the two countries would trade most goods and services without trade barriers, such as tariffs. The negotiations are led by a moderator, a representative from the fictional organization Global Trade Council.

Background

Atlantica

- Atlantica has the larger economy of the two nations. It imports many products from foreign countries.

- Atlantica has placed tariffs on some goods, such as agricultural products, in order to protect its own key industries from competition.

- Atlantica has many laws that are designed to ensure fair treatment of its workers and protection of the environment. These restrictions help make Atlantica's products more expensive than those produced in many other countries.

Pacifica

- Pacifica has historically imported few products.

- Pacifica has an enormous workforce with a very low standard of living.

- Pacifica needs foreign investment to grow its economy and has recently encouraged such foreign investment.

- Pacifica has few protections for its workers or the environment.

❷ The Discussions

The two countries have negotiated a proposed trade agreement. Now trade representatives from each country must meet separately to discuss the proposal.

Trade representatives from each country need to decide whether their nation will approve the agreement or request changes. If trade representatives want any changes to the agreement, they must discuss those changes. During their discussions, trade representatives should consider the Background information on the previous page, the Proposed Trade Agreement in the box at right, and the following questions:

● What kinds of trade conditions and barriers are reasonable for both countries?

● What does each nation stand to gain or lose with this agreement?

● Should a country approve an agreement that does not address all of its concerns?

❸ The Decision

After each side has decided whether or not it will approve the trade agreement, the two nations should come together to make an official decision. Led by the moderator, each country should present its position. If both sides approve the agreement as written, the negotiations are complete. If either nation requests changes, it must get the approval of the other side before the agreement can be modified. If the sides are unable to agree, the negotiations have failed.

❹ Debriefing

After trade representatives finish their negotiations, write a detailed explanation of the decision. Did the negotiations succeed or fail? What was each side's reasoning for its decision?

Proposed Trade Agreement between Atlantica and Pacifica

1. Tariffs on motor vehicles, electronics, textiles, and agricultural products will end immediately. All other tariffs will be phased out over the next 10 years.

2. Intellectual property rights (patents, copyrights, and trademarks) will be protected.

3. Each nation will enforce only its own environmental laws, not those of the other country.

4. Pacifica will not establish a minimum wage for its workers.

5. Atlantica-based companies can open factories and businesses in Pacifica.

6. Labor unions may not be organized in Pacifica-based businesses owned by Atlantica companies.

7. Atlantica workers will not receive any guarantees that their jobs will be protected.

Connecting Online

Quiz and Review

GOV 101
Examine key concepts in this chapter.

ONLINE QUIZZES
Take a practice quiz for each section in this chapter.

Activities

eActivities
Complete Webquests and Internet research activities.

INTERACTIVE FEATURES
Explore interactive versions of maps and charts.

KEEP IT CURRENT
Link to current events in U.S. government.

Partners

American Bar Association Division for Public Education
Learn more about the law, your rights and responsibilities.

Center for Civic Education
Promoting an enlightened and responsible citizenry committed to democratic principles and actively engaged in the practice of democracy.

Online Textbook

ONLINE SIMULATIONS
Learn about U.S. government through simulations you can complete online.

STUDENT CASEBOOK
Take notes electronically on Interactive Chapters.

Comprehension and Critical Thinking

SECTION 1 *(pp. 486–495)*

1. a. Review Key Terms For each term, write a sentence explaining its significance or meaning: authoritarian, coalition.

  b. Compare How does the role of a chief executive differ in presidential and parliamentary systems of government?

  c. Evaluate Identify a benefit and a drawback of both the presidential and the parliamentary systems of government.

SECTION 2 *(pp. 498–505)*

2. a. Review Key Terms For each term, write a sentence explaining its significance or meaning: totalitarianism, communism.

  b. Compare and Contrast Compare and contrast the authoritarian governments of the Soviet Union and China. How are they similar? How are they different?

  c. Predict Chinese leaders are trying to balance authoritarian rule, economic growth, and slow political reform. Given the events that took place in the Soviet Union during the late 1980s and early 1990s, do you think there will be any significant changes to China's government in the next five years? in the next 20 years?

SECTION 3 *(pp. 508–515)*

3. a. Review Key Terms For each term, write a sentence explaining its significance or meaning: market economy, command economy, mixed economy, capitalism, socialism.

  b. Contrast How do capitalism and socialism differ?

  c. Evaluate How does the role of government in the U.S. economic system compare to the role of government under socialism? under communism?

FOCUS ON WRITING

Expository Writing *Expository writing gives information, explains why or how, or defines a process. To practice expository writing, complete the assignment below.*

Writing Topic: The Effectiveness of Different Political and Economic Systems

4. Assignment Based on what you have read in this chapter, write a paragraph that ranks the effectiveness of different political and economic systems. You may wish to use the criteria of protection of human rights or promoting the common good as the basis for your decision. What other criteria would you use to evaluate different political and economic systems?

State and Local Government

Who provides many of the services you rely on every day? How can individual citizens influence public policies? What helps to guarantee that your rights as an individual are respected?

Answers to all of these questions can be found in state and local government. Your state and local governments are in place to provide essential public services, represent the interests of citizens, and protect citizens' civil rights. In this chapter you will learn how the various levels of state and local government are organized, what their powers are, and what services they provide to you as a citizen.

> **Interactive Feature** ✳
>
> **Essential State and Local Services**
> Explore what essential services state and local governments provide to citizens and how those services are delivered.
>
> **THINK** central **Interactive**
> thinkcentral.com
> **KEYWORD:** SGO SLG

Table of Contents

Elected officials lead the nation's state and local governments. Above, members of the Oregon Senate are shown meeting in session. At left, Mayor Martin Chávez of Albuquerque, New Mexico, discusses city government with visiting students.

Student Casebook

Use your Student Casebook to take notes on the chapter and to complete the simulations.

States and the National Government

Reading Focus

As you have learned, the word *federalism* is used to describe the relationship between the national and state governments. State governments function under the national constitution and a state constitution. State constitutions share important similarities as well as strengths and weaknesses.

CASE STUDY **The Nullification Crisis**
Learn about the crisis that developed when South Carolina tried to disregard a federal law.

WHAT YOU NEED TO KNOW Learn about the powers of states within the United States and how state constitutions organize state government.

SIMULATION **Amending the State Constitution** Use your knowledge to debate a proposed amendment to your state constitution.

Student Casebook

Use your Student Casebook to take notes on the section and to complete the simulation.

The outcome of the nullification crisis is shown in this mid-nineteenth-century political cartoon. President Andrew Jackson (center left) stands in triumph over a defeated John C. Calhoun of South Carolina (far left).

1828 — **1829** — **1830** — **1831** — **1832** — **1833** — **1834**

May 1828
A tariff on British imports is signed into law. Southerners call it the Tariff of Abominations.

July 1832
In response to southern protest, Congress passes a reduced tariff.

November 1832
South Carolina passes the Ordinance of Nullification, declaring the federal tariff void in the state.

December 1832
President Jackson issues the Nullification Proclamation, which declares the actions of South Carolina illegal.

March 1833
A compromise tariff gradually lowers the tariff to pre-1828 levels—ending the crisis.

The Nullification Crisis

Decades before the Civil War, the national government and the states disagreed over the issue of states' rights. One state decided to challenge the national government by declaring a federal law null and void. The ensuing crisis put American federalism to the test.

The Buildup

In 1828, Congress raised a tariff, a tax on imported or exported goods, on British imports in order to make similar products manufactured in the northern states seem less expensive. Southern states had long argued that tariffs benefited the North at the expense of the South. Prices of goods remained high in the South, where the 1828 tariff became known as the Tariff of Abominations.

The protest over the tariff raised the issue of whether a state had the right to disregard federal law. The issue hit at the heart of the government, dividing even President Andrew Jackson and his vice president, John C. Calhoun. President Jackson argued that the federal government must have supremacy over the states. Calhoun promoted the theory that a state had the right to nullify federal laws that the state judged to be unconstitutional or against its best interests.

Although a new tariff passed in 1832 lowered the rates of the previous tariff, the change was not enough to satisfy the state of South Carolina. Its legislature made a monumental decision: It voted to test the doctrine of nullification.

The Crisis

In November 1832 the South Carolina legislature passed the Ordinance of Nullification. The ordinance declared the 1828 and 1832 tariffs to be "null, void, and no law, nor binding upon this State, its officers or citizens."

South Carolina's ordinance put national unity in crisis. President Jackson and others in the federal government believed that if a state could nullify federal laws, it would threaten the very existence of the nation. In December 1832 President Jackson issued the Nullification Proclamation, in which he declared South Carolina's ordinance to be illegal. He argued that federal laws were too important to be canceled by the opinion of one state. "Were we mistaken, my countrymen, in attaching this importance to the Constitution of our country?" Jackson wrote. "Did we pledge ourselves to the support of an airy nothing—a bubble that must be blown away by the first breath of disaffection?"

An Uneasy Resolution

The federal government and South Carolina remained in a standoff until the following year, when a compromise tariff resolved the crisis. The new law gradually reduced the tariff rates over several years.

The issue of states' rights, however, remained unsettled. It fueled debates about slavery, which in turn contributed to the Civil War. In the end, national unity prevailed. In 1869 the Supreme Court declared in the landmark decision *Texas* v. *White* that the United States was "an indestructible Union composed of indestructible States."

The dispute over states' rights remains at the heart of many issues today. From civil rights to gun control, some Americans argue that states should be permitted to form their own policies, rather than being subject to federal laws.

What Do You Think?

1. Should the federal government pass laws that affect different parts of the country in different ways? Explain your answer.

2. Should states have the right to nullify federal laws? Why or why not?

3. Describe a situation from current events that is similar to the nullification crisis. How would you resolve the conflict?

States in the Federal System

The Case Study about the nullification crisis illustrates the ways in which the federal system shapes the relationship of the states to the national government. Now you will learn how federalism shapes the relationships of the states to one another.

Key Terms
guarantee clause
fundamental law
statutory law

Relations with the Federal Government

Federalism is the sharing of powers between the national government and the state governments. Remember that the U.S. Constitution grants specific powers, such as the power to regulate immigration, to the federal government. These powers are known as delegated powers. All other powers are either reserved for the states or the people or are held concurrently by the national and state governments. The power to establish local governments, for example, is a reserved power because only states may take this action. The power to tax, however, is a concurrent power, because both states and the federal government may levy taxes.

Although they had outlined these powers in the Constitution, the Framers realized that conflicts would arise between the national government and the states. To resolve such conflicts, the Framers included the supremacy clause in Article VI, Section 2, of the Constitution. This clause declares the Constitution and the laws of the federal government to be the "supreme Law of the Land." This means state governments may not ignore federal laws or the U.S. Constitution or contradict them with their own laws or constitutions. As you have read, federal supremacy sometimes strains the relationship between the states and the federal government.

REAL-WORLD EXAMPLE

CASE STUDY LINK

Twenty-first Century Nullification The United States nearly faced another nullification crisis as recently as 2003. In that year, a small group of lawmakers in the New Hampshire House of Representatives introduced HB 1246, titled "An Act Nullifying the USA Patriot Act." The legislation declared that New Hampshire would no longer recognize the USA Patriot Act, the federal law enacted following the September 11 terrorist attacks. A crisis over possible nullification was averted, however, when a New Hampshire House committee deemed HB 1246 "inexpedient [unwise] to legislate."

Applying Information Why do you think HB 1246 was considered unwise to legislate?

Relations with Other States

A state's relationship to the federal government is only one part of the overall influence of the federal system on the states. After all, states must also interact with one another. The Constitution establishes guidelines for these relationships too.

Chiefly, the Constitution promotes a cooperative relationship between the states. One important way it does so is through the full faith and credit clause, found in Article IV, Section 1. The full faith and credit clause requires that each state recognize the civil laws and acts of the other states. For example, a driver's license issued by one state is valid in all the other states, even if standards for issuing a license, such as training requirements, are different. Each state must also honor the decisions of the courts in the other states.

READING CHECK Identifying the Main Idea How do states relate to one another in the U.S. federal system?

State Constituions

As you learned by reading the first three chapters of this book, the United States has a long tradition of limited government and democracy. One way that tradition is maintained is through Article IV, Section 4, of the U.S. Constitution—the **guarantee clause**—which "guarantee[s] to every State in [the] Union a Republican Form of Government." Although the clause does not define *republican*, it is generally understood to mean that the state governments will be structured like the national government—they will be limited and representative. These ends were achieved through the ratification of each state's constitution.

Beyond the guarantee clause, however, the U.S. Constitution does not provide guidelines for how state and local governments should be organized. Rather, each state government is conferred legitimacy and authority by its own state constitution. Each state constitution also outlines a specific framework for state and local government.

Qualities of State Constitutions

State constitutions are as different as the states themselves. Some state constitutions are longer than the U.S. Constitution, and others are shorter. Some have retained the same wording since the 1700s, and others have been rewritten many times.

Despite these differences, state constitutions have similarities as well. For example, each state constitution expresses basic civic principles and practices. Every state constitution also protects civil rights through a bill of rights. These bills of rights help to ensure that majority rule does not infringe upon minority rights. Additionally, every state constitution prescribes respect for the equality of citizens and provides for due process of law.

The fundamental goal of every state constitution is also essentially the same—to establish the system of government for the state. Although each state government is different, each is similar in key ways. Every state constitution provides for a limited state government in which power is shared among a legislative, executive, and judicial branch, for example.

Changes to State Constitutions

Another similarity of state constitutions is that most have changed dramatically over the years. The U.S. Constitution has been amended only 27 times in its entire history. In contrast, state constitutions have been amended more than 5,900 times—more than one amendment every year for each state.

Characteristics of State Constitutions

In general, state constitutions are

- **Long.** The average is 28,600 words. The U.S. Constitution, with amendments, is about 7,400 words long.

- **Frequently amended.** The average is 100 amendments. The U.S. Constitution has 27 amendments.

- **Frequently rewritten.** The average is 3 constitutions. Louisiana, with 11, has had the most.

- **Overly detailed and inflexible.** Excessive detail leaves state constitutions unable to adapt during times of change.

REAL-WORLD EXAMPLE

State Bills of Rights For the most part, state bills of rights simply reinforce the rights guaranteed to U.S. citizens by the U.S. Bill of Rights. For example, Michigan's bill of rights guarantees state citizens freedom of speech and the press. However, like many state bills of rights, the Michigan bill of rights also contains provisions not found in the U.S. Bill of Rights. For example, the Michigan bill of rights guarantees state citizens who have been victims of crime the right to be present at all court proceedings at which the accused will also be present.
Applying Information How are the rights guaranteed by the national government similar to the rights guaranteed by state governments?

One reason for this distinction is that amending a state constitution is easier than amending the U.S. Constitution. Consider the process for amending the Oregon Constitution. In Oregon the legislature proposes an amendment to the state constitution by a majority vote. The amendment is approved if a majority of the voters vote in favor of it at the next election. Oregon voters themselves may also propose an amendment by gathering enough signatures on a petition. This power, known as the initiative, is a power that Oregon voters share with voters in 16 other states.

Not only are state constitutions frequently amended, most have been completely rewritten at least once—and some many times. Louisiana, for example, has had 11 constitutions, and Georgia has had 10. On the other hand, Massachusetts and several other states still have their original state constitutions. In fact, the Massachusetts Constitution, ratified in 1780, is the world's oldest constitution that still remains in effect.

Constitutional Problems and Solutions

Given the frequency with which they have been amended and rewritten, it is reasonable to conclude that state constitutions are imperfect in comparison to the U.S. Constitution. Problems with state constitutions result from the kinds of provisions they contain, their length, and their age. Solving these problems often involves amending the documents or even rewriting them altogether.

CONSTITUTIONS AND AMENDMENTS*

QUICK FACTS

State	Year of Statehood	Current Constitution	Number of Amendments	Number of Constitutions
Alabama	1819	1901	772	6
Illinois	1818	1971	11	4
Louisiana	1812	1974	129	11
Maryland	1788	1867	219	4
Massachusetts	1788	1780	120	1
Michigan	1837	1964	25	4
New Mexico	1912	1912	151	1
New York	1788	1895	219	4
North Carolina	1789	1971	34	3
Ohio	1803	1851	161	2
Oregon	1859	1859	238	1
Pennsylvania	1787	1968	30	5
South Carolina	1788	1896	485	7

*as of 2006

Problems The average state constitution is 28,600 words long—almost four times as long as the U.S. Constitution. One reason state constitutions tend to be longer than the U.S. Constitution is that they contain different types and quantities of provisions.

The U.S. Constitution contains **fundamental law**, meaning law that determines the basic political principles of a government. Many state constitutions, however, contain both fundamental law and **statutory law**. Statutory law is very detailed and specific. For example, the Minnesota Constitution contains a provision that citizens do not need a license to sell produce grown in their gardens. Because state constitutions are so easily amended, they contain many examples of statutory law—details you would not find in the U.S. Constitution. Another problem related to this excessive detail is that portions of many state constitutions have become obsolete.

Solutions Many people believe that state constitutions should focus exclusively on fundamental law and contain less detail. Between 1950 and 1970, forty-five states revised their constitutions. Some states chose to completely rewrite their constitution. Other states used the amendment process to change their constitution. Kansas, for example, has one of the shortest state constitutions, at about 11,900 words. Kansans have revised their constitution through amendment rather than by rewriting it completely. Kansans can vote on up to five amendments at a time, at regularly scheduled general elections or at special elections called by the state.

READING CHECK **Comparing and Contrasting** How are state constitutions similar to and different from the U.S. Constitution?

Section 1 Assessment

THINK central **Online Quiz**
thinkcentral.com
KEYWORD: SGO SLG HP

Reviewing Ideas and Terms

1. **a. Identify** What powers does the U.S. Constitution grant to state governments?
   b. Explain Is a contract signed in one state legally binding in another state? Why or why not?
   c. Elaborate State why the supremacy clause and the full faith and credit clause are important to the U.S. system of government.

2. **a. Recall** From what source do state governments receive their legitimacy and authority?
   b. Contrast What distinguishes **fundamental law** from **statutory law**?
   c. Evaluate Why do you think state constitutions have been revised so frequently, compared with the U.S. Constitution?

Critical Thinking

3. **Draw Conclusions** In your opinion, is the amount of detail in state constitutions a strength, a weakness, or both? Explain your answer.

CASE STUDY LINK You answered the following questions at the end of the Case Study. Now that you have completed Section 1, think about and answer the questions again. Then compare your answers with your earlier responses. Are your answers the same or different?

4. Should the federal government pass laws that affect different parts of the country in different ways? Explain your answer.

5. Should states have the right to nullify federal laws? Why or why not?

6. Describe a situation from current events that is similar to the nullification crisis. How would you resolve the conflict?

Amending the State Constitution

Student Casebook

Use your Student Casebook to complete the simulation.

Will the citizens of your state make English the state's official language?

In a democracy, government officials must balance majority rule with minority rights when writing and enforcing laws. Consider the issue of English as an official language. In this simulation, use what you learned in Section 1 to debate and then vote on a fictional amendment to your state constitution that would make English the state's official language.

Roles

- Supporters of the English-language amendment
- Opponents of the English-language amendment
- Concerned citizens

❶ The Situation

The state legislature has recently decided to allow the people to vote on an amendment to the state constitution. If approved by the voters, the amendment will make English the official language of the state. In the final weeks before the election, a citizens' group has called for a debate on the amendment. Groups both for and against the amendment will take questions from concerned citizens in an open forum to be televised throughout the state.

The Proposed Amendment

The United States has always benefited from the rich diversity of its people. Throughout American history, the thread binding individuals of differing backgrounds has been the English language. English has permitted diverse individuals to discuss, debate, and agree on controversial issues. Therefore, we add the following new article to our state constitution, on approval of the voters and by proclamation of the governor:

- English is the official language of our state.

- All official actions will be conducted in English only.

- Government will be required to preserve, protect, and enhance English as the official language, prohibiting discrimination against persons using English, and permitting private lawsuits to enforce the official English amendment to our state constitution.

❷ The Debate

Your teacher will moderate a public debate between supporters and opponents of the proposed amendment. The purpose of the debate is to provide voters with enough information to make an informed decision on the amendment in the upcoming election.

Sample Arguments in Favor of the Amendment

The amendment will

- protect the majority culture in the state
- encourage immigrants to learn English
- save the government money by reducing the costs of providing services in multiple languages

Sample Arguments against the Amendment

The amendment will

- limit cultural diversity in the state
- prevent recent immigrants from communicating effectively with the government and others
- conflict with the principle of respect for minority rights

❸ The Election

As voters in a state election, vote either "yes" or "no" on the proposed amendment. When casting your vote, be sure to consider all the points mentioned in the classroom debate.

❹ Debriefing

After the votes are tallied, think about the factors you considered before you cast your vote. Write a letter to the editor, explaining how the election results relate to the concepts of majority rule and minority rights.

English as an Official Language in the United States

- Of the 50 states, 26 currently have a law making English the official state language.
- Six states made the law through constitutional amendment. Twenty states made the law through a statute.
- The U.S. Congress has debated making English the official language of the United States. A federal law has never been passed.

PRIMARY LANGUAGE SPOKEN AT HOME

Vietnamese 2%
Other 6%
Spanish 8%
English 84%

Costs and Benefits to the State

- Of the $35.5 billion spent by the state government last year, $1.2 million was spent providing services in languages other than English. This figure represents less than one one-hundredth of 1 percent of the state's budget.
- Non-English-speaking and English-speaking households contributed to the state's gross domestic product at roughly the same rate.

State Government

Reading Focus

State governments, like the federal government, divide power among legislative, executive, and judicial branches. In terms of their structure and functions, these state branches mirror the branches of the federal government. Also like the federal government, state governments must find funding for expensive yet essential programs and services.

CASE STUDY **Teen Driving Laws** Learn about how and why states have moved toward stricter laws concerning teenagers and driving.

WHAT YOU NEED TO KNOW Learn about how the powers of state governments are spread among three branches. Learn how the legislative, executive, and judicial branches function. Then read about state government finances.

SIMULATION **Budgeting and Public Policy** Use your knowledge to debate how best to spend a small surplus in the state's budget.

Student Casebook

Use your Student Casebook to take notes on the section and to complete the simulation.

DRIVER EDUCATION STUDENT DRIVER

Each state passes its own laws regulating drivers and driver education.

Teen Driving Laws

Motor vehicle crashes are the leading cause of death among 15- to 20-year-olds in the United States. In recent years many states have passed new laws restricting teenage drivers. These laws aim to reduce driving-related accidents and deaths involving teenagers.

Tragedy in Georgia

On July 1, 2003, Joshua Brown was 17 years old and on top of the world. He was a recent graduate of Cartersville High School in Cartersville, Georgia, and a star athlete. In the fall, Joshua planned to attend music school in Boston. On the night of July 1, in one tragic instant, everything changed. While driving on a wet road, Joshua lost control of his car and collided with a tree. He died several days later.

In their grief, Joshua's parents approached their state senator to ask for a new law mandating training for teenage drivers. They believed better driver education might have saved their son's life. The proposal was passed by Georgia's legislature and signed into law by the governor. Known as Joshua's Law, the new legislation went into effect on January 1, 2007.

Georgia Driving Laws

Even before Joshua's Law, teenage drivers in Georgia faced strict laws. The licensing system in Georgia includes a learner's permit, followed by a restricted license for drivers between 16 and 18 years of age. With a restricted license Georgia teens may not drive between 12 a.m. and 6 a.m. For the first six months they may not have teenage passengers other than siblings.

Joshua's Law added another important element to Georgia's system: It made driver education mandatory for 16-year-olds wishing to apply for an unrestricted license. In addition to driver education, teens must complete 40 hours of supervised driving, including 6 hours at night. Teenagers who choose not to complete driver education must wait until age 17 to apply for an unrestricted license. Supervised driving is mandatory for all teen drivers.

The results of Georgia's teen driving laws are promising. The Georgia Department of Driver Services reported that after the first laws went into effect in 1997, speed-related crashes among teenage drivers dropped by 44.5 percent.

Other States, Other Laws

In the United States, driving laws are the responsibility of the states. For this reason, driving laws vary widely. For example, in some states, teenagers can drive without supervision at age 14 and a half. In other states, teens must wait until they are 16 and a half before they are even allowed to get behind the wheel.

During the last two decades, many states have taken steps to protect teenage drivers. In the 1980s Maryland, California, and Oregon were among the first states to institute graduated licensing systems. Graduated licensing systems require a learner's permit period, often combined with a period of restricted driving. Only later is an unrestricted license issued, in some states as late as 18 years of age.

Today 46 states and the District of Columbia have a three-stage graduated licensing system. Like Georgia, other states using such systems have reduced crashes involving teenagers. Michigan and North Carolina, for example, have both reported about a 25-percent reduction in crashes involving 16-year-old drivers.

What Do You Think?

1. Do you think graduated licensing systems are a good idea? Explain your answer.
2. What are your opinions of the arguments for and against strict teen driving laws?
3. How else could society promote teenage driver safety?

WHAT YOU NEED TO KNOW

Organization of State Governments

governor
citizen legislatures
professional legislatures
line-item veto
executive clemency
Missouri Plan

Driving laws, like those discussed in the Case Study, are products of state government. In this section you will learn that, much like the federal government, state governments divide and balance power among three branches. Although the structures and powers of these branches are similar from state to state, there are differences as well.

All but one state legislature is bicameral, meaning the legislature has two houses. In most states the lower house is called the house of representatives, and the upper house is called the senate. Nebraska is the only state with a unicameral, or one-house, legislature. Nebraskans adopted the one-house legislature during the Great Depression in an attempt to reduce the costs of running the government. The state never returned to a bicameral system.

Other differences between state legislatures also exist. The total number of legislators differs from state to state, ranging from as few as 49 in Nebraska to as many as 424 in New Hampshire. Terms of office and session lengths also vary among state legislatures. Overall, however, state legislative branches are quite similar to one another and to the U.S. Congress.

Structures and Powers of State Governments

State constitutions divide power among legislative, executive, and judicial branches.
The structures and powers of these branches differ from state to state.

Arkansas
Governor: Has "supreme executive power" under the state constitution
General Assembly: Part-time; meets for 60 days every other year
Judiciary: Seven supreme court justices elected to eight-year terms; also appellate court, circuit courts, and district courts

Florida
Governor: Chief executive works with three elected cabinet members
Legislature: House and Senate pass laws that affect every Floridian; considered the most powerful branch
Judiciary: Supreme court is highest, then court of appeals, circuit courts, and county courts

Georgia
Governor: Strong budgetary powers; four-year term, limit two consecutive terms
General Assembly: House and senate with two-year terms, no term limits; meets 40 days each year
Judiciary: Include supreme court and lower superior courts, where most important trials occur

Illinois
Executive: State departments and agencies led by governor; elected to four-year term, no term limits
Legislative: House and senate with two-year terms; meet annually to pass laws
Judicial: Seven supreme court justices elected to 10-year terms; 1 appellate court and 22 circuit courts

State executive branches are also similar to each other and to the executive branch of the federal government. In all 50 states, voters elect a **governor** to serve as chief executive of state government. Although the first state constitutions limited governors' powers in order to prevent the concentration of power in the hands of one person, today's state constitutions grant governors sufficient power to lead a truly separate and equal branch of government. Forty-three states also have a lieutenant governor whose duties, relative to the governor's, are like those of the U.S. vice president. Yet unlike the vice president, who is elected on the same ticket as the president, many lieutenant governors are independently elected.

Similarities also exist between the state judicial branches and the federal judicial branch. Like the federal judiciary, the states have two types of courts—trial courts and appellate courts. State courts handle different types of cases than federal courts do, however. Federal courts handle cases involving federal laws, while state courts handle cases involving state laws. In fact, because there are far more state laws than federal laws, state and local courts handle some 99 percent of all court cases in the United States.

READING CHECK **Comparing and Contrasting** What are two similarities and two differences between the federal government and the state governments?

RESPONSIBILITIES OF LEADERSHIP

Governors are the chief executives of the state governments. Like all leaders, however, governors are only as powerful as the team that supports them. To exercise effective leadership, governors must engage in teamwork and consensus building—skills that are important for all citizens to develop and use.

Maryland
Governor: Four-year term; leads 24-member cabinet; submits annual budget
General Assembly: House and Senate pass laws, create executive depts; meets annually, no term limits
Judiciary: Court of appeals is highest; then court of special appeals, circuit courts, district courts

New Mexico*
State: House can impeach any state officer or judge by majority vote. Senate tries impeachments and convicts with a two-thirds vote.
Tribal: Native American tribal governments exercise legitimate power over tribal territories. Powers and responsibilities are similar to those of state government.

Ohio
Executive: Article III establishes five offices, including a governor, who enacts and enforces laws.
Legislative: Under Article II, the two-house General Assembly creates and changes laws.
Judicial: Under Article IV, the supreme court and lesser courts interpret laws.

South Carolina
Governor: Oversees the faithful execution of laws; assisted by cabinet and other executive officers.
General Assembly: House and Senate meet annually; committees key to process
Judiciary: Supreme court; General Assembly elects chief justice and four associate justices to 10-year terms

*Native American tribal governments exist in New Mexico and in at least 38 other states.

State Legislative Branches

Wyoming's Citizen Legislature The Wyoming legislature is one of the last true citizen legislatures in the United States. In odd-numbered years, Wyoming legislators meet in a general session that may last for a maximum of only 40 days. The legislature also meets for a 20-day budget session in even-numbered years. Legislators receive $125 per day in salary and $80 per day for expenses. They are not eligible for state employee benefits such as retirement or health insurance.

Applying Information Why do you think Wyoming has chosen to retain its citizen legislature?

ACADEMIC VOCABULARY

grant to permit as a right

All 50 state governments include a legislative branch that makes the state's laws. In most states the state legislative body is simply called the legislature, though in some states it is known as the General Assembly, the Legislative Assembly, or the General Court. You might think of your state legislature as a smaller, state-specific version of the U.S. Congress. In many respects this is true, though differences exist as well. The key characteristics of state legislatures are outlined below.

Types of Legislatures

Generally speaking, state legislatures can be divided into two types—citizen legislatures and professional legislatures. The two types are distinguished by session frequency and length, legislator salaries, and terms of office. Twenty-two state legislatures exhibit characteristics of both types and, as such, defy classification.

Citizen legislatures are also often called part-time legislatures. Citizen legislatures sometimes meet in session as infrequently as once every other year and for a period of about two months. Salaries are very small, and terms of office may be shorter than those in other states. Service in a citizen legislature is designed to be a part-time job. Unless they are independently wealthy, legislators must hold another job to earn a living. Seventeen state legislatures can be classified as citizen legislatures.

As the duties of state government have grown increasingly complex, 11 states have formed **professional legislatures**. Sessions of a professional legislature are usually held annually and often last for much of the year. Legislators' salaries typically reflect the full-time nature of the job, and legislative terms may be longer. In states with a professional legislature, legislators usually do not have other jobs while they are serving in the legislature.

How State Legislatures Work

State legislatures work much like the U.S. Congress does, with a few important differences. State legislatures also have duties similar to those of the U.S. Congress, though, of course, on a smaller scale.

Powers Recall that under the U.S. federal system, those powers not granted to the federal government are reserved for the states or for the people. State legislatures possess all of these reserved powers that are not given to another branch of state government by the state constitution and that are not denied to the legislature by the state constitution or the U.S. Constitution. A broad range of powers are extended to state legislatures in this way.

Writing laws is, of course, the primary power of state legislatures. Often, laws dealing with important or controversial issues are first passed in state legislatures. When a law becomes a trend across many states, the U.S. Congress may consider enacting the law on a national level. In this way, state legislatures can influence national policy. In addition, state legislatures have powers that serve as checks on the other branches of state government. Important legislative checks include the power to approve appointments and to impeach or remove from office state officeholders of any branch.

Organization Like the U.S. Congress, state legislatures are led by presiding officers with substantial leadership powers. These officers fill leadership posts that resemble those in Congress. As in Congress, too, these leaders assign bills to committees, appoint legislators to committees, and control floor debates.

Just as they do at the national level, committees perform the main legislative work of the states. This work primarily consists of considering and reporting on proposed bills. The power of committees varies from state to state. In some states, legislative committees resemble U.S. congressional committees in their scope and influence. In other states, committees are not nearly as strong as in the U.S. Congress, making it relatively easy to get a bill considered on the floor without committee approval.

Process The lawmaking process at the state level is similar to the process at the national level. First, a member of the legislature introduces a bill. The bill is then assigned to a committee, which considers the bill. If the committee approves the bill, it is debated on the floor and a vote is taken.

Sometimes different versions of a bill will be passed in the upper and lower houses of the state legislature. When this occurs, a joint committee drafts a compromise bill, which again goes to both houses for a vote. If passed, the new bill goes to the executive branch, where it is either signed into law or vetoed.

READING CHECK **Summarizing** What are the major powers and duties of the legislative branch of state government?

Term-Limitation Movement As more states adopted professional legislatures, a movement to maintain a common characteristic of citizens legislatures began. Throughout the 1990s, in what became known as the term-limitation movement, 21 states enacted laws limiting the number of terms legislators could serve. Visit **thinkcentral.com** to begin a Webquest exploring the impact of this political trend.

THINK central Webquest

thinkcentral.com
KEYWORD: SGO SLG

State Legislatures

QUICK FACTS

- Each state has one, though with various names (General Assembly, Legislative Assembly, General Court, the legislature).

- Forty-nine are bicameral. Only Nebraska's is unicameral.

- Seventeen are citizen (or part-time) legislatures, and 11 are professional (or full-time). Twenty-two defy classification.

- All possess those powers reserved for the states by the U.S. Constitution and not denied by the U.S. or state constitutions.

- Each state legislature functions much like the U.S. Congress.

State legislatures, like the Vermont House, are lively centers of debate.

State Executive Branches

The executive branch of the state government includes several important offices. The terms, salaries, roles, and powers of these offices—and the qualifications required to hold them—vary from state to state.

The Governor

The governor is the chief executive of the state government. The officeholder fills a role comparable to that of the U.S. president.

Roles and Powers Today's state governors have many roles and powers. They oversee the <u>enforcement</u> of state laws and help develop the state's policy agenda. They act as ambassadors for their states by attempting to attract businesses and by promoting state products. Recently, governors have even taken on national issues such as education and immigration. Often, presidential candidates are former governors who have risen to the national stage.

In addition to these roles, governors hold certain other powers given to them by their state's constitution. Governors may appoint the heads of some state agencies and departments. Governors also typically play a major role in the creation of the state's budget. Finally, much as the president is the commander in chief of the armed forces, the state governor has the power to mobilize the state's units of the National Guard.

Governors may exercise checks on the other branches of government. They can veto bills passed by the legislature, for example. Most governors also have the power of the **line-item veto**, which allows them to reject specific parts of legislation while signing the rest of a bill into law. Governors also have powers of **executive clemency**. These powers include the power to grant pardons and commutations, which you read about in Chapter 6.

Qualifications and Election Each state's constitution lists the official qualifications for becoming governor. Most states require that the governor be a U.S. citizen. Candidates must also have resided in the state for a certain length of time. Age requirements vary, but typically a governor must be at least 30 years of age.

The characteristics of people elected as governors vary along with the political culture of a state. Most governors, for example, have been white men in their late forties. Increasingly, though, women and minorities are winning governor's races.

Governors in all states are elected by popular vote. In most states, a candidate needs only a plurality of votes to win the election. A plurality means that the candidate receives the most votes of all the candidates, even if that amount is less than a majority of the votes cast. In a handful of states, a candidate for governor needs a majority vote to win election.

ACADEMIC VOCABULARY

enforcement the act of carrying out

REAL-WORLD EXAMPLE

Governors as Presidents Governors have greater success as presidential candidates than any other group of politicians, including members of the U.S. Congress. In fact, 19 presidents once served as governor of a U.S. state or territory. Most recently, in 2000 George W. Bush was elected president after having served as governor of Texas. Before him, Bill Clinton was elected president in 1992 after having served as governor of Arkansas.

Applying Information Why do you think so many former governors have been elected president?

The Governorship

Roles
- Enforce state laws
- Set policy agenda
- Promote the state

Powers
- Appointment
- Budget proposal
- National Guard mobilization
- Veto/line-item veto
- Executive clemency

Qualifications
- U.S. citizen
- State resident
- Typically 30 years old or older

Terms
- Usually four years
- Often a two-term limit

Salary
$70,000 to $206,500

Governors, like Missouri's Matt Blunt, occupy a highly visible position in state government.

Terms and Salaries Forty-eight state governors are elected to four-year terms. In New Hampshire and Vermont, governors are elected to two-year terms. Many governors are limited to serving two terms in office. Virginia allows its governor to serve only one term.

Governors' salaries vary from state to state. As of 2007, California has the highest salary at $206,500 per year, though the governor declined to accept the full amount. Maine's governor is the lowest paid, with an annual salary of $70,000. Most states provide the governor with an official residence. Governors also typically receive compensation for travel and related expenses.

Other Executive Offices

Most states elect a lieutenant governor who is next in line to assume the governorship. The lieutenant governor often leads the state senate, plays a role in public policy, and advises the governor. Many lieutenant governors are eventually elected governor themselves.

In most states a secretary of state is responsible for record keeping and for administering state elections. These duties may include maintaining a list of registered voters, for example. A state treasurer manages the state's money by collecting taxes and making many different types of payments on behalf of the state. Finally, an attorney general serves as the state's chief lawyer. He or she advises state officials and interprets state laws as necessary. Legal opinions issued by the attorney general are influential in shaping state laws. These officeholders, in cooperation with the governor and other executive branch officials, work to ensure that the policies and laws of the state are faithfully carried out.

READING CHECK **Summarizing** How are state executive branches organized?

REAL-WORLD EXAMPLE

Federal and State Freedom-of-Information Laws The U.S. Freedom of Information Act (FOIA) requires federal government agencies to comply with most citizen requests for government information. Enacted in 1966, the law applies to all departments and more than 70 agencies in the executive branch. Each state has its own freedom-of-information and open-meeting laws as well. The procedure for filing a FOIA request involves writing a letter to the appropriate department or agency, listing precise details about the information being sought.

Applying Information Freedom-of-information laws are also sometimes called sunshine laws. Why do you think this is so?

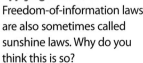

State Judicial Branches

As discussed in Chapter 8, all cases involving federal law or the federal government are handled in the federal court system. Most laws that affect people's everyday lives are passed not by the federal government, however, but by the states. Therefore, most court cases are heard in state courts or in local courts also established by the state. In 2004, more than 36 million cases of all types were filed in state courts throughout the United States.

The State Court System

State courts handle cases involving state laws—including both criminal and civil laws. Civil laws deal with the relationships between people. For example, civil law cases include divorce, adoption, property ownership, contracts, wills, and many other issues. Criminal cases involve laws related to public order. Most criminal cases are also tried in state courts.

A typical state court system contains two basic types of courts: trial courts and appellate courts. Most criminal cases begin their journey through the court system in a trial court. At this level an official known as the district attorney prosecutes cases. Before a trial even begins, however, the case must be reviewed by a grand jury, a group of ordinary citizens who have been called to serve as jurors. The grand jury decides whether the state has enough evidence to put a person on trial for a crime. If the grand jury decides there is enough evidence, a petit jury (also known as a trial jury) will hear the case in a trial court.

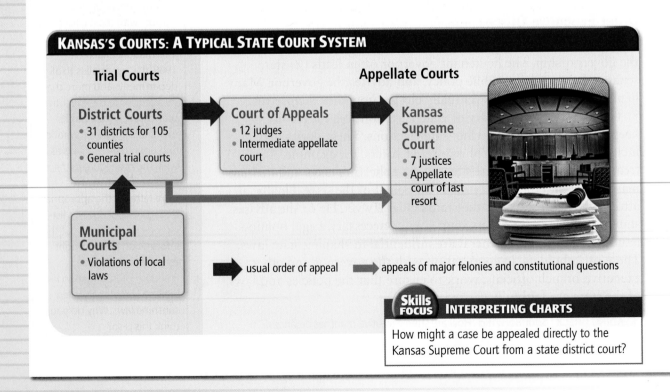

KANSAS'S COURTS: A TYPICAL STATE COURT SYSTEM

Trial Courts

District Courts
- 31 districts for 105 counties
- General trial courts

Municipal Courts
- Violations of local laws

Appellate Courts

Court of Appeals
- 12 judges
- Intermediate appellate court

Kansas Supreme Court
- 7 justices
- Appellate court of last resort

→ usual order of appeal   → appeals of major felonies and constitutional questions

Skills FOCUS INTERPRETING CHARTS

How might a case be appealed directly to the Kansas Supreme Court from a state district court?

If the trial court finds the person guilty, he or she may appeal the decision to the state's intermediate appellate court. The intermediate appellate court, often called the court of appeals, stands between the trial courts and the state's appellate court of last resort—the state supreme court. The function of the appellate courts is generally not to hear the case anew but rather to determine whether the lower court correctly interpreted and applied the law. Most often the determination of the intermediate appellate court is final, though many cases do still make their way to the state supreme court.

Cases of state law may usually be appealed only within the state court system. Sometimes, however, court cases do move from the state court system to the federal court system. This can only happen if the state case involves a possible violation of federal law or the U.S. Constitution. For a state case to move to the federal courts, it must first be heard in the state supreme court.

Selection of Judges

As you might imagine, how we choose the people who serve as judges has a powerful impact upon the effectiveness of the state courts. Therefore, the process for selecting judges is extremely important and can become very politically controversial.

Unlike the judges of the federal courts, who are all appointed, judges in state courts may be either elected or appointed. In states where judges are appointed, the governor or the legislature—or a combination of the two—makes the judicial appointment. When making appointments, a governor usually appoints judges who are members of his or her own party.

In states where judges are elected, names appear on the ballot in a regular election or a judicial election. Although this system may seem fairer than appointment, it has disadvantages as well. Voter turnout in the election of judges is usually lower than in other elections. Judges in office usually do not face an opponent when running for re-election. Therefore, once elected, a judge can be difficult to unseat.

About half of the states use some form of the **Missouri Plan**, which combines methods of election and appointment, to select judges. Under the Missouri Plan, the state bar association helps a nonpartisan commission create a list of potential judges. The list is based upon the merit and qualifications of the potential judges, not upon politics. The governor then appoints one of the candidates on the list. At the next election, usually a year later, the voters decide whether the judge should remain in office. If the people vote "no," the selection process begins over again.

READING CHECK **Identifying the Main Idea** Why are the state judicial branches so important to U.S. government?

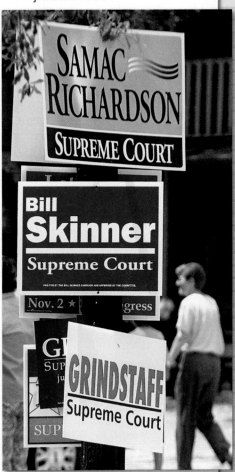

The majority of states allow for the election of at least some judicial officials.

REAL-WORLD
EXAMPLE
CASE STUDY LINK

Regulating Drivers State governments pass driver regulations, such as Joshua's Law from the Case Study, in order to keep citizens safe. One of the newest kinds of driver regulations being considered by states concerns drivers older than 65. Studies indicate that older drivers are three times less likely to cause an accident than are 18- to 24-year-olds. Yet because of their age, drivers older than 65 are more likely to be severely injured in any accident that does occur. **Applying Information** What is one argument for and one argument against regulating older drivers?

State Services and Finances

State governments must provide many services. To do so, they must raise billions of dollars in revenue and create detailed budgets.

State Services

The federal government has only those powers granted to it by the U.S. Constitution. Therefore, the states are responsible for providing many essential government services.

What are some services provided by state governments? State governments build schools, provide textbooks, pay teachers, and decide what students should learn. State governments administer programs like Medicaid, a health care service for people in need. State governments maintain highways and establish guidelines for licensing drivers. State governments establish a state police force to provide for public safety. State governments also work for environmental conservation and the management of state-owned lands.

State Revenues

Where do state governments get the money to pay for the services they provide? You probably know some sources of state government money, such as taxes. Other revenue sources may surprise you.

Taxes Most states collect an income tax, though rates vary from state to state. Only Alaska, Florida, Nevada, South Dakota, Texas, Washington, and Wyoming have no state income tax. These states must raise revenue in other ways.

Sales taxes are another source of state government revenue. The sales tax is assessed as a percentage of the sales price whenever a good or service is bought. Sales tax rates differ from state to state and are as high as 7 percent in some states.

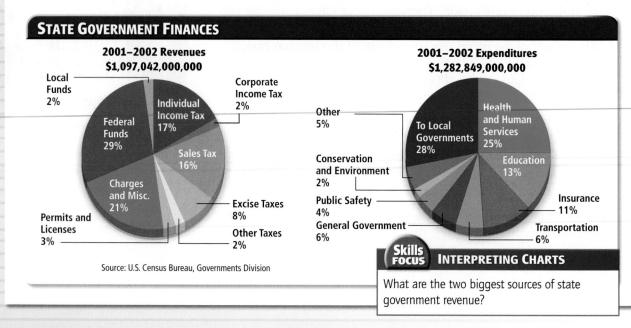

STATE GOVERNMENT FINANCES

2001–2002 Revenues
$1,097,042,000,000

- Local Funds 2%
- Federal Funds 29%
- Individual Income Tax 17%
- Corporate Income Tax 2%
- Sales Tax 16%
- Charges and Misc. 21%
- Permits and Licenses 3%
- Excise Taxes 8%
- Other Taxes 2%

2001–2002 Expenditures
$1,282,849,000,000

- Other 5%
- To Local Governments 28%
- Health and Human Services 25%
- Conservation and Environment 2%
- Education 13%
- Public Safety 4%
- General Government 6%
- Insurance 11%
- Transportation 6%

Source: U.S. Census Bureau, Governments Division

Skills FOCUS INTERPRETING CHARTS

What are the two biggest sources of state government revenue?

Other Revenues In addition to taxes, sources of state revenue include user fees, federal grants, borrowing, and state lotteries.

- User fees include highway tolls and tuition at state colleges. Fees ensure that those who use services, pay for those services.

- The federal government provides grants to states. Some grants are for specific programs. Other grants are for general use.

- States borrow money by selling bonds. People buy state bonds and, after a time, receive their money back with interest.

- Many states run a lottery. Some states raise as much as 2 to 3 percent of their total revenue in this way.

State Budget Officers While most state governors are charged with the task of preparing their state's budget, no governor undertakes the task without assistance from trained financial professionals. Visit **thinkcentral.com** to begin a Webquest exploring the important role played by the state budget officers.

thinkcentral.com
KEYWORD: SGO SLG

State Budgets

Accurately projecting revenues is an important first step in the state budget process. Then the governor develops a budget proposal detailing how the state should spend its money. Legislators debate the budget proposal and make revisions. The final budget bill is then sent back to the governor for approval. The final budget is a reflection of the state's overall public policy goals.

Many states require a balanced budget, though exceptions are often made for projects like highway construction. Economic cycles, however, can make balancing a budget difficult. For this reason many states set money aside for economic downturns.

READING CHECK **Summarizing** How do states pay for the services they provide?

thinkcentral.com
KEYWORD: SGO SLG HP

Section 2 Assessment

Reviewing Ideas and Terms

1. **a. Describe** How are state governments organized?
   b. Analyze Describe one advantage and one disadvantage of Nebraska's unicameral legislature.

2. **a. Identify** What are the main differences between **citizen legislatures** and **professional legislatures**?
   b. Explain How do state legislatures sometimes influence national policy?

3. **a. Define** What is the **line-item veto**?
   b. Compare and Contrast How is the governor's role similar to and different from that of the president?

4. **a. Describe** How is a state court system structured?
   b. Evaluate What is the **Missouri Plan**? Is it a fair method for selecting state judges? Why or why not?

5. **a. Identify** What are three state services?
   b. Make Inferences Why is it important for states to accurately project revenues?

Critical Thinking

6. **Draw Conclusions** Why are state governments critically important to citizens?

CASE STUDY LINK You answered the following questions at the end of the Case Study. Now that you have completed Section 2, think about and answer the questions again. Then compare your answers with your earlier responses. Are your answers the same or different?

7. Do you think graduated licensing systems are a good idea? Explain your answer.

8. What are your opinions of the arguments for and against strict teen driving laws?

9. How else could society promote teenage driver safety?

SIMULATION

Budgeting and Public Policy

Student Casebook

Use your Student Casebook to complete the simulation.

What state programs will receive additional funding?

State budget officers must make difficult decisions when deciding how to distribute the state's money. By funding certain programs and not others, state budget officers play an important role in shaping public policy. The final state budget becomes one of the clearest expressions of the state's goals and priorities. Use what you have learned and the information provided to simulate a hearing involving five state departments and the state budget committee.

Roles

- State budget committee members
- Parks department representatives
- Corrections department representatives
- Public health department representatives
- Transportation department representatives
- Education department representatives
- State citizens

❶ The Situation

After providing for all of the must-haves in the budget, officials identify $1 billion of left over funding for the state. The state budget committee is holding a hearing to decide how the money should be spent. Representatives from five state agencies will approach the committee to request funding for specific projects. The state budget committee must decide how to allocate the total $1 billion of additional funds. The committee may fund all or a portion of any combination of programs, provided the total expenditure does not exceed $1 billion.

State Agency Proposals

- **Parks Department** A recent flood severely damaged several state parks and historic areas. The parks department is requesting $500 million to restore them.

- **Corrections Department** State prisons are at capacity. The corrections department is requesting $500 million to build new facilities so that it can avoid releasing prisoners before their sentences end.

- **Public Health Department** A flu epidemic is expected during the upcoming winter. The public health department is requesting $500 million to restock flu vaccine.

- **Transportation Department** Traffic jams in the state capital have reached an all-time high and are keeping customers away from retail stores. The transportation department is requesting $500 million to improve the city's public-transit system.

- **Education Department** Students have been leaving the state to attend medical school, which is limiting the number of medical professionals available across the state. The education department is requesting $500 million to establish a new medical school at the state university.

❷ The Budget Hearing

The seven-member state budget committee will hold a hearing on how to spend the extra money. The committee must decide how to allocate the $1 billion among the five departments making requests. The committee members must consider the following when making their determination:

- the merit of each department's plan

- the governor's public-policy goals

- public opinion

At the hearing, representatives from each department will present a detailed proposal. Representatives will also present their most convincing arguments for funding their specific projects. Following the departmental presentations, several citizens will come forward to express their opinions to the committee.

❸ The Decision

Based on the presentations, the state budget committee will issue its decision on how to award funding. Which departments will receive funding?

❹ Debriefing

After the state budget committee announces its decision, write a report that evaluates the decision and answers the following questions:

- How does the committee's decision reflect the governor's public-policy goals?

- How does the committee's decision reflect public opinion?

- What does the committee's decision indicate about the state's policy goals?

PUBLIC OPINION POLL

Are you worried about the upcoming flu season?

Yes	20%
No	60%
Not Sure	20%

Is there a shortage of doctors in the state?

Yes	40%
No	40%
Not Sure	20%

Would you support a new prison in your town to ease overcrowding?

Yes	10%
No	80%
Not Sure	10%

Is traffic congestion a problem in your area?

Yes	40%
No	50%
Not Sure	10%

Are state parks a valuable resource?

Yes	80%
No	10%
Not Sure	10%

The Governor's Public-Policy Goals

- To encourage people and businesses to move to the state

- To encourage current citizens and businesses to remain in the state

- To protect the health and safety of citizens

- To improve the state university system

Local Government and Citizen Participation

Reading Focus
A variety of local governments provide many of the services you rely on every day. These services are paid for by local, state, and federal revenue. Direct citizen participation in government is often easiest at the local level.

CASE STUDY **Land Use in Easton, Maryland** Learn how the government in one Maryland town addressed the issue of land use.

WHAT YOU NEED TO KNOW Learn about local governments and the services they provide. Examine ways in which citizens can become involved in government.

SIMULATION **Conducting the City's Business** Use your knowledge to debate the issues and make decisions at a fictionalized city council meeting.

Student Casebook

Use your Student Casebook to take notes on the section and to complete the simulation.

Local governments must balance preservation and progress. Easton, Maryland, officials limited large-scale construction (top) hoping to preserve the town's picturesque downtown (bottom).

Land Use in Easton, Maryland

Easton, Maryland, is a small town on the eastern shore of the Chesapeake Bay. In 2006 the population of Easton was about 14,000. When several companies announced plans to build large new stores in town, the local government stepped in before the town's character would be changed forever.

A Balancing Act

Local governments across the United States must routinely make decisions about acceptable uses for local land. Often these decisions are a difficult balancing act. Local governments must weigh interests of public safety and the environment, for example, against economic growth and new opportunities for residents. The case of Easton, Maryland, illustrates how local governments can manage land use and development issues.

Easton residents are proud of their town's historic buildings and residential character. In 1999 several national retailers proposed Easton as the location for three "big-box" stores—so called because of their enormous size and cookie-cutter shape. The three proposed stores would have over half a million square feet of shopping space. Some residents wondered how such development would affect their quality of life.

Residents had plenty of questions about the impact of big-box development. Would the roads be able to handle the extra traffic? Would the local police be able to maintain standards of public safety? How would the new stores affect the local environment and natural resources? What effect would the new stores have on smaller, locally owned businesses? Would the new stores change Easton's small-town charm? Would the stores provide needed jobs? Would the stores offer greater variety, lower prices, and added convenience for residents?

Local Government Weighs In

Easton's government played an important role in addressing residents' questions about bringing big-box stores to town. First, in September 1999 the town government ordered a moratorium, or waiting period, that temporarily prevented the start of construction of any big-box stores. The moratorium was intended to give town officials time to decide how best to proceed.

During the moratorium, Easton residents and government officials held public hearings to discuss the effects of large-scale development. The town also commissioned a study examining the same topic. In the end, it was determined that stores larger than 65,000 square feet would bring more harm than good to Easton.

Acting on the findings, in December 1999 the Easton Planning and Zoning Commission issued a recommendation to prohibit the construction of any retail store in excess of 65,000 square feet. A few months later, the Easton Town Council adopted Ordinance 399, which formally prohibited stores larger than 65,000 square feet within the town's borders.

Questions surrounding development occur throughout the United States. As in Easton, local governments play an important role in addressing these questions. Many local governments decide that economic growth and the other benefits of development outweigh the negative effects. Other local governments, like Easton's town government, take action to restrict development they believe will hurt their communities.

What Do You Think?

1. Why might government favor development? Why might government oppose development?

2. Who should have the final say about development: government, landowners, or voters? Explain your answer.

3. What factors should local governments consider when deciding land-use issues?

Local Government

While there is just one national government and only 50 state governments, there are about 88,000 local governments in the United States. Every American lives under the jurisdiction of one or more local governments. In this section you will learn about the types of local governments and how those governments function.

Key Terms

counties
parishes
boroughs
townships
municipalities
incorporation
mayor-council system
council-manager system
commission system
special districts
zoning laws
initiative
referendum
recall

Types of Local Governments

The U.S. Constitution does not mention local governments. For this reason, local governments are created by states. Local governments extend state power to a manageable level and come in many forms.

Counties and Townships All states are divided into **counties**. Except for parts of New England, counties are the most basic unit of local government. In Louisiana counties are called **parishes**, and in Alaska they are called **boroughs**. County government originated in colonial times as a way to govern areas in which people lived far away from one another.

Most of the nation's 3,000 or so counties are governed by an elected county board. A typical county board has five members serving four-year terms. The board members meet regularly to exercise the county's executive and legislative powers.

In some states, particularly in the Midwest and Middle Atlantic regions, counties are divided into **townships**. In these areas, township governments assist the county in the delivery of services to rural areas. There are about 16,500 townships in the United States.

Layers of Government

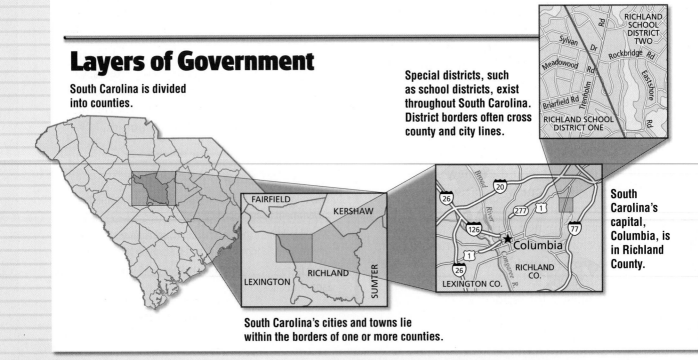

South Carolina is divided into counties.

Special districts, such as school districts, exist throughout South Carolina. District borders often cross county and city lines.

South Carolina's capital, Columbia, is in Richland County.

South Carolina's cities and towns lie within the borders of one or more counties.

Cities and Towns In addition to the country's counties and townships, people have formed **municipalities**—the nation's cities, towns, and villages. There are nearly 20,000 municipalities in the 50 states. A state gives its municipalities their legal authority through a process called **incorporation**.

Three main forms of municipal government are in use in the United States. In the **mayor-council system**, citizens elect a mayor to serve as the chief executive and a city council to serve as the local legislature. In a **council-manager system**, the city council appoints a city manager to be the chief executive. In this system, the mayor's role is to lead the city council. In a **commission system**, a group of elected commissioners lead city departments and set local policies.

In Connecticut, Rhode Island, and parts of Massachusetts, towns replace counties as the most basic unit of local government. In these areas, a unique system of government is used. Under this system, a board of selectmen of three to five members presides over town meetings and manages the town's affairs.

Special Districts The greatest number of local governments are special districts. **Special districts** provide a single service, such as water or transportation, to a defined area. The most familiar type of special-district government is the school district, responsible for running the public schools in an area. Of the 48,878 special-district governments in the United States, 13,522 are school districts.

Services of Local Government

Local governments provide a wide range of services to their residents. Counties typically provide the most essential services. These services include providing for public safety through police and fire departments; maintaining public roads; operating welfare programs, hospitals, and jails; keeping records of deeds, marriage licenses, and other legal documents; and supervising elections.

Municipal governments provide services in addition to those provided by county governments. These services include running libraries and recreation facilities and operating garbage collection and waste treatment facilities. As you read in the Case Study on Easton, Maryland, city and town governments are also involved in deciding land-use issues. Most cities and towns pass zoning laws to regulate land use. Through **zoning laws**, cities and towns can keep factories away from residential areas, for example.

Finances of Local Government

As with state and federal government, the costs of operating local governments can be quite high. Local governments, therefore, must raise large sums of money to function. To raise this money, local governments assess taxes and collect fees. As you read in Chapter 4, local governments also receive state and federal grants.

WEBQUEST

Local Legislative Process
Just as Congress creates laws at the national level and state legislatures create laws at the state level, county, city, and town councils create laws at the local level. Local laws are usually called ordinances. Visit **thinkcentral.com** to begin a Webquest examining how laws are created at the local level.

THINK central — Webquest

thinkcentral.com
KEYWORD: SGO SLG

REAL-WORLD EXAMPLE

Charters and Charter Amendment State governments grant powers to local governments through official documents called charters. Charters frequently spell out what services a local government is authorized to provide. In some states, if a service is not listed in the charter, a municipality must have its charter amended to authorize the service. Procedures for charter amendment vary by state. In Oklahoma, a charter amendment may be approved by voters in a local election. In other states, such as Virginia, a charter amendment must be approved by the state legislature.
Applying Information What is one advantage of each system of charter amendment?

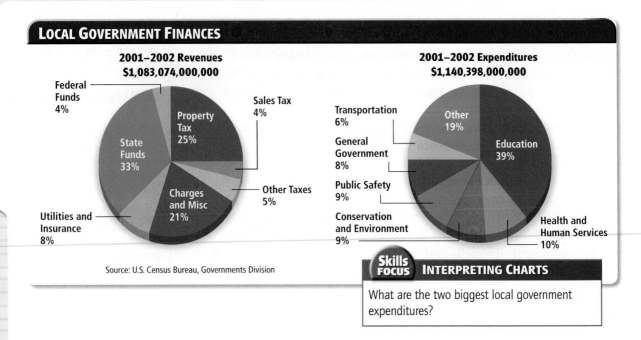

LOCAL GOVERNMENT FINANCES

2001–2002 Revenues
$1,083,074,000,000

- Federal Funds 4%
- Property Tax 25%
- Sales Tax 4%
- State Funds 33%
- Other Taxes 5%
- Charges and Misc 21%
- Utilities and Insurance 8%

Source: U.S. Census Bureau, Governments Division

2001–2002 Expenditures
$1,140,398,000,000

- Transportation 6%
- Other 19%
- General Government 8%
- Education 39%
- Public Safety 9%
- Conservation and Environment 9%
- Health and Human Services 10%

Skills FOCUS **INTERPRETING CHARTS**

What are the two biggest local government expenditures?

REAL-WORLD EXAMPLE

CASE STUDY LINK

Generating Local Revenue While large-scale development might permanently alter the character of a community, it can also contribute revenue to the local economy. One large national retailer reported collecting more than $12.8 billion in state and local sales taxes in 2007 and paying millions more in property taxes.
Applying Information How might large-scale development be beneficial to a local community?

Local governments collect property taxes annually. These taxes on land, homes, cars, and business property are the biggest source of local government revenue. Organizations such as schools and churches, however, typically do not pay property taxes. This means that, for example, towns built around universities may have trouble raising enough revenue to support their local government.

Other local revenue sources include sales and income taxes. These taxes are charged in addition to state and federal taxes. Some cities also tax corporations in their jurisdiction. Municipalities can also raise money through user fees. If citizens demand lower taxes, user fees are often increased to make up the difference. Finally, local governments may raise money by selling municipal bonds.

In addition to locally generated revenues, local governments receive funds from their state government and the federal government. These funds are called intergovernmental revenue. Included in this category are grants. Nearly half of local government revenues come from federal and state grants.

READING CHECK **Identifying Supporting Details** How do local governments pay for the services they provide?

Participating in State and Local Government

As you have read, your state and local governments provide many of the services you use every day. How those services are paid for and distributed is largely determined by your elected officials. To have a say in this process, you must become an active citizen.

Participatory Citizenship

Democracy works best when citizens monitor public policy and take action to make their interests known. This active involvement in government is called participatory citizenship. What are some ways Americans can participate in government? Citizens who are at least 18 years old may vote in elections and run for public office. Citizens of all ages may volunteer in their communities or testify before state or local boards.

Direct Democracy

Some forms of participatory citizenship even have the force of law. For example, the **initiative** process allows citizens to propose and enact state and local laws directly. The process begins when a certain number of voters signs a petition to support a bill. The bill is then passed to the state legislature or directly to the state's voters for approval. Initiatives are allowed in 24 states, including Ohio.

A **referendum** is a popular vote on a proposal that has already been considered by the legislature. Many state constitutional amendments must be approved by referendum, for example. Some form of referendum is allowed in every state except Alabama.

The **recall** process allows citizens to remove government officials from office before the end of a term. Like an initiative, the recall process begins when voters request a special recall election. Recalls of state officials are allowed in only 18 states, whereas recalls of local officials are allowed in at least 29 states.

READING CHECK **Identifying the Main Idea** How can U.S. citizens participate in state and local government?

Participatory Citizenship

Two forms of direct democracy—initiative and recall—begin with citizens collecting signatures on a petition. In the photo, Lorain, Ohio, residents sign a petition to recall a local government official.

Section 3 Assessment

THINK central **Online Quiz**

thinkcentral.com
KEYWORD: SGO SLG HP

Reviewing Ideas and Terms

1. **a. Identify** What are three sources of local government revenue?
    b. Contrast What are the main differences between a **mayor-council system**, a **council-manager system**, and a **commission system** of city government?
    c. Elaborate Why do you think there are so many **special districts** in the United States?

2. **a. Describe** What is participatory citizenship?
    b. Interpret Why do you think legislators sometimes send controversial bills for a **referendum**?
    c. Design How would you suggest that a person become involved in state and local government?

Critical Thinking

3. **Draw Conclusions** Do you think active citizen participation in state and local government is important? Why or why not?

CASE STUDY LINK You answered the following questions at the end of the Case Study. Now that you have completed Section 3, think about and answer the questions again. Then compare your answers with your earlier responses. Are your answers the same or different?

4. Why might government favor development? Why might government oppose development?

5. Who should have the final say about development: government, landowners, or voters? Explain your answer.

6. What factors should local governments consider when deciding land-use issues?

Conducting the City's Business

What will be decided at this week's city council meeting?

Student Casebook

Use your Student Casebook to complete the simulation.

City councils meet to make decisions that affect their local communities. These decisions range from the ordinary to the unusual. Use what you have learned and the information provided to complete a simulated city council meeting.

Roles

- Mayor
- Council members
- Football players
- North End resident
- Fire chief
- Citizen who regularly crosses Main and Elm streets
- Citizen against excessive stoplights
- President of ABC Gardeners
- Previous client of XYZ Gardeners
- West End resident
- Unemployed factory workers

❶ The Situation

It is 7:00 p.m. on Tuesday. Inside the Elmsville City Hall the city council has just called its weekly meeting to order. On tonight's agenda are five items. Elmsville citizens fill the seats and wait their turn to address the council on the agenda items that concern them.

❷ The Meeting

Elmsville has a mayor-council system of government. The mayor therefore runs the city council meeting, but in a nonvoting capacity. If there is a tie, the mayor casts the deciding vote. Follow this process to conduct the meeting:

- Use the agenda on the next page to conduct the meeting.
- The mayor calls the meeting to order and presents the first agenda item.
- Concerned citizens present speeches to the council and answer council members' questions. Citizens should prepare notes before the meeting. Refer to the data boxes for information about each agenda item.
- Council members debate the agenda item. The mayor presides over this debate.
- When debate ends, the mayor calls for a vote on the item. The council may approve, reject, or table the item for later consideration.
- The above process is repeated until all agenda items have been addressed and all votes have been taken.

❸ Debriefing

The *Elmsville Gazette* always runs an article recapping the events at each week's city council meeting. Write that article for tomorrow's edition.

Elmsville City Council Agenda

1. Proclamation congratulating the Elmsville High School football team on winning the state championship
2. A review of the plans for a new fire station in the North End
3. Funding for the installation of a new stoplight at the intersection of Main Street and Elm Street
4. Awarding the landscaping contract for Hampton Park
5. Permit for the construction of a factory in the western part of town

Elmsville High Football Team Proclamation

The Elmsville Eagles had never won a state football championship. This year, led by star quarterback Tommy Parker, they clinched the title, to the joy of the entire town.

West End Factory Construction

- The West End factory would create 300 jobs in Elmsville.
- The only available site for the factory is in the West End in what is now a mainly residential area.
- The factory would need to operate 24 hours a day.
- A neighboring city is trying to lure the factory to a location there.

Funding for Main Street Stoplight

- Eight accidents have taken place at the intersection of Main Street and Elm Street in the past year.
- One accident at the intersection resulted in a fatality.
- Stoplights cost $50,000 to install and $10,000 per year to maintain.
- Elmsville already has more stoplights than other towns its size.

Proposed North End Fire Station

- There have been three fires in Elmsville this year.
- Elmsville's only fire station is located in the southern part of town. Some citizens believe the response times to the North End are too long.
- Building a new fire station will cost at least $5 million.

Landscaping Contract for Hampton Park

- XYZ Gardeners would charge $500 per month to maintain Hampton Park.
- ABC Gardeners would charge $300 per month for the same services. However, ABC has a reputation for being unreliable.

Connecting Online

Visit thinkcentral.com for review and enrichment activities related to this chapter.

THINK central

KEYWORD: SGO SLG

Quiz and Review

GOV 101
Examine key concepts in this chapter.

ONLINE QUIZZES
Take a practice quiz for each section in this chapter.

Activities

eActivities
Complete Webquests and Internet research activities.

INTERACTIVE FEATURES
Explore interactive versions of maps and charts.

KEEP IT CURRENT
Link to current events in U.S. government.

Partners

American Bar Association Division for Public Education
Learn more about the law, your rights and responsibilities.

Center for Civic Education
Promoting an enlightened and responsible citizenry committed to democratic principles and actively engaged in the practice of democracy.

Online Textbook

ONLINE SIMULATIONS
Learn about U.S. government through simulations you can complete online.

STUDENT CASEBOOK
Take notes electronically on Interactive Chapters.

Click for More

Read more about key topics online.

Comprehension and Critical Thinking

SECTION 1 *(pp. 520–525)*

1. a. Review Key Terms For each term, write a sentence that explains its significance or meaning: fundamental law, statutory law.

b. Compare and Contrast What are some common features of state constitutions? In what ways do state constitutions differ from one another?

c. Rate In your opinion, is it better to amend a state constitution many times or to rewrite it completely? Explain your answer.

SECTION 2 *(pp. 528–539)*

2. a. Review Key Terms For each term, write a sentence that explains its significance or meaning: citizen legislatures, professional legislatures, line-item veto, Missouri Plan.

b. Compare How do the structure and functions of state governments resemble those of the national government?

c. Elaborate Why do you think citizen legislatures are becoming less common in the United States?

SECTION 3 *(pp. 542–547)*

3. a. Review Key Terms For each term, write a sentence that explains its significance or meaning: counties, municipalities, incorporation, mayor-council system, council-manager system, commission system, special districts, zoning laws, initiative, referendum, recall.

b. Explain What important functions do local governments serve in citizens' lives?

c. Develop In your opinion, what is the best way for citizens to actively participate in government? Explain your answer.

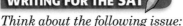
WRITING FOR THE SAT

Think about the following issue:

Selecting judges can be complicated. State judges are either elected by the voters, appointed by the governor, or a combination of the two. In about half of the states, under some form of the Missouri Plan, a commission creates a list of judicial candidates. The governor then appoints a judge from that list. One year later, the voters decide whether the judge should remain in office. In contrast, in the federal court system, the president appoints judges for life.

4. Assignment In your opinion, what is the best method for selecting judges to serve on a state court? Write a short essay in which you develop your position on this issue. Support your point of view with reasoning and facts.

REFERENCE SECTION

American Flag Etiquette

The American flag is a symbol of the nation. It is recognized instantly, whether as a big banner waving in the wind or a tiny emblem worn on a lapel. The flag is so important that it is a major theme of the national anthem, "The Star-Spangled Banner." One of the most popular names for the flag is the Stars and Stripes. It is also known as Old Glory.

The Meaning of the Flag

The American flag has 13 stripes—7 red and 6 white. In the upper-left corner of the flag is the union—50 white five-pointed stars against a blue background.

The 13 stripes stand for the original 13 American states, and the 50 stars represent the states of the nation today. According to the U.S. Department of State, the colors of the flag also are symbolic:

> Red stands for courage.
> White symbolizes purity.
> Blue is the color of vigilance, perseverance, and justice.

Displaying the Flag

It is customary not to display the American flag in bad weather. It is also customary for the flag to be displayed outdoors only from sunrise to sunset, except on certain occasions. In a few special places, however, the flag is always flown day and night. When flown at night, the flag should be illuminated.

Near a speaker's platform, the flag should occupy the place of honor at the speaker's right. When carried in a parade with other flags, the American flag should be on the marching right or in front at the center. When flying with the flags of the 50 states, the national flag must be at the center and at the highest point. In a group of national flags, all should be of equal size and all should be flown from staffs, or flagpoles, of equal height.

The flag should never touch the ground or the floor. It should not be marked with any insignia, pictures, or words. Nor should it be used in any disrespectful way—as an advertising decoration, for example. The flag should never be dipped to honor any person or thing.

Saluting the Flag

The United States, like other countries, has a flag code, or rules for displaying and honoring the flag. For example, all those present should stand at attention facing the flag and salute it when it is being raised or lowered or when it is carried past them in a parade or procession. A man wearing a hat should take it off and hold it with his right hand over his heart. All women and hatless men should stand with their right hands over their hearts to show their respect for the flag. The flag should also receive these honors during the playing of the national anthem and the reciting of the Pledge of Allegiance.

The Pledge of Allegiance

The Pledge of Allegiance was written in 1892 by Massachusetts magazine (*Youth's Companion*) editor Francis Bellamy. (Congress added the words "under God" in 1954.)

> *I pledge allegiance to the flag of the United States of America and to the Republic for which it stands, one nation under God, indivisible, with liberty and justice for all.*

Civilians should say the Pledge of Allegiance with their right hands placed over their hearts. People in the armed forces give the military salute. By saying the Pledge of Allegiance, we promise loyalty ("pledge allegiance") to the United States and its ideals.

ECONOMICS HANDBOOK

Learn the basic concepts of economics, how the laws of demand and supply operate to set prices, the different types of business organizations, the role of government in the economy, and why nations engage in international trade.

Overview
The Constitution and the U.S. Market Economy

The U.S. economy is mostly a market economy. A **market economy** is one in which the government intervenes relatively little in economic decisions about what, how, and for whom goods and services are produced and which factors of production are owned by individuals. The U.S. Constitution supports our market economy by promoting and regulating trade, controlling the money supply, protecting the right to enter into contracts, and protecting private property rights.

Economists list six characteristics of a market economy. These characteristics are

- **Private property** Factors of production (land, labor, and capital) and the goods and services produced in the economy are largely owned by private individuals and institutions rather than the government.

- **Freedom to choose** Private individuals have the freedom to open any business—and to produce and sell any goods or services—they choose. Individuals are free to work where they want to and buy the goods and services they want.

- **Self-interest** Business owners are often motivated by self-interest to make the most profit they can. Likewise, self-interest typically motivates workers to choose their employment and earn the highest wages or salary they can and motivates consumers to get the most products for their money.

- **Competition** Competition is economic rivalry among sellers of the same or similar products. It encourages producers to improve existing products—or develop new ones—to attract customers and profits.

- **System of markets and prices** Markets are where buyers and sellers of goods and services meet. Prices—the amount buyers pay and sellers receive—for goods and services are set in the marketplace by the forces of demand and supply.

- **Limited government** In a competitive market economy, the government has little reason to intervene. The U.S. government, however, does provide public goods, such as national defense; a definition of and protection for property rights; and a legal system in which individuals can enforce their property rights.

MARKET ECONOMY PROVISIONS IN THE U.S. CONSTITUTION

Characteristic	Art. I, Sec. 8	Art. I, Sec. 9	Art. I, Sec. 10	4th Amend.	5th Amend.	9th Amend.	10th Amend.	14th Amend.
Private property	✓	✓	✓	✓	✓			✓
Freedom to choose	✓	✓	✓					
Self-interest	✓							
Competition	✓							
System of markets and prices	✓							
Limited government		✓	✓	✓	✓	✓	✓	✓

The study of the choices that people make to satisfy their needs and wants is called **economics**. A person who studies these economic choices is called an **economist**. The first step to understanding economics and the economic choices you make is to develop an economic way of thinking.

Making Economic Decisions

How does an economist view the world? Economists pay attention to decisions—who makes decisions and how decisions are made.

Who Makes Decisions? In economic terms, there are two large groups of economic decision makers. The people who decide to buy things are called **consumers**. The people who make the things that satisfy consumers' needs and wants are called **producers**. In the U.S. market economy, consumers choose what to buy and producers choose what to provide and how to provide it. This network of decisions is the basis of all economic systems.

How Are Decisions Made? Economic choices are based on needs and wants, which reflect desires for certain goods and services. Economists classify as **needs** those goods and services that are necessary for survival, such as food, clothing, and shelter. **Wants** are those goods and services that people consume beyond what is necessary for survival—such as CDs, plasma TVs, and RSS feeds.

Economic decisions involve goods and services. **Goods** are physical objects that can be purchased. Pizzas, cars, and cell phones are examples of goods. **Services** are actions or activities done for others for a fee. Lawyers, plumbers, nurses, and insurance agents perform services. The term *product* often refers to both goods and services.

Economic Resources

An economist sees things, such as trees, factories, assembly robots, and people as economic resources. A resource is anything that people use to fulfill their needs or wants.

Resources used to produce goods and services are called **factors of production**. Economists group factors into four categories: land, labor, capital, and entrepreneurship.

- **Land, or Natural Resources** Natural resources are found in or on the earth or in the earth's atmosphere. Examples of natural resources are farmland, rivers, oil fields, coal mines, sunlight, wind, and rain. A natural resource is considered a factor of production only when it is scarce and some payment is necessary for its use.

- **Labor, or Human Resources** Labor consists of any human effort or contribution—whether physical or mental—exerted in the production process. Today labor may also be referred to as human capital or—especially in the field of information technology (IT)—as intellectual capital. Assembly-line workers, store clerks, IT technicians, professional athletes, physicians, video game designers, and nurses all are human capital.

- **Capital, or Capital Resources** The manufactured materials used to make goods and provide services are called capital resources. Capital includes capital goods and the money used to purchase capital goods. **Capital goods** are the buildings, structures, machinery, and tools used in the production process. Department stores, factories, dams, port facilities, computers, hammers, and surgical scalpels are examples of capital goods. Capital goods are used to make consumer goods. **Consumer goods** are the finished goods and services that people buy.

Some products can be either capital goods or consumer goods, depending on how they are used. A street bike bought for personal use is a consumer good. The same bicycle is a capital good, however, when a New York City messenger service purchases it for use in making deliveries.

- **Entrepreneurship** Finally, the management and organizational skills involved in raising capital to start a new business or introduce a new product are called **entrepreneurship**. Entrepreneurs—people who display entrepreneurship—put together combinations of other factors of production to create something of value. Entrepreneurs are also risk takers—they risk economic failure in return for the possibility of financial gain.

Technology Technology is not a factor of production. **Technology** is using knowledge, tools, techniques, processes, and methods to make existing products more efficiently or to create new products. For example, computer technology has dramatically changed how work—and how much work—is done. Around the world, in today's manufacturing plants, computers manage many production processes by controlling robots on assembly lines.

Each producer of goods and services—in trying to meet a need or a want—strives to find the combination of land, labor, capital, entrepreneurship, and technology that will both satisfy consumers and provide a satisfactory economic return. Occasionally, however, a producer finds that a resource is not available or has become scarce.

Economic Scarcity

All resources are limited. People's wants, however, are unlimited. This combination of limited resources and unlimited wants results in a condition known as **scarcity**. Scarcity is the most basic problem of economics because it forces people to make decisions about how to use resources effectively.

In economics, the idea of scarcity has two parts. First, a particular resource may be considered scarce if society's wants for that resource are greater than the amount of the resource available. Second, a resource may be considered scarce if it has more than one valuable use to society.

Many factors contribute to scarcity. Low amounts of rainfall may lead to poor harvests and therefore to a scarcity of fruits and vegetables at grocery stores. Today, for example, fresh water is a scarce resource in some places, while Web developers are a scarce resource in other places.

Identifying Economic Questions

Scarcity requires people to make decisions. People must decide how to **allocate**, or distribute, resources to satisfy the greatest number of needs and wants. To allocate resources effectively, an economic system or a society must address three basic questions:

● what to produce

● how to produce

● for whom to produce

Every society, large or small, must answer these questions. How a society answers them helps determine the best allocation of resources to meet that society's needs and wants.

Productivity

When a society has answered the economic questions, it tries to ensure that its scarce resources are used as effectively as possible. To measure if resources are being used wisely, people study productivity. **Productivity** is the level of output that results from a given level of input. Productivity measures efficiency, or using the smallest amount of resources in producing the greatest amount of output. For example, BigBike Motorcycles may use assembly lines using a **division of labor**, where each worker assembles, over and over, only one or a few parts of each bike. Division of labor allows for **specialization**, under which workers gain expertise and efficiency in their assigned tasks. With this system, BigBike employs 600 people who can assemble 200 motorcycles per day. BigBike's productivity, at 200 motorcycles per day, is about 1 new motorcycle every 4 minutes.

BigBike's president knows that to be competitive, the company must be more productive and more efficient. One way to increase productivity might be to have small groups of workers building motorcycles as a team. Each team would build one bike from start to finish along the assembly line. BigBike might find that teams could produce 400 motorcycles a day with the same 600 employees. Using the team approach, BigBike can build one motorcycle every 2 minutes!

Many of today's jobs have been made more efficient through automation, which is the use of computers and machines to replace workers. Machines work faster and longer—therefore at a lower cost per unit—than a person can.

The goal of a business is to produce the greatest amount of its goods or services at the lowest possible **cost of production**. The cost of production is the total cost of the materials, labor, and other costs related the production of that good or service. The producer asks, "What mix of resources will give me the most outputs—products—with the fewest inputs? How do I know which resources to choose and which ones not to use?" These questions may be answered by analyzing questions of trade-offs and opportunity costs.

Trade-offs and Opportunity Costs

Choosing among alternative uses for available resources forces people to make choices. If a resource is used to produce one good or service, that same resource cannot be used to produce or consume some other good or service. One resource is sacrificed for another. In economic terms this sacrifice is called a **trade-off**. The cost of this trade-off—the value of the next best alternative given up to obtain that item—is called the **opportunity cost**.

You face trade-offs and opportunity costs every day. You may, for example, want to upgrade your cell phone and want to buy some new clothes. Both purchases cost the same. Unfortunately, you have only enough money at the moment to make one purchase. You must make a trade-off—an economic choice—because you cannot afford to buy both. If you spend money on clothes, your alternative choice—a new phone—is the opportunity cost of buying new clothes.

Your phone-or-clothes choice is an example of a simple, two-item choice. Most choices, however, involve several trade-offs. When resources are used to build an office building, the trade-off is not between the building and one other use of the resources. All of the workers, equipment, and financial input used to build the building could be used to build several combinations of homes, condominiums, schools, and shopping centers. These same factors of production might also be used in ways other than construction. For example, investors might decide to put their money into real estate development. The land might be used as a city park instead of a restaurant. There may be many trade-offs within a set of choices, but only one of these—the next best choice—is considered the opportunity cost.

Value

Consumers and producers determine the worth of items in an exchange by assigning goods and services a **value** that can be expressed as an amount of money, or a price. The value of a product may be determined by its scarcity. Suppose, for example, that you collect rare jazz records. The value of your music collection is determined by how much someone else will pay you for your records.

Value is also determined by a product's **utility**, or usefulness to a person. Utility can be more difficult to determine than scarcity, because one person may find a product useful while another finds the product to be of no use. Do diamonds and water have utility? Yes, both are useful. Water is necessary to life, and diamonds are both a popular gemstone and an important tool in some industries. Water has utility but is not, for most people, scarce. Diamonds have both utility and scarcity.

The combination of scarcity and utility is the basis for determining value. Once values are determined, producers and consumers can decide the relative worth of the goods and services in an exchange.

Interdependence

To have successful exchange, each party must be able to provide goods and services that the other wants but does not have. An exchange depends on unmet needs and wants.

Can you, by yourself, produce everything you need? Are you self-sufficient? People, and societies or nations, are **self-sufficient** when they can fulfill all their needs without outside assistance. True self-sufficiency is rare, however, because resources are limited and self-sufficiency requires a tremendous supply of tools, equipment, and raw materials. In addition, self-sufficiency demands extensive skills and knowledge in a variety of fields.

As a result, people tend to specialize in certain areas of production and rely on others for the additional goods and services they need. This reliance between economic actors is called **interdependence**. Interdependence means that events or developments in one region of the world or part of the economy influence events or developments in other regions or sectors. Interdependence obviously offers benefits, but it also poses the threat of economic vulnerability. For example, if the supply of an important resource, such as imported oil, is cut, the economic consequences to the U.S. economy could be devastating.

Assessment

1. **Describe** Compile a list of your needs and wants and prioritize the items on your list. Discuss your list with classmates and defend your decisions if necessary.

2. **Explain** Explain your opportunity costs when choosing between needs and wants on your list, including how you assigned a value to each item.

Section 2
The Laws of Demand and Supply

The free exchange of goods and services between buyers and sellers is called the **market**. In a market economy, consumers—individually and all together—influence what goods and services are produced and the prices for which those goods and services are sold.

As a consumer, your role in the marketplace is governed by basic economic concepts, such as demand and supply. In this section, you will learn about demand and supply, how the laws of demand and supply interact in the marketplace, and what forces shape the demand for and supply of products.

Voluntary Exchange

The principle of voluntary exchange is what drives a market economy. A **voluntary exchange** is the unconditional and mutually beneficial transfer of goods or services between buyer and seller. For the exchange to work, the buyer must have an idea of how much to pay—and the seller must have an idea of how much to charge—for the product. When both parties are satisfied with the terms of the transaction, the exchange will take place and both parties will feel they are better off than they were before the exchange.

Demand

In economic terms, the concept of **demand** means the total amount of a good or service consumers are willing and able to buy at *all possible prices* at a given time. Demand is different from the **quantity demanded**, which is the amount of a good or service that consumers are willing and able to buy at any *particular price* at a given time. The time period must be specific and limited because market circumstances can change over time and affect demand for a product.

Law of Demand

In a free-enterprise system, price is the key variable affecting demand. Specifically, there is an inverse relationship between price and the quantity demanded. This relationship is described by the **law of demand**, which states that an increase in a good's price causes a decrease in the quantity demanded and that a decrease in price causes an increase in the

quantity demanded. Three other factors can also influence demand. These factors are

- **Income Effect** The amount of money, or income, that people have available to spend on goods and services is referred to as their **purchasing power**. Any increase or decrease in consumers' purchasing power caused by a change in price is called the income effect.

- **Substitution Effect** The substitution effect—the tendency of consumers to substitute a similar, lower-priced product for a relatively more expensive product—helps explain the relationship between price and the quantity demanded.

- **Diminishing Marginal Utility** In economic terms, utility is the usefulness of a product, or the amount of satisfaction that an individual receives from consuming a product. With diminishing marginal utility, as more units of a product are consumed, the satisfaction received from consuming each additional unit declines. At some point, consumers cannot use any more of a product. Even if a good or service is free, people will not consume all the units produced—they just do not want any more. This limit to a product's utility is a limit to consumers' demand.

Demand Schedules

One way to show the relationship between the price of a product and the quantity that consumers demand is a demand schedule, such as the one below. Demand schedules list the quantity of goods that consumers are willing and able to buy at a series of possible prices.

DEMAND SCHEDULE

Price ($)	Quantity Demanded
500	110
400	160
300	260
200	380
100	520

SIMPLE DEMAND CURVE

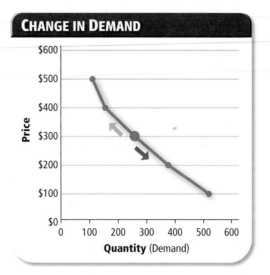

CHANGE IN DEMAND

Demand Curves

A simple demand curve is a graphic way to show the relationship between the price of a good or service and the quantity of the good or service demanded by consumers. A demand curve plots on a graph the information from a demand schedule. Any demand schedule can be converted into a demand curve.

Look at the demand curve on this page. Each point on the curve represents a specific combination of quantity demanded (on the *x* axis) and price (on the *y* axis). The curve slopes downward because consumers will buy more goods and services at lower prices than they will at higher prices.

Changes in Demand

As you have learned, a demand curve illustrates a product's market during a specific period of time. The demand curve is a snapshot of a market, such as the motorcycle market for which BigBike makes its products. Because the snapshot is taken at one point in time, the only factor causing a change in demand for motorcycles is the one shown in the graph above: price. At the time this snapshot of the motorcycle market was taken, nothing but a change in price could cause a change in the quantity of motorcycles demanded.

Shifts in the Demand Curve

Markets do not stand still, so new snapshots of demand must be taken periodically. Indeed, the passage of time allows factors other than price—called determinants of demand—to

influence demand significantly. In economic terms, these factors can shift the entire demand curve of a product, such as the one shown on the next page, instead of simply causing movement along the demand curve. Determinants of demand include:

- **Consumer Tastes and Preferences** Changes in consumer preferences or tastes, such as people buying touring motorcycles instead of automobiles, can have an impact on demand for products.

- **Market Size** Changes in the size of a market tend to shift demand—whether the change is caused by an increase in the population or a change in demographics, such as an increase in older buyers.

- **Income** In general, when income increases, people have more money to spend. Increased spending results in a greater demand for goods and services.

- **Prices of Substitute Goods** Goods that can be purchased to replace similar goods when prices rise are called substitute goods. Margarine is an example of a substitute good. When the price of butter increases, some people buy less butter and use margarine instead.

- **Prices of Complementary Goods** Complementary goods are goods that are used with other goods, such as paintbrushes with paint. As the price of a gallon of paint increases, the quantity of paint demanded decreases—and so does the quantity of paintbrushes demanded.

● **Consumer Expectations** Consumers sometimes make purchases in anticipation of having more money from a new job or a salary increase. Similarly, consumers may delay purchases if they think their income will decline for some reason.

CHANGE IN QUANTITY DEMANDED

Keep in mind that change in any one of these determinants can cause a change in the overall demand of a good or a service.

Elasticity of Demand How much does the quantity demanded decrease when a product's price increases, or increase when the price drops? Businesspeople answer these questions by determining the elasticity of demand for their products. **Elasticity of demand** is the degree to which changes in a product's price affect the quantity demanded of the product by consumers.

Demand for a product can be elastic or inelastic. **Elastic demand** exists when a small change in a good's price causes a major, *opposite* change in the quantity demanded. Factors that affect a good's elasticity include that the product is not a necessity, that there are readily available substitutes for the product, and that the product's cost represents a large portion of consumers' income.

Inelastic demand for a product is when a change in a good's price has little impact on the quantity demanded. Factors contributing to inelastic demand include that the product is a necessity, there are few or no good substitutes for the product, or the product's cost represents a small portion of consumers' income.

Supply

In economic terms, supply is more than just the available selection of a good or service. **Supply** is the quantity of goods and services that producers offer at various possible prices during a given time period. During the winter months, for example, jacket manufacturers offer a certain quantity of jackets at each price. The **quantity supplied** is the amount of a good or service that a producer is willing to sell at each *particular* price.

Law of Supply

As with demand, price is a key factor affecting the quantity supplied in a free-market system. The quantity supplied is directly related to the prices that producers can charge for their products. This relationship is described by the law of supply. The **law of supply** states that producers supply more goods and services when they can sell them at higher prices and they supply fewer goods and services when they must sell them at lower prices.

Profit Motive After producers have paid all of their costs, the amount of money remaining from the sale of its product is called **profit**. A business makes a profit when its revenues—the money received from the sale of its goods—are greater than its costs of production. These costs include employee wages and salaries, rent, interest on loans, and bills for electricity, raw materials, and any other goods and services used to manufacture a product. To make a profit, producers must provide products that consumers want at prices consumers are willing and able to pay.

Profit and Markets The profit motive has a far-reaching effect in free-enterprise markets. It not only governs how individual companies make decisions but it also helps direct the use of resources in the entire market.

For example, if a company finds that demand is low for its new product, a T-shirt with a built-in sound-sensitive graphic display, it may lower the price of the shirt to attract more buyers. If, even after lowering the price of the shirt, the company still barely makes enough money to pay its costs of production, it may decide to decrease—or end—production of the sound-activated T-shirts.

At the same time, the low sales and profits from these T-shirts signal to other makers that consumer demand in the market for sound-sensitive T-shirts is low and not profitable.

SIMPLE SUPPLY CURVE

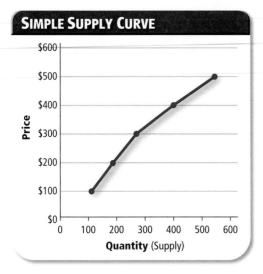

CHANGE IN SUPPLY

Other manufacturers may reduce production of such shirts and use their resources to make more-profitable products. The low demand also discourages new manufacturers from entering the market because they cannot expect to make good profits. In this way, profits help direct the use of resources.

Supply Schedules

As with demand, the tool that shows the relationship between the price of a good or service and the quantity that producers will supply is a supply schedule, such as the one shown below. This schedule lists each quantity of a product that producers are willing to supply at various market prices.

SUPPLY SCHEDULE

Price ($)	Quantity Supplied
100	110
200	190
300	280
400	400
500	540

Supply Curves

Supply curves, similar to demand curves, show the relationship between the price of a good or service and the quantity of the product

supplied. A supply curve, such as the one shown above, plots on a graph the information from a supply schedule.

Each point plotted on the graph represents a specific combination of price and quantity supplied. The curve slopes upward, reflecting the greater quantity that producers will supply at higher prices. Note that the upward-sloping supply curve is the opposite of the downward-sloping demand curve.

Changes in Supply

Supply curves show a product's market for a specific period of time. Study the Change in Supply curve, above, and note that price is the only factor affecting the quantity supplied.

Producers must consider their costs of production when deciding how much of a good or service to supply to the market. Costs of production are described as fixed, variable, total, and marginal costs.

- **Fixed Costs** Production costs that do not change as the level of output changes are called fixed costs. Fixed costs include salaries, rent, property insurance premiums, interest on loans, and local and state property taxes. Fixed costs also include depreciation, or the reduction in value because of wear and tear, on machines and other capital goods.

- **Variable Costs** Unlike fixed costs, variable costs do change as the level of output changes. Variable costs include payments for raw materials and the wages of hourly or contract workers.

Total Costs The sum of fixed and variable production costs is a company's total costs. At zero output a firm's total costs are equal to its fixed costs. As soon as production begins, however, so do variable costs. This in turn raises the company's total costs. Labor costs—wages and benefits—are a part of variable costs. Producers often have no control over raw material costs, so they may lower their variable costs—and their total costs—by reducing wages and other labor costs.

Marginal Costs To make production decisions, producers also need to know their marginal costs. **Marginal costs** are the additional variable costs of producing one more unit of output. Marginal costs allow the business to determine the profitability of increasing or decreasing production by a few units.

Supply Shifts

Supply, like demand, is affected over time by factors other than price. In economic terms, these factors—called determinants of supply—can shift the entire supply curve of a product, such as shown in the graph below, instead of simply changing the quantity supplied along the supply curve. A shift in the supply curve means that a different quantity of motorcycles is supplied at *each and every* price. The determinants of supply include the following:

Prices of Resources One factor that can shift supply is a change in the price of resources. Any change in the price of a resource directly affects a business's production costs.

CHANGE IN QUANTITY SUPPLIED

Government Actions The three main government actions that affect supply are taxes, subsidies, and regulation.

Technology New technology usually makes production more efficient, which lowers the costs of production.

Competition Competition—a larger number of suppliers—tends to *increase* supply, while a lack of competition tends to *decrease* supply. Remember that suppliers can leave as well as enter a market, which tends to decrease supply.

Prices of Related Goods The supply for one good often is connected to the supply for related goods. This means that changes in a product's price can affect the supply of the product's related goods. Suppose a farmer can grow the related goods wheat, corn, soybeans, and hay profitably. As you may know, ethanol is often made from corn. As demand for corn increases, so does its price. Farmers can make more money growing corn, so the supply of corn will increase—and the supply of the related goods may decrease.

Producer Expectations Suppliers sometimes make current production decisions based on their projected future income. The expectations of future changes in price can affect how much of their product they supply to the market now.

A change in any one of these determinants can cause a change in the overall supply of a good or a service. Any change in the overall supply of—or demand for—a good or service is likely to be reflected in the price you, as a consumer, pay for that good or service.

Elasticity of Supply Similar to elasticity of demand, **elasticity of supply** is the degree to which changes in price affect the quantity supplied. **Elastic supply** exists when a small change in a good's price causes a major change in supply. **Inelastic supply** exists when a change in a good's price has little impact on the quantity supplied.

Assessment

1. **Explain** What is the difference between demand and quantity demanded? Between supply and quantity supplied?

2. **Elaborate** Explain how profits are related to the laws of demand and supply.

Consumers and producers each act in their own best interest. As a consumer, for example, you usually want to buy pizza at low prices—you want to get the most pizza for your money. Pizza producers, meanwhile, supply more pizza when they can receive the highest price for it and make a good profit.

Economic self-interest thus leads consumers and producers to have different goals when they enter the marketplace. How do consumers and producers communicate with each other to decide on a level of production that satisfies a consumer's desire for affordable pizza and the producers' desire to make a profit? The answer is the price system.

The Price System

Prices are the way in which producers tell consumers how much it costs to make and distribute a product. The price of a pizza tells you, the consumer, "If you want this amount of pizza, you have to pay this price." If you buy the pizza, your message to producers is "Yes, I want this much pizza at this price." If you do not buy pizza, your response is "No, I do not want this much pizza at this price."

When consumers buy a product at the established price, producers may be satisfied and maintain current production levels and prices. On the other hand, producers may try to increase their profits by raising pizza prices. If consumers do not accept the price increase, they will buy fewer pizzas.

Similarly, if consumers choose not to buy a product at the established price, producers must determine whether they can reduce their prices and still make a profit. If they can, producers tell consumers—by reducing prices—that the product is more attractive.

Benefits of the Price System

Using the price system as a form of communication between producers and consumers has several benefits. It provides

- information
- incentives
- choice
- efficiency
- flexibility

Information Producers and consumers can gather information through the price system. For example, prices of resources tell producers how much they must pay to make their products. If producers did not have this information, businesses would make random decisions about what to produce because they would have no idea whether one product would be more profitable than another.

At the same time, consumers—who want to make informed buying decisions—can gather information through the price system. Consumers need to know the prices of goods. Without prices, consumers would have no way of knowing how the cost of a sweater compares with the price of a jacket. Prices inform consumers of the relative worth of the goods and services they purchase.

Incentives The price system also provides producers and consumers with incentives to participate in the market. High prices, when combined with low costs, generally encourage producers to supply more goods and services. This reflects the law of supply—that high prices encourage increases in the quantity supplied while low prices encourage reductions in the quantity supplied.

Low prices, meanwhile, give consumers an incentive to buy more goods and services. This reflects the law of demand, which states that high prices encourage reductions in the quantity demanded while low prices encourage increases in the quantity demanded. If there were no price incentives, producers and consumers would have an extremely difficult time exchanging goods and services.

Choice By encouraging participation in markets, the price system also increases the choices available in those markets. The greater the incentive to supply products to the marketplace, the greater the choice of products supplied. In competing with each other, manufacturers create hundreds of different products, trying to match consumer preferences and generate the most profit. As a result, consumers can select from a wide range of goods and services in the marketplace.

Efficiency The price system supports efficiency in two ways. First, it provides for the appropriate allocation of resources. Prices tell producers what consumers want to buy.

High prices encourage producers to use resources to make what consumers want. Low prices lead producers to stop using resources to make goods that consumers do not want. The pricing system tells producers how best to use their resources—natural, human, and capital—to meet consumer demand.

Second, the price system encourages efficiency by delivering information to producers and consumers quickly. Prices immediately signal the value of a good in relation to other goods. Producers can easily compare the prices of resources, and consumers can do the same for goods and services. As a result, both groups can make decisions quickly and efficiently.

Flexibility One of the price system's greatest strengths is its ability to deal with change. The supply and demand of goods changes almost constantly. A hit movie or music video can increase consumer demand for a particular hair or clothing style overnight. Sudden events such as floods, ice storms, and work stoppages can reduce the supply of crops or manufactured goods. The price system accommodates and reflects these changes quickly.

Limitations of the Price System

In general, the price system is effective in coordinating the decisions of consumers and producers in a free-market economy. The system does have some limitations: The market does not account for the costs of externalities or public goods, and, in some circumstances, the price system may become unstable.

Externalities The production of goods sometimes results in side effects, called externalities, for people not directly connected with the production or consumption of the goods. An **externality** is an effect that an economic activity has on people and businesses that are neither producers nor consumers of the good or service being produced. Externalities can be negative or positive.

Public Goods The price system also fails to assign to all consumers the cost of public goods. A **public good** is any good or service that is consumed by all members of a group, regardless of who has actually paid for it. Public goods include national defense, the judicial system, highways, and education. If the government did not require people to pay

for these goods and services through taxes, some people who enjoyed the benefit of these public goods would not pay for them.

Instability Although the price system's ability to adapt to change is generally considered a benefit, this flexibility can make the system somewhat unstable. A drastic drop in prices might cause some companies to go out of business. A large price increase in a necessity may make it so expensive that most people cannot afford it. Even less dramatic price swings can prevent the market from functioning smoothly because producers and consumers cannot rely on stable prices when making business or purchasing decisions.

Determining Prices

If the price system is a type of unspoken language, how can you see its influence on the decisions of producers and consumers? You can see the price system at work most clearly in *how* it determines the quantities and prices of goods and services in the marketplace.

Equilibrium The price system helps producers and consumers reach a situation called market equilibrium. **Market equilibrium** occurs when the quantity supplied and the quantity demanded for a product are equal at a given price. At the market equilibrium point the needs of both producers and consumers are satisfied and the forces of supply and demand are in balance.

Study the Market Equilibrium graph on the next page. The point at which the two curves intersect is the market equilibrium. How does the price system actually steer producers and consumers toward the equilibrium point? The process does not take place instantly. In fact, a certain amount of trial and error may be necessary, as producers change prices and quantities of the goods and services supplied. This adjustment process works to eliminate surpluses and shortages—situations in which the forces of supply and demand are not in balance.

Surpluses A **surplus** exists when the quantity supplied exceeds the quantity demanded at a specific price. A surplus tells a producer that it is charging too much for its product. After re-examining costs, a business may decide it can lower its price and still make a profit. The lower price increases the quantity demanded and decreases the quantity supplied,

MARKET EQUILIBRIUM

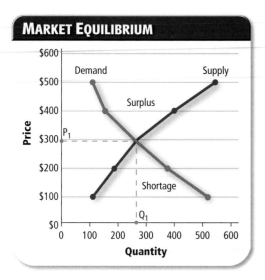

SETTING A NEW EQUILIBRIUM

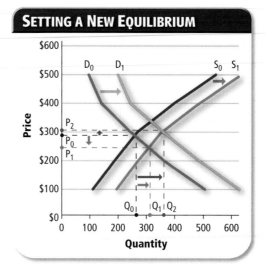

eliminating the surplus and steering the market toward the equilibrium point.

Shortages A **shortage** exists when the quantity demanded exceeds the quantity supplied at a specific price. A shortage tells a producer that it is charging too little for its goods or services. All other things being equal, the producer will usually raise its price. The higher price decreases the quantity demanded and increases the quantity supplied, eliminating the shortage and steering the market back toward equilibrium.

Remember, while each individual producer considers its own circumstances, the same process of price determination is taking place in every other producer in the marketplace. Over time, the price system steers all producers and consumers toward market equilibrium.

Shifts in Equilibrium

As you learned in Section 2, a variety of factors can shift a product's entire demand or supply curve. Changes in consumer tastes and preferences, market size, income, prices of related goods, and consumer expectations can all shift demand. Similarly, changes in government actions, technology, competition, producer expectations, and the prices of resources and related goods can all shift supply. When *either* the demand or the supply curve shifts, the equilibrium point also shifts.

For an illustration, study the Setting a New Equilibrium graph above. The market equilibrium for cell phones, for example, is set by curves D_0 and S_0 at point Q_0 and P_0. Suppose that new technology allows BigTalk

Phones to make a less expensive cell phone. This new product shifts the supply curve from S_0 to S_1. The new market equilibrium is at the intersection of D_0 and S_1, or at point Q_1 and P_1. Note that price P_1 is lower than price P_0.

BigTalk's advertising would likely increase the consumer demand for its new phones. Consumers would buy more BigTalk phones at every possible price, so the demand curve also shifts to the right from D_0 to D_1.

What happens to the market equilibrium point? It moves from Q_0 and P_0 to point Q_2 and P_2, at the new intersection of the demand and supply curves. The new equilibrium price is about $305, and the new equilibrium quantity is about 370 units of phones. The quantity of phones demanded and the quantity supplied are equal at a new equilibrium price.

Setting Prices

The price system has a number of limitations. It does not accurately determine who should pay the costs of externalities like pollution. Nor does it accurately distribute the costs and benefits of public goods like national defense. The system's occasional instability can also complicate efforts of producers and consumers to predict prices and plan for the future.

To address these limitations, governments sometimes intervene in the marketplace. Governments assign the costs of public goods by having citizens pay for them through taxes. Similarly, governments can assign the costs of externalities—for example, by making companies reduce the amount of pollution they emit and pay for any damage it causes.

To keep the market functioning smoothly, governments sometimes set prices—through price ceilings and price floors—to protect the market from dramatic price swings. Governments may also ration goods.

Price ceilings A **price ceiling** is a government regulation that establishes a maximum price for a particular good. Producers cannot charge prices above this set level. Rent controls—a government limit on the amount a landlord can charge to rent an apartment—are an example of price ceilings.

Price floors Price floors are more common than price ceilings. A **price floor** is a government regulation that establishes a minimum level for prices. Base prices for agricultural crops and the minimum wage are examples of price floors.

Consequences of Setting Prices Most economists oppose using price ceilings and price floors. Interfering in the normal market interaction between demand and supply can cause unintended imbalances and may prevent markets from reaching equilibrium. Price ceilings can result in shortages, while price floors may result in surpluses.

Rationing

Sometimes the supply of a good is so low that a government rations the good. **Rationing** is a system in which a government or other institution decides how to distribute a product. Under a rationing system, a good is distributed on the basis of policy decisions rather than on the market system of supply and demand.

Rationing Is Rare Rationing rarely occurs in a free-enterprise system. In the United States, rationing has occurred mainly during wars and other crises. During World War II, for example, the U.S. government rationed goods such as tires, gasoline, meat, butter, and coffee. To coordinate its rationing efforts, the government distributed coupon books that allowed citizens to buy specific amounts of rationed goods.

Consequences of Rationing Opponents of rationing argue that it is unwise economic policy because a rationing system is unfair, is expensive, and creates black markets. Rationing is unfair because it distributes goods and services unfairly by favoring one person or group over another.

Another criticism of rationing is that it is costly to put into effect. A government must not only determine who is to receive rationed goods and in what amounts but also must print and distribute ration coupons. In addition, the government must have a way to enforce the rationing program to ensure that people do not receive more rationed goods than they should. These tasks can use significant amounts of human resources and financial capital.

The final problem with rationing is that it fosters black markets. In a black market, goods are exchanged at prices that are higher than officially established prices. Although rationing programs succeed in distributing goods among consumers, they do not completely satisfy consumer demand. These people's demand for tickets is not satisfied.

Assessment

1. **Explain** How does the market interaction of demand and supply set prices?

2. **Predict** Copy the following table showing how increases (I) and decreases (D) in demand and supply affect equilibrium. Fill in the remaining answers. Use a question mark if the change cannot be predicted.

Demand	Supply	Equilibrium Price	Equilibrium Quantity
I		I	I
D			
	I	D	I
	D		
I	I	?	I
D	D		
I	D		
D	I		

3. **Elaborate** How is ticket scalping a type of black market?

Business and Business Organizations

The U.S. free-enterprise system allows potential business owners to select the type of organization that best suits their needs. The most common forms of business organizations in the United States are sole proprietorships, partnerships, and corporations.

Sole Proprietorships

Sole proprietorships are the most common and simplest form of business organization. A **sole proprietorship** is a business owned and managed by one person. This type of business has advantages and disadvantages.

Advantages A sole proprietor makes all the business decisions, enjoys any business profits, and can sell or transfer the business at any time. There are no special taxes on a sole proprietorship—the owner draws profits from the business and pays taxes on his or her individual income. Finally, sole proprietorships are easy to set up and face few legal requirements.

Disadvantages A sole proprietorship owner can be held personally liable for all the debts, taxes, and liabilities of the business. This means the owner's home, savings, and personal property may be seized to satisfy the business's debts.

Also, because investors do not usually invest in sole proprietorships, owners often have to find other sources of start-up or expansion capital. A final disadvantage of sole proprietorships is lack of longevity, or the length of time the business operates. Because sole proprietorships depend on the health, commitment, and competence of one person, they have a shorter life span than other types of business organizations.

Partnerships

A **partnership** is a business owned and controlled by two or more people who share in the business's profits and are responsible for its losses. A partnership is formed when two or more people agree to operate a business together. Partnerships come in two basic forms: general partnerships and limited partnerships. In a **general partnership**, partners have equal decision-making authority.

Each partner also has unlimited liability. Unlimited liability means that general partners, like sole proprietors, are responsible for paying all of the debts and financial losses of the business. General partners' personal assets—money and property—are at risk if the business fails.

In a **limited partnership**, some partners join as investors and provide capital in exchange for a share of the profits. They are called limited partners because they do not take an active role in operating the business or making business decisions. As a result, a limited partner's liability is limited to the amount of his or her investment. The general partners, who run the business, must pay the rest. Limited partners can be individuals, businesses, or other organizations.

Partnerships, like sole proprietorships, have advantages and disadvantages. These advantages and disadvantages are common to both kinds of partnerships.

Advantages of Partnerships Like sole proprietorships, partnerships are easy to set up, are subject to few regulations, and require relatively little capital to start. A partnership also pays all its business expenses, such as supplies and employment taxes, from its revenue, and partners then share in the profits of the business. Each partner pays taxes on his or her individual income—there are no separate taxes on the partnership. Other advantages of partnerships include:

- Specialization—Specific business duties can be assigned to each partner, which allows each partner to put his or her skills and talents to the best use.

- Shared decision making—Unlike sole proprietors, who make business decisions by themselves, partners can minimize business mistakes by consulting with each other on business matters.

- Shared business losses—Partners share any business losses, which may allow the business to survive circumstances that would ruin a sole proprietorship.

- Access to capital—Creditors may be more likely to lend capital, whether for starting the business or expanding it, to partnerships because the risk of loss is spread among several people.

Partnership Disadvantages Some of the problems of sole proprietorships also affect partnerships, but they are often less severe because they are shared. Disadvantages of partnerships include:

- Unlimited liability—Each general partner is responsible for all debts incurred by the business. As a result, general partners may sacrifice personal property to cover the debts of a failed business.

- Potential for conflict—Disagreements, such as conflicts involving personalities, management styles, or business goals, may arise and cause the business to fail.

- Lack of longevity—Finally, the life of a partnership depends on the willingness and ability of the partners to continue working together. Illness, death, conflict among partners, and other problems can end the partnership. If the problems cannot be solved, the business must be dissolved.

Corporations

A corporation is a business that is legally separate from the people who own and run it. Under the law, corporations are treated as "persons," with many of the same rights and responsibilities that individuals have.

Corporate Structure The structures of specific corporations may vary, but in any corporation, the board of directors is the most important decision-making body. The board determines how the corporation will develop and what policies it will follow.

The board also selects corporate officers. Corporate officers typically are experienced managers hired to make day-to-day decisions and advise the board about the future. They also carry out the board's policies and plans.

Corporate Finances The board of directors also decides how the corporation will raise funds. The most common way for corporations to raise funds is to sell shares of **stock.** Each share represents partial ownership of the business. Owners of stock, called **shareholders**, want the company to do well so that their shares increase in value and they will receive part of the profits. The profits paid to shareholders are called **dividends.** Dividends are a "return," or profit, on a person's investment.

Corporations issue two kinds of stock—common and preferred. Common stock gives shareholders a voice in how the company is run and entitles them to share in any dividends the corporation may generate.

Preferred stock provides guaranteed dividends—paid before any given to holders of common stock—but does not give shareholders any voice, however small, in running the corporation.

Corporations also raise money by issuing **corporate bonds.** A bond is a certificate issued by a corporation in exchange for money borrowed from an investor. While stock represents ownership in a corporation, corporate bonds indicate that the corporation is in debt to the bondholder. A bondholder does not own any part of the company.

Corporation Advantages Corporations have two sets of advantages. One set is enjoyed by the stockholders, and the other is enjoyed by the business itself.

For stockholders, the major advantage is limited liability. If a corporation fails, the loss to its stockholders is limited to the amount they invested—what they paid for their stock. A shareholder's personal property and assets cannot be seized to pay corporate debts. The corporate structure also gives stockholders flexibility, allowing them to take back all or part of their investment by selling shares. A stockholder, generally, can sell shares at any time, provided that someone will buy them.

A second advantage is the separation of ownership from management. Shareholders do not make day-to-day decisions about company activities. Instead, the corporation hires individuals who are skilled at operating a business to make the employment, marketing, production, and other decisions. A corporation also can hire other specialists, such as lawyers and accountants, to advise management.

A third advantage for a corporation is the relative ease with which capital can be raised. Unlike sole proprietorships and partnerships, which generally rely on collateral to gain credit, corporations can raise money by expanding ownership through the sale of stock. Bonds allow corporations to borrow from individuals as well as from institutions such as banks. A corporation, therefore, has many more potential sources of capital than does a sole proprietorship or a partnership.

The final advantage for a corporation is longevity. A corporation often continues to exist after the deaths of its founders and original management. This long life span is possible because the corporation's structure is not dependent on one or a few individuals, as in a sole proprietorship or partnership. A corporation's ownership changes constantly as stock is bought and sold and as corporate directors, officers, and employees quit, retire, and are hired and fired. These changes could force a proprietorship or partnership to close, but a corporation is most likely to continue.

Corporation Disadvantages There are a number of disadvantages to the corporate form of business. Most of them affect the company itself rather than the stockholder.

First, a corporate charter can be expensive and difficult to obtain. Costs vary from state to state, but attorney fees and any filing expenses required by the state may total several thousand dollars.

Second, the federal and state governments regulate corporations much more closely than they do sole proprietorships and partnerships. For example, corporations follow extensive and complex regulations in order to sell their stock. They must also publicize financial information to keep shareholders and possible investors informed about the business.

A third disadvantage for a corporation is the slow process of decision making. In a corporation—particularly a large one—decisions are made only after extensive study of the issues by specialists and discussion among managers. Proposals pass through a chain of command before final decisions are made. The process can be further slowed if top-level managers and the board of directors disagree over matters such as hiring practices and production goals.

Stockholder Issues The main disadvantage for stockholders is lack of control. Although stockholders—the owners of the business—technically can influence the company, their power generally is limited. Annual shareholder meetings offer a chance to vote on company policies, but most stockholders own only a small percentage of shares, making it difficult to influence policy and corporate objectives. In addition, stockholders have no power to influence a corporation's day-to-day activities.

Shared Issues Some people claim that there is a disadvantage that applies both to the corporation and to its stockholders. These people argue that corporate profits are taxed twice—once as corporate profits and again as dividends. Corporate profits are taxed because legally the corporation is treated as if it were an individual. If these after-tax profits are then distributed to shareholders as dividends, the government views these payments as income for the stockholder. Therefore, the shareholder must also pay income tax on this money.

Nonprofit Organizations

Most businesses exist to produce profits for their owners. However, some businesses, called **nonprofit organizations**, provide goods and services while pursuing charitable, educational, or other goals, such as operating a hospital or a local theater. Nonprofit organizations are usually structured like corporations, but they do not seek profits for their owners.

Nonprofit organizations include a wide variety of community and civic organizations, such as churches, schools, hospitals, and cooperatives. Nonprofit groups also include labor, professional, political, environmental, humanitarian, arts, and business associations, such as the International Red Cross, Oxfam, United Way, Habitat for Humanity, and your local Better Business Bureau.

Labor and Labor Unions

Producers sometimes cut costs of production by reducing workers' wages and benefits or by ignoring workplace health and safety issues. In the past, many workers relied upon labor unions to protect their interests. A **labor union** is an organization formed by workers to negotiate with employers for better wages, improved working conditions, and job security. Today, for several reasons, unions are struggling to maintain membership and securing the needs of workers.

Unions Past and Present

Historically, most unions began as small groups of workers organized to protect their rights, health, and safety in the workplace. These groups often joined together in a local union—people who worked for a particular company or in a particular geographic area.

During the 1800s, government generally favored business interests over those of labor unions. Over time, unions grew larger and stronger, and the government's attitude toward unions changed during the first decades of the 1900s when the country entered a period of social and political reform. Congress and state legislatures passed laws protecting the rights of workers. New laws limited the hours in a workday, regulated workplace safety, outlawed child labor, and required business owners to pay fair wages to workers.

In recent decades U.S. labor unions have experienced significant declines in union membership. Reasons offered for the decline include the success that unions have had in achieving their goals, management and corporate opposition to labor unions, changes in employment and demographic patterns, globalization and other changes in competition, and legislative changes that make it harder for unions to organize.

Other government actions have also affected unions. For example, in 1981, the Professional Air Traffic Controllers Organization (PATCO), the union representing U.S. air traffic controllers, went on strike. President Ronald Reagan fired the striking controllers and hired replacements. Before the PATCO strike, employers did not often fire striking workers and replace them. One result of the government's action that continues today was to reduce the effectiveness of a strike as a weapon to achieve workers' goals.

Unions have responded to the drop in membership by addressing new issues of concern to workers, such skill training, career development, and quality of life in the workplace. Unions are also trying to organize workers who have not been part of the labor movement, such as workers in the construction and janitorial services sectors of the economy.

Unions and Management

Labor unions have traditionally focused on issues that affect workers on a daily basis. The major issues usually discussed include:

- Wages and fringe benefits—Wages are set by labor contracts and vary according to position and how long a worker has been employed. Fringe benefits are nonwage payments, such as sick days, holidays, and vacation days; health and life insurance; and savings and retirement programs.

- Job security—Unions often seek contracts that increase job security through a system often based on the number of years a worker has been employed by the firm.

- Union security—In its broadest sense, union security provides workers with the right to organize and join a union. This right is enforced by the National Labor Relations Board (NLRB), which was created by Congress in the National Labor Relations Act (NLRA) in 1935.

Union representatives and management usually arrive at a contract agreement by using one or more of the following processes:

- Collective bargaining—During collective bargaining, union and management representatives meet to discuss their goals and offer solutions and compromises. In most cases, collective bargaining results in a contract settlement.

- Mediation—In mediation, negotiators call in a respected and neutral third party, or mediator, to listen to the arguments of both sides and suggest ways in which an agreement may be reached.

- Arbitration—Arbitration also involves assistance of an outside negotiator. An arbitrator, like a mediator, is a neutral third party. Unlike in mediation, however, an arbitrator's decision is legally binding.

If unions and management are unable to reach an agreement, unions may resort to a strike, in which they call for union members to stop working until contract demands are met. Three tactics commonly used by striking unions are picketing, boycotting, or a combination of both.

Management may take several actions in response to a strike, including hiring new workers to replace the striking workers. Management may hold a lockout, in which the employer closes the company's doors until an agreement is reached. Management may also seek an injunction, or a court order that legally prohibits the workers from striking.

Assessment

1. **Compare and Contrast** How are sole proprietorships, partnerships, and corporations similar? How are they different?

2. **Elaborate** Why might the success of the union movement have led to decreased levels of union membership?

Section 5
Economic Performance and the Role of Government

In a market economy, producers, consumers, and government officials need to know how well—or poorly—the economy is performing. Economists and other experts monitor a variety of economic indicators and statistics to measure the performance of the economy.

Measuring Economic Performance

To measure strengths and weaknesses in the economy, economists use measures such as gross domestic product, gross national product, and the consumer and producer price indexes to track production, income, and consumption in the economy.

Gross domestic product (GDP) is the dollar value of all the final goods and services produced by a nation's economy in a calendar year. GDP increases or decreases in response to shifts in demand and supply. Gross domestic product is often given as "real GDP," which is GDP adjusted for price changes over some period of time. For example, economists may want to track the growth in GDP for the years 2005 to 2012. Generally, they would use 2005 prices as the base level and would show GDP levels for each subsequent year in terms of those 2005 prices.

To measure prices and price changes over time, economists use price indexes. A price index is a measure of the average prices of a group of goods relative to a base year. Examples of price indexes are the consumer price index and the producer price index. The **consumer price index** (CPI) is a measure of the average change over time in prices paid by urban consumers for a market basket of consumer goods and services. The **producer price index** (PPI) measures the change over time in selling prices received by domestic producers of goods and services.

Another important measure of the economy is the gross national product. **Gross national product** (GNP) is GDP plus all the income earned outside the United States by U.S. citizens and businesses, plus all the income earned by foreign citizens and businesses in the United States.

Economists use GDP, GNP, and price indexes to track business cycles in the economy. A **business cycle** is any significant increase or decrease in the GDP or GNP from normal levels. Business cycles have four parts—expansion, peak, contraction, and trough. The graph below shows a typical business cycle in a market economy.

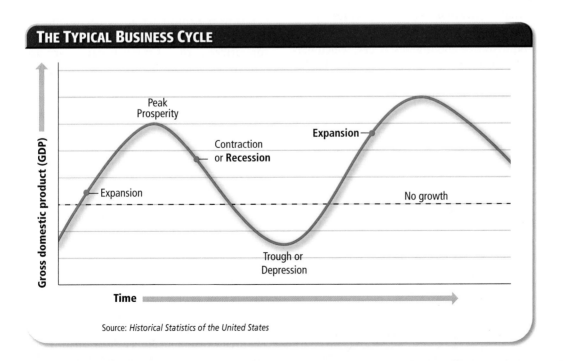

THE TYPICAL BUSINESS CYCLE

Peak
Prosperity

Contraction
or **Recession**

Expansion

Expansion

No growth

Trough or
Depression

Gross domestic product (GDP)

Time

Source: *Historical Statistics of the United States*

The Constitution and Economics

The Constitution provides the basis for the government to promote economic prosperity in our economic system. For example, in Article I, Congress is given the power to lay and collect taxes, coin money, regulate interstate and foreign commerce, and promote science and the arts. The Constitution also recognizes and protects the right of individuals to enter into contracts and to buy, sell, transfer, and dispose of private property.

Further, the Fourth Amendment protects persons and their property against unreasonable search and seizure—upon which a person's right to personal and business privacy is based. Finally, the Fifth Amendment prohibits government from depriving anyone of his or her property without due process of law, or from taking anyone's property for public use without just compensation.

Government Actions

Governments at all levels—local, state, and federal—act to regulate business, provide public goods, and promote economic well-being. The federal government also acts to stabilize the national economy and to respond to failures of the market system. Local, state, and federal government actions can affect demand for and the supply of goods and services. The tools of government action include taxes, subsidies, and regulation.

Taxes Higher taxes reduce a consumer's ability to buy goods and services, which may reduce demand for a good or service. Higher taxes also add to a business's production costs, which may affect supply because higher taxes may mean higher costs and less profit.

Subsidy A government payment of money or benefits to individuals or private businesses is a **subsidy**. Subsidies may increase a consumer's ability to buy goods and services. Subsidies to businesses lower costs of production and encourage businesses to supply more of a product than would be offered without the subsidy. Subsidies and taxes have opposite effects on supply.

Regulations To protect the public, the government passes regulations, or rules, about how companies conduct business. Complying with regulations may increase companies' production costs and prevent producers from supplying as many goods or services as they otherwise would. Government regulation is often a response to failures of the market system. It has four main purposes—preventing abuses, protecting consumers, limiting negative externalities, and promoting competition.

Providing Public Goods

Governments provide public goods and services, such as streets, national defense, and disaster response. These goods and services are available to all citizens, even though some of them may not be used by everyone.

Governments at all levels share the funding and distribution of public goods. Because the price system fails to assign the cost of public goods among all consumers, government spreads the cost of these goods to all citizens.

Recently, governments at all levels have begun to privatize public goods. Privatization refers either to the sale of government property to or providing certain government services—such as garbage collection or operating county hospitals—by private businesses.

Supporters of privatization argue that government should not compete with private business. Private firms, they argue, operate certain industries more efficiently than government can. Supporters also point out that government can use proceeds from the sale of public property to reduce its costs and pay off some of its debt.

Opponents of privatization want public goods to remain under government control. Government provides these goods and services for citizens, they argue, because private industry is unable or unwilling to. Unlike businesses, government also has—or has access to—the kinds and quantities of resources needed to meet the requirements and circumstances of providing public goods.

Promoting Economic Well-Being

The third major economic role of government is to promote economic well-being. The government does this by improving people's standard of living and redistributing wealth.

Improving the Standard of Living The standard of living for a nation, state, or region reflects how people live and how many goods and services they consume. For example, medical care programs, such as the State Children's Health Insurance Program (SCHIP),

Medicare, and Medicaid provide health insurance to some children, older Americans, and people with low incomes who might not have medical care. This improves the standard of living of all these people.

Redistributing Wealth Some government programs reduce the gap between rich and poor through transfer payments. A **transfer payment** is when the government collects money from one group of citizens and distributes, or transfers, it to another group.

Transfer payment programs are usually specific aid programs that distribute income to anyone who qualifies. These programs may provide income for households or finance medical care, higher education, housing, and job training or retraining programs.

Some private businesses and public agencies also receive transfer payments to ensure the continued service or production of certain goods. The government, for example, assumes some of the costs of some types of mass transportation, which ensures that these public services are available and affordable for many citizens who depend on them.

Stabilizing the Economy

Federal, state, and local governments all regulate business, provide public goods, and promote economic well-being. The federal government acts mostly alone to stabilize the economy by moderating the business cycle and responding to market failures.

Moderating the Business Cycle The U.S. economy generally follows a pattern, with periods of economic prosperity followed by periods of economic slowdown, or recession. This sequential rising and falling of the economy is called the **business cycle**.

Periods of economic expansion may be accompanied by inflation. **Inflation** is an increase in overall prices that results from rising wages, an increased money supply, and too many dollars spent on too few goods and services. Government policies, especially monetary and fiscal policies, are described in more detail in the next section.

Responding to Market Failures In addition to moderating the business cycle, the government tries to ensure economic stability by limiting the effects of market failures. Four types of market failures are externalities, the inability or unwillingness of private enterprise to produce some public goods, inadequate business competition, and consumers' inadequate knowledge of market conditions. You read earlier how government limits externalities by regulating businesses, and it provides the public goods that private enterprises do not. How does it address the other two types of market failures?

Inadequate business competition occurs when one or a few businesses dominate a field and control the price and supply of a good, as in the case of a monopoly. Governments may respond to a lack of competition by prohibiting or dissolving business mergers or monopolies.

As for the fourth type of market failure, the government responds to consumers' inadequate knowledge of market conditions by making information available to the public. For example, two agencies that provide information to consumers are the Consumer Products Safety Commission (CPSC), which is charged with protecting the public from injury or death from consumer products, and the Securities and Exchange Commission (SEC), which protects investors; maintains fair, orderly, and efficient markets; and facilitates capital formation.

Government and the Public

What are the consequences of government policies and regulations? Government actions can affect all aspects of production and consumption, including prices, services, profits, and productivity.

Prices Government regulation may cause prices to increase. For example, a city may require real estate developers to pay a fee to offset part of the city's cost of extending water and sewage lines to the new area, and may also require that a portion of the land be used as a park. The utility fee means that each house would be more expensive to build, and the greenspace requirement might reduce the number of homes built on the land. As a result, houses in the development would be more expensive than they would be without the government requirements. In fact, government regulation often leads to increased production costs or reduced supplies of the product, both of which lead to higher consumer prices.

On the other hand, the utility fee makes the developer—and people who buy a home in the development—pay a share of the cost of the services they get. The park requirement gives everyone in the city a new park to enjoy.

Services Different types of government regulation can affect services in different ways. In some cases, regulation can encourage greater levels of service. Suppose that BigView Cable TV wants to offer 163 cable channels to subscribers. Regulations, however, require the cable company to provide 258 channels. If BigView wants the contract, it must offer the larger number of channels to consumers.

Other forms of regulation reduce service. For example, if regulations force producers to supply goods or services at a lower price than they otherwise would, producers may reduce service to avoid losing money. A regulation that limits the amount of money a county pays for certain medical treatments at the county hospital may, if the cost of the treatment increases, lead the hospital operator to reduce the availability of that service or eliminate the service entirely.

Profits Private companies' profits may increase when government regulations result in higher prices and make it more difficult for new companies to enter a particular market. That is, less competition usually means higher profits. Regulations tend to lower companies' profits because regulation increases the costs of doing business, and not all costs can be passed on to consumers.

Productivity Government regulation may cause productivity to decline. As workers spend time meeting government regulations instead of producing goods and services, the amount of goods and services produced per worker declines and productivity suffers. For example, government regulations that require that food processing machinery be cleaned every four hours instead of every eight hours means that workers at the food processing plant will spend twice as much time cleaning the machines and less time making food.

Assessment

1. **Describe** In what ways can the U.S. Constitution be considered an economic document as well as a political one?
2. **Elaborate** Should government provide any public goods or services, or should highways, national defense, and health protection be provided by the private sector? Support your answer with examples and reasons.

THE CIRCULAR FLOW OF RESOURCES AND MONEY

This chart is a simplified model of the flow of resources, products, and money payments in the U.S. economy.

Federal Government
The government provides services (and sometimes money payments) to households and businesses. The government pays businesses for products and households for labor.

Businesses
Businesses sell products to households and the government. Businesses pay wages and salaries to individuals and taxes to the government.

Households (Individuals)
Households provide resources (labor, land) to businesses and government. Households pay businesses for products and taxes to the government.

At the national level, government promotes economic stability with two economic tools. The first is monetary policy, implemented by the Federal Reserve System, and the second is the fiscal policy—government taxing and spending—of the federal government.

The Federal Reserve System

In 1913 Congress set up the Federal Reserve System as the nation's central bank. Referred to as the Fed, the Federal Reserve System operates 12 district Federal Reserve Banks. These banks handle all the banking needs of the federal government, and they put most U.S. currency into circulation. The Fed is also the banker's bank. A member bank can go to its district Federal Reserve bank to borrow funds to meet unexpected cash demands.

The major goal of the Fed, however, is to promote the goals of economic growth and stability. The Fed tries to achieve this goal through the use of monetary policy.

The Fed and Monetary Policy

The Federal Reserve System uses monetary policy to promote economic stability. **Monetary policy** is the manipulation of the amount of money and credit in private hands in the economy. By controlling the money supply, the Fed can promote or slow economic growth. For example, by regulating the money supply and the interest rates charged for credit, the Fed influences aggregate demand.

Aggregate demand measures demand for all products in the economy and is the total of all planned expenditures at a particular time. Like demand, aggregate demand requires that consumers be willing and able to buy a product, but it measures demand for all goods and services in the U.S. economy rather than for a particular product.

The Fed measures both the money supply and aggregate demand in order to develop a monetary policy. Based on the amount of money and the spending habits of people across the United States, the Fed adopts either an easy-money policy or a tight-money policy.

Easy-money Policy An easy-money policy increases the money supply. The goal of an easy-money policy is to expand the money supply, increase aggregate demand, create jobs and reduce unemployment, and promote economic growth.

The Fed usually adopts an easy-money policy during a recession because the economy needs a financial boost to move it toward recovery. By charging banks lower interest to borrow money, the Fed makes more money available to banks. When banks pay less in interest on their funds, they are able to lower the interest rates they charge their customers.

When banks charge lower interest rates for loans, people and businesses borrow more money in order to pay for more goods and services. Increased borrowing and increased spending in turn stimulate economic growth as businesses increase production and hire more workers. Businesses then expand by investing new capital.

How does an easy-money policy affect consumers? Suppose that the Fed charges a lower interest rate to banks, and as a result, bank interest rates on car loans drop from 8 percent to 6.5 percent. Because interest rates are lower, a consumer may decide that he or she can afford to borrow money to buy a car. As other consumers make similar decisions, demand for cars increases. Automobile producers provide more cars and borrow money to expand their businesses. These workers have new income and further stimulate aggregate demand.

Tight-money Policy A tight-money policy slows business activity and helps stabilize prices. During times of inflation the Fed may determine that too much money is circulating and credit is too accessible. To restrict the money supply and thus limit credit, the Fed adopts a tight-money policy. A tight-money policy is characterized by higher interest rates and a smaller money supply, both of which are designed to reduce aggregate demand and slow economic growth. The effect on consumers will be the opposite of the effect of an easy-money policy.

Monetary Policy Tools

The Fed has three main tools it uses to carry out its monetary policy. These tools are open-market operations, the discount rate, and reserve requirements.

Open-market Operations Trading in securities, usually U.S. Treasury bills, allows the Fed to increase or decrease the money supply and to provide the government with the cash it needs to finance public goods and services. Treasury bills, also called T-bills, are short-term debt obligations—similar to bonds—of the U.S. government.

The Federal Open Market Committee (FOMC) decides to buy or sell government securities based on the monetary policy set by the Board of Governors. Open-market operations involve buying and selling T-bills. If the Fed wants to lower the money supply, it sells T-bills. The money spent on the T-bills is taken out of the money supply. If the Fed wants to increase the money supply, it buys T-bills back from investors, putting more money into circulation.

Discount Rate The discount rate is the interest rate the Fed charges banks to borrow money. When the Fed changes this rate, it signals commercial banks that the Fed wants to loosen or tighten the money supply. For example, when the Fed lowers the discount rate, banks may borrow and loan more money. That helps the economy grow. Raising the discount rate has the opposite effect.

Reserve Requirements Finally, the Fed makes use of the reserve requirement, which is a percentage of member banks' total net transaction accounts. In other words, the Fed determines the amount of money in deposit accounts in all member banks and requires banks to hold back a percentage of that total. By lowering the reserve requirement, the Fed frees up banks to loan more money. By raising the reserve requirement, the Fed forces banks to keep more of their money in reserve.

Timing Whichever tools the Fed uses to adjust monetary policy, timing the change is always an important consideration. First, the Fed must determine the current state of the economy. Second, the Fed must decide whether to increase or decrease the money supply and to provide the government with the cash it needs to finance public goods and services.

Monetary Policy Limitations The enormous size of the U.S. economy presents several obstacles to the Fed in carrying out a monetary policy. The five main challenges facing the Fed are economic forecasts, time lags in developing and carrying out monetary policy, priorities and trade-offs, lack of coordination among government agencies in forming economic policies, and conflicting opinions about monetary policy.

Fiscal Policy

Another tool the government can use to influence the economy is fiscal policy, or government spending, taxing, and borrowing policies used to achieve desired levels of economic performance.

Government revenue is all the money the government collects in taxes to pay for programs such as road construction, national defense, and health care programs. The government may also use tax policy to influence the behavior of individuals. For example, the federal and state governments might increase taxes on tobacco and alcohol products to discourage people from consuming large quantities of these goods. Governments can choose among three basic types of taxes, proportional, progressive, and regressive. Each type of tax affects different taxpayers in different ways, depending on the tax rate—the percentage of a person's income that goes toward taxes.

Collecting Taxes

Governments rely on a combination of proportional, progressive, and regressive taxes to collect funds. The largest sources of tax revenue are

- individual income taxes,
- corporate income taxes,
- Social Security taxes,
- property taxes, and
- sales taxes.

Fiscal Policy Strategies

Taxes are an important part of fiscal policy. The five chief fiscal policy tools are

- taxation,
- tax incentives,
- government spending,
- public transfer payments, and
- progressive income taxes.

Taxation Congress may use taxation to regulate aggregate demand in the private sector. If businesses begin to lay off employees, the workers reduce their spending. As other people make similar choices—because they have been laid off or because they anticipate losing their jobs—aggregate demand declines and the economy moves toward recession.

To reduce unemployment, Congress might decrease taxes, which increases people's disposable incomes and allows businesses to retain more of their profits. Additional money encourages more total spending and higher aggregate demand.

To help limit inflation, Congress might raise taxes. Higher taxes decrease disposable income and a corporation's profits. Higher taxes also slow business activity and reduce the chances of inflation, or "too much money chasing too few goods."

Tax Incentives A second fiscal policy tool is tax incentives. Tax incentives are targeted tax breaks the government gives to businesses to encourage investment in new capital.

One major tax incentive is the investment tax credit, which permits firms to deduct from their corporate income taxes a percentage of the money they spend on new capital. To help reduce unemployment, Congress raises the investment tax credit, encouraging businesses to spend more money on expansion and thereby increase aggregate demand. To help reduce inflation, Congress decreases the investment tax credit to restrict business activity and thus lower aggregate demand.

Government Spending A third tool of fiscal policy is government spending. To help reduce inflation, Congress may cut government spending, resulting in lower aggregate demand and slower business activity.

To help reduce unemployment, on the other hand, Congress can increase government spending for goods and services. Higher spending on education, national defense, and the nation's infrastructure increases aggregate demand and employment opportunities.

Public Transfer Payments Some tax dollars are redistributed to nonproductive sectors of the economy through public transfer payments. *Nonproductive* in this context means that no goods or services are created in exchange for these government payments.

Transfer payments form a safety net of social programs for the people in the United States.

A significant type of transfer payment is unemployment compensation. When unemployment rises, more people are eligible for this payment. Governments provide these funds to a larger percentage of the population. Later, when the unemployment rate drops, fewer people need this compensation and governments are able to reduce the amount of money they spend on these payments.

Many federal public transfer payments also stabilize aggregate demand. Social Security payments and veterans' benefits, for example, provide income to elderly and disabled citizens. Likewise, health insurance through Medicare and Medicaid injects billions of dollars into the economy each year.

Progressive Income Taxes Personal income tax and corporate income tax both are intended to be progressive taxes because higher incomes are taxed at higher rates. As higher incomes of individuals and firms place them in higher tax brackets, individuals and firms pay a greater percentage of their incomes in taxes. As taxes increase, disposable income—income after taxes—does not increase by the same percentage as your total income. By reducing such increases in disposable incomes, higher tax rates reduce the increase in aggregate demand that might come with rapidly rising incomes.

During recessions, on the other hand, incomes tend to fall. Many individuals and firms are taxed at lower rates because they earn less and therefore are in lower tax brackets. The lower tax rates reduce the possibility of a drop in aggregate demand.

Limitations on Fiscal Policy Although fiscal policy is designed to regulate aggregate demand in the economy, putting policies to work is not always a smooth process. The four most important limitations are timing problems, political pressures, unpredictable economic behaviors, and lack of coordination among government policies.

Assessment

1. **Describe** How does the Fed promote economic stability through monetary policy?

2. **Elaborate** How do the tools of fiscal policy promote economic growth and stability?

Section 7
The U.S. Economy and International Trade

Why do nations engage in trade? Two factors provide a basis for international trade. First, international trade is voluntary. Nations choose which resources and products to trade. Second, nations pursue trade that increases their wealth in terms of goods, services, or resources.

Specialization and Trade

Specialization and economic interdependence are the basis for international trade. Specialization may happen because certain resources are unique to a nation. For example, coffee grows best in tropical or subtropical regions. As a result, much of the world's coffee comes from tropical or subtropical countries such as Brazil, Colombia, and Vietnam. Countries outside the coffee-growing region, such as Switzerland and Canada, must import all their coffee.

Without international trade, a nation can consume only the goods and services it produces. Specialization offers a nation the opportunity to specialize—become efficient—in the production of a few goods and services and to trade them for whatever goods and services that nation cannot supply to its people. This trade provides opportunities for improvements in the standard of living.

Absolute and Comparative Advantage

The factors of production are distributed unequally throughout the world. This uneven distribution means that a nation must trade to improve its citizens' standard of living. What a nation decides to produce is determined by the economic concepts of absolute advantage and comparative advantage.

Absolute Advantage A nation or region has an **absolute advantage** in producing a good when it is more efficient in producing that good—can produce it at a lower cost—than any other nation or region. In other words, the country uses fewer resources to produce something than another country. Advanced technology may also give a nation an absolute advantage over other nations. For example, Brazil and Costa Rica both produce coffee, cocoa, and lumber. If Brazil can produce each at a lower cost—whether due to a technological advantage or more accessible resources—Brazil has an absolute advantage over Costa Rica for these items.

Comparative Advantage The fact that Brazil has an absolute advantage over Costa Rica in producing these goods does not mean that Brazil will produce everything and Costa Rica will produce nothing. Which items each nation produces is determined by knowing where each nation may have a comparative advantage. A nation has a **comparative advantage** when it can produce its goods at a lower opportunity cost than another nation. Recall that opportunity cost is the value of the next-best alternative action that is not taken. The comparative advantage is found by determining where the largest absolute advantage occurs for each item. Comparative advantage allows each nation to benefit—use its resources more efficiently and raise its standard of living—through specialization and international trade. Study the Comparative Advantage table on the next page.

Buying and Selling Money

When nations begin to trade, international trade is similar to any other market. Buyers in one nation want to purchase products from sellers in other nations. Whose currency will be used carry out these transactions?

In 2007 there were about 200 nations in the world, each with its own government and national currency. Each nation accepts its own currency, such as the U.S. dollar, Chinese yuan, and Japanese yen, as payment for goods and services within its borders. The euro—the currency for the European Union (EU), an economic and political association of European countries—is accepted as a common currency for its 27 members. For most international trade, however, each nation must determine the value of its currency in relation to other currencies.

One way to establish the relative value of currencies is to buy and sell them in a marketplace, just like any other good. Markets known as foreign exchange markets exist for this purpose—the buying and selling of currency. For most currencies, foreign exchange markets set foreign exchange rates.

COMPARATIVE ADVANTAGE

Nation	Shirts	Skirts	Opportunity Cost of Shirts	Opportunity Cost of Skirts
Country A	120	100	0.83 (100 skirts for 120 shirts)	1.2 (120 shirts for 100 skirts)
Country Z	60	90	1.5 (90 skirts for 60 shirts)	0.67 (60 shirts for 90 skirts)
Total (no trade)	180/2=80	190/2=95	(Because each country spends half its time making shirts and half making skirts)	
Total (with trade)	120	90		

Absolute and Comparative Advantage In this example, Country A uses its resources to make shirts and Country B its resources to make skirts. Country A has an absolute advantage in both products.

Country A has a comparative advantage in making shirts because it gives up only 0.83 skirt for each shirt it makes (100 skirts for 120 shirts), whereas Country Z must give up 1.5 skirts to make each shirt (90 skirts for 60 shirts). On the other hand, Country Z has a comparative advantage in making skirts, because it must give up only 0.67 shirt for each skirt, while Country A must give up 1.2 shirts to make each of its skirts.

So even though Country A has an absolute advantage in producing both goods, it would benefit from trade with Country Z. Country A should specialize in making shirts and Country Z should specialize in making skirts. Even though it appears that there is a net loss of 5 skirts with specialization and trade, Country A could give up making 6 shirts to make up the 5 skirts. That would still mean the world would have 114 shirts—a gain of 34 shirts over the original production—with no loss of skirts.

Foreign Exchange Rates

When a business in one country imports items, it pays for them in its own currency. The business in the other country that exports the items wants to be paid in its own currency. Through foreign exchange markets, one currency can be converted into another currency. When the value of one currency in relation to another is determined, an exchange rate has been established.

Foreign exchange rates are expressed in two ways. For the United States, for example, the first way is to give the U.S. dollar value for each unit of foreign currency. On a particular day, one euro might be worth $1.4685, which means that an item that sells for 1 euro in Italy would sell for $1.47 in the United States. At the same time, 1 Japanese yen (JY) might be worth $0.008935—less than a penny.

The second way to express the foreign exchange rate is the amount of another nation's currency that equal one dollar. At the exchange rates above, $1 = 0.6809 euros, which means that an item selling for $10 in the United States would sell for 6.81 euros. At the same time, $1 = 111.88 yen.

Exchange Rates and Trade

As in any market, prices of currency—exchange rates—rise and fall in response to the forces of demand and supply. Most currencies float—rise or fall—on exchange markets without restriction against each other. Demand and supply usually operate without government involvement. Governments do, however, intervene occasionally in exchange markets to keep their own currency, or other currencies, from rising or falling too much.

A government may control its currency float by limiting the values within which its currency rises or falls. Governments also buy or sell their currency in the exchange markets. This intervention affects demand for or supply of the currency and affects its exchange rate.

Decrease in Exchange Rate When a nation's currency weakens, its value decreases in terms of other currencies. This weakening is called devaluation or depreciation of the currency. When a nation's currency depreciates, its products become cheaper to other nations. In the example above, the dollar might weaken from $1 = 111.88 JY to $1 = 102 JY, which means that $1 would buy goods worth only 102 yen instead of goods worth 111.88 yen. At that rate, an item for which you might have paid $350 would, after the devaluation, cost you about $383.90.

This depreciation or weakening in the dollar means that goods and services imported from Japan are relatively more expensive than they were before the rate changed. When goods and services imported from a country become more expensive, the quantity of those goods and services demanded by U.S. consumers will decrease. Companies and individuals who make their living by importing and selling goods and services will suffer a decline in their businesses.

At the same time, however, the decline in the dollar's strength means that Japanese consumers will spend only 102 yen to buy a dollar's worth of goods instead of spending 111.88 yen. Goods imported into Japan from the United States—goods exported by U.S. businesses and individuals—will be less expensive. As a result, Japanese consumers will tend to purchase more U.S. products. The weaker dollar, then, helps U.S. companies that make and sell goods for export to Japan.

Increase in Exchange Rate On the other hand, when a nation's currency increases in value compared to other nations' currencies, strengthening, or appreciation, has occurred. The effect on imports and exports is the opposite of what happens when the currency weakens. Appreciation of a nation's currency means that consumers in other countries will find the products of that nation becoming more expensive. At the same time, consumers in that nation will find the goods and services imported from other nations will become relatively less expensive.

Balancing Trade and Payments

Nations conduct their business in much the same way as individuals do. Nations buy more than they sell in international trade during certain years and sell more than they buy in other years. Nations that buy more than they sell in foreign trade must finance their purchases by accumulating debt or by allowing other nations to hold their currency.

Balance of Payments A nation's **balance of payments** is a year-long accounting record of all the payments and receipts among its own individuals, businesses, and governments and all the individuals, businesses, and governments of other nations. A balance of payments account gives information about the trading relationship between a nation and all its trading partners.

For example, the U.S. balance of payments is divided into two major categories: the current account and the capital account. The current account shows the dollar value of goods and services the United States bought

from and sold to others, the income that U.S. multinational corporations (MNCs) earned in other countries, and the income that foreign MNCs earned in the United States.

The capital account portion of the balance of payments tracks the movement of money or capital between nations. Like individuals, governments and corporations move their funds to financial institutions that offer higher interest rates accompanied by safety, liquidity, and convenience. For example, if U.S. interest rates are relatively higher than interest rates in other countries, foreign capital is likely to flow into the United States. If interest rates are relatively low in the United States, foreign capital likely will be invested in other nations.

When both the current and capital accounts are totaled, the total expenditures in other nations will rarely be exactly balanced by the receipts from other nations. If a nation's expenditures exceed its receipts, it has a balance-of-payments deficit. When its receipts exceed its expenditures, it has a balance-of-payments surplus.

Balance of Trade The difference in value between a nation's imported products and its exported products is known as its **balance of trade**. The balance of trade account has historically been the most important factor in determining a nation's balance of payments.

For example, when a nation exports more than it imports, it has a trade surplus, or favorable balance of trade. When a nation imports more than it exports, it has a trade deficit, or unfavorable balance of trade.

U.S. Trade Deficit Only in three of the years since 1970 has the United States had a balance of trade surplus. For example, in 2006 the U.S. balance of trade deficit in goods and services was $758.5 billion. It will be more than $710 billion in 2007. Causes of this deficit include higher energy prices, consumer demand for imported goods, and the growth and expansion of the U.S. economy.

A nation's economic growth—investment in new businesses, plants, equipment, and employees—is usually paid for by money that people save. Banks lend these funds to growing businesses. However, people in the United States save less than people in other countries. As a result, much of the U.S. economic expansion is financed by money borrowed from countries such as China and Japan.

Trade Barriers and Cooperation

In theory, international free trade leads to economic efficiency and growth. However, a nation's trade policy may be affected by powerful individuals, international businesses, concerns about labor conditions, and international organizations. These economic and political factors, plus competition for resources, lead nations to restrict the free exchange of goods across national borders.

Common Trade Barriers Government actions—often urged by businesses or unions—to protect domestic industries or jobs from foreign competition are called trade barriers. Trade barriers include tariffs, import quotas voluntary restrictions, and embargoes.

- **Tariffs** Any tax on imports is a **tariff**. Tariffs can be either revenue tariffs, which are designed to raise money for government, or protective tariffs, which are designed to restrict the number of foreign goods sold in a country. A protective tariff is designed to protect domestic industries from foreign competition. By raising the prices of imported goods, protective tariffs reduce the quantity of foreign goods demanded.

- **Import Quotas and Voluntary Restrictions** Governments may use import quotas and trade restrictions to decrease imports. These regulations help domestic industries sell their products by limiting the amount of a specific product that can be imported. An import quota, which sets a fixed amount of an item that can be imported, is a law. A voluntary trade restriction is a binding agreement between two nations that does not require legislative action. Quotas and voluntary trade restrictions are often directed at specific goods from specific nations.

- **Embargoes** An embargo is a formal act of government restricting or stopping one or more imports from or exports to a specific country. Historically, embargoes have been used for political rather than economic reasons. For example, President George W. Bush placed an embargo on the sale of military arms and technology to Venezuela. The reason for the embargo, according to the U.S. State Department, was that Venezuela was not cooperating fully with U.S. efforts to fight terrorism.

Other Trade Barriers Other trade barriers include licensing requirements and extensive paperwork, which can interrupt the free flow of goods between countries. Some nations require firms to obtain a license before they can import goods. By restricting the number of licenses, these nations ensure that fewer foreign goods are imported.

Free Trade Versus Protectionism

Free trade is international trade that is not subject to government regulation or other barriers. Free trade supporters believe that goods and services should flow freely between nations according to trade agreements.

Not everyone supports free trade, however. Some people believe in **protectionism**—the use of trade barriers to protect domestic industries. Both protectionists and free trade supporters use arguments that include protecting infant industries, specialization, national security, and fair trade.

Infant Industries Protectionists argue that a nation's "infant," or new, industries should be protected from foreign competition until they are well established. By restricting imports of the goods produced by these new industries, the government allows the "infants" to build a strong domestic market. Developing nations may use this argument to protect their infant industries against competition from multinational corporations or other nations.

Free-trade advocates believe that the decreased competition resulting from trade barriers encourages inefficiency; that is, the protected businesses have less reason to be efficient. Free-trade supporters also claim that these temporary protective measures are often extended indefinitely because of the political pressures that businesses exert on government. Once protected, always protected, they argue.

Job Protection Another protectionist argument is that by reducing foreign competition, U.S. businesses compete better in the domestic market. They also hire more U.S. workers. Free-trade supporters, on the other hand, claim that trade restrictions actually reduce the employment of U.S. workers because U.S. trade barriers historically have led other nations to erect their own barriers to U.S. trade. These barriers reduce U.S. exports to other countries, which ultimately costs U.S. workers their jobs.

Standard of Living Protectionists argue that trade barriers protect the high wages and standard of living in the United States. Trade barriers are needed, they say, because lower-paid labor in other nations gives those nations an unfair advantage in world markets.

Supporters of free trade believe that the high wages and high standard of living in the United States can be maintained without barriers. Businesses can pay high wages and produce competitively priced products because of U.S. workers' skills and efficiency levels.

Specialization Advocates of protectionism argue that free trade encourages economies to overspecialize. Overspecialization, they argue, can hurt a nation's economy when the world market for a product changes. For example, a nation may grow only one kind of cash crop or manufacture only one kind of computer chip. If the market for those products changes, that nation and its citizens would suffer an economic setback. Protectionists urge nations not to overspecialize and to produce as wide a variety of products as possible.

Supporters of free trade recognize that an economy based on a single product is not as strong as a diversified economy, such as that of the United States. However, they argue that, overall, free trade benefits the world economy and that competition guarantees the best product at the best price.

National Security and Fair Trade Arguments

Both protectionists and free-trade supporters offer two final arguments. One is based on national security, the other on the need for fair trade agreements.

National Security Protectionists argue that the more the United States depends on foreign sources of supply for vital products, such as oil, the more vulnerable the nation is in time of war or international crisis. Certain industries must be protected from competition in order to preserve national security. Free-trade supporters agree that vital industries must be protected. But, they say, too many industries believe that their products are vital to national security, and nonessential industries use this argument to seek protection.

Fair Trade Protectionists also argue that few, if any, nations allow truly free trade. They believe that the United States should establish

barriers that match those of other nations. Free-trade supporters support negotiations to eliminate—or at least reduce—all trade barriers instead of erecting even more.

Rarely is a government's trade policy completely protectionist or completely free trade. Most nations' policies are based on a variety of international and domestic factors, including both economic and political factors. In the United States, government officials monitor the nation's international trade and react to policy changes in other nations.

Cooperation

Nations do cooperate with each other to reduce trade barriers in order to reap economic and political benefits from international trade. Examples of cooperation include reciprocal trade agreements, regional trade organizations, and international trade agreements.

Reciprocal Trade Agreements In 1934, Congress enacted the Reciprocal Trade Agreements Act (RTAA), which gave the president authority—without congressional approval—to conclude tariff-reduction agreements with individual foreign countries. The act led to agreements that reduced U.S. tariffs and was the basis for the 1947 General Agreement on Tariffs and Trade (GATT).

Since 1930, Congress has had the power to grant normal trade relations (NTR) status to U.S. trading partners. When the United States lowers tariffs with one NTR trading partner, all nations with the same status benefit. Congress has the final authority to grant and to revoke NTR status.

Regional Trade Organizations Many nations form regional trade organizations or alliances to reduce or eliminate trade barriers among member nations. Such benefits, however, usually are limited to the member nations and may have negative consequences on nations that are not a part of the alliance.

One major regional trade group is the European Union (EU), an economic and political association of 27 European countries stretching from Sweden and Finland to Greece and Cyprus. The amount of trade in goods and services between the EU and the United States makes that trade relationship the largest bilateral trading relationship in the world. Similar economic and political associations include the Association of Southeast Asian Nations (ASEAN) and the African Union.

International Trade Agreements The most significant international trade agreement of the post–World War II period was GATT, the multinational trade agreement that lasted from 1947 until 1995. In 1995, GATT was replaced by the World Trade Organization (WTO). To encourage international free and fair trade, WTO has trade rules that its 151 members, including the United States, are supposed to follow. It also serves as a forum for nations to negotiate trade agreements and settle trade disputes.

The United States is a member of two other international trade agreements. The North American Free Trade Agreement (NAFTA) is an international trade agreement among Mexico, Canada, and the United States. The Dominican Republic–Central America Free Trade Agreement (CAFTA-DR) includes the United States, El Salvador, Guatemala, Honduras, Nicaragua, Dominican Republic, and Costa Rica. The goal of both NAFTA and CAFTA-DR is to create free-trade zones among the member countries by reducing or eliminating tariffs and other trade barriers.

NAFTA went into effect on January 1, 1994. Before its adoption, the agreement was the subject of vigorous debate about whether it would help or hurt the U.S. economy. Since NAFTA was adopted, debate has continued on a variety of issues, including environmental protection and NAFTA's effects on economic growth, trade and investment, immigration, productivity, and wages.

CAFTA-DR, which was approved by Congress and signed by president George W. Bush in 2005, has been the subject of similar disagreements. A final assessment of the overall effects of both agreements may take many years as the economies of the member nations adjust to new international business and trading relationships.

Assessment

1. **Explain** How do changes in foreign exchange rates affect the U.S. economy?

2. **Evaluate** Do you favor protectionism, free and fair trade, or a combination of the two? Describe and support your position.

U.S. Imports and Exports under NAFTA

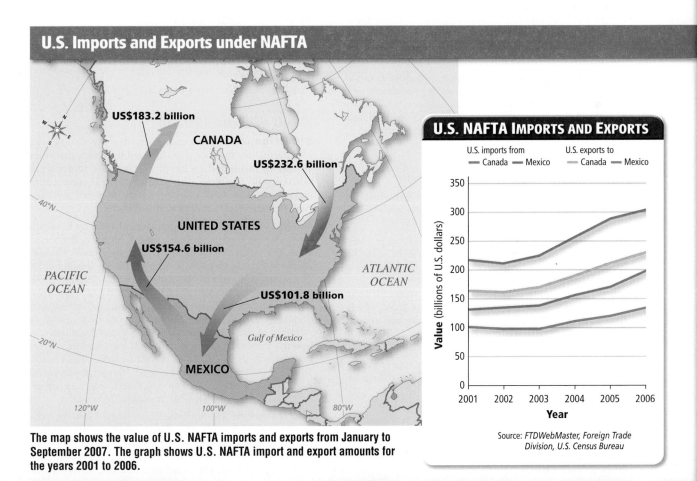

The map shows the value of U.S. NAFTA imports and exports from January to September 2007. The graph shows U.S. NAFTA import and export amounts for the years 2001 to 2006.

Source: *FTDWebMaster, Foreign Trade Division, U.S. Census Bureau*

Supreme Court Decisions

Abrams v. United States (1919)

Significance: This case, along with *Schenck v. United States*, determined that the government has the right to limit speech when such speech poses a "clear and present danger" to national security.

Background: Jacob Abrams and others were convicted, under an amendment to the Espionage Act of 1917, of inciting resistance to the war effort during World War I. The men had distributed leaflets that criticized U.S. involvement in the Russian Revolution and encouraged munitions workers to strike, claiming the arms made for use by U.S. forces during World War I were also being used against Russian Bolsheviks.

Decision: The Court decided 7–2 that the amendment was constitutional and upheld the convictions of the men. In the dissenting opinion, Justice Oliver Wendell Holmes wrote that the government failed to prove the leaflets posed any real danger, and he encouraged the Court to take its responsibilities to the First Amendment more seriously.

Adarand Constructors v. Peña (1995)

Significance: The Court ruled that racial classifications used to grant government contracts must be able to pass a test of "strict scrutiny" in order to be constitutional.

Background: Adarand Constructors had submitted a bid to be a subcontractor on a highway project being funded by the U.S. Department of Transportation. Although Adarand's bid was the lowest, another firm received the contract because it was certified as a minority business and the main contractor would receive extra government funds if it hired businesses owned by "socially and economically disadvantaged individuals."

Decision: The Court ruled 5–4 that race alone is not a sufficient condition to classify a person or company as disadvantaged and that race-based classifications "must serve a compelling government interest, and be narrowly tailored to further that interest" to be nondiscriminatory and, therefore, constitutional.

Alden v. Maine (1999)

Significance: This ruling upheld the principle of "sovereign immunity" in that private citizens cannot sue a state in that state's courts.

Background: A group of probation officers brought a suit in federal court, claiming their employer—the state of Maine—had violated overtime provisions of the federal Fair Labor Standards Act. The federal court dismissed the case, ruling that states are immune from private suits in federal court. The officers then took the suit to state court, which ruled that the state had immunity against private suits in state court. Maine's supreme court upheld the ruling.

Decision: The Court ruled 5–4 that Congress does not have the power to override the powers of the states in cases that do not involve the powers given specifically to Congress in the Constitution.

Baker v. Carr (1962)

Significance: Through this decision, the Court ruled that the judiciary branch may involve itself in hearing cases about political matters.

Background: Voters from Tennessee sued their state in federal court, arguing that the way the state drew boundary lines between representative districts created unequal representation within the legislature and, therefore, unequal protection under the laws of the state. Tennessee argued that the federal court did not have jurisdiction to hear the case.

Decision: By a 6–2 margin, the Court decided that the federal court did have the right to hear the case and that the voters had the right to sue over the issue.

Brandenburg v. Ohio (1969)

Significance: The government's power to limit the First Amendment right of speech was restricted by this ruling.

Background: Clarence Brandenburg was a Ku Klux Klan leader convicted under an Ohio law that outlawed speech that advocated "crime, sabotage, violence, or unlawful methods of terrorism." Brandenburg claimed his First Amendment rights were violated by this law.

Decision: The Court's unanimous opinion was that the law did violate Brandenburg's free speech rights. The ruling said speech can be prohibited if it is "directed at inciting or producing imminent lawless action" and if it is "likely to incite or produce such action." Since the law did not take into account whether the speech would actually incite lawless action, it was overly broad and unconstitutional.

Brown v. Board of Education of Topeka, Kansas (1954)

See **Landmark Supreme Court Cases**, *p. 333*.

Buckley v. Valeo (1976)

See **Landmark Supreme Court Cases**, *p. 273*.

Bush v. Gore (2000)

Significance: The question before the Court was whether ballots that could not be read by voting machines should be recounted by hand. The broader issues were whether the Supreme Court can overrule state court decisions on state laws and whether an appointed judiciary can affect the results of democratic elections.

Background: The 2000 presidential election between Democrat Al Gore and Republican George W. Bush was close. The winner would be determined by votes in Florida. People in Florida voted by punching a hole in a ballot card. The votes were counted by a machine that detected these holes. According to that count, Bush won the state by a few hundred votes and the Florida Elections Commission declared Bush the winner. However, about 60,000 ballots were not counted because the machines could not detect a hole in the ballot. Gore argued in the Florida Supreme Court that these votes should be recounted by hand. The Florida Supreme Court ordered counties to recount those votes. Bush appealed to the U.S. Supreme Court, which issued an order to stop the recount while it made a decision.

The Decision: The Supreme Court voted 5–4 to end the hand recount of votes. The Court ruled that the Florida Supreme Court ordered a recount without setting standards for what was a valid vote. Different vote counters might use different standards. The Court said that this inconsistency meant that votes were treated arbitrarily (based on a person's choice, rather than on standards). This arbitrariness violated the due process clause and the equal protection clause of the Constitution.

City of Boerne, Texas v. Flores (1997)

Significance: In 1993 Congress enacted the Religious Freedom Restoration Act (RFRA) to protect the right of citizens to the free exercise of their religion. Under RFRA state and local laws, such as zoning ordinances, were made subject to the federal legislation.

Background: The archbishop of San Antonio wanted to expand a church in Boerne, Texas. City authorities denied him permission, saying that the church was in a historical district governed by an ordinance that prohibited new construction. The archbishop sued, claiming the city had violated his rights under the RFRA. The local authorities argued that the RFRA was unconstitutional because it invalidated the local preservation ordinance.

Decision: By a 6–3 vote, the Court struck down the RFRA as an unconstitutional use of Congress's enforcement powers. The Court has the exclusive power to say which rights are guaranteed by the Constitution. Congress cannot add to or take away from those rights.

Civil Rights Cases (1883)

Significance: This ruling struck down the Civil Rights Act of 1875 and allowed private businesses to discriminate based on race or color.

Background: Five separate cases were combined under this one decision. Even though the Civil Rights Act was law, individuals and businesses continued to discriminate against African Americans. In these cases, African Americans were denied the same accommodations that whites were provided.

Decision: The case was decided by a vote of 8–1. The Court ruled that Congress could make laws preventing only states, not private individuals or companies, from discriminating.

Clinton v. City of New York (1998)

Significance: The Supreme Court ruled that the Line Item Veto Act of 1996, which allowed the president to void or cancel certain provisions of appropriations bills without having to veto the entire bill, was unconstitutional.

Background: President Bill Clinton used a line item veto to cancel a provision of the Balanced Budget Act of 1997 that waived the government's right to collect taxes the state of New York had levied against Medicaid providers. The city of New York and several hospital organizations sued, claiming that the Constitution does not give the president the power to alter laws that had been duly passed by Congress. Clinton's line item veto of a provision in the Tax Payer Relief Act of 1997 brought a similar suit by the Snake River farmers' cooperative. Both suits were consolidated by a U.S. district court, which ruled in favor of the plaintiffs.

Decision: The Supreme Court upheld the lower court's ruling 6–3. In its opinion, the Court stated that the act violated the presentment clause in Article I of the Constitution, which outlines the process by which a bill becomes a law. Under the presentment clause, the Court wrote, the president must either approve or reject legislation that passes both houses of Congress. The president does not have the power to alter legislation without congressional approval.

Cruzan v. Director, Missouri Department of Health (1990)

Significance: This ruling helped define who may refuse medical treatment. Although the issue is still undecided, this case began a series of efforts to provide legislative and judicial guidelines for the "right to die."

Background: The parents of comatose patient Nancy Cruzan wanted to remove her life-support system. The Missouri Department of Health ruled that Cruzan had not previously made clear her desire to refuse medical treatment in the event of brain damage.

Decision: By a 5–4 margin, the Court ruled that Cruzan's parents could not remove her from life support because she had not clearly expressed her desires previously. The Court stated that it was Nancy's demands, not her parents' wishes, that the state must respect in such cases.

Engel v. Vitale (1962)

Significance: This case involved the specific issue of organized prayer in schools and the broader issue of the relationship between government and religion under the First Amendment. The question was whether a state that composes a prayer that students must say at the beginning of the school day is in violation of the First Amendment.

Background: The state of New York recommended that public schools begin the day by having students recite a prayer and wrote a prayer for students to say. A group of parents sued to stop the official prayer, saying that it was contrary to their beliefs and their children's beliefs. The parents said the law was unconstitutional, arguing that the state prayer amounted to "establishing" religion.

Decision: By a 6–1 margin the Court agreed with the parents and struck down the state law. Justice Hugo Black wrote that under the First Amendment, ". . . it is no part of the business of government to compose official prayers for any group of the American people to recite as a part of a religious program carried on by government."

Furman v. Georgia (1972)

Significance: The ruling in this case forced states to re-examine their laws on capital offenses in order to ensure that the death penalty was not used in an arbitrary and discriminatory manner.

Background: William Henry Furman was burglarizing a house when the owner returned home. As Furman tried to escape, he tripped and the gun he was carrying went off, killing one of the residents. Furman was convicted of murder and was sentenced to death.

Decision: The Court consolidated two other death penalty cases (*Jackson v. Georgia* and *Branch v. Texas*) in its decision. Justice Potter Stewart, writing for the majority, wrote that in examining these and similar cases, the Court found that the death penalty was often applied in an arbitrary fashion and that there appeared to be a racial bias against African American defendants when the death sentence was issued. In these cases, the imposition of the death penalty was cruel and unusual punishment in violation of the Eighth and Fourteenth amendments. Over the next few years, many states revised their death penalty laws to address the Court's concerns.

Gibbons v. Ogden (1824)

See **Landmark Supreme Court Cases,** *p. 132.*

See **Landmark Supreme Court Cases,** *p. 132.*

Gideon v. Wainwright (1963)

See Landmark Supreme Court Cases, *p. 24.*

Gitlow v. New York (1925)

Significance: The Fourteenth Amendment was used to extend the reach of First Amendment rights to the states. Previous Court decisions had held that the Bill of Rights applied only to the federal government and that federal courts could not strike down states' laws that restricted their citizens' constitutional rights.

Background: Benjamin Gitlow was arrested for distributing a manifesto that called for the establishment of a socialist government. He was found guilty of breaking a state law that made it a crime to advocate overthrowing the government by force.

Decision: While the Court upheld Gitlow's conviction, it stated in its decision that the rights of freedom of speech and freedom of the press were protected by the due process clause of the Fourteenth Amendment, which the states had to follow. This reasoning was later used by the Court in such cases as *Gideon v. Wainwright.*

Goss v. Lopez (1975)

Significance: The Court ruled in this case that suspending a student from school without a hearing is a violation of a student's Fourteenth Amendment right of due process.

Background: Dwight Lopez and several other students in Columbus, Ohio, were suspended from school for 10 days for destroying school property and disrupting the learning environment. Ohio state law at the time allowed schools to suspend students without a hearing.

Decision: The Supreme Court upheld the district court's ruling that stated since the state of Ohio had chosen to extend the right of an education to its citizens, it could not take away that right without some form of due process in some form of a hearing.

Gratz v. Bollinger and Grutter v. Bollinger (2003)

Significance: These cases considered whether a university violates the Constitution by using race as a factor for admitting students to its undergraduate school and its law school. The rulings affect use of affirmative action programs in higher education. The decisions gave colleges guidelines as to what is permitted and what is not.

Background: Jennifer Gratz and Barbara Grutter are both white. They challenged the University of Michigan's affirmative action admissions policies. Gratz said the university violated the Constitution by considering race as a factor in its undergraduate admissions programs. Grutter claimed the University of Michigan Law School also did so.

Decisions: In *Gratz* the Court ruled 6–3 that the undergraduate program—which gave each minority applicant an automatic 20 points toward admission—was unconstitutional. Chief Justice William Rehnquist's opinion held that the policy violated the equal protection clause because it did not consider each applicant individually. It was almost an automatic preference based on the minority status of the applicant. The result was different when the Court turned to the affirmative action policy of Michigan's Law School, which used race as one factor for admission. In *Grutter*, by a 5–4 margin, the Court held that the Law School's policy did not violate the equal protection clause. Justice Sandra Day O'Connor wrote for the majority that "truly individualized consideration demands that race be used in a flexible, non-mechanical way . . . Universities can . . . consider race or ethnicity . . . as a 'plus' factor."

Gregg v. Georgia (1976)

Significance: This ruling upheld the constitutionality of capital punishment, provided that a set of objective guidelines is followed when imposing the death penalty, an appeals process is in place to review those guidelines, and the judge or jury can consider mitigating circumstances when assessing punishment.

Background: Following the Court's ruling in *Furman* v. *Georgia* (1972), states began revising their laws to ensure that the death penalty would not be applied in a discriminatory fashion. Under these new laws, Troy Leon Gregg was convicted of murder and sentenced to die.

Decision: In a 7–2 decision, the Court ruled that the death penalty, in certain circumstances, was not cruel and unusual punishment. The Court wrote that if a jury is given objective standards to use when assessing the death penalty and if the jury's decision is subject to appeal, the death penalty can be considered constitutional. The Court stated that the jury must be able to consider mitigating circumstances when deciding whether to impose the death penalty.

Hamdi v. Rumsfeld and Rasul v. Bush (2004)

Significance: These cases addressed the balance between the government's powers to fight terrorism and the Constitution's promise of due process. Each case raised a slightly different question: (1) Can the government hold U.S. citizens for an indefinite period as "enemy combatants" and not permit them access to U.S. courts? (2) Do non–U.S. citizens captured overseas and jailed at Guantánamo Bay, Cuba, have the right to ask U.S. courts to decide if they are being held legally?

Background: Detaining U.S. Citizens: In *Hamdi* v. *Rumsfeld*, Yaser Hamdi, a U.S. citizen, was arrested in Afghanistan in 2001. The U.S. military said Hamdi was an enemy combatant and claimed that it has the authority to hold enemy combatants captured on the battlefield and prevent them from returning to the battle. Hamdi's attorney said Hamdi deserved the due process rights that other Americans have, including a hearing in court to argue that he was not an enemy combatant.

Detaining Non–U.S. Citizens at Guantánamo Bay: The prisoners in *Rasul* v. *Bush* also claimed they were wrongly imprisoned. They wanted a court hearing, but Guantánamo Bay Naval Base is on Cuban soil. Cuba leases the base to the United States. In an earlier case, the Court had ruled that "if an alien is outside the country's sovereign territory, then . . . the alien is not permitted access to the courts of the United States to enforce the Constitution."

Decisions: In *Hamdi*, the Court ruled 6–3 that Hamdi had a right to a hearing. Justice Sandra Day O'Connor wrote that "a state of war is not a blank check for the president when it comes to the rights of the nation's citizens." The government decided not to prosecute Hamdi. In *Rasul*, also decided 6–3, Justice John Paul Stevens wrote that the prisoners had been held for more than two years in territory that the United States controls. Thus, even though the prisoners are not on U.S. soil, they can ask U.S. courts if their detention is legal.

Heart of Atlanta Motel v. United States (1964)

Significance: The ruling upheld the public accommodations clause of the Civil Rights Act of 1964. It enforced the right of African Americans to receive access to the same accommodations as whites.

Background: The owner of the Heart of Atlanta Motel routinely discriminated against African Americans. He claimed that his business was not an interstate business and therefore not subject to regulation by congressional acts.

Decision: In a unanimous decision, the Court declared that as a business that served people from across state boundaries, the Heart of Atlanta Motel was in fact an interstate business and that therefore congressional acts did apply.

In Re Debs (1895)

Significance: The Court upheld the right of the federal government to halt strikes organized by union workers.

Background: Railway union official Eugene V. Debs had organized a strike of union workers. The government ordered him to halt the strike, and a court held him in contempt when he refused. Debs fought his conviction.

Decision: In a unanimous decision, the Court declared that the federal government did have the power to order Debs to halt the strike.

Korematsu v. United States (1944)

Significance: This case addressed the question of whether government action that treats one racial group differently than others violates the equal protection clause of the Fourteenth Amendment.

Background: When the United States declared war on Japan in 1941, about 112,000 Japanese Americans lived on the West Coast. About 70,000 of these Japanese Americans were citizens. In 1942, anti-Japanese sentiment and fears that Japanese Americans could aid a Japanese attack against the United States caused the U.S. government to order most of the Japanese Americans to move to internment camps. Fred Korematsu, a Japanese American and an American citizen, did not go to the camps as ordered. He stayed in California, was arrested, and was then sent to a camp in Utah. Korematsu sued, claiming the government acted illegally when it sent people of Japanese descent to camps.

Decision: By a 6–3 margin the Supreme Court said the orders moving the Japanese Americans into the camps were constitutional. Justice Hugo Black wrote the opinion for the Court. He said that the unusual demands of wartime security justified the orders. However, he made it clear that distinctions based on race are "inherently suspect" and that laws based on race must withstand "strict scrutiny" by the courts.

Lochner v. New York (1905)

Significance: This decision established the Supreme Court's role in overseeing state regulations. For more than 30 years, *Lochner* was used as a precedent in striking down state laws such as minimum-wage laws, child labor laws, and regulations on banking and transportation.

Background: In 1895 the state of New York passed a labor law limiting bakers to working no more than 10 hours per day or 60 hours per week. The law was intended to protect the health of bakers, who worked in hot and damp conditions and breathed in large quantities of flour dust. In 1902 Joseph Lochner, the owner of a small bakery in New York, claimed that the state law violated his Fourteenth Amendment rights by unfairly depriving him of the liberty to make contracts with employees.

Decision: This case was decided in favor of Lochner. The Court judged that the Fourteenth Amendment protected the right to sell and buy labor and that any state law restricting that right was unconstitutional. The Court rejected the argument that the limited workday and workweek were necessary to protect the health of bakery workers.

Mapp v. Ohio (1961)

Significance: In this ruling the Court declared that evidence discovered in the process of an illegal search could not be used in state courts.

Background: While searching for a bombing suspect, police found evidence of a separate crime in the house of Dollree Mapp. The police did not have permission to enter the home, nor did they have a search warrant. Upon conviction for the separate crime, Mapp appealed her case to the Supreme Court.

Decision: The Court stated that evidence obtained by searches and seizures in violation of the Constitution is inadmissible in court.

Marbury v. Madison (1803)

See Landmark Supreme Court Cases, *p. 75.*

McCulloch v. Maryland (1819)

See Landmark Supreme Court Cases, *p. 107.*

Miranda v. Arizona (1966)

See Landmark Supreme Court Cases, *p. 309.*

Muller v. Oregon (1908)

Significance: A landmark for cases involving social reform, this decision established the Court's recognition of social and economic conditions as a factor in making laws.

Background: In 1903 Oregon passed a law limiting workdays to 10 hours for female workers in laundries and factories. In 1905 Curt Muller's Grand Laundry was found guilty of breaking this law. Muller appealed, claiming that the state law violated his freedom of contract (the Supreme Court had upheld a similar claim in *Lochner v. New York*). The state of Oregon argued that the state had the power to protect its citizens' health, safety, and welfare.

Decision: This case was decided by a vote of 9–0 upholding the Oregon law. The Court agreed that women's well-being was in the state's public interest and that the 10-hour law was a valid way to protect their well-being.

Near v. Minnesota (1931)

Significance: Along with *New York Times v. United States* (1971), this case upheld the freedom of the press from "prior restraint," the attempt to prevent the press from publishing a story.

Background: Jay M. Near was a newspaper publisher in Minneapolis who had printed stories claiming that some local politicians had links to organized crime. He also accused some public officials of taking bribes and other crimes. Officials got an injunction against Near to keep him from publishing his newspaper.

Decision: The Court ruled that the Minnesota law was unconstitutional and noted that protection against the prior restraint of the press was one of the key rights guaranteed by the First Amendment. This established the precedent that, except in rare cases, the government did not have the right to censor or prohibit a publication in advance.

New Jersey v. T.L.O. (1985)

Significance: In this ruling, the Court declared that searches of juveniles on school grounds are not subject to the same standards of "reasonableness" and "probable cause" that protect other citizens.

Background: T.L.O. was a 14-year-old who was caught smoking in the girls' bathroom of her school. A principal at the school questioned the girl and searched her purse, finding marijuana and other drug paraphernalia.

Decision: In a 5–4 decision, the Court ruled that the reasonableness of a search depended on context, and that one's expectation of privacy is diminished in a school setting.

New York Times v. Sullivan (1964)

Significance: In this key case concerning freedom of the press, the Court established the concept of "actual malice," which requires proof that a publisher knowingly printed false statements, in deciding libel and defamation cases.

Background: In 1960 a full-page advertisement in the *New York Times* stated that the arrest of Martin Luther King Jr. in Alabama on perjury charges was an attempt to curb King's efforts to end segregation in the South. The ad detailed some actions taken against civil rights activists at the hands of the Montgomery, Alabama, police. Some of the claims were inaccurate. Montgomery city commissioner L. B. Sullivan filed a libel suit against the *Times*, claiming that the allegations against the police were an attack on him, since his duties included supervision of the police department. Sullivan won $500,000 in an Alabama court judgment.

Decision: In a unanimous decision, the Court ruled that the First Amendment protects all statements about the conduct of public officials, even if the statements are false. In order to win a libel case, a public official must show either that the publisher acted with "actual malice," meaning the false statements were printed even though the publisher knew the statements were false, or that the publisher acted in "reckless disregard" of the truth.

New York Times v. United States (1971)

Significance: In this ruling the Court dismissed the idea of "prior restraint," or attempting to stop an action before it happens, by the government as unconstitutional.

Background: The *New York Times* began publishing a series of papers, called the Pentagon Papers, that were critical of the government's handling of the Vietnam War. The government attempted to stop publication of the papers with a court order, citing national security.

Decision: The Court declared that the government could not stop publication of the Pentagon Papers. Although the government did have the right to stop publication if it could prove the danger to national security, the Court said that in this case the government had not met the burden of proof.

Northern Securities Co. v. United States (1904)

Significance: In this ruling the Court declared that the federal government had the right to break up companies if their formation was illegal.

Background: The Northern Securities Company held stock in several major railroads. Although President Theodore Roosevelt claimed the company was a trust and illegal under the Sherman Antitrust Act, some disagreed that the idea of trusts extended into the realm of owning stocks.

Decision: In a 5–4 decision, the Court ruled that the formation of the company was illegal and that the federal government had the power to disband it.

Planned Parenthood of Southeastern Pennsylvania, et al. v. Casey (1992)

Significance: In this ruling the Court upheld its decision in *Roe v. Wade* (1973) of the right to elective abortion, but the Court allowed the state of Pennsylvania to impose restrictions of notification and consent upon minors.

Background: In 1988 and 1989 Pennsylvania revised its abortion control laws to require that minors receive consent from a parent and that married women notify their husbands before having an abortion. The laws were challenged by several abortion clinics and physicians.

Decision: In a 5–4 decision, the Court upheld its previous ruling of *Roe v. Wade*—that women have the right to an abortion in the first trimester of pregnancy—but provided that a state may allow that minors must have the consent of one parent 24 hours before the procedure. The Court struck down the part of the Pennsylvania laws that required married women to notify their husbands, saying that it could be an "undue burden" upon the woman.

Plessy v. Ferguson (1896)

See Landmark Supreme Court Cases, *p. 237*.

Powell v. Alabama (1932)

Significance: The right to legal counsel in a capital case was guaranteed by the Court's ruling in this case.

Background: Nine African American youths were accused of raping two women on a train passing through Alabama. All nine were quickly tried, found guilty, and sentenced to die. Although Alabama law required that the defendants have access to legal counsel, the attorneys appointed to the cases did not consult with their clients before the trial and did little more to represent the defendants at their trial.

Decision: The Court ruled that the men were denied their right to due process because they were not given a reasonable amount of time with their attorneys in order to build an adequate defense to the charges against them.

Regents of the University of California v. Bakke (1978)

Significance: With this ruling, the Court held that while affirmative action programs are constitutional, a quota system based on race is not.

Background: Allan Bakke had applied to the University of California Medical School at Davis but was denied admission twice. Bakke sued the school, stating that he was a victim of "reverse discrimination" because he was white. Minority students, whose college grades and test scores were not as good as Bakke's, were being admitted through the school's affirmative action program, which set aside sixteen places in each incoming class for minorities.

Decision: The Court ruled that the university's racial quota system violated the Civil Rights Act of 1964. However, the Court wrote, using race as one of several factors in the admissions process was acceptable.

Reno v. American Civil Liberties Union (1997)

Significance: First Amendment protections similar to those granted to the press were extended to the Internet as a result of this case.

Background: The Communications Decency Act was passed in 1996 as an attempt to protect minors from "obscene or indecent" material on the Internet. There were several lawsuits challenging the act.

Decision: The Court declared that the act was unconstitutional because it was too broad in its restrictions. In a unanimous decision, the Court ruled that the law did not clearly define "indecent" material or limit its restrictions so that they did not apply to adults. Also, the Court wrote that the types of government regulations placed on broadcast media do not apply to the Internet.

Roe v. Wade (1973)

Significance: This case established a woman's right to an abortion as part of the constitutional right of privacy.

Background: The case was brought in the name of Jane Roe against the anti-abortion laws of Texas. Until this case, states had widely varying laws about the availability of abortions, some prohibiting them altogether.

Decision: In a 7–2 decision, the Court said that elective abortions must be available to any woman in her first three months of pregnancy. Because of the variety of moral opinions about when life begins, the Court ruled in this case that a fetus does not have the same rights as an infant.

Schechter Poultry Corporation v. United States (1935)

See Landmark Supreme Court Cases, *p. 203.*

Schenck v. United States (1919)

See Landmark Supreme Court Cases, *p. 61.*

Scott v. Sandford (1857)

Significance: This ruling denied enslaved African Americans U.S. citizenship and the right to sue in federal court. The decision also struck down the Missouri Compromise and increased the controversy over the expansion of slavery in new states and territories.

Background: John Emerson, an army doctor, took his slave Dred Scott with him to live in Illinois and then Wisconsin Territory, both of which had banned slavery. In 1842 the two moved to Missouri, a slave state. Scott later sued for his freedom according to the Missouri legal principle of "once free, always free." The principle meant that a slave was entitled to freedom if he or she had once lived in a free state or territory.

Decision: The Court ruled that slaves did not have the right to sue in federal courts because they were considered property, not citizens. The Court also ruled that Congress did not have the power to abolish slavery because that power was not strictly defined in the Constitution.

Stromberg v. California (1931)

Significance: The concept that the First Amendment also protects "symbolic speech" was first realized in this case.

Background: The state of California had a law making it illegal to fly a red flag, which was considered a symbol of communism. Yetta Stromberg was a teacher at a summer youth camp that was run by several groups, some of which were Communist or were sympathetic to the Communist cause. In 1929 Stromberg was arrested because she led a group in a daily ceremony at the camp in which a red flag was raised and saluted.

Decision: In a 7–2 decision, the Court ruled that the law was unconstitutional. In the majority opinion, Chief Justice Charles Evans Hughes wrote that to outlaw a peaceful demonstration or display is "repugnant to the guarantee of liberty" in the Constitution.

Texas v. Johnson (1989)

Significance: This ruling answered the question of whether the First Amendment protects burning the American flag as a form of symbolic speech.

Background: At the 1984 Republican National Convention in Texas, Gregory Lee Johnson doused an American flag with kerosene during a demonstration as a form of protest. Johnson was convicted of violating a Texas law that made it a crime to desecrate the national flag. The Texas Court of Criminal Appeals reversed the conviction because, it said, Johnson's burning of the flag was a form of symbolic speech protected by the First Amendment. The state then appealed to the U.S. Supreme Court.

Decision: The Court ruled for Johnson, 5–4. Justice William Brennan wrote that Johnson was within his constitutional rights when he burned the flag in protest. The Court concluded that Johnson's burning the flag was a form of symbolic speech protected by the First Amendment.

Texas v. White (1869)

Significance: In this case, the Court ruled that Texas never legally left the Union during the Civil War and that states do not have the right to secede from the Union.

Background: Following the Civil War, the Reconstruction government of Texas attempted to reclaim $10 million in U.S. bonds that had been issued to Texas in 1851. The bonds had been used by the Confederate Texas government to buy munitions and supplies from George W. White and others during the war. The question was whether Texas had remained a state during the Civil War and, therefore, had the right to have the Supreme Court hear the case.

Decision: In a 5–3 decision, the Court ruled that the Constitution does not give states the right of secession. In the majority opinion, Chief Justice Salmon P. Chase wrote that "the Constitution, in all its provisions, looks to an indestructible Union, composed of indestructible States." Therefore, Chase wrote, the union between Texas and the United States was "indissoluble."

Tinker v. Des Moines Independent Community School District (1969)

Significance: This ruling established the extent to which public school students can take part in political protests in their schools. The question the case raised is whether, under the First Amendment, school officials can prohibit students from wearing armbands to symbolize political protest.

Background: Some high school and junior high school students in Des Moines, Iowa, decided to wear black armbands to protest the Vietnam War. Two days before the protest, the school board created a new policy that students who wore an armband to school and refused to remove it would be suspended. Three students, including Mary Beth Tinker and John Tinker, wore armbands and were suspended. They said their First Amendment right to freedom of speech had been violated.

Decision: By a 7–2 margin, the Court agreed with the students. Justice Abe Fortas wrote for the majority that students do not "shed their constitutional rights to freedom of speech . . . at the schoolhouse gate." Fortas admitted that school officials had the right to set rules. However, their rules must be consistent with the First Amendment.

United States v. American Library Association (2003)

Significance: This case deals with the constitutionality of the Children's Internet Protection Act (CIPA). This federal law was designed to protect children from being exposed to pornographic Web sites while using computers in public libraries. The question before the Court was whether a public library violates the First Amendment by installing Internet-filtering software on its public computers.

Background: CIPA applies to public libraries that accept federal money to help pay for Internet access. These libraries must install filtering software to block pornographic images. Some library associations sued to block these filtering requirements. They argued that by linking money and filters, the law required public libraries to violate the First Amendment's guarantees of free speech. The libraries argued that filters block some non-pornographic sites along with pornographic ones. That, they said, violates library patrons' First Amendment rights.

Decision: Chief Justice William Rehnquist authored a plurality opinion. He explained that the law does not require any library to accept federal money. A library can choose to do without federal money. If the library makes that choice, they do not have to install Internet filters. Rehnquist said that filtering software's tendency to block some non-pornographic sites was not a constitutional problem. Adult patrons could simply ask a librarian to unblock a blocked site, or they could have the filter disabled entirely.

United States v. E.C. Knight Co. (1895)

Significance: The Court declared local manufacturing to be out of the scope of the interstate commerce regulatory power of Congress.

Background: The E.C. Knight Company had a virtual monopoly on sugar refining in the United States. The federal government sued the company under the Sherman Antitrust Act in an attempt to break this monopoly and allow other companies to refine sugar.

Decision: The Court ruled that although the act was legal, it did not apply to manufacturing. Justice Melville Fuller said that manufacturing was not interstate commerce and could therefore not be regulated by Congress.

United States v. Nixon (1974)

See **Landmark Supreme Court Cases**, *p. 171.*

Vernonia School District v. Acton (1995)

Significance: The ruling allowed schools to administer random drug tests to all students who wanted to play sports.

Background: In an effort to reduce drug use, particularly among student athletes, the Vernonia School District of Oregon started a program for random urinalysis drug testing for students participating in sports. Student athlete James Acton refused to participate in drug testing, stating that the policy invaded his right to privacy and was an illegal search and seizure.

Decision: In a 6–3 decision, the Court ruled that while on school property, students are subject to greater control of personal rights than free adults. Furthermore, concern over the safety of minors under governmental supervision outweighs the minimal intrusion into a student's privacy.

Wabash, St. Louis & Pacific Railroad v. Illinois (1886)

Significance: This ruling removed the states' power to regulate railroad rates. It reasserted the authority of Congress over interstate commerce and led to the creation of the Interstate Commerce Commission.

Background: The state of Illinois passed a law attempting to regulate the shipping rates of railroads that passed through the state, including the Wabash, St. Louis & Pacific line. In an attempt to operate without regulation, the railroad company sued the state.

Decision: The Court struck down the Illinois law, saying that the state was able to regulate businesses that operated only within its boundaries. Businesses that operated between states were subject to federal regulation.

Wallace v. Jaffree (1985)

Significance: This ruling declared that a state law authorizing a moment of silence for prayer violated the First Amendment's establishment clause.

Background: An Alabama law allowed teachers to set aside time each day for a moment of "silent meditation or voluntary prayer." A parent of three children enrolled at a Mobile, Alabama, school sued the state, complaining that the law amounted to forcing prayer upon the students.

Decision: The Court ruled 6–3 that the Alabama law was unconstitutional. In its opinion, the Court wrote that even though prayer was considered voluntary, the state statute was designed to endorse religion and was "not motivated by any clear secular purpose."

Watkins v. United States (1957)

Significance: This decision limited the inquiry powers of Congress. Congress was expected not to engage in law enforcement (an executive function), nor to act as a trial agency (a judicial function), but to inquire only as far as was necessary for its function.

Background: John Watkins was a labor union officer who appeared before the House Un-American Activities Committee. Although he was willing to answer personal questions about himself and others whom he knew to be members of the Communist Party, he would not answer questions about past members of the Communist Party. He was held in contempt of Congress.

Decision: In a vote of 6–1, the Court threw out the charge of contempt against Watkins. Congress, it said, did not have the right to invade the private lives of individuals.

Weeks v. *United States* (1914)

Significance: In this case, the Court established that police must have a warrant before seizing items from a private home and determined that illegally obtained evidence is inadmissible in court.

Background Fremont Weeks was convicted of using the U.S. mail to distribute lottery tickets, which was against Missouri gambling laws. The conviction was based on papers that police seized when they entered Weeks's home without a warrant. Weeks sued the police and demanded the return of his papers.

Decision: In a unanimous decision, the Court ruled that Weeks's Fourth Amendment right against unlawful search and seizure had been violated. The Court also ruled that evidence obtained illegally cannot be used in court proceedings, establishing what is now known as the exclusionary rule.

West Virginia State Board of Education v. *Barnette* (1943)

Significance: In this case, the Court overruled an earlier decision and held that requiring children at public schools to recite the Pledge of Allegiance is unconstitutional.

Background: The West Virginia State Board of Education required that a salute to the American flag be performed by all teachers and students in the state's schools. Anyone who refused to participate could be expelled. Walter Barnette, a Jehovah's Witness, challenged the law, saying that members of his religion were prohibited from saluting or pledging to political institutions or symbols. Barnette was going up against a precedent set in a similar case, *Minersville School District* v. *Gobitis* (1940), in which the Court had ruled that a mandatory flag salute was constitutional and that the government had an interest in promoting "national cohesion," which was the "basis of national security."

Decision: Following the ruling in the *Gobitis* case, there were many incidents of violence and discrimination against Jehovah's Witnesses. Many Jehovah's Witnesses were brutally assaulted or driven from their homes. In response to attacks on Jehovah's Witnesses, several newspapers and legal experts began to publish statements critical of the Supreme Court's handling of the case, leading a couple of the justices to re-examine their decisions. When Barnette's case came before the Court just three years later, the vote was 6–3 saying that a compulsory flag salute was prohibited by the First Amendment's guarantee of free speech. In the majority opinion, Justice Robert H. Jackson wrote that "no official, high or petty, can prescribe what shall be orthodox in politics, nationalism, religion, or other matters of opinion or force citizens to confess by word or act their faith therein."

Whitney v. *California* (1927)

Significance: In this case, the Court ruled that states have the right to regulate speech that represents a "clear and present danger" to the government.

Background: Charlotte Anita Whitney was accused of teaching the violent overthrow of the government and was convicted of promoting "terrorism as a means of accomplishing change" for her part in establishing the Communist Labor Party in California. She claimed the group was formed to promote political ideas, not to advocate violence.

Decision: The Court, in a unanimous decision, upheld Whitney's conviction. Justice Terry Sanford wrote that the state has the right to punish those who abuse their freedom of speech to "incite crime, disturb the public peace, or endanger the foundations of organized government and threaten its overthrow." In his concurring opinion, Justice Louis Brandeis wrote that only the clear, present, and imminent threats of "serious evils" could justify suppression of speech.

Wisconsin v. *Yoder* (1972)

Significance: The Court ruled that a law requiring that Amish children attend school past the eighth grade violated their First Amendment right to freedom of religion.

Background: Three children from Amish families stopped attending a New Glarus, Wisconsin, school after they finished the eighth grade. The children's parents claimed that attending high school went against their religious beliefs. The parents were charged with violating a Wisconsin law that required all children attend school until the age of 16. The Amish families' religious beliefs also prohibited them from going to court to settle a dispute, but a Lutheran minister became interested in the case and formed a group to represent the Amish families.

Decision: The Court ruled unanimously that a person's freedom of religion outweighed the state's interest in requiring that children attend school past the eighth grade. Chief Justice Warren Burger wrote in the majority opinion that the education provided in secondary school was "in sharp conflict with the fundamental mode of life mandated by the Amish religion."

Worcester v. *Georgia* (1832)

Significance: This ruling made Georgia's removal of the Cherokee illegal. However, Georgia, with President Andrew Jackson's support, defied the Court's decision. This case showed the limits of the Court's power to enforce a decision if it chose not to use further legal action to compel cooperation. As a result, American Indian peoples continued to be forced off lands protected by treaties.

Background: The state of Georgia wanted to remove the Cherokee people from lands they held by treaty. Samuel Worcester, a missionary who worked with the Cherokee Nation, was arrested for failing to take an oath of allegiance to the state and to obey a Georgia militia order to leave the Cherokee's lands. Worcester sued, charging that Georgia had no legal authority on Cherokee lands.

Decision: This case was decided in 1832 by a vote of 5–1 in favor of Worcester. Chief Justice John Marshall spoke for the Supreme Court, which ruled that the Cherokee were an independent political community. The Court decided that only the federal government, not the state of Georgia, had authority over legal matters involving the Cherokee people.

Facts about the States

STATE	CAPITAL	YEAR of STATE-HOOD	AREA (square miles)	2005 POPULATION	African American	Asian American	Caucasian	Hispanic	Native American	Other
Alabama	Montgomery	1819	52,419	4,557,808	26.4	0.8	71.4	2.2	0.5	0.9
Alaska	Juneau	1959	663,267	663,661	3.6	4.5	70.7	4.9	15.8	5.3
Arizona	Phoenix	1912	113,998	5,939,292	3.5	2.1	87.6	28	5	1.7
Arkansas	Little Rock	1836	53,179	2,779,154	15.8	0.9	81.3	4.4	0.7	1.3
California	Sacramento	1850	163,696	36,132,147	6.8	12.1	77.2	34.7	1.2	2.8
Colorado	Denver	1876	104,094	4,665,177	4.1	2.5	90.3	19.1	1.1	1.9
Connecticut	Hartford	1788	5,543	3,510,297	10.1	3.1	85.1	10.6	0.3	1.4
Delaware	Dover	1787	2,489	843,524	20.4	2.6	75.3	5.8	0.4	1.4
Florida	Tallahassee	1845	65,755	17,789,864	15.7	2.0	80.6	19	0.4	1.3
Georgia	Atlanta	1788	59,425	9,072,576	29.6	2.6	66.4	6.8	0.3	1.1
Hawaii	Honolulu	1959	10,931	1,275,194	2.2	41.8	26.5	7.9	0.3	29.2
Idaho	Boise	1890	83,570	1,429,096	0.6	1.0	95.5	8.9	1.4	1.4
Illinois	Springfield	1818	57,914	12,763,371	15.1	4.0	79.5	14.0	0.3	1.2
Indiana	Indianapolis	1816	36,418	6,271,973	8.8	1.2	88.7	4.3	0.3	1.6
Iowa	Des Moines	1846	56,272	2,966,334	2.3	1.4	95.0	3.5	0.3	0.9
Kansas	Topeka	1861	82,277	2,744,687	5.9	2.1	89.4	8.1	1.0	1.7
Kentucky	Frankfort	1792	40,409	4,173,405	7.5	0.9	90.4	1.9	0.2	1.1
Louisiana	Baton Rouge	1812	51,840	4,523,628	33.3	1.4	64.1	2.8	0.6	0.8
Maine	Augusta	1820	35,385	1,321,505	0.7	0.8	96.9	1.0	0.6	0.9
Maryland	Annapolis	1788	12,407	5,600,388	29.1	4.6	64.5	5.4	0.3	1.6
Massachusetts	Boston	1788	10,555	6,398,743	6.8	4.6	87.0	7.7	0.3	1.4
Michigan	Lansing	1837	96,716	10,120,860	14.3	2.2	81.4	3.7	0.6	1.4
Minnesota	St. Paul	1858	86,939	5,132,799	4.1	3.4	89.9	3.5	1.2	1.5
Mississippi	Jackson	1817	48,430	2,921,088	36.8	0.7	61.3	1.7	0.5	0.6
Missouri	Jefferson City	1821	69,704	5,800,310	11.5	1.3	85.4	2.6	0.5	1.4
Montana	Helena	1889	147,042	935,670	0.4	0.5	91.1	2.4	6.4	1.6
Nebraska	Lincoln	1867	77,354	1,758,787	4.3	1.5	92.1	6.9	0.9	1.2
Nevada	Carson City	1864	110,561	2,414,807	7.5	5.5	82.5	22.8	1.4	3.0
New Hampshire	Concord	1788	9,350	1,309,940	0.9	1.7	96.2	2.1	0.2	0.9
New Jersey	Trenton	1787	8,721	8,717,925	14.5	7.0	76.9	14.9	0.3	1.3
New Mexico	Santa Fe	1912	121,589	1,928,384	2.4	1.3	84.7	43.3	10.1	1.6
New York	Albany	1788	54,556	19,254,630	17.5	6.7	73.9	16.0	0.5	1.6
North Carolina	Raleigh	1789	53,819	8,683,242	21.8	1.7	74.1	6.1	1.3	1.1
North Dakota	Bismarck	1889	70,700	636,677	0.7	0.7	92.4	1.5	5.2	0.9
Ohio	Columbus	1803	44,825	11,464,042	11.9	1.4	85.2	2.2	0.2	1.2
Oklahoma	Oklahoma City	1907	69,898	3,547,884	7.7	1.5	78.6	6.3	8.1	4.1
Oregon	Salem	1859	98,381	3,641,056	1.8	3.4	90.9	9.5	1.4	2.3
Pennsylvania	Harrisburg	1787	46,055	12,429,616	10.5	2.2	86.2	3.8	0.2	0.9
Rhode Island	Providence	1790	1,545	1,076,189	6.1	2.7	89.1	10.3	0.6	1.6
South Carolina	Columbia	1788	32,020	4,255,083	29.4	1.1	68.3	3.1	0.4	0.9
South Dakota	Pierre	1889	77,116	775,933	0.8	0.7	88.7	2.0	8.6	1.2
Tennessee	Nashville	1796	42,143	5,962,959	16.8	1.2	80.7	2.8	0.3	1.0
Texas	Austin	1845	268,581	22,859,968	11.7	3.2	83.3	34.6	0.7	1.1
Utah	Salt Lake City	1896	84,899	2,469,585	0.9	1.9	93.8	10.6	1.3	1.4
Vermont	Montpelier	1791	9,614	623,050	0.6	1.0	96.9	1.0	0.4	1.1
Virginia	Richmond	1788	42,774	7,567,465	19.9	4.4	73.8	5.7	0.3	1.6
Washington	Olympia	1889	71,300	6,287,759	3.5	6.3	85.3	8.5	1.6	3.0
West Virginia	Charleston	1863	24,230	1,816,856	3.2	0.6	95.2	0.8	0.2	0.8
Wisconsin	Madison	1848	65,498	5,536,201	5.9	1.9	90.2	4.3	0.9	1.0
Wyoming	Cheyenne	1890	97,814	509,294	0.9	0.6	94.8	6.7	2.4	1.3
Washington, D.C.	–	–	68	550,521	57.7	3.0	37.4	8.5	0.3	1.6

[1]Totals may not equal 100 percent since the Hispanic population may be any race and also may be listed in other categories.

| STATE | 2008 VOTE | | | | | |
| | BARACK OBAMA (D) | | JOHN McCAIN (R) | | OTHER CANDIDATES | |
	Popular Vote	Electoral College	Popular Vote	Electoral College	Popular Vote	Electoral College
Alabama	811,764	0	1,264,879	9	15,903	0
Alaska	122,485	0	192,631	3	6,984	0
Arizona	948,648	0	1,132,560	10	24,978	0
Arkansas	418,049	0	632,672	6	26,037	0
California	7,441,458	55	4,554,643	0	228,478	0
Colorado	1,216,793	9	1,020,135	0	36,867	0
Connecticut	1,000,994	7	628,873	0	19,532	0
Delaware	255,394	3	152,356	0	4,578	0
Florida	4,143,957	27	3,939,380	0	60,888	0
Georgia	1,843,452	0	2,048,244	15	28,805	0
Hawaii	324,918	4	120,309	0	7,105	0
Idaho	235,219	0	400,989	4	15,470	0
Illinois	3,319,237	21	1,981,158	0	70,700	0
Indiana	1,374,039	11	1,345,648	0	31,367	0
Iowa	818,240	7	677,508	0	20,324	0
Kansas	499,979	0	685,541	6	20,857	0
Kentucky	751,985	0	1,048,462	8	26,061	0
Louisiana	780,981	0	1,147,603	9	29,475	0
Maine	421,484	4	296,195	0	13,637	0
Maryland	1,612,692	10	956,663	0	32,884	0
Massachusetts	1,891,083	12	1,104,284	0	53,071	0
Michigan	2,867,680	17	2,044,405	0	81,414	0
Minnesota	1,573,354	10	1,275,409	0	61,606	0
Mississippi	520,864	0	687,266	6	10,156	0
Missouri	1,442,180	0	1,445,812	11	37,400	0
Montana	229,725	0	241,816	3	15,489	0
Nebraska	329,132	1	448,801	4	11,919	0
Nevada	531,884	5	411,988	0	21,254	0
New Hampshire	384,591	4	316,937	0	6,120	0
New Jersey	2,085,051	15	1,545,495	0	39,352	0
New Mexico	464,458	5	343,820	0	10,752	0
New York	4,363,386	31	2,576,360	0	80,372	0
North Carolina	2,123,390	15	2,109,698	0	25,419	0
North Dakota	141,113	0	168,523	3	6,351	0
Ohio	2,708,685	20	2,501,855	0	84,946	0
Oklahoma	502,294	0	959,745	7	0	0
Oregon	978,605	7	699,673	0	36,108	0
Pennsylvania	3,192,316	21	2,586,496	0	61,446	0
Rhode Island	296,571	4	165,391	0	7,805	0
South Carolina	862,449	0	1,034,896	8	23,624	0
South Dakota	170,886	0	203,019	3	7,997	0
Tennessee	1,085,720	0	1,477,405	11	33,438	0
Texas	3,521,164	0	4,467,748	34	56,398	0
Utah	327,670	0	596,030	5	28,670	0
Vermont	219,105	3	98,791	0	5,413	0
Virginia	1,958,370	13	1,726,053	0	32,340	0
Washington	1,750,848	11	1,229,216	0	56,814	0
West Virginia	301,438	0	394,278	5	11,986	0
Wisconsin	1,670,474	10	1,258,181	0	36,998	0
Wyoming	80,496	0	160,639	3	5,194	0
Washington, D.C.	210,403	3	14,821	0	1,349	0
Total	67,127,153	365	58,521,300	173	1,672,131	0

The Presidents

George Washington

Thomas Jefferson

	NAME	PARTY	STATE[1]	YEARS in OFFICE	AGE on taking OFFICE	VICE PRESIDENT(S)
1	George Washington (1732–1799)	none	Virginia	1789–1797	57	John Adams
2	John Adams (1735–1826)	Federalist	Massachusetts	1797–1801	61	Thomas Jefferson
3	Thomas Jefferson (1743–1826)	Republican[2]	Virginia	1801–1809	57	Aaron Burr, George Clinton
4	James Madison (1751–1836)	Republican	Virginia	1809–1817	57	George Clinton, Elbridge Gerry
5	James Monroe (1758–1831)	Republican	Virginia	1817–1825	58	Daniel D. Tompkins
6	John Quincy Adams (1767–1848)	Republican	Massachusetts	1825–1829	57	John C. Calhoun
7	Andrew Jackson (1767–1845)	Democratic	Tennessee (South Carolina)	1829–1837	61	John C. Calhoun, Martin Van Buren
8	Martin Van Buren (1782–1862)	Democratic	New York	1837–1841	54	Richard M. Johnson
9	William Henry Harrison (1773–1841)	Whig	Ohio (Virginia)	1841	68	John Tyler
10	John Tyler (1790–1862)	Whig	Virginia	1841–1845	51	none
11	James K. Polk (1795–1849)	Democratic	Tennessee (North Carolina)	1845–1849	49	George M. Dallas
12	Zachary Taylor (1784–1850)	Whig	Louisiana (Virginia)	1849–1850	64	Millard Fillmore
13	Millard Fillmore (1800–1874)	Whig	New York	1850–1853	50	none
14	Franklin Pierce (1804–1869)	Democratic	New Hampshire	1853–1857	48	William R. King
15	James Buchanan (1791–1868)	Democratic	Pennsylvania	1857–1861	65	John C. Breckinridge
16	Abraham Lincoln (1809–1865)	Republican	Illinois (Kentucky)	1861–1865	52	Hannibal Hamlin, Andrew Johnson
17	Andrew Johnson (1808–1875)	Democratic	Tennessee (North Carolina)	1865–1869	56	none
18	Ulysses S. Grant (1822–1885)	Republican	Illinois (Ohio)	1869–1877	46	Schuyler Colfax, Henry Wilson
19	Rutherford B. Hayes (1822–1893)	Republican	Ohio	1877–1881	54	William A. Wheeler
20	James A. Garfield (1831–1881)	Republican	Ohio	1881	49	Chester A. Arthur
21	Chester A. Arthur (1829–1886)	Republican	New York (Vermont)	1881–1885	51	none

[1] State of residence when elected; state of birth shown in parentheses if born in another state
[2] The Republican Party of the third through sixth presidents is not the Republican Party of Abraham Lincoln, which was founded in 1854.

Andrew Jackson

Abraham Lincoln

Theodore Roosevelt

Woodrow Wilson

Franklin D. Roosevelt

John F. Kennedy

	NAME	PARTY	STATE[1]	YEARS in OFFICE	AGE on taking OFFICE	VICE PRESIDENT(S)
22	Grover Cleveland (1837–1908)	Democratic	New York (New Jersey)	1885–1889	47	Thomas A. Hendricks
23	Benjamin Harrison (1833–1901)	Republican	Indiana (Ohio)	1889–1893	55	Levi P. Morton
24	Grover Cleveland (1837–1908)	Democratic	New York (New Jersey)	1893–1897	55	Adlai E. Stevenson
25	William McKinley (1843–1901)	Republican	Ohio	1897–1901	54	Garret A. Hobart, Theodore Roosevelt
26	Theodore Roosevelt (1858–1919)	Republican	New York	1901–1909	42	Charles W. Fairbanks
27	William Howard Taft (1857–1930)	Republican	Ohio	1909–1913	51	James S. Sherman
28	Woodrow Wilson (1856–1924)	Democratic	New Jersey (Virginia)	1913–1921	56	Thomas R. Marshall
29	Warren G. Harding (1865–1923)	Republican	Ohio	1921–1923	55	Calvin Coolidge
30	Calvin Coolidge (1872–1933)	Republican	Massachusetts (Vermont)	1923–1929	51	Charles G. Dawes
31	Herbert Hoover (1874–1964)	Republican	California (Iowa)	1929–1933	54	Charles Curtis
32	Franklin D. Roosevelt (1882–1945)	Democratic	New York	1933–1945	51	John Nance Garner, Henry A. Wallace, Harry S Truman
33	Harry S Truman (1884–1972)	Democratic	Missouri	1945–1953	60	Alben W. Barkley
34	Dwight D. Eisenhower (1890–1969)	Republican	Kansas (Texas)	1953–1961	62	Richard M. Nixon
35	John F. Kennedy (1917–1963)	Democratic	Massachusetts	1961–1963	43	Lyndon B. Johnson
36	Lyndon B. Johnson (1908–1973)	Democratic	Texas	1963–1969	55	Hubert H. Humphrey
37	Richard M. Nixon (1913–1994)	Republican	California	1969–1974	56	Spiro T. Agnew, Gerald R. Ford
38	Gerald R. Ford (1913–2006)	Republican	Michigan (Nebraska)	1974–1977	61	Nelson A. Rockefeller
39	Jimmy Carter (1924–)	Democratic	Georgia	1977–1981	52	Walter F. Mondale
40	Ronald Reagan (1911–2004)	Republican	California (Illinois)	1981–1989	69	George H. W. Bush
41	George H. W. Bush (1924–)	Republican	Texas (Massachusetts)	1989–1993	64	J. Danforth Quayle
42	William J. Clinton (1946–)	Democratic	Arkansas	1993–2001	46	Albert Gore Jr.
43	George W. Bush (1946–)	Republican	Texas (Connecticut)	2001–2009	54	Richard B. Cheney
44	Barack Obama (1961–)	Democratic	Illinois (Hawaii)	2009–	47	Joe Biden

The United States of America: Political

Strait of Juan de Fuca

Puget Sound

Franklin D. Roosevelt Lake

Seattle
Tacoma
Olympia ★
Spokane

WASHINGTON

Portland

Pend Oreille

Flathead Lake

Salem ★

Columbia River

Eugene

OREGON

Great Falls

Helena ★

MONTANA

Missouri River

Fort Peck Lake

Billings

Yellowstone River

NORTH DAKOTA

Lake Sakakawea

Bismarck

Goose Lake

Cape Mendocino

Shasta Lake

Boise

Sun Valley

IDAHO

Snake River

Pocatello

Yellowstone Lake

WYOMING

Lake Oahe

SOUTH DAKOTA

Pierre

Rapid City

Sacramento River

Pyramid Lake

Reno
Carson City
Lake Tahoe

NEVADA

Ogden

Great Salt Lake

Salt Lake City
Provo

Utah Lake

UTAH

Green River

Cheyenne

NEBRASKA

Platte River

Berkeley
Oakland
San Francisco
San Francisco Bay

Sacramento ★

San Jose

Monterey Bay

San Joaquin River

Fresno

CALIFORNIA

Boulder
Vail
Aspen
Denver ★
Colorado Springs

COLORADO

Pueblo

Arkansas River

KANSAS

35°N

Las Vegas

Lake Mead

Colorado River

Lake Powell

Santa Barbara
Ventura
Los Angeles
Long Beach
Riverside
Palm Springs
Anaheim
Santa Ana
San Diego

Channel Islands

Salton Sea

Flagstaff

ARIZONA

Phoenix ★

Taos

Santa Fe ★

Albuquerque

NEW MEXICO

OKLAHOMA

Canadian River

Oklahoma City ★

Amarillo

Lawton

PACIFIC OCEAN

Gila River

Casa Grande

Tucson

Las Cruces

El Paso

Lubbock

Brazos River

Midland
Odessa

Abilene

Fort Worth

TEXAS

Pecos River

Colorado River

30°N

Gulf of California

To understand the relative locations of Alaska and Hawaii, as well as the vast distances separating them from the rest of the United States, see the world map.

Amistad Reservoir

Rio Grande

Austin

San Antonio

HAWAII

Kauai
Niihau
Oahu
Honolulu
Molokai
Maui
Lanai
Kahoolawe

PACIFIC OCEAN

22°N
155°W
160°W

Hilo
Hawaii

19°N

0   75   150 Miles
0   75   150 Kilometers
Projection: Mercator

ARCTIC OCEAN

RUSSIA

Arctic Circle

Bering Strait

Nome

Yukon River

St. Lawrence Island

St. Matthew Island

Fairbanks

CANADA

ALASKA

Nunivak Island

Anchorage
Valdez

Skagway

MEXICO

Corpus Christi

Laredo

Padre Island

Bering Sea

Attu Island

55°N
50°N
170°E
180°

0   250   500 Miles
0   250   500 Kilometers
Projection: Albers Equal Area

Gulf of Alaska

Kodiak Island

Juneau ★

Alexander Archipelago

55°N

140°W
150°W
160°W
170°W

PACIFIC OCEAN

ALEUTIAN ISLANDS

125°W

120°W

CANADA

MINNESOTA
Grand Forks
Fargo
Duluth
Superior
Marquette
Sault Ste. Marie
Lake Superior

WISCONSIN
Minneapolis
St. Paul
Green Bay
Madison
Milwaukee
Sioux Falls

MICHIGAN
Lake Michigan
Lake Huron
Grand Rapids
Saginaw
Lansing
Detroit
Ann Arbor

IOWA
Sioux City
Cedar Rapids
Davenport
Des Moines
Rockford
Chicago
Gary
South Bend
Fort Wayne

MISSOURI
Kansas City
Kansas City
Topeka
St. Louis
East St. Louis
Jefferson City
Lake of the Ozarks
Springfield

ILLINOIS
Peoria
Springfield
Indianapolis

INDIANA
Dayton
Cincinnati

OHIO
Toledo
Cleveland
Youngstown
Akron
Columbus

Lake Erie
Lake Ontario
Buffalo
Rochester
Syracuse
Albany

NEW YORK

PENNSYLVANIA
Pittsburgh
Harrisburg
Allentown
Philadelphia
Susquehanna River

St. Lawrence River
Lake Champlain
Burlington
Montpelier
Augusta

MAINE
Portland
VT
NH
Concord
Manchester
Boston
Worcester
Providence
Cape Cod
MA
Springfield
Hartford
CT
RI
Bridgeport
New Haven
Yonkers
Long Island Sound
Long Island
Jersey City
Newark
New York City
Trenton
Camden
NJ
Atlantic City
Dover
DE
Baltimore
MD
Annapolis
Washington D.C.
Delaware Bay

WEST VIRGINIA
Charleston

VIRGINIA
Richmond
Newport News
Norfolk
Virginia Beach
Chesapeake Bay

ATLANTIC OCEAN

40°N
70°W
35°N

Frankfort
Louisville
Evansville
Lexington
Ohio River

KENTUCKY
Lake Barkley

MISSOURI

Keystone Lake
Tulsa
Fayetteville
Springfield
Kentucky Lake
Nashville
Knoxville
Asheville

Greensboro
Durham
Raleigh
Winston-Salem

NORTH CAROLINA
Charlotte
Cape Hatteras

ARKANSAS
Little Rock
Pine Bluff
Memphis

TENNESSEE
Chattanooga
Huntsville
Greenville

SOUTH CAROLINA
Columbia
Charleston

MISSISSIPPI
Vicksburg
Jackson
Meridian

ALABAMA
Birmingham
Montgomery

GEORGIA
Atlanta
Macon
Columbus
Savannah
Savannah River
Sea Islands

Shreveport
Beaumont
Houston
Galveston
Dallas
Toledo Bend Reservoir

LOUISIANA
Baton Rouge
New Orleans
Mobile
Pensacola
Biloxi
Chandeleur Islands

Tallahassee
Gainesville
Jacksonville
Chattahoochee R.

FLORIDA
Orlando
Tampa
St. Petersburg
Lake Okeechobee
Cape Canaveral
Fort Myers
Fort Lauderdale
Miami
Cape Sable
Florida Keys
Straits of Florida

BAHAMAS

30°N
25°N
80°W
75°W

Gulf of Mexico

N W E S

95°W
90°W
85°W

Red River
Mississippi River
Missouri River
Minnesota River
Red River

Lake Texoma
Lake Eufaula

Legend:
- ✪ National capital
- ★ State capitals
- ● Other cities

0 100 200 Miles
0 100 200 Kilometers
Projection: Albers Equal Area

World: Political

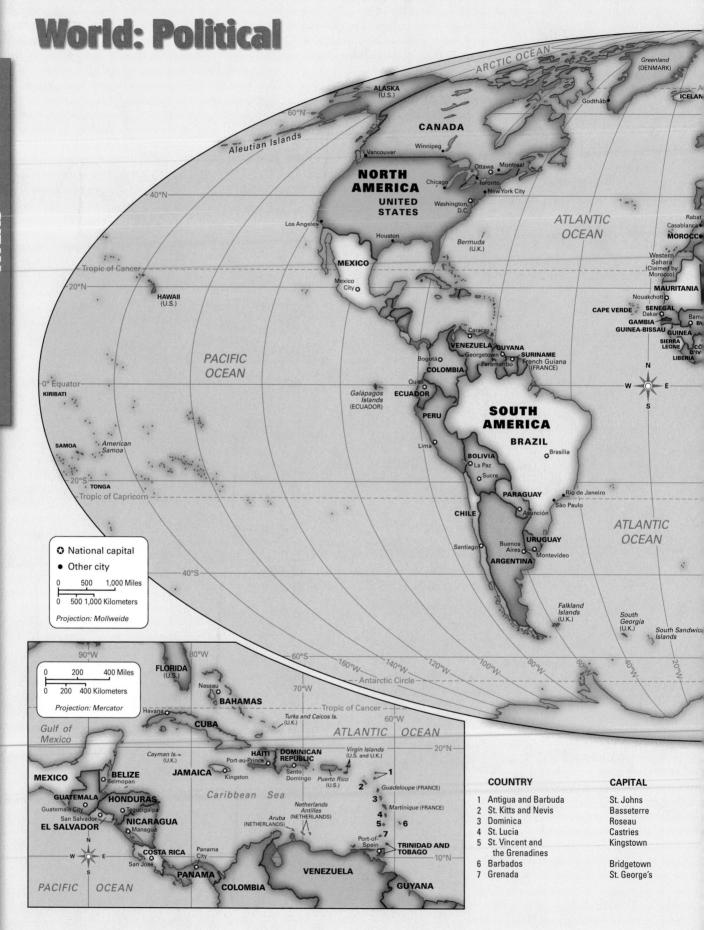

ARCTIC OCEAN

Greenland
(DENMARK)

ICELAN

ALASKA
(U.S.)

60°N

CANADA

Aleutian Islands

Winnipeg

Vancouver

Godthåb

Ottawa   Montreal

NORTH
AMERICA

Chicago   Toronto
New York City

40°N

UNITED
STATES

Washington,
D.C.

ATLANTIC
OCEAN

Rabat
Casablanca

MOROCC

Los Angeles

Houston

Bermuda
(U.K.)

Western
Sahara
(Claimed by
Morocco)

MEXICO

Tropic of Cancer

20°N

Mexico
City

MAURITANIA

Nouakchott

CAPE VERDE   SENEGAL
Dakar

HAWAII
(U.S.)

Bama
Bl

GAMBIA
GUINEA-BISSAU   GUINEA

Caracas

SIERRA   CÔ
LEONE   D'IV

VENEZUELA   GUYANA

Georgetown   SURINAME

LIBERIA

Paramaribo   French Guiana
(FRANCE)

N

Bogotá

COLOMBIA

W   E

PACIFIC
OCEAN

0° Equator

Quito

ECUADOR

S

KIRIBATI

Galápagos
Islands
(ECUADOR)

PERU

SOUTH
AMERICA

Lima

BRAZIL

Brasília

SAMOA

American
Samoa

BOLIVIA

Rio de Janeiro

La Paz

Sucre

20°S

TONGA

PARAGUAY

São Paulo

Tropic of Capricorn

Asunción

ATLANTIC
OCEAN

CHILE

○ National capital

● Other city

0   500   1,000 Miles

0   500 1,000 Kilometers

Projection: Mollweide

Santiago

URUGUAY

Buenos
Aires

Montevideo

ARGENTINA

40°S

Falkland
Islands
(U.K.)

South
Georgia
(U.K.)

South Sandwic
Islands

60°S   160°W   140°W   120°W   100°W   80°W   60°W   40°W   20°W

Antarctic Circle

90°W   80°W

FLORIDA
(U.S.)

Tropic of Cancer   60°W

0   200   400 Miles

Nassau

Turks and Caicos Is.
(U.K.)

70°W

20°N

0   200   400 Kilometers

BAHAMAS

ATLANTIC   OCEAN

Projection: Mercator

Havana

Gulf of
Mexico

CUBA

Cayman Is.
(U.K.)

HAITI   DOMINICAN
REPUBLIC

Port-au-Prince

Virgin Islands
(U.S. and U.K.)

1

MEXICO   BELIZE

Belmopan

JAMAICA

Kingston

Santo
Domingo

Puerto Rico
(U.S.)

2

Guadeloupe (FRANCE)

GUATEMALA   HONDURAS

Caribbean Sea

3

Guatemala City   Tegucigalpa

Martinique (FRANCE)

San Salvador   NICARAGUA

Netherlands
Antilles
(NETHERLANDS)

4

EL SALVADOR

Managua

N

Aruba
(NETHERLANDS)

5   6

W   E

7

S

Port-of-
Spain

TRINIDAD AND
TOBAGO

COSTA RICA

Panama
City

San José

PANAMA

PACIFIC   OCEAN

VENEZUELA

10°N

COLOMBIA

GUYANA

COUNTRY	CAPITAL
1 Antigua and Barbuda	St. Johns
2 St. Kitts and Nevis	Basseterre
3 Dominica	Roseau
4 St. Lucia	Castries
5 St. Vincent and the Grenadines	Kingstown
6 Barbados	Bridgetown
7 Grenada	St. George's

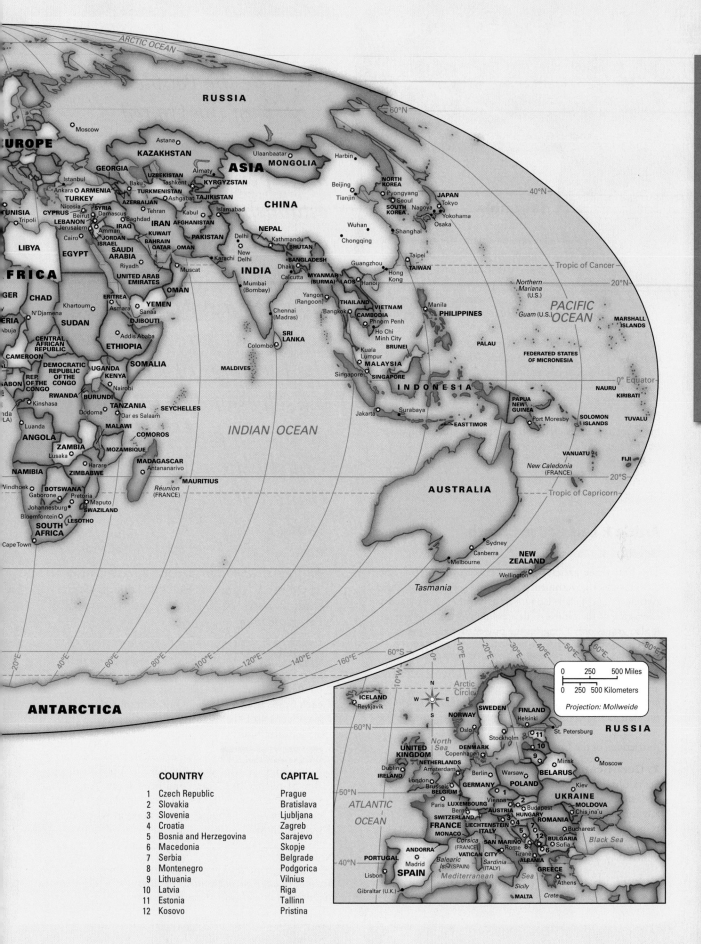

ARCTIC OCEAN

RUSSIA

EUROPE

Moscow

Astana

KAZAKHSTAN

Ulaanbaatar

MONGOLIA

Harbin

GEORGIA

Almaty

ASIA

Istanbul

Ankara ARMENIA

Baku

UZBEKISTAN

Tashkent

KYRGYZSTAN

Beijing

NORTH
KOREA

JAPAN

Tokyo

TURKEY

Nicosia

AZERBAIJAN

Ashgabat

TAJIKISTAN

Tianjin

Pyongyang

Seoul

Nagoya

Yokohama

CYPRUS

Damascus

TURKMENISTAN

CHINA

SOUTH
KOREA

Osaka

SYRIA

Tehran

Beirut

Baghdad

Kabul

Islamabad

Wuhan

Shanghai

LEBANON

Jerusalem

IRAQ

AFGHANISTAN

Delhi

NEPAL

Kathmandu

BHUTAN

Chongqing

Taipei

Amman

JORDAN

KUWAIT

PAKISTAN

New
Delhi

BANGLADESH

Guangzhou

TAIWAN

Tropic of Cancer

ISRAEL

BAHRAIN

QATAR

Cairo

Riyadh

OMAN

Karachi

INDIA

Dhaka

Hong
Kong

LIBYA

EGYPT

SAUDI
ARABIA

UNITED ARAB
EMIRATES

Muscat

Mumbai
(Bombay)

Calcutta

MYANMAR
(BURMA)

LAOS

Hanoi

Northern
Mariana
(U.S.)

PACIFIC
OCEAN

20°N

CHAD

OMAN

Yangon
(Rangoon)

VIETNAM

Guam (U.S.)

MARSHALL
ISLANDS

KHARTOUM

ERITREA

YEMEN

Sanaa

Chennai
(Madras)

THAILAND

Bangkok

Manila

PHILIPPINES

N'Djamena

SUDAN

Asmara

DJIBOUTI

CAMBODIA

Phnom Penh

PALAU

FEDERATED STATES
OF MICRONESIA

CENTRAL
AFRICAN
REPUBLIC

Addis Ababa

ETHIOPIA

Colombo

SRI
LANKA

Ho Chi
Minh City

BRUNEI

Kuala
Lumpur

MALAYSIA

CAMEROON

DEMOCRATIC
REPUBLIC
OF THE
CONGO

UGANDA

SOMALIA

MALDIVES

Singapore

SINGAPORE

INDONESIA

0° Equator

NAURU

KIRIBATI

GABON

REP.
OF THE
CONGO

Nairobi

KENYA

RWANDA

BURUNDI

Kinshasa

TANZANIA

SEYCHELLES

SOLOMON
ISLANDS

TUVALU

Luanda

Dodoma

Dar es Salaam

MALAWI

COMOROS

INDIAN OCEAN

PAPUA
NEW
GUINEA

Port Moresby

ANGOLA

ZAMBIA

MOZAMBIQUE

MADAGASCAR

Jakarta

Surabaya

EAST TIMOR

VANUATU

FIJI

Lusaka

Harare

Antananarivo

New Caledonia
(FRANCE)

20°S

NAMIBIA

ZIMBABWE

MAURITIUS

Réunion
(FRANCE)

AUSTRALIA

Tropic of Capricorn

Windhoek

BOTSWANA

Gaborone

Pretoria

Johannesburg

Maputo

SWAZILAND

LESOTHO

SOUTH
AFRICA

Bloemfontein

Cape Town

Sydney

Canberra

NEW
ZEALAND

Melbourne

Wellington

Tasmania

20°E 40°E 60°E 80°E 100°E 120°E 140°E 160°E 60°S

ANTARCTICA

80°N 40°N

	COUNTRY	CAPITAL
1	Czech Republic	Prague
2	Slovakia	Bratislava
3	Slovenia	Ljubljana
4	Croatia	Zagreb
5	Bosnia and Herzegovina	Sarajevo
6	Macedonia	Skopje
7	Serbia	Belgrade
8	Montenegro	Podgorica
9	Lithuania	Vilnius
10	Latvia	Riga
11	Estonia	Tallinn
12	Kosovo	Pristina

0 250 500 Miles
0 250 500 Kilometers
Projection: Mollweide

ICELAND

Reykjavik

SWEDEN

FINLAND

Helsinki

NORWAY

Oslo

Stockholm

St. Petersburg

RUSSIA

60°N

UNITED
KINGDOM

North
Sea

DENMARK

Copenhagen

Minsk

Moscow

Dublin

IRELAND

NETHERLANDS

Amsterdam

Berlin

Warsaw

BELARUS

London

GERMANY

POLAND

Kiev

50°N

Brussels

BELGIUM

LUXEMBOURG

Vienna

UKRAINE

ATLANTIC
OCEAN

Paris

Bern

AUSTRIA

HUNGARY

Budapest

MOLDOVA

Chișinău

SWITZERLAND

FRANCE

LIECHTENSTEIN

ITALY

ROMANIA

Bucharest

MONACO

SAN MARINO

Rome

BULGARIA

Black Sea

Sofia

ANDORRA

Corsica
(FRANCE)

VATICAN CITY

Tirane

ALBANIA

PORTUGAL

Madrid

Balearic
Is. (SPAIN)

Sardinia
(ITALY)

GREECE

Lisbon

SPAIN

Athens

Gibraltar (U.K.)

Sicily

MALTA

Crete

Mediterranean
Sea

Arctic
Circle

40°N

10°W 0° 10°E 20°E 30°E 40°E 50°E 60°E 70°E 80°E

The United States Constitution

Preamble

Short and dignified, the Preamble explains the goals of the government under the Constitution. These goals include ensuring justice and peace, providing protection against foreign enemies, promoting the general well-being of the people, and securing liberty for current and future generations. The phrase "We the People" has become a signature of American democracy. The Framers firmly established the people's authority by creating a republic, a government in which people exercise their sovereignty by electing representatives to govern them. "To form a more perfect Union" means that the new government will provide greater cooperation among the states than was outlined in the Articles of Confederation.

Article I: Legislative Branch

Section 1. Congress

The first three articles of the Constitution divide the powers of U.S. government among three separate branches. Article I establishes Congress, a bicameral legislature consisting of the House of Representatives and the Senate. It also grants only Congress the power to make laws.

Section 2. The House of Representatives

1. Elections Members of the House of Representatives are elected to serve two-year terms. A person is eligible to vote for representatives if he or she is eligible to vote for the state house with the most members. Who can vote for state legislators is entirely up to each state, subject to the restrictions of the Constitution and federal law.

2. Qualifications A representative must be at least 25 years old, a U.S. citizen for at least seven years, and a resident of the state he or she represents. Subject to constitutional limits, each state determines for itself the requirements for legal residence. Most representatives live not only in the state but also in the district from which they were chosen.

We the People of the United States, in Order to form a more perfect Union, establish Justice, insure domestic Tranquility, provide for the common defense, promote the general Welfare, and secure the Blessings of Liberty to ourselves and our Posterity, do ordain and establish this Constitution for the United States of America.

Article I

Section 1.

All legislative Powers herein granted shall be vested in a Congress of the United States, which shall consist of a Senate and House of Representatives.

Section 2.

1. Elections The House of Representatives shall be composed of Members chosen every second Year by the People of the several States, and the Electors in each State shall have the Qualifications requisite for Electors of the most numerous Branch of the State Legislature.

2. Qualifications No Person shall be a Representative who shall not have attained to the Age of twenty five Years, and been seven Years a Citizen of the United States, and who shall not, when elected, be an Inhabitant of that State in which he shall be chosen.

Note: *The parts of the Constitution that have been lined through are no longer in force or no longer apply because of later amendments. The titles of the sections and articles are added for easier reference.*

3. Number of Representatives Representatives and direct Taxes shall be apportioned among the several States which may be included within this Union, according to their respective Numbers, ~~which shall be determined by adding to the whole Number of free Persons, including those bound to Service for a Term of Years, and excluding Indians not taxed, three fifths of all other Persons.~~ The actual Enumeration shall be made within three Years after the first Meeting of the Congress of the United States, and within every subsequent Term of ten Years, in such Manner as they shall by Law direct. The Number of Representatives shall not exceed one for every thirty Thousand, but each State shall have at Least one Representative; ~~and until such enumeration shall be made, the State of New Hampshire shall be entitled to choose three, Massachoosetts eight, Rhode-Island and Providence Plantations one, Connecticut five, New-York six, New Jersey four, Pennsylvania eight, Delaware one, Maryland six, Virginia ten, North Carolina five, South Carolina five, and Georgia three.~~

4. Vacancies When vacancies happen in the Representation from any State, the Executive Authority thereof shall issue Writs of Election to fill such Vacancies.

5. Officers and Impeachment The House of Representatives shall choose their Speaker and other Officers; and shall have the sole Power of impeachment.

Section 3.

1. Number of Senators The Senate of the United States shall be composed of two Senators from each State, ~~chosen by the Legislature thereof,~~ for six Years; and each Senator shall have one Vote.

2. Classifying Terms Immediately after they shall be assembled in Consequence of the first Election, they shall be divided as equally as may be into three Classes. The Seats of the Senators of the first Class shall be vacated at the Expiration of the second Year, of the second Class at the Expiration of the fourth Year, and of the third Class at the Expiration of the sixth Year, so that one third may be chosen every second Year; ~~and if Vacancies happen by Resignation, or otherwise, during the Recess of the Legislature of any State, the Executive thereof may make temporary Appointments until the next Meeting of the Legislature, which shall then fill such Vacancies.~~

3. Qualifications No Person shall be a Senator who shall not have attained to the Age of thirty Years, and been nine Years a Citizen of the United States, and who shall not, when elected, be an Inhabitant of that State for which he shall be chosen.

3. Number of Representatives The number of representatives given to each state shall be based on its population, determined by a general census every 10 years. Each state shall have at least one representative.

"Those bound to Service" refers to indentured servants. "Three fifths of all other Persons" refers to enslaved African Americans. Slaves made up a large part of the population in several southern states. Counting all the slaves would have given the southern states much greater representation in Congress, but because some taxes were based on population it would have also increased taxes. Southern states wanted to count all slaves for representation purposes but none for taxation. Northern states objected. In the Three-Fifths Compromise, delegates agreed that all whites plus three-fifths of the slave population would be counted for both representation and taxation. Native Americans were not counted.

The requirement that there shall be no more than one representative for every 30,000 persons no longer has practical force. There is now one representative for about every 650,000 persons. The Reapportionment Act of 1929 fixed the permanent size of the House at 435 members, with each state having at least one representative.

4. Vacancies If a vacancy occurs in a House seat, that state's governor must call a special election to fill it. However, if the next regularly scheduled election is to be held soon, the governor may allow the seat to remain empty rather than call a special election.

5. Officers and Impeachment The House chooses an officer called the Speaker to lead meetings. The House alone has the power to bring impeachment charges against government officials.

Section 3. The Senate

1. Number of Senators Each state has two senators who serve six-year terms and have one vote each. The Constitution at first provided that each state legislature should select the state's senators, but the Seventeenth Amendment changed this provision by allowing the voters of each state to choose their own senators.

2. Classifying Terms Senators are elected to six-year terms. Every two years, one-third of the senators are elected and two-thirds remain in office. This arrangement, called overlapping terms of office, makes the Senate a continuing body, unlike the House, whose entire membership is elected every two years. The Seventeenth Amendment changed the method of filling vacancies. In case of a vacancy, the seat is to be filled by a special election called by the governor. However, state law may allow the governor to appoint a successor to serve until that election is held.

3. Qualifications A senator must be at least 30 years old, a U.S. citizen for at least nine years, and a resident of the state from which he or she is elected.

4. Role of Vice President The vice president serves as president of the Senate. However, he or she votes only when a tie vote occurs.

5. Officers The Senate elects an officer called the president pro tempore, or temporary president, to lead meetings when the vice president is absent.

6. Impeachment Trials The phrase "on Oath or Affirmation" means that senators are placed under oath when trying impeachment cases, just as jurors are in a regular court trial. The provision that the chief justice, and not the vice president, presides over the Senate in an impeachment trial probably grows out of the fact that a conviction would make the vice president the president.

7. Punishment for Impeachment If an impeached person is found guilty, he or she is removed from office and forbidden to hold federal office again. The Senate cannot impose any other punishment, but the person may also be tried in regular courts. Two presidents, Andrew Johnson and Bill Clinton, were impeached but were not removed from office.

Section 4. Congressional Elections

1. Regulations Each state legislature may decide the time, place, and method for electing members of Congress from their state.

2. Sessions In Europe rulers could keep parliaments from meeting simply by not calling them together. This is the reason for the requirement that Congress must meet at least once a year. The Twentieth Amendment changed the date of the opening day of the session to January 3.

Section 5. Rules and Procedures

1. Quorum Each house determines if its members are legally qualified to serve and have been elected fairly. A quorum is the minimum number of legislators required to carry on business. Discussion and debate can take place whether a quorum is present or not, as long as a quorum comes in to vote. However, any member may demand a "quorum call." If a quorum is not present, the house must adjourn or the sergeant at arms can be ordered to round up absent members.

2. Rules and Conduct When acting on motions to expel a member, either house of Congress may consider other matters bearing on that member's fitness for office. Each house makes its own rules, can punish its members, and can expel a member with a two-thirds vote.

3. Records The House Journal and the Senate Journal are published at the end of each session of Congress. They list all the bills and resolutions considered during the session, as well as every vote. All messages from the president to Congress also are included. The journals are the only publications required by the Constitution and are considered the official documents for the proceedings of Congress.

4. Role of Vice President The Vice President of the United States shall be President of the Senate, but shall have no Vote, unless they be equally divided.

5. Officers The Senate shall choose their other Officers, and also a **President pro tempore**, in the Absence of the Vice President, or when he shall exercise the Office of President of the United States.

6. Impeachment Trials The Senate shall have the sole Power to try all Impeachments. When sitting for that Purpose, they shall be on Oath or Affirmation. When the President of the United States is tried, the Chief Justice shall preside: And no Person shall be convicted without the Concurrence of two thirds of the Members present.

7. Punishment for Impeachment Judgment in Cases of Impeachment shall not extend further than to removal from Office, and disqualification to hold and enjoy any Office of honor, Trust or Profit under the United States: but the Party convicted shall nevertheless be liable and subject to Indictment, Trial, Judgment and Punishment, according to Law.

Section 4.

1. Regulations The Times, Places and Manner of holding Elections for Senators and Representatives, shall be prescribed in each State by the Legislature thereof; but the Congress may at any time by Law make or alter such Regulations, except as to the Places of choosing Senators.

2. Sessions ~~The Congress shall assemble at least once in every Year, and such Meeting shall be on the first Monday in December, unless they shall by Law appoint a different Day.~~

Section 5.

1. Quorum Each House shall be the Judge of the Elections, Returns and Qualifications of its own Members, and a Majority of each shall constitute a Quorum to do Business; but a smaller Number may adjourn from day to day, and may be authorized to compel the Attendance of absent Members, in such Manner, and under such Penalties as each House may provide.

2. Rules and Conduct Each House may determine the Rules of its Proceedings, punish its Members for disorderly Behaviour, and, with the Concurrence of two thirds, expel a Member.

3. Records Each House shall keep a Journal of its Proceedings, and from time to time publish the same, excepting such Parts as may in their Judgment require Secrecy; and the Yeas and Nays of the Members of either House on any question shall, at the Desire of one fifth of those Present, be entered on the Journal.

4. Adjournment Neither House, during the Session of Congress, shall, without the Consent of the other, adjourn for more than three days, nor to any other Place than that in which the two Houses shall be sitting.

Section 6.

1. Salary The Senators and Representatives shall receive a Compensation for their Services, to be ascertained by Law, and paid out of the Treasury of the United States. They shall in all Cases, except Treason, Felony and Breach of the Peace, be privileged from Arrest during their Attendance at the Session of their respective Houses, and in going to and returning from the same; and for any Speech or Debate in either House, they shall not be questioned in any other Place.

2. Restrictions No Senator or Representative shall, during the Time for which he was elected, be appointed to any civil Office under the Authority of the United States, which shall have been created, or the **Emoluments** whereof shall have been increased during such time; and no Person holding any Office under the United States, shall be a Member of either House during his **Continuance** in Office.

Section 7.

1. Tax Bills All Bills for raising Revenue shall originate in the House of Representatives; but the Senate may propose or concur with Amendments as on other Bills.

2. Lawmaking Every Bill which shall have passed the House of Representatives and the Senate, shall, before it become a Law, be presented to the President of the United States: If he approve he shall sign it, but if not he shall return it, with his Objections to that House in which it shall have originated, who shall enter the Objections at large on their Journal, and proceed to reconsider it. If after such Reconsideration two thirds of that House shall agree to pass the Bill, it shall be sent, together with the Objections, to the other House, by which it shall likewise be reconsidered, and if approved by two thirds of that House, it shall become a Law. But in all such Cases the Votes of both Houses shall be determined by yeas and Nays, and the Names of the Persons voting for and against the Bill shall be entered on the Journal of each House respectively. If any Bill shall not be returned by the President within ten Days (Sundays excepted) after it shall have been presented to him, the Same shall be a Law, in like Manner as if he had signed it, unless the Congress by their Adjournment prevent its Return, in which Case it shall not be a Law.

4. Adjournment While in session, neither the House of Representatives nor the Senate may go into recess for more than three days without the approval of the other house. Both houses of Congress must always meet in the same location.

Section 6. Payment

1. Salary The Senate and the House of Representatives each set their members' salaries. Members of Congress are technically immune from arrest while going to and from congressional business, although this has little importance today. Members of Congress, like anyone else, may be arrested for breaking the law. Congressional immunity from charges of libel and slander remains important. Immunity under the speech and debate clause means that members of Congress may say whatever they wish in connection with congressional business without fear of being sued.

2. Restrictions These provisions prevent members of Congress from creating jobs to which they can later be appointed, from raising the salaries (emoluments) of jobs they hope to hold in the future, and from holding office in other branches of government during their term (continuance) in Congress.

Section 7. How a Bill Becomes a Law

1. Tax Bills All tax bills must originate in the House. This rule has little importance today. The Senate can amend a tax bill to such an extent that it no longer resembles the original bill.

2. Lawmaking A bill passed by both houses of Congress goes to the president for the president's approval. If the president disapproves, or vetoes, the bill, it must be returned to Congress within 10 days, not including Sundays, along with a statement of the president's objections. Congress can override the president's veto, thus making the bill a law, with a two-thirds majority vote in each house. The president can allow a bill to become law without signing it merely by letting 10 days pass while Congress is in session. However, a bill sent to the president during the last 10 days of a congressional session cannot become law unless it is signed. If a bill reaches the president near the end of the session, the bill may simply be held unsigned. When Congress adjourns, the bill is killed. This practice is known as a pocket veto.

3. Role of the President This clause covers joint resolutions, measures that Congress often passes to deal with temporary or ceremonial matters. A joint resolution passed by Congress and signed by the president has the same force of law as a bill. However, concurrent and simple resolutions do not have the force of law and are not submitted to the president.

Section 8. Powers Granted to Congress

1. Taxation Congress has the power to establish and collect taxes, duties, and excises. Duties are taxes on goods coming into the United States. Excises are taxes on the sale, use, or production of goods as well as on some business procedures or privileges. *Imposts* is a general tax term that includes both duties and excises.

2. Credit In order to help finance the government, Congress has the power to borrow money.

3. Commerce This section, called the commerce clause, gives Congress authority over commercial activity with foreign nations and within the country. Commerce "among the several States" is usually refered to as interstate commerce.

4. Naturalization and Bankruptcy Congress has the power to set up rules regarding naturalization, the process by which a foreign-born person may become a U.S. citizen. Congress also has the power to make laws covering bankruptcy.

5. Money From this clause, Congress gets its power to charter national banks, to establish the Federal Reserve System, and to print money. This clause also gives Congress the power to set the exchange rate for foreign money and standards for measurement and weight.

6. Counterfeiting Congress has the power to make laws to prosecute those found guilty of counterfeiting money or securities. Securities are government bonds.

7. Post Office Congress has the power to establish a postal system. Post roads include all routes by which mail travels.

8. Patents and Copyrights Under this clause, Congress has the power to grant patents and copyrights. A patent gives inventors the exclusive right to control the production and sale of their inventions. A copyright gives authors and composers the exclusive right to control the publication, reproduction, and sale of their work. Patents and copyrights expire after a period of time.

9. Courts Congress has the power to create federal courts. Examples of courts "inferior to the supreme Court" include district courts and courts of appeals.

10. International Law Congress, rather than the states, has jurisdiction over crimes committed at sea and crimes committed within the United States that are against the laws of other nations.

3. Role of the President Every Order, Resolution, or Vote to which the Concurrence of the Senate and House of Representatives may be necessary (except on a question of Adjournment) shall be presented to the President of the United States; and before the Same shall take Effect, shall be approved by him, or being dis-approved by him, shall be repassed by two thirds of the Senate and House of Representatives, according to the Rules and Limitations prescribed in the Case of a Bill.

Section 8.

1. Taxation The Congress shall have Power To lay and collect Taxes, **Duties**, **Imposts** and **Excises**, to pay the Debts and provide for the common Defense and general Welfare of the United States; but all Duties, Imposts and Excises shall be uniform throughout the United States;

2. Credit To borrow Money on the credit of the United States;

3. Commerce To regulate Commerce with foreign Nations, and among the several States, and with the Indian Tribes;

4. Naturalization and Bankruptcy To establish an uniform Rule of **Naturalization**, and uniform Laws on the subject of Bankruptcies throughout the United States;

5. Money To coin Money, regulate the Value thereof, and of foreign Coin, and fix the Standard of Weights and Measures;

6. Counterfeiting To provide for the Punishment of counterfeiting the **Securities** and current Coin of the United States;

7. Post Office To establish Post Offices and **post Roads**;

8. Patents and Copyrights To promote the Progress of Science and useful Arts, by securing for limited Times to Authors and Inventors the exclusive Right to their respective Writings and Discoveries;

9. Courts To constitute Tribunals inferior to the supreme Court;

10. International Law To define and punish Piracies and Felonies committed on the high Seas, and Offences against the Law of Nations;

11. War To declare War, grant **Letters of Marque and Reprisal**, and make Rules concerning Captures on Land and Water;

12. Army To raise and support Armies, but no Appropriation of Money to that Use shall be for a longer Term than two Years;

13. Navy To provide and maintain a Navy;

14. Regulation of the Military To make Rules for the Government and Regulation of the land and naval Forces;

15. Militia To provide for calling forth the Militia to execute the Laws of the Union, suppress Insurrections and repel Invasions;

16. Regulation of the Militia To provide for organizing, arming, and disciplining, the Militia, and for governing such Part of them as may be employed in the Service of the United States, reserving to the States respectively, the Appointment of the Officers, and the Authority of training the Militia according to the discipline prescribed by Congress;

17. District of Columbia To exercise exclusive Legislation in all Cases whatsoever, over such District (not exceeding ten Miles square) as may, by Cession of particular States, and the Acceptance of Congress, become the Seat of the Government of the United States, and to exercise like Authority over all Places purchased by the Consent of the Legislature of the State in which the Same shall be, for the Erection of Forts, Magazines, Arsenals, dock-Yards, and other needful Buildings;—And

18. Necessary and Proper Clause To make all Laws which shall be necessary and proper for carrying into Execution the foregoing Powers, and all other Powers vested by this Constitution in the Government of the United States, or in any Department or Officer thereof.

Section 9.

1. Slave Trade ~~The Migration or Importation of such Persons as any of the States now existing shall think proper to admit, shall not be prohibited by the Congress prior to the Year one thousand eight hundred and eight, but a Tax or duty may be imposed on such Importation, not exceeding ten dollars for each Person.~~

2. Habeas Corpus The Privilege of the **Writ of Habeas Corpus** shall not be suspended, unless when in Cases of Rebellion or Invasion the public Safety may require it.

11. War Only Congress can declare war. However, the president, as commander in chief, has engaged the United States in wars without a declaration by Congress. Letters of marque and reprisal are documents that authorize private vessels to attack enemy ships during time of war. This practice is now prohibited by international law.

12. Army and **13. Navy** Congress has the power to establish and fund the nation's armed forces. The two-year limit on funding is designed to ensure civilian control over the military by requiring that Congress pass a new military budget every two years.

14. Regulation of the Military Congress has the power to make laws regulating the armed forces. Today these laws are covered in the Uniform Code of Military Justice, which went into effect in 1951 and has been amended several times over the years.

15. Militia Congress can regulate the calling forth of state militias. Congress has given the president power to decide when a state of invasion or uprising exists. At such times, the president can call out the militia, now known as the National Guard.

16. Regulation of the Militia The federal government shares the cost and maintenance of the National Guard. National Guard units are normally under the command of the state governor, but the president has the power to take command of any or all Guard units in a state of emergency.

17. District of Columbia The District of Columbia was created out of land ceded by the states of Virginia and Maryland. This clause grants Congress the power to govern the District of Columbia and federal properties on which forts, naval bases, arsenals, and other federal works or buildings are located. Congress also has the power to purchase land from the states for federal use.

18. Necessary and Proper Clause The famous necessary and proper clause, also known as the elastic clause, gives Congress implied powers to deal with many matters not specifically mentioned in the Constitution. As times have changed, this clause has allowed Congress to pass needed laws without amending the Constitution.

Section 9. Powers Denied Congress

1. Slave Trade This clause prevented Congress from regulating the importation of slaves into the United States for a period of 20 years. In 1808, after the expiration of this restriction, Congress outlawed the foreign slave trade. Slavery, however, remained legal in some parts of the United States until 1865.

2. Habeas Corpus A writ of habeas corpus is an order that commands people who have a person in their custody to bring that person into court to explain why he or she is being held. If their explanation is unsatisfactory, the judge can rule that the detention is illegal and order the prisoner released. This right, however, can be suspended by Congress in some rare circumstances.

3. Illegal Punishment This clause prevents Congress from passing bills of attainder or ex post facto laws. A bill of attainder is an act passed by a legislature to punish a person without a trial. An ex post facto law is one that provides punishment for an act that was not illegal when the act was committed.

4. Direct Taxes A capitation is a tax collected equally from everyone. It is also called a head tax or a poll tax. The Supreme Court once held that this section prohibits an income tax. The Sixteenth Amendment set aside the Court's decision and gave Congress the right to collect income tax.

5. Export Taxes This clause forbids Congress from taxing goods exported from the states.

6. No Favorites Congress cannot make laws concerning trade that favor one state over another. Ships going from one state to another need not pay taxes to do so.

7. Public Money Government money cannot be spent without the consent of Congress. This clause gives Congress the "power of the purse" and provides Congress with an important check on presidential power. Congress must issue financial statements periodically.

8. Titles of Nobility Congress cannot give anyone a title of nobility, such as countess or duke. The clause also prohibits federal officials from accepting a gift, office, payment, or title from a foreign country without the consent of Congress.

Section 10. Powers Denied the States

1. Restrictions The states are not allowed to make agreements or treaties with foreign countries, nor are they allowed to issue their own currency. Both of these powers are exclusive to the national government. Other powers that are denied Congress are denied the states as well.

2. Import and Export Taxes Without the consent of Congress, a state cannot tax goods entering or leaving the state, except for small fees to cover inspection costs. Profits from a tax on interstate commerce go to the federal government.

3. Peacetime and War Restraints States are prevented from levying taxes on ships based on the ships' cargo capacity, maintaining a standing army or navy, making treaties with foreign countries, or waging war without the approval of Congress. Only the federal government may make treaties and carry out measures for national defense.

3. Illegal Punishment No **Bill of Attainder** or **ex post facto Law** shall be passed.

4. Direct Taxes No **Capitation**, or other direct, Tax shall be laid, unless in Proportion to the Census or enumeration herein before directed to be taken.

5. Export Taxes No Tax or Duty shall be laid on Articles exported from any State.

6. No Favorites No Preference shall be given by any Regulation of Commerce or Revenue to the Ports of one State over those of another; nor shall Vessels bound to, or from, one State, be obliged to enter, clear, or pay Duties in another.

7. Public Money No Money shall be drawn from the Treasury, but in Consequence of Appropriations made by Law; and a regular Statement and Account of the Receipts and Expenditures of all public Money shall be published from time to time.

8. Titles of Nobility No Title of Nobility shall be granted by the United States: And no Person holding any Office of Profit or Trust under them, shall, without the Consent of the Congress, accept of any present, Emolument, Office, or Title, of any kind whatever, from any King, Prince, or foreign State.

Section 10.

1. Restrictions No State shall enter into any Treaty, Alliance, or Confederation; grant Letters of Marque and Reprisal; coin Money; emit Bills of Credit; make any Thing but gold and silver Coin a Tender in Payment of Debts; pass any Bill of Attainder, ex post facto Law, or Law impairing the Obligation of Contracts, or grant any Title of Nobility.

2. Import and Export Taxes No State shall, without the Consent of the Congress, lay any Imposts or Duties on Imports or Exports, except what may be absolutely necessary for executing it's inspection Laws: and the net Produce of all Duties and Imposts, laid by any State on Imports or Exports, shall be for the Use of the Treasury of the United States; and all such Laws shall be subject to the Revision and Control of the Congress.

3. Peacetime and War Restraints No State shall, without the Consent of Congress, lay any Duty of Tonnage, keep Troops, or Ships of War in time of Peace, enter into any Agreement or Compact with another State, or with a foreign Power, or engage in War, unless actually invaded, or in such imminent Danger as will not admit of delay.

Article II

Section 1.

1. Terms of Office The executive Power shall be vested in a President of the United States of America. He shall hold his Office during the Term of four Years, and, together with the Vice President, chosen for the same Term, be elected, as follows:

2. Electoral College Each State shall appoint, in such Manner as the Legislature thereof may direct, a Number of Electors, equal to the whole Number of Senators and Representatives to which the State may be entitled in the Congress: but no Senator or Representative, or Person holding an Office of Trust or Profit under the United States, shall be appointed an Elector.

3. Former Method of Electing President The Electors shall meet in their respective States, and vote by Ballot for two Persons, of whom one at least shall not be an Inhabitant of the same State with themselves. And they shall make a List of all the Persons voted for, and of the Number of Votes for each; which List they shall sign and certify, and transmit sealed to the Seat of the Government of the United States, directed to the President of the Senate. The President of the Senate shall, in the Presence of the Senate and House of Representatives, open all the Certificates, and the Votes shall then be counted. The Person having the greatest Number of Votes shall be the President, if such Number be a Majority of the whole Number of Electors appointed; and if there be more than one who have such Majority, and have an equal Number of Votes, then the House of Representatives shall immediately choose by Ballot one of them for President; and if no Person have a Majority, then from the five highest on the List the said House shall in like Manner choose the President. But in choosing the President, the Votes shall be taken by States, the Representation from each State having one Vote; A quorum for this purpose shall consist of a Member or Members from two thirds of the States, and a Majority of all the States shall be necessary to a Choice. In every Case, after the Choice of the President, the Person having the greatest Number of Votes of the Electors shall be the Vice President. But if there should remain two or more who have equal Votes, the Senate shall choose from them by Ballot the Vice President.

4. Election Day The Congress may determine the Time of choosing the Electors, and the Day on which they shall give their Votes; which Day shall be the same throughout the United States.

5. Qualifications No Person except a natural born Citizen, or a Citizen of the United States, at the time of the Adoption of this Constitution, shall be eligible to the Office of President; neither shall any Person be eligible to that Office who shall not have attained to the Age of thirty five Years, and been fourteen Years a Resident within the United States.

Article II: The Executive Branch

Section 1. The Presidency

1. Terms of Office The president is the chief of the executive branch. It is the job of the president to enforce the laws. The Framers set up the electoral system, which differs greatly from out electoral process today.

2. Electoral College Although the Constitution does not use the term *electoral college*, that body is established in this clause. The electoral college is a group of electors chosen in every state to select the president and vice president. The number of electors each state has is equal to that state's number of representatives and senators in Congress.

3. Former Method of Electing President Originally, electors voted for two individuals, but did not specify which was to be president and which was to be vice president. The person who received the most votes became president, while the runner-up became vice president.

In the election of 1800, candidates Thomas Jefferson and Aaron Burr received the same number of votes. The tie threw the election into the House of Representatives, which chose Jefferson to become president. The Twelfth Amendment, ratified in 1804, changed the procedure for electing the president and vice president.

4. Election Day The day for choosing electors was set by Congress as the Tuesday after the first Monday in November of every fourth year. Casting of electoral votes is then held the Monday after the second Wednesday in December.

5. Qualifications The president must have been born a U.S. citizen, be at least 35 years old, and have been a resident of the United States for at least 14 years. The youngest person elected president was John F. Kennedy, who was 43 years old when he was inaugurated. Theodore Roosevelt was 42 when he assumed office after the assassination of William McKinley.

6. Succession The vice president becomes president if the president dies, resigns, or leaves office before the end of the term. Congress has the power to provide for the succession of the presidency if both the president and vice president are unable to serve. The Twenty-fifth Amendment, ratified in 1967, clarified this clause to specify the order and conditions of succession.

7. Salary The president's salary cannot be raised or lowered during his or her term of office. This ensures that Congress cannot attempt to influence the president by threatening to lower or promising to raise his or her salary. In 1999 Congress voted to set future presidents' salaries at $400,000 per year, plus an annual $50,000 expense account.

8. Oath of Office This clause establishes the official presidential oath of office. It does not state who shall administer the oath to the newly elected president. President George Washington was sworn in by Robert R. Livingston, then a state official in New York. After that, it became customary for the chief justice of the United States to administer the oath.

Section 2. Presidential Powers

1. Military Powers The president serves as commander in chief of the armed forces, including state militias when they are in service to the national government. The president may establish executive departments, known as the cabinet.

In addition, the president has the power to grant pardons and reprieves. A pardon forgives a person for his or her crime and eliminates the punishment. A reprieve postpones the carrying out of a person's sentence.

2. Treaties and Appointments However, the Framers of the Constitution intended that in some matters, the Senate should serve as an advisory body for the president. The president can make treaties with foreign nations and appoint various government officials, including Supreme Court justices. Two-thirds of the senators present must approve before a treaty is confirmed, and high appointments require approval of more than half the senators present. Executive agreements, or pacts with foreign governments on minor matters, do not require Senate approval.

3. Vacancies This clause grants the president the power to fill vacancies without the Senate's approval if the Senate is not in session. Known as recess appointments, they must be approved by the Senate by the end of the next session.

6. Succession In Case of the Removal of the President from Office, or of his Death, Resignation, or Inability to discharge the Powers and Duties of the said Office, the Same shall devolve on the Vice President, and the Congress may by Law provide for the Case of Removal, Death, Resignation or Inability, both of the President and Vice President, declaring what Officer shall then act as President, and such Officer shall act accordingly, until the Disability be removed, or a President shall be elected.

7. Salary The President shall, at stated Times, receive for his Services, a Compensation, which shall neither be increased nor diminished during the Period for which he shall have been elected, and he shall not receive within that Period any other Emolument from the United States, or any of them.

8. Oath of Office Before he enter on the Execution of his Office, he shall take the following Oath or Affirmation:—"I do solemnly swear (or affirm) that I will faithfully execute the Office of President of the United States, and will to the best of my Ability, preserve, protect and defend the Constitution of the United States."

Section 2.

1. Military Powers The President shall be Commander in Chief of the Army and Navy of the United States, and of the Militia of the several States, when called into the actual Service of the United States; he may require the Opinion, in writing, of the principal Officer in each of the executive Departments, upon any Subject relating to the Duties of their respective Offices, and he shall have Power to grant **Reprieves** and **Pardons** for Offences against the United States, except in Cases of Impeachment.

2. Treaties and Appointments He shall have Power, by and with the Advice and Consent of the Senate, to make Treaties, provided two thirds of the Senators present concur; and he shall nominate, and by and with the Advice and Consent of the Senate, shall appoint Ambassadors, other public Ministers and Consuls, Judges of the supreme Court, and all other Officers of the United States, whose Appointments are not herein otherwise provided for, and which shall be established by Law: but the Congress may by Law vest the Appointment of such inferior Officers, as they think proper, in the President alone, in the Courts of Law, or in the Heads of Departments.

3. Vacancies The President shall have Power to fill up all Vacancies that may happen during the Recess of the Senate, by granting Commissions which shall expire at the End of their next Session.

Section 3.

He shall from time to time give to the Congress Information of the State of the Union, and recommend to their Consideration such Measures as he shall judge necessary and expedient; he may, on extraordinary Occasions, convene both Houses, or either of them, and in Case of Disagreement between them, with Respect to the Time of Adjournment, he may adjourn them to such Time as he shall think proper; he shall receive Ambassadors and other public Ministers; he shall take Care that the Laws be faithfully executed, and shall Commission all the Officers of the United States.

Section 4.

The President, Vice President and all civil Officers of the United States, shall be removed from Office on Impeachment for, and Conviction of, Treason, Bribery, or other high Crimes and Misdemeanors.

Article III

Section 1.

The judicial Power of the United States shall be vested in one supreme Court, and in such inferior Courts as the Congress may from time to time ordain and establish. The Judges, both of the supreme and inferior Courts, shall hold their Offices during good Behavior, and shall, at stated Times, receive for their Services a Compensation, which shall not be diminished during their Continuance in Office.

Section 2.

1. General Authority The judicial Power shall extend to all Cases, in Law and Equity, arising under this Constitution, the Laws of the United States, and Treaties made, or which shall be made, under their Authority;—to all Cases affecting Ambassadors, other public Ministers and Consuls;—to all Cases of admiralty and maritime Jurisdiction;—to Controversies to which the United States shall be a Party;—to Controversies between two or more States —between a State and Citizens of another State; — between Citizens of different States;—between Citizens of the same State claiming Lands under Grants of different States, and between a State, or the Citizens thereof, and foreign States, Citizens or Subjects.

2. Supreme Authority In all Cases affecting Ambassadors, other public Ministers and Consuls, and those in which a State shall be Party, the supreme Court shall have original Jurisdiction. In all the other Cases before mentioned, the supreme Court shall have appellate Jurisdiction, both as to Law and Fact, with such Exceptions, and under such Regulations as the Congress shall make.

Section 3. Presidential Duties

This clause outlines several presidential duties, including addressing Congress, calling special sessions and adjourning Congress, meeting with foreign dignitaries, enforcing the laws of Congress, and commissioning civilian and military officials. The president gives a State of the Union message to Congress each year. During the 1800s presidents often called Congress into session. Today Congress is in session most of the time. No president has ever had to adjourn Congress. The responsibility to "take Care that the Laws be faithfully executed" puts the president at the head of law enforcement for the national government. Every federal official, civilian or military, gets his or her authority from the president.

Section 4. Impeachment

The impeachment process is outlined in the duties of the legislature in Article I. Section 4 states that the president, vice president, and all other government officials can be impeached, tried, and convicted for abuse of power.

Article III: The Judicial Branch

Section 1. Federal Courts and Judges

The Constitution gives federal courts the power to hear cases between the government and individuals and between private parties. The creation of only the Supreme Court is spelled out in the Constitution, but Congress is given the power to establish lower courts. The Constitution makes every effort to keep the courts independent of both the legislature and the president. The guarantee that judges shall hold office during "good Behaviour" means that, unless they are impeached and convicted, they can hold office for life. This protects judges from any threat of dismissal by the president during their lifetime. The rule that a judge's salary may not be reduced prevents Congress from using salary to influence judges.

Section 2. Authority of the Courts

1. General Authority This clause identifies cases over which federal courts have jurisdiction. The right of the federal courts to handle cases "arising under this Constitution" is the basis of the Supreme Court's right to declare laws unconstitutional. This right of judicial review was established in *Marbury* v. *Madison* (1803) in an opinion written by Chief Justice John Marshall. The Eleventh Amendment, ratified in 1795, set aside the phrase "between a State and Citizens of another State." A citizen of one state cannot sue another in federal court.

2. Supreme Authority The Supreme Court has original jurisdiction in cases affecting the representatives of foreign countries and in cases in which a state is a party, meaning that cases of this kind go directly to the Supreme Court. In other kinds of cases, the Supreme Court has appellate jurisdiction. This means that the cases are tried first in a lower court and may come up to the Supreme Court for review. Congress cannot take away or modify the original jurisdiction of the Supreme Court, but it can take away the right to appeal to that Court or fix the conditions needed to present an appeal.

3. Trial by Jury With the exception of impeachment, people accused of a federal crime are guaranteed the right to a trial by a jury in a federal court in the state in which the crime occurred.

Section 3. Treason

1. Definition The Framers included a specific definition of treason, the only crime so defined in the Constitution, in order to prevent the misuse of such charges. According to the Constitution, treason consists of plotting war against the United States or giving "Aid and Comfort" to enemies of the United States. No person can be convicted of treason against the United States unless he or she confesses in open court or unless two witnesses testify that he or she has committed a treasonable act.

2. Punishment The punishment that Congress has set for those convicted of treason ranges from a minimum of five years in prison and/or a $10,000 fine to a maximum of death. The phrase "no Attainder of Treason shall work Corruption of Blood" means that the family of a traitor does not share the guilt.

Article IV: Relations among States

Section 1. State Acts and Records

This section requires each state to honor the laws, records, and court decisions of all other states.

Section 2. Rights of Citizens

1. Citizenship This clause means that citizens traveling from state to state are entitled to all the rights and freedoms that automatically go to the citizens of those states. Some privileges, such as the right to vote, do not automatically go with citizenship but require a period of residence and perhaps other qualifications.

2. Extradition If a person commits a crime in one state and flees to another state, the governor of the state in which the crime was committed can demand that the fugitive be returned. The process of handing over an accused person is called extradition.

3. Fugitive Slaves A "Person held to Service or Labour" was a slave or an indentured servant, a person bound by contract to serve someone for several years. This part of the Constitution no longer has any force, since slavery was abolished in the United States in 1865.

Section 3. New States

1. Admission This clause grants Congress the authority to admit new states to the Union. New states cannot be formed by dividing or joining existing states without the consent of the state legislatures and Congress.

3. Trial by Jury The Trial of all Crimes, except in Cases of Impeachment, shall be by Jury; and such Trial shall be held in the State where the said Crimes shall have been committed; but when not committed within any State, the Trial shall be at such Place or Places as the Congress may by Law have directed.

Section 3.

1. Definition Treason against the United States, shall consist only in levying War against them, or in adhering to their Enemies, giving them Aid and Comfort. No Person shall be convicted of Treason unless on the Testimony of two Witnesses to the same overt Act, or on Confession in open Court.

2. Punishment The Congress shall have Power to declare the Punishment of Treason, but no **Attainder of Treason shall work Corruption of Blood**, or Forfeiture except during the Life of the Person attainted.

Article IV

Section 1.

Full Faith and Credit shall be given in each State to the public Acts, Records, and judicial Proceedings of every other State. And the Congress may by general Laws prescribe the Manner in which such Acts, Records and Proceedings shall be proved, and the Effect thereof.

Section 2.

1. Citizenship The Citizens of each State shall be entitled to all Privileges and Immunities of Citizens in the several States.

2. Extradition A Person charged in any State with Treason, Felony, or other Crime, who shall flee from Justice, and be found in another State, shall on Demand of the executive Authority of the State from which he fled, be delivered up, to be removed to the State having Jurisdiction of the Crime.

3. Fugitive Slaves No Person held to Service or Labour in one State, under the Laws thereof, escaping into another, shall, in Consequence of any Law or Regulation therein, be discharged from such Service or Labour, but shall be delivered up on Claim of the Party to whom such Service or Labour may be due.

Section 3.

1. Admission New States may be admitted by the Congress into this Union; but no new State shall be formed or erected within the Jurisdiction of any other State; nor any State be formed by the Junction of two or more States, or Parts of States, without the Consent of the Legislatures of the States concerned as well as of the Congress.

2. Congressional Authority The Congress shall have Power to dispose of and make all needful Rules and Regulations respecting the Territory or other Property belonging to the United States; and nothing in this Constitution shall be so construed as to Prejudice any Claims of the United States, or of any particular State.

Section 4.

The United States shall guarantee to every State in this Union a Republican Form of Government, and shall protect each of them against Invasion; and on Application of the Legislature, or of the Executive (when the Legislature cannot be convened), against domestic Violence.

Article V

The Congress, whenever two thirds of both Houses shall deem it necessary, shall propose Amendments to this Constitution, or, on the Application of the Legislatures of two thirds of the several States, shall call a Convention for proposing Amendments, which, in either Case, shall be valid to all Intents and Purposes, as Part of this Constitution, when ratified by the Legislatures of three fourths of the several States, or by Conventions in three fourths thereof, as the one or the other Mode of Ratification may be proposed by the Congress; Provided that no Amendment which may be made prior to the Year One thousand eight hundred and eight shall in any Manner affect the first and fourth Clauses in the Ninth Section of the first Article; and that no State, without its Consent, shall be deprived of its equal Suffrage in the Senate.

Article VI

All Debts contracted and Engagements entered into, before the Adoption of this Constitution, shall be as valid against the United States under this Constitution, as under the Confederation.

This Constitution, and the Laws of the United States which shall be made in Pursuance thereof; and all Treaties made, or which shall be made, under the Authority of the United States, shall be the supreme Law of the Land; and the Judges in every State shall be bound thereby, any Thing in the Constitution or Laws of any State to the Contrary notwithstanding.

The Senators and Representatives before mentioned, and the Members of the several State Legislatures, and all executive and judicial Officers, both of the United States and of the several States, shall be bound by Oath or Affirmation, to support this Constitution; but no religious Test shall ever be required as a Qualification to any Office or public Trust under the United States.

2. Congressional Authority Congress has the power to make laws for territories, public lands, and property of the United States that does not fall under the jurisdiction of any of the states.

Section 4. Guarantees to the States

This section requires that the federal government make sure that every state has a republican form of government, a government in which the people elect representatives to govern. The Supreme Court ruled that Congress, not the courts, must decide whether a government is republican. According to the Court, if Congress admits a state's senators and representatives, that action indicates that Congress considers the government republican. The legislature or governor of a state can request federal aid to deal with riots or other internal violence.

Article V: Amending the Constitution

Amendments to the Constitution may be proposed by a two-thirds vote of each house of Congress or by a national convention called by Congress at the request of two-thirds of the states. To become part of the Constitution, amendments must be ratified by the legislatures of three-fourths of the states or by conventions in three-fourths of the states. The Framers of the Constitution purposely made it difficult to put through an amendment. Congress has considered more than 7,000 amendments but has passed and submitted to the states only 33. Of these, only 26 have been ratified. Only one amendment, the Twenty-first, was ratified by state conventions. All the others were ratified by state legislatures. The Constitution sets no time limit during which the states must ratify a proposed amendment.

Article VI: Supremacy of National Government

This article begins by promising that all debts and obligations made by the United States before the adoption of the Constitution will be honored. The young nation had borrowed large sums of money during the Revolutionary War and in its formative years, so this clause promised that the new government would pay off those debts.

This article also establishes the supremacy of the national government. One of the biggest problems facing the delegates to the Constitutional Convention was the question of what would happen if a state law and a federal law conflicted. This portion of the Constitution, known as the supremacy clause, answers that question. The supremacy clause has been called the linchpin of the Constitution—that is, the part that keeps the entire structure from falling apart. The clause simply means that when state laws conflict with national laws, the national laws are superior. It also means that to be valid, a national law must be in agreement with the Constitution.

The Constitution requires both federal and state officials to give supreme allegiance to the Constitution of the United States, rather than to the constitution of any state. This article also forbids any kind of religious test for holding office.

Article VII: Ratification

The Constitution was signed by George Washington and the other Framers on September 17, 1787. The next step was for the states to ratify the Constitution. The Articles of Confederation called for all 13 states to approve any revision to the Articles. The Constitution required that 9 out of the 13 states ratify the document. The first state to ratify was Delaware, on December 7, 1787. Almost two and a half years later, on May 29, 1790, Rhode Island became the last state to ratify the Constitution.

One of the conditions set by several states for ratifying the Constitution was the inclusion of a bill of rights to protect the basic rights of the people. The first 10 amendments, known as the Bill of Rights, were proposed on September 25, 1789, and ratified on December 15, 1791. Originally, the amendments applied only to the federal government, but the Fourteenth Amendment declares that no state can deprive any person of life, liberty, or property without "due process of law." The Supreme Court has interpreted those words to mean that most of the Bill of Rights applies to the states as well.

Article VII

The Ratification of the Conventions of nine States, shall be sufficient for the Establishment of this Constitution between the States so ratifying the Same.

Done in Convention by the Unanimous Consent of the States present the Seventeenth Day of September in the Year of our Lord one thousand seven hundred and Eighty seven and of the Independence of the United States of America the Twelfth In witness whereof We have hereunto subscribed our Names,

George Washington—
President and deputy from Virginia

Delaware
George Read
Gunning Bedford Jr.
John Dickinson
Richard Bassett
Jacob Broom

Georgia
William Few
Abraham Baldwin

Maryland
James McHenry
Daniel of St. Thomas
 Jenifer
Daniel Carroll

Massachusetts
Nathaniel Gorham
Rufus King

Connecticut
William Samuel Johnson
Roger Sherman

New Hampshire
John Langdon
Nicholas Gilman

New York
Alexander Hamilton

New Jersey
William Livingston
David Brearley
William Paterson
Jonathan Dayton

North Carolina
William Blount
Richard Dobbs Spaight
Hugh Williamson

Pennsylvania
Benjamin Franklin
Thomas Mifflin
Robert Morris
George Clymer
Thomas FitzSimons
Jared Ingersoll
James Wilson
Gouverneur Morris

South Carolina
John Rutledge
Charles Cotesworth
 Pinckney
Charles Pinckney
Pierce Butler

Virginia
John Blair
James Madison Jr.

Attest:
William Jackson,
 Secretary

Amendment I

Congress shall make no law respecting an establishment of religion, or prohibiting the free exercise thereof; or abridging the freedom of speech, or of the press; or the right of the people peaceably to assemble, and to petition the Government for a redress of grievances.

Amendment II

A well regulated Militia, being necessary to the security of a free State, the right of the people to keep and bear Arms, shall not be infringed.

Amendment III

No Soldier shall, in time of peace be quartered in any house, without the consent of the Owner, nor in time of war, but in a manner to be prescribed by law.

Amendment IV

The right of the people to be secure in their persons, houses, papers, and effects, against unreasonable searches and seizures, shall not be violated, and no Warrants shall issue, but upon probable cause, supported by Oath or affirmation, and particularly describing the place to be searched, and the persons or things to be seized.

Amendment V

No person shall be held to answer for a capital, or otherwise infamous crime, unless on a presentment or **indictment** of a **Grand Jury**, except in cases arising in the land or naval forces, or in the Militia, when in actual service in time of War or public danger; nor shall any person be subject for the same offence to be twice put in jeopardy of life or limb; nor shall be compelled in any criminal case to be a witness against himself, nor be deprived of life, liberty, or property, without due process of law; nor shall private property be taken for public use, without just compensation.

Amendment I

Freedom of Religion, Speech, and the Press; Rights of Assembly and Petition

This amendment forbids Congress to set up or in any way provide for an official state church. It has been interpreted to forbid government endorsement of or aid to religious doctrines. In addition, Congress may not pass laws limiting worship, speech, or the press. Congress also may not keep people from meeting peacefully or from asking for relief from unfair treatment.

Amendment II

Right to Bear Arms

This amendment was created to ensure that state militias would continue as an armed means of defense and to ensure that individual citizens had a right to own firearms. When the Bill of Rights was drafted, Americans were convinced of the need for the militias to protect "the security of a free State." Today the United States has a strong national military and no longer depends on state militias. Some citizens believe the amendment should be read to apply only to well-regulated militias. However, many Americans cherish the Second Amendment's promise of the right to "keep and bear Arms."

Amendment III

Housing of Soldiers

This amendment grew directly out of an old complaint against the British, who had forced people to take soldiers into their homes. This amendment forbids the government from housing troops in private homes during times of peace. During war, troops can occupy private homes only with legal permission. The practice of quartering soldiers in private homes is rare today.

Amendment IV

Search and Arrest Warrants

This measure does not forbid authorities to search, to seize goods, or to arrest people. It requires, in most cases, that authorities first obtain a search warrant from a judge.

Amendment V

Rights in Criminal Cases

This amendment provides protections for people accused of a crime. It guarantees that no one has to stand trial for a federal crime unless he or she has been indicted, or accused, by a grand jury. A grand jury is a special panel selected to decide whether there is enough evidence against a person to hold a trial. A capital crime is one punishable by death. An infamous crime is one punishable by death or imprisonment. A person cannot be put in double jeopardy, or tried twice, for the same offense in the same jurisdiction. But a person may be tried a second time if a jury cannot agree on a verdict, if a mistrial is declared for some other reason, or if the person requests a new trial.

This amendment also guarantees that people cannot be forced to testify against themselves. The statement that no person shall be deprived of life, liberty, or property "without due process of law" is one of the most important rules of the Constitution. It expresses the idea that a person's rights are not subject to the uncontrolled power of government. This amendment also forbids the government from taking property without fair payment.

Amendment VI

Right to a Fair Trial

This amendment protects the rights of people on trial. It provides that a person accused of a crime must have a prompt, public trial by an open-minded jury. Accused individuals must be informed of the charges against them and must be allowed to question those who have accused them. Accused persons must have a lawyer to defend them if they want one. If a criminal defendant is unable to afford a lawyer, the Supreme Court has held that a lawyer must be appointed to represent the accused individual.

Amendment VII

Rights in Civil Cases

In the Sixth Amendment, the Framers of the Constitution provided for jury trials in criminal cases. In the Seventh Amendment, they provided for such trials in civil suits where the amount contested exceeds $20. The amendment applies only to federal courts. But most state constitutions also call for jury trials in civil cases.

Amendment VIII

Bails, Fines, and Punishments

Bails, fines, and punishments must be fair and humane. The phrase "cruel and unusual punishments" has been used to challenge the death penalty. The Supreme Court has ruled that the death penalty may be imposed if certain standards are applied to guard against arbitrary results in capital cases.

Amendment IX

Rights Retained by the People

Some people feared that the listing of some rights in the Bill of Rights would be interpreted to mean that other rights not listed were not protected. This amendment was adopted to prevent such an interpretation.

Amendment X

Powers Retained by the States and the People

This amendment was adopted to reassure people that the national government would not replace the states' governments. The Tenth Amendment confirms that the states or the people retain all powers not given to the national government. For example, the states have authority over such matters as marriage and divorce.

Amendment VI

In all criminal prosecutions, the accused shall enjoy the right to a speedy and public trial, by an impartial jury of the State and district wherein the crime shall have been committed, which district shall have been previously ascertained by law, and to be informed of the nature and cause of the accusation; to be confronted with the witnesses against him; to have compulsory process for obtaining witnesses in his favor, and to have the Assistance of Counsel for his defence.

Amendment VII

In suits at common law, where the value in controversy shall exceed twenty dollars, the right of trial by jury shall be preserved, and no fact tried by a jury, shall be otherwise reexamined in any Court of the United States, than according to the rules of the common law.

Amendment VIII

Excessive bail shall not be required, nor excessive fines imposed, nor cruel and unusual punishments inflicted.

Amendment IX

The enumeration in the Constitution, of certain rights, shall not be construed to deny or disparage others retained by the people.

Amendment X

The powers not delegated to the United States by the Constitution, nor prohibited by it to the States, are reserved to the States respectively, or to the people.

Amendment XI

Passed by Congress March 4, 1794. Ratified February 7, 1795.

The Judicial power of the United States shall not be construed to extend to any suit in law or equity, commenced or prosecuted against one of the United States by Citizens of another State, or by Citizens or Subjects of any Foreign State.

Amendment XII

Passed by Congress December 9, 1803. Ratified June 15, 1804.

The Electors shall meet in their respective states and vote by ballot for President and Vice-President, one of whom, at least, shall not be an inhabitant of the same state with themselves; they shall name in their ballots the person voted for as President, and in distinct ballots the person voted for as Vice-President, and they shall make distinct lists of all persons voted for as President, and of all persons voted for as Vice-President, and of the number of votes for each, which lists they shall sign and certify, and transmit sealed to the seat of the government of the United States, directed to the President of the Senate;—the President of the Senate shall, in the presence of the Senate and House of Representatives, open all the certificates and the votes shall then be counted;— The person having the greatest number of votes for President, shall be the President, if such number be a majority of the whole number of Electors appointed; and if no person have such majority, then from the persons having the highest numbers not exceeding three on the list of those voted for as President, the House of Representatives shall choose immediately, by ballot, the President. But in choosing the President, the votes shall be taken by states, the representation from each state having one vote; a quorum for this purpose shall consist of a member or members from two-thirds of the states, and a majority of all the states shall be necessary to a choice. ~~And if the House of Representatives shall not choose a President whenever the right of choice shall devolve upon them, before the fourth day of March next following, then the Vice-President shall act as President, as in case of the death or other constitutional disability of the President.~~—The person having the greatest number of votes as Vice-President, shall be the Vice-President, if such number be a majority of the whole number of Electors appointed, and if no person have a majority, then from the two highest numbers on the list, the Senate shall choose the Vice-President; a quorum for the purpose shall consist of two-thirds of the whole number of Senators, and a majority of the whole number shall be necessary to a choice. But no person constitutionally ineligible to the office of President shall be eligible to that of Vice-President of the United States.

Amendment XI

Lawsuits against States

This amendment makes it impossible for a citizen of one state to sue another state in federal court. The amendment resulted from the 1793 case of *Chisholm* v. *Georgia*, in which a man from South Carolina sued the state of Georgia over an inheritance. Georgia argued that it could not be sued in federal court, but the Supreme Court ruled that the state could be sued. Georgia then led a movement to add this amendment to the Constitution. However, individuals can still sue state authorities in federal court for depriving them of their constitutional rights.

Amendment XII

Election of the President and Vice President

The Twelfth Amendment, which provides that members of the electoral college, called electors, vote for one person as president and another as vice president, resulted from the election of 1800. At that time, each elector voted for two persons, not specifying which was to be president and which vice president. The person who received the most votes became president; the runner-up became vice president. In 1800, candidates Thomas Jefferson and Aaron Burr received the same number of votes. The tie threw the election into the House of Representatives. The House eventually chose Jefferson.

Amendment XIII
Abolition of Slavery

Section 1. Slavery Banned

President Abraham Lincoln's Emancipation Proclamation of 1863 had declared slaves free in the Confederate states still in rebellion. This amendment completed the abolition of slavery, banning slavery throughout the United States. Involuntary servitude, being forced to work against one's will, is still allowed as punishment for a crime.

Section 2. Enforcement

This section gives Congress the power to make other laws in order to carry out the provisions of this amendment.

Amendment XIV
Civil Rights

Section 1. Citizenship Defined

The principal purpose of this amendment was to make former slaves citizens of both the United States and the state in which they lived. The amendment also forbids states to deny equal rights to any person. The terms of the amendment clarify how citizenship is acquired. All persons naturalized, or granted citizenship, according to law are U.S. citizens. Anyone born in the United States is also a citizen, regardless of the nationality of his or her parents, unless they are diplomatic representatives of another country or enemies during a wartime occupation. This amendment does not grant citizenship to American Indians on reservations, but Congress later passed a law that did so. By living in a state, every U.S. citizen automatically becomes a citizen of that state as well.

The phrase "due process of law" has been construed to forbid the states to violate most rights protected by the Bill of Rights. It has also been interpreted as protecting other rights by its own force. The statement that a state cannot deny anyone "equal protection of the laws" has provided the basis for many Supreme Court rulings on civil rights. For example, the Court has outlawed segregation in public schools. The justices declared that "equal protection" means a state must make sure all children, regardless of race, have an equal opportunity for education.

Section 2. Voting Rights

This section proposes a penalty for states that refuse to give the vote in federal elections to all who qualify. States that restrict voting can have their representation in Congress cut down. This penalty, however, has never been used. Parts of this section have been set aside by the Nineteenth and Twenty-sixth amendments.

Section 3. Rebels Banned from Government

This section is of historical interest only. Its purpose was to keep federal officials who joined the Confederacy from becoming federal or state officers again. Congress could vote to overlook such a record.

Amendment XIII

Passed by Congress January 31, 1865. Ratified December 6, 1865.

1. Slavery Banned Neither slavery nor **involuntary servitude**, except as a punishment for crime whereof the party shall have been duly convicted, shall exist within the United States, or any place subject to their jurisdiction.

2. Enforcement Congress shall have power to enforce this article by appropriate legislation.

Amendment XIV

Passed by Congress June 13, 1866. Ratified July 9, 1868.

1. Citizenship Defined All persons born or naturalized in the United States, and subject to the jurisdiction thereof, are citizens of the United States and of the State wherein they reside. No State shall make or enforce any law which shall abridge the privileges or immunities of citizens of the United States; nor shall any State deprive any person of life, liberty, or property, without due process of law; nor deny to any person within its jurisdiction the equal protection of the laws.

2. Voting Rights Representatives shall be apportioned among the several States according to their respective numbers, counting the whole number of persons in each State, ~~excluding Indians not taxed~~. But when the right to vote at any election for the choice of electors for President and Vice-President of the United States, Representatives in Congress, the Executive and Judicial officers of a State, or the members of the Legislature thereof, is denied to any of the ~~male~~ inhabitants of such State, ~~being twenty-one years of age~~, and citizens of the United States, or in any way abridged, except for participation in rebellion, or other crime, the basis of representation therein shall be reduced in the proportion which the number of such ~~male~~ citizens shall bear to the whole number of ~~male~~ citizens ~~twenty-one years of age~~ in such State.

3. Rebels Banned from Government No person shall be a Senator or Representative in Congress, or elector of President and Vice-President, or hold any office, civil or military, under the United States, or under any State, who, having previously taken an oath, as a member of Congress, or as an officer of the United States, or as a member of any State legislature, or as an executive or judicial officer of any State, to support the Constitution of the United States, shall have engaged in insurrection or rebellion against the same, or given aid or comfort to the enemies thereof. But Congress may by a vote of two-thirds of each House, remove such disability.

4. Payment of Debts The validity of the public debt of the United States, authorized by law, including debts incurred for payment of pensions and bounties for services in suppressing insurrection or rebellion, shall not be questioned. But neither the United States nor any State shall assume or pay any debt or obligation incurred in aid of insurrection or rebellion against the United States, ~~or any claim for the loss or emancipation of any slave~~; but all such debts, obligations and claims shall be held illegal and void.

5. Enforcement The Congress shall have the power to enforce, by appropriate legislation, the provisions of this article.

Amendment XV

Passed by Congress February 26, 1869. Ratified February 3, 1870.

1. Voting Rights The right of citizens of the United States to vote shall not be denied or abridged by the United States or by any State on account of race, color, or previous condition of servitude.

2. Enforcement Congress shall have the power to enforce this article by appropriate legislation.

Amendment XVI

Passed by Congress July 2, 1909. Ratified February 3, 1913.

The Congress shall have power to lay and collect taxes on incomes, from whatever source derived, without apportionment among the several States, and without regard to any census or enumeration.

Amendment XVII

Passed by Congress May 13, 1912. Ratified April 8, 1913.

The Senate of the United States shall be composed of two Senators from each State, elected by the people thereof, for six years; and each Senator shall have one vote. The electors in each State shall have the qualifications requisite for electors of the most numerous branch of the State legislatures.

When vacancies happen in the representation of any State in the Senate, the executive authority of such State shall issue writs of election to fill such vacancies: *Provided*, That the legislature of any State may empower the executive thereof to make temporary appointments until the people fill the vacancies by election as the legislature may direct.

~~This amendment shall not be so construed as to affect the election or term of any Senator chosen before it becomes valid as part of the Constitution.~~

Section 4. Payment of Debts

This section ensured that the Union's Civil War debt would be paid but voided debts run up by the Confederacy during the war. The section also states that slaveholders would not be reimbursed for slaves who were freed.

Section 5. Enforcement

This section gives Congress the power to make other laws needed to help enforce the terms of this amendment.

Amendment XV

African American Suffrage

Section 1. Voting Rights

African Americans who had been enslaved became citizens under the terms of the Fourteenth Amendment. The Fifteenth Amendment does not specifically say that the freed slaves must be allowed to vote. The states are free to set qualifications for voters, but the amendment states that a voter cannot be denied the ballot because of race.

Section 2. Enforcement

This section gives Congress the power to make other laws needed to help enforce the terms of this amendment.

Amendment XVI

Income Taxes

In 1894 Congress passed an income tax law, but the Supreme Court declared the law unconstitutional. This amendment authorizes Congress to levy such a tax.

Amendment XVII

Direct Election of Senators

This amendment takes the power of electing senators from the state legislature and gives it to the people of the state. If a Senate seat becomes vacant, the governor of the state must call an election to fill the vacancy. However, state law may allow the governor to appoint a successor to serve as senator until that election is held.

Amendment XVIII

Prohibition of Liquor

Throughout the history of the United States, several groups had fought to outlaw alcohol. These groups asserted that alcohol hurt families, promoted crime, and caused health problems. By 1917, more than half the states had passed some form of law restricting alcohol use. The Eighteenth Amendment was ratified in 1919, and Congress passed a law known as the Volstead Act to enforce the amendment. However, prohibition was repealed 14 years later by the Twenty-first Amendment.

Amendment XIX

Women's Suffrage

This amendment officially guarantees the right for women to vote throughout the United States. Amendments giving women the right to vote were introduced in Congress for more than 40 years before this one was passed.

Amendment XX

Terms of the President and Congress

Section 1. Presidential Terms

Sometimes called the Lame-Duck Amendment, this amendment moved the date that newly elected presidents and members of Congress take office closer to election time. A lame duck is a government official who continues to serve in office though not re-elected to another term. Before the Twentieth Amendment came into force, defeated senators and representatives continued to hold office for four months before their successors took over. Originally, the Constitution stated that a newly elected president and Congress would not take office until March 4. Members of Congress now take office during the first week of January, and the president takes office on January 20.

Section 2. Meeting of Congress

This section sets the start of the congressional term at noon on January 3, unless Congress chooses another date.

Section 3. Succession of Vice President

This section provides a clear order of succession in case the president-elect dies before taking office or is unable to take office. If the vice president–elect is unable to succeed the president-elect, Congress is then authorized to determine who shall act as president. To date, none of these situations have occurred.

Amendment XVIII

Passed by Congress December 18, 1917. Ratified January 16, 1919. Repealed by Amendment XXI.

1. Liquor Banned After one year from the ratification of this article the manufacture, sale, or transportation of intoxicating liquors within, the importation thereof into, or the exportation thereof from the United States and all territory subject to the jurisdiction thereof for beverage purposes is hereby prohibited.

2. Enforcement The Congress and the several States shall have concurrent power to enforce this article by appropriate legislation.

3. Ratification This article shall be inoperative unless it shall have been ratified as an amendment to the Constitution by the legislatures of the several States, as provided in the Constitution, within seven years from the date of the submission hereof to the States by the Congress.

Amendment XIX

Passed by Congress June 4, 1919. Ratified August 18, 1920.

1. Voting Rights The right of citizens of the United States to vote shall not be denied or abridged by the United States or by any State on account of sex.

2. Enforcement Congress shall have power to enforce this article by appropriate legislation.

Amendment XX

Passed by Congress March 2, 1932. Ratified January 23, 1933.

1. Presidential Terms The terms of the President and the Vice President shall end at noon on the 20th day of January, and the terms of Senators and Representatives at noon on the 3d day of January, of the years in which such terms would have ended if this article had not been ratified; and the terms of their successors shall then begin.

2. Meeting of Congress The Congress shall assemble at least once in every year, and such meeting shall begin at noon on the 3d day of January, unless they shall by law appoint a different day.

3. Succession of Vice President If, at the time fixed for the beginning of the term of the President, the President elect shall have died, the Vice President elect shall become President. If a President shall not have been chosen before the time fixed for the beginning of his term, or if the President elect shall have failed to qualify, then the Vice President elect shall act as President until a President shall have qualified; and the Congress may by law provide for the case wherein neither a President elect nor a Vice President shall have qualified, declaring who shall then act as President, or the manner in which one who is to act shall be selected, and such person shall act accordingly until a President or Vice President shall have qualified.

4. Succession by Vote of Congress The Congress may by law provide for the case of the death of any of the persons from whom the House of Representatives may choose a President whenever the right of choice shall have devolved upon them, and for the case of the death of any of the persons from whom the Senate may choose a Vice President whenever the right of choice shall have devolved upon them.

5. Ratification Sections 1 and 2 shall take effect on the 15th day of October following the ratification of this article.

6. Ratification This article shall be inoperative unless it shall have been ratified as an amendment to the Constitution by the legislatures of three-fourths of the several States within seven years from the date of its submission.

Amendment XXI

Passed by Congress February 20, 1933. Ratified December 5, 1933.

1. Eighteenth Amendment Repealed The eighteenth article of amendment to the Constitution of the United States is hereby repealed.

2. Liquor Allowed by Law The transportation or importation into any State, Territory, or Possession of the United States for delivery or use therein of intoxicating liquors, in violation of the laws thereof, is hereby prohibited.

3. Ratification This article shall be inoperative unless it shall have been ratified as an amendment to the Constitution by conventions in the several States, as provided in the Constitution, within seven years from the date of the submission hereof to the States by the Congress.

Amendment XXII

Passed by Congress March 21, 1947. Ratified February 27, 1951.

1. Term Limits No person shall be elected to the office of the President more than twice, and no person who has held the office of President, or acted as President, for more than two years of a term to which some other person was elected President shall be elected to the office of President more than once. But this Article shall not apply to any person holding the office of President when this Article was proposed by Congress, and shall not prevent any person who may be holding the office of President, or acting as President, during the term within which this Article becomes operative from holding the office of President or acting as President during the remainder of such term.

Section 4. Succession by Vote of Congress

This section gives Congress the power to pass laws in the event of the death of candidates for president and vice president, if a situation occurs in which the election must be determined in Congress. However, such a law has never been passed.

Amendment XXI

Repeal of Prohibition

Section 1. Eighteenth Amendment Repealed

Enforcing prohibition proved to be virtually impossible. Law enforcement and federal officers found it difficult to keep up with the bootleggers and liquor smugglers, and the illegal liquor business became the foundation of organized crime. By the 1930s many people began to see prohibition as a failed experiment. This amendment repealed the Eighteenth Amendment.

Section 2. Liquor Allowed by Law

This section grants each state the power to regulate the transportation, distribution, and sale of liquor within the state, and bars the importation of alcohol into states that have passed laws against it.

Section 3. Ratification

To date, the Twenty-first Amendment is the only amendment Congress has submitted to the states for ratification by state conventions.

Amendment XXII

Limitation of Presidents to Two Terms

From the time of President George Washington's administration, it was a custom for presidents to serve no more than two terms in office. Franklin D. Roosevelt, however, was elected to four terms. This amendment provides that no person can be elected president more than twice. Also, no one who has served as president for more than two years of someone else's term can be elected more than once. Therefore, the longest time that any president can serve is 10 years.

Amendment XXIII

Suffrage in the District of Columbia

Until the ratification of the Twenty-third Amendment, the people of Washington, D.C., could not vote in presidential elections. This amendment gives the District of Columbia the same number of electors as the least populous state, so Washington, D.C., has three electoral college votes.

Amendment XXIV

Poll Taxes

This amendment forbids making voters pay a poll tax before they can vote in a national election. A poll tax, or head tax, is a tax collected equally from everyone. Some states once used such taxes to keep poor people and African Americans from voting. The Supreme Court has interpreted the Fourteenth Amendment as forbidding the imposition of a poll tax in state elections.

Amendment XXV

Presidential Disability and Succession

Section 1. Succession of Vice President

This section clarifies Article II, Section 1, Clause 6, to specify the order and conditions of succession.

Section 2. Vacancy of Vice President

This section provides for filling a vacancy in the vice presidency. Before this amendment, vice presidential vacancies remained unfilled until the next presidential election. In 1973 Gerald R. Ford became the first person chosen vice president under the terms of this amendment. In 1974 President Richard M. Nixon resigned and Ford became president. Nelson A. Rockefeller then became vice president under the new procedure. For the first time, the United States had both a president and vice president who had not been elected to their offices.

2. Ratification ~~This article shall be inoperative unless it shall have been ratified as an amendment to the Constitution by the legislatures of three-fourths of the several States within seven years from the date of its submission to the States by the Congress.~~

Amendment XXIII

Passed by Congress June 16, 1960. Ratified March 29, 1961.

1. District of Columbia Represented The District constituting the seat of Government of the United States shall appoint in such manner as Congress may direct:

A number of electors of President and Vice President equal to the whole number of Senators and Representatives in Congress to which the District would be entitled if it were a State, but in no event more than the least populous State; they shall be in addition to those appointed by the States, but they shall be considered, for the purposes of the election of President and Vice President, to be electors appointed by a State; and they shall meet in the District and perform such duties as provided by the twelfth article of amendment.

2. Enforcement The Congress shall have power to enforce this article by appropriate legislation.

Amendment XXIV

Passed by Congress August 27, 1962. Ratified January 23, 1964.

1. Voting Rights The right of citizens of the United States to vote in any primary or other election for President or Vice President, for electors for President or Vice President, or for Senator or Representative in Congress, shall not be denied or abridged by the United States or any State by reason of failure to pay poll tax or other tax.

2. Enforcement The Congress shall have power to enforce this article by appropriate legislation.

Amendment XXV

Passed by Congress July 6, 1965. Ratified February 10, 1967.

1. Succession of Vice President In case of the removal of the President from office or of his death or resignation, the Vice President shall become President.

2. Vacancy of Vice President Whenever there is a vacancy in the office of the Vice President, the President shall nominate a Vice President who shall take office upon confirmation by a majority vote of both Houses of Congress.

3. Written Declaration Whenever the President transmits to the President pro tempore of the Senate and the Speaker of the House of Rep-resentatives his written declaration that he is unable to discharge the powers and duties of his office, and until he transmits to them a written declaration to the contrary, such powers and duties shall be discharged by the Vice President as Acting President.

4. Removing the President Whenever the Vice President and a majority of either the principal officers of the executive departments or of such other body as Congress may by law provide, transmit to the President pro tempore of the Senate and the Speaker of the House of Representatives their written declaration that the President is unable to discharge the powers and duties of his office, the Vice President shall immediately assume the powers and duties of the office as Acting President.

Thereafter, when the President transmits to the President pro tempore of the Senate and the Speaker of the House of Representatives his written declaration that no inability exists, he shall resume the powers and duties of his office unless the Vice President and a majority of either the principal officers of the executive department or of such other body as Congress may by law provide, transmit within four days to the President pro tempore of the Senate and the Speaker of the House of Representatives their written declaration that the President is unable to discharge the powers and duties of his office. Thereupon Congress shall decide the issue, assembling within forty-eight hours for that purpose if not in session. If the Congress, within twenty-one days after receipt of the latter written declaration, or, if Congress is not in session, within twenty-one days after Congress is required to assemble, determines by two-thirds vote of both Houses that the President is unable to discharge the powers and duties of his office, the Vice President shall continue to discharge the same as Acting President; otherwise, the President shall resume the powers and duties of his office.

Amendment XXVI

Passed by Congress March 23, 1971. Ratified July 1, 1971.

1. Voting Rights The right of citizens of the United States, who are eighteen years of age or older, to vote shall not be denied or abridged by the United States or by any State on account of age.

2. Enforcement The Congress shall have power to enforce this article by appropriate legislation.

Amendment XXVII

Originally proposed September 25, 1789. Ratified May 7, 1992.

No law, varying the compensation for the services of the Senators and Representatives, shall take effect, until an election of representatives shall have intervened.

Section 3. Written Declaration

This section provides that the vice president succeeds to the presidency if the president voluntarily admits in writing that he or she is unable to serve. This section also provides for the president to declare himself or herself ready to resume office.

Section 4. Removing the President

This section creates a procedure for the involuntary removal of a president from office in cases in which he or she is disabled and unable to fulfill the duties of the executive office. If the vice president and a majority of the heads of the executive departments in the president's cabinet, or a special body appointed by Congress to determine whether the president is fit for duty, declare the president unable to serve, the president can be removed from office and the vice president becomes acting president. This might occur in a situation where the president is incapacitated and unable to provide a written declaration as provided for in Section 3. It is also possible that a president could be removed from office in cases of serious mental illness or emotional instability or if it can be shown there is a conflict of interest that might jeopardize national security.

The president may return to serving as chief executive by submitting to Congress a written declaration stating that he or she is now fit to resume the duties of the office. If the vice president and cabinet are not satisfied with the president's condition, they may issue another declaration stating that they believe the president is still unfit for duty. Congress must then meet within 48 hours to decide whether the president may return to office. Under the terms of this section, Congress must make its decision within 21 days. A two-thirds vote from both houses is required to declare the president unfit. The vice president continues to serve as president unless Congress either rules that the president may return to duty or allows 21 days to pass without reaching a decision. To date, this section of the Twenty-fifth Amendment has not been invoked.

Amendment XXVI

Suffrage for 18-Year-Olds

During the Vietnam War, many young Americans were distressed that they were eligible for the draft at age 18 but were unable to vote for the leaders who were making policy on how the military was used. This amendment lowered the voting age from 21 to 18.

Amendment XXVII

Congressional Pay Raises

Any increase in congressional pay does not go into effect until after the next regular election of the House of Representatives. This amendment prevents members of Congress from giving themselves a pay raise. Originally proposed as part of the Bill of Rights, the measure was not passed until 1992.

Historical Documents

MAGNA CARTA, 1215

Vocabulary

relief a payment made by the heir of a deceased tenant to a lord for the privilege of succeeding to the tenant's estate

barony land held by a baron

fief in feudalism, land given to a noble in return for a pledge of loyalty and military service

ward a child who is not ready to inherit the title and responsibilities due him or her

rancour bad feeling

laity people who are not clergy

patent protected

In the early 1200s King John of England angered the nobility when he imposed high taxes. The nobles joined forces with the archbishop of Canterbury and in 1215 forced the king to sign Magna Carta (Latin for "Great Charter"). The main point established by Magna Carta was that the king, like all other people in England, was subject to the rule of law. The document also established the due process of law and the right to a fair and speedy trial as basic rights enjoyed by all people in England. These principles endured as part of English law and became part of American law in the Bill of Rights.

1. In the first place have granted to God, and by this our present charter confirmed for us and our heirs for ever that the English church shall be free, and shall have its rights undiminished and its liberties unimpaired . . . We have also granted to all free men of our kingdom, for ourselves and our heirs for ever, all the liberties written below, to be had and held by them and their heirs of us and our heirs.

2. If any of our earls or barons or others holding of us in chief by knight service dies, and at his death his heir be of full age and owe relief he shall have his inheritance on payment of the old relief, namely the heir or heirs of an earl 100 for a whole earl's barony, the heir or heirs of a baron 100 for a whole barony, the heir or heirs of a knight 100s, at most, for a whole knight's fee; and he who owes less shall give less according to the ancient usage of fiefs.

3. If, however, the heir of any such be under age and a ward, he shall have his inheritance when he comes of age without paying relief and without making fine.

40. To no one will we sell, to no one will we refuse or delay right or justice.

41. All merchants shall be able to go out of and come into England safely and securely and stay and travel throughout England, as well by land as by water, for buying and selling by the ancient and right customs free from all evil tolls, except in time of war and if they are of the land that is at war with us . . .

42. It shall be lawful in future for anyone, without prejudicing the allegiance due to us, to leave our kingdom and return safely and securely by land and water, save, in the public interest, for a short period in time of war—except for those imprisoned or outlawed in accordance with the law of the kingdom and natives of a land that is at war with us and merchants (who shall be treated as aforesaid).

62. And we have fully remitted and pardoned to everyone all the ill-will, indignation and rancour that have arisen between us and our men, clergy and laity, from the time of the quarrel. Furthermore, we have fully remitted to all, clergy and laity, and as far as pertains to us have completely forgiven, all trespasses occasioned by the same quarrel between Easter in the sixteenth year of our reign and the restoration of peace. And, besides, we have caused to be made for them letters testimonial patent of the lord Stephen archbishop of Canterbury, of the lord Henry archbishop of Dublin and of the aforementioned bishops and of master Pandulf about this security and the aforementioned concessions.

63. An oath, moreover, has been taken, as well on our part as on the part of the barons, that all these things aforesaid shall be observed in good faith and without evil disposition. Witness the above-mentioned and many others. Given by our hand in the meadow which is called Runnymede between Windsor and Staines on the fifteenth day of June, in the seventeenth year of our reign.

SKILLS FOCUS ANALYZING PRIMARY SOURCES

1. **Describe** What are the main ideas in the first paragraph of Magna Carta?

2. **Make Inferences** What does Magna Carta tell you about the relationship between kings and nobles under the feudal system?

MAYFLOWER COMPACT, 1620

In 1620 the Pilgrims left England, bound for Virginia. A storm blew the Mayflower *off course, and the Pilgrims made landfall in what is now Massachusetts. In Virginia the Pilgrims would have come under the laws governing that colony, but in Massachusetts there were no laws. So the Pilgrims drew up a framework for self-government.*

We whose names are underwritten, the loyal subjects of our dread Sovereign Lord King James, by the Grace of God of Great Britain, France and Ireland, King, Defender of the Faith, etc.

Having undertaken, for the Glory of God and advancement of the Christian Faith and Honour of our King and Country, a Voyage to plant the First Colony in the Northern Parts of Virginia, do by these presents solemnly and mutually in the presence of God and one of another, Covenant and Combine ourselves together into a Civil Body Politic, for our better ordering and preservation and furtherance of the ends aforesaid; and by virtue hereof to enact, constitute and frame such just and equal Laws, Ordinances, Acts, Constitutions and Offices, from time to time, as shall be thought most meet and convenient for the general good of the Colony, unto which we promise all due submission and obedience. In witness whereof we have hereunder subscribed our names at Cape Cod, the 11th of November, in the year of the reign of our Sovereign Lord King James, of England, France and Ireland the eighteenth, and of Scotland the fifty-fourth. Anno Domini 1620.

Vocabulary

covenant enter into a binding agreement

SKILLS FOCUS ANALYZING PRIMARY SOURCES

Identify What was the central agreement of the Mayflower Compact, and where were the settlers when they signed it?

ENGLISH PETITION OF RIGHT, 1628

The Petition of Right was presented to King Charles I by the British Parliament in 1628. The petition complained that certain actions of the king violated rights that were granted in Magna Carta.

They do therefore humbly pray your most excellent Majesty, that no man hereafter be compelled to make or yield any gift, loan, benevolence, tax, or such like charge, without common consent by act of parliament; and that none be called to make answer, or take such oath, or to give attendance, or be confined, or otherwise molested or disquieted concerning the same or for refusal thereof; and that no freeman, in any such manner as is before mentioned, be imprisoned or detained; and that your Majesty would be pleased to remove the said soldiers and mariners, and that your people may not be so burdened in time to come; and that the aforesaid commissions, for proceeding by martial law, may be revoked and annulled; and that hereafter no commissions of like nature may issue forth to any person or persons whatsoever to be executed as aforesaid, lest by color of them any of your Majesty's subjects be destroyed or put to death contrary to the laws and franchise of the land.

Vocabulary

benevolence a tax levied by the king for no particular reason

disquieted disturbed

franchise rights

SKILLS FOCUS ANALYZING PRIMARY SOURCES

Summarize What is Parliament demanding from the king?

MASSACHUSETTS BODY OF LIBERTIES, 1641

Vocabulary

presse person forced into service

chattel personal property

In 1641 the Massachusetts General Court established the Massachusetts Body of Liberties, the first legal code established by colonists in New England.

We do therefore this day religiously and unanimously decree and confirm these following Rights, liberties and privileges concerning our Churches, and Civil State to be respectively impartial and inviolably enjoyed and observed throughout our Jurisdiction for ever.

1. No man's life shall be taken away, no man's honour or good name shall be stained, no man's person shall be arrested, restrained, banished, dismembered, nor any ways punished . . . unless it be by virtue or equity of some express law of the Country warranting the same, established by a general Court . . .

2. Every person within this Jurisdiction, whether Inhabitant or foreigner shall enjoy the same justice and law . . .

5. No man shall be compelled to any public work or service unless the presse be grounded upon some act of the general Court . . .

8. No man's Chattel or goods of what kind soever shall be pressed or taken for any public use or service, unless it be by warrant grounded upon some act of the general Court, nor without such reasonable prices and hire as the ordinary rates of the Country do afford.

SKILLS FOCUS **ANALYZING PRIMARY SOURCES**

Interpret Under what circumstances could a person's property be seized?

ENGLISH BILL OF RIGHTS, 1689

Vocabulary

prerogative privilege

quartering providing lodging or living places for people

elude avoid

forfeitures the compulsory surrender of property or money as a penalty

In 1689, after the change of government known as the Glorious Revolution, Parliament passed the English Bill of Rights. This act ensured that Parliament would have power over the monarchy. The bill also protected the rights of English citizens. This part of the document contains a list of royal wrongdoings that would no longer be permitted.

By assuming and exercising a power of dispensing with and suspending of laws and the execution of laws without consent of Parliament; . . .

By levying money for and to the use of the Crown by pretence of prerogative for other time and in other manner than the same was granted by Parliament;

By raising and keeping a standing army within this kingdom in time of peace without consent of Parliament, and quartering soldiers contrary to law; . . .

And excessive bail hath been required of persons committed in criminal cases to elude the benefit of the laws made for the liberty of the subjects;

And excessive fines have been imposed;

And illegal and cruel punishments inflicted;

And several grants and promises made of fines and forfeitures before any conviction or judgment against the persons upon whom the same were to be levied;

All which are utterly and directly contrary to the known laws and statutes and freedom of this realm . . .

SKILLS FOCUS **ANALYZING PRIMARY SOURCES**

Draw Conclusions Which of the rights listed in the document do we enjoy today?

THE SECOND TREATISE ON GOVERNMENT, 1690

English philosopher John Locke believed that all people were born equal—with natural rights of life, liberty, and property—and that the purpose of government was to protect those rights. He also believed that people consented to be ruled by a government, whose power was limited by law.

To understand political power right, and derive it from its original, we must consider, what state all men are naturally in, and that is, a state of perfect freedom to order their actions, and dispose of their possessions and persons, as they think fit, within the bounds of the law of nature, without asking leave, or depending upon the will of any other man.

A state also of equality, wherein all the power and jurisdiction is reciprocal, no one having more than another; there being nothing more evident, than that creatures of the same species and rank, promiscuously born to all the same advantages of nature, and the use of the same faculties, should also be equal one amongst another without subordination or subjection . . .

Men being, as has been said, by nature, all free, equal, and independent, no one can be put out of this estate, and subjected to the political power of another, without his own consent. The only way whereby any one divests himself of his natural liberty, and puts on the bonds of civil society, is by agreeing with other men to join and unite into a community for their comfortable, safe, and peaceable living one amongst another, in a secure enjoyment of their properties, and a greater security against any, that are not of it. This any number of men may do, because it injures not the freedom of the rest; they are left as they were in the liberty of the state of nature. When any number of men have so consented to make one community or government, they are thereby presently incorporated, and make one body politic, wherein the majority have a right to act and conclude the rest . . .

And thus every man, by consenting with others to make one body politic under one government, puts himself under an obligation, to every one of that society, to submit to the determination of the majority, and to be concluded by it; or else this original compact, whereby he with others incorporates into one society, would signify nothing, and be no compact, if he be left free, and under no other ties than he was in before in the state of nature. For what appearance would there be of any compact? What new engagement if he were no farther tied by any decrees of the society, than he himself thought fit, and did actually consent to? This would be still as great a liberty, as he himself had before his compact, or any one else in the state of nature hath, who may submit himself, and consent to any acts of it if he thinks fit . . .

Whosoever therefore out of a state of nature unite into a community, must be understood to give up all the power, necessary to the ends for which they unite into society, to the majority of the community, unless they expressly agreed in any number greater than the majority. And this is done by barely agreeing to unite into one political society, which is all the compact that is, or needs be, between the individuals, that enter into, or make up a commonwealth. And thus that, which begins and actually constitutes any political society, is nothing but the consent of any number of freemen capable of a majority to unite and incorporate into such a society. And this is that, and that only, which did, or could give beginning to any lawful government in the world . . .

But submitting to the laws of any country, living quietly, and enjoying the privileges and protection under them, makes not a man a member of that society: this is only a local protection and homage due to and from all those, who, not being in a state of war, come within the territories belonging to any government, to all parts whereof the force of its laws extends . . . Nothing can make any man so, but his actually entering into it by positive engagement, and express promise and compact. This is that, which I think, concerning the beginning of political societies, and that consent which makes any one a member of any common-wealth.

HISTORICAL DOCUMENTS

SKILLS FOCUS ANALYZING PRIMARY SOURCES

1. **Recall** According to Locke, what is the basis for government?

2. **Interpret** Why would people give up their "natural liberty" in order to join a community?

PENNSYLVANIA CHARTER OF PRIVILEGES, 1701

William Penn wrote the Pennsylvania Charter of Privileges to establish a government for the colony and to grant individual rights to the colonists. Penn wanted to base his government on the ideals of equality and tolerance.

BECAUSE no People can be truly happy, though under the greatest Enjoyment of Civil Liberties, if abridged of the Freedom of their Consciences, as to their Religious Profession and Worship . . . I do hereby grant and declare, That no Person or Persons, inhabiting in this Province or Territories, who shall confess and acknowledge One almighty God, the Creator, Upholder and Ruler of the World; and profess him or themselves obliged to live quietly under the Civil Government, shall be in any Case molested or prejudiced, in his or their Person or Estate, because of his or their conscientious Persuasion or Practice, nor be compelled to frequent or maintain any religious Worship, Place or Ministry, contrary to his or their Mind, or to do or suffer any other Act or Thing, contrary to their religious Persuasion.

AND that all Persons who also profess to believe in Jesus Christ, the Savior of the World, shall be capable (notwithstanding their other Persuasions and Practices in Point of Conscience and Religion) to serve this Government in any Capacity, both legislatively and executively, he or they solemnly promising, when lawfully required, Allegiance to the King as Sovereign, and Fidelity to the Proprietary and Governor, and taking the Attests as now established by the Law.

SKILLS FOCUS ANALYZING PRIMARY SOURCES

Explain Does the Charter of Privileges grant freedom of religion? Why or why not?

VIRGINIA DECLARATION OF RIGHTS, 1776

Thomas Jefferson drew upon the Virginia Declaration of Rights for the opening paragraphs of the Declaration of Independence. Virginia's declaration was widely copied by the other colonies and became the basis of the Bill of Rights. Written by George Mason, the declaration was adopted by the Virginia Constitutional Convention on June 12, 1776.

A Declaration of Rights made by the representatives of the good people of Virginia, assembled in full and free convention which rights do pertain to them and their posterity, as the basis and foundation of government.

Section 1. That all men are by nature equally free and independent and have certain inherent rights, of which, when they enter into a state of society, they cannot, by any compact, deprive or divest their posterity; namely, the enjoyment of life and liberty, with the means of acquiring and possessing property, and pursuing and obtaining happiness and safety.

Section 2. That all power is vested in, and consequently derived from, the people; that magistrates are their trustees and servants and at all times amenable to them.

Section 3. That government is, or ought to be, instituted for the common benefit, protection, and security of the people, nation, or community; of all the various modes and forms of government, that is best which is capable of producing the greatest degree of happiness and safety and is most effectually secured against the danger of maladministration. And that, when any government shall be found inadequate or contrary to these purposes, a majority of the community has an indubitable, inalienable, and indefeasible right to reform, alter, or abolish it, in such manner as shall be judged most conducive to the public weal.

SKILLS FOCUS ANALYZING PRIMARY SOURCES

Identify According to this document, what is the source of a government's power?

COMMON SENSE, 1776

In January 1776, colonists were divided about their relationship with Great Britain. Then Thomas Paine published Common Sense, *a pamphlet that stated in easy-to-understand terms why the colonies should break free from Britain. This widely read document strengthened support for revolution.*

Any submission to, or dependence on, Great Britain, tends directly to involve this continent in European wars and quarrels, and set us at <u>variance</u> with nations who would otherwise seek our friendship, and against whom we have neither anger nor complaint. As Europe is our market for trade, we ought to form no partial connection with any part of it. 'Tis the true interest of America to steer clear of European contentions, which she can never do while by her dependence on Britain she is made the weight in the scales of British politics.

Vocabulary

variance odds

> **SKILLS FOCUS** **ANALYZING PRIMARY SOURCES**
>
> **Interpret** According to Paine, what is a major problem with remaining under British rule?

VIRGINIA STATUTE FOR RELIGIOUS FREEDOM, 1786

The Virginia Statute for Religious Freedom, written by Thomas Jefferson and passed by Virginia's legislature in 1786, was an early statement of the rights of citizens to worship freely without experiencing coercion from government. The act was an inspiration to writers of the Bill of Rights.

To compel a man to furnish contributions of money for the <u>propagation</u> of opinions which he disbelieves, is sinful and tyrannical; that even the forcing him to support this or that teacher of his own religious persuasion, is depriving him of the comfortable liberty of giving his contributions to the particular pastor . . . that our civil rights have no dependence on our religious opinions, any more than our opinions in physics or geometry; that therefore the <u>proscribing</u> any citizen as unworthy the public confidence by laying upon him an incapacity of being called to Offices of trust and <u>emolument</u>, unless he profess or renounce this or that religious opinion, is depriving him injuriously of those privileges and advantages to which in common with his fellow-citizens he has a natural right . . .

Be it enacted by the General Assembly, That no man shall be compelled to frequent or support any religious worship, place, or ministry whatsoever, nor shall be enforced, restrained, molested, or <u>burthened</u> in his body or goods, nor shall otherwise suffer on account of his religious opinions or belief; but that all men shall be free to profess, and by argument to maintain, their opinion in matters of religion, and that the same shall in no wise diminish enlarge, or affect their civil capacities.

. . . Yet we are free to declare, and do declare, that the rights hereby asserted are of the natural rights of mankind, and that if any act shall be hereafter passed to repeal the present, or to narrow its operation, such act shall be an infringement of natural right.

Vocabulary

propagation spread

proscribing forbidding or prohibiting

emolument payment

burthened loaded down

> **SKILLS FOCUS** **ANALYZING PRIMARY SOURCES**
>
> **Elaborate** Why is Jefferson's Statute for Religious Freedom important today?

HISTORICAL DOCUMENTS

HISTORICAL DOCUMENTS

Vocabulary

stile (style) title

jurisdiction authority

emolument compensation

In 1777, during the Revolutionary War, the Continental Congress adopted the Articles of Confederation, which created a national government for the newly formed United States. This government allowed the states to have more power than the central government, a situation that would lead to problems later.

To all to whom these Presents shall come, we the undersigned Delegates of the States affixed to our Names send greeting. Whereas the Delegates of the United States of America in Congress assembled did on the fifteenth day of November in the Year of our Lord One Thousand Seven Hundred and Seventy seven, and in the Second Year of Independence of America agree to certain articles of Confederation and perpetual Union between the states of New Hampshire, Massachusetts Bay, Rhode Island and Providence Plantations, Connecticut, New York, New Jersey, Pennsylvania, Delaware, Maryland, Virginia, North Carolina, South Carolina and Georgia in the Words following . . .

I. The <u>Stile</u> of this Confederacy shall be "The United States of America".

II. Each state retains its sovereignty, freedom, and independence, and every power, <u>jurisdiction</u>, and right, which is not by this Confederation expressly delegated to the United States, in Congress assembled.

III. The said States hereby severally enter into a firm league of friendship with each other, for their common defense, the security of their liberties, and their mutual and general welfare, binding themselves to assist each other, against all force offered to, or attacks made upon them, or any of them, on account of religion, sovereignty, trade, or any other pretense whatever.

IV. The better to secure an perpetuate mutual friendship and intercourse among the people of the different states in this union, the free inhabitants of each of these states, paupers, vagabonds and fugitives from Justice excepted, shall be entitled to all privileges and immunities of free citizens in the several states . . .

VI. No State, without the consent of the United States in Congress assembled, shall send any embassy to, or receive any embassy from, or enter into any conference, agreement, alliance or treaty with any King, Prince or State; nor shall any person holding any office of profit or trust under the United States, or any of them, accept any present, <u>emolument</u>, office or title of any kind whatever from any King, Prince or foreign State; nor shall the United States in Congress assembled, or any of them, grant any title of nobility . . .

VIII. All charges of war, and all other expenses that shall be incurred for the common defense or general welfare, and allowed by the United States in Congress assembled, shall be defrayed out of a common treasury, which shall be supplied by the several States in proportion to the value of all land within each State, granted or surveyed for any person, as such land and the buildings and improvements thereon shall be estimated according to such mode as the United States in Congress assembled, shall from time to time direct and appoint. The taxes for paying that proportion shall be laid and levied by the authority and direction of the legislatures of the several States within the time agreed upon by the United States in Congress assembled.

IX. The United States in Congress assembled, shall have the sole and exclusive right and power of determining on peace and war . . . of sending and receiving ambassadors [and] entering into treaties and alliances . . .

XIII. Every state shall abide by the determinations of the United States in Congress assembled, on all questions which by this Confederation are submitted to them.

SKILLS FOCUS ANALYZING PRIMARY SOURCES

1. **Summarize** What powers were granted to Congress by the Articles of Confederation?

2. **Predict** What are some possible problems that might arise from this compact?

FEDERALIST PAPER No. 10, 1787

The Federalist Papers *were a series of essays written in favor of ratifying the United States Constitution. The essays were written by James Madison, Alexander Hamilton, and John Jay. In* Federalist Paper *No. 10, Madison addressed critics who said that the United States was too large to be governed by a strong central government. Critics claimed there were too many interest groups, or "factions," to be ruled by a democratically elected government. Madison acknowledged the presence and problem of factions. He argued however, that the republican form of government under the Constitution was best able to deal with the problem by helping different factions negotiate solutions.*

By a faction, I understand a number of citizens, whether amounting to a majority or a minority of the whole, who are united and actuated by some common impulse of passion, or of interest, adversed to the rights of other citizens, or to the permanent and aggregate interest of the community . . .

The latent causes of faction are thus sown in the nature of man; and we see them everywhere brought into different degrees of activity, according to the different circumstances of civil society. A zeal for different opinions concerning religion, concerning government, and many other points, as well of speculation as of practice; an attachment to different leaders ambitiously contending for pre-eminence and power; or to persons of other descriptions whose fortunes have been interesting to the human passions, have, in turn, divided mankind into parties, inflamed them with mutual animosity, and rendered them much more disposed to vex and oppress each other than to cooperate for their common good . . .

The inference to which we are brought is, that the *causes* of faction cannot be removed, and that relief is only to be sought in the means of controlling its *effects* . . .

A republic, by which I mean a government in which the scheme of representation takes place, opens a different prospect, and promises the cure for which we are seeking. Let us examine the points in which it varies from pure democracy, and we shall comprehend both the nature of the cure and the efficacy which it must derive from the Union.

The two great points of difference between a democracy and a republic are: first, the delegation of the government, in the latter, to a small number of citizens elected by the rest; secondly, the greater number of citizens, and greater sphere of country, over which the latter may be extended . . .

The effect of the first difference is, on the one hand, to refine and enlarge the public views, by passing them through the medium of a chosen body of citizens, whose wisdom may best discern the true interest of their country, and whose patriotism and love of justice will be least likely to sacrifice it to temporary or partial considerations. Under such a regulation, it may well happen that the public voice, pronounced by the representatives of the people, will be more consonant to the public good than if pronounced by the people themselves, convened for the purpose . . .

It clearly appears, that the same advantage which a republic has over a democracy, in controlling the effects of faction, is enjoyed by a large over a small republic—is enjoyed by the Union over the States composing it. Does the advantage consist in the substitution of representatives whose enlightened views and virtuous sentiments render them superior to local prejudices and to schemes of injustice? It will not be denied that the representation of the Union will be most likely to possess these requisite endowments. Does it consist in the greater security afforded by a greater variety of parties, against the event of any one party being able to outnumber and oppress the rest? In an equal degree does the increased variety of parties comprised within the Union increase this security? Does it, in fine, consist in the greater obstacles opposed to the concert and accomplishment of the secret wishes of an unjust and interested majority? Here again, the extent of the Union gives it the most palpable advantage.

Vocabulary

latent hidden
animosity dislike
vex anger
discern understand or recognize
convened brought together

SKILLS FOCUS   ANALYZING PRIMARY SOURCES

1. **Recall** According to Madison, what is the best solution to keep factions from dividing the nation?

2. **Evaluate** What advantage does a republic have over a pure democracy?

FEDERALIST PAPER No. 51, 1788

Vocabulary

agency power

magistracies officials

inexpedient not advisable

emoluments compensation

encroachments violations of another's rights

commensurate equal

auxiliary extra

This essay, written by James Madison, outlines reasons that the division of power written into the Constitution would keep the government from infringing on citizens' rights.

In order to lay a due foundation for that separate and distinct exercise of the different powers of government, which to a certain extent is admitted on all hands to be essential to the preservation of liberty, it is evident that each department should have a will of its own; and consequently should be so constituted that the members of each should have as little agency as possible in the appointment of the members of the others. Were this principle rigorously adhered to, it would require that all the appointments for the supreme executive, legislative, and judiciary magistracies should be drawn from the same fountain of authority, the people, through channels having no communication whatever with one another. Perhaps such a plan of constructing the several departments would be less difficult in practice than it may in contemplation appear. Some difficulties, however, and some additional expense would attend the execution of it. Some deviations, therefore, from the principle must be admitted. In the constitution of the judiciary department in particular, it might be inexpedient to insist rigorously on the principle: first, because peculiar qualifications being essential in the members, the primary consideration ought to be to select that mode of choice which best secures these qualifications; secondly, because the permanent tenure by which the appointments are held in that department, must soon destroy all sense of dependence on the authority conferring them.

It is equally evident, that the members of each department should be as little dependent as possible on those of the others, for the emoluments annexed to their offices. Were the executive magistrate, or the judges, not independent of the legislature in this particular, their independence in every other would be merely nominal.

But the great security against a gradual concentration of the several powers in the same department, consists in giving to those who administer each department the necessary constitutional means and personal motives to resist encroachments of the others. The provision for defense must in this, as in all other cases, be made commensurate to the danger of attack. Ambition must be made to counteract ambition. The interest of the man must be connected with the constitutional rights of the place. It may be a reflection on human nature, that such devices should be necessary to control the abuses of government. But what is government itself, but the greatest of all reflections on human nature? If men were angels, no government would be necessary. If angels were to govern men, neither external nor internal controls on government would be necessary. In framing a government which is to be administered by men over men, the great difficulty lies in this: you must first enable the government to control the governed; and in the next place oblige it to control itself. A dependence on the people is, no doubt, the primary control on the government; but experience has taught mankind the necessity of auxiliary precautions . . .

The constant aim is to divide and arrange the several offices in such a manner as that each may be a check on the other—that the private interest of every individual may be a sentinel over the public rights . . .

But it is not possible to give each department an equal power of self-defense. In republican government, the legislative authority necessarily predominates. The remedy for this inconveniency is to divide the legislature into different branches; and to render them, by different modes of election, and different principles of action, as little connected with each other as the nature of their common functions and their common dependence on society will admit.

SKILLS FOCUS   ANALYZING PRIMARY SOURCES

1. **Summarize** According to Madison, why are members of the judicial branch free from the influence of those who appointed them to office?

2. **Make Inferences** Why does Madison believe it necessary to divide power among separate branches of government?

CIVIL DISOBEDIENCE, 1846

American writer and philosopher Henry David Thoreau was one of the key figures of the transcendentalist movement in the mid-1800s. Opposed to the government's support of slavery, Thoreau refused to pay a tax to the state of Massachusetts and was arrested in 1846. After spending a night in jail, Thoreau wrote the essay known as "Resistance to Civil Government" or "Civil Disobedience."

I heartily accept the motto—"That government is best which governs least"; and I should like to see it acted up to more rapidly and systematically. Carried out, it finally amounts to this, which also I believe—"That government is best which governs not at all"; and when men are prepared for it, that will be the kind of government which they will have. Government is at best but an expedient; but most governments are usually, and all governments are sometimes, inexpedient. The objections which have been brought against a standing army, and they are many and weighty, and deserve to prevail, may also at last be brought against a standing government. The standing army is only an arm of the standing government. The government itself, which is only the mode which the people have chosen to execute their will, is equally liable to be abused and perverted before the people can act through it . . .

This American government—what is it but a tradition, though a recent one, endeavoring to transmit itself unimpaired to posterity, but each instant losing some of its integrity? It has not the vitality and force of a single living man; for a single man can bend it to his will. It is a sort of wooden gun to the people themselves; and, if ever they should use it in earnest as a real one against each other, it will surely split. But it is not the less necessary for this; for the people must have some complicated machinery or other, and hear its din, to satisfy that idea of government which they have. Governments show thus how successfully men can be imposed on, even impose on themselves, for their own advantage. It is excellent, we must all allow; yet this government never of itself furthered any enterprise, but by the alacrity with which it got out of its way. *It* does not keep the country free. *It* does not settle the West. *It* does not educate. The character inherent in the American people has done all that has been accomplished; and it would have done somewhat more, if the government had not sometimes got in its way. For government is an expedient by which men would fain succeed in letting one another alone; and, as has been said, when it is most expedient, the governed are most let alone by it. Trade and commerce, if they were not made of India rubber, would never manage to bounce over the obstacles which legislators are continually putting in their way . . .

But, to speak practically and as a citizen, unlike those who call themselves no-government men, I ask for, not at once no government, but *at once* a better government. Let every man make known what kind of government would command his respect, and that will be one step toward obtaining it.

After all, the practical reason why, when the power is once in the hands of the people, a majority are permitted, and for a long period continue, to rule, is not because they are most likely to be in the right, nor because this seems fairest to the minority, but because they are physically the strongest. But a government in which the majority rule in all cases cannot be based on justice, even as far as men understand it. Can there not be a government in which majorities do not virtually decide right and wrong, but conscience?—in which majorities decide only those questions to which the rule of expediency is applicable? Must the citizen ever for a moment, or in the least degree, resign his conscience to the legislator? Why has every man a conscience, then? I think that we should be men first, and subjects afterward. It is not desirable to cultivate a respect for the law, so much as for the right. The only obligation which I have a right to assume, is to do at any time what I think right . . .

Vocabulary

expedient convenience

perverted corrupted

posterity generations to come

alacrity eagerness

inherent inborn

fain gladly; willingly

SKILLS FOCUS ANALYZING PRIMARY SOURCES

1. **Describe** According to Thoreau, what is wrong with majority rule?

2. **Elaborate** Thoreau writes that his only obligation "is to do at any time what I think right." Do you agree? Explain.

SENECA FALLS DECLARATION OF SENTIMENTS, 1848

Vocabulary

usurpations seizures

tyranny unjust rule

candid fair

remuneration payment

precept example

franchise the vote

The first women's rights convention in the United States met in 1848 in Seneca Falls, New York. The delegates adopted a series of resolutions stating their belief in the equality of men and women. Their Declaration of Sentiments appeals to the principles of freedom and equality set forth in the Declaration of Independence.

When, in the course of human events, it becomes necessary for one portion of the family of man to assume among the people of the earth a position different from that which they have hitherto occupied, but one to which the laws of nature and of nature's God entitle them, a decent respect to the opinions of mankind requires that they should declare the causes that impel them to such a course.

We hold these truths to be self-evident: that all men and women are created equal; that they are endowed by their Creator with certain inalienable rights; that among these are life, liberty, and the pursuit of happiness; that to secure these rights governments are instituted, deriving their just powers from the consent of the governed . . .

The history of mankind is a history of repeated injuries and usurpations on the part of man toward woman, having in direct object the establishment of an absolute tyranny over her. To prove this, let facts be submitted to a candid world.

He has never permitted her to exercise her inalienable right to . . . [vote] . . .

He has taken from her all right in property, even to the wages she earns . . .

He has monopolized nearly all the profitable employments, and from those she is permitted to follow, she receives but a scanty remuneration. He closes to her all the avenues to wealth and distinction . . .

He has denied her the facilities for obtaining a thorough education, all colleges being closed against her . . .

Resolved, That all laws which prevent woman from occupying such a station in society as her conscience shall dictate, or which place her in a position inferior to that of man, are contrary to the great precept of nature, and therefore, of no force of authority.

Resolved, That it is the duty of the women of this country to secure to themselves their sacred right to the elective franchise . . .

SKILLS FOCUS **ANALYZING PRIMARY SOURCES**

Identify According to this document, what rights have been denied to women?

EMANCIPATION PROCLAMATION, 1863

Vocabulary

repress to forcefully restrain

garrison to station troops

After the Union victory at the Battle of Antietam, President Abraham Lincoln decided to issue the Emancipation Proclamation, which freed all enslaved people in states under Confederate control. The proclamation, which went into effect on January 1, 1863, was a step toward the Thirteenth Amendment (1865), which ended slavery in all of the United States.

That on the 1st day of January, in the year of our Lord 1863, all persons held as slaves within any state or designated part of a state, the people whereof shall then be in rebellion against the United States, shall be then, thenceforward, and forever free; and the executive government of the United States, including the military and naval authority thereof, will recognize and maintain the freedom of such persons and will do no act or acts to repress such persons, or any of them, in any efforts they may make for their actual freedom . . .

And I further declare and make known that such persons of suitable condition will be received into the armed service of the United States to garrison forts, positions, stations, and other places, and to man vessels of all sorts in said service. And upon this act, sincerely believed to be an act of justice, warranted by the Constitution upon military necessity, I invoke the considerate judgment of mankind and the gracious favor of Almighty God.

SKILLS FOCUS **ANALYZING PRIMARY SOURCES**

Interpret Aside from their freedom, what right is being granted to former slaves?

THE GETTYSBURG ADDRESS, 1863

On November 19, 1863, Abraham Lincoln addressed a crowd gathered to dedicate a cemetery at the Gettysburg battlefield. His short speech, which appears below, reminded Americans of the ideals on which the Republic was founded.

Fourscore and seven years ago our fathers brought forth on this continent a new nation, conceived in liberty and dedicated to the proposition that all men are created equal.

Now we are engaged in a great civil war, testing whether that nation or any nation so conceived and so dedicated can long endure. We are met on a great battlefield of that war. We have come to dedicate a portion of that field as a final resting-place for those who here gave their lives that that nation might live. It is altogether fitting and proper that we should do this.

But in a larger sense, we cannot dedicate—we cannot consecrate—we cannot hallow—this ground. The brave men, living and dead, who struggled here have consecrated it far above our poor power to add or detract. The world will little note nor long remember what we say here, but it can never forget what they did here. It is for us, the living, rather, to be dedicated here to the unfinished work which they who fought here have thus far so nobly advanced.

It is rather for us to be here dedicated to the great task remaining before us—that from these honored dead we take increased devotion to that cause for which they gave the last full measure of devotion; that we here highly resolve that these dead shall not have died in vain; that this nation, under God, shall have a new birth of freedom; and that government of the people, by the people, for the people shall not perish from the earth.

Vocabulary

fourscore eighty
consecrate to make holy

LINCOLN'S SECOND INAUGURAL ADDRESS, 1865

On March 4, 1865, President Lincoln laid out his approach to Reconstruction in his second inaugural address. As the excerpt below shows, Lincoln hoped to peacefully reunite the nation and its people.

At this second appearing to take the oath of the Presidential Office there is less occasion for an extended address than there was at the first. Then a statement somewhat in detail of a course to be pursued seemed fitting and proper. Now, at the expiration of four years, during which public declarations have been constantly called forth on every point and phase of the great contest which still absorbs the attention and engrosses the energies of the nation, little that is new could be presented . . .

On the occasion corresponding to this four years ago all thoughts were anxiously directed to an impending civil war. All dreaded it, all sought to avert it. While the inaugural address was being delivered from this place, devoted altogether to saving the Union without war, urgent agents were in the city seeking to destroy it without war—seeking to dissolve the Union and divide effects by negotiation. Both parties deprecated war, but one of them would make war rather than let the nation survive, and the other would accept war rather than let it perish, and the war came . . .

With malice toward none, with charity for all, with firmness in the right as God gives us to see the right, let us strive on to finish the work we are in, to bind up the nation's wounds, to care for him who shall have borne the battle and for his widow and his orphan, to do all which may achieve and cherish a just and lasting peace among ourselves and with all nations.

Vocabulary

deprecated made little of
malice desire to cause injury; hatred

Vocabulary

paradoxical
contradictory

existential real

estrangement
alienation

conniving
conspiring

While protesting segregation in Birmingham, Alabama, Martin Luther King Jr. was arrested and held in jail for several days. The following is an excerpt from a letter that King wrote in response to a full-page ad in a local newspaper, taken out by eight clergymen, denouncing the protests as unjustified.

You express a great deal of anxiety over our willingness to break laws. This is certainly a legitimate concern. Since we so diligently urge people to obey the Supreme Court's decision of 1954 outlawing segregation in the public schools, at first glance it may seem rather <u>paradoxical</u> for us consciously to break laws. One may well ask: "How can you advocate breaking some laws and obeying others?" The answer lies in the fact that there are two types of laws: just and unjust. I would be the first to advocate obeying just laws. One has not only a legal but a moral responsibility to obey just laws. Conversely, one has a moral responsibility to disobey unjust laws. I would agree with St. Augustine that "an unjust law is no law at all."

Now, what is the difference between the two? How does one determine whether a law is just or unjust? A just law is a man-made code that squares with the moral law or the law of God. An unjust law is a code that is out of harmony with the moral law. To put it in the terms of St. Thomas Aquinas: An unjust law is a human law that is not rooted in eternal law and natural law . . . All segregation statutes are unjust because segregation distorts the soul and damages the personality. It gives the segregator a false sense of superiority and the segregated a false sense of inferiority. Segregation, to use the terminology of the Jewish philosopher Martin Buber, substitutes an "I-it" relationship for an "I-thou" relationship and ends up relegating persons to the status of things. Hence segregation is not only politically, economically and sociologically unsound, it is morally wrong and awful. Paul Tillich said that sin is separation. Is not segregation an <u>existential</u> expression of man's tragic separation, his awful <u>estrangement</u>, his terrible sinfulness? Thus it is that I can urge men to obey the 1954 decision of the Supreme Court, for it is morally right; and I can urge them to disobey segregation ordinances, for they are morally wrong.

An unjust law is a code inflicted upon a minority which that minority had no part in enacting or creating because they did not have the unhampered right to vote. Who can say that the legislature of Alabama which set up the segregation laws was democratically elected? Throughout the state of Alabama all types of <u>conniving</u> methods are used to prevent Negroes from becoming registered voters and there are some counties without a single Negro registered to vote despite the fact that the Negro constitutes a majority of the population. Can any law set up in such a state be considered democratically structured?

These are just a few examples of unjust and just laws. There are some instances when a law is just on its face and unjust in its application. For instance, I was arrested Friday on a charge of parading without a permit. Now there is nothing wrong with an ordinance which requires a permit for a parade, but when the ordinance is used to preserve segregation and to deny citizens the First Amendment privilege of peaceful assembly and peaceful protest, then it becomes unjust.

I hope you can see the distinction I am trying to point out. In no sense do I advocate evading or defying the law as the rabid segregationist would do. This would lead to anarchy. One who breaks an unjust law must do it openly, lovingly . . . and with a willingness to accept the penalty. I submit that an individual who breaks a law that conscience tells him is unjust, and willingly accepts the penalty by staying in jail to arouse the conscience of the community over its injustice, is in reality expressing the very highest respect for the law.

SKILLS FOCUS ANALYZING PRIMARY SOURCES

1. **Summarize** Explain the distinction King makes between a just and an unjust law.

2. **Evaluate** How do King's ideas compare to such founding-era documents as the Virginia Declaration of Rights, the Declaration of Independence, the Massachusetts Body of Liberties, and the *Federalist Papers*?

English and Spanish Glossary

MARK	AS IN	RESPELLING	EXAMPLE
a	alphabet	a	*AL-fuh-bet
ā	Asia	ay	AY-zhuh
ä	cart, top	ah	KAHRT, TAHP
e	let, ten	e	LET, TEN
ē	even, leaf	ee	EE-vuhn, LEEF
i	it, tip, British	i	IT, TIP, BRIT-ish
ī	site, buy, Ohio	y	SYT, BY, oh-HY-oh
	iris	eye	EYE-ris
k	card	k	KAHRD
ō	over, rainbow	oh	OH-vuhr, RAYN-boh
ú	book, wood	ooh	BOOHK, WOOHD
ȯ	all, orchid	aw	AWL, AWR-kid
ȯi	foil, coin	oy	FOYL, KOYN
aú	out	ow	OWT
ə	cup, butter	uh	KUHP, BUHT-uhr
ü	rule, food	oo	ROOL, FOOD
yü	few	yoo	FYOO
zh	vision	zh	VIZH-uhn

*A syllable printed in small capital letters receives heavier emphasis than the other syllable(s) in a word.

Phonetic Respelling and Pronunciation Guide

Many of the key terms in this textbook have been respelled to help you pronounce them. The letter combinations used in the respelling throughout the narrative are explained in the phonetic respelling and pronunciation guide at left. The guide is adapted from *Merriam-Webster's Collegiate Dictionary, Eleventh Edition; Merriam-Webster's Biographical Dictionary;* and *Merriam-Webster's Geographical Dictionary.*

A

absentee ballot a ballot submitted on or before election day by a voter who cannot be present on election day (p. 271)
voto ausente voto emitido el día de la votación o el día anterior por un votante que no puede ir a votar en persona (pág. 271)

administration the group of people who work for the executive branch under a specific president (p. 181)
administración grupo de personas que trabajan para el poder ejecutivo bajo el mandato de un presidente específico (pág. 181)

affirmative action a policy that requires employers and institutions to provide opportunities for members of certain historically underrepresented groups (p. 339)
acción afirmativa política que requiere que los empleadores y las instituciones den oportunidades a miembros de ciertos grupos que históricamente han estado poco representados (pág. 339)

Albany Plan of Union (1754) first plan for uniting the colonies; proposed by Ben Franklin (p. 38)
Plan de Unión de Albany (1754) primer plan para unificar a las colonias; propuesto por Benjamín Franklin (pág. 38)

amnesty a general pardon for offenses committed by a group of offenders (p. 174)
amnistía conceder a un grupo de transgresores un perdón general por los delitos cometidos (pág. 174)

Antifederalists a group of people who opposed the adoption of the U.S. Constitution (p. 58)
antifederalistas grupo de personas que se opuso a la adopción de la Constitución de Estados Unidos (pág. 58)

apartheid a system of racial segregation and oppression that was practiced in South Africa when the country's white minority dominated the country (p. 494)
apartheid sistema de segregación racial y opresión practicado en Sudáfrica cuando la minoría blanca dominaba el país (pág. 494)

appellant a person who files an appeal (p. 230)
apelante persona que presenta una apelación (pág. 230)

appellate jurisdiction the authority of some courts to review decisions made by lower courts (p. 221)
jurisdicción apelativa autoridad de algunas cortes para revisar las decisiones tomadas en cortes inferiores (pág. 221)

apportionment the distribution of seats in the House of Representatives among the states (p. 124)
distribución forma en la que están repartidos los puestos de la Cámara de Representantes entre los estados (pág. 124)

appropriation a congressional act or bill that sets aside funds for a specific purpose (p. 125)
asignación de fondos ley o proyecto de ley del Congreso que separa fondos para un propósito específico (pág. 125)

Articles of Confederation (1777) the document that created the first central government for the United States; it was replaced by the Constitution in 1789 (p. 48)
Artículos de la Confederación (1777) documento que creó el primer gobierno central de Estados Unidos; fue reemplazado por la Constitución de 1789 (pág. 48)

authoritarian a form of government in which power is concentrated in the hands of a single leader or small group (p. 488)
autoritario forma de gobierno en la cual el poder está concentrado en las manos de un dirigente único o de un grupo pequeño (pág. 488)

B

bail money pledged by a person accused of a crime that he or she will return to court for trial (p. 306)
fianza dinero entregado por una persona acusada de un crimen como garantía de que volverá a la corte para someterse a juicio (pág. 306)

bankruptcy a legal process by which persons who cannot pay money they owe others can receive court protection and assistance in settling their financial problems (p. 229)
bancarrota proceso legal a través del cual las personas que no pueden pagar el dinero que deben a otras pueden recibir protección y asistencia judicial para resolver sus problemas económicos (pág. 229)

bench trial a trial in which a judge, not a jury, hears and decides the case (p. 311)
juicio de estrado juicio en el cual un juez, y no un jurado, escucha y decide sobre el caso (pág. 311)

bias errors introduced by polling methods that lead to one outcome over others (p. 253)
parcialidad errores provocados por métodos de votación que producen un resultado en mayor medida que otros (pág. 253)

bicameral consisting of two houses (p. 33)
bicameral que consiste de dos cámaras (pág. 33)

bill of attainder a law that punishes a person without trial (p. 135)
ley de extinción de derechos civiles ley que castiga a una persona sin someterla a juicio previo (pág. 135)

Bill of Rights the first ten amendments to the U.S. Constitution concerning basic individual liberties (p. 60)
Declaración de derechos primeras diez enmiendas hechas a la Constitución de Estados Unidos, relacionadas con las libertades individuales fundamentales (pág. 60)

bills proposed laws (p. 140)
proyectos de ley ley que es considerada (pág. 140)

bipartisan made up of members from both major political parties (p. 201)
bipartidista formado por miembros de los dos partidos políticos más importantes (pág. 201)

block grants federal grants given to state and local governments for broad purposes, such as welfare, community development, public health, or education (p. 113)
subsidio en bloque fondo federal concedido a los gobiernos estatales y locales para que lo utilicen en objetivos amplios, como por ejemplo asistencia social, desarrollo de la comunidad, salud pública o educación (pág. 113)

bond a financial instrument by which a borrower agrees to pay back borrowed money, plus interest, at a future date (p. 208)
bono herramienta financiera mediante la cual un prestatario accede a devolver un dinero prestado, más un interés, en una fecha futura (pág. 208)

boroughs the name used in Alaska for counties (p. 544)
boroughs nombre que se da a los condados en Alaska (pág. 544)

bourgeoisie the people who own the means of production in a capitalist system (p. 512)
burguesía grupo de personas que es dueño de los medios de producción en el sistema capitalista (pág. 512)

briefs written arguments filed by the parties in an appeal (p. 230)
escritos argumentos escritos presentados por las partes en una apelación (pág. 230)

bureaucracy a type of organization, either in government or the private sector, having the following features: a clear formal structure, a division of labor, and a set of rules and procedures by which it operates (p. 192)
burocracia tipo de organización, ya sea en el gobierno o en el sector privado, que tiene las siguientes características: una estructura formal clara, división del trabajo y un conjunto de reglas y procedimientos con los cuales opera (pág. 192)

bureaucrats administrators and skilled, expert workers who carry out many specific tasks of the bureaucracy (p. 193)
burócratas administradores y trabajadores calificados y expertos que llevan a cabo muchas tareas específicas de la burocracia (pág. 193)

C

cabinet the leaders of the executive departments, who also act as advisers to the president (p. 88)
gabinete líderes de los departamentos ejecutivos, que también son consejeros del presidente (pág. 88)

capitalism an economic system based on the private ownership of the means of production and distribution, and individuals and businesses make most economic decisions (p. 511)
capitalismo sistema económico basado en la propiedad privada de los medios de producción y distribución en el que los individuos y las empresas toman la mayoría de las decisiones económicas (pág. 511)

capital punishment the death penalty (p. 306)
pena capital castigo de muerte (pág. 306)

categorical grant a federal grant that can only be used for a specific purpose, or category, of state and local spending; these grants usually require that the state contribute money in addition to the national money (p. 113)
subsidio para fines específicos subsidio federal que solo puede ser usado para un propósito específico dentro de los gastos estatales o locales; estos subsidios en general requieren que el estado contribuya con dinero agregándolo al dinero otorgado a nivel nacional (pág. 113)

caucus a meeting of party members who select the candidates to run for election (p. 269)
caucus reunión de los miembros de un partido para seleccionar a los candidatos a participar en una elección (pág. 269)

charter colonies colonies based on a grant of land by the British Crown to a company or a group of settlers (p. 35)
colonia por fueros colonia basada en la cesión de tierras por parte de la corona británica a una compañía o a un grupo de colonos (pág. 35)

checks and balances a system in which each branch of government is able to limit the power of the other branches (p. 73)
equilibrio de poderes sistema mediante el cual cada rama del gobierno puede limitar el poder de las otras ramas (pág. 73)

chief executive another title for the president, who holds the executive's power to run government programs and implement laws that are passed by Congress (p. 163)
jefe del ejecutivo otro título para el presidente, quien tiene el mando del poder ejecutivo para llevar a cabo los programas de gobierno y para implementar las leyes aprobadas por el Congreso (pág. 163)

chief of staff the official who manages the everyday operations of the White House Office or who may serve as the primary presidential adviser who controls all access to the president and helps map political strategy (p. 181)
jefe del estado mayor funcionario que administra las operaciones diarias de la Casa Blanca o que puede ser el principal consejero presidencial que controla todos los accesos al presidente y que contribuye en la planificación de la estrategia política (pág. 181)

chief of state another title for the president, takes on the role of the symbolic figurehead of the United States (p. 163)
jefe de estado otro título para el presidente, que cumple el papel de cabeza simbólica de Estados Unidos (pág. 163)

citizen legislatures state legislatures that meet only occasionally and for brief sessions, and whose members are paid a small salary for their service; also called "part-time legislatures" (p. 532)
asambleas legislativas ciudadanas asambleas legislativas estatales que se reúnen solo ocasionalmente y por sesiones breves, y cuyos miembros reciben un pequeño salario por su servicio; también llamadas "asambleas legislativas de tiempo parcial" (pág. 532)

civil disobedience the nonviolent refusal to obey the law as a way to advocate change (p. 335)
desobediencia civil negativa no violenta a obedecer la ley como una manera de exigir un cambio (pág. 335)

civil law the category of law that covers private disputes between people over property or relationships (p. 304)
derecho civil categoría de ley que cubre los conflictos entre personas en lo privado, ya sea en cuanto a la propiedad o las relaciones (pág. 304)

civil liberties the basic freedoms to think and to act that all people have and that are protected against government abuse (p. 281)
libertades civiles libertades fundamentales de acción y de pensamiento que tienen todas las personas y que están protegidas contra abusos del gobierno (pág. 281)

civil rights the rights that involve equal status and treatment and the right to participate in government (p. 281)
derechos civiles derechos que implican la igualdad social, el trato igualitario para todas las personas y el derecho a participar en el gobierno (pág. 281)

civil rights movement a mass movement in the 1950s and 1960s to guarantee the civil rights of African Americans (p. 334)
movimiento por los derechos civiles movimiento masivo de las décadas de 1950 y 1960 para garantizar los derechos civiles de los afroamericanos (pág. 334)

civil service the group of nonmilitary government workers who carry out the work of the federal government (p. 194)
funcionariado grupo de trabajadores no militares del gobierno que llevan a cabo el trabajo del gobierno federal (pág. 194)

closed primary a primary election in which only voters registered as party members can vote in selecting that party's candidates (p. 270)
primarias cerradas elecciones primarias en las que solo los votantes que son miembros inscritos del partido pueden votar para elegir a sus candidatos (pág. 270)

cloture the vote to end debate of a bill in the Senate (p. 147)
límite del debate voto para terminar el debate sobre un proyecto de ley en el Senado (pág. 147)

coalition a temporary alliance of political parties formed for political purposes (p. 492)
coalición alianza temporal entre partidos políticos formada para propósitos políticos (pág. 492)

collective security the attempt at keeping international peace and order (p. 442)
seguridad colectiva intento de mantener la paz y el orden a nivel internacional (pág. 442)

command economy an economic system in which the government decides what goods and services are produced (p. 510)
economía dirigida sistema económico en el cual el gobierno decide los bienes y los servicios que se producen (pág. 510)

commander in chief another title for the president, who serves as commander of the nation's military forces (p. 163)
comandante en jefe otro título para el presidente, que es el comandante de las fuerzas militares de la nación (pág. 163)

commerce clause Article I, Section 8, Clause 3, of the Constitution which outlines the commerce powers granted to Congress (p. 129)
cláusula de comercio Artículo 1, Sección 8, Cláusula 3 de la Constitución, que explica los poderes para el comercio otorgados al Congreso (pág. 129)

commission system a form of municipal government in which a group of elected commissioners lead city departments and set local policies (p. 545)
sistema de comisiones forma de gobierno municipal en la cual un grupo de comisionados elegidos dirigen los departamentos de la ciudad y establecen las políticas locales (pág. 545)

Committee of the Whole a measure taken in the House of Representatives in which all representatives become members of a single committee, allowing the House to function when many members are absent (p. 153)
comisión plenaria medida tomada en la Cámara de Representantes mediante la cual la totalidad de los miembros se convierten en un solo comité, lo que permite el funcionamiento de la Cámara cuando muchos miembros están ausentes (pág. 153)

communism a political and economic system based on the writings of Karl Marx in which the state controls the production and distribution of goods, and social classes and private ownership are discouraged (p. 502)
comunismo sistema político y económico basado en las teorías de Karl Marx, en el cual el estado controla la producción y distribución de bienes, y se desalientan las clases sociales y la propiedad privada (pág. 502)

commute to reduce a person's sentence (p. 175)
conmutar reducir la sentencia de una persona (pág. 175)

concurrent jurisdiction cases that fall under jurisdiction of both state and federal courts (p. 221)
jurisdicción concurrente casos que caen bajo la jurisdicción tanto de cortes federales como de cortes estatales (pág. 221)

concurrent power the power that is shared by both the federal and state governments (p. 100)
poder concurrente poder que es compartido por el gobierno federal y los gobiernos estatales (pág. 100)

concurrent resolutions measures in which both houses of Congress address matters that affect the operations of both chambers (p. 150)
resoluciones concurrentes medidas en las cuales las dos cámaras del Congreso tratan asuntos que afectan las operaciones de ambas cámaras (pág. 150)

concurring opinions statements by Supreme Court justices who agree with the overall conclusion in the case, but stress some different or additional legal point (p. 241)
opinión concurrente acuerdo redactado por jueces de la Corte Suprema que concuerdan con la conclusión general de un caso, pero enfatizan algún razonamiento legal adicional o diferente (pág. 241)

confederal system an alliance of independent states manifesting a degree of national unity through a central government (e.g., the United States under the Articles of Confederation) (p. 18)
sistema confederal alianza de estados independientes que manifiestan un grado de unidad nacional a través de un gobierno central de poderes unidos (por ejemplo, Estados Unidos bajo los Artículos de la Confederación) (pág. 18)

conference committee a joint committee formed from both houses to resolve differences between the House and Senate versions of a bill (p. 154)
comité de conferencia comisión mixta formada por miembros de ambas cámaras para resolver las diferencias entre las versiones de un proyecto de ley de la Cámara de Representantes y del Senado (pág. 154)

constituents the people of a particular geographic area who are represented by a lawmaking body (p. 123)
electores personas de un área geográfica en particular que están representadas por un cuerpo legislativo (pág. 123)

containment U.S. policy adopted in the late 1940s to stop the spread of Communism by providing economic and military aid to countries opposing the Soviet Union (p. 474)
contención política estadounidense adoptada hacia fines de la década de 1940 para detener la expansión del comunismo y que proveía ayuda económica y militar a los países que se oponían a la Unión Soviética (pág. 474)

cooperative federalism (1930–1960) an era of federalism during which the national and state government shared functional authority in broad policy areas; also called "marble cake" federalism (p. 109)
federalismo cooperativo (1930–1960) época del federalismo durante la cual el gobierno nacional y el estatal compartieron autoridad funcional en amplias áreas políticas; también llamada federalismo de "pastel marmolado" (pág. 109)

council-manager system a form of municipal government in which the city council appoints a city manager to be the chief executive to handle the day-to-day operations of the city government while the mayor's role is to lead the city council (p. 545)
sistema de concejo-administración forma de gobierno municipal en la cual el concejo municipal designa a un administrador municipal para que sea el jefe ejecutivo y maneje las operaciones diarias del gobierno de la ciudad, mientras que la función del alcalde es dirigir el concejo municipal (pág. 545)

Council of Economic Advisers (CEA) the group of advisers charged with providing the president with expert analysis of the economy and also assisting in forming economic policy (p. 183)
consejo de asesores económicos (CEA, por sus siglas en inglés) grupo de asesores que se ocupan de proporcionar al presidente análisis expertos de la economía y también de asistir en la creación de las políticas económicas (pág. 183)

counties subdivisions of state government formed to carry out state laws, collect taxes, and supervise elections (p. 544)
condados subdivisiones del gobierno estatal formadas para aplicar leyes estatales, recaudar impuestos y supervisar las elecciones (pág. 544)

courts-martial hearings held for the trial of military personnel accused of violating military law (p. 232)
tribunal militar audiencias llevadas a cabo para el juicio de personal militar acusado de desobedecer la ley militar (pág. 232)

creative federalism (1960–1980) the period in which the national government channeled federal funds to local governments and citizen groups to address problems that states could or would not address; also called "picket fence" federalism (p. 109)
federalismo creativo (1960–1980) período en el cual el gobierno nacional destinó fondos federales a los gobiernos locales y a los grupos ciudadanos para tratar los problemas que los estados no podían o no querían tratar; también llamado federalismo de "valla" (pág. 109)

criminal law the category of law that deals with crimes and their punishments (p. 304)
derecho penal categoría de la ley que se ocupa de los crímenes y sus castigos (pág. 304)

cyber-surveillance searches of wireless communications (p. 410)
cibervigilancia búsquedas dentro de las comunicaciones inalámbricas (pág. 410)

de facto segregation segregation in fact; separation of races that occurs without laws requiring segregation (p. 332)
segregación de facto segregación de hecho; separación de razas que sucede sin leyes que requieran la segregación (pág. 332)

defendant the person against whom a complaint is filed (p. 221)
acusado persona contra la cual se presenta una acusación (pág. 221)

defense alliance an agreement to come to another nation's aid in the event of an attack (p. 442)
alianza defensiva acuerdo para brindar ayuda a otra nación en caso de un ataque (pág. 442)

deficit a condition in which government revenues are lower than expenses (p. 129)
déficit condición en la cual los ingresos del gobierno son más bajos que los gastos (pág. 129)

de jure segregation separation of races by law (p. 330)
segregación por ley separación de las razas determinada por ley (pág. 330)

democratization U.S. foreign policy of promoting the establishment of democratic governments in other nations (p. 478)
  democratización política exterior estadounidense de promover el establecimiento de gobiernos democráticos en otras naciones (pág. 478)

demographic a population group defined by a specific characteristic or set of characteristics (p. 363)
  grupo demográfico grupo de la población definido por una caracterís tica específica o por un conjunto de características (pág. 363)

denaturalization the legal process by which a naturalized citizen has his or her citizenship revoked (p. 343)
  desnaturalización proceso legal a través del cual se revoca la ciudadanía de un ciudadano naturalizado (pág. 343)

deportation the legal process of forcing a noncitizen to leave a country (p. 346)
  deportación proceso legal que consiste en forzar a un no ciudadano a abandonar el país (pág. 346)

desegregation the process of ending the formal separation of groups based on race (p. 332)
  integración proceso que pone fin a la separación formal de grupos basada en la raza (pág. 332)

détente a policy of relaxing of tensions between the United States and the Soviet Union (p. 475)
  détente política de reducción de tensiones entre Estados Unidos y la Unión Soviética (pág. 475)

deterrence the policy of building up the U.S. armed forces in order to discourage acts of military aggression by other nations (p. 473)
  disuasión política de fortalecer las fuerzas armadas estadounidenses para desalentar los actos de agresión militar por parte de otras naciones (pág. 473)

devolution (1980–present) the modern trend in federalism in which more power is given back to the states; also known as "new federalism" (p. 110)
  devolución (1980–presente) tendencia moderna del federalismo en la cual se devuelve más poder a los estados; también conocida como "nuevo federalismo" (pág. 110)

dictatorship a system of rule in which one person, a dictator, or a small group of people can hold unlimited power over government, which is usually controlled by force. (p. 15)
  dictadura sistema de gobierno en el que una persona, un dictador, o un grupo pequeño de personas puede ejercer un poder ilimitado sobre el gobierno, el cual es generalmente controlado por la fuerza (pág. 15)

diplomacy the art of negotiating with foreign governments (p. 163)
  diplomacia arte de negociar con gobiernos extranjeros (pág. 163)

diplomatic recognition the presidential power to formally recognize the legitimacy of a foreign government (p. 172, 453)
  reconocimiento diplomático poder presidencial para reconocer formalmente la legitimidad de un gobierno extranjero (págs. 172, 453)

direct democracy a form of government in which citizens met regularly in a popular assembly to discuss issues of the day, pass laws, and vote for leaders (p. 16)
  democracia directa forma de gobierno en la que los ciudadanos se reúnen con regularidad en una asamblea popular para hablar de los temas del día, aprobar leyes y votar por los dirigentes (pág. 16)

direct primary a primary, or first, election in which the party's candidate for office is chosen directly by voters (p. 269)
  primaria directa elección primaria, o primera, en la cual los votantes eligen directamente al candidato del partido para un cargo (pág. 269)

direct tax a tax an individual pays directly to the government (p. 128)
  impuesto directo impuesto que los individuos pagan directamente al gobierno (pág. 128)

discharge petition a measure taken in the House of Representatives to force a bill out of committee (p. 152)
  petición de descargo medida que se toma en la Cámara de Representantes para hacer que una ley salga de un comité (pág. 152)

discretionary spending spending subject to the annual budget process (p. 209)
  gastos arbitrarios gastos expuestos al proceso anual de presupuestos (pág. 209)

dissenting opinions statements written by Supreme Court justices who disagree with the majority's decision; these opinions do not have a direct legal impact on the case but they can influence future judgments (p. 241)
  opinión discrepante escrito de jueces de la Corte Suprema que están en desacuerdo con la decisión mayoritaria; estas opiniones no tienen un impacto legal directo en el caso pero pueden influenciar decisiones futuras (pág. 241)

divine right of kings the theory that a monarch rules by the sanction, or approval, of God (p. 10)
  derecho divino teoría de que un monarca reina con la sanción, o aprobación, de Dios (pág. 10)

docket the list of cases to be heard before a court (p. 240)
  lista de casos calendario de casos que verá una corte (pág. 240)

doctrine of nullification the belief that the states had the right to cancel federal laws with which they disagreed (p. 106)
  doctrina de anulación creencia de que los estados tenían el derecho de cancelar las leyes federales con las cuales estaban en desacuerdo (pág. 106)

doctrine of secession the idea that a state had the right to separate from the Union (p. 106)
  doctrina de secesión idea que propone que un estado tenía el derecho de separarse de la Unión (pág. 106)

double jeopardy being made to stand trial twice for the same offense (p. 311)
  doble riesgo ser juzgado por segunda vez por el mismo delito (pág. 311)

dual federalism (1790–1930) the time period during which national and state governments were seen as equal authorities, operating over separate areas of influence, and the authority of national government was generally limited to the expressed powers listed in the Constitution; also called "layer cake" federalism (p. 104)
  federalismo doble (1790–1930) período de tiempo en el que el gobierno nacional y el estatal eran vistos como autoridades iguales, que operaban sobre áreas de influencia separadas, y la autoridad del gobierno nacional estaba generalmente limitada a los poderes expresados en la Constitución; también llamado federalismo de "pastel en capas" (pág. 104)

due process following established and complete legal procedures (p. 283)
  debido proceso seguir los procedimientos legales establecidos y completos (pág. 283)

ENGLISH AND SPANISH GLOSSARY

economic sanctions the policy of withholding money or banning trade with a country and its allies in order to bring about social or political change in that country (p. 443)
sanciones económicas política de retener el dinero o de prohibir el comercio con un país y sus aliados para que haya un cambio social o político en ese país (pág. 443)

electoral college the body of 538 people elected from the 50 states and the District of Columbia to cast the official votes that elect the president and vice president (p. 89)
colegio electoral cuerpo de 538 personas elegidas de los 50 estados y el Distrito de Columbia que votan oficialmente para elegir al presidente y al vicepresidente (pág. 89)

electorate the body of people entitled to vote (p. 261)
electorado personas que tienen derecho a votar (pág. 261)

embassies diplomatic centers that nations maintain in other countries around the world (p. 442)
embajadas centros diplomáticos que las naciones mantienen en otros países alrededor del mundo (pág. 442)

endorse to publicly declare support for a particular candidate in an election (p. 257)
refrendar declarar públicamente el apoyo para un candidato en particular en una elección (pág. 257)

English Bill of Rights (1689) document signed by King William that stated that English monarchs would no longer be able to enact laws, raise taxes, or keep an army without Parliament's consent (p. 34)
Declaración de Derechos inglesa (1689) documento firmado por el rey Guillermo en el cual establecía que los monarcas ingleses ya no podrían aprobar leyes, recaudar impuestos o tener un ejército sin el consentimiento del Parlamento (pág. 34)

equality the principle that all people possess a fundamental, moral worth that entitles them to fair treatment under the law and equal opportunity in all aspects of life—political, social, and economic (p. 21)
igualdad principio que sostiene que todas las personas poseen un valor fundamental y moral que les da derecho a un trato justo ante la ley y a oportunidades iguales en todos los aspectos de la vida: político, social y económico (pág. 21)

equal protection clause the part of the Fourteenth Amendment to the U.S. Constitution that requires states to apply the law the same way for one person that they would for another person in the same circumstances (p. 326)
cláusula de igualdad de protección parte de la Decimocuarta Enmienda de la Constitución de Estados Unidos, que requiere que los estados apliquen la ley a una persona de la misma manera en que lo harían para otra persona en las mismas circunstancias (pág. 326)

establishment clause the part of the First Amendment of the U.S. Constitution that declares that government cannot take actions that create an official religion or support one religion over another (p. 286)
cláusula de establecimiento parte de la Primera Enmienda de la Constitución de Estados Unidos que declara que el gobierno no puede actuar para crear una religión oficial ni apoyar a una religión por encima de otra (pág. 286)

exclusionary rule the rule that evidence obtained illegally may not be used against a person in a trial (p. 298)
regla de exclusión regla que afirma que las pruebas obtenidas ilegalmente no pueden ser usadas contra una persona en un juicio (pág. 298)

exclusive jurisdiction the sole right to hear and decide a certain type of case, depending either on the subject matter of a case or the parties involved (p. 221)
jurisdicción exclusiva derecho único de escuchar y decidir sobre cierto tipo de casos, dependiendo tanto del tema del caso como de las partes involucradas (pág. 221)

executive agreements arrangements or compacts the U.S. president makes with foreign leaders or foreign governments (p. 85)
acuerdos ejecutivos acuerdos o pactos entre el presidente de Estados Unidos y el líder o gobierno de otra nación (pág. 85)

executive clemency powers that allow a governor to grant pardons and commutations (p. 534)
clemencia ejecutiva poderes que permiten a un gobernador conceder perdones y conmutaciones de penas (pág. 534)

executive departments agencies of the federal government responsible for carrying out laws, administering programs, and making regulations in their particular area of responsibility (p. 184)
departamentos ejecutivos agencias del gobierno federal responsables de formular leyes, administrar programas y establecer regulaciones en su área específica de responsabilidad (pág. 184)

Executive Office of the President the group of advisers and assistants to the president (p. 181)
Oficina Ejecutiva del Presidente grupo de asesores y asistentes del presidente (pág. 181)

executive orders formal, signed statements from the president that instruct or guide executive officials and have the force of law (p. 170)
órdenes ejecutivas comunicados formales firmados por el presidente que instruyen o guían a los funcionarios ejecutivos y que tienen fuerza de ley (pág. 170)

executive privilege the power that allows a president to refuse to release information to Congress or a court (p. 170)
privilegio ejecutivo poder que permite al presidente negarse a dar a conocer información al Congreso o a una corte (pág. 170)

exit poll a survey of a randomly selected fraction of voters after they have voted (p. 253)
encuesta a boca de urna encuesta realizada a una fracción de votantes seleccionada al azar después de que han votado (pág. 253)

expatriation the legal process of giving up one's citizenship (p. 343)
expatriación proceso legal de renunciar a la propia ciudadanía (pág. 343)

ex post facto laws laws that criminalize an action that took place in the past and that was legal at that time; *ex post facto* is a Latin phrase meaning "from after the fact" (p. 135)
ley *ex post facto* ley que penaliza una acción que ocurrió en el pasado y que era legal en aquel tiempo; *ex post facto* es una frase en latín que quiere decir "de después del hecho" (pág. 135)

expressed powers the powers explicitly granted to Congress by the Constitution (p. 98)
poderes expresados poderes explícitamente otorgados al Congreso por la Constitución (pág. 98)

factors of production the basic resources that make up an economy; the three main factors of production are land and natural resources, labor, and capital (p. 510)
factores de producción recursos básicos que forman una economía; los tres factores principales de producción son la tierra y los recursos naturales, el trabajo y el capital (pág. 510)

federal debt the total amount of money that the government has borrowed and not yet repaid (p. 209)
deuda pública cantidad total de dinero que el gobierno pidió prestado y todavía no ha devuelto (pág. 209)

Federal Election Commission (FEC) government commission formed to enforce the Federal Election Campaign Act (p. 371)
Comisión Electoral Federal (FEC, por sus siglas en inglés) comisión del gobierno formada para hacer cumplir la Ley Federal de Campañas Electorales (pág. 371)

federalism the form of political organization in which power is divided among a central government and territorial subdivisions; in the United States, among the national, state, and local governments (p. 76)
federalismo forma de organización política en la cual el poder está dividido entre un gobierno central y subdivisiones territoriales; en Estados Unidos, entre el gobierno nacional, el estatal y el local (pág. 76)

Federalist Papers a collection of essays on the principles of government written in defense of the Constitution in 1787 and 1788. (p. 59)
Federalist Papers colección de ensayos sobre los principios de gobierno escritos en defensa de la Constitución en 1787 y 1788. (pág. 59)

Federalists group of people who supported the adoption of the U.S. Constitution and a strong national government (p. 58)
federalistas grupo de personas que apoyaban la adopción de la Constitución de Estados Unidos y un gobierno nacional fuerte (pág. 58)

federal mandates regulations that the national government imposes on state and local governments (p. 113)
mandatos federales regulaciones que el gobierno nacional impone sobre los gobiernos estatales y el locales (pág. 113)

federal system a form of political organization in which power is divided among a central government and territorial subdivisions; in the United States power is shared among the national, state, and local governments (p. 17)
sistema federal forma de organización política en la cual el poder está dividido entre un gobierno central y subdivisiones territoriales; en Estados Unidos el poder es compartido por el gobierno nacional, el estatal y el local (pág. 17)

filibuster the tactic used when opponents of a measure seek to prevent it coming up for a vote in the Senate by refusing to stop talking in hopes of stalling action long enough that the rest of the Senate will be forced to move on to other business (p. 147)
obstruccionismo táctica usada cuando los opositores a una medida buscan evitar que se vote en el Senado, para lo cual se niegan a dejar de hablar con la esperanza de retrasar la acción lo suficiente como para que el resto del Senado sea forzado a tratar otros asuntos (pág. 147)

First Continental Congress (1774) a meeting of colonial delegates in Philadelphia to decide how to respond to the abuses of authority by the British government (p. 40)
Primer Congreso Continental (1774) reunión de los delegados coloniales en Filadelfia para decidir cómo responder a los abusos de autoridad por parte del gobierno británico (pág. 40)

fiscal federalism a system of spending, taxing, and providing grants in the federal system (p. 113)
federalismo fiscal sistema de gastos, recaudación de impuestos y otorgamiento de subsidios del sistema federal (pág. 113)

fiscal policy a government's policy of taxation and spending (p. 211)
política fiscal política de gastos y de recaudación de impuestos de un gobierno (pág. 211)

527 group a tax-exempt organization created to influence an election by attempting to influence voters' opinions about candidates or issues without directly calling for a candidate's election or defeat (p. 374)
grupo 527 organización exenta de impuestos creada para influenciar la opinión de los votantes sobre los candidatos o los temas de una elección sin promover directamente la victoria o la derrota de un candidato (pág. 374)

floor leader the representative of each party elected to help manage the actions and strategy of their party in the House of Representatives (p. 140)
portavoz representante de cada partido elegido para ayudar a dirigir las acciones y la estrategia de su partido en la Cámara de Representantes (pág. 140)

focus group a small gathering of people whose response to something is used to predict the response of a larger population (p. 359)
grupo de discusión grupo pequeño de personas cuya respuesta a algo se usa para predecir la respuesta de una población más grande (pág. 359)

food security an adequate food supply at the national, household, and individual level (p. 480)
seguridad alimentaria suministro adecuado de alimentos a nivel nacional, doméstico e individual (pág. 480)

foreign policy a nation's plans and procedures for dealing with other countries (p. 163, 440)
política exterior plan de un país para tratar con otros países (págs. 163, 440)

foreign service U.S. State Department employees who work in foreign countries (p. 451)
servicio diplomático empleados del Departamento de Estado de Estados Unidos que trabajan en otros países (pág. 451)

Framers delegates of the Constitutional Convention who developed the framework for the government and wrote the Constitution (p. 52)
redactores delegados de la Convención Constitucional que desarrollaron el esquema para el gobierno y redactaron la Constitución (pág. 52)

freedom of association the right to join with others, share ideas, and work toward a common purpose (p. 294)
libertad de asociación derecho a reunirse con otras personas, a compartir ideas y a trabajar con un propósito en común (pág. 294)

freedom of expression the right of citizens to hold, explore, exchange, express, and debate ideas (p. 393)
libertad de expresión derecho de los ciudadanos a tener, explorar, intercambiar, expresar y debatir ideas (pág. 393)

free enterprise an economic system in which individuals and businesses are free to engage in economic activity with a minimum of government interference (p. 25)
libre empresa sistema económico en el que los individuos y las empresas son libres para emprender actividades económicas con mínima interferencia del gobierno (pág. 25)

free exercise clause the part of the First Amendment of the U.S. Constitution that guarantees each person the right to hold any religious beliefs they choose (p. 288)
cláusula de libre ejercicio parte de la Primera Enmienda de la Constitución de Estados Unidos, que garantiza el derecho de las personas de practicar cualquier creencia religiosa que elijan (pág. 288)

full faith and credit clause provision of the Constitution that requires each state to honor the public acts, official records, and judicial proceedings of every other state (p. 101)
cláusula de plena fe y crédito disposición de la Constitución de Estados Unidos que establece que cada estado debe respetar los actos públicos, los registros oficiales y los procedimientos judiciales de los otros estados (pág. 101)

fundamental laws the laws, similar to the U.S. Constitution, that outline the fundamental political principles of a government (p. 525)
derecho fundamental leyes, parecidas a las de la Constitución de Estados Unidos, que delinean los principios políticos fundamentales de un gobierno (pág. 525)

Fundamental Orders of Connecticut (1639) a framework of laws agreed to by settlers of the Connecticut colonies that put limits on the power of government and gave all free men the right to choose judges (p. 34)
Órdenes Fundamentales de Connecticut (1639) esquema de leyes acordado por los pobladores de las colonias de Connecticut que puso límites al poder del gobierno y dio a todos los hombres libres el derecho a elegir jueces (pág. 34)

gerrymandering the drawing of district boundaries for political advantage (p. 139)
manipulación de distritos proceso de demarcar los límites de los distritos con el propósito de obtener una ventaja política (pág. 139)

government the formal structures and institutions through which a territory and its people are ruled (p. 7)
gobierno estructuras e instituciones formales mediante las cuales se gobierna un territorio y su población (pág. 7)

government corporations government agencies that are organized and run like businesses but are owned in whole or in part by the federal government (p. 202)
empresas públicas agencias del gobierno que están organizadas y dirigidas como empresas pero que pertenecen en su totalidad o en parte al gobierno federal (pág. 202)

governor the chief executive of a state government (p. 531)
gobernador jefe ejecutivo de un gobierno estatal (pág. 531)

grand juries panels of citizens set up to hear evidence of a possible crime and to recommend whether the evidence is sufficient to file criminal charges (p. 228)
jurado de acusación grupo de ciudadanos que se reúnen para considerar si las pruebas de un posible delito son suficientes para presentar cargos penales (pág. 228)

grants-in-aid federal funds given to state and local governments for specific projects (p. 113)
subsidios fondos federales otorgados a los gobiernos estatales y locales para llevar adelante proyectos específicos (pág. 113)

grass roots the lowest level of an organization or society (p. 258)
bases nivel más bajo de una organización o sociedad (pág. 258)

Great Compromise (1787) an agreement worked out at the Constitutional Convention establishing that a state's population would determine representation in the lower house of the legislature, while each state would have equal representation in the upper house (p. 53)
Gran Compromiso (1787) acuerdo resuelto en la Convención Constitucional que establece que la población de un estado determinaría la representación en la cámara baja de la legislatura, mientras que cada estado tendría igualdad de representantes en la cámara alta (pág. 53)

gridlock the inability to govern effectively due to separation of powers or a conflict between political parities (p. 89)
punto muerto incapacidad de gobernar con efectividad debido a la separación de poderes o a los conflictos entre partidos políticos (pág. 89)

guarantee clause Article IV, Section 4, of the U.S. Constitution that guarantees that every state will have a republican form of government, with a structure similar to that of the national government (p. 523)
cláusula de garantía Artículo IV, Sección 4 de la Constitución de Estados Unidos que garantiza que cada estado tendrá una forma republicana de gobierno, de estructura similar al gobierno de la nación (pág. 523)

hard money money that is donated to an individual campaign (p. 268)
dinero duro dinero donado a una campaña individual (pág. 268)

ideal conception of something in its most perfect form (p. 21)
ideal concepto de algo en su forma más perfecta (pág. 21)

impeachment the process of charging officials in the executive and judicial branches with wrongdoing and bringing them to trial (p. 125)
juicio político proceso de acusar a funcionarios de las ramas ejecutiva o judicial de haber obrado mal y llevarlos a juicio (pág. 125)

implied powers the powers assumed by the government that are not specifically listed in the Constitution (p. 98)
poderes implícitos poderes asumidos por el gobierno que no están específicamente mencionados en la Constitución (pág. 98)

income tax a tax on a person's or corporation's income (p. 207)
impuesto sobre la renta impuesto sobre los ingresos de una persona o una empresa (pág. 207)

incorporation the process by which municipalities are given their legal authority by the state (p. 545)
  incorporación proceso por el cual el estado da autoridad legal a los municipios (pág. 545)

incorporation doctrine the concept that certain protections of civil rights are essential to the due process of the law (p. 283)
  doctrina de incorporación concepto de que ciertas protecciones de los derechos civiles son esenciales para el debido proceso de la ley (pág. 283)

independent agencies government agencies that operate separately from the executive departments and are established to address issues that have become too complicated or require too much specialized knowledge to handle through regular legislation (p. 200)
  agencias independientes agencias del gobierno que operan separadas de los departamentos ejecutivos y que se establecen para tratar con temas que se han vuelto muy complicados o que requieren un conocimiento muy especializado para manejarlos mediante la legislación común (pág. 200)

independent candidate a candidate who is not associated with any political party (p. 264)
  candidato independiente candidato que no está asociado a ningún partido político (pág. 264)

independent executive agencies government agencies established to oversee and manage a specific aspect of the federal government (p. 200)
  agencias ejecutivas independientes agencias del gobierno establecidas para supervisar y administrar un aspecto específico del gobierno federal (pág. 200)

independent regulatory commissions government agencies established to regulate some aspect of the economy (p. 201)
  comisiones reguladoras independientes agencias del gobierno establecidas para regular algún aspecto de la economía (pág. 201)

indictment a formal complaint of criminal wrongdoing (p. 305)
  acusación denuncia formal de una conducta delictiva (pág. 305)

indirect tax a tax levied on one person but passed on to another for payment to the government; tariffs are examples of indirect taxes (p. 128)
  impuesto indirecto impuesto que recauda el gobierno y que se exige a una persona pero no a otra; los aranceles son ejemplos de impuestos indirectos (pág. 128)

inherent powers those delegated powers of the Constitution that are assumed to belong to the national government because it is a sovereign state (p. 99)
  poderes inherentes poderes delegados por la Constitución que se supone que pertenecen al gobierno nacional porque es un estado soberano (pág. 99)

initiative the process that allows citizens to propose and enact state and local laws directly (p. 547)
  iniciativa proceso que permite a los ciudadanos proponer y aprobar leyes estatales y locales directamente (pág. 547)

interest group an organization of people with common interests that tries to influence government and its policies (p. 255)
  grupos de interés organizaciones con intereses comunes que intentan influir en las decisiones y políticas del gobierno (pág. 255)

internationalist foreign policy that promotes cooperation between nations (p. 441)
  internacionalista política exterior que promueve la cooperación entre naciones (pág. 441)

Iroquois Confederation alliance of six Native American nations (the Mohawk, Oneida, Onondaga, Cayuga, Seneca, and Tuscarora) formed in 1570 to end wars between the nations and to resist European takeover (p. 38)
  Confederación iroquesa alianza de seis naciones indígenas norteamericanas (los mohawk, los oneida, los onondaga, los cayuga, los seneca y los tuscarora) formada en 1570 para dar fin a las guerras entre las naciones y para resistir en conjunto ante los europeos (pág. 38)

isolationism a policy of avoiding involvement in foreign affairs (p. 440)
  aislacionismo política de evitar la participación en los asuntos exteriores (pág. 440)

issue ads advertisements that support or oppose candidates' views without specifically calling for their election or defeat (p. 372)
  propagandas temáticas anuncios que apoyan los puntos de vista de los candidatos o se oponen a ellos sin defender específicamente la victoria o la derrota del candidato en las elecciones (pág. 372)

Japanese American internment the imprisonment of about 120,000 Japanese Americans during World War II (p. 323)
  campos de internamiento de japoneses americanos encarcelamiento de aproximadamente 120,000 japoneses que habitaban en Estados Unidos durante la Segunda Guerra Mundial (pág. 323)

Jim Crow laws segregation laws aimed mainly at African Americans that were passed in the late 1800s and early 1900s; named after a popular racist song (p. 329)
  leyes de Jim Crow leyes de segregación dirigidas principalmente hacia los afroamericanos que fueron aprobadas a finales del siglo XIX y principios del siglo XX; el nombre proviene de una canción racista popular (pág. 329)

joint committees special committees formed from members of the House of Representatives and the Senate to address broad issues that affect both chambers (p. 141)
  comités mixtos comités especiales formados por miembros de la Cámara de Representantes y del Senado para tratar una variedad de temas que afectan a ambas cámaras (pág. 141)

joint resolution a congressional measure used in certain out-of-the-ordinary circumstances and has the force of law if passed by both houses of Congress and signed by the president (p. 150)
  resolución conjunta medida del Congreso usada en alguna circunstancia fuera de lo común y que tiene fuerza de ley si es aprobada por ambas cámaras del Congreso y firmada por el presidente (pág. 150)

judicial activism the concept that the Constitution should be interpreted more broadly, as an evolving document, something that subsequent generations can interpret consistent with changing values and circumstances (p. 224)
  activismo judicial concepto que propone que la Constitución debe interpretarse de manera más amplia, como un documento que evoluciona, algo que las generaciones subsiguientes puedan interpretar reflejando el cambio de los valores y las circunstancias (pág. 224)

ENGLISH AND SPANISH GLOSSARY

judicial restraint the concept that a judge should interpret the Constitution according to the Framers' original intentions (p. 224)
contención judicial concepto que plantea que un juez debe interpretar la Constitución de acuerdo con la intención original de los redactores (pág. 224)

judicial review the power of the judicial branch to check the power of the legislative and executive branches by declaring their acts unconstitutional (p. 74)
recurso de inconstitucionalidad poder de la rama judicial de verificar el poder de las ramas legislativa y ejecutiva por medio de la declaración de la inconstitucionalidad de sus actos (pág. 74)

jurisdiction a court's authority to hear and decide a case (p. 221)
jurisdicción autoridad de una corte para escuchar y decidir un caso (pág. 221)

jus sanguinis (YOOS SANG-gwuh-nuhs) the principle of citizenship by parentage; a Latin phrase meaning "law of the blood" (p. 343)
jus sanguinis principio de la ciudadanía por parentesco; frase en latín que significa "ley de la sangre" (pág. 343)

jus soli (YOOS SOH-lee) the principle of citizenship by birthplace; a Latin phrase that means "law of the soil" (p. 343)
jus soli principio de la ciudadania basada en el lugar de nacimiento; enfrase en latín que significa "ley del pais natal" (pág. 343)

just war theory the idea that a state may justly go to war under certain specific circumstances and must limit its conduct according to certain standards (p. 445)
teoría de la guerra justa idea que sostiene que un estado puede entrar en guerra con razón bajo ciertas circunstancias específicas y que debe limitar su conducta según ciertas normas (pág. 445)

labor unions organizations of workers who do the same job or work in related industries (p. 256)
sindicatos laborales organizaciones de trabajadores que hacen el mismo trabajo o trabajan en industrias relacionadas (pág. 256)

laissez-faire the idea that there should be minimal government involvement in economic affairs; *laissez-faire* is French for "to let alone" (p. 511)
laissez-faire idea que propone que la participación del gobierno en los asuntos económicos debe ser mínima; *laissez-faire* es una frase en francés que significa "dejar algo en paz" (pág. 511)

leadership PACs political action committees that are separate from the officeholder's campaign organization (p. 373)
comités de liderazgo comités de acción política que están separados de la organización de campaña del titular (pág. 373)

legitimacy right and proper (p. 10)
legitimidad correcto y apropiado (pág. 10)

libel a defamatory statement that appears in print (p. 289)
difamación afirmación falsa que aparece en medios impresos (pág. 289)

liberal democracy a form of democracy that protects the rights of the minority (p. 23)
democracia liberal forma de democracia que protege los derechos de la minoría (pág. 23)

liberty the ability of people to act and think as they choose, so long as their choices do no harm to the liberty or well-being of others (p. 21)
libertad capacidad de las personas de actuar y pensar como quieran, siempre y cuando sus acciones no dañen la libertad o el bienestar de los demás (pág. 21)

limited government the principle that the powers and functions of government are restricted by the U.S. Constitution and other laws (p. 71)
gobierno limitado principio que sostiene que los poderes y las funciones del gobierno están restringidos por la Constitución de Estados Unidos y otras leyes (pág. 71)

line-item veto the power that allows a governor to reject specific parts of legislation while signing the rest of a bill into law (p. 534)
veto de partidas específicas poder que permite al gobernador rechazar partes específicas de una ley y aun así aprobar el resto del proyecto (pág. 534)

lobbying contacting a public official to persuade the official to support the group's interests (p. 258)
cabildeo contactar a un funcionario público para convencerlo de que apoye los intereses de un grupo (pág. 258)

M

magistrate judges district court officials responsible for overseeing some of the early hearings of a criminal trial at which routine matters are carried out, and who may also hear misdemeanor criminal cases and certain civil cases (p. 229)
jueces de audiencia preliminar funcionarios de las cortes de un distrito responsables de supervisar algunas de las primeras audiencias de un juicio penal en las que se llevan a cabo asuntos de rutina, y que también pueden oír casos de delitos menores y ciertos casos civiles (pág. 229)

Magna Carta (1215) a charter agreed to by King John of England that granted nobles certain rights and restricted the king's powers (p. 33)
Carta Magna (1215) carta de libertades, firmada por el rey Juan de Inglaterra, que concedió a los nobles ciertos derechos y restringió el poder del rey (pág. 33)

majority opinion the Supreme Court's ruling in a case that is signed by at least five of the nine members of the Supreme Court (p. 241)
opinión de la mayoría decisión de la Corte Suprema en un caso, firmada por al menos cinco de los nueve miembros de la Corte (pág. 241)

majority rule a basic principle of democracy that decisions are made by a majority, by getting more than half of the votes cast (p. 23)
gobierno de la mayoría principio básico de la democracia que propone que las decisiones son tomadas por una mayoría, al obtener más de la mitad de los votos (pág. 23)

mandatory spending spending mandated by laws and not subject to the annual budget process (p. 209)
gastos preceptivos gastos mandados por ley y no expuestos al proceso anual de presupuestos (pág. 209)

market economy an economic system in which individuals and businesses make most decisions on what goods and services to produce based on their own understanding of the needs and wants of others (p. 510)

economía de mercado sistema económico en el que los individuos y las empresas toman la mayoría de las decisiones sobre los bienes y los servicios que producen basándose en su propio entendimiento de las necesidades y los deseos de los demás (pág. 510)

marshals law enforcement officers who provide security and police protection at federal courthouses, transport prisoners, help track down and arrest people accused of crimes, and provide protection to witnesses in federal cases (p. 230)

alguaciles funcionarios de la ley que brindan seguridad y protección policial en las cortes federales, transportan prisioneros, ayudan a perseguir y a arrestar a personas acusadas de crímenes y brindan protección a los testigos de los casos federales (pág. 230)

mass media any means of communication that provides information to a large audience, including magazines, radio, television news, and news on the Web (p. 250)

medios de comunicación masiva cualquier medio de comunicación que proporciona información a un gran público; entre ellos se encuentran las revistas, la radio, los noticieros de televisión y las noticias de la web (pág. 250)

mayor-council system a form of municipal government in which citizens elect a mayor to serve as the chief executive and a city council to serve as the local legislature (p. 545)

sistema de alcalde-concejo forma de gobierno municipal en la que los ciudadanos eligen a un alcalde que es el jefe del poder ejecutivo y a un concejo que es la legislatura local (pág. 545)

minority rights the political rights held by groups that make up less than half of the population (p. 23)

derechos de la minoría derechos políticos de grupos que tienen menos de la mitad de la población (pág. 23)

Miranda warnings a list of certain constitutional rights possessed by those accused of crimes; includes the right to remain silent and the right to have an attorney present during questioning (p. 308)

advertencia Miranda lista de ciertos derechos constitucionales que poseen las personas acusadas de cometer delitos, entre ellos el derecho a permanecer en silencio y el derecho a que haya un abogado presente durante el interrogatorio (pág. 308)

misdemeanor a minor crime (p. 229)

delito menor falta de poca importancia (pág. 229)

Missouri Plan a method of selecting state judges in which a state committee prepares a list of qualified candidates and the governor appoints a judge from this list (p. 537)

plan Missouri método para elegir jueces estatales en el que un comité estatal prepara una lista de candidatos calificados y el gobernador nombra a un juez de esa lista (pág. 537)

mixed economy an economic system that combines elements of traditional, market, and command economies (p. 511)

economía mixta sistema que combina elementos de la economía tradicional, la economía de mercado y la economía dirigida (pág. 511)

monarchy a form of government in which political power is exercised by a single ruler, such as a king or a queen, who exercises absolute authority under the claim of divine or hereditary right (p. 15)

monarquía forma de gobierno en la que el poder político es ejercido por un gobernante único, como por ejemplo un rey o una reina, quien ejerce la autoridad apelando al derecho divino o heredado (pág. 15)

monetary policy a government's policy of regulating the money in circulation and the interest rates at which money is borrowed (p. 211)

política monetaria política del gobierno para regular el dinero que hay en circulación y la tasa de interés a la cual se presta dinero (pág. 211)

Monroe Doctrine (1823) President James Monroe's statement forbidding further colonization in the Americas and declaring that any attempt by a foreign country to colonize would be considered an act of hostility (p. 472)

Doctrina Monroe (1823) declaración del presidente James Monroe en la que se prohibía, a partir de entonces, la colonización futura del continente americano y en la que se advertía que cualquier intento de colonización por parte de otro país se consideraba un acto hostil (pág. 472)

multiparty system a system of government in which several political parties compete for control of the government (p. 262)

sistema multipartidista sistema de gobierno en el que varios partidos políticos compiten por el control del gobierno (pág. 262)

municipalities the nation's cities, towns, and villages; units of local government that are incorporated by the state and have a large degree of self-government (p. 545)

municipalidades ciudades y pueblos de la nación; unidades de gobierno local incorporadas por los estados y que tienen un alto grado de autonomía (pág. 545)

National Security Council (NSC) the group of the top military, foreign affairs, and intelligence officials in the president's administration that focuses on U.S. national security (p. 182)

Consejo Nacional de Seguridad (NSC, por sus siglas en inglés) grupo de los funcionarios militares, de asuntos exteriores y de inteligencia con mayor jerarquía de la administración del presidente, centrado en la seguridad nacional de Estados Unidos (pág. 182)

National Security Letter (NSL) a form of administrative subpoena that is used by the U.S. Federal Bureau of Investigation (p. 410)

Carta de Seguridad Nacional (NSL, por sus siglas en inglés) forma de citatorio administrativo usado por la Oficina Federal de Investigaciones de Estados Unidos (pág. 410)

naturalization the legal process by which an immigrant becomes a citizen (p. 343)

naturalización proceso legal por el cual los inmigrantes se convierten en ciudadanos (pág. 343)

ENGLISH AND SPANISH GLOSSARY

necessary and proper clause Article I, Section 8, Clause 18, of the Constitution, which gives the national legislature the power to "make all laws that are necessary and proper" to exercise the powers granted by the Constitution; also known as the "elastic clause" (p. 128)
cláusula necesaria y justa Artículo I, Sección 8, Cláusula 18 de la Constitución, la cual concede a la legislatura nacional el poder de "hacer todas las leyes que sean necesarias y justas" para ejercer los poderes concedidos por la Constitución; también conocida como "cláusula elástica" (pág. 128)

negative campaigning attacking an opponent during a political campaign (p. 360)
campaña negativa atacar a un oponente durante una campaña política (pág. 360)

New England Confederation an alliance formed in 1643 by the Plymouth, Connecticut, Massachusetts Bay, and New Haven colonies in order to defend themselves from threats posed by Native Americans and by settlers from nearby Dutch colonies (p. 38)
Confederación de Nueva Inglaterra alianza formada en 1643 por las colonias de Plymouth, Connecticut, massachussets Bay y New Haven para defenderse de las amenazas que representaban los indígenas norteamericanos y los pobladores de las colonias holandesas (pág. 38)

new federalism (1980–present) modern era in federalism in which authority that rested with the national government is being returned to the states; also called "devolution" (p. 110)
nuevo federalismo (1980–presente) era moderna del federalismo en la que la autoridad que correspondía al gobierno federal es devuelta a los estados; también llamado "devolución" (pág. 110)

New Jersey Plan (1787) a proposal to created a unicameral legislature with equal representation of states instead of representation by population (p. 53)
Plan de Nueva Jersey (1787) propuesta para crear una asamblea legislativa unicameral que contara con la misma representación por parte de cada estado, sin basarse en el tamaño de su población (pág. 53)

nomination process the process of naming candidates for elective office (p. 261)
proceso de nominación proceso de nombrar a los candidatos para cargos electos (pág. 261)

Northwest Ordinance (1787) legislation passed by Congress to establish a plan for settling the Northwest Territory, which included areas that are now in Illinois, Indiana, Michigan, Ohio, Minnesota, and Wisconsin (p. 49)
Ordenanza del Noroeste (1787) ley aprobada por el Congreso para establecer un plan para colonizar el Territorio del Noroeste, que incluía las áreas de lo que es hoy Illinois, Indiana, Michigan, Ohio, Minnesota y Wisconsin (pág. 49)

objectivity freedom from bias and outside factors that may influence the results of a poll (p. 253)
objetividad ausencia de parcialidad y de factores externos que podrían influenciar los resultados de una encuesta (pág. 253)

Office of Management and Budget (OMB) the organization set up to develop and implement the federal budget, legislation, government regulations, the management of government finances, and the purchase of goods, services, and property for the entire government (p. 183)
Oficina de administración y presupuesto (OMB, por sus siglas en inglés) organización establecida para desarrollar e implementar el presupuesto federal, la legislación, las regulaciones del gobierno, la administración de las finanzas del gobierno y la compra de bienes, servicios y propiedades para todo el gobierno (pág. 183)

oligarchy rule by a few small groups of people, usually members of the military or the economic elite (p. 16)
oligarquía gobierno de unos pocos grupos pequeños de personas, generalmente miembros del ejército o de una élite económica (pág. 16)

one-party system a system of government in which a single political party controls government (p. 262)
sistema unipartidista sistema de gobierno en el que un solo partido político controla el gobierno (pág. 262)

open primary a primary election in which any registered voter may vote in either party's primary election (p. 270)
primarias abiertas elecciones primarias en las que cualquier votante inscrito puede votar en la elección primaria de cualquier partido (pág. 270)

original jurisdiction the authority of a court to be the first court to hold trials in certain kinds of cases (p. 221)
jurisdicción de primera instancia autoridad de una corte para ser la primera corte en ver cierto tipo de casos (pág. 221)

oversight the power of Congress to check up on the executive branch and to make sure it is following the laws Congress has passed (p. 126)
supervisión poder del Congreso para controlar la rama ejecutiva y para asegurarse de que sigue las leyes que aprobó el Congreso (pág. 126)

pardon an official act by the president or by a governor forgiving a person convicted of a crime and freeing that person from having to serve out his or her sentence (p. 174)
indulto acción oficial por parte del presidente o de un gobernador en la que se perdona a una persona condenada por un delito y se le libera de tener que cumplir el resto de su sentencia (pág. 174)

parishes the name used in Louisiana for counties (p. 544)
parroquias nombre usado en Louisiana para los condados (pág. 544)

parliamentary system a form of government in which the chief executive is the leader whose party holds the most seats in the legislature after an election or whose party forms a major part of the ruling coalition (p. 19)
sistema parlamentario forma de gobierno en la que el jefe del ejecutivo es el dirigente cuyo partido tiene la mayor cantidad de puestos en la legislatura después de una elección o cuyo partido forma una parte importante en la coalición de gobierno (pág. 19)

party-building activities political party activities, such as voter registration drives and television ads supporting the party's principles, that do not support specific candidates but instead promote the party (p. 371)
  actividades partidistas actividades de un partido político, como organizar inscripciones de votantes e idear anuncios de televisión que apoyan los principios del partido, que no apoyan a candidatos específicos, pero que fomentan el partido (pág. 371)

party caucus a meeting of all the House members from a particular party held to elect party officers (p. 140)
  caucus partidario reunión de todos los miembros de la cámara de un partido en particular para elegir a los funcionarios del partido (pág. 140)

payroll tax money that is withheld from a person's paycheck by his or her employer (p. 207)
  retenciones de la nómina dinero que retiene el empleador del salario de una persona (pág. 207)

Petition of Right (1628) a document signed by Charles I of England that limited the powers of the English monarch (p. 33)
  Petición de Derechos (1628) documento firmado por el rey Carlos I de Inglaterra que limitó los poderes de la monarquía inglesa (pág. 33)

plaintiff the person making a legal complaint in court (p. 221)
  demandante persona que presenta una querella en una corte (pág. 221)

plain view doctrine legal rule that allows a law enforcement officer to seize, without a warrant, evidence and contraband found in plain view during a lawful observation (p. 406)
  doctrina de plena vista norma jurídica que permite a un oficial de la ley tomar, sin una orden, pruebas o contrabando hallado a simple vista durante una observación legítima (pág. 406)

platform a political party's stand on important issues and the party's general principles (p. 356)
  plataforma postura de un partido político sobre los temas importantes y los principios generales del partido (pág. 356)

plurality when a candidate in an election has more votes than any other candidate (p. 271)
  mayoría relativa cuando un candidato en una elección tiene más votos que cualquier otro candidato (pág. 271)

pocket veto a means by which the president can reject a bill, when Congress is not in session, by not signing it (p. 155)
  veto indirecto recurso que tiene el presidente para rechazar un proyecto de ley en un momento en que el Congreso no esté en sesión al no firmarlo (pág. 155)

police power a government's ability to regulate behavior for the common good (p. 301)
  poder policial capacidad del gobierno de regular el comportamiento para el bien común (pág. 301)

policy any decision made by government in pursuit of a particular goal (p. 7)
  política cualquier decisión tomada por el gobierno en busca de una meta en particular (pág. 7)

political action committee (PAC) an organization created to raise and contribute money legally to the campaigns of political candidates (p. 255)
  comité de acción política (PAC, por sus siglas en inglés) organización creada para recaudar dinero y contribuir legalmente con dinero a las campañas de los candidatos políticos (pág. 255)

political party an organized group that seeks to win elections in order to influence the activities of government (p. 87, 261)
  partido político grupo organizado que busca ganar elecciones para lograr cierta influencia en las actividades del gobierno (págs. 87, 261)

political socialization the process by which people acquire political beliefs (p. 250)
  socialización política proceso por el cual las personas adquieren creencias políticas (pág. 250)

political spectrum the difference in political views held by the different political parties (p. 261)
  espectro político diferencia en las opiniones políticas que sostienen los distintos partidos políticos (pág. 261)

politics the process by which government makes and carries out decisions (p. 9)
  políticas proceso por el cual el gobierno toma decisiones y las lleva a cabo (pág. 9)

poll a survey of people scientifically selected to provide opinions about something (p. 252)
  encuesta sondeo hecho a personas seleccionadas científicamente para proporcionar opiniones sobre algo (pág. 252)

poll tax a tax levied on someone who wants to vote (p. 337)
  impuesto electoral impuesto exigido a alguien que quiere votar (pág. 337)

poll watchers volunteers that a party or candidate sends to polling places to ensure that the election there is run fairly (p. 381)
  observadores electorales voluntarios que envía un partido o candidato a los centros electorales para asegurarse de que la elección es llevada a cabo correctamente (pág. 381)

poll workers people hired by local election officials to manage voting on election day (p. 381)
  trabajadores electorales personas contratadas por los funcionarios electorales locales para administrar la votación el día de las elecciones (pág. 381)

popular sovereignty the idea that government is created by and subject to the will of the people (p. 70)
  soberanía popular idea que sostiene que el gobierno es creado por el pueblo y sujeto a la voluntad de él (pág. 70)

power a government's authority to make and enforce policies and laws (p. 7)
  poder la autoridad del gobierno de establecer y ejectuar leyes y políticas (pág. 7)

precedent an earlier court decision that guides judges' decisions in later cases (p. 224)
  precedente decisión previa de una corte que guía las decisiones de los jueces en casos posteriores (pág. 224)

precinct the smallest unit of area for administering elections and local voting (p. 264)
  distrito electoral la unidad de área más pequeña para administrar elecciones y votaciones locales (pág. 264)

preemptive strike the use of force before a potential attack occurs (p. 477)
  golpe preventivo la posibilidad de usar fuerza antes que ocurra un ataque (pág. 477)

prejudice a negative opinion formed without just grounds or a reasonable investigation of the facts (p. 322)
  prejuicio opinión negativa formada sin motivos justos o sin una investigación razonable de los hechos (pág. 322)

presidential doctrines foreign policy statements made by the president that guide the direction of U.S. foreign policy (p. 453)
doctrinas presidenciales declaraciones sobre política exterior hechas por el presidente que guían la dirección de la política externa de Estados Unidos (pág. 453)

presidential system a form of government headed by a president who is elected by the people for a limited term of office and whose powers are balanced by an elected legislature (p. 18)
sistema presidencial forma de gobierno encabezada por un presidente elegido por el pueblo, por un período de mandato limitado y cuyos poderes son equilibrados por una legislatura electa (pág. 18)

president of the Senate a position held by vice president of the United States, who presides over debate in the Senate chamber (p. 145)
presidente del Senado posición que tiene el vicepresidente de Estados Unidos, quien preside el debate en la cámara (pág. 145)

president pro tempore the official who presides over the Senate in the absence of the vice president (p. 145)
presidente pro tempore funcionario que preside el Senado en ausencia del vicepresidente (pág. 145)

prior restraint government action that seeks to prevent materials from being published (p. 292)
censura previa acción del gobierno que busca evitar la publicación de materiales (pág. 292)

probable cause the reason for a search or an arrest, based on the knowledge of a crime and the available evidence (p. 297)
causa probable razón para una búsqueda o un arresto, basada en el conocimiento de un delito y la evidencia disponible (pág. 297)

procedural due process the requirement that government follow certain procedures before punishing a person (p. 301)
derecho al debido proceso requerimiento de que el gobierno siga ciertos procedimientos antes de castigar a una persona (pág. 301)

professional legislatures state legislatures that hold lengthy, annual sessions, and whose members are paid a full-time wage (p. 532)
legislaturas profesionales legislaturas estatales que mantienen largas sesiones anuales y cuyos miembros reciben un salario de tiempo completo (pág. 532)

progressive tax a tax whose rates increase as the amount that is subject to taxation increases (p. 207)
impuesto progresivo impuesto cuya tasa aumenta a medida que aumenta la cantidad sujeta al pago del impuesto (pág. 207)

proletariat the working class, whose members Karl Marx believed were oppressed by the bourgeoisie (p. 512)
proletariado clase trabajadora cuyos miembros eran oprimidos por la burguesía según la creencia de Karl Marx (pág. 512)

propaganda information designed to shape public opinion (p. 252)
propaganda información diseñada para influir en la opinión pública (pág. 252)

proportional tax a tax that is applied at the same rate against all income (p. 208)
impuesto proporcional impuesto que se aplica a la misma tasa sobre todo el ingreso (pág. 208)

proprietary colony a colony that was based on a grant of land by the English monarch to a proprietor, or owner, in exchange for a yearly payment (p. 34)
colonia de propietario colonia basada en el otorgamiento de tierras por la corona inglesa a un propietario, o dueño, a cambio de un pago anual (pág. 34)

public defenders lawyers appointed by the court to represent in criminal trials defendants who cannot afford to hire legal counsel (p. 229)
defensores públicos abogados designados por la corte para representar a los acusados que no pueden pagar un abogado contratado en los juicios penales (pág. 229)

public opinion the aggregation of views shared by a segment of society on issues of interest or concern to people (p. 249)
opinión pública total de los puntos de vista compartidos por un segmento de la sociedad con respecto a los temas de interés o que preocupan a las personas (pág. 249)

public policy the choices the government makes and the actions it takes in response to a particular issue or problem (p. 249)
política pública decisiones y acciones que toma el gobierno en respuesta a un tema o problema en particular (pág. 249)

Publius the pen name that Framers Alexander Hamilton, James Madison, and John Jay used when writing the *Federalist Papers;* Latin for "public man" (p. 59)
Publius seudónimo que usaban los redactores Alexander Hamilton, James Madison y John Jay cuando escribían los *Federalist Papers;* es un término en latín que significa "hombre público" (pág. 59)

quorum the minimum number of members needed to legally conduct business (p. 153)
quórum número mínimo de miembros que se necesitan para que un cuerpo legislativo entre en funcionamiento (pág. 153)

quota a fixed number or percentage (p. 339)
cuota número fijo o porcentaje (pág. 339)

R

racism discrimination and unfair treatment based on race (p. 322)
racismo discriminación y trato injusto basados en la raza (pág. 322)

ratified formally approved (p. 48)
ratificar aprobar formalmente (pág. 48)

reapportionment the redistribution of seats in the House of Representatives among the states based on the results of the census (p. 139)
redistribución nueva repartición de los puestos de la Cámara de Representantes entre los estados basada en los resultados de un censo (pág. 139)

recall the process that allows citizens to remove government officials from office before the end of a term (p. 547)
destitución proceso que permite a los ciudadanos retirar a un funcionario del gobierno de su cargo antes del fin de su mandato (pág. 547)

redistricting the process of drawing new boundaries for legislative districts (p. 384)
reestructuración de distritos proceso a través del cual se trazan nuevos límites para los distritos legislativos (pág. 384)

redress of grievances to remove the cause of a complaint and make things right (p. 398)
reparación de agravios retirar la causa de una querella y enmendar la situación (pág. 398)

referendum a popular vote on a proposal that has already been considered by the legislature (p. 547)
referéndum voto popular sobre una propuesta que ya ha sido considerada por la legislatura (pág. 547)

regressive tax a tax that has a greater impact on lower-income earners than on upper-income earners (p. 207)
impuesto regresivo impuesto que tiene un mayor impacto en los grupos de ingresos más bajos que en los grupos de ingresos más altos (pág. 207)

repeal to cancel or revoke a law by a legislative act (p. 81)
revocar cancelar una ley por medio de una acción legislativa (pág. 81)

reprieve a postponement in the carrying out of a prison sentence (p. 174)
conmutación retraso en el cumplimiento de una sentencia de cárcel (pág. 174)

republic an indirect form of democracy in which people elect representatives to make decisions on their behalf (p. 16)
república forma indirecta de democracia en la que el pueblo elige a los representantes para que tomen decisiones en su nombre (pág. 16)

reservation an area of public land set aside by the government for Native Americans (p. 323)
reserva área de tierra pública separada por el gobierno para los indígenas americanos (pág. 323)

reserved powers the powers that are not specifically granted to the federal government nor denied to the states that are reserved for the states (p. 99)
poderes reservados poderes que no están específicamente otorgados al gobierno federal ni denegados a los estados y que se reservan para los estados (pág. 99)

reverse discrimination discrimination against the majority group (p. 339)
discriminación inversa discriminación contra el grupo mayoritario (pág. 339)

rider an addition to a bill that often has little relationship to the bill's main topic; the goal of a rider may be to add an unpopular provision to a bill that is likely to be passed so that the addition may "ride" along with the bill that is passed, or a rider may be designed to kill a bill by attaching an unpopular provision to that bill (p. 150)
anexo agregado a un proyecto de ley que generalmente tiene poca relación con el tema principal; el objetivo de un anexo puede ser agregar una disposición poco popular a un proyecto de ley que es probable que sea aprobado, lo que permite que la disposición poco popular sea "anexada", o bien, matar un proyecto de ley al agregar un anexo poco popular (pág. 150)

right of assembly the right to form and join groups, and to gather for any peaceful and lawful purpose (p. 398)
derecho de asamblea el derecho de establecer y unirse a grupos y de juntarse para cualquier fin que sea legal y tranquilo (pág. 398)

roll-call vote a vote in which each member of Congress is required to publicly state his or her vote; also called a record vote (p. 153)
votación por lista votación en la que se requiere que cada miembro del Congreso declare públicamente su voto; también llamado voto registrado (pág. 153)

royal colonies colonies directly controlled by the English king through appointed governors who served as the colonies' chief executives (p. 35)
colonia real colonias directamente controladas por el rey inglés mediante un gobernadores designados que eran jefes ejecutivos de las colonias (pág. 35)

rule of law principle that every member of a society, including the ruler or government, must follow the law (p. 71)
imperio de la ley principio que sostiene que cada miembro de la sociedad, incluyendo el gobernante o el gobierno, debe respetar la ley (pág. 71)

sample the group of people who take part in a poll (p. 252)
muestra grupo de personas que participan de una encuesta (pág. 252)

sampling error a poll's margin of error, or uncertainty level (p. 253)
error de muestreo margen de error de una encuesta, o nivel de incertidumbre (pág. 253)

search within the meaning of the Fourth Amendment, any action by government to find evidence of criminal activity (p. 405)
registro dentro del sentido de la Cuarta Enmienda, cualquier acción del gobierno que sirva para hallar evidencia de actividad criminal (pág. 405)

search warrant a document that gives police legal authority to search private property (p. 298)
orden de registro documento que da a la policía la autoridad legal para registrar la propiedad privada (pág. 298)

Second Continental Congress (1775) a meeting of colonial delegates in Philadelphia to decide how to react to fighting between colonists and British troops at Lexington and Concord (p. 40)
Segundo Congreso Continental (1775) reunión de los delegados de las colonias en Filadelfia para decidir cómo reaccionar ante la lucha entre los colonos y las tropas británicas en Lexington y Concord (pág. 40)

sedition a legal term for speech or actions that inspire revolt against the government (p. 290)
sedición término legal para discursos o acciones que inspiren revueltas en contra del gobierno (pág. 290)

segregation the separation of racial groups (p. 329)
segregación separación en grupos raciales (pág. 329)

seizure occurs when authorities keep something, such as an object or a person, within the meaning of the Fourth Amendment (p. 405)
confiscación ocurre cuando las autoridades toman algo para sí, como un objeto o una persona, dentro de la acepción de la Cuarta Enmienda (pág. 405)

select committees temporary committees in the House of Representatives formed to carry out specific tasks that are not already covered by existing committees (p. 141)
comités selectos comités temporales de la Cámara de Representantes para hacer tareas específicas que no han sido ya cubiertas por los comités existentes (pág. 141)

selective exclusiveness legal doctrine that states that when the commerce at issue requires national, uniform regulation, only Congress may regulate it (p. 430)
exclusividad selectiva doctrina legal que establece que cuando el comercio en disputa requiere una regulación nacional uniforme, sólo el Congreso puede regularlo (pág. 430)

self-government the belief that ordinary people could aspire to rule themselves and do so as political equals (p. 22)
autogobierno creencia de que las personas comunes podrían aspirar a gobernarse a sí mismas y a hacerlo en igualdad política (pág. 22)

Senate majority leader the person elected by the majority party who serves as the spokesperson and main strategist for the majority party in the Senate (p. 145)
líder de la mayoría del Senado persona elegida por el partido mayoritario para ser el vocero y estratega principal para el partido mayoritario del Senado (pág. 145)

senatorial courtesy the tradition that a senator from the same state as a nominee to a federal district court and the same political party as the president can block a nomination for virtually any reason (p. 224)
cortesía parlamentaria tradición de que un senador del mismo estado que un candidato a un tribunal federal de primera instancia y del mismo partido político que el presidente puede impedir un nombramiento virtualmente por cualquier razón (pág. 224)

Seneca Falls Convention (1848) the first women's rights convention held in the United States (p. 330)
Convención de Seneca Falls (1848) primera convención celebrada en Estados Unidos por los derechos de la mujer (pág. 330)

seniority rule the tradition in the Senate in which the chair of a committee is given to the most senior majority Senator on that committee (p. 146)
regla de antigüedad tradición en el Senado que permite que la presidencia de un comité se otorgue al senador con más antigüedad del partido mayoritario del comité (pág. 146)

separate-but-equal doctrine the policy that laws requiring separate facilities for racial groups were legal so long as the facilities were "equal" (p. 329)
doctrina de "separados pero iguales" política de que las leyes que requerían lugares separados para los grupos raciales eran legales mientras los lugares fueran "iguales" (pág. 329)

separation of powers division of government powers among the executive, legislative, and judicial branches (p. 72)
separación de poderes división de los poderes del gobierno en las ramas ejecutiva, legislativa y judicial (pág. 72)

Shays's Rebellion (1786–1787) the revolt led by former Revolutionary War captain Daniel Shays to prevent judges in Massachusetts from foreclosing on the farms of farmers who could not pay taxes the state had levied (p. 49)
Rebelión de Shays (1786–1787) revuelta liderada por el antiguo capitán de la Guerra de Independencia, Daniel Shays, para evitar que los jueces de Massachusetts confiscaran las granjas de los agricultores que no podían pagar los impuestos que el estado exigía (pág. 49)

slander a spoken defamatory statement (p. 289)
calumnias declaraciones difamatorias falsas y orales (pág. 289)

social contract theory a theory of society in which government is a contract between a government and the governed to provide protection and support for the people; under this theory, a government is legitimate only so long as the people voluntarily agree to hand over their power to the state (p. 11)
teoría del contrato social teoría de la sociedad en la que el gobierno es un contrato entre el gobierno y los gobernados para proporcionar protección y apoyo; bajo esta teoría, un gobierno es legítimo sólo mientras las partes estén de acuerdo en entregar su poder al estado (pág. 11)

socialism a political and economic system in which the government controls resources and industries (p. 512)
socialismo sistema político y económico en el que el gobierno controla los recursos y las industrias (pág. 512)

soft money money that is given to a political party rather than to a specific candidate (p. 268)
dinero blando dinero otorgado a un partido en vez de a un candidato específico (pág. 268)

sound bite a very brief segment of a speech or statement usually broadcast on the radio or television (p. 362)
extracto segmento muy breve de un discurso o de una declaración, generalmente transmitido por la radio o la televisión (pág. 362)

sovereign immunity the principle that a sovereign government cannot be taken to court unless it agrees to be sued (p. 231)
inmunidad soberana principio que propone que un gobierno soberano no puede llevarse a un tribunal a menos que esté de acuerdo en ser demandado (pág. 231)

sovereignty ultimate, supreme power in a state; in the United States, sovereignty rests with the people (p. 8)
soberanía poder absoluto y supremo de un estado; en Estados Unidos, la soberanía es del pueblo (pág. 8)

Speaker of the House the presiding officer of the House of Representatives (p. 140)
Presidente de la Cámara funcionario que preside la Cámara de Representantes (pág. 140)

special districts units of local government created to provide a single service, such as water, housing, or transportation, to a defined area (p. 545)
distritos especiales unidades del gobierno local creadas para proporcionar un servicio específico, como por ejemplo agua, vivienda o transporte, para un área definida (pág. 545)

special needs test the standard that a search of a person's body may be considered reasonable under the Fourth Amendment if the search serves some safety or security need for society (p. 408)
criterio de urgencias especiales la norma que el registro del cuerpo de una persona se puede considerar legítimo, bajo la cuarta enmienda, si el registro cumple con alguna urgencia que afecta la tranquilidad y seguridad del pueblo (pág. 408)

spoils system the practice of awarding government jobs as political rewards to people who supported the president's policies or the president's election campaign (p. 194)
tráfico de influencias práctica a través de la cual se conceden empleos en el gobierno como recompensas políticas a las personas que apoyaron las políticas del presidente o la campaña electoral del presidente (pág. 194)

Stamp Act (1765) law passed by the English Parliament that required a government tax stamp on paper goods and all legal documents, such as contracts and licenses (p. 39)

Ley del Sello (1765) ley aprobada por el parlamento inglés que requería que se aplicara un sello fiscal del gobierno en los artículos de papel y en todos los documentos legales, como contratos y licencias (pág. 39)

standing committees permanent committees of the House of Representatives that address the major areas in which most proposed laws fall, such as agriculture, the budget, and the armed services (p. 141)

comités permanentes comités permanentes de la Cámara de Representantes que se ocupan de las áreas importantes de las que tratan la mayoría de las leyes propuestas, como la agricultura, el presupuesto y las fuerzas armadas (pág. 141)

state a political unit made up by a group of people that lives within a clearly defined territory (p. 7)

estado unidad política formada por un grupo de personas que viven dentro de un territorio claramente definido (pág. 7)

statutory laws all laws put forth by a lawmaking government body (p. 525)

leyes legisladas todas las leyes aprobadas por un cuerpo de legisladores del gobierno (pág. 525)

stump speech a standard speech that candidates give during a political campaign (p. 360)

discurso de campaña discurso estándar que dan los candidatos durante una campaña política (pág. 360)

subpoenas legal documents that require a person to testify in a certain matter (p. 134)

citación documento legal que requiere a una persona que testifique sobre un asunto en particular (pág. 134)

substantive due process the idea that laws themselves must be fair and just since all people have inalienable rights that cannot be taken away from them (p. 302)

proceso sustancial previsto idea de que todas las leyes deben ser justas de por sí, dado que todas las personas tienen derechos inalienables que no pueden quitárseles (pág. 302)

succession the process of succeeding, or coming after someone (p. 166)

sucesión proceso de suceder, o de venir después de alguien (pág. 166)

suffrage the right to vote (p. 330)

sufragio derecho al voto (pág. 330)

supermajority any majority that is larger than a simple majority, such as three-fifths, two-thirds, or three-fourths (p. 80)

mayoría calificada cualquier mayoría que sea más grande que una mayoría simple, como por ejemplo tres quintos, dos tercios o tres cuartos (pág. 80)

suspect classification a classification or distinction in a law that is based on race or national origin (p. 327)

clasificación sospechosa clasificación o distinción en una ley basada en la raza o en la nacionalidad de origen (pág. 327)

swing states those states where support for each candidate in an upcoming election is about equal (p. 360)

estados clave estados en los que el apoyo para cada candidato de una próxima elección es aproximadamente igual (pág. 360)

symbolic speech the communication of ideas through symbols and actions (p. 292)

discurso simbólico comunicación de ideas mediante símbolos y acciones (pág. 292)

Terry stop legal rule that allows a law enforcement officer to stop a person based upon "reasonable suspicion" that a person may have been engaged in criminal activity; from the ruling in the Supreme Court case *Terry* v. *Ohio* (1968) (p. 408)

detención de Terry regla legal que permite a un oficial de la ley detener a una persona basándose en una "sospecha razonable" de que la persona puede haber estado involucrada en una actividad criminal; de la resolución de la Corte Suprema en el caso *Terry* versus *Ohio* (1968) (pág. 408)

theocracy a form of authoritarian government in which the government is ruled by religious leaders (p. 500)

teocracia forma de gobierno autoritario en la que el gobierno es dirigido por líderes religiosos (pág. 500)

third party any political party in a two-party system besides the two major ones (p. 264)

tercer partido cualquier partido político en un sistema bipartidista además de los dos partidos principales (pág. 264)

Three-Fifths Compromise (1787) an agreement stating that three-fifths of the slave population would be counted when determining a state's population for representation in the lower house of Congress (p. 54)

Compromiso de los tres quintos (1787) acuerdo que establecía que las personas esclavizadas serían contadas como tres quintos de persona cuando se determinara la población de un estado para determinar la representación en la cámara baja del Congreso (pág. 54)

totalitarianism a form of government in which the political authority exercises absolute and centralized control over all aspects of life (p. 500)

totalitarismo forma de gobierno en la cual la autoridad política ejerce un control absoluto y centralizado sobre todos los aspectos de la vida (pág. 500)

townships divisions of counties in the Midwest and Middle Atlantic regions that assist the county in the delivery of services to rural areas (p. 544)

municipalidades divisiones de condados en las regiones del Medio Oeste y del Atlántico medio que asisten al condado en la entrega de servicios a las zonas rurales (pág. 544)

trade association a business group that represents certain industries or parts of industries (p. 256)

asociación comercial grupo de empresas que representa a ciertas industrias o a partes de industrias (pág. 256)

traditional economy an economic system in which individuals produce the goods they need or barter with others to obtain those goods (p. 510)

economía tradicional sistema económico en el cual los individuos producen los artículos que necesitan o que cambian por otros para obtener los que necesitan (pág. 510)

treason the crime of making war against the United States or giving "aid and comfort" to its enemies (p. 290)

traición crimen que consiste en entrar en guerra contra Estados Unidos o en dar "ayuda y comodidad" a sus enemigos (pág. 290)

trust territory a colony or territory placed under administration by another country or countries (p. 465)

territorio en fideicomiso colonia o territorio que está bajo la administración de otro país o países (pág. 465)

ENGLISH AND SPANISH GLOSSARY

two-party system a system of government in which two political parties compete for control of the government (p. 262)
sistema bipartidista sistema de gobierno en donde dos partidos políticos compiten por el control del gobierno (pág. 262)

unconstitutional a law or government action that is found to violate any part of the Constitution; an unconstitutional law or act is deemed illegal and cannot be enforced or carried out by the government (p. 74)
inconstitucional ley o acción del gobierno que viola cualquier parte de la Constitución; una ley o un acto inconstitucional se considera ilegal, y el gobierno no puede llevarla a cabo ni hacerla cumplir (pág. 74)

undocumented alien someone living in the United States without authorization from the government (p. 346)
extranjero indocumentado alguien que vive en Estados Unidos sin la autorización del gobierno (pág. 346)

unenumerated rights certain fundamental rights, such as the right to privacy, that are not expressly mentioned in the Constitution but that have been recognized by the U.S. Supreme Court (p. 418)
derechos sin enumerar ciertos derechos fundamentales, como el derecho a la privacidad, que no están mencionados expresamente en la Constitución pero que han sido reconocidos por la Corte Suprema de Estados Unidos (pág. 418)

unitary system a form of government in which all authority is vested in a central government from which regional and local governments derive their powers (p. 17)
sistema unitario forma de gobierno en la que toda la autoridad es conferida a un gobierno central del que provienen los poderes de los gobiernos regionales y locales (pág. 17)

UN Security Council division of the United Nations charged with maintaining international peace and security (p. 463)
Consejo de Seguridad de la ONU división de las Naciones Unidas encargada de mantener la paz y la seguridad internacional (pág. 463)

veto a refusal by the president or a governor to sign a bill into law (p. 73)
veto negativa por parte del presidente o de un gobernador para no firmar un proyecto de ley (pág. 73)

Virginia Declaration of Rights (1776) a declaration of citizens' rights issued by the Virginia Convention (p. 41)
Declaración de Derechos de Virginia (1776) declaración de los derechos de los ciudadanos dictada por la Convención de Virginia (pág. 41)

Virginia Plan (1787) the plan for government in which the national government would have supreme power and a legislative branch would have two houses with representation determined by state population (p. 53)
Plan de Virginia (1787) plan de gobierno en el que el gobierno nacional tendría poder supremo y la rama legislativa tendría dos cámaras con la representación determinada por la población del estado (pág. 53)

ward a voting district made up of several precincts (p. 264)
subdivisión distrito electoral formado por varios distritos electorales más pequeños (pág. 264)

whips the representatives of each party whose duty is to encourage fellow party members to vote as the party leadership wants (p. 140)
coordinador representante de cada partido cuya función es alentar a los compañeros del partido a votar como quieren los dirigentes del partido (pág. 140)

White House Office the key assistants and deputy assistants to the president that handle much of the daily business in the White House (p. 181)
funcionarios de la Casa Blanca asistentes clave y suplentes del presidente que manejan gran parte de la actividad diaria de la Casa Blanca (pág. 181)

write-in candidates political candidates who announce that they are running for an office and ask voters to write in their names on the ballot (p. 268)
candidato por inserción escrita candidatos políticos que anuncian que se postulan para un cargo y que les piden a los votantes que escriban su nombre en la cedula electoral (pág. 268)

writ of certiorari (SUHR-SHUH-RAR-EE) an order by a higher court seeking review of a lower court case (p. 240)
orden de revisión de sentencia orden de un tribunal superior para revisar un caso de un tribunal menor (pág. 240)

writ of habeas corpus a court order that forces the police to present a person in court to face charges; *habeas corpus* is a phrase in Latin meaning "you have the body" (p. 135)
orden de habeas corpus orden judicial que obliga a la policía a presentar a una persona ante un tribunal para enfrentar los cargos; *habeas corpus* es una frase en latín que significa "tiene el cuerpo" (pág. 135)

zoning laws laws that are designed to regulate land use (p. 545)
leyes de zonificación leyes que son diseñadas para regular el uso de la tierra (pág. 545)

Index

E

INDEX

Credits and Acknowledgments

Photo Credits